THE MARK TWAIN PAPERS

Mark Twain's Letters
Volume 5: 1872–1873

THE MARK TWAIN PAPERS AND WORKS OF MARK TWAIN
is a comprehensive edition for scholars of the private papers
and published works of Mark Twain (Samuel L. Clemens).

THE MARK TWAIN LIBRARY
is a selected edition reprinted from the Papers and Works for
students and the general reader. Both series of books are published
by the University of California Press and edited by members of the

MARK TWAIN PROJECT
with headquarters in The Bancroft Library,
University of California, Berkeley.

Editorial work for all volumes is jointly supported by grants from the

NATIONAL ENDOWMENT FOR THE HUMANITIES,
an independent federal agency,
and by public and private donations,
matched equally by the Endowment, to

THE FRIENDS OF THE BANCROFT LIBRARY

THE MARK TWAIN PAPERS

Letters to His Publishers, 1867–1894
Edited with an Introduction by Hamlin Hill
1967

Satires & Burlesques
Edited with an Introduction by Franklin R. Rogers
1967

Which Was the Dream? and Other Symbolic
Writings of the Later Years
Edited with an Introduction by John S. Tuckey
1967

Hannibal, Huck & Tom
Edited with an Introduction by Walter Blair
1969

Mysterious Stranger Manuscripts
Edited with an Introduction by William M. Gibson
1969

Correspondence with Henry Huttleston Rogers, 1893–1909
Edited with an Introduction by Lewis Leary
1969

Fables of Man
Edited with an Introduction by John S. Tuckey
Text established by Kenneth M. Sanderson and Bernard L. Stein
Series Editor, Frederick Anderson
1972

Notebooks & Journals, Volume I (1855–1873)
Edited by Frederick Anderson, Michael B. Frank,
and Kenneth M. Sanderson
1975

Notebooks & Journals, Volume II (1877–1883)
Edited by Frederick Anderson, Lin Salamo, and Bernard L. Stein
1975

Notebooks & Journals, Volume III (1883–1891)
Edited by Robert Pack Browning, Michael B. Frank, and Lin Salamo
General Editor, Frederick Anderson
1979

Letters, Volume 1: 1853–1866
Editors: Edgar Marquess Branch, Michael B. Frank,
and Kenneth M. Sanderson
Associate Editors: Harriet Elinor Smith,
Lin Salamo, and Richard Bucci
1988

Letters, Volume 2: 1867–1868
Editors: Harriet Elinor Smith and Richard Bucci
Associate Editor: Lin Salamo
1990

Letters, Volume 3: 1869
Editors: Victor Fischer and Michael B. Frank
Associate Editor: Dahlia Armon
1992

Letters, Volume 4: 1870–1871
Editors: Victor Fischer and Michael B. Frank
Associate Editor: Lin Salamo
1995

Letters, Volume 5: 1872–1873
Editors: Lin Salamo and Harriet Elinor Smith
1997

THE WORKS OF MARK TWAIN
Roughing It
Edited by Franklin R. Rogers and Paul Baender
1972

What Is Man? and Other Philosophical Writings
Edited by Paul Baender
1973

A Connecticut Yankee in King Arthur's Court
Edited by Bernard L. Stein,
with an Introduction by Henry Nash Smith
1979

The Prince and the Pauper
Edited by Victor Fischer and Lin Salamo,
with the assistance of Mary Jane Jones
1979

Early Tales & Sketches, Volume 1 (1851–1864)
Edited by Edgar Marquess Branch and Robert H. Hirst,
with the assistance of Harriet Elinor Smith
1979

The Adventures of Tom Sawyer · Tom Sawyer Abroad
Tom Sawyer, Detective
Edited by John C. Gerber, Paul Baender, and Terry Firkins
1980

Early Tales & Sketches, Volume 2 (1864–1865)
Edited by Edgar Marquess Branch and Robert H. Hirst,
with the assistance of Harriet Elinor Smith
1981

Adventures of Huckleberry Finn
Edited by Walter Blair and Victor Fischer,
with the assistance of Dahlia Armon and Harriet Elinor Smith
1988

Roughing It
Editors: Harriet Elinor Smith and Edgar Marquess Branch
Associate Editors: Lin Salamo and Robert Pack Browning
1993

THE MARK TWAIN LIBRARY

No. 44, The Mysterious Stranger
Edited by John S. Tuckey and William M. Gibson
1982

The Adventures of Tom Sawyer
Edited by John C. Gerber and Paul Baender
1982

Tom Sawyer Abroad · Tom Sawyer, Detective
Edited by John C. Gerber and Terry Firkins
1982

The Prince and the Pauper
Edited by Victor Fischer and Michael B. Frank
1983

A Connecticut Yankee in King Arthur's Court
Edited by Bernard L. Stein
1983

Adventures of Huckleberry Finn
Edited by Walter Blair and Victor Fischer
1985

Huck Finn and Tom Sawyer among the Indians, and Other Unfinished Stories
Foreword and Notes by Dahlia Armon and Walter Blair
Texts established by Dahlia Armon, Paul Baender, Walter Blair, William M.
Gibson, and Franklin R. Rogers
1989

Roughing It
Editors: Harriet Elinor Smith and Edgar Marquess Branch
Associate Editors: Lin Salamo and Robert Pack Browning
1996

OTHER MARK TWAIN PROJECT PUBLICATIONS

The Devil's Race-Track: Mark Twain's Great Dark Writings
The Best from Which Was the Dream? *and* Fables of Man
Edited by John S. Tuckey
1980

Union Catalog of Clemens Letters
Edited by Paul Machlis
1986

Union Catalog of Letters to Clemens
Edited by Paul Machlis,
with the assistance of Deborah Ann Turner
1992

Samuel L. Clemens, 1872. Printed on a silk doily.
Mark Twain Papers, The Bancroft Library (CU-MARK).

THE MARK TWAIN PAPERS

General Editor, ROBERT H. HIRST

Contributing Editors for this Volume
VICTOR FISCHER
MICHAEL B. FRANK
KENNETH M. SANDERSON

A Publication of the Mark Twain Project
of The Bancroft Library

MARK TWAIN'S
LETTERS
VOLUME 5 ❧ 1872 – 1873

Editors
LIN SALAMO
HARRIET ELINOR SMITH

UNIVERSITY OF CALIFORNIA PRESS
Berkeley · Los Angeles · London
1997

University of California Press
Berkeley and Los Angeles, California

University of California Press, Ltd.
London, England

Manufactured in the United States of America

Library of Congress Cataloging-in-Publication Data

(Revised for vol. 5)

Twain, Mark, 1835–1910.
Mark Twain's letters.

(The Mark Twain papers)
Vol. 5: editors, Lin Salamo and Harriet Elinor Smith
Includes bibliographical references and indexes.
Contents: — v. 1. 1853–1866 — v. 2. 1867–1868 — [etc.] — v. 5. 1872–1873.
1. Twain, Mark, 1835–1910—Correspondence.
2. Authors, American—19th century—Correspondence.
3. Humorists, American—19th century—Correspondence.
I. Branch, Edgar Marquess, 1913–   II. Frank, Michael B.
III. Sanderson, Kenneth M.
IV. Roy J. Friedman Mark Twain Collection (Library of Congress).
V. Title.   VI. Title: Letters.   VII. Series.
VIII. Series: Twain, Mark, 1835–1910.   Mark Twain papers.
PS1331.A4   1987   818'.409 [B]   87-5963
ISBN 0-520-03669-7 (v. 2 : alk. paper)   ISBN 0-520-03670-0 (v. 3 : alk. paper)
ISBN 0-520-20360-7 (v. 4 : alk. paper)   ISBN 0-520-20822-6 (v. 5 : alk. paper)

Editorial work for this volume has been supported by a generous gift to the
Mark Twain Project of The Bancroft Library from the

BARKLEY FUND

and by matching and outright grants from the

NATIONAL ENDOWMENT FOR THE HUMANITIES,
an independent federal agency.

Without that support, this volume could
not have been produced.

Contents

Acknowledgments

THIS VOLUME in the Mark Twain Papers, like the fourteen volumes that precede it, was made possible by the National Endowment for the Humanities, an independent federal agency. The Endowment has funded editorial work on Mark Twain's writings, without interruption, since 1966, making both outright and matching grants to the Mark Twain Project of The Bancroft Library. The Endowment provided funds for the present volume partly by matching a substantial gift to the Project from the Barkley Fund. We thank both the Endowment and the trustees of the Barkley Fund for their timely and generous support.

More than half of the Endowment's recent grants to the Project were made feasible by gifts from individuals and foundations, each of which has been matched dollar for dollar. We wish to thank the following major donors to the Project, who have all given generously to it (often more than once) during the past few years: William H. Alsup; Jonathan Arac; Mr. and Mrs. John P. Austin; The Behring-Hofmann Educational Institute; Lawrence I. Berkove; Paul Berkowitz; The House of Bernstein, Inc.; Kevin J. and Margaret A. Bochynski; J. Dennis Bonney; Edgar Marquess Branch; Edmund G. and Bernice Brown; Class of 1938, University of California, Berkeley; June A. Cheit; Chevron Corporation; Jean R. and Sherman Chickering Fund; Chronicle Books; William A. and the late Mildred Clayton; Dana T. Coggin; Don L. Cook; Dow Chemical Corporation Foundation; Victor A. Doyno; Dorothy Eweson; the late Alice C. Gaddis; Launce E. Gamble; John C. Gerber; Dr. and Mrs. Orville J. Golub; Marion S. Goodin; Susan K. Harris; the late James D. Hart; William Randolph Hearst Foundation; Hedco Foundation; Heller Charitable & Educational Fund; Janet S. and William D. Hermann; Mr. and Mrs. Stephen G. Herrick; Kenneth E. Hill; Hal Holbrook; James M. Hotchkiss, Jr.; Fred Kaplan; Ralph H. Kellogg; Dr. Charles C. Kelsey; Holger Kersten; Koret Foundation; Horst and Ursula Kruse; Irene and Jervis Langdon, Jr.; David C. Mandeville; Mark Twain Circle; Mark Twain Foundation; Robert Massa; the late Robert N. Miner; F. Van Dorn Moller; Jane Newhall; Jeanne G. O'Brien and the late James E. O'Brien; Hiroshi Okubo; the late David Packard; The Pareto Fund; Constance Crowley Hart Peabody; Connie J. and David H. Pyle; the late Catherine D. Rau; Verla K. Regnery Foundation; Deane and Peggy Robertson; John W. and Barbara Rosston; Virginia C. Scardigli; Michael Shelden; John R. Shuman; L. J. Skaggs and Mary C. Skaggs Foundation; Marion B. and Willis S. Slusser; Miriam and Harold Steinberg Foundation; Jeffrey Steinbrink; Thomas More Storke Fund; Koji Tabei; Mrs. Joseph Z. Todd; Gretchen Trupiano; the late John Russell Wagner; Mrs. Paul L. Wattis; and Alvin Ziegler.

We are likewise grateful to the following donors for their timely gifts to the Project, all of which have also been matched by the Endowment: Dr. John E. Adams; Sid and Jan Allison; Paul Alpers; Mr. and Mrs. Ward Anderson; Harold Aspiz; Roger Asselineau; John Edward Back; Julia Bader; Nancy and Howard G. Baetzhold; Brenda J. Bailey; Dwight L. and Nancy J. Barker; Benjamin Samuel Barncord; Mr. and Mrs. Donald P. Barron; David Barrow; Trenton Don Bass; Jay D. Bayer; H. H. Behrens; Barbara Belford; John B. and Ann W. Bender; the late Dr. Leslie L. Bennett and the Bennett Family Trust; Carol C. Bense; JoDee Ann Benussi; Mary K. Bercaw; Hannah M. Bercovitch; Alice R. Berkowitz; James R. Bernard; Roger Berry; R. J. Bertero; Marilyn R. Bewley; David Bianculli; Diane B. Bickers; Diane Birchell; John Bird; Donald P. Black and Robert L. Black, M.D., in memory of their father, Harold A. Black; W. Edward Blain; William Makely in memory of Walter Blair; Burton J. Bledstein; Mary Boewe; Dennis A. Bohn; Dr. Richard J. Borg; Harold I. and Beulah Blair Boucher; Betsy Bowden; Mr. and Mrs. Philip E. Bowles; Boone Brackett, M.D.; Philip and Katherine Bradley; Sandra Wentworth Bradley; The Brick Row Book Shop; Earl F. Briden; Richard Bridgman; the late Stanley Brodwin; Timothy Buchanan; Louis J. and Isabelle Budd; Linda E. Burg; Richard Byrd; Gerald K. Cahill; Mr. and Mrs. Grant W. Canfield; Lawrence G. Carlin; Clayton C. Carmichael; Professor James E. Caron; Paul Carrara; CD Squared; C. D. Christensen; Patricia Christensen; Fred Clagett; Mrs. Wanda Clark; Edwina B. Coffing; Hennig Cohen; Marvin M. Cole; James L. Colwell; Bob Comeau; Mrs. Shirley Larson Cook; Nancy Cook; Alice and Robert Cooper; Wayne and Germaine Cooper; Cornell

University Library; Ruth Mary Cordon-Cradler; Joan and Pascal Covici, Jr.; James M. Cox; Frederick Crews; Harry W. Crosby; Charles L. Crow; Sherwood Cummings; Sally J. Letchworth in memory of Susan Letchworth Dann; Beverly (Penny) David; Carlo M. De Ferrari; Edgar and Elinor De Jean; Theresa Demick; Mrs. Wilma Cox DeMotte; Barbara Deutsch; Jean Pond Dever; Joseph E. Doctor; Carl Dolmetsch; William G. Donald; Edgar L. Dow; Marie S. Doyle; Jon A. Dubin; William J. Duhigg, Jr.; Richard A. and Sherry T. Dumke; Dennis Eddings; Matthew J. Ehrenberg; Sanford S. Elberg; Everett Emerson; Allison R. Ensor; William W. Escherich; Ann Cahill Fidanque; Joel M. Fisher; Shelley Fisher Fishkin; Gerald L. and Norma J. Flanery; George R. Flannery; Willis and Maria P. Foster; Margaret Anne Fraher; the Reverend Don Fraser; Peter L. Friedman, M.D., Ph.D.; Friends of Caxton; Robert E. Futrell; Louis G. Gambill; Joe Gannon; Michael D. Gastaldo; Guy G. Gilchrist; Jay E. Gillette; Jerry S. Gilmer, Ph.D.; Dorothy Goldberg; Gloria R. Goldblatt; Stephen L. Golder; Lowell Gorseth; Shoji Goto; Mr. William J. Graver; C. Gordon Greene; Ralph J. Gregory; Kenneth L. Greif; Jean F. Guyer; Frank W. Hammelbacher; Peter E. Hanff; Robert N. and Arlene R. Hansen; John Mitchell Hardaway; Mr. and Mrs. Robert T. Harnsberger; Mrs. Mercedes Haroldson; Paul C. Harris, Jr.; William N. Harrison; Peter D. Hart; Mr. and Mrs. David P. Hawkins; Miss Quail Hawkins; Juan C. Hayes; E. Dixon Heise; Katherine Heller; Katherine Heller and Rolf Lygren Fund; Betty and Carl Helmholz; H. Sleet Henderson; Judith B. Herman; Aurora and Jim Hill; Charles J. Hitch; Sandra Hjorth; Mary Jo Hobart-Parks; Elizabeth Hoem; Mrs. Carl J. Hoffman; Raymond Holbert; Patricia A. Holland; Professor and Mrs. Richard H. Holton; Walter Hoops; Jason G. Horn; George J. Houle; Professor Kay S. House; Goldena Howard; Lawrence Howe; George Lowman Howell; W. Robert Howell; David S. Hubbell, M.D.; Justine Hume; Hiroyoshi Ichikawa; Masago Igawa; M. Thomas Inge; Jane A. Iverson; Iwao Iwamoto; Dr. Janice Beaty Janssen; Robert Jenkins, M.D., Ph.D.; Alastair Johnston; Yoshio Kanaya; Nick Karanovich; Lawrence Kearney; Dan Keller Technical Services; Dennis and Hene Kelly; Lynn Kelly; Dr. Derek Kerr; Howard Kerr; Harlan Kessel; Dr. David B. Kesterson; Mr. and Mrs. Dudley J. Kierulff; Dr. J. C. B. Kinch; John K. King Books; Michael J. Kiskis; Paul and Elisa Kleven; Jeremy Knight; Robert and Margarete Knudsen; Larry Kramer; Leland Krauth; Mr. and Mrs. S. L. Laidig; Lucius Lampton,

M.D.; Baldwin G. and Ormond S. Lamson; Mr. and Mrs. H. Jack
Lang; J. William and Jeanne Larkin; Jennifer Signe Larson; Roger K.
Larson, M.D.; Richard W. LaRue; Jacklyn Lauchland-Shaw; Mary-
Warren Leary; Philip W. Leon; Andrew Levy; Joan V. Lindquist; Wil-
liam S. Linn; Robert Livermore; Albert Locher; Joseph H. Towson for
Debbie L. Lopez; Frederic B. Lovett; George J. Houle in memory of
Matthias (Matt) P. Lowman; Lolita L. Lowry; Karen A. Lystra; Peter
McBean; Senior United States District Judge Thomas J. MacBride,
Eastern District of California; Patricia Murphy McClelland; William J.
McClung; Joseph B. McCullough; Mac Donnell Rare Books; Coleman
W. McMahon; Hugh D. McNiven; Laura McVay; Wilson C. Mc-
Williams; James H. Maguire; George F. Mahl; Thomas A. Maik; Steven
Mailloux; Linda Maio; Mila Mangold; Michael Maniccia; Mark Twain
Society, Inc.; Miss Jean E. Matthew; Ronald R. Melen; Dr. Jeffrey A.
Melton; Thomas M. Menzies; Eileen N. Meredith; Elsa Meyer Miller
in memory of Elsa Springer Meyer; Jay and Elise Miller; Victoria
Thorpe Miller; Michael Millgate; R. E. Mitchell, M.D.; Tokuhiro
Miura; Dr. and Mrs. I. W. Monie; James M. Moore; Rayburn S. Moore;
Frank and Gabrielle Morris; Ron Morrison; Steven G. Morton; Ann
Elizabeth and Robert Murtha; Charles J. Naber; Alan Nadritch; Ma-
koto Nagawara; Koichi Nakamura; Suzanne Naiburg; Frances M. Neel;
Fred M. Nelsen; David A. Nelson; Leta H. Nelson; Ralph G. Newman,
Inc.; Robert S. Newton; Emily V. Nichols; Cameron C. Nickels; Sandy
Niemann; Charles A. Norton; Patrick and Cathy Ober; Harold P. and
Olive L. Oggel; the Olive L. Oggel Trust: Terry, Steve, and Jeff Oggel;
Terry and Linda Oggel; Koji Oi; Peter K. Oppenheim; Chris Orvin; R.
Overbey; David C. Owens; Hershel Parker; Kenneth D. and Nancy J.
Parker; Mary Jane Perna; Frederick D. Petrie; Linda Propert; Randall
House Rare Books; R. Kent Rasmussen; Allen Walker Read; Reader's
Digest Foundation; Robert Regan; Miss Elizabeth Reid; Maryanne and
Thomas Reigstad; Richard W. Reinhardt; Arno W. Reinhold; Elinor
Reiss; Louise Burnham Rettick; James Richardson; Hans J. Riedel;
Mrs. Barbara H. Riggins; The Riverdale Press; Taylor Roberts; Dr.
Verne L. Roberts; Mrs. Kip Robinson; Mr. and Mrs. S. R. Rose; Ber-
nard M. Rosenthal; Norman J. and Claire S. Roth; Brandt Rowles;
Sharon L. Ruff; Linda Haverty Rugg; Lynne M. Rusinko; Barbara
Ryan; Susan J. Sager; Mrs. Leon E. Salanave; Kenneth M. Sanderson;
Mrs. Elaine R. Santoro; Gary D. Saretsky; Elinor P. Saunders; Evelyn

H. Savage; Barbara E. Schauffler; Katherine Schmidt; Thelma Schoonmaker; Timothy and Sue Schulfer; Judith A. Sears; Lucy W. Sells; Caroline Service; Carol Sharon; Virginia M. Shaw; Thomas J. Shephard, Sr.; Laura Beth Sherman; Polly A. Siegel; Oscar Alan Sipes; Michael J. and Marsha C. Skinner; Ward B. Skinner, D.D.S.; Richard Skues; David E. E. Sloane; Mr. and Mrs. Robert T. Slotta in memory of Caroline Thomas Harnsberger; Elinor Lucas Smith; Jonathan C. Smith; Gene Snook; David N. Socholitzky; Colleen A. Spadaro; Marseille Spetz, M.D.; Ronald M. Spielman; Betty Jean and Jim Spitze; Marjorie H. Sproul; Verne A. Stadtman; J. D. Stahl; George A. Starr; Horace D. Stearman; Richard T. Stearns; Dwight C. Steele; Carol Steinhagen; Jody Steren; Albert E. Stone; Janet P. Stone; Louis Suarez-Potts; Edward W. Swenson; Eleanor H. Swent; G. Thomas Tanselle; Barbara W. Taylor; Harry Tennyson; Jeffrey and Evelyne Thomas; Burt Tolerton; Eloyde J. Tovey; Col. Robert T. Townsend; Dorothy Tregea; Frederic B. Tankel in memory of Donald G. Tronstein; Masao Tsunematsu; Edward L. Tucker; Charles S. Underhill; Marlene Boyd Vallin; Thomas S. Van Den Heuvel; Patrick J. Vaz; Ellen M. and Michael Vernon; Robert W. Vivian; Sally Walker; Willard D. Washburn; Jeanne H. Watson; Abby H. P. Werlock; Mr. and Mrs. F. A. West; John and Kim Wheaton; John Wiesemes; T. H. Wildenradt; Christine Williams; Ilse B. Williams; Frederick B. Wilmar; the late James D. Wilson; Merilynn Laskey Wilson; Herbert A. Wisbey, Jr.; Edward O. Wolcott; Harold A. Wollenberg; Thomas R. Worley; Tom and Amy Worth; Laurel A. and Jeffrey S. Wruble; Jin-Hee Yim; Mary A. Young; David Joseph and Yoko Tanabe Zmijewski; Jim Zwick; and Kate Zwirko.

Despite the great financial stringency of recent years, the University of California has continued to provide a home, and support, for the Project. For their help in securing repeated exemptions from indirect costs (thus materially reducing the cost of editing borne by the Endowment grants) we wish especially to thank Linda R. Rutkowski, Lynn E. Deetz, and Joseph Cerny, Vice Chancellor for Research. For both tangible and intangible support we also thank C. D. Mote, Jr., Vice Chancellor for University Relations, and Carol T. Christ, the Vice Chancellor and Provost. The newest members of the Mark Twain Project's Board of Directors have likewise been indispensable to its survival within the larger institution. We thank especially Peter Lyman, University Librarian, Charles B. Faulhaber, Director of The Bancroft Library, and Peter E.

Hanff, now Deputy Director after more than five years as Acting Director of The Bancroft, as well as Jo Ann Boydston, Don L. Cook, Frederick Crews, Michael Millgate, George A. Starr, G. Thomas Tanselle, and Elizabeth Witherell. Each has contributed significantly, though in different ways, to our ability to remain "stubborn for a long time" about editing Mark Twain's papers and works.

Our thanks go as well to the Council of The Friends of The Bancroft Library for their continued moral support of this enterprise: Cindy Arnot Barber, chair; William P. Barlow, Jr., Peggy Cahill, Kimo Campbell, Dorian Chong, Gifford Combs, Charles B. Faulhaber, Carol Hart Field, Rita Fink, Ann Flinn, Victoria Fong, Roger Hahn, Peter E. Hanff, E. Dixon Heise, Martin Huff, Lawrence Kramer, Allan Littman, Robert Livermore, William Petrocelli, Bernard M. Rosenthal, George Sears, Julia Sommer, Katharine Wallace, and Thomas B. Worth. We owe special thanks as well to Kelly Penhall-Wilson and Leela Virassammy, past and present coordinators for The Friends.

We are grateful for moral as well as practical support from our many colleagues in the Library, especially Charles B. Faulhaber and Peter E. Hanff, already mentioned. For wisdom, advice, and uncounted acts of assistance we also thank Willa K. Baum, Bonnie L. Bearden, D. Steven Black, Anthony S. Bliss, Walter V. Brem, Jr., Bonnie Hardwick, Cynthia A. Hoffman, Timothy P. Hoyer, David Kessler, Ann Lage, Lauren Lassleben, Mary L. Morganti, Jacqueline M. Mundo, Paul T. Payne, Daniel Pitti, Merrilee Proffitt, Teri A. Rinne, William M. Roberts, Patrick J. Russell, Paul Shen, Susan E. Snyder, Andrew C. Spalaris, and Jack von Euw. Jo Lynn Milardovich and the hard-working staff of the Interlibrary Borrowing Service helped us to obtain many rare and remote works that proved essential to the annotation. We are also indebted to Daniel L. Johnston and Marnie L. Jacobsen of the Library Photographic Service for cheerfully filling, with unvarying excellence, our requests for photographs.

All editors of Mark Twain are permanently indebted to the generations of scholars who pioneered in the tasks of locating, copying, collecting, and publishing his letters—particularly Albert Bigelow Paine and his successors as Editor of the Mark Twain Papers: Bernard DeVoto, Dixon Wecter, Henry Nash Smith, and Frederick Anderson. Paine's *Mark Twain: A Biography* (1912) and *Mark Twain's Letters* (1917) are still indispensable works of scholarship, and are sometimes the only known source for letters reprinted here. Wecter's *Mark Twain to Mrs. Fairbanks* (1949) and *The Love Letters of Mark Twain* (1949) were the first editions to publish Mark Twain's letters in accord with modern scholarly standards for annotation and transcription, although just eleven years later, Henry Nash Smith and William M. Gibson's *Mark Twain–Howells Letters* (1960) established new and even higher standards. Frederick Anderson assisted Smith and Gibson in that work and, until his death in 1979, served as Series Editor for the Mark Twain Papers, which included among its first volumes Hamlin Hill's *Mark Twain's Letters to His Publishers, 1867–1894,* and Lewis Leary's *Mark Twain's Correspondence with Henry Huttleston Rogers, 1893–1909,* published in 1967 and 1969, respectively. We have profited from all of these books in ways too numerous to bear mention in the notes.

The Mark Twain Papers in The Bancroft Library are the archival home for nearly a third of the three hundred letters published in the present volume. Mark Twain's own private papers were brought to the University of California in 1949—a result of Dixon Wecter's irresistible persuasiveness and the accommodating generosity of Clara Clemens Samossoud. Subsequent gifts and purchases over the years have added substantially to this massive cache of private documents. For gifts of letters and other documents used in this volume we are grateful to the late Violet Appert, Mrs. Dorothy Clark, Robert Daley, Marie S. Doyle, Mr. and Mrs. Robert M. Gunn, the late Mrs. Eugene Lada-Mocarski, Jervis Langdon, Jr., Mrs. Robert S. Pennock, and Mrs. Bayard Schieffelin. One letter (4 August 1873 to Edmund H. Yates) was purchased with funds from the James F. and Agnes R. Robb Memorial Fund in The Bancroft Library. Special thanks go also to William P. Barlow, Jr., for affording us unlimited access to his vast and ever-growing collection of manuscript and book auction catalogs, which are not infrequently the sole available source for letter texts included here, or in the previous four volumes of *Mark Twain's Letters.* We are likewise indebted to Todd M. Axelrod, executive director of the Gallery of History in Las Vegas, who generously gave us direct access to the nearly one hundred and thirty letters he has collected (four letters in this volume alone, several more in each of the previous volumes).

All other original letters published here are owned, and have been made available to the editors both directly and in photocopy, by the following repositories or individuals, to whom we and the reader are indebted: Amherst College, Amherst, Massachusetts; Mr. and Mrs. Fred D. Bentley, Sr.; the Boston Public Library and Eastern Massachusetts Regional Public Library; the British Library; the Buffalo and Erie County Historical Society Archives; the Cincinnati Historical Society; Columbia University; the Connecticut Historical Society and the Connecticut State Library, Hartford; the James S. Copley Library, La Jolla, California; Robert Daley; Chester L. Davis, Jr.; the East Sussex Record Office; the Detroit Public Library; Robert M. Dorn; the Folger Shakespeare Library, Washington, D.C.; Russell Freedman of Second Life Books, Lanesborough, Massachusetts; the Houghton Library of Harvard University; David Howland; the Henry E. Huntington Library, San Marino, California; the Rare Book and Special Collections Library of the University of Illinois, Urbana; the University of Iowa; the late Victor and Irene Murr Jacobs; Nick Karanovich; the Seymour Library of Knox College, Galesburg, Illinois; the Linderman Library of Lehigh University, Bethlehem, Pennsylvania; the Library of Congress; the Litchfield Historical Society, Litchfield, Connecticut; the Mark Twain Archives and Center for Mark Twain Studies at Quarry Farm, Elmira College; the Mark Twain Birthplace State Historic Site, Stoutsville, Missouri; the Mark Twain Home Foundation, Hannibal, Missouri; the Mark Twain House, Hartford; the Massachusetts Historical Society, Boston; the Moray District Council, Elgin, Scotland; the Pierpont Morgan Library, New York City; Rosemary Morris and Marjory Anderson; the Henry W. and Albert A. Berg Collection of The New York Public Library, Astor, Lenox and Tilden Foundations; the New York Historical Society, New York City; the Newberry Library, Chicago; the Historical Society of Pennsylvania, Philadelphia; Princeton University; Reed College, Portland, Oregon; the Rush Rhees Library of the University of Rochester, Rochester, New York; Routledge and Kegan Paul, London; Charles W. Sachs of the Scriptorium, Beverly Hills; Saint Mary's Seminary, Perryville, Missouri; Bruce Schwalb; the University of Southern California, Los Angeles; the Harriet Beecher Stowe Center, Hartford; the Strathclyde Regional Archives, Glasgow; the Harry Ransom Humanities Research Center of the University of Texas, Austin; Jean Thompson; the Vassar College Library, Poughkeepsie, New York; Middlebury College, Middlebury, Vermont; the Clifton Waller Barrett Library at the University of Virginia, Charlottesville; the Western Reserve Historical Society, Cleveland; the Memorial Library of the University of

Wisconsin, Madison; the Beinecke Rare Book and Manuscript Library, Yale University; Washington University, St. Louis.

A great many librarians and scholars have assisted us in transcribing, annotating, and tracing the provenance of these letters. We owe particular thanks to the following: John Ahouse, Curator of American Literature, University of Southern California, Los Angeles; Harold Augenbraum, Director, Mercantile Library of New York; Frederick W. Bauman, Manuscript Reference Librarian, Library of Congress; Lawrence I. Berkove, Department of English, University of Michigan, Dearborn; Amy Bolt, Reference Librarian, Library of Michigan, Lansing; Lisa Browar, formerly Assistant Director for Rare Books and Manuscripts and Acting Curator of the Berg Collection, The New York Public Library, now head of the Lilly Library, Bloomington; Michaelyn Burnette, Humanities Librarian, Collection Development and Reference Services Department, University of California, Berkeley; Undine Concannon, Archivist, Madame Tussaud's, London; Marianne Curling, Curator, and Beverly Zell, Photograph Librarian, Mark Twain House, Hartford; Margaret Daley, Liverpool Record Office; Michael Donnelly, Archives Assistant, Maritime Archives and Library, Merseyside Maritime Museum, Liverpool; Gina Douglas, Librarian and Archivist, Linnean Society of London; Inge Dupont, Head of Reader Services, Pierpont Morgan Library, New York City; Eric Flounders, Cunard Line, London; Patricia Higgins, Researcher, Offley, Hitchin, Hertfordshire; Sara S. Hodson, Curator of Literary Manuscripts, Huntington Library, San Marino, California; Margaret D. Hrabe, Public Services Assistant, Special Collections/Manuscripts, Alderman Library, University of Virginia; Julian Hunt, Local Studies Librarian, County Library and Museum, Buckinghamshire; JoAnne Jager, Local History Librarian, Lansing Public Library; Marilyn Kierstead, Special Collections Librarian, Reed College Library, Portland, Oregon; E. Bruce Kirkham, Department of English, Ball State University, Muncie, Indiana; John Lancaster, Head of Special Collections, and Donna Skibel, Archives Associate, Amherst College Library; Robert A. McCown, Special Collections and Manuscripts Librarian, University of Iowa; Karen Mix, Special Collections, Mugar Library, Boston University; Virginia Moreland, College Librarian, Agnes Scott College, Decatur, Georgia; Leslie A. Morris, Curator of Manuscripts, and Melanie Wisner, Houghton Reading Room, Houghton Library, Harvard University; Kelly Nolin, Reference Librarian, Connecticut Historical Society; John D. O'Hern, Director and Curator, Arnot Art Museum, Elmira; Kermit J. Pike, Library Director, Western Reserve Historical Society, Cleveland; Diana Royce, Librarian, Stowe-Day Library, Harriet Beecher Stowe Center, Hartford; P. R. Saunders, Curator, Salisbury and South Wiltshire Museum; Gary Scharnhorst, Department of English Language and Literature, University of New Mexico, Albuquerque; Jeffrey Kaimowitz, Curator, and Alesandra M. Schmidt, Assistant Curator, Reference and Manuscripts, Watkinson Library, Trinity College, Hartford; Martha Smart, Reference Assistant, Connecticut Historical Society, Hartford; Michael Shelden, Department of English, Indiana State University, Terre Haute; Virginia Smith, Reference Librarian, Massachusetts Historical Society, Boston; Linda Stanley, Manuscripts and Archives Curator, Historical Society of Pennsylvania, Philadelphia; E. Gordon Williams, Liverpool Shipwreck and Humane Society; Diane Wishinski, State of Vermont Department of Libraries, Montpelier; Vincent Giroud, Curator of the MacDonald Collection, Danielle C. McClellan, Public Services Assistant, Stephen Parks, Curator of the Osborn Collection, and Patricia Willis, Curator of the Yale Collection of American Literature, Beinecke Rare Book and Manuscript Library, Yale University; Laetitia Yeandle, Manuscripts Librarian, Folger Shakespeare Library.

Throughout the typesetting and physical production of this volume we have had essential guidance and assistance from the University of California Press. We are especially appreciative of Sam Rosenthal, who saw the book through the intricacies of the production process; Doris Kretschmer, our sponsoring editor; and Sandy Drooker, who designed and prepared the dust jacket. As in the past, we have benefited from the punctilious work of the expert and knowledgeable staff at Wilsted & Taylor Publishing Services, Oakland, California. We again thank Christine Taylor and LeRoy Wilsted, and we renew those thanks for Kimberly Cline, typesetter par excellence, as well as Jennifer Brown, Jeff Clark, Melissa Ehn, Nancy Evans, Stephen Fraser, Melody Lacina, Beth Lee, Julie Lefevre, Rosemary Northcraft, and Heather Rudkin. Allen McKinney of Graphic Impressions in Emeryville, California, together with his assistant Tom Beidler, again provided the exceptionally fine halftones for the photographs published here.

We thank David Chesnutt for his thoughtful, careful, and highly appreciative inspection of this volume for the Modern Language Association's Committee on Scholarly Editions, whose seal of approval appears on the copyright page.

Finally, we express our abiding gratitude to colleagues and former colleagues in the Mark Twain Project for their indispensable help at every stage of editing and production. Richard Bucci traveled to several archives in the East, where he expertly compared original letter manuscripts with our transcriptions. Robert Pack Browning helped secure formal permission to publish letters owned by other institutions and individuals. Victor Fischer provided authoritative guidance and limitless patience in helping us to establish the texts. Michael B. Frank contributed his expertise in styling and checking the annotation, and he was among those who carefully proofread the entire volume. Kenneth M. Sanderson applied his exceptional skill in reading Mark Twain's handwriting to improve the accuracy of the transcriptions. The *Union Catalog of Clemens Letters* (1986) and the *Union Catalog of Letters to Clemens* (1992), edited by Paul Machlis—the latter with the assistance of Deborah Ann Turner—were essential to the preparation of this volume. Four student interns participated in both research for, and proofreading of, the texts published here: David G. Briggs, Anh Bui, Ashley R. D'Cruz, and Louis Suarez-Potts. Brenda Bailey, administrative assistant to the Project, shielded us from the bureaucracy and the telephones, always with her customary efficiency and good cheer.

L. S.   H. E. S.

Introduction

THIS VOLUME OPENS on 2 January 1872, with Clemens traveling the Midwest in the eleventh week of his winter lecture tour. Although chafing to be done with "this lecturing penance" (p. 14), he could not manage a home visit with Olivia and fourteen-month-old Langdon until 25 January, eight days before his second wedding anniversary. In late February, after a half dozen more performances, "the most detestable lecture campai[g]n that ever was" (p. 43) was at last over.

The 309 letters gathered here, well over half of them never before published, document in intimate detail the events of 1872 and 1873, during which the Clemenses prospered from the royalties on *Roughing It* (over ten thousand dollars in the first three months), rejoiced at the birth of a healthy daughter and mourned the loss of their son shortly thereafter, and began building the house in Hartford in which they would live contentedly for nearly two decades. Meanwhile, Clemens's professional life flourished, as he became established among the leading writers and journalists of his day. The letters shed light on his friendships with many prominent people, among them Whitelaw Reid, the new editor in chief of the New York *Tribune,* the most influential newspaper in America; Bret Harte, at the peak of his fame; William Dean Howells, the highly respected editor of the *Atlantic Monthly;* Thomas Nast, the crusading political cartoonist of *Harper's Weekly;* and Charles Dudley Warner, his congenial neighbor and the coauthor of *The Gilded Age.* At the same time, Clemens was earning an international reputation. By the end of 1873, when this volume closes, he had made three trips across the Atlantic, spending a total of eight and a half months in Great Britain, where he reveled in his success as both an author and a lecturer.

During the first half of 1872 Clemens was occupied with several literary projects. In late February *Roughing It* was published, and despite his early anxiety about its critical reception, brisk sales and "sufficient testimony, derived through many people's statements" made him feel "at last easy & comfortable about the new book" (p. 69). Another project, a book about the South African diamond mines planned in 1870 with John Henry Riley as surrogate traveler and collaborator, was first postponed, and then—with Riley fatally ill—abandoned. In the meantime Clemens made short work of revising *The Innocents Abroad* and two collections of sketches for publication in England by George Routledge and Sons, who, with their edition of *Roughing It*, were now established as his official English publishers. Casting about for a new project, Clemens followed a suggestion from Joseph Blamire, the Routledges' New York agent, to write a book about England. On 21 August he embarked for London, intending to spend several months sightseeing and quietly gathering information. Within days of his arrival, however, he was overwhelmed with "too much company—too much dining—too much sociability" (p. 155). Welcomed everywhere as a literary lion and flooded with invitations to lecture, he was astounded and gratified to discover that he was "by long odds the most widely known & popular American author among the English" (p. 197). In November he sailed for home, having decided to postpone an English lecture series and any further research on his book until he could return the following spring, accompanied by Olivia.

Back home in Hartford, Clemens turned his attention to topical issues, firing off letters and articles to the New York *Tribune*, the Hartford *Evening Post*, and the Hartford *Courant* in which he commented—with characteristic humor—on subjects as wide ranging as street repair, safety at sea, incompetent juries, and political corruption. His most significant pieces were two long letters on the Sandwich Islands, written in January 1873 in response to an invitation from Whitelaw Reid. The attention these letters received led to several lecture invitations, and in February Clemens revived his Sandwich Islands talk for enthusiastic audiences in New York, Brooklyn, and New Jersey.

Clemens's next major project reflected his heightened interest in social issues and took him in a new direction, away from personal narrative and toward fiction. Inspired by newspaper reports of government corruption and scandal in New York and Washington, he set to work, in collaboration with his friend Charles Dudley Warner, on a political satire: *The Gilded Age*. Writing with a rare enthusiasm, the two authors completed their manuscript in about four months. By early May the American Publishing Company had agreed to issue the book, and arrangements for simultaneous publication in England had been made with the Routledges.

On 17 May, Clemens again sailed for England, this time accompanied by Olivia (on her first trip abroad), ten-month-old Susy and her nursemaid (Nellie Bermingham), Olivia's childhood friend Clara Spaulding, and a secretary, Samuel C. Thompson. To his original objectives—research and lecturing—Clemens had added two further missions: to secure a valid British copyright on *The Gilded Age* by establishing residency in Great Britain, and to correspond for the New York *Herald*.

In London the Clemens party was busy with excursions, sightseeing, and dinners. Clemens held court in their rooms at the Langham Hotel, and was often seen about town or at clubs in company with Joaquin Miller, the eccentric poet. Anthony Trollope, Robert Browning, and other prominent English and American visitors came to call or issued invitations. After seven hectic weeks in London, the Clemenses fled north in search of rest and quiet, visiting Scotland and Ireland for several weeks.

In October Clemens kept his promise to lecture, appearing for a week in London before large and appreciative audiences with his talk on the Sandwich Islands. By this time, however, Olivia was "blue and cross and homesick"—and newly pregnant (p. 457). But Clemens's business in London was by no means concluded: the English publication of *The Gilded Age* had been delayed. He therefore accompanied Olivia home in late October, returning immediately to London for a third time to "finish talking" (p. 472). Comfortably settled again at the Langham Hotel, he now had his old San Francisco friend Charles Warren Stoddard as a secretary and amiable companion. Clemens lectured from 1 to 20 December, soon replacing the Sandwich Islands lecture with "Roughing It," which was equally well received by London's "bully audiences" (p. 521). By the end of the year—with both the American and English editions of *The Gilded Age* in print, but with his English book still in abeyance—Clemens was making preparations to return home. "Thirteen more days in England, & then I sail!" he wrote Olivia on 31 December. "If I only *do* get home safe, & find my darling & the Modoc well, I shall be a grateful soul. And if ever I do have another longing to leave home, even for a week, please dissipate it with a club" (p. 543).

L. S. H. E. S.

Editorial Signs

THE EDITORIAL conventions used to transcribe Mark Twain's letters were designed, in part, to enable anyone to read the letters without having to memorize a list. The following is therefore offered less as a necessary preliminary than as a convenient way to look up the meaning of any convention which, in spite of this design, turns out to be less than self-explanatory. Only the editorial conventions used in this volume are given here, since each new volume will require a slightly different list. New or newly modified conventions are identified by an asterisk (*). Not included are the typographical equivalents used to transcribe Mark Twain's own signs and symbols in manuscript. For those equivalents, and for a more discursive explanation of editorial principles, see the Guide to Editorial Practice, pp. 695–722.

EDITORIAL HEADING

From . . .	Clemens is named in the heading only when he wrote jointly with someone else.
. . . with a note to . . .	Used when two persons are addressed in the same letter, but Clemens intended the second to read *only* the briefer part, or "note."
per . . .	Precedes the name or identity of the amanuensis or agent who inscribed the document sent or received.
2? May	On this day—give or take a day.
1–3 May	On any day (or days) within this span.
1 and 2 May	On both days.

(MS)   The source document is the original letter, almost invariably Clemens's holograph manuscript.

(*damage emended*)   The source document has sustained significant damage, and the transcription therefore includes, without brackets, emendation to restore the affected text.

(MS facsimile)   The source document is a photographic facsimile of the MS, not the MS itself.

(Paraphrase)   The source document preserves some of the *words* of the original letter, but is manifestly not a deliberate transcription of it.

(Transcript)   The source document is a printed, handwritten, or typed (TS) transcription of the letter, not necessarily made at first hand.

LETTER TEXT

NEW-YORK   Extra-small small capitals with no initial capitals signify printed text *not* originated by Clemens, such as letterhead or the postmark.

(SLC)   *Italicized* extra-small small capitals within an oval border transcribe monograms or initials printed or embossed on personal stationery.

Feb. 13,   Text above a dotted underscore was inscribed in a printed blank in the original document.

· · · ·   Editorial ellipsis points (always centered in an otherwise blank line) signify that an unknown amount of the original letter is judged to be missing.

Ruled borders are an editorial device to represent the edge of a document, usually printed or partly printed, such as a telegram blank or newspaper clipping.

A two cance- deletions,   Cancellation is signified by slashes for single characters (and underscores), rules for two or more characters.

Well, *I* pass.   A hairline rule signifies a mock, or pretended, cancellation: words lightly and distinctively crossed out, easily read, and often still necessary to the sense.

marking it ˄up˄   Insertion is signified by a single caret for single characters, two carets for two or more characters.

shaded words   Gray background identifies text originated and inscribed by someone other than Clemens—or by Clemens himself when he altered or signed what his amanuensis wrote.*

[ ]   Author's square brackets are transcribed this way to avoid any confusion with editorial brackets.

[ ]   Editorial square brackets enclose [*editorial description*]; words or characters omitted by the writer an[d] now interpolated by [the] editors; and text modified by description, such as [*in margin:* All well].

◊iamond   The diamond stands for a character, numeral, or punctuation mark the editors cannot read because it is physically obscured or obliterated. It *never* stands for the space between words.

double‑
hyphen   The hyphen is to be retained. Single hyphens at the ends of lines therefore signify division only.

Sam*ˡ*   Superscript ell is always italicized to prevent confusion between one (^{1}) and ell (^{ˡ}). The sign ⸺ transcribes a paraph or flourish.*

✉————   The envelope and full-measure rule signal that everything transcribed below them was written, stamped, or printed on the envelope or on the letter itself at the time of transmission or receipt.

| Signifies the end of a line in the source document.

To James Redpath
2 January 1872 • Logansport, Ind.
(*MTL*, 1:193–94, and three others)

Logansport, Ind. Jan. 2.

Friend Redpath—

Had a splendid time with a splendid audience in Indianapolis last night—a perfectly jammed house, just as I have all the time out here. I like the new lecture but I hate the "Artemus Ward" talk & won't talk it any more. No man ever approved that choice of subject in my hearing, I think.[1]

Give me some comfort. If I am to talk in New York am I going to have a good house? I don't care now to have any appointments canceled. I'll even "fetch" those Dutch Pennsylvanians with this lecture.[2]

Have paid up $4,000 indebtedness.[3] You are the last on my list. Shall begin to pay you in a few days & then I shall be a free man again.[4]

Yours,

Mark.

[1] On the evening of 1 January Clemens arrived in Indianapolis and delivered "Roughing It in Nevada," based on selections from his forthcoming book. The next day the Indianapolis *Journal* reported that he had addressed "a large, refined, and very appreciative audience, with the single exception of one young lady, who looked on mournfully while her neighbors were convulsed with laughter" ("Personal" and "Mark Twain," 2 Jan 72, 4). Clemens had delivered this "new lecture"—the third since the start of his tour on 16 October—no more than a dozen times, and since its introduction on 7 December he had twice rewritten it, once after performing what he called "the germ of it" on 7 and 8 December (*L4*, 514), and again after the Chicago *Tribune* published a detailed synopsis of it on 20 and 24 December. While reworking "Roughing It" he fell back on his previous offering, "Artemus Ward, Humorist," intermittently through 27 December. That lecture, first performed on 23 October, had received some stinging criticism from local reviewers, which no doubt reinforced his decision to replace it. Redpath prepared a new "Lyceum Circular" announcing "Roughing It," with extracts from several early reviews so that lecture committees could "advertise it properly" (*L4*, 562). This new circular must have been available by 31 December, for on 1 January the Indianapolis *Journal* quoted one of its extracts in a lecture announcement ("Amusements," 4; *L4*, 478, 480 n. 3, 481–82 n. 18, 482–83 n. 1, 486, 488 n. 1, 511–25 passim). For Clemens's 1871–72 lecture schedule, and a facsimile of the circular for "Roughing It," see *L4*, 557–63.

[2] On 11 December Clemens had expressed his concern to Redpath about the turnout expected for his 24 January lecture in New York City, asking George Fall to confirm that his appointment was indeed for a *"regular course"* selling *"season tickets"* (*L4*, 514). Redpath and Fall surely did so, perhaps in a letter Clemens replied to here, but failed to "comfort" him (see also 26 Jan 72 to Redpath). The previous October, Clemens had been unable to "fetch" the "chuckle-headed Dutch" of Bethlehem and Allentown, Pennsylvania, with the first lecture of his tour, "Reminiscences of Some un-Commonplace Characters I have Chanced to Meet" (*L4*, 472 n. 1, 474, 475 n. 1). He was now engaged to appear in seven other Pennsylvania towns, beginning with Kittanning on 12 January.

[3] Within the last two weeks, Clemens had paid the balance owed on $12,500 borrowed from Jervis Langdon in 1869 to purchase an interest in the Buffalo *Express*. He had also sent $300 to Olivia for their quarterly house rent and $300 to his mother in Fredonia (*L4*, 338–39 n. 3, 526–27).

[4] The Boston Lyceum Bureau charged its lecturers a 10 percent commission on all fees they collected from local committees. Clemens's fees for the 1871–72 season, as recorded in his lecture appointment book, totaled $9,690 through the end of January. Not recorded there were the fees for his last three lectures, all in February, but they evidently added $200 to his total. He paid the commission in two installments, sending $704.69 on 13 January and $260 on 7 March, at the same time withholding $24.31 for unusual expenses he said the bureau itself should bear (Redpath and Fall, 1–16; 13 Jan 72 to OLC; 7 Mar 72 to Redpath and Fall; Eubank, 132).

To John Henry Riley
4 January 1872 • Dayton, Ohio
(MS: NN-B)

Dayton, O., Jan. 4.[1]

Friend Riley—

Heaven prosper the Minister to S. A! Amen.[2]

"This is my thought"—as the Injuns say (but only in novels.)[3] The first day of March—or the 4th or 5th at furthest—I shall be ready for you.[4] I shall employ a good, appreciative, genial phonographic reporter who can listen first rate, & enjoy, & even throw in a word, now & then. Then we'll all light our cigars every morning, & with your notes before you, we'll talk & yarn & laugh & weep over your adventures, & the said reporter shall take it *all* down—& so, in the course of a week or so, we'll

have you & Du Toits Pan[5] & Du Toits other household & kitchen furniture all pumped dry—& away you go for Africa again & leave me to
work up & write out the book at my leisure (of which I have abundance—
very.)
How's that?
Don't say any thing about the book.
Never mind ~~Baby~~ Babe—~~the~~ his book won't hurt—opposition's the
life of trade—but of course I'd rather be out *first*. Why *didn't* you get my
letter & stay there longer.[6]

Ys

Mark.

[1] Clemens lectured in Logansport on 2 January and in Richmond, Indiana, on
3 January. His 4 January lecture in Dayton elicited "hearty laughter and frequent
applause" from a "full house," according to the Dayton *Journal*, which also described the speaker as "slightly awkward in his movements," with a

> slow-tongued and droll manner, which seem to be rather natural with him than put on
> for the occasion. His wit runs into the extravagant style, consisting of exaggerated facts,
> nonsense and absurdities; but to use his own expression, he tacks on the nonsense to
> make the facts take. ("Mark Twain's Lecture," 5 Jan 72, no page)

A Dayton correspondent of the Cincinnati *Gazette* noted on 4 January:

> Mark Twain arrived here this afternoon, putting up at the Beckel House, and writing
> in the register, in a tolerable hand, "Sam'l L. Clemens, Hartford, Conn." He was as-
> signed to room 169, and not a few admirers of the genial humorist passed the door, and
> gazed wistfully at it. Mark Twain had a whopping house to-night. He announced this
> as "my first and last appearance in Dayton," from which it may be inferred that he is
> going out of the lecture or show business. ("From Dayton," letter dated 4 January, 5
> Jan 72, 1)

[2] Riley was Clemens's intended collaborator on a book about the South African diamond fields (*L4*, 168 n. 2, 252–53 n. 1). By October 1871 he had returned
from South Africa with a commission as consul general from the Orange Free
State to the United States. He wrote Clemens from Washington on 3 December:

> I returned to Phil[a] from California on the 23[d] ult., and remained there till over
> Thanksgiving Day, and then on the 1st inst came back here. I just missed your ev'g of
> lecture at the Academy of Music, Phila [on 20 November], but bro Charlie and sisters
> Mary & Sophie were there.
>   I have perfected my idea of a Diamond sifting and washing machine but have done
> nothing yet towards getting it patented.
>   I am here doing nothing but corresponding for the ALTA   Have not yet been to
> the State Depart to be recognized as Consul Gen., but will attend to that the coming
> week. Cole says a mission to the Dutch Republics of S. A. must be created and that I
> must go out as U.S. Minister.
>   We shall see but I'd like to know what I am to do in the meantime and when you
> are going to be ready for the book work. I am pretty nearly [at] the end of the money

that old Sutro gave me in San Fran and will get nothing from the ALTA till the end of the present month. Let's hear from you. Direct to Lock-box 78 P.O. Washington. . . . You know that I have no Com. clerkship this session. (CU-MARK)

Senator Cornelius Cole of California was known to both Riley and Clemens. Riley was again corresponding for the San Francisco *Alta California*, but had not regained his position as clerk for a senate committee and was running out of money, despite what Adolph Sutro had given him (see also 11 June 72 to Sutro, n. 2). By 16 December Riley's credentials as consul general had been "recognized by the President" and "by the State Department" ("Telegraphic Notes," New York *Tribune*, 16 Dec 71, 1; "Washington Correspondence," letter dated 16 December, Carson City *State Register*, 3 Jan 72, 2). Riley explained to a correspondent of the Chicago *Times* that

> he accepted the commission tendered to him for the purpose of being able to speak officially for that government while here. Instead of retaining it, he will probably transfer it to the proper hands here, and return to Africa clothed with diplomatic authority to establish such relations with Orange as shall result in securing a lasting friendship with the United States, if not an alliance that will eventually give us a permanent foothold in the "diamond republic." ("South African Diamonds," dispatch dated 18 December, Chicago *Times*, 21 Dec 71, 1)

Clemens was replying not just to Riley's 3 December letter, but to a follow-up letter (now lost), sent because he had failed to reply sooner.

[3] Although this remark appears to refer to James Fenimore Cooper, the quotation has not been found in his works.

[4] A concession to Riley's urgency, since Clemens had previously put off beginning their book until May (*L4*, 467). Work did not, after all, begin as planned (see 27 Mar 72 to Riley).

[5] Du Toit's Pan was among the largest and best-known mining camps in the newly discovered diamond fields. It lay a few miles southeast of what is now Kimberley, South Africa, in the province of Griqualand West, just over the border from the Orange Free State. In less than a year's time it had acquired a population of sixteen thousand (Albert E. Coleman, 333; *Annual Cyclopaedia 1871*, 2).

[6] In 1871, Jerome L. Babe's "letters from the diamond fields of South Africa" to the New York *World* "first made the American people aware of their immense importance" ("Literary Notes," New York *World*, 1 July 72, 2). Babe's *South African Diamond Fields* (New York: David Wesley and Co.) would be just over a hundred pages long, in paper covers, when it was published in late June 1872. Since Riley did not mention Babe on 3 December, he must have done so in the missing follow-up letter. Clemens's letter urging Riley to prolong his stay in Africa is also lost. "Opposition (or competition) is the life of trade" was clearly proverbial for Clemens, yet this letter precedes by more than thirty years what had been identified as the first American use of the phrase (Mieder, Kingsbury, and Harder, 109, 441).

To Olivia L. Clemens
enclosing a letter (not sent) to J. H. Barton
4 January 1872 • Dayton, Ohio
(MS: CU-MARK)

ₐThe draft for $125 is enclosed.

────────────ₐ

Dayton, 4ᵗʰ—

Livy, old sweetheart, sent you another book today—Edwin of Deira.[1]

Have accepted Warner's friend's invitation—though I *always* decline private houses.

No, on second thoughts I don't *dare* to do it. A lecterurer ̶d̶e̶r̶ dreads a private house—Oh, more than he dreads 200 miles of railway travel. I must tear up my letter of acceptance.[2] In *spite* of yourself you respect their unholy breakfast hours—you can't *help* it—& then you feel drowsy & miserable for two days & you give two audiences a very poor lecture. No, I don't dare go there. I like to be perfectly free—more than that: perfectly *lawless*. Will you read this to Warner & get him to drop the Doctor a line thanking him for the invitation but "ₐkind of" explaining that the necessities of my trade make acceptance impossible? Hotels are the only proper places for lecturers. When I am ill natured I so enjoy the freedom of a hotel—where I can ring up a domestic & give him a quarter & then break ̶c̶h̶a̶i̶r̶s̶ furniture over him—then I go to bed calmed & soothed, & sleep as peacefully as a child. Would the doctor's henchmen stand that? Indeed no.

I tell you Annies & Sammy's fresh & genuine delight make squandering watches a coveted & delicious pleasure. I don't know when I have enjoyed anything so really & so heartily as Annie's letter. I wish the watch had been seven times as large, & much more beautiful.[3]

The's printed joke is *splendid*. Oh I *would* love to see Sue & The & Clara in our dear, dear Nook Barn. Hang it, though, I'll miss it all, I just know. My ̶d̶e̶l̶u̶g̶e̶ darling, I deluge you now with all my love—bail it out on them second-hand when they come.[4]

I know there are other things I ought to write, but it is so late & I am so sleepy.

Expect to put a check in this for $125—making $550 to you since ~~just be~~ (& including) Danville, Ill.[5] Telegraph receipt, if I put in the check.

With a world of love. Oh, the letters! *Never* get done writing business letters till long past midnight.

Lovingly

Sam*l.*

[*postscript is cross-written:*]

P.S.—me sick? The idea! I would as soon expect a wooden image to get sick. I don't know what sickness is.

[*enclosure:*]

Dayton, O., Jan. 4.

D*r* J. H. Barton[6]

Dear Sir—

It seems an odd thing to do, since I am a stranger, but Warner W tells me to just drop you a line saying I am coming, & then just invade your premises without further ceremony. But I'll try & not be quite *that* abrupt. I will have at least the grace to thank you very kindly & cordially for your proffered hospitality; & I shall likewise telegraph you about what hour I shall arrive, to the end that if anything has in the meantime interfered with your plans you can transfer me to the hotel & everything will be all right.

Ys Very Truly

Sam*l.* L. Clemens

You, see, Livy dear, I *wanted* to, but I didn't *dare*.

Sam*l.*

[1] This epic poem about Britain's first Christian king was written by the Scottish poet Alexander Smith (1830–67). Clemens probably sent the first American edition, which was in his library in 1910 (Boston: Ticknor and Fields, 1861; Gribben, 2:648).

[2] He desisted: see the enclosure.

[3] Clemens had selected the watches as Christmas gifts for his niece and nephew, Annie and Samuel Moffett (*L4*, 507, 510 n. 2).

4 Susan and Theodore Crane, as well as Olivia's close friend Clara Spaulding, had been visiting her in Hartford since late December. Clemens had not yet received Olivia's letter announcing their arrival (*L4*, 523 n. 2). Theodore Crane's "printed joke" has not been identified, although Clemens was more explicit about it in his next letter to Olivia, on 7 January. "Nook Barn" was presumably a nickname for the "imposing brick Gothic house" (Van Why, 7) at the corner of Forest and Hawthorn streets which the Clemenses had rented from John and Isabella Beecher Hooker since October 1871. Olivia commented to Annie Moffett, "You'd know this house was built by a Beecher. It's so queer" (*MTBus*, 123). The Hookers had built their house on a more than one-hundred-acre farm property that Hooker and his brother-in-law, Francis Gillette, purchased in 1853. It was known as "Nook Farm" because the Park River "curved about the southern part of it in such a way as to leave some thirty or forty acres within the nook" (Hooker, 170).

5 Clemens had lectured in Danville, Mattoon, and Paris, Illinois, and in Indianapolis, Logansport, and Richmond, Indiana, before arriving in Dayton. He earned $125 for each lecture, except the one in Richmond, for which he received $100. The inserted postscript at the top of the letter shows that he did enclose the check, now lost (Redpath and Fall, 9–12).

6 A resident of Lock Haven, Pennsylvania, where Clemens would lecture on 16 January. Barton had for twenty years been what he characterized as a "most intimate friend" of Charles Dudley Warner. In 1855 he may have been Warner's associate in a Philadelphia real estate business, Barton and Warner. In 1873 it was Barton who first noticed that *The Gilded Age* seemed to use the name of one of his associates, George Escol Sellers, for that irrepressible speculator, Colonel Eschol Sellers (Barton to Sellers, 26 Dec 73, PPAmP, in Hill 1962, 108; Lounsbury, ix).

To William Dean Howells
per Telegraph Operator
7 January 1872 • Wooster, Ohio
(MS, copy received: MH-H)

855

NO. 44.

HALF RATE MESSAGES.

THE WESTERN UNION TELEGRAPH COMPANY REQUIRE THAT ALL MESSAGES RECEIVED FOR TRANSMISSION SHALL BE WRITTEN ON THE BLANKS OF THE COMPANY, UNDER AND SUBJECT TO THE CONDITIONS PRINTED THEREON, WHICH CONDITIONS HAVE BEEN AGREED TO BY THE SENDER OF THE FOLLOWING HALF RATE MESSAGE.

O. H. PALMER, SEC'Y.   WILLIAM ORTON, PRES'T.[1]

~~11~~ 547   1050

DATED   Wooster Ohio   7   187 2

RECEIVED AT   Jan 7[2]

TO   W D Howells

Editor Atlantic Monthly.

Please telegraph the following to Bret Harte immediately at my cost[3] W A Kendall the poet writes that he is friendless & moneyless & is dying by inches as you know doctors say he must return to California & by sea wants to sail the fifteenth will you petition the steamship company for a pass for him & sign my name & ᴷHowells & the other boys to it & forward said pass to Kendall at three twenty three Van Buren[4] street Brooklyn I will send him fifty dollars get him some money if you can I do not know him but I know he is a good fellow and has hard luck[5]

S L Clemens

114 paid

½

Twx

[1] Oliver Hazard Palmer (1814–84) was a lawyer, former judge, Civil War veteran, and, since 1863, the secretary and treasurer of the Western Union Tele-

graph Company. William Orton (1826–78) became president of the company in July 1867. Among other changes, early in 1870 he "pushed into operation the sending of messages at half rates at night" (*NCAB*, 7:502). The "855" written at the top of the printed form was a record number indicating the count of telegrams received. The numbers "547" and "1050" were probably the time of receipt and time of delivery in Boston—presumably in the morning, since this was a half-rate message sent at night. At the bottom of the telegram, the operator noted that the "114" words of the message (address and signature were not counted) had been paid for at "½" rate, and appended his telegraphic initials, or "sign" (Gabler, 52, 80; New York *Times:* "Improving the Telegraph," 30 Oct 70, 6; "Gen. Oliver Hazard Palmer," 4 Feb 84, 2; *Western Union*, 3, 28, 40; James D. Reid, 487, 535, 547–56).

²On 6 January Clemens left for Wooster, where he was to lecture that evening (see the next letter, n. 3). The "7" on the line above and the "Jan 7" here show that the telegram was sent from Wooster and received in Boston on the same date. Clemens probably sent it after his lecture, in the early morning hours of 7 January.

³Howells became "chief-editor" of the *Atlantic Monthly* on 1 July 1871 (Howells 1979a, 375). Although he and Clemens first met in late 1869, they had only recently become better acquainted, dining several times in November 1871 with Thomas Bailey Aldrich and Ralph Keeler and, on at least one occasion, with James T. Fields and Bret Harte as well (*L3*, 382 n. 6; *L4*, 485–86 n. 3, 489). Howells first met Harte and his family in February 1871, when they were his house guests for a week, during which time Harte met and was lionized by the Boston literati. On 6 March 1871 Harte accepted a one-year, $10,000 contract to write a dozen stories for the *Atlantic* and other journals published by James R. Osgood—a contract that would soon end and would not be renewed. Clemens may well have been unsure about where to find Harte at this time, for in 1871 the Hartes moved frequently among several addresses in New York City, Rye (New York), and Newport (Rhode Island). As one of Harte's editors, Howells was likely to be informed of his current whereabouts (Merwin, 222–29, 232–33).

⁴The numbers below "Van Buren" were added by the receiving operator to indicate that the name had been counted as two words (*Western Union*, 16).

⁵William Andrew Kendall (1831?–76), a native of Massachusetts, had been a schoolteacher in Petaluma, California, before moving to San Francisco in about 1861 to pursue a literary career. He worked first as an editor for the *Golden Era*, to which he contributed poems signed "Comet Quirls," then from about 1865 to 1868 as a reporter and editor on the *Morning Call*. The "tall, black-eyed, long-haired poet" remembered by Charles Warren Stoddard (Stoddard 1907, 642) published his poems chiefly in San Francisco journals like the *Evening Bulletin, Puck*, and the *Californian*. In November 1868 he published *The Voice My Soul Heard*, a sixteen-page pamphlet containing two admonitory poems about the vanity of wealth and earthly power. It is not known when Kendall traveled to New York. Despite their years in common as San Francisco journalists (1864–66), Clemens claimed not to "know" Kendall; in any event, he did not remember him. Joaquin Miller's 1892 recollection of having seen both men in the offices of the *Golden Era*—along with several other celebrities—is not conclusive, even if accurate. Harte, however, had known Kendall and his work, and had included

three of his poems in the notoriously choosy *Outcroppings: Being Selections of California Verse* (1866). The much more catholic selection in Mary Richardson Newman's *Poetry of the Pacific* (1867) also included three. During Harte's tenure as editor of the *Overland Monthly* from 1868 to 1871, he published five Kendall poems in the magazine. Clemens's effort to enlist the charity of Harte, Howells, and "the other boys" (presumably other members of the *Atlantic* fraternity) was successful. In December 1872, a well-informed reporter for the San Francisco *News Letter and California Advertiser* wrote:

> When Mr. Kendall lay sick and destitute in New York last year, he appealed to Mr. Harte to relieve his distress; that gentleman and Mr. Clemens (Mark Twain) headed a subscription paper with which they visited their acquaintance in New York, and raised the funds necessary to relieve Mr. Kendall and pay his passage to California. At Mr. Harte's solicitation, the Pacific Mail Company allowed Mr. Kendall a first-class passage upon a second class ticket. W. A. Kendall had the claim of previous acquaintance upon Mr. Harte for these favors. He had known him in California. It appears that Kendall has been what we are constrained in accuracy to call a "literary bummer" in California for some years. He had made a precarious livelihood by writing in the papers, and wrote rhymes. At least one of these (and we think two or three) Mr. Harte admitted to the *Overland*—apologizing to his friends for their quality, but accepting them, with the knowledge of his publishers, as a distinct charity. ("W. A. Kendall," 21 Dec 72, 8)

Kendall apparently sailed from New York on 31 January aboard the Pacific Mail Steamship Company's *Henry Chauncey,* arriving in San Francisco (after changing ships in Panama) on 6 March aboard the *Alaska:* he is probably the "J. H. Kendall" and "W. H. Randall" on the passenger lists published in New York and San Francisco newspapers. He survived in San Francisco until 1876, but "as a sort of literary waif . . . utterly prostrated in health . . . poor and destitute, living on weekly contributions from newspaper men," according to an obituary in the San Francisco *Chronicle*. He committed suicide in January 1876, leaving a note that reflected with great bitterness on "these last eight years." For Kendall's further efforts to enlist Clemens's help, see 13 Mar 73 to Howells (San Francisco *Chronicle:* "Poor Kendall," 20 Jan 76, 1; "A Forgotten Poet," 14 July 89, 8; "Poem by W. A. Kendall," San Francisco *Evening Bulletin,* 7 Nov 68, 1; Kendall 1868, 1869a–d, 1870; Miller; Harte 1866, 74–85; Newman, 99–106; Langley: 1862, 224; 1863, 209; 1865, 255; 1867, 280; "Passengers Sailed," New York *Tribune,* 1 Feb 72, 3; "Shipping Intelligence," San Francisco *Morning Call,* 7 Mar 72, 4).

To Olivia L. Clemens
7 January 1872 • Wooster, Ohio
(MS: CU-MARK)

Wooster, Jan 7.[1]

Livy darling, did these clothes ever come? If so you ought to have informed me. If they did, forward the enclosed note to the tailors, along with the bill (have Orion get you a check for $89 & enclose that, too—I am out of money.) If they *didn't* come, write & tell ~~them so~~ *Redpath* so (36 Bromfield st) & enclose ~~th~~ my letter & the draft to *him* & let him see the tailors.[2]

I hired a locomotive for $75 yesterday, to keep from having to get up at 2 in the morning;[3] then I gave away $50 to a sick & needy poet,[4] & so I am about out of cash.

I enclose a couple for Theodore—but both of them put together ain't as good as that child's-trumpet story.[5]

I have been figuring. My lecture business, up to the end of January, yields about $10,000—& yet, when I preach Jan. 30, it is ~~wh~~ well I am so close to Hartford, for I would not have money enough to get home on.[6] It has all gone & is going, for those necessaries of life—debts. Every night the question is, Well, who does *this* day's earnings belong to?—& away it goes. I *do* hate lecturing, & I shall try hard to have as little as possible of it to do hereafter. The rest of my earnings will go to Ma & Redpath, principally[7]—& then what are *we* going to do, I don't reckon? *You* gave that $50 to the poet, honey, for that was the money I was going to buy you a Christmas present with. How do you like such conduct as those?

Lecturing is hateful, but it *must* come to an end yet, & *then* I'll see my darling, whom I love, love, *love.*

Love to all that jolly household & that dear old Susie.[8]

Saml.

✉————————————————————————

Mrs. S. L. Clemens | cor Forest & Hawthorne | Hartford | Conn [*postmarked:*] WOOSTER O. JAN 10

[1] After his 4 January lecture in Dayton, Clemens spoke the next evening in Columbus before a full and "appreciative" house:

> Whenever he paused, placed his left arm akimbo and his right elbow in his left hand and began to gesticulate slowly with his right hand, the next word or words he uttered was the funny point toward which all that he had been saying just before tended, and which forced the audience into convulsions. It is impossible to imitate on paper his gestures and manner of speaking. One must hear him to realize the effect of what he says. ("Mark Twain's Lecture," Columbus *Ohio State Journal*, 6 Jan 72, 4)

The *Ohio State Journal* also reprinted (without attribution) a synopsis of the lecture from the Chicago *Tribune* of 20 December, slightly altered and updated, as if it were a transcription of the Columbus lecture. "If the report don't correspond with the lecture," the *Journal* quipped, "it is the fault of the lecturer" (Columbus *Ohio State Journal:* "'Mark Twain'" and "Notes and Comments," 6 Jan 72, 1; "'Mark Twain,'" Chicago *Tribune*, 20 Dec 71, 4; *L4*, 519).

[2] The bill and Clemens's "enclosed note" have not been found, presumably because Olivia sent them to Redpath or to the tailors, both of whom were in Boston. Clemens probably bought the clothes referred to in November 1871, when he was last in that city.

[3] That is, to travel from Columbus, Ohio, to Wooster in order to lecture on the evening of 6 January. According to the Wooster *Republican*, Clemens lectured successfully to a "fair audience" and mentioned his railroading difficulties:

> Failing to make connection at Crestline [forty miles west of Wooster] he hired an engine to bring him to Wooster. He introduced his subject, "Roughing It," by a very humorous description of his trip from Crestline to Wooster. The gentleman from Wooster, of regal appearance, who accompanied him and is said to have palmed himself off as the Grand Duke, enjoys the joke immensely, but denies its foundation in fact. ("Lecture of Mark Twain," 11 Jan 72, 2)

The "gentleman from Wooster" was very likely Clemens's official host there, attorney Charles M. Yocum (Redpath and Fall, 11–12; "Attorneys," Wooster *Republican*, 11 Jan 72, 1).

[4] See the previous letter, n. 5.

[5] The enclosures have not been found, but were evidently printed jokes like the one Crane had just sent Clemens (4 Jan 72 to OLC).

[6] Actually, Clemens did not "get home" to Hartford for more than a few days until after his 1 February lecture in Troy, New York, when he returned for a three-week break. He lectured on 30 January in Jersey City, and on 31 January in Paterson, New Jersey. For his lecture income, see 2 Jan 72 to Redpath, n. 4.

[7] See 2 Jan 72 to Redpath, n. 3, and *L4*, 504 n. 4.

[8] Susan Crane.

To James Redpath
7 January 1872 • Wooster, Ohio
(MS: Axelrod)

Wooster Jan ~~5~~ 7.

Dear Redpath—

Paterson wails. Weeps for Feb. 1. I telegraphed them to fix a date with you—in January if possible; in Feb if it couldn't be helped. But *my* understanding of things is that I am at Troy Feb. 1. I wish Paterson was the day before or the day after Jersey City—though a loafing ~~in~~ day in New York is no great hardship.[1]

Did you expunge that backward march to Scranton~~+~~?[2]

Ys

Mark

Can't go on the new list of lecturers for next year yet.

⟨⊠⟩————————————————————————————

[letter docketed:] Clemens Sam L. | Wooster O | Jan. 9 '72[3]

[1] The date of the Paterson, New Jersey, lecture had been in dispute with the lecture committee since August 1871, but was finally set by Redpath for 31 January 1872, the day after Clemens's lecture in Jersey City (*L4*, 456 n. 7, 502 n. 6, 503 n. 1). Redpath explained his management of the dispute in a long letter of 18 January, which reached Clemens in Baltimore on 23 January (CU-MARK):

BOSTON, Jan[y] 18 187 2.

S L Clemens, Esqr.,—Travelling:
 Dear Mark— When you reach Paterson, N. J., you will find, possibly,—probably—an indignant Secretary, who threatens, I think—for his language seems to smell of gunpowder—to complain to you of our course in refusing to give him February 1. As his statements will probably end in an appeal for an abatement of fee, I write now to say—*Dont abate;* & then to explain the case—as it stands. He thinks there are "inconsistencies" in our correspondence & possibly he thinks so from the fact that we had to be careful to conceal the engagement you promised Troy, Feb 1;—& *you* forgot that agreement, I guess, when you telegraphed to Paterson about a February date some time since.
 Here are the facts:—
Aug 26 We promised them February 1 in these words:—
 "*Twain*—Feb 1, or a date within 2 or 3 days of it[.] He may insist on closing his list in
  January. If so, your date w[d] have to be moved back a little into ~~February~~
  ᴀJanuary,"
 On *Sept 1* we wrote again:—
 "*Twain*—Feb 1 or thereabout. Presume you noted our remarks about Mark Twain's
  date"—in previous letter.

————————————

 When we made out your book, you had already instructed us to put nothing in February. We therefore did not enter the Paterson date in your book at all, intending— as Fall you remember explained to you previously, to move it back into January.
 You went to Albany. There the hero of Troy besieged you, & finaly carried you by assault. You told him that Feb 1 w[d] do.
 Well, Troy had telegraphed for Feb. 8. We telegraphed you. You answered with a "word with a bark to it—No[.]" Hearing no more from you on Troy we supposed Troy pledged for Feb 1. We wrote to them & found that they had "entered" you on their course & had advertised you for Feb 1. We then wrote to Paterson to change their date. They did not answer us. They wrote you. You know your reply. We w[d] have been glad to let Paterson have Feb 1, of course; there was no reason why we sh[d] not oblige them if we c[d] as well as not—or in fact at all; *but* your promise to Troy, their acceptance & announcement of Feb 1 closed the door agst Paterson.
 When the Paterson man therefore wrote to us that you had consented to Feb 1, we simply said you had doubtless forgotten an "arrangement" for that date which you had previously made, & that, owing to it, you c[d] not come Feb 1. So they change. We did not think it best to explain about Troy—as it was none of their business and it w[d] only have made them ~~so~~ angry that Troy sh[d] be preferred even altho it had the right of priority[.]
 Now, when you read the correspondence over, in the light of these facts, you will see we did our level best both for Paterson & you. Does Roughing it still go smoothly?
         Yours truly
          Jas Redpath

[2]Clemens had lobbied for eliminating the Scranton lecture as early as 23 November (*L4*, 502), but Redpath was unable to do so. Clemens lectured as scheduled on 29 January, following a few days at home in Hartford. The Scranton engagement might have been more logically scheduled in mid-January with other lectures in central Pennsylvania.

[3]In the hand of the Boston Lyceum Bureau's clerk, George H. Hathaway, who in this case misread the date of the letter.

To Olivia L. Clemens
8 January 1872 • Salem, Ohio
(MS: CU-MARK)

Salem, Jan. 8.[1]

Livy darling, I got your dispatch announcing safe arrival of all the checks.[2]

Well, slowly this lecturing penance drags toward the end. Heaven knows I shall be glad when I get far away from these country communities of wooden-heads. Whenever I want to go ƿ away from New England again, lecturing, please show these letters to me & bring me to my senses. How I do chafe & sweat when I count up the Dutch audiences I have yet to play the fool before.

I want to *see* you—writing is no good. Speed the day! I *love* you, darling.

Sam[*l*].

✉————————————————————————————

Mrs. Sam[*l*]. L. Clemens | Cor. Forest & Hawthorne sts | Hartford | Conn.
[*postmarked:*] SALEM O. JAN 9

[1]The Salem *Republican* judged that Clemens's 8 January lecture "as a whole" did not meet expectations. It praised "some passages of fine description and word painting," but complained that "no one could tell when he told the truth or when he was indulging in fiction, and when he was half through, his hearers had lost confidence in his sayings, and did not *expect* to be told anything on which they could rely" (10 Jan 72, transcript in CU-MARK courtesy of William Baker).

[2]See 4 Jan 72 to OLC, n. 5.

To Olivia L. Clemens
10 January 1872 • Steubenville, Ohio
(MS: CU-MARK)

Steubenville, Jan. 9.

Livy Darling, I am stopping at the Female Seminary—70 of the girls were at the lecture last night, & a mighty handsome lot they were.[1]

These windows overlook the Ohio—once alive with steamboats & crowded with all manner of traffic; but now a deserted stream, victim of the railroads. Where be the pilots. They were starchy boys, in my time, & greatly envied by the youth of the West. The same with the Mississippi pilots—though the Mobile & Ohio Railroad had already walked suddenly off with the passenger business in my day, & so it was the beginning of the end.[2]

I am reading "The Member from Paris" a very bright, sharp, able French political novel, very happily translated. It is all so good & so Frenchy that I don't know where to mark.[3] I have read & sent home The Golden Legend, The New England Tragedies, Edwin of Deira, Erling the Bold, & a novel by the author of John Halifax—forgotten the name of it.[4]

DID MY CANVASSING BOOK, FULL OF LECTURE MSS REACH YOU FROM PARIS? You do not mention it.[5]

There is no life in me this morning—have slept too long & hard. Love to all those dear fellows under the roof, & cords & cords of love to you, Livy my darling.

Sam¹.

✉———————————————————————————————

Mrs. Sam*¹*. L. Clemens | Cor. Forest & Hawthorne sts | Hartford | *Conn.*
[*return address:*] IF NOT DELIVERED WITHIN 10 DAYS, TO BE RETURNED TO [*postmarked:*] STEUBENVILLE O. JAN 11

[1]Clemens wrote on 10 (not 9) January, the morning after he lectured to a "large audience" for the YMCA course in Steubenville (Steubenville *Gazette:* "Here and There," 12 Jan 72; "New Advertisements," 5 Jan 72, both no page). Clemens noted in his lecture appointment book that his Steubenville hosts wanted him "to stop at Seminary like Gough" (Redpath and Fall, 12). The Steubenville Female Seminary (1829–98) occupied several buildings on an extensive

landscaped site overlooking the Ohio River. It offered its students an unusually strong academic program, and was regarded as the "educational and social center of a large community. Statesmen, authors, musicians and lecturers of international fame were frequent guests" ("The Steubenville Female Seminary," Steubenville *Herald*, 29 Sept 1926, no page; Weisenburger, 174).

²Competition between railroads and steamboats on the Ohio was first joined in 1854; by 1857, with the advent of daily passenger trains between Cincinnati and St. Louis, the railroads had won. During the same period the Mobile and Ohio Railroad and the New Orleans, Jackson, and Great Northern Railroad were extended northward paralleling the Mississippi. Continuous rail service between Cincinnati and New Orleans was in place by 1859 and was expected to "take a large passenger business from the steamers," according to a Cincinnati report on commerce. With the interruption caused by the war, however, "rail service improved so slowly on this route that twenty years were to pass before the position of steamboats on the Mississippi below Cairo was seriously threatened" (Hunter, 485–86). Clemens dealt briefly with the same events in chapter 15 of *Life on the Mississippi:*

> First, the new railroad stretching up through Mississippi, Tennessee, and Kentucky, to Northern railway centres, began to divert the passenger travel from the steamers; next the war came and almost entirely annihilated the steamboating industry during several years . . . ; and finally, the railroads intruding everywhere, there was little for steamers to do, when the war was over, but carry freights; so straightway some genius from the Atlantic coast introduced the plan of towing a dozen steamer cargoes down to New Orleans at the tail of a vulgar little tug-boat; and behold, in the twinkling of an eye, as it were, the association and the noble science of piloting were things of the dead and pathetic past! (SLC 1883, 191–92)

³*The Member for Paris: A Tale of the Second Empire* by "Trois-Étoiles" (Boston: J. R. Osgood and Co., 1871) was not a translation; it was written by English journalist Eustace Clare Grenville Murray (1824–81), who was living in exile in Paris to avoid prosecution in an 1869 libel case (Griffiths, 430–31).

⁴Besides Alexander Smith's *Edwin of Deira*, mentioned previously (4 Jan 72 to OLC), Clemens listed Longfellow's *Golden Legend* (1851) and *New-England Tragedies* (1868), which he is known to have owned, respectively, in an 1862 and a first edition. His library would also include the 1870 American edition of Robert Michael Ballantyne's *Erling the Bold: A Tale of the Norse Sea-Kings* (1869). The novel by Dinah Maria (Mulock) Craik, author of *John Halifax, Gentleman* (1856), may have been *Christian's Mistake* (1865), which Clemens owned in an 1871 reprint by Harper and Brothers (Gribben, 1:43, 162, 420). Olivia had already received *The Golden Legend*. On 7 January she had written Clemens the following letter (CU-MARK), directing it to Bellefonte, Pennsylvania, where she expected him to lecture on 15 January (see 17 Jan 72 to Redpath, n. 3):

(LLC)

                                                              Hartford Jan 7ᵗʰ 1872
My Youth
        You have seemed so near and dear to me, if any thing more than usually so, since last evening— Clara and I got to talking of you and I felt so rich in you and thankful for you, I could not help going to the tin box when I went to my room it is never very safe for me to go there, however I did not read any of the oldest love letters, only some that were written since we were married, when you were in New York after the

baby was born—how sweet the memory ~~connected with~~ ˏof allˏ our love life is—often when I get to thinking of you I would like to have a good cry, a happy, thankful cry it would be—but at such times it is hard not to be able to put out my hand and touch you— Last night I had a vivid dream of your return, a natural dream, in my sleep I did all the things that I should have done waking if you had returned to me, put my hand in yours, stroked your hair, did every thing that should make me really conscious of your presence— Youth don't you think it is very sweet to love as we love?

This morning Theodore, Clara and I went to church. Mr Twichell gave us a good ~~av~~ a *very good* sermon—of course I thought much of you and wanted you— When I went in ⟩ & saw that it was the communion service, my heart sank because I do feel so unfit to go to the table of communion, yet cannot bear to go away from it— Mr Twichells gave such an *earnest* invitation to all those who were feeling cold and far away from God and discouraged to stay and get comfort, that I could not come away— I staid and of course my prayers were for you and myself and our boy— Oh a Father and Mother do have so much to pray for, so very much that they need guidance in— I do love Joseph Twichell, he is a good man—a Godly man— I love to hear him preach and pray— I feel at home there— Clara says she was never in a strange church where she felt so much at home as she did there—

Darling if you are not going to be able to come home the 25ᵗʰ if any lecture has been appointed for that evening be sure and tell me—because I am so depending on that time— If Redpath has not already filled up those three evenings 25ᵗʰ, 26ᵗʰ & 27ᵗʰ I wish you would telegraph him not ~~do~~ to do it, I think we should like to look upon each other's faces by that time— Don't you? I wish that there was a train after you lecture that would bring you in here at one or two o'clock—you should not walk out and carry your carpet bags—

Evening—
We had a long and very pleasant call from Mr Perkins this afternoon—he told us a good deal about his moose hunting experience in Nova Scotia this winter— Mrs Perkins has gone to Boston to be gone two or three days—

I think The Golden Legend is beautiful   I wonder you did not mark it still more than you have, but I am so very glad you marked it at all, I do so heartily enjoy the books that you have marked— I have not yet rec'd the one that you gave the Syracuse City Missionary, telling him to send it to me— I cannot afford to lose any thing that you have marked, so hope he will not fail to send it— Do you get my letters regularly? I suppose of course you do though, as you say nothing to the contrary— The baby is well and as sweet as can be only not as devoted to his Mother as she would like to have him— You will see a change in the little fellow— With the same old love Livy—

Olivia mentioned lawyer Charles E. Perkins and his wife, Lucy, who lived on Woodland Street, just beyond the Nook Farm neighborhood (*L3*, 294 n. 4; Geer 1872, 108; Van Why, 7). For the book given to the "Syracuse City Missionary," James P. Foster, see *L4*, 507–8 n. 3.

⁵Clemens had lectured in Paris, Illinois, on 30 December. From there he may have sent home the manuscript for any of three lectures used on his tour—"Reminiscences," "Artemus Ward," or even "Roughing It"—protected by the nearly seventy leaves of a "canvassing book" (salesman's prospectus) for *Roughing It*, a copy of which he had received from Bliss by 27 November. No manuscript for "Reminiscences" and only one page of the "Artemus Ward" lecture are known to survive; about two dozen pages of miscellaneous notes for the "Roughing It" lecture are in the Mark Twain Papers (*L4*, 479 n. 2, 500 n. 2; SLC 1871j). It is barely possible that Clemens was referring instead to manuscripts for a projected "volume of 'Lecturing Experiences,'" one of which he sent home at this time, either from or shortly after leaving Paris (see the next letter, n. 6).

To Olivia L. Clemens
10 and 11 January 1872 • Wheeling, W. Va.,
and Pittsburgh, Pa.
(MS: CU-MARK)

Wheeling, 10th
Livy darling, it was perfectly splendid—no question about it—the liv-
est, quickest audience I almost ever saw in my life.[1]
M̸

Pittsburgh 11th.
This was the largest audience ever assembled in Pittsburgh to hear a lecture, some say. Great numbers were turned away—couldn't get in; stage
was jam-full; ~~three~~ all the private boxes full—~~bo~~ Seems to me there were
three tiers of them.[2]

Sweetheart I sent the $300 draft purposely for Hooker—came near
having it drawn in his name——however it is no matter.[3]

Am so glad you are having such jolly sociable times with our Elmira
folks & the Clemenses & the neighbors.[4] I would give the *world* (if I had
another one like it,) to be out of this suffering lecture business & at home
with you,—for I love you, Livy darling.

If I had been at Mrs. Stowe's reading[5] & they wanted any help, I
would have read about "Fat-Cholley Aitheřns" & the rest of my little
darkey's gossip. I think I could swing my legs over the arms of a chair &
that boy's spirit would descend upon me & enter into me. I am glad Warner likes the sketch. I must keep it for my volume of "Lecturing Experiences"—but I'm afraid I'll have to keep it a good while, for I *can't* do
without those unapproachable names of the Aithens family—nor "Tarry
Hote,"—nor any of those things—ɟ & if I were to print the sketch *now* I
should have the whole "fo'-teen" after me.[6]
As

Well, love in abundance to you—& to the cubbie & the folks.[7]
Sam'.

◼━━

Mrs. Sam¹. L. Clemens | Cor Forest & Hawthorne | Hartford | Conn.
[*return address:*] IF NOT DELIVERED WITHIN 10 DAYS, TO BE RETURNED TO [*post-marked:*] PITTSBURGH PA. JAN 1◇

¹According to the Wheeling *Intelligencer,* "The hall was crowded with the most intelligent and refined people of the city, who had a high appreciation of the lecture, if we may judge from the almost continuous laughter and applause that greeted it." The lecturer

> very much resembles the pictures that are meant to represent him in his great book, "Innocents Abroad," except that he don't wear the check trowsers on the lecture stand that he wore in the holy land. He is a youngish looking man of somewhere about thirty-five, not handsome, but having a bright and intelligent look, and eyes with a merry twinkle that put him at once *en rapport* with an audience, and that have a fashion of snapping just as he comes to the crisis of the joke. He was dressed very neatly in a black suit, the upper garment being black frock coat, closely buttoned. He is clean shaven except a heavy dark moustache; and his manner of wearing his hair, which is abundant, shows that he is his own tonsorial artist. His style of oratory is not unlike that of Artemus Ward. He has the same dry, hesitating, stammering manner, and his face, aside from the merry light in his eyes, is as grave as the visage of an undertaker when screwing down the coffin lid. He appears to labor under some embarrassment in not knowing just how to dispose of his arms and hands, but this only heightens the drollery of his manner, and may be merely a "stage trick." ("Mark Twain," 11 Jan 72, 4)

The reviewer for the Wheeling *Register* reported, "We passed an hour or two in his company after the lecture and after listening to his inexhaustible fund of stories, his exquisite humor and style, cannot but feel that the world would be better if we had more Mark Twains." Before Clemens finally left for Pittsburgh on the afternoon of 11 January he also received a large group of Wheeling citizens who were "anxious to make the acquaintance of the man whose pilgrimage had so delighted them." To them he mentioned his family association with Wheeling through Sherrard Clemens (1820–80), a congressman for the Wheeling district in the 1850s, as well as "other distant relatives in the city" (Wheeling *Register,* 11 Jan 72 and 12 Jan 72, quoted in "Mark Twain Lectured in Wheeling a Century Ago," Richwood *West Virginia Hillbilly,* 21 Apr 1973, 1, 14; *L1,* 346 n. 6).

²For two reviews of the Pittsburgh lecture, see 13 Jan 72 to OLC.

³On 28 December Clemens sent Olivia a check for $300, but neglected to say that it was intended as payment for their quarterly rent (*L4,* 526–27 n. 3). John Hooker's receipt, dated 5 January (CU-MARK), indicates that Olivia made the payment in any case, as she must have reported in a letter of 5 or 6 January (now lost).

⁴Some of the "jolly sociable times" with Clara Spaulding, the Cranes, Orion and Mollie Clemens, and various neighbors must have been mentioned in Olivia's lost letter of 5 or 6 January, which presumably also described Harriet Beecher Stowe's reading (see the next note). The Clemenses' Nook Farm neighbors included several interrelated households. On Forest Street, for instance, besides John and Isabella Beecher Hooker, lived their eldest daughter, Mary

Hooker Burton, and her husband, lawyer Henry Eugene Burton; Francis Gillette (1807–79), senator from Connecticut in 1854 and 1855, and his wife, Elisabeth Hooker Gillette (1813–93), John Hooker's sister; their daughter, Elisabeth (Lilly) Gillette Warner, and her husband, George H. Warner, Charles Dudley Warner's younger brother. Charles Dudley and Susan (Lee) Warner, Hartford residents since 1860, lived across from the Hooker house, on Hawthorn Street. Calvin Ellis Stowe (1802–86), a retired professor of theology, and his wife, Harriet Beecher Stowe, had moved into their dream house, Oakholm, near the southern edge of Nook Farm, in 1864, but the house proved hard to maintain, and they left it in 1870; they would not again become permanent residents of the neighborhood until 1873, when they purchased attorney Franklin Chamberlin's house at 1 Forest Street (*L2*, 146 n. 5; *L3*, 143 n. 11, 407 n. 3; *L4*, 313 n. 9, 456 nn. 1, 6, 505 n. 8, 523–24 n. 2; Andrews, 5, 6; Van Why, 4, 20–21, 42, 72; "Nook Farm Genealogy," 15, 30; "Hartford Residents," Gillette Family, 1–2; Geer: 1870, 276; 1872, 41, 44, 63, 79, 133; 1873, 129).

[5] Harriet Beecher Stowe read selections from her latest book, *Sam Lawson's Oldtown Fireside Stories* (1872), at Hartford's Seminary Hall on the evening of 5 January to "an exceedingly friendly and appreciative audience," according to the Hartford *Courant*. "No writer has so well portrayed the life of a rural New England town, and Mrs. Stowe is entirely familiar with the appropriate pronunciation and inflection." The reading was a benefit for the reconstruction of a church in Mandarin, Florida, where Mrs. Stowe maintained a winter home (Hartford *Courant:* "Readings by Mrs. Stowe," 1 Jan 72, 2; "Mrs. Stowe's Reading," 6 Jan 72, 2).

[6] Clemens's projected "volume of 'Lecturing Experiences'" never materialized, at least in part because of the inherent difficulties of the theme, which he had recognized as early as 1869:

> Lecturing experiences, deliciously toothsome and interesting as they are, must be recounted only in secret session, with closed doors. Otherwise, what a telling magazine article one could make out of them. I lectured all over the States, during the entire winter and far into the spring, and I am sure that my salary of twenty-six hundred dollars a month was only about half of my pay—the rest was jolly experiences. (SLC 1869b)

He waited almost three years to publish his sketch; it appeared in the New York *Times* on 29 November 1874 as "Sociable Jimmy," with the following preface:

> [I sent the following home in a private letter, some time ago, from a certain little village. It was in the days when I was a public lecturer. I did it because I wished to preserve the memory of the most artless, sociable, and exhaustless talker I ever came across. He did not tell me a single remarkable thing, or one that was worth remembering; and yet he was himself so interested in his small marvels, and they flowed so naturally and comfortably from his lips that his talk got the upperhand of my interest, too, and I listened as one who receives a revelation. I took down what he had to say, just as he said it—without altering a word or adding one.] (SLC 1874d)

The "certain little village" was Paris, Illinois, where Clemens lectured on 30 December, and stayed over, probably until the morning of 1 January (*L4*, 527–30). The extensive "Aithens family" was undoubtedly that of Josiah F. and Catharine Athon of Paris. Josiah Athon, listed as a fifty-three-year-old "hotel keeper" in the 1870 county census, then had nine children (five boys and four girls) living at home. William, the eldest, aged thirty-one, was listed in the census as a "hotel clerk" and further identified by an 1879 local history as the "accommodating clerk" at the Paris House hotel, where Clemens stayed. Charles, aged eight, was probably the "Fat-Cholley" mentioned in Clemens's letter. In the published sketch, "Sociable Jimmy" himself may have been young William Evans, whose family—one of the few black families in Paris—lived next door to the Athons. William was six or seven years old at the time of Clemens's visit (information courtesy of Nicole Remesnick; Hammond, 239–40; *History of Edgar County*, 590). Clemens had "Jimmy" explain that "Dey's fo'-teen in dis fam'ly 'sides de ole man an' de ole 'ooman—all brothers an' sisters. But some of 'em don't live heah." He also conflated the landlord father and his son William, the clerk, and disguised both family and place names: "the landlord—a kindly man, verging toward fifty"—was "Bill Nubbles," and the fictional towns of "Ragtown" and "Dockery" were named rather than the boy's "Tarry Hote" (Terre Haute, Indiana, about twenty-five miles east of Paris). Clemens also indicated that he had written the names of the Athon family on the flyleaf of his copy of Longfellow's *New-England Tragedies*, one of the books he said on 10 January had already been "sent home" (SLC 1874d; 10 Jan 72 to OLC, n. 4; Redpath and Fall, 9–10; *L4*, 128–29 n. 3).

⁷ A copy of the "Lyceum Circular" that Redpath and Fall recently distributed for Clemens (2 Jan 72 to Redpath, n. 1) has been housed with this letter at least since it was purchased from Jacques and Clara Clemens Samossoud in 1952. The letter does not mention the document, but Clemens probably enclosed it. Redpath and Fall sent Clemens a small supply of circulars on 22 January, care of William A. Sherman, corresponding secretary of the New York Mercantile Library Association (CU-MARK), but the folds in the copy with this letter show that it was never part of that later package (Mercantile Library, "Officers . . . for 1871–72"). For the full text of the enclosure, see *L4*, 562–63.

To Olivia L. Clemens
12 January 1872 • Kittanning, Pa.
(MS: CU-MARK)

Kittanning, 12ᵗʰ
Livy darling, this is a filthy, stupid, hateful Dutch village, like *all* Pennsylvania—& I have got to lecture to these leatherheads tonight—but

shall leave for ~~Putt~~ Pittsburgh at 3 in the morning, & spend Sunday in
that black but delightful town.

   Am up for dinners & things there.[1] I *love* you, Livy darling.

                                                                     Sam*l*.

☒——

Mrs. Sam*l* L. Clemens | Cor Forest & Hawthorne | Hartford | Conn. [*return address:*] IF NOT DELIVERED WITHIN 10 DAYS, TO BE RETURNED TO [*postmarked:*] PITTSBURGH PA. JAN 10◊

[1] No reviews of Clemens's performance in Kittanning have been found. With
no lecture scheduled on the weekend, Clemens planned to make the thirty-five-
mile rail journey back to Pittsburgh early on Saturday morning, 13 January. His
favorable impression of Pittsburgh dated from his successful lectures there in
November 1868 and November 1869 (*L2*, 282–83, 298; *L3*, 382 n. 2).

To Olivia L. Clemens
13 January 1872 • Pittsburgh, Pa.
(MS: CU-MARK)

$*150*.

                                                        Pittsburgh, Jan. 13.
Livy darling, just been sending you a long dispatch. *All* the papers speak
highly, but I have duplicates of only 2 (enclosed.)[1]

   Livy dear, don't send any patent rubbish to me—send it to Bliss—
the whole thing is in his hands.[2]

   I send Redpath $700[00] today[3] & you $150. Please acknowledge.

   Most lovingly & in a great hurry

                                                                     Sam*l*.

ₐI enclosed the autograph for Mrs. Hooker.ₐ[4]

[*enclosure:*][5]

TSBURGH DAILY GAZETTE

NEWS.

y reference to a card on
l be seen that the Da-
ted a Board of Direc-
ear that will compare
pard in the city. The
dent and Cashier are
positions, and will no
e places to the entire
iders.

lunteer
erary paper, the
n commenced in
own & Co. It
and promises
cess. It will
t, poetry, edi-
nd a depart-
of soldiers, in
pe given to mat-
varrants and the
rs and their wid-
laws relating to
e especially fitted
s one of them has
cted witn the press
a very prominent
ecialty of claim and
imber contains the
g tale called Fletch-
of the Crescent, by
umber of complete
new enterprise has

iesale Grocers, Nos.
nd Avenue.
se, so well estab-
at present enlarg-
ilities for supplying
new customers.
been entered into
that may be made
ly engaged very
ess, in connection
ave the exclusive

MARK TWAIN.

Roughing It at Library Hall.

Mark Twain gave his new lecture "Roughing
it" at Library Hall last night. The audience
upon the occasion, evinced in a melancholy
degree the truth of the oft quoted assertion
that the "public are fickle," for when the
genial humorist and man who, by his own
confession, says he *can* tell a lie, but *wont*, appeared in our city the last time there were
many who registered secret and open vows
that they never would hear him again being so
influenced, partly from the fact that his lecture then was not altogether so brilliant as
was anticipated, and partly perhaps
because of the exhaustion produced from
the merriment occasioned by the few "humorous remarks" he then did make. The vows were
doubtless meant to be kept, and may be they
were; but somehow there seemed to be no di-
minution of the familiar faces at Library Hall
last night, and the company being further increased by a large concourse who do not generally find attraction in the lecture hall, the
consequence was that Mark was greeted with
an immeasurably larger audience than he
heretofore looked upon in Pittsburgh, and one
which in every respect has never perhaps been
excelled. Some of the people dropped in on
Wednesday evening, it is said to "be in time
to get a seat." We don't endorse that, but certainly a great many dropped in quite early
last evening and they kept coming until there
was no room in the parquette, nor in the parquette circle, nor in the balcony, nor in the
gallery away back, and then the is ailles were
filled with ladies and gentlemen standing and
the boxes, even the highest tier could hold no
more, and the stage last of all provided accommodation for over a hundred. There
would still have been many more in attendance but they couldn't get in nor within ear-
shot of the speaker, and they formed a mournful procession on the retreat.

The lecturer was somewhat late in coming
and in response to the occasional expressions
of impatience from the audience, Mr. W. N.
Howard about eight o'clock announced that
he had arrived in the city but half an hour
previous and was then winding his devious

BOOTBL
THE mo
healthy c
THE firs
march on
MUD, ir
tery, was
AN OLI
Second a
moved to
THE Ri
of makin
be held
two o'cl
THE ME
been on a
city yest
Western
principal
THE ne
indicatin
names c
can be
fice, on
AN OL
on Wed
press tr
was mov
man's inju
THE pray
dent and all
and for the
temperance.
The Christian
gaged in Chri
WE receiver
ed army office
Texas, the fol
just read yo
tribute to the
The memorial
THE meat s
corner of Six
yesterday, wh
sum of money
dollars taken
trator of the t
THE winter

s called "Heart's
atural leaf, which
ining the popular
. Their line of gro-
most complete and
aking this into con-
vith the established
e and square dealing
ecessarily bespeak for
patronage from their
recommend them very
y to new ones. Give
holesale stores, Nos. 130
.

Letters

e Pittsburgh postoffice

Pine Flats, Pa., 3c; N. H.
Ohio, 3c; Mary Braun,
, 3c; W. G. Brownson,
eo. W. Conn, Florence,
ham, Cunningham, Pa.,
anday Creek, Pa., 1c;
iladelpia, Pa., 3c;
Pa., 3c; Josephine
nia, 1c; Mrs. M. E.
; Ewing Searight,
repaugh, Philadel-
owler, Chicago, Ill.,
omerfield P. O., Ohio,
Spring Valley, N. Y.,
Parker's Landing, Pa.,
n, Sharpsburgh, Pa., 1c;
ille, Mo., 1c; Mr. Hunter,
Lafayette Gas Co., Lafay-
, Huff & Co., Chestnut
Pa., 3c; Mrs. McDonough,
, 3c; Lizzie Plankinton,
Millie Peterson, Mans-
es Buffner, Blairsville,
, Beaver Falls, Pa., 1c;
earfield, Pa., 3c; Isaac
O., Pa., 3c; J. B. Taylor,
Wade, Baltimore, Md.,
Brighton, Pa,, 3c.
H. STEWART, P. M.

e Pulpit.

shop of W. W.
et, a pulpit made
marbleized, and
late design. Mr.
oldest and most ex-
all kinds of marble
marbelizing pro-
ere his customers
ry kind of work for
ocess secures a bet-
finish than is pos-
the marble itself.
that any

way through Pittsburgh's thoroughfares to
the hall. Twenty minutes later a small man
with half-shut, dreamy eyes, and a queer,
comical expression of countenance, as if its
possessor was in doubt whether to laugh
or cry, the mouth on the upper side
rimmed in with a short, thick, sandy-
colored moustache and the chin barren of any
hirsute adornment—a little man arrayedin a
black dress suit and supporting a glittering
diamond ring on one finger, quietly edged his
way through the crowd on the stage, and so
quickly that he stood in the centre of the
small space reserved for the lecturer before
the audience knew what the movement
meant. He introduced himself as Mark
Twain, adopting as he said that method of
getting in all the facts before proceeding with
the details of his discourse.

The audience then for an hour and a quarter
were treated to a literary compound of brilliant description and hard material facts,
giving the romance and reality of "roughing
it" in Nevada, and all picturesquely inter-
woven with jokes and happy strokes of wit,
which came so frequent and were so transparent that the merriment seemed hardly for
an instant to cease. And then the most con-
summate stroke as all was that of which five
reporters were made the victims—five inde-
fatigable pencil destroyers, who for all that
hour and a quarter, repressing every outflow
of humor, had sedately toiled at their craft
and retired elate with the prospects of the
rich feast in store for their readers to-day—
prospects which were, alas, dispelled by a
call from the genial joker himself, who
suavely preferred his request for a suppres-
sion of the "notes" taken, for the good of the
community and the happiness of himself, as
he "traveled some on those remarks." A
brother journalist could not be denied, and
thus the vision melted away.

Mr. Clemens seemed to be in his happiest
vein last night, and never in matter or manner compressed more that was enjoyable. His
"roughing it" in the lecture field has evidently given him a new insight into popular feeling, of which he has not been slow to avail
himself. The effort financially to the managers, happily to the lecturer, and enjoyably
in the highest degree to the people, was a signal success, which has doubly increased the
hold of the humorist on popular favor in this
community.

The next lecture of the course will be delivered on Tuesday evening next by Olive Logan, who will talk of "Nice Young Men."

POLICE NOTES.

Brief Mention of Criminalities.

The little girl Victoria Sinigo, who was in
the lock-up last night before last on a charge of
otorder taken to the House of

16th; at Oil Cit
and St. Mary's
January 24th.
have been air
whom this noti
attend.

ON Wednes
Robert McDon,
severely bitten
belonging to on
Chess, Smythe
moned and dre
is said the dog
ber of other r
that an informa
owner of the b

IN the prese
street, it is w
many collisions
vehicles to rec
terday aftern/
light spring w
horse and d
of the stre
fortunate
man, bea

THE S
firmed
case o
road
is sh
the
ed,
rec
fre
—I
wh

Ye
CRIMINAL
The first case
that of John Gap
sault and batter
with a knife. T
guilty.
Gap was then
charge—that of a
tery, in the kno
Evan Evans. The
ple assault and b
ferred in both case
The next case t
Haner, charged w
striking James Wi
is on trial.
Trial 1
Commonwealth
Wm. Smith,
James Vaus,
Jno. Wagoner,
Jos. Cullinan,
Michael Graham,

Mrs. Sam*l*. L. Clemens | Cor Forest & Hawthorne | Hartford | Conn.

[*return address:*] IF NOT DELIVERED WITHIN 10 DAYS, TO BE RETURNED TO [*post-marked:*] PITTSBURGH PA. JAN 10

¹Clemens's "long dispatch" (presumably a telegram) has not been found or further identified. Only the Pittsburgh *Gazette* review of Clemens's 11 January lecture survives with the letter (see note 5). The other enclosed review may have been the one in the Pittsburgh *Commercial*, possibly written by his friend William C. Smythe (19 Apr 72 to Bliss, n. 2). It is transcribed here in its entirety:

MARK TWAIN.

The Lecture Last Evening.

    Library Hall was crowded to repletion last evening to listen to Mark Twain's lecture, "Roughing It." The gentleman did not arrive in the city until a short time before the hour announced for his appearance, and the consequence was that the large audience was kept in waiting for some time before Mr. Twain made his appearance. He was preceded by Mr. Howard, of the Lecture Committee, who announced that the next lecture of the course would be delivered on Tuesday evening by Olive Logan, when she will discourse on "Nice Young Men."

    On making his appearance Mr. Twain introduced himself in a very humorous manner. He then gave some very interesting descriptions of life in Nevada, its mountains[3] lakes and rivers; the inhabitants, soil, birds, beasts, &c., which were most pleasantly interwoven with a series of telling jokes, humorous hits and, apparently, unconsciously delivered sallies of wit which convulsed the entire audience in the most uproarious laughter. To publish one of the lecturer's humorous points would be but to debar a host of the readers of the COMMERCIAL in other cities in this vicinity, where Mr. Clemens will appear, from enjoying them as they fall from the lecturer's lips.

    All present last evening appeared to thoroughly enjoy "Roughing it" and manifested their delight in the most effective manner. Mr. Clemens lectures in Kittanning to-night. (12 Jan 72, 4)

²Clemens had been granted a patent for "Mark Twain's Elastic Strap" in December 1871. In a postscript to her letter of 30 and 31 December, Olivia reported that his "patent right documents" had come (*L4*, 524); in a later letter she may have offered to send them to him (*L4*, 453, 462–64; see 20 July 72 to Bliss, n. 2).

³Clemens was paying the first installment of the Boston Lyceum Bureau's commission (see 2 Jan 72 to Redpath, n. 4). He actually sent $704.69—as he noted in his lecture appointment book—in at least two drafts (see the next letter; Redpath and Fall, 11).

⁴The autograph for Isabella Beecher Hooker has not been found. Clemens wrote this sentence in the bottom margin with the paper reversed.

⁵Clemens cut the enclosure from page 4 of the Pittsburgh *Gazette* of 12 January 1872. It is reproduced here in two parts, although the original clipping is one piece. The *Gazette* mentioned that as many as five reporters made stenographic records of the lecture, but they were suppressed at Clemens's particular request (see also the Pittsburgh *Commercial* review quoted in note 1). According to a later report, one newspaper ignored the request:

    Mark Twain's lecture was stenographed by a Pittsburg reporter and published. Mark took his little shot-gun and called on the reporter. The reporter said that he had been instructed to take it. "Yes," said Mark, "and if my pocket book had been on the table you would have been instructed to take that too, I suppose." ("Personal," Buffalo *Express*, 26 Jan 72, 2)

Even before this report appeared, the Pittsburgh *Gazette* of 15 January abandoned its friendly view of Clemens, taking umbrage at his threat not to lecture in Pittsburgh again:

MARK TWAIN will hardly ever again come to the city as a lecturer. We are duly sorry for the city. He thinks the newspaper reporters are little better than thieves, because they stole the *good* (?) points out of his recent lecture and published them. Mark is a much over-estimated clown. He has little originality and less genuine humor. He would hardly fill the bill for a police reporter on a first class journal, and yet he would aspire to the position of Horace Greeley, should that wise sage fall out of service. His lecture sounds well to those who never read the almanac literature of the day and we do not wonder that he is anxious that no word he speaks on the stage should be published, for "comparisons are odious." We bid him a cordial good-bye, and hope some better stuff may be brought out during the season by our lecture giving committee to compensate for the gross fraud perpetrated on the intellectual community by introducing such a mountebank as Mark Twain, who now, so far as his literary reputation is concerned, like a swan is singing (at 75 dollars per song) before he dies. Let him rest. ("Brevities," 15 Jan 72, 4)

Although Clemens must have seen this item before he left the city on 16 January, his next comment about Pittsburgh is unclouded by any trace of the dispute (see 19 Apr 72 to Bliss).

To James Redpath and George L. Fall
13 January 1872 • Pittsburgh, Pa.
(MS: CLjC)

₄$124.69.
——⌁⌁——ᴀ

Pittsburgh, Jan. 13.

Redpath & Fall
    Gentlemen:
    Enclosed please find N. Y. draft in your favor for $124.69.[1]
       Please acknowldg—

                      Ys
                  S. L. Clemens.

◻️⃠————————————————————————————————

[*letter docketed:*] *1/16.72* [*and*] *Clemens* Saml L. | Pittsburg Pa | Jan. 13 '72

---

[1] See the previous letter, n. 3.

To Olivia L. Clemens
16 January 1872 • Pittsburgh, Pa.
(MS: CU-MARK)

16th

Livy darling, in the course of an hour I shall ⅋ take the train for Lock Haven. It goes at 3 in the morning.[1] I must do some packing, bill-paying & so forth, & this note is merely to tell you that I love you, & that if ever I get through with this tour alive I never want to take another, even for a month. I love you, darling.

Sam[l].

✉—————————————————————————————

Mrs Sam[l]. L. Clemens | Cor Forest & Hawthorne | Hartford | Conn. [*return address:*] IF NOT DELIVERED WITHIN 10 DAYS, TO BE RETURNED TO [*postmarked:*] PITTSBURGH PA. JAN 16

[1] His lecture of 15 January at Bellefonte, Pennsylvania, having been canceled (see the next letter), Clemens had extended his stay in Pittsburgh another day. On the evening of 16 January he lectured in Lock Haven, Pennsylvania, where he also received the following letter from Olivia (CU-MARK), written on 9 January in reply to his 4 January letter from Dayton:

(LLC)

    My Darling

        I have been so interupted that nearly all the time that I had set apart for a visit with you is gone— Sue and Theodore and Clara have gone out for a ride— I have been having a good time with baby part of the day today, he is a glorious little fellow—he has his second tooth, he has twice today said something very like *Papa*— I talk papa at him a good deal of the time——

        Evening

        Have had a *perfect* evening at the Warners, I hope yet that you will go to Dr. Bartons, Mr Warner says it is not their habit to get up in the morning, they never do— soberly he says, just tell them that you don't want to be called & it will be all right— I wish you could escape one of those forlorn hotels, besides I think it would be so pleasant for you to see them as you have mutual friends——but of course Darling just as you feel—

        Oh it is so sweet to love you, I like to do it— I have ever so much to write you, but I am feeling just a little light headed tonight, so think I best go to bed—it is nearly eleven——

                        Good night my youth—
                        with just a bit of love
                        Livy—

To James Redpath
17 January 1872 • Lock Haven or Milton, Pa.
(MS: IaU)

Jan. 17.[1]

Dear Red—

No, I can't lecture anywhere outside of New England in Feb., except it be in Troy, on the 1st. Wouldn't talk in Utica or Newburgh either, for twice the money.[2]

Was glad Bellefonte backed—wish some more would.[3] The fewer engagements I have from this time forth, the better I shall be pleased.

Ys

Mark.

✉—————————————————————————————

[*letter docketed:*] *Clemens* Saml L. | Jan. 17 / 72

[1]Clemens was probably writing from Milton, where he lectured on 17 January, but it is possible that he was still in Lock Haven, which was only about fifty miles by rail northwest of Milton (Redpath and Fall, 11; *Appletons' Hand-Book*, 162).

[2]Clemens wished to stay close to home as Olivia neared the end of her pregnancy. No lecture was scheduled in Newburgh, New York. A note in Clemens's appointment book indicates that a tentative lecture engagement in Utica, New York, for 2 February, was canceled (Redpath and Fall, 15).

[3]Clemens had been scheduled to lecture in Bellefonte, Pennsylvania, on Monday, 15 January. When the committee "backed," he remained in Pittsburgh for a long weekend instead (Redpath and Fall, 11).

To Olivia L. Clemens
20 January 1872 • Harrisburg, Pa.
(MS: CU-MARK)

Harrisburgh, 20th.

Livy darling, I am here to stay over Sunday.[1]

Sent Ned House's letter back to you for preservation. *Give it to*

Orion & let him hand it to Bliss to be read—then let Bliss send it back to you. Don't forget.[2]

Had a magnificent time at Lancaster last night. Stormy night, but brilliant, crowded audience. I wrote a new, long clause jammed it into the lecture & talked it off from memory without missing a word—a mistake would have been ghastly. All these late places insist on my coming back.[3]

I enclose a poem—or rather, two poems. The woman's poem is exquisite—Mr. Longfellow's is not to be mentioned in the same day with it. But Mr. L. has not plagiarized. If he had been stealing from this woman he would not ¢ have overlooked one of her finest points—the one where the old Monk's simple sense of *duty* makes him spring up & go to his charitable work when the bells ring——Longfellow makes him drag himself reluctantly away in answer to a plain call "within his breast"— a call so worded as to give the instant impression that he recognized in it a command, (& a *promise*, almost,) from the Vision.[4]

I have seen this beautiful old legend put into all manner of poetical measure, but never so touchingly & effectively as this woman has done it. Show it to Warner.

So Joe is in N. York. I will write him.[5]

Slee writes that Larned thinks he has sold his interest in the Express & wants to pay my notes.[6]

Only a few days, my old darling, & I shall have you in my arms. I *love* you Livy darling.

Saml.

✉ ————————————————————————

Mrs. Saml. L. Clemens | Cor Forest & Hawthorne | Hartford | Conn. [*return address:*] IF NOT DELIVERED WITHIN 10 DAYS, TO BE RETURNED TO [*postmarked:*] HARRISBURG PA. JAN 20

[1] Clemens lectured in Harrisburg on 18 January, drawing mixed reviews from the local press. The Harrisburg *Telegraph* deemed his performance "the roughest excuse for a lecture we ever heard":

> The peculiar drawling style of the lecturer does not add to the interest of the subject— many of the jokes were very far-fetched, and the lecture itself was as devoid of interesting matter as it well could be. It was indeed all "chaff," hardly a good seed in the lot. Any person hearing Mark Twain once won't desire to hear him again. ("Mark Twain's lecture . . . ," 19 Jan 72, 3)

At the other extreme, the Harrisburg *Evening Mercury* called it "a grand success oratorically and facetiously" ("Amusement Notes," 19 Jan 72, 1). The temperate

Harrisburg *Patriot* found that the lecture afforded "much agreeable amusement" and described at length the crush in the hall: "The only vacant space left when the lecturer commenced was his mouth, and that nobody crowded down his throat was astonishing" ("Local Intelligence," 19 Jan 72, clipping in CU-MARK). Clemens lectured on Friday, 19 January, in Lancaster (see note 3); with no lecture scheduled for 20 or 21 January, he returned to Harrisburg for the weekend.

² Edward H. House's letter has not been found. It probably concerned the book about Japan which, through Clemens, he had offered the American Publishing Company in May 1871. House had been in Japan since 1870, teaching English at the University of Tokyo and corresponding for the New York *Tribune* (see, for example, "Progressive Japan," New York *Tribune*, 12 Feb 72, 3, from "E. H. H.," the *Tribune*'s "REGULAR CORRESPONDENT"). He did not return to America until March 1873 (*L4*, 149–50 n. 3, 388, 389 n. 1; House to Whitelaw Reid, 20 and 21 Mar 73, Whitelaw Reid Papers, DLC; see 3 May 73 to Bliss, n. 2).

³ "Mark Mark Twain as the sensation of our course of lectures," said the Lancaster *Intelligencer.* Clemens held a capacity crowd "in rapt admiration of his beautiful descriptions of scenery or convulsed them with laughter by his humorous sketches. His manner is admirably suited to his subject and matter, and his strong clear voice enabled all to hear him distinctly" ("Mark Twain's Lecture," 20 Jan 72, 2). According to the Lancaster *Evening Express*, he "paid Lancaster the compliment of saying that he never appeared before a finer and more appreciative audience, and added that if he could always have such audiences he would stick to lecturing as a profession" ("Mark Twain had the pleasure . . . ," 23 Jan 72, 2).

⁴ The original enclosures have not been found. The "woman's poem" remains unidentified. Longfellow's poem was "The Legend Beautiful," which was the "Theologian's Tale" in the second installment of *Tales of a Wayside Inn* (1863–74). Clemens may have clipped the poem from the pages of the *Atlantic Monthly*, where it first appeared in December 1871; it did not appear in book form until May 1872, when it was reprinted by James R. Osgood and Company in *Three Books of Song*. The *Atlantic*'s text is transcribed in Appendix B. Longfellow's monk, called to attend to the poor at the convent gate, hesitates to leave the splendid "Vision" of Christ which has visited him in his cell. Clemens refers to the climactic verse: "Then a voice within his breast/ Whispered, audible and clear/ As if to the outward ear:/ 'Do thy duty; that is best;/ Leave unto thy Lord the rest!'" (Longfellow 1871, 659; "Advance Book-Notes," *Publishers' and Stationers' Weekly Trade Circular* 1 [23 May 72]: 464).

⁵ Clemens's old Nevada friend and employer, Joseph T. Goodman, proprietor of the Virginia City *Territorial Enterprise*, left Virginia City in December 1871, accompanied by his wife, Ellen, for a visit to Washington, New York, and other eastern cities. The Goodmans did not leave New York until 1 April 1872; doubtless they were able to see Clemens in February or March. Goodman had last visited Clemens in the spring of 1871 in Elmira during the composition of *Roughing It* (Virginia City *Territorial Enterprise*: "Gone East," 13 Dec 71, 3; "Home Again," 25 Apr 72, 3; Goodman to SLC, 24 Mar 72, CU-MARK; *L4*, 378, 379 n. 2; *RI 1993*, 840–42).

⁶ John D. F. Slee, the "very able" young businessman who since May 1870 had been a partner in J. Langdon and Company, had often advised Clemens about his financial affairs, including the $3,000 loan he made to his Buffalo *Express* associate, Josephus N. Larned, in April 1870 (*L4*, 157 n. 1). On 20 January 1872 the Buffalo *Express* editorial page included Larned's "Personal" announcement: "Having sold my interest in the EXPRESS PRINTING COMPANY to my recent partner, George H. Selkirk, I retire to-day from the editorial management of the EXPRESS" (2). Larned's retirement after thirteen years' association with the *Express* was closely followed by his election as Buffalo's superintendent of education. Selkirk, president of the Express Printing Company, which published the Buffalo *Express*, was now sole owner, having also purchased Clemens's shares in March 1871 (*L3*, 401–2 n. 2; *L4*, 81–82, 109, 140 n. 2, 338–39 n. 3; "Charter Election," Buffalo *Express*, 7 Feb 72, 4).

🌿

NO LETTERS written between 20 and 26 January 1872 have been found. After his weekend in Harrisburg, Clemens moved on to Carlisle, Pennsylvania, where his lecture of 22 January "was more largely attended than any of the previous ones of the course"; attendance was estimated at six hundred ("The lecture . . . ," Carlisle *Herald*, 25 Jan 72, no page; Fatout 1960, 171). He was in Baltimore on 23 January, speaking to a "thronged" hall. The Baltimore *Sun* noted that his "comical appearance as he entered alone, at once excited laughter, and his gestures and speech, which are of an apparently lazy character, with his humor and paradoxical ideas, kept his audience in the best humor for over one and a half hours" ("Mark Twain in the Maryland Institute," 24 Jan 72, 1). In Baltimore, apparently, lecture manager T. B. Pugh approached Clemens about delivering a second Philadelphia lecture on 9 February (Clemens had already lectured there on 20 November). Clemens gave him no definite response, but the next day (24 January), when he reached New York, he telegraphed Redpath to tell Pugh that he "could not lecture again in Phila this Season" (Pugh to SLC, 26 Jan 72, CU-MARK; *L4*, 497; see also 20 Jan 73 to Pugh).

Clemens's New York lecture was a benefit for the Mercantile Library, founded in 1820 by a group of mercantile clerks. By 1871, with about thirteen thousand subscribers and one hundred and twenty thousand volumes, it had become "the fourth in size of the libraries of this country, and the largest lending-library in America" (Hassard, 353). Borrowing privileges were available even to nonmembers for only five dollars a year, and they were free to editors of the press. Its main reading room and reference and circulating collection were housed at Clinton Hall on Astor Place (Hassard, 361; Disturnell, 115; Moses King 1893, 328). Clemens's friend John Rose Greene Hassard reported in *Scribner's Monthly*, "Of Mark Twain's *Innocents Abroad* the library has 115 copies, all of which are constantly in use and ordered in advance" (Hassard, 363).

The lecture was to be Clemens's first appearance in New York City since May 1867, when, with great trepidation, he had first addressed an eastern audience. Despite the success of that first lecture, he was again understandably anxious about having a "good house" in New York, as he had more than once expressed to Redpath in recent weeks (2 Jan 72 to Redpath, n. 2; *L2*, 40–44). His fears were to prove groundless: the lecture was unusually well noticed in advance by the press, insuring a large attendance. Not only did the Mercantile Library Association place advertisements in the major New York newspapers, there were items in the news and editorial columns as well. On 18 January the *Tribune* provided an important endorsement—something it did not customarily do for lecturers—with a paragraph on its editorial page mentioning the "extraordinary success" of the "Roughing It" lecture: "It is said to be the most entertaining of all his productions for the lyceum" (18 Jan 72, 4). And on the day of the lecture, again on its editorial page, the *Tribune* predicted "one of the best audiences of the season," while the *Evening Express* carried the following notice in its news columns: "**The Mercantile Library Association** appeal for a large house, at Steinway Hall, tonight, with Mark Twain and one of the most amusing of his efforts. They invest the profits in the Library, and look to the public to buy tickets" ("Mark Twain's lecture . . . ," New York *Tribune*, 24 Jan 72, 4; New York *Evening Express*, 24 Jan 72, 3). The result was that Steinway Hall was filled literally to overflowing with a crowd of "over 2,000" (see the enclosure with the next letter). The New York *Times* reviewer noted:

> The effort—which seemed to require no effort at all on the part of the humorous story-teller—was all about "Roughing It" out in Nevada, the land of sage hens, Mexican bloods, mountain sheep, alkali dust and duels. The lecturer related his narrative to a crowded house. He was repeatedly applauded. . . . The lecture was a decided success, and much gratified all who heard it. ("Mark Twain's Lecture," 25 Jan 72, 5)

The New York *Herald* reported, "Everybody appeared to have gone expecting to be amused, and if uproarious mirth might be taken as an evidence, their expectations were thoroughly fulfilled" ("Mark Twain's Lecture," 25 Jan 72, 3).

After the lecture, Clemens stayed at the St. Nicholas Hotel, then returned home to Hartford, probably on 25 January, for several days ("Prominent Arrivals," New York *Tribune*, 25 Jan 72, 8).

🐦

To James Redpath
26 January 1872 • Hartford, Conn.
(AAA 1924c, lot 98)

Home, 26th

. . . .

Oh, no, they couldn't afford more than $150, so we've done 'em a charitable good deed. The statements in this notice were made to me on the platform at the close of the lecture, by the President of the Mercantile Library Asso'n, while trying to have me repeat the lecture;[1] and as Col. John Hay was the only other person listening, he necessarily wrote this notice & besides he is the only man in New York who can speak so authoritatively about "the true Pike accent."[2] I outdrew Dickinson & Gough everywhere[3]

. . . .

Mark

[*enclosure:*]

MARK TWAIN AT STEINWAY HALL.

If there are those who fondly think that the popularity of the American humoristic school is on the decline, they would have been bravely undeceived by a visit to Steinway Hall last night. The most enormous audience ever collected at any lecture in New-York came together to listen to "Mark Twain's" talk on "Roughing it." Before the doors were opened $1,300 worth of tickets had been sold, and for some time before Mr. Clemens appeared the house was crammed in every part by an au-

dience of over 2,000. A large number were turned away
from the door, and after the close of the evening's entertainment the officers of the Library Association warmly
urged Mr. Clemens to repeat his lecture for the benefit
of those who were disappointed.

It was not only financially that the lecture was successful. There was never seen in New-York an audience
so obstinately determined to be amused. There was
hardly a minute of silence during the hour. Peals of
laughter followed every phrase, the solemn asservera-
tions of the lecturer that his object was purely instructive and the investigation of the truth increasing the
merriment. At several points of the lecture, especially
the description of Mr. Twain's Mexican Plug, the
Chamois of Nevada, and the Washoe Duel, the enjoyment of the audience was intemperate.[4] A singular
force and effectiveness was added to the discourse by
the inimitable drawl and portentous gravity of the
speaker. He is the finest living delineator of the true
Pike accent, and his hesitating stammer on the eve of
critical passages is always a prophecy—and hence,
perhaps, a cause—of a burst of laughter and applause.
He is a true humorist, endowed with that indefinable
power to make men laugh which is worth, in current
funds, more than the highest genius or the greatest
learning.

[1]Clemens probably telegraphed Redpath about his New York success soon
after the lecture, on 24 or 25 January. Redpath evidently replied that Clemens's
fee ought to have been higher than $150, which was only $15 more than his average fee for the season (his fees ranged from $100 to $250, with about half at
$125). Clemens's lecture was the final one in a series of six sponsored by the Mer-
cantile Library Association: he had been preceded by Secretary of the Treasury
George S. Boutwell, Olive Logan, Senator Carl Schurz, Frederick Douglass, and
Wendell Phillips. The association's president in 1871–72, Arthur W. Sherman,
may have been the source for Clemens's information that, until his lecture, the
course had been losing money. In an essay written later in the year but wisely
left unpublished (see 18 July 72 to Redpath, n. 5), Clemens said:

The New York Mercantile Library Association got up a "good old-fashioned" course
that was perfectly saturated with morals & instruction, & at the end of it came out wise
& holy, but—in debt. I went there with my "degrading influence," & with a single stalwart effort cleared off the debt & left twelve or fifteen hundred dollars in the committee's
coffers. (SLC 1872k, 11–12†, first inscription, all revisions here suppressed.)

The association's annual report stated that the lectures "were in the main well
attended, and one of them (that by Mr. Clemens) attracted one of the largest
audiences ever assembled at a lecture in New York City. The net proceeds of the
lectures, $816.31, . . . were used in the purchase of books" (Mercantile Library,
15, "Officers . . . for 1871–72"; Redpath and Fall, 1–14).

[2]These four words appear seven lines from the end of the review that Clemens

enclosed, probably as a clipping from page 5 of the New York *Tribune* for 25 January (but see the textual commentary). John Hay and Clemens had probably known each other since 1867; they had certainly become well acquainted since Hay joined the New York *Tribune* editorial staff in the fall of 1870. Like Clemens, Hay could claim thorough familiarity with the native Pike speech pattern and character: he had grown up in Warsaw, Illinois, on the banks of the Mississippi River, just upriver from Clemens's own Hannibal and from the Pike County areas of Missouri and Illinois. By the late 1860s, the "Pike" was already established in American literature as a distinct type—the unlettered, unorthodox, "uncouth Westerner, the antithesis of the man of the East" (Pattee, 84)—but the sudden vogue for Pike literature in the early 1870s grew out of one poem, Bret Harte's "Plain Language from Truthful James," first published in the *Overland Monthly* in September 1870 and widely reprinted. Hay's *Pike County Ballads and Other Pieces* was published in May 1871, just four months after Harte's collected *Poems*, and included the immensely popular "Little-Breeches" and "Jim Bludso." Hay would later say that the ballads were unique among his works, his only literary exploitation of the Pike dialect and the "peculiar Pike county mind," and he would claim that they were all written "within a week" in November 1870 (Eggleston 1902)—a claim somewhat belied by his letters of the period. Both Hay and Clemens had chafed at being accused of imitating Harte's dialect verses, so Hay's praise of Clemens as the "finest" delineator of the "true" accent probably carried with it an implied judgment of Harte, who was a native of Albany, New York (see *L4*, 269–70, 299–300 n. 1, 303–5). Indeed, according to an account written by Hay's close friend Clarence King, Hay had written the ballads in reaction to Harte's unsatisfactory attempts at Pike dialect—"to see how a genuine Western feeling, expressed in genuine Western language, would impress Western people" (Clarence King, 737). In July 1873, in the notebook he dictated in London, Clemens called Bret Harte's dialect sketches "underwrought," claiming that Harte, despite being "called the great master of dialect," was ignorant of the Pike dialect, in one sketch mixing "about 7 dialects . . . all in the one unhappy Missouri mouth" (*N&J1*, 553; MacMinn; *L4*, 250 n. 7, 338; Hay: 1870; 1871a–b; 1908, 2:5, 7–8; Harte 1870, 1871; "Notes on Books and Booksellers," *American Literary Gazette and Publishers' Circular* 16 [2 Jan 71]: 61; Clarence King; "Hay and Harte," Boston *Evening Transcript*, 16 May 71, Supplement, 1; Pattee, 83–91; Carkeet, 325–26; for the genesis of Clemens's friendship with Hay and their interest in vernacular writing see *L4*, 292–93 n. 3, and *RI 1993*, 804, 825, 828–30).

[3] John Bartholomew Gough, famed for his temperance lectures, and Anna E. Dickinson were top performers on the lecture circuit. Gough's lecture schedule has not been reconstructed in detail, but at this point in the 1871–72 season Dickinson is known to have lectured in the same city or town as Clemens some twenty-four times, preceding Clemens in eighteen cases. In New York City, Dickinson had preceded Clemens on 9 January, delivering her popular "Joan of Arc" lecture; Gough preceded Clemens on 15 January, lecturing on "Eloquence and Orators." Dickinson had been a client of Redpath's in 1870–71; Gough was to become one in July 1872 (Chester, 86, 101–3; "Amusements," New York *Tribune*, 8 Jan 72, 7; "Lectures," New York *Times*, 15 Jan 72, 7; *Lyceum:* 1870, 2; 1871, 21; 1872, 3).

[4] For the Mexican Plug, see chapter 24 of *Roughing It*. The "Chamois of Ne-

vada" was not used in the book, but can be recovered from a synopsis of an earlier lecture performance, published in the Lansing (Mich.) *State Republican* on
21 December:

> It's the noblest hunting ground on earth. You can hunt there a year and never find any-
> thing—except mountain sheep; but you can't get near enough to them to shoot one.
> You can see plenty of them with a spyglass. Of course you can't shoot mountain sheep
> with a spyglass. It is our American Shamwah (I believe that is the way that word is
> pronounced—I don't know), with enormous horns, inhabiting the roughest mountain
> fastnesses, so exceedingly wild that it is impossible to get within rifleshot of it. (Lorch,
> 313)

The "Washoe Duel" was also left out of the book, but Clemens reprised it in
"How I Escaped Being Killed in a Duel," published in England in December
1872 (SLC 1872b; 11 Sept 72 to OLC, n. 10).

To James Redpath
27 January 1872 • Hartford, Conn.
(MS: MH-H)

(*LLC*)

Hartford, 27th

Dear Redpath—

√ 1. Say *no* to New York.

√ 2. Say *no* to Englewood.

☞ 2/9 3. Since Danbury is not a positive engagement, say *no* to
Danbury. [*in margin:* Ithaca has written me. Please say to Ithaca that I
cannot come.]¹

√ 4. Since Amherst *is* a positive engagement, we must say yes
to it, but it looks like the infernalest misfortune that I have got to go there
& talk after being out of practice three whole weeks.² I shall make a botch
of it, for I use no notes whatever, & my memory is execrable. Cannot you
beg off from it?—putting it on the ground of a charity to us.

Thank God it is nearly over. I haven't a cent to show for all this long
campaign. Squandered it thoughtlessly paying debts.³

Ys

Mark

✉───

[*letter docketed:*] *Twain* Mark Hartford Cn Jan. 27. '72 [*and in pencil:*]
Drawer

¹The Mercantile Library Association had evidently written Redpath to request a second lecture. Clemens did not repeat his lecture for the association in 1872, but within a year he had agreed to lecture for it twice—on 5 and 10 February 1873—and for what he then thought were significantly better terms (see 24 Jan 73 to Redpath, n. 2). He also did not lecture in Englewood, New Jersey, or in Ithaca, New York, but he did in Danbury, Connecticut. Clemens's instructions were annotated—probably by two hands—at the Boston Lyceum Bureau. The marks are in pencil, except for "2/9" in ink, the latter note probably indicating that 9 February was the proposed date for the Danbury lecture. The lecture was soon firmly scheduled for 21 February: advertisements for it began appearing on 7 February ("Reading Notices," Danbury *News*, 7 Feb 72, 2).
²Until the Danbury lecture date was settled, Clemens's only scheduled engagements were in Troy, New York, on 1 February and in Amherst, Massachusetts, on 27 February.
³See 2 Jan 72 to Redpath, n. 3.

❧

No LETTERS written between 27 January and 3 February 1872 have been found. On Sunday afternoon, 28 January, Clemens may well have attended a performance of the Jubilee Singers, touring on behalf of Fisk University in Nashville. They "sang a half a dozen times at the Asylum Hill church Sunday school concert in the afternoon. The notice was very brief but the large house was nearly filled, and their singing created a sensation rarely equalled" ("The Jubilee Singers," Hartford *Courant*, 29 Jan 72, 2; see 10 Mar 73 to Hood and Routledge and Sons). Clemens's first lecture after his three or four days at home was on 29 January in Scranton, Pennsylvania. His by-now well-worn gambit of introducing himself was the most successful part of the lecture, according to the reviewer in the Scranton *Republican*, who added, "The audience enjoyed the evening's entertainment, and if his concluding remarks had been as funny as his opening, they would have been sorry that the lecturer closed in less than an hour" ("Mark Twain's Lecture," 1 Feb 72, 6). On 30 January Clemens lectured in Jersey City, New Jersey, to an overflowing house, once again introducing himself:

> Mark immediately stepped to the front of the platform and announced that the next monthly meeting of the Young Men's Christian Association would take place on February 8th, and then it was supposed that instead of being the lecturer of the evening, he was the member of the association upon whom devolved the duty of introducing that gentleman. His next announcement quickly dissipated that idea however, and he said that the next lecture of the

course would be no lecture at all, but a grand vocal and instrumental concert, on Feb. 15th. He then continued, "I will now introduce the lecturer of the evening, a gentleman whose great learning, historical accuracy, devotion to science, and veneration for the truth are only equalled by his high moral character and majestic presence." He then disclaimed any discourtesy in thus introducing himself, and added that he had an insurmountable antipathy to being introduced in the regulation style. He was satisfied that it must be very uncomfortable for the lecturer to be standing around the platform while some other man was performing the operation; he always preferred to do the introduction himself, and then he was sure to get in the facts. A gentleman [out] west undertook the task of introducing him on one occasion, and knowing that he disliked having compliments showered upon him, he did the introduction in this style; "I don't know anything about this man except two things, one is, he has never been in the penitentiary, and the other is, I don't know the reason why." (Jersey City *American Standard*, 31 Jan 72, 1)

The Jersey City *Evening Journal* judged that "Mark is no orator":

He don't pretend to be, but he is an amusing talker with a droll drawl, a nasal twang, and an indescribably odd fashion of "standing around" and moving his hands and his features as if he didn't know what to do with them. He is a mixture of Artemus Ward, Baron Munchausen and—Mark Twain, with Mark preponderating. He made people laugh, and that was what he came for, but we would rather read his fun than have it from him by word of mouth. ("Twain Talk," 31 Jan 72, 1)

After the lecture, Clemens undoubtedly took the ferry back to New York, checking into the St. Nicholas for the night ("Prominent Arrivals," New York *Tribune*, 31 Jan 72, 8; "Morning Arrivals," New York *Evening Express*, 31 Jan 72, 3). The next day he recrossed the river to lecture in Paterson, New Jersey. The Paterson *Press* found him to be "about all that could have been reasonably expected," and summarized some features of the lecture:

He gave a beautiful and eloquent description of Lake Tahoe, . . . set like a crystal mirror in a frame of pine and snow clad mountains, and where the only game was mountain-sheep that could never be shot, and—seven up; not that he approved of card playing, which in fact he thought decidedly immoral— unless you could make a little something at it! The "Dead Sea" of the Pacific was also fully described, its striking peculiarity being very strong lye (the Dead Sea's or the story's). The "specialty" of the "Mexican Plug," the alkali and sage-bush desert, the peculiarities of the climate, the singular mode of dealing out "justice," the enormity of duelling and Mark's own aversion to and cure for the same, etc., etc., were all dwelt on and described in the same tone as the scenes depicted in the "Innocents Abroad," with that inimitable mixture of fact and fancy, seriousness and fun, absurd pathos and sentiment, that have established "Twain" as one of the most successful of humorists. ("City and Vicinity," 1 Feb 72, 3)

If Clemens followed the suggestion of his lecture appointment book, he stayed the night at Paterson's Franklin House hotel (Redpath and Fall, 13–14; Boyd, 181). The next day, 1 February, he lectured to a "jammed" house in Troy, New York, and kept the audience "convulsed with laughter." After drawling out his customary self-introduction, he referred to the subject of his lecture (which had not been named in advance notices):

> I don't *know*, ladies and gentlemen, what lecture I am advertised to deliver to-night—I have not enquired. I have delivered several lectures this Winter— and can deliver them all to you this evening if you wish it, but if I had my choice I should deliver the one entitled "Roughing It." ("'Roughing It' by Mark Twain," Troy *Press*, 2 Feb 72, 3)

Clemens was doubtless back in Hartford in time to celebrate his second wedding anniversary on 2 February. And he was probably able to see the first copies of *Roughing It*: 304 copies were received from the bindery on 30 and 31 January (APC, 74).

❧

To Alvin J. Johnson
3 February 1872 • Hartford, Conn.
(Wingate 1872, 67)

Hartford, Conn., Feb. 3d, 1872.

Mr. A. J. Johnson—Dear Sir: Domestic duties deny my wife the pleasure of coming, but I shall be glad to do what in me lies to worthily represent the family.[1]

Mark Twain.

[1] Olivia Clemens was just a few weeks away from the birth of her second child, and she also had house guests: Clara Spaulding and probably Clara's sister, Alice—presumably the "domestic duties" referred to here. Clemens was replying, at the latest possible moment, to an invitation from Alvin Jewett Johnson (1827– 84) and his wife, Lucia (née Warner), to attend a celebration of Horace Greeley's sixty-first birthday, that same evening "between the hours of Nine and Eleven,"

in their home at 323 West Fifty-seventh Street in New York City (Wingate 1872, 2, 16, 51). Johnson, an intimate friend of Greeley's, was a prosperous publisher of subscription books, particularly textbooks, scientific works, and reference works like the much-reprinted *Johnson's New Illustrated Family Atlas*. The evening began with a small dinner party for Greeley's closest friends. Clemens, who had met Greeley in December 1870 and corresponded briefly with him in 1871, was invited to the reception following the dinner. The New York *World* reported that it brought together "one of the largest and most remarkable companies of men and women of letters" ever seen in New York: "Several hundred persons were present, and the ample parlors were soon crowded with animated talkers" ("Horace Greeley's Sixty-first Birthday," New York *Tribune*, 5 Feb 72, 5, reprinting the New York *World* of 4 Feb 72). Journalist Charles Frederick Wingate, known to Clemens since 1870, produced a detailed commemorative pamphlet about the party. He recalled that at about ten o'clock,

> the hall door suddenly opened, and a whole crowd of guests came in together, bringing with them a fresh gust of cold air from out doors. These consisted of a party that had come all the way from New England, either from Worcester, Springfield, or Hartford. They had had a jolly time on their trip down, and arrived just at the height of the entertainment. Among their number was Samuel Bowles, the vigilant and intrepidly independent editor of the Springfield *Republican*, who was received by Mr. Greeley with a cordial "Why, how are you, Sam?" and replied with a no less hearty "How are you, Horace?" His tall form was conspicuous among the crowd, and he found numerous acquaintances on all sides. With him came ex-Governor [Joseph R.] Hawley, editor of the *Hartford Courant* a fine, sturdy, intelligent-looking man, with mustache and imperial a little like those of the Emperor Napoleon. Mark Twain was also with the party, besides other journalists. (Wingate 1872, 43–44)

Wingate observed that Bret Harte, Mark Twain, and John Hay "formed a trinity of wit such as has rarely been found under one roof." They were "looked upon as lions of the occasion, and each at once became the bright particular star of a group of admiring and attentive listeners" (Wingate 1872, 42, 43). In addition to the guests already mentioned, the company included Phineas T. Barnum (1810–91), who had written to Clemens at least once—on 17 December 1870 (CU-MARK)—but probably had not as yet met him; Mary Louise Booth (1831–89), editor in chief of *Harper's Bazar* since its inception in 1867; Noah Brooks, an editor on the New York *Tribune* since 1871, but well-known to Clemens from his years in California; William Conant Church, editor with his brother, Francis P. Church, of both the *Army and Navy Journal* and the *Galaxy;* Dr. Titus Munson Coan (1836–1921), then "literary editor of the *Independent*" (Wingate 1872, 44), who probably wrote the *Independent's* 11 April review of *Roughing It* (see *RI 1993*, 886); David G. Croly, managing editor of the New York *World;* Anna E. Dickinson, currently on a two-day break in her lecture schedule (Chester, 104); Mary Mapes Dodge (1831–1905), the associate editor of *Hearth and Home* and soon to be editor in chief of *St. Nicholas* magazine (1873); Edward Eggleston, author of *The Hoosier Schoolmaster* (issued in book form in December 1871 by Orange Judd and Company) and currently editor in chief of *Hearth and Home;* John Elderkin (1841–1926), editor of the *American Booksellers' Guide* and one of the founding members of the Lotos Club (to which Clemens would be elected in 1873); Murat Halstead (1829–1908), editor and principal owner of the Cincinnati *Commercial;* Frank Leslie, pioneer publisher of illustrated journals, known to Clemens since at least December 1868; Whitelaw Reid, second in command to Greeley on the New York *Tribune;* and Richard Henry Stoddard (1825–1903), an established poet and recently appointed editor of the *Aldine.* On 5 April, Greeley thanked Johnson for the party, observing that to "meet Brett Harte, John Hay, and Mark Twain under the same roof with Samuel Bowles, Murat Halstead, and Joseph R. Hawley, should be reckoned an event in almost any one's life, even though he were not privileged then and there to greet likewise Anna Dickinson and Mary L. Booth" (Wingate 1872, 57–58, 1–67 passim; *RI 1993*, 825–26, 849–50, 852, 866, 868; *L4*, 102–3; *L2*, 298, 300 n. 4; Chester, 104; New York *Tribune:* "Books of the Week," 23 Dec 71, 8; "Horace Greeley's Sixty-first Birthday," 5 Feb 72, 5, reprinting the New York *World* of 4 Feb 72; "Alvin J. Johnson," 23 Apr 84, 5; "Greeley," New York *Evening Express,* 5 Feb 72, 4; "Mr. Horace Greeley's Birthday—Celebration by His Friends," New York *Times,* 4 Feb 72, 1; "Personal," Hartford *Courant,* 6 Feb 72, 2; "New York," Boston *Advertiser,* 5 Feb 72, 1).

❧

NO LETTERS written between 3 and 13 February 1872 have been found. The Greeley birthday party ended about midnight, and Clemens remained in New York at least overnight. He was listed among the guests at the St. Nicholas Hotel in the New York *Evening Express* of Monday, 5 February ("Morning Arrivals," 3), probably because he had arrived late on Saturday, either just before or just after the Greeley birthday party (the newspaper did not publish on Sundays). It is likely that he returned to Hartford on 4 February or shortly thereafter, but his activities for the next week or so are undocumented. In fact, Clemens's presence in Hartford is demonstrable only on Saturday, 10 February, when he purchased a pair of "patent Congress Gaiters" from Casper Kreuzer, a Hartford bootmaker (receipt in CU-MARK; Geer 1871, 173).

Before he left New York City, Clemens may have visited the medium James Vincent Mansfield. (Taking into account Clemens's lecture schedule, the visit must have occurred after 24 January and before 27 February, when Clemens mentioned his experience with "spirit mediums in New York" at a reception in Amherst, Massachusetts.) Mansfield, listed only as a "writer" in the New York City directory, had been for at least fifteen years a "writing medium of great celebrity" (Hardinge, 186), who conducted a mail-order spiritualism business from his home at 361 Sixth Avenue in New York City, "Terms, $5 and four three-cent stamps" ("Mediums and Magnetic Physicians," *Woodhull and Claflin's Weekly,* 18 May 72, 13). His extraordinary apartment was described by one visitor as "an enormous baby house in which 10,000 bits of glass and china had been arranged with no other purpose than to produce an overpowering glare of dazzle" ("Off the Beaten Track," New York *World*, 25 Feb 72, 3). His specialty, according to P. T. Barnum, was "the answering of sealed letters addressed to spirits":

> Mr. Mansfield does not engage to answer all letters; those unanswered being too securely sealed for him to open without detection. To secure the services of the "Great Spirit-Postmaster," a fee of five dollars must accompany your letter to the spirits; and the money is retained whether an answer is returned or not. . . .
> Time and again has Mansfield been convicted of imposture, yet he still prosecutes his nefarious business. (Barnum, 59–60)

In 1882, in writing chapter 48 of *Life on the Mississippi*, Clemens would fictionalize his session with Mansfield (called "Manchester" in the book), explaining, "I called on him once, ten years ago, with a couple of friends, one of whom wished to inquire after a deceased uncle." In the manuscript draft of the chapter, before revision, Clemens himself was the client, and the spirit contact was Henry Clemens, killed in a steamboat explosion in 1858. The accompanying "friends" have not been identified:

> I remember Mr. Manchester very well. I called on him once, ten years ago, with a couple of friends, to inquire after ~~my brother, lost on the Pennsylvania in~~ ˄a distant relative, killed in a cyclone.˄ I asked the questions, & my ~~brother~~ ˄late relative˄ wrote down the replies by the hand of the medium,—I mean the medium *said* it was my ~~brother.~~ ˄relative.˄˄

The séance concluded with Clemens's comical attempts to make the spirit state when and how he died. Clemens told the medium

> that when my ~~brother~~ ˄relative˄ was in this poor world, he was endowed with an extraordinary intellect & an absolutely defectless memory, & it seemed great pity that he had not been allowed to keep some shred of these. . . . But I explained that if I had had the slightest idea that I was really conversing with a departed human being, I would not have uttered any light word whatever, but would have spoken in all cases reverently. I added that while I could not say I had *not* been talking with my ~~brother,~~ ˄relative,˄ I was at least quite able to say I did not *believe* I had been talking with him.
> This man had plenty of clients—has plenty yet. He receives letters from spirits located in every part of the spirit world, & delivers them all over this country through the United States mail. These letters are filled with advice— advice from "spirits" who don't know as much as a tadpole—& this advice is religiously followed by the receivers. ~~Of course every man in the world is in~~

~~one way or another a fool, & is well aware of it; but why should he be~~ *this* ~~kind of a fool?~~ (SLC 1882, 18–19, 29–32†)

In 1866, in San Francisco, Clemens had attended spiritualist demonstrations, and lampooned the new "wildcat religion" in several newspaper sketches (SLC 1866a–e). His visit to Mansfield came at a time of renewed interest in spiritualism, fanned by the recent publication of Robert Dale Owen's *The Debatable Land between This World and the Next* (New York: G. W. Carleton and Co., 1872) (H. Wilson 1871, 761; *L1*, 80–86; *N&J2*, 310–11 n. 41; Kerr, 110, 114, 164–68; SLC 1883, 481–85; Branch 1950, 144–46; "New Publications," New York *Tribune*, 26 Dec 71, 6; "New Publications," New York *Times*, 27 Jan 72, 2).

❧

To Mary Mason Fairbanks
13 February 1872 • Hartford, Conn.
(MS: CSmH)

Hartford 13[th].

Dear Mother—

At last I am through with the most detestable lecture campai[g]n that ever was—a campaign which was one eternal worry with contriving new lectures & being dissatisfied with them. I think I built & delivered 6 different lectures during the season[1]—& as I lectured 6 nights in the week & never used notes, you may fancy what a fatiguing, sleepy crusade it was. My last effort suited them in New York, & so I come out satisfactorily at the very fag-end of the course. Pity but it could have happened sooner.

The building of a new lecture robbed me of my visit to you, upon which I had long been calculating. But there was no help for it. I worked all night at Erie, & all next day, & still wrote by candle-light from Erie to Toledo in the cars & got through at midnight—but was so killed up that I had to fall back on my old lecture for a night or two.[2] And then after all, the Chicago Tribune *printed* my new speech in full & I had to sacrifice ~~all my~~ most of my sleeping time for 5 days & nights in the getting up of an entirely *new* lecture.

So you can see that letter writing has been among the impossibilities with me for the last four months. I have wanted to write you, many a time, but there wasn't life enough in me for that or anything else. Under the circumstances, my conscience almost held me guiltless. When you get into the lecture field you will appreciate these hardships; but until that time I fear you will only laugh at them.

I lectured eleven or twelve thousand dollars' worth, paid off all my debts, squandered no end of money, & came out of the campaign with less than $1500 to show for all that work & misery.³ I ain't going to ever lecture any more—unless I get in debt again. Would you?

[I killed a man this morning. He asked me when my book was coming out.]⁴

Our baby is flourishing wonderfully. He is as white as snow, but seel seems entirely healthy,ⱼ, & is very fat, & chubby, & always cheerful & happy-hearted—can say "Pa" & knows enough to indicate which parent he means by it (which is Margaret the nurse.)⁵ He can't walk, though 16 months old; but that is not backwardness of development physically, but precocity of del development intellectually, so to speak, since it is development of inherited indolence, acquired from his father—(indolence is an intellectual faculty I believe?)

Livy is doing finely—getting a little bit stronger all the time. She is taking German lessons from an Irishwoman (the party who does our washing)⁶—& she drives out without counting the miles. So, bodily & mentally she is growing.

We have the Spaulding girls with us from Elmira, & also the Gleasons from the Water Cure.⁷ I wish we had you & your tribe.

We are to go to Elmira early in March & stay 2 months—& then we not only hope to see you there, but bring you here with us when we return.⁸ We would go to see *you*, but our servants will not permit us to be absent more than 2 months. They have so signified.⁹

Love to the household. Do you forgive

Yr eldest

Sam¹?

¹Clemens actually delivered five "different lectures," if the three versions of "Roughing It" are counted (see 2 Jan 72 to Redpath, nn. 1, 2). In June 1871, before the season even began, he had written and discarded two additional lectures: "An Appeal in behalf of Extending the Suffrage to Boys" and "D. L. H." (*L4*, 398, 402 n. 12, 413, 414).

²Clemens had intended to spend Sunday, 10 December, visiting the Fair-

bankses in Cleveland, on his way between Erie, Pennsylvania, and Toledo, Ohio (*L4*, 513).

[3] See 2 Jan 72 to Redpath, nn. 3, 4.

[4] Clemens was evidently impatient with the delay between the arrival of the first copies of *Roughing It* from the bindery, on 30 January, and the start of actual distribution, probably on 19 February, when a copy was deposited with the Library of Congress. Books were certainly available before 23 February, when the earliest known review appeared in the Utica (N.Y.) *Morning Herald and Daily Gazette* (1) (possibly written by Ezekiel D. Taylor, Jr., city editor of the newspaper and a cousin of Olivia's [*L4*, 29 n. 4]). Publication was not officially announced until 29 February. Bliss may have delayed distribution out of a mistaken belief that he needed to wait for the second volume of the English edition to secure British copyright (*RI 1993*, 876–77).

[5] The nursemaid Margaret had served the Clemenses since 1871 in Buffalo, Elmira, and Hartford (*L4*, 412 n. 3, 504, 505 nn. 6, 8).

[6] Unidentified.

[7] The guests were Olivia's girlhood friends Alice and Clara Spaulding, and the proprietors of the Elmira Water Cure, doctors Rachel Brooks Gleason and Silas O. Gleason, who, presumably, were taking an interest in Olivia's pregnancy. Clara had arrived on 29 December; Clemens's reference is the first and only indication of Alice's presence (*L3*, 182–83 n. 6; *L4*, 335 n. 2, 523 n. 2).

[8] See 2? Mar 72 to Fairbanks, n. 2, for Fairbanks's response to this plan.

[9] Besides Margaret, the identifiable servants included coachman Patrick McAleer and (probably) his wife, the former Mary Reagan of Elmira, and Ellen, the cook or housekeeper (15 May 72 to OC and MEC, nn. 4, 7–8; "Coachman Many Years for Mark Twain," Hartford *Courant*, 26 Feb 1906, 6).

To James Redpath
13 February 1872 • Hartford, Conn.
(Will M. Clemens, 28; Libbie, lot 62; AAA 1926a, lot 132)

Hartford, Feb. 13.

. . . .

If you could get that N. Y. Tribune notice of my lecture copied in full into one or two of the biggest Boston papers it would be the next best thing to achieving a Boston triumph.[1]

. . . .

Success to Fall's carbuncle & many happy returns.

. . . .

Mark

¹For the New York *Tribune* review by John Hay, see 26 Jan 72 to Redpath. When Clemens lectured in Boston the previous November, he got a warm reception from his audience but only a tepid one from the press, and therefore felt he had not had a "Boston triumph" *(L4,* 484–85). If Redpath succeeded in having Hay's notice reprinted in some Boston paper, it was neither the *Evening Transcript* nor the *Advertiser.* Redpath may have been preparing the next issue of the *Lyceum Magazine* (dated July, but available in June), which included both a list of lecturers available and "Lyceum Circulars" for more than thirty of them. Circulars consisted very largely of quotations from press notices. No circular for Mark Twain was included, but he was listed with two lecture subjects ("Roughing It" and a "New lecture, not yet named"), even though Redpath explained that "Mr. Clemens has not decided yet whether he shall enter the field this season or not. We shall be able to announce in July his decision to correspondents who apply for him" (*Lyceum* 1872, 5).

🍃

NO LETTERS written between 13 and 23 February 1872 have been found. Presumably Clemens spent most of this period at home in Hartford. After almost three weeks of rest, on 21 February he did travel to Danbury, Connecticut, in order to lecture that evening. The Danbury *News* (a weekly) reviewed the performance on 28 February:

> The lecture on Wednesday night was a failure and a disappointment. The audience went prepared to get a somewhat entertaining sketch of Western life, and material for considerable cachinatory enjoyment. The peculiar awkward appearance of the lecturer and the saddening drawl in his speech were calculated to handsomely bring out his humor, but exerted a depressing influence upon his information, and altogether the evening was so dreadfully tedious, and the humor was so wickedly sparse, that the people became tired, and not a few disgusted. The Opera House was crowded, many of those present coming from out of town, and some of them a distance of fifteen miles with teams.
>
> Mr. Twain is not a beautiful man. His hair is carroty, his gait shambling, and but one of his eyes appeared to be fully alive to the importance of the occasion. He looks like a person who had served long and faithfully in a brick yard without any fore-piece to his cap. ("Mark Twain," 2)

Although Danbury is only fifty miles south of Hartford, rail service was apparently routed through Norwalk, almost doubling the distance (*Appletons' Hand-Book,* 70, 71). Clemens was probably obliged to stay overnight in Danbury, returning to Hartford on 22 February.

🍃

To James Redpath
23 February 1872 • Hartford, Conn.
(Transcript and paraphrase: AAA/Anderson 1935, lot 121)

A. N. s. "Mark", 1 p., small 8vo, n.p. [February 23, 1872], to James Redpath, about 25 words; inviting Redpath to breakfast. The reverse bears the address, reading as follows: "From Mark Twain. James Redpath Esq Allyn House. Wake him up & deliver immediately."[1]

---

[1] Redpath's presence in Hartford has not been explained. His visit with Clemens must have been limited to breakfast, since by noon of 23 February Clemens was on his way to New York City to attend a dinner at the St. James Hotel given by the publishers of the *Aldine*, an illustrated literary monthly, self-described as a "typographic art journal." (In 1871 Clemens had sent his regrets for a similar occasion on 15 March ["The Aldine Dinner," New York *Tribune*, 16 Mar 71, 5].) The dinner, presided over by Vice-President Schuyler Colfax, a former printer, celebrated "the increased prosperity of the Aldine, the accession of Mr. R. H. Stoddard to its editorial management, and other matters relating to American art and literature" ("New York," Boston *Advertiser*, 27 Feb 72, 2). It brought together about fifty guests, primarily publishers, journalists from the New York, Boston, and Philadelphia press, artists, and writers. The *Aldine*'s publisher, James Sutton, and editor, Richard Henry Stoddard, were present, as well as Whitelaw Reid, John Hay, William F. G. Shanks, and Samuel Sinclair, city editor and publisher, respectively, of the New York *Tribune*. Others present included: Robert Shelton Mackenzie (1809–81), literary and drama critic of the Philadelphia *Press;* poet and stockbroker Edmund Clarence Stedman (1833–1908), whose long friendship with Clemens may have dated from this dinner; the Reverend Thomas De Witt Talmage, whom Clemens had attacked in "About Smells" in his May 1870 *Galaxy* column; traveler and author Bayard Taylor (1825–78); sculptor Launt Thompson, whom Clemens had urged Elisha Bliss to consult about illustrator Edward F. Mullen in December 1870; and Charles F. Wingate. According to the *Tribune*, Clemens, when called upon, "excused himself from making a speech by a felicitous speech of some length, abounding with touches of humor peculiar to himself" ("The Aldine Dinner," 26 Feb 72, 8). The *Tribune* did not reproduce the speech, but the Cleveland *Leader* printed the text on 1 March, and a more complete version appeared in the Elmira *Advertiser* on 18 March. Clemens used his account of "Jim Wolf and the Tom-Cats"—and Wolf's statement, "I could have ketched them cats if I had had on a good ready"—to explain his inability to make an impromptu speech (SLC 1867b, 1872i). The speech was "received with shouts of laughter," according to the Cleveland *Leader* ("'Mark Twain,'" 1 Mar 72, 3). Clemens stayed at the St. James Hotel for at least one night; he was back home in Hartford by 26 February

(New York *Tribune:* "The Aldine Dinner," 24 Feb 72, 5; "Prominent Arrivals,"
24 Feb 72, 8; *L4,* 123–24, 281, 282 n. 1, 337 n. 1).

To James Redpath and George L. Fall
per Telegraph Operator
26 February 1872 • Hartford, Conn.
(MS, copy received: OrPR)

BLANK NO. 1.

THE WESTERN UNION TELEGRAPH COMPANY.

THE RULES OF THIS COMPANY REQUIRE THAT ALL MESSAGES RECEIVED FOR
TRANSMISSION, SHALL BE WRITTEN ON THE MESSAGE BLANKS OF THE COMPANY,
UNDER AND SUBJECT TO THE CONDITIONS PRINTED THEREON, WHICH CONDITIONS
HAVE BEEN AGREED TO BY THE SENDER OF THE FOLLOWING MESSAGE.

THOS. T. ECKERT, GEN'L SUP'T,[1]   WILLIAM ORTON, PRES'T,}   NEW YORK.
NEW YORK.   O. H. PALMER, SEC'Y,

DATED   Hartford Conn   187 2

RECEIVED AT   Feb 26

TO   Redpath & Fall
       36 Bromfield st

Am not going to Boston.[2] How in the name of God does a man
find his way from here to Amherst & when must he start give
me full particulars or send a man with me. If I had another engagement I would rot before I would fill it.[3]

S. L. Clements

FROM BRANCH OFFICE, BASEMENT OLD STATE HOUSE

49 paid
Hdx

✉️

[*telegram docketed:*] *G.L.F.* [*and*] *Clemens* S. L. | Hartford Conn | Feb.
26 | '72 [*and by Fall:*] Leave Hartford at ~~½~~ ₍two₎ afternoon Reach Spring-
field at ~~three~~ ten minutes past three. Leave Springfield at four. Reach
Palmer at half past four. change cars. Leave Palmer at five fifty five.
Reach Amherst at seven.

[1] Thomas Thompson Eckert (1825–1910) supervised the organization of the
Union military telegraph system during the Civil War, rising to the rank of

brigadier-general. Appointed assistant secretary of war in July 1866, he resigned in February 1867 to become general superintendent of the eastern division of Western Union.

²The purpose of Clemens's canceled trip to Boston is not known (see also 3 Mar 72 to Redpath).

³Clemens was scheduled to deliver his last lecture of the season, at Amherst College, the next day. Fall's instructions (presumably telegraphed to Clemens) show that it would take him five hours to reach his destination, even though it was only about forty miles north of Hartford. The *Amherst Student* reported, "We do not know whether the audience had expected too much of the funny Mark Twain from reading his funny book, or whether two hours of nonsense is more than people care for at once, or not, but true it is that they had heard enough of him when he was done" (5 [9 Mar 72]: 38). The Amherst *Record* concurred, calling the lecture "a first-class failure," despite "some good hits . . . nearly all of it we had already read, and it seemed rather stale to us" ("Mark Twain's Lecture," 28 Feb 72, 4). In a separate report, the *Record* noted:

> After the lecture last evening a choice collation consisting of oysters, tongue, cold meats, and the like, was served at the Amherst House for recuperating the bodily vigor of Mark Twain, the numerous ushers, and other officials, together with a few invited guests. The occasion was very enjoyable to all parties, and, in the opinion of some, Mark appears to better advantage at the festive board than upon the platform. He kept the company in the best of humor by narrating some of his experiences in piloting on the Mississippi and with spirit mediums in New York. ("A Collation," 28 Feb 72, 4)

Clemens's experience with "spirit mediums" may have been as recent as the last three or four weeks (see pp. 41–43).

To Mary Mason Fairbanks
2? March 1872 • Hartford, Conn.
(MS: CSmH)

Hartford

Dear Mother—

The photographs are excellent—they are on exhibition on the mantel piece. You never looked so much like yourself in a picture before.[1]

Thank you cordially for forgiving my remissness with so much magnanimity.[2] I still regret the hard luck that compelled me to go on writing new lectures instead of enjoying a recuperating day of loafing under your roof.

Livy says you wrong the innocent to punish ~~to~~ the guilty when you refuse to come to see ~~m~~ us because of my rascality or my ill luck. She says it isn't right to punish *her* in this unfair & wholesale way. And she is right, too. You just pack up & come along.

We are getting to work, now, packing up, & fixing things with the
servants, preparatory to migrating to Elmira, & so I will cease writing
& go to *superintending.* I don't mind superintending, but I hate to help
do the work.
            Lovingly, & with love to all the household,
                                    Your son
                                    Sam*.*
Wrote Charley to-day—Hudson, *N. Y. Suppose* it is N. Y., but don't
know.[3]

[1] Clemens replied to Fairbanks's letter of 28 February (see the next note). The
photographs Fairbanks enclosed have not been found. Her letter was postmarked in Cleveland on 29 February; Clemens probably received and answered
it within a day or two of that date.
[2] Fairbanks's forgiveness was contained in her letter of 28 February (CU-
MARK), a response to Clemens's 13 February letter. The delay in responding
may have been caused, in part, by the death of her father-in-law, Zabad Fairbanks (b. 1790), on 12 February at Fair Banks (Cleveland *Herald:* "Death
of Mr. Z. Fairbanks," 13 Feb 72, 2; "Funeral of Mr. Z. Fairbanks," 14 Feb
72, 4; Fairbanks, 318). The tone of her remarks was more reproachful than
magnanimous:

                                    Fair Banks Feb. 28th/72
    My dear *unreliable* boy, but much more reliable daughter!
        I hardly know where to take up the broken thread. I feel as if you had been to
    Europe.
        I did n't mind your not writing. Livy's pleasant letter was the sweetest peace-
    offering you could have sent me. I know by experience how much there is to hinder our
    letters, even to those to whom our loving thoughts fly quickest. All that had been reck-
    oned up and no balance brought in against you. I heard of you here and there and every-
    where. I knew your weariness and your annoyances. Mother-like I so often wished for
    you, that you might *sleep all day* in my house, where no one could find you. That you
    might have just what you wanted for breakfast—as many cups of coffee as you wanted,
    with two sugar bowls to one cup. Oh! I was full of tenderness for you, and when Livy
    wrote that you would make Cleveland for Sunday before Toledo, I was in ecstasy! I fixed
    your room, and then I *un-fixed* it! I forced the green-house and I forced the kitchen. I
    added up and subtracted and divided the time you were to be here, that I might make
    the most of it, for you and for me and for all of us who were so glad of your coming. Mr.
    Fairbanks *judiciously* suggested that I must not be *too sanguine!* I *withered* him with
    rebuke for such distrust! Did I not know you—*?*? With all your eccentricity, had you
    ever broken faith with me? I took a new dignity upon myself at thought of *my* confidence
    in you, and *your* certain justification of it. This was the role I filled the week *before* you
    went to Toledo. The week following, the play was *withdrawn* and the house closed. The
    subject is not commented upon in my presence. My husband ~~does have~~ had a peculiar
    way of reading aloud any notice he saw of "Mark Twain" in Columbus—"Mark Twain"
    in Pittsburg,—points from which *Cleveland* has always been very accessible *heretofore.*
    I would n't notice him. It was enough for me to know way down in my inner heart, that
    the boy I had so doted upon had outgrown me. It did not make the matter any better to
    "put myself in his place"—for I know that if *I* had been on a lecture circuit, I would
    have disappointed my audience, before I would ~~him~~ have ~~mi~~ passed him—or I would
    have treated them to "Casabianca" or "Hohenlinden"— It is all passed now—I have

resumed my regular duties, but there is a little *sore spot in my heart*, and it throbs whenever any one says "when is Mr. Clemens coming to see you?" I think I shall do with the
next questioner, what you did with your *book catechizer*—kill him! I have n't seen the
book yet—Frank has it & will send it me when he has read it. I hear pleasant things of
it from others.

Mr. Fairbanks is in Chicago an or St. Louis this week— Frank & Mary are nicely
fixed at the Weddell. Allie still reigns supreme in the Gaylord house. Charlie is at school
in Hudson. That boy is going to make his mark, if he is my son— I do not mean by hard
work or close study—but he is *so bright*. His father is as foolish about him as I am. He
says he asked you to write Charlie. I concluded you would feel as you did when Mrs.
Crocker asked you to write for her son's paper— However you have no business to feel
so, and a half dozen lines from you would be extremely flattering to Charlie. He is going
on to New-York during one of his vacations to make Nast's acquaintance. He is his
ardent admirer. Mollie is circulating around the grounds with the little Sterling's from
town. I think they are skating on one of the ponds[.] She is as much of a darling to me
as ever although fifteen— She stays so *natural*. She was trying to justify something
which she had done to which I objected. She said "Oh Mama you are too strict with
me." I said "why Mollie I really feel that you are too much indulged. You pursuade me
against my judgment." ["]Oh! Mama, I'm all right, for I'm just as *good principled* as I
can be."

G Do you remember the old "grand pa" of our household? He has lived with us
over a year. Two Three weeks ago he was stricken with paralysis and two weeks since
he died. We have now only three at our table, except when we can bring a friend to us
which we are always glad to do. We are more & more delighted with our home, the
winter beauties charm us if possible more than the summer.

During holiday week we invited some three hundred of our friends— Everybody
was kind enough to say it was one of the most agreeable parties of the season. Dancing
in the green-house. It was the evening after the Duke's reception at Mr. Stone's and I
had a pretentious courtly note from his Secretary Counsellor Machin acknowledging an
invitation to the Grand Duke & his suit to lunch, & regretting that his inability to accept
private hospitality. Mr. Stone compromised with the Mayor and first invited personal
friends and then opened his house at 10 P.M to the Council and friends.

Mr. Duke was very gracious to me and talked very easily & pleasantly of our visit
to Yalta. How vividly it recalled all the ridiculous things of that momentous day, when
we sweltered in our good clothes up through the Russian parks. Poor Bloodgood Cutter
lost a coat that day!

You are coming to Elmira in March—that will be a delight to all concerned. If it
concerned me I should rejoice too, for I have wished for a sight of Livy's face—and I
have something of a grand Mother's love for the white-faced baby who calls his nurse
Pa. Alas! like Jeptha I have made a vow. I come from a proud clan, and henceforth *you*
must find me within my castle walls. You propose to take me home with you from Elmira[.] *What* do you take me for? Read Acts 16th—last clause of verse 37th. Paul and I
are of one mind.

We have been saying all winter we were going to New-York, but we are loth to
leave home.

We shall probably go before warm weather, because then we wish to be at home
to our friends.

A bushel of love to Livy & Langdon and for yourself all you choose to come for
Mother.

I shall write soon to Livy. None of these *hard* words are for her

In addition to her teen-aged son and daughter, Charles Mason and Mary Paine
(Mollie), Fairbanks mentioned her stepdaughter, Alice (Allie) Fairbanks Gaylord; her son-in-law, William H. Gaylord; her stepson, Frank Fairbanks, a partner in his father's Cleveland *Herald*, who had married the former Mary Walker
in November, and was apparently living at Cleveland's Weddell House; and

Eliza P. (Mrs. Timothy D.) Crocker, one of the *Quaker City* passengers, who had written to Clemens on 6 February 1871 soliciting a contribution for a monthly paper, the *Velocipede*, printed by her sixteen-year-old son, Otis D. Crocker (CU-MARK). Also mentioned: the Cleveland visit of Grand Duke Alexis Aleksandrovich on 26–28 December 1871 (see 5 Dec 72 to the editor of the Hartford *Evening Post*, n. 6); Amasa Stone, Jr. (1818–83), wealthy Cleveland banker and builder, and future father-in-law of John Hay; W. T. Machin, identified by the newspapers as the Russian councillor of state; Frederick W. Pelton, mayor of Cleveland in 1871 and 1872; Bloodgood Haviland Cutter, the "Poet Lariat" of *The Innocents Abroad*, who, with other *Quaker City* passengers, visited Tsar Aleksandr II in Yalta in August 1867, and left his "bombazine coat," stuffed with poems, at the palace (Frederick W. Davis to SLC, 25 Apr 1906, CU-MARK); and two often-recited poems, "Casabianca" by Felicia Dorothea Hemans (1793–1835) and "Hohenlinden" by Thomas Campbell (1777–1844). Jephthah's history is told in Judges 11 and 12; the last clause of Acts 16:37 reads, "but let them come themselves and fetch us out" (*L2*, 80–85, 132 n. 10, 134–35 n. 2, 311 n. 10; *L3*, 187 n. 5; *L4*, 302 n. 1; Fairbanks, 552, 754–55; *Cleveland Directory*, 162, 403; Rose, 183, 208–9, 261, 275, 303, 381, 407; Cleveland *Herald:* "The Grand Duke Alexis," 27 Dec 71 and 28 Dec 71, 4).

[3] Clemens may have misdirected his letter. Charles Fairbanks, who would turn seventeen on 27 March, was probably attending Western Reserve Academy, a preparatory school associated with Western Reserve College, in Hudson, Ohio, about twenty miles southeast of Cleveland. Clemens docketed the envelope of Fairbanks's letter, "Ch. Fairbanks | Nast.," indicating that he intended to write to Thomas Nast on Charles's behalf (CU-MARK†; 10 Dec 72 to Nast; Fairbanks, 755; Rose, 104, 386).

To James Redpath
3 March 1872 • Hartford, Conn.
(MS: ViU)

Hartford 3[d]

Dear Redpath—

~~Dear~~ I have seen a picture of the church as it is to be, & it ~~with a~~ will be a queer looking thing but very beautiful. ~~The~~ They find they can't house the horses under the church, but that is the *only* item left out of the programme.[1]

Tell Fall to send me my bill in detail.[2] Am not going to be able to go to Boston. Leave for Elmira in a few days, for the summer.[3]

                                        Ys
                                        Mark.

[✉]————————————————————————————————

[letter docketed:] Clemens S. L. | Hartford Conn | Mch. – 72 *[and by Redpath:]* Over *[and on the back:]* Send down to Smith & ask how much this w^d make in the Magazine reading matter & take the copy back | R⁴

[1] Clemens had described the Reverend Thomas K. Beecher's eccentric but humane plan for the new home of his Park Congregational Church, to which the Langdons belonged, in "A New Beecher Church" in the July 1871 *American Publisher* (SLC 1871g). He had no doubt seen the picture of the "proposed pile" which Beecher sent to Olivia in December, through her brother, Charles Langdon. "It satisfies my eye—almost perfectly," wrote Beecher, "& if we can ever get any figures from the Stone quarries, we shall be able to wade in intelligently" (Beecher to OLC, 6 Dec 71, CU-MARK). Horatio Nelson White of Syracuse provided architectural plans for the building, and in March the trustees of the church solicited construction bids. On 2 April the Elmira *Advertiser* reported, "The work of taking down the old Park Church and rebuilding the new one will be commenced in a few weeks" ("Sunday Meetings," 4). The new church was completed in the fall of 1876 (*L4*, 411 n. 3, 440 n. 2; Cotton, 16; Elmira *Advertiser:* "Notice to Builders," 27 Mar 72, 3; "City and Neighborhood," 10 Jan 73, 4; *Park Church*, 8).

[2] See 7 Mar 72 to Redpath and Fall.

[3] Clemens had already told Redpath in his 26 February telegram that his Boston trip was canceled. The Clemenses' departure for Elmira—where Olivia could spend the final days of her pregnancy at her mother's home (and, possibly, call on the services of Dr. Rachel Gleason)—would be delayed until mid-month. It would be a spring visit: they returned to Hartford in late May and in early July went to New Saybrook, Connecticut, for the rest of the summer.

[4] Redpath's note, written on the back of Clemens's letter, referred to an enclosure, now lost. (Smith has not been identified.) Clemens probably sent a copy of "A New Beecher Church" (SLC 1871g), which Redpath evidently considered reprinting in his next *Lyceum Magazine* (available by 5 June). The magazine had greatly expanded in the three years since its inception, and now contained a "Literary Department" devoted to original and reprinted articles about lecturers and lecturing. Clemens's article was evidently a candidate for this department because it was a good advertisement for Beecher, who would join Redpath's 1872–73 season roster for the first and only time, offering lectures entitled "Man Revealed by Music," "The Negative Illusion," "Property," and an unnamed "spic-span new lecture" (*Lyceum* 1872, 2; "Lectures," Boston *Globe*, 6 June 72, 8; Eubank, 295–320). Although the magazine did not reprint anything by Clemens, he soon included "A New Beecher Church" in two collections of sketches published in May by Routledge and Sons, *A Curious Dream* and *Mark Twain's Sketches* (see 31 Mar 72 to Osgood, n. 4).

To James Redpath and George L. Fall
7 March 1872 • Hartford, Conn.
(MS: MH-H)

Home Mch. 7.

Dear Afflicted:

Fall does the carbuncles, Redpath does the boils—hire me to do an abscess & Nasby a tumor, or a wen, or something picturesque, like a goitre, for instance, & let's ~~g~~ open the Lyceum Course at Music Hall[1] with an exhibition, with appropriate music & a cold lunch. It would be the sensation of the season/, if Redpath's boils are ~~happily~~ ˌstrikinglyˌ situated. We could get some surgeon to take the baton & lecture while the panorama moves.

But we must come down to the serious affairs of life. I dock your bill about $25 to feed ~~fe~~ fat an ancient grudge I bear[2] the Bureau! To get from Columbus, Ohio, to the next awfully out-of-the-way place, I had to hire a locomotive & pay *$75* for it.[3] If the Fall had adhered to my written stipulations that next place wouldn't have been in my list at all. So I divide up the expense & make you pay a third of it, though my conscience continually urges me to mulct you the full amount, every time I think of the vexation, the profanity & the unspeakable indignation of that long day & the talking to the dullest & stupidest of audiences that memorable night. A place so out of the way that my usual telegraphing cost me $18 that day!

Enclosed please find check for $260 instead of $284.31.

But Lord bless you, being now avenged & satisfied, I will harbor vindict/itude no longer, but upon ~~rep~~ receˌipt of notice that this course is considered unkind & wrongful treatment by you, will hasten to forward the additional $24.31 immediately at once without delay.[4]

Ys ever

Sam*ˡ*. L. Clemens.

✉————————————————————————————————

[*letter docketed:*] *3/8.72* [*and*] Clemens Saml. L. | Hartford Conn | Mch. 7 '72

[1] Boston's largest auditorium. Clemens lectured there on 1 November 1871 (*L4*, 422 n. 7, 484–85).
[2] Shylock's words in *The Merchant of Venice*, act 1, scene 3.
[3] See 7 Jan 72 to OLC, n. 3.
[4] On 8 March the lyceum bureau acknowledged Clemens's check as payment "in full for commissions on engagements for season 1871 & '72" (CU-MARK).

To Orion Clemens
7 March 1872 • Hartford, Conn.
(MS: CU-MARK)

Evening, Mch. 7.

My Dear Bro:

I cannot let you think that I overlook or underestimate the brotherly goodness & kindness of your motive in your assault upon Bliss. I would have you feel & know that I fully appreciate *that*, & value it. The fact that I contemn the *act* as being indefensible, does not in the least blind me to the virtue of the *motive* underlying it, or leave me unthankful for it. Livy & I have grieved sincerely over the thought of the depression & distress this matter is doubtless causing you, & Livy's first impulse naturally (for her,) was to go straight down to your house & tell you to cast the whole thing aside & forget it, & consider that there are sunshine & cheer left in the world, & the ability in you & all of us to find them & enjoy them. And she would have gone if she could. Her idea is correct: forget it. There is no profit it remembering unpleasant things. Remember only that it has wrought one good: It has set you free from a humiliating servitude; a thing to be devoutly thankful for, God knows.[1]

Being now free of all annoyance or regret in this matter, I hasten to say so.

Affectionately yr Bro.

Sam.

[1] Orion had apparently accused Bliss of fraud in the way he produced *Roughing It*—by cutting corners on the quality of the engravings, paper, printing, and binding (see 15 May 72 to OC and MEC, n. 6). In consequence he was fired or resigned as editor of the *American Publisher*, a job that had grown irksome to him because of Bliss's refusal to grant him the independence he thought he deserved. His "humiliating servitude" must have continued until the April issue was ready

for the printer: his name appeared there on the masthead for the last time. Although Clemens evidently considered Orion's "assault upon Bliss" to be an "indefensible" act of disloyalty to his own employer and his brother's publisher, he did not dismiss Orion's charges, but soon sought clarification from Bliss (20 Mar 72 to Bliss [draft]; *L4*, 364 n. 1).

🌿

NO LETTERS written between 7 and 16 March 1872 have been found. Clemens's activities during the period are not easily documented. He was certainly in Hartford as late as Tuesday, 12 March, when he had a painful conference with his publisher, Elisha Bliss (20 Mar 72 to Bliss [draft]). In addition, on that evening, Clemens was expected at a party at the Hartford home of Joseph R. Hawley. Lilly Warner (1838–1915) mentioned the party in a letter to her husband, George H. Warner (1833–1919). Warner was often away from home in his capacity as secretary and treasurer of the American Emigrant Company, which sold land to settlers and provided services for immigrants from overseas. Lilly Warner remained at home, on Forest Street in Nook Farm, with her two children, Frank (b. 1867) and Sylvia (1871–74). In later years, she wrote for the *St. Nicholas* magazine, and occasionally did professional illustrating (Salsbury, 435; Elisabeth G. Warner, 1, 15; Geer 1872, 133; letterhead of George H. Warner to T. Max Smith, 22 Feb 77, CtHSD). She wrote on 11 March:

> My dearest George—
> Three envelopes from you this morning—one from Crestline & two from Chicago—so you were safely there—but what a provoking delay. And now how perfectly provoking that you are away when Mary Foote & Mr. Hague are here & Hattie has a lovely little party for them tomorrow night. I am so *so* sorry—it spoils half the pleasure. Yesterday was a great ice-storm & nobody stirred out of this house for church— Charley went, & came in to tell me he found Mary & Mr. H. at Joe's. They came Sat. night, & Mr. H. goes Wednes—Mary the last of the week. She stays to get some dresses fitted. Mr. H. came home a week ago & is to go back the latter part of April, accompanied by his sweet little *wife*. I have just been down to call on them, & am much pleased with his face & manner. He is handsomer than his photog.—such fine color— Hattie has asked us—the Burtons, Clemens, Charley & Sue, Perkinses, & Bolles of Springfield, & Jewells tomorrow eve'g, at 7 o'cl. & it will be ever so pleasant—all but your not being there. (CU-MARK)

The party, at the home of Hartford *Courant* editor Joseph Roswell Hawley (1826–1905) and his wife, the former Harriet ("Hattie") Foote (1831?–86), was for Mrs. Hawley's sister, Mary Ward Foote (1846–98), and her fiancé, mining engineer James Duncan Hague (1836–1908). The guests included Henry Eugene and Mary Hooker Burton; Charles Dudley and Susan Warner; Charles and Lucy Perkins; Marshall Jewell, governor of Connecticut, and his wife, Esther; "Bolles of Springfield" was, presumably, Samuel Bowles, editor of the Springfield (Mass.) *Republican (L3,* 97 n. 5, 267 n. 1, 269 n. 4, 294 n. 4; "Nook Farm Genealogy," Foote Addenda, vi).

By 14 March Clemens and Olivia (and, of course, Langdon, undoubtedly accompanied by his nurse, Margaret) were at the St. Nicholas Hotel in New York City. They apparently left the city on the morning of Saturday, 16 March, arriving in Elmira late that day, as noted by the Elmira *Advertiser:* "For the time being Mark Twain is 'roughing it' in this city. He arrived here on Saturday evening with his family, and will remain for several weeks" ("City and Neighborhood," 19 Mar 72, 4; "Prominent Arrivals," New York *Tribune,* 15 Mar 72, 8; "Morning Arrivals," New York *Evening Express,* 15 Mar 72, 3).

🦅

To Unidentified
16 March–28 May 1872 • Elmira, N.Y.
(MS: Howland)

[one-third of MS page (between 5 and 24 words) missing][1]

PIT—splendid is the word. But I never have seen him on the platform at all—never have heard him lecture.

Our people all like his lecturing; but you asked for *my* opinion, individually, & so I have to confess ignorance.[2]

Ys Truly
Saml L. Clemens.

---

[1] All that survives of this letter is the bottom portion of a leaf, inscribed on one side. If the original letter consisted of this single sheet, then only the dateline and salutation (perhaps five words) and a line or two of text (up to about ten

words) may be missing. If, however, the letter ran to several pages, then twenty-four words or so may be missing from this side of the sheet, in addition to any preceding pages. The letter's contents suggest that it was written from Elmira (see the next note). In addition, it is on stationery found in only four other letters, all written from Elmira between 27 March and 17 May 1872.

2 The letter seems to be a response to a query about the Reverend Thomas K. Beecher's lecturing ability. "Our people" presumably refers to the Langdon and Crane households. Beecher's Sunday evening sermons in the Elmira Opera House and his occasional lectures elsewhere had achieved some celebrity since 1868, and he would lecture for the Boston Lyceum Bureau in the 1872–73 season. On 24 March he lectured about the 1872 presidential election in the Opera House (*L3*, 57 n. 9; Elmira *Advertiser:* "City and Neighborhood," 4 Feb 70, 4; "Our Seven Churches," 19 Oct 70, 4; "Mr. Beecher for President," 25 Mar 72, 4; "Opera House Meetings," Elmira *Saturday Evening Review,* 5 Feb 70, 4; 3 Mar 72 to Redpath, n. 4).

To William Dean Howells
18 March 1872 • Elmira, N.Y.
(MS: MH-H)

Elmira, Mch. 18.

Friend Howells—

We are very much obliged for the book—which came today. We bought it & read it some time ago, but we prize this copy most on account of the autograph.¹ I would like to send you a copy of *my* book, but I can't get a copy myself, yet, because 30,000 people who have bought & paid for it have to have preference over the author. But how is that for 2 months' sale?² But I'm going to send you one when I get a chance.³ We have just arrived here on a 2 months' holiday. I shove my love at you & the other Atlantics & Every Saturdays.

Yr friend
Mark.

¹ Howells had sent a copy of *Their Wedding Journey* (Boston: James R. Osgood and Co., 1872) inscribed "To Mr. Samuel L. Clemens with the regards of W. D. Howells. Cambridge, March 15, 1872" (Gribben, 1:335). Serialized in the *Atlantic Monthly* from July through December 1871, the novel was published in

book form on 19 December. On 30 December Olivia mentioned that she had begun reading it (Howells 1979a, 387 n. 4; *L4*, 523 n. 2).

²Canvassers began taking orders for *Roughing It* as early as 7 December, so Clemens's reference here to "2 months' sale," suggesting a starting point in mid-January, is inaccurate. In later statements the American Publishing Company as well as Clemens counted sales from the beginning of February—that is, after receipt of the first bound books (advertisement, *American Publisher* 2 [June 72]: 6; 20 Apr 72 to Redpath, n. 4). Bliss made sure that the impressive results of the canvass were reported in the newspapers. By 8 February, according to the Hartford *Courant*, twenty thousand orders had been received ("Brief Mention," 8 Feb 72, 2). On 23 February the Hartford *Evening Post* reported that the book was selling "very rapidly": "25,000 orders have been received, and six hundred or eight hundred copies are being shipped per day" ("Our Publishing Companies," 23 Feb 72, 2). On 1 March the Elmira *Advertiser* called it "the most popular book of the season, if not of the century," adding, "It is almost impossible— at any rate it is exceedingly difficult—to procure books fast enough to supply the demand" ("Roughing It," 4; *RI 1993*, 875, 876, 890; see also 21 Mar 72 to Bliss, n. 2).

³See 20 Mar 72 to Bliss (draft), n. 7.

To Orion Clemens
19 March 1872 • (1st of 2) • Elmira, N.Y.
(MS: CU-MARK)

Ⓛ

Born, in Elmira, N.Y., at 4.25 AM March 19, 1872, to the wife of Saml. L. Clemens, of Hartford, Conn., a daughter. Mother & child doing exceedingly well. Five-pounder.[1]

In witness whereof, &c,

Sam*ˡ*. L. Clemens.

[*one-quarter of MS page (about 15 to 20 words) cut away*][2]

✉———————————————————————————

Orion Clemens Esq | 54 College street | Hartford | Conn [*on the flap:*]
Ⓛ [*postmarked:*] ELMIRA N Y. MAR 19

[1]Olivia Susan (Susy) Clemens was named for her grandmother, Olivia Lewis Langdon, and her aunt, Susan Langdon Crane. Like her brother, she seems to

have been somewhat premature: the Twichells were "taken aback by the sudden news of the nativity at Elmira" (19–22 Mar 72 to the Twichells, n. 1; SLC 1876–85, 2). Among the first friends notified of the birth were Abel and Mary Mason Fairbanks, who—with their fifteen-year-old daughter, Mary (Mollie)—were at the St. Nicholas Hotel in New York City on 20 March, perhaps having just traveled from Cleveland in response to a telegram from Clemens. (If so, their detour to New York City added about sixteen hours of rail travel to their journey.) In any case, they arrived at the Langdon home soon after 20 March and stayed for several days, returning to New York by 26 March. Clemens did not immediately make a public announcement of the birth, as he had for Langdon in November 1870—somewhat to his regret, because of Langdon's precarious health ("Morning Arrivals," New York *Evening Express*, 20 Mar 72 and 26 Mar 72, 3; *L4*, 227–28, 235–36, 238). Nonetheless, the news found its way into the press. The earliest notice that has been found appeared in the Buffalo *Courier* on 29 March: "This birth is recorded in a New York paper: Clemens—In Elmira, N. Y., March 10, a daughter to the wife of Mark Twain, the humorist. Weight, ten pounds" ("Personal," 1). The "New York paper" has not been identified. The Hartford correspondent of the Boston *Globe* also reported, in a dispatch dated 30 March, "Mark Twain's last, is a daughter about two weeks old" ("Connecticut," 2). These items were then picked up by a number of western papers (for example: "Mrs. Mark Twain . . . ," Salt Lake City *Deseret Evening News*, 10 Apr 72, 4; "Personals," San Francisco *Chronicle*, 11 Apr 72, 1; "Personal," San Francisco *Evening Bulletin*, 13 Apr 72, 4; "Mark Twain's last . . . ," Virginia City *Territorial Enterprise*, 14 Apr 72, 3; "Miscellaneous Items," Sacramento *Union*, 20 Apr 72, 8).

²The bottom quarter of the page has been cut away, possibly because it contained some personal message to Orion.

To Orion Clemens
19 March 1872 • (2nd of 2) • Elmira, N.Y.
(MS: CU-MARK)

Mch. ~~18~~ 19.

Dear Bro—

All well & flourishing. Enclosed please find check for $100.¹

Yr Bro

Sam.

¹This note was written on the same graph-lined paper as the previous letter and may have been enclosed with it, along with the check, now lost.

To Frank Mayo
19–22 March 1872 • Elmira, N.Y.
(MS: NN)

Ⓛ

Born in Elmira, N. Y., at 4.25 A.M., March 19, 1872,[1] to the wife of Sam*ʹ*. L. Clemens, of Hartford, Conn., a daughter. Mother & child doing superbly.
A true copy:
Sam*ʹ*. L. Clemens.[2]

[1] Clemens apparently sent out birth announcements over a period of days, from 19 March (as evidenced by the postmark on the announcement sent to Orion) to about 22 March: Joseph T. Goodman replied from New York on 24 March to an announcement probably sent on 21 or 22 March (CU-MARK), and Abraham Reeves Jackson of Chicago, the "Doctor" in *The Innocents Abroad*, acknowledged receipt of an announcement dated 21 March (Jackson to SLC, 27 Mar 72, CU-MARK; *L2*, 65–66).

[2] Actor Frank Maguire Mayo was one of a group of Clemens's western cronies who met in New York City on 26 March and toasted the birth of the "charming, rosy, wee-bit of a baby girl" (Farington). (The group included Joseph T. Goodman; Frank Farington, local reporter on the Gold Hill [Nev.] *News* and the Virginia City *Union* in the mid-1860s, now correspondent of the Virginia City *Territorial Enterprise*, who was en route to Europe and Japan; and Clement T. Rice, a New York insurance agent who, as "the Unreliable," had been Clemens's journalistic rival in Virginia City in the 1860s.) Mayo (1839–96) was born in Boston, but emigrated to California at the age of fourteen. By 1856 he had begun his acting career, and over the next several years appeared in San Francisco and Sacramento and toured the mining camps. From 1863 to June 1865 he was a leading actor at Maguire's Opera House in San Francisco, and he probably met Clemens during that period—perhaps through Goodman, a close mutual friend. Returning to the East in the summer of 1865, he became a leading actor on the Boston and New York stages, with a repertoire of classical roles and contemporary character parts. (He appeared in Hartford, for example, on 28 February 1872 in Wilkie Collins's *Man and Wife*.) In the summer of 1872 Mayo became the manager of the Rochester, New York, Opera House, where, in September, he opened in *Davy Crockett*, a role he would perform over two thousand times. In September 1894 Clemens gave Mayo the dramatization rights to *Pudd'nhead Wilson*. The play opened in April 1895, with Mayo in the title role. He died the following year while taking it on a western tour (Doten, 2:812, 905, 994; "Among the Saints," Gold Hill [Nev.] *News*, 12 Mar 72, 3; "Passengers Sailed," New York *Tribune*, 28 Mar 72, 3; "Farington," Virginia City *Virginia Evening Chronicle*, 31 May 72, 3; *RI 1993*, 651–52; Joseph T. Goodman to Frank Mayo, 15 June 65,

Alice Fischer Papers, NN; Hartford *Courant:* "Amusements," 28 Feb 72, 3;
"Man and Wife," 29 Feb 72, 2; "Personal," Hartford *Evening Post,* 17 July 72,
2; *HHR,* 139 n. 2, 219–20).

To Joseph H. and Harmony C. Twichell
19–22 March 1872 • Elmira, N.Y.
(MS: PBL)

Born, in Elmira, N.Y., at 4.25 A.M., March 19, 1872, to the wife
of Saml. L. Clemens, of Hartford, Conn., a daughter. Mother & child
doing exceedingly well.
    In witness whereof, &c.,

                                            Samˡ. L. Clemens.[1]

Wrote Buffalo ⎫
about Lawson.[2] ⎭

✉——————————————————————————————————————

[*letter docketed in pencil:*] Susie

[1] This birth announcement was probably directed to the Twichells: the postscript about Lawson suggests that the addressee was a Hartford resident (see the
next note), and the docket appears to be in the hand of Harmony Twichell. Joseph Twichell replied in a letter of 2 April, in which he also sent his regards to
Thomas K. Beecher ("*T. K. B.*"):

                                            Hartford. April 2ⁿᵈ 1872
    Dear Mark,
        We were so taken aback by the sudden news of the nativity at Elmira that really
    we could not find breath for a speedy remark on the subject. And since we put off speech
    in the first moment, later silence has not signified. You deprived us of a luxury we had
    much reckoned on by your confounded precipitation. We had supposed that we should
    have ample scope to wait and wonder, and surmise and hope and expect, but lo,
    you cut us off from even a single hour of sweet uneasiness by your desperate
    earliness. The little maid ought to be called "Festina"—the hasty or hastening one.
    Well, God grant she may keep well ahead of all the worlds worst troubles as long as she
    lives.
        We greet and salute and bless her. And to her dear mother we send our best love. Now
    that we have had Livy among us, we find her absence irksome, and want her back.
    Indeed, about the first thing we thought of when your bulletin announced the birth was
    that now you would return sooner than you had been proposing. Is it so?
        By the way, Mark, you are not going to be in New York in the next few days, are you?

For, you see, I am going down Saturday to stay till the following Wednesday—and going alone. So that we could get at least one regular old classic and attic night together in case we were there together. Again, our love to Livy.

Yours as ever

J. H. Twichell

Regards to *T. K. B.*

P.S. A telegram just received upsets my plan of going to New York as within described. I shall not be there till Tuesday (CU-MARK)

[2] Presumably the Twichells had asked Clemens to inquire among his Buffalo associates about journalist George Dudley Lawson, whose dubious career would soon be public knowledge. Lawson was news editor of the Hartford *Courant* in 1871 (at least until mid-August), and then was temporarily connected with the Hartford *Evening Post*. He married Lottie B. Hale of Hartford on 12 March (Geer 1871, 175; "Centennial Anniversary of the Birth of Sir Walter Scott," Hartford *Times*, 16 Aug 71, 2; "New England," Boston *Globe*, 20 Apr 72, 6; "Marriages," Hartford *Courant*, 15 Mar 72, 3). The Hartford correspondent of the Boston *Globe* sketched Lawson's history in a dispatch dated 30 March and published on 2 April:

> Hartford's latest sensation is the sudden departure from town of Mr. George D. Lawson, a well-known newspaper man, to avoid arrest for bigamy. Lawson is well known to the journalistic fraternity of Boston, having been connected with the Advertiser four or five years ago. He appeared in this city in January, 1871, and during his residence here was connected with two of the city dailies. He was a fellow of unprecedented cheek, and in a short time had made himself known to nearly everybody in town. Being a Canadian, he was very active in forming a brigade of the order of Alfredians here, and was elected Grand Commander, or something of that sort, of the body. He was hand and glove with the Caledonians, for whom he was orator at the celebration of the Scott centenary. He became connected with the Knights of Pythias, and nobody knows how many other organizations. He had not been in town long before he had ingratiated himself with a respectable family with whom he boarded, and after paying his addresses to their daughter for several months married her. A few days ago a letter was received from Buffalo, saying Lawson had a wife and two children in that city. The attention of the grand jurors was called to the case, and Lawson would have been arrested had he not suddenly left town, to the sorrow of his new-made wife and numerous creditors.
>
> By his own story, Lawson had lead a roving and adventurous life. He was the son of a prominent citizen of Port Dover, Ontario, who has represented his district several times in the Ontario Parliament. He was educated at the University of Toronto, where he took his degree in 1857, and soon after left home, and, after engaging in several occupations, became a confirmed Bohemian.
>
> He was employed on various Canadian and western papers until the breaking out of the war, when he went to California and resided there several years, being at one time city editor of the Alta California. In 1867 he went to China, as he claims, as private secretary to J. Ross Browne, and, quarreling with that gentleman, was turned off to find his way back to America, with a small amount of money in his pocket. By native wit and what money he had, he managed to secure his passage on various vessels to England, and thence sailed for Boston, where he arrived with twenty eight cents in his pocket, after his journey of 25,000 miles, more or less.
>
> His career in Boston is not entirely unknown to many of your readers. He left your city under unpleasant circumstances, and, after some rough life on the plains and brief engagements on newspapers in Cheyenne, Omaha, Detroit, Indianapolis, Buffalo and Pittsburg, and some reporting for Brick Pomeroy in New York, turned up in Hartford. His sojourn here was unusually long for one of his roving disposition. Lawson was a man of more than average parts, and as the moralists say, had he turned his talents to

good account would have made his mark in the profession. His last newspaper work was a series of articles for the Post on the Portland strike. He was accused by one of the State papers of having received $500 from the owners of the quarries for coloring his articles to their advantage, and, although he denied the charge, did not entirely free himself from suspicion. ("Connecticut," 2)

Lawson's connection with J. Ross Browne, minister to China from March 1868 to July 1869, has not been documented, nor was Lawson listed in directories of the period for Boston, Buffalo, Pittsburgh, or New York City. Between 1861 and 1867, his name appeared in the San Francisco directory only once, in 1865, as an agent for the humor monthly *Puck* (Langley 1865, 271, 364; Browne, 329–31, 344, 351; *L4*, 102 n. 9; "The Story of a Bohemian—The Latest Sensation," Elmira *Advertiser*, 12 Apr 72, 2). On 6 April 1872 the Buffalo *Courier* (whose editor, David Gray, was Clemens's good friend) reprinted the Boston *Globe* dispatch, prefacing it with what may be a reference to the letter of inquiry which Clemens wrote:

> Many in Buffalo will remember a flashy young man who made himself conspicuous some time since in the position of local editor of one of the daily papers of the city—a man who had an abundance of superficial talent, but even more cheek, and in a still greater degree a facility in contracting and not discharging pecuniary obligations. Before printing the following story about him, written by the Hartford correspondent of the Boston *Globe*, we will say that inquiries were sent here concerning his matrimonial antecedents, the answer to which, had it reached Hartford in time, would have secured his arrest. ("A Bohemian Bigamist," 2)

In July the Hartford *Evening Post* noted that Lawson had reappeared, on the staff of the daily Baltimore *American* ("Personal," 17 July 72, 2).

To Unidentified
19 March–8 May 1872 • Elmira, N.Y.
(MS: NN)

.   .   .   .

"S. L. Clemens, Elmira, N. Y.," ~~witholl~~ will find me without any trouble.

Our tribe is rather unusually well, nowadays[1]

.   .   .   .

[1] All that survives of this letter is the top third of one page, numbered "3," cut or torn from a folder and inscribed on one side. The stationery is of a type Clemens used intermittently in 1872. He must have written this letter from Elmira in the spring, when his "tribe," including Langdon and newborn Susy, were

healthy. On 20 April, for instance, he wrote to Redpath: "Our tribe are flourish-ing—the new cub most of all." Clemens and Olivia visited the Fairbankses in Cleveland from 9 to 14 May, and upon their return to Elmira found Langdon suffering from a bad cold. He was still unwell when they left Elmira on 28 May.

To Elisha Bliss, Jr.
20 March 1872 • Elmira, N.Y.
(MS, draft, not sent: CU-MARK)

Elmira, Mch. 20/72

Friend Bliss—

The more I think over our last *t* Tuesday's[1] talk about my copyright or royalty, the better I am satisfied. But I *was* troubled a good deal, when I went there, for I had worried myself pretty well into the impression that I was getting a smaller ratio of this book's profits than ~~I had~~ ˌthe spirit of our contract had authorized me toˌ promiseḍ myself; indeed, I was so nearly convinced of it that ~~if I had not known you so well, or~~ if you had not been so patient ~~& good tempered~~ with my ~~wool-gatherings~~ & perplexities, & taken the pains to show me by facts & figures & ar-guments that my present royalty gives ˌmeˌ fully half & possibly even more than half the net profits of the book, I would probably have come to the settled conviction that such was not the case, & then I should have been ~~about as~~ dissatisfied, ˌ ~~a man as could be found in the country. I think few men could have convinced me that I am getting full half the profits, in the state of mind I then was, but you have done it, & I am glad of it, for after our long & pleasant intercourse, & the confidence that has existed between us,~~ ˌI am glad you convinced me, forˌ I would ~~have been~~ sorry indeed to have come away ˌfrom your house,ˌ feeling that I had put such entire trust & confidence in you ~~& the company~~ to finally lose by it. ~~And I am glad that you convinced me by good solid arguments & figures instead of mere plausible generalities, for that was just & business-like, & a conviction grounded in that way is satisfying & permanent. So~~ ˌButˌ everything is plain & open, now. ~~I knew I was entitled to half the profits, & you will not blame me for coming frankly forward & consulting you~~

when I felt a little unsure about it. And after thinking it over, & I feel
that, the result being the same, you will not mind ˄readily assent to the˄
altering the ˄of our˄ contract in such a way that it shall express that I am
to receive half the profits.[2] I am sorry the idea occurs to me so late, but
that, of course, is of no real consequence. Any friend of mine can represent me in the matter. Twichell ˄Charley Warner˄ will do as well as another.[3] Let Twichell attend to it. However, I suppose he has his hands
about full; & perhaps he isn't much experienced in this sort of thing.
Then let Charles Perkins do it. Contracts are in *his* line, at any rate. It is
too complicated for anybody but a lawyer to handle, anyhow; I could not
even conduct it myself. I will write him. ˄ask him to do it.˄

                            ˄See page 6.˄[4]

   I am at last easy & comfortable about the new book. I have sufficient
testimony, derived through many people's statements to my friends, to
about satisfy me that the general verdict gives "Roughing It" the preference over "Innocents Abroad." This is rather gratifying than otherwise. The *reason* given is, that they like a book about America because
they understand it better. It is pleasant to believe this, because it isn't a
great deal of trouble to write books about one's own country. Miss Anna
Dickinson says the book is unprecedentedly popular—a strong term,
but I believe that was it.[5]
   We are all well & flourishing—all four of us.[6]
                                        Ys
                                        Clemens.

   (Request added to send 25 23 ½ morr moroccos to friends of mine
named.)[7]
[*on back as folded:*]
½ profit letter to Bliss.

───────────

   [1] Tuesday, 12 March, while Clemens was still in Hartford.
   [2] Clemens carefully preserved this seven-page draft as a record of the letter he
actually sent, which was a fair copy (see the next letter). Orion's recent charges
of fraud in the production of *Roughing It* (see 7 Mar 72 to OC) had prompted
Clemens to question the royalty he was receiving for it. He had signed a contract
stipulating a 7½ percent royalty on the retail price (2½ percent more than he had
received for *The Innocents Abroad*), on Bliss's explicit assurance that this per-

centage was equivalent to "half the profits" (contract of 15 July 70, CU-MARK, in *L4*, 565–66). Orion's revelations about production shortcuts had led Clemens to suspect that Bliss's costs were actually less than he claimed, and that the publisher's profit was therefore greater than the agreed-upon half. In 1875 Clemens summarized the situation for his friend Charles Henry Webb:

> I came to the conclusion that an assertion of Bliss's which had induced me to submit to a lower royalty than I had at first demanded, was an untruth. I was going to law about it; but after my lawyer (an old personal friend & the best lawyer in Hartford) [Charles Perkins] had heard me through, he remarked that Bliss's assertion being only verbal & not a part of a written understanding, my case was weak—so he advised me to leave the law alone——& charged me $250 for it. (8 Apr 75, NBuU-PO, in *MTLP*, 86)

The present letter was an attempt to force Bliss to follow the logic of his own "facts & figures & arguments" and to amend the contract to state explicitly that Clemens was entitled to half the profit on the book. Such a revision would give Clemens grounds for a lawsuit if he could also prove that Bliss had overstated his manufacturing costs. Bliss evidently declined to amend the contract. Clemens decided to sue anyway, but dropped his suit long before it ever reached court, probably by late June. His sense of grievance persisted, however, and in 1906 he claimed that 7½ percent "hardly represented a sixth of the profits" (AD, 23 May 1906, CU-MARK, in *MTE*, 155; 15 May 72 to OC and MEC; 11 June 72 to Sutro, n. 1; *RI 1993*, 807–8, 878–81).

[3] Warner earned a law degree from the University of Pennsylvania in 1858, and for two years practiced law in Chicago.

[4] When Clemens reached this point, halfway down page 5, he left the rest of the page (and the verso) blank, apparently because he stopped to make a fair copy of what he had written and revised so far. He then began on a fresh sheet, page 6, and completed the letter with virtually no revision.

[5] This report of Dickinson's remark does not appear in either of the two known transcriptions of the fair copy that Clemens sent (see the next letter). It is possible that both transcriptions omitted it coincidentally, but somewhat more likely that Clemens himself did so, intentionally or otherwise, when he made the fair copy. Dickinson must have made her remark to the Langdons when she stayed with them after lecturing in Elmira on 1 March. In turn she heard from them about another recent visitor, Frederick Douglass, who lectured in Elmira on 23 February and stayed the night in the Langdon home (Elmira *Advertiser:* "Anna E. Dickinson," 2 Mar 72, 4; "Personal" and "City and Neighborhood," 23 Feb 72, 4). In a 30 March letter to her mother, Dickinson wrote:

> At Elmira I had a delightful time, as always, with my friends the Langdons.— Mrs. L. sent her love to thee & her hope that thee would yet come to see her.—
> What a gap *his* death has made in the house!— She was telling me of Frederick Douglass coming into the house,—taking her hand, & then the tears so choking & blinding him, as to make him drop her hand & go out to the streets.
> "Thirty years ago" said he, "when it was an invitation to the incendiary, your husband took me home, sick, nursed, & cared for, & tended me as a Mother, & now it is his son who invites me, in days when hospitality yet costs something to give."
> And certainly it does. Mrs. L. told me that *three* of her girls refused to wait at the table, & of course got their congee, & when Frederick was leaving [he] asked Charlie to go with him to the hotel.— He stayed one night, & the next was to leave at 4 in the morning, & so did not wish to disturb them, & would go to the little hotel at the De-

pot,—as Charlie was bidding him good-by & was driving off, Frederick put his hand
on his arm, & said "Will you please come in with me." "Of course," said Charlie, I
went, "& found that if I hadn't the wretched little rat who keeps the hotel would have
said *no* to him. Fortunately he's in my debt & had to mind his P's & Q's."
      Pretty state of affairs in this day, generation & region. (Anna Dickinson to
Mary E. Dickinson, 30 Mar 72, Anna E. Dickinson Papers, DLC)
      [6]Presumably Clemens had already sent Bliss an announcement of Susy's
birth.
      [7]Clemens did not reproduce for himself his list of twenty-three friends who
were to receive copies of *Roughing It* in half-morocco bindings. The list he sent
with the fair copy has been lost, presumably because Bliss passed it on to someone at the American Publishing Company. It must have included William Dean
Howells and Abraham Reeves Jackson, to whom Clemens promised copies on
18 and 21 March, respectively, and possibly James Redpath and Adolph Sutro
as well. The company's 15 April statement shows that on 30 March Clemens
was charged $48.92 for "R. I. H.M. 23 & Express prepaid," plus $2.40 for two
cloth-bound copies delivered to Orion Clemens, and $1.80 for one in half-
morocco sent to Jane Clemens (CU-MARK; 18 Mar 72 to Howells; Jackson to
SLC, 27 Mar 72, CU-MARK; 23 Apr–14 May 72 to Bliss, n. 1; 11 June 72 to
Sutro, n. 2).

To Elisha Bliss, Jr.
20 March 1872 • Elmira, N.Y.
(MS draft and transcripts: CU-MARK,
WU, and Anderson Galleries 1917, lot 85)

Private.[1]

                                                                Elmira, Mch. 20/72
Friend Bliss—
      The more I think over our last Tuesday's talk about my copyright
or royalty, the better I am satisfied. But I *was* troubled a good deal, when
I went there, for I had worried myself pretty well into the impression
that I was getting a smaller ratio of this book's profits than the spirit of
our contract had authorized me to promise myself; indeed, I was so
nearly convinced of it that if you had not been so patient with my perplexities, & taken the pains to show me by facts & figures & arguments
that my present royalty gives me fully half & possibly even more than
half the net profits of the book, I would probably have come to the settled
conviction that such was not the case, & then I should have been dissatisfied. I am glad you convinced me, for I would be sorry indeed to have

come away from your house feeling that I had put such entire trust & confidence in you to finally lose by it. But everything is plain & open, now. And after thinking it all over, I feel that, the result being the same, you will readily assent to the altering of our contract in such a way that it shall express that I am to receive half the profits. Any friend of mine can represent me in the matter. Charley Warner will do as well as another. I will ask him to do it.

I am at last easy & comfortable about the new book. I have sufficient testimony, derived through many people's statements to my friends, to about satisfy me that the general verdict gives "Roughing It" the preference over "Innocents Abroad." This is rather gratifying than otherwise. The *reason* given is, that they like a book about America because they understand it better. It is pleasant to believe this, because it isn't a great deal of trouble to write books about one's own country.

We are well & flourishing—all four of us.

Yrs
Clemens

[*list missing*]

[1]The manuscript of this letter has not been found, but it was undoubtedly a fair copy of Clemens's original heavily revised draft (the previous letter). The present text is based on that draft and two transcriptions of the fair copy, only one of which (a typescript) is relatively complete. For details about differences in wording and punctuation in the draft and transcriptions, see the textual commentary. Notes on the draft are not repeated here.

To Elisha Bliss, Jr.
21 March 1872 • Elmira, N.Y.
(MS: CtY-BR)

Elmira, Mch. 21.

Friend Bliss—

At last I have sat down in earnest & looked the new book through— & my verdict is, better a long sight *leave the Jumping Frog out*. There is too much fun in the book as it is. For Heaven's sake let us not *add* to it. Don't hesitate about it but just *take the Frog out*. What *we* want, is that the book ~~she~~ should be *the best we can make it.* We seriously injure it by putting in the *f* Frog.[1] Such is the settled belief of

Ys

Clemens.

P. S. After all the preparations for putting this book on the market right you have let yourself get caught in a close place with a short edition. That wasn't like you.[2]

---

[1] The "new book" was the printer's copy for a collection of sketches which, in December 1870, Clemens had prepared and contracted to publish with Bliss. By 5 January 1871 he had drawn up a table of contents and prepared most or all of the printer's copy for thirty-eight sketches, but by 27 January he had postponed further work on it until after *Roughing It* was published. As Clemens wrote *Roughing It,* he removed from the sketchbook printer's copy one or more unpublished sketches, as well as five previously printed ones, incorporating them into his narrative. And although he probably did no substantial work on the sketchbook in late 1871 or early 1872, he may have added a few sketches from the Buffalo *Express* and the *American Publisher* (*ET&S1,* 595 n. 141). Bliss had again suggested an addition to the contents: "The Celebrated Jumping Frog of Calaveras County." Ever since Clemens purchased the plates of his *Jumping Frog* book in December 1870, Bliss had consistently favored—and Clemens had just as consistently opposed—including its title sketch in the new sketchbook. Clemens's preference was to reprint it in a pamphlet with only a few other pieces, as he ultimately did in 1874 with *Mark Twain's Sketches. Number One.* The present letter indicates that Clemens had brought the printer's copy for the sketchbook with him to Elmira, intending to ready it again for publication. Within the next few days, however, he accepted an offer from George Routledge and Sons to reprint his sketches in England. He used the printer's copy he had on hand, doubling its size with some two or three dozen additional sketches and sending the whole to England (see 31 Mar 72 to Osgood, n. 4). Bliss seems to have made no objection to deferring the American sketchbook once again: apparently by mutual consent, *Mark Twain's Sketches, New and Old* was not published until 1875 (*L4,* 281, 282–83 n. 5, 295–96, 319; *RI 1993,* 826–28; *ET&S1,* 571–86, 589–90, 608, 611; SLC 1865c, 1867a, 1874c, 1875).

[2] The Chicago *Tribune* reported on 17 March:

> Owing to the immense rush for Mark Twain's new book, "Roughing It," from all parts of the country, the publishers have been unable to manufacture them fast enough to meet the demand; but we are assured by Messrs. F. G. Gilman & Co., general agents for the Northwest, that they are increasing their facilities for manu[f]acture, and will soon be able to fill all orders promptly. The thousands of our citizens who have subscribed will soon receive the book at the hands of their gentlemanly canvassers. ("Mark Twain," 5)

A similar report appeared in the Elmira *Advertiser* on 24 March ("In Great Demand," 4). The binding records of the American Publishing Company show that from February through June 1872, at least 10,000 copies a month were bound, the peak coming in May with 16,905 copies. Since 30,000 orders had been received by 18 March, but only 23,695 copies were bound by the end of the month,

Bliss's "edition" was indeed "short" (APC, 74–76, 109; 18 Mar 72 to Howells; *RI 1993*, 890, gives 24,676 copies for March because it includes 981 copies bound on 1 and 2 April).

To John Henry Riley
27 March 1872 • Elmira, N.Y.
(MS: ViU)

Elmira, Mch. 27

Friend Riley—

I don't really know what the phonographer's work is going to be worth. Your story ought to make some 3,000 pages of MSS when he has written it up in full from his shorthand notes—that is to say, 3,000 *folios* of a hundred words each. It may make a good deal more, & *can't* ~~well~~ make less. I want to pay him *by the day* while *taking* the notes; & *by the folio* while *copying* them. I will pay him $3 a day & *board & lodge* him, while he is taking the notes; or, $5 a day & he board & lodge himself— which latter I prefer.

To *copy* the notes (which he can do after he⸍ returns home as well as he could do it here,) is worth anywhere from *5 to 10 cents a folio* (from $150 to $300 for the copying, altogether). About 70 folios ~~a day~~ is a fair average day's work⸍, in copying.

I should ~~wanted~~ it stipulated that the copying should be done & the MSS put into my hands within a given time.

RECAPIT:

$3 or $5 a day while *taking notes;* ~~5 to n~~ Not less than 5 nor more than 10 cents a folio for *copying*⸍ them.

How's that? Can you try for a bargain on those figures & let me know if you fail?

We want a good, *appreciative listener*—find a reporter who is *that.* Get your man to take down a yarn for you & see if he knows enough to enjoy your good points. It is really ⸌much⸌ more important than perfect reporting—though we don't want the latter to be much short of perfect.

If you find your Washington man won't do, try Philada.

If a reporter don't like the terms I offer, *get him to make a proposition.*

I am making large & necessary outlays, now, & ~~am~~ must get things ciphered down as cheaply as possible.

Telegraph me, when you start, & I will receive you.[1]

Ys

Mark.

Preserve this letter for me—have kept no copy—as it relates to business it ought not to be destroyed.

[1] These arrangements for the South African diamond mine book were probably not carried far, for within a few weeks Riley was known to be critically ill (15 May 72 to Bliss).

To James R. Osgood
31 March 1872 • Elmira, N.Y.
(MS: NjP)

THE M^cINTYRE COAL COMPANY   PRESIDENTS OFFICE

ELMIRA, N.Y. Sunday —187 2[1]

J. R. Osgood Esq

Dr Sir:

Indeed I *would* like to publish a volume of sketches through your house,[2] but unfortunately my contracts with my present publisher tie my hands & prevent me.[3] I have just made up quite a portly volume of them for Routledge & Sons, London,[4] but I have to leave my own countrymen to "suffer & be strong"[5] without them. Much love to the boys.[6]

Ys Truly

Saml. L. Clemens.

[1] For the date of this letter, see note 4. The McIntyre Coal Company was a subsidiary of J. Langdon and Company, of which Charles Langdon was president (*L4*, 451–52 n. 1).

[2] In 1855 James Ripley Osgood (1836–92) was a clerk in the Boston publishing firm of Ticknor and Fields. When William Ticknor died in 1864, Osgood became a junior partner; when Howard M. Ticknor retired in 1868, the firm became Fields, Osgood, and Company; and after James T. Fields retired in December 1870, the remaining partners (Osgood, John S. Clark, and Benjamin H. Ticknor) immediately reorganized as James R. Osgood and Company. They in-

herited a prestigious list of American and British authors, including Lowell, Longfellow, Holmes, Whittier, Emerson, and Harriet Beecher Stowe, as well as Dickens and Tennyson. Osgood had significantly enhanced that list, adding many of Clemens's friends: Bret Harte, John Hay, William Dean Howells, Charles Dudley Warner, and Thomas Bailey Aldrich. Clemens tried in February 1875 to give Osgood his sketchbook, only to be frustrated by his 1870 contract with Bliss. Osgood did not succeed in publishing a book by Mark Twain until 1877, with *A True Story, and the Recent Carnival of Crime*. Osgood and Company also published several very successful magazines: the *Atlantic Monthly* and *Every Saturday*, as well as the *North American Review* and *Our Young Folks* ("Copartnership Notice," *Every Saturday*, n.s. 2 [14 Jan 71]: 2; Edgar, 341, 344; Austin, 38–39; *ET&S1*, 619; see also 7 Jan 72 to Howells, n. 3).

³Clemens was bound to publish his books exclusively with the American Publishing Company, both by his *Roughing It* contract and by two additional contracts signed on 6 and 29 December 1870. The first of these, for the South Africa diamond mine book, was about to be redrawn because of Riley's fatal illness. The second, for a book of sketches, would not be fulfilled until 1875 (see the previous letter, n. 1; 11 June 72 to Sutro, n. 1; *L4*, 565–68; *ET&S1*, 435–36).

⁴George Routledge and Sons had been courting Clemens since 1868, when they paid him generously (as he recalled thirty years later) for the right to publish "Cannibalism in the Cars" in the *Broadway: A London Magazine*, a short-lived journal they had founded—in part—to foster good relations with American writers. In April 1870 they published a new edition of *The Celebrated Jumping Frog of Calaveras County, And other Sketches*, which included "Cannibalism in the Cars" as "a New Copyright Chapter," probably with the author's sanction (SLC 1868e, 1870a). Then in February 1872 they paid Clemens a token fee of £37 ($185) for the right to "simultane" *Roughing It*. They issued it in two volumes, fully protected by British copyright, thereby establishing themselves as his authorized English publishers. Almost immediately thereafter, probably in late February or early March, they suggested issuing a British edition of his sketches. This "portly volume," as Clemens called it, became in fact two volumes: *A Curious Dream; and Other Sketches*, containing fifteen sketches that no one had yet reprinted in England, and *Mark Twain's Sketches*, containing sixty-six sketches in all, including the fifteen in *A Curious Dream*. Except for "Cannibalism in the Cars," none of these sketches was protected by British copyright. Even so, the Routledges paid Clemens another £37 for the two sketchbooks, which they soon received from their printer: 10,000 copies of *A Curious Dream* on 8 May, and 6,000 copies of *Mark Twain's Sketches* on 10 May. Both volumes were in fact "Selected and Revised by the Author," as their title pages claimed (SLC 1872a, e). Clemens was able to prepare the book quickly because he already had with him a substantial number of sketches that he had earlier prepared for Bliss (see 21 Mar 72 to Bliss, n. 1). He expanded the contents twofold by using copies of the Routledge 1870 *Jumping Frog* as well as two small collections of his sketches—*Eye Openers* and *Screamers*—which John Camden Hotten of London had published without his consent, in late 1871 (SLC 1871a, e). Clemens deleted some sketches that he did not write, and revised and corrected many others—generally toning down his language to suit his notion of a British audience. He probably wrote this letter to Osgood just before (or perhaps just after) the Routledges' New York agent, Joseph Blamire, shipped the printer's copy to London. The Routledges required three weeks to set a book in type and print

it, as their contract for *The Gilded Age* specified. It is therefore likely that Clemens wrote the letter on Sunday, 31 March, and sent off his printer's copy on that day or the next. Blamire could then have forwarded it on any of several ships that left New York on 3 April and reached England between 12 and 15 April, in time for books to be ready on 8 and 10 May. The possibility remains, however, that Clemens wrote the letter one week earlier, on 24 March, three days after telling Bliss he had "looked the new book through" (*RI 1993*, 876–77; *L4*, 85 n. 2, 411 n. 6, 432 n. 2; *ET&S1*, 550–53, 590 n. 129; Appendix D; "Shipping Intelligence," New York *Tribune*, 15 Apr 72 and 16 Apr 72, 2).

   ⁵From the last verse of Longfellow's "Light of Stars," collected in *Voices of the Night* (1839): "Oh, fear not in a world like this, / And thou shalt know erelong, / Know how sublime a thing it is / To suffer and be strong" (Longfellow 1902, 4).

   ⁶Clemens's *Atlantic* and *Every Saturday* acquaintances (see 7 Jan 72 to Howells, n. 3).

No LETTERS written between 31 March and 19 April 1872 have been found. Mary Mason Fairbanks wrote to Olivia soon after her return to Cleveland, fondly recalling the three children she had enjoyed seeing in Elmira: newborn Susy; her brother, Langdon; and their cousin Julie, Charles and Ida Langdon's daughter, then just four months old.

                                                      Cleveland April 1ˢᵗ/72
   My Dear Livy
      I have had you and your little kittens in my mind all the morning, and the impulse has just seized me, to sit down before I take up my sewing, and tell you two or three of my thoughts. First and foremost I have an unconquerable yearning to hold your babies, and *cuddle* them. That however seems out of question— I am glad I have seen you and them. Mollie and I talk of you all. She seems *infatuated* with the children, and has given Allie [a] most minute and graphic account of the three. How I do wish it was the fashion to travel in balloons—or better still that I was one of the 'genii' of Arabian days—I'd have you all spread around here before you knew anything about it. It is such a pleasant, funny dream to me—this *quartette* of yours. I think of something each day, which I would have said—or some question I would have asked— But sometime when you are strong and the children clamor to come to Cleveland, then we will say all that must remain unsaid till then. I suppose it would be counted *barbarism* to suggest that a trip might benefit *you*, leaving the babies to grow larger. I tried to say that to you. I wish your physician & nurse would prescribe it.

      Another suggestion I wanted to make, or rather a request—that you send your "Youth" to recuperate a few days, and get him out of your way. It seemed to me that he was just ready to have ague, and wanted the tonic of open air[.] The spring is coming to us now freighted with freshness— Willie

Gaylord says nothing so rejuvenates him as a day and a night at "Fair Banks"— If Samuel Clemens will come now, anytime, I will engage Will to play Billiards with him, and give him the range of the fifteen acres— If he gets blue we'll read to him from "Roughing it."

Tell him I want to talk with him when he is making a plan for his new book. I read two or three elegant extracts yesterday to Mr. F. from Holmes "Poet at the Breakfast Table"—and he said "that sounds like Clemens in his best moods." I'm just crazy to have him write one book of *polite literature*—I want him to show the world more of his rich, brilliant imaginings.

But I never make one of these suggestions, without feeling as if perhaps you both wondered at my *Partington* presumption. Of course you cannot write to me now, but your husband can be your amanuensis.

Mollie said the evening we rode away from your house, "I love everybody in that house." So do I.

Mother Fairbanks

"*Partington* presumption" probably refers to Benjamin P. Shillaber's garrulous and opinionated Mrs. Partington, rather than Sydney Smith's Dame Partington (Hart 1983, 688).

By 11 April Clemens was able to take a respite from family life, for on 12 April the New York *Tribune* noted his presence at the Astor House (where David Ross Locke was a fellow guest). He probably made the trip with his brother-in-law, Charles Langdon, who was sailing for England on 13 April (and would remain abroad until July), although Langdon registered at the St. Nicholas Hotel. Clemens joined Langdon at the St. Nicholas on 12 April, and presumably saw him off the next day. He may also have been able to see Joseph Twichell, who had planned to arrive in the city on Tuesday, 9 April (19–22 Mar 72 to the Twichells, n. 1). Clemens was again reported at the Astor House on 16 April, indicating, perhaps, that he had left the city and returned. If so, he might have gone to Hartford to consult his lawyer, Charles Perkins, about his royalty dispute with Bliss (see 20 Mar 72 to Bliss [draft], n. 2). He must have remained in New York no more than another day or two before making the ten-hour trip back to Elmira ("Morning Arrivals," New York *Evening Express*, 12, 13, and 17 Apr 72, 3; New York *Tribune:* "Prominent Arrivals," 12 Apr 72 and 17 Apr 72, 8; "Passengers Sailed," 15 Apr 72, 2; "Personal," New York *World*, 13 Apr 72, 7; "Going to Europe," Elmira *Advertiser*, 9 Apr 72, 4; 19–22 Mar 72 to the Twichells, n. 1; Langdon, Jr.).

To Francis E. Bliss
19 April 1872 • Elmira, N.Y.
(MS: Bentley)

Elmira, Apl. 19.

Friend Frank—

What is your *new* number? I only know 149 Asylum.[1]

W^m. C. Smythe (whose letter I enclose) is a splendid ~~on~~ old friend of mine. He is city editor of the principal Pittsburgh paper—a city *where I drew the largest audience ever assembled in Pittsburgh to hear a lecture.* Send him a book. I want a *big* sale in Pittsburgh.[2]

Ys

Mark.

✉

[*letter docketed:*] √ [*and*] Saml. Clemens | Elmira | April 19/72

[1] Clemens had just received two statements from the American Publishing Company, evidently accompanied by a note (now lost) from Frank Bliss, Elisha Bliss's son and treasurer of the company, mentioning that the company had a new address. It now occupied "more spacious and eligible" offices at 116 Asylum Street, having moved from 149 Asylum ("New Quarters," *American Publisher* 2 [May 72]: 4). One of the statements, an accounting of his *Innocents Abroad* sales, (mistakenly) dated 1 April, was written on 116 Asylum Street letterhead, which Clemens must not have noticed. The "accompanying statement" of his personal account was written on 149 Asylum Street letterhead and dated 15 April (Francis E. Bliss to SLC, 15 Apr [misdated 1 Apr] 72, CU-MARK; American Publishing Company to SLC, 15 Apr 72, CU-MARK).

[2] The enclosure has not survived. Smythe had impressed Clemens as a "dry, sensible genius" when they first met at a banquet for Clemens in Pittsburgh on 30 October 1869 (*L3*, 376, 378, 382 n. 5). Smythe was then with the Pittsburgh *Dispatch*. Clemens jotted Smythe's name and "Commercial, Pittsburg" in his lecture appointment book for 1871–72, probably after seeing him in that city between 11 and 14 January (Redpath and Fall, 16; Boone: 1871, 470; 1872, 452). This request—and the one in the next letter, to Redpath—signaled a change in Clemens's attitude toward publicizing *Roughing It*. As he told David Gray many years later, he had feared at the time of publication "that it would be considered pretty poor stuff, & that therefore I had better not let the press get a chance at it" (10 June 80, NHyF, in *RI 1993*, 797). Now, reassured by praise from friends and impressive sales figures, he was willing for it to receive more critical attention (see the next letter, n. 4, and 4 Mar 73 to Bliss; see also *RI 1993*, 797–98, 882–90).

To James Redpath
20 April 1872 • Elmira, N.Y.
(MS: ViU)

Elmira, Apl. 20.

Dear Red—

Warrington's article was delicious. *I* want to go for Timothy one of these days—& shall.[1]

Our tribe are flourishing—the new cub most of all. I was very sorry to hear such sad news of Fall's family, & sincerely hope the calamity will proceed no farther.[2]

I hope to see you all when I come up to the Jubilee.[3] I am practicing a little solo in hopes of getting a chance to sing there.

Could you jam this item into the Advertiser? I hate to see our fine success wholly uncelebrated:

Mark Twain's new book, "Roughing It" has sold 43,000 copies in two months & a half. Only 17,000 copies of "The Innocents Abroad["]] were sold in the first two ~~months~~ & a half months.[4]

I ordered a copy to be sent to you a couple of weeks ago. If it has been delayed, let me know.[5]

Ys Ever

Mark.

[*letter docketed:*] *Twain* Mark | Elmira N.Y. apr. 20 72 [*and*] BOSTON LY- CEUM BUREAU. REDPATH & FALL. APR 22 1872

[1] "Warrington" was William Stevens Robinson (1818–76), the Boston correspondent of the Springfield *Republican* from 1856 until his death, and also the influential clerk of the Massachusetts House of Representatives from 1862 to 1873. Redpath, his long-time friend and fellow ardent abolitionist, had called him "the bravest public man in New England, without any exception" (Redpath 1875, 153). The article that Redpath had evidently sent Clemens was a letter from Robinson to the *Republican*, published on 22 March, which included his reply to a bitterly sarcastic attack on him in "Topics of the Time" in the April issue of *Scribner's Monthly*, manifestly written by its founding editor, Dr. Josiah Gilbert Holland (1819–81) (Holland 1872b). Holland had pursued brief careers as a doctor and teacher in the 1840s, and was for many years an editor on the Springfield *Republican* (and therefore Robinson's boss). He was also the very popular author of a half-dozen novels, narrative poems, and didactic essays,

which he often signed with the pen name "Timothy Titcomb." Redpath and Clemens both knew that Holland had recently attacked humorous lecturers in a "Topics of the Time" column entitled "Triflers on the Platform," in the February *Scribner's* (Holland 1872a). The rejoinder that Clemens found "delicious" said, in part:

> The doctor knows that although his position in the literary and political world is appreciated well enough, only here and there a man has thought it worth while to express an accurate opinion about him. . . . Of course I have occasionally said what occurred to me in relation to his jejune style of lecturing and writing; but I have been on the whole reticent, for excellent reasons, concerning this aspect of the case. "What's done he partly may compute," but he can never know what I have "resisted." . . . The diffusion of the alphabet and of what is called popular intelligence, has compelled the advent of a class of men, not literary men in a proper sense of the word, but men who are able to put the 26 letters into new and often into grammatical forms of prose and verse. Holland is one of these men; the Country Parson another; Tupper another. There are thousands of them. They are embalmed in Allibone, who takes notice of everything that gets between pasteboard covers, but they have no part in literature. It is no use to say in reply to this that there is no accounting for tastes, and that if a man or a woman says he thinks Dr Holland a better essayist than Higginson or a greater poet than Lowell, he has a right to his opinion. A man is at liberty to prefer Browning to Tennyson, for instance, or George Eliot to Thackeray. So a man may say he prefers Holland to Gail Hamilton, or vice versa. But the preference must be within or without the lines of recognized literary excellence or else criticism and comparison go for nothing. (William Stevens Robinson)

Robinson mentioned Andrew K. H. Boyd (1825–99), a Scottish minister known as the "Country Parson," whose facile essays were widely read in America; Martin Farquhar Tupper, author of the popular *Proverbial Philosophy* (1838); Samuel Austin Allibone, compiler of the comprehensive *Critical Dictionary of English Literature and British and American Authors* (1858–71); and editor and essayist Mary Abigail Dodge (1833–96), who used the pseudonym "Gail Hamilton." Referring to religious orthodoxy and salvation, which Holland had discussed in the April *Scribner's* article, Robinson concluded, "If I were to venture to advise Holland I should say to him that he had better not only free his mind of cant, but his head of conceit, and if then he feels the less need of being saved he will be much more worth saving than he is now." Clemens would shortly draft his own reply to Holland (see 18 July 72 to Redpath, n. 5).

²The calamity has not been identified. George Fall's own poor health would force his retirement in 1873 and lead to his death at age thirty-seven in May 1875 (*L4*, 11 n. 4).

³Clemens may have attended the Boston World's Peace Jubilee and International Musical Festival in late June or early July (see p. 112).

⁴No such item has been found in the Boston *Advertiser.* Clemens's figure (43,000) represented orders *received* to date but not yet all filled, since Bliss's edition was "short" (21 Mar 72 to Bliss, n. 2). (By the end of April Bliss was still at least five thousand orders behind: the American Publishing Company's royalty statement of 1 May, covering the "sale of 'Roughing It' since its issue," reported 37,701 copies sold [enclosure with 8 May 72 to Perkins].) Clemens's reference to "two months & a half" suggests that he was not counting sales from the book's formal issue date on 29 February or from its copyright date of 19 February, but from the delivery of the first bound books on 30 January. The bindery records generally support his comparison with *The Innocents Abroad:* by mid-

October 1869, two and a half months after that book's issue, only 12,671 copies had been bound, and by the time of the first quarterly accounting on 1 November 1869, 16,409 books had been bound (APC, 45–48, 106; *L3*, 287 n. 1; *RI 1993*, 876).
⁵See 23 Apr–14 May 72 to Bliss.

To Charles Dudley and Susan L. Warner
22 April 1872 • Elmira, N.Y.
(MS: CU-MARK)

Elmira, Apl. 22.

We have read two ~~b~~Back-logs aloud since we came here,¹ & a thoroughly grateful audience have insisted both times that I write & cordially thank the author—a thing which I was glad enough to do. Mrs. C. reminded me of it again as I started to bed—hence my non-forgetfulness this time.

Livy desires me to write Mrs. Warner in her place, too, since she has not "got down to her work" yet. I have no news save of the household. The new baby flourishes, & groweth strong & comely apace. She keeps one cow "humping herself" to supply the bread of life for her— & Livy is relieved from duty. ~~Livy is very inefficient in some respects.~~ Langdon has no appetite, but is brisk & strong. His teeth don't come— & neither does his language.

Livy drives out a little, sews a little, walks a little—is getting along pretty satisfactorily.

Peace be with you!

I write this note only on condition that it shall not inflict the duty of answering it. I fancy you have writing enough to do, Warner, without bothering with letters.

~~Ys~~ Yrs. Truly
S.L. Clemens

[*on a separate sheet:*]

I have told this lady² to apply to you—though I doubted if you really had time to do the work,

Ys
Clemens

[*enclosure 1:*]

Lansing, Mich.,

April 18th 1872.

S. L. Clemens,

  Hartford, Conn.,

    Sir,

      In pursuance of our design to bring the Woman Suff. question favorably, before the people of Mich., during the present year, we wish to obtain a Play for public representations. I wrote to Mr Locke[3] in reference & enclose his reply. Can you meet our wishes? We will of course, pay any reasonable amt., you may think due such service. Permit me to suggest certain characters as likely to *draw* if well acted. Our object is to make money for the state organization purposes, &, at the same time, to present the question to the people in a popular form. Give us a good play M[r] Clemens, & we will not let your reputation suffer by the manner in which we will deal with it. We intend to present it in all towns large & small throughout the state. If you cannot serve us in this matter will you suggest some one who can & will? Hoping to hear favorably from you at an early day I am,

Resp'y Yours,

(Miss) Mathilde Victor,

Cor. Sec. M. W. S. Ass[n]

A minister of the Fulton or Robert Laird Collyer pattern[4] *rabidly* opposed—a negro—a dutchman & an Irishman, also opposed. A saloon keeper & a young & green graduate of "Yale" or some other college excluding women, also opposed—a reformed drunkard, favorably inclined—a strong minded woman—all the better if an old maid, a strong advocate of the movement—a gay young miss on the rampage after a husband, very much opposed—an old farmer—a regular ol broadhorn very bitter—a young popinjay—just shedding his pin-feathers, opposed. Mixing & mingling these characters with a due proportion of friends & advocates, will I think, give us a drama that will be of much service to us.

[*enclosure 2:*]

Toledo, O., April 15 1872

Miss Mathilde Victor
   Cor Sec &c
   It will be impossible for me to write you a play as you desire,
my time being all occupied

Respectfully

D R Locke

P.S.—I am not certain but that Mark Twain would do it, as he is not
busy at this present time   Write him and say that I suggested him   He
is thoroughly in sympathy with th[e] cause and Can do it (if he will)
splendidly

L

His address is
   Samuel L Clemens
   Hartford Conn

✉

Chas. Duncan Warner Esq⁵ | Editor "Courant" | Hartford | Conn. [*return
address:*] IF NOT DELIVERED WITHIN 10 DAYS, TO BE RETURNED TO [*postmarked:*]
ELMIRA N Y. APR 23

  ¹Warner's "Back-Log Studies" were a combination of informal essay and recreated dialog that attempted to capture the intimacy, good humor, and wit of
fireside conversation in the Nook Farm community. The first appeared in *Scribner's Monthly* in July 1871. Then, after a hiatus of six months, the rest appeared
once a month from February through July 1872. Clemens had probably read
aloud the March and April installments, the latter having particular interest because it introduced the character of "Our Next-Door Neighbor," clearly a portrait of Clemens himself (Andrews, 174–76):

> I ought to explain who our next-door neighbor is. He is the person who comes in
> without knocking, drops in in the most natural way, as his wife does also, and not sel-
> dom in time to take the after-dinner cup of tea before the fire. Formal society begins as
> soon as you lock your doors, and only admit visitors through the media of bells and
> servants. It is lucky for us that our next-door neighbor is honest. (Charles Dudley War-
> ner 1872, 696)

  ²Clemens enclosed a request addressed to him by Mathilde Victor, the corresponding secretary of the Michigan Woman Suffrage Association, which in
turn enclosed David Ross Locke's note to Victor of 15 April 1872.

  ³David Ross Locke, an editor and part owner of the Toledo *Blade*, was well
known by his pseudonym, "Petroleum V. Nasby," as a humorist and platform

performer. He had expressed his strong convictions in favor of female suffrage in his successful lecture "The Struggles of a Conservative on the Woman Question," first delivered during the 1869–70 lecture season (*L3*, 56 n. 1, 389 n. 4).

[4] Justin Dewey Fulton (1828–1901), a Baptist clergyman, was pastor of Boston's Tremont Temple from 1863 to 1873. He was a forceful and opinionated preacher, known for his opposition to women's suffrage, drinking, and the theater. Robert Laird Collier (1837–90), a Unitarian minister associated with churches in Chicago and Boston in the 1860s and 1870s, was a well-known preacher and writer. He lectured for Redpath's Boston Lyceum Bureau from 1869 to 1871, one of his topics being "Woman's Place" (*Lyceum:* 1869, 1; 1870, 2; *Annual Cyclopaedia 1890*, 641).

[5] Clemens conflated Charles Dudley Warner's name with that of Captain Charles Duncan, organizer of the 1867 *Quaker City* excursion (*L2*, 24 n. 2).

To Francis E. Bliss
23 April–14 May 1872 • Elmira, N.Y.
(Parke-Bernet 1954b, lot 290)

[letter from James Redpath, missing][1]

Please send James Redpath a ½ morocco copy, Frank, & oblige

Yrs

Mark.

Address 36 Bromfield St. Boston[2]

[1] The auction catalog that supplies the text of Clemens's note states that it was written "at the foot" of a letter from Redpath, which it describes merely as "regarding" *Roughing It*. Redpath's letter was probably a negative reply to Clemens's 20 April inquiry about whether he had received a copy of the book, "ordered . . . to be sent a couple of weeks ago." If Redpath was among the twenty-three people to whom Bliss shipped books on 30 March at Clemens's order, he evidently failed to receive his copy (20 Mar 72 to Bliss [draft], n. 7). The present request could not have been written earlier than 23 April, one day after Redpath received Clemens's 20 April letter (which was docketed on 22 April), nor later than 14 May, the day before Clemens asked Bliss to send Redpath "another" half-morocco copy.

[2] The address of the Boston Lyceum Bureau.

To Charles E. Perkins
8 May 1872 • Elmira, N.Y.
(MS: CtHMTH)

J. LANGDON,	OFFICE OF J. LANGDON & CO. MINERS AND DEALERS IN
J. D. F. SLEE,	ANTHRACITE AND BITUMINOUS COALS. 6 BALDWIN ST.
T. W. CRANE,	
C. J. LANGDON.	ELMIRA, N.Y., May 8 187 2

Chas E Perkins Esq[1]
  D[r] Sir:
       I have received F. E. Bliss's check for $10,562.13, for sales of "Roughing It" first 3 months. Will you please acknowledge (to him) the receipt of the check, & accompany it with the necessary protest?[2] Or you can attac‖h it to this note & mail to him.
                                    Ys Truly
                                    Sam[l]. L. Clemens.

Please preserve the enclosed note.
[*enclosure:*]

AGENTS WANTED FOR STANDARD WORKS.	OFFICE AMERICAN PUBLISHING COMPANY,
E. G. HASTINGS, PRES'T.	NO. 116 ASYLUM STREET,
E. BLISS, JR., SEC'Y.	
F. E. BLISS, TREAS.	HARTFORD, CONN., May 1 18 72

Dr Clemens
       The sale of "Roughing It" since its issue has been as follows,

In cloth	22,543 cops	
copyright 7½%	.26¼ =	5,917.53

In Library & clo gt[3]	13,952 cops	
copyright 7½%	.30 =	4,185.60

In Half morroco	1176 cops	
copyright 7½%	.37² =	441.00

In Full morroco	30 cops	
	60 =	18.00

The Total I enclose ch for	$10,562.13.

please send me a receipt for same & oblige. A *splendid* showing I think.
Father has been home sick for nearly 2 weeks now but will be better soon
I hope, he has worked altogether too hard of late & worn himself out.
                                                                Yrs truly
                                                                FE. Bliss.

[1] Charles Enoch Perkins (1832–1917), a nephew of Harriet Beecher Stowe and
of Henry Ward Beecher, began practicing law in Hartford in 1855 with his father,
Thomas Clap Perkins (1798–1870), one of the original settlers of Nook Farm. In
1875 Clemens described the younger Perkins, who acted as his attorney until
late 1882, as "an old personal friend & the best lawyer in Hartford" (20 Mar 72
to Bliss [draft], n. 2). Known for his encyclopedic knowledge of civil law and his
companionable nature, he also served as president of the Connecticut State Bar
Association and of the Hartford County Bar Association (Van Why, 8, 72;
MTBus, 204; "C. E. Perkins Dead, Prominent Lawyer for Half Century," Hartford *Courant*, 9 Jan 1917, 1, 7).
    [2] Clemens wanted Perkins to acknowledge the royalty payment, but under
"protest"—that is, without conceding that "half profits" equaled 7½ percent.
Clemens's contention that the two were not equal was the basis for the lawsuit he
had asked Perkins to prepare against the American Publishing Company (20
Mar 72 to Bliss [draft], n. 2; 15 May 72 to OC and MEC, n. 6). The Blisses must
have thought that the amount of this first royalty check was impressive enough
to use in promoting the book: on Monday, 6 May, the Hartford *Courant* published the following item, which was widely reprinted:

> "Mark Twain's" copyright on sales of his new book "Roughing It," for three months
> ending May 1, amounts to the handsome sum of $10,562.13, and his publishers, the
> American Publishing company of this city, forwarded him a check for the whole amount
> on Saturday. The book is having a good sale, over 40,000 copies having been sold the
> first three months. ("Brief Mention," 2)

    [3] That is, the "Library Style" leather binding and the "Gilt Edge" cloth bind-
ing, both of which sold for $4.00. Clemens's 7½ percent royalty earned him $.30
per copy on these. The standard cloth binding ($3.50), the half-morocco ($5.00),
and the full-morocco ($8.00) bindings earned him $.2625, $.375, and $.60, respectively (publisher's announcement and advertising leaflet for *Roughing It*,
KU-S).

To Olivia Susan (Susy) Clemens
9 May 1872 • Cleveland, Ohio
(MS: CtHMTH)

Fair Banks,[1]
May 9.

My Dear Daughter:

Your grandmother Fairbanks joins your mother & me in ~~much~~ great love to yourself & your brother Langdon.

We are enjoying our stay here to an extent not expressible save in words of syllables beyond your strength. Part of our enjoyment is derived from sleeping tranquilly right along, ~~the same~~ & never listening to see if you ~~are snufflin~~ have got the snuffles afresh or the grand duke up stairs has wakened & wants a wet rag. And yet no doubt *you*, both of you, prospered just as well all night long as if you had had your father & mother's usual anxious supervision. Many's the night I've lain awake till 2 oclock in the morning reading Dumas & drinking beer, listening for the slightest sound you might make, my daughter, & suffering as only a father can suffer, with anxiety for his ~~off~~ child. ‚Some day you will thank me for this.‚

$

Well, good bye to you & to all the loving ones who are trying to supply the paternal place. My child, be virtuous & you will be happy,[2]

Yr father
Sam*l*. L. Clemens.

[1]Clemens and Olivia, accompanied by Jane Lampton Clemens, were visiting the Fairbanks home, built in 1870 near Lake Erie in East Cleveland. The visit had been urged on Olivia by Fairbanks in her letter of 1 April, after her own recent visit to the Clemens family in Elmira (see pp. 74–75). The Clemenses probably left Elmira on 8 May, making the trip to Cleveland by taking the New York and Erie Railway to Dunkirk, New York, and the Lake Shore Railway to Cleveland—about three hundred and thirty miles and ten hours of rail travel. Jane Clemens must have joined them at the Dunkirk junction, just three miles north of Fredonia, where she had lived with the Moffett family since April 1870. The Clemenses returned to Elmira on 14 May (*L4*, 118 n. 2, 301, 302 n. 5).

[2]Clemens quoted Benjamin Franklin, who wrote—in the last paragraph of a letter of 9 August 1768 to John Alleyne, in which he expressed his approval of early marriages—"Be in general virtuous, and you will be happy" (Franklin,

837). Clemens published his own twist on this maxim—"Be virtuous and you will be eccentric"—in an 1869 Buffalo *Express* sketch, "The Latest Novelty" (SLC 1869c). By the time he had published *Following the Equator*, he had further transformed it: "Be good & you will be lonesome" (SLC 1897, frontispiece).

To Orion and Mary E. (Mollie) Clemens
15 May 1872 • Elmira, N.Y.
(MS: CU-MARK)

THE M^cINTYRE COAL COMPANY   PRESIDENTS OFFICE

ELMIRA, N.Y. May 15 187 2

My Dear Bro & ~~B~~ Sister—

We arrived last night from Cleveland. Your letter was a great comfort to us, since it speaks so ~~cleer~~ cheeringly of Mollie & the rest of the household affairs.[1] We find Langdon enjoying a heavy cough & the suffering & irritation consequent upon developing six teeth in nine days. He is as white as alabaster, and is weak; but he is pretty jolly about half the time.[2] The new baby is as fat as butter, & wholly free from infelicities of any kind. She weighed 4¼ pounds at birth—weighs about 9 now.

Livy is pretty well, but yesterday's ~~ju~~ journey told upon her considerably—together with the bad news—she heard none of it till last night—I had kept it from her.[3] She feels grateful to you & Mollie, & unquestionably to Mary Burton likewise.

~~Mary~~ Margaret's testifies that Ellen is hard to get along with. That would be evidence enough, without any other, for it must be a hard case indeed that Margaret couldn't get along with. The case is overwhelming, backed up as it is by so much other good evidence. Therefore I want you to discharge Ellen, & pay her ~~x one week's more wages than is coming to her in lieu of two~~ the usual *one* week's ~~notice to quit. But~~ ʌjust what is coming to her—which will be $40 next Saturday.ʌ I want her to leave the premises without ʌunnecessaryʌ delay—& I want you to *lock every drawer* & keep a sharp lookout against her purloining anything. This is only a mere precaution—nothing more—I would take it against *anybody* I did not know.[4]

Hire the cook Mrs. Burton speaks of,—the Apthorp's[5] girl's cousin, if I remember rightly.

The latest & best lawn mower costs $25. Buy one.

Ask Chas. Perkins if he wants you to give him points in my lawsuit. But give ɥ̸ none otherwise.[6]

I send $100 for *house money*. Pay no bills except such as you make yourself. Let all others wait. I will find out what is coming to Ellen so you can pay her off.

Yr Bro
Sam.

Maɟ́ enjoyed Cleveland & is flourishing.

We saw Sammy & Annie a moment but did not stop at Fredonia.

P. S. Let Patrick[7] select the mower himself.

If Ellen stays till Saturday, there will be $~~44~~ ˄$40.˄ coming to her. Therefore, pay her $~~44.~~ $40. (~~i. e. a week extra,~~) ˄(& no more,)˄ & let her go at once.

Sam

If you need more money, write.

OVER.

Now Livy is not willing to pay Ellen a week's extra wages in lieu of a week's notice to quit, but *I* am. Therefore, if she wants it, pay her $44, & make no words about it.[8]

Sam.

✉——————————————————————————————

Orion Clemens Esq | Cor Forest & Hawtho[r]ne sts | Hartford | Conn. [*return address:*] RETURN TO J. LANGDON & CO., ELMIRA, N. Y., IF NOT DELIVERED WITHIN 10 DAYS. [*postmarked:*] ELMIRA N Y. MAY 15

[1]Orion and Mollie Clemens had been staying at the Hartford house since at least 11 May, preparing it for the return of the Clemenses (MEC and OC to SLC and OLC, 17 May 72, CU-MARK). Their letter is not known to survive.

[2]In his response to the present letter, written on 17 May, Orion commented that "Langdon's picture is very fine," noting that "for his age . . . Langdon writes a good hand" (see note 6). Clemens had evidently sent Orion and Mollie a photograph of Langdon, ostensibly inscribed by him. A photograph of Langdon taken at eighteen months, probably another print of the one Clemens sent, is reproduced in Appendix F.

[3]The "bad news" was trouble with the household staff, discussed in the next paragraph.

[4]Margaret, the children's nursemaid, had accompanied the Clemenses to Elmira. Ellen was probably not housekeeper and cook Ellen White, who had been employed in Buffalo and Elmira in 1870 and 1871. She was more likely the cook

hired in late 1871, who, as Mollie mentioned in her 17 May letter (see note 8), had at least one child (*L4*, 358, 412 n. 3, 491, 504, 506 n. 8).

⁵ Miss E. D. Apthorp lived nearby, at 15 Hawthorn Street (Geer 1872, 27).

⁶ See 20 Mar 72 to Bliss (draft), n. 2. Orion wrote a long reply, which he may have enclosed with his and Mollie's letter of the same date (note 8):

Hartford, May 17, 1872.

My Dear Brother:—

I don't know how to approach Perkins. I didn't know you had commenced a law suit. My plan did not contemplate a law suit by you. I suppose it is a suit for damages. I did not think there was any chance for enough to be made that way to justify such a proceeding. My plan would have been to use the fraud you can prove concer[n]ing the printing of Roughing It to give a court of chancery jurisdiction so as to protect you against Bliss interfering with your putting your next book into some other publisher's hands precisely as if no contracted existed concer[n]ing it between you and Bliss. He could interfere in only one of two ways.

1. By injunction, ˏto stop the publishing.ˏ This makes him a plaintiff in chancery, and it is a settled chancery principle that he who seeks relief in that court must come into it with clean hands. Hᶿis hands are not clean. They are stained with fraud.

2. By waiting till your book is published and then suing you for damages. This makes him a plaintiff on the law side, but you can still take it into chancery by an injunction against the further proceeding of ᶁ ˏtheˏ court of law on the ground of the prevention of a multiplicity of suits, and alleging fraud and deception. Chancery abhors fraud.

In the meantime, while waiting for him to assume the role of plaintiff, which is a difficult position, because the plaintiff has every thing to prove, you prepa keep an eye on the paper manufacturer, on Hinckley, book keeper at Bliss's, on the book binders, and on the foremen of the press and book rooms of the Churchman, so that in case of sickness, or prospect of removal from the state, you may get an order from the chancellor to have their testimony taken for preservation on the ground of a probable lawsuit. Imagine the effect of such an order on Bliss when he finds Hinckley subpoenaed to testify as to ˏborrowed engravings,ˏ the amount of paper received from the paper mill for the publis Roughing It; the testimony of the paper man as to its quality; of the Churchman pressman as to the country newspaper style of printing the cuts ˏ&c.ˏ; of the binder as to the quality of the binding, and how many he bound so. Bliss can see then that there is only needed to be added the testimony of some prominent ˏengravers, book binders, andˏ book publishers in the trade, at Boston or ˏandˏ New York, to overwhelm with devastating ruin the subscription business and the American Publishing Company in particular,—ˏbesides inevitably beating them in the suit if there should be a if they should sue, your case would be one of the "*causes celebre.*" It would be seized upon with keen relish by newspapers favorable to the trade, and no the testimony published. All this Bliss must foresee as soon as ˏwhen, he sees the course indicated as soon as an excuse offers to ta ˏto, "perpetuate the evidence" of—say Hinckley. This ˏindirect, quiet threat would be so terrible that he would never bring a suit against you if you simply went quietly along and ˏwrote, your next book and which you have contracted with him to publish, and put it into the hands of somebody else to publish just as if you had never made any contract at all with Bliss to publish it.

Affly your Bro.,
Orion.

For his age I should think Langdon writes a good hand, though his teething seems to have made him nervous. Hope he will soon be well. Rejoiced to hear so favorably from the youngest. Langdon's picture is very fine, and he is a handsome boy.

[*on a separate scrap of paper:*]

If you will let me open a law office here, and put me on a salary of ˏ($100 a month same as at Bliss's), $1200 a year for two or three years, I will watch study all the points of your case with such zeal, and watch your witnesses so closely, and so ˌso, take advantages when opportunity occurs, that I would insure you the full enjoyment of your rightful profits of the next book. I should think Perkins might take me as a partner.—though I suspect his practice to have been mainly on the law side, and that an oversight is not impossible with him in that practice.

If it didn't cost too much to consult the best lawyer in New York I would like to have you see if my plan ˌin the accompanying letter, wouldn't strike him as about the proper one. (CU-MARK)

[7] Patrick McAleer, who had been with the family since their Buffalo residence, was dismissed soon after this, apparently for drinking; he was replaced by a man named Downey (*L4*, 55 n. 5; 20–23 July 72 to MEC). Clemens would happily rehire McAleer in the spring of 1874 (8 May 74 to Charles E. Perkins, CtHMTH; 10 June 74 to OC and MEC, CU-MARK).

[8] Mollie answered Clemens's letter:

At your house. May 17, 1872.

Dear Brother & Sister—

Yours of the 15th just received. I would have written the first of the week, to tell you that every thing was passing off pleasantly nowˌ,, but was not equal to the task.ˌ

Ellen has treated Mary & Patrick, *meanly*, over and over again & day after day.

I saw in two hours after coming in the house that she was getting her temper up against me, because I did not say any thing to Patrick & Mary. Saturday morning I had a talk with her and she said she could not live in the same house with the others, then before we were through said she would stay if I wanted her until Mrs Clemens came home. But that she was thinking of leaving here when you went away—only Mrs Clemens said her wages could go on and she could have her child here. I told her I would see about it. Soon she came in and said she would leave, and would give me a weeks notice. I very coolly, said very well Ellen: Finish your work this morning and you can go this afternoon to look [for] a place. She went, and I believe is at Mrs Twitchells. She was in a rage Sunday morning; but no one crossed her, so she had to cool off by whipping her boy. She left Sunday after breakfast[.] I would have kept her three days to cleane her room and finish the house, washing—but it would have been a three days of trouble to all. I think Mary will prove a treasure to Livy. She is very neat, quick, willing and amiable. She did not stop one moment Monday & Tuesday—from cleaning Ellens part of the house. Ellen said she intended to wait til just before you came to clean her department so one cleaning would do.

I do not believe Ellen was honest, but of course I could not tell, if she were to carry off half in the house as I knew not what your house contained. You will have to see for yourselves when you come. Mary says she has never seen the buttons for the pillow cases in all her cleaning.

The horse, cow, dog, cats, birds, and the rest of us, are at peace with all mankind now; so do not give a thought to affairs here, only to say what you would like to have done.

We will settle with Ellen. Will not get the mower now; have used Mrs Burtons this week.

The beds, need some plants which we will get, if you do not come soon.

For my part I would not want a cook—but will see about the one you refer to— or some other if we cannot get her—and try to have one in by the time you come.

Livy you cannot think how much Orion is enjoying the milk & cream. He carries a quart bottle full for his noon meal, and uses all he wants at breakfast & dinner. He gets up at five, and works upon—upon—I now call it, his idol, until breakfast which he takes alone (generally) at six. I think he looks better already for the grateful change: and I am better.

Write and tell us *any thing* you want attended to.

Please be sure and let us know when you will be here, so we can make arrangements accordingly[.]

Poor darling Langdon, I am so sorry he is having such a hard time—but after all it is well his teeth are coming now before the weather gets warmer. His picture is beautiful—and the ˏother˷ angel, must I say Jennie*ₐ*, ⱥ give her showers of kisses for us.˷ O this long letter! I'll stop. Love to all.

Affly

Mary E. Clemens.

Orion's "idol," as Mollie termed it, was probably the paddle wheel invention he had been working on for some years (*L4*, 396 n. 3, 457–58 n. 1). Mollie also alluded to her daughter, Jennie, who had died in 1864. Orion completed the letter, writing in the margin of the first page:

> Ellen came this afternoon for her things, and Mollie paid her $34, all she claimed, and took her receipt, from March 14 to May 12. Mollie says tell Miss Clara Spaulding that the "Spanish" Doctor proved to be an Irishman unable to talk Spanish. The engagement to Miss Eaton was only one of three in Hartford, all of which went to pieces and he went to Savannah.
>
> We are glad Ma went with you, and that Livy is getting well over the fatigue. ⱶ Our love to our nephew and niece and the rest of the family. (CU-MARK)

Miss Eaton was living in the George H. Warner household for periods of time in 1871 and 1872, employed in sewing work. She may have been related to Mrs. E. M. Eaton, who ran the Hartford boarding house at which Orion and Mollie Clemens lived in the same years (Elisabeth G. Warner, 2; Elisabeth G. Warner to George H. Warner, 13 Nov 71 and 3 June 72, CU-MARK; *L4*, 445 n. 2; 19 Mar 72 to OC [1st]).

To James Redpath
15 May 1872 • Elmira, N.Y.
(MS: MB)

Elmira, May 15.

My Dear Redpath—

Thank you with all my heart.[1] I want to send a copy to the Boston literary correspondent of the N.Y. Tribune—Louise Chandler Moulton, isn't it?[2] I will have it sent to you⸀. Will you give it to her with my compliments?[3]

Ys

Mark.

[1] Clemens's thanks may have been for Redpath's efforts in promoting *Roughing It* to the Boston press. On 1 May an appreciative review in the Boston *Evening Transcript* pointed out the "serious side to Mark Twain's genius" and praised the

book's "eloquent and almost poetical" descriptions and masterful character sketches ("Mark Twain's New Book," 3; 20 Apr 72 to Redpath; *RI 1993*, 887).

[2] Ellen Louise Chandler Moulton (1835–1908) began her literary career at an early age, publishing her first collection of sketches and poems in 1854. After her marriage in 1855 to William U. Moulton (d. 1898), a Boston journalist and publisher, she lived in Boston, where her Friday gatherings attracted luminaries of art, music, and literature. A frequent contributor to literary journals, she achieved a notable success with the first of several volumes of juvenile literature, *Bed-Time Stories*, in 1873. She was well respected as the *Tribune*'s Boston literary correspondent from 1870 to 1876. Extracts from her letters "were copied all over the United States, and they came to be looked upon as a sort of authorized report of what was doing in the intellectual capital of the country" (Whiting 1910, 58).

[3] Redpath may have given Moulton this note as well: it was later laid into her half-morocco copy of *Roughing It* (see the textual commentary).

To Francis E. Bliss
15 May 1872 • Elmira, N.Y.
(MS: CtY-BR)

Elmira, May 15.

Friend Frank—

Please send another ½ morocco copy right away, to *James Redpath, 36 Bromfield st., Boston*. He knows what I want him to do with it among the newspaper people.

I enclose Riley's letter. The simple fact is, that the cancer has ~~him~~ fast hold of his vitals & he can live but a little while.[1] Nine physicians have tried their hands on him, but the cancer has beaten the lot. I shall go down & see him day after tomorrow.[2]

Ys

Mark.

[1] The enclosed letter from Riley is not known to survive, but on 16 May Riley wrote again, and Clemens apparently passed that letter on to Frank Bliss as well. (The provenance of Riley's letter suggests that it was once in the files of the American Publishing Company.) In his 16 May letter, Riley acknowledged receipt of a letter from Clemens written in Cleveland on 13 May, and mentioned that he was undergoing "electro-galvanic" treatments:

> But I am satisfied that it all has simmered down to a simple contest between Cancer and Constitution and I have to take the chances on my cast iron Constitution coming out ahead. This is my only hope. In the meantime I am fit for nothing, and have to fight off care and anxiety as they are not good for my well being I am told.

Try your level best *to get on and see me as soon as you can* for so far my intuition has
not failed me, and I would not insure my bearing up against this, many—let's say YEARS
for luck—much longer.

Wishing myself as I was this time one year ago, and hoping you are quite well with
all your cares and troubles.

I remain
Yours Riley.

Come as soon as you can. (CtY-BR)

²Clemens was unable to make this visit to Philadelphia (11 June 72 to Sutro).

From Olivia L. and Samuel L. Clemens
to Annie E. Moffett
17 May 1872 • Elmira, N.Y.
(MS: NPV)

Elmira May 17ᵗʰ 1872

Dear Annie

I send you by express today black silk to make an underskirt and
lining for your grenadine. I was afraid that you might not find what
would suit you in Fredonia—

If you should not have goods enough send to Mollie Fairbanks a
sample of the goods and she will get you more.¹ I know that it takes an
immense amount of cloth to trim dresses as they trim them nowadays
and I have been afraid since I came home that I ought to have bought 30
yards—

The babies are both of them ~~w pretty~~ quite well, Susie is a healthy
little thing and Langdon is as well as his teeth will let ˏhimˏ be

All I made out of the Innocents Abroad was $25,000, & I sunk it in
the Buffalo Express—& meantime I have made $25,000 lecturing & in
other miscellaneous work—& that I have spent—at least a good deal of
it. So far, I have only received $10,500 out of the new book. I have about
$30,000 in bank, & Livy about the same. So you see we are not nearly
so rich as the papers think we are.²

The new nurse has ~~gone~~ come, & ~~Livy~~ Margaret is gone.³ All, well,

Lovingly—
Sam.

presumably seen in the newspaper and asked about: "Mark Twain made $150,000 by his 'Innocents Abroad,' and expects $200,000 from 'Roughing It.' What innocent would't wander for $150,000, and who would't rough it for $200,000?" (Fredonia *Censor,* 15 May 72, 3). This item, which probably derived from a longer version published in the Buffalo *Courier* of 10 May ("Personal," 1), was widely circulated by the newspaper exchanges. Clemens issued a corrective in the Hartford *Courant:*

> Petroleum V. Nasby, it is said, makes forty-four thousand dollars per annum by lecturing and by his notable letters. Mark Twain made one hundred and fifty thousand dollars by his "Innocents Abroad," and expects two hundred thousand dollars for "Roughing It." It is well worth while to be verdant and to have been rough at those figures.—*Exchange.*
> This is a fair sample of the absurd items that go the rounds at regular intervals. To make $44,000, Nasby would have to lecture nearly three hundred nights in the year, and receive $150, over and above all expenses, for every lecture. He probably does not make $10,000 in a year, by lectures. Mark Twain has received, to date, a little over $22,000 for "Innocents Abroad," and is likely to receive very nearly the same sum for the first six months of "Roughing It," which is not very rough on Mark, but a long way short of the figures in the item quoted. ("Nasby and Twain," 6 June 72, 2)

Clemens chose not to mention to the Moffetts the money Olivia had inherited from her father, which was tied up in a variety of investments; as of September 1873 her assets would total over $237,000 ("In Memoriam," Elmira *Saturday Evening Review,* 13 Aug 70, 5; Charles J. Langdon to OLC, 3 Sept 73, CU-MARK).

[3] Margaret's replacement was probably the nursemaid, Ellen (Nellie) Bermingham, who would accompany the Clemenses to New Saybrook, Connecticut, in July.

To Mary E. (Mollie) Clemens
20 May 1872 • Elmira, N.Y.
(MS: CU-MARK)

Elmira, Monday.

Dear Mollie—

Just a hasty note to say, get the ~~girl~~ ‸cook‸ ~~th~~ Mrs. Burton speaks of if you can.[1]

Also, have the ~~ca~~ cot bed taken out of the little room (off the first floor bedroom) & put it in my study. Leave the book case in the study till we come.

We shall start home about Thursday or Friday noon.[2] Will telegraph.

Affly

Sam.

✉—————————————————————————————————

Mrs. Orion Clemens | Cor Forest & Hawthorne | Hartford | Conn. [*return address:*] IF NOT DELIVERED WITHIN 10 DAYS, TO BE RETURNED TO [*postmarked:*] ELMIRA N Y. MAY 21

[1] See 15 May 72 to OC and MEC.
[2] The Clemenses' return to Hartford would be delayed until Wednesday, 29 May (see p. 97).

To Orion and Mary E. (Mollie) Clemens
22 May 1872 • Elmira, N.Y.
(MS: CU-MARK)

(L)

Elmira, Wednes[y]

Dear Bro & Sister:

We are delayed because we have but one nurse. ₍That is, ~~one~~ only one that can go to Hartford with us.)ₐ However, one of mother's second-girls wants to have the place & is gone to see if her mother is willing she shall go so far from home. If it proves all right we shall start about Monday—but doubtless not sooner.

Aff'ly
Sam.

~~P. S.~~

✉—————————————————————————————————

Orion Clemens Esq | Cor Forest & Hawthorne sts | Hartford, | Conn. [*postmarked:*] ELMIRA N Y. MAY 22

To William Dean Howells
22–29? May 1872 • Elmira, N.Y.
(Broadley, 229)

. . . . .

Since penning the foregoing the "Atlantic" has come to hand with
that most thoroughly & entirely satisfactory notice of "Roughing it,"[1] &
I am as uplifted & reassured by it as a mother who has given birth to a
white baby when she was awfully afraid it was going to be a mulatto.[2] I
have been afraid & shaky all along, but now unless the N. Y. "Tribune"
gives the book a black eye, I am all right.[3]

With many thanks

Twain

[1] Howells's review appeared in his "Recent Literature" column in the *Atlantic
Monthly* for June, which was available as early as 22 May ("City and Neighborhood," Elmira *Advertiser*, 23 May 72, 2). Clemens seems likely to have acquired
the *Atlantic* as soon as it was available, certainly before his departure from Elmira on 29 May. Howells found the book "singularly entertaining":

> We can fancy the reader of Mr. Clemens's book finding at the end of it (and its six
> hundred pages of fun are none too many) that, while he has been merely enjoying him-
> self, as he supposes, he has been surreptitiously acquiring a better idea of the flush times
> in Nevada, and of the adventurous life generally of the recent West, than he could pos-
> sibly have got elsewhere. The grotesque exaggeration and broad irony with which the
> life is described are conjecturably the truest colors that could have been used, for all
> existence there must have looked like an extravagant joke, the humor of which was only
> deepened by its nether-side of tragedy. The plan of the book is very simple indeed, for
> it is merely the personal history of Mr. Clemens during a certain number of years, in
> which he crossed the Plains in the overland stage to Carson City, to be private secretary
> to the Secretary of Nevada; took the silver-mining fever, and with a friend struck "a
> blind lead" worth millions; lost it by failing to comply with the mining laws; became
> local reporter to a Virginia City newspaper; went to San Francisco and suffered extreme
> poverty in the cause of abstract literature and elegant leisure; was sent to the Sandwich
> Islands as newspaper correspondent; returned to California, and began lecturing and
> that career of humorist, which we should all be sorry to have ended. The "moral" which
> the author draws from the whole is: "If you are of any account, stay at home and make
> your way by faithful diligence; but if you are of 'no account,' go away from home, and
> then you will *have* to work, whether you want to or not."
>
> A thousand anecdotes, relevant and irrelevant, embroider the work; excursions and
> digressions of all kinds are the very woof of it, as it were; everything far-fetched or near
> at hand is interwoven, and yet the complex is a sort of "harmony of colors" which is not
> less than triumphant. The stage-drivers and desperadoes of the Plains; the Mormons
> and their city; the capital of Nevada, and its government and people; the mines and
> miners; the social, speculative, and financial life of Virginia City; the climate and char-

acteristics of San Francisco; the amusing and startling traits of Sandwich Island civilization,—appear in kaleidoscopic succession. Probably an encyclopædia could not be
constructed from the book; the work of a human being, it is not unbrokenly nor infal-
libly funny; nor is it to be always praised for all the literary virtues; but it is singularly
entertaining, and its humor is always amiable, manly, generous. (Howells 1872)
    [2] Howells recalled that this remark was made about his review of *The Innocents
Abroad*. Albert Bigelow Paine followed Howells's error and quoted the remark
as "When I read that review of yours, I felt like the woman who was so glad her
baby had come white" (*MTB*, 1:390n; Howells 1910, 3; *MTHL*, 1:6–7; see 19
Apr 72 to Bliss, n. 2).
    [3] See 18 June 72 to Moulton.

To Francis E. Bliss
26 May 1872 • Elmira, N.Y.
(MS: Daley)

                                                             Elmira, May 26.
Friend Frank—
    Please send ½-moroccos to
                        ⎧   Hon. W^m· H. Clagett,
                        ⎪   Washington, D.C.[1]
                        ⎨   and
                        ⎪   Thos. Nast, artist,
                        ⎩   ~~Care Harp~~
                              Morristown, N. J.[2]

✉——

[*letter docketed:*] √ [*and*] S. Clemens | May 26, 1872

    [1] Clemens had known William Horace Clagett in Keokuk, Iowa, and encoun-
tered him again in Nevada in 1861. Clagett figured in chapter 27 of *Roughing It*
as one of Clemens's companions on the trip to the Humboldt mining district. In
August 1871, while reading over the printer's copy in Hartford, Clemens added
to chapter 27 a parenthetical reference to Clagett's recent election to Congress.
Clagett served as a Republican delegate from Montana Territory from December
1871 to March 1873 (*L1*, 123 n. 1, 240 n. 1; *RI 1993*, 180, 627, 868).
    [2] Thomas Nast had been a staff artist with *Harper's Weekly* since 1862, but pre-
ferred to work out of his home studio. In 1871, uneasy about threats he had received because of his attacks on the Tweed Ring, he relocated his family to Morristown, where in March 1872 he bought a house. In December he would
mention to Clemens that he came in to the New York editorial offices only once
a week (*L4*, 373 n. 1; Paine 1904, 84, 120–21, 179–81, 206; 17 Dec 72 to Nast,

n. 1). The copy of *Roughing It* sent to Nast was inscribed on the flyleaf, probably by one of the Blisses rather than by Clemens himself: "Thomas Nast | With warm regards | of the Author | June 1872" ⟨Anderson Auction Company 1911, lot 33; see *L4*, 216 n. 3).

🌳

No LETTERS written between 26 May and 11 June 1872 have been found. On Sunday, 26 May, as Susan Crane noted in her journal, ten-week-old Susy was baptized. Two days later Clemens, Olivia, eighteen-month-old Langdon, and Susy—accompanied by Theodore Crane and by at least one nursemaid—started back to Hartford, by way of New York City. They probably left Elmira on the noon train, scheduled to arrive in Jersey City at 9:15 that evening. There they boarded the steam ferry for the one-mile crossing to New York City. After one night at the St. Nicholas Hotel, the Clemens household continued on to Hartford by train, arriving on Wednesday evening, 29 May (22 May 72 to OC and MEC; Susan L. Crane to Albert Bigelow Paine, 25 May 1911, ODaU; "Erie Railway," Elmira *Advertiser*, 28 May 72, 2; Disturnell, 175–76, 268, 269; "Morning Arrivals," New York *Evening Express*, 29 May 72, 3; "Prominent Arrivals," New York *Tribune*, 30 May 72, 8). The "heavy cough" that Langdon had developed in Elmira had now become cause for alarm (15 May 72 to OC and MEC). Lilly Warner wrote her husband on Friday, 31 May:

> The Clemens came Wed. eve'g—telegraphing for Dr. Taft to be at the house, the boy being taken very sick. He was better again yesterday. I went to see Mrs. C. but Mark came in instead—ever so cordial & pleasant—his wife was worn out, & a little, & he was'nt going to let her get up all day. He says the baby girl is perfectly healthy & no care or trouble. Langdon requires all their care. (CU-MARK)

In 1885, thirteen-year-old Susy set down the story as she had heard it from her parents:

> When in Elmira Langdon began to fail but I ‚think‚ mamma did not know just what was the matter with him. At last it was time for Papa to return to Hartford and Langdon was real sick at that time, but still mamma decided to go with him thinking the journey might do him good. But [when] they reached Hartford he became very sick and his trouble proved to be diptheria. He died about a week after mamma & papa reached Hartford. After that mamma became very very ill, so ill that there seemed great danger of death, but with a great deal of good care she recovered. (Olivia Susan Clemens, 31)

Lilly Warner described these events in two letters to her husband
(CU-MARK). On Monday, 3 June, she wrote:

> The little Clemens boy has at last finished his weary little life. For two or three
> days his cold grew worse, till at last, Sat'dy, it was pronounced to be diptheria,
> & at 9 o'cl. yesterday morning he gave up his life-long struggle to live & died
> quietly in his mother's arms. Of course everybody thinks what a mercy that
> he is at rest—but his poor devoted mother is almost heart-broken. It is always
> so, I believe—those children that are the most delicate & ~~the~~ need the most
> care—that everybody else wants to have die—are the most missed &
> mourned by their mothers. . . . Mr. Clemens was all tenderness but full of
> rejoicing for the baby—said he kept thinking it was'nt death for him but the
> beginning of life. She will see it all by & by, but can't yet, & it is such a mercy
> that they have the little baby. She is strong & well, & an uncommonly pretty
> little baby.

In a second letter, written on 3 and 5 June (Monday and Wednesday),
she continued:

> It has been such a lovely June day—bright & cool—as sweet as that one we
> never can forget, six years ago. That little white form lying at rest over across
> the street has seemed to hallow it. All yesterday & today it has seemed as if
> birds & flowers & sunshine—everything—were rejoicing over that dear little
> fellow's escape from sorrow & pain. . . .
>   *Wednes. Morning.* I couldn't possibly send you a letter yesterday,—&
> none came from you. After breakfast I went up in the grove to get ferns &
> flowers for little Langdon. . . . The plan then was to have funeral services at
> the house early in the evening, & for Mr. Orion Clemens & Mr. & Mrs. Crane
> (the sister of Mrs. Livy C. & her husband) who came right on, Monday, go
> back—by the steamboat train—taking the little boy with them. Mrs. Clemens
> had at last given up going, overcome by the wishes of the Dr. & everybody
> else. We all felt that it would be almost wild for her to go in her poor state of
> health—but she felt at first that she must. We staid by the fountain a good
> while, after walking ~~a good while~~ down along the slope, & then, coming home,
> I found the time had been changed to 2 o'cl. & they were going by the river
> boat. So there was no time to think of anything else. Aunt Belle [Isabella
> Beecher Hooker] has been a great comfort to them—was with them Sat. night
> & has been nearly ever since, taking charge of things in her energetic & most
> kind way. Joe Twichell read from the Bible & made a simple & most appro-
> priate prayer, we all of the neighborhood sitting in the parlor. It began to rain
> hard at noon, & was a regular storm when the carriges started off. Poor Mrs.
> Clemens had to go right back to her room, but several of the friends went to
> the boat. I staid last of all & put things back in their own places, & then came
> home to my own precious little well children. Oh, how sweet & lovely the baby
> seemed & how my heart ached for those who must give up theirs.

Langdon was taken to Elmira and buried in the Langdon plot at Wood-lawn Cemetery, close by his grandfather Jervis (Taylor, 2278–80). A death mask of the child was made, and preserved by the grieving parents. Olivia would write to Mollie Clemens on 7 July, "Seeing the Mothers with their children does make me so homesick for Langdon—it seems as if I could not do without him— Mollie don't let that green box in the closet of the study be touched it has ʌthe cast of͏ʌ Langdon's face in it—" (CU-MARK). The mask was rediscovered in 1938 and presented to the Mark Twain Museum in Hannibal, Missouri. It may have been the basis for the plaster bust of Langdon executed by Buffalo sculptor Augusta C. Graves (1842–1925), now at the Arnot Art Museum in Elmira (Sweets, 1). Although the plaster bust is undated, a letter from New York sculptor Joseph Graef, dated 21 July 1872, establishes that Clemens was making inquiries about "having a childs bust executed in marble" at that time (CU-MARK). Presumably the commission was given to Graves shortly afterward.

In an autobiographical dictation of 1906, Clemens made a rare reference to Langdon, commenting on Susy's 1885 statement, "When in Elmira Langdon began to fail but I think mamma did not know just what was the matter with him":

> I was the cause of the child's illness. His mother trusted him to my care and I took him [for] a long drive in an open barouche for an airing. It was a raw, cold morning, but he was well wrapped about with furs and, in the hands of a careful person, no harm would have come to him. But I soon dropped into a reverie and forgot all about my charge. The furs fell away and exposed his bare legs. By and by the coachman noticed this, and I arranged the wraps again, but it was too late. The child was almost frozen. I hurried home with him. I was aghast at what I had done, and I feared the consequences. I have always felt shame for that treacherous morning's work and have not allowed myself to think of it when I could help it. I doubt if I had the courage to make confession at that time. I think it most likely that I have never confessed until now. (AD, 22 Mar 1906, in *MTA*, 2:230–31)

In 1911, in a letter to Albert Bigelow Paine, Susan Crane transcribed her journal entries for the days before and after Langdon's death:

Quarry Farm
Elmira.

Dear Mr Paine,
    On reading your question in regard to the date of Langdons death, I thought, "Yes it was on Sunday June 3, 1872— But decided to be sure and

looked in the old memorandum book to find the following which I give you to show that we were both one day wrong, and to give you the atmosphere of that event in small measure.

On looking at the small calendar in the book I found June 3, 1872 was Monday.

Fri May 24, 1872 Langdon "has a severe cold

25th Last night I had Langdon in our room, today he is miserable.

26 Sun Little Susy, was baptized.

27 Monday Langdon feeble.

28 Tues Theodore started for New York with Livy & Mr Clemens"—

It was considered safe to start with him, indeed he was bright and cheerful on the trip. He would not accept much care from the new nurse—which made it seem wise for Mr Crane to go. On his return he told me how Langdon smiled upon him and patted his shoulder as he carried him to the ferry from the train. Patted his friend with that beautiful hand, the miniature of his father's, so fair and shapely, with palm always open, as if he cared to lay hold of no material good. He seemed all spirit. Wed, Thurs, Fri, Sat, passed—we heard of the safe arrival in Hartford, and rested in the assurance that the child was doing well because the last days we did not here, as I remember.

Sun 2nd reads—

> "arranged the wildflowers for the church. Soon after we learned that little Langdon's frail life had gone out—

Mon 3. "Theodore and I started at 8⁰⁰ last eve, reaching Hartford at 12m today. Coming to a house of sorrow, with sad hearts, for the child was very dear to us.

Tues 4. "After a short simple service, we started with the body of little Langdon, for home that it might be laid to rest beside father. It was hard to leave Livy in her desolation, but she said it was best.

Wed 5. We arrived in the sunlight, and with dear friends laid the pure beautiful sleeper near his grandfather just as the sun was going down."

Livy was worn and feeble, and could not leave Susy—nor could Mr Clemens leave Livy—therefore they sent the little body to lovers by the hands of lovers.

Mr Beecher—and our old friend Mr Robinson took the white casket in their arms in a buggy, to the old home where you were that dark Sunday. In that same room where Mr Clemens & Livy were married the beautiful child was laid, surrounded by all our best beloved friends—while Mr Beecher offered prayer—

I recall how we lingered to look at that unusually beautiful face, and how conscious we were of the absent parents—

Yes, the drive was in Elmira, but we never thought of attributing Langdon's death to that drive, as I remember. It is true he took cold, but was so much better, that the physician said he was perfectly able to take that journey.

After he arrived in Hartford diphtheria developed— Mr Clemens was often inclined to blame himself unjustly— (25 May 1911, ODaU)

🍂

To Adolph H. Sutro
11 June 1872 • Hartford, Conn.
(MS: Jacobs)

Hartford, June 11.

Friend Ɫ Sutro—

Yes, I know poor Riley's condition, from his letters to me, & although he has been loath to confess the entire seriousness of his disorder, I felt fully convinced that he would never get over it.[1] I shall send him a check for $100 by this mail.[2]

I have been trying for weeks to get down there to see him, but my family affairs would not permit it. Our eldest child remained precariously sick for more than two months, & finally died a week ago. My wife's health is such that I can hardly be able to absent myself from home for some time yet.[3]

Yr friend
Saml L. Clemens.

✉

[*letter docketed:*] *1872.* | Sam'l Clemens. | [*rule*] | Hartford, Conn. | June 11, 1872. | [*rule*] | As to Mr. Riley [*and*] Ans June 30/72

[1] Acting on this conviction, on 22 June Clemens signed a new contract with Elisha Bliss which superseded his 6 December 1870 contract for the diamond mine book (*L4*, 566–68). The new contract (reproduced in Appendix D) gave Clemens the option of publishing the book under another pseudonym, or substituting for it a new book, since it had now become

doubtful whether the information to be received from Mr J. H Riley the party sent to Africa will on account of his ill health be sufficient to enable the sd Clemens to write a book on the subject, or if „it, is sufficient for that purpose whether it will be sufficient for him to write a book which he will be satisfied to put his own nom de plume (Mark Twain) to. . . .

In case the health of sd Riley should be such as to render it utterly impossible for the said Clemens to write the book on the Diamond Fields at all, then he shall be freed from his agreement to write a book on that subject but shall proceed to prepare the other book at once—viz the one upon which he is to appear as author and on which he is to receive 10% copyright.

This new contract, in which Bliss first granted Clemens a 10 percent royalty, may signal an end to their dispute over the 7½ percent royalty on *Roughing It*. It was not fulfilled until June 1879, when Clemens and Bliss agreed that *The Adventures of Tom Sawyer* (1876), for which no contract had been drawn up, would be used to satisfy the Riley contract retroactively (8 May 72 to Perkins, n. 2; Hill 1964, 130–32; see 28 July 72 to Bliss, n. 2).

[2] Mining entrepreneur Adolph Sutro, Riley's occasional employer in recent years, had responded to an appeal from Riley by sending him a check for $100 and visiting him at home in Philadelphia. On 9 June Sutro wrote to Clemens on Riley's behalf. In the same letter, he acknowledged the mention of his tunnel in chapter 52 of *Roughing It* (he may have received one of the half-morocco copies sent out at Clemens's order at the end of March): "I have read your book with pleasure and I think it is a capital production. I am much obliged for the kind notice you gave me" (Robert E. Stewart, 157; 20 Mar 72 to Bliss [draft], n. 7). Complete transcriptions of the texts of Sutro's letter of 9 June, and of his response to the present letter, dated 30 June, survived until at least 1958; their present location is unknown (Robert E. Stewart, 156–57; Stewart and Stewart, 105, 215, 222; *L4*, 264–65 nn. 1, 3, 340 n. 7; *RI 1993*, 360, 866–67).

[3] Clemens never made the projected trip to Philadelphia to visit Riley.

To William Dean Howells
15 June 1872 • Hartford, Conn.
(MS: NN-B)

Hartford, June 15.

Friend Howells—

Could you tell me how I could get a copy of your portrait as published in Hearth & Home? I hear so much talk about it as being among the finest works of art which have yet appeared in that journal, that I feel a strong desire to see it. Is it suitable for framing? I have written the publishers of H & H time & again, but they say that the demand for the portrait immediately exhausted the edition & now a copy cannot be had, even for the European demand, which has now begun.[1] Bret Harte has been here,[2] & says his family would not be without that portrait for any consideration. He says his children get up in the night & yell for it.[3] I would give anything for a copy of that portrait to put up in my parlor. I have Oliver Wendell Holmes's & Bret Harte's, as published in Every Saturday,[4] & of all the swarms that come every day to gaze upon them, none go away that are not softened & humbled & made more resigned to the will of God. If I had yours to put up alongside of them, I believe the combination would bring more souls to earnest reflection, & ultimate conviction of their lost condition, & ~~infallible~~ than any other kind of warning would. Where in the nation *can* I get that portrait? Here are heaps of people that want it, ~~tha~~—that *need* it. There is my uncle. *He* wants a copy. He is lying at the point of death. He has *been* lying at the point of death for two years. He wants a copy—& I want him to *have* a copy. ~~If it will not~~ And I want you to send a copy to the man that shot my dog. I want to see if he is dead to every human instinct.

Now you send me that portrait. I am sending you mine, in this letter; & am glad to do it, for it has been greatly admired. People who are judges of art, find in the execution a grandeur which has not been equalled in this country, & an expression which has not been approached in *any*.

Ys Truly

S. L. Clemens.

P. S.—62,000 copies of Roughing It sold & delivered in 4 months.

[enclosure:][5]

SALT LAKE TRIBUNE,
PUBLISHED EVERY SATURDAY,
=SALT LAKE CITY, UTAH.
PRICE:
$5.00 per year (currency); $2.50 per half
year; single copies 10 cents; clubs,
5 copies, $20.00, (invariably
in advance.)

All communications should be addressed to
FRED. T. PERRIS, Manager.

MARK TWAIN.

A good many of our readers will
recognize the likeness given above as
that of a personal acquaintance. We
were in conversation only yesterday
with a gentleman of this city, Mr. P.
Launan, who regaled us with anecdotes of the famous humorist, remarking that, while contributing to the *Enterprise* his *Slaughter-house* was about
the first thing "Mark wrote up."
"The Innocents Abroad" will long retain its unique and unrivaled place
in literature, but among the short
sketches from his wonderful pen we
have not seen anything better than
the following :

A NEVADA FUNERAL.

BY MARK TWAIN.

[1] Howells's portrait appeared on the cover of the 30 March 1872 issue of *Hearth and Home* (see the illustration on p. 107). (The 9 November issue would include a brief biography of Clemens and a portrait reengraved from the London *Graphic* of 5 October.) *Hearth and Home* was an illustrated household and agricultural weekly founded in 1868; its editorial staff included Harriet Beecher Stowe (briefly) and Mary Mapes Dodge. The magazine, whose readership was limited to "a leisure-class of well-to-do people, pottering with amateur horticulture and interested in literature and art," was a "financial failure from the beginning" (Eggleston 1910, 131). It was sold to publishers Orange Judd and Company in October 1870. Edward and George Cary Eggleston took over as editor and managing editor in August 1871; the latter succeeded his brother as editor in mid-1872. The magazine advertised itself as "one of the most beautiful Journals in the world," each volume containing "about $25,000 worth of splendid engravings, finely printed, and of a highly pleasing and instructive character" (*Hearth and Home* 4 [30 Mar 72]: 260). *Hearth and Home* was purchased by the New York *Graphic* in 1874 and ceased entirely in December 1875 (Eggleston 1910, 146; Mott 1957, 99–100; *Hearth and Home* 4 [30 Mar 72]: 243, and 4 [9 Nov 72]: 836; 5 Oct 72 to Fitzgibbon).

[2] Lilly Warner mentioned Harte's visit in a letter of 13 June to her husband: "I've had a short call from Mr. Clemens—Mark—on his way back from the carriage shed. He is going to the station at a quarter of 5, for Bret Harte, who is coming to visit him. I hope somehow I shall get a sight at him" (CU-MARK). The Hartford *Courant* of 14 June also mentioned Harte's stay ("Brief Mention," 2). The visit may account for the appearance of Harte's name in the 1872 Hartford directory (published in July), where he was listed as "poet, author, b. Forest." The *Publishers' and Stationers' Weekly Trade Circular* of 12 September drew attention to the listing and suggested that Harte was "put down as a boarder at the house of Mr. Clemens" (2:259). The false entry may have been instigated by Clemens as a joke (Geer 1872, 7–8, 25, 74). In 1907 Clemens recalled the reason for Harte's visit:

> When Harte had been living in New York two or three months he came to Hartford and stopped over night with us. He said he was without money, and without a prospect; that he owed the New York butcher and baker two hundred and fifty dollars and could get no further credit from them; also he was in debt for his rent and his landlord was threatening to turn his little family into the street. He had come to me to ask for a loan of two hundred and fifty dollars. I said that that would relieve only the butcher and baker part of the situation, with the landlord still hanging over him; he would better accept five hundred, which he did. He employed the rest of his visit in delivering himself of sparkling sarcasms about our house, our furniture, and the rest of our domestic arrangements. (AD, 4 Feb 1907, CU-MARK, in *MTE*, 273–74)

Harte wrote to Clemens on 17 June (CU-MARK), after his Hartford visit, apparently in response to a letter from Clemens which has not been found:

217 E. 49th St

June 17th.

My dear Clemens,

Many thanks for your kindly concern, my dear fellow, but for notwithstanding all these delays in the processes the result was all right. Slote bro't a note (wh. as Pegotty says "is rhyme though not intentioned") and his cheque, and I found Butterworth the next day.

I liked Slote greatly. He is very sweet, simple and sincere. I think he is truly "white" as you say, or quite "candid" as Mr Lowell would say in his Latin-English.

I enclose your diamond stud, wh. I wore in the cars. My general style and tone wont admit of jewelry, and when a gentleman with a black moustache in the smoking car called me "Pard," and asked me to join him at draw poker and a remarkably over-dressed young lady offered me a seat in her carriage home I concluded to take the diamond off.

Let me hear from you about Bliss. Tell Mrs Clemens I deputize you to kiss the baby for me, as I havent yet been able to perform the osculatory act for mine own.

You ought to be very happy with that sweet wife of yours and I suppose you are. It is not every man that can cap a hard, thorny, restless youth with so graceful a crown, and you are so lucky that, like the Barmacide, I almost tremble for you.

Let me hear from you soon

Always Yours
Bret Harte

M^r. S. L. Clemens

Clemens's old *Quaker City* friend Daniel Slote (of Slote, Woodman and Company of New York City), who sometimes acted as his banker, had evidently given Harte a "cheque" for the promised loan. "Butterworth" was probably Harte's importunate butcher: George G. Butterworth was listed in the 1872 New York directory as a purveyor of game. Harte slightly misquoted a remark of Daniel Peggotty's from chapter 63 of *David Copperfield*. Clemens was serving as an intermediary between Harte and Elisha Bliss in negotiating a book contract. The "Barmecide" provided the illusory feast to the beggar in the *Arabian Nights* (*L4*, 6 n. 6, 248–49, 397–98 n. 1; George R. Stewart, 197, 206–7, 209; Duckett, 51, 76–78, 87–89; H. Wilson 1872, 173; see 28 July 72 to Bliss, n. 2).

[3] Harte had married Anna Griswold in 1862, and by this time they had three children—Griswold (b. 1863), Francis King (b. 1865), and newborn Jessamy, born on 31 May 1872 (*L2*, 40 n. 2; Jesse Benton Frémont to Thomas Starr King, 16 Oct 73, CSfCP, in Frémont, 356; Duckett, 81; Harte to "Zander," 5 June 72, CU-BANC).

[4] Holmes's portrait, engraved by William J. Linton, appeared on the cover of *Every Saturday* on 30 December 1871, supplemented inside by a graceful appreciation of his work. Harte's portrait, also executed by Linton, had appeared on the cover nearly a year earlier, on 14 January 1871. The accompanying biographical sketch made much of the "delicacy and cultivation" captured in the portrait: "The writings of Mr. Harte must account to all tolerably sensible people for such a face as this; and acquaintance with this face cannot but heighten the enjoyment with which they will turn again to his stories and poems" (42; Hamilton, 169). Both portraits are reproduced on the next page.

[5] Clemens enclosed a clipping from the front page of the Salt Lake City *Tribune* of 27 May 1872, presumably sent by a western friend. It is shown here at 85 percent of actual size. The *Tribune* had reproduced Clemens's portrait to illustrate "A Nevada Funeral," an extract reprinted from the Buck Fanshaw episode in chapter 47 of *Roughing It*. The poorly executed engraving was apparently based on an 1869 photograph by Gurney and Son of New York (*L3*, 503). Someone, possibly Clemens, drew double underlines under the first eight words of the introductory paragraph. Patrick H. Lannan, mentioned in the paragraph, was the proprietor of the City Market in Virginia City in 1863. From 1883 to 1901 he was one of the owners of the Salt Lake City *Tribune*. Nevada journalist Alf Doten

Portrait of William Dean Howells in *Hearth and Home* for 30 March 1872. See 15 June 72 to Howells.

Portrait of Oliver Wendell Holmes, engraved by William J. Linton, in *Every Saturday* for 30 December 1871.

Portrait of Bret Harte, engraved by Linton, in *Every Saturday* for 14 January 1871.

described him in 1899 as "one of the best and most popularly known former
Comstockers" who had dabbled in journalism in Virginia City (Doten, 3:2228;
Malmquist, 73–74, 202; Kelly, 247). Clemens's early *Territorial Enterprise* article
on Lannan's slaughterhouse has not been identified.

To Louise Chandler Moulton
18 June 1872 • Hartford, Conn.
(MS: DLC)

Forest street
Hartford, June 18.

Dear Mrs Moulton—

(I will explain the seeming ostentation of the above date, since it is
framed as it is for the express purpose of *avoiding,* ostentation, & at the
same time *snubbing* the English affectation which has led the owner of
this property to give it a fanciful name, as if it were a ducal seat;[1] I do
not occupy the whole of Forest street, but only an unnumbered &
impossibly-to-be-designated section or corner of it.)

I am *content,* now that the book has been praised in the Tribune—
& so I thank you with all that honest glow of gratitude that comes into a
mother's eyes when a stranger praises her child.[2] Indeed, it is my sore
spot that my publisher, in a frenzy of economy, has sent not a copy of my
book to any newspaper to be reviewed, but is only always *going* to do it—
so I seem to be publishing a book that attracts not the slightest mention.
It is small consolation to me when he says, "Where is the use of it?—the
book is 4 months & one week old, we are printing the 75th thousand, &
are still behind the orders." If I say, "If you had had the book noticed in
all the papers ₐyouₐ would be now printing the 150th thousand, maybe,"
the wisdom falls upon a sodden mind that refuses to be enlightened.[3] But
I am content, now, & I thank you.

And I thank you also for expressing your kindly & thoroughly welcome sympathy for our irreparable loss. We did feel such a jubilant pride
in our boy. You know how honest is the conviction that the child that is

gone was the one only spirit that was perfect. When we shall feel "reconciled," God only can tell. To us it seems a far away time, indeed.

Yours Very Sincerely

Sam*¹*. L. Clemens.

¹The Hookers' "fanciful name" for their house has not been found. For the
Clemenses' facetious name, see 4 Jan 72 to OLC.

²Moulton's review of *Roughing It* appeared in her column, "Literary Notes,"
in the New York *Tribune* of 10 June 1872:

> For pure fun, I know of nothing which has been published this year to compare with
> "Roughing It," by Mark Twain (Samuel S. Clemens), a New-England, though not a
> Boston, issue. It is a large and handsome book, full of the funniest possible illustrations.
> In his preface the author penitently deplores the fact that there *is* information in the
> volume, concerning an interesting episode in the history of the Far West—the rise,
> growth, and culmination of the silver-mining fever in Nevada. . . . Having thus dep-
> recated censure for any misplaced wisdom which may be gleaned from his pages, the
> author commences his irresistible tale. It is funny everywhere; perhaps it is funniest of
> all when he sojourns in Salt Lake City, and learns to understand the Mormons through
> the revelations of their Gentile neighbors. (Moulton)

Moulton then paraphrased or quoted several episodes from the book.

³This criticism of Bliss is clearly disingenuous, since the responsibility for
withholding review copies, at least until April, was Clemens's alone (see 19 Apr
72 to Bliss, n. 2). For reviews of the book see *RI 1993*, 882–90.

To Joseph L. Blamire
21 June 1872 • Hartford, Conn.
(MS: ViU)

Hartford 21ˢᵗ·

Joseph L. Blamire Esq¹

Dʳ Sir:

We are very much obliged for the books,² & shall take pleasure in
reading them to the youngster.

I have just finished revising the Innocents & shall forward it to you
Monday.³

I expect to be in N.Y. next Wednesday, at the house of my friend
Slote, of 121 William street,⁴ & will try hard to look in on you.

I will write the prefaces as you suggest & forward them to you.⁵

Very Truly Yrs

S. L. Clemens.

[1] Blamire was the New York agent for Clemens's London publishers, George Routledge and Sons; his office was at 416 Broome Street. The firm had maintained a New York City office since 1854 (Welland, 15).

[2] Unidentified.

[3] Clemens, writing on Friday, had marked a copy of the first American edition of *The Innocents Abroad* to serve as printer's copy for the Routledges' authorized edition. Collation reveals that he made over four hundred revisions—removing slang, toning down the humor, and making his narrator less ignorant and bumptious. These changes were in part a response to English reviews of the book—in particular, one in the London *Saturday Review*, which (for example) declared, "Mr. Mark Twain here verges on buffoonery" (30 [8 Oct 70]: 467–68; see also the London *Athenaeum*, 24 Sept 70, 395–96; both reviews are reprinted in Anderson and Sanderson, 36–43; see Hirst, 365–77; *L4*, 267, 268 n. 4, 283; Arthur L. Scott). The Routledges, who had made quick work of the two sketchbooks in the spring, were able by 24 August to announce their "Author's English Edition" of *Innocents* (*ET&S1*, 591; 31 Mar 72 to Osgood, n. 4; SLC 1869a, 1872c, f).

[4] Daniel Slote's blank-book and stationery manufacturing firm—Slote, Woodman and Company—was located at 119 and 121 William Street; his home address was 28 West Forty-ninth Street (H. Wilson 1872, 1122).

[5] Blamire's prompting letter is not known to survive. For Clemens's prefaces to the English edition of *The Innocents Abroad*, see the next letter, and 16 or 17 July 72, and 21 July 72, all to Blamire.

To Joseph L. Blamire
23 June 1872 • Hartford, Conn.
(MS: ViU)

Hartford 23[d]

Joseph L Blamire Esq
    D[r] Sir

I ~~will~~ enclose preface for Roughing It. I suppose it will do just as it is for two volumes if you divide the book.[1]

Will try not to forget to ship the revised Roughing It today.

Ys Truly

S L Clemens.

[*enclosure:*]

Preface to the English Edition.[2]

———

Messrs. Geo Routledge & Sons pay me ~~coy~~ copyright on my books. The moral grandeur of this thing cannot be overestimated in an age like

ours, when even the sublimest natures betray the taint of earth, & the noblest & ˄the˄ purest among us will steal. ~~at J. C. H.~~[3]
This firm is truly an abnormal firm. ~~Other firms republish my books & refine & instruct & uplift whole tribes & peoples with them, yet never pay the benefactor a cent.~~ If there is another in foreign parts with similar instincts I have not ~~heard of it.~~ ˄had personal dealings with it.˄

My appreciation of ~~this~~ the moral singularity ˄I am lauding˄ is attested by the fact that at ~~their~~ the request of ~~Messrs G R & S Rout-ledge~~ ˄this house˄ ˄this publishing house˄ I have ~~sat up ni~~ wrought diligently, here in oppressive midsummer, until I have accomplished a thorough revision & correction of this book for republication in England, in defiance of the opinions of ~~eminent physicians that~~ ˄the great & wise˄ historian Josephus,[4] that "during the enervating season of summer, all persons so delicately constituted as authors & preachers ought to refrain from arduous employments ˄of any kind˄ & do nothing but worship nature, breathe the pure atmosphere of woods & mountains, & fool around."

Mark Twain.

[1] Clemens absentmindedly wrote "Roughing It," here and below, when he meant to write "Innocents Abroad." Despite the intention expressed in his previous letter to Blamire, Clemens enclosed only one preface. The Routledges did divide the book into two parts—*The Innocents Abroad* and *The New Pilgrims' Progress*—and soon pressed for a second preface (10 July 72 to Blamire, n. 1).

[2] Within a few weeks Clemens decided to revise this preface (21 July 72 to Blamire).

[3] This canceled reference to publisher John Camden Hotten is apparently the vestige of an earlier version, now lost. Hotten's piracies had recently become a subject of public controversy: in mid-May Hotten and the Routledges had begun to skirmish—in letters published in the London *Spectator*—over the issue of unauthorized versions of Mark Twain's sketches (see 20 Sept 72 to the editor of the London *Spectator*, n. 7).

[4] Clemens had recently invoked the Jewish historian Flavius Josephus (A.D. 37–?100) to humorous effect in his 1871 sketch, "A Brace of Brief Lectures on Science" (Part 2), and in chapter 22 of *Roughing It*. Clemens's library included a copy of the two-volume 1829 edition of *The Genuine Works of Josephus*, although it is not known when he acquired it (SLC 1871i; Gribben, 1:361).

No LETTERS written between 23 June and 9 July 1872 have been found. Clemens had expressed his intention of being in New York City on 26 June, perhaps staying with Dan Slote (21 June 72 to Blamire), but no mention of his presence in the city has been found until 1 July, when the New York *Tribune* listed him among the previous day's arrivals at the St. Nicholas Hotel. About this time, Clemens may also have made his long-planned junket to the Boston World's Peace Jubilee and International Musical Festival (20 Apr 72 to Redpath), although he is not mentioned in accounts of the festival. (He did, however, purchase monogrammed stationery from a Boston stationer sometime during this period: see 25–27? July 72 to MEC, n. 1.) The festival ran from 17 June to 4 July, attracting up to one hundred thousand visitors a day. A vast temporary coliseum was built for concerts of soloists and bands from all over the world, and a chorus of twenty thousand voices was featured. James R. Osgood and Company were among the principal underwriters of the event, and Osgood himself presided over the Press Reception Committee. Clemens referred to the Jubilee in one of his June 1873 New York *Herald* letters, but his ambiguous remark does not confirm his own attendance: having failed to secure a seat for a concert at the Albert Hall in London, he noted that it was supposed "to seat 13,000 people, and surely that is a thing worth seeing—at least to a man who was not at the Boston Jubilee" (SLC 1873r; "Prominent Arrivals," New York *Tribune*, 1 July 72, 8; Boston *Advertiser:* "Amusements," 17 June 72, 1; "The World's Jubilee and International Musical Festival," 17 June 72, Supplement, 1; "The Last Days," 6 July 72, 1).

Clemens was certainly home by 5 July, when the family packed up precipitately to flee the summer heat. The next day, with Orion and Mollie once again in charge of the Hartford house, Clemens, Olivia, infant Susy, and the nursemaid Nellie removed to the waterside resort of Fenwick Hall at Saybrook Point, just north of New Saybrook (now Saybrook), Connecticut, two hours by rail from Hartford (11 Aug 72 to Fairbanks; OLC to MEC, 12 July 72, CU-MARK; Holman, 3, 46). Completed in 1871, Fenwick Hall was in its second season. The "splendid" hotel

> was built at Saybrook Point at the mouth of the Connecticut. A company had been formed . . . and $100,000 of stock taken principally by Hartford men, to improve the fine location afforded at that point for building up a favorable watering place. The land was divided into villa lots, and parcelled out among the stockholders. . . . The building . . . is an elegant and spacious frame edifice furnished with all modern improvements. . . . Saybrook Point is essen-

tially a Hartford enterprise and Hartford people take pride in its success. ("Connecticut," Boston *Globe*, 19 June 72, 2)

Many Hartford residents stayed for the entire summer, while others went for weekends or to attend the Saturday evening "hops." Swimming, boating, and picnicking, as well as billiards and bowling, were available ("Opening of Fenwick Hall," Hartford *Courant*, 26 June 72, 2). Olivia wrote to Mollie Clemens on 7 July:

> We are very comfortably fixed here, much more so than I thought we should be from Mr Clemens discription— The air is delightful, the coolness is a pleasant coolness not chilliness. The only disagreableness is that there are so many Hartford people here, but then I stay closely in the room— (CU-MARK)

Unlike Olivia, Clemens was a very visible participant in the daily activities, as revealed in an account that appeared in the Hartford *Courant* later in July:

> There is no more pleasant way of spending a morning than sitting on the cool and spacious verandah of the Fenwick and watching the myriads of sail moving slowly over the broad expanse of water before you. For a lazy man it is delicious. Mark Twain does it every day when he is not playing billiards or setting up ten-pins. By the by, the genial humorist is a great favorite with the ladies, and really the lion of the house. The other day, while scoring at the bowling alley and becoming dreadfully mixed, he exclaimed to a party of ladies around him, in his well-known, drawling tone, "Ladies, I be-lie-ve I do-on't kno-ow any more about this ga-ame than you do." Another story is told at his expense. A charming young lady from the west, to whom Mr. Clemens was introduced, said, "I met you in Buffalo a few years ago, Mr. Clemens. Don't you remember me?" "Yes-s-s, perfectly," said Mark. "You were sitting on the curbstone, with a pa-a-ir of ear-rings on." "Sir![''] said she, and moved off with the air of an offended duchess. ("Fenwick Hall," 29 July 72, 2)

Clemens also took part in the *tableaux vivants* staged in the hotel's parlor, entertaining the guests on the evening of 29 July with "an inimitable personation of Mrs. Jarley," the wax-works exhibitor in Dickens's *Old Curiosity Shop* ("Brief Mention," Hartford *Courant*, 31 July 72, 2). Three leaves of his script for that entertainment survive in the Mark Twain Papers. Clemens, as Mrs. Jarley, seems to have provided a running narration for the *tableaux*, interspersing personal remarks, such as the following:

> Then I married a scrub by the name of Mark Twain—one of these ritin mejums. Mark T warn't his *real* name—but if all I've heard is true, he had good

reasons for not trottin out his other one. He wouldn[']t steal—Oh, no—a man with a mug like that wouldn't steal—but people noticed that when he came around it was pooty difficult to make their things stay wher they put 'em. And I always noticed myself that his clothes warn't any particular size, & they had more different marks in 'em than was *necessary.* (SLC 1872m, 7–8†)

Clemens's literary activity during his Saybrook stay may have produced more than the Jarley script. Isabel V. Lyon, his secretary from 1902 to 1909, later recalled his response to an inquiry about "when & where" he began to write *The Adventures of Tom Sawyer:*

> he spoke with tenderness of the boy and the playmates and the pranks which inspired Tom Sawyer. . . . He said that during all the years between boyhood and a summer spent in Saybrook, Connecticut—"about 1872"—when he definitely began to write a book about those boys, he had "never lost sight of the magic and freedom and careless young life on the river." (Isabel V. Lyon to W. T. H. Howe, 28 Nov 1934, NN-B)

❦

To Francis E. Bliss
9–12 July 1872 • New Saybrook, Conn.
(MS: MoPeS)

This is from my sister, Mrs. P. A. Moffett. Will you attend to it, Frank,?

The former bill was $4.15. How was that?

Ys
Clemens.

P. A. MOFFETT.

Fredonia July 8./72.

My dear Brother:

Sammy succeeded in getting only three subscribers before he left home. It seems the Dunkirk agent did canvass this village but not very thoroughly, so there is still a chance for Sammy. He thinks he can get more names when he comes back. I rec'd a letter from Mrs. Beecher to-day, telling me of his safe arrival Saturday morning about six o'clock.[1]

He filled up one of the publisher's blanks before he left and intended writing to them himself but was so busy celebrating the 4th he could not find time. I thought I would bother you this time and next time he could write directly to them. I cannot send the money because I do not know how much will be deducted from the regular price of the books. I suppose they will be willing to collect from the express company as they did before.[2]

I wish you and Livy would write and let us know how[3]

.   .   .   .

I have a cold in my head. Ma and Annie are as well as usual.

✉—————————————————————————————

[*letter docketed:*] S. Clemens | July 8th 72.

   [1] The reason for eleven-year-old Samuel Moffett's trip has not been discovered, nor has Mrs. Beecher been identified.

   [2] Sammy was canvassing for the American Publishing Company, selling books (almost certainly *Roughing It*) to subscribers on the basis of a prospectus. He then ordered the books from the company at a discount that at this time was 50 percent of the "regular" (retail) price. Pamela was apparently submitting an order for three books on Sammy's behalf, and expected him to pay as he had done with his earlier order (which had totaled $4.15), by giving the money to the express company upon delivery. The American Publishing Company would then "collect from the express company." When Sammy distributed the books, his subscribers would pay him the full retail price. Clemens's puzzlement over the "former bill" of $4.15 was understandable: that total was not possible if Sammy ordered one or two books at a 50 percent discount off the four possible retail prices (8 May 72 to Perkins, n. 3; *L4*, 253 n. 2; Hill 1964, 5–6, 178–79; Lehmann-Haupt, 251–52; *Facts*, 149; "Conditions," *Roughing It* prospectus, CU-MARK; *HF*, 844).

   [3] Pamela's letter breaks off abruptly at this point, with both sides of one leaf covered (the remaining sentences are a postscript written along the margin of the first page). Clemens wrote his message at the top of the first page and forwarded the letter to Frank Bliss, probably on 9 or 10 July, but certainly by 12 July, when Olivia wrote to Mollie Clemens, "I enclose you part of Pamela's letter, Mr Clemens tore off the rest and sent it to Mr Bliss as it was on business, so this is all that I have seen of the letter" (CU-MARK). The balance of Pamela's letter has not been found.

To Joseph L. Blamire
10 July 1872 • New Saybrook, Conn.
(MS: Routledge)

GEORGE ROUTLEDGE & SONS, PUBLISHERS,
BOOKSELLERS, AND IMPORTERS, 416 BROOME
STREET, CORNER OF ELM STREET.

NEW YORK, ... 187 ......

Hartford, Conn, July 10ᵗʰ 1872

Received from Messrs George Routledge and Sons of London by the hands of their American Agent Joseph L. Blamire of 416 Broome street, New York, the sum of Two Hundred and Fifty Dollars in payment for a copy of my book "Innocents Abroad" with revisions, additions, and preface (or prefaces) made by me for them at their request for republication of said book in London.[1] And I do hereby sell to said George Routledge and Sons all right and title to said additions, revisions, preface or prefaces for republication in London, England; but this payment carries with it no privilege or right whatsoever for the importation or sale of said book into or within the United States of America, nor does it prevent me from using the said revisions, additions, or prefaces in the United States of America should I at any time desire to use the same in my American Edition of said Book.[2]

Samˡ. L. Clemens.

Fenwick Hall, Saybrook Pt, July 10.[3]

Joseph L. Blamire Esq

Dʳ Sir: Am spending the summer at this quiet ₄ watering place, & am not feeling a bit industrious; but I like your suggestion so much that I mean to write the other preface at the very earliest feasible moment—& I thank you for it, too.[4]

Ys Truly

Samˡ L. Clemens

---

[1] Blamire had enclosed this receipt for Clemens to sign in a letter dated 9 July (CU-MARK), in which he replied to a letter from Clemens of 6 July, now lost:

Samuel L. Clemens Esq.
Dear Sir:
    Your favor of 6th is duly at hand. In reply I have to say that I received all
right the copy of "Innocents Abroad" and sent it promptly to London; (I have no doubt
but a part of it will be already in type by the time you receive this letter, as the steamer
by which I sent it arrived at Queenstown on the evening of the 7th inst.) and I now have
the pleasure of enclosing you our cheque for Two Hundred and Fifty Dollars in payment, which I think you will find correct.
    I wish that (notwithstanding the advice which the learned Historian Josephus
gives to Authors, Preachers, and such like for their guidance in summer weather) you
could get time to write us an additional preface; the one you sent it seems to me will do
capitally for one of the volumes and I think our People will be pleased with it, but they
write me that they think it indispensable that *each of the vols.* should have a separate
preface. I think a preface somewhat general in its character and bearing date July 1872
would be desirable; a little talk *with the English Public* about the objects of the tour, the
Circumstances that gave rise to it, the peculiarities of American humor, some allusion
to Artemus Ward who was a great favorite with them, or any other topic that might
suggest itself to you as a fitting subject for a homely, unconventional chat would come
very well from you just now; I think you could very well write a couple of pages of
something that would come to them with a domestic, home feeling, and that would tend
to endear your writings to them and so lead to mutual profit and pleasure in the not
distant future.
    I enclose a receipt which I will feel obliged if you will sign and return to me for
transmission to London.

                                                & remain Dear Sir
                                                v truly yr's
                                                Joseph L. Blamire
                                                ag[t] for Geo Routledge & Sons

²Clemens never used the revised English text in later American editions, although he authorized the Routledge volumes as the basis for Christian Bernhard
Tauchnitz's Continental edition in 1879 (Tauchnitz to SLC, 19 Feb 79, CU-
MARK; SLC 1879a).
    ³The postmarks on Blamire's 9 July letter show that it arrived in Hartford on
the morning of 10 July and was forwarded to New Saybrook that same evening.
It is possible that Clemens did not receive it, however, until the next morning,
and that he subscribed the date "July 10" in order to match the date at the head
of the receipt.
    ⁴Clemens's first preface—along with his marked copy of *The Innocents
Abroad*—had been shipped on the steamship *Idaho*, which left New York on 26
June and arrived in Queenstown on 7 July. The Routledges must have sent Blamire a cablegram almost immediately, confirming receipt of the book and requesting a second preface (see note 1; 10 July 72 to Blamire, n. 1; "Departure of
Foreign Mails," New York *Tribune*, 25 June 72, 2). On 13 July Blamire cabled
back, "Twain promises second preface" (ViU).

To Francis E. Bliss
11 July 1872 • New Saybrook, Conn.
(Henkels 1930c, lot 351)

FENWICK HALL. D. A. ROOD, PROPRIETOR.

NEW SAYBROOK, CONN., July 11, 187 2

Friend Frank—

Is your father at home? & does he ever come down here. I have heard from Bret Harte[1]

.   .   .   .

but I can't leave here very well just now as our child is not well.

Mark.

[1] Clemens had been trying to bring Elisha Bliss and Harte together to discuss publishing a book by Harte since mid-June (15 June 72 to Howells, n. 2). Harte's letter to Clemens of 6 July, written from his sister's family hotel in Morristown, New Jersey, has been found only as a fragmentary quotation in an auction catalog:

> I don't know what to say about going to Saybrook[.] The baby has been dangerously sick, and we shall not be able to leave here until she is better . . . until Mrs Harte finds the wet-nurse, who, the Dr. says is essential . . . I have spent much of my holiday season running to the Doctor's . . . (distant about 3 miles) and going to the city wet-nurse hunting. (AAA 1925a, lot 322)

To Colt's Patent Fire Arms Manufacturing Company
12 July 1872 • New Saybrook, Conn.
(MS: Ct)

Fenwick Hall,
Saybrook Pt. July 12.

Gentlemen:

A friend of mine who is connected with an insignificant foreign government, officially, writes me to call upon you & "inquire the cost of a Gattling gun complete, including duplicates of certain portions necessary (in a country where repaŕirs will be impossible,) & 25,000 rounds of ammunition comprising the different cartridges used."[1]

As I shall probably not return home to Hartford till the warm weather is over, I have thought it best to make this inquiry through the mail. An early reply will greatly oblige—

Ys Truly

Sam*ᶦ*. L. Clemens.

¹This request might have come from John Henry Riley, who had been appointed consul general to the United States from the Orange Free State. Colt's Patent Fire Arms Manufacturing Company, incorporated in 1855 in Hartford, began manufacturing the Gatling gun in 1866, when it was officially adopted by the United States Army. This revolutionary rapid-fire gun had been invented in 1862 by Richard Jordan Gatling (1818–1903) of North Carolina, who became a Hartford resident in 1870 (Geer 1872, 67, 289).

To Joseph L. Blamire
16 or 17 July 1872 • New Saybrook, Conn.
(MS: ViU)

·   ·   ·   ·

[*enclosure:*]¹

To the English Reader.

A long introductory speech would not become me, a stranger. So I will only say, in offering this revised edition of my book to the English reader, that it is nothing more than a simple record of a pleasure excursion among foreign peoples with whom he is doubtless much better acquainted than I am. I could not have made it learned or profound, if I had tried my best. I have only written of men & things as they seemed to me: & so it is very likely that the reader will discover that my vision was often inaccurate. I did not seriously expect anybody to buy the book when it was originally written—& that will account for a good deal of its chirping complacency & ˌfreedom fromˌ restraint: the idea that nobody is listening, is apt to seduce a body into airing his small thoughts & opinions with a rather juvenile frankness. But no matter, now. I have said enough to make the reader understand that I am not offering this work to him as either law or gospel, upon any point, principle, or subject; but only as a trifle to occupy himself with when he has nothing to do & does not wish to whistle.

The naive ecstasies of an innocent on his first ⌀ voyage, become, in print, a matter of serious concern to a part of the great general world— to-wit, the part which consists of that Innocent himself. Therefore, as nearly unnecessary as this book is, I feel a solicitude about it. Any American likes to see the work of his hands achieve a friendly reception in the mother country, & it is but natural—natural, too, that he should prize its kindly reception there above the same compliment extended by any people other than his own. Our kindred blood & our common language, our kindred religion & political liberty, make us feel nearer to England than to other nations, & render us more desirous of standing well there than with foreign nationalities that are foreign to us in all particulars. So, without any false modesty, or any consciousness of impropriety, I confess to a desire that Englishmen should read my book. That a great many Englishmen have already read it, is a compliment which I mention in this place with what seems to me to be legitimate & justifiable gratification.

Respectfully,

The Author.

Hartford, U. S.,⎫
  July, 1872. ⎬

[1]Clemens's cover letter for this enclosure has not been found. The enclosure itself is the promised second preface for the English edition of *The Innocents Abroad* (10 July 72 to Blamire). It was a fair copy, as comparison with a partial draft still in the Mark Twain Papers shows (SLC 1872j). Blamire must have sent the manuscript immediately to England, on 17 or 18 July, on any of several ships that arrived at Queenstown between 26 and 29 July. The document reached England in time to be set into type and printed with the first 4,000 copies of the *second* volume of the English edition, *The New Pilgrims' Progress*, completed on 1 August. The first volume, *The Innocents Abroad*, was not completed until 24 August ("Shipping Intelligence," New York *Tribune*, 27 July 72 and 30 July 72, 3; Routledge Ledger Book 4:632, Routledge; see 21 July 72 to Blamire). Blamire also wrote to Clemens almost immediately, probably sending him a secretarial copy of his first preface and suggesting that he might want to reconsider it in light of what the second preface now contained. Since Clemens received that letter on 20 July and replied on 21 July, it seems unlikely that Blamire received the second preface much earlier than 17 or 18 July, or that Clemens sent it before 16 or 17 July.

To James Redpath
18 July 1872 • New Saybrook, Conn.
(MS: NN-B)

Fenwick Hall—
New Saybrook,
July 18.

Dear Redpath—

It *is* pleasant to be called for by so many towns so early in the season, but I have decided not to lecture all at all this season; but shall spend the fall & winter either in England or in Florida & Cuba.[1] I never shall lecture again more than one month in one season, & then only in the large cities—this, of course, is supposing that I remain pecuniarily able to follow such a course.[2]

Why yes—I *do* want you to say one thing about me in that article. I *very much* desire it. It is this: that I have been offered *$10,000* to lecture *one month*, next winter, before the associations of the principal cities, or $5,000 for 12 nights[3]—& have declined both offers because I am under contract to write a book[4] & shall not get it done as soon as I desire, if I drift off to other things.

Can you say that? Because I am "going for" Timothy Titcomb in one of the magazines & I would like him to chaw over that little evidence that "buffoons & triflers" are not scorned by *every*body.[5]

My wife is hurrying me to dinner. We are summering here all season.

Yrs,
Mark.

⊠————————————————————————————————

[letter docketed:] Clemens S. L. | New Saybrook | July 18th '72. *[and]* BOS-
TON LYCEUM BUREAU. REDPATH & FALL. JUL 23 1872

¹Clemens's interest in visiting Cuba—ravaged since 1868 by a war of rebellion against the Spanish government—may have been roused by Whitelaw Reid and Bret Harte, who had been guests on a cruise to the island in January. Clemens apparently hoped to gather material for a book ("A Distinguished Excursion Party," New York *Tribune*, 26 Jan 72, 5; see 21 July 72 to Blamire, n. 3).
²Clemens was replying to a letter of 12 July from Redpath (CU-MARK):

Dear Mark:

About *biz* first: Will you? or Wont you? Lecture committees are getting importunate about you. We have $7000 or $8000 of engagements recorded for you—"if he lectures." And this is only July 12! Here are ‚is‚ a list ‚of cities applying‚ as entered: Baltimore, Ithaca, Brooklyn, Elmira, Toledo, Bay City, Elizabeth, Jacksonville, Brooklyn, Minneapolis, New burg, Watertown, Rockford, Monmouth, Brooklyn, Baltimore, Titusville, Cambridgeport, St Pauls, Lawrence (Kansas) Waterloo (Ia) Palmyra, Natick, Monmouth, Lancaster (Pa) Evansville, Pittsburg, New Bedford, Cairo, Middletown, Lewiston, Phila, St Louis, St Paul, Poughkeepsie, Brooklyn, New York City, Jersey City, Stamford, Buffalo, Brooklyn again, Brockport, Sing Sing, Cincinnatti, Jersey City again, Plainfield, Toledo, Athol Depot, Boston. This is a heavy list for so early in the season. Wherever the same town is repeated the 2ᵈ or 3ᵈ application came from different parties.

As soon as we can say that you *will* lecture the list can be extended & dates fixed. What say? We want to announce yr subject as well as the fact that you *will* lecture. When will you decide?

———————

Is there anything particularly disagreeable that you wd like said about you in the N. Y. Independent? I rushed off an article called "The Americans who Laugh" & made the first on Nasby as his publisher here importuned me. It is just published & I want to go for you next.

I have been so thoroughly played out with heat & things that I believe I did not write to say that I was perfectly delighted with your "Roughing It."—But, there, if I go on you won't care about reading my article & if I have stood 400 of your pages there is no reason why you shdn't stand a column from me.

Yours in a parboiled "state of nature,"

Jas Redpath

[3] Redpath's article, signed "Berwick" (a pen name derived from his birthplace of Berwick-upon-Tweed, in England near the Scottish border), appeared in the New York *Independent*, a religious weekly, on 11 July. Redpath warmly championed "the men who laugh and who make their fellows laugh" as possessors of a "rare and divine" gift especially effective in exposing prejudice, superstition, and political folly (Redpath 1872a). No further articles in the proposed series have been discovered. Clemens included the information about his lucrative lecture offers in "An Appeal from One That Is Persecuted" (see note 5). The lecture offers have not been documented.

[4] See 11 June 72 to Sutro, n. 1.

[5] J. G. Holland (Timothy Titcomb) first decried the lecture circuit's "buffoons and triflers" in the *Atlantic Monthly* for March 1865. He enlarged on this theme in the March 1871 issue of *Scribner's Monthly*, blaming the lecture bureau system for the growing number of "literary jesters and mountebanks" to be found on lyceum rosters (Holland: 1865, 366; 1871, 560). (Redpath reprinted the latter article, with his own rebuttal, in the 1871 *Lyceum Magazine* [Redpath 1871].) More recently, Holland had returned to the attack in "Triflers on the Platform" in the February 1872 *Scribner's Monthly*, rousing Clemens to tell Redpath on 20 April that he would "go for Timothy one of these days." Holland singled out Artemus Ward as a particularly pernicious influence on the lyceum:

> Artemus Ward "lectured;" and he was right royally paid for acting the literary buffoon. He has had many imitators; and the damage that he and they have inflicted upon the institution of the lyceum is incalculable. The better class that once attended the lecture courses have been driven away in disgust, and among the remainder such a greed for

inferior entertainments has been excited that lecture managers have become afraid to offer a first-class, old-fashioned course of lectures to the public patronage. Accordingly, one will find upon nearly every list, offered by the various committees and managers, the names of triflers and buffoons who are a constant disgrace to the lecturing guild, and a constantly degrading influence upon the public taste. Their popularity is usually exhausted by a single performance, but they rove from platform to platform, retailing their stale jokes, and doing their best and worst to destroy the institution to which they cling for a hearing and a living. . . . Wit and humor are always good as condiments, but never as food. The stupidest book in the world is a book of jokes, and the stupidest man in the world is one who surrenders himself to the single purpose of making men laugh. . . . When our lyceums . . . at last become agents of buffoonery and low literary entertainments, they dishonor their early record and the idea which gave them birth. Let them banish triflers from the platform, and go back to the plan which gave them their original prosperity and influence. (Holland 1872a, 489)

In July Holland followed up with "The Literary Bureaus Again" (Holland 1872c). This article goaded Clemens into "going for" Holland, in a nineteen-page essay entitled "An Appeal from One That Is Persecuted," which, however, he never published. The "Appeal" shows that Clemens took Holland's remarks personally: "He *must* mean me in those paragraphs, because the language fits me like my own skin" (SLC 1872k, 10†). In reply he claimed that Holland had overlooked the real villain:

It is *not* I & my craft that des bankrupt & destroy the lecture societies, but it is Dr Holland himself & the other "first-class old fashioned" disseminators of "instruction" that do it. . . . Dr Holland says the buffoons charge so much for their services that they have are breaking up the lecture system by making the thing unbearably expensive. How *can* he talk so when with the memory of bleeding Jersey City in his mind, where he charged a hundred dollars and had only a hundred & fifty people in the house? I shudder to think what might have happened to that lyceum if I ˌif one or two "literary buffoons"ˌ had not happened along in the nick of time and drummed up ~~twenty-five hundred people~~ ˌtwo or three thousand people, who were willing to be have their taste "degraded" but did not need any threadbare "instruction." The real truth is, that the doctor & his people go about the country massacreing lecture associations, & the buffoons follow after and resurrect them. It sounds strangely enough to hear Dr Holland ab accusing *us* of killing the lecture business. . . . He moves through the lecture field a remorseless intellectual cholera; & wherever he goes—figuratively speaking,—"death & hell follow after."

Dr Holland's plaintive complainings and ~~thin~~ ˌillogicalˌ reasoning aside, what do these things ~~most~~ more probably betoken? Simply, that in the old ignorant times, people had ˌlittle or, nothing to read, & so they talked nothing but crops & the weather, & *needed* a little ˌtedious, miscellaneous "instruction;" ~~even from rather~~ but in these days when newspapers and free libraries cram everybody to suffocation with instruction on every possible subject, the thing their overburdened heads pine for is the wholesome *relief* ˌin the shape, of amusement, entertainment, care-~~conquering,~~-banishing, laughter—*not* a further stuffing at the hands of a blessed old perambulating sack of chloroform. . . . But ˌDr.ˌ Holland's day has gone by. Holland, to speak candidly & without malice or any shade of ill feeling, is the very incarnation of the Commonplace. Now that That is to say, when he is on the platform,ˌ ~~or in the editorial chair.~~ ˌspelling out his manuscript., Now that will not do in these ~~vigorous~~ ˌprogressive &ˌ exacting times. Why will he not take a seat peaceably in the rear, along with the rest of the condemned mediocre instructors, & stop wailing?

And just to glorify myself & the other buffoons, & just to make him feel how unjust he is toward us when he says we are killing the lecture business, I will state here that I am one of two "literary buffoons" who were a few days since offered $10,000 apiece to lecture *one month*, or $5,000 apiece to lecture twelve nights. The other buffoon

has accepted, I believe, but I—what sacrifice ~~do you suppose I am about to make?~~ ₐam
I about to make?ₐ ~~Anxious as I am to accept, & t~~Tempting as the offer is, I hereby withdraw totally from the field ₐ(declining in good earnest,)ₐ & tender this splendid month's
work to the Raw-Head-&-Bloody-Bones of the lecture arena, Dʳ ~~Timothy Titcomb~~
Holland, the Moral Instructor! There is a noble magnanimity in this act, if I do say
it myself, that shouldn't. (And I should think the ₐdoctorₐ would sink into the earth
for shame, after the way in which he has treated me & the other "literary triflers.") Now
the public shall see how that speculator ~~will finish~~ will come out with a lecturer of the
only true & legitimate stamp. (SLC 1872k, 10–19†)

Clemens's defensive statements and sarcasms failed to address the most troubling part of Holland's view—his dismissal of all claim by the "triflers" to be
taken seriously in literary matters. Clemens remained sensitive on this point: a
year later, in his letter of 20 April 1873 to Whitelaw Reid, he asserted—again
defensively—"I am not a man of trifling literary consequence."

To Elisha Bliss, Jr.
20 July 1872 • New Saybrook, Conn.
(MS: ViU)

Fenwick Hall
20ᵗʰ·

Friend Bliss—

Been looking for Harte here. If he comes, will let you know.[1] If he
comes, he may run up to Hartford with me.

What does Lockwood say about the patent?[2]

Ys

Clemens.

[*letter docketed:*] Saml. Clemens | July 20ᵗʰ 72

[1] See 28 July 72 to Bliss, n. 2.
[2] Henry C. Lockwood of Baltimore, inventor of an "elastic waist strap," had
secured an interest in the manufacture of Clemens's adjustable garment strap as
a result of his patent dispute with Clemens in the fall of 1871. Bliss was charged
with pursuing the strap's manufacture, which was never accomplished; nothing
is known of his dealings with Lockwood (*L4*, 465–66 nn. 1, 5).

From Samuel L. and Olivia L. Clemens
to Mary E. (Mollie) Clemens
20 or 21 July 1872 • New Saybrook, Conn.
(MS and transcript: Davis, and Davis 1977b, 3)

Dear Mollie:
Send to Moore, Weeks & Co. 12 & 14 Market street & buy a lot of their Swiss condensed milk for babes. You will have to take a sort of wholesale quantity, for they will not retail. You can keep most of it at the house & send us 3 or 4 cans a week with the clothes. ~~Did you get the hat trunk~~[1]

Yrs
Sam

OVER
Dear Mollie
Mr Clemens is determined that I shall bathe so I shall *have* to ask you to get me a bathing suit—they advertize them ready made caps & all— I would like quite a pretty one then I can keep it for this purpose for all time— [*about 10 or 12 unrecovered words deleted*]~~+~~ Mr Clemens is going to make me take sitz baths too so I shall have to trouble you for that black and white wrapper that hangs on the left in my closet   I use it for sitz baths— My back is troubling me some is the reason that Mr C. is taking these vigorous measures—
Susie is quite well

Lovingly Livy—

[*on new page:*]
Dear Mollie
More things I shall have to trouble you for— You will think there is no end to my commissions and I do not know as there will be   I do not know whether I wrote you that the piece of flannel that you sent is not the one that I need; I ought to have written that there were three pieces there instead of two   I would now like the coarsest of the two that are left—and I wish when you are down town some day you would ~~send~~ get me four yards of white flannel   I want good but I don't care to have it of the finest— I would like my worsted work that is in the book case drawer.

I would like the two ~~ski~~ short flannel skirts that are cut out and are in the same drawer with the squares of flannel in the sewing room— I would like you to see the size silk that the work is done with ˏon the short skirts,ˏ and send me the same size— ~~I w~~ I want my best black silk and my white polonaise if it is done up— The black silk is in the trunk at the left hand of my closet door, you might put things in the bottom of the trunk and send it, the dress could not be packed very tight as it would crush the crape—but please send the hat trunk too so that we can return our dirty clothes in it— Mollie I am *so sorry* to bother you with all these things but I do not know what else to do— There is no hurry about any of them so take your own time, do not go down town when it is hot and uncomfortable—

Of course you did right about Emily[2] I want to answer your letter at length but this must go to the mail— I shall not want her back with ~~se~~ such a ~~hap~~ habit as that—how dreadful for an old woman like her—

Will you put in the trunk the jet pin that is on the cushion in the guest room—if I should break this one I should have none to wear while geting it mended—

Susie is well— I do not know when we shall be at home it is cool & comfortable here— Love to Orion—

Lovingly Livy—

Will you send some of the crape that is on the shelf in my closet?——

✉—————————————————————————————————

O.K. at Clemens[3] | Cor. Forest & Hawthorne | Hartford, Conn. [*postmarked:*] NEW SAYBROOK CONN. JUL ◊◊ 1872

[1] A bill dated 22 July from the Hartford grocers Moore, Weeks and Company records the purchase of a case of condensed milk for $12.50 and establishes the probable date of Clemens's letter (CU-MARK). The "hat trunk" was used to send the Clemenses' dirty laundry from Fenwick Hall to Mollie at the Hartford house.

[2] A seamstress employed at the Hartford house, not further identified (OLC to MEC, 10? July 72, CtHMTH, and 12 July 72, CU-MARK).

[3] Clemens addressed almost all of the envelopes he sent to the Hartford house during the summer in this manner—referring, presumably, to Orion Clemens— even though the enclosed notes were invariably written to Mollie. Olivia addressed her notes more conventionally to "Mrs Orion C." or "Mrs Orion."

To Mary E. (Mollie) Clemens
20–23 July 1872 • New Saybrook, Conn.
(MS: CU-MARK)

Dear Mollie—
Please send me 50 of my visiting cards.
Have Downey put up a bell in his house right away & carry the wire
to our bedroom window—& another ~~one to y~~ wire to your bedroom window, while the plumber is at it.[1]
I want Ed & Orion to borrow fire arms from Burton[2] & watch for
that man & lay a snare for him & kill him. And I want the police to hound
him down. I will pay $100 for his ‸capture &‸ conviction.[3]

Ys affly

Sam

O. K. | At Clemens's | Cor Forest & Hawthorne | Hartford | Conn. [*return address:*] IF NOT DELIVERED WITHIN 10 DAYS, TO BE RETURNED TO [*postmarked:*] NEW SAYBROOK CONN. JUL 2◊ 1872 [*written in top margin of first page of letter, in MEC's hand:*]

	30	25	25
~~12~~	13	35	35
	20	~~30~~ 35	40
	~~90~~ 95	100	

[1] Downey, Patrick McAleer's replacement, apparently served as both coachman and handyman until the spring of 1874. He may have been either John or Patrick Downey, both listed in the Hartford directory as laborers employed or residing on Forest Street (Geer: 1872, 57; 1873, 58). His house—perhaps a carriage house—seems to have been adjacent to the Burton property on Forest Street, which was next door to the Hooker house rented by the Clemenses. The alarm bell was installed according to Clemens's instruction (OC to SLC, 2 Aug 72, CU-MARK; 8 May 74 to Charles E. Perkins, CtHMTH).

[2] Probably Henry Eugene Burton. "Ed" has not been identified. Only the first digit of this letter's postmark ("2") is visible. Since Orion was out of town from 23 July until the morning of 29 July, the letter seems likely to have been written before his departure—between 20 and 23 July (OC to SLC, 2 Aug 72, CU-MARK).

[3] Presumably, Clemens had learned of the presence of a prowler in the neighborhood from Orion or Mollie in a letter now lost. On 2 August Orion sent him a detailed account of the man's frightening activities since "the early part of July"

(CU-MARK). Both the Clemens household and the adjacent Burton household, as well as Miss Apthorp at 15 Hawthorn Street, were disturbed by the prowler, who was finally arrested on 4 August, as reported in the Hartford *Courant:*

An unknown scallawag has bothered the police and frightened a good many people, especially women, by going about all parts of the city and spying through the window blinds of dwelling houses in the night season. . . . In one locality a vigilance committee was organized, the men in the neighborhood sitting up nights to catch him. . . . Yet he has evaded capture, and has at last been discovered by an accident. His name is William Jackson, and he is about twenty-two years of age. He was arrested as a vagrant on Sunday. . . . The police officers, who saw that he was half-witted, held some conversation with him, and he said that he was a detective, and had been sent here from Providence to find a woman who had left that city. He then proceeded to detail his mode of operation, saying that whenever he saw a light in a dwelling house, he always took the precaution to look through the window, lest some crime should be committed that it was his duty, as an officer, to ferret out. This admission led the officers to a further investigation, and the result proved that he was the man they had for three months been looking after. He has gone to the workhouse for sixty days. ("Arrested at Last," 6 Aug 72, 2)

To Joseph L. Blamire
21 July 1872 • New Saybrook, Conn.
(MS: ViU)

Fenwick Hall,
Saybrook, Conn,
21[st.]

Joseph Ɫ L. Blamire Esq
Dʳ Sir:

I snatched this off yesterday when I got your letter; & I made it as brief as possible—as being in better taste than either a long introduction to so reserved & dignified a people as the English. Tell me if you think it will do. Make any suggestions that strike you. By the way: Suppose we destroy that other introduction—it is not in at all in good taste.[1]

Please send those books & papers[2] *here*—shall be here all summer. Too hot in Hartford.

I have declined a proposition to lecture a month for $10,000, & shall spend my winter either in the rural part of England or in Cuba & Florida—the latter most likely.[3]

Yrs
Clemens.

[*enclosure 1:*]
 ˄Please use this if it be *possible*—
do try hard, anyway.
      Tear up the other.   S. L. C.˄

Preface to the English Edition.

At the request of Messrs. George Routledge & Sons, I have made a patient & conscientious revision of this book for republication in England, ~~& I feel satisfied that I have eliminated~~ & have weeded out of it ˄nearly, if not quite, all of˄ the most palpable & inexcusable of its blemishes. At the same time I have wrought into almost every chapter additions which ~~seemed to me judicious~~ cannot fail to augment the attractions of the book, ~~or~~ or diminish them. I have ~~not~~ done my best to make this revised volume acceptable to the reader; & so, since I am as other men are, it would gratify me indeed to win his good opinion.
Respectfully,
The Author.

Hartford, U.S., July 1872.

[*enclosure 2:*]
Substitute ˄for this˄ enclosed, ~~for~~

Preface to the English Edition

Messrs George Routledge and Sons pay me copyright on my books. The moral grandeur of this thing cannot be overestimated in an age like ours, when even the sublimest natures betray the taint of earth, and the noblest and the purest among us will steal.

This firm is truly an abnormal firm. If there is another in foreign parts with similar instincts I have not had personal dealings with it.

My appreciation of the moral singularity I am lauding is attested by the fact that at the request of this publishing House I have wrought diligently, here in oppressive midsummer, until I have accomplished a thorough revision and correction of this book for republication in England, in defiance of the opinion of the great and wise historian Josephus, that "during the enervating season of summer, all persons so delicately constituted as authors and preachers ought to refrain from

arduous employments of any kind and do nothing but worship nature,
breathe the pure atmosphere of woods and mountains, and fool around."
Mark Twain

[1] On 18 or 19 July, after receiving and then forwarding the second preface for
the English edition of *Innocents*, Blamire seems to have recognized that the two
prefaces undercut each other. He evidently sent Clemens a secretarial copy of
the first, urging him to reconsider it. This letter shows that Clemens did exactly
that. He enclosed a new, shorter version of his first preface, together with the
secretarial copy—now canceled—and an instruction to tear up the original, already in London. Two days later Blamire sent the Routledges the revised preface
and Clemens's covering letter:

> 416 BROOME ST., NEW YORK, July 23 187 2
>
> Per S.S. "Nebraska"
>   July 24/72
> Messrs G. R. & Sons
>   London
>   D[r]. Sirs
> Herewith please find Mark Twain's preface for one of the Vols. of Innocents also his
> letter to me.
> Duplicates will be sent by Thursday's boat with my letter, & I have no doubt will reach
> you as early as (or before) this original. (ViU)

The *Nebraska* departed from New York on Wednesday, 24 July, and arrived at
Queenstown early on 5 August. "Thursday's boat" was the *City of Bristol*, which
arrived only three hours after the *Nebraska*. The Routledges proceeded with the
typesetting and printing of the first volume, *The Innocents Abroad*, which was
completed by 24 August (more than three weeks after the second volume) and
contained this revised preface ("Shipping Intelligence," New York *Tribune*, 6
Aug 72 and 7 Aug 72, 3; Routledge Ledger Book 4:632, Routledge; SLC 1872c).
[2] Unidentified.
[3] Blamire replied to this remark in a letter of 26 July:

> Certainly I must admit that so far as the Climate is concerned it will be pleasanter for
> you in winter either in Cuba or Florida, but if you do not wish to tempt the English
> Climate in winter I do hope you will find it convenient to spend next summer (or a
> greater part thereof in England); if so I think I can safely promise you on behalf of
> Messrs Routledge—Father & three Sons—a real, genuine, hearty welcome—such as
> will make you feel (during the time that you are in London at least) at home with them
> & all around you. Will you do me the favor to allow me to mention in one of my early
> letters to them that they may expect you; I feel sure they w[d] be pleased to see you at any
> time of the year but it w[d] be pleasanter for you in summer & they w[d] also have more
> opportunity of being with you. (CU-MARK)

Blamire wrote again on 6 August, by which time Clemens may have already made
his decision:

> I cannot resist the temptation of saying that I think a Book on Great Britain w[d] be ever
> so much more interesting than one on Cuba at present; besides, would you feel like
> trusting y[r] self there just now? Suppose they nabbed you & shut you up like they did
> Howard, that w[d] not be satisfactory to you or to yrs truly. (CU-MARK)

Blamire alluded to the case of Dr. John E. Howard (or Houard), an American-born resident of Cuba who had been arrested and court-martialed by Spanish authorities for aiding the insurgents. Howard was "sentenced to eight years hard labor in a chain-gang, and the confiscation of all his property," and was transported to Spain in chains in March 1872 ("Howard or Houard," New York *Times*, 2 Apr 72, 5). Howard was eventually pardoned and returned to New York in late August 1872. By 7 August Clemens had decided on the English trip ("The War in Cuba," New York *Times*, 24 Mar 72, 1; "Dr. Houard's Sufferings," New York *Tribune*, 22 Aug 72, 3; 7 Aug 72 to Bliss).

To Mary E. (Mollie) Clemens
22 or 23 July 1872 • New Saybrook, Conn.
(MS: CU-MARK)

Dear Mollie—
　　Please send me a few of my photographs—I mean the Imperial size.
　　　　　　　　　　　　　　　Yr Bro
　　　　　　　　　　　　　　　　　Sam.

✉———————————————————————————

O. K. | S. L. Clemens' residence | Cor Forest & Hawthorne | Hartford.
[*postmarked:*] NEW SAYBROOK CONN. JUL 23 1872

To Mary E. (Mollie) Clemens
24 or 25 July 1872 • New Saybrook, Conn.
(MS: CU-MARK)

Dear Mollie—
　　Please send all my individual washing to the steam laundry (or rather, notify them to come & get it,) till you find a washerwoman who is more talented than this one. This one don't even turn down a vest collar—or wash it, either, I may add.

The dirty clothes were expressed to you Monday. Will so telegraph you after breakfast——

Much obliged for the photos, cards & things.

Afly

Sam.

✉——————————————————————————————————

O. K. | ₌At₌ C̶o̶r̶ Clemens'ₛ—Cor Forest & Hawthorne sts | Hartford | Conn. [*postmarked:*] NEW SAYBROOK CONN. JUL 25 1872

To Mary E. (Mollie) Clemens
25–27? July 1872 • New Saybrook, Conn.
(MS: CU-MARK)

Dear Mollie—

The Boston package is monogram paper. *Did you pay for it? Or is there a bill with it?*

Please open it & send 3 quires of the white & 3 ″ of the gray paper, & a sufficient number of the 2 kinds of envelops.[1]

Ys

Sam

[1] Clemens had purchased a ream of stationery—ten quires each of two types, with matching envelopes—from the Boston stationers Lowell and Brett at a cost of $42.50. The paper was paid for on delivery at the Hartford house on 24 July (Lowell and Brett receipted invoice dated 24 July 72, CU-MARK). The present letter has been dated conjecturally within two or three days of the delivery. The gray stationery, first found in Clemens's letter of 2 August to Mollie, has a grid pattern, and is engraved with an ornate "SLC" monogram; the matching envelope bears Lowell and Brett's embossment. This is the first personal monogram found in Clemens's letters, and it may have been his own design: a scrap of paper preserved in the Mark Twain Papers has his outline drawing of the monogram. The white stationery has the same monogram rendered in three colors. Both stationeries were used frequently from August through December 1872, and occasionally in early 1873. See the illustration on the next page.

Monogram design in Clemens's hand, and the monogram printed on graph-lined stationery. Mark Twain Papers, The Bancroft Library (CU-MARK).

To Elisha Bliss, Jr.
28 July 1872 • New Saybrook, Conn.
(MS: NN)

Fenwick Hall,
Sunday.

Friend Bliss:

I shall be up about Aug 1ˢᵗ· Will copyright returns be ready?[1]

Harte would like to bring his family to Mount Holyoke for a few weeks. Can ̠in August, I suppose. Can he get rooms?[2]

20 per cent dividend is *good*.[3] Will attend to all my money matters when I come up.

Ys
Clemens.

[*letter docketed:*] √ [*and*] Saml Clemens | *July 29, 72*

[1] The royalty statement would not be ready when Clemens visited Hartford (see the next note), but was sent to him at Fenwick Hall on 5 August. It showed sales of 28,611 copies of *Roughing It* for the second quarter (May through July), and 3,431 of *The Innocents Abroad* (for April through July), for total royalties of $8,485.17, of which $5,000 had already been disbursed to Clemens on 24 June (OC to SLC, 2 Aug 72, CU-MARK; Bliss to SLC, 5 Aug 72, CU-MARK; check

dated 24 June 72, signed by F. E. Bliss, CtHMTH; receipt dated 24 June 72, signed by SLC, CtY-BR).
[2]Clemens relayed a request from Harte's most recent letter, postmarked 25 July. Harte also mentioned receiving two letters, now lost, in which Clemens had evidently continued his efforts (still with little success) to arrange for Bliss to publish a book by Harte (CU-MARK):

> Grand View House,
> Morristown N.J.
>
> My dear Clemens:
>
> Thanks for your two letters. That was a seductive picture you gave of Fenwick Hall—particularly to one who doesn't know how to play billiards and has spent most of his days trying to evade the companionship of people greatly older than himself. I fear, however, that the sea side is not "indicated," as the Doctors say, in Mrs Hartes case. She has hardly got over her last summer at Newport and longs for mountain air. I'm afraid that this will mean Mt. Washington or the Cattskills or some other remoteness, unless I can find something tonic nearer at hand. I think that Holyoke or Mt. Tom would have fitted. Will there be any chance there about 1st August or later? Save Mrs Harte's persistent weakness and my own attempts to do work in an atmosphere and surroundings that inculcate laziness as a moral virtue we are doing pretty fairly here at Morristown. The wet-nurse—who is a well disposed mammal—is bringing up the baby wonderfully, and we have lost at least all present anxiety, whatever you may see in the future.
>
> This is a capital place for children. The air, without being at all bracing is pure and sweet; the scenery pretty and pastoral; the house—a very comfortable family hotel kept by my sisters husband—is 2½ miles from Morristown and 1½ hours from New York. It is near enough to the city to permit me, when I get quite desperate with the sleepy *dolce far niente* air, to rush to my empty house on 49th st for a days quiet work there—for work here is almost impossible. Could not you and I find some quite rural retreat this summer where we could establish ourselves (after your Elmira or Buffalo fashion) in some empty farm house a mile or two away from our families, and do our work, with judicious intervals of smoking, coming home to dinner at abt 3 P.M?—Think of it.
>
> I've not yet directly heard from Bliss, but I fancy he will write to me after you have answered that note you enclosed. I'll get at the book as soon as this press of unfinished work is done.
>
> When you write, address in "Care of E.P. Dutton & Co 713 Broadway, cor Washington Place"; its about as direct and much more certain than this Morristown P.O. Regards to Mrs Clemens & love to baby
>
> Ever Yours
> Bret Harte

Bliss replied to Clemens on 31 July, saying in part:

> Friend Clemens,
> Yours at hand.
> Will make up copyright a/c right away. Will take two or three days to get *books posted up*—then all ready, dont come for that time— How about Hartes book. Can you give me any light on the subject? Has he been at Saybrook? He wrote me, that after hearing from you I should probably hear from him, but no word yet. Am a little anxious to know, so as to shape my course for operations
> Will write at once to Holyoke Mt for prospect for rooms & report at once   Let me have a line from you if possible at once about the Book (CU-MARK)

Mount Holyoke and Mount Tom, overlooking the Connecticut River, were in a popular summer resort area of Massachusetts about thirty miles north of Hartford. Mount Washington is a peak in the White Mountains in northern New

Hampshire. It is not known whether Bliss and Harte saw each other before 8 September, when they met in New York and signed a contract in which Harte agreed to deliver, and Bliss to publish, "the manuscript for a book, upon a subject to be agreed upon by the parties hereto, . . . as soon as practicable, but as soon as the 1st day of January next." Bliss agreed to an advance of $1,000 on a royalty of 7½ percent, half of which he paid to Harte on 8 September, and the other half on 19 September. Harte was slow to meet his side of the bargain, taking several years to produce the manuscript for *Gabriel Conroy*, his only full-length novel. Clemens recalled in 1907 that

> Bliss could get plenty of promises out of Harte but no manuscript—at least no manuscript while Harte had money or could borrow it. He wouldn't touch the pen until the wolf actually had him by the hind leg; then he would do two or three days' violent work and let Bliss have it for an advance of royalties. . . . The book was nearing a finish, but, as a subscription-book, its value had almost disappeared. He had advanced to Harte thus far—I think my figures are correct—thirty-six hundred dollars, and he knew that he should not be able to sleep much until he could find some way to make that loss good; so he sold the serial rights in "Gabriel Conroy" to one of the magazines for that trifling sum. (AD, 4 Feb 1907, CU-MARK, in *MTE*, 280–81)

Gabriel Conroy was issued by the American Publishing Company in September 1876, and by November 1878 had sold only 3,332 copies (American Publishing Company contract, CLU-S/C, information courtesy of Gary Scharnhorst; Duckett, 102–3, 109; APC, 90; Charles E. Perkins to Anna E. Dickinson, 26 June 74, Anna E. Dickinson Papers, DLC; *Appletons' Hand-Book*, 97–98). Harte would remind Clemens more than once that his contract with Bliss had benefited Clemens himself. On 24 December 1875 Harte wrote him, "Do you remember that some years ago when Bliss wanted a book from me for his House, you told him you would use your influence provided he did the decent and honorable thing to you in some contested point of business?" (CU-MARK, in Duckett, 97). And on 1 March 1877 he wrote, "You afterwards admitted to me that a disputed question of one or two thousand dollars was settled in your favor by *virtue of that contract so made*" (CU-MARK, in Duckett, 135). Since Clemens's efforts to use his influence with Harte occurred between June and August 1872, it is likely that the "contested point of business" was the royalty dispute over *Roughing It*, and that the benefit Clemens derived was at least in part Bliss's agreement to pay a 10 percent rather than a 7½ percent royalty on his next book, as stipulated in the contract Clemens and Bliss signed on 22 June. Harte's reference to "one or two thousand dollars" has not been explained, but that amount might have been the difference between half profits and 7½ percent on some portion of the sale of *Roughing It* (11 June 72 to Sutro, n. 1; 20 Mar 72 to Bliss [draft], n. 2; 8 May 72 to Perkins, n. 2).

³ "The American Publishing Company has declared a quarterly dividend of twenty per cent" ("Brief Mention," Hartford *Courant*, 17 July 72, 2; see 4 Mar 73 to Bliss, n. 4).

To Mary E. (Mollie) Clemens
30 July 1872 • New Saybrook, Conn.
(MS: CU-MARK)

FENWICK HALL. D. A. ROOD, PROPRIETOR.

NEW SAYBROOK, CONN., July 30 187 2

Dear Mollie—
    The Satchel arrived. But we are often on short allowance of con-
densed milk. Send us about 10 cans, now, & after that send us a can or
two whenever you send clothes—& this will keep us supplied.
    All flourishing.

                                              Yrs affly
                                                  Sam

✉

O. K. | Cor. Forest & Hawthorne | Hartford. [*return address:*] From
S. L. Clemens. [*postmarked:*] NEW SAYBROOK CONN. JUL 31 1872

To Mary E. (Mollie) Clemens
2 August 1872 • New Saybrook, Conn.
(MS: CU-MARK)

SLC

                                              Fenwick, 2ᵈ. Aug.
Dear Mollie:
    I wish Orion would go, some time within the next fortnight, &
get the price of clean *screened* Lehigh coal—& *then* go to Hatch & Tyler¹
& if their price is similar, tell them to put *ten tons of screened Lehigh* into
our cellar. And then I want ɏ Downey to take particular note of how
much of a pile it makes. *I* think it will fill the cellar; & I think that when
I bought 36 tons of Hooker last fall, I bought more than the whole front
yard would hold.
    Ɫ Some day when you are down ∥ town, I wish you would buy me a

dozen pairs of *very* fine, soft, white cotton socks—~~not those~~ Lisle thread, but cotton. *All* my present socks appear to have darns on them. I infinitely prefer holes.

Livy keeps delighting herself over the little garment you made for ⅄ Susie, & so I judge she is as well pleased as possible with it.

Ys affy
Sam.

⋈ ───

O. K. | Cor Forest & Hawthorne | Hartford | Conn [*return address:*] From. S. L. Clemens [*postmarked:*] NEW SAYBROOK CONN. AUG 3 1872

[1]Hatch and Tyler, wholesale and retail coal dealers in Hartford, provided "Lehigh, Lackawanna, Wilkesbarre and other coals . . . for domestic use" (Geer 1872, 150; "Coal," Hartford *Courant*, 23 July 72, 3).

To Mary E. (Mollie) Clemens
per Telegraph Operator
5 August 1872 • Saybrook Point, Conn.
(MS, copy received: CU-MARK)

BLANK NO. I.

CONNECTICUT RIVER TELEGRAPH COMPANY.

THE RULES OF THIS COMPANY REQUIRE THAT ALL MESSAGES RECEIVED FOR TRANSMISSION, SHALL BE WRITTEN ON THE MESSAGE BLANKS OF THE COMPANY, UNDER AND SUBJECT TO THE CONDITIONS PRINTED THEREON, WHICH CONDITIONS HAVE BEEN AGREED TO BY THE SENDER OF THE FOLLOWING MESSAGE.

GERSHOM B. HUBBELL, SUP'T,⎱ 4 F. W. RUSSELL, PRES'T, ⎱ HARTFORD.[1]
HARTFORD, CONN. ⎰   J. A. SMITH, JR., SEC'Y,⎰

DATED Saybrook Point, Ct.   187

RECEIVED AT 8.14—Aug 5″

TO Mrs Orion

Cor. Forest & Hawthorn sts.

Send carriage to depot about ten 10 this morning.[2]

S. L. Clemens

9 collect

s

✉—————————————————————————

Mrs Orion | Cor Forest & Hawthorn | NO. 4 | CHARGES. 30 & 25 Dly [*return address:*] WESTERN UNION TELEGRAPH CO. | WILLIAM ORTON, PRES'T.

[1] Hubbell, Russell, and Smith were directors as well as officers of the Connecticut River Telegraph Company, founded in 1867 (Geer 1872, 290).
[2] The purpose of Clemens's trip to Hartford is not known.

To Charles M. Underhill
6 August 1872 • New Saybrook, Conn.
(MS: NN-B)

(SLC)

Fenwick Hall,
New Saybrook, Conn
Aug. 6/72.

C. M. Underhill Esq[1]
D[r] Sir:
My next payment to T. A. Kennett falls due on the 9th inst.
Will you please attend to it for me, & pay the money to Kennett's
brother, in the clothing store.[2]
The payment is $2,500—& with interest is $2,815[00]—so Theodore
writes me—(he has all the papers in Elmira.)
I believeing that upon receiving this money Kennett is to transfer
some more of the Express stock, but hanged if *I* know.
I enclose draft for $2,000, & will get Theodore to forward a draft
for $815 from Elmira.[3]

Ys Truly
Sam[l]. L. Clemens

[*on back of second sheet:*]
Wrote on 2 sheets of paper without knowing it.[4]

✉—————————————————————————

C. M. Underhill Esq | 221 Main street | Buffalo | N. Y. | Coal office. [*on
flap:*] (SLC) [*postmarked:*] NEW SAYBROOK CONN. AUG 8 1872

[1] Charles Munson Underhill (b. 1839) was a graduate of Genesee College in
Lima, New York. He had been a teacher (with his brother-in-law, John D. F.

Slee) in Fulton, New York, before entering the coal trade. In 1870, when Slee became a partner in the Langdon firm in Elmira, Underhill succeeded him as general salesman of the Buffalo Anthracite Coal Association, an affiliate of J. Langdon and Company. In the 1880s, when Underhill was western manager of J. Langdon and Company, he was more than once the Clemenses' host for overnight stays in Buffalo (Reigstad, 1, 5–6; *L3*, 119 n. 4; Charles S. Underhill to Thomas Tenney, 23 July 1981, CU-MARK).

  ²Clemens still owed Thomas A. Kennett $5,000 of the original $25,000 he had paid for the one-third interest in the Buffalo *Express* purchased in August 1869. Kennett, now in a New York City banking and brokerage firm, had reminded Clemens in a note of 13 July that the annual payment was due. His brother was, presumably, merchant tailor Henry Kennett, employed in the family business at 273 Main Street in Buffalo (*L3*, 294 n. 2; *L4*, 338–39 n. 3; Kennett to SLC, 13 July 72, CU-MARK; *Buffalo Directory* 1872, 392).

  ³Theodore Crane, a partner in J. Langdon and Company, informed Clemens on 16 August, "The money $2815 has been paid over to Kennett and he has transferred to you 25 shares of stock—we have the receipt" (CU-MARK). Clemens had, in fact, resold his Buffalo *Express* interest to George H. Selkirk in March 1871 for $15,000, so the stock shares, as they were signed over by Kennett, were to be transferred to Selkirk. Selkirk was then permitted to retransfer the shares to Clemens as security for his own indebtedness. No record has been found of Clemens's payment of the final $2,500 owed to Kennett, which was due in August 1873. Selkirk had still not managed to pay Clemens in full by January 1878, when Clemens learned that the *Express* shares he was holding as security were worthless (*L4*, 338–39, n. 3; Charles J. Langdon to SLC, 7 Jan 78, CU-MARK; Selkirk to SLC, 17 Jan 78, CU-MARK). Many years later Clemens would recall his dealings with Kennett—whom he misnames "Kinney"—in an autobiographical dictation:

  I have some little business sense now, acquired through hard experience and at great expense; but I had none in those days. I had bought Mr. Kinney's share of that newspaper (I think the name was Kinney) at his price—which was twenty-five thousand dollars. Later I found that all that I had bought of real value was the Associated Press privilege. I think we did not make a very large use of that privilege. It runs in my mind that about every night the Associated Press would offer us five thousand words at the usual rate, and that we compromised on five hundred. Still that privilege was worth fifteen thousand dollars, and was easily salable at that price. I sold my whole share in the paper—including that solitary asset—for fifteen thousand dollars. Kinney (if that was his name) was so delighted at his smartness in selling a property to me for twenty-five thousand that was not worth three-fourths of the money, that he was not able to keep his joy to himself, but talked it around pretty freely and made himself very happy over it. . . . He was a brisk and ambitious and self-appreciative young fellow, and he left straightway for New York and Wall Street, with his head full of sordid and splendid dreams—dreams of the "get rich quick" order; dreams to be realized through the dreamer's smartness and the other party's stupidity. . . .
  Kinney went to Wall Street to become a Jay Gould and slaughter the innocents. Then he sank out of sight. I never heard of him again, nor saw him during thirty-five years. Then I encountered a very seedy and shabby tramp on Broadway—it was some months ago—and the tramp borrowed twenty-five cents of me. To buy a couple of drinks with, I suppose. He had a pretty tired look and seemed to need them. It was Kinney. His dapperness was all gone; he showed age, neglect, care, and that something which in-

dicates that a long fight is over and that defeat has been accepted. (AD, 16 Feb 1906, CU-MARK†, published in part in *MTA*, 2:118–19)

[4]Clemens began his letter on the outside of one folder of stationery and inadvertently continued it on the inside of a second folder.

To Elisha Bliss, Jr.
7 August 1872 • New Saybrook, Conn.
(MS: CtY-BR)

Saybrook, Aug 7/72
Friend Bliss—

This is to acknowledge receipt of copyright to Aug. 1, $8,485.17, less $5,000 ~~previously~~ advanced to me by you before it was due.[1]

I have written strongly to Anna Dickinson.[2]

How about Harte's rooms?[3]

Hurry up your figuring on the volume of sketches,[4] for I leave for England in 10 or 12 days to be gone several months.

Ys

Clemens

[*letter docketed:*] S. L. Clemens | Saybrook | Conn | Aug 7/72 [*and*] *auth* [*and*] Sam'l Clemens | For Year *1872*

[1] See 28 July 72 to Bliss, n. 1.

[2] Anna E. Dickinson, having decided to "write a book, and get a pot of money" (as she reportedly told Whitelaw Reid), was considering signing with Bliss and the American Publishing Company (Chester, 131). With Charles Dudley Warner's endorsement ("I think it is a good company. But it has been made by Mark Twain's books. It had not much luck before"), Dickinson wrote to Bliss (Warner to Dickinson, 11 July 72, Anna E. Dickinson Papers, DLC). On 23 July she informed Clemens that she had demanded "a guarantee of $10,000 at the rate of 7½ per ct. . . . I shall be indebted to you if you will impress it upon the mind of your friend that I wont write the book for less" (CU-MARK). Clemens's "strongly" worded response to Dickinson has not been found. He may have described the merits of the company, or, perhaps, discouraged her peremptory demand of a $10,000 guarantee. Dickinson had previously published only one book, *What Answer?* (1868), a melodramatic romance that had little success. Over the next two years, she continued to solicit opinions about Bliss's company

and royalty arrangements. In June 1874 she told Clemens that she was "simmering over a book" that she hoped would meet Bliss's "approbation." No agreement was ever reached, however, even though Bliss offered her an 8 percent royalty (Dickinson to SLC, 23 June 74, CU-MARK; Charles E. Perkins to Dickinson, 26 June 74, Anna E. Dickinson Papers, DLC). Dickinson's next book, *A Paying Investment*, was published in 1876 by James R. Osgood and Company (Chester, 106, 166, 173; Charles Dudley Warner to Dickinson, 31 July 73, and George H. Warner to Dickinson, 29 May 74, both in Anna E. Dickinson Papers, DLC; Dickinson to SLC, 1 July 74, CU-MARK).

³See 28 July 72 to Bliss, n. 2.

⁴Clemens still expected to fulfill his December 1870 contract with the American Publishing Company for a collection of sketches, despite having diverted to the Routledge sketchbooks the printer's copy he had originally prepared for Bliss (21 Mar 72 to Bliss, n. 1).

To Mary E. (Mollie) Clemens
per Telegraph Operator
8 August 1872 • (1st of 2) • Saybrook Point, Conn.
(MS, copy received: CU-MARK)

BLANK NO. 1.

CONNECTICUT RIVER TELEGRAPH COMPANY.

THE RULES OF THIS COMPANY REQUIRE THAT ALL MESSAGES RECEIVED FOR TRANS-MISSION, SHALL BE WRITTEN ON THE MESSAGE BLANKS OF THE COMPANY, UNDER AND SUBJECT TO THE CONDITIONS PRINTED THEREON, WHICH CONDITIONS HAVE BEEN AGREED TO BY THE SENDER OF THE FOLLOWING MESSAGE.

GERSHOM B. HUBBELL, SUP'T,}   217   F. W. RUSSELL, PRES'T,} 9^{30}
HARTFORD, CONN.   J. A. SMITH, JR., SEC'Y,}   HARTFORD.

DATED   Saybrook Pt Ct 8   187 2

RECEIVED AT   Aug 8

TO   Mrs O Clemens

Cor Forest & Hawthorne

Please stir up that infernal¹ Steam Laundry

*

Sam'l L Clemens

7 Collect 30 L & n

Infernal

*

✉┤───

Mrs O Clemens | NO. 2̲1̲7̲ | CHARGES. 3̲0̲ & 2̲5̲ Dly [*return address:*] WESTERN UNION TELEGRAPH CO. | WILLIAM ORTON, PRES'T.

[1] Having slightly miswritten "infernal," the operator marked it with an asterisk and rewrote it clearly at the foot of the telegram.

To Mary E. (Mollie) Clemens
8 August 1872 • (2nd of 2) • New Saybrook, Conn.
(MS: CU-MARK)

Fenwick 8th

Dear Mollie—

Please send the Enclosed check to Kellogg & Co.[1]

All well. I am going to England in a week from now.[2]

Ys

Sam.

✉┤───

O. K. | Cor. Forest & Hawthorne | Hartford | Conn. [*postmarked:*] NEW SAYBROOK CONN. AUG 9 1872

[1] The "Enclosed check" does not survive. E. C. C. Kellogg and Company were Hartford gunsmiths who advertised themselves as "Locksmiths, *Bellhangers*, grinding and polishing, and General Jobbing. Ammunition and Fishing Tackle, &c." (Geer 1872, 84). A receipt in the Mark Twain Papers, dated 6 August, for "Hanging Bell," suggests that Kellogg and Company installed the prowler alarm recently requested by Clemens (20–23 July 72 to MEC, n. 1).

[2] Clemens's actual departure date, 21 August, would be determined by Joseph Blamire's advice (see the next letter, n. 1).

To Orion Clemens
11 August 1872 • New Saybrook, Conn.
(MS: CU-MARK)

(SLC)

Fenwick Hall,
Saybrook, Conn.,
Aug. 11, 1872.

My Dear Bro:

I shall sail for England in the Scotia, Aug. 21.[1]

But what I wish to put on record now, is my new invention—hence this note, ~~whch~~ which you will preserve. It is this—a *self-pasting scrap=book*,—good enough idea if some juggling tailor does not come along & ante-date me a couple of months, as in the case of the elastic vest-strap.[2]

The nuisance of keeping a scrap book is: 1. One never has paste or gum tragicanth handy; 2. Mucilage won't stick, or stay, 4 weeks; 3. Mucilage sucks out the ink & makes the scraps unreadable; 4. To daub & paste 3 or 4 pages of scraps is tedious, slow, nasty & tiresome. My idea is this: Make a scrap book *with leaves veneered or coated with gum-stickum* of some kind; wet the page with sponge, brush, rag or tongue, & ~~dap~~ dab on your scraps like postage stamps.

Lay on the gum in columns of stripes, thus:

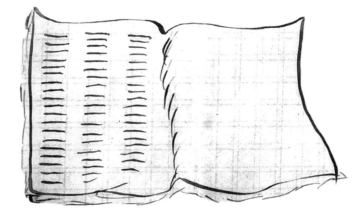

Each stripe of gum the length of say 20 M's, small pica, & as broad as your finger; a blank ₍about₎ as b̶r̶s̶ broad as your finger between each 2 stripes—so in wetting the paper you need not wet any more of the gum than your scrap or scraps will cover—then you may shut up the book & the leaves won't stick together.

Preserve, also, the envelop of this letter—postmark ought to be good evidence₍ of the date of this great humanizing & civilizing invention.

I'll put it into Dan Slote's hands & tell him he must send you all over America to urge its use upon stationers & booksellers—so don't buy into a newspaper.³ The name of this thing is "Mark Twain's Self-Pasting Scrap-book."⁴

All well here. Shall be up 2 P M Tuesday. Send the carriage.⁵

Yr Bro.

S. L. Clemens

✉———————————————————————————

Orion Clemens Esq | Cor. Forest & Hawthorne sts | Hartford | Conn [*return address:*] From Sam*ˡ*. L. Clemens [*postmarked:*] NEW SAYBROOK CONN. AUG 1◊ 1872 [*docketed by OC:*] Received and opened by M E Clemens, Aug 13, 1872. Read by me August 13, 1872.

¹ Joseph Blamire had written to Clemens on 9 August, replying to a letter of 7 August, now lost:

> Of course it wᵈ have been better if you cᵈ have started a month earlier; still if you get there early in September, you will I think, see a good deal of country life, before the folks begin to return to Town; As far as my recollection goes they spend August & September mostly in the country; Parliament will I think be prorogued this year about the 12ᵗʰ inst. & then the flight to the country & sea side which had begun probably in July will be completed.
>
> As to the Steamship line you will meet by all odds, the best class of People, in the Cunard *Wednesday* line, (they have 2 lines, one leaving New York on Wednesdays, the other on Saturdays; by the Wednesday line they charge $100⁰⁰ or $120⁰⁰ gold according to location of room; by their Saturday line they charge much the same as other less aristocratic lines of Steamships, say $80 gold; I wᵈ by all means if you care for the best society, go by one of their Wednesday Steamers. In coming this way, I wᵈ if I were you, take a different line; the Cunard line, leaving N. Y. on Wednesdays do not carry Steerage Passengers either way, all other English lines (*including their ₍Cunards₎ Saturdays line* carry them both ways) & there is where the best fun of a westwardly voyage comes in; the steerage Passengers are obliged to keep their division of the ship, but the Cabin Passengers, go where they choose & I know that you wᵈ enjoy some of the Evening Scenes amazingly. . . .
>
> I should say then go by a Cunard Boat leaving N. Y. on WEDNESDAYS & return by a Cunard Boat of their other line, leaving Liverpool on TUESDAYS. . . .
>
> I don't think you wᵈ see any thing particularly worth your while among the Steerage passengers from this side, but among the passengers coming here—elated as they often are, with their new & brighter prospects, there are sometimes rich scenes.

The Crack Steamer of the Cunard Line is the Scotia, to sail August 21ˢᵗ· If I can do anything for you about your passage command me.

I will either give to you in N. Y. or send you a letter of introduction to our folks, of the very simplest kind that I can write₍·₎ (CU-MARK)

On 15 August Blamire assured Clemens that he had received his check for $150, with which he had "secured *the best Room that was left* on the Scotia" (Blamire to SLC, 15 Aug 72, CU-MARK).

² See 20 July 72 to Bliss, n. 2. The wording of Clemens's oblique reference to Lockwood ("some juggling tailor") has not been explained.

³ Since leaving his position as editor of the *American Publisher* in March 1872, Orion had been unemployed, but his brother had apparently agreed to underwrite a new career. In May, Orion had suggested that Clemens set him up in a law practice in Hartford. Then in late July, Orion left on a week-long trip to investigate buying into a country newspaper. On 26 July he wrote to Mollie from Vermont:

The Rutland Independent man wants to start a daily, and wants an editor; but I am afraid the Daily would die at the end of the presidential campaign.

The best thing I have seen on my whole route is the Rutland Herald. It has a daily of 900, and a weekly of 2500 circulation, and a net income of about $7,000, and no job office—just one press and the material for the paper. The weekly is 79 years old, and the daily 7 years old. It has is owned by a smart business man. I look upon an a purchase of an interest in it by Sam in his own name as an investment as sure as bank stock, and as certain as investment can be to bring him his 7 per cent. One person told me the owner asked $15,000, and another that he asked $30,000 for it. If I could get a third interest, and a salary of a hundred dollars a month, I could pay Sam his interest, and still have a nice income left. The owner took the names of Davis & McKee to write to them. (CU-MARK)

Davis has not been identified. William McKee was a former employer of Orion's on the St. Louis *Missouri Democrat*. On 2 August, after his return, Orion reported to Clemens, "I wrote Thursday morning to the Vergennes man to ask him the lowest he would take for his office—if $1600; and to Pittsfield Sun to know the lowest he would take—if $2,000. I am going down to the Churchman this afternoon to seek work till the matter is settled" (CU-MARK). Orion's inquiries about the Vergennes *Vermonter* and the Pittsfield (Mass.) *Sun* (both weeklies) came to nothing, nor is there any indication that he found work at the *Churchman*, an Episcopal weekly published in Hartford. His visit to Rutland, however, would lead to a job offer in the spring of 1873 (7 Mar 72 to OC, n. 1; 15 May 72 to OC and MEC, n. 6; *L2*, 198 n. 1; 5 May 73 to OC and MEC, n. 1; Rowell, 14, 48, 109; Mott 1938, 69).

⁴ Several months would pass before Clemens was able to apply for a patent on his "Improvement in Scrap-Books": he signed a descriptive statement on 15 April 1873, filed the application on 7 May, and was granted patent number 140,245 on 24 June (SLC 1873k). Although he deferred manufacture for several years, he ultimately placed the scrapbook in the hands of his friend Daniel Slote. The first extant statement from Slote, Woodman and Company is dated 12 January 1878 and covers the last six months of 1877. It shows domestic and foreign sales of 26,310 scrapbooks, with Clemens's profit totaling $1,071.57 (Scrapbook 10:33, CU-MARK). The scrapbook—known as "Mark Twain's Patent Self-Pasting Scrap Book," "Mark Twain's Adhesive Scrap Book," or simply "Mark Twain's Scrap Book"—proved to be Clemens's only profitable patent, providing a modest but steady income. Albert Bigelow Paine stated that it was still being

sold in 1912 ("Slote, Woodman & Co.," New York *Herald*, 19 July 78, 8; "Daniel Slote," New York *Tribune*, 14 Feb 82, 2; Daniel Slote and Company to Charles L. Webster and Company, 21 Dec 89, CU-MARK; *MTB*, 1:457).

[5]The purpose of Clemens's trip to Hartford on Tuesday, 13 August, has not been discovered.

To Mary Mason Fairbanks
11 August 1872 • New Saybrook, Conn.
(MS: CSmH)

Fenwick Hall
Saybrook, Conn.,
Aug. 11.

Dear Mother:

What a brief note it was! Now how did we know where you were? Been waiting ever so patiently to learn that you had reached home again, so that we could write you.[1] Indeed, part of that is true. But the main reason why I, individually, have not written, is,—laziness. I never was afflicted with it before, but now that I have tried it, I adore it.

Our Susie is doing famously *here*, but the case was different in Hartford, the moment the warm weather set in. We had to pack our trunks mighty suddenly, the 5th of July & rush down here—& none too soon, for the succeeding week wilted Hartford children away like a simoom. This place is on the Sound,[2] 2 hours from Hartford, & is delightfully cool & comfortable—never an hour of heat, day or night. Mrs. Langdon will reach here in a day or two, & she & Livy will remain till cool weather—but I sail in the Scotia, Aug. 21st for Europe—England, rather—to be gone several months. If I find I am to be away very long, shall return by & by & take Livy over. I confine myself to England & Scotland. I wish you would come over there; & if you can't, I wish you would make Livy a real good visit.

You must remember us lovingly to our friends in Cleveland, & especially the Severances[3]—Mrs. S's. letter to us when we lost our boy touched us & so warmed our hearts toward her. I say these things to you because we have replied to none of the many letters of condolence we received, writing was so painful.

Susie is bright & strong & we love her so that no sacrifice seems too much to make for her; though I feel that we *must* look up a less expensive article of condensed milk for her. Good-bye.

Lovingly, Yr Son

Saml.

[1] Abel and Mary Mason Fairbanks had been traveling in California and Nevada (they were in Virginia City in late June). Mrs. Fairbanks, who sometimes used the pseudonym "Myra," contributed sketches about the trip to the Cleveland *Herald*. They were later reprinted as *Cleveland to San Francisco* (n.d.) (*L2*, 166 n. 4; Fairbanks, 552; "Editorial Visit," Virginia City *Virginia Evening Chronicle*, 26 June 72, 3).

[2] Long Island Sound.

[3] Emily and Solon Long Severance of Cleveland were part of the small group of Clemens's favored companions on the 1867 *Quaker City* trip (*L2*, 63, 66).

To Mary E. (Mollie) Clemens
per Telegraph Operator
16 August 1872 • Saybrook Point, Conn.
(MS, copy received: CU-MARK)

BLANK NO. I.

CONNECTICUT RIVER TELEGRAPH COMPANY.

THE RULES OF THIS COMPANY REQUIRE THAT ALL MESSAGES RECEIVED FOR TRANS-MISSION, SHALL BE WRITTEN ON THE MESSAGE BLANKS OF THE COMPANY, UNDER AND SUBJECT TO THE CONDITIONS PRINTED THEREON, WHICH CONDITIONS HAVE BEEN AGREED TO BY THE SENDER OF THE FOLLOWING MESSAGE.

GERSHOM B. HUBBELL, SUP'T,⎫   *I02*   F. W. RUSSELL, PRES'T, ⎫ HARTFORD.
HARTFORD, CONN.   ⎭   J. A. SMITH, JR., SEC'Y,⎭

DATED   Saybrook Pt, Ct.   187 2

RECEIVED AT   12.20 Aug 16

TO   Mrs O. Clemens

Cor. Forest & Hawthorn st.

Send down all my white pants

S. $ L. Clemens

6 p'd 30

s

To Orion or Mary E. (Mollie) Clemens
16 or 17 August 1872 • New Saybrook, Conn.
(MS: CU-MARK)

51.
                                              Hartford, July 18. 1872[1]
S. L. Clemens,
    Bought of W. K. Holt.
1 bbl. Flour, Haxall,[2] $.16⁰⁰
[*in pencil on the back:*] S. L. Clemens.

Pay this, if correct.
    S. L. Clemens

⊠———————————————————————————————

O. K. | Cor. Forest & Hawthorne | Hartford | Conn [*postmarked:*] NEW
SAYBROOK CONN. AUG 17 1872

[1] Clemens wrote his note at the bottom of a bill from William K. Holt, a Hartford flour dealer, either on the day he mailed it or possibly the day before (Geer
1872, 79). The envelope address shows that he sent it either to Orion or to Mollie
(see 20 or 21 July 72 to MEC, n. 3).
[2] The Haxall flour mill, founded by Phillip and William Haxall in 1809, was
in Richmond, Virginia (Kuhlmann, 48–49).

To Olivia L. Clemens
19 August 1872 • Hartford, Conn.
(MS: NN-B)

(SLC)
                                              Midnight Aug 18.
Livy darling, when these lines reach you I shall still be ~~na~~ near enough
at hand to blow a loving kiss to you over the few intervening acres of soil,
& you will be near enough to intercept it before its expression has cooled
in the morning breeze.[1]

While this moon lasts it will be easy, on shipboard or on shore, to look up at the vague shapes in it & recal our last night on the verandah when they were our only witnesses. And as long as we are separated we can still regard the waxing & waning phases of this moon & commune with each other through her across the waste of seas, sending & receiving messages that shall ignore distance & count the accumulated meridians of longitude as nothing.

Livy darling, I love you, truly & tenderly, & you ₫ alone— And am now & shall always be, Your most affectionate husband—

Sam*.*

To my dear little wife. (I have used the *worthiest* paper.)[2]

[1]Clemens had left New Saybrook on the first leg of his trip to England. Although he may have sent this letter from New York City, his reference here to being near to Olivia suggests that he stayed at the Hartford house on the night of 18 August. He probably arrived in New York on 19 August, since his presence at the St. Nicholas Hotel was reported on 20 August ("Prominent Arrivals," New York *Tribune*, 8; "Morning Arrivals," New York *Evening Express*, 3).
[2]Clemens wrote on the white stationery, monogrammed in red, gold, and black, which he had purchased earlier in the summer (25–27? July 72 to MEC, n. 1).

To Olivia L. Clemens
20 August 1872 • New York, N.Y.
(MS: Davis, Jr., and CU-MARK)

Dan Slotes, 20ᵗʰ PM.[1]

Livy darling, my hands are still full of business, but I have a few minutes respite just now. It just occurs to me—how could *you* sleep on the shelf they call a berth, in a steamer? The thing is impossible. You would prefer your bath-tub at home, with a newspaper under you to soften it. I have been to the bank & bought exchange on London, & have reserved a handful of British gold for emergencies between here & the banking house in London. I enclose triplicate No. 2 & will give Charley No. 3, & carry No. 1 with me.[2] Preserve yours—it is to protect me in case I lose

No. I. I have bought a hat, & some books & other traps. I go aboard the ship at noon tomorrow. Presently I am going out to dine with John Hay, & the Harper's Drawer man & Will M. Carleton the bal farm-ballad writer.[3] Bret Harte talks of going to Saybrook for a week. With ever so much love, my darling.

Y Sam*.*

[*enclosure:*][4]

[*on the back:*]
Pay Sam* L. Clemens
—or order
    E. Zeidler

Room *15.* | Mrs. S. L. Clemens— | Fenwick Hall | Saybrook | Conn.
[*postmarked:*] NEW YORK AUG 20 6 PM

[1]Clemens wrote this letter on the backs of two advertising flyers printed by Slote, Woodman and Company, Blank Book Manufacturers, while at the company's office, 119 and 121 William Street.

[2]Charles Langdon and his wife, Ida, arrived at the St. Nicholas late on 20 August. Langdon delivered two boxes of cigars to Clemens, sent by Theodore Crane ("Morning Arrivals," New York *Evening Express*, 21 Aug 72, 3; Crane to SLC, 16 Aug 72, CU-MARK).

[3]William A. Seaver (1813?–83) had written the "Editor's Drawer" in *Harper's New Monthly Magazine* since April 1867. Born in New York State, he was for a time editor of the Buffalo *Courier*. In the early 1860s he went to New York City, where he edited a church journal and wrote correspondence for several newspapers. In addition to his column in *Harper's*, he wrote the personal columns in *Harper's Weekly* and *Harper's Bazar*. According to the obituary writer for the New

York *Times*, Seaver was "an admirable story-teller," and "displayed the finest taste in dinners, and was counted a judge of wines without a superior" ("William A. Seaver," 8 Jan 83, 5; Durfee, 691). Will M. Carleton (1845–1912) was born on a farm in Michigan. After graduating from Hillsdale College in 1869 he worked as an editor for the Hillsdale (Mich.) *Standard* and the Detroit *Tribune*. In the 1871 *Harper's Weekly* he published a series of four "Farm Ballads," whose simple language and homely sentiments gave them wide popularity (Carleton 1871a–d). A collection of his poems, *Farm Ballads* (1873), sold forty thousand copies in eighteen months. On 21 August the New York *Tribune* announced, "Samuel L. Clemens, esq. (Mark Twain), sails for England to-day, for a visit of several months. He was entertained last night at the Union League Club by a party distinguished in literature and politics" ("Personal," 21 Aug 72, 5). This dinner, perhaps arranged by Hay, may have been Clemens's introduction to both Seaver and Carleton. The other guests, if any, have not been identified.

⁴The exchange document that Clemens enclosed ("triplicate No. 2"), issued by Henry Clews and Company, located at 32 Wall Street, survives in the Mark Twain Papers. It is reproduced photographically at 50 percent of actual size. It has not been explained why this check (for about $1,275) was issued to "E. Zeidler," who in turn endorsed it to Clemens. Ernest Zeidler is identified as a porter in the New York directory, and it is possible that Clemens entrusted him with this banking errand (Wilson 1872, 1325).

To Olivia L. Clemens
29 August 1872 • SS *Scotia* en route from
New York, N.Y., to Liverpool, England
(MS: CU-MARK)

(SLC)

Off Queenstown, Ireland,
Aug. 29/72.

Livy darling, I have little or nothing to write, except that I love you & think of you night & day, & wonder where you are, & what you are doing, & how the Muggins¹ comes on, & whether she ever speaks of me—& whether mother² is cheerful & happy. I hope & trust & pray that you are all well & enjoying yourselves—but I can't say that I have been enjoying myself, greatly, lost in a vast ship where our 40 or 50 passengers flit about in the great dim distances like vagrant spirits. But latterly our small clique *have* had a somewhat better time of it, though if one is absent there can be no whist.

I have given the purser a ten-dollar telegram of 3 words to send to

you from Queenstown,[3] & also my journal in 2 envelops[4]—& now I'll
rush & give him this—consider, my dear, that I am standing high on the
stern of the ship, ⩔ looking westward, with my hands to my mouth,
trumpet fashion, yelling across the tossing waste of waves, "I LOVE
YOU, LIVY DARLING!"

Saml.

✉——————————————————————————————

[*in ink:*] Mrs. Sam*l*. L. Clemens | Cor. Forest & Hawthorne sts. | Hart-
ford, | Conn. [*in upper left corner, boxed:*] U. S. of America. [*on flap:*]
(SLC) [*postmarked:*] QUEENSTOWN A AU30 72 [*and*] NEW YORK SEP 10 PAID ALL
[*docketed by OLC:*] 1st

¹Susy Clemens. In games such as cribbage or dominoes, if a player fails to
record a score, his opponent may call him a "muggins" and claim the score for
himself.
²Mrs. Langdon was staying with Olivia in New Saybrook (11 Aug 72 to
Fairbanks).
³At 8 A.M. on 30 August the *Scotia* arrived at Queenstown, where Clemens's
telegram (now lost) was sent, and this letter mailed. The ship reached Liverpool
the next day ("European Marine News," New York *Times,* 31 Aug 72, 8; "Home
Arrivals," London *Times,* 2 Sept 72, 9).
⁴In preparation for writing a book about England, Clemens kept a journal in
"Francis' Highly Improved Manifold Writer," which used "Carbonic Paper" to
create duplicates of each page. The material in the journal is discursive, unlike
the sketchy and elliptical notes he usually recorded in his notebooks—none of
which are extant for this period. All of the journal text that has survived is transcribed in Appendix C.

To Olivia L. Clemens
1 September 1872 • Liverpool, England
(MS: CU-MARK)

(SLC)

Liverpool, Sunday.

Livy darling, I wonder if you are back home yet; & I wonder how the
Muggins is & what she looks like.[1] I seem only a stone's-throw from you,
& cannot persuade myself that this is a foreign land & that an ocean rolls
between us. I feel very near to you.

I have just finished a long & laborious conning of newspapers & pasting extracts & jotting down trivialities in my journal, & now comes my *bete noir*—for I must shave.

I will put in another 20 minutes cutting out my journal to enclose with this. It seems to take a power of time to cut out those flimsy leaves.[2]

Kiss mother & the baby for me & accept of the world of love I bear you sweetheart.[3]

Sam*l*.

✉—————————————————————————————————

[*in ink:*] Mrs. Saml. L. Clemens | Cor Forest & Hawthorne sts | Hartford | Conn. [*in upper left corner:*] U.S. of America. | [*flourish*] [*on flap:*] LIV-ERPOOL ADELPHI HOTEL COMPANY LIMITED LIVERPOOL [*postmarked:*] F F LIVER-POOL 2 SP 72 2 [*and*] NEW YORK SEP 14 PAID ALL

[1] Clemens told Mrs. Fairbanks that Olivia, Susy, and Mrs. Langdon planned to stay in Saybrook "till cool weather" arrived; they probably left during the first week of September (11 Aug 72 to Fairbanks; OLC to MEC, 27 Aug 72 and 28 Aug 72, CU-MARK).

[2] Clemens pasted the "extracts" into a scrapbook (Scrapbook 9, CU-MARK). See, for example, Appendix B, enclosure with 25 Jan 73 to Reid, nn. 6, 8. The journal pages were very thin to facilitate the copying process (see Appendix C).

[3] Mrs. Langdon evidently accompanied her daughter back to Hartford, remaining until Clemens's return in November (Julia Beecher to Olivia Lewis Langdon, 15 Oct 72, CtHMTH; 26 Nov 72 to JLC and PAM).

❀

No LETTERS written between 1 and 11 September 1872 have been found. Clemens probably spent two nights in Liverpool, 31 August and 1 September, and on 2 September, the day he mailed the previous letter, boarded the train for London. On the train, according to his own recollection in 1907, he sat opposite a man reading *The Innocents Abroad*, whose failure to laugh at the book, or even smile, "affected me dismally. It gave me a longing for friendly companionship and sympathy":

> Next morning this feeling was still upon me. It was a dreary morning, dim, vague, shadowy, with not a cheery ray of sunshine visible anywhere. By half past nine the desire to see somebody, know somebody, shake hands with somebody and see somebody smile had conquered my purpose to remain a stranger in London, and I drove to my publisher's place and introduced my-

self. The Routledges were about to sit down at a meal in a private room up-
stairs in the publishing house, for they had not had a bite to eat since breakfast. I helped them eat the meal; at eleven I helped them eat another one; at
one o'clock I superintended while they took luncheon; during the afternoon
I assisted inactively at some more meals. . . .

In the evening Edmund Routledge took me to the Savage Club, and there
we had something to eat again; also something to drink; also lively speeches,
lively anecdotes, late hours, and a very hospitable and friendly and contenting
and delightful good time. (SLC 1907, 3–4)

Contemporary newspaper reports make it clear that Clemens misremembered both the name of the club and the day when he was introduced to literary and artistic London: the dinner actually took place at
the Whitefriars Club on Friday, 6 September (see the next letter and 22
Sept 72 to Conway [2nd]). According to Albert Bigelow Paine, "From
that night Mark Twain's stay in England could not properly be called a
gloomy one." Routledge, Tom Hood, and

all literary London, set themselves the task of giving him a good time. Whatever place of interest they could think of he was taken there; whatever there
was to see he saw it. Dinners, receptions, and assemblies were not complete
without him. The White Friars' Club and others gave banquets in his honor.
He was the sensation of the day. When he rose to speak on these occasions he
was greeted with wild cheers. (*MTB*, 1:461)

🦍

To Olivia L. Clemens
11 September 1872 • London, England
(MS: CU-MARK)

(GR&S)   THE BROADWAY, LUDGATE, LONDON, E.C.[1]

Sept. 11— 187 2

Livy darling, I was getting positively uneasy until this morning,
when I got your two ~~fr~~ first letters (one dated Aug. 20 & one Aug. 28).[2] I
was going to telegraph you today, to ask what the matter was. But now I
am all right. You are well, Mother[3] is with you & the Muggins is jolly &
knows what her hands are made for. I would like very much to see you
all just now.

Confound this town, time slips relentlessly away & I accomplish next to nothing. Too much company—too much dining—too much sociability. (But I would rather live in England than America—which is treason.) Made a speech at the Whitefriars Club[4]—very good speech—but the shorthand reporters did not get it exactly right & so I do not forward it. No that is not it. I neglected to buy copies of the papers.[5] The only places I have been to in this town are the ᴧChrystal Palace, theᴧ Tower of London & Old St. Paul's.[6] Have not even written in my journal for 4 days—don't get time. Real pleasant people here.

Left Londay day before yesterday with Osgood the Boston publisher[7] & spent all day yesterday driving about Warwickshire in an open barouche. It is the loveliest land in its summer garb! We visited Kenilworth ruins, Warwick Castle[8] (pronounce it *Warrick*) and the Shakspeare celebrities in & about Stratford-on-Avon—(pronounce that *a* just as you would the a in *Kate*).[9] Go down to Brighton tomorrow with Tom Hood. (Tell Warner a Philadelphia paper, just arrived, abuses Hood for not separating his own feeble name from his father's great fame by calling himself "Thomas Hood the Younger"—& the joke of it is that the son's name is *not* ~~Tom~~ Thomas, but simply *Tom*, & so there was no *Tom* Hood the *elder*.)[10]

Indeed Charley's letter[11] is in the last degree comforting—*isn't* it? Charley's a good brother, & I don't know how we ever could get along with our money matters without him.

~~Young~~

I send all my love to you & our dear babies[12]—& to Mother.

Saml.

"~~The Broadway,~~
~~Ludgate Hill~~
~~London.~~"

✉ Mrs. S. L. Clemens | Cor Forest & Hawthorne | Hartford | Conn. [*in upper left corner:*] U.S. of America | [*flourish*] [*across envelope end:*] Did Charley send the ~~$500~~ $600 from Arnot's Bank?[13] [*on flap:*] G. ROUTLEDGE & SONS BROADWAY LUDGATE HILL E C [*postmarked:*] J I LONDON II SP 72 [*and*] NEW YORK SEP 24 PAID ALL.

[1] Clemens used the stationery of George Routledge and Sons.
[2] None of Olivia's letters to Clemens in this period is known to survive.
[3] Mrs. Langdon.

[4] The Whitefriars Club was "founded in 1868 by a band of journalists, actors, and artists, who met together in mutual regard and gracious friendship to discuss the affairs of the universe over a tankard and a pipe" (Watson, 125). At the club's Friday dinners,

> some leading light in literature, science, or art is invited to open a "conversation" on a selected topic; after which a pleasant couple of hours are spent in discussing or talking round the subject. . . . The meetings are well attended by authors, journalists, and members of kindred professions; and *confrères* from across the Atlantic or elsewhere are frequently present as guests. (Sims, 3:160)

[5] The newspapers that first reported Clemens's speech of 6 September at the Whitefriars Club dinner, probably on the following day, have not been identified. One of them must have been the source, however, for articles that appeared in the South London *Press* and the London *Court Journal* (weekly publications) on 14 September, both of which began with the following explanation: "Within the last few days the celebrated humorist Mark Twain has arrived in England, and he was on Friday evening present at dinner with the members of the Whitefriars Club, at the Mitre Tavern" ("Mark Twain at the Whitefriars Club," South London *Press*, 14 Sept 72, 4; "'Mr. Mark Twain, I Believe,'" London *Court Journal*, 14 Sept 72, 1081). According to the *Press*, which printed an apparently complete version of his speech, Clemens was the guest of Tom Hood. Among the "members and friends" present were George and Edmund Routledge, as well as Ambrose Bierce (see note 9), "of the *San Francisco News Letter*, himself a well-known American humorist":

> In the course of the evening, the chairman took occasion to propose the health of their visitor in eloquent terms, dwelling on the fact that it was often the privilege of the Whitefriars to welcome men of ability belonging to the great brotherhood of brains—men who, not having greatness thrust upon them, had achieved positions of eminence in the literary world, and they felt peculiar pleasure in welcoming one who had won more than an European reputation—one who was recognized on both sides of the Atlantic by his genius, by his peculiar humour, and as possessing those special claims to consideration which it was the delight of the club to acknowledge. The toast was drunk with enthusiasm.
>
> Mr. Mark Twain responded after his peculiar fashion, amidst roars of laughter, with an effect of which the simple words convey but little idea, so much depended on the quaint and original manner of the speaker.

Clemens delivered a humorous speech in which he claimed it was he who found Dr. Livingstone, while Henry M. Stanley got "all the credit" (SLC 1872n; see 25 Oct 72 to OLC). In response the club extended the "privilege of honorary membership to their distinguished visitor during his stay in England—a mark of respect which had been accorded to few strangers" ("Mark Twain at the Whitefriars Club," South London *Press*, 14 Sept 72, 4).

[6] The Crystal Palace, an immense glass and iron exhibition hall, was built in Hyde Park for the Great Exhibition of 1851, and moved afterward to Sydenham, a suburb of London. It was destroyed by fire in 1936. In September 1872 its attractions included a fine-arts gallery, technology and natural history collections, an aquarium, fountains and fireworks displays, and orchestral and band concerts (Weinreb and Hibbert, 215–16, 853; advertisement, London *Times*, 9 Sept 72, 1). The Tower of London, the "most perfect medieval fortress in Britain," was begun by William the Conqueror and enlarged over the next two centuries, serving as a palace, prison, and place of execution, and housing such

valuables as the royal armory, mint, Public Records, and Crown Jewels (Weinreb and Hibbert, 871). "Old St. Paul's" was the usual designation of the large Norman cathedral built in the late eleventh century and destroyed in 1666 by the Great Fire. In his English journal Clemens wrote a humorous account of his visit to the site, on which stood "new" St. Paul's, a church completed in 1710 from a design by Christopher Wren (Appendix C; Weinreb and Hibbert, 756–59).

[7] Osgood was traveling in England, having sailed from New York in mid-August ("Personal," New York *Tribune*, 15 Aug 72, 5).

[8] Kenilworth Castle, one of the finest "baronial ruins" in England, is five miles from the town of Warwick. Founded about 1120, it was greatly enlarged and improved in the sixteenth century by the earl of Leicester. His lavish entertainment there of Queen Elizabeth was immortalized by Sir Walter Scott in *Kenilworth* (1821). Cromwell's officers destroyed most of the structure; only the gatehouse was still in use, by its present owner, the earl of Clarendon (Baedeker 1901, 256–57; Murray 1890, 222). Warwick Castle, in Warwick on the banks of the Avon, is a picturesque structure dating from Saxon times, although most of the residential sections were built in the fourteenth and fifteenth centuries. On display were paintings, old armor, and other "curiosities" (Baedeker 1901, 255). In 1886 Clemens used Warwick Castle for the opening scene in *A Connecticut Yankee in King Arthur's Court* (*CY*, 5–6, 47).

[9] In a letter to the San Francisco *Alta California* dated 3 October, Ambrose Bierce described his own visit to Shottery, a village near Stratford, where "Ann Hathaway, aged twenty-five, wooed and won Will Shakspeare, aged eighteen":

> I cannot say I was much interested in Ann and her affairs. The visitors' book here was very much more to my mind; and therein, among a multitude of famous autographs I found those of General Sherman and Mark Twain. I could not repress a smile as I read the name of the grim, heartless, and unimaginative warrior recorded at this shrine of pure sentiment—a sentiment, too, of the sicklier sort. From Mark something like this was to be expected. I had met him a few evenings before in London. We had dined together at one of the literary clubs, and in response to a toast Mark had given the company a touching narration of his sufferings in Central Africa in discovery of Dr. Livingstone! It was, therefore, not surprising that he should have penetrated as far as Shottery. He was probably looking for Sir John Franklin. (Bierce)

[10] The given name of Tom Hood (1835–74), the son of poet and humorist Thomas Hood (1799–1845), was the same as his father's, and the title pages of some of his works identify him as "Thomas Hood, the younger," but he was commonly known as "Tom." Educated at Oxford, he published his first poem in 1853. From 1856 to 1859 he worked on the Liskeard *Gazette*, and in 1860 took a position as a clerk in the war office. Since May 1865 he had been the editor of *Fun*, for which he not only wrote material but drew and engraved illustrations. In 1865 he published a three-volume novel, and in 1869, *Rules of Rhyme, a Guide to English Versification*. He began publishing his annual anthologies of humor in 1867. *Tom Hood's Comic Annual for 1873*, available by 7 December 1872, included an original sketch by Mark Twain, "How I Escaped Being Killed in a Duel" (SLC 1872b). In 1894 Clemens recalled that Hood had encouraged him to write down the story after hearing him tell it at a dinner party (advertisement, *Fun*, 7 Dec 72, 240; "Mark Twain and the Reporter," Buffalo *Express*, 1 Apr 94, part 2:15).

[11] Charles Langdon's letter to Olivia is not known to survive.

[12] Since Langdon Clemens had died in June, Clemens may have been referring to his niece, Julia Langdon, in addition to Susy Clemens.
[13] John Arnot was president of the Chemung Canal Bank in Elmira (Boyd and Boyd, 59).

To Henry Lee
13 September–11 November 1872 • London, England
(Dawson's Book Shop 1938, item 161)

161. **CLEMENS, SAMUEL.** Note on his visiting card, reading "All right, my boy, I've nobody to invite. Yours sincerely, S.L.C." Contained in original envelope, addressed in Clemens' own hand to Henry Lee of London.[1]

[1] Henry Lee (1826–88) was a self-educated naturalist. He played a large role in the construction of the Brighton Aquarium—which had opened for the first time on 10 August—and became its resident naturalist in December. In addition to providing informative "Aquarium Notes" for visitors, he collected his own specimens for study and published several books and articles on biological topics, aimed primarily at a general audience. Lee also owned a fur business, listing himself as a "skinner, furrier, & beaver cutter" in the London directory (*London Directory*, 1053; Boase, 2:352; "Opening of the Brighton Aquarium," London *Morning Post*, 12 Aug 72, 2; "Obituary," London *Times*, 3 Nov 88, 9). Clemens probably first met Lee on 12 September, when he visited Brighton with Edmund Routledge and Tom Hood as Lee's guest. He could have written this note anytime thereafter until his departure from London on 11 November. For Clemens's affectionate description of Lee, see Appendix C.

To James R. Osgood
13–18 September 1872 • London, England
(Rendell 1970, item 35)

(SLC)

                                                                 The Langham[1]
Dear Osgood[2]

Enclosed is a photo.[3] Hope to send a better one when our latest come up from that Brighton place.[4] Here's to you!

·   ·   ·   ·

¹ The Langham Hotel, in Portland Place, was built in 1864,

> in the style of a Florentine palace on seven floors, with 600 rooms including many private suites. It was magnificently furnished in white, scarlet and gold. There were 15,000 yards of carpet and the plaster-relief ceilings and mosaic flooring were by Italian craftsmen. (Weinreb and Hibbert, 445–46)

Although greatly damaged in the Second World War, the building still stands, housing offices and studios of the British Broadcasting Corporation (Weinreb and Hibbert, 446).

² This letter was written after Clemens's Brighton excursion, and presumably in time to reach Osgood in London before his departure on 19 September (Weber, 130).

³ The photograph does not survive, but was almost certainly the "London picture" taken by Charles Watkins (5 Oct 72 to Fitzgibbon), the only known print of which was inscribed to "Mr. Sandifer." (A "Jabez Sandifer," otherwise unidentified, is listed in the 1873 *London Directory* [2147].) It is reproduced in Appendix F.

⁴ While in Brighton on 12 September Clemens had several photographs taken at the studio of W. and A. H. Fry, "Art Photographers and Miniature Painters": four poses are known to be extant. Clemens, Lee, and Routledge also sat for a group photograph, and on one of the surviving copies, each man signed his name under his picture. All of the surviving Brighton poses are reproduced in Appendix F.

To Olivia L. Clemens
15 September 1872 • London, England
(MS: Davis, Jr.)

(SLC)

London, Sep. 15.

Livy darling everybody says lecture—lecture—lecture—but I have not the least idea of doing it—certainly not at present. Mr. ~~Dob~~ Dolby, who took Dickens to America, is coming to talk business to me tomorrow, though I have sent him word once before, already, that I can't be hired to talk here, because I have no time to spare.¹

There is too much sociability—I do not get along fast enough with work. ~~On~~ Tomorrow I lunch with Mr. Toole & a member of Parliament—Toole is the most able Comedian of the day.[2] And then I am done for a while. On Tuesday[3] I mean to hang a card to my key-box, inscribed "Gone out of the City for a week"—& then I shall go to work & work hard. One can't be caught in a hive of 4,000,000 people *,*, like this.

I have got such a perfectly delightful razor. I have a notion to buy some for Charley, Theodore,[4] & Slee—for I *know* they have no such razors there. I have got a neat little watch chain for Annie[5]—$20.

I love you my darling. My love to all of you.

Sam*l*.

✉—

Mrs. Sam*l*. L. Clemens | Cor Forest & Hawthorne sts | Hartford | Conn. [*in upper left corner:*] U.S. of America | [*flourish*] [*on flap:*] (SLC) [*postmarked:*] LONDON W 3 SP16 72 [*docketed by OLC:*] Sep 15/—

[1]Clemens did not lecture in England until the fall of 1873. George Dolby (d. 1900), a theatrical manager, was hired to escort Dickens on his reading tour in Britain in April–June 1866. The ailing and high-strung Dickens found Dolby not only an efficient manager but an amiable companion, and they became friends. Dolby accompanied Dickens on his second tour in Britain (January–May 1867), his American tour (December 1867–April 1868), and his final tour, again in Britain (October 1868–April 1869), which ended prematurely when Dickens became too ill to go on. Dolby published his memories of these days "on the road" with his "Chief" in *Charles Dickens As I Knew Him*, calling the tours "the most brilliantly successful enterprises of their kind that were ever undertaken" (Dolby 1885, vii; Page, 120–35). In 1900 Clemens recalled Dolby as a "gladsome gorilla" who was "large & ruddy, full of life & strength & spirits, a tireless and energetic talker, & always overflowing with good-nature & bursting with jollity" (SLC 1900, 34, in *MTA*, 1:140; see also Ollé).

[2]The "member of Parliament" was probably Douglas Straight (25 Sept 72 to OLC). John Lawrence Toole (1830–1906) was a renowned comic actor and theatrical manager. As a young man, he was employed as a wine merchant's clerk when Dickens saw him in an amateur play and urged him to pursue a stage career. His professional debut occurred in 1852.

[3]Tuesday, 17 September.

[4]Charles Langdon and Theodore Crane.

[5]Annie Moffett.

To Arthur Locker
17 September 1872 • London, England
(MS: NElmC)

(SLC)

Langham Hotel
Sept 17.

Dear Sir:[1]
I believe the sketch in "Men of the Time" is accurate—indeed, I furnished the facts myself. Nothing in the way of addition or correction occurs to me now, & so I have only [to] thank you very kindly for the courtesy of offering me the opportunity—[2]

& subscribe myself
Yrs faithfully
Sam¹. L. Clemens.

Arthur Locker Esq.

[1]Arthur Locker (1828–93) was educated at Oxford. From 1852 to 1861 he lived in Australia and India, became a journalist, and wrote several tales and plays. After his return to England he wrote for various newspapers and magazines, and from 1865 to 1870 "contributed reviews" to the London *Times* ("Mr. Arthur Locker," London *Times*, 26 June 93, 10). In mid-1870 he became the chief editor of the London *Graphic*, an illustrated weekly founded in December 1869, and held that position until 1891. He also wrote several novels (Boase, 2:468; Griffiths, 378).
[2]Locker was writing a brief sketch of Clemens's life for the *Graphic*, basing it on the entry in *Men of the Time: A Dictionary of Contemporaries*, issued by the Routledges in 1872. The entry did contain one error, which Clemens probably would have corrected had he seen the printed text: it listed "Flush Times in the Silver-mines, and other Matters" among his works (*Men of the Time*, 227). He had proposed this title to Bliss on 10 July 1871, but within four months had renamed his book *Roughing It* (*L4*, 431). Locker's article, "Two American Humorists—Hans Breitmann and Mark Twain," appeared in the *Graphic* on 5 October, illustrated with engravings of both authors (Clemens's portrait is reproduced on the next page; for Breitmann's, see Appendix F). The first paragraph contained a brief biography of Breitmann (Charles Godfrey Leland: see 6 July 73 to Fairbanks, n. 5), and the second gave an outline of Clemens's life, correctly listing his major published works to date, and concluding:

Mr. E. P. Hingston, in his preface to "The Innocents Abroad," gives a lively description of the then editor of the *Enterprise*. "In Mark Twain," he says, "I found a flower of the wilderness, tinged with the colour of the soil; the man of thought and the man of action rolled into one, humorist and hard-worker, Momus in a felt hat and jack-boots." As a humorist, Mr. Clemens shows the same quaint exaggerative spirit as the late Artemus Ward, though less dependent on bad spelling for his fun. Judging by the wide circulation of his works, he is highly popular both here and in his native country. (Locker 1872)

Portrait of Clemens in the London *Graphic* (5 Oct 72, 324). See 17 Sept 72 to Locker.

To the Editor of the London *Spectator*
20 September 1872 • London, England
(London *Spectator*, 21 Sept 72)

TO THE EDITOR OF THE "SPECTATOR."

SIR,—I only venture to intrude upon you because I come, in some sense, in the interest of public morality, & this makes my mission respectable. Mr. John Camden Hotten, of London,[1] has, of his own individual motion, republished several of my books in England. I do not protest against this, for there is no law that could give effect to the protest;[2] &, besides, publishers are not accountable to the laws of heaven or earth in any country, as I understand it. But my little grievance is this: My books are bad enough just as they are written; then what must they be after Mr. John Camden Hotten has composed half-a-dozen chapters & added the same to them? I feel that all true hearts will bleed for an author whose volumes have fallen under such a dispensation as this. If a friend of yours, or if even you yourself, were to write a book & set it adrift among the people, with the gravest apprehensions that it was not up to what it ought to be intellectually, how would you like to have John Camden Hotten sit down & stimulate his powers, & drool two or three original chapters on to the end of that book? Would not the world seem cold & hollow to you? Would you not feel that you wanted to die & be at rest? Little the world knows of true suffering. And suppose he should entitle these chapters "Holiday Literature," "True Story of Chicago," "On Children," "Train up a Child, & Away he Goes," & "Vengeance," & then, on the strength of having evolved these marvels from his own consciousness, go & "copyright" the entire book, & put in the title-page a picture of a man with his hand in another man's pocket, & the legend "All Rights Reserved." (I only *suppose* the picture; still it would be a rather neat thing.) And, further, suppose that in the kindness of his heart & the exuberance of his untaught fancy, this thoroughly well-meaning innocent should expunge the modest title which you had given your book, & replace it with so foul an invention as this, "Screamers & Eye-Openers," & went & got *that* copyrighted, too.[3] And suppose that on top of all this, he continually & persistently forgot to offer you a single penny or even send you a copy of your mutilated book to burn. Let one suppose all this.

Let him suppose it with strength enough, & then he will know something about woe. Sometimes when I read one of those additional chapters constructed by John Camden Hotten, I feel as if I wanted to take a
broom-straw & go & knock that man's brains out. Not in anger, for I feel
none. Oh! not in anger; but only to see, that is all. Mere idle curiosity.

And Mr. Hotten says that one *nom de plume* of mine is "Carl Byng."
I hold that there is no affliction in this world that makes a man feel so
down-trodden & abused as the giving him a name that does not belong
to him.[4] How would this sinful aborigine feel if I were to call him John
Camden Hottentot, & come out in the papers & say he was entitled to it
by divine right?[5] I do honestly believe it would throw him into a brain
fever, if there were not an insuperable obstacle in the way.

Yes—to come back to the original subject, which is the sorrow that
is slowly but surely undermining my health—Mr. Hotten prints unrevised, uncorrected, & in some respects, spurious books, with my name
to them as author, & thus embitters his customers against one of the most
innocent of men.[6] Messrs. George Routledge & Sons are the only English
publishers who pay me any copyright, & therefore, if my books are to
disseminate either suffering or crime among readers of our language, I
would ever so much rather they did it through that house, & then I could
contemplate the spectacle calmly as the dividends came in.[7]—I am, Sir,
&c.,

SAMUEL L. CLEMENS ("MARK TWAIN").

London, September 20, 1872.

[1] John Camden Hotten (1832–73) went to work for a bookseller at age fourteen
and developed an abiding interest in books. After spending several years in the
United States, he returned to England in 1856 and became a bookseller and publisher. He was soon one of London's best-known publishers, with an extensive
list that included Dickens, Swinburne, and Blake, works of antiquarianism,
popular histories, cheap editions of standard works, humor, and poetry. He
compiled and issued his own *Dictionary of Modern Slang, Cant, and Vulgar Words*
in 1859, and wrote, compiled, or translated many other works. He also published erotica, some of which he sold in limited or subscription editions, and
some, like James Glass Bertram's *Flagellation and the Flagellants: A History of the
Rod in All Countries* (1869), through his regular list (Marcus, 69–70; advertisements at end of SLC 1871e and Hingston 1871). In the 1860s, in the absence of
any international copyright convention, Hotten began reprinting the works of
popular American writers, like Emerson, Lowell, Whitman, Holmes, Artemus
Ward, and Hans Breitmann. In the early 1870s he expanded his American list
to include Mark Twain, Bret Harte, Joaquin Miller, and Ambrose Bierce. Most
of these writers were reprinted without their consent, and of course without pay-

ment. In an unpublished diatribe against Hotten, written sometime between late November 1872 and June 1873, Clemens set down his own version of the publisher's career:

He began life as a bookseller's clerk in London, under the name of John Hotten. By & by his employer discovered a sign up a back street with this legend on it: "JOHN HOTTEN, BOOKSELLER."
So his clerk had hired clerks of his own, & was driving a private trade without his employer's knowledge. Right enough, perhaps. But when it transpired that John Hotten had *stolen* his stock of books from his employer, he made a sudden journey to America to escape the consequences. He was in exile here for some time. Then he turned up in England again & chose a new victim. Who? A former benefactor, of course. This was a benefactor who had an excellent business location, & John Camden Hotten (he had added the "Camden," now) wanted it. He found that the lease was almost out, & he entered into a secret treaty for it with the owners. And he came near getting it, too, before the occupant found it out. . . .
At the present day Hotten is an extensive publisher of cheap literature, at 74 Piccadilly, London, & has & yet, large as his business really is, the man has not a speaking acquaintance personal friend whom a respectable person could dare to associate with. There are so many people who desire to pull his nose that it is next to impossible to find him in his shop. (SLC 1872–73, 5–7†)

Clemens had himself recently visited Hotten's office. On 7 September Hotten wrote Ambrose Bierce, "Tom Hood has just been here with 'Mark Twain.' Mark was introduced to me as 'Mr Bryce,' & he looked as glum and as stern as any member of the Bryce family I ever saw."

I suppose the joke w^d have succeeded, but I at once brought out my portrait of Mark Twain, & this did the business, altho "Bryce" intensified his sternness & swore— at least he asseverated—he was of that *ilk* to the last. But the likeness! My goodness me, I never saw anything like it! (CU-BANC)

Hood also mentioned the failed ruse in a letter to Bierce of 9 September: "Hotten was too sharp for he twigged Mark, and not sharp enough because he said so before we had time to commit ourselves" (CU-BANC). Bierce was at this time on the staff of Hood's comic newspaper, *Fun;* by his consent, Hotten was his English publisher (see Grenander 1978, 459–60).

[2] Hotten was not legally required to obtain an author's permission or pay a royalty when reprinting works first published in the United States. He had published unauthorized editions of *The Innocents Abroad,* the *Jumping Frog* book, and the *(Burlesque) Autobiography* (SLC 1870b–d, 1871c–d); compiled two collections of Mark Twain's newspaper pieces, *Eye Openers* and *Screamers* (SLC 1871a, e); and included several selections by Mark Twain in humor anthologies, like *Practical Jokes with Artemus Ward* (Hotten 1870a–b, 1872a; *ET&S1,* 549–55, 586–89).

[3] In his edition of *Mark Twain's (Burlesque) Autobiography,* Hotten had included a two-part piece entitled "On Children," comprising two sketches printed in the Buffalo *Express* over the pseudonym "Carl Byng" (see the next note): "How to Train up a Child" and "'Train up a Child, and Away He Goes'" (SLC 1871c; Byng 1870b, 1871). He then reprinted the two pieces in *Screamers,* together with another Byng piece, "Holiday Literature" (Byng 1870a). Also included in *Screamers* were "Almost Incredible—True Story of Chicago" (whose author is unidentified) and "Vengeance." In June 1872 Hotten claimed to have belatedly learned that "Vengeance" was the work of the "editor of *Cassell's Mag-*

azine" (George Manville Fenn, 1831–1909), who had "announced himself as the author" after seeing the book in print. Hotten thereupon "withdrew it from my collection," removing it from later printings of *Screamers* (Hotten 1872b; *BAL* 3333). Neither Hotten nor Clemens had true British copyright on this reprinted material. The title pages of *Screamers* and *Eye Openers* did include the words "All Rights Reserved"—a "conventional device to reserve right of translation and republication in countries that shared an international copyright agreement with Great Britain" (*ET&S1*, 597 n. 143).

⁴Between November 1870 and late January 1871 several sketches signed "Carl Byng" appeared in the Buffalo *Express*. A study of these texts indicates that Clemens did not write them, and that they may have been the work of Josephus N. Larned, Clemens's editorial colleague on the newspaper (*L4*, 306 n. 3). Hotten introduced the sketch "Holiday Literature" in *Screamers:* "The following criticism of Mother Goose, by Carl Byng—which is another name for Mark Twain, we imagine—will repay perusal" (Hotten 1871). And in his letter published in the London *Spectator* on 8 June 1872 he reiterated the claim that "Carl Byng" was "another *nom de plume*" of Clemens's (Hotten 1872b; see also note 6). Clemens consistently rejected as "spurious" all sketches by Carl Byng, regardless of how Hotten identified them (London *Spectator*, 8 June 72, 722, in *ET&S1*, 594).

⁵In an unpublished manuscript that Clemens probably wrote in mid-September 1872, "To the Superintendent of the Zoological Gardens," he pretended to offer

> for your inspection & purchase one of the most remarkable creatures which nature has yet produced. For the sake of convenience I call it the John Camden Hottentot. It is not a bird, it is not a man, it is not a fish, it does not seem to be in all respects a reptile. It has ₰ ‚the‚ body & features of a man, but ~~none of the ins~~ scarcely any of the instincts that belong to such a structure. It will answer to its name, & come with the greatest alacrity to do a mean thing, but will hide away in its lair, with every indication of distress, if it is required to be in any wise accessory to a virtuous action. (SLC 1872o, 1–2†)

Although Clemens did not publish this fulmination, the Hottentot conceit appeared again in an anonymous burlesque review on 23 November in the London *Figaro*, a satiric semiweekly journal. Purporting to be a notice of *John Camden Hotten: The Story of His Life*, a (fictive) biography by Henry M. Stanley, the article revealed that Hotten was the son of a "famous Hottentot chieftain," and that he had run away to England and "dropped the 'tot' at the end of his name." Hotten's career was also discussed, "especially his famous discoveries of American humorists,"

> which he commenced a few years ago, and continues to the present day, with such great success. The story of Hotten's discovery of Bret Harte is now as familiar as a household word, and the persistent way in which he unearthed Mark Twain, who disguised himself under all manner of *aliases*, is equally well known. . . . Mr. Stanley gives Mr. Hotten full credit for his discoveries in this direction; but complains that the Piccadilly publisher does not pay his humorists for discovering them. . . . It costs Mr. Hotten time and labour and money to discover the Transatlantic humorists; and we do not see why he is so indebted to them. If they would discover themselves, it would be a very different matter; but they do not. ("Stanley on Hotten," clipping in CU-MARK)

⁶Clemens's assessment of Hotten's publishing practices would be echoed in the succinct obituary included in the *Annual Cyclopaedia* for 1873:

June 14.—HOTTEN, JOHN CAMDEN, an enterprising but somewhat notorious publisher of London, who republished American novels very largely, altering them, without notice to the authors, to suit his ideas, and often announcing anonymous books of inferior merit, as by popular authors; died in London. (*Annual Cyclopaedia 1873*, 597–98)

[7] Clemens's struggle to retain control of the contents of his English sketch-books had first become public in May of 1872, when the Routledges wrote the London *Spectator* to protest a negative review of Hotten's *Screamers*, which "singled out half of the nonauthorial pieces for its dispraise" (*ET&S1*, 591–92; "Mark Twain," London *Spectator*, 18 May 72, 633–34). On 1 June the *Spectator* retracted its assertion that Clemens had authored the sketches in question, and announced that the Routledges would soon issue "a volume of sketches . . . authenticated and revised by the author himself," *Mark Twain's Sketches* (London *Spectator*, 1 June 72, 698; SLC 1872e). Hotten responded, pointing to the curious fact that the sketches in the new Routledge collection had derived from his own *Eye Openers* and *Screamers:* Clemens had revised Hotten's edited texts for the Routledges, in effect "pirating his own pirate" (*ET&S1*, 593–96). In his unpublished attack on Hotten, Clemens admitted that "Hotten cleanses me carefully before spreading me before the British public, but ~~I suppose it rather benefits me than otherwise I doubt~~ I suspect he leaves more dirt by contact of his person than he removes from me by his labor" (SLC 1872–73, 18–19†). This may account for his willingness to accept some of Hotten's otherwise unwelcome changes. After the present letter was published, Hotten again defended himself against Clemens's accusations, in a letter which appeared in the *Spectator* on 28 September (Hotten 1872c):

SIR,—It was unkind of "Mark Twain" to write you that note last week concerning myself. You may, perhaps, remember that in June last you permitted me to say in your journal that a so-called "revised edition" of "Mark Twain's" sketches, recently issued here by another publisher "consisted simply of my own revised editions transposed; in fact, my little books seem to have been sent to some one in New York who returned the sketches intact, but with the arrangement a little altered;" and in proof, I further stated that certain very forcible expressions which I left out as unnecessary were also curiously left out in the "revised edition," and certain new titles given by me turned up in a most unaccountable manner in the new "author's revised edition"; and the punctuation, English orthography, and even our printer's errors all appeared in the new "author's revised edition" in a way that was simply marvellous—in a way the like of which I never before remember as occurring to an "author's revised edition." As no denial of my statement has ever appeared in your journal, I suppose its truth will not now be challenged.

But "in the interest of public morality," "Mark Twain" complains that I have "composed half-a-dozen chapters and added the same to his books." Perhaps, in the interest of common-sense, you will allow me to say that I have done nothing of the kind. "Mark Twain" instances five papers as my composition. Whether American humourists as fathers are different from other men I cannot say, but in this instance "Mark Twain" has forgotten his own children. Three of these stories appeared in his own paper, the *Buffalo Express*, and the others were very generally circulated under his name, without a single denial appearing. Any one interested in the authorship can see the American originals at my office.

"Mark Twain" says that the name "Carl Byng" does not belong to him. I can only say that his brother journalists in New York State must be labouring under an extraordinary delusion, seeing that they *always* treat "Carl Byng" *as* "Mark Twain," and "Mark" himself has never once corrected them, although the statement that the two names refer to one man must have come before him some hundreds of times. The articles signed "Carl Byng," I may just mention, invariably appear in Mr. Clemens' paper, the *Buffalo Express*. But his taste for many *noms de plume* was curiously displayed only the other day. When Mark Twain called upon me with one of the greatest humourists of Fleet Street, I gave the former a hearty welcome as "Mr. Clemens, the famous 'Mark Twain,'" but observing that he looked glumpy, his companion took me on one side, and in a hurried manner explained to me that "Mr. Twain" would be much better pleased if addressed as "Mr. Bryce." I did so, and he seemed greatly cheered up. We talked of the old and modern schools of humour, and after accepting a little book as a present, "Mr. Bryce" left me, and made his way back to Fleet Street.

There is one misapprehension I trust you will allow me to clear up. I have in three years written thrice to Mr. Clemens, but never received one answer. As late as January last I wrote, offering equitable payment for any work he might do for me; and the editor of my English edition of the "Innocents Abroad" [Edward P. Hingston] has also, I believe, been unable to get an answer. To any American author who may either write or edit for me, I will make payment to the best of my ability; but if it is left for me to gather up newspaper trifles, trifles cast off and forgotten, and left to me to obtain a market for their sale in a collected form, with the cheerful probability of another edition appearing at one-sixth of my price,—for such non-copyright raw material, liable to such a contingency, I am not prepared to pay anything, and I do not think any man in his senses would pay.

When "Bret Harte's" agent called upon me a few days since with a new copyright story, we at once came to terms.—I am, Sir, &c.,

JOHN CAMDEN HOTTEN.

(See also Hotten to SLC, 3 Feb 72, Letterbook 6:18, Chatto and Windus.) Hotten was already in the process of producing yet another unauthorized collection of Mark Twain's sketches, which he began to advertise in October or early November. Clemens was now so exasperated by the appearance of spurious works credited to him that he paid Hotten another visit on 8 November, with an offer to revise the new sketchbook. Hotten cordially accepted, but Clemens, suddenly called home, was unable to carry out his revisions. Hotten issued *The Choice Humorous Works of Mark Twain*, an "immense volume," in March 1873 (*ET&S1*, 600–601). By the fall of 1873, however, when Clemens returned to England for his December lecture series, Hotten had died, and his successor, Andrew Chatto (now in partnership with W. E. Windus), again offered Clemens the chance to revise his sketches. In a letter of 25 November 1873, Chatto wrote:

> I am sincerely anxious to establish more cordial relations as between Author & Publisher, than have hitherto existed, between you and our firm, and I beg to submit to you a set of the sheets of a volume of your writings, in order that you may (as I understand you expressed a desire to do) correct certain portions of the contents. (Letterbook 6:707, Chatto and Windus)

The volume in question was *Choice Humorous Works*, which Clemens agreed to revise, using a set of folded and gathered sheets. In addition to deleting seventeen sketches (including all those by Carl Byng), he made extensive corrections on many more (for a full description of these revisions, see *ET&S1*, 603–7). The corrected sheets, which Clemens completed before returning home in January 1874, served as printer's copy for altering the plates of *Choice Humorous Works* to produce a new edition of that title, issued in April. The sheets are preserved in the Rare-Book Division of the New York Public Library (SLC 1873b, 1874a).

To Olivia L. Clemens
22 September 1872 • London, England
(MS: CU-MARK)

London, Sept. 22.

Livy darling, I am making tolerably fair progress, & am at last getting my sight-seeing systematized. I am running the legs off myself, but to-morrow & next day I am going to devote to my diary. It will bring me up a good long way.

I have been carrying English paper money loosely in my pocket, just as I always did with greenbacks, & I have come to grief. I find I have lost it all out, some time or other, don't know when—only noticed it to-day. Lost anywhere from £30 to £40.[1] Stupid business.

Published that blast at Hotten yesterday. I met Mrs. George Turner & Nellie on the stairs yesterday—wasn't expecting to see them here.[2]

This is no worn-out field. I can write up some of these things in a more different way than they have been written before.

Made a speech at the Savage Club last night. Had a very good time there.[3]

Welly-well-well, I ỵ wish you were *here* instead of half a world away, sweetheart. Tell me how you are. I love you Livy darling, I do assure you, with all my heart.

Sam'.

[✉] ——————————————————————————————

[*in ink:*] Mrs. Sam'. L. Clemens | Cor Forest & Hawthorne | Hartford | Conn. [*in upper left corner:*] U.S. of America. | [*flourish*] [*on flap:*] (SLC)
[*postmarked:*] LONDON · W 6 SP23 72 [*and*] NEW YORK OCT 5 PAID ALL

[1] About one hundred fifty to two hundred dollars. Clemens recalled this incident in 1907, mistakenly placing the dinner within a day or two of his arrival in England:

We broke up at two in the morning; then I missed my money—five 5-pound notes, new and white and crisp, after the cleanly fashion that prevails there. Everybody hunted for the money but failed to find it. How it could have gotten out of my trousers-pocket was a mystery. . . . After I had gone to bed in the Langham hotel I found that a single pair of candles did not furnish enough light to read by with comfort, and so I rang, in order that I might order thirty-five more, for I was in a prodigal frame of mind on account of the evening's felicities. The servant filled my order, then he proposed to carry away my clothes and polish them with his brush. He emptied all the pockets, and among other things he fetched out those five 5-pound notes. Here was another mystery! . . . He said it was very simple; he got them out of the tail-coat pocket of my dress suit! I must have put them there myself and forgotten it. Yet I do not see how that could be, for as far as I could remember we had had nothing wet at the Savage Club but water. As far as I could remember. (SLC 1907, 4–5)

[2] Judge George Turner (1829–85), whom Clemens had known in Nevada in 1861 and 1862 when Turner was chief justice of the territory, was visiting London with his wife, Sarah, and their daughter, Nellie. Since the mid-1860s he had been practicing law in San Francisco (*L1*, 128–29 n. 2; "Suicide of George Turner," San Francisco *Evening Bulletin*, 13 Aug 85, 1). Clemens noted in his English journal that "Judge Turner & family . . . hailed me from a box in the Lyceum theatre" (Appendix C). And in mid-October he called on the Turners, where he met his old friend and fellow writer J. Ross Browne. Browne wrote to his wife on 16 October, "I met Mark Twain a day or two ago at Judge Turner's. He is just the same dry, quaint old Twain we knew in Washington. I believe he is writing a book over here. He made plenty of money on his other books—some of it on mine" (Browne, 399; *L2*, 230–31 n. 7). Browne evidently believed that *The Innocents Abroad* and *Roughing It* had been modeled on his own travel writings, such as *Yusef* (1853) and *Adventures in Apache Country* (1869), which had many of the same "tricks of humor" and "journalistic appeals" as Clemens's works, but had received far less recognition (Blair, 158). Joaquin Miller, for example, believed that Browne had been a strong influence on Clemens, asserting that "it is clear to the most casual reader that if there had been no *Yusef* there would have been no *Innocents Abroad*" (quoted in Browne, xix).

[3] See the next two letters. The Savage Club was founded in 1857 as a private but informal "place of reunion" for a "little band of authors, journalists, and artists" (Watson, 17). Moncure Conway, in a letter to the Cincinnati *Commercial*, explained that

> no man can belong to it who has not produced some successful work in art or literature, or gained some success on the stage, and the number of these is limited to a hundred. Membership of the Savage Club has been vainly sought by Lords who had done nothing. The members dine together every Saturday at a *table d'hôte*, the hour being fixed at five, so that the actors and others may repair to the theaters. (Conway 1872)

Some believed that the club took its name from poet and playwright Richard Savage (d. 1743), whose claim of illegitimate birth, maternal ill-treatment, and subsequent poverty (made famous in an account by Samuel Johnson) are now considered apocryphal. Journalist and novelist George Augustus Sala, on the other hand, asserted that "we dubbed ourselves Savages for mere fun" and "practised a shrill shriek or war-whoop, which was given in unison at stated intervals" (Watson, 21).

To Moncure D. Conway
22 September 1872 • (1st of 2) • London, England
(Anderson Galleries 1920a, lot 47)

47. CLEMENS (SAMUEL L.). Autograph Manuscript of his Speech before the Savage Club made in 1872. Written on 11 sheets of various sizes, in pencil. Autograph post card, addressed to M. D. Conway,[1] saying that he sends a rough draft of the speech.[2]

[1] Moncure Daniel Conway (1832–1907)—whom Clemens may have first met the previous evening—was born in Virginia and raised as a Methodist. He graduated from Dickinson College at age seventeen, and served for a time as a Methodist preacher. He soon rejected Methodism, however, and entered Harvard Divinity School, becoming pastor of the Unitarian Church in Washington upon graduation. Dismissed because of his antislavery views, he was next called to the First Congregational Church in Cincinnati. While in Ohio he wrote for several periodicals, and edited *The Dial, A Monthly Magazine for Literature, Philosophy, and Religion.* He then moved to Concord, Massachusetts, where he edited the *Commonwealth,* an antislavery newspaper. Shortly after traveling to England in 1863 to lecture for the Northern cause, he accepted the pastorate of South Place Chapel in Finsbury, a London suburb. Conway continued to write for various magazines and newspapers, and in 1870 published *The Earthward Pilgrimage* (London: John Camden Hotten). Since 1870 his correspondence for the Cincinnati *Commercial,* on virtually all topics of current interest—politics, the arts and sciences, fashionable events—had earned him a wide reputation as a journalist (Burtis, 129–30, 246).

[2] In this paraphrased "post card," almost certainly written on Sunday, 22 September, Clemens explained that he was sending an eleven-page draft of his speech of 21 September at the Savage Club, presumably in response to a request from Conway. He made a few revisions in his manuscript and enclosed it with the next letter, of the same date.

To Moncure D. Conway
22 September 1872 • (2nd of 2) • London, England
(MS and transcript: NNC and Conway 1872)

(SLC)

The Langham, Sunday.

Dear Sir:

I have worried through, after a fashion—a heavy job, & roughly done—but memory will enable you to read it.[1] I have marked the Marble Arch, & the Hyde Park & the Statuary of Leicester Square, ₍"Mabille,"₎ &c, with a star (*) so that you could explain the allusions—an American reader would not understand them. They wouldn't comprehend anything about it. I have appended one footnote myself to the reference to the Albert Memorial.[2]

Lost a wad of bank bills out of my vest pocket last night on my way home—£40—suppose I did it taking out my watch—& just as luck goes, in this life, it is an even bet that the least deserving scalawag in London found it.[3]

Hoping to be able to ₫ drop in on you before you go out of town or soon after your return, I am

Ys Truly
Saml L. Clemens.

[*enclosure:*][4]

Mr. Chairman & gentlemen, it affords me sincere pleasure to meet this distinguished club, a club which has extended its hospitalities & its cordial welcome to so many of my countrymen. I hope you will excuse these clothes.[5] I am going to the theatre: that will explain these clothes. I have other clothes than these.[6] Judging human nature by what I have seen of it, I suppose that the customary thing for a stranger to do when he stands here is to make a pun on the name of this club, under the impression, of course, that he is the first man that that idea has occurred to. It is a credit to our human nature—not a blemish upon it; for it shows that underlying all our depravity (& God knows, & *you* know we are depraved enough) & all our sophistication, & untarnished by them, there is a sweet germ of innocence & simplicity still. When a stranger says to me, with a glow of inspiration in his eye, some gentle innocuous little thing about "Twain" & "one flesh," & all that sort of thing, I don't try to crush that man into the earth—no. I feel like saying: "Let me take you by the hand, sir; let me embrace you; I have not heard that pun for weeks." We *will* deal in palpable puns. We *will* call parties named "King" Your Majesty, & we will say to the Smiths that we think we have heard that name before somewhere. Such is human nature. We can not alter this. It is God that made us so for some good & wise purpose. Let us not repine. But though I may seem strange, may seem eccentric, I mean to refrain from punning upon the name of this club, though I could make a very good one if I had time to think about it—a week.

I can not express to you what entire enjoyment I find in this first visit to this prodigious metropolis of yours. Its wonders seem to me to be limitless. I go about as in a dream—as in a realm of enchantment— where many things are rare & beautiful, & all things are strange & marvelous. Hour after hour I stand—I stand spell-bound, as it were—& gaze upon the statuary in Leicester Square.[7] I visit the mortuary effigies of noble old Henry the Eighth, & Judge Jeffreys,[8] & the preserved Gorilla, & try to make up my mind which of my ancestors I admire the most. I go to that matchless Hyde Park & drive all *around* it, & then I start to enter it at the Marble Arch—&—am induced to change my mind.[9] It is a great benefaction—is Hyde Park. There, in his Hansom cab, the invalid can go—the poor sad child of misfortune—& insert his nose between the railings, & breathe the pure health-giving air of the country & of heaven. And if he is a swell invalid, who isn't obliged to depend upon parks for his country air, he can drive inside—if he owns his vehicle. I drive round & round Hyde Park, & the more I see of the edges of it the more grateful I am that the margin is extensive.

And I have been to the Zoological Gardens.[10] What a wonderful place that is! I never have seen such a curious & interesting variety of wild animals in any garden before—except "Mabille."[11] I never believed before there were so many different kinds of animals in the world as you can find there—& I don't believe it yet. I have been to the British Museum.[12] I would advise you to drop in there some time when you have nothing to do for—five minutes—if you have never been there. It seems to me the noblest monument that this Nation has yet erected to her greatness. I say to her, *our* greatness—as a Nation. True, she has built other monuments, & stately ones, as well; but these she has uplifted in honor of two or three colossal demigods who have stalked across the world's stage, destroying tyrants & delivering Nations, & whose prodigies will still live in memories of men ages after their monuments shall have crumbled to dust—I refer to the Wellington & Nelson columns, &—the Albert Memorial.*

The Library at the British Museum I find particularly astounding. I have read there hours together & hardly made an impression on it. I revere that library. It is the author's friend. I don't care how mean a book is, it always takes one copy.[13] And then, every day that author goes there to gaze at that book, & is encouraged to go on in the good work. And what a touching sight it is of a Saturday afternoon to see the poor toil-worn clergymen gathered together in that vast reading-room cabbaging sermons for Sunday!

You will pardon my referring to these things. Everything in this monster city interests me, & I can not keep from talking, even at the risk of being instructive. People here seem always to express distances by parables. To a stranger it is just a little confusing to be so parabolic—so to speak. I collar a citizen, & I think I am going to get some valuable information out of him. I ask him how far it is to Birmingham, & he says it is twenty-one shillings & sixpence. Now, we know that don't help a man any who is trying to learn. I find myself down town somewhere, & I want to get some sort of idea of where I am—being usually lost when alone—& I stop a citizen & say: "How far is it to Charing Cross?" "Shilling fare in a cab," & off *he* goes. I suppose if I were to ask a Londoner how far it is from the sublime to the ridiculous, he would try to express it in coin.

But I am trespassing upon your time with these geological statistics & historical reflections. I will not longer keep you from your orgies. 'Tis a real pleasure for me to be here, & I thank you, for the name of the Savage Club is associated in my mind with the kindly interest & the friendly offices which you lavished upon an old friend of mine who came among you a stranger, & you opened your English hearts to him & gave him welcome & a home—Artemus Ward.[14] Asking that you will join me, I give you his memory.[15]

*Sarcasm.—The Albert Memorial is the finest monument in the world, & celebrates the existence of as commonplace a person as good luck ever lifted out of obscurity.[16]

[1] Clemens referred to his enclosure, a "rough draft" of the speech he had delivered the previous evening at the Savage Club. Conway included it in a letter of 24 September to the Cincinnati *Commercial:*

> On the occasion of his first appearance at the Club he came attended by his publisher, the genial and clever Mr. [Edmund] Routledge. Fortunately the chairman of the evening was the inimitable Toole, the wittiest actor in London. Mark Twain was given the seat of honor at his side, and when the repast was over, Toole arose and invited us to fill our glasses. A large proportion of the fifty or sixty persons present did not know that any distinguished guest was present until this unusual invitation to fill glasses was given. The necessity of repairing to the theaters has made it the rule that there shall be no toasts or speeches to prolong the dinners, except at the Christmas or anniversary banquet. All now set themselves to know what was up. Toole then said: "We have at our table Mark Twain." At these words a roar of cheers arose, and for some moments the din was indescribable. Toole then proceeded in a penitent way to confess that for a year or two he had been cribbing from Mark Twain in a way that must now, he feared, suffer a humiliating exposure. When now and then he had indulged in an innocent "gag," he had had friends rush to him behind the scenes or on the streets with "Toole, that was capital; your own, I suppose?" Now invariably when he had been so greeted the thing happened to be Mark Twain's. So all he could say was: "Oh—ah—well—ahem—glad you liked it." He could not exactly make out how it was, but when he did put in a bit of originality, his friends seemed very rarely to come and inquire whether it was his own or not. Toole's deferential gravity and innocent look is always amusing, but his fooling in this speech was unusually funny. When Mark Twain arose, the contrast between him and the clever, comic actor beside him was singular. The one is small, with a jolly, blooming countenance, full of quickness, eye ever on the alert; the American tall, thin, grave, with something of the look of a young divinity student fallen among worldlings. (Conway 1872)

According to a "private letter" quoted in the New York *Tribune,* "Mark was the guest of Mr. Lee." Nearby sat Watts Phillips (1825–74), a dramatist and novelist; Andrew Halliday (1830–77), an essayist and dramatist; and Tom Hood ("Mark Twain at the Savage Club," 8 Oct 72, 8).

[2] Clemens's speech manuscript has not been found. His enclosure is therefore transcribed from the text in the Cincinnati *Commercial,* which was typeset from that manuscript (Conway 1872). Where Clemens said he had inserted a "star" (asterisk) to identify allusions needing explanation, Conway interpolated explanations in square brackets (see the textual commentary). For "Mabille" and the Albert Memorial, see notes 11 and 16.

[3] See 22 Sept 72 to OLC, and note 15.

[4] Conway introduced Clemens's speech as follows:

> Being one of the Savages, I have the happiness of laying before your readers Twain's speech, of which the Londoners are in hopeless ignorance, but, alas, it loses much by being transferred to paper. In its proper setting, related to its immediate environment, and delivered with a solemn and dry suavity, quite indescribable, it struck others present besides myself as the best after-dinner speech we had ever heard.
> The speaker had on full evening dress—swallow-tail coat, white cravat, and all that,—to wear which to the club dinner calls down upon the wearer considerable chaff, until it be meekly apologized for. This fact will explain the opening sentences of Twain's speech, which were uttered with deprecating lowliness. (Conway 1872)

[5] Conway inserted the comment "—and here the speaker's voice became low and fluttering—" after "hope."

[6] Here Conway added, "The manner in which these words were uttered produced a great deal of merriment."

[7] Conway, as Clemens suggested in his letter, explained the joke: "[Great laughter—Leicester Square being a horrible chaos, with the relic of an equestrian statue in the center, the King being headless and limbless, and the horse in little better condition.]" This statue of George I in armor, "modelled by C. Burchard in about 1716," was "sold for £16 in 1872 and removed from the Square" (Weinreb and Hibbert, 817–18).

[8] Clemens might have seen the statue of Henry VIII at St. Bartholomew's Hospital in Smithfield, situated in a niche over the principal entrance gateway: in his London guidebook he underlined "Henry VIII" in a description of the statue, and noted in the margin, "Why not Rahere?" (Rahere was the founder of the hospital) (Pardon, 96†). A wax effigy of Henry VIII was on display at Madame Tussaud's as well (information from Madame Tussaud's). George Jeffreys, first Baron Jeffreys of Wem (1648–89), was an English judge notorious for his brutal and unjust treatment of defendants charged after the Monmouth rebellion of 1685, during trials known as the "bloody assizes." No statue or effigy of Jeffreys that Clemens could have seen has been identified.

[9] Here Conway explained, "[Cabs are not admitted in Hyde Park—nothing less aristocratic than a private carriage.]"

[10] The Zoological Gardens in Regent's Park were opened in 1828 (Weinreb and Hibbert, 978). Clemens described his 15 September visit there with Henry Lee in his English journal (Appendix C).

[11] Despite Clemens's mention of marking "Mabille" with an asterisk, Conway did not add an explanation for it. The Jardin Mabille in Paris was one of the most frequented of the public *bals d'été*, recommended to the tourist "on account of the gay, brilliant, and novel spectacle they present. The rules of decorum are tolerably well observed, but it need hardly be said that ladies cannot go to them with propriety." At Mabille,

> on Tuesdays, Thursdays, and Saturdays, when the admission is 5 fr., many handsome, richly dressed women of the 'demi-monde' and exquisites of the boulevards assemble here, while on the other evenings, when the admission is 3 fr., and women enter without payment, the society is still less respectable. (Baedeker 1874, 51)

In chapter 14 of *The Innocents Abroad* Clemens mentioned having made a brief visit to the Jardin Mabille in 1867.

[12] Clemens went to the British Museum with Lee, as he recorded in his journal (Appendix C). A six-month ticket to use the Reading Room, issued on 18 September to "Mr Samuel L. Clemens | Langham Hotel," survives in the Mark Twain Papers. The museum, first housed in Montagu House on Great Russell Street, opened in 1759. Its original holdings comprised antiquities, works of art, and books formerly belonging to Sir Hans Sloane, Robert Harley (earl of Oxford), and the Cotton family. The collection, continually enlarged by purchases and gifts, eventually outgrew the available space, necessitating the construction of a new museum building on the same site, completed in 1847 (Weinreb and Hibbert, 89–91).

[13] Conway explained, "[A copy of every book printed in Great Britain must by law be sent to the British Museum, a law much complained of by publishers.]" This law had been in effect since the passage of the Literary Copyright Act of 1842 (Copinger, 18, 73).

14 Clemens's friend and fellow humorist Artemus Ward achieved a triumphant success in London in 1866 with his comic lecture on the Mormons. Conway claimed in his *Autobiography* that "never was American in London so beloved." Ward made the Savage Club his headquarters, and became its "life and soul":

> Yet all those brilliant articles in "Punch," all those unforgettable dinners, lasted but six months, and the entertainments in Egyptian Hall only seven weeks. When it was learned that the most delightful of men was wasting away under rapid consumption even while he was charming us, the grief was inexpressible. (Conway 1904, 2:136–37)

Conway conducted Ward's funeral in March 1867: "The chapel in Kensal Green Cemetery was filled to its utmost capacity. All the chief actors and actresses, writers of plays, literary men and women, were present, and sorrow was in every face." From that time Conway "enjoyed the friendship of many connected with the stage, and became a member of the Savage Club" (Conway, 2:137). In the early paragraphs of his Cincinnati *Commercial* article Conway reminisced about Ward and compared Clemens to him, suggesting that Clemens was "not simply a humorist, like Artemus, . . . but a shrewd observer, capable of making grave criticisms on general subjects" (Conway 1872). Clemens had delivered a lecture on Ward during his 1871–72 tour (2 Jan 72 to Redpath, n. 1; *L4*, 478–82).

15 Conway concluded his article:

> In deep silence, and with much feeling, the company present rose and drank to this sentiment. Then, after some moments, the new-comer was heartily cheered, and the members went up to make his acquaintance. Soon after Mark Twain went off to the Gayety Theater with some friends, and saw Byron's play, "Good News," and "Ali Baba," (a new extravaganza,) in both of which Toole appeared, and in the latter of which he had the most absurd gag, crying out: "As Mark Twain says in the 'Jumping Frog,' 'Lie on, Macduff, and thingumbobbed be he,'" &c. Afterward the party supped with Mr. Straight, M.P.
>
> I am sorry to learn from a note received from Mark Twain to-day that the pleasant evening did not end so happily after all. On returning to his hotel (the Langham) he discovered that he had dropped—he thinks on taking out his watch—a roll of bank notes amounting to forty pounds. He only fears that the meanest scalawag in London may have found them. (Conway 1872)

See 22 Sept 72 to OLC, n. 1.

16 Although Clemens wrote Conway that he had "appended one footnote," Conway rendered the footnote as a separate paragraph enclosed within square brackets in the body of the text. In his *Autobiography* Conway recalled a more amusing version of Clemens's remarks:

> After speaking of Hyde Park he got off a satire so bold that it quite escaped the Englishmen. "I admired that magnificent monument [i.e. to the Prince Consort] which will stand in all its beauty when the name it bears has crumbled into dust." The impression was that this was a tribute to Albert the Good, and I had my laugh arrested by the solemnity of those around me. Indeed, one or two Americans present with whom I spoke considered it a mere slip, and that Mark meant to say that the Prince's fame would last after the monument had crumbled. (Conway 1904, 2:143)

The 175-foot-high monument to Albert, prince consort of England (1819–61), on the south side of Kensington Gardens, had just been completed in July 1872, except for the statue of the prince, which was added in 1876. Designed by George Gilbert Scott, the memorial took ten years to plan and construct, at a cost of one hundred and twenty thousand pounds. Its Gothic canopy is inlaid with polished stones, mosaics, and enamels. The base comprises seven tiers of statuary, executed by ten different artists and sculptors (Weinreb and Hibbert, 11–12). Clemens described the monument at some length in his journal (Appendix C).

To T. B. Pugh
23 September 1872 • London, England
(MS: PHi)

London, Sept. 23.

My Dear Pugh:

I snatch a moment, in a desperate hurry, to say that it won't be possible for me to talk in the Star course.[1] I have not even the vaguest notion of lecturing next winter—otherwise I would accept your proposition at once. Wishing you ~~g~~ every good fortune, I am

Ys Sincerely

Sam*. L. Clemens

[1] Thomas B. Pugh's "Star Course of Lectures and Concerts," now beginning its fourth season, featured the most famous performers of the day, and was so popular that "every seat in the great Academy of Music" was filled "as soon as the tickets could possibly be passed out to the waiting crowd" (Pond, 543). Pugh arranged Clemens's appearance in Philadelphia in December 1869, and again in November 1871. In January 1872 he had tried unsuccessfully to engage Clemens for yet another lecture there (*L3*, 415–16; *L4*, 239–40 n. 1, 399, 401 n. 4; see p. 31).

To Olivia L. Clemens
25 September 1872 • London, England
(MS: CU-MARK)

(SLC)

London, Sept. 25.

Livy darling, got yours of 8th tonight, & was amused to see how you always complain of being "~~st~~ sleepy & stupid" when you write, & I am

always "in haste—dinner ready"——so Mother Fairbanks says, anyway. Glad to hear good accounts of the Muggins—*don't* let her be carried
always, but make her crawl—& help herself all she can.

Been to hear the Messiah, to-night, sung by Titiens & a chorus of
several hundred.[1] A box was placed at our disposal a week ago. There
are 350 private boxes in that magnificent Albert Hall,[2] & they are all
larger & in every way more comfortable than our stage-boxes at home.
The house seats 10,000, & wherever you sit you can see about two-thirds
of the people. Mind, it seats 10,000 *roomily*—*we* would put 20,000 in the
same space.

Sir John Bennett, the sheriff of London,[3] called, in our box & invited me to a trial at the Old Bailey[4] tomorrow, & also to the election for
Lord Mayor on Saturday, & also to the Sheriff's dinner on the same
day—not a private dinner, strictly speaking, for there are to be 450 others present.[5] I was to have dined with him & the Newgate judges,[6] to-day,
at the Old Bail/ey, but did not know it. Mr. Douglas Straight, Member
of Parliament,[7] na made the appointment, but he misunderstood me, for
I told him I had a previous engagement. Sir John Bennett said they
waited dinner some time for me & were considerably disappointed, for
they had all read the Innocents & hadeld thems & had traveled over the
same ground, & held themselves under obligations to the author of the
best book of travel extant. He said that at the Lord Mayor's banquet
some time ago[8] a number of big-wigs made my books the subject of an ø
hour's laudation. Very pleasant—isn't it? I had lost my pencil, & sadly
needed one—so he gave me his; & as it is gold, or silver, or something
of the kind, & has a gold pen in it, I am very much obliged.

The Duke of Wellington & the Duchess of Cambridge (the Queen's
cousin) were in the neighboring royal box, with a prince Sob Somebody.
The Duke has white hair & is the picture of the Great Duke his father.[9]

I enclose a couple of pennies which were made for me in the mint
to-day. Also an Emeu's feather.[10] Observe that an emeu's feather is a double feather on a single stem.

I do love you Livy darling, & I do most powerfully want to see you.
Good-bye sweetheart.

                                                              Sam*l.*

Let øOrion or Warner publish the Enclosed.[11]

✉──

Mrs. S. L. Clemens | Cor. Forest & Hawthorne | Hartford | Conn. [*in upper left corner:*] U.S. of America. | [*flourish*] [*on flap:*] (SLC) [*postmarked:*] LONDON · W I SP26 72 [*and*] NEW YORK OCT 7 PAID ALL

---

[1] On 25 September Teresa Titiens (or Tietjens) (1831–77), an internationally known Hungarian soprano, sang in a one-time production of Handel's most popular oratorio, *Messiah* (1742), which featured a "band and chorus of 700 performers" (advertisement, London *Times*, 25 Sept 72, 1).

[2] The Royal Albert Hall, directly across Kensington Road from the Albert Memorial, was designed by Captain Francis Fowke of the Royal Engineers. The work was completed in 1871, after his death, by Colonel H. Y. Darracott Scott. The elliptically shaped hall is covered by a dome 135 feet high. In June 1873 Clemens described it in a New York *Herald* letter as "a huge and costly edifice, but the architectural design is old, not to say in some sense a plagiarism; for there is but little originality in putting a dome on a gasometer" (SLC 1873e; Weinreb and Hibbert, 11; Kent, 4).

[3] Sir John Bennett (1814–97) was the leading watchmaker in London. He served as a member of the common council for the ward of Cheap (1862–89), as a member of the London school board (1872–79), and as one of two sheriffs of London and Middlesex (1871–72). On 14 March 1872 he was knighted at Buckingham Palace (Boase, 4:361).

[4] The Old Bailey Sessions House, named for the street on which it stood, housed the Central Criminal Court. It was built in 1774 to replace its predecessor, erected in 1539. The sheriffs had chambers there. Although the courts were nominally open to the public, the sheriffs—together with the aldermen—had the privilege of issuing tickets of admission "on the occasion of great trials" (Pardon, 95; Weinreb and Hibbert, 133, 783).

[5] The election of the lord mayor, chief magistrate of the Corporation of London and chairman of its two governing bodies (the Court of Aldermen and the Court of Common Council), usually takes place on Michaelmas Day, 29 September. In 1872, however, this day fell on a Sunday, so the election was held on Saturday, 28 September. The sheriffs, who are elected on Midsummer Day (24 June), take the oath of office on Michaelmas Eve, 28 September. The event is then celebrated by an inauguration banquet in the evening (Weinreb and Hibbert, 480–81, 783; "Election of Sheriffs," London *Times*, 25 June 72, 10; "Election of Lord Mayor," London *Morning Post*, 30 Sept 72, 2). See the next two letters.

[6] Clemens evidently referred to the criminal judges who presided at the Old Bailey, which was connected to Newgate Prison by an underground passage. Built in 1783, Newgate housed defendants awaiting trial and convicts sentenced to death; it was demolished in 1902 to make way for a new Central Criminal Court. There had been a prison on this site, at Newgate Street and Old Bailey, since the twelfth century (Pardon, 95; Weinreb and Hibbert, 544–46). Clemens may not have visited Newgate Prison in 1872, but he certainly did so in 1873, during his next visit: on 9 September 1873, in a letter to the Cincinnati *Commercial*, Moncure Conway reported the following conversation between a warder

at Newgate and an American visitor, identified only as a "Quakeress." The warder said:

"I was showing our place the other day to a remarkably intelligent American who admired our arrangements exceedingly, only he thought we were too lenient. That gentleman said that the great mistake in America was leniency. 'Would you believe it,' said he, 'we caught a rascal in America the other day whom we ought immediately to have burned, and we only hung him. But we are coming to our senses, and are now making arrangements to burn certain men for whom the gallows is too good.'"

"Will thee be good enough to tell me the name of the American gentleman who made that remark to thee?" said the Quakeress.

"Ah, yes," said the warder reflectively; "let me see—it was a Mr. Mark Twain."

The lady gave a smile of relief and went off. I am happy to say that Mr. Mark Twain is now at the Langham Hotel, busily at work on a book about the English, wherein, I venture to predict, he will give a readable account of his conversations at Newgate, of which I have been able to report only one sentence. (Conway 1873)

[7] Douglas Straight (1844–1914) became a successful barrister at a young age, and was involved in several sensational criminal cases. Under the pseudonym "Sidney Daryl" he wrote short stories, many of them reminiscences of his school days at Harrow, and between 1867 and 1877 published several volumes, including *Routledge's Hand-Book of Quoits and Bowls* (1868). In 1870 he was elected the Conservative member of Parliament for Shrewsbury, retaining the seat until 1874. He served as a judge in India from 1879 until 1892, when he was knighted. In his later years he turned to journalism: from 1896 until 1909 he edited the London *Pall Mall Gazette*. According to his biographer, Straight was "one of the most popular men in London," well liked for the "brisk bonhomie and humour of his conversation" (Griffiths, 541; *BBA*, s.v. "Straight, Sir Douglas").

[8] The lord mayor's banquet, hosted by the new lord mayor on the occasion of his succession to office and held annually in the Guildhall since 1501, was (and still is) a major social event attended by hundreds of distinguished guests. Until the twentieth century it took place after the Lord Mayor's Show on 9 November; now it is held on the following Monday (Weinreb and Hibbert, 481–84; Baedeker: 1878, 62; 1900, 135; 10 Nov 72 to OLC).

[9] The present duke of Wellington was Arthur Richard Wellesley (1807–84), a lieutenant general in the army who had served as a member of Parliament (1830–52). His father, the first and "Great Duke," was Arthur Wellesley (1769–1852), celebrated for his rout of the French at Waterloo in 1815. The duchess of Cambridge was Augusta Wilhelmina Louisa of Hesse Cassel (1797–1889), who in 1818 married the duke of Cambridge, Adolphus Frederick (1774–1850), the seventh son of George III. The duchess was a first cousin of George III, Queen Victoria's grandfather. Their son, George William Frederick Charles (1819–1904), inherited his father's title in 1850, but his 1847 marriage to an actress was not considered legal (being in contravention of the Royal Marriage Act of 1772), and so his mother retained the title of duchess (Burke 1904, clxxxii–clxxxvi, 1606; Cokayne, 2:497–99).

[10] The enclosures are now lost. The Royal Mint was on Little Tower Hill. According to *Routledge's Guide to London*, it was

an elegant and extensive building. . . . designed and executed, in the Grecian style of architecture, by Robert Smirke, jun. . . . The interior is arranged in the most appropriate and systematic manner; and the various engines and machines for the making of gold and silver coin are constructed in the very first style of ingenious excellence. Steam-engines of vast power give motion to the machinery. (Pardon, 147)

[11]Clemens enclosed a clipping (now lost) of his 20 September letter to the London *Spectator.* Charles Dudley Warner reprinted the letter in the Hartford *Courant* on 7 October ("Mark Twain and His English Editor," 2). Orion Clemens was evidently now working on the Hartford *Evening Post,* "the pleasantest berth he had ever had in his life," as Clemens later described it (see AD, 5 Apr 1906, CU-MARK, in *MTA*, 2:322–23; 5 May 73 to OC and MEC, n. 1). The *Post* did not reprint the *Spectator* letter. On 10 October, however, it published a brief article (possibly by Orion) which argued that "the justice of an international copyright is manifest." After summarizing Clemens's grievances against Hotten, it reprinted an item from the Manchester *Guardian* giving the gist of Clemens's "extremely humorous letter to The Spectator" and quoting his remark that no author would like Hotten to "sit down and stimulate his powers and drool out two or three original chapters" for his book (10 Oct 72, 2).

To Elisha Bliss, Jr.
28 September 1872 • London, England
(MS: CU-MARK)

London, Sept. 28.

Friend Bliss—

I have been received in a sort of tremendous way, tonight, by the brains of London, assembled at the annual dinner of the Sheriffs of London—mine being (between you & me) ~~bet~~ being a name which was received with a flattering outburst of spontaneous applause when the long list of guests was called.[1]

I might have perished on the spot but for the friendly support & assistance of my excellent friend Sir John Bennett—& I want you to paste the enclosed in a couple of the handsomest copies of the Innocents & Roughing It, & send them to him., His address is—

"Sir John Bennett
Cheapside
London."

Yrs Truly
S. L. Clemens.

I have informed him they are coming.[2]

✉——————————————————————————

[letter docketed:] S. L. Clemens | London | Sep 28ᵗʰ | 1872.

[1] See the next letter.
[2] The enclosures are not known to survive. Bliss evidently sent the books to Clemens for inscription, and Clemens then gave them to Bennett. The copy of *Roughing It* has not been found, but a copy of *The Innocents Abroad* (first edition, second issue, bound in morocco leather with gilt edges) survives in the collection of the Mark Twain House (CtHMTH), inscribed as follows:

> To Sir John Bennett
> With the warm regards of
> The Author—
> Sam*ⁱ*. L. Clemens
> Mark Twain.
>
> ———
>
> Nov. 7, 1872.
>
> ———

To Olivia L. Clemens
28 September 1872 • London, England
(MS: CU-MARK)

(SLC)

London, Saturday
Night, Sept. 28.

Livy darling, it has been a splendid night. I was at the installation in Guildhall, to-day, of the new Sheriffs & Lord Mayor of London.[1] Tonight I was at the great dinner given by the news Sheriffs of London to the several guilds & liverymen of London. When I arrived nobody seemed to know me—so I passed modestly in, & took the seat assigned to me. There was a vast crowd present at the dinner. In accordance with ancient custom, a man got up & called the names of all that immense mass of guests, beginning with the new Sheriff (a tremendous office in London) & called a horde of great names, one after another, which were received in respectful silence—but when he came to my name along with the rest, there was such a storm of applause as you never heard.[2] The applause continued, & they could not go on with the list. I was never so taken aback in my ̸n life—never stricken so speechless—for it was totally unlocked-for on my part. I thought I was the humblest in that great titled assembl̸eage—& behold, ̶m̶y̶ mine was the *only* name in the long list that called forth this splendid compliment.

I did not know what to do, & so I sat still & did nothing. By & by the new sheriff, in his gorgeous robes of office, got up & proposed my health, & accompanied it with the longest & most extravagantly complimentary speech of the evening, & appointed me to ̶r̶e̶p̶ respond to the toast to "literature."[3] Imagine my situation, before that great audience, without a single word of preparation—for I had expected nothing of this kind—I did not know I was a lion. I got up & said whatever came first, & made a good deal of a success—for I was the only man they consented to ̶h̶e̶r̶ ̶c̶l̶ hear *clear through*—& they applauded handsomely. Indeed I wish I had known beforehand the good-will they had for me—I would have prepared a terrific speech. Even the fact that I was placed at the head of the table between Sir Antoine Baker[4] & Sir John Bennett had not prepared me for this ovation. I think it was a sort of lame speech I made, but it was ̸p splendidly received.[5] I love you, Livy darling.

Saml.

[*enclosure 1:*]

(This was sent to me by Douglas Straight, M.P. during the dinner—S.L.C.)

My dear Clemmens—

What do you think of this "*Saturnalia*," as far as you've got? The ceremony is peculiar but is of ancient date. It came over with the "Conqueror" and has been "*too much*" for us all ever since, consequently it has been continued. You see by the applause they "read Mark Twain & inwardly digest him."[6]

Yours

Douglas Straight

[*on back of note as folded:*]
Mark Twain
   Esq

[*enclosure 2:*]

[*on back of calling card:*]
Dear Twain—
will you stand for Literature if the Sheriff gives it? you can speak in your own language & the Press will understand every word.
J.B.[7]

[*in ink:*] Mrs. S. L. Clemens | Cor. Forest & Hawthorne | Hartford | Conn. [*in upper left corner:*] U. S. of America. | [*flourish*] [*on flap:*] (SLC) [*postmarked:*] LONDON. W 7 SP30 72 [*and*] NEW YORK OCT. ◊◊ PAID ALL.

[1] The London *Times* reported this ceremony, in which the liverymen, or guild members, chose a new lord mayor, and the new sheriffs took the oath of office:

On Saturday, according to a time-honoured custom at Michaelmas, the Liverymen of the City of London were convened in the Guildhall to elect a member of the Court of Aldermen to the office of Lord Mayor for the ensuing civic year, beginning on the 9th of November. Sir Sills John Gibbons, the Lord Mayor, went in state from the Mansion-house, at 11 o'clock, to preside at the ceremony, escorted by the Sheriffs, and, as usual, preceded by trumpeters. Prior to the election, the new Sheriffs, Mr. Alderman White and Mr. Frederick Perkins, were publicly inducted into office in the presence of the Lord Mayor and Aldermen, attended by the high officers of the Corporation, the retiring Sheriffs all wearing their official robes, and the Liverymen assembled in the Hall. The new Sheriffs, with their friends and Under-Sheriffs, had previously met at the Guildhall Tavern, and had proceeded thence to the Hall for the purpose of making the requisite declarations on assuming office. ("Election of Lord Mayor," 30 Sept 72, 11)

Clemens's new friend, Sir John Bennett, was one of the retiring sheriffs. The new sheriffs were Thomas White (1818–83), a wine merchant who had been an alderman since 1871, and Frederick Perkins (b. 1826), who since 1859 had served five terms as the mayor of Southampton. The new lord mayor was Sir Sydney Hedley Waterlow (1822–1906), a stationer and printer who had served as a common councilman, alderman, and sheriff of London (1866–67); he was knighted in 1867 (Boase, 3:1317; "The New Sheriffs," London *Morning Post*, 30 Sept 72, 2; "Election of Lord Mayor," London *Times*, 30 Sept 72, 11). Clemens described the installation and election ceremonies in his journal (Appendix C). The London *Telegraph* reported:

With an unctuous relish for the quaint traditionary forms, . . . each and all who took part in the scene strove laudably to preserve its curious interest and historic dignity in the eyes of strangers. The auspicious rumour that an American man of letters had come to see what he should see was buzzed about; and when it became known that this illustrious visitor was "Mark Twain," one of the latest and most successful of those comic writers who dissemble their graces and accomplishments beneath a humorous eccentricity of spelling, and who discover a truly international spirit in their mingling of Yankee rhetoric with Cockney rhymes, great was the desire to identify the face of the distinguished *littérateur.* To so shrewd an observer as Mr. Clemens ("Mark Twain" being only a *nom de plume*), there must have been much that was both amusing and instructive in Saturday's ceremonial. ("Civic Changes," 30 Sept 72, 3)

[2] Attending the sheriffs' dinner at the Freemasons' Tavern were about two hundred and fifty guests, of whom the London *Times* listed forty-six, among them "Mr. Samuel L. Clemens ('Mark Twain')" ("Election of Lord Mayor," 30 Sept 72, 11). According to Albert Bigelow Paine, Clemens was talking with Bennett while the roll call of guests was being read:

All at once the applause broke out with great vehemence. This must be some very distinguished person indeed. He joined in it with great enthusiasm. When it was over he whispered to Sir John:
"Whose name was that we were just applauding?"
"Mark Twain's." (*MTB*, 1:463)

[3] Sheriff Thomas White

proposed "Success to Literature," coupled with the popular name of Mark Twain [cheers]. Who had ever read Mark Twain's works could have done otherwise than admire him [cheers]. He was glad to be able to say that the gentleman so favourably known in England as Mark Twain was present and that he had kindly consented to respond for the toast [great cheering]. ("Election of Lord Mayor & Swearing in of Sheriffs," London *Observer*, 29 Sept 72, 6, clipping in CU-MARK)

[4] Clemens mistook the name: he meant Sir Antonio Brady (1811–81), who began his civil-service career as a clerk and eventually became the first superintendent of the new contract department of the admiralty. Brady retired in March 1870, and three months later was knighted. Thereafter he devoted himself to social, educational, and religious reform. His interest in paleontology led him to recover, from an area near his residence, a large collection of mammalian remains, later deposited in the British Museum of Natural History.

[5] The London *Observer* of 29 September printed the following text of Clemens's speech, whose splendid reception was no doubt aided by the conviviality of the occasion:

Mr. S. L. CLEMENS (Mark Twain), who was very indistinctly heard, was understood to say—Messrs. Sheriffs, Ladies, and Gentlemen: Though I have had no previous notice, I am ready for you this time [laughter]. I beg to thank you very heartily for the expression of goodwill which you have displayed towards me [hear]. It was only an hour ago that I was told that I should be called upon to respond to a toast with which I was told that my name would be coupled. I am, therefore, not very well prepared to respond to the kind manner in which my name has been referred to. It would not, perhaps, be becoming in me to trouble you very much on an occasion like the present. Indeed, I am not prepared to do so. I have been taken so much by surprise that I do not know that I can adequately speak to the toast with which you have so kindly coupled my name [cries of Go on]. The toast to which I have been called upon to respond is one in which I take a great interest—one with which I have had some slight connection [laughter]. I regret that you did not tell me that I was to speak to such a toast as this. Had you given me even twenty-four hours' notice instead of half an hour, I should have prepared a speech respecting literature which I am certain would have proved very acceptable to you—in fact a speech which I believe would have made your hair stand on end [laughter]. I must only hope that under these circumstances you will excuse me. I beg you will understand that I have no lack of words, I have no want of ideas, and that I have no want of method in putting those ideas together in a sufficiently chaste manner to meet the public gaze [cheers]. All I want is time [laughter]. Had you given sufficient time I might have prepared a speech such as I hope and believe would have proved satisfactory [renewed laughter]. As I have told you, literature is a subject in which I take some interest, but you will admit it is a subject which cannot be treated upon very offhand or readily [hear]. If you take me by surprise in this manner, and if I do not reply in adequate terms, you have yourselves to blame and not me [laughter]. I should like very much to express myself properly on an occasion like the present, and I think, if I were disposed, I might keep you all the night long [cries of All right and Go on]. I could do so, but I had better not; at least I am sure you think so [laughter, and cries of Speak louder]. It is impossible for me to speak louder. I have been at this table so long, and the wines have been so good and so various, that I have become to be perhaps too emotional [laughter]. I should be glad to speak louder if I could, but I do not know that I can do so under the circumstances. I am not a person who is inclined to talk nonsense. Therefore I like to leave to some one better prepared to say what I have got to speak about [hear, hear]. I have crossed the Atlantic with the intention of doing some good. I hope you will allow me to do that good in my own collected and reflective way [hear, hear]. Instead, therefore, of butchering a subject in which I feel much interest, and respecting which I do not like to speak without some reflection, I beg you will allow me to leave it to other gentlemen who may be better prepared to do justice to the matter. I have only to say, ladies and gentlemen, in conclusion, that I thank you very much for the cordial reception you have given to the toast and to myself this evening [cheers]. (SLC 1872q)

The London *Times* noted, "Mr. Clemens, the American humourist, 'Mark Twain,' acknowledged, in an amusing speech, the toast 'Success to Literature,' with which his name had been associated" ("Election of Lord Mayor," 30 Sept 72, 11).

    [6]From the collect for the second Sunday in Advent in *The Book of Common Prayer:* "Blessed Lord, who hast caused all holy Scriptures to be written for our learning; Grant that we may in such wise hear them, read, mark, learn, and inwardly digest them" (Blunt, 73–74).

    [7]In 1907 Clemens recalled his "first experience of a banquet in a foreign country"—clearly the present occasion, although he forgot that he was unprepared to speak:

I was there by appointment, to respond to a regular toast, of which there were nine! Nine to be responded to, and mine in the place of honor—the last! It was a large distinction to confer upon a stranger, and I was properly proud of it; sorry for it too, for it broke my heart to wait so long; if I had had a hatful of hearts it would have broken them all. When at last the long, long, exhausting wait was ended, and my turn was come, and my gratitude rising up and pervading and supporting and supporting my whole system, a disaster befell: Sir John Bennett rose, uninvited, and began to speak. The indignation of the weary house burst out with the crash of an avalanche—a crash made up of shouts of protest and disapproval, powerfully aided and reinforced by deafening pounding of the tables with empty champagne bottles. But no matter—the gallant Sir John stood serene on the distant edge of the smoke and storm of battle and visibly worked his jaws and his arms, undismayed—and in silence, of course, for neither he nor any other man could hear a word that he was saying. He was one of the two out-going sheriffs, and it was said that he always made speeches at the great banquets; that he was never invited to make them; that no one had ever been able to find out whether they were good or bad, or neither, because nobody had ever heard one of them, since the tempest of resentment always broke out with his rising and never ceased until he finished his pantomime and sat down again. (AD, 29 Aug 1907, CU-MARK†)

To Olivia L. Clemens
3 October 1872 • London, England
(MS: CU-MARK)

(SLC)

London, Oct. 3.

Livy darling, it is indeed pleasant to learn that Orion is happy & progressing. Now if he can only *keep* the place, & continue to give satisfaction, all the better. It is no trouble for a man to get any situation he wants—by working at first for nothing—but of course to hold it firmly against all comers—after the wages begin—is the trick.[1]

Somebody has sent me some Philadelphia papers whereby I see that poor old faithful Riley is dead. It seems too bad.[2]

Mrs. Hooker's solemn retirement from public life is news which is as grateful as it is humorous—but ~~her~~ the tremendousness of her *reason* for retiring (because "her work is done" & her great ~~lesson~~ end accomplished,) surpasses the mere humanly humorous—it is the awful humor of the gods. For all these long months, this pleasant lady, under the impression that she was helping along a great & good cause, has been blandly pulling down the temple of Woman's Emancipation & shying the bricks at the builders; for all these long months she has moved sublimely among the conventions & congresses of the sex ~~like the~~ a very Spirit of Calamity; & whatsoever principle she breathed upon oratorically, perished; & whatsoever convert she took by the hand, that convert returned unto his sin again; & ~~upo~~ unto whatsoever political thing she lavished her love upon, there came sickness, & suffering, & speedy death; after all these long months, wherein she never rested from making enemies to her cause save when she was asleep, she retires serenely from her slaughter-house & says, in effect, Let the nations sing hosannah, el let the spinning spheres applaud—I have My—my work is done!

She is a good woman—she *is* a good woman—but it ƒ is so like her to ad do these things—she does derive such a satisfaction from everything her tangled brain conceives & her relentless hand demolishes. Well, anyway, I am glad she is out of "public life," ʄ & I have no doubt that all of her best friends are, also.[3]

Livy darling, I have been shopping & bought you a cloak, & if I don't lose it I will fetch it home to you. I shall probably buy no other present while here—they are too troublesome—but after hunting London over for a present for you, I found this thing & I liked it.

Been to Oxford for a day & a half—& if you *could* only see that piece of landscape (between here & Oxford) in its summer garb, you would have to confess that there is nothing even in New England that equals it for pure loveliness, & nothing outside of New England that even remotely approaches it. And if you could see the turf in the quadrangles of some of the colleges, & the Virginian creeper that pours its cataract of green & golden & crimson leaves down a quaint old gothic tower of Magdalen College—clear from the topmost pinnacle it comes flooding down over pointed windows, & battered statues, & grotesque stone faces projecting from the wall—a wasteful, graceful little Niagara graceful, gorgeous little Niagara[4]—& whosoever looks upon it will miss his train sure. That was the darlingest, loveliest picture I ever saw.

Good-bye Sweetheart, good-bye. Good-bye Sweetheart, good-bye.[5] I love you.

                                                          Sam*l*.

P.S. Mr. Tyler of Hatch & Tyler, promised to send you your winter supply of coal—at $7 I think. Send to him when you need it.[6]

✉

[*in ink:*] Mrs. S. L. Clemens | Cor Forest & Hawthorne | Hartford | Conn. [*in upper left corner:*] U.S. of America | [*rule*] [*on flap:*] ⓈⓛⒸ [*postmarked:*] LONDON · W 3 OC 3 72

[1]See 25 Sept 72 to OLC, n. 11.
[2]Clemens's correspondent has not been identified. John Henry Riley died of

cancer on 17 September in Philadelphia (Philadelphia *Inquirer:* "Died," 18 Sept 72 and 19 Sept 72, 4; "Obituary," 23 Sept 72, 2). According to the San Francisco *Alta California,* Riley's death "was the result of a cancer that started from a slight wound inflicted on the inside of his cheek by a fork while eating, the impulse being given accidentally by a stranger striking his elbow in a restaurant" ("Death of J. H. Riley," 18 Sept 72, 1).

[3] No public announcement of Isabella Beecher Hooker's intended retirement has been found, so presumably Olivia learned of it from Hooker herself, or from a mutual friend in the Nook Farm community. (John Hooker was in London in September 1872, but there is no evidence that he and Clemens had any contact with each other.) In any event, Clemens's pleasure was premature: Hooker continued her efforts on behalf of women's suffrage throughout her lifetime. His disapproval probably resulted from her association, since January 1871, with Victoria Claflin Woodhull (see 26 Nov 72 to JLC and PAM, n. 3). Woodhull's advocacy of "free love" and women's right to equality in sexual matters had shocked Hooker's family and associates, "who considered this new alliance to be a dangerous one for both the movement and a 'respectable' member of the Beecher and Hooker families" (Margolis, 29–31; Hartford *Courant:* "Hartford Personals," 14 Sept 72, 2; "Brief Mention," 30 Sept 72, 2; for an extended discussion of Hooker's record as a feminist, see Andrews, 134–43). Clemens's later remarks about Hooker were highly complimentary. In 1907, shortly after her death, he recalled:

> Isabella Beecher Hooker threw herself into the woman's rights movement among the earliest, some sixty years ago, and she labored with all her splendid energies in that great cause all the rest of her life; as an able and efficient worker she ranks immediately after those great chiefs, Susan B. Anthony, Elizabeth Cady Stanton, and Mrs. Livermore. When these powerful sisters entered the field in 1848 woman was what she had always been in all countries and under all religions, all savageries, all civilizations—a slave, and under contempt. The laws affecting women were a disgrace to our statutebook. Those brave women besieged the legislatures of the land, year after year, suffering and enduring all manner of reproach, rebuke, scorn and obloquy, yet never surrendering, never sounding a retreat; their wonderful campaign lasted a great many years, and is the most wonderful in history, for it achieved a revolution—the only one achieved in human history for the emancipation of half a nation that cost not a drop of blood. They broke the chains of their sex and set it free. (AD, 1 Mar 1907, CU-MARK†)

[4] Magdalen College, founded in 1458, is noted for its 145-foot tower, completed in 1505 (Murray, 304). Clemens used nearly identical wording to describe the college in his English journal (Appendix C).

[5] Clemens quoted the refrain from a popular love song of the same title, composed in the 1850s by John Liptrot Hatton (1809–86), with words by Folkestone Williams (Edmondstoune Duncan, 298–99).

[6] See 2 Aug 72 to MEC.

To Henry Lee
4 October 1872 • London, England
(MS: Axelrod)

Oct. 4—night.
One o'clock tomorrow—all right. Will do my level best
not to forget it. The best way will be not to *get up* till
one. If you don't find me at breakfast, skip right up in
the lift. Thanks.
Yrs
Clemens.

POST CARD

THE ADDRESS ONLY TO BE WRITTEN ON THIS SIDE.

TO

Henry Lee, Esq
43 Holland street
Blackfriars Road,
London, S. E.

[*postmarked:*] LONDON · W 7 OC 5 72 [*and*] LONDON · E. C BA OC 5 72

To Charles Dudley Warner
5 October 1872 • London, England
(MS: CU-MARK)

London Oct. 5.

My Dear Warner—
By the enclosed it appears that I have an unknown friend in England. I was an ass to make a speech at such an awfully swell affair at 15

minutes notice$, but then the mere mention of my name, when according to ancient custom they called over the list, before soup,—my name being No. 75 in a list of 250 guests, called forth a spontaneous welcome (the other names being received without this demonstration) that well= nigh took my breath away. I was so completely knocked out of time that I did not even know enough to get up & bow—a thing that makes me ashamed every time I think of it. So when they invented that toast I responded with alacrity. I made a good speech, too, ~~but~~ & it was received in a way that was exceedingly delightful; but it was execrably reported, & so I am disseminating the report that some impostor personated me there.[1] If they had only reported one or two of the twenty other speeches made there, & butchered *them*, I could have stood it—but to be *alone* in my humiliation!

I am having a very cheerful time here (though of course you will know enough to tell my wife that I write in a rather sad ~~va~~ vein.) She gives me pleasant news of you & Mrs. Warner, for which I thank her. My warm regards to you both.

Ys Truly

S. L. Clemens.

[*enclosure:*][2]

> THE SCOTTISH CORPORATION AND MR. STANLEY AND MARK TWAIN.— MARK TWAIN AT THE SHERIFFS' DINNER.
> (FROM OUR LONDON CORRESPONDENT.)
> LONDON, WEDNESDAY EVENING.
> I understand that the Scottish Corporation have been endeavouring to get Mr. Stanley to be present at their annual festival on Saint Andrew's Day, but that his having to be in America in November will prevent him.[3] It is anticipated that Mark Twain will be both present at the dinner and make a speech.[4] It may well be hoped that if he should make a speech, the reporters will endeavour to do him more justice than they did on the occasion of the Sheriff's dinner. Mark Twain speaks very well. He has a good loud, telling voice, which he seems to know well how to manage. On Saturday he spoke under much disadvantage. It was outrageous to call upon a stranger to respond to a toast at a moment's notice. When the company sat down to dinner, there was no notice of having such a toast as "Success to

> Literature." He would have been fully justified
> in declining to be unceremoniously put forward.
> Twain was too much the gentleman to refuse.
> The speech was, nevertheless, the best of the
> evening. It abounded in capital points, not one
> of which was done justice to by the reporters.
> I cannot account for this.

[*in ink:*] Chas. Dudley Warner Esq | Cor. Forest & Hawthorne sts | Hart-
ford | Conn. [*in upper left corner:*] U.S. of America. | [*flourish*] [*on flap:*]
(SLC) [*postmarked:*] LONDON-W 7 OC 7 72 [*and*] NEW YORK OCT 20 PAID ALL

[1] Clemens's speech at the sheriffs' dinner of 28 September, as reported in the
London *Observer* the next day, is quoted in full in 28 Sept 72 to OLC, n. 5.
[2] The following article by George H. Fitzgibbon, Clemens's "unknown
friend," appeared in the Darlington *Northern Echo* on 3 October 1872 (Fitzgibbon 1872). Fitzgibbon no doubt sent a clipping of it to Clemens, who in turn
enclosed it in this letter (see the next letter, n. 1). Warner reprinted the item in
the Hartford *Courant* on 22 October ("Mark Twain in London," 2). The actual
clipping has not been found: it is simulated here from the *Northern Echo*, reset
line for line.
[3] See 25 Oct 72 to OLC and 3 Nov 72 to Redpath, n. 6.
[4] Clemens left England before the St. Andrew's Day dinner on 30 November,
but he attended the event during his return visit in 1873 and responded to the
toast to "The Ladies" (see 28 Nov 73 to Fitzgibbon; "The Scottish Corporation,"
London *Morning Post*, 2 Dec 72, 2).

To George H. Fitzgibbon
5 October 1872 • London, England
(MS: CtHMTH)

(SLC)

The Langham Oct. 5. PM

My Dear Sir:
    I thank you very heartily for saying that good word for me.[1] I don't
know when that ˏSt Andrewsˏ dinner is to come off, but if it transpires
before the middle of November, & if I am invited; & if they give me a
toast to respond to & two days to get ready in, I would just as soon dis-

charge a little instruction from my system as not—& I'll give you a *verbatim* copy!

I thank Mrs. Fitzgibbon for reminding me, though indeed I had not forgotten, about the photos. They only came yesterday (I had to write & hurry up Mr. Watkins)[2]—& he goodnaturedly begged pardon & said it was owing to his card-maker's dilatoriness; & that if the world had had to wait on that man to build the Ark, we wouldn't have had the flood yet!

I believe I was to send four photos—but if there are too many, burn the rest, or put them in the British Museum. And I was to send the London picture,—which was very well, for only 2 of the Brighton ones have arrived thus far.[3] I sent one home[4] & rushed the other off (along with a London one,) to Miss Florence Stark[5]—for you know & I know that she didn't put a great deal of confidence in me, & I was anxious to bolster up my credit. She has written me a pleasant note & confessed her suspicions, & now I think she believes in me. She is a very charming little lady, I think. The picture in the Graphic is very good. It was made from the London photo.[6]

With the kindest regards to you & to all your pleasant household,

ₐI amₐ Ys faithfully

Saml. L. Clemens.

G. FitzGibbon Esq

[1] See the article enclosed with the previous letter, written by Fitzgibbon for the Darlington *Northern Echo.* Fitzgibbon must have sent Clemens the clipping, with a letter that does not survive. Very little is known about George Hyett Fitzgibbon, except that he corresponded for the *Echo,* reporting on events in London—including Parliamentary proceedings—in irregular letters headed "From Our London Correspondent." A remark of Clemens's in a letter to Fitzgibbon, indicating that he had planned to write an article for the London *Observer,* suggests that he may have been associated with that weekly (12 June 73 to Fitzgibbon; 28 Nov 73 to Fitzgibbon, n. 2). Clemens probably met Fitzgibbon at the sheriffs' inauguration dinner on 28 September, and by the date of this letter had apparently been to his home in Islington, a northern London suburb, and become acquainted with his wife and two daughters (*London Directory,* 2057; Fitzgibbon to SLC, 27 Dec 72, CU-MARK; Dixon Wecter asserted that Fitzgibbon was an associate of the Routledges', but offered no evidence: see *MTMF,* 175 n. 1).

[2] Clemens posed for photographer Charles Watkins, at 54 Chancery Lane, soon after his arrival in London; only one pose from this session is known to be extant (it is reproduced in Appendix F). Since Clemens must have provided a

print of the photograph some days earlier for the engraver of the *Graphic* portrait (see note 6), the batch of photographs that arrived "yesterday" was a reorder. By 14 September Watkins had given a copy to at least one London journalist, and on 1 November John Camden Hotten would order a hundred copies for resale (see 23 Dec 73 to OLC, n. 3).

[3] Clemens evidently enclosed four prints of the Watkins photograph.

[4] A copy of the Brighton photograph of Clemens, Henry Lee, and Edmund Routledge, mounted on a card measuring 4³⁄₁₆ by 6½ inches, survives in the Mark Twain Papers and is reproduced in Appendix F (13–18 Sept 72 to Osgood, n. 4). It is addressed in Clemens's hand on the back: "U.S. of America | Mrs. S. L. Clemens | Cor. Forest & Hawthorne | *Via* Queenstown | Hartford | Conn. | S. L. Clemens" (CU-MARK†). Since there is no postage on the card, however, it is unclear whether it was actually mailed. Clemens may have sent one of the portraits of himself instead.

[5] This friend of the Fitzgibbons' has not been identified. Clemens would visit Miss Stark and her family in Ventnor, on the Isle of Wight, in December 1873 (30 Dec 73 to Fitzgibbon).

[6] See 17 Sept 72 to Locker, n. 2. The engraved portrait of Clemens in the *Graphic* for 5 October 1872 is a reverse image of the Watkins photograph.

To Moncure D. Conway
6 October 1872 • London, England
(MS: NNC)

(*SLC*)

The Langham, Oct. 6.

My Dear Sir:

It is with sincere regret that I lose the opportunity of going with you to Stratford & enjoying the hospitality of Mr. Flower,ₛ, so kindly offered; but one engagement is piled on top of another to that degree that I find myself in inextricable fetters for some weeks to come—not a day clear ₁, that I can see from this till the hour I expect to sail. I have delayed answering your note, in the hope that I might manage to shake myself free in some way, but without avail. I hope you will thank Mr. Flower heartily for me, & in return may your Stratford sojourn be as pleasant as I know that mine would have been.[1]

Ys faithfully

Samˡ. L. Clemens.

[1] The invitation to visit Stratford-upon-Avon apparently came, through Conway, from Edward Fordham Flower (1805–83), a prosperous retired brewery

owner. Flower started the family business in 1832 and retired in 1862. He had served four times as mayor of Stratford-upon-Avon, most recently in 1864. He and his wife, the former Celina Greaves (1805?–84), enjoyed entertaining Americans at their residence, the Hill, built in 1855 (Boase, 1:1071). Clemens and Olivia were able to make the Stratford visit in 1873, although their host then was Flower's eldest son, Charles E. Flower (14 July 73 to Flower).

To Olivia L. Clemens
12 October 1872 • London, England
(MS: CLjC)

LANGHAM HOTEL, PORTLAND PLACE, LONDON. W. Oct. 12.
I have been thinking & thinking, Livy darling, & I have decided that one of 2 or 3 things *must* be done: either you must come right over here for 6 months; or I must ‚go‚ right back home 3 or 4 weeks hence & both of us come here April 1ˢᵗ & stay all summer. But I am not going abroad any more without you. It is too dreary when the lights are out & the company gone. Don't particularly want to *talk* to you, for I do hate talking—much prefer reading & smoking—but I simply need & want the *company* there is in your ⸿ presence—I want to know & be⫽ conscious that you are *around*—close at hand. I don't think you have ever understood my penchant for silence & how much I enjoy a person's mere *presence* without the bore of *speech*. You may have observed that I do dearly love to go to bed & lie ~~their~~ there steeped in the comfort of reading—& I have observed that you will not permit a body to get any satisfaction out of that sort of thing, but you always *interfere*. Here, I lie & read every night till 1 or 2 oclock. It would be perfect bliss if you were at my side— (& perfectly quiet & peaceable)‚—(even asleep)—but without you I am free to admit that it is only a poor lame sort of enjoyment.

The courts ‚of justice‚ I cannot see till the first week in November— & there are other things that date along there—& besides it will take that long to get an answer to this. So I wait. If you ~~can~~ prefer to come over now & stay till the middle of next summer, telegraph me & come right along. If you prefer & will *promise* to come April 1 & spend the entire summer, ~~telegraph me & I~~ write me & I will no doubt ~~skip~~ ‚start‚ along home about ~~10ᵗʰ or~~ 12ᵗʰ or 15ᵗʰ November.

About one thing there is no question whatever—& that is, one mustn't tackle England in print with a mere superficial knowledge of it. I am by long odds the most widely known & popular American author among the English & the book will be read by pretty much every Englishman—therefore for my own sake it must not be a poor book.

In the course of a week or ten days the Routledge's will send you that cloak through their N. Y. house.[1]

Good bye sweetheart—I love you.

Saml.

If you should con

✉──

Mrs. S. L. Clemens | Cor Forest & Hawthorne | Hartford | Conn. [*in upper left corner:*] US. of America. | [*rule*] [*on flap:*] THE LANGHAM [*postmarked:*] LONDON · W 6 OCI2 72 [*and*] NEW YORK OCT 2◊ PAID ALL

[1] The Routledges' New York agent was Joseph Blamire.

To Unidentified
18 October 1872 • London, England
(MS: Axelrod)

LANGHAM HOTEL, PORTLAND PLACE, LONDON. W.

Oct. 18.

Sir:

I think it will be 2 or 3 weeks before I shall really know whether I can lecture in Great Britain or not.[1] So I am obliged to be thus indefinite in my reply. I certainly shall lecture about 8 or 10 times in this country if other & more necessary business shall permit.

Ys Truly

Sam<i>l</i>. L. Clemens.</div>

[1] See 15 Sept 72 to OLC. Clemens's plans were uncertain while he awaited a reply from Olivia to his letter of 12 October.

To Henry Lee
25 October 1872 • London, England
(MS: ViU)

Friday

Dear Lee—

Can't. I am in the family way with 3 weeks undi-
gested dinners in my system, & *ƒ* shall just roost here
& diet & purge till I am delivered. Shall I name it after
you?

Yr friend
Saml. L. Clemens.

Dam John Camden Hotten.[1]

POST CARD

THE ADDRESS ONLY TO BE WRITTEN ON THIS SIDE.

TO

Henry Lee Esq
43 Holland street
Blackfriars Road
London, S.E.

[*postmarked:*] LONDON ◊◊ 3 OC25 72 5

[1] See 20 Sept 72 to the editor of the London *Spectator*.

To Olivia L. Clemens
25 October 1872 • London, England
(MS: CU-MARK)

London, Oct. 25.

Livy darling, I have been bumming around in a vagrant sort of way, to-day, through the Seven Dials & such places. Nothing remarkable, except a street of *second-hand shoes*—every cellar full, & more displayed on the sidewalk. Scrawny people & dirty & ragged ones rather abundant, but *they're* no sight.[1]

The truth is, there *are* no sights for me—I have seen them *all* before, in other places. It does seem to me that there is *nothing* under the sun that ~~does~~ ͵is͵ not a familiar old friend to my eye. Consequently I do just as little sightseeing as possible, but try to see as many *people* as I can. If I could take notes of all I hear *said,* I should make a most interesting book—but of course these things are interminable—only a shorthand reporter could sieze them.

I don't get letters from you, my child, any oftener than you do from *me, I* believe—so there, now.

I am using a note-book a little, now, & journalizing when I *can.*[2]

Between you & me, & the gatepost, Stanley lacks a deal of being a gentleman—tho' I say it that shouldn't, seeing we have been intimate & I have been of assistance to him & he has been of assistance to me.[3] In the first place he denies his nationality—denies it *strongly*—swears he is an American. Now that is bad. ~~And be as~~ As soon as he opeńed his mouth to talk *I* in private, I *felt* that he was a foreigner—the moment he spoke a dozen sentences in public, I *knew* he was a foreigner. Nobody here appears to know it for certain, but he will be detected at once, in America. Now, my dear, he has been honored here as very few ꝑ strangers were ever honored in England, & yet he shows the meanest ungrateful spirit. Because everybody did not rise up at first & believe in him (a thing *not* to be expected till he had fully proved himself,) he has ever since resented it. At last when ꝑ all England, with the Queen at the head came forward & frankly owned their error, he was not great-souled enough to say let bygones be bygones, but continued to go about snarling at England & the English.[4]

I think the most tremendous piece of manliness of modern times was the conduct of the Royal Geographical Society last Monday. After all the blackguarding that Stanley has ⊄ heaped upon them at dinners & on railway platforms, they came forward superbly & said your achievement merits the Victoria Medal, & you shall have it—& they gave him a grand dinner—& although there were but 119 plates, you should have seen the sort of men they were & heard their names called.[5] In the ante‑room, when the company were assembling, every time I was introduced to a man his name nearly took my breath away. They were the renowned men of Great Britain's army, navy & schools of science; & every broad ribbon that encircled their necks & every star & cross that blazed upon their breasts was a memento of some great thing their *brains* had done. Titled they were—~~most~~ ₐa great many, of them—men of ancient family & noble blood, but it was their *brains* that gave them celebrity. Well, you must know that here, men are seated at table strictly according to their *rank*—so the idiot son of an earl would sit above the Speaker of the House of Commons—& so on. But as Americans have *no* rank, it is proper to place us either *above* or *below* the nobles. Courtesy rather forbids the latter, & so we get good ~~com~~ seats. They usually set the table in this form: The chairman sits where the cross is. The Pres‑ident of the Geographical Society, Major General Sir Henry Rawlinson,[6] sat there; ₐStanley &ₐ the Lord Mayor of London[7] & a lot of lords & Admirals & gen‑erals on his right; & our Secretary of legation[8] on his left; then the famous Sir Bartle Frere;[9] then our Ex-Secretary McCøullough;[10] then some more ⊄ gran‑dees. I sat opposite the President (•) & was flanked by various dignitaries. Now you see, I could look into Stanley's & Rawlinson's faces, & mark every expres‑sion. And when Sir Henry R. stood up & made the  most manly & magnificent apology to Stanley for himself & for the Society that ever I listened to, I thought the man rose to the very pinnacle of human nobility;[11] & if I had been Stanley I would have made Rome howl with ~~an app~~ a burying of the hatchet that should have been yet grander & more magnanimous or I would have perished on the spot. But that spaniel got up & wagged his unwilling tail through a reluctant acceptance of the apology[12] & then went right on & opened the old sore & flung the same old taunts out of his wounded self-love that made him make such a poor little shabby dog of himself at the Brighton dinner![13] And now again he is at it in Glasgow yesterday.[14] I am really & truly gla/d this fellow is *not* American—though indeed he *must* have learned his puppyism with us. He did a stupendous thing in Africa, but he will blacken his fair renown forever & come to be treated with contempt yet.

Don't let any of this Stuff get into print, Livy darling. Every day I get invitations to lecture in the cities & towns of England & Scotland— & the gratifying feature of it is that they come not from speculators or cheap societies, but from self-elected committees of *gentlemen,* who want to give me their hospitality in return for the pleasure & they say my pen has given them. When *gentlemen* condescend in this way in England, it means a very great deal. An English gentleman never does a thing that may in the slightest degree detract from his dignity.

Well, I must get at my journal—so good night & the pleasantest of dreams, my darling wife.

Saml.

[*in ink:*] Mrs. S.L. Clemens | Cor Forest & Hawthorne | Hartford | Conn [*in upper left corner:*] America. | [*flourish*] [*postmarked:*] LONDON · W 7 OC26 72 [*and*] NEW YORK NOV 6 PAID ALL

[1] Seven Dials was a circular area, between Soho Square and Drury Lane, from which radiated seven streets. A column in the center, removed in 1773, had contained a clock with seven faces (or only six, according to at least one authority). The surrounding district, a notorious slum that Dickens described in *Sketches by Boz* (1836–37), was largely cleared away when Charing Cross Road was built in the 1880s (Kent, 577–78; Weinreb and Hibbert, 139, 779).

[2] Clemens's notebook, as opposed to his journal (Appendix C), is not known to survive.

[3] Clemens had met journalist and explorer Henry M. Stanley (1841–1904) in 1867, as he recalled in 1906: "I knew Stanley well for thirty-seven years—from the day that he stenographically reported a lecture of mine in St. Louis, for a local newspaper, until his death in 1904" (AD, 20 Nov 1906, CU-MARK†). Stanley reported Clemens's Sandwich Islands lecture in the St. Louis *Missouri Democrat* for 28 March 1867 (1 Feb 94 to Frank Fuller, CtY; Henry M. Stanley). The mutual assistance Clemens mentioned has not been explained; it seems unlikely that Stanley's article, although complimentary, was part of it, since Clemens consistently objected to newspaper dissemination of his lectures.

[4] Stanley was born John Rowlands, in Wales. His reluctance to acknowledge his nationality resulted from the unhappy circumstances of his childhood. His mother abandoned him at birth, and his father died a short time later. He was

cared for by his maternal grandfather, passed into foster care at his grandfather's death, and then, at age six, was sent to a workhouse, where he was brutally treated, but managed nevertheless to receive some education. He ran away at age fifteen, after attacking the sadistic schoolmaster, and in 1859 emigrated to New Orleans. There he was adopted by a merchant, Henry Morton Stanley, whose name he assumed. His successful career as a journalist began during the Civil War. In 1869 he received an assignment from the New York *Herald* to search for the Scottish missionary David Livingstone, who had disappeared in Africa several years earlier. After enduring great hardship, he succeeded in November 1871, and returned to England on 1 August 1872 expecting praise and recognition. Instead, he was greeted by the jealousy and disbelief of the British geographical establishment. The popular press discredited and abused him, even alleging that he was a fraud and that the letters he had brought from Livingstone were forgeries. Some newspapers treated Stanley more fairly, however, and his achievement was soon universally acknowledged. On 16 August Stanley spoke in Brighton at a meeting of the Geographical Section of the British Association for the Advancement of Science, receiving an "exceptionally hearty and enthusiastic" response. The London *Morning Post* reported, "The men of science in England have fully and formally recognised the success and applauded the energetic services of the now unquestioned discoverer of Dr. LIVINGSTONE" ("London, Monday, August 19, 1872," 19 Aug 72, 4). On 27 August Queen Victoria sent Stanley a gold snuffbox set with diamonds, and on 10 September she granted him a ten-minute audience at Dunrobin, in northern Scotland, the seat of the duke of Sutherland. Stanley, however, remained permanently bitter about his initial rejection (Hird, 15–20, 27, 33–34, 44, 68–89, 105–19; Farwell, 81–85; Anstruther, 148–55; "The British Association," London *Morning Post*, 17 Aug 72, 2). Clemens noted in his English journal on 15 September, "Been around to see Stanley. He dined with the Queen last Saturday," and commented on the effect of the queen's approval (Appendix C).

    [5] The Royal Geographical Society honored Stanley with a banquet at Willis's Rooms, St. James Square, on the evening of 21 October. The attendance was low, as the president explained, because many of the members had not yet returned from their country residences. Although the rules of the society stipulated that the Victoria Medal be awarded in the spring, they were set aside for Stanley, an honor never before paid to an explorer. Stanley had some cause for complaint against the society, however. Its president, Sir Henry Rawlinson (see the next note), had launched a rival expedition in February 1872, ostensibly to ensure Livingstone's safety, but in reality hoping to precede Stanley and thus prevent him from receiving credit. When Rawlinson was forced in May 1872 to acknowledge Stanley's success, he mistakenly announced that Livingstone had rescued Stanley from starvation, and not the other way around. The British public, already confused by conflicting reports, was confirmed in regarding Stanley as a somewhat ridiculous figure (Anstruther, 122–32, 141–44, 156; Hird, 106; London *Morning Post:* "The Livingstone Relief Expedition," 16 Aug 72, 6; "Dinner to Mr. Stanley," 22 Oct 72, 2).

    [6] Sir Henry Creswicke Rawlinson (1810–95), president of the Royal Geographical Society since the spring of 1871, had served with the British Army in India and Persia, where he became interested in oriental studies. He had been the British consul general in Persia, and a two-time member of Parliament. In

addition, he was a renowned Assyriologist and one of the first scholars to decipher the cuneiform alphabet.

7 London's lord mayor for 1871–72 was Sir Sills John Gibbons (1809–76), a hop merchant (Boase, 1:1137). When his term expired in November, he would be replaced by Sir Sydney Waterlow.

8 Benjamin Moran (1820–86) was born in Pennsylvania and in his early years wanted to be a writer. He had lived in England since 1853, and since that time worked for the American legation—first as a clerk, later as assistant secretary of legation, and, since 1864, as secretary. He described Clemens's appearance at the dinner in his journal: "Among the celebrities of the day who were present was 'Mark Twain.' He is a wiry man, with brown, crisp, wiry hair; a narrow forehead, Roman nose, and sinister expression, and does not seem to know more than ~~,~~as much as, would hurt him" (Moran, 33:203).

9 Sir Henry Bartle Frere (1815–84) was born in Wales and went to India in 1834. He earned distinction as a competent colonial administrator, serving as governor of Bombay from 1862 to 1867. He returned to England in 1867 when appointed a member of the Indian council. He was about to leave for Zanzibar, where late in 1872 he negotiated a treaty with the sultan of Zanzibar to suppress the slave trade, a mission given new urgency by Livingstone's recently published reports from Africa ("Sir Bartle Frere's Mission," London *Morning Post*, 28 Oct 72, 6). Frere would succeed Sir Henry Rawlinson as president of the Royal Geographical Society in 1873.

10 Hugh McCulloch (1808–95) was born in Maine. He was trained as a lawyer, but in 1835 began a distinguished career as a banker in Indiana. From 1863 to 1865 he was comptroller of currency in Washington, and then served as secretary of the treasury (1865–69). He was now a partner in the London banking house of Jay Cooke, McCulloch and Company.

11 Rawlinson called Stanley's journey "one of the most brilliant exploits in the whole history of African travel," and claimed that "the memory of it would remain to after ages as an example of what a man could do when his heart was in the right place, and when he was animated by a high sense of duty and loyalty." He then referred to the incident of the previous May (see note 5), explaining that at the time he was

aware that ample supplies had already been sent from the coast to Dr. Livingstone, and therefore he thought he was quite authorised in saying that if the two travellers met at Ujiji, Livingstone would relieve Stanley, rather than Stanley Livingstone. With the full knowledge he now possessed and which the public possessed a few months after, he saw that he was wrong, and he regretted extremely that he had made use of that expression. (Cheers.) He was now convinced that Livingstone was destitute of supplies, and that Mr. Stanley arrived at a most fortunate time for his relief. He would say more: he had a strong feeling that to Mr. Stanley Dr. Livingstone owed his life. ("Dinner to Mr. Stanley," London *Morning Post*, 22 Oct 72, 2)

12 Stanley's remarks, as reported in the London *Morning Post*, were not as negative as Clemens suggested. His speech was primarily devoted to praising Livingstone, especially his heroic efforts to abolish the African slave trade. He said he had come

home with this account of the great traveller, and, as he had foreseen, and had told Dr. Livingstone—his story was doubted. . . . He (Mr. Stanley) had . . . found every one as it were in a cloud. Everybody seemed to have some particular delusion on the subject of the great African traveller, but now all that was cleared away, and this was a time for a general shaking of hands.

Stanley then "thanked the Geographical Society—first, for the present banquet; next, for the medal they had conferred upon him; and next for the hearty reception they had accorded him" ("Dinner to Mr. Stanley," 22 Oct 72, 2).

[13] Clemens alluded to an unfortunate incident that occurred on 17 August at a dinner in Brighton hosted by the Brighton and Sussex Medico-Chirurgical Society. Despite his warm reception the previous day by the Geographical Section, Stanley had been affronted by some of the remarks of the president, who, "with questionable taste," claimed that Stanley's route "was an open track easily travelled by caravans," and, at the conclusion of the meeting, "went out of his way to observe that they did not want sensational reports, but correct scientific observations" ("The British Association," London *Morning Post*, 20 Aug 72, 2). At the 17 August dinner, therefore, Stanley was quick to take offense when, responding to the toast to "The Visitors," he heard a guest give a "derisive laugh." He at once abandoned the "humorous and cheerful style in which he had been speaking," and protested that "he had not come there to be laughed at, and that he had had quite enough gratuitous sneering of late without their adding to it":

> Alluding to the insinuations which had been made against him at the meeting of the Geographical Section on the previous day, that he had indulged rather too much in "sensationalism," he assured them that it was not to get the thanks of England or the English people that he had gone out to discover Livingstone, but as a matter of professional duty. They might call it what they liked; but if the finding of Livingstone in the heart of Africa after he had been given up for lost had not something of the "sensational" in it, then he did not know the meaning of the word. But why was it that his statements were questioned? Was it because he was an American, and for that reason that he should be rewarded with gratuitous sneering? . . . If that was to be the way in which he was to be treated he would at once withdraw from their company. No sooner had Mr. Stanley said these words than he left the room, and repaired to his apartments. ("The British Association," London *Morning Post*, 20 Aug 72, 2)

[14] At a banquet in Glasgow on 23 October, Stanley complained of his treatment at Brighton, saying it "harasses my feelings every time I think of it" (Farwell, 86).

To Mary Mason Fairbanks
2 November 1872 • London, England
(MS: CSmH)

The Langham Hotel,
London, Nov. 2.

Dear Mother—Of course I know you are a grandmother now & I send my loving regards to the new cub & my loud & long continued applause to the parents.[1] (Applause is what *they* want, you know, because this is a fresh thing to *them,* but you or me, now, would prefer not quite so much pow-wow & a little more condolence.)

How have I been received? Just the same as if I were a Prodigal Son getting back home again.[2] These English men & women take a body right into the inner sanctuary, as it were—& when you have broken bread & eaten salt with them once it amounts to *friendship*. With a person they don't know, it is said, ˏthatˏ becoming acquainted is a slow & careful piece of work—but I am speaking of ~~per~~ myself whom they *do* know—all of them. But there's not a particle of gush, not a bit of constraint, or acting, or embarrassment, or the infliction of embarrassment upon *you*—with the introductory bow you appear to drop into a vacancy in that social circle as comfortably & easily as if you were a plug that had been specially made for it. You honestly do just as you honestly please, & nobody takes any offense. In about 4 weeks, here, one learns to quit questioning people's motives & trying to hunt out slights. He finds that these folks do not doubt each other's truth, & that it does not occur to them to ascribe ill motives to each other. Of course this is by no means universal, but it amounts to the rule, I think. So when you hear a person blackguarding everybody & impugning everybody's motives it arrests your attention.

I have had such a gorgeous time that I am all out of order, now, & can't digest my food any more than a tin soldier could. But I don't mind it. I go to the dinners, public & private, & steer clear of wine & food, & so I have just as good a time as ever chaffing & talking & making little speeches.

Been out to a stag hunt at the country village of Wargrave-near₌ Henley-on-the-Thames (I believe that is about all of its name)—for several days. I hunted that stag in a wagon—but I didn't catch him. Neither did the red-coated, pigskin-breeched hunters—but it was fine to see the 250 scour over the hills & fields & sail over the hedges & fences like so many birds.[3]

One day we dined & breakfasted with a splendid fox-hunting squire named Broom in his quaint & queer old house that has been occupied 500 years—& on his table cutlery I noticed something like that,

 & presently ~~remin~~ figured out that it was a sprig of broom (the gentleman's name). I knew that the broom-sprig~~n~~g (plant-à-genèt) was the cognizance & gave name to the Plantagenet kings, & ˏIˏ so I just asked him facetiously if he wasn't a Plantagenet—but bless you he didn't notice the facetiousness of it, & simply said he

was.[4] And his genealogical tree shows it, too. ~~If Solon Severance will come over here we'll make this man king—~~ Why ̶I̶ it had all the seeming of hob-nobbing ~~in~~ with the Black Prince[5] in the flesh!—for this fellow is of princely presence & manners, & 35 years old. Now years ago it used to be a curious study to me, to follow the variations of a family name down through a ɸPeerage or a biography from the Roll of Battle-Abbey[6] to the present day—& manifold & queer were the changes, too. But here within 2 miles of Mr. Broom, lives a family named Abear who still own & farm the same piece of ground their ancestors have owned & farmed for nine hundred & fifty years![7]—without ever a break in the succession or a change of ownership!—& without ever a change of the style or pronunciation of the family name from King Alfred's[8] days to these! There is but one other case of the kind in England—*another* small farmer—for both families were always mere plebeian, undistinguished yeomen, albeit theirs is the longest & by all odds the purest & *straightest* lineage in Great Britain, the queen's not excepted. People drop in, over yonder, & say "Good morning, Abear," just as other folks walked over ˌtheˌ same ground & said "Good morning Abear," in the days of the Saxon Heptarchy.[9] But it is *Broom*, now, instead of Plantagenet.

Please don't let a word of this letter get into print—these things are from private conversations & the footprints must be all covered up carefully before they see the light. Americans have the reputation here of not sufficiently respecting private conversations.

Now if you'll come over here in the spring with Livy & me, & spend the "ˌLondon Season" (the summer,) you will have just the loveliest time you ever had in your life, & you will come to the conclusion that rural England is too absolutely beautiful to be left out doors—ought to be under a glass case. The Mayor of Stratford-on-Avon[10] would make us at home & they say he lives like ̶a̶ the finest of fine old English gentlemen. As I was too busy to visit him now, I reserved the invitation. Come! Will you? We'll dig up Shakspeare & cart him over to our side a spell.

Make Charley study drawing. Don't fool away a good artist trying to make an inferior something else of him. Send my love to Mollie—& pray, you & all of you, the heads of th[e] house & the household,[11] accept of measureless quantities of the same.

> ̶$̶ Yr Son,
> Sam*l.*

¹Fairbanks's stepdaughter, Alice, married William H. Gaylord in January 1871. On 25 August 1872 she gave birth to a son, Paul Fairbanks Gaylord, who died on 8 September 1873 (*L2*, 132 n. 10; *L4*, 301 n. 1; Fairbanks, 552).

²Upon his return from "a far country," the Prodigal Son was fed on "the fatted calf" (Luke 15:11–32).

³The picturesque village of Wargrave, in Berkshire about thirty miles from London, was so small that it was evidently identified by its proximity to Henley-on-Thames, three miles down the river (Page and Ditchfield, 3:191; Vincent, 296–97, 433). Clemens's host for the hunt is unidentified. Clemens could have attended either of two recent staghunts in the area, both within twelve miles of Wargrave: on 29 October "the hunting season with her Majesty's staghounds was opened with the first public meet at Salt Hill, near Slough," and on 1 November a second hunt took place at Maidenhead. The opening-day hunt was a colorful event, overseen by Sir Richard Boyle, the earl of Cork, master of the queen's staghounds. The road in the vicinity was "thronged with equestrians of both sexes, carriages, traps, and pedestrians, and presented a lively spectacle" (London *Morning Post:* "Her Majesty's Staghounds," 30 Oct 72, 3; "Hunting Appointments," 26 Oct 72, 3; Burke 1904, 374).

⁴The name "Plantagenet" derived from *planta genista,* sprig of broom, the emblem of Geoffrey, count of Anjou and son-in-law of Henry I. The Plantagenets succeeded to the English throne with the accession of Henry II in 1154; their royal dynasty ended with the death of Richard III in 1485. According to at least one source, the "sign of the *Planta genista* originated the surname of *Broom*" (Baring-Gould, 96), and, in accord with Clemens's sketch of the family device, the crest of the Brome, Broom, and Broome families is described as "an arm couped at the elbow and erect, . . . holding in the hand . . . a bunch of broom vert" (Fairbairn, 1:77). One possible (but somewhat unlikely) candidate for the "splendid fox-hunting squire named Broom" is Captain Arthur Broome, listed in an 1877 Berkshire directory as the tenant (but not the owner) of Remenham Lodge near Henley-on-Thames (*Berkshire Directory,* 672). Captain Broome was the author of *History of the Rise and Progress of the Bengal Army,* published in Calcutta in 1850, and therefore must have been older than Clemens's Broom, described below as thirty-five years old. The Broom family is not mentioned in *A Concise Topographical Account of . . . Berkshire* (Lysons and Lysons), in *Return of Owners of Land, 1873,* or in *The Victoria History of the County of Berkshire* (Page and Ditchfield), which describes in detail the ownership history of all the manor houses in the area.

⁵Edward (1330–76), eldest son of Edward III and father of Richard II, so called because he wore black armor.

⁶A list compiled in the fourteenth century (the original of which is no longer extant) of families that came over to England with William the Conqueror.

⁷The manor of Bear-Place, in the parish of Wargrave, "is said to have been formerly in the A'Bears, a family still existing, and supposed to be of great antiquity; but their names are not to be found at the Heralds' College, nor among the Tower Records" (Lysons and Lysons, 411).

⁸Alfred the Great (849–?901), king of the West Saxons.

⁹A name given by sixteenth-century historians to the seven kingdoms of Angles and Saxons in England during the fifth through ninth centuries.

¹⁰Edward F. Flower, a former mayor of Stratford (6 Oct 72 to Conway, n. 1).

[11]Fairbanks's son, Charles, wanted to become an artist (2? Mar 72 to Fairbanks, nn. 2, 3; 10 Dec 72 to Nast, n. 2). Clemens also sent greetings to her
sixteen-year-old daughter, Mollie; their father, Abel; and presumably to her
stepchildren, Frank and Alice, both of whom had married and set up their own
households (*L2*, 134 n. 1, 259 n. 1; Fairbanks, 552, 754–55).

To James Redpath
3 November 1872 • London, England
(Transcripts: CtLHi; Will M. Clemens, 29)

Langham Hotel,
London, Nov. 3

Dear Redpath—

Good for Andrews—new name to me.[1] But I knew perfectly well
that Briggs was first rate for the platform.[2] All the readers I ever saw were
idiots when it came to selecting humorous pieces for recitation. Andrews
must be of a superior race of them.

Josh's letter was good—I sent it to Tom Hood.[3] I meant to refer to
it in a speech in answer to a regular toast at the annual dinner of the
Whitefriars Club & the chairman had done me the honor to make me his
guest & appointed me a seat at his right hand & as I know nearly all of
the Whitefriars I expected to have a gorgeous time.[4] But I got it into my
head that Friday was Thursday & so I staid in the country stag-hunting
a day too long & when I reached the club last night nicely shaved & gotten up regardless of expense, I found that the dinner was *the night before*.

I would like to stay here about fifteen or seventy-five years, a body
does have such a good time.

I am revamping, polishing & otherwise fixing up my lecture on
Roughing It & think I will deliver it in London a couple of times about
a month from now, just for fun.[5] Have received invitations & large offers
from pretty much all the big English & Scottish towns, but have declined, not being fond of railroading. I haven't been 50 miles from London yet & don't intend to budge from it till I budge homewards.

So Stanley gets $50,000 for 100 nights.[6] That is as it *should* be. They
charge $2 to hear Parepa[7] sing 2 pieces (15 minutes, all told) & if you
charged a dollar to hear one of us fellows squawk, it would become the

fashion to hear us & then the gates of hell could not prevail against us—
we would *always* have a full house.

When I yell again for less than $500 I'll be pretty hungry.[8] But I
haven't any intentions of yelling at any price.

How does Bret Harte make it? Give me the early news.[9]

Ys ever,
Mark

[*letter docketed:*] BOSTON LYCEUM BUREAU. REDPATH & FALL. NOV 25 1872

[1] The letter from Redpath to which this letter replied is not known to survive.
William S. Andrews (1841–1912) was a New York actor and platform speaker.
On 14 October 1872, in Boston's Tremont Temple, he delivered a lecture for
Redpath's Boston Lyceum Bureau entitled "Dialect Humor," which included at
least one reading from Mark Twain's works—almost certainly "Buck Fanshaw"
from chapter 47 of *Roughing It*. (Andrews would recite this excerpt on 22 November 1872 at a reception for Henry M. Stanley at the Lotos Club in New York,
and it became a popular entertainment at the club.) Although the Boston appearance was advertised as an "Extra Lecture"—not part of the regular Boston
series—Andrews toured with "Dialect Humor" during the 1872–73 and 1873–
74 seasons, sponsored by Redpath's bureau. In the *Lyceum Magazine* for the latter season he was described as

> one of the best trained and most talented recitationists now living. The most popular
> comedians and humorists of the day,—the best actors of New York, as well as "Nasby"
> and "Mark Twain,"—and the press of every city in which he has appeared, have united
> in extolling his histrionic powers. His lecture gives specimens of nearly all the dialects
> of the United States and several dialects of the British people. Every dialect is illustrated
> by a humorous story or poem. He made a decided hit in Boston on his first appearance.
> (*Lyceum* 1873, 3)

Andrews was born in Texas but moved to New York at an early age, where in
1860 and 1861 he worked as an actor at Niblo's Garden. During the Civil War he
served on the staff of General Ambrose Burnside, and at its conclusion he returned to the stage, successfully enacting both tragic and comic roles. He also
served as the deputy collector of internal revenue for Brooklyn, was twice elected
a New York State assemblyman (in 1868 and 1881), and in later years became an
influential politician (Boston *Evening Transcript:* "Lectures," 14 Oct 72, 2; "Dialect Humor," 15 Oct 72, 4; Elderkin, 21–22; *Lyceum:* 1872, 2; 1873, 3; "William
S. Andrews Dies," New York *Times,* 30 Dec 1912, 7; Harlow and Hutchins, 170–
73).

[2] In his now-lost letter Redpath may have mentioned author and journalist
Charles Frederick Briggs (1804–77), although no evidence has been found that
he ever appeared on the platform. Briggs published his first novel, *The Adventures of Harry Franco,* in 1839. He edited *Putnam's Magazine* for two separate
stints, wrote for the New York *Times,* contributed "witty pieces" to *Knickerbocker Magazine,* and from 1870 to 1873 worked as financial editor on the Brooklyn *Union* (Blair and Hill, 177).

³Redpath had forwarded a letter written to the Boston Lyceum Bureau by Josh Billings (Henry Wheeler Shaw), a popular humorist and homespun philosopher whom Clemens had known since at least November 1869 (*L3*, 397 n. 3). In the 9 November issue of *Fun* Hood commented on the American preference for humorous lectures, noting that "the article is not always to be got," and then quoted the following passage from Billings's letter: "Who is the coming man among the humorists? There is no one I know of who has yet begun to make a reputation for the business. The publick will find out that good phools are skase" (Hood 1872a).

⁴See 11 Sept 72 to OLC, nn. 4, 5. The chairman has not been identified.

⁵Clemens did not deliver this lecture in London until December 1873.

⁶Stanley arranged with a New York agent, Frederick Rullman, to lecture sixty times for $30,000 during the 1872–73 season in the United States, with an option for an additional forty at the same price ($500 each), if Rullman so desired; the total for one hundred appearances would have been $50,000. Stanley performed so poorly, however, at his first two lectures in New York, on 3 and 4 December, that Rullman canceled the last two because he did "not find the enterprise remunerative" (New York *Tribune:* "Lectures and Meetings," 7 Dec 72, 8; "Amusements," 3 Dec 72, 10, and 4 Dec 72, 7). Although most of the tour was evidently called off, Stanley lectured occasionally over the next few months—appearing in Boston, for example, on 16 and 18 December, and in Washington on 13 January. Many years later he lectured more successfully in the United States, briefly in 1886 (when Clemens introduced him in Hartford and Boston), and at greater length during the 1890–91 season (Farwell, 91–92; H. Wilson 1872, 1042; "Amusements," Boston *Evening Transcript*, 13 Dec 72 and 17 Dec 72, 3; "Personal," Hartford *Courant*, 3 Dec 72, 2; Pond, 263–80).

⁷Euphrosyne Parepa-Rosa (1836–74), an English operatic soprano.

⁸Tickets for Clemens's lectures during the 1871–72 season cost fifty cents, or occasionally seventy-five cents for reserved seats. He usually received from $100 to $150 per lecture (occasionally as much as $250), well below the amount paid to the most popular performers (*L4*, 398–402).

⁹Clemens could not have heard the "early news" about Harte's winter lecture tour, which Redpath's bureau was arranging, until he returned home in late November, and it must have been a surprise when he did. Harte and Redpath had ended their business relationship, suddenly and very publicly, on Wednesday, 13 November, when Harte, having canceled his first scheduled lecture on 12 November in Hartford, also declined to appear the next evening in Boston. The Hartford *Evening Post* reported the Hartford cancellation on the day he was scheduled to appear, noting that "a private letter from Mr. F. Bret Harte, poet and author, received in this city last evening announced that, 'owing to the pressure of literary engagements' he should not be able to lecture in Hartford this evening as announced" ("Postponement of Bret Harte's Lecture," 12 Nov 72, 2). The Boston cancellation had louder repercussions. According to the Boston *Globe*,

> The name and fame of Mr. Francis Bret Harte were not such as to collect a very large audience in Music Hall last evening, and those who assembled to listen to such remarks as the man who was once pronounced the "representative American novelist" might be inspired to make on "The Argonauts of '49" were disappointed, for, to use the words of Mr. Redpath, in his spicy little speech of apology, "for the third time the Heathen Chinee insulted a Boston audience." "The first time," said Mr. Redpath, "was at Cambridge, when he promised to deliver a first-rate poem, and read a second-rate one; the

second time was when he promised to read to the Grand Army of the Republic, and sent a third-rate poem; and the third time is this evening, when he does not come at all. His engagement with us was made last June for the thirty-first of October, a date afterwards changed at his request. On Saturday, he telegraphed to us, asking that his lecture here and at Hartford should be either postponed or cancelled. We wrote to him immediately, telling him that his lecture could not be postponed, and requesting him to telegraph to us forthwith. This he did not do, but yesterday we received a letter saying that his lecture must be either postponed or cancelled as he could not come, and immediately cancelled his engagement. It is our rule, whenever we are compelled to disappoint our ticket-holders, to substitute a better lecturer than the one whose name we withdraw, and, in accordance with this custom, I invite your attention this evening to Dr. Oliver Wendell Holmes." ("Bret Harte as a Breaker of Engagements," Hartford *Evening Post*, 15 Nov 72, 2, reprinting the Boston *Globe* of 14 Nov 72)

Holmes did lecture that evening in Harte's place, and Redpath managed to announce the last minute change in at least one Boston paper ("Boston Lyceum. Special Announcement!" Boston *Evening Transcript*, 13 Nov 72, 2). On 15 November the editorial page of the New York *Tribune* rushed to defend Harte against Redpath's unusual public wrath, asserting that he had "been unavoidably prevented from delivering his lecture at Boston on Wednesday night last" (4). That assertion, and the explanation Harte offered to Hartford ("the pressure of literary engagements"), do not entirely square with the fuller explanation Harte sent on 16 November to the Boston *Advertiser* (one of the newspapers that had published Redpath's angry "remarks"):

> For the last two years Messrs. Redpath and Fall of the Lyceum Bureau have repeatedly solicited me to enter the lecture field under their auspices. I finally acceded, and in August last in an interview with Mr. Redpath stated very clearly the conditions, and the only conditions, under which I would lecture. On the first of November I received from them a list of engagements whose conditions were totally at variance with those I had named. I at once informed them by letter that I would not accept them, and reiterated my former demand. To this I received no reply, but on the 9th of November, four days before the date of my Boston engagement, not wishing to disappoint a gathered audience pending these purely private and personal negotiations, I telegraphed to Messrs. Redpath and Fall that they must postpone that date. They replied by telegraph the same day that it was impossible, adding that Hartford (my first engagement) would accept my conditions. I at once wrote to them that until *all* my engagements were made equally satisfactory, they must postpone or cancel both, and that I would not permit Hartford to be forced, at the last moment, into accepting conditions of which they had not been previously aware. To this I added that the Boston fire, then burning, was a sufficient excuse for postponement—an excuse that afterward in the case of two distinguished lecturers was considered valid and not particularly "insulting" to a Boston audience.
>
> With a perfect understanding of these details, and with my letter in his pocket, Mr. James Redpath rose before an audience *which he had permitted to gather to hear a man who he knew would be absent,* charged me with insulting them, depreciated the wares he had asked permission to peddle exclusively—all in the most extraordinary performance, I trust, ever given before a New England lyceum.
>
> I have only to add that it is still my intention to lecture before a Boston audience, but not for Mr. Redpath, nor of him. (Harte 1872)

Harte's letter was published on 20 November (2). Two days later, Redpath replied to it, also in the *Advertiser.* He repeated the assertion that it was in June that Harte first wrote to him offering to lecture in Boston "on the 30th of October if we agreed to his terms, which we promptly did accept." Harte in turn accepted that date "on the first of July" (Redpath 1872b). Harte had still not agreed to a lecture tour, but by August his reluctance was apparently overcome by the need for cash, and he met (as he said) with Redpath to spell out terms. On 1 September Redpath agreed to postpone Harte's Boston engagement until 13 November, presumably with the same terms Harte had earlier proposed. Redpath did not accept Harte's bargaining over the terms of his lecture tour as grounds for failing to appear, as previously agreed, in Boston:

> We received no notification whatever from him of his intention not to lecture in Boston until the Saturday preceding the lecture—*before* the fire. It was in these words: "N. Y., Nov. 9, Redpath and Fall: Must postpone Boston lecture on 13th. Bret Harte." Just so much and nothing more. Not a syllable of explanation. Although we telegraphed at once, and, in a letter sent by that evening's mail, urged him to *telegraph* us on Monday if he could *not* keep the engagement, we received not a word from him until Tuesday, when he not only refused to appear, but made—or seemed to make—his intention of lecturing in Boston *at all* conditional on the readjustment of fees in western Massachusetts, New York, Pennsylvania and Maryland. Moreover, the letter showed that his lecture had never been written. (Redpath 1872b)

This bruising quarrel—which was noticed, commented on, and partly reprinted in newspapers around the country—led Redpath to bring suit against Harte, who ultimately agreed, in October 1875, to pay him $205 in compensation (Harte to James R. Osgood, 6 Oct 75, ViU, in Harte 1997). Harte nonetheless persisted in his plans to lecture during the winter, in many cases making "new and distinct agreements and engagements with each of the Lyceums that Redpath & Fall had treated with previously as my agents," as he reminded George Fall on 29 November 1873 (CU-BANC, in Harte 1997). He appeared in Boston, sponsored by the American Lecture Bureau (possibly the same as the American Literary Bureau), on 13 December 1872, exactly one month after his canceled engagement. Upon arrival he was nearly imprisoned for failing to pay a tailor's bill. John S. Clark, of Osgood and Company, was Harte's host in Boston and "gave his individual note on demand to liquidate the bill and release the prisoner" ("An Embarrassing Predicament," New York *Evening Express*, 19 Dec 72, 1, reprinting the Boston *Saturday Evening Gazette* of 14 Dec 72; "Lecture," Boston *Evening Transcript*, 13 Dec 72, 2; 22 Mar 73 to Larned, nn. 2, 3).

To W. A. Turner
3 November 1872 • London, England
(MS: CtHMTH)

The Langham Hotel,
Nov. 3.

Dear Sir:[1]

My time is so occupied that I cannot venture to trench upon it ~~lie~~

literarily. Pray overlook my delay in answering—I have been away from the city.

Ys Truly

S. L. Clemens.

And please excuse the pencil—no ink in my room.

✉

[*in ink:*] W. A. Turner Esq | The Laurels, Pendleton, | Manchester. [*postmarked:*] LONDON · W 2 NO 4 72 [*docketed in ink:*] Mark Twain | [*flourish*]

¹ Turner has not been identified.

To Susan L. Crane
4–11 November 1872 • London, England
(*MTB*, 1:470)

.   .   .   .

If you & Theodore[1] will come over in the spring with Livy & me, & spend the summer,[2] you shall see a country that is so beautiful that you will be obliged to believe in fairy-land. There is nothing like it elsewhere on the globe. You should have a season ticket & travel up & down every day between London & Oxford & worship nature.

And Theodore can browse with me among dusty old dens that look now as they looked five hundred years ago; & puzzle over books in the British Museum that were made before Christ was born; & in the customs of their public dinners, & the ceremonies of every official act, & the dresses of a thousand dignitaries, trace the speech & manners of all the centuries that have dragged their lagging decades over England since the Heptarchy fell asunder. I would a good deal rather live here if I could get the rest of you over.

.   .   .   .

¹Crane.
²This letter was written sometime between 4 November, when Clemens received Olivia's cablegram saying she was willing to return with him in the spring, and 11 November, when he left London for Liverpool on the first leg of the trip home (see the next letter).

To Henry Lee
5 November 1872 • London, England
(MS: Axelrod)

ₐMidnight—just from Inauguration Dinner.ₐ¹

[*in pencil:*]

Langham, Tuesday,

Dear ₱ₗee—

Cable telegram from my wife, saying "Come home",—therefore I sail in first steamer after Lord Mayor's dinner on the 9ᵗʰ,² & return with my family in April, to spend the summer.

Linnean Society dinner, O.K..³

Yrs

S. L. Clemens

P. S.—*Tight.*⁴

¹Clemens attended an inauguration dinner for the lord mayor elect (Sir Sydney Waterlow) on the evening of Monday, 4 November. His engraved invitation, requesting the "favor of an early answer," survives in the Mark Twain Papers. The banquet, held in the hall of the Stationers' Company, was attended by about a hundred guests ("The Lord Mayor Elect," London *Times*, 5 Nov 72, 10).
²Olivia's telegram does not survive. Clemens sailed from Liverpool on the Cunard steamship *Batavia*, bound for New York via Boston, on Tuesday, 12 November, having left London the previous day.
³Lee was a member of the Linnean Society of London, founded in 1788 to commemorate Swedish naturalist Carl Linnaeus and promote the study of natural history. In 1829 the society became the repository for Linnaeus's library and collection of specimens. Lee, who also belonged to the society's dining club, brought Clemens as his dinner guest on the evening of 7 November; both men signed the book in which the club's minutes were recorded (Weinreb and Hibbert, 460–61; Linnean Club Minute Book, entry for 7 Nov 72, Linnean Society of London Archives; information from the Linnean Society of London).
⁴By the end of the letter Clemens's handwriting had become a loose scrawl.

To the Editor of the London *Daily News*
5 November 1872 • London, England
(London *Daily News*, 6 Nov 72)

TO THE EDITOR OF THE DAILY NEWS.[1]

SIR,—With your kind permission, I desire to say to those societies in London & other cities of Great Britain under whose auspices I have partly promised to lecture, that I am called home by a Cable telegram. I shall spend, with my family, the greater part of next year here, & may be able to lecture a month during the autumn upon such scientific topics as I know least about, & may consequently feel least trammelled in dilating upon.—Yours respectfully,

MARK TWAIN.

Langham Hotel, Nov. 5.

[1] On 5 November Clemens sent the same announcement to the editors of at least three London newspapers. It appeared, with trivial variations, on 6 November in the *Daily News*, and on 7 November in the *Morning Post* and the *Times*. The *Daily News* was edited by Frank Harrison Hill. The editor of the *Morning Post* was William Hardman. John T. Delane (1817–79) had made the *Times* the "leading journal of Europe" since assuming the editorship in 1841 (*Newspaper Press Directory*, 17; 10 Dec 73 to the editor of the London *Morning Post*, n. 1; 21 Dec 73 to OLC, n. 1).

To Jane Lampton Clemens and Pamela A. Moffett
6 November 1872 • London, England
(MS: NPV)

London, Nov. 6, 1872.

My Dear Mother & Sister:

I have been so everlasting busy that I *couldn't* write—& moreover I have been so unceasingly lazy that I couldn't have written, anyhow. I came here to take notes for a book, but I haven't done much but attend dinners & make speeches. But I have had a jolly good time & I do hate to go away from these English folks. They make a stranger feel entirely at home—& they laugh so easily that it is a comfort to mak[e] after-dinner speeches here. I have made hundreds of personal friends; & last night in the crush at the opening of the New Guildhall Library & Museum, it I was surprised to meet a familiar face every few steps. Nearly 4,000 people, of both sexes, came & went during the evening, & so I had a good opportunity to make a great many new acquaintances.[1]

Livy is willing to come here with me next April & stay several months—so I am going home next Tuesday. I would sail on Saturday, but that is the day of the Lords Mayor's ‚annual‚ grand state dinner, when they say 900 of the great men of the city sit down to table, a great many of them in their fine official & court paraphernalia, & so I must not miss it. However, I may yet change my mind & sail Saturday.[2]

I am looking at a fine magic lantern which will cost a deal of money, & if I buy it Sammy may come & learn to make the gas & work the machinery, & paint pictures for it on glass.[3] I mean to give exhibitions for charitable purposes in Hartford & charge a dollar a head.

I watched them weave the enclosed. A machine does it all—& almost without watching.[4]

In a hurry,

Ys affly

Sam.

---

[1] A costly new building had been erected to house the Guildhall Library and Museum. On 6 November the London *Daily News* announced:

> The new Library and Museum which the Corporation of London has established for the use of its citizens, . . . is sufficiently near completion to have been publicly opened last evening. . . . The Library and Museum, as is now well known, is a home of literature and art for the great City of London. . . . The first essential of the modern *conversazione*—a crush, unmitigated and continued—was of course scrupulously observed. . . . The crowd was densest in the Library, where the Lord Chancellor was to declare the building open.

After the lord chancellor (Roundell Palmer) made his speech, the guests were able to "move about, to enjoy Mr. Fred Godfrey's band, to pay one's respects to Gog and Magog, and attempt ices, fruits, and cooling drinks" ("Opening of the City Library and Museum," London *Daily News*, 6 Nov 72, 2; Kent, 431). Fourteen-foot wooden statues of the legendary giants Gog and Magog, carved in 1708, adorned the Guildhall, adjoining the new library (Kent 358–59, 362; Weinreb and Hibbert, 344).

[2] If Clemens had sailed on Saturday, 9 November (instead of on 12 November), he would have had Henry M. Stanley as a fellow passenger (London *Times:* "Cunard Line," 8 Nov 72, 2; "The Discovery of Dr. Livingstone," 11 Nov 72, 7; for the lord mayor's dinner see 10 Nov 72 to OLC).

[3]Clemens seems to be describing a stereopticon, rather than the relatively simple "magic lantern." The magic lantern was a projector with two lenses, between which an operator "placed slips of glass bearing transparent photographs or paintings," causing them to be "thrown in a magnified form on the wall or screen opposite to the lantern." The stereopticon was "an improved form of magic lantern, consisting essentially of two complete lanterns matched and connected," allowing the "pictures shown to pass from one to the next by a sort of dissolving effect which is secured by alternate use of the two lenses"; containers of oxygen and hydrogen were attached to the device with "flexible tubes for separately conveying these gases to the burners and mixing them only as they are needed to supply light" (Whitney and Smith, 3:3350, 5:5935). Clemens apparently considered buying this complicated apparatus for his nephew, Samuel Moffett, but ultimately purchased a steam engine for him and bought the stereopticon for himself, shipping both items from London through Joseph Blamire, the Routledges' New York agent (see 26 Nov 72 to JLC and PAM; 5 Dec 72 to JLC and family; Blamire to SLC, 6 Jan 73, CU-MARK). When Clemens and Olivia went to Europe in 1878 they lent the stereopticon to Frank Warner, the young son of Lilly and George Warner, who gave a show with it for his family and friends (Elisabeth G. Warner, 104; "Nook Farm Genealogy," 30).

[4]The enclosed weaving sample does not survive; Clemens may have obtained it at the Guildhall opening, where many of the trade companies, perhaps including the mercers, had "curiosities" on display ("Opening of the City Library and Museum," London *Daily News*, 6 Nov 72, 2).

To Mary Mason Fairbanks
6 November–10 December 1872 • London, England,
or Hartford, Conn.
(Transcript: CtHSD)

· · · ·

Indeed Susie Crane *is* an angel,[1] & it is such a comfort to me to know that if I *do* chance to wind up in the fiery pit hereafter, she will flutter down there every day, in defiance of law & the customs of the country & bring ice & fans & all sorts of contraband things under her wings & sit there by the hour cheering me up, & then go back home not caring two cents that her scorched feathers, & dilapidated appearance & brimstone smell are going to get her into trouble & cause her to be shunned by all proper angels as an eccentric and disreputable saint. I can believe a good deal of the bible but I never will believe that a heaven can be devised that will keep Susie Crane from spending the most of her time in Hell trying to comfort the poor devils down there.

It sounds extravagant, but if I don't believe it I wish I may be hanged in a minute. Sue *couldn't* enjoy heaven if there was supplicating suffering in sight,. Hell *is* in sight; because we all know that Lazarus saw Dives & heard him beseech a drop of water—which Lazarus declined to furnish.[2]

When Susie Crane gets to her final rest, you mark my words, the first party she will go for will be that same John W. Dives, you hear me!

· · · · ·

[1] This fragment of a letter to Fairbanks survives only in a transcription by Julia Beecher, who copied it into a letter that her husband, Thomas K. Beecher, wrote on 13 December 1872 to Ella L. Wolcott, one of his parishioners and a close family friend. Beecher ended his portion of the letter, "Julia will insert a squib of Mark Twain's—that bears many perusals—& I am yours as ever," and Mrs. Beecher introduced her transcription as an "Extract from Mark Twains letter to Mrs. Fairbanks." Fairbanks had evidently sent the Beechers this portion of Clemens's letter (or a copy of it), knowing they would enjoy his description of their mutual friend Susan Crane. Wolcott was traveling in the Midwest in late 1872. After visiting her brother in Cleveland, she went in November to Jacksonville, Illinois, where Beecher's letter of 13 December was directed (*L3*, 13 n. 4, 243–44 n. 6; *L4*, 191 n. 1; Boyd and Boyd, 219; Thomas K. Beecher to Ella L. Wolcott, 25 Nov 72 and 13 Dec 72, CtHSD; Wolcott, 389–90, 413–14). Clemens's image of Susan Crane as an angel was clearly a response to a remark Fairbanks had made to him in a letter of 26 October (CU-MARK). Since this letter would have taken at least eleven days to reach him, he could have answered her no sooner than 6 November from London—nor any later than about 10 December (if he delayed responding until after his return to Hartford), in order for the Beechers to have included his words in a letter of 13 December. (By 10 December, in fact, he had received another letter from Fairbanks: see 10 Dec 72 to Nast.) Fairbanks wrote:

My dear "Savage"   Fair Banks   Oct. 26th

I wrote you a note a few days ago, but Mr. Fairbanks thinks he forgot to put on more than an ordinary stamp. We are not accustomed to *foreign* correspondence. As the newspaper begins to talk about you now and you seem to be the fashion, I can afford to send you the second letter, but I stipulate right here for an early and a double answer.

Who do you think ate our wild ducks, last Friday and gathered our flowers, and said pretty things about our home? Susie Crane and her husband. Was n't it nice in them to come, and to be so pleased with everything, and to make us so happy? Is n't Susie an angel—I know there are places for wings on her shoulders—and I begin to see new loveliness in Theodore. We talked of you and we all concluded you were worth loving. The day they left brought "Joaquin" Miller to rhapsodize over Fair Banks. He spent a night with us and I like the man as I had *not* thought to. He won us in spite of prejudice and newspapers. Is he a villain! He certainly has genius in rich measure—and he has grown so delicate & gentle and unaffected. He has dropped the barbaric element and is ambitious to seem a refined gentleman. He has shorn his Absalom locks, he wears kid gloves and black neck-tie. What do you believe of his domestic life? He adores you and England.

They are treating you handsomely in England—we are glad—and everybody is watching you here—and I your anxious mother am stretching my neck over all the great audience. I know you'll say and do your *best* and *simplest* things. Don't write newspaper letters of anything you are to put in a book, will you? Your next book, make a *fresh* surprise. Joaquin Miller says, "write to Twain & thank him for his letter to Hutton the Publisher.["]

Your little "after dinner" at the Club was *nice*. Keep doing the *nice* things. Say nothing irreverent—make your wit exquisite (as you know how) not broad—touch lightly, rather tenderly upon *departed* goodness, even if it was not greatness (see Albert memorial), and then I'll just settle back to my knitting and dream of your glory.

Good bye—I shall send no more cautions nor suggestions till I hear from you.

I am always your loving Mother,

M. M. F.

For Clemens's letter to Hotten ("Hutton") see 20 Sept 72 to the editor of the London *Spectator.* For his " 'after dinner' at the Club" see 22 Sept 72 to Conway (2nd). The speech had been reprinted in Abel Fairbanks's Cleveland *Herald* on 19 October.

²In the Bible parable, Lazarus, the sick beggar, finds comfort after death in "Abraham's bosom," while Dives, the rich man who ignored him, is tormented by thirst. It is Abraham, not Lazarus, who denies Dives relief, explaining that the "great gulf" between the saved and the damned prevents any contact (Luke 16:19–31).

To the Editor of the London *Telegraph*
per Unidentified
8 November 1872 • London, England
(MS: ViU)

Langham Hotel

Nov. 8ᵗʰ 1872[1]

___

To the Editor of
"The Daily Telegraph"[2]

___

Sir,

With your kind permission I desire to say to those Societies in London and other cities of Great Britain, under whose auspices I have partly promised to lecture, that I am called home by a Cable Telegram.

I shall spend with my family, the greater part of next year here, and may be able to lecture a month during the Autumn upon such scientific topics as I know least about & may consequently feel least trameled in dilating upon

Yours respectfully
Mark Twain

[*letter docketed:*]
My Dear Macdonell[3]

Perhaps this may amuse you.
DLJ[4]

[1] Since Clemens's 5 November letters to the *Daily News*, the *Morning Post*, and the *Times* survive only in printed form, it is not known whether Clemens hired a copyist to make the duplicates he needed. But by 8 November he had found some help: except for the signature, the present letter is entirely in the hand of an unidentified amanuensis. This letter was not published, however, either in the London *Telegraph* or in any other London newspaper that has been found.

[2] Edward Levy (later Levy Lawson, 1833–1916) was the influential editor of the politically liberal London *Telegraph*, a widely read newspaper known for "the promptitude, the fullness, and the variety of its telegraphic advices" (*Newspaper Press Directory*, 17; Griffiths, 362–63). Levy began his journalism career as a drama critic on the London *Sunday Times*. He was appointed editor of the *Telegraph* in 1856 by his father (the proprietor), and his vivid treatment of the news brought to the newspaper a wide readership. Clemens later met Levy, probably through Anthony Trollope (see 6 July 73 to Fairbanks, n. 11).

[3] James Macdonell (1842–79) was Levy's "confidential helper." He began his newspaper career in Scotland at age sixteen, and in 1865 went to work on the *Telegraph*. He was also a regular contributor to *Fraser's Magazine*, *Macmillan's Magazine*, and the *North British Review* (Griffiths, 388–89).

[4] Unidentified.

To Olivia L. Clemens
10 November 1872 • London, England
(MS: CU-MARK)

London, Nov. 9, 1872
Midnight.

Livy darling, it was flattering, at the Lord Mayor's dinner,[1] tonight, to
have the nation's honored favorite, the Lord High Chancellor of England,[2] in his vast wig & gown, with a splendid, sword-bearing lackey,
following him & holding up his train, walk me arm-in-arm through the
brilliant assemblage, & welcome me with all the enthusiasm of a girl, &
tell me that when affairs of state oppress him & he can't sleep, he always
has my books at hand & forgets his perplexities in reading them! And
two other be-g be-wigged & gowned great state judges of England told
me the very same thing.

And it was pleasant in such an illustrious assemblage to overhear
people talking about me at every step, & always complimentarily—&
also to have these grandees come up & introduce themselves & apologize
for it. You will heartily enjoy your English welcome when you come
here. With a world of love,

Saml.

✉

[*in ink:*] Mrs. S. L. Clemens | Cor Forest & Hawthorne | Hartford |
Conn. [*in upper left corner:*] America. | [*flourish*] [*postmarked:*] LONDON ·
W 7 NO 11 72 [*and*] NEW YORK NOV 23 PAID ALL

[1] On Saturday, 9 November, "Sir Sydney Waterlow, the new Lord Mayor, was
escorted from the Guildhall to Westminster, with all the accustomed pomp, to
be presented to the Barons of the Exchequer, in accordance with ancient usage."
When the grand procession, known as the Lord Mayor's Show, arrived at Westminster, the new mayor took his oath of office. In the evening, the "usual State
banquet was given by the Lord Mayor and the Sheriffs of London and Middlesex
at Guildhall. The Lord Mayor received the guests on their arrival in the new
Library. Covers were laid for between 800 and 900" ("Lord Mayor's Day," London *Times*, 11 Nov 72, 10; Weinreb and Hibbert, 482–84).
[2] Sir Roundell Palmer, Lord Selborne (1812–95), became lord chancellor on
15 October 1872. He was educated at Oxford, where he performed brilliantly,
and entered the practice of law in 1837. He served as solicitor-general (1861),

attorney general (1863–66), and was twice lord chancellor (1872–74, 1880–85). Knighted in 1861, he was made Baron Selborne of Selborne in October 1872.

To the Royal Humane Society
20 November 1872 • SS *Batavia* en route from
Liverpool, England, to Boston, Mass.
(Boston *Advertiser*, 26 Nov 72)

ON BOARD CUNARD STEAMER BATAVIA, ⎫
At Sea, November 20, 1872. ⎬
To the Royal Humane Society:—[1] ⎭

Gentlemen,—The Batavia sailed from Liverpool on Tuesday, November 12. On Sunday night a strong west wind began to blow, & not long after midnight it increased to a gale. By four o'clock the sea was running very high; at half-past seven our starboard bulwarks were stove in & the water entered the main saloon; at a later hour the gangway on the port side came in with a crash & the sea followed, flooding many of the staterooms on that side. At the same time a sea crossed the roof of the vessel & carried away one of our boats, splintering it to pieces & taking one of the davits with it. At half-past nine the glass was down to 28.35, & the gale was blowing with a severity which the officers say is not experienced oftener than once in five or ten years. The storm continued during the day & all night, & also all day yesterday, but with moderated violence.

At 4 P. M. a dismasted vessel was sighted.[2] A furious squall had just broken upon us & the sea was running mountains high, to use the popular expression. Nevertheless Captain Mouland[3] immediately bore up for the wreck (which was making signals of distress), ordered out a life-boat & called for volunteers. To a landsman it seemed like deliberate suicide to go out in such a storm. But our third & fourth officers & eight men answered to the call with a promptness that compelled a cheer. Two of the men lost heart at the last moment, but the others stood fast & were started on their generous enterprise with another cheer. They carried a long line with them, several life buoys, & a lighted lantern, for the atmosphere was murky with the storm, & sunset was not far off.

The wreck, a barque, was in a pitiable condition. Her mainmast was naked, her mizen-mast & bowsprit were gone, & her foremast was but a stump, wreathed & cumbered with a ruin of sails & cordage from the fallen fore-top & fore-top gallant masts & yards. We could see nine men clinging to the main rigging. The stern of the vessel was gone & the sea made a clean breach over her, pouring in a cataract out of the broken stern & spouting through the parted planks of her bows.

Our boat pulled 300 yards & approached the wreck on the lee side. Then it had a hard fight, for the waves & the wind beat it constantly back. I do not know when anything has alternately so stirred me through & through & then disheartened me, as it did to see the boat every little while get *almost* close enough & then be hurled three lengths away again by a prodigious wave. And the darkness settling down all the time. But at last they got the line & buoy aboard, & after that we could make out nothing more. But presently we discovered the boat approaching us, & found she had saved every soul,—nine men. They had had to drag those men, one at a time, through the sea to the life-boat with the line & buoy—for of course they did not dare to touch the plunging vessel with the boat. The peril increased now, for every time the boat got close to our lee our ship rolled over on her & hid her from sight. But our people managed to haul the party aboard one at a time without losing a man, though I said they would lose every single one of them—I am therefore but a poor success as a prophet. As the fury of the squall had not diminished, & as the sea was so heavy it was feared we might lose some men if we tried to hoist the life-boat aboard, so she was turned adrift by the captain's order, poor thing, after helping in such a gallant deed. But we have plenty more boats, & very few passengers.

To speak by the log, & be accurate, Captain Mouland gave the order to change our ship's course & bear down toward the wreck at 4.15 P. M.; at 5.15 our ship was under way again with those nine poor devils on board. That is to say, this admirable thing was done in a tremendous sea & in the face of a hurricane, in *sixty minutes by the watch,*—& if your honorable society should be moved to give to Captain Mouland & his boat's crew that reward which a sailor prizes & covets above all other distinctions, the Royal Humane Society's medal, the parties whose names are signed to this paper will feel as grateful as if they themselves were the recipients of this great honor. Those who know him say that Captain Mouland has risked his life many times to rescue shipwrecked men—in the days when he occupied a subordinate position—& we hopefully trust that the seed sown then is about to ripen to its harvest now.

The wrecked barque was the Charles Ward, Captain Bell, bound from Quebec to Scotland with lumber.[4] The vessel went over on her beam-ends at 9 o'clock Monday morning, & eleven men were washed overboard & lost. Captain Bell & eight men remained, & these our boat saved. They had been in the main rigging some thirty-one hours, without food or water, & were so frozen & exhausted that when we got them aboard they could hardly speak, & the minds of several of them were wandering. The wreck was out of the ordinary track of vessels, & was 1500 miles from land. She was in the centre of the Atlantic. Our life-boat crew of volunteers consisted of the following: D. Gillies, third officer; H. Kyle, fourth do.; Nicholas Foley, quartermaster; Henry Foley, do.; Nathaniel Clark, do.; Thomas Henry, seaman; John Park, do.; Richard Brennan, do.

The officers tell me that those two quartermasters, the Foley brothers, may be regarded as a sort of *permanent volunteers*—they stand always ready for any splendid deed of daring.

John Park is a sturdy young sailor, but young as he is I overheard him say, "Well, that's the *third* time I've been out on that kind of an expedition." And then he added, with a kindly faith in his species that did him no discredit, "But it's all right; I'll be in a close place like that myself, some day, & then somebody will do as much for me, I reckon."

When our lifeboat first started away on her mission it was such a gallant sight when she pinnacled herself on the fleecy crest of the first giant wave that our party of passengers, grouped together on deck, with one impulse broke out into cheer upon cheer. Officer Gillies said afterwards that about that time the thought of his wife & children had come upon him & his heart was sinking a bit, but the cheers were strong brandy & water to him & his heart never "went back on him" any more. We would have cheered their heads off only it interrupted the orders so much. Really & truly, these men while on their enterprise were safe at no time except when in the open sea between the vessels; all the time that they were near either the wreck or our own ship their lives were in great peril.

If I have been of any service toward rescuing these nine shipwrecked human beings by standing around the deck in a furious storm, without any umbrella, keeping an eye on things & seeing that they were done right, & yelling whenever a cheer seemed to be the important thing, I am glad, & I am satisfied. I ask no reward. I would do it again under the same circumstances. But what I *do* plead for, & earnestly & sincerely, is that the Royal Humane Society will remember our captain & our life-boat crew; &, in so remembering them, increase the high honor & esteem in which the society is held all over the civilized world.

In this appeal our passengers *all* join with hearty sincerity, & in testimony thereof will sign their names. Begging that you will pardon me, a stranger, for addressing your honored society with such confidence & such absence of ceremony, & trusting that my motive may redeem my manner,

    I am, gentlemen,
                                              Your ob't servant,
[Signed]   MARK TWAIN (Samuel L. Clemens),
                                              Hartford, Conn.

We the undersigned, passengers by the steamer Batavia, eye⸗ witnesses of the action described by Mr. Clemens, are glad of this opportunity of expressing our admiration of the gallantry displayed by the volunteers of the lifeboat, & the cool judgment & skill of Captain Mouland in directing the affair, & we feel sure that never has a case more deserving of honorable recognition been brought before the notice of the Royal Humane Society.

C. F. Wood, England.[5]
Edward W. Emerson, Concord, Massachusetts.[6]
Rev. Edmund K. Alden, Boston, Massachusetts.
C. J. Dobell, Albion, Edwards Co., Illinois.
Rev. Henry W. Biggs, Chillicothe, Ohio.
Rev. George E. Street, Exeter, New Hampshire.
E. G. Moss, New York.
Lafayette Devenny, Cincinnati, Ohio.
Sidney D. Palmer, New York.
George K. Kinney, Cincinnati, Ohio.
Colton Greene, Memphis, Tennessee[7]
A. A. Dorion, Lower Canada, Montreal.
James Hall, State Geologist, Albany, New York.[8]
C. C. Walworth, Boston, Massachusetts.
Mrs. C. C. Walworth, Boston, Massachusetts.
Mrs. C. M. Walworth, Boston, Massachusetts.

Mrs. L Devenny, Cincinnati, Ohio.
Mrs. A. B. Denmead, Cincinnati, Ohio.
Mrs. E. G. Moss, New York.

[1] The Boston *Advertiser* published this letter on 26 November, the day after the *Batavia* arrived in Boston, describing it as a communication "from [Mark Twain's] pen, furnished to the Daily Advertiser" ("A Daring Deed," 4). The typesetter for the *Advertiser* was probably working from an amanuensis copy, since the original manuscript (now lost) was presumably sent to the Royal Humane Society in London. The society was instituted in 1774 "to collect and circulate the most approved and effectual methods for recovering persons apparently drowned or dead; to suggest and provide suitable apparatus for, and bestow rewards on, those who assist in the preservation and restoration of life" (Royal Humane Society). It was supported by voluntary contributions.

[2] That is, at 4 P.M. on Tuesday, 19 November.

[3] John Elsey Mouland, captain of the *Batavia*, was born in Hampshire in 1828 and earned his master mariner's certificate in Cork in 1852. He assumed his first post on a Cunard vessel, the *Arabia*, in 1858. During the Civil War he served on at least two "blockade runners"—ships that attempted to evade the Union blockade of southern ports to deliver arms and other goods to the Confederacy. On 26 May 1862 he was on the *Cambria* when it was captured by Federals while trying to enter the port of Charleston with a load of rifles, saltpeter, and medicines. He later served on the *Hibernia* (1863–64), a ship in the Atlantic Irish Royal Mail Steam Navigation Company. In 1864 he returned to Cunard, on the *China*, but for several years also worked intermittently for other companies. On 3 September 1872 he assumed command of the *Batavia*, built in 1870 (*Lloyd's Register*, 493; Wise, 63, 292, 307; New York *Tribune*: "Operations of the Blockading Squadron," 3 June 62, 8; "Ocean Steamers," 21 Dec 60, 3; "Ocean Steamers," 21 Oct 63, 5; "Shipping Intelligence," 26 May 70, 3; "Shipping Intelligence," 19 Aug 72, 3; "Arrivals," New York *Herald*, 15 Sept 72, 12; information from the Cunard Line; see also 22 Jan 73 to Mouland).

[4] The boat, under Captain I. F. Bell, was actually bound for Sunderland, England, a seaport twelve miles southeast of Newcastle, having left Quebec on 2 November ("A Daring Deed," Boston *Advertiser*, 26 Nov 72, 4).

[5] See 26 Nov 72 to JLC and PAM.

[6] Edward Waldo Emerson (1844–1930) was the son of Ralph Waldo Emerson. In 1871, after two years at Harvard Medical School, he went to Berlin to continue his studies. Having worked for a time at a London hospital, he was now returning home. He described the voyage in a letter to his sister:

> Who do you think turned up among the passengers? Verily Mark Twain. He is a curious looking bird and has or very probably affects a very broad and rustic speech and a drawl not exactly Yankee but rather like a Western man. He seems a simple, countrified, serious man and you at once think of his book and think here really is an innocent abroad. His manner is just the right one to make his conversation amusing and reminds one of the descriptions of his friend Artemus Ward, i.e., he would appear to be serious and stumble into his jokes with an air of pathetic innocence. (Edward W. Emerson to Ellen Emerson, no date, Forbes and Finley, 32)

[7] See 3 Dec 72 to Mouland, n. 2.

⁸James Hall (1811–98), a renowned geologist and paleontologist, was the author of *New York State Natural History Survey: Paleontology* (8 vols. in 13, 1847–94). Except for Wood, Emerson, Greene, and Hall, no attempt has been made to identify the passengers who signed this letter; none of those remaining unidentified is known to have had any further connection with Clemens.

From Samuel L. Clemens and Others
to John E. Mouland
23 November 1872 • SS *Batavia* en route from
Liverpool, England, to Boston, Mass.
(MS: ViU)

The Passengers to Capt. Mouland¹

Of On Board Steamer "Batavia," ⎫
At Sea, Nov. 23, 1872. ⎬

Sir: You have brought us safely through a remarkable voyage, & one which once or twice seemed to promise disastrous results to ship & passengers. Your courageous bearing & your cheery words & countenance, all through the storms that beset us, inspired us with a hope & a confidence that not even the deliberate villainy of the barometer could vanquish. When we were uneasiest & our perils seemed at the highest, the reflection that you were at your post on deck brought with it an inspiriting ¢ sense of security; & after you had braved that gale, up there, through all that terrific morning of the 18ᵗʰ November, & we had remained in dismal suspense hearsed in the saloon, it was sunshine to see your face again when you introduced the wave that smashed the bulwarks & flooded the cabins; & it was cordial wine to hear you say, with cheery indifference to truth, that there was "no danger."

For a large part of two days & nights you were wholly without food or sleep; you lost the ends of your fingers & never missed them, you were so busy issuing orders & fighting the hurricane; & by only a hairsbreadth you escaped annihilation by the wave that accomplished the starboard damage——& then we would have been in a state of things. We are sailors enough to know & appreciate the necessity to us all of your intelligent head ꝑ̶ and your superb seamanship in thr those th troubled hours—we are sailors enough for that, although it is doubtful if one of us can tell the mizzen-foretops'l-jib-boom from the binnacle gaskets of the main-to'⸗ gallan'mast bulkhead. You went through a good deal, Captain, but you brought the ship through along with you, & you never lost a single spar except the two life-boats—one of which was splintered & washed overboard by a wave that was hunting for the main-royals, & the other was turned adrift because sound judgment dictated that course. And we speak the simple, grateful truth when we say that we all recognize & appreciate the great qualities which you have manifested, & the happy success achieved by their exercise—& when we add that we respect & honor & esteem you without stint or measure, our hearts speak through our lips.

You did a brave, good ~~dead~~ deed when you went instantly to the aid of the shipwrecked crew of the "Charles Ward," Nov. 19th. Without a moment's hesitation you took the serious responsibility of halting ~~the~~ ₓyourₓ ship in a fierce gale of wind & a turbulent sea, & adventuring a boat's-crew of gallant volunteers in the service of humanity. Your masterly management of the rescuing enterprise was conspicuous throughout; & to you, the head & chief here, the crew of the wreck owe their first obligations for their restoration to the world of the living.

We shall separate to-morrow; but no matter how widely our diverging paths may sunder us, our memories of you will still bloom & bear pleasant fruit through the accumulating years; & whenever we think of you or hear the friendly music of your name, we'll warm right up & say Here's luck & long life to the "old man!"

C. C. Walworth ⎱
Chairman of meeting of passengers ⎰
Edward W. Emerson ˄
Secretary

Saml. L. Clemens, (Mark Twain.) ⎫
——⩙——
ₓChairman of Committee on Address. ⎭
——〜——
˄

James Hall
C. F. Wood.
E. K. Alden
Colton Greene

Lafayette Devenny	Cincinnati Ohio
Mrs. L. Devenny.	" "
Miss A. B. Denmead.	Cincinnati Ohio.
Mrs E. G. Moss.	New York.
E. G Moss	" "
Mrs C. C Walworth,	Boston,
Miss E. M. Walworth.	Boston. Mass.
George E. Street.	Exeter. N. H.
Edmund John Dobell	Albion Edwards Co Ill[s]
M[rs] Jenny Dobell	do do
Henry W Biggs	Chillicothe Ohio
Mrs C. L. Biggs	Do Do
Sidney D Palmer	New York
George K Kinney	Cincinnati Ohio
Edward Corn –	Burslem – England
A. A. Dorion.	Montreal. Canada—
Sarah Gregory	
Johanna Ross	

[1] Although Clemens and his fellow passengers addressed this letter to Mouland, they also planned to have it published with the previous letter. The original manuscript was evidently given to Mouland, and a copy of it given to the Boston *Advertiser*, where the two letters appeared under the same headline, "A Daring Deed." The *Advertiser* added a brief explanation before the present (second) letter: "A meeting of the passengers was held after the rescue, officers appointed, and a committee to draw up an address. Of course the task was intrusted to the genial humorist, and the result was as follows" (26 Nov 72, 4).

From Mary E. (Mollie) Clemens and Samuel L. Clemens to Jane Lampton Clemens and Pamela A. Moffett
26 November 1872 • Hartford, Conn.
(MS: NPV)

Hartford Nov 26. 1872.

Dear Folks,

I will write only a note to say Sam has arrived safely and in good health after being gone three months & a week; and of passing through the most terriffic S[t]orm of a week—and just before reaching Hartford of a narrow escape of a car wreck as there were ties fastened on the track in two places.[1] Give thanks for his safe delivery at home   Mrs Langdon leaves Friday; and we expect to get away next week.

Sam brought an English gentleman with him for the night and has just carried him to the train. Mr Wood is on his way to New Zealand.[2] Had a Fejeee Islander with him as servant. Sam says Livy shall not cross Mrs Hookers threshold and if he talks to Mrs H he will tell her in plain words the reason.[3]

Mrs Geo Warner is within three weeks of confinement and Sunday was taken with something like apoplexy, ⸗ or spasms—but today is a little better; so there is hope of her life.[4]

Write us soon.

There is a great deal more I could say but I am taking "the epizootic" and my eyes and nose both run faster than my pen.[5]

Love to all.

Affly M. E. C.

Dear Mother & Sister—Very glad to get home—& shall be glad to return to England in May. In London I bought a steam engine for Sammy's Christmas present. Bought it second-hand & had it thoroughly repaired. Paid $80, gold, for it. It cost about $4 $140 when new. Sammy must learn how to run it before he blows himself up with it. He must contrive work for it to do, & hunt up all sorts of applications for its power. It is a very excellent little toy, & can be made to do a stout job of work. It will arrive from London before long, & go straight to Fredonia. I bought no other presents for anybody, because there are so many of us I didn't know where to begin—& as Sammy can't be allowed to read, I thought he ought to have some amusement.[6]

Love to you all.

[1] On Monday morning, 25 November, Clemens left the *Batavia* in Boston, whence the ship proceeded to New York. He took an express train for Hartford, which narrowly escaped derailment near Enfield, Connecticut, about fifteen miles north of Hartford:

About three-quarters of a mile from the bridge the express train coming south on the west track, about seven o'clock Monday evening, met a pile of ties. The engineer saw them, and by his presence of mind and the Westinghouse brake was able to stop the train before the crash so that no damage was done. ("A Villain's Work," Hartford *Courant*, 27 Nov 72, 2)

The attempt on Clemens's train, and similar attempts on three later trains the same evening (one of which was derailed), were the work of an "insolently drunk" man who was ejected from a train for refusing to pay sufficient fare ("A

Villain's Work," Hartford *Courant*, 27 Nov 72, 2; "From Europe," Boston *Evening Transcript*, 25 Nov 72, 4).

[2] C. F. Wood wrote to Clemens in 1907:

Dear Fellow Traveller of 35 years ago. You will remember our voyage in the "Batavia" from Liverpool to Boston—our "battened down" existance for two days during the storm, our games of Euchre to keep up the spirits of the more dejected passengers, and our looking on at the rescue of the survivors of the crew of the "Charles Ward." I was on my way out for a cruise in the South Seas and you on our arrival at Boston, kindly took me to your home at Hartford. I know you are much enjoyed, but I sh[d] like to call & see you & press your hand once more. (3 July 1907, CU-MARK)

In 1875 Wood described his travels in *A Yachting Cruise in the South Seas:* "Early in November, 1872, I left Liverpool by the Cunard line, and crossing the American continent by the Great Pacific Railway, sailed from San Francisco for New Zealand, calling at the Sandwich Islands." He explained that he was "induced to publish these few imperfect sketches of my last cruise by the belief that any facts relating to the manners and customs of these islanders, should not be allowed to perish" (C. F. Wood, "Preface," 1).

[3] In a September 1872 speech to a convention of Boston spiritualists, Victoria Woodhull, Isabella Beecher Hooker's close ally in the women's rights movement, accused Henry Ward Beecher (Hooker's half-brother) of committing adultery with Elizabeth Tilton, one of his parishioners. Woodhull reiterated the charge in the 2 November issue of *Woodhull and Claflin's Weekly*, objecting not so much to the relationship itself, but to Beecher's hypocrisy in condemning free love from the pulpit while practicing it in private. Beecher and Tilton remained silent, refusing to deny or admit the truth of the charge. Hooker, unable to believe in her brother's innocence, defended Woodhull. The rest of the Beecher family (except for Catharine, Beecher's oldest sister) ostracized Hooker, and Clemens seems to have followed suit. The Beecher scandal became a *cause célèbre* in August 1874, when Theodore Tilton sued Beecher for alienation of affections. Beecher's trial ended in a hung jury in July 1875, but in February 1876 a church council reviewed the case and officially exonerated him (Andrews, 35–41; Clark, 207–9, 220–21; Oliver, 117–49; Shaplen, 199, 260–62; *L2*, 14; Woodhull). Victoria Claflin Woodhull (1838–1927) was born in Ohio, and in her early years collaborated with her family in selling patent medicines and telling fortunes. At age fifteen she married Dr. Canning Woodhull, whom she divorced in 1864. She subsequently formed a liaison with James H. Blood (and may have legally married him), but in 1876 she divorced him as well. In January 1870 she and her sister, Tennessee Claflin, opened a profitable stock brokerage in New York with the help of Cornelius Vanderbilt, and in May of the same year the sisters founded *Woodhull and Claflin's Weekly*, which advocated equal rights for women and a single standard of free love for both sexes. In part because of these views, Henry Ward Beecher often attacked her from the pulpit, citing her as an example of vice. In May 1872 Woodhull became the presidential nominee of the Equal Rights Party, with Frederick Douglass as her running mate (Shaplen, 133–38, 157, 269; Marberry 1967, 15, 27, 188).

[4] Lilly Warner recovered, and gave birth to her third surviving child, Margaret (known as "Daisy"), on 23 December (Elisabeth G. Warner, 1).

[5] The term "epizootic," which technically meant a type of equine influenza, was used informally for human illnesses such as the common cold. Mollie was evidently treating herself with a homeopathic medication, designed to cure by exacerbating her symptoms.

[6]Clemens's nephew, Samuel Moffett, suffered from an unidentified problem with his eyes which prevented him from reading. The steam engine did not arrive in Fredonia until January 1873 (*L4*, 332; 22 Jan 73 to PAM).

To the Editor of the *Literary World*
December 1872 • Hartford, Conn.
(MS: CtY-BR)

[*written in margins of the printed page:*][1]

Dear Sir—The other charge ˄(see 4th column on this page)˄ is playful,[2] but I'm not sure that the author of this "boy's journal" hadn't been reading page 637 of the "Innocents Abroad," at some time or other.[3] But the truth is, a deliberate plagiarism is seldom made by any person who is not an ass; but unconscious & blameless plagiarisms are made by the best of people every day: Considering the fact that billions of people have been thinking & writing every day for 5 or 6,000 years, I wonder that any man of the present day ˄ever˄ dares to consider a thought original with himself.[4]

Very Truly Yrs
Mark Twain.

[1]Clemens wrote this letter to the editor of the *Literary World: A Review of Current Literature* in the margins of page 106 of the December 1872 issue. (The entire page is photographically reproduced in Appendix F.) This Boston monthly was founded in 1870 and survived until 1904. Its editor and publisher from 1870 to 1877, Samuel R. Crocker, "used to have a literary connection with the book firm of Ticknor & Fields," and had been the "Boston correspondent of several journals of other cities" ("Boston Correspondence," Hartford *Courant*, 24 Feb 72, 1). He

> had been trained as a lawyer; but he was widely read and had a flair for literary criticism, a studious habit, and tremendous industry. The *World* was his personal organ, but such were his versatility, breadth of interests, and voracity that it became a fairly well-rounded literary paper. . . . [Crocker's] reviews, though "friendly" as a rule, were apparently honest and fairly discriminating. The *World* was informative, conservative, and inclined to dullness.
>
> Crocker's health declined in 1876, and in the following year he became hopelessly insane; he died in a hospital in 1878. (Mott 1957, 454–56)

Crocker, who was not personally acquainted with Clemens, had written a negative review in April 1871 of *Mark Twain's (Burlesque) Autobiography and First Romance*, which Clemens had almost certainly read (Crocker 1871; see *L4*, 381 n. 1).

²Clemens meant to refer to the third (and last) column on the page, which included a "playful" note about plagiarism from "F. B. P." (The item was circled in pencil, possibly not by Clemens.) "F. B. P." compared Mark Twain's account of mourning at the grave of Adam in chapter 53 of *The Innocents Abroad* with "an old French story" about a similar absurd lamentation over the untimely death of the poet Pindar. Crocker published Clemens's rebuttal in the "Notes and Queries" column of the next issue, prefaced with the remark, " '*Mark Twain*,' *Hartford, Conn.*, comments upon the humorous attempt of 'F. B. P.,' in our last issue, to convict him (M. T.) of plagiarism" (Crocker 1873).

³Clemens drew a box around the extract from a "boy's journal," in the first column of the *Literary World* page. The extract was quoted in a review of *What Katy Did: A Story* (Boston: Roberts Brothers, 1872), the first of three "Katy" books by Sarah Chauncy Woolsey (1835–1905), who, under the pseudonym "Susan Coolidge," wrote a number of popular children's books. Crocker praised the book for its "exquisite naturalness, its fidelity to average child-life," and the "pleasant humor" of passages like the journal (Crocker 1872). Clemens points out the similarity of Woolsey's concept to his own (fictional) boyhood journal, included in chapter 59 of *The Innocents Abroad*.

⁴In December 1879 Clemens returned to his concept of "unconscious plagiarism" ("we all unconsciously worked over ideas gathered in reading and hearing, imagining they were original with ourselves") in a graceful speech honoring Oliver Wendell Holmes (SLC 1879b).

To the Editor of the San Francisco *Alta California*
3 December 1872 • Hartford, Conn.
(MS: MH-H)

Hartford, Dec. 3, 1872.

To the Editor of the $ Alta:¹

Sir: Certain gentlemen here in the east have done me the honor to make me their mouthpiece in a matter which should command the interest & the sympathy of many Californians. They represent that the veteran Capt. Ned Wakeman is lying paralyzed & helpless at his home near your city,² & they beg that his old friends on the Pacific coast will take his case do toward him as they would gladly do, themselves, if they were back, now, in San Francisco—that is, take the old mariner's case in hand & assist him & his family to the pecuniary aid they stand in such sore need of. His house is mortgaged for $5,000 & he will be sold out of h & turned shelterless upon the world in his broken in January unless this is done. I have made voyages with the old man when fortune was a friend to him, & am aware that he gave with a generous heart & a willing hand to all the needy that came in his way;[3] & now that twenty years of rough toil on the watery highways of the far west find him wrecked & in distress, I am sure that the splendid generosity which has made the name of California to be honored in all lands will come to him in such a shape that he shall confess that the seeds he sowed in better days did not fall upon unfruitful soil.

Will not some of the old friends of Capt. Wakeman, in your city, take this matter in hand and do by him as he would surely do by them were their cases reversed?[4]

Very Truly Yours,
Mark Twain.

Hartford, Conn., Dec. 3.

[1] Clemens intended this letter to be published in the San Francisco *Alta California*, where it appeared on the front page of the 14 December issue under the headline "Appeal for Capt. Ned Wakeman—Letter from 'Mark Twain.'" If Clemens also sent a covering letter to his friend John McComb, supervising editor on the *Alta*, it does not survive.

[2] The appeal for aid for Edgar (Ned) Wakeman came from Vernon Seaman of Newburgh, New York, "an old friend and former purser with Captain Wakeman" (Wakeman-Curtis, 376). Wakeman was stricken suddenly by paralysis in July 1872 while at sea. Over the next several months, he made a partial recovery at his home in Oakland, California, but never regained his health; he died in 1875 at age fifty-seven (Wakeman-Curtis, 361, 377; Vernon Seaman to SLC, 7 Jan 73, CU-MARK).

[3] Clemens made only one voyage with Captain Wakeman, traveling from San Francisco to Nicaragua in December 1866 aboard the steamer *America* under Wakeman's command. He encountered Wakeman only one other time, in July 1868 in Panama while en route from San Francisco to New York. Finding Wakeman's *America* anchored in the harbor, Clemens spent a convivial evening in his company, entertained by some of his imaginative yarns. He later described Wakeman:

> He was a great, burly, handsome, weatherbeaten, symmetrically built and powerful creature, with coal black hair and whiskers, and the kind of eye which men obey without talking back. He was full of human nature, and the best kind of human nature. He was as hearty and sympathetic and loyal and loving a soul as I have found anywhere; and when his temper was up he performed all the functions of an earthquake, without the noise. . . . He had never had a day's schooling in his life, but had picked up worlds and worlds of knowledge at second-hand, and none of it correct. He was a liberal talker, and inexhaustibly interesting. In the matter of a wide and catholic profanity he had not his peer on the planet while he lived. . . . He knew the Bible by heart, and was profoundly and sincerely religious. (AD, 29 Aug 1906, CU-MARK, in *MTE*, 244–45)

Wakeman's place in Mark Twain's imagination and in his writing is thoroughly examined in *N&J1*, 241–43 (*RI 1993*, 677–78; *L1*, 370 n. 8; *L2*, 242 n. 1 *top*; SLC 1868d).

⁴Clemens's appeal "set the ball in motion," and over the next two weeks, $4,750 was raised to liquidate the Wakemans' mortgage. The donors included Darius O. Mills and William C. Ralston ("Captain Wakeman's Decks Cleared," San Francisco *Chronicle*, 28 Dec 72, 3). Mary L. (Mrs. Edgar) Wakeman wrote gratefully to Clemens on 19 January 1873, "Our home is once more our own, and we feel the kind and prompt assistance extended by the Capt's. California friends, is to be attributed to that letter" (CU-MARK).

To Olivia Lewis Langdon
3 December 1872 • Hartford, Conn.
(MS: CtHMTH)

                                                   Home, Dec. 3.
Dear Mother:

We have not heard of your arrival, but we judge that you must have reached home, ∮ before this, else some of the people there would be inquiring into it by telegraph, maybe. I was uneasy & uncomfortable a good while, the day you left, for I dreaded some more railroad obstructions—& I was not over the discomfort till we got your dispatch next morning—& *then* it occurred to me that as you went down in a *daylight* train no obstructor would be muggins enough to try to throw it off the track.¹

You left your muff here & we are going to send it to you by mail—would do it today, but are out of prepaid envelops. We have been pretty homesick for you, & even my potent presence was not sufficient to keep Livy from missing you day & night & talking about it.

Send Sue & The. along—we want them ever so much. The *little* Susie needs them, too.² She has a marvelous cold—as bad a one as I ever had myself, I think. It pulls her down at a wonderful rate. She is nothing now but skin & bones & flesh.

I ∦ went to work on my English book yesterday & turned out 36 pages of ~~on~~ satisfactory manuscript, but the baby kept me awake so much last night that today I find the inspiration is vanished & gone, right in the middle of my subject.

Clara may as well get ready, for she has to go with us to England in May.³

How stands Elmira on the Beecher Scandal?⁴ Miss Catherine

Beecher[5] tells us that Mr. Moulton[6] *did* go after a MS., to Mr. Beecher, & ~~suexspe~~ expecting that he "would be mad," took a pistol with him. The poor old soul was in considerable trouble, evidently, & fully appreciated the damaging effect of *one* statement in the Woodhull arraignment being a *fact*. She was sorry a sweeping assertion of the untruth of the said arraignment would not do—because of that unlucky pistol business. However, she said Beecher didn't give up the paper.[7] The Twichells now tell us that ~~th~~ a full year ago the Tiltons (both the he one & the she one)[8] gave to Mr. Beecher an absolute denial of all these slanders, & that that paper is still in Mr. B.'s possession.[9]

Very well, then. The Twichells say, with us, that that paper ought at once to be printed. Whoever feels uncertain about the truth or falsehood of those slanders (& I would extremely like to know who feels certain) is suffering shame & defilement, & is continuing to carry a filthy subject in his mind, to his further defilement, when possibly the Beecher party are all the while able to sweep away his doubts & purify his mind with a breath. *I* think the silence of the Beechers is a hundred fold more of an *obscene publication* than ~~the~~ that of the Woodhulls,[10]—~~for~~ & the said silence is a thousand-fold more potent in convincing people of the truth of that scandal than the evidence of fifty Woodhulls could be. *Silence has given assent* in all ages of the world—it is a law of *nature*, not ethics—& Henry Ward Beecher is as amenable to it as the humblest of us. You will find presently that the general ~~verdict~~ ˄thought˄ of the nation will gradually form itself into the verdict that there is *some* fire somewhere in all this smoke of scandal.

Mrs. Hooker has gone down to see Mr. Beecher—moved thereto by a talk with Miss Catharine, it$ is said.[11]

Mother dear, the autumn leaves are *exquisite*, & so is the frame that encloses them—& more prized than all is the mother-love of which they are the expression. The gift occupies the middle of my study mantel, & is flanked by your & father's[12] portraits in the lovely blue velvet mounting—Livy's birthday gift to me. These things give the study a dainty air that marvelously assists composition.

Nasby has just gone—been here an hour on a flying visit.[13]

Love to you & to all the household.

> Yr son
> Sam*l*.

¹See 26 Nov 72 to JLC and PAM.

²Susan and Theodore Crane, and Susy Clemens.

³Clara Spaulding, a close friend of Olivia's, had agreed to accompany the Clemenses to England. Susan Crane later recalled:

> Miss Clara Spaulding had long desired to go abroad. Mrs. Clemens desired her company, for there had never been any break in the friendship beginning in early girlhood—Mr. Spaulding, with large means was happy to send the daughter to whom he was devoted.
> It proved to be one of the experiences where friends can travel many months together, with increasing devotion. (Susan L. Crane to Albert Bigelow Paine, 2 June 1911, Davis 1956, 3)

⁴See 26 Nov 72 to JLC and PAM, n. 3.

⁵Author and educator Catharine Beecher was seventy-two years old. She came out of retirement in August 1870 to serve as principal of the Hartford Female Seminary, the school she had founded in 1827, but resigned in February 1871. Beecher was not listed in the Hartford directory in the 1870s. She may have been living with any of her numerous family, perhaps in Hartford or Brooklyn (Trumbull, 1:648–49; Stowe, 133–36; information about Hartford Female Seminary courtesy of the Connecticut Historical Society).

⁶Francis D. Moulton (1836–84) had been an intimate friend of Theodore Tilton's since they were classmates at the College of the City of New York. After Moulton graduated in 1854, he accepted a position with Woodruff and Robinson, a mercantile establishment, becoming a partner in the firm in 1861. His wife, a niece of one of his partners, was a member of Henry Ward Beecher's Plymouth Church, although Moulton himself was not. In December 1870 Tilton confided in Moulton, who thereafter acted as a mediator between Tilton and Beecher over the next four years. During Beecher's trial Moulton's testimony was crucial, and in 1874 Beecher brought a charge of criminal libel against him, but later dropped it ("The Mutual Friend Dead," New York *Times*, 5 Dec 84, 8; Hibben, 193, 213, 283).

⁷Victoria Woodhull's "arraignment" (her version of the "Beecher Scandal") appeared in the 2 November 1872 issue of *Woodhull and Claflin's Weekly*. Claiming that her information came largely from the Tiltons themselves, she reported that in December 1870 Elizabeth Tilton had confessed her adultery with Beecher to her husband. Beecher then visited Mrs. Tilton and "compelled or induced" her to "sign a statement he had prepared, declaring, that . . . there had never been any criminal intimacy between them." Theodore Tilton was outraged, and asked Moulton to retrieve the statement for him: "My friend took a pistol, went to Mr. BEECHER and demanded the letter of Mrs. TILTON, under penalty of instant death." This was the "*fact*" that Catharine Beecher acknowledged. Contrary to her statement, however, Beecher did "give up the paper" to Moulton, who put it in his safe (Woodhull, 13–14; Clark, 215–20). In December 1872 Mrs. Tilton confirmed that two years earlier she had

> signed a paper *which he* [Beecher] *wrote*, to clear him in case of trial. . . . I found on reflection that this paper was so drawn as to place me most unjustly against my husband, and on the side of Mr. Beecher. . . . Mr. Moulton procured from Mr. B. the statement which I gave to him in my agitation and excitement, and now holds it. (*Beecher Trial*, 6–7)

Mrs. Tilton changed her mind again during Beecher's trial and wrote another statement denying his guilt.

[8] Theodore Tilton (1835–1907) gained experience as a journalist on the New York *Tribune*. Later, as a reporter for the New York *Observer* (a Presbyterian weekly), he took down Beecher's sermons in shorthand. In 1855 he married Elizabeth Richards (1834–97), a Sunday school teacher at Plymouth Church, with Beecher performing the ceremony. The following year he became managing editor of the *Independent*, a Congregationalist weekly. In this position he gained a national reputation, transforming the religious journal into one of broad appeal. In addition, he edited the Brooklyn *Union*. In December 1870 he was dismissed from both these positions when he and Henry C. Bowen, who owned both journals, had a disagreement over the Beecher affair. Elizabeth Tilton for a time edited *Revolution*, a suffragist publication, and both she and her husband were active in the Equal Rights Association. Theodore Tilton's journalism career, as well as his marriage, was ruined by the Beecher scandal. He left the country in 1883, and lived in Paris on the meager wages he earned from writing novels and poetry.

[9] The Twichells may have heard an inaccurate rumor about a peculiar and equivocal "disavowal" signed in April 1872 by Tilton, Beecher, and Henry C. Bowen, in an attempt to "remove all causes of offense existing between us, real or fancied, and to make Christian reparation for injuries done or supposed to be done" (Oliver, 251). The document capped a tangled series of events: Tilton's accusation against Beecher, Bowen's initial encouragement of Tilton (fueled by his own enmity toward the minister), Bowen's abrupt reversal of position and dismissal of Tilton, and Tilton's subsequent lawsuit for breach of contract—settled by Bowen for $7,000. Tilton's statement read, in part:

> I, Theodore Tilton, do, of my own free will and friendly spirit toward Henry Ward Beecher, hereby covenant and agree that I will never again repeat, by word of mouth or otherwise, any of the allegations, or imputations, or in[n]uendoes contained in my letters hereunto annexed. (Oliver, 251–52)

This document was not made public until the spring of 1873, when someone furnished a copy of it to the press (Oliver, 230–54; Clark, 208).

[10] As soon as Woodhull's account appeared in her *Weekly* (see note 7), she and her sister were arrested and charged with sending obscene literature through the mail, a federal offense. They were freed on bail a month later, then tried and acquitted in June 1873 (Marberry 1967, 112–13, 127, 147).

[11] On 27 November Isabella Hooker had written to Beecher, proposing to "appear in his pulpit and take sole charge of the services to read a paper she would write 'as one commissioned from on high.' . . . She named a meeting place and demanded that Henry come to see her." Theodore Tilton came instead of Beecher, and (according to Moulton's later testimony) silenced Hooker by threatening to expose a past adultery of hers. Tilton reported his action to Beecher, who "was delighted with it" (Andrews, 38).

[12] Jervis Langdon, who died in August 1870.

[13] Petroleum V. Nasby (David Ross Locke) was on his way to Middletown, Connecticut, where he lectured on the evening of 3 December ("Local Personals," Hartford *Courant*, 4 Dec 72, 2).

To John E. Mouland
3 December 1872 • Hartford, Conn.
(MS: ViU)

(SLC)

Hartford, Dec. 3.

Dear Captain:
　You must d̶o̶w̶ run down next voyage & see us, if you can.[1] Telegraph me what hour you will arrive & I'll go to the station & fetch you
home. Mr. Wood stayed all night with us & then joined the General[2] in
New York & they went ∅ West together. I wanted the General to stop
with us, too, but his business made it impossible.
　The American papers say the Royal Humane Society ought to give
me a medal for "standing around on deck without any umbrella," &c.[3] I
e̶x̶suspect they mean a leather one.
　My wife is anxious that you should be put in command of the biggest Cunarder afloat, & then she thinks s̶h̶e̶ the sea-sickness will deal less
harshly by her. I hope͵, also, that͵ you'll have a particularly big ship next
m̶ May, for I *am* afraid my wife is going to have a hard time with sea͵
sickness.

Yrs Faithfully
Sam*ᴵ*. L. Clemens
Cor. Forest & Hawthorne sts.
Hartford.

Capt. Mouland—
(forgot the initials͵)—as usual.)

　[1] Mouland responded to this invitation on 21 January 1873 (22 Jan 73 to Mouland, n. 1).
　[2] General Colton Greene of Memphis, Tennessee, had been a passenger on the
Batavia in November (20 Nov 72 to the Royal Humane Society). A South Car-
olinean by birth, he "accumulated a sizable fortune in merchandising" at a
young age and eagerly gave "his time, ability, and money to the cause of the
South" (Adamson, 4). He was an advisor to Governor Claiborne F. Jackson of
Missouri during the pivotal early days of the Civil War, when Jackson attempted
to swing the state to the Confederacy, and rose to the rank of brigadier general
in the Confederate army. Later he settled in Memphis, where in the 1870s "the
elegant General" became a social arbiter by virtue of "his extensive European

travel and command of languages. . . . Handsome and charming as he was, he never married; he never divulged anything about his origin except that he was born in South Carolina—a mystery still talked about in Memphis" (McIlwaine, 236; Adamson, 1–4; Heitman, 2:177). Clemens included a recollection of C. F. Wood and Greene aboard the *Batavia* in his November 1881 notebook:

> Met gentleman who had been in the Batavia—it reminded me of how Gen Green & I were each refusing the only seat in the fiddle one night when Wood came in & jocularly remarked that while we did the polite he would reap the advantage of a careful coarser training—took the seat & got shot in the back by a sea that nearly broke him in two. (*N&J2*, 403–4)

[3]Clemens quoted his own published letter of 20 November to the Royal Humane Society: "If I have been of any service toward rescuing these nine shipwrecked human beings by standing around the deck in a furious storm, without any umbrella, . . . I am satisfied. I ask no reward." Clemens's claim that the "American papers" recommended a medal for him has not been substantiated. The Cleveland *Leader*, however, did return to the subject on 30 November:

> Mark Twain and Charles Sumner have each had an experience in saving life at sea. Mark says he stood around without an umbrella, and yelled at the proper time. On the strength of this he asks the Royal Humane Society to reward those who were active in the good work. Mr. Sumner, on the steamship, made a speech at the table, and solicited aid for the shipwrecked and those who saved them. The results were most happy. The Senator goes to Washington and Mark to his profitable fancies. ("Passing Events," 2)

Senator Charles Sumner (1811–74) of Massachusetts arrived in New York from Liverpool on 26 November aboard the steamship *Baltic*, which had passed through the same Atlantic storms as the *Batavia*. He had headed a committee of passengers who raised a cash reward for the crewmen involved in rescuing the survivors of another distressed ship, the *Assyria* ("Marine Disasters," New York *Tribune*, 27 Nov 72, 1).

To Jane Lampton Clemens and Family
5 December 1872 • Hartford, Conn.
(MS: NPV)

Hartford De 5.

Dear Folks—

Livy is so tired she makes me write the letter she meant to write herself. She wants you all to visit us during this winter; & can best accommodate two of you at a time—so she wants two of you (whichever 2 you please,) to come, choosing the date of your coming to suit yourselves, & letting us know what hour to expect you.

We have a letter from Annie today & an excellent photograph.

Orion has taken a house in Sigourney street, & will begin to move in tomorrow.[1]

We shall like to have a couple of you here for Christmas, if you feel like coming.[2]

I don't hear anything of Sammy's engine, but it will be along presently. It will have cost about $140 in greenbacks by the time it gets through the custom house, & I think it will be a very useful & entertaining toy.[3] I took it in preference to a magic lantern I was going to buy for him. The lantern & fixtures took up too much room—got disgusted with it—it was too much like importing a stock of dry-goods.

Love to all.

Ys

Sam.

[1] Orion and Mollie Clemens's stay at 55 Sigourney Street in Hartford would be short-lived. By 1 May 1873 Orion was working in Rutland, Vermont, and Mollie was apparently staying with the Moffett household in Fredonia (Schuyler Colfax to OC, 15 Feb 73, CU-MARK; 5 May 73 to OC and MEC, n. 1).

[2] See 20 Dec 72 to JLC and family.

[3] See 26 Nov 72 to JLC and PAM.

To Whitelaw Reid
5 December 1872 • Hartford, Conn.
(New York *Tribune*, 7 Dec 72)

To the Editor of The Tribune.[1]

SIR: This Missouri case is a bad business.[2] You know that none but sailors can untackle a ship's boats, & get them into the water right side up; & you know that at a perilous time the frantic passengers won't give the sailors a chance to do this work successfully. Now, don't you believe that if every vessel carried several life-rafts (like the life-stages of Western steamboats)[3] lashed upon their upper decks, with axes cleated to them which the insanest passenger could use in cutting their fastenings, that many lives would be saved? If the rafts were thrown overboard, & the crazy passengers thrown after them, the sailors might then work at the hampering & complicated tackle of the boats with some method &

some show of success. They could launch them right side up, & go & take the people from the rafts.

In time of danger you cannot successfully launch a boat, even on the quiet waters of the Mississippi, until you have driven all the human cattle into the river first. I'm an old boatman & I speak by the card.[4]

    Yours truly,

Hartford, Dec. 5.   SAML. L. CLEMENS.

[*enclosure:*][5]

> Twelve persons were saved in one boat and four in another; all the rest were of no account in the rescue of the drowning, burning people. If there had been skillful management by the ship's crew, there might have been little or no loss of life. But the boats were unskillfully handled and dangled in mid-air, pouring their passengers into the sea, or were shattered against the side of the ship. Five or six boats were not enough for a passenger steamship like the Missouri, and though it is true that a heavy sea was running at the time, it is a disgrace to science and civilization to say that it is impossible to lower safely a boat under such circumstances. Organization and discipline would have done wonders in this particular, even though the boats were insufficient. If there is no tackle or other machinery by which a boat can be got from a ship's deck to the sea alongside without wreck or swamping, in humanity's name let ingenuity and skill be brought to bear on that single point before we hear of any more inventions to increase speed or alleviate the mere discomforts of the sea-voyage.

[1]Clemens's letter was printed as part of a 7 December New York *Tribune* story, "The Missouri Disaster," under the subheading "Mark Twain on Launching Ships' Boats," with the *Tribune's* preface: "Mr. Mark Twain, in a private letter which we venture to publish below, incloses the following extract from a TRIBUNE editorial on the Missouri disaster, and adds the appended comment" (7 Dec 72, 5; for the enclosed "extract" see note 5). Whitelaw Reid had become managing editor of the newspaper, under Horace Greeley, in mid-1869, and Clemens had since maintained a friendly relationship with him, benefiting from his willingness to publish Clemens's letters to the editor on topical subjects of his

own choice. In addition, Reid had often made complimentary mention on the editorial page of Clemens, who undoubtedly found such endorsement from the country's most prestigious daily newspaper very gratifying. Since May 1872 Reid had acted as editor in chief of the newspaper, with John Hay as his second in command, freeing Greeley to pursue his campaign for the presidency. Defeated on 5 November, Greeley resumed the editorship, but fell ill almost immediately with inflammation of the brain and died on 29 November, precipitating a fight for control of the newspaper which Clemens would follow closely. Reid was the editorial heir apparent, but owned virtually no stock in the paper and lacked the financial means to buy enough of a share to secure his position. The crisis was not resolved until 23 December (see 10 Dec 72 to Nast, n. 4, and pp. 261–62; *L3*, 265 n. 1; *L4*, 227–29, 270–72, 288–93, 382–86, 417–18; Baehr, 105–16, 119–22; Vogelback 1954, 374–77; New York *Tribune:* "A Card," 15 May 72, 4; "Re-election of Grant," 6 Nov 72, 1; "A Card," 7 Nov 72, 4; "Mr. Greeley's Last Hours," 30 Nov 72, 1).

2On 22 October 1872 the steamer *Missouri*, traveling from New York to Havana, burned at sea during a gale. Only one of its lifeboats was successfully launched, and of the eighty-nine passengers and crew on board, only sixteen survived. In early December, a court of inquiry found that "the Missouri was not provided with a sufficient number of boats, and such boats as she had were so secured as to be found difficult to be lowered," and that "on the alarm of fire all was confusion; that there was no discipline, no organization, or combined effort to save life; that each man acted independently to save his own life, and that no attempt was made to save the life of the female passengers" (New York *Tribune:* "The Missouri Disaster," 5 Dec 72, 2; "Horrors of Travel," 31 Oct 72, 1; "The Burning of the Missouri," 1 Nov 72, 1; "A Voice from the Sea," 5 Dec 72, 4).

3Strictly speaking, the steamboat "stage" was a "hanging gangplank for reaching from boat to shore," not an independently maneuverable raft (Bates, 119). But seamen used "floating *stages*, and *stages* suspended by the side of a ship, for calking and repairing" (Whitney and Smith, 5:5887; Way, 267).

4To "express oneself with care and nicety" (*OED*, 2:888), as, for example, in *Hamlet:* "We must speak by the card, or equivocation will undo us" (act 5, scene 1).

5The actual enclosure, a clipping of part of an editorial in the *Tribune* of 5 December entitled "A Voice from the Sea" (4), has not survived. Its text is reproduced here in a line-for-line transcription. The *Tribune* reprinted the clipping, with only trivial differences, along with the present letter.

To the Editor of the Hartford *Evening Post*
5 December 1872 • Hartford, Conn.
(Hartford *Evening Post*, 6 Dec 72)

To The Editor of The Post:[1]—Mayor Hall appears to be coming to the surface as frequently & as persistently, now, as if he had never been in disgrace & glad to hide his despised head. The hardihood of this creature is beyond comprehension. Out of a jury of twelve men, seven are of the opinion that he is an oath-breaker & a thief; *all* men, in their secret hearts believe him to be an oath-breaker & a thief. And one thing is *certain*—a long black list of robberies which he could have prevented by withholding his signature he did not so prevent. If he knew these bills were frauds, he was a knave; if he failed to know it, he was a fool. I wonder which character he prefers?[2]

Very well. When a distinguished English historian is coming over to visit us, who is it that pushes himself forward to receive him publicly? Longfellow?—Bryant?—Holmes? No—this precious Mayor Hall.[3] When Stanley discovers Livingstone, England does him honor through some graceful personal attentions from the queen of the empire. When he arrives here do we vie with a foreign nation in appreciation of our citizen, & call upon the most exalted personage in the land to smoke a friendly cigar with him & say, "Well done, lad?" Oh, no—we take a pair of tongs & lead out our uncanny Mayor Hall & have *him* extend the people's welcome.[4] When the great editor dies & the nation mourns, do we select a gentleman to convey to the chief magistrate of the union the public desire that he shall honor himself & the dead with his presence at the funeral? Not at all. We permit our fragrant Mayor Hall, freely & un-snubbed, to crawl out of his sewer & insult the president of the United States, both in the language of the invitation & the source from whence it emanates.[5]

Just once, the people rose up & pushed this creature aside & saved us a national shame. Otherwise he would have stepped out from among the foul ring of New York thieves & offered the insult of his welcome to the son of an emperor who has always honored & befriended us. And it was fortunate for Mayor Hall that he was snubbed into inaction at that time; for the people were not in a patient mood, then, & if he had ventured to thrust himself & his speech upon the nation's imperial guest his face would have become a public spittoon in fifteen minutes by the watch.[6]

Is there no keeping this piece of animated putridity in the background? If the Second Advent shall transpire in our times, will he step forward, hat in hand, &——. But of course the man is equal to anything.

Yours truly,   M. T.

Hartford, Dec. 5.

[1]Clemens may have directed this semi-anonymous letter to the *Post* because Orion had recently obtained a position on the editorial staff (25 Sept 72 to OLC, n. 11). The editor in chief at this time was probably Henry Thompson Sperry (1837–1912), part owner of the newspaper and president of the Evening Post Association. Sperry was certainly the editor by July 1873, and had presumably held the post since July 1872, when Isaac Hill Bromley (1833–98) resigned. It is not known if Sperry and Clemens were personally acquainted (Trumbull, 1:611; Geer: 1872, 37, 124, 290; 1873, 127, 293; "Editorial Announcement," Hartford *Evening Post*, 16 July 72, 2).

[2]Abraham Oakey Hall (1826–98) overcame early poverty, earning the money for his education by writing for newspapers. He attended the University of the City of New York and Harvard law school, and received further training in law offices in New York and New Orleans. In 1851 he was admitted to the New York bar; that same year he was appointed assistant district attorney of New York County. He served as district attorney from 1855 to 1858 and again from 1862 to 1868, gaining a reputation as an energetic and effective prosecutor. In 1864 he became a member of New York's powerful Tammany Hall, and, through its influence and his association with William ("Boss") Tweed and the Tweed Ring, became mayor in 1868 and was easily reelected in 1870. Literate, social, and meticulous in dress, he was known as "Elegant Oakey." In July 1871 the New York *Times* began to escalate its campaign to expose Hall's corrupt administration, charging that the city's debt had ballooned while Hall rubber-stamped millions of dollars of fraudulent bills submitted by Tammany contractors. The *Times*'s daily attacks were reinforced by Thomas Nast's scathing cartoons in *Harper's Weekly*. A committee of outraged citizens demanded Hall's resignation in November 1871. An attempt to prosecute him ended in March 1872 in a mistrial, when one of the jurors died. His retrial in October 1872 resulted in another mistrial, with five jurors voting for acquittal and seven for conviction. Hall maintained his innocence throughout, claiming to have authorized payments without questioning their validity and without fraudulent intent. He was tried again on similar charges in December 1873 and was found innocent, but his political career was ended. Clemens had previously commented on the Tweed Ring's dep-

redations in a satirical article written for the New York *Tribune* in September 1871, "The Revised Catechism," in which "St. Hall's Garbled Reports" were cited as prized texts "for the training of the young" in the new municipal morality (SLC 1871h; see Vogelback 1955). He apparently soon concluded that Hall was more "fool" than "knave": in a burlesque of Tammany frauds in chapter 33 of *The Gilded Age*, he stated, "The controller and the board of audit passed the bills, and a mayor, who was simply ignorant but not criminal, signed them" (SLC 1873–74, 303; "The Committee of Seventy Demands Mayor Hall's Resignation," New York *Tribune*, 29 Nov 71, 1; New York *Herald:* "Second Trial of Mayor Hall," 24 Oct 72, 4; "Mayor Hall's Trial—The Lessons of the Past," 2 Nov 72, 7; "A. Oakey Hall Is Dead," New York *Times*, 8 Oct 98, 1; Paine 1904, 140–46, 166–76; Hershkowitz, 177–84, 209, 217, 222–23).

[3] James Anthony Froude (1818–94) arrived in the United States on 9 October 1872 on a lecture tour connected with the publication of the first volume of *The English in Ireland in the Eighteenth Century* (3 vols., 1872–74). The Lotos Club, whose members reputedly "watched the wharves for the arrival of distinguished strangers from Europe" (Elderkin, 13), honored him with a reception on 12 October. Mayor Hall, who served as president of the club from 1870 until May 1872 (when Whitelaw Reid succeeded him), was one of several speakers. He referred facetiously to the welcome accorded Froude by the city and suggested:

> If he will take a walk to-morrow perhaps we will get him up a few first-class street brawls. I have the authority of THE TRIBUNE for saying that street brawls on Sunday are very common. [Laughter.] I may say in passing, and I believe it to be so, TRIBUNE or no, that there is no such thing as murder in this city. We have street brawls and homicides and misadventures, but old-fashioned grudge murder we hand over to London and Boston. ("James Anthony Froude. Reception by the Lotos Club," New York *Tribune*, 14 Oct 72, 5)

Members and guests at the reception included John Bigelow (1817–1911), former U.S. minister to France; Samuel J. Tilden (1814–86), chairman of the New York State Democratic Committee; David G. Croly of the New York *World;* William C. Church of the *Galaxy;* Edward Eggleston; Bret Harte; John Hay; Josiah Holland; Joaquin Miller; and Edmund Yates. On 29 October the New York *Times* referred to the occasion:

> The manager of the *Tribune* [Whitelaw Reid] and Mayor Hall were the principal "speakers" at a thing called a "reception," recently foisted upon Mr. Froude at an obscure "club" in this City. Hall and Greeley's representative are samples of Reformers on the Greeley-Fenton pattern. Probably Mr. Froude never found himself in such company before, but he is expert at whitewashing, and he will have plenty of room for his skill in the objects which he met at the "club" alluded to. ("'Reform,'" 1)

Reuben E. Fenton (1819–85), U.S. senator from New York, was one of the leaders of the anti-Grant faction. The *Times's* allusion to Froude's skill at "whitewashing" probably referred to his appreciative portrait of Henry VIII in the *History of England from the Fall of Wolsey to the Death of Elizabeth* (12 vols., 1856–70), and to the opinions he expressed in his most recent work, which were seen as an attempt to vindicate England's policies toward Ireland (Dunn, 2:266–70, 370–87; New York *Tribune:* "New-York City," 10 Oct 72, 8; Elderkin, 11–12, 18–20; Cortissoz, 1:235–36; Paine 1904, 208; see also 1 Feb 73 to Reid, n. 2).

[4] Henry M. Stanley arrived in New York from Europe on 20 November. The next day Mayor Hall addressed a message to the city council, asking it to pass "joint resolutions of welcome" and recommending that an "opportunity upon some appointed day be afforded to our citizens of giving, under civic auspices, a popular welcome to Mr. Stanley in the City Hall" ("Honors to Mr. Stanley," New York *Tribune*, 25 Nov 72, 2). The publication of Hall's message, before the council had considered it, occasioned "severe comment": "The matter was characterized as a misdemeanor and an infringement upon the dignity of the legislative branch of the City Government" ("Municipal Matters," New York *Tribune*, 27 Nov 72, 2). On 22 November the Lotos Club gave Stanley a reception, at which Mayor Hall was one of the speakers (New York *Tribune:* "Arrival of Mr. Stanley," 21 Nov 72, 5; "Stanley Welcomed," 23 Nov 72, 5; for Queen Victoria's reception of Stanley, see 25 Oct 72 to OLC, n. 4; see also 30 Nov 72 to Redpath, n. 6).

[5] On 1 December, two days after Horace Greeley's death, Mayor Hall sent a telegram to George Maxwell Robeson, secretary of the navy:

> Having the honor of your personal acquaintance, I telegraph you to say that the civic authorities will join the private societies and citizens in a public funeral on Wednesday, from the City Hall, to the late Mr. Greeley, and the idea is universal that should the President attend, and the authorities hereby respectfully invite him, his attendance would popularly be regarded the most magnanimous, graceful, and faction-assuaging event of the country.

Robeson replied the next day that President Grant had decided to attend the funeral even before receiving Hall's telegram ("The President to Attend the Funeral," New York *Tribune*, 3 Dec 72, 1).

[6] Grand Duke Alexis Aleksandrovich (1850–1908), the third son of Tsar Aleksandr II, sailed into New York harbor with a fleet of Russian ships on 19 November 1871, on the first leg of an extensive tour of the United States. In April, as soon as unofficial reports of the upcoming visit appeared in the press, a committee of prominent citizens had begun preparations for an elaborate reception. Mayor Hall was not on the committee, nor did his name appear on the list of those attending the climactic event of the prince's stay, a banquet and ball at the Academy of Music on 29 November ("The Grand Duke's Arrival," New York *Tribune*, 20 Nov 71, 1; New York *Times:* "An Imperial Visitor," 21 Apr 71, 1; "The Coming Reception of the Grand Duke Alexis," 27 Apr 71, 2; "The Russian Grand Duke," 18 Oct 71, 2; "The Prince's Ball," 30 Nov 71, 1).

To Albert W. Whelpley
5 December 1872 • Hartford, Conn.
(MS: OCHP)

(SLC)

Hartford Dec. 5/72

Dr Sir:[1]

Dan Slote tells me to drop you this line & sign my name to it, & you will understand it—a thing which I do with great pleasure.

Ys Truly

Saml. L. Clemens

Mark Twain.

Ѧ To A. W Whelpley Esq

✉——————————————————————————

Albert W Whelpley Esq | Care Robt. Clarke & Co | Cincinnati | Ohio [*on flap:*] (SLC) [*postmarked:*] HARTFORD DEC 5 ◊◊◊

[1]Whelpley (1831–1900) was born in New York City, but moved to Cincinnati in the 1850s. He was associated with the publishing house of Robert Clarke Company, primarily as a salesman, until 1886, when he became the librarian of the Cincinnati Public Library. Upon his death he left a large collection of letters, poems, and other material by well-known nineteenth-century political and literary figures. Many of the letters, such as this one, were addressed personally to him (Greve, 2:440–41; Cincinnati Public Library, 87).

To Thomas Nast
10 December 1872 • Hartford, Conn.
(MS: NjP)

Hartford, Dec. 10

My Dear Nast—

As the best way of coming at it, I enclose my "mother Fairbanks's" letter[1]—the last page of it refers to you. We think the whole world of Mrs. Fairbanks (wife of proprietor of Cleveland Herald)—she was a pilgrim with me in the Innocents Abroad. H~~r~~ Her son Charley I have written you about, before, & you sent him an autograph from your pencil which set him up wonderfully. Now *I* think it a glorious thing to be a boy's idol, for it is the only worship one can *swear* to, as genuine—& I have no doubt you feel a good deal as I do about it. Therefore I send Charley Fairbanks to you without distrust or fear[2]—satisfied that the few minutes he robs you of will be an inspiration to him & will be transmitted in the works of his hands to the next generation—& just as well satisfied that you will place that loss, with little regret, along with many another like it, labeled, "Bread cast upon the Waters."[3]

Nast you, more than any other man, have won a prodigious victory for Grant—I mean, rather, for Civilization & progress;—those pictures were simply marvels; & if any man in the land has a right to hold his head ~~&~~ up & be honestly proud of his share in this year's vast events that man is unquestionably yourself. We all do sincerely honor you & are proud of you.[4]

Ys Ever
Mark Twain.

[1]Not extant.

[2]After learning from Mary Mason Fairbanks in March that her son was an "ardent admirer" of Nast's, Clemens had evidently written to Nast on his behalf (2? Mar 72 to Fairbanks, nn. 2, 3). Nast again replied graciously to this second plea (17 Dec 72 to Nast, n. 1).

[3]Ecclesiastes 11:1.

[4]In May 1872 Horace Greeley was nominated to run for president on the Liberal Republican ticket against Republican incumbent Ulysses S. Grant; in July he was endorsed by the Democratic party, whose policies he had long de-

nounced. Nast took every opportunity to satirize Greeley's personal eccentricity and political waywardness in his *Harper's Weekly* cartoons, waging a "Campaign of Caricature" that was largely instrumental in securing Grant a second term in the 5 November election (Paine 1904, 220, 227–29, 235–39, 241–42, 246–64). Although Clemens's remarks here clearly show his support of the Republican party and Grant, he avoided expressing his views in print during the campaign. He did, however, publish an anonymous humorous sketch in the Hartford *Courant* of 20 July—"The Secret of Dr. Livingstone's Continued Voluntary Exile"—which concluded with a jibe at Greeley's turncoat politics. In the sketch, the newly discovered Livingstone is given a summary of the news of the preceding five years, and decides to remain in Africa upon learning, to his disgust, that "Greeley is the democratic candidate for President of the United States, and all rebeldom hurrahs for him" (SLC 1872*l*). Charles Dudley Warner gleefully accepted Clemens's contribution, writing him on 19 July: "Thank you for that jolly drive on Horace. It's first chop and will be printed tomorrow" (CU-MARK).

To Mary Hunter Smith
10 December 1872 • Hartford, Conn.
(MS: Karanovich)

(SLC)

Hartford Dec. 10.

My Dear Friend—[1]

Your letter of Nov. 6[2] has this day reached me, by the way of London. I left there ~~4~~ only a day or two after you wrote it, so I met it somewhere in mid-ocean.

I am sorry it failed to come to hand while I was on the other side; I would have brought the package with pleasure. However, unless you ~~are~~ want it right away I can bring it yet, because I am going back there in May. If you were an Englishman that would be time enough, but Americans are not quite so patient.

Sincerely Yrs
Sam*ˡ*. L. Clemens.

✉

Mrs. Mary Hunter Smith, | 1215 Chesnut street | St Louis | Mo. [*postmarked:*] HARTFORD CONN. DEC 11 ◇◇◇

¹Mary Berkeley Hunter Smith (b. 1830?) could claim cousinship to Clemens: her younger sister, Ella Hunter, was married to James Andrew Hays Lampton, half-brother of Jane Lampton Clemens. Smith was married to Arden Richard Smith (b. 1825?), an Englishman who settled in St. Louis about 1849 and became an editor on the St. Louis *Missouri Republican*. By 1869 he was listed in the St. Louis directory as a principal in the firm of Scott and Smith, auctioneers. The Smiths' son, who took the name Edwin Hunter Pendleton Arden (1864–1918), became a prominent actor and playwright. The St. Louis address on the envelope accompanying this letter—1215 Chesnut Street—was near the residence of the Moffett-Clemens household in the late 1860s, at 1312 Chesnut Street. In 1886, in writing to Clemens, Arden Smith would refer to their "old Missouri acquaintance and the family friendship" (Smith to SLC, 2 Dec 86, CU-MARK; *St. Louis Census*, 291; *L1*, 15 n. 7, 19 n. 3; *Inds*, 330; Edwards, 705, 723).

²Not extant.

To Thomas Nast
17 December 1872 • Hartford, Conn.
(MS: Thompson)

(SLC)

Hartford, Dec. 17.

My Dear Nast—

I thank you heartily for your kindness to me & to my friend Charley.¹

The Almanac has come,² & I have enjoyed those pictures with ɰ all my soul & body. Perkins's plagiarism of Doestick's celebrated Niagara drunk is tolerable—that is, for a man to write whose proper place is in an asylum for idiots. Pity that I should say it who am his personal acquaintance.³

ᵡYour "Mexico" is a fifty-years' history of that retrograding chaos of a country portrayed upon the ɸ space of one's thumb-nail, so to speak; & that sphynx in "Egypt" charms me—I wish I could draw that old head in that way.⁴

I wish you *could* go to England with us in May. Surely you could never regret it. I do hope my publishers can make it pay you to illustrate my English book. Then I should have good pictures. They've got to improve on "Roughing It."[5]

Ys Ever

Sam* l*. L. Clemens.

[1]Nast had written from Morristown, New Jersey, on 15 December (CU-MARK):

My dear Mark

I shall be glad to see my young "adorer," but I am not to be found in New-York usually, I only go in once a week, to see to things, and do all my work at home. My day in, is usually Friday, but I would recommend inquiry at "Harper's" first, as to my whereabouts, as it happens, that I am sometimes summoned in hot haste by telegram. Poor deluded boy! he needs but to behold, to be completely cured of his infatuation. But send him along. There are trains in and out, quite frequently, and I shall receive your young friend as a friend of mine.

If you can ever spare the time, I should like to see you out here very much. It is nearly thirty miles from New-York, and the air is really very fine. I moved here on account of health. I have had catarrh for three years, and this air is highly recommended for such complaints. But I am afraid I dont give myself half a chance to get well again, as I keep at work so constantly. . . .

I hope to see a book from you, before long, of your English travels. How much I should like to go with you and illustrate it. I think we would have fun, and I might forget to have the catarrh and the blues for awhile. The recollections of my European trip eleven years ago, give me great pleasure still. Thanking you, for your eulogistic remarks about my work, I remain

Yours truly

Th: Nast.

Despite seventeen-year-old Charles Fairbanks's early ambitions of becoming an artist, after finishing his schooling he began a career in journalism on his father's Cleveland *Herald*. His introduction to Nast nevertheless developed into a lifelong friendship. He became to some extent Nast's protégé, lived with him for a time, collaborated with him in 1892–93 on the short-lived *Nast's Weekly* (Fairbanks supplying the text, Nast the pictures), and named his second son, born in 1879, after him (Paine 1904, 263, 510, 539–40; "Charles M. Fairbanks, Newspaper Man, Dies," New York *Times*, 30 May 1924, 15; Fairbanks, 755).

[2]*Th. Nast's Illustrated Almanac for 1873*—the second in Nast's series of almanacs for Harper and Brothers—reprinted Mark Twain's "Story of the Good Little Boy Who Did Not Prosper," first published in the *Galaxy* in May 1870. Nast had considered including it in his previous almanac (*L4*, 373–74 n. 2; Nast 1871; Nast 1872, 22–28; SLC 1870h).

[3]Nast reprinted a sketch by Eli Perkins (Melville De Lancey Landon, 1839–1910) entitled "New-Year's Calls," in which the author, during a series of social calls, becomes progressively tipsier, signified by his comically disordered syntax. The sketch reminded Clemens of a widely reprinted comic letter by Mortimer Neal Thomson, "Doesticks on a Bender," about a visit to Niagara Falls, which first appeared in 1854 and introduced Q. K. Philander Doesticks to the public. Clemens had known Thomson since 1867. His acquaintance with Landon is undocumented, but he expressed his opinion of Landon's work in the margins of a

copy of *Saratoga in 1901*, published by Sheldon and Company in August 1872. He labeled the book "The Droolings of an Idiot," noted insipid or stolen jokes, and railed at the author as "this foetus," "this humbug, this sham," and "this cur" (Landon, 99, 104, 129†; Nast 1872, 17–21; Thomson, 26–32; *L4*, 216 n. 1; *Publishers' and Stationers' Weekly Trade Circular* 2 [22 Aug 72]: 168, 178; Gribben, 1:394–95).

⁴For each month of the almanac, Nast provided a humorous drawing depicting a different country or continent, integrated with the appropriate astrological sign. "Mexico," picturing a native sitting backward on a crab (Cancer), was the headpiece for June; the Sphinx, representing "Africa," and a scorpion (Scorpio) figured in the headpiece for October (Nast 1872, 10, 14). The drawings are reproduced below.

⁵Nast traveled to Europe in March 1873, but returned in June without, apparently, having seen Clemens abroad. Clemens soon proposed to Bliss that Nast illustrate his next book, *The Gilded Age* (Paine 1904, 274–76; 4 Mar 73 to Bliss; for the English book see 30 Dec 73 to Fitzgibbon, n. 2).

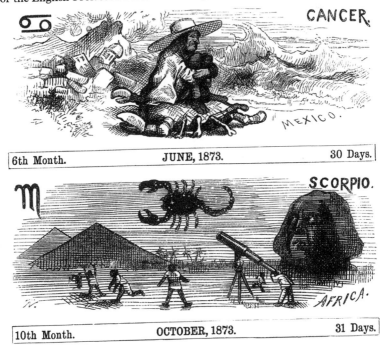

Calendar illustrations from *Th. Nast's Illustrated Almanac for 1873*. See note 4.

From Olivia L. and Samuel L. Clemens
to Jane Lampton Clemens and Family
20 December 1872 • Hartford, Conn.
(MS: NPV)

ₐP. S. I put in the clothes to fill up thinking you might use them for Sammy.

Livy.ₐ

Hartford Dec. 20ᵗʰ 1872

Dear Ma, Pamela, Annie & Sammie

A Merry Christmas and a very Happy New Year to you all— We send you our Christmas box of remembrance— I hope that Sammy's Engine will reach Fredonia [by] Christmas so that he can add that to his other things— The slippers are for him from Aunt Mollie she worked them—

Annie the little Ermine tippet your Uncle Sam bought in England, also the little silver flower for the hair— We did so want to get you aﬀ muff to go with the tippet, but we could hardly afford it this year, however we shall remember that you need one—

The gold chain as you will see by the mark ₐon the boxₐ was purchased in England—

Sammy's chain will serve as a guard for his watch but it is not intrinsically valuable being only a composition— Ma the laces are for you as you will know, and Pamela the spoons for you— The handkerchiefs for Annie—

We took dinner last night with Orion and Mollie and had an exceedingly pleasant time, they are very cozily situated— Yesterday was the Aniversary of their wedding—¹

We are so glad the that Ma and Annie are coming, we want the other two, after their visit is made—² I must leave a little room for Mr Clemens

With love affectionately yours

Livy Clemens

Your eldest son & daughter are exceedingly cosily situated, & ∅Qₐrion is as happy as a martyr when the fire won't burn.

Wish you all a merry Christmas & many happy returns. I have been aggravating the baby by showing her another baby in a hand-glass whom she can't find behind it. Goodbye. Am justing off to the station after Sue.[3]

Ys

Sam

[1] Orion and Mollie Clemens had been married for eighteen years.

[2] This visit was delayed until late January (see 22 Jan 73 to PAM). Twenty-year-old Annie Moffett spent the holiday in Quincy, Illinois, at the home of her aunt and uncle, Sally and Erasmus M. Moffett (Annie Moffett to PAM, 25 Dec 72, CU-MARK; *MTBus*, 19, 26). The "other two" were Pamela and Samuel Moffett.

[3] Susan Crane.

To Joseph H. Twichell
20–22 December 1872 • Hartford, Conn.
(MS: CtY-BR)

Ɫ P. S. Enclosed⎫
is the money. ⎭

To-day, PM.

Dear Twichell—

I wrote a note to Dr Bushnell & abused you like a pickpocket—Oh I did give it to you![1]

Now ȼ you go straight off & get that book & take it to him this and try to make your peace & get yourself forgiven.[2] And tell him we Clemenses thank ₌him₌ just as sincerely & as cordially as we can for letting us down so gently & so kindly. And you must say that although mother has returned to Elmira,[3] *we* are still here & shall be very glad indeed to try to make the new acquaintanceship as pleasant as if it bore the generous flavor of age.

Now you go & make *another* lot of blunders, you splendid old muggins!

Come around, you & Harmony, & I will read to you my (bogus) *protest of the Publishers against the proposed foreign copyright.*[4]

Yrs Ever

Mark.

Good ∅ news—Susie Crane is here! Come & see her—help us worship her.

[*cross-written:*]
Return the Doctor's letter to me.
[*enclosure:*]

Hartford Dec 20 1872

S. L. Clemens Esq
   Dear Sir
      You blame yourself over much. I am the one who is principally in fault—neither you nor Twichell. I had no right to be joking my poverty so hard as to make it appear that I cannot buy a five dollar book. I can if I do not buy too many. My joke was in my customary vein. When I have nothing better to say I talk of my poverty—which bears it excellently well

      Now I see no way to make the matter easy, since you take it so much to heart,, but to ask that you will let T. give me the book. Only he must not do it "by post"; for I want the chance to wreak my —— thanks on him for his services.

      Meantime, if another storm in my eyes does not prevent, I and my wife will be able to make our long projected call on Mrs Langdon, as the valued friend of my valued friend T. K. Beecher, and suffer no awkward feeling on account of the present. We shall ¢ also be allowed to claim the very pleasant new acquaintance of Mrs & Mrs Clemens, doing it the more freely for our deed of charity in accepting the book

Most resignedly Yours
Horace Bushnell

Put my signature to the petition a long way down and let the literary gentle[m]en have their lead—this of course.[5]

---

[1]Clemens's "note" has not been found. Horace Bushnell (1802–76) was the minister of Hartford's North Church of Christ (later Park Congregational Church) from 1833 to 1859. He was also the author of a number of controversial but influential theological works and volumes of sermons, many written in his retirement, notably *Christian Nurture* (1861), which urged the religious training of children, and *The Vicarious Sacrifice* (1866), which formulated his theory of the "moral influence" of Christ's Atonement. Bushnell was both friend and mentor to Twichell: it was Bushnell who in 1865 recommended Twichell for the pastorate at the newly formed Asylum Hill Congregational Church, and whose unconventional theological views—with their rejection of strict Calvinism and emphasis on perceiving spirituality in man and in nature—Twichell soon embraced (Trumbull, 1:389–90; Strong, 47, 57–59; Andrews, 25–30).

[2]Twichell had somehow confounded Clemens's attempt to give a book to

Bushnell (see the enclosure with this letter). Clemens here rectified the situation by enclosing the money for Twichell to purchase the book. The present letter has been assigned a date of 20 December or shortly thereafter, since Clemens probably wrote to Twichell soon after receiving Bushnell's letter.

³On 29 November (26 Nov 72 to JLC and PAM).

⁴Only a fragment of Clemens's "(bogus) *protest*" has survived, in a manuscript of just over five pages, written on the blue-lined wove paper (bearing an "E. H. MFG. CO." embossment) which Clemens used from December 1872 to May 1873. Clemens had the publishers address Congress as follows:

> 1. Ever since literature was invented, publishers have thriven at the expense of authors, & all righteous governments have protected them in it. Would you break down this ancient & honorable precedent? Would you strike at the root of freedom? Would you undermine the Constitution?
>
> 2. While a publisher can publish only 100 books a year & clear $50,000, almost any author is able to write one book in two years & clear $700 on it. What more can they want? Have these men no bowels? Would you—*can* you—abet them in a pernicious lust for money which moves them to aspire in their grasping desires to the selling of their labors to *two* hemispheres? God forbid! . . .
>
> 5. If we stole from the shoemakers, the blacksmiths, the distillers of Europe, you might stay our thieving hands with justice—but reflect, good Congressmen, we only steal from authors. We do not steal bread or clothes or whisky, we only steal brains. We do not steal anything that a man can carry in his pocket, we only steal the hard-earned results of years of study, & travel, expenditure of money & unceasing labor of hand & brain. (SLC 1872x, 2–3, 6–7†)

Clemens was apparently reacting to recent efforts to pass a more comprehensive copyright law. On 11 December 1871, a bill "for securing to authors in certain cases the benefit of international copyright, advancing the development of American literature, and promoting the interests of publishers and book-buyers in the United States" had been introduced in the House by Samuel S. Cox, representative from New York (*Congressional Globe* 1872, 2:29). It was referred to the House Library Committee, which solicited the views of prominent American publishers. Despite significant disagreement among themselves, the publishers were able to draft a document recommending that foreign authors be allowed to obtain copyright "upon the same terms and conditions as are now required of an American author" ("The International Copyright Movement—Meeting of Publishers—Appointment of a Committee to Go to Washington," New York *Times*, 7 Feb 72, 8). The copyright bill languished in committee throughout 1872, however, and was finally reported adversely in February 1873: "In the opinion of the committee such legislation was inexpedient. . . . The committee was discharged from further consideration of the subject" (*Congressional Globe* 1873, 2:1164).

⁵In September 1875, having been urged by Howells to express his views on the copyright issue, Clemens asserted that he had lost the "old petition, (which was brief)," and added, "The only man who ever signed my petition with alacrity, & said that the fact that a thing was *right* was all-sufficient, was Rev. Dᴿ˙ Bushnell" (18 Sept 75 to Howells, NN-B, in *MTHL*, 1:100; Howells to SLC, 11 Sept 75, *MTHL*, 1:98). The copyright petition that Bushnell signed was clearly not the "bogus" one mentioned above, but a real petition intended to influence the legislative debate (see the previous note). The real petition was probably not

entirely "lost": an eight-page manuscript, "Petition. (Concerning Copyright.),"
which survives in the Mark Twain Papers, is probably the draft of the document
Bushnell signed. It has been published (with a supplied date of 1875) in Appendix N of *Mark Twain: A Biography* (SLC 1872y).

🌿

No LETTERS written between 22 December 1872 and 3 January 1873
have been found, but Clemens seems to have remained in Hartford
throughout the period. Following his return from England on 25 November, he had begun to draft chapters for his English book, a project
that doubtless claimed some of his time in late 1872 and early 1873. By
10 February he had prepared a substantial amount of material—or so he
claimed to a New York correspondent of the Chicago *Tribune* (not further
identified):

> Clemens is now occupied with his fourth book, "John Bull," of which he
> has written nearly one-third. Those who have seen the MS. say it will be in-
> describably funny. He looks at the native Britons at such a variety of angles,
> and detects them in so many grotesque positions, that they ought to be able
> to laugh at themselves as presented by "Twain." (Colstoun 1873a)

"John Bull" (or "Upon the Oddities and Eccentricities of the English,"
as John Camden Hotten referred to it in March) was never completed,
and the "nearly one-third" of the whole does not survive as a coherent
manuscript (Hotten 1873, xxxvii). In fact, when all the surviving materials that may have been part of the manuscript are combined, they still
do not constitute a third of a typical six-hundred-page subscription
book. Only two chapters that Clemens is likely to have written before
his return trip to England in May 1873 have been identified. The first,
"A Memorable Midnight Experience," was published in *Mark Twain's
Sketches. Number One*, identified as "From the Author's Unpublished
English Notes" (SLC 1874c, 3–8; see Appendix C). The second, "Some
Recollections of a Storm at Sea," is a fictionalized account of the rescue
effected during Clemens's Atlantic crossing on the *Batavia* in November
1872. Clemens sent Mary Mason Fairbanks the manuscript in January
1876, to assist in one of her charitable projects, and evidently identified
it as "Being an Extract from Chapter III, of a Book Begun Three Years
Ago, But Afterwards Abandoned"—the description she used when
printing it in "The Bazaar Record," a pamphlet advertising her chari-

table event (Storkan, 1; SLC 1876). (Two additional pieces, "Rogers" and "Property in Opulent London," could also have been written at this time: see 30 Dec 73 to Fitzgibbon, n. 2.)

By the end of 1872 Clemens had already become interested in a new project, to be written in collaboration with Charles Dudley Warner: a satirical novel about the corrupt state of American politics, published at the end of 1873 as *The Gilded Age*. All accounts agree that the authors conceived of the project soon after Clemens's return from England. By late December or early January Clemens had begun writing the opening chapters, as Albert Bigelow Paine explained in his version of how the project was conceived:

> At the dinner-table one night, with the Warners present, criticisms of re-cent novels were offered, with the usual freedom and severity of dinner-table talk. The husbands were inclined to treat rather lightly the novels in which their wives were finding entertainment. The wives naturally retorted that the proper thing for the husbands to do was to furnish the American people with better ones. This was regarded in the nature of a challenge, and as such was accepted—mutually accepted: that is to say, in partnership. On the spur of the moment Clemens and Warner agreed that they would do a novel together, that they would begin it immediately. This is the whole story of the book's origin; so far, at least, as the collaboration is concerned. Clemens, in fact, had the beginning of a story in his mind, but had been unwilling to undertake an extended work of fiction alone. He welcomed only too eagerly, therefore, the proposition of joint authorship. His purpose was to write a tale around that lovable character of his youth, his mother's cousin, James Lampton—to let that gentle visionary stand as the central figure against a proper background. The idea appealed to Warner, and there was no delay in the beginning. Clem-ens immediately set to work and completed 399 pages of the manuscript, the first eleven chapters of the book, before the early flush of enthusiasm waned. (*MTB*, 1:476–77)

Paine's account, which is doubtless substantially correct, differs in only its details from the much earlier recollection of Stephen A. Hub-bard (d. 1890), a colleague of Warner's on the Hartford *Courant* (*L3*, 97 n. 5), whose version of the story must have come from Warner himself:

> It happened that one evening, when the Twains had the Warners at a family dinner, something was said about the success of "Innocents Abroad." There-upon both Mrs. Clemens and Mrs. Warner began to twit Mark Twain; they made all manner of good-natured fun of his book, called it an accidental hit, and finally ended up by defying him to write another work like it. . . .
>
> In high good humor Mark Twain turned to Mr. Warner. "You and I will show these ladies that their laughter is unseemly and a 'cracking of thorns

under a pot,'" he cried. "We'll get together and write a story, chapter by chapter every morning, and we will so interweave our work that these wives of ours will not be able to say which part has been written by Mark Twain and which by Charles D. Warner; for once a week we will gather in my library and read the story to them as it has progressed under our pens."

What was spoken in jest was acted upon in the spirit of jest, Mr. Warner agreeing to meet Mark Twain every morning for an hour or two, so that together they could write a story somewhat on the lines of "Innocents Abroad." After they had been at work on their little joke for a little while, they became thoroughly interested in it, and then, when Mark Twain proposed to introduce the character of Col. Sellers in the story, both he and Mr. Warner grew actually enthusiastic over it, and their wives confessed their deep interest in it as it was read to them as the writing progressed.

So the jest was carried on until the story was about half finished, if I remember correctly, when it suddenly occurred to Mark Twain that it might be worth publishing; if it interested the wives of the authors, it ought to interest the public. Therefore, Twain approached his publishers and told them that he and Mr. Warner were jointly writing a book, and he wondered whether he could make arrangements with them to publish it. They jumped at the proposition. (E. J. Edwards)

A similar account, possibly also by Hubbard, was reported in December 1876 by the Hartford correspondent of the New York *Graphic* ("Eminent Authors at Home," 23 Dec 76, 377, clipping in Scrapbook 8:5, CU-MARK).

Charles Warren Stoddard recalled a slight variant of this story, apparently as told by Clemens in London in late 1873:

Mark and Charles Dudley Warner were walking to church one Sunday in Hartford. Said Warner: "Let us write a novel!" Mark wondered what in the world there was to write a novel about, but promised to think the matter over, and proceeded to do so. On the way home it was decided that Mark should begin and write till he got tired, and that there should be a gathering of the wives and Joe Twichell—the clerical chum—for the reading of the same. He wrote a dozen chapters and read them to the domestic critics.

"Do you catch the idea?" said Mark to Warner. The latter thought he did, and took up the thread of the narrative where Mark dropped it, and spun on until he felt fagged. (Stoddard 1903, 70–71)

None of the three accounts mentions the novel's satirical theme, which may have occurred to Clemens as early as July 1870, when he dined in Washington with Senator Samuel Clarke Pomeroy of Kansas (among others) and afterward told Olivia, "I have gathered material enough for a whole book!" (*L4*, 167, 168 n. 4). And Washington politics could also have been the subject of a project he discussed with David Gray before deciding in April 1871 that Joseph T. Goodman was the right collaborator to "do the accurate drudgery and some little other writing"—a book he was certain would be "an *awful* success" (*L4*, 386). In any event, once Clemens began to draft the early chapters he seems to have warmed to his theme, inspired by political events reported in late 1872 and early 1873, like the Tweed Ring inquiries, the investigation for bribery of Senator Pomeroy, and the Crédit Mobilier scandal (*Annual Cyclopaedia 1873*, 394–96; French, 87–95; 7 Mar 73 to the staff of the New York *Tribune;* for further discussion of the genesis and composition of *The Gilded Age*, see French, 25–37, and Hill 1964, 72–75; see also 17? Apr 73 to Reid, n. 1).

In early January Clemens may also have worked on the manuscript of *The Adventures of Tom Sawyer*, a story he had begun to write at Fenwick Hall the previous summer (see p. 114). On page 23 of that manuscript (the first page of chapter 2), he inserted in the top margin, in part: "Never forget the splendid jewelry that illuminated the trees on the morning of Jan. 9, '73. ~~Brigh~~ Brilliant sun & gentle, swaying wind—deep, crusted snow on ground—all the forest gorgeous with gems" (SLC 1982).

The work that Clemens published at this time was closely linked to events at the New York *Tribune*. The unexpected death of Horace Greeley on 29 November 1872 had cast the newspaper into turmoil (5 Dec 72 to Reid, n. 1). Whitelaw Reid remained the acting editor in chief, but a faction of powerful stockholders—headed by William Orton of the Western Union Company, who had purchased the majority shares in the *Tribune* from its publisher, Samuel Sinclair—planned to offer the post to Schuyler Colfax, vice-president during Grant's first term (but not renominated with Grant) and therefore a political enemy of Greeley's. On 16 December Reid resigned, when his defeat seemed inevitable, inspiring many of his *Tribune* colleagues—including John Hay—to resign with him. Then Colfax, whose reputation had already been tainted by the Crédit Mobilier scandal, unexpectedly declined (or was forced to decline) the editorship. In a surprising turn of events, Reid was able to purchase Orton's controlling interest with money borrowed from wealthy investors, chief among them Jay Gould. On 23 December, in an unsigned editorial, Reid in effect declared himself in charge of the *Tribune*—as both editor and proprietor—and announced his intention to make the newspaper "what Horace Greeley would have made it if God had spared him,—a frank and fearless newspaper, . . . detesting neutrality in politics as the refuge of the weak-minded and the timid, but keeping its independence as the best title to honor and usefulness" ("The Tribune," New York *Tribune,* 23 Dec 72, 4). On that same day Clemens wrote a satirical poem for the Hartford *Evening Post,* entitled "The New Cock-Robin" (SLC 1872y), in mocking imitation of the nursery rhyme "Who Killed Cock Robin?" In reply to the repeated question *"Who's to be Editor of the Tribune?"* Clemens proposed a different candidate in each verse. The third verse read:

> *I,* says Whitelaw Reid!
> On great Pegasus, my steed,
> I charged the felon Tweed!
> Of all his filthy breed,
> That with a ghoul-like greed
> On our credit's corpse did feed,
> The metropolis I freed.
> Of Reform I took the lead—
> To the West, with ardent speed
> Bent my way. And in the hour of need,
> In Cincinnati sowed the seed
> Of a movement that decreed
> Corruption's death. Alas! the reed—
> Oh, weaker still!—the *weed*—
> We leaned on, broke—indeed
> The time was past, I rede,
> For "Liberal" virtue to succeed.
> Now I promise naught. I'm key'd
> Up to honor's pitch. I'll bleed
> Before I'll ever draw a bead
> In monopoly's defence. Give heed
> To my words. On which basis Whitelaw Reid
>   Is content to be that Editor.

(Chicago *Tribune:* "The New York Tribune," 17 Dec 72, 8, and 20 Dec 72, 8; "The Tribune Transformation," Elmira *Advertiser,* 20 Dec 72, 2, reprinting the New York *World* of 18 Dec 72; Buffalo *Courier:* "The New York Tribune Again," 25 Dec 72, 1, reprinting the New York *Evening Post* of 23 Dec 72; "The Tribune Ownership," 28 Dec 72, 4; Vogelback 1954, 375–83; Baehr, 116–23; Bingham Duncan, 47–48.)

Reid immediately set to work to reestablish the *Tribune's* reputation and finances. On 26 December he asked Charles Dudley Warner to "write me something . . . in your peculiar vein." Two days later he made a similar request of Bret Harte (Whitelaw Reid Papers, DLC). On 28 December Reid also wrote to Clemens (CU-MARK):

Private

My Dear Twain:

    I want very much to have *The Tribune* recognised at once as the medium of communication with the public to which men of note in letters or politics naturally resort. Why wont you write me something, no matter what, over your own signature within the next week? Say your say on any topic on which you want to say it. I cannot pay you the prices which those subscription publishers pay, but I can pay enough to make it worth your while, and you will value a great deal more than the money the fact that you are doing a kindness to

Faithfully Yours,
Whitelaw Reid

Clemens responded on 3 January, first with a telegram at 11:06 A.M., and again later in the day with a letter enclosing the requested article.

❦

To Whitelaw Reid
per Telegraph Operator
3 January 1873 • (1st of 2) • Hartford, Conn.
(MS, copy received: DLC)

BLANK NO. I.

292

THE WESTERN UNION TELEGRAPH COMPANY.

NO. 23   THE RULES OF THIS COMPANY REQUIRE THAT ALL MESSAGES   1106
RECEIVED FOR TRANSMISSION SHALL BE WRITTEN ON THE MESSAGE BLANKS OF THE COMPANY, UNDER AND SUBJECT TO THE CONDITIONS PRINTED THEREON, WHICH CONDITIONS HAVE BEEN AGREED TO BY THE SENDER OF THE FOLLOWING MESSAGE.

G. H. MUMFORD, SEC.[1] T. T. ECKERT, GEN. SUPT., NEW YORK. WILLIAM ORTON, PREST.

DATED,   Hartford Ct   3 REC'D AT 145 BROADWAY,

TO   Whitelaw Reid   Jany 3 1873.

    Ed Tribune

Will write the article today.

    Mark Twain

  4 5. Paid

  OK

[1] George Hart Mumford (1840–75) graduated from Harvard University; he was admitted to the bar in 1864. Since 1865 he had worked for the Western Union Telegraph Company, spending several years in charge of its business on the Pacific Coast. In 1872 he succeeded his uncle, Oliver H. Palmer, as secretary of the company, becoming vice-president shortly thereafter ("Obituary," New York *Times*, 27 July 75, 4; James D. Reid, 503–4, 506).

To Whitelaw Reid
3 January 1873 • (2nd of 2) • Hartford, Conn.
(MS: DLC)

My Dear Reid—

The Lord knows I grieved to see the old Tribune wavering & ready to tumble into the common slough of journalism, & God knows I am truly glad you saved it. I hope you will stand at its helm a hundred years.

To speak truly, *I* would rather those islands remained under a native king, if I were there, but you can easily see that that won't suit those planters.[1] Mr. Burlingame told me privately that if he were minister there he would have the American flag flying on the roof of the king's palace in less than two weeks. And he was in earnest, too. He hungered for those rich islands.[2]

Telegraph me if you want another column of this stuff—for I dasn't fool away a day at work that may not be needed, for I am pretty busy.[3]

Yrs

Mark.

[letter docketed:] 3 Jan. 1872. 1873.

[1] The death of King Kamehameha V (b. 1830) on 11 December 1872, and the publication of his obituary in the New York *Tribune* on 2 January 1873, had prompted Clemens to write about the Sandwich Islands ("Death of King Kamehameha," 2 Jan 73, 5). The manuscript for his article is not known to survive, but it was dated 3 January and published in the *Tribune* on 6 January: see Appendix B for the full text. Clemens had corresponded from the islands for the

Sacramento *Union* from March until July 1866, and found the raw material for this *Tribune* letter (and the second one, published three days later) in the notebooks he kept during his trip (*N&J1*, 91–237), as well as in the *Union* letters themselves, which in the summer of 1871 he revised for *Roughing It* (*RI 1993*, 861–62). He concluded his first article with a brief paragraph in which he asked why Prince William Lunalilo (1835–74), the "true heir to the Sandwich Islands throne," was being ignored by the *Tribune* correspondents "as if he had no existence and no chances." Clemens had seen Lunalilo during his visit to the islands, and considered him "a splendid fellow, with talent, genius, education, gentlemanly manners, generous instincts, and an intellect that shines as radiantly through floods of whisky as if that fluid but fed a calcium light in his head" (Appendix B; *RI 1993*, 715). Although Lunalilo, whom the Legislative Assembly elected king on 8 January 1873, was known to favor American over British influence, many American sugar growers pressed for an even closer tie to the United States, believing that annexation would greatly increase their profits by eliminating high import duties on sugar. Native Hawaiians were strongly opposed to annexation, however, which did not occur until 1898, when Hawaii became a U.S. territory (Kuykendall and Gregory, 225–33, 285–89; "The Sandwich Islands," New York *Tribune*, 8 Jan 73, 9).

[2]Anson Burlingame, then U.S. minister to China (1861–67), befriended Clemens in Honolulu in June 1866 (*L1*, 345–46 n. 5, 347–48; see also *L2*, 238 n. 1). In 1870 Clemens eulogized Burlingame as "a great man—a very, very great man" (SLC 1870e).

[3]The editorial page of the *Tribune* expressed approval of Clemens's first article on the day it appeared:

> Mr. Mark Twain, in a letter to THE TRIBUNE, gives some curious facts touching a subject which is just now attracting a great deal of notice. The humorous and grotesque features of life in the Sandwich Islands are naturally those which first caught his attention; but he might have made for this letter the same apology which he made for his latest book, that, in spite of all he could do, it contained a great deal of information. Mr. Clemens, as those who know him will testify, is not only a wit, but a shrewd and accurate observer; and so our readers will find, in the pithy communication published to-day, not merely food for laughter but subjects for reflection. (6 Jan 73, 4)

Reid must have requested "another column," for Clemens soon wrote a second one. On 20 April he claimed that he had set aside *The Gilded Age* "in the midst of a chapter & put in two whole days i̶n̶ on the S. I. letters" (20 Apr 73 to Reid).

To Whitelaw Reid
per Telegraph Operator
6 January 1873 • Hartford, Conn.
(MS, copy received: DLC)

BLANK NO. 1.

1608

THE WESTERN UNION TELEGRAPH COMPANY.

NO. 75　　　THE RULES OF THIS COMPANY REQUIRE THAT ALL MESSAGES　　945

RECEIVED FOR TRANSMISSION SHALL BE WRITTEN ON THE MESSAGE BLANKS OF THE COM-PANY, UNDER AND SUBJECT TO THE CONDITIONS PRINTED THEREON, WHICH CONDITIONS HAVE BEEN AGREED TO BY THE SENDER OF THE FOLLOWING MESSAGE.

G. H. MUMFORD, SEC.　T. T. ECKERT, GEN. SUPT., NEW YORK.　WILLIAM ORTON, PREST.

DATED,　Hartford 6　　　　　　　　　REC'D AT 145 BROADWAY,

TO　Whitelaw Reid　　　　　　　　Jan 6ᵗʰ. 1873.

Editor – Tribune –

Have mailed second & concluding paper[1]

Mark Twain

6pdx Jos

---

[1] See Appendix B for the full text of this second Sandwich Islands letter, published in the *Tribune* on 9 January.

To Ira F. Hart
per Olivia L. Clemens
12 January 1873 • Hartford, Conn.
(MS facsimile: Tollett and Harman, item 29)

HARTFORD, Jan. 12 187*2*-3.[1]

DEAR SIR:[2]

I THANK YOU VERY MUCH FOR YOUR INVITATION, BUT AM COM-
PELLED TO DECLINE IT, AS I AM NOT LECTURING AT ALL THIS SEASON,
ₐexcept the lectures in New York⏤ & Brooklyn,ₐ[3] OTHER DUTIES
RENDERING THIS COURSE NECESSARY.

YOURS TRULY,

MARK TWAIN.

Dear Sir

It will be impossible for me to reconsider the matter of lecturing in
Elmira & Towanda.[4] I have now more work to do than I can possibly
accomplish between this & middle of April—[5]

S. L. C

[1] Olivia revised this printed form, evidently at Clemens's direction. All of the
writing is in her hand, including the appended note and signature.

[2] Ira F. Hart, a physician on the Board of Health and treasurer of the Academy
of Medicine in Elmira, was the likely addressee. Hart had been a member of the
Young Men's Christian Association since 1858 and was its corresponding secretary in 1872 and 1873. He had earlier served as Clemens's host for the YMCA-
sponsored lecture in Owego, New York, on 4 January 1870. And in January 1874
(or late December 1873) he again invited Clemens to lecture in Elmira (*L3*, 416;
"The Twain Lecture," Owego *Times*, 6 Jan 70, 3; Boyd and Boyd, 37, 46, 47, 48,
122; OLC to Ira F. Hart, 10 Jan 74, CU-MARK).

[3] As the next letter suggests, Clemens's two Sandwich Islands letters had
brought invitations to lecture. As of this date he had tentatively agreed to lecture
in New York City and in Brooklyn (24 Jan 73 to Redpath).

[4] Towanda, Pennsylvania, is about twenty-five miles southeast of Elmira.
Hart's connection with Towanda has not been explained.

[5] Clemens was determined to finish *The Gilded Age* before his departure for
England, which was ultimately postponed until mid-May.

To John M. Hay
12 January 1873 • Hartford, Conn.
(MS: OCIWHi)

Hartford, Jan 12

Dear Hay—

Bliss is going to send "Roughing It" to the Tribune today, so he says. If you ever do any book reviews for the paper, I wish you'd & Reid would arrive at an amicable arrangement whereby you can have an hour or two to write a review of that book in, ~~for you understand it~~ & a week's holiday afterward to rest up in—for you know the people in it & the spirit of it better than an eastern man would.[1] I shall hope so, at any rate. ˏThat is I mean I hope you'll write it—that is what I am *trying* to mean.ˏ

Don't answer this letter—for I know how a man hates a man that's made him write a letter.

I have half a notion of preaching a Sandwich Island lecture in N. Y., (being invited thereto by several parties at rather seductive figures). ˏ~~Tribune letters, you know.~~ˏ ˏI published 2 letters on the Islands in the Tribune last week.ˏ[2] ⁋ But I am pretty busy & may not do it. Still, what I am trying to say, is, that if I *do* do it, I will *then* call upon you & get the answer to this letter——so don't write.

Ys Truly

Sam*ˡ*. L. Clemens

✉—————————————————————————————————

Col. John Hay | Tribune Editorial staff | New York. | [*flourish*] [*return address:*] IF NOT DELIVERED WITHIN 10 DAYS, TO BE RETURNED TO [*postmarked:*] HARTFORD

[1] With sales now lagging, Clemens and Bliss evidently hoped that a *Tribune* review from a sympathetic critic would boost the book's popularity (*RI 1993*, 882–92; 19 Apr 72 to Bliss, n. 2; see also 26 Jan 72 to Redpath, n. 2). Reid did not assign the review to Hay, however, as he explained to Bliss on 26 January (Whitelaw Reid Papers, DLC):

Dear Sir:

I received the copy of Mark Twain's book of which you speak, and have asked our Mr Ripley to give it early attention. . . . he may be able to make such a notice as will be gratifying to you. In that case it will be none the less so to myself, since Clemens has few warmer friends or heartier admirers than

Very truly yours
Whitelaw Reid

E. Bliss, Jr. Esq.
   116 Asylum St.
   Hartford
     Conn.

George Ripley (1802–80) received a degree from Harvard Divinity School in 1826 and served as an ordained minister for fifteen years. In 1841, together with his wife, sister, and several others, he founded the Brook Farm Institute, a short-lived experimental community near Boston. He had been the literary critic for the *Tribune* since 1849. Clemens was not at all pleased with his review: see 2 Feb 73 to OLC.

²Clemens may have thought that Hay was out of town when the Sandwich Islands letters appeared (Appendix B).

To Whitelaw Reid
13 and 17 January 1873 • Hartford, Conn.
(MS: DLC)

ₐP. S. I always write too much for a business man to read. But I've scratched some out. And interlined more.ₐ

Hartford, Jan. ₁₂ ₐ13ₐ.

My Dear Reid:

Your check for $100 for Sandwich Island letters is received, & is plenty.[1]

You made some small alterations here & there in the MS. for which I was sincerely grateful—they happened to [be] things I regretted to have said, when the MS. was gone & it was too late.[2]

I do hope to have an occasional moment to scribble an article in, but it can hardly be often, for I am so hard at work that I am obliged to decline a twenty-night lecture offer that would pay me $12,000.[3] I would have to decline it if it paid me $20,000, for books pay considerably better. ₐlecturing & forego all miscellaneous literary pleasures.ₐ

John Hay has been doing a couple of royal lectures. I think he just lays over anything in the guild.[4] ₐIt is but the opinion of a Border Ruffian from Pike—but then I'm "on it" myself.ₐ[5]

Have just bought the loveliest building-lot in Hartford—544 feet
front on the Avenue & 300 feet deep[6]—ₓ(paid for it with first six months
of "Roughing It"—how's that?)[7] &ₓ the house will be built while we are
absent in England[8]—& then by & by, whenever you fellows will run up
I'll make it awful lively for you, I swear!

Ys Ever

Mark.

Jan. 17.—But it appears I've *got* to lecture, after all—at least I am wavering & am *almost* ready to give in—but I'll have to talk only a mighty
few times if I talk at all. On "Sandwich Islands"—& you must not report
me like Fields—you'd desolate my richest property.[9]

[1] Reid had written Clemens on 11 January (CU-MARK):

> My Dear Twain:
>   The letters were admirable, the second especially, I think, is as good as any-
> thing you have ever done.
>   Is the enclosed cheque fair?
>   And wont you do something more for us when you see a chance? It wont hurt you
> a bit to freshen up people's recollection of you as a newspaper writer. If you only knew
> enough of Cuba and Santo Domingo to give us similar pictures! But pray seize upon
> some fresh topic, and write again.
>   With many thanks,
>
> Very truly yours,
Whitelaw Reid

[2] These "small alterations" are not recoverable, since the manuscripts for the
Sandwich Islands letters in the *Tribune* are not known to survive.

[3] This offer, yielding a per-lecture fee more than twice Clemens's highest fee
($250) during his 1871–72 lecture tour, has not been independently corrobo-
rated, although Samuel C. Thompson, Clemens's secretary from mid-May to
mid-July 1873, recalled that Clemens told him of a similar proposal:

> A bureau (Pond's ‚Redpaths?‚ I think) got him to deliver a lecture on the Islands at the
> Academy of Music, New York, five evenings for $.500.00 each. At the end they offered
> him the same rate for thirty nights in the leading cities. He refused. The manager of-
> fered to increase the pay; but he refused. (Thompson, 78)

Redpath's Boston Lyceum Bureau (James B. Pond was one of the partners who
took over Redpath's bureau in 1875) did not manage Clemens's February 1873
lectures in New York City and Brooklyn, and was almost certainly not the source
of the $12,000 offer (*L4*, 401 n. 4; Redpath 1876; 24 Jan 73 to Redpath, n. 1).

[4] Clemens had probably not attended any of Hay's lectures but may have read
newspaper accounts of them. The first, which Hay used in the Midwest in the
fall, was originally called "Phases of Washington Life." By the evening of 13
January, when he delivered it in New York's Steinway Hall for the Mercantile
Library Association, he had decided to call it "The Heroic Age in Washington"
(possibly prompted by the Chicago *Tribune*, which had suggested "The Heroic
Age of America" or "The Character of Lincoln" as titles). This lecture praised

the fortitude of the country's statesmen, especially Lincoln, during the Civil War (Thayer, 1:346–47; "Amusements," Chicago *Tribune*, 19 Nov 72, 8; "Washington in War Times," New York *Tribune*, 14 Jan 73, 4). On 20 December Hay delivered a second lecture, entitled "Day-Break in Spain," at Association Hall in New York for the Young Men's Christian Association. He described how the "Church and the Crown" had gained "absolute control" over the country, and expressed his belief that the Spanish people were now making "rapid progress toward true and orderly democracy." The New York *Tribune* review of the lecture praised it as "brilliant, noble, and compact with information" ("Day-Break in Spain," 21 Dec 72, 4).

⁵A "Border Ruffian" was literally "a member of the pro-slavery party in Missouri who in 1854–58 crossed the border into Kansas to vote illegally"; here Clemens used it to mean merely "troublemaker." To be "on it" meant to be skilled in something, or to understand it (Mitford M. Mathews, 1:165, 2:1160; Ramsay and Emberson, 160; 26 Jan 72 to Redpath, n. 2).

⁶The Clemenses had been planning to build a house in Hartford since early March 1871, seven months before relocating there and renting the Hooker residence. In mid-November 1871, while Clemens was away lecturing, Olivia inspected a lot in the Nook Farm area owned by Hartford attorney Franklin Chamberlin (1821–96), who had purchased a large tract of land from Nook Farm's founders in 1864. The following month she discussed other possibilities with friends and neighbors. The lot the Clemenses had just purchased from Chamberlin for $10,000 was apparently not the one Olivia had previously considered (see 22 Jan 73 to Mouland for a slightly different report of its dimensions). According to the deed, dated 16 January 1873, its northern boundary ran westward along Farmington Avenue from a point 350 feet west of Forest Street to the river (the north branch of Park River); its western boundary was the river itself; and its eastern boundary ran south to the land of Francis Gillette. Chamberlin later sold adjoining small portions of land to the Clemenses. The first of these, for which they paid $1,000 on 22 March 1873, was a small wedge along their eastern boundary, measuring 25 feet on the north, "about 300 feet" on the east and west, and 40 feet on the south (Land Records, Town of Hartford, 148:632–63; Van Why, 5, 7; *L4*, 338, 347, 371, 523–24 n. 2; Schwinn, 1:5; Salsbury, 424; Elisabeth G. Warner to George H. Warner, 14 Nov 71, CU-MARK; 16 Mar 81 to PAM, NPV).

⁷The first quarterly royalty payment that Clemens received for *Roughing It*, on 8 May 1872, was for $10,562.13, representing a 7½ percent copyright on 37,701 books; by 5 August he had received an additional $7,863.37, for 28,611 books. By January 1873 the book had earned him about $20,600 (8 May 72 to Perkins; 20 Apr 72 to Redpath, n. 4; Elisha Bliss, Jr., to SLC, 5 Aug 72, CU-MARK; *RI 1993*, 890–91).

⁸George and Lilly Warner, who were building a house on Forest Street immediately south of the Clemenses' lot, recommended their own architect, Edward Tuckerman Potter (1831–1904), who had designed St. John's Episcopal Church in East Hartford, the Church of the Good Shepherd in Hartford, and the Church of Heavenly Rest in New York, as well as many other churches and private residences. The house he planned for the Clemenses was in a style described as "High Victorian Gothic." Potter was assisted by a junior partner, Alfred H. Thorp (1843–1917), who had studied in Paris under Honoré Daumet. Thorp

served as the primary site supervisor during construction, which had begun by the time the Clemenses left for England in May. Charles E. Perkins represented them in their absence, mediating between the architects and the general contractor, John B. Garvie (Landau, 8, 111, 136, 147, 152, 381; Salsbury, 6, 9; *MTB*, 1:481; Van Why, 4–5, 55–56; Schwinn, 1:21; Geer 1872, 67, 215; information courtesy of Marianne Curling of the Mark Twain House).

[9] On 4 January the *Tribune* printed a "nearly in full" account of James T. Fields's "Masters of the Situation," a lecture on "reminiscences and characteristics of eminent men" delivered at New York's Association Hall on 3 January for the Young Men's Christian Association. On 15 January the *Tribune* also published a verbatim transcription of the lecture in the "Lectures and Letters— Extra Sheet," a publication separate from the daily issue, which also included reprintings of Clemens's Sandwich Islands letters. Clemens regularly protested "infernal synopses" of his own lectures (*L4*, 522; New York *Tribune:* "Masters of the Situation," 4 Jan 73, 1, 8; "Ready To-Day: Tribune Lecture Extra. No. 2," 15 Jan 73, 6; original printing of the "Extra Sheet," CU-MARK).

To Whitelaw Reid
14 January 1873 • Hartford, Conn.
(New York *Tribune*, "Lectures and Letters—Extra Sheet," after 15 Jan 73)

. . . .

I am one who regards missionary work as slow & discouraging labor, & not immediately satisfactory in its results. But I am very far from considering such work either hopeless or useless. I believe that such seed, sown in savage ground, will produce wholesome fruit in the third generation, & certainly that result is worth striving for. But I do not think much can reasonably be expected of the first & second generations. It is against nature. It takes long & patient cultivation to turn the bitter almond into the peach. But we do not refrain from the effort on that account, for, after all, it pays.[1]

. . . .

[1] Before sending the previous letter (delayed until 17 January) Clemens learned—probably from a 14 January advertisement—that his Sandwich Islands letters were to be reprinted the next day in the *Tribune*'s "Extra Sheet." He evidently decided to take the opportunity to revise one of his remarks about missionaries in his first letter, printed on 6 January. He mailed this correction to Whitelaw Reid; the note that must have accompanied it does not survive. Reid

responded on 15 January: "Your correction about the missionaries only arrived to day, unfortunately just 24 hours too late even for our extra sheet. But I will have the correction made tonight and a new plate cast for what we print hereafter" (Whitelaw Reid Papers, DLC; "We shall publish . . . ," New York *Tribune*, 14 Jan 73, 4). The first issue of the "Extra" was printed from the same plates as the original 6 January printing, and the text was therefore identical. Later issues of the "Extra," however, contained this additional paragraph (see Appendix B for the earlier version of the text: the addition was inserted after the paragraph "These people . . . pardonable way."). This later issue (printed sometime after 15 January) is thus the source of the text that Clemens forwarded to Reid, presumably on 14 January.

To William Bowen
17 January 1873 • Hartford, Conn.
(MS: TxU-Hu)

(SLC)

Hartford, Jan. 17.

Dear Will:

I am deeply grieved to hear of the death of our ˄my˄ little namesake; & our own great loss makes me able to sympathise with you & Mollie & know what you feel.[1] Otherwise I would not speak, but hold my peace—for words are empty at such times; they are but the shadow of consolation without the substance; they bring no relief, they can suggest no comfort.

So we can only say, we feel for you & with you—& so saying, we leave you to the healing charity of Time, that in its own good season takes the pain from all wounds & leaves only the scar to remind us rather of the kindly mercy wrought in our behoof than the pain we suffered.

With the love of other days,

Your friend
Saml. L. Clemens.

[1] William Bowen of St. Louis was Clemens's closest boyhood friend and fellow Mississippi River pilot. The reference to the death of "my little namesake" seems to suggest that the letter was written in January 1872, since Bowen family records indicate that Mary Clemens Bowen, the Bowens' youngest child, was

born in July 1871 and died in January 1872 (*L4*, 53 n. 1; Hornberger, 7 n. 11). Clemens was not in Hartford on 17 January 1872, however, and his mention of "our own great loss" seems a clear reference to the death of Langdon Clemens on 2 June 1872.

To James Redpath
17 January 1873 • Hartford, Conn.
(Anderson Galleries 1926, lot 413,
and AAA/Anderson 1929, lot 22)

Home, Jan. 17, 1873.

. . . .

$1000 wouldn't pay me to memorize that lecture, & I won't re-deliver the Sandwich Islands lecture there[1]—besides, I may talk the latter in N. Y. & Brooklyn for the Mercantile Library . . . I haven't got a bit of time to fool away lecturing.

. . . .

[1]Clemens was probably replying to the following letter of 16 January from George L. Fall (IaU):

Dear Sir:
    Pugh, Philadelphia offers 400 $ for a lecture in his course, and gives you these dates to select from:—
    Feb 17th
        20th
    Mch 6th
        10th
        15th
    Please telegraph us early in morning, your answer, as Pugh is pressed for time. Redpath in NY.
    Yours truly   Redpath & Fall

Clemens may have telegraphed a briefer answer before following up with the present letter. The lecture that he was unwilling "to memorize" has not been identified. He had delivered his Sandwich Islands lecture in Philadelphia, in T. B. Pugh's "Star Course," on 7 December 1869 (*L3*, 485).

To T. B. Pugh
20 January 1873 • Hartford, Conn.
(MS: PHi)

₍Private.

═══════₍

Hartford, Jan. 20.

Dear Pugh =

It will be better for you & better for the Star lecturers when you get entirely disgusted ~~witte~~ with the present stupid system & carry out your ~~design~~ ₍idea₍ which you mentioned to me last year[1]—viz., taking all the stars in₍to₍ your own hands exclusively & running them yourself in every big city, placing tickets at $1, & giving the said stars about one= third of the gross proceeds—& never exhibiting in second-rate cities ex- cept to break journeys. You needn't go 100 miles west of the Atlantic seaboard to make that profitable. There isn't pluck enough in the whole gang of lecture bureau$x to run a one-horse circus. They all *mean* well enough; but that isn't sufficient. I talk ₍Sandwich Islands₍ once or twice in N. Y. about Feb. 1; Beecher talks once, Gough once.[2] Why such a menagerie as we 3, ought to run *ten nights each* in N. Y. *You* could talk 3 such cards there that long & charge a dollar a head & make the very chil- dren cry for tickets. Under such circumstances would any of us care what became of the ~~stupid~~ absurdity that at present goes under the name of the lecture "system?" Hardly. We never would talk outside of a big city, because we'd never have any need to. And you bet your life the thing a man would be proudest of & put on the most frills about, would be, that he "belonged to Pugh's Menagerie." And the very first time *you* forgot ₍yourself₍ & tried to ring in an Olive Logan or Lilian Edgarton on the public as being anything else but shameless intruders upon the platform & ~~the~~ exquisitely commonplace at that, all your elephants would hoist their trumpets into the air & vamos the ranche![3] Just think how you could lay out those seven ~~50-~~ ₍30-₍cent courses in Boston by charging a dollar a head & trotting out your swell literary giraffes & Cardiff Giants one after the other!—[4] No use to make them promise they wouldn't leave you for other agents—ha, you couldn't hire them to do it! I'm sound on this question.

Ys Ever

S. L. Clemens.

[1] Evidently in Baltimore on 23 January 1872 (see p. 31).

[2] Clemens was still negotiating the dates of his appearances for the Mercantile Library, which also sponsored Henry Ward Beecher's talk on "The Unconscious Influence of Democratic Principles" at Steinway Hall on 20 January, and John B. Gough's "rewritten lecture called 'Will It Pay?'" scheduled for 27 January (Gough failed to appear). Gough's lecture was advertised on 20 January as the "concluding Lecture of the Mercantile Library Course" ("Lectures and Meetings," New York *Tribune*, 20 Jan 73, 3, and 27 Jan 73, 8; "Personal," Hartford *Courant*, 29 Jan 73, 2).

[3] Olive Logan, an author and former actress, was one of the most popular women lecturers, reputedly earning as much as fifteen thousand dollars a year on the platform. On 18 December 1872 she lectured on "Successful People" at Association Hall in New York. In 1906 Clemens claimed that unlike the "Anna Dickinson kind" of female lecturer, who "had something to say; and could say it well," Logan represented "a new kind of female lecturer," who "hadn't anything to say, and couldn't have said it if they had had anything to say; women who invaded the platform to show their clothes. They were living fashion-plates" (AD, 11 Apr 1906, CU-MARK†). Another of the "new kind" of lecturer was the "glamorous" Lillian S. Edgarton, the "pearl of the platform," who appeared in the Mercantile Library course at Steinway Hall on 6 January 1873, speaking on "Gossip—Its Causes and Cure" (*L4*, 9 n. 3; *NCAB*, 6:276; Eubank, 136; "Other Lectures," New York *Tribune*, 18 Dec 72, 5; "Amusements," New York *Times*, 6 Jan 73, 7; Odell, 9:119, 335; Fatout 1960, 98, 101, 147).

[4] In February 1872 P. T. Barnum announced his ownership of the "only living giraffes on this continent, having just succeeded in landing two of these beautiful creatures in good condition" ("New-York City," New York *Tribune*, 2 Feb 72, 8). The Cardiff Giant, a three-thousand-pound human figure carved from gypsum, was secretly buried and then "discovered" in 1869 on a farm near Cardiff, New York, and subsequently exhibited as a "petrified man" until the hoax was discovered (*DAH*, 1:313).

To John E. Mouland
22 January 1873 • Hartford, Conn.
(MS: ViU)

(SLC)

Hartford, Jan. 22.

My Dear Capt—

I am just as glad you got the gold medal, "old man," as if I'd got it myself—I am THOROUGHLY glad. And I am glad the officers & men were so handsomely treated by the Humane Society.[1] You say "a money reward to each man & - - - pay to the officers." I can't make out that word; is it "extra pay," or is it "two years' pay?"—or what is it? Be sure & write or telegraph me, because I want to give the item to the N. Y. Tribune, & I want to get it right.[2] Don't forget it—don't neglect it.

Well, they couldn't have conferred the gold medal on a better man, anyway. But by George, when I think how Wood & the General[3] & I did swell around that perilous upper deck & help give orders it makes me marvel at our own intrepidity!

I am to lecture in N. Y. the last day of this month & the first day or two of Feb.[4] And after that I'm going to peg away at my book[5] & be ready to sail for England in May. My wife said, weeks ago, when we were reading about the immensity & the palatial splendors of some of the other ships, "Well, it is no matter, we will not sail with anybody but Capt. Mouland." So that thing is settled, & entirely to my satisfaction, too. Ah, & won't we cut tobacco & smoke pipes & have a general good time? I rather think so.

Now "old man," try hard to get down here next trip. It is only *4* hours from Boston—not 6. You leave there at 9 AM & reach here at 1 PM; or you leave there at 3 PM & get here at 7. Be sure & telegraph me when you start, so that I can meet you at the station & cart you out.[6]

I am very much obliged to that Humane Society. When I lecture in London I mean to offer them the proceeds in a quiet way, for I think the Society is supported by voluntary contributions.[7]

I have just bought a lovely piece of ground, 544 feet front on the Avenue here, and 320 feet deep & shall have a house built in the midst of it while we are absent in England[8]—& then we'll have a blow-out there every time you can run down from Boston.

Don't forget about that information as to the officers' reward.

Faithfully Yours,

Sam*ˡ*. L. Clemens.

[1]Clemens first described Mouland's heroic rescue of the crew of the shipwrecked *Charles Ward*, suggesting that Mouland and his crew should receive a medal, in his letter of 20 November 1872 to the Royal Humane Society. On 3 December he invited Mouland to visit him in Hartford. Mouland replied (CU-MARK):

R M S "Batavia"

Jany 21ˢᵗ 1873

Boston

My very Dear Friend

    I Rec^d your kind note in L'pool, & had determined to take advantage of it this trip, but now at the last moment I find it impossible—today customs business, tomorrow shift my ship under the — grain elevator, & Friday customs clearance again & I sail from the wharf at 6 am Saturday on up of tide—so Thursday would be the only time & it is 6 hours from here to Hartford & 6 back   I am *miserably* disapointed for I anticipated a pleasant visit, & hoped to prolong my acquaintance with you but I *promise* you, I will be with you the very first opportunity—& I hope when you return to Europe you will give me a chance of doing the hospitalities of the ship for you & your Lady— What a reputation you have given me—you have made me quite famous   I got a gold medal & vote of thanks from the Humane society & my crew & officers a silver medal & thanks besides a money reward of 7£ to each man & Injun pay to the officers— I hope soon to be able to show you the medal   Again regretting not to be able to take advantage of your kind offer & hoping you are in good health, I Remain with Sincere thanks & Regards Yours

Faithfully

John E Mouland

Sam*ˡ*. L Clemens Esq

please reply if possible

Although Clemens did not realize it, Mouland's gold medal came not from the Royal Humane Society, but from the Liverpool Shipwreck and Humane Society, to which his recommendation was evidently referred. Founded in 1839, the Liverpool society still grants awards "to recognise the actions of persons instrumental in saving, or attempting to save, human life from danger" (Liverpool Shipwreck and Humane Society 1994, 2, 4). The society's annual report for the year ending 1 July 1873 recorded the following:

To Captain John E Mouland, s.s. "Batavia", a GOLD MEDAL; and SILVER MEDALS to Mr David Gillies, 3rd officer; Mr Haslett Kyle, 4th officer; Nicholas Foley and Henry Foley, quartermasters; Richard Brennan, Nathanial Clarke, John Park, and Thomas Henry, seamen, for a most gallant and skilful rescue of nine survivors of the crew of the "Charles Ward", which was dismasted and waterlogged and almost torn to pieces by the fearful violence of the winds and waves in the Atlantic, on the 20th November, 1872. The weather was so bad that they could not hoist up the lifeboat after the rescue, and it had to be abandoned. (Liverpool Shipwreck and Humane Society 1873, 11)

²If Mouland answered Clemens's question his letter is now lost. Clemens's "item" (published as "British Benevolence" in the New York *Tribune* on 27 January) said that the officers received "a money reward suited to their official grade" (see 25 Jan 73 to Reid, n. 2, and Appendix B). The meaning of Mouland's original words, "Injun pay," has not been discovered.

³See 26 Nov 72 to JLC and PAM, n. 2, and 3 Dec 72 to Mouland, n. 2.

⁴These dates were changed (see p. 295).

⁵The manuscript for *The Gilded Age*.

⁶Between late January and mid-May the *Batavia* was assigned to the Liverpool-Boston route. Mouland visited the Clemenses twice before their departure for England in May, during the two periods when he was in the country on layovers. The first visit took place at the end of February, and the second sometime between 7 and 11 April ("Brief Mention," Hartford *Courant,* 28 Feb 73, 2; "News Summary," Brooklyn *Eagle,* 14 Apr 73, 2; Boston *Transcript:* "Steamboats," 25 Jan 73, 7, and 28 Feb 73, 7; "Transcript Marine Journal," 25 Feb 73, 5, and 7 Apr 73, 5; "Shipping," New York *Times,* 16 May 73, 7; 26 Apr 73 to Greene).

⁷No record has been found of any donation from Clemens to the Royal Humane Society or to the Liverpool Shipwreck and Humane Society.

⁸See 13 and 17 Jan 73 to Reid, nn. 6, 8.

To Pamela A. Moffett
22 January 1873 • Hartford, Conn.
(MS: CU-MARK)

Home, 22ᵈ PM

Dear Sister:

Ma & Annie have just come—7 PM. They have been steadily on the road, 31 hours,, & are rather tired, but will be all right in the morning.[1]

Ma says Sammy can't run the engine because alcohol is expensive. I have given ma twenty dollars for Sammy to buy alcohol with—& so you can let him have the money as he needs it & ma will pay you. Let him get a mechanic to repair the engine where it leaks.[2]

Yrs Lovingly
Sam.

[1] If Jane Clemens and Annie Moffett spent "31 hours" on the road from Fredonia, they may have stopped overnight in New York. The trip would normally have taken about nineteen hours by train, with good connections ("Traveler's

Guide," Fredonia *Censor,* 22 Jan 73, 4; Jervis Langdon, Jr., 3–4; Baedeker 1893, 198).
  ² See 26 Nov 72 to JLC and PAM.

To James Redpath
24 January 1873 • Hartford, Conn.
(MS: NN)

                                                            Hartford, Jan. 24.
Dᴿ Redpath—

  I am already booked for Mercantile Library, Steinway Hall Feb. 5ᵗʰ & 10ᵗʰ, Brooklyn Academy 7ᵗʰ & Jersey City 8ᵗʰ—Sandwich Islands— the old lecture a little bit altered, & (I think) a little bit improved. Shall close it seriously instead of with a joke—which I *know* is the best way, but I have never had pluck enough to do it, heretofore. It used to win in San Francisco, where I wasn't afraid.¹

  Just had a letter saying the Mercantile understand (in effect) that the term "gross proceeds" signifies "*net* proceeds." Rather thin, isn't it? My telegram in reply will make *my* understanding of the phrase tolerably plain.² I was indignant, at first, but now it seems too conflagrationally funny (coming from some 1500 or 3,000 business men, clerks, &c.,₍[]₎ for anger.

  I hated to decline Pugh's offer; (~~not, entire~~ didn't do it entirely be- cause this lecture was old, there, for that's no excuse in so large a city,)— but it really wouldn't pay me to go anywhere for $400.³ I am very sorry I engaged to talk in N. Y.—it costs me valuable time—time worth more money than they can put into their houses. Am glad I shall see you if you stay there till Feb. 10.⁴

                                                            Ys Ever
                                                            Mark.

[✉]——

[*letter docketed:*] *Clemens* S. L. | Hartford | Jan. 24 '73.

[1]Clemens lectured on the Sandwich Islands at Steinway Hall in New York on 5 and again on 10 February, at the Academy of Music in Brooklyn on 7 February, and at the Tabernacle in Jersey City on 13 (not 8) February. The "old lecture" was "Our Fellow Savages of the Sandwich Islands," which he had used during his 1869–70 tour, itself a revised version of his original Sandwich Islands lecture, dating from 1866–67 and revived briefly in 1868. The new, "altered" lecture included some remarks about the recently elected king, Lunalilo, and ended "seriously" with a passage on the beauty of the islands—probably a new addition:

> The land I have tried to tell you about lies out there in the midst of the watery wilderness, in the very heart of the almost soilless solitudes of the Pacific. It is a dreamy, beautiful, charming land. I wish I could make you comprehend how beautiful it is. It is a land that seems ever so vague and fairy like when one reads about it in books, peopled with a gentle, indolent, careless race.
>
> It is Sunday land. The land of indolence and dreams, where the air is drowsy and things tend to repose and peace, and to the emancipation from labor, and turmoil, and weariness, and anxiety of life. ("Mark Twain," Brooklyn *Eagle*, 10 Feb 73, 4)

For reviews of Clemens's lectures, see pp. 295–96; a composite lecture text may be found in Fatout 1976, 4–15 (*L1*, 344 n. 1, 361–67, 372–73; *L2*, 40–44, 213 n. 4, 217 n. 1; *L3*, 375–442).

[2]Neither the letter from the Mercantile Library Association nor Clemens's telegram is known to survive. Clemens expected to receive "half the gross proceeds" for his two lectures in New York City (OLC to Olivia Lewis Langdon, 19 Jan 73, CtHMTH). The misunderstanding was not resolved to his satisfaction: according to Orion, in November he claimed that the association had

> kept back $700 he ought to have had from his two lectures in Steinway Hall last winter. There were 2000 or 2500 people at each lecture. He was to have had half and they were to pay all expenses. The tickets were a dollar and they paid him $1300 for the two lectures. Now they want him to lecture again and he wants to tell them they are thieves. (OC to MEC, 3 Nov 73, CU-MARK)

Although reserved seats were one dollar, an unknown number of unreserved seats had cost only seventy-five cents (New York *Tribune:* "Lectures and Meetings," 4 Feb 73, 7; "Of course . . . ," 5 Feb 73, 4).

[3]See 17 Jan 73 to Redpath, n. 1.

[4]Redpath had been in New York since 5 January ("Home News," New York *Tribune*, 6 Jan 73, 8). It is not known if he remained there long enough to see Clemens.

To Whitelaw Reid
25 January 1873 • Hartford, Conn.
(MS: DLC)

ˌ*Personal*ˏ

Jan. ~~24~~ 25ᵗʰ·

My Dʳ· Reid—

Warner was by when I got this news, & so no doubt he will have it in the form of a small item in tomorrow's Courant.[1]

I meant to make three stickfuls of it for you, but I got fond of it & so it has strung out to a couple of columns.[2] I am so awfully busy getting ready to lecture in New York that I ought *not* to have "got fond of it." But it's all right; everybody likes the Cunarders, though nobody *knows* anything about them.

Let the boys follow my copy—there's only 2 italicised words.

Yrs

Mark.

[*letter docketed:*]

Mr Reid: This is a very entertaining letter—on the reward to the sailors who effected a rescue described by Mark Twain—on British benevolence generally, and winding up with a strong puff of the Cunard line.

There is some part of it cut out on the 17th p. which I think it ~~was~~ rather a pity to leave out. Perhaps Mr. C. thought it might be considered irreverent.[3]

WCW[4]

---

[1] The "news"—the subject of Clemens's enclosed article for the New York *Tribune*—was the awarding of a gold medal and money to John Mouland and his crew (see 22 Jan 73 to Mouland, n. 1). Warner's item appeared in the Hartford *Courant* of 27 January ("A Reward Well Earned," 2).

[2] The manuscript that Clemens enclosed is not known to survive; it was published as "British Benevolence" in the *Tribune* on 27 January: see Appendix B for the full text. A composing stick contained about two inches of handset type; thus "three stickfuls" equaled six column inches of material, or about five hundred words in the seven-point type commonly used in the *Tribune* (Pasko, 378, 529). A *Tribune* editorial published the same day as the article explained:

Mark Twain was on board the Cunard steamer Batavia when the gallant crew of that vessel picked up at sea, hazarding their lives, the survivors of the foundered bark Charles Ward. Readers of THE TRIBUNE will recollect his blood-stirring account of the rescue, at which he so nobly "assisted"—as the French have it. They will be glad to hear the sequel of the whole matter, which is related by Mark Twain in a characteristic letter, herewith published. The award of the gold medal and other things therewith connected give our correspondent occasion to reel off a pleasant skein of gossip about worthier topics than will be found in what he calls "the daily feast of Congress corruption and judicial rottenness." (27 Jan 73, 4)

³Clemens's legible cancellation probably occurred in the section subtitled "WHAT THE CUNARD CO. DID FOR OUR HEROES." It is not known whether it was restored in the printed text.

⁴William C. Wyckoff (1832–88), science editor of the *Tribune* since 1869 (Wilson and Fiske, 6:630).

To Michael Laird Simons
27 and 28 January 1873 • Hartford, Conn.
(MS: NN-B)

(SLC)

Hartford, Jan. 27.

Dear Sir:¹

I regret the delay, but I have been driven for time to even ~~turn~~ eat in, lately.

I have furnished the data to Chas. Dudley Warner & he ~~wise~~ will hurry up my biographical sketch.²

I only know of 2 portraits of me—both wood. The one enclosed (which I have cut from a western newspaper) first appeared in the Aldine³ & they have probably sold an electrotype to the paper I speak of. But the picture is too large anyway, I suppose. The other portrait appeared in the London "Graphic" in September, & was excellent, but it is even larger than the Aldine cut.⁴ So I enclose a first-rate photograph, with an autograph on it, as you suggest.⁵

As for selections, I would suggest—from "Roughing It":

The Pony Rider (descriptive)—page 71⁶

The South Pass ("   )   "   100

From The "Innocents Abroad":
  [*"*]*European Guides*" (humorous)—290[7]
  ♭

—————

        Also Humorous:—viz:
{ *The Jumping Frog*
{ *The Good Little Boy who didn't prosper.*
These are both in the small volume entitled "The Jumping Frog &
other Sketches,"[8] & I think all my books are in your principal public
library. If not, I ¢ will send a set to you if you desire it.

There is another humorous sketch which I like—"*Baker's Cat,*" page
439, "Roughing It."

And there is (th also humorous—& if not pathetic—*the author weeping
over Adam's Grave*—page 567 Innocents Abroad.
        Also "*Buck Fanshaw's Funeral,*" page 328 "Roughing It."[9]
        But I must wait and take another look, for these selections seem
cumbersomely long.

        P. S.—28.—
        These are only suggestions, nothing more. They are cumbersomely
long, & you may be able to select something that will not crowd your
space so much. I have suggested both di descriptive & humorous writing—that is to say the serious *&* the humorous, because ¢ humor cannot
do credit to itself without a good background of gravity & of earnestness.
Humor unsupported rather hurts its author in the estimation of the
reader. Will you please present me in the two lights?
                                        Ys Truly
                                        Sam*l*. L. Clemens
                                        Mark Twain.

M. L. Simons Esq

[*enclosures:*]

[1] Michael Laird Simons (1843–80) began his journalism career with the Philadelphia *Inquirer* and later worked for the Philadelphia *Evening Telegraph*, contributing to various literary journals as well. He was active in establishing the Reformed Episcopal church, and edited several historical and religious works (Wilson and Fiske, 5:535).

[2] Simons had written to ask assistance in preparing a "biographical sketch" of Clemens to be included in a revision of the *Cyclopaedia of American Literature*, originally edited by Evert A. and George L. Duyckinck and first published in 1856. The new edition, "edited to date by M. Laird Simons," appeared in fifty-two parts in 1873–74, and was published in two volumes in 1875. Warner prepared an article for it, based on the eleven pages of autobiographical "data" that Clemens provided him (now at the Pierpont Morgan Library in New York), but preferred "as a matter of taste . . . *not* to appear as the writer of the sketch" (Warner to Simons, 22 May 73, ODaU; SLC 1873f; Charles Dudley Warner 1875).

[3] The portrait of Clemens in the *Aldine* for April 1871 (4:52), reproduced on p. 285 as an enclosure, was engraved on wood by John C. Bruen from an 1870 photograph taken by Mathew Brady (*L4*, 416 n. 2). The "western newspaper" has not been identified.

[4] The *Graphic* portrait appeared in the issue for 5 October 1872 (5 Oct 72 to Fitzgibbon). It is reproduced on p. 162.

[5] The "first-rate photograph" was taken by Edward H. Paige of Buffalo and first exhibited in his gallery in the spring of 1870. The print that Clemens signed and enclosed is not known to survive, so the enclosure is reproduced above from

the engraving made for the *Cyclopaedia* (Duyckinck and Duyckinck, 2:951; several original prints of this photograph are extant, and are reproduced in *L4*, 132, 136, 163).

⁶The page numbers throughout the letter refer to the American Publishing Company's first editions. Calling it "the finest piece of writing I ever did," Clemens suggested to Elisha Bliss in March 1871 that he print the pony-rider passage (from chapter 8) in the *American Publisher* as an advertisement or foretaste of *Roughing It* (*L4*, 368). Simons included the pony-rider extract in his *Cyclopaedia* article, but not the description of South Pass (from chapter 12).

⁷From chapter 27 of *The Innocents Abroad*, also reprinted in the *Cyclopaedia*.

⁸Clemens referred to his first book, *The Celebrated Jumping Frog of Calaveras County, And other Sketches* (SLC 1867a), whose title sketch had first appeared in the New York *Saturday Press* for 18 November 1865 (SLC 1865c). The collection does not include "The Story of the Good Little Boy Who Did Not Prosper," which was first published in the *Galaxy* for May 1870, and was reprinted by Hotten the following year in *Screamers*. In March 1872 Clemens revised Hotten's pirated text for inclusion in *Mark Twain's Sketches* (SLC 1870h, 1871e, 1872e; 31 Mar 72 to Osgood, n. 4; 20 Sept 72 to the editor of the London *Spectator*, n. 7).

⁹The story of Jim Baker's cat, Tom Quartz, first appeared in the Buffalo *Express* on 18 December 1869 (SLC 1869e), and Clemens later revised it for inclusion in chapter 61 of *Roughing It*. Both versions were preceded, however, by an unpublished draft entitled "Remarkable Sagacity of a Cat," probably written in June 1868 (*RI 1993*, 705; SLC 1868c). Scotty Briggs's interview with a "fledgling" minister to arrange Buck Fanshaw's funeral occurs in chapter 47. The "*author weeping over Adam's grave*" is from chapter 53 of *Innocents;* it was the third extract that Simons selected for his article.

To the Public
28 January 1873 • Hartford, Conn.
(Hartford *Evening Post*, 28 Jan 73)

With the present new-laid ten inches of snow for a text, one might preach a pithy sermon upon the distress this vigorous winter has brought, in Hartford, to many a fireside where there is no fire. But no doubt it is sufficient to say that Mr. Hawley knows of a great many widows & little children here who suffer from cold & hunger every day & every night, & yet the means he is able to gather up fall far short of being enough to relieve them. He has made some strong appeals for aid, through the press, & they have been responded to with considerable liberality; but still the empty mouths & the fireless hearths are so many that he is pretty well discouraged. His appeals are not in behalf of able-bodied tramps who are too lazy to work, but in behalf of women & children— women broken down by illness & lack of food, & children who are too young to help themselves. If I were to go into details & tell what Father Hawley knows about these blameless unfortunates, the purse-strings of this benevolent old city would relax with one impulse, & the trouble would be at an end.[1]

Now several of us have conceived the idea that we might raise a thousand dollars for Father Hawley's clients through the medium of a lecture to be given at Allyn Hall next Friday night by the undersigned. I am thoroughly & cheerfully willing to lecture here for such an object, though I would have serious objections to talking in my own town for the benefit of my own pocket—we freebooters of the platform consider it more graceful to fly the black flag in strange waters & prey upon remote & friendless communities.

We desire that *all* the proceeds of the lecture shall go into Father Hawley's hands; therefore we called for volunteers to pay the expenses of hall rent, advertising, &c., & his excellency the governor of the state promptly offered to foot the whole bill, but as a dozen other prominent citizens demanded a chance, we let them have it, for there is nothing mean about us. When we appeal for liberality in others we are willing to be generous ourselves. One of the first merchants of Hartford, one of her most capable & energetic business men, has shouldered the whole work of advertising & managing the business details of our enterprise, & it will be done well. He gives to it, for nothing, time which is worth a great many dollars a day to him.[2]

The price of our tickets will be one dollar each, all over the house— & reserved seats can be secured at Brown & Gross's[3] without extra charge. We hear of parties who are taking from ten to fifty of them, & we receive the news with high gratification—we place the tickets at double price for several reasons. One is, the lecture itself being worth nearly twenty-five cents, the ticket purchaser would really be *giving* only about twenty-five to the charity if the tickets were fifty cents; but by making the price a dollar, the purchaser has a chance to make a good honest undefiled contribution of seventy-five to charity. The idea is mine—none but an old business head would have thought of an attraction like that. Another reason for high prices is, that charity is a dignified & respectworthy thing, & there is small merit about it & less grace when it don't cost anything. As a general thing, charity entertainments are the cheapest that are offered to the public,—& that is paying but a poor compliment to the public. One would suppose that the idea was to get the thing down to a figure that would enable the hungry poor to attend their own entertainments & support themselves. Now that cannot be right—it cannot be either just or generous.

Lucca charges $4 a ticket, & so my first idea was to put our tickets at $4, too, & run opposition. But friends said, no, there was a difference—Lucca sings.[4] I said, very well, I would sing, too. I showed them what I could do. But they still objected, & said that a mere disturbance was not singing. So I have come down to a dollar; but I do it with reluctance.

I must not deceive any one; therefore I will say, in parenthesis, as it were, that I am going to deliver a lecture that I delivered here before the Young Men's Institute two or three years ago—a lecture on the Sandwich Islands.[5] I do this because Father Hawley's need is so pressing that I have not time to prepare a new lecture; I happen to be just fixed & primed for this Sandwich Island talk, for the reason that I have been rubbing it up to deliver before the New York Mercantile Library some ten days hence. Now we offer these following terms: all who have not already heard the lecture can pay a dollar & come in; & all who have heard it before can commute for two dollars apiece, & remain at home if they prefer. In which case the police will be instructed not to disturb them. But if they come to the hall they must behave, & not cry over old jokes that merely made them sad when they heard them before.

We would like to have a thousand dollars in the house; we point to the snow & the thermometer; we call Hartford by name, & we are not much afraid but that she will step to the front & answer for herself.[6]

Will the other papers please copy?[7]

MARK TWAIN

Hartford, Jan. 28.

[1] This letter is a public plea for charity—an advertisement for a benefit lecture that Clemens had agreed to deliver in Hartford's Allyn Hall on 31 January. David Hawley (1809–76) was a farmer until 1851, when he was hired by the City Mis-

sion Board to do humanitarian work in Hartford. Since then he had concerned himself with the "ministration of temporal charities," devoting much of his time to visiting the poor (Trumbull, 1:538; "A Good Man Gone," Hartford *Courant,* 1 Feb 76, 2). In 1906 Clemens recalled that he was a

> man whose pity went spontaneously out to all that suffer. . . . He was not a clergyman, nor an officer in any church; he was merely a plain, ordinary Christian; but he was so beloved—not to say worshiped—by all ranks and conditions of his fellow-citizens that he was called "Father" by common consent. It was a title of affection, and also of esteem and admiration; and his character and conduct conferred a new grace and dignity upon that appellation. (AD, 21 Nov 1906, CU-MARK†)

²Marshall Jewell (1825–83) was governor of Connecticut from 1869 to 1870 and from 1871 to 1873. The prominent citizens responded to Joseph Twichell's plea from his pulpit on 26 January, the Sunday before the lecture. The manager of the enterprise was John S. Ives, co-owner of a dry-goods store ("Mark Twain's Lecture," Hartford *Evening Post,* 1 Feb 73, clipping in Scrapbook 6:129, CU-MARK; Geer: 1872, 81, 212; 1873, 258).

³A bookstore on Asylum Street, near Allyn Hall, owned by Flavius A. Brown and William H. Gross (Geer 1872, 27, 38, 71, 210).

⁴Pauline Lucca (1841–1908), an Austrian operatic soprano of Italian descent who had made her American debut in New York in September 1872, won great popularity during her 1872–74 United States tour. She was scheduled to sing the role of Marguerite in Gounod's *Faust* in Hartford on 29 January. The most expensive tickets, for reserved seats in the "Parquet and Parquet Circle," cost four dollars ("Roberts Opera House," Hartford *Courant,* 27 Jan 73, 3; Odell, 9:316–17, 421, 441–42).

⁵Clemens had given "Our Fellow Savages of the Sandwich Islands" in Hartford on 23 November 1869 (*L3,* 407 n. 8).

⁶About fifteen or sixteen hundred people attended Clemens's lecture, which yielded net proceeds of fifteen hundred dollars. His performance was very well received. According to the Hartford *Evening Post,*

> The audience listened with great attention throughout, evidently enjoying the lecturer's eloquence, his vivid descriptions, and his serious comments, and the wit, humor and jokes, about equally. If the lecturer had been himself among the audience he could hardly have judged better of the variety that would be pleasing. Perhaps we might make a single exception. There may have been a trifle too much cannibal.
>
> In the serious passages of the lecture the audience showed their appreciation by their still, intent listening. There was much useful, curious, and even startling information concerning the people. The natural beauties, charming climate, and wonderful volcano were painted in glowing words with a pleasing voice and manner. ("Mark Twain's Lecture," 1 Feb 73, clipping in Scrapbook 6:129, CU-MARK)

This review may have been written by Orion Clemens, who was working for the *Evening Post* at this time (25 Sept 72 to OLC, n. 11).

⁷Both the Hartford *Courant* and the Hartford *Times* reprinted this letter on 29 January ("The Poor of Hartford and the Sandwich Islands," Hartford *Courant,* 2; "The Poor of Hartford—Card from Mark Twain," Hartford *Times,* 2).

To the Staff of the New York *Tribune*
30 January 1873 • Hartford, Conn.
(MS: NN)

Hartford, Jan. 30.

Gentlemen—

Can you send me a couple of copies of my ~~letter~~ Tribune letter of a few days ago concerning British liberality & the awarding of the Humane Society's gold medal to Capt. Mouland?[1]

Ys Truly

Mark Twain

[1] "British Benevolence," published in the *Tribune* on 27 January (Appendix B). See 2 Feb 73 to OLC.

To Whitelaw Reid
per Telegraph Operator
1 February 1873 • Hartford, Conn.
(MS, copy received: DLC)

BLANK NO. I.

596

THE WESTERN UNION TELEGRAPH COMPANY.

NO. 7Fa   I   THE RULES OF THIS COMPANY REQUIRE THAT ALL MESSAGES   12.40
RECEIVED FOR TRANSMISSION SHALL BE WRITTEN ON THE MESSAGE BLANKS OF THE COMPANY, UNDER AND SUBJECT TO THE CONDITIONS PRINTED THEREON, WHICH CONDITIONS HAVE BEEN AGREED TO BY THE SENDER OF THE FOLLOWING MESSAGE.

G. H. MUMFORD, SEC.   T. T. ECKERT, GEN. SUPT., NEW YORK.   WILLIAM ORTON, PREST.

DATED,   Hartford Ct   I   REC'D AT 145 BROADWAY,
TO   Whitelaw Reid   Feb I   1873.

Editor Tribune

Andrews[1] and I will go to the club without going first to the hotel[2]

S L Clemens

~~14pd Jx~~

[1] William S. Andrews (3 Nov 72 to Redpath, n. 1).

[2] Reid had written to Clemens on 26 January, on Lotos Club stationery (CU-MARK):

My Dear Twain:

Wont you come to New York next Saturday, and "be dined" as the guest of the Lotos? The members of the Club will give you a hearty welcome, and I will see that your dinner is not wholly indigestible. You will have to endure the solemnity of my society during the dinner, but at its close you can find some relief.

Very truly Yours,
Whitelaw Reid

Reid was the current president of the Lotos Club, founded in 1870 "to promote social intercourse among journalists, literary men, artists and members of the musical and dramatic professions, and such merchants and professional gentlemen of artistic tastes and inclinations as would naturally be attracted by such a club," on the model of the famous Savage Club of London (Elderkin, 9; 5 Dec 72 to the editor of the Hartford *Evening Post*, n. 3). On Saturday evening, 1 February, Clemens attended a dinner given in his honor and delivered a speech that "set the key for a good deal of the sarcastic drollery which prevailed on many occasions":

He said that he did not like to make any personal allusions, but that the profane conversation he had been compelled to listen to from Whitelaw Reid, John Hay, Samuel Bowles and Henry Watterson had frightened away all the pious thoughts he had concocted for the solemn occasion. He spoke of Mr. Reid as a man who had grown so accustomed to editing a newspaper that he could not distinguish between truth and falsehood; and that John Hay had written so many ribald verses that he (Twain) was always compelled to disown his acquaintance when presiding at meetings of the Young Men's Christian Association. . . . He closed with an apology for discontinuing his harangue; saying that those anxious to hear the remainder of it might step down stairs, where he had stationed a number of agents, and purchase tickets for his Wednesday evening [5 February] lecture, adding, "I make it a rule of life never to miss any chances, especially on occasions like these, where the opportunity for converting the heathen is luxuriously promising." As may be surmised, Mr. Twain was not let off without a dreadful scoring in which he was denounced as an impostor. Much of his history was ventilated. (Elderkin, 15–16)

Clemens checked into the St. Nicholas Hotel that evening and stayed for much of the next two weeks in New York (see p. 295). On 13 February the Lotos Club elected him a member, and he evidently remained one until his death (Charles Inslee Pardee to SLC, 13 Feb 73, CU-MARK).

To Olivia L. Clemens
2 February 1873 • New York, N.Y.
(MS: CU-MARK)

No. 2.[1]

Sunday.

It is a good long time since the 2[d] of February[2] became more to me than other days—a good long time since it became set apart in the calendar as the high chief day of the 365; & I think that if our mutual satisfaction in it & in the momentous fact it keeps in remembrance continues to grow as it has grown since 1870, we shall by & by become not merely the lovingest couple in the land but the happiest. I think our gales of happiness, with lulls of depression between, are quieting down day by day, & will presently be resolved into a calm great deep of love & peace, untouched by any ruffling breeze, & unshadowed by any vagrant passing cloud.

I am keeping the great anniversary in the solitude of the hotel; & not boisterously, for th last night's whirlwind of excitement has swept the all spirit out of me & I am as dull & lifeless as if h I had just come waked out of a long, stupefying sleep.

I find that the Tribune review of Roughing It was written by the profound old stick who has done all the Tribune reviews for the last 90 years. The idea of setting such an oyster as that to prating about Humor! This is "journalism." They would think me absurd if I ⌀ were to suggest that they hire Josh Billings[3] to write a critique on the Iliad, but it does not occur to them that he is as thoroughly competent to do it as is th⌀is old ˌTribune, fool to criticise a book of humor.[4] What a curious idea it is to have only one book reviewer connected with a great newspaper. It would be just as consistent to hire a clerk to keep their books, write their editorials, cook their food & do their washing. *No* man has an *appreciation* so various that his judgment is good upon all varieties of literary work. If they were to set *me* to review Mrs. Browning, it would be like asking you to deliver judgment upon the merits of a box of cigars:[5] to you, one or two whiffs of the aroma would be the utmost that your senses could enjoy, but there are millions of better qualified persons who would know that the whole box brimmed with delight. I will preach a small discourse upon this absurdity o̸ one of these days.

I would just as soon see you & the Muggins as not. In fact I would walk a good long way to see you & the Muggins, although you are both constantly in my mind & heart, & that is having you pretty near neighbors. I love you both, ever, ever, every̸ so much.

Sam.

Love to Ma & Annie.[6]

If ⱥ 2 Tribunes comes̸ with the "~~God~~ Gold Medal" letter in them, cut them out & mail one to the Glasgow Herald, Scotland & the other to G. Fitz Gibbon, 1 Wellesley Terrace, ⱥUpper street. Islington, London, England.[7]

✉——————————————————————————————

Mrs. Sam[1]. L. Clemens | Hartford | Conn [*return address:*] IF NOT DELIVERED WITHIN 10 DAYS, TO BE RETURNED TO [*postmarked:*] MAILED ST. NICHOLAS HOTEL, FEB 2 ◊◊◊◊ [*and*] NEW YORK FEB 2

[1] This is evidently the second of two letters Clemens wrote to his wife from New York on 1 or 2 February, the first of which is not known to survive.

[2] The Clemenses' wedding anniversary.

[3] Henry Wheeler Shaw.

[4] The *Tribune* review of *Roughing It* appeared on 31 January. Clemens had no doubt learned from Hay at the Lotos Club dinner that he had not been asked to review it, as Clemens had requested, and that Reid had assigned George Ripley instead (12 Jan 73 to Hay, n. 1). Ripley offered little serious criticism, but instead quoted liberally from the book, concluding that it "may be regarded as one of the most racy specimens of Mark Twain's savory pleasantries" (Ripley, 6).

[5] Olivia's fondness for Elizabeth Barrett Browning's poetry, which Clemens considered "marvelous ravings," was a running joke (*L3*, 95; see also *L3*, 26, 241; *L4*, 72).

[6] Jane Clemens and Annie Moffett had begun their visit on 22 January (22 Jan 73 to PAM).

[7] Clemens was unsuccessful in arranging for the reprinting of "British Benevolence" in the Darlington (England) *Northern Echo*, which employed his friend Fitzgibbon, or in the Glasgow *Herald*. His contact on the *Herald* may have been William Jack (b. 1834), the editor from 1870 to 1875, who was also a fellow of St. Peter's College, Cambridge (1859–71), and a professor of natural philosophy at Owen's College, Manchester (1866–70) (*BBA*, s.v. "Jack, William"). No association between Jack and Clemens has been documented, however.

No LETTERS written between 2 and 15 February 1873 have been found. For much of that time Clemens stayed at the St. Nicholas Hotel, in order to be near his lecture venues in New York City (5 and 10 February) and Brooklyn (7 February). He returned to Hartford briefly on 8 February, and again on 11 February, traveling from there to Jersey City on 13 February for his appearance that evening ("Personal Intelligence," New York *Herald*, 2 Feb 73 and 10 Feb 73, 7; John Hay to William A. Seaver, 10 Feb 73, RPB). All four lectures were resoundingly successful. On 5 February the following enthusiastic endorsement appeared on the editorial page of the New York *Tribune:*

> Of course none of our readers will forget that it is to-night Mr. Mark Twain gives for the first time, in Steinway Hall, that new lecture upon the Sandwich Islands, which is expected to exhaust the sum of the learning, the sentiment and the science at present existing in the world in regard to that interesting subject. Many people have visited that fascinating archipelago, but none took the precaution of carrying with them the eyes of Mr. Clemens. The consequence is that those who go to Steinway Hall to-night will get entirely new views of Kanaka civilization, even though they may have resided at Honolulu from their youth up. It must never be forgotten that Mr. Clemens is not only a great humorist, but a great observer and a deep philosophical thinker. (5 Feb 73, 4)

The *Tribune* also reviewed the lecture favorably, remarking on Clemens's apparently "unconscious drollery," and noting that "his hearers never laugh in the wrong place. Perhaps this is because he never indicates either by voice or manner what he thinks the right place for a laugh; and hence his audience has to listen sharply." The reviewer concluded:

> After you have laughed at his wild extravagances for an hour, you are astonished to perceive that he has given you new and valuable views of the subject discussed. Every sentence may be burlesque, but the result is fact. And what insures his success as a teacher is that his manner is so irresistibly droll that it conquers at the first moment the natural revolt of the human mind against instruction. ("Mark Twain's Lecture," 6 Feb 73, 5)

The New York *World* described the audience's reaction:

> It is within bounds to say that Steinway Hall has scarcely ever had within its walls so large a number as was last night assembled to hear Mr. Clemens (better known as Mark Twain) tell what he knew about the Sandwich Islands. Every seat was occupied, and when the lecturer began there was not room for

the entrance of a single additional person. The platform was equally crowded. Frequent applause and bursts of laughter greeted the numerous telling "points" of fun or wit, though the audience bestowed a similar appreciative attention upon the more serious portions of the lecture. (" 'Mark Twain,' " 6 Feb 73, 8)

Fortunately for the "more than a thousand people" who were "turned away because there was no chance to get in" on 5 February, Clemens appeared again at Steinway Hall on 10 February ("A Crowded House," Boston *Times*, 7 Feb 73, clipping in CU-MARK). The reviewer for the Brooklyn *Eagle* made only the briefest of general observations—noting that the audience at the Academy of Music was large, and that "at the close of the lecture Mr. Clemens went off the stage as he came on, with well feigned awkwardness, and amid loud applause"—but included a lengthy synopsis, of the type that Clemens tried repeatedly to prevent ("Mark Twain," 10 Feb 73, 4; see 13 and 17 Jan 73 to Reid). The Jersey City *Evening Journal* also reported a "large audience" at the Tabernacle, and reported that "Mark's genial countenance shone with good humor, which communicated itself to the audience at once":

> It is useless to attempt to follow Twain through his lecture here, for he must be heard to be appreciated. His humor is peculiar, and depends much upon the peculiar style of his delivery. The audience laughed and laughed, until their sides ached, and this seemed to be eminently satisfactory to the hero of the "Innocents Abroad." ("Mark Twain on the Sandwich Islands," 14 Feb 73, 1)

Sometime during these days in New York, Clemens had the chance to visit with his old California friend John McComb, an owner and supervising editor of the San Francisco *Alta California*. McComb had been largely responsible for getting him the assignment to cover the *Quaker City* excursion. A mutual friend, Frank Soulé, wrote to Clemens on 31 March from the *Alta*'s editorial rooms: "McComb has just come in. He speaks in the most enthusiastic terms of you, and his hob-nobbing with you in N. Y." (CU-MARK; *L1*, 361; *L2*, 12 n. 1). And on 6 April, Joseph T. Goodman wrote Clemens just after returning from a recent stay in San Francisco:

> Old John McComb returned from the East during my sojourn, and he devoted one entire afternoon to recounting his intercourse with you in New York. What infinite appreciation and recollection he has! I don't believe you said a single good thing but what he repeated literally—and then his eyes would

sparkle and he would laugh in that unctious way of his till he would shake the building like a mastodon turbulent with merriment. (CU-MARK)

Clemens probably returned to Hartford on 14 February, the day after his final lecture, in Jersey City.

To James Hammond Trumbull
15 February 1873 • Hartford, Conn.
(MS: CtHi)

Hartford, Feb. 15

J H Trumbull Esq[1]
 Dr. Sir:

  I shall be very glad indeed to meet with the Club as a member on next Monday Evening, & am thankful, too.[2]

  And I willingly "excuse the informal character" of the notice—am even *grateful* for it; for if you had started in to make it formal you might have got it in Sanscrit,[3] & that would just simply have made trouble with

Ys Truly

Saml. L. Clemens

[1] James Hammond Trumbull (1821–97), a historian, philologist, and bibliographer, served as Connecticut's secretary of state from 1861 to 1866, and for many years as librarian of the Watkinson Library in Hartford. In addition to compiling and editing numerous works of history and biography, he was an authority on the history and languages of New England Indian tribes.

[2] The Hartford Monday Evening Club (which Trumbull had helped found in January 1869) gathered fortnightly to hear and discuss an original essay presented by one of its members. Clemens attended the meeting of 17 February 1873 and heard Congregational clergyman Nathaniel J. Burton read an essay entitled "Individualism." Samuel C. Thompson recalled a comment of Clemens's about the club: "At the meetings . . . they generally discuss some learned subject, too deep for me; but I have to take my turn, and Dr. Burton especially gets into a gale of laughter at my attempts to contribute" (Thompson, 77). Clemens delivered his first essay—"The License of the Press"—on 31 March 1873. He remained a club member until his death (Cheney, 3, 11, 13, 14, 28).

[3] Albert Bigelow Paine described Trumbull as "the most learned man that ever lived in Hartford. He was familiar with all literary and scientific data, and ac-

cording to Clemens could swear in twenty-seven languages." It was he who "prepared the variegated, marvelous cryptographic chapter headings" for *The Gilded
Age* (*MTB*, 1:477–78 n. 1; see French, 272–73).

From Olivia L. and Samuel L. Clemens
to Olivia Lewis Langdon
17 February 1873 • Hartford, Conn.
(MS: CtHMTH)

(SLC)

Hartford Monday

Mother dear

Why don't we hear from Clara? I *do* hope she is not going to dis-
apoint us— I wish some of you could see her and persuade her to write
us—

I shall be *dreadfully* disapointed if she does not go—

Does Mrs Spaulding go next month?—[1]

I am hungry to see you when are you coming? So many things that
I want to talk with you about—

I hope Sue will not get sick in her fair work—yet I am afraid of it—
I wish she could come on again—[2]

I think it would be pleasant to have cousin Ed come if Anna comes
with you and Hattie, but after all, I don't know where I could put
him—[3]

Love to all—

Susie[4] has had a cold for two days and feels rather fretful.

With deepest love

your daughter

Livy—

The baby. & I send love to you, mother. I would like to write & tell
you all about her—& I sat down here intending to do it—but it isn't any
use; I can't write; been mooning ~~alone~~ along all day forcing myself to
write, & now by head is thicker & muddier than ever. If I were to ∅ have
an idea at such a time as this it would overstrain my intellect. So for fear
I *should* have one by accident, I will say good by mother, & go out & walk
off some of this accumulating imbecility.

Yr son   Saml

[1] By early December, Clara Spaulding had agreed to accompany the Clemenses to England, but had evidently not yet written to confirm those plans. Clara's mother, Mrs. Henry C. Spaulding, preceded her daughter to Europe, leaving New York on 22 March. Clara left with the Clemenses on 17 May (3 Dec 72 to Langdon, n. 3; "There will be . . . ," Elmira *Advertiser*, 22 Mar 73, 4).

[2] Susan Crane was preparing for the Orphans' Home Fair, sponsored by several churches in Elmira, which raised over five thousand dollars from the sale of food, handicrafts, books, and household items, and the display of art works loaned by local residents. Olivia obviously wrote this letter before the fair began its four-day run on 18 February. The "Hartford Monday" of her dateline might therefore have been 3, 10, or 17 February. But Clemens was in New York on 3 and 10 February, and thus could not have added his paragraph on either of those days, leaving 17 February as the most likely date of joint composition. The Cranes had visited the Clemenses in December ("Orphans' Home Fair," Elmira *Advertiser*, 18, 19, 21, 22 Feb 73, 4; 3 Dec 72 to Langdon).

[3] Olivia's first cousins Edward L. Marsh and Anna Marsh Brown were the children of Mrs. Langdon's twin sister, Louisa Lewis (Mrs. Sheppard) Marsh. Harriet Lewis (later Paff), the daughter of Mrs. Langdon's brother Huron, and an intimate friend of Olivia's, was visiting Elmira at this time, and helped with the Orphans' Home Fair. She and Mrs. Langdon went to stay with the Clemenses in Hartford during the last week of March, remaining until 24 April (*L4*, 43; "Lewis Genealogy"; *L3*, 23 n. 2; "Orphans' Home Fair," Elmira *Advertiser*, 19 Feb 73, 4; 22 Apr 73 to Reid [3rd], n. 1). In 1897 Lewis recalled this visit:

> I spent a month with them at the time Mr C. and Mr. Warner were writing Gilded Age together— Each would write during the day in his own study, and in the early twilight Mr. W. would come over and he & Mr C. with no light save that given by the glowing grate would talk about the book, and later when the lights were brought in, each would read what he had written, so that I heard nearly all of that book before it went to the printers. After the reading we would all go home with Mr. Warner, and his wife—a fine musician—would play for us until the lateness of the hour compelled us to return home. (Paff, 9)

[4] Susy Clemens.

To Whitelaw Reid
18 February 1873 • Hartford, Conn.
(Transcript and MS: New York *Tribune*,
22 Feb 73, and DLC)

Mark Twain's success, at Steinway Hall,[1] has brought him any quantity of invitations to lecture, but his literary contracts confine him at home, & he will not be able to lecture any more this season.

Private:

Home, Feb. 18.

My Dear Reid—

Can you put the above in?[2] I'm *flooded*—& Shanks & The Tribune are largely to blame for it![3] I want a chance to do something beside decline lecture invitations this year. I think I have had *20* from New York city alone. Come—put ~~it~~ the above paragraph (or the substance of it) in & make grateful,

Ys faithly
Clemens

[letter docketed:] *1873*

[1] See pp. 295–96.

[2] Someone at the *Tribune*, possibly Reid, tore off the top portion of this letter and sent it to the newspaper's composing room. That part of the original manuscript is not known to survive. The text is taken from the *Tribune* for 22 February, and therefore may not be a verbatim transcription of Clemens's original words.

[3] William Franklin Gore Shanks (1837–1905) had been the city editor of the *Tribune* since 1871. He began reporting for the Louisville *Journal* and *Courier*, and was a Civil War correspondent and then an editorial writer for the New York *Herald*. After working as the managing editor for *Harper's Weekly Magazine* and then as city editor of the New York *Times*, he joined the *Tribune* staff in 1870 as a foreign correspondent. Clemens playfully blamed Shanks, whom he may have met at the *Aldine* dinner in February 1872, for so frequently printing his work in the *Tribune* (23 Feb 72 to Redpath, n. 1).

To Elisha Bliss, Jr.
25 February 1873 • Hartford, Conn.
(MS: CtY-BR)

Home, 25th

Friend Bliss—

~~Str~~ Stir Frank up—he is getting 3 or 4 weeks behindhand with his statement.[1]

Man in New York wants permission to print a hundred copies or so

of the Jumping Frog, "merely for distribution among friends." He don't
say how many he wants to print for sale, though![2]

Ys

Clemens

⊠———————————————————————————

[*letter docketed:*] √ [*and*] S. L. Clemens | Hartford. Feb. 25. 1873.

[1] Frank Bliss often sent Clemens the American Publishing Company's quarterly royalty statements.

[2] Clemens was the sole owner of the rights to his first book, *The Celebrated
Jumping Frog of Calaveras County, And other Sketches* (SLC 1867a), having purchased the copyright from its publisher, Charles H. Webb, in December 1870
(*L4*, 269, 274, 281). The person seeking permission to reprint it has not been
identified.

To Elisha Bliss, Jr.
26 February 1873 • Hartford, Conn.
(MS: CU-MARK)

Hartf^d Feb. 26.

Friend Bliss—

All right. Make it March 1—& then go back to the old system &
make the next statement *May* 1. You see it was your delay that strung it
out to Nov. 26; ⟨never⟩ it *should* have been Nov. 1.[1]

I̸n inclose proxy.[2]

Can get sketches ready any time, but shall wait awhile, as I have
good hopes of finishing a book which I am working like a dog on—a
book which ought to outsell the sketches, & doubtless will. ₍It will make
a pretty lively sensation I bet you.₎[3]

Ys

Mark.

⊠———————————————————————————

[*letter docketed:*] √ [*and*] S. L. Clemens | Feb 26/73 | Hartford Ct | Author

¹The letter from Bliss to which Clemens replied is not known to survive. The two American Publishing Company quarterly statements extant for 1872 are dated 1 May and 5 August, indicating the next statements were due on 1 November 1872 and 1 February 1873. Only one statement survives from 1873, dated 1 May, but Bliss clearly did send one on or about 1 March (8 May 72 to Perkins; Elisha Bliss, Jr., to SLC, 5 Aug 72 and 1 May 73, CU-MARK; 4 Mar 73 to Bliss).

²The enclosed proxy, which Bliss had presumably requested from Clemens as a voting stockholder in the American Publishing Company, does not survive (4 Mar 73 to Bliss, n. 5).

³Clemens was at work on *The Gilded Age*. He did not issue a book of sketches through Bliss until 1875 (21 Mar 72 to Bliss, n. 1).

To Elisha Bliss, Jr.
28 February 1873 • Hartford, Conn.
(Transcript and paraphrase: Heritage, item 199)

Hartford, Feb. 28.

Friend Bliss—

[*paraphrase: Twain discusses delays in receiving statements from his publisher, states that he is* "so infatuated" *with his new book,* The Gilded Age] that I hate to lay the pen down a moment, [*paraphrase: and adds that he is leaving for Europe shortly, as he wants to publish simultaneously in England and America.*]¹

Clemens.

¹By publishing *The Gilded Age* "simultaneously" in both countries Clemens could acquire a valid British copyright. There was disagreement in the courts on the question of whether an author needed to be a British resident at the time of publication, but to take every precaution against having his book pirated Clemens intended to remain in England until publication was accomplished (Copinger, 60–66; French, 259–60).

To Louisa I. Conrad
March 1873 • Hartford, Conn.
(MS: CU-MARK)

ₐFor Miss Louise Conrad.[1]

─────

With the kindest regards of
   "Mark Twain.".ₐ
                              ⓈⓁⒸ

RECIPE FOR MAKING A SCRAPBOOK
UPON THE CUSTOMARY P̶A̶ PLAN.

Some rainy afternoon, get out the pasteboard box you keep your
scraps in, & look over your collection. This will occupy some hours.
Next day, buy a handsome folio scrap-book, with leaves of all shades &
varieties of color—also get a bottle of mucilage˳ ⅋̶ Now work an hour &
cover two or three pages with choice selections; & then be called suddenly away. After a day or two, prepare to resume. You will now find that
the pages are hopelessly warped; ₐthat₎ the mucilage has soaked through
& made the print almost illegible, & that colored leaves are a hateful
thing in a scrapbook.[2]

Now buy a new w̶h̶i̶ book, with pure white, stiff leaves—& get one
ounce of good gum tragicanth. Leave a dozen flakes of the gum soaking
in a gill of water over night; in the morning, if the gum is too thick &
stiff, add water, but precious little of it, for the paste should not be thin.
Paste in a page or two of scraps, & then iron them dry & smooth̸, or else
leave the book under pressure.

You will be satisfied with your work this time. Now w̶o̶r̶k̶ labor with
enthusiasm for three days, heaving in poetry, theology, jokes, obituaries,
politics, tales, recipes for pies, poultices, puddings,—shovel them in
helter-skelter, & every-which-way, first-come-first-served—but *get them
in.* During the next few days, cool down a little; during the next few,
cool down altogether & quit.

While the next six months drift by, cut out scraps occasionally &
throw them loosely in between the leaves of the scrap-book, & say to
yourself that some day you will paste them. Meantime, mislay your gum
tragicanth & lose your brush.

By & by that scrapbook will begin to reproach you every time your eye falls upon it; it will accuse you, it will deride your indolence; it will get to intruding itself with studied & offensive frequency & persistence; it will rob you of your peace by day & your rest by night. It will haunt your very dreams, & say: "Look at me & the condition I am in."

And at last that day will come which is inevitable in the history of all scrap-books—you will carry it up to the grave-yard of musty, dusty, discarded & forgotten literature in the garret; & when next you see it you will be old, & sad, & scarred with the battle of life, & will say, "Ah, well= a-day, it is but the type of all the hopeful efforts & high ambitions of the morning & the noontide of my pilgrimage—each so gallantly begun, & each in turn so quickly humbled & broken & vanquished!"

Yr friend,
Sam*ˡ*. L. Clemens.

Hartford, March 1873.[3]

[1] Clemens became acquainted with Louisa Conrad during his visit to St. Louis in March 1867. In January 1869 he described her to Olivia as "a most estimable young lady. . . . She was [a] near neighbor of ours, & my mother & sister are very fond of her, & of all her family" (*L3*, 19).

[2] Clemens was granted a patent for an "Improvement in Scrap-Books" on 24 June 1873 (11 Aug 72 to OC, n. 4).

[3] Mollie Clemens had evidently solicited Clemens's contribution on Conrad's behalf, and then forwarded it to her, with a letter that is not known to survive. On 7 July 1873 Conrad wrote to thank Mollie:

> Your letter was a real treasure, and Mr. Clemmens' contribution to my scrap-book an exquisite tribute, for which I am a thousand times grateful. I esteem it a high honor that his signature should adorn my book, and his beautiful composition places it with my choicest jems. (CU-MARK)

To Henry Wheeler Shaw (Josh Billings)
March? 1873 • Hartford, Conn.
(Shaw 1873, 4)

Dear Josh.—I think a very great deal of you, as a personal friend, of long standing; I admire you as a philosopher; I actually revere you as almost the only specimen remaining with us, of a species of being that used to be common enough—I mean an honest man.

Therefore you can easily believe that if I don't write the paragraphs you desire for your department of the paper, it is not because there is any lack in me of either the will or the willingness to do it.[1]

No, it is only because my present literary contracts, & understandings, debar me.

I am thus debarred for three years to come.[2]

But after that—however, you wouldn't want to wait, perhaps.

I wish we could compromise; I wish it would answer for you to write one of these books, for me, while I write an almanac for you.[3]

But this will not do, because I cannot abide your spelling.

It does seem to me that you spell worse every day.

Sometimes your orthography makes me frantic.

It is out of all reason that a man, seventy-five years of age, should spell as you do.[4]

Why do you not attend a night-school?

You might at least get the hang of the easy words.

I am sending you a primer by this mail which I know will help you, if you will study it hard.

Now is the most favorable time you have had in seventy years, now that you are just entering your second childhood.

It ought to come really easy to you.

Many people believe that in the dominion of natural history, you stand without a peer.

It is acknowledged on all sides that you have thrown new light on the mule, & also on other birds of the same family; that you have notably augmented the world's admiration of the splendid plumage of the kangaroo—or possibly it might have been the cockatoo—but I know it was one of those bivalves, or the other; that you have uplifted the hornet, & given him his just place among the flora of our country; & that you have aroused an interest never felt before, in every fur-bearing animal, from the occult rhinoceros clear down to the domestic cow of the present geologic period.[5]

These researches ought not to die; but what can you expect?

Yale University desires to use them as text books in the natural history department of that institution, but they cannot stand the spelling.

You will take kindly what I am saying; I only wish to make you understand that even the profoundest science must perish & be lost to the world, when it is couched in such inhuman orthography as yours.

Even the very first word in your annual is an atrocity; *"Allminax"* is no way to build that word.

I can spell better than that with my left hand.

In answer to your other inquiry I say no, decidedly.

You can't lecture on "Light" with any success.

Tyndall has used up that subject.[6]

And I think you ought not to lecture on "Nitro-Glycerine, with Experiments"—the cost of keeping a coroner under salary would eat up all the profits.

Try "Readings"—they are all the rage now. And yet how can you read acceptably when you cannot even spell right?

An ignorance so shining & conspicuous as yours— Now I have it— go on a jury.[7]

That is your place.

Your friend,

Mark Twain.

[1] Shaw had apparently asked Clemens to contribute something to his column in the *New York Weekly*, "Spice-Box," which had first appeared in the May 1867 issue. He printed Clemens's "refusal" (the present letter) instead, in his column for 28 July, introducing it as follows:

> Among the most valued of our private correspondents is Mark Twain.
> We received a letter of love from him lately, and we see no harm in making some extracts from it, and laying them before our readers.
> The letter is strictly a private one, but we admire Mark so much that we don't think he will be angry at us if we make public property of a portion of it. (Shaw 1873; Kesterson, 24)

Shaw did not mention the date of the letter, which is conjecturally assigned to March: see note 8. Several peculiar spellings have been emended—for example, "Tharefore" and "beleave"—on the assumption that they were errors, or even deliberate revisions by Billings, who relied on phonetic spelling for comic effect. (The style of one-sentence paragraphs, also characteristic of Billings but not of Clemens, cannot be remedied.) The possibility remains, however, that Clemens himself introduced the misspellings to burlesque his friend's method.

[2] Clemens clearly expected his letter to appear in print. His claim of being "debarred" from writing "paragraphs" had little basis in fact. His *Roughing It* contract, drawn up in July 1870, merely stipulated that during the book's "preparation and sale" he was "not to write or furnish manuscript for any other book," unless it was for the American Publishing Company (*L4*, 565). Nevertheless, Elisha Bliss preferred Clemens to write exclusively for that company.

[3] Shaw's series of comic annuals, *Josh Billings' Farmer's Allminax*, had sold hundreds of thousands of copies since 1869. Clemens had hoped to rival these with "Mark Twain's Annual—1871," but Bliss opposed the scheme (*L4*, 209, 212, 213–14 n. 2, 218).

4 Shaw was born in April 1818.

5 Nature was among Billings's favorite topics. His essay "Sum Natral History" was a comic discussion of insects. In "Josh Billings on the Muel" he wrote, "The mule is haf hoss, and haf Jackass, and then kums tu a full stop, natur diskovering her mistake. . . . Tha are like sum men, very korrupt at harte" (Shaw: 1866, 13–14; 1868, 14–19; see also Kesterson, 58–59). Billings had lectured frequently on "Milk and Natral Histry" (though playfully avoiding the nominal topic), and for the 1872–73 season "The Pensiv Cockroach" was one of his advertised lectures (*L4*, 227 n. 1 *bottom; Lyceum* 1872, 2).

6 John Tyndall (1820–93) was a British physicist and well-known popularizer of modern science. He made major contributions to the understanding of magnetism and diamagnetism, heat, sound, and light. In the winter of 1872–73 he delivered a series of lectures in the United States, renowned for their lucidity and ingenious experimental illustrations. The lectures were published in the "Tribune Lecture Extra No. 1" in mid-January 1873 and, in mid-March, were collected in book form as *Lectures on Light* (New York: D. Appleton and Co.) (New York *Tribune:* "Lectures and Meetings," 15 Jan 73, 7; "New Publications," 14 Mar 73, 6).

7 This comment suggests that Clemens wrote the present letter in March, when developments in a prominent murder case led him to suggest publicly that ignorance was a prerequisite for jury duty: see the enclosure with 7 Mar 73 to Reid (2nd).

To Willard M. White
3 March 1873 • Hartford, Conn.
(Transcript: CtY)

Hartford, Conn., March 3, 1873.

Mr. White,¹—Dear Sir:

There is nothing that a just & right feeling man rejoices in more than to see a mosquito imposed on & put down, & brow-beaten & aggravated,—& this ingenious contrivance will do it.² And it is a rare thing to worry a fly with, too. A fly will stand off & curse this invention till language utterly fails him. I have seen them do it hundreds of times. I like to dine in the air on the back porch in summer, & so I would not be without this portable net for anything; when you have got it hoisted, the flies have to wait for the second table. We shall see the summer day come when we shall all sit under our nets in church & slumber peacefully, while the discomfited flies club together & take it out of the minister.

There are heaps of ways of getting priceless enjoyment out of these charming things, if I had time to point them out & dilate on them a little.

Mark Twain.

[1] White (1843–1923) was born in nearby Canton, Connecticut. He graduated from Amherst College in 1872, shortly after Clemens lectured there on 27 February. In 1862 he had enlisted in the Twenty-second Regiment of the Connecticut Volunteers, serving until 7 July 1863. He graduated from Boston University Law School in 1875, was admitted to the bar that same year, and until 1880 practiced law in Boston. From 1880 until 1897 he worked in the oil business in Pennsylvania, eventually moving to Boise, Idaho, where he built electric power plants. White had helped to organize the Amherst lecture series in which Clemens appeared, presumably the occasion of their becoming acquainted (Amherst alumni obituary, courtesy of John Lancaster, Amherst College Library).

[2] In November 1872 White obtained patent number 133,279 for a Mosquito-Net Frame, designed for attachment to a bed (*Official Gazette*, 2:584). He must have asked Clemens for his help in promoting his "ingenious contrivance," for this letter was published in an advertising circular which is now the sole source for the text. Two other endorsements, both dated 1 March 1873, were also included: one from W. H. H. Murray, who spoke two weeks before Clemens in the Amherst lecture series, and another from Edward Hitchcock, M.D., an Amherst faculty member ("Course of Lectures in College Hall, Amherst," Amherst College Library, PH in CU-MARK, courtesy of Thomas A. Tenney).

To Elisha Bliss, Jr.
4 March 1873 • Hartford, Conn.
(MS: ViU)

Hartf^d, Mch. 4/73

Friend Bliss—

Statement rec'd for quarter ending Mch 1, & check for $1,656.69 for royalties on Innocents Abroad & Roughing It.

So Roughing It sells less than twice as many in a quarter as Innocents, a book which is getting gray with age.[1] The fault is mainly in the engravings & paper, I think.[2] That, & the original lack of publicity. I believe I have learned, now, that if one don't secure publicity & notoriety for a book the instant it is issued, no amount of hard work & faithful advertising can accomplish it later on. When we look at what Roughing

It sold in the first 3 & 6 months, we naturally argue that it would have sold ~~from~~ full 3 times as many if it had gotten the prompt & early journalistic boost & notoriety that the Innocents had.[3]

Recognizing the importance, now, of this ~~early~~ prompt notoriety (which I was *afraid* of & didn't want until we were dead sure of 50,000 subscriptions to R. I.—but which I am not afraid of now,) I have conceived a plan which ~~wh~~ will advertise the next book from Maine to the Marquesas ˏfree of expenseˏ before the proofsheets are all read. But I'll fix that, myself.

Now Nast appears to be doing nothing in particular. I want him, solitary & alone, to illustrate ~~the~~ this next book, it being an essentially *American* book, & he will enjoy doing it. Nast only has just one *first-class* talent ˏ(caricature,)ˏ & no more ˏ~~(caricature)~~ˏ —but this book will exercise that talent, I think. I think he will be glad to do this work below his usual terms. If you say so *I will write him.* Tell me what you think, & tell me about the total amount you think it best to put in the *drawing* of the illustrations.[4]

I wish you would say nothing about ~~an~~ a new book from me for the spring (or rather next fall) issue, because as soon as I can get some more stock at easy figures, I want it. I want to be a Director, also.[5]

Ys
Clemens.

How [many] copies have been sold of Innocents? And how many of R. I.? Get it from the official figures.[6]

[letter docketed:] √ *[and]* S. L. Clemens | Mar. 4/73

[1] The American Publishing Company's statement for 1 March is not known to survive. The bindery records, however, indicate that in the quarter ending on that date, 3,684 copies of *Roughing It*, but only 2,045 copies of *The Innocents Abroad*, were bound (APC, 109). The number of copies actually sold would have been slightly lower.

[2] See 7 Mar 72 to OC, n. 1.

[3] Clemens had been reluctant to send out review copies of *Roughing It* (19 Apr 72 to Bliss, n. 2). In contrast, when *The Innocents Abroad* was published in August 1869, Bliss had distributed "from 1 to 2,000 copies" to newspapers, and the book was widely—and favorably—reviewed (*L3*, 293 n. 1, 323 n. 1, 328 n. 1*top;* see 13 and 17 Jan 73 to Reid, n. 7).

[4] Thomas Nast did not contribute any drawings to *The Gilded Age.* Bliss hired several well-known but presumably less costly artists instead—although in at

least one advertisement for the book he made the implausible claim that the illustrations cost nearly $10,000 (see 10? July 73 to Warner, n. 3; *MTLP*, 75 n. 2; *RI 1993*, 881–82).

[5] In January 1873 Clemens owned $5,000 of American Publishing Company stock, on which he received a 10 percent dividend for the preceding quarter. He sold the stock in 1881, having never received another dividend. No record has been found of an additional purchase. Clemens became a director of the company in 1873, and—except for 1878–79, when he was in Europe—retained the position until sometime in 1881 (Elisha Bliss, Jr., to SLC, 7 Jan 73, CU-MARK; Hill 1964, 124; Geer 1872–82).

[6] As of 1 March 1873, a total of 77,654 copies of *Roughing It* and 103,907 copies of *The Innocents Abroad* had been bound (APC, 106–7, 109).

To Whitelaw Reid
per Telegraph Operator
7 March 1873 • (1st of 2) • Hartford, Conn.
(MS, copy received: DLC)

BLANK NO. 1.

792

THE WESTERN UNION TELEGRAPH COMPANY.

NO. 4Fa   THE RULES OF THIS COMPANY REQUIRE THAT ALL MESSAGES   209
RECEIVED FOR TRANSMISSION SHALL BE WRITTEN ON THE MESSAGE BLANKS OF THE COMPANY, UNDER AND SUBJECT TO THE CONDITIONS PRINTED THEREON, WHICH CONDITIONS HAVE BEEN AGREED TO BY THE SENDER OF THE FOLLOWING MESSAGE.

G. H. MUMFORD, SEC.   T. T. ECKERT, GEN. SUPT., NEW YORK.   WILLIAM ORTON, PREST.

DATED,   Hartford Ct ⎫   REC'D AT 145 BROADWAY,

TO   Whitelaw Reid ⎭   March ⌀ 7 1873.

"Tribune"

Leave It out. The man Is the second advent In disguise god help us. we dont want to crucify the saviour twice handrunning[1]

Saml L Clemens

23 paid

Rd Kr

---

[1] On 6 March Clemens had sent Reid an article about convicted murderer William Foster for publication in the *Tribune*. On 7 March, after writing and suppressing an addition to it (enclosed in the next letter), he sent the present telegram requesting that it be withdrawn. No text of the withdrawn article survives, but Clemens provided glimpses of it in the first paragraph of the next letter and in the first sentence of its enclosure.

To Whitelaw Reid
7 March 1873 • (2nd of 2) • Hartford, Conn.
(MS: DLC and NN)

7th Mch

My Dear Reid—

Hang it, I fooled away a good deal of valuable time over the enclosed, & then, just as I was sending it off to the telegraph office it occurred to me that in confessing that imprisonment for life was a heavier
penalty after all than that mush-&-milk jury really wanted to inflict, I
had knocked the bottom out of my article & was whooping for the enemy. So of course I crossed it all out & sent the brief dispatch which you
doubtless got.[1]

Tear up this stuff—but read it first—it isn't bad. Read the last page,
anyway. God knows I was intended for a statesman. I can solve any political problem that ever was started.

Love to Hay & Brooks[2] & Hazzard.

Ys

Clemens

[*enclosure, page 1:*]

₍66₎

₍I73₎[3]

₍Telegram. Send it at once.₎

Hartford Feb Mch. 7

Whitelaw Reid
    Editor Tribune
      New York.

Leave out the girl and add this as a postscript:

Since writing that, I have read Foster's Plea in T read the Foster petitions in Thursday's Tribune.[4] The lawyers' opinions do not disturb me,
because I know that those same gentlemen could make as far stronger
far abler ₍an₎ argument in favor of Judas Iscariot; which is a great deal
for me to say, for I never can think of Judas Iscariot without losing [*page
2:*] my temper. To my mind Judas Iscariot was nothing but a low, mean,
premature Congressman. The attitude ₍of the jury₎ does unsettle a body,

I must admit; and it seems plain that they would have modified their verdict to murder in the ~~first~~ second degree if the judge's charge had permitted of it.[5] But when I come to the petitions of Foster's friends & find out Foster's true character, the generous tears will flow, I cannot help it. How easy it is to get a wrong impression of a man. I perceive that from childhood up, this one has been a sweet, docile thing, full of pretty ways & [*top of page 3: 284,*] gentle impulses, the charm of the fireside, the admiration of society, the idol of the ~~s~~ Sunday-school. I recognize in him the divinest nature that has ever glorified any mere human being. I perceive that the sentiment with which he regarded temperance was a thing that amounted to frantic adoration. I ,freely, confess that it was the most natural thing in the world for such an organism as this to get drunk & insult a stranger & then beat his brains out with a car hook because he did not seem to admire it. Such is Foster. And to think that we came so near losing him![6] How do we know ~~that~~ [*page 4:*] but that he is the Second Advent? And yet, after all, if the jury had not been hampered in their choice of a verdict I ,think I, could consent to lose him.

The humorist who invented trial by jury played a colossal practical joke upon the world, but since we have the system we ought to try to ~~believe~~ respect it. A thing which is not thoroughly easy to do, when we reflect that by command of the law a criminal juror must be an intellectual vacuum attached to a melting heart & perfectly maccaronian bowels of compassion. [*page 5:*]

I have had no experience in making laws or amending them, but still I cannot understand ~~whe~~ why, when it takes twelve men to inflict the death penalty upon a ~~man, it~~ ,person, it, should take any less than twelve more to undo their work. If I were a legislature, & had just been elected & had not had time to sell out, I would put the pardoning & commuting power ~~ut~~ into the hands of twelve able men instead of dumping so huge a burden upon the shoulders of one poor petition-persecuted individual.

S. L. C.

~~Hartf~~ Paid—472—$9.49.

[*letter docketed:*]

Col Hay:
I haven't read this. Please look through it & tell me whether you think it would do to publish together with his letter and dispatch.

WR

[*and*]
I think it will do to publish alone.

H[7]

[1] The previous letter.
[2] Noah Brooks (1830–1903) joined the *Tribune* in 1871, but Clemens had known him in California. He began his newspaper career in Boston at the age of eighteen; six years later he went west, eventually settling in California, where he founded the Marysville *Appeal*. During the Civil War he served as Washington correspondent for the Sacramento *Union*, and after the war he became managing editor of the San Francisco *Alta California*. It was during this time (1865–66) that he and Clemens became acquainted, initially through their mutual friend Bret Harte. Brooks was still an editor on the *Alta* when Mark Twain's letters from the *Quaker City* appeared there in 1867 and 1868 (*L2*, 17 n. 1; "Noah Brooks Dead," New York *Times*, 18 Aug 1903, 7; Brooks, 98).
[3] These numbers were Clemens's word count for the first page of the suppressed telegram he enclosed (66), followed by a total for the first two pages (173). He did not count the dateline and address (or the signature on the fifth page) because the telegraph company did not charge for these essential elements. The "284" at the top of the third page is an accurate word count up through that page, and the last line on the fifth page gives an accurate total for the whole (472 words, costing $9.49: that is, $.25 for the first ten words, plus $.02 per word for the rest).
[4] The *Tribune* for Thursday, 6 March, contained more than a page of petitions and testimonials from prominent lawyers and clergymen, as well as family, friends, and other supporters of convicted murderer William Foster, all attesting to his upright character and calling upon Governor John A. Dix to commute his death sentence to life imprisonment. In May 1871 Foster had been found guilty of the first-degree murder of merchant Avery D. Putnam. Foster had insulted a female streetcar passenger (presumably the "girl" of Clemens's original article). When Putnam came to her defense, the men exchanged angry words, and Foster

struck Putnam in the head with an iron bar, or "car hook," which resulted in his death several days later (Wilson 1870, 983; New York *Tribune:* "Foster's Plea," 6 Mar 73, 3–4; "The Moral of the Foster Case," 22 Mar 73, 6; see also Willson).

[5] Among the petitions in the 6 March *Tribune* were several from jurors who believed Foster's crime had not been premeditated, but, as a result of the judge's instructions, were under the impression that the law did not permit them to convict him of second-degree murder. They had therefore accompanied their verdict with a plea for mercy, assuming that it would dissuade the judge from imposing the death penalty ("Foster's Plea," New York *Tribune,* 6 Mar 73, 3).

[6] Clemens assumed (as did the *Tribune*) that Governor Dix would commute Foster's sentence. But Dix denied the petition on 14 March, and Foster was hanged a week later (New York *Tribune:* "Foster's Case," 6 Mar 73, 6; "The End of the Foster Case," 15 Mar 73, 6; "The Moral of the Foster Case," 22 Mar 73, 6).

[7] Reid's private secretary, Donald Nicholson, first recorded Reid's instructions using an abbreviated reporter's shorthand (a modified form of the system devised by Isaac Pitman), then translated those notes into longhand (probably signing Reid's initials) so that John Hay could read them and reply (Baehr, 220). Hay's recommendation was followed: under the title "Foster's Case," the enclosure (beginning "I have read") was published facing the editorial page for 10 March (5). Neither Clemens's covering letter nor the previous dispatch was included. A *Tribune* editor marked the manuscript with instructions to the typesetters: he altered the salutation to read *"To the Editor of the Tribune"*; crossed out Clemens's opening thirteen words ("Leave out . . . that,"); wrote "stet" at the top of each sheet (pages 1, 3, and 5) to nullify Clemens's cancel marks; altered the signature to "MARK TWAIN"; and added "Hartford, March 7, 1873." beneath it.

To the Staff of the New York *Tribune*
7 March 1873 • Hartford, Conn.
(MS: NN)

                                                             Hartford, 7th
Gentlemen—
   Please send 2 Credit Mobilier Extra sheets[1] to
                                             Yours &c
                                             Mark Twain

[1] On 7 March, the *Tribune* advertised for sale an

extra sheet of eight pages, a complete résumé of the entire CREDIT MOBILIER IN-VESTIGATION. The reports which have for two months cumbered the papers are carefully condensed, winnowed of extraneous matter, and presented in a clear and intelligent shape without note or comment. ("New Publications," 6)

Clemens probably intended to draw on this account for his portrayal of corrupt politicians in *The Gilded Age*. The Crédit Mobilier of America was a banking corporation chartered (under a different name) in 1863, through which the capitalists who were building the transcontinental railway (Union Pacific Railroad) pocketed exorbitant profits from 1867 to 1869 from government financing that greatly exceeded actual construction costs. Legislation permitting these actions had been passed in 1867 and 1868 by senators and representatives who had been bribed with gifts of valuable railroad stock. The Crédit Mobilier scandal became public late in the 1872 presidential campaign, and was investigated by House and Senate committees during the winter of 1872–73. Although the Senate ultimately took no punitive action, and the House censured only two of its members, the reputations of many politicians were damaged by the allegations of corruption (*DAH*, 2:84–85; Smith, 289–90; *Annual Cyclopaedia 1873*, 671–80).

To Tom Hood and George Routledge and Sons
10 March 1873 • Hartford, Conn.
(Pike, 14–15)

Hartford, March 10.

To Tom Hood, Esq., & Messrs. George Routledge & Sons, London:

Gentlemen:

The Jubilee Singers are to appear in London, & I am requested to say in their behalf what I know about them—& I most cheerfully do it.[1]

I heard them sing once, & I would walk seven miles to hear them sing again.[2] You will recognize that this is strong language for me to use, when you remember that I never was fond of pedestrianism, & got tired of walking, that Sunday afternoon, in twenty minutes, after making up my mind to see for myself & at my own leisure how much ground his grace the Duke of Bedford's property covered.[3]

I think these gentlemen & ladies make eloquent music—& what is as much to the point, they reproduce the true melody of the plantations, & are the only persons I ever heard accomplish this on the public platform. The so-called "negro minstrels" simply mis-represent the thing; I do not think they ever saw a plantation or ever heard a slave sing.

I was reared in the South, & my father owned slaves,[4] & I do not know when anything has so moved me as did the plaintive melodies of the Jubilee Singers. It was the first time for twenty-five or thirty years

that I had heard such songs, or heard them sung in the genuine old way—
& it is a way, I think, that white people cannot imitate—& never can,
for that matter, for one must have been a slave himself in order to feel
what that life was & so convey the pathos of it in the music. Do not fail
to hear the Jubilee Singers. I am very well satisfied that you will not regret it.

Yours faithfully,
Saml. L. Clemens.
Mark Twain.

[1] The Jubilee Singers of Fisk University in Nashville, Tennessee, had undertaken an extended singing tour in 1871 to raise money for their school. The third
year of their tour took them to Great Britain, where they performed from May
1873 until May 1874, raising nearly ten thousand pounds. According to their
agent, Gustavus Pike, the eleven singers—eight of them former slaves—won
acclaim for the "spiritual and religious power of the songs of the slaves of the
South, and thus touched the hearts of the Christian people everywhere and secured their sympathy and liberal aid" (Pike, vi–viii, 31, 38, 193). Tom Hood,
the editor of *Fun*, published extracts from Clemens's letter on 26 April, explaining that it had been "brought over by the agent in advance" of the arrival of the
Jubilee Singers (Hood 1873). Several other prominent men supplied similar endorsements, including Henry Ward Beecher and George MacDonald (Pike, 13).
Pike retained the letter and published it in his account of the 1873–74 tour.
Clemens probably addressed his letter to the Routledges, as well as to Hood, to
increase its chances for publication. Perhaps he hoped they would print it in
their magazine, the *Broadway*—which, however, ceased publication in early
1873.

[2] It is not known for certain when Clemens first heard the Jubilee Singers, but
it may have been on the afternoon of 28 January 1872, when they performed at
a Sunday school concert at Joseph Twichell's Asylum Hill Congregational
Church and, according to the Hartford *Courant*, created "a sensation rarely
equalled":

> It is the first time that we at the north have heard the genuine songs of their race, exe-
> cuted with their faith and their feeling. It was like a revelation. . . . One heard in those
> strange and plaintive melodies the sadness and the hope of a trusting and a really joyous
> race. ("The Jubilee Singers," 29 Jan 72, 2)

Clemens had another opportunity to hear the singers in Hartford on 17 December 1872 ("Brief Mention," Hartford *Courant*, 13 Dec 72, 2). In any case, it is
certain that he heard them twice during his stay in England. Samuel C. Thompson recalled going with him to purchase tickets for one of their London concerts:

> He felt in all his pockets and got the money. But just as the clerk was sweeping it into
> the drawer some one called out "Don't take that money." "Isn't it the right amount?"
> said Clemens. "Isn't this Mr. Clemens?" said the manager. "You can't pay any money
> to go to this concert. Give him the best seats in the hall." Going out Clemens explained
> that he had written an article in a London paper drawing attention to the fact that now

the public would have an opportunity to compare the conventional "negro minstrels" with the genuine negroes of the South and their singing. After the concert Clemens said he had never before seen a cultured English audience so enthusiastic in applause. (Thompson, 85–86)

On 16 July Clemens heard the singers again at a private garden party (see 11 July 73 to Smith, n. 2). Nearly two years later, on 8 March 1875, Clemens recalled one of these London performances in a letter to Theodore F. Seward, then the Jubilee Singers' musical director ("Mark Twain and the Jubilee Singers," Boston *Evening Journal*, 13 Mar 75, 4, in Martin, 2–3):

> Dear Sir—I am expecting to hear the Jubilee Singers to-night, for the fifth time (the reason it is not the fiftieth is because I have not had fifty opportunities), and I wish to ask a favor of them. I remember an afternoon in London, when their "John Brown's Body" took a decorous, aristocratic English audience by surprise and threw them into a volcanic eruption of applause before they knew what they were about. I never saw anything finer than their enthusiasm. Now, John Brown is not in this evening's programme; cannot it be added? It would set me down in London again for a minute or two, and at the same time save me the tedious sea voyage and the expense. I was glad of the triumph the Jubilee Singers achieved in England, for their music so well deserved such a result. Their success in this country is pretty well attested by the fact that there are already companies of imitators trying to ride into public favor by endeavoring to convey the impression that they are the original Jubilee Singers.
> Very truly,
> SAMUEL L. CLEMENS
> (Mark Twain.)

³Sometime during his 1872 trip to England, Clemens had evidently accompanied Hood on a visit to Woburn Abbey, the principal seat of the duke of Bedford. The present duke, Francis Charles Hastings Russell (1819–91), had succeeded his cousin in May 1872. The house, built in 1747 on the foundations of a Cistercian abbey, was near the village of Woburn in Bedford County. Its sixty acres of gardens and pleasure grounds and thirty-five hundred acres of deer park, one of the largest in England, were open to the public (Burke 1904, 137–38; Murray, 459–60).

⁴For Clemens's recollections of the slaves his father owned, see *Inds*, 89, 104, 327, 346.

To William Dean Howells
13 March 1873 • Hartford, Conn.
(MS: ViU)

Hartf^d, Mch 13.

Friend Howells—

This is from the man Kendall whom we once shipped out to California to die, but who baseley went back on us.¹ For he still lives, as

Harte knows to his cost, since this is the same ~~virtuous~~ ‚hypercritical‚ Kendall who "exposed" ~~the said~~ Harte in the San Francisco Chronicle.[2]

He seems to still afflict me with his perilous friendship—wants me to get him a show in the Eastern Magazines. I have had his poems on hand for a month, intending to return them to him "with thanks," but have neglected it so long that it requires cheek to do it, now—& besides this ill-constructed chronic starveling needs charitable treatment more than he deserves. He is down, & although I would *like* to hit him, even in that position it seems like "going for" crippled game & I sort of hate to do it.

Now you will probably not want his poetry—& if so, just be kind enough to mail it back to him, either with or without explanations, for I would dearly like to see him get up your private history with Kendallian embellishments & deliver it seething hot in the Chronicle—& indeed I have so set my heart upon this ~~than~~ that I cannot think you will have the heart to disappoint me. I would do as much for you, any time.

But if you should prefer to print the poetry, do so; but in that case I beg that you will "improve" it here & there, as Harte used to do for him, & that will answer the same purpose & produce the same result. I wait with impatience, not to say feverish greed.[3]

Yrs
Clemens.

[1] Clemens evidently enclosed a letter from poet W. A. Kendall, along with the poems mentioned in the next paragraph. (For Clemens's previous efforts on Kendall's behalf, see 7 Jan 72 to Howells.)

[2] On 15 December 1872 Kendall published an attack on Harte in the San Francisco *Chronicle,* belittling his talent and accusing him of embezzling funds intended for contributors to the *Overland Monthly* (Kendall 1872). On 26 December Harte enclosed a copy of Kendall's article in the following letter (CU-MARK):

Sturtevant House
Decem. 26th/72

My dear Clemens,

    I have been lately pretty well abused from unexpected sources but I think the enclosed caps the climax. Do you remember the man to whom you gave $50; for whom I raised $60 and procured by begging a first class passage to San Francisco and to whom I sent anonymously $25, when I was rather poor myself? Well—this is the reptile! And worse than all, this is the second or third time that he has thus requited me.

    Now, what, in the name of all that is diabolically mean, am I to do. I dont mind his slander; that I can refute—but how am I to make this dog, know that he is a dog and not a man?

    You wrote me from London that you had heard that Osgood had taken £50 from Hotten and given him the copyright of my new book. I believe Osgood did it for the best, but as I had no idea of condoning that pirate Hotten's offenses for £50, I repudiated it at once. I told Osgood not to send him advanced sheets of my new story and to say that Mr Harte annulled the contract. He did so—and I see by the Spectator that Hotten has quietly reproduced all the book except that story, without even paying the £50, and further has had the advantage of his previous announcement that he was "authorized by Mr Harte &c". Further the book contains somebody else's story foisted upon me. But that'll do today. I'll see you I hope on the 3^d. I saw your brother-in-law at Elmira the other day

Yours

Harte

Harte had seen the review in the London *Spectator* for 7 December 1872 (1557–58) of Hotten's *Stories of the Sierras*, which included Joaquin Miller's "Last Man of Mexican Camp," together with eight stories and poems by Harte. (His "new story" has not been identified.) Harte had been in Elmira on 23 December (when he saw Charles Langdon) to deliver his lecture, "The Argonauts of '49" ("Bret Harte," Elmira *Advertiser*, 24 Dec 72, 4). He expected to see Clemens on 3 January in Hartford, where he was scheduled to lecture that evening (22 Mar 73 to Larned, n. 3). A week after Kendall's attack on Harte was published, the San Francisco *News Letter and California Advertiser* remarked on his ingratitude, claiming that not even a dog would "gnaw the hand that fed" it, as Kendall had done ("W. A. Kendall," 21 Dec 72, 8; see also 7 Jan 72 to Howells, n. 5). In 1878, after Clemens had quarreled with Harte, he told Howells that John Carmany, publisher of the *Overland*, as well as the contributors had believed Kendall's charge (27 June 78 to Howells, MH-H, in *MTHL*, 1:235; information courtesy of Gary Scharnhorst).

³Harte must have revised Kendall's poetry before publishing it in *Outcroppings* and the *Overland Monthly* (Harte 1866; 7 Jan 72 to Howells, n. 5). Howells never published Kendall in the *Atlantic*.

To William Bowen
20 March 1873 • Hartford, Conn.
(MS: TxU-Hu)

Hartf^d, Mch. 20.

Dear Will——

Am very much obliged to Mr. Bent for the copy of his lecture, & shall read it with interest.[1]

Can't come out there & lecture. Can't lecture anywhere—detest the business with all my heart. Am not a free man, anyway. Been offered everything, from $500 up to $800 a night for 20 or 30 nights,[2] & my wife said *No*—for which I was not sorry & did not weep.

We ~~said~~ sail for England May 17 & return in October—meantime we hope the most aggravating part of the house will be built & off our minds.[3]

Ys Ever

Sam.

[1] Clemens had evidently received—either from Bowen or from Silas Bent—a copy of Bent's *Gateways to the Pole: An Address Delivered before the St. Louis Mercantile Library Association, January 6th, 1872, upon the Thermal Paths to the Pole, the Currents of the Ocean, and the Influence of the Latter upon the Climates of the World* (St. Louis: 1872). Bent (1820–87) was an oceanographer and former naval officer who, like Bowen, lived in St. Louis. His thesis—that currents maintained an open sea around the North Pole—was not accepted by other authorities on polar exploration.

[2] See 13 and 17 Jan 73 to Reid, n. 3.

[3] See 13 and 17 Jan 73 to Reid, nn. 6, 8.

To Josephus N. Larned
22 March 1873 • Hartford, Conn.
(MS: NBuHi)

HARTFORD, Mch. 22 187*2*–3.

DEAR SIR:[1]

    I THANK YOU VERY MUCH FOR YOUR INVITATION, BUT AM COMPELLED TO DECLINE IT, AS I AM NOT LECTURING AT ALL ~~THIS~~ ₍this or next₎ SEASON, OTHER DUTIES ₍& inclinations & lazinesses₎ RENDERING THIS COURSE NECESSARY.

YOURS TRULY,

MARK TWAIN.

₍Care of₎ "American Literary Bureau,*'* Cooper Institute, N. Y.," is Bret Harte's business address.[2] He ought to take with a Buffalo audience, I should think. He has an excellent lecture this season, & reads it execrably. The newspapers say he reads finely, & so I am willing to give you your choice between the criticisms.[3] *I* wouldn't be a bit afraid to put him in a regular course.[4]

I wish you had told me when Selkirk's next payment is due to me while you were writing—I think it is due this month.[5]

I can't call any good lecture-cards to mind just at this moment, & I have no lists by me; but if you will drop a line to the American Lit. Bureau, N. Y., & to James Redpath, 36 Bromfield street Boston, they'll furnish you full lists, & David Gray[6] & you together would have no trouble in making a selection.

Ys Truly

Sam[l]. L. Clemens.

[1] Larned, Clemens's former partner on the Buffalo *Express*, had evidently written in his role as chairman of the lecture committee of the Young Men's Association of Buffalo (20 Jan 72 to OLC, n. 6; "Young Men's Association Lecture Course," Buffalo *Courier*, 7 Jan 73, 3; *Buffalo Directory*, 49).

[2] According to an announcement in the Buffalo *Courier* for 23 December 1872, the American Literary Bureau was "arranging a western lecturing tour" for Harte, a reference to his upcoming appearances in Kansas and Missouri in the fall of 1873 ("Personal," 1). This bureau, owned by James K. Medbery, had handled many of Clemens's engagements during his 1868–69 lecture tour (Merwin, 241; *L3*, 353 n. 2, 481).

[3] Clemens had heard Harte deliver his lecture, "The Argonauts of '49," in Hartford on 3 January. According to the Hartford *Times*,

> The lecture was full of brilliant points. Some of them were too neatly presented—too quietly exposed—to "rake down the crowd." Only his stories and anecdotes secured a full and hearty appreciation. But, as these constituted a large part of his discourse, the performance, as a whole, cannot be said to have lacked an appreciative reception. Certainly nobody who witnessed the mirth of that audience could have any doubt on *that* point. Nevertheless it is a fact—as was casually remarked by Mark Harte—no, we mean Bret Twain, who, with two other choice spirits, flocked in and secured seats in one of the private boxes—that in order to bag the game, every time, when one shoots at an American audience, he must put in a good deal of powder behind his shot, and make his "p'ints" stick out so *very* plain, that you can almost hang your hat on 'em. ("The Argonauts of '49," 4 Jan 73, 1)

Although not all of Harte's other winter engagements have been discovered, he is known to have appeared in Springfield (25 November 1872), Albany (3 December), Boston (13 December), New York (16 December), Elmira (23 December), Washington, D.C. (7 January 1873), Pittsburgh (9 January), and in Toronto, Montreal, and Ottawa, as well as Ogdensburg, New York (February–March) (Merwin, 239–41; Harte 1926, 18–20; Hartford *Courant:* "Brief Mention," 25 Nov 72, 2; "Personal," 11 Mar 73, 2; "Bret Harte," Elmira *Advertiser*, 24 Dec 72, 4). Harte's performances were in general well received; for example, the New York *Tribune* praised his Steinway Hall appearance as

> a most gratifying and genuine success. . . . Such delicate humor, such fine, airy fancy, such close and conscientious painting of character, is rare to the lecture platforms. . . . The lecture of last night was not only good writing, but good talking also. . . . Mr. Harte's manner is easy and colloquial, and his voice, while not very strong, is clear and well managed. ("California's Golden Age," 17 Dec 72, 8)

In the fall of 1873, while touring in the Midwest, Harte wrote his wife that the critics "may be right—I dare say they are—in asserting that I am no orator, have no special faculty for speaking—no fire, dramatic earnestness, or expression" (Harte to Anna Harte, 19 Oct 73, Harte 1926, 26).

[4] Someone, possibly Larned, arranged for Harte to speak in Buffalo. On 27 March the Buffalo *Courier* announced that Harte would lecture on 31 March (with no sponsor mentioned), but the engagement was canceled. His "first appearance before a Buffalo audience" took place on 7 December 1874, sponsored by the Young Men's Christian Association (Buffalo *Courier:* "Bret Harte Coming," 27 Mar 73, 2; "The Argonauts of '49," 8 Dec 74, 2).

[5] On 1 March 1871 George H. Selkirk had purchased Clemens's one-third interest in the Buffalo *Express* for $15,000, to be paid over five years. Selkirk did not complete payment on schedule, however (see *L4*, 338–39 n. 3).

[6] Poet, coeditor of the Buffalo *Courier,* and close friend of Clemens's (*L4*, 102 n. 9).

To Elisha Bliss, Jr.
26 March 1873 • Hartford, Conn.
(MS: CU-MARK)

26th

Friend Bliss—

I leave in the morning (IF nothing happens to prevent) for the West, to be gone until I sail for Europe, middle of May—but shall finish the book before I sail.[1]

And now I am reminded, &c, &c. See enclosed letter. Old California acquaintance. They *never* die, & they all write books on Californian geology, geography, ˌ&ˌ Indianology & enlarge upon everything *except* the main chief product of that country which is Damphoology. And they all run to me to find a publisher for them.

Please tell this man—well tell him anything you please. I have just written him a note & told him where to find you.

Ys

Clemens

✉———————————————————————————

[*letter docketed by Bliss:*] Came with Wm Gouverneur Morris letter[2] [*and in unidentified hand:*] √ [*and*] S. L. Clemens 1873 | *Mar 26th*

[1]Clemens was planning a trip to Elmira, which he postponed. By the time he left Hartford, on 8 May, he had finished *The Gilded Age* (12 May 73 to Redpath, n. 1).

[2]The enclosed letter from William Gouverneur Morris (1832–84) is not known to survive, and no information has been found about his acquaintance with Clemens. Although Morris never published a book, he won a prize from the Mechanics' Institute of San Francisco for "An Essay on the Manufacturing Interests of California," published in 1872. A native of New York, Morris earned a law degree at Howard University in 1855 and soon thereafter went to California. During the Civil War he served in the Second Regiment of California Cavalry, and since 1869 had been U.S. marshal for the District of California (Menefee, 141–44; "Oregon," Sacramento *Union*, 18 Feb 84, 2).

To William Bowen
28 March 1873 • Hartford, Conn.
(MS: TxU-Hu)

Mch. 28.

Dear Will—
 Bless your heart, child, is thy servant a muggins, that he should travel 1200 miles by rail when there ain't anybody to *make* him do it? Skasely.[1]
  My London address will be:
   Care Geo. Routledge & Sons
Many Publishers,
thanks my The Broadway
boy. Write me Ludgate Hill
there. Ys Ever London, E. C.
   Sam.

[1]Bowen had evidently pressed Clemens to lecture in St. Louis, despite his earlier refusal (20 Mar 73 to Bowen).

To Whitelaw Reid
28 March 1873 • Hartford, Conn.
(MS: DLC)

Hartfd, Mch. 28

My Dear Reid—

Cheque for $15 received. Bless you I'll write short Foster articles all the time[1]—you pay more for them than you do for *Ł* long ones about Cunard Companies & gold medals, which you don't pay anything for! But I'm not finding any fault—I wrote for the love of it.[2]

Hope to spend Saturday previous to May 17 in New York. ~~Sl~~ Self & family of 4 persons[3] sail for England May 17 to stay four months. Shall have my book done & take a copy in MS over & publish simultaneously in England.[4] Some people think I have no head for business, but it is a lie.

I have a nice putrid anecdote that Hay will like. Am preserving it in alcohol—in my person.

Ys Truly
Saml. L. Clemens

[*letter docketed:*]

Dear Hay: I think you can make a nice min'. ¶ about the personal and literary news in this. Please return it. WR[5]

---

[1] See 7 Mar 73 to Reid (2nd). On 26 March Reid's secretary, Donald Nicholson, sent Clemens this check "for your letter on the Foster case" (Whitelaw Reid Papers, DLC).

[2] The *Tribune* had published "British Benevolence" on 27 January (see Appendix B). Reid responded to this good-natured hint by sending a check on 2 April, remarking, "I am sorry the Cunard business was overlooked" (Whitelaw Reid Papers, DLC).

[3] Olivia, Susy, Susy's nursemaid (Nellie), and Clara Spaulding.

[4] See 28 Feb 73 to Bliss, n. 1. The English edition of *The Gilded Age* was typeset from proofsheets of the American edition. It is possible, but not likely, that a fair copy of the manuscript served as printer's copy for the last nine chapters (see 27 July 73 to Bliss, n. 2).

[5] Donald Nicholson first took down this note from Reid to John Hay in shorthand, and then transcribed it in longhand. (For an example of Nicholson's shorthand, see 7 Mar 73 to Reid [2nd].) Reid recommended that Hay write an edito-

rial paragraph to be set in minion type (the equivalent of seven-point type), the smaller of the two sizes used on the editorial page (Pasko, 70, 378). Reid replied to Clemens on 2 April, "We are going to have a little paragraph about your book and trip in a few days. Good luck go with you" (Whitelaw Reid Papers, DLC). The paragraph corrected a mistaken report that Bret Harte was about to sail for Europe, adding the observation that since

> one of our Great American Humorists is due in Great Britain and Mr. Harte cannot go, Mr. Mark Twain will sail on the 17th of May, taking with him the MS. of his new volume, which will be published simultaneously in both worlds. It has sometimes been insinuated that Mr. Clemens is not a good business man. He authorizes us to contradict this in the most unreserved manner. ("It has been . . . ," New York *Tribune*, 2 Apr 73, 4)

To the Editor of the Hartford *Courant*
30 March 1873 • Hartford, Conn.
(Hartford *Courant*, 31 Mar 73)

To the EDITOR *of the* COURANT:—[1]

About noon yesterday the Rev. George H. Bigler, one of the oldest & most esteemed citizens of Farmington, left his home in that village to visit his married daughter, Mrs. Eli Sawyer, of Hartford. He came in an open two-horse wagon, & was accompanied by his wife, his youngest son, Thomas, aged 18; his grandchild, Minnie Sawyer, aged 8; & two neighbors, Simon & Ellsworth Oglethorpe, brothers, the former a lawyer & the latter formerly postmaster of Farmington. When the wagon arrived at the junction of Farmington avenue & Forest street, in this city, the guard of warning who should have been on duty there was absent from his post; the party in the wagon glanced up at the semaphore telegraph on the top of Mr. Chamberlin's house,[2] & strangely enough but one of its arms was visible & that was pointing directly north, signifying "No danger." So they turned into Forest street & proceeded on their way. In a little while they found themselves hopelessly entangled among the grading & gas-laying improvements, which have been going on in that street since the inauguration of the Christian Era. They shouted for help & presently made themselves heard; passers-by ran to the vicinity, & as soon as they comprehended the state of the case an alarm was sounded (it is due to Mr. Joseph W. Milligan, grocer, to say that he was the first to get to a fire alarm station & turn the key) & within a few minutes all the bells in the city were clamoring. Thousands & tens of thousands of people gathered to the scene of danger & openly sympathized with the persons in peril. They could do no more, for it would have been foolhardy in the extreme to venture into the street, the mud being at that place from thirty to ninety feet deep on a level, to say nothing of the water.

The wagon made another start, & plowed along desperately until it reached the monument (the first one from Farmington avenue—the one erected to a street commissioner during the middle ages for promising to quit repairing the street—which he basely violated & hence the vindictiveness of the inscription on the shaft). Here, as is known, there is more water than mud; the nearest life-boat station in this part of the street is the one located in front of Mr. George Warner's (new) premises. Captain Hobson & his crew of nine men at once launched a life-boat & started on their errand, notwithstanding it was Sunday & would cause remark; but the wind was blowing a gale by this time, & as it was just the turn of the tide, every thing was against the gallant boys. The boat was swept to leeward of the monument & shivered to atoms against the marble column erected in 1598 to the memory of a Sabbath school procession which disappeared at that spot, dressed with unusual care in the best clothes they had, & were never heard of afterward. Fragments of the life-boat crew washed ashore this morning in the extreme southern end of Forest street, nearly three hundred yards from the scene of the disaster. The party in the wagon were well nigh desperate now. But when hope seemed darkest Capt. Duncan MacAllister of the canal boat George Washington arrived with a ship's compass, a chronometer fifteen minutes slow, & a sack of sea-biscuit & hove them aboard the vehicle, while cheers rent the air from the surging multitude that lined the sidewalks. The Rev. Mr. Bigler & his party seemed greatly encouraged after a brief luncheon. (These crackers were from Johnson & Peterson's bakery & are acknowledged to be the best in this market.) Mr. Bigler now bore away sou-west-by-west-half-west, but his weather harness got fouled, his port check-rein fetched away, & his wagon broached to & went ashore at the base of the monument erected five years ago to commemorate the 1868th annual alteration of the grade. Here the starboard horse began to disappear; Mr. Simon Oglethorpe at once cut away the main rigging, & the animal continued his journey to China. Within five minutes the other horse followed him. There was a heavy sea on by this time, of mud & water mixed, & every third colossal poultice of it that rolled along made a clean breach over the wagon & left the occupants looking like the original Adam before the clay dried.

Hope now departed at once & forever, & it was heartrending to hear the castaways plead for a little drop of limpid water; they were willing to die, they were ready to die, but they wanted to wash first. There was not a dry eye in the vicinity. The awful moment came at last; a great sea of sable mush swept the wagon from stem to stern, then the vehicle plunged once, twice, three times, & disappeared beneath the state with all its precious freight on board.

This is a sad case. I am not writing this letter in order to make a great to-do about the loss of a few unnecessary country people in Forest street, for of course that is too common a thing to excite much attention; but I have an object which makes my letter of moment.

In the first place I wish to discourage the building of monuments in Forest street. Every few years the street commissioner goes out there & deposits sixteen feet of gas pipe (on top of the ground) & straightway the property-holders set up a majestic monument to remember it by. Every year he changes the grade & plagiarizes original chaos, & they monumentalize that. Every now & then somebody gets off soundings there & never comes back to dinner any more, & up goes another monument. The result is that what solid ground there is in that street is all occupied by monuments, now, & it makes no end of trouble. There is only one solid spot left, & I discover that a new length of gas pipe has just been dumped in the street & the ground ravaged in the vicinity, preparatory to burying that piece of tube one of these years. Now, will they not want to commemorate that bit of official energy? You know, yourself, that they will, & away goes the last square yard of firm soil in Forest street. If there had been fewer monuments to get shipwrecked against, the Farmington people & the life-boat crew might all be with us yet.

Secondly, I think there ought to be more lanterns standing on barrels, & more sentinels roosting on the fences along Forest street, to warn strangers.

Thirdly, I think there ought to be at least three more life-boat stations on that street, & a number of miscellaneous rafts, with provisions & literature lashed on them, distributed along here & there.

Fourthly, I think there ought to be a chart of the street made, with the soundings marked on it.

Fifthly, I think the war office ought to establish a signal station in Forest street & put in the Probabilities,[3] "Danger signals are ordered for the lakes, the Gulf of Mexico, the Atlantic seaboard & Forest street, Hartford—the one at Forest street to be nailed up with fifteen inch spikes & remain permanent in all weathers."

Then I shall enjoy living in this soft, retired street even more than I do now, perhaps.

M. T.

Sunday, March 30.

[1] Clemens often placed items in the Hartford *Courant* through Charles Dudley Warner, one of its editors. Its editor in chief was Joseph R. Hawley, a former governor of Connecticut now serving as a U.S. congressman (*L3*, 97 n. 5).

[2] Except for Franklin Chamberlin and George Warner (mentioned in the second paragraph), the characters in this mock drama are not listed in the Hartford directory for 1872–73, and are presumably fictitious.

[3] A standard feature of the *Courant*'s "Weather" column (see, for example, "The Weather," 31 Mar 73, 3).

To Charles F. Wingate
2 April 1873 • Hartford, Conn.
(MS: CtHMTH)

(SLC)

Hartford, Apl. 2.

Dear Sir:[1]

I shall be here at home some three weeks yet, & possibly longer. I cannot ⹁therefore⹁ tell exactly when I shall be ~~at~~ in New York. But I stop at the St Nicholas Hotel always, ⧸ & if you should glance at the T̸ hotel arrivals in the Tribune you would see when I come, & then I would be glad if you dropped in. The reason I cannot be more positive as to the day I shall leave here is, that I am finishing a book[2] & I find it impossible to tell exactly when I am going to get it done.

Very Truly Yrs
Sam*^l*. L. Clemens.

Chas. F. Wingate Esq

[1]Charles Frederick Wingate (Carlfried; 1848–1909), a New York correspondent for the Springfield (Mass.) *Republican* and for the Boston *Globe*, had prepared a pamphlet commemorating the celebration of Horace Greeley's sixty-first birthday in February 1872, which Clemens had attended (3 Feb 72 to Johnson, n. 1). In May of that year he became the editor of the *Paper Trade Journal*. In 1875 he edited *Views and Interviews on Journalism*, which included interviews with twenty-seven prominent journalists, among them Whitelaw Reid, Samuel Bowles, Murat Halstead, Henry Watterson, George W. Smalley, and David G. Croly (*L4*, 102–3; Wilson and Fiske, 6:564; "Personals," Boston *Globe*, 5 June 72, 5; Wingate 1875).

[2]*The Gilded Age.*

To William C. Cornwell
5–15? April 1873 • Hartford, Conn.
(*Globe* 1 [May 73]: 28–29)

. . . .

I don't know of any correction that I can offer. I perceive that the writer has discovered my besetting weakness, which is unreflecting & rather ungraceful irritability.

It isn't a pleasant trait.

I *have* some pleasant ones, but modesty compels me to hide them from the world, so no one gets the benefit of them but myself.[1]

. . . .

[1]Clemens was reacting to a brief unsigned article, "Mark Twain as a Buffalo Editor," published in the first number of *The Globe: A Magazine of Literary Record and Criticism*. The anonymous author had evidently worked on the Buffalo *Express* in 1869, when Clemens became one of its editors and owners, and although he praised "the fresh, agreeable editorial paragraphs that bore, so unmistakably, the stamp of Twain's matchless sarcasm and humor," he also gave a frank portrait of him:

A quiet, reserved and irritable man, he gave his fellow citizens little opportunity to annoy him with their attentions or questions. Although courteous upon all occasions he was wont to turn a cold shoulder to the staring Paul Prys. The writer has often seen some luckless offending individual scourged beneath the stinging lash of his sarcasm. Mr. Clemens is a bitterly sarcastic man—humorists, as a rule are so—and his uncurbed independence of expression often leads him into unpleasant encounters. His editorial career, when he was one of the proprietors of the Buffalo *Express* illustrated this quality to a very notic[e]able extent. The manner in which he wielded the journalistic sceptre was more that of an impatient autocrat than an humble American citizen. (*Globe* 1 [Apr 73]: 6)

William Caryl Cornwell (1851–1932) was the editor and illustrator of the *Globe*, which named his brother Edward L. Cornwell as its publisher. (In 1869, when Clemens probably met him, Cornwell was a bank clerk, and more recently had been a bookkeeper for the Third National Bank of Buffalo.) The first issue of their magazine appeared in Buffalo on 3 April, and William Cornwell evidently sent Clemens a copy, asking for comment. If Clemens replied promptly, he probably wrote this letter before mid-April; he certainly wrote it before 29 April, because the next day the contents of the second issue of the *Globe* (published on 2 May) were reported to include "A Letter from Mark Twain to the *Globe*" ("The Globe," Buffalo *Courier:* 4 Apr 73, 2; 30 Apr 73, 2; 2 May 73, 2). Only the extract that the *Globe* printed is known to survive, introduced by Cornwell himself:

> We have received a letter from Mr. Clemens, from which, although it is addressed to the Editor personally, we cannot but make a very brief but very characteristic extract. He says in reference to the article concerning himself in the April number of the *Globe:* . . .
>
> Those who know Mr. Clemens can testify to the thorough good fellowship and unfailing good humor which make him so pleasant a companion, as well as to the staunch adherence which he manifests as a friend.
>
> During his stay among us afflictions in his family prevented an extended intercourse, but those who did meet the distinguished humorist will never forget to be his friends. ("Editor's Portfolio," *Globe* 1 [May 73]: 28–29)

Although the *Globe* continued publication until March 1875, Cornwell did not go on to become a journalist, but remained in banking. In 1877 he became a cashier for the Bank of Buffalo, which he then managed until 1892. In the latter year he organized the City Bank of Buffalo, becoming its president. Two years later he helped found the New York State Bankers' Association, serving as its first president. Cornwell enjoyed painting for recreation throughout his life, and in 1910 invented a new method for reproducing works of art on glass. No further communication between him and Clemens is known (Severance, 231; *Buffalo Directory:* 1869, 43, 260; 1871, 303; 1872, 38).

To Unidentified
7 April 1873 • Hartford, Conn.
(MS: MA)

Hartford, Apl. ⫽ 7/73.

Dʳ· Sir:

Enclosed is page 15 of ~~the~~ my first effort in the lecture field, if you desire it. Subject, "Sandwich Islands"—delivered in San Francisco Oct.

2, 1866, & 150 times since—& altered a little from time to time, as the
MS. betrays.[1]

Ys Truly
Sam*ʲ*. L. Clemens
Mark Twain.

[*enclosure:*][2]

15

~~but he will be scorched hereafter, for all that. If the Bishop saves
Harris alone, his mission will be a gorgeous success.~~[3] * The Bishop's
church has other members ~~besides these~~, of course, & is making
some progress, but ~~is~~ it is not doing what ~~we might~~ ˄be˄ ˄the vulgar˄
term˄ed˄ a land office business, by any means. ˄Officers & men British ships˄ won't go.˄ ˄But to return to Bish cch.˄

The Episcopalians scowl upon the Bishop's ˄nondescript˄
Church ˄& officers British ships˄,—the Puritans scowl upon it—&
the Catholics, with whom he wᵈ fraternise, flout it. ~~It is the wildest
of all wildcat religions,~~ ˄In Cali phraseology it is wildcat— These
things compel us to conclude that the Bish religion is wild˄, & if there
is any of the pay rock of saving grace in its main lead, they haven't
struck it yet in the lower level.

In that genuine good-

[*on the back in pencil:*]

˄Harris is not popular.˄

The former Min Finance—I think he was—~~was a S~~ & Mr.
Wyllie—was a Scotsman & able & highly respected—had passion
for writing statistics[4]—old Moffett[5] another Scotsman down on
him—dream—

<hr>

[1] Clemens relied on this method of dealing with autograph seekers at least
three times in April (see the next two letters). The manuscript of the 1866 Sandwich Islands lecture that Albert Bigelow Paine had in 1910 was surely not complete, but it probably included both a fair copy of about forty pages (half its
original length) and several shorter sequences of five and ten pages, each of
which was clearly written earlier than the fair copy. On the assumption that virtually all of what Paine had is now in the Mark Twain Papers (SLC 1866h), it is
likely that the sequence of pages from which this page "15" came was already
lost in 1910, not because Clemens "tore it up" (as he told Frank Fuller in 1894),
but because he had given it away to autograph seekers (1 Feb 94 to Fuller, CtY-
BR†; *MTB*, 3:1601–3; *MTS* 1923, 7–20).

[2] The enclosure was written almost entirely in black ink (now faded to brown),
with most of its revisions and all of the final paragraph in pencil. These revisions,

the use of nonstandard abbreviations ("Bish," "cch.," "Cali"), and the elliptical sentence structure of this passage all combine with the evidence of ink and paper to show that this page belonged to an early draft of the lecture, not very far removed from the raw working notes on which it was obviously based:

> Bishop Staley ˏof the Epis cchˏ importation
> King belong to his church
> (So everybody SAYS ˏother Mish boys—strong
> Am. feeling.ˏ
> Harris belongs ˏTHE EXPERIMENT.ˏ—scorch for all
> that.
> Church has other members—some progress.
> Episcopalions scowl upon it
>   These things force the conclusion that
> Bishop's religion is *wildcat!*—& if there is any
> pay rock
> In that genuine good-fellowship
>   PAUSE.
> White folks excellent—happy
> Longing go home—gen affluent
>   not bad (SLC 1866h†)

[3] Thomas Nettleship Staley (1823–98) was an Anglican bishop sent from England in 1862 to head the newly formed Hawaiian Reformed Catholic church. He soon secured King Kamehameha IV and Queen Emma, as well as other high chiefs and government figures, as members of his church, thereby antagonizing the long-established Protestant and Roman Catholic missions. Clemens sided with the Protestant missionaries (Americans) against Staley, who was inclined to dismiss as ineffectual their efforts to convert the native population (*RI 1993*, 719–20). Charles Coffin Harris (1821–81) settled in the Sandwich Islands in 1850, where he was a businessman and lawyer. Between 1863 and 1872 he served under King Kamehameha V as attorney general, minister of finance, and minister of foreign affairs. Harris was among Bishop Staley's earliest converts, a fact which, together with his natural vanity and pomposity, earned him a permanent role as Clemens's whipping boy. Clemens consistently called attention to his pretentiousness—first in his 1866 letters to the Sacramento *Union*, then in *Roughing It*, and again most recently in his 9 January 1873 *Tribune* letter (*RI 1993*, 718; *L4*, 278–79; Appendix B).

[4] Robert C. Wyllie (1798–1865) was likewise one of Staley's early converts. Born in Scotland and educated as a physician, he lived for many years in South America and Mexico, earning a fortune from various commercial enterprises. In 1844 he went to the Sandwich Islands as secretary to the new British consul general. From 1845 until his death he played a major role in the government, serving as minister of foreign affairs under kings Kamehameha III, Kamehameha IV, and Kamehameha V (Kuykendall and Gregory, 169–70; Alexander, 340–41).

[5] Unidentified.

To Unidentified #1
7–30? April 1873 • Hartford, Conn.
(MS: MH-H)

40̰ ̷3 ̷1
[*in pencil:*] ˌObject coul[d]n't been to convert, because already converted.ˌ

[*in ink:*] The Bishop has said that the ~~natives~~ missionaries have done more harm than good, & that the natives would ~~be~~ have been far better off if they had never ~~come~~ ˌgone, there—which is to say that idolatry, & human sacrifices, and possible cannibalism, and wars, & famines, & the cruelties & barbarities practised upon the masses in former times by the chiefs, were far better than the education & civilization, & the peace & plenty & liberty & happiness conferred in later times upon these natives by the missionaries. In the face of

[*cross-written on the page:*][1]
Original MS. of
first lecture.
Written, October, 1866.
San Francisco.
Yrs Truly
Sam*ʲ*. L. Clemens
Mark Twain.

April, 1873.

---

[1] Like the page enclosed with the previous letter, this one clearly belonged to an early draft of the Sandwich Islands lecture. It was written on what is almost certainly the same wove paper stock, albeit lacking the embossment (which appears only on pages torn from the top half of a full sheet). It too is in black ink (faded to brown) with two penciled revisions: the insertion of "0" in the page number "40" and the addition of one sentence at the top of the page. As in the previous case, the original sequence of pages to which this page belonged does not survive, but Clemens's subject is clearly Bishop Staley's habit of belittling the work of the American missionaries. The date of this letter has not been precisely determined. Nevertheless, because Clemens's explanation here of the

manuscript page was less complete than on 7 April, and because he wrote directly on the page instead of enclosing a covering note, it seems likely that it was at least the second time he had replied in this way to an autograph seeker, and that the letter was written sometime between 7 April and the end of the month.

To Unidentified #2
7–30? April 1873 • Hartford, Conn.
(MS: NN-B)

ᴧ58ᴧ   88̶ 53̶

ᴧupᴧ a dome of bloody ᴧlikeᴧ lava as large as a small cottage, & this bursts & sends a million sparkling gems aloft that shed a blinding radiance around—& from the midst of the exploding dome a filmy veil of light green flame flashes out & floats away like a disembodied soul,—& then the monstrous mass crushes back into the lake & attests its ponderous weight by the deep, funnel-like depression it makes in the surface. In a few moments a black crust of cooling lava forms upon the lake like a cream, & over it dance a myriad of beauti-

[*cross-written on the page:*][1]
Will this do? Though it isn't a "sentiment" strictly speaking. It is original MS of first lecture. Delivered October, 1867 in San Francisco.[2]

> Yrs Truly
> Sam[l]. L. Clemens
> Mark Twain.
>
> April, 1873.

[1] Like the previous two pages of lecture manuscript that Clemens mailed, this page was originally written in black ink (faded to brown), then revised in pencil: the insertion of the page number "58," the deletion of "88," and the insertion of "like" were all in pencil, as were the two lines striking through the entire page. Although the paper stock is different from the previous two pages, it has the same dimensions as those and a dozen others from the same manuscript, now in the Mark Twain Papers (SLC 1866h). None of the immediately surrounding pages is known to survive, but it is apparent that Clemens was describing Kilauea volcano, a well-known highlight of his lecture from its very first performance in San Francisco. The date of Clemens's letter is again uncertain, but see the next note.

²The year was 1866, not 1867. Clemens's error may mean that some time had passed since he wrote the two previous letters, in both of which he correctly dated his lecture.

To Whitelaw Reid
9 April 1873 • Hartford, Conn.
(MS and transcript: DLC and New York *Tribune*, 11 Apr 73)

PRIVATE.

9ᵗʰ ~~Mch.~~ Apl.

My Dear Reid—

Thanks for check & also the promised notice.¹

I wish you would step on board a steamer & refresh your memory as to how a ship's boats look & how useless such things are in a heavy sea. *You* know that in such a sea if your ship were going down you would not dream of such folly as taking to a ship's boat if you could get a life= raft. A few editorials on this subject might draw attention to it & accomplish something, but I can't do anything with communications. I mean to go & worry Mr. Plimsoll or get somebody else to do it, when I get to England—*he* can get the life-raft adopted.

Ys

Clemens

P. S. I might not have the cheek, only he gave me a pretty high-toned compliment in one of his London newspaper letters on my Humane Society letter.²

[*enclosure:*]³

To the Editor of The Tribune.

SIR: When the Mississippi was burned at sea some time ago, & nearly all her boats were smashed in the effort to cast them loose, or were swamped the instant they struck the water, I wrote you a private letter (which you published) suggesting that ships be provided with life-rafts instead of these almost useless boats.⁴ I did not expect that the Government would jump at the suggestion, & I was not disappointed. The Government had business on hand at the time which would benefit not only our nation but the whole world—I mean the project of paying Congressmen over again for work which they had already been paid to do; that is to say, the labor of receiving Crédit Mobilier donations & forgetting the circumstance.[5] But that shining public benefit being accomplished, why cannot the Government listen to me now?

The Atlantic had eight boats, of course—all steamers have. Not one of the boats saved a human life. The great cumbersome things were shivered to atoms by the seas that swept over the stranded vessel.[6] And suppose they had not been shivered, would the case have been better? Would not the frantic people have plunged pell-mell into each boat as it was launched & instantly swamped it? They always do. But a life-raft is a different thing. All the people you can put on it cannot swamp it. Nobody understands davit-falls but a sailor, & he don't when he is frightened; but any goose can heave a life-raft overboard, & then some wise man can throw him after it. The sort of life-raft I have in my mind is an American invention, consisting of three inflated horizontal rubber tubes, with a platform lashed on top. These rafts are of all sizes, from a little affair the size of your back door, to a raft 22 feet long & six or eight feet wide. As you remember, no doubt, two men crossed the Atlantic from New-York to London, some years ago, on one of these rafts of the latter size.[7] That raft would carry 120 men. Nine such rafts would have saved the Atlantic's 1,000 souls, & these rafts (fully inflated & ready for use) would not have occupied as much room on her deck as four of her lubberly boats; hardly more than the room of three of her boats, indeed. Her boats were probably 30 feet long, seven feet deep, & seven or eight feet wide at the gunwales.

You could furnish a ship with medium & full-sized rafts—an equal number of each—& pile them up in the space now occupied by four boats, & then you could expect to save all her people, not merely a dozen or two. They would sail away through a storm, sitting high & dry from two to four feet above the tops of the waves. In addition to the rafts, the ship could carry a boat or two, for promiscuous general service, & for the drowning of old fogies who like old established ways. You could attach a raft to a ship with a ten fathom line & heave it overboard on the lee side in the roughest sea (& it can't fall any way but right side up), & there it will lie & ride the waves like a duck till it receives its freight of food & passengers—& then you can cut the line & let her go. But if you launch a boat, it usually falls upside down; & if it don't, the people crowd in & swamp it. Boats have sometimes gone away safely with people & taken them to land, but such accidents are rare.

I am not giving you a mere landsman's views upon this raft business; they are the views of several old sea captains & mates whom I have talked with, & their voice gives them weight & value. Our Government has so many important things to attend to that we cannot reasonably expect it to bother with life-rafts, & we cannot reasonably expect the English Government to bother with them because this admirable contrivance is a Yankee invention, & our mother is not given to adopting our inventions until she has had time to hunt around among her documents & discovered that the crude idea originated with herself in some bygone time— then she adopts it & builds a monument to the crude originator. England has our life-raft on exhibition in a museum over there (the raft that made the wonderful voyage),[8] & heaps of people have gone in every day for several years & paid for the privilege of looking at it. Perhaps many a bereaved poor soul whose idols lie stark & dead under the waves that wash the beach of Nova Scotia may wish, as I do, that it had been on exhibition on board the betrayed Atlantic.

MARK TWAIN.

Hartford, Conn., April 8, 1873.

[*letter docketed:*] I have marked the article minion, must. WCW[9] [*and in unidentified hand:*] *1873*

[1] See 28 Mar 73 to Reid, nn. 2, 5.

[2] Samuel Plimsoll (1824–98), member of Parliament for Derby since 1868, worked tirelessly for legislation to improve safety in the shipping industry. Born in Bristol to parents of limited means, Plimsoll began work as a clerk in a brewery, but rose eventually to become a wealthy London coal merchant. In January 1873 he published *Our Seamen: An Appeal* (London: Virtue and Co.), a strongly worded but not wholly accurate attack on unscrupulous ship owners and underwriters. The public outcry that resulted led ultimately to the Merchant Shipping Act of 1876, which instituted, among other reforms, the use of the "Plimsoll mark," the line on a ship's hull indicating the waterline when it is safely loaded (Masters, 17–18, 36–37, 52–62, 107–9, 121–25, 193, 224, 269). Clemens's "Humane Society letter" appeared in the *Tribune* on 27 January (Appendix B). Plimsoll's "high-toned compliment" has not been found.

[3] As the docket to this letter indicates, Clemens enclosed the manuscript (now lost) of a letter to the *Tribune*, which published it on 11 April (5) under the title "Life-Rafts. How the Atlantic's Passengers Might Have Been Saved," the sole source of the following text. An untitled editorial comment, probably written by William C. Wyckoff, John Hay, or Reid himself, appeared the next day:

It is to be hoped that the admirable appeal for the use of Life-Rafts, which we published yesterday from the pen of Mark Twain, will not be permitted to fall without response. The general apathy is astonishing in relation to a matter so full of vital interest to every one. The questions of ship-building, of the education of officers, of the training and organization of crews, are all highly important in respect to their influence upon the safety of travel by sea. But these are all matters of time, and discussion, and experiment. The adoption of Life-Rafts suggested by our valued correspondent as a portion of the indispensable equipment of every sea-going vessel, is a thing to be tried at once, without the least delay. It would cost little, in expense or in space. It need not necessarily exclude the present provision of life-boats, but every vessel should be forced to carry rafts enough to save all the lives on board, and then, as Mr. Clemens magnanimously observes, "the ship could carry a boat or two for promiscuous general service, and for the drowning of old fogies who like old established ways." (New York *Tribune*, 12 Apr 73, 6)

On 20 August 1873, Reid remarked to Charles Henry Webb:

> Mark Twain has always been remarkable until of late for the care with which he avoided wearing out his welcome with the public, and it seemed to me one of the elements of his success[.] I should like to suggest another point in which Twain has made a big success. The best things he has done have seemed to have some definite good end in view. For instance his letter about rafts instead of lifeboats attracted more attention and brought him more praise than any thing he has done of late years. The letter about the Cunarders in the same vein was equally successful. (Correspondence of Charles Henry Webb, DLC, TS in CU-MARK)

[4] See 5 Dec 72 to Reid. Clemens meant the *Missouri*, not the *Mississippi*.

[5] See 7 Mar 73 to the staff of the New York *Tribune*, n. 1.

[6] On the morning of 1 April 1873, in what the *Tribune* described as "the most terrible sea-disaster of the century," the steamer *Atlantic*, bound for New York out of Liverpool, struck a submerged rock on the coast of Nova Scotia while making an unscheduled detour to Halifax for refueling ("A Fearful Calamity," 2 Apr 73, 1). The ship quickly sank, carrying with it the only lifeboat launched. A total of 481 died, out of 931 passengers and crew; the survivors were rescued by lifelines to the shore and by local boats. A court of inquiry censured the captain of the *Atlantic* and suspended him for two years for miscalculating the ship's speed, neglecting to obtain soundings, and failing to keep a "proper and vigilant lookout" (Springfield [Mass.] *Republican*, 19 Apr 73, 5; Adams, 507–11).

[7] Clemens described this raft, named the *Nonpareil*, in a letter to the San Francisco *Alta California* dated 6 June 1867:

> This raft is a thing made of three cylinders, 25 feet long, each, and 26 inches in diameter, made fast together, side by side. We have all heard of shipwrecked men drifting for days and days together, in mid-ocean, on such contrivances not very dissimilar to this, but why any man should want to start for Europe on one, when he could travel in a ship and still have a reasonable hope of never getting there, is a mystery to me. . . . The Captain rigged five sails on his little hen-coop, and took forty days' rations of water and provisions for himself and his two men. He expects to reach Havre in twenty-five to thirty days, but somehow the more I looked at that shaky thing the more I felt satisfied that the old tar was on his last voyage. He is going to run in the usual route of the ships, and somebody will run over him some murky gray night, and we shall never hear of the bold Prussian any more. (SLC 1867c)

The raft (which was actually 12½ feet wide) first attempted to leave New York on 4 June, but was delayed until 12 June; it made the crossing to Southampton in forty-three days without serious incident ("Arrival of the American Liferaft," London *Times*, 26 July 67, 10; "The Voyage of the Life-Saving Raft 'Nonpareil,'" New York *Times*, 3 Dec 67, 3).

[8] The *Nonpareil* was put on display at the Crystal Palace ("The Voyage of the Life-Saving Raft 'Nonpareil,'" New York *Times*, 3 Dec 67, 3; see 11 Sept 72 to OLC, n. 6).
[9] William C. Wyckoff.

To Mary Mason Fairbanks
16 April 1873 • Hartford, Conn.
(MS: CSmH)

Hartford, Apl. 16.

Dear Mother—

Laziness, ~~ham~~ obstructed by work, is my excuse,—not want of desire to write you, or lack of affection.[1] Every since I arrived from England, several months ago, Chas Dudley Warner & I have been belting away every day on a *partnership novel.* I have worked 6 days a week—good full days—& laid myself up, once. Have written many chapters twice, & some of them three times—have thrown away 300 clean pages of MS. & still there's havoc to be made when I enter on the final polishing. Warner has been more fortunate—he won't lose 50 pages.

¶ Three more chapters will end the book. ~~We~~ I laid out the plan of the *boss* chapter, the climax chapter, yesterday, & Warner will write it up to-day; I wrote it up yesterday, & shall work & trim & polish at it to-day—& to-night ˌwe shall read, &ˌ the man who has written it best is all right—the other man's MS. will be torn up. If *neither* succeeds, we'll both write the chapter over again.

Every night for many weeks, Livy & Susie Warner have collected in my study to hear Warner & me read our day's work; & they have done a power of criticising, but have always been anxious to be on hand at the reading & find out what has been happening to the dramatis personae since the previous evening. They both pleaded so long & vigorously for Warner's heroine, that yesterday Warner agreed to spare her life & let her marry—he meant to kill her. I killed my heroine as dead as a mackerel yesterday (but Livy don't know it yet). Warner may or may not kill her to-day (this is in the "boss" chapter.) We shall see. I wish you had been here all this time to criticise. The book will issue ¢ in the end of summer—here & in England spasmodically—I tote over a copy of the MS May 17.[2]

I'm not half done [with] this letter, but I have an itching desire to get back to my chapter & shake up my heroine's remains. We're all well. Livy will write.

Affectionately

Yr Son

Sam[l].

P. S.—(Night.) My climax chapter is the one accepted by Livy & Susie, & so my heroine, Laura, remains dead.

I have also written another chapter, in which I have brought Clay Hawkins home from California & the Chinchas, made Washington tear up the tax bill, & started him & Col. Sellers home, to appear no more in the book. Do you think that was best? Or would it have been better to let Sellers go over into Pennsylvania, first, & give Philip a lift with his mining troubles? He could have passed through Philadelphia, then, & had a chance to see Ruth (poor Ruth!) & the Boltons.[3]

Sam

[1] In an undated letter postmarked 14 April, Fairbanks had chided the Clemenses for their failure to write (CU-MARK):

My dear Hartford children—

Why do I hear nothing from you? So often of late have my thoughts turned questioningly towards you only to come back *unanswered*, that I am constrained to send this little messenger out of my ark, in search of you.

Of course the breezes of rumor give me unreliable items of "Mark Twain" here & "Mark Twain"—but what is that, when I am wondering *how* you are—how Livy is—how Susie is—what your hopes are—what your fears, if any—the nameless yearnings we have a right to feel for those we love.

My own season is peaceful. Mr. Fairbanks and I have passed a quiet but a happy winter, looking hopefully to a summer reunion—when the vacations send our children home. Do you still hold to the plan of going abroad in May? How very much I wish you could spend the summer with us. We would domicile you in the little cottage at the gate where you might receive us or shut us out. I suppose however you would scorn such plebian hospitality now.

Pray give me hope that sometime you'll come down from the heights of Plantagenet dinners to drink a glass of milk with us.

Love & kisses for Livy and the wee Susie who is now a young lady of something more than twelve-months.

Faithfully Yours

Mother Fairbanks

[2] In chapter 60 of *The Gilded Age* Laura is reported to have turned "to that final resort of the disappointed of her sex, the lecture platform," only to suffer humiliation on her first appearance. She is found dead a few days later from

"heart disease" (SLC 1873–74, 547, 551). Clemens expected the English edition to issue "simultaneously" rather than "spasmodically."
[3]Clay Hawkins, Washington Hawkins, and Colonel Sellers all resolve their affairs and go home in chapter 61. Ruth Bolton recovers from her serious illness and agrees to marry Philip Sterling, who has barely escaped financial ruin by discovering coal on her father's land, in chapters 62 and 63.

To David G. Croly
17 April 1873 • Hartford, Conn.
(MS facsimile: New York *Graphic*, 22 Apr 73)

· · · ·

Hartford, Apl. 17.

Ed. Graphic:[1]

Your note is received. If the following two lines which I have cut from it are your ⱨ natural hand-writing, then I understand you to ask me

"for a farewell letter
in the name of the American
people."[2] Bless you, the joy of the American
people is just a little premature; I haven't gone yet. And what is more, I am not going to stay, when I do go.

Yes, it is too true. I am only going to remain beyond the seas six months—that is all. I love stir & excitement; & so the moment the spring birds begin to sing, the zephyrs to sigh, the flowers to bloom, & the stagnation, the pensive melancholy, the lagging weariness of summer to threaten, I grow restless, I get the fidgets; I want to pack off somewhere where there's something going on. But you know how that is—you must have felt that way. This very day I saw the signs in the air of the coming dulness, & I said to myself, "How glad I am that I have already chartered the steamer Batavia ˄a steamship˄ to tow me & my party over on my life= raft."[3] There was absolutely nothing in the morning papers. You can see for yourself what the tell telegraphic headings were:

BY TELEGRAPH

A Colored Congressman in Trouble.

Excitement at Albany.

Five Years Imprisonment.

Wall Street Panicky.

Two Failures and Money at 150 Per Cent.

Two Criminal Cases.

Arrested for Highway Robbery.

The Assault on the Gas Collector.

A Striker Held for Murder in the Second Degree.

The Murderer King Dangerously Sick.

Lusignani, the Wife Murderer, to be Hung.

Two would-be Murderers to be Hung.

Incendiarism in a Baptist Flock.

A Fatal Mistake.

Washing Away of a Railroad.

Ku-Klux Murders.

A SHOCKING DISASTER.

A Chimney Falls and Buries Five Children—Two of them Already Dead.

The Modoc Massacre.

RIDDLE'S WARNING.

A Father Killed By His Son.

A Bloody Fight in Kentucky.

An Eight-Year Old Murderer.

A Grave-Yard Floating Off.

A LOUISIANA MASSACRE.

A Court House Fired, and Negroes Therein Shot While Escaping.

Two to Three Hundred Men Roasted Alive!

A Lively Skirmish in Indiana.

A TOWN IN A STATE OF GENERAL RIOT.

A PARTY OF MINERS BESIEGED IN A BOARDING HOUSE.

TROOPS AND POLICE FROM INDIAN-APOLIS ASKED FOR.

BLOODY WORK EXPECTED.

Furious Amazon Leaders.

A HORRIBLE STORY.

A NEGRO'S OUTRAGE.

A SUFFERING AND MURDERED WO-MAN TERRIBLY AVENGED.

A Man 24 Hours Burning, and Carved Piece-meal.

The items under those headings all bear date yesterday, Apl. 16 ₍refer to your own paper,₎,[4]—$\cancel{I}$ & I give you my word of honor that that string of commonplace stuff was everything there was in the telegraphic columns that a body could call news. Well, said I to myself, this is getting pretty dull; this is getting pretty dry; there don't appear to be anything going on anywhere; has this progressive nation gone to sleep? Have I got to stand another month of this torpidity before I can begin to browse among the lively capitals of Europe?

₍But never mind—things may revive while I am away.₎

During the last two months my next-door neighbor, Chas. Dudley Warner, has dropped his "Back-Log Studies,"[5] & he & I have written a

bulky novel in partnership. He has worked up the fiction & I have shov-
eled ˌhurledˌ in the facts. I consider it one of the most astonishing novels
that ever was written. Night after night I sit up reading it over & over
again & crying. It will be published early in the fall, with plenty of pictures. Do you consider this an advertisement?—& if so, do you charge
for such things, when a man is your friend & is an orphan?

Drooping, now, under the solemn peacefulness, the general stagnation, the profound lethargy that broods over the land, I am

Ys Truly

Sam*ˡ*. L. Clemens

ˌMark Twain.ˌ

¹Clemens's letter survives only as a photolithograph of the original manuscript, published on 22 April 1873 in the New York *Graphic*, a new illustrated
daily newspaper of eight pages which had begun publication on 4 March. The
original probably included a personal salutation and message to Croly, not reproduced in the *Graphic* (see Appendix F). Founded by a Canadian firm of engravers who invented and patented a photolithographic process (which, as the
term implies, used photochemical means to transfer images to lithographic
plates), the *Graphic* was able to produce accurate illustrations of newsworthy
events as quickly as typeset text, without the time and expense previously required to make engravings by hand. David Goodman Croly (1829–89), the editor of the *Graphic*, had been managing editor of the New York *World* until his
resignation in late 1872. Clemens knew him, as did their mutual acquaintance
Charles Wingate, who had recently tried to set up an appointment with Clemens.
All three had attended the Greeley birthday dinner in February 1872 (2 Apr 73
to Wingate; 3 Feb 72 to Johnson, n. 1). Croly was born in Ireland but grew up
in New York. In 1855 he became a reporter for the New York *Evening Post*, but
soon took a job on the *Herald*. In 1858 he moved to Illinois, where he founded
the Rockford *News*. Returning to New York in 1860, he joined the staff of the
World and two years later became its managing editor. From March 1873 until
1878 he edited the *Graphic*. Croly was an unusual journalist who had already
written several books, including *Miscegenation* (1864), in which he advocated
interracial marriage as the best means to advance civilization, and *The Truth
about Love: A Proposed Sexual Morality Based upon the Doctrine of Evolution, and
Recent Discoveries in Medical Science* (1872), in which he defended the Oneida
Community (Mott 1950, 502; "The Daily Graphic . . . ," New York *Tribune*, 5
Mar 73, 4; Eder, 627–28; "Personal," Buffalo *Courier*, 21 Dec 72, 1; Wingate
1875, 325).

²The *Graphic*'s facsimile (reproduced in Appendix F) confirms that Clemens
cut these words out of Croly's "note" (now lost) and pasted them into his own
manuscript, adding the quotation marks.

³Evidently an allusion to Clemens's crusade to supply ships with life rafts (see
9 Apr 73 to Reid).

⁴Clemens cut these newspaper headlines from page 3 of the Hartford *Evening
Post* for 16 April 1873. He chose only the most sensational—ignoring, for ex-

ample, "Educational Question in Brooklyn" and "Delayed Mail for Europe."
He evidently pasted these snippets to his letter manuscript in an order largely of
his own choosing, omitting the intervening text to heighten the comic effect. The
Graphic did not reproduce this part of his letter as a photofacsimile, but instead
prepared a type facsimile of it, perhaps to make it more legible than the original.
Comparison with the *Post* headlines shows that the *Graphic's* typesetters introduced minor errors in punctuation. Since the actual document Clemens sent has
not been found, the headlines as he actually pasted them in place cannot be exactly reproduced here. The *Graphic's* type facsimile is not reproduced because
of its several errors. This transcription therefore supplies a new type facsimile,
based on the real *Post* headlines and the arrangement of them as published in the
Graphic, correcting its errors but not simulating the *Post* typography quite as well
as the *Graphic* typesetters were able to do in 1873.

    [5] In December 1872 Warner published *Backlog Studies* (Boston: James R. Os-
good and Co.), a collection of essays, many of which had first appeared in *Scribner's Monthly* ("Jas. R. Osgood & Co.'s New Holiday Books," *Publishers' and
Stationers' Weekly Trade Circular* 2 [5 Dec 72]: 635; 22 Apr 72 to the Warners,
n. 1).

To Whitelaw Reid
17? April 1873 • Hartford, Conn.
(MS: DLC)

Friend Reid—

    How's that,?— for the present? *Can't* hit on an entirely satisfac-
tory title, somehow—but we want a mere mention, *now,*—with either
exceedingly complimentary additions, or pitiless abuse accompanied
with profanity. We shall be down there within a fortnight. We think a
pretty good deal of this novel I can tell you; even the paper it is written
on cost eleven dollars.

Ys

<u>Mark.</u>

[*letter docketed by Reid:*]
Dear Hay:

    Here's a chance for a rollicking bit of minion. It shld be *must* for
Saturday.[1]

WR

[and in unidentified hand:]
Hartford   }
18 Apr, 1873.[2]

[1] Clemens's enclosure does not survive, but clearly was a suggested text for a notice of his forthcoming book, soon to be entitled *The Gilded Age.* The letter and its enclosure were probably used by John Hay to prepare the following item, which appeared in minion type (equivalent to seven-point type) in the *Tribune* for Saturday, 19 April (6):

> Beaumont and Fletcher may now retire as instances of genius working in double harness. Mark Twain and Chas. Dudley Warner have written a novel in partnership! It will be published about the end of the Summer, and will be octavo in form and profusely illustrated. The book deals with the salient features of our American life of to-day; and, as might easily be divined, is in the nature of a satire. It is known to contain all the profound philosophy, the sound learning, and geological truth which are found in "Innocents Abroad" and "Roughing It," and even more of practical wisdom and agricultural suggestion than are contained in "My Summer in a Garden." It is no holiday work. It deals with every aspect of modern society, and we are authorized to announce that the paper on which it is written cost eleven dollars.

The collaboration of playwrights Francis Beaumont (1584–1616) and John Fletcher (1579–1625) was proverbial. *My Summer in a Garden* was the collection of humorous essays which established Warner as a writer of note (Boston: J. R. Osgood and Co., published in November 1870 [*L4,* 294 n. 1]). The *Tribune* notice may also have drawn some information from a letter that Warner wrote to Reid on 7 April:

> Maybe it's a great piece of presumption, but Mark and I are writing a novel, and can so nearly see the end of it that it is safe to speak of it. No one here, except our wives, knows anything of it. We conceived the design early in the winter, but were not able to get seriously at work on it till some time in January. If there is any satire on the times in it, it won't be our fault, but the fault of the times. We have hatched the plot day by day, drawn out the characters, and written it so that we cannot exactly say which belongs to who; though the different styles will show in the chapters. This may be a good feature, giving the reader relief, and it may be it will only bother him. It is, under the circumstances, rather a novel experiment. (Cortissoz, 1:273)

"It *is* an experiment," Reid replied, "still it has been successful two or three times abroad, and you and Twain will make it successful if anybody can here. Besides it seems to me that you and he were well calculated to fit into and supplement each other's work. Good luck attend you both" (10 Apr 73, Whitelaw Reid Papers, DLC).

[2] The docket recorded the date of receipt. The letter was probably written on 17 April.

To Whitelaw Reid
20 April 1873 • Hartford, Conn.
(MS: DLC)

Private & conf.

Hartford, 20^{th,}

My Dear Reid, you have manifestly tried to do us a good turn on the novel, but in speaking facetiously instead of seriously, I am afraid you have hurt us. I wanted you to do us a genuine good turn & give us a fair & ǥ square good send-off. I have not allowed my publisher to know the book was a novel; Warner has foreborne to mention it in his paper; I have kept ₐmyₐ brother quiet (he is an editor,)—& all because we wanted the *first* mention to come from the *Tribune,* so that it might start from the most influential source in the land & start *right.*

And now you give us a notice which ~~the~~ carries the impression to the minds of other editors that we are people of small consequence in the literary world, & indeed only triflers; that a novel by us is in no sense a literary event. Half the papers in America will not see that you were meaning to say a pleasant word for us & simply chose an unfortunate way of doing it: they will merely see that you give us a stickful of pleasantry down in a corner—& every man of ~~in~~ them will take his cue from you, (as they all do) & will act accordingly.[1] You paid my life-raft article a grave, dignified compliment, full of Tribune *character,* & straightway all the papers see that my suggestion was sensible—& you know they never would have so regarded it if you had kept silence or had chaffed the article.[2]

Now I hold that a̸ novel from us is a literary *event,* (though it may sound pretty egotistical) & it deserved from you two stickfuls of *brevier,* gravely worded, & an honorable place in your chief editorial columns. I am not a man of trifling literary consequence. The *voluntary* & unsought subscriptions to my next book already run up into thousands—though no man knows what the book is to be, or what subject it will treat of. These people simply say, "I don't care—put my name down." Now you know that that is unusual. "Roughing It" had 43,000 subscribers already booked, the day it issued from the press. The "Innocents Abroad" (now 3½ years old) sold 12,000 copies this last year—sells ~~£ 2,000~~ 1000 a month right along—which looks as if it had entered permanently into the ~~let~~ literature of the country.[3] These things all mean this: that I have a good reliable audience in this country—& it is the biggest one in America, too, if I do say it myself. So a novel from me alone would ~~be a literary event, &~~ ₐbe a good deal in the nature of a literary event, &ₐ the Tribune, to be just, should have made it so ɪ appear, I think.

In confidence I wish to say that young Bennett has been trying for several months to get me to write for the Herald, & some time ago sent a man up here to argue the case with me. Sent a telegram from Europe the other day asking when he will see me there. The ₐ day after I told his ~~man~~ ₐmessenger, NO, & said I was writing a book & couldn't break into it with newspaper work, you dropped a line asking for Sandwich Island letters & I put down this novel in the midst of a chapter & put in two whole days ~~in~~ on the S. I. letters. The spirit of the novel got into them & they had a good public reception.[4] Now confound you when I want you to do something for me, you shove my novel at the world as if neither it nor its father amounted to much! This isn't fair—I swear it is not fair.

Now this Christian Union notice[5] of an absolutely worthless book, will make many & many a newspaper man say ɪₗaudatory things of the bantling. Such a notice from you of our novel would have been truthful & would have launched us into absolutely certain success. If our novel isn't worth ten such messes of ill-digested stuff as this Metropolisville thing, I will agree to eat it, without condiments. Our novel will have some *point* to it & will *mean* something, & *I* think it will not be snubbed & thrown aside, but will make some men talk, & may even make some people *think*. But of course my saying so does not make it so. All I claim is that it is the literary event of the season—& that I stick to. Your notice of it is not ten hours old, in Hartford, & yet it is talked of here more now than ~~an other~~ another man's book would be in a week—& not because I live here for I ~~an~~ am not known here.

I think you fellows meant well by us—indeed you could have had no reason to mean otherwise—but you could have given us a splendid send= off & not stepped outside the proprieties of the occasion in any way. I am sorry to make you read so long a letter, but Lord knows that what your paper says about a book of mine is a serious thing to me. I fancy that what able people sa might say about your Essay upon journalism was a matter of solicitude with you.⁶ So, under the circumstances you must overlook the length of this screed.

ʌ / ʌTitle,ʌ
"The Gilded
Age."⁷

Yr friend
Samˡ. L. Clemens.

Now just see if you can't do us a real outspoken good turn that will leave a strong wholesome impression on the public mind—& then command our services, if they can be of use to you. Title of novel is, "The Gilded Age."

[*enclosure:*]⁸

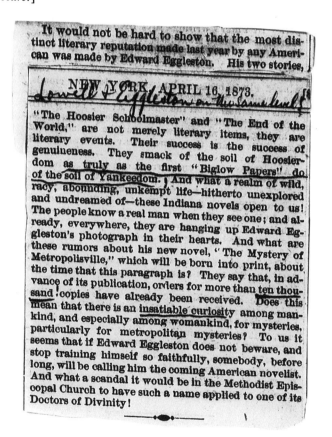

> It would not be hard to show that the most distinct literary reputation made last year by any American was made by Edward Eggleston. His two stories,
>
> NEW YORK, APRIL 16, 1873.
>
> "The Hoosier Schoolmaster" and "The End of the World," are not merely literary items, they are literary events. Their success is the success of genuineness. They smack of the soil of Hoosier-dom as truly as the first "Biglow Papers" do of the soil of Yankeedom. And what a realm of wild, racy, abounding, unkempt life—hitherto unexplored and undreamed of—these Indiana novels open to us! The people know a real man when they see one; and already, everywhere, they are hanging up Edward Eggleston's photograph in their hearts. And what are these rumors about his new novel, "The Mystery of Metropolisville," which will be born into print, about the time that this paragraph is? They say that, in advance of its publication, orders for more than ten thousand copies have already been received. Does this mean that there is an insatiable curiosity among mankind, and especially among womankind, for mysteries, particularly for metropolitan mysteries? To us it seems that if Edward Eggleston does not beware, and stop training himself so faithfully, somebody, before long, will be calling him the coming American novelist. And what a scandal it would be in the Methodist Episcopal Church to have such a name applied to one of its Doctors of Divinity!

¹Clemens was alarmed by the New York *Tribune* notice of 19 April (see the previous letter, n. 1). It appeared in the bottom right corner of the editorial page

(6), set in minion, rather than in the slightly larger brevier (equivalent to eight-point type), which was "generally used for editorial matter" (Pasko, 70). The principal *Tribune* editorials were set in brevier, with minion used for briefer notes on the same page covering topics of less importance. Clemens's alarm was prompted by the facetious tone of the notice, not merely its minion ranking, and is largely explained by his sensitivity to the slightest hint that he was not to be taken seriously. Significantly, he thought the notice implied that he and Warner were only "triflers," the same word that stung when Josiah G. Holland used it to belittle him as a lecturer (see 18 July 72 to Redpath). Warner was coeditor of the Hartford *Courant*. Orion Clemens had been on the editorial staff of the Hartford *Evening Post* since around mid-September 1872, a position he was about to leave (25 Sept 72 to OLC, n. 11; 5 May 73 to OC and MEC, n. 1).

²See 9 Apr 73 to Reid, n. 3, and the enclosure with the letter.

³Clemens's claim about the early sales of *Roughing It* is inaccurate: orders for "43,000 subscribers" were not on hand until over two and a half months after the first books came from the bindery (18 Mar 72 to Howells, n. 2; 20 Apr 72 to Redpath, n. 4). Clemens also exaggerated the sales of *The Innocents Abroad:* only 8,409 copies were bound in 1872, and 2,731 in January–April 1873, for an average of fewer than 700 per month (*RI 1993*, 890; APC, 106–7).

⁴James Gordon Bennett, Jr., became managing editor of the New York *Herald* in 1866 and succeeded his father as editor in chief in June 1872. In 1867 the younger Bennett secured four unsigned letters from Clemens on the *Quaker City* voyage (only one of them identified as his), and enlisted his services the following winter as an anonymous correspondent from Washington (*L2*, 55 n. 3, 106–7 n. 2, 115–16, 160). Clemens may have dismissed Bennett's messenger the day before he received Reid's letter of 28 December 1872 asking for an article "on any topic" (see p. 263), or on 4–5 January, before he received Reid's telegram (now lost) requesting a second article on the Sandwich Islands (3 Jan 73 to Reid [2nd]; 6 Jan 73 to Reid). By late December he had evidently begun to write *The Gilded Age*.

⁵See the enclosure and note 8.

⁶Reid had delivered a lecture at the University of the City of New York on 4 April 1872, addressing a proposal to create a school of journalism. His speech was reported at length in the *Tribune* and published from his manuscript in *Scribner's Monthly* for June ("Schools of Journalism," New York *Tribune*, 5 Apr 72, 1–2; Whitelaw Reid; Cortissoz, 1:236–37). Reid was publicly and privately committed to raising the professional level of journalism in the United States.

⁷Clemens squeezed in and circled the title here because his first mention, on the bottom of his final page, was cramped for lack of space and difficult to read.

⁸Clemens cut this clipping from the *Christian Union* of 16 April 1873 (7:301). This weekly (begun in 1867 as the *Church Union*) had been edited since 1870 by Henry Ward Beecher, and during his tenure evolved from a religious journal into a "general family periodical" (Mott 1957, 422–24). One of the current members of its editorial staff was Edward Eggleston (1837–1902), a former lay preacher in the Methodist church who had become a popular success as an author and editor, publishing *The Hoosier Schoolmaster* in 1871 and *The End of the World* in 1872. His *Mystery of Metropolisville*, a melodramatic novel about a real-estate boom in Minnesota, was serialized in *Hearth and Home* beginning in 1872. Orange Judd

and Company issued it as a book in early April 1873 (Hart, 224; "Alphabetical List of Books Just Published," *Publishers' Weekly* 3 [12 Apr 73]: 378). James Russell Lowell (1819–91), the author of two collections of *Biglow Papers* (1848 and 1867), was the dean of American dialect versifiers, as Clemens explicitly acknowledged in his scornful remark on the clipping itself: "Lowell & Eggleston on the same level!" Clemens was not alone in deprecating Eggleston's latest book. William Dean Howells had reviewed his first two books with some enthusiasm in the *Atlantic*, but did not review *Mystery of Metropolisville*, later calling it "disappointing . . . for though it showed a good sense of character and the story was interesting, it was not so fresh as The Hoosier Schoolmaster, and it had not such poetic elements as The End of the World. It was not an advance; it was something of a retrogression" (Howells 1874, 745–46). Clemens himself referred to the book somewhat less scornfully in March 1879 (*N&J2*, 303).

From Samuel L. Clemens and Charles Dudley Warner
to Ainsworth R. Spofford
21 April 1873 • Hartford, Conn.
(MS: DLC)

Hartford, Apl. 21

1873.

A R Spofford Esq[1]

D[r] Sir:

Enclosed please find title-page, which please enter in our names, as per to-day's letter, enclosing fees, &c.[2]

Ys Truly

Saml. L. Clemens

Chas. D. Warner.

[1]Ainsworth R. Spofford had been the librarian of Congress since 1864; he and Clemens may have become acquainted in Washington during the winter of 1867–68 (*L4*, 207 n. 1).

[2]Clemens's other letter "enclosing fees" is not known to survive, nor is the title page that he enclosed here. Spofford filled in and returned the following (CU-MARK):

To Whitelaw Reid
22 April 1873 • (1st of 3) • Hartford, Conn.
(MS: DLC)

Apl. 22.

My Dear Reid:

Cheque received for $12¹—for which this is acknowledgm'ᵗ

All right! You go ahead & give us that other notice. Bilious? I was more than bilious—I was *scared*. When a man starts out in a new role, the public always says he is a fool & won't succeed. So I wanted to make every knife cut that could *help* up us succeed, anyway.²

Why of *course* the Tribune would make Hartford talk,—& the rest of the country, for that matter—else why would I be so solicitous about what the Tribune said? That is just the point—I want the Tribune to say it *right* & say it powerful——& then I will answer for the consequences.

The consequence will be that all other papers will *follow suit*—as

ˌwhich ˌ you know, as ⫽ well as I do. And then our game is made & our venture launched with a fair wind instead of a baffling one.

Ys

Clemens

[*enclosure:*]³

> The best piece of news, in the literary way, for many a day, is the announcement that Mark Twain and Charles Dudley Warner have written a novel in partnership! It will be published about the end of the summer, and will be octavo in form and profusely illustrated. The book deals with the salient features of our American life of to-day; and, as might easily be divined, is in the nature of a satire.

¹On 21 April Reid had forwarded a check "for your life-raft letter" (Whitelaw Reid Papers, DLC; see 9 Apr 73 to Reid).

²Reid evidently responded (probably in a telegram, now lost) to Clemens's "bilious" letter of 20 April by offering to publish another, more satisfactory, notice of *The Gilded Age*.

³This enclosed clipping was cut from the Springfield (Mass.) *Republican* of 22 April 1873 (7) by Warner, who wrote "Springfield Rep." on it and gave it to Clemens. Clemens added his own comment before sending it to Reid. The item seems to be based on the *Tribune* notice of 19 April to which Clemens took exception.

To Whitelaw Reid

22 April 1873 • (2nd of 3) • Hartford, Conn.
(MS: DLC)

22ᵈ

My Dear Reid—

Now *that* notice is bully! ~~Wh~~ If any man is deceived by that, he will be deceived in the happy direction, at any rate—& ⫽ that is what we want. All right, now!¹

Ys

Mark.

[*letter docketed:*] 24 Apr. 1873 | Hartford

[1] It is possible that Clemens misdated his letter by one day, and that he wrote after seeing the *Tribune*'s second notice of *The Gilded Age,* published (in minion) on 23 April in the upper right quarter of the editorial page (4). It is somewhat more likely, however, that Reid telegraphed the text before publication to Clemens, who wrote this reply late on 22 April, so that it was not docketed until 24 April. The notice read:

> The work upon which Mark Twain and Mr. Charles Dudley Warner have been engaged for the past year is likely to prove the chief literary event of the season. Its first mention in THE TRIBUNE has excited great attention and interest, and we are able now to announce its name. It is called "The Gilded Age"—a name which gives the best promise of the wealth of satire and observation which it is easy to expect from two such authors. It is an unusual and a courageous enterprise for two gentlemen who have already won honorable distinction in other walks of literature, to venture upon untrodden paths with a work so ambitious and so important as this is likely to be. In one sense there is nothing to fear. An immense audience is already assured beforehand; and it is fair to conclude that writers who have displayed so much wit, insight, and delicate and fanciful observation, in former works, will not be unprovided with the equipment which is necessary to successful fiction. The new novel will be eagerly looked for and enormously read, and we hazard little in predicting that it will contain as much food for thought as for laughter.

To Whitelaw Reid
22 April 1873 • (3rd of 3) • Hartford, Conn.
(MS: DLC)

Hartf[d], Apl. 22.

My Dear Reid:

Warner hasn't finished up & isn't going to get away for a week or more yet—& I guess I'm in the same boat. But the main bar with me is that my wife is pretty ill with diphtheria, & will not be on her feet for some little time. So we have to lose the chance of a good time at the Lotos, for which I am very truly sorry.[1]

Yrs

S. L. Clemens.

✉———————————————————

[*letter docketed:*] *1873*

[1] Clemens replied to the following invitation from Reid, dated 21 April: "If you and Warner are coming here next week, why not arrange to be in town Sat-

urday night at the Lotos Club? It is the closing dinner of the season, and you should meet plenty of people you like" (Whitelaw Reid Papers, DLC). No other surviving documents mention that Olivia was ill, and only two days later, on 24 April, she and Susy accompanied Mrs. Langdon and Hattie Lewis on their return to Elmira. Nevertheless, she may have been experiencing early symptoms of the quinsy she developed in Elmira (Elisabeth G. Warner to George H. Warner, 24 Apr 73, CU-MARK; 17 Feb 73 to Langdon, n. 3; 25 and 26 Apr 73 to OLC; 5 May 73 to OC and MEC).

To Unidentified
25 April ?1873 • Hartford, Conn.
(Parke-Bernet 1971, lot 207)

Hartford, April 25.

. . . .

any N.Y. book store can furnish you a Mormon Bible[1]

. . . .

[1]Clemens seems to have been answering a question prompted by his ridicule of the Mormon bible in chapter 16 of *Roughing It*. Since he was not in Hartford in April 1872, this letter fragment has been assigned to 1873, although it may have been written in 1874, or even later.

To Olivia L. Clemens
25 and 26 April 1873 • Hartford, Conn.
(MS: Davis)

Home, P.M.

Livy Ð darling, ₐas Warner says "ₐThe child is born, & his name is Mary Jane!"[1] Which is to say, that just as Eliza[2] called me to dinner I put the last touch to the chapter where Phil strikes the coal mine——so we the book is really *done*,—all except the tedious work of correcting, dove= tailing & revamping. A fearful load went off my mind with the discovery of that coal vein. Now I want you to ask the boys to find out from Fulton one thing—to-wit: When one is after a coal vein in a tunnel, & that vein is well canted up, or stands perpendicular, does water always burst out when they strike into the vein (if below the water level, of course,) & *is the bursting out of the water a* SIGN *that they've struck the main lead?*[3]

It is always the case in silver mining.

The place is pretty lonely without you & the muggins—am sorry now that I let mother & Hattie go.[4] I didn't intend to, but I got to thinking of something else—as sometimes happens to me. I love you, my child.

The copyright has come. Also, propositions from a couple of publishers.[5]

Love to all, & mostly to you & Susie-su & *old* Sue[6] & the rest.

Sam*l*.

[*new page:*]

26th

Can't write you a line today, honey—too busy. Hoped my telegram to say all well would catch you in N. Y. yesterday morning, but I am afraid Downey started down a little late—w[h] was chiefly my fault. Got Elmira dispatch.[7] Glad.

House comes Tuesday.[8]

I love you, honey.

Saml.

✉

Mrs. Saml L. Clemens | Elmira | N. Y. [*return address:*] IF NOT DELIVERED WITHIN 10 DAYS, TO BE RETURNED TO [*postmarked:*] HARTFORD CT. APR 2◊ 8 PM

[1]Clemens alluded to the story of a minister whose grandiose predictions of masculine achievement for a baby he was about to christen were momentarily upset when he learned, at the last moment, that the baby was a girl. Clemens evidently first heard the story from Warner, but by 1885, when it became one of his favorite pieces for oral delivery, he was crediting the version told by Bram Stoker (SLC 1890–99, 1–2; *N&J3*, 195, 268, 353, 357, 369; *MTS* 1910, 149–50).

[2]A Hartford servant, not further identified.

[3]The "boys" were Charles J. Langdon, Theodore Crane, and John D. F. Slee, partners in J. Langdon and Company, coal merchants (*L4*, 140 n. 2, 157). Fulton was evidently a company employee, otherwise unidentified. Clemens must have received the confirmation he sought, since the appearance of water remained the sign of Philip Sterling's triumph in chapter 62, the penultimate chapter of *The Gilded Age*.

[4]Susy Clemens, Mrs. Langdon, and Harriet Lewis.

[5]For the copyright, see 21 Apr 73 to Spofford, n. 2. The "propositions" from

publishers have not been identified, but one might have come from Isaac E. Sheldon (see 3 May 73 to Bliss, n. 1).

[6] Susy Clemens and Susan Crane.

[7] Clemens evidently telegraphed Olivia at the New York hotel (probably the St. Nicholas) where she stayed overnight before proceeding to Elmira. Her "Elmira dispatch" undoubtedly reported her safe arrival on 26 April.

[8] In 1890 Clemens recalled that Edward H. House, who had been living in Japan since 1870, "came with a couple of Japanese boys and stayed a few days in my house in Hartford. Charles Dudley Warner & I had just finished 'The Gilded Age,' & House read it in manuscript" (SLC 1890, 6†; see also 17 May 73 to Warner, n. 2). House probably arrived as planned, on Tuesday, 29 April, and stayed until at least 1 May, when he wrote to Whitelaw Reid from Hartford that he was "with Mark Twain for a day or two, and enjoying myself" (Whitelaw Reid Papers, DLC).

To Colton Greene
26 April 1873 • Hartford, Conn.
(MS: MoHH)

Hartford, Apl. 26.

My Dear General—

Thank you heartily, you splendid old reconstructed profane rebel conundrumist!

The "old man" has been down again & spent two days with me—he came fortified—brought 6 bottles of Scotch whisky—& all he drank while here was two glasses.[1]

We talked a deal about you & your disheartening habit of cursing & swearing at the table while the ladies & the ministers needed quiet & silence wherein to coax their sustenance to go down—& stay.

Well, the builders have been at work digging cellar a week, now, & so it does really look as if a year from to-day (as per contract) the architect might ~~really~~ be able to say, "Mr. Clemens your shanty is ready." And then—or sooner if you can—I want you to come![2]

Good-bye—

Yrs

S. L. Clemens.

[1] See 22 Jan 73 to Mouland, n. 6.

[2] John B. Garvie, the general contractor, and John R. Hills, the masonry con-

tractor, built the house from plans by Edward T. Potter and Alfred H. Thorp. The Clemenses were not able to occupy it until the fall of 1874, and even then it was still unfinished (*MTB*, 1:520; "Twain Home Given Builders' Pictures," unidentified Hartford newspaper, 18 May 1931, PH in CU-MARK). It is not known whether Greene ever visited the Clemenses.

To Olivia L. Clemens
26 April 1873 • Hartford, Conn.
(MS: CU-MARK)

Apl. 26th, 10.30 PM.

Livy darling, I have finished trimming & revamping all my MS, & to= day we began the work of critically reading the book, line by line & numbering the chapters & working them in together in their appropriate places. It is perfectly fascinating work. All of the first eleven chapters are mine, & when I came to read them right straight along without breaking, I got really interested; & when I got to Sellers's eye-water & his clock & his fireless stove & his turnip dinner, I could hardly read for ~~Lau~~ laughing. The turnip dinner is powerful good—& is satisfactory now.[1]

Warner failed on his description of Laura as a school-girl—as a *picture* of her, I mean. He had simply copied Miss Woolson's pretty description almost word for word—the plagiarism would have been detected in a moment. I told him so—he saw it & yet I'm hanged if he didn't hate to lose it because there was a "nip" & a pungency about that woman's phrases that he hated to lose—& so did I, only they weren't ours & we couldn't take them.[2] So I set him to create a picture & he went at it. I finally took ~~a~~ paper & pencil, had a thought, ‸(as to phraseology)‸ & scratched it down. I had already told him what the *details* of the picture should be, & so only choice language was needed to dress them in. ~~My pi~~ Then we read our two efforts, & mine being rather the best, we used it.[3] And so it *ought* to have been the best. If I had been trying to describe a picture that was in *his* mind, *I* would have botched it.

We both think this is going to be no slouch of a novel, as Solomon said to the Hebrew Children.

Dined with Warner yesterday—at home today—lunch with Twichell noon tomorrow. The kitties are very frisky, now. They & the old cat
sleep with me, nights, & have the run of the house. I wouldn't take thousands of dollars for them. Next to a wife whom I idolise, give me cat—
~~&~~ ₐan₍ *old* cat, with kittens. How is the muggins, now, by the way. It is
very melancholy here, but I don't notice it. I'm pretty sad, but I'm used
to it—it can't phaze *me*. I'm an old hand at grief. Grief makes me hump
myself when I'm *alone*, but that is taking advantages. When my family
is around I am superior to it.

But I am not grieving tonight, honey. I've pegged away all day till
this hour & done a big day's work, & I feel as gay as a hymn. ~~It is bed
time,~~

Got a French version of the Jumping Frog—fun is no name for it.[4]
I am going to translate it *literary̸ally*, ₐFrench₍ construction & all, (apol-
ogising in parenthesis where a word is too many for me) & publish it in
the Atlantic as the grave effort of a man who does not know ₎ẇ but what
he is as good a French scholar as there is—& sign my name to it, without
another word. It will be toothsome reading.

Good bye my darling, I love you & I love the muggins. It is bed time,
now—I got to go ₐdown₍ & roust out the cats.

Saml.

Mrs. Sam*ˡ*. L. Clemens | Elmira | N. Y. [*return address:*] IF NOT DELIVERED
WITHIN 10 DAYS, TO BE RETURNED TO [*postmarked:*] HARTFORD CT. APR ◊◊ 11 AM

---

[1] See chapters 7, 8, and 11 of *The Gilded Age*.
[2] The "pretty description" by Constance Fenimore Woolson (1840–94) has
not been identified (but see French, 295 n. 13). Woolson, James Fenimore Cooper's grandniece, was born in New Hampshire but spent her early years in Ohio.
In the 1860s and early 1870s she published poems, stories with regional settings,
and travel sketches in *Harper's Monthly*, the *Galaxy*, and the *Atlantic Monthly*,
among other journals.
[3] *The Gilded Age*, chapter 6.
[4] Thérèse Bentzon (Marie-Thérèse Blanc), in the first of two articles about
American humorists, introduced Mark Twain to French readers in the 15 July
1872 issue of *Revue des deux mondes* (Blanc). She included her own translation
of the "Jumping Frog" tale, which (according to a critic in 1910) was "remarkably accurate" but lacked the spirit of the original—hardly surprising, given her
evident failure to fully appreciate the subtleties of Mark Twain's humor. In her
opinion, the tale was

one of his most popular little stories—almost a type of the rest. It is, nevertheless, rather difficult for us to understand, while reading the story, the "roars of laughter" that it excited in Australia and in India, in New York and in London; the numerous editions of it which appeared; the epithet of "inimitable" that the critics of the English press have unanimously awarded to it. (Henderson, 303, 304, 308)

She concluded, "Soon we will be accustomed to an American language whose delectable freedom is not to be disdained, anticipating the more delicate and more refined qualities which time will no doubt bring to it" (Tenney, 4; Blanc, 335; see also Wilson).

[5] Clemens soon wrote this sketch, but he did not publish it in the *Atlantic Monthly* (7 July 73 to Bliss, n. 1).

To John E. Mouland
29 April 1873 • Hartford, Conn.
(Transcript: CU-MARK)

Hartford, April 29.

Dear Capt.

The bearer is my friend and London helpmeet, Mr. Samuel C. Thompson. He would like to sail with us, May 17th in the "Batavia" & I would exceedingly like it myself. I hope that the ship is not so full but that a shelf can be found for him to dispose himself upon.[1]

My wife and I send warm regards.

Your friend

Mark Twain.

Capt. Jno. E. Mouland
  Steamer Batavia.

[1] The text of this letter is preserved only in Samuel Chalmers Thompson's unpublished autobiography (written between 1918 and 1921), together with his account of meeting Clemens and offering to act as his stenographic secretary during the upcoming trip to England. Thompson (b. 1848) was born in Georgia. At sixteen he went to sea on a whaling ship. Upon his return he attended the University of Georgia, and then Trinity College in Hartford. He worked briefly as a reporter for the New York *Tribune* in the summer of 1872, and then "obtained [a] position of teacher at Vernor Episcopal Institute, East Windsor Hill, eight miles above Hartford," where his friend Azel Stevens Roe, Jr., was also employed teaching music (Thompson, 72–73). Roe was a California acquaintance of Clemens's who had visited him in Hartford in mid-January (Thompson, 1, 4, 32, 53, 59, 203; *L3*, 253 n. 2; OLC to Olivia Lewis Langdon, 19 Jan 73, CtHMTH). According to Thompson, his first meeting with Clemens occurred

soon after that visit, probably in mid-March, when Clemens "came out to give us a lecture in the school hall; but a blizzard blocked the gathering. . . . He, Roe and I passed the hours till bed time in solemn discourse. . . . He and Dudley Warner were now colaborating on 'The Gilded Age,' a chapter a day." Thompson further recalled:

> Clemens complained of forgetfulness; lost much by not writing things down at once; thought of learning short hand, but found the only way to learn would be to hire a teacher to live with him till he mastered it. . . . Also he wished he could have with him the coming summer in England a suitable person to help take notes. An Englishman would not notice things that would strike Americans as peculiar. And in some cases a substitute could go when he wanted to go somewhere else. Having been a sailor I had thought of taking a healthful summer holiday by shipping before the mast for a voyage or two, and doing a little sight seeing about the ports. But it occurred to me that I might get up short hand and go for the summer with Clemens if he wanted me. He seemed pleased at the idea. I had occasion to run down to New York. Monson's was the leading system in shorthand. He was in Park Row. I had a talk with him and got a copy of his work. . . . I put in all my spare time for six weeks, teaching and timing myself. . . . Then I went again to see Clemens. Dudley Warner was with him in his study, manu-script all around, hurrying to finish "The [G]ilded Age.["] . . . He wanted me to go over in the same steamer, and all the state rooms had been engaged weeks before, his on the Cunarder "Batavia." Warner suggested that Clemens write to the Captain, Mouland. The latter [and] Clemens were chummy. The Captain had visited him and he preferred to cross by the Batavia when possible. (Thompson, 76–78)

Clemens "wrote and handed" the present letter to Thompson: "In New York I took my letter to the Captain and he went over to the main office and got me a birth in the last state room aft on the port side" (Thompson, 79–80). Thompson taught himself a system of shorthand developed by James E. Munson (1835–1906), who had published the first edition of his *Complete Phonographer* in 1866 (New York: Robert H. Johnston and Co.). Munson had been a law reporter since 1857, and later became the official stenographer for the Superior Court of New York. He based his shorthand on the phonetic symbols invented by Isaac Pit-man, which he modified to "adapt the system to the requirements of the re-porter" (Munson, title page, iii, v; Westby-Gibson, 138; see also *L2*, 311 n. 8).

To Olivia L. Clemens
1 May 1873 • Hartford, Conn.
(Transcript: CU-MARK)

May 1.

Livy dear, are you really well? No letter today—only 2 since you have been gone, & it seems to me that I have written 15 or 16—16 I think.

Love to the muggins—et sa mere.

Saml.

✉———————————————————————————————

Mrs Saml L. Clemens | Elmira | N. Y.[1]

[1]The source for this letter is a typed transcript of the original manuscript, whose location is no longer known. Although the address is transcribed at the head of the letter, it must have been taken from an envelope (or possibly from the verso of a postcard). None of the letters Olivia wrote to her husband in 1873 is known to survive.

To Elisha Bliss, Jr.
3 May 1873 • Hartford, Conn.
(Transcript: WU)

Home   May 3/73

Friend Bliss—

We shall doubtless be ready to talk business by about Tuesday, Wednesday, or, at latest, Thursday—& we shall be in a hurry too— shan't have long to talk. So, think it all over—Sheldon & Co think we will make a serious & damaging mistake if we try to sell a novel by subscription.[1] Try & be ready, also to recommend to me another Hartford subscription publisher to get out a telling book on Japan, for I suppose you have got your hands about full. I want you to recommend a man who will appreciate a good thing & know how to push it.[2]

Yrs

Clemens

[1]Clemens wrote on Saturday. His "hurry" seems to have been prompted, at least in part, by his plan to leave for Elmira (by way of New York City), which he did on Thursday, 8 May—the same day he and Warner finally met with Bliss to sign the contract for *The Gilded Age*. Bliss agreed to a 10 percent royalty (5 percent to each author) on the retail price of every book sold (see Appendix D and 16 July 73 to Bliss, n. 2). London publisher George Routledge was also in Hartford that day and may have joined them to discuss arrangements for the English edition. The manuscript itself was probably not delivered to Bliss until late May, after Warner had revised it ("Brief Mention," Hartford *Courant*, 8 May 73, 2; 12 May 73 to Redpath, n. 1; 16 July 73 to Bliss). Isaac E. Sheldon's prediction of failure in publishing "a novel by subscription" was merely the received

wisdom at this time, both among trade and subscription publishers. When Bliss issued *The Gilded Age* in December 1873, it became the first novel published by subscription. In April 1871 Clemens had proposed writing "quite a respectable novel" for publication by Sheldon, who had been encouraging: "I like the idea & it would sell well if it were a good story & had a quiet vein of humor as well as the tragic interest of a story. I do not see why you could not write such a story" (*L4*, 375, 376 n. 1). The "story" in question was probably a version of *The Gilded Age*, which Clemens then thought of writing with Joseph T. Goodman. The present letter shows that he must have talked with Sheldon again, this time about the novel he and Warner had actually written. Bliss was predisposed to regard Sheldon as a rival, having objected to his publication, in March 1871, of *Mark Twain's (Burlesque) Autobiography and First Romance* (SLC 1871b) as a violation of his own exclusive contract with Clemens (see *L4*, 320–21 n. 1). That rivalry may have influenced his decision to agree to the 10 percent royalty. In general, subscription publishers paid authors far more than did trade publishers, as Warner implicitly acknowledged on 19 April when he informed James R. Osgood of his own, presumably temporary, defection from the retail trade: "Mark Twain and I have been writing a novel the last two months, but it will have to go into the subscription trade here, and we hope that our high art will be rewarded with several dollars" (CtHMTH; see also Hill 1964, 6–13, 71).

[2]On 3 May 1871 Clemens had urged Bliss to consider publishing a book that Edward H. House was writing about Japan. Bliss was interested, but the project was not pursued until House evidently revived it during his recent visit to Clemens, in late April. Despite Clemens's suggestion here, by late 1873 Bliss had reached an agreement with House, who wrote him from Japan on 25 November that the "MSS. progresses with reasonable rapidity, and as there seems to be ample time, I am seeing through a new series of observations, in order to make it additionally accurate and complete" (ViU). Ultimately, however, the American Publishing Company did not publish House's book (see *L4*, 388, 389 n. 1; 25 and 26 Apr 73 to OLC, n. 8).

To Orion and Mary E. (Mollie) Clemens
5 May 1873 • Hartford, Conn.
(MS: CU-MARK)

Home, Monday

Dear Sister & Bro:

Your letters received today—am very glad indeed for the news they brought. We finished revamping & refining the book tonight—ten days' labor. ⸿ It is near midnight & we are just through.

I like Orion's editorials. I like their gentlemanly dignity & refinement as much as their other virtues.[1] The English papers[2] will soon stop I fear—I subscribed till May 1[st.] Will subscribe for one for Orion when I get to London if I don't forget it.

Am very sorry to hear Ma is sick. Livy is down. In Elmira. Quinzy. Very bad attack of it. Just heard it to-day.[3] The baby is well.

                              Good-bye
                               Lovingly
                                Sam

✉️

Orion Clemens Esq | Bardwell House | Rutland | Vermont [*return address:*] IF NOT DELIVERED WITHIN 10 DAYS, TO BE RETURNED TO [*postmarked:*] HARTFORD CT. MAY 6 1 PM

---

[1] The letters from Orion and Mollie have not been found, but Orion's presumably reported on his position with the newly established Rutland (Vt.) *Globe*, which he had agreed to edit from its first issue, published on 1 May. On 18 April the Hartford *Courant* had announced, "Mr. Clemens, brother of 'Mark Twain,' who has been editorially connected with the *Evening Post* of this city for some time past, is about to take the editorial direction of a new daily to be established in Rutland, Vt." ("Brief Mention," 2). Orion may have written any of the editorials printed in the *Globe* in early May—for example: "The Globe's Politics" and "The Indian Policy" on 1 May (2); "The Smitten Gould" on 2 May (2); and "Cruelty to Animals" and "Editorial Notes" on 5 May (2)—but none can be attributed to him with certainty. (He might also have sent Clemens drafts of proposed editorials that were never published.) During Orion's editorship (from May possibly through mid-July) the *Globe* made no mention of him, and published no other work identifiable as his. Orion had been interested in Rutland newspapers since his visit there in July 1872, when he learned that the owner of the weekly Rutland *Independent* wanted to start a daily newspaper (see 11 Aug 72 to OC, n. 3). As of 1 May this unidentified owner gave up the *Independent* and began to publish both the daily and the weekly *Globe*. In 1906 Clemens recalled Orion's experience in Rutland:

A new Republican daily was to be started in Rutland, Vermont, by a stock company of well-to-do politicians, and they offered Orion the chief editorship at three thousand a year. He was eager to accept. His wife was equally eager—no, twice as eager, three times as eager. My beseechings and reasonings went for nothing. I said:

"You are as weak as water. Those people will find it out right away. They will easily see that you have no backbone; that they can deal with you as they would deal with a slave. You may last six months, but not longer. Then they will not dismiss you as they would dismiss a gentleman: they will fling you out as they would fling out an intruding tramp."

It happened just so. (AD, 5 Apr 1906, CU-MARK, in *MTA*, 2:323)

By late July Orion was already negotiating for a different position, this time on the Oil City (Pa.) *Derrick* ("Personal," Buffalo *Courier,* 18 Apr 73, 1; Gregory, 692; OC to MEC, 21 July 73 and 22 July 73, CU-MARK).

[2] Unidentified.

[3] Mollie may have been in Rutland with Orion, but it seems more likely that she was staying temporarily with Clemens's family in Fredonia. Clemens's comment on his mother's health evidently replied to news from Mollie, to whom Orion was expected to forward this letter. Olivia's quinsy (a severe throat inflammation) was treated by Dr. Henry Sayles. Her infection may have begun in Hartford, but if so, it was misdiagnosed as diphtheria, which is also characterized at first by a sore throat (OLC to Olivia Lewis Langdon, 23 and 26 May 73, CtHMTH; 22 Apr 73 to Reid [3rd]).

To James Redpath
12 May 1873 • Elmira, N.Y.
(Mark Twain Quarterly, 5:19)

Elmira, May 12.[1]

Dear Redpath:

We sail from New York next Saturday in the Batavia—shan't be in Boston before sailing.

Shall return next October. May possibly lecture in 3 or 4 large eastern cities—but nowhere else.[2]

Too late to write me here. London address will be care of

Geo. Routledge & Sons
The Broadway
Ludgate Hill London E. C.

Yrs Ever,
Mark.

[1] Clemens left Hartford on 8 May, after signing the contract for *The Gilded Age,* and stopped briefly in New York, where he met with Edward T. Potter (his architect) and John B. Garvie (his builder) to discuss plans for the new house. He probably arrived in Elmira late on 9 May (Elisabeth G. Warner to George H. Warner, 8 May 73, CU-MARK).

[2] Clemens did not lecture again in the United States until March 1874; see 17 Dec 73 to Redpath, n. 2.

To Charles Dudley Warner
13 May 1873 • Elmira, N.Y.
(MS: PBL)

H̶a̶r̶t̶f̶ Elmira, 13th

My Dear Warner:

There was no use for "about 600 pages" in the contract, & the putting them there was foolish surplusage. I want Bliss to *take them out.* That will leave it that we contract to furnish to him the MS of a book called the Gilded Age—& that is entirely sufficient. There never was n̶ any sense in sticking in that stupid reference to the number of pages. D̶o̶n̶'̶t̶ ̶y̶o̶u̶ If you suggest the a̶u̶t̶ alteration while the MS. is still in your hands there won't be any trouble or anything disagreeable.[1]

The baby was sick & kept us u̶p̶ ̶a̶l̶l̶ ˍawake seven-tenths of theˍ night—seems better today. Livy rusty—I too.

Ys in haste (of packing up)

Saml. L. Clemens

ˍCare Geo. Routledge & Sons
Publishers—
The Broadway,
Ludgate Hill
London, E. C.,ˍ

Never mind Lackland. In his prosperity—then in his adversity—& finally in his lunatic death i̶n̶ ̶a̶ ̶h̶o̶u̶s̶e̶ ̶o̶f̶ ̶d̶ by the side of the corpse of his only friend—he is perhaps better suited to the stage than a book.[2]

---

[1] The contract remained unchanged (Appendix D). Clemens's sensitivity on this minor point probably owes something to his frustration in 1871, when he had difficulty producing enough manuscript to make *Roughing It* six hundred pages long (*RI 1993*, 872–73).

[2] Major Lackland figures in chapter 10 of *The Gilded Age*, where he is reported to have died "wholly alone and friendless," leaving "certain memoranda" that show Laura is not the natural child of Mr. and Mrs. Hawkins (SLC 1873–74, 100–101). Since Lackland does not die "by the side of the corpse of his only friend," it seems likely that Warner declined the advice in the present letter and revised the chapter to resolve whatever problem he had identified, eliminating in the process this melodramatic detail. Warner would have made his changes on

the manuscript itself, or possibly on the proofs (see Hill 1965, 142). None of the proofs, and only five pages of manuscript, are known to survive from chapter 10 (the changes would have been on pages 258–63, and the first surviving page is 264).

From Olivia L. and Samuel L. Clemens
to Olivia Lewis Langdon
17 May 1873 • SS *Batavia* at New York, N.Y.
(MS: CtHMTH)

Darling Mother—

Mrs Fairbanks has just left us—she spent the night on ship board with us— Claras letter to Allie will tell you all the news—[1] We saw Mrs Brooks for a few moments—[2] We feel as happy as possible and as hopeful of a successful voyage— Capt. Mouland is perfectly delightful and does everything for our comfort— The baby had a good nights sleep— I am glad there is no bidding good bye to be done here it would be very hard—

All your thoughts of us must be pleasant thoughts for I am sure we shall do well—

Mother Fairbanks was such a comfort to us—

Good bye, mother dear, we are just backing away from the pier.[3] Shall send this back by the pilot. Love.

Sam*l*.

[1] On 16 April Mrs. Langdon had invited Mary Mason Fairbanks to come to New York to see off the Clemens party on 17 May:

> Have you an intention to go to New York this spring, if so cannot you arrange to come to us and to go on to New York with Sam*l* and Livia when they sail[?] It would delight me and them very much if you could do so.—I do not think I shall be equal to going, but Charlie will go with them doubtless and perhaps some others of the family. (CtHMTH)

Clemens, Olivia, and Susy and her nurse (Nellie), along with Clara Spaulding, left Elmira accompanied by Fairbanks (and probably Charles Langdon) on 15 May, arriving in New York late the same day or very early the next. On the night of 16 May, Fairbanks stayed with Olivia in her cabin aboard the *Batavia*, while Clemens spent the night at the St. Nicholas Hotel; Clara probably stayed on board as well. Allie was Alice Spaulding, Clara's older sister (17 May 73 to Warner, n. 5; "Prominent Arrivals," New York *Tribune*, 17 May 73, 12; *L3*, 182 n. 6).

²Fidele A. Brooks, the wife of New York merchant Henry J. Brooks, was a close friend of the Langdons' (*L2*, 276 n. 10).

³The sixth member of the Clemens party, Samuel C. Thompson, met them on shipboard. He recalled that "some passengers from Pittsburgh told me they heard Clemens was to be one of them, had watched the gangway and decided that I was he. It seemed a curious coincidence at first. But I happened to be the only other passenger with moustache and thick bushy hair" (Thompson, 82). In 1909 Clemens recalled the impression Thompson made:

> I can see him now. It was on the deck of the *Batavia*, in the dock. The ship was casting off—with that hubbub, & confusion, & ~~tramping~~ & rushing of sailors, & shouting of orders, & shrieking of boatswains' whistles which marked the departure-preparations in those days. . . . Every individual was in storm-rig—heavy clothes of sombre hue & melancholy to look upon, but new, & designed & constructed for the occasion, & strictly in accordance with sea-going etiquette—anything wearable on *land* being distinctly & odiously out of the question!
>
> Very well. On that deck, & gliding placidly among those honorably & properly upholstered groups, appeared Thompson, young, grave, long, slim, with an aged & fuzzy plug hat towering high on the upper end of him & followed by a gray linen duster which flowed down without break or wrinkle to his ancle-bones!
>
> He came straight to us & shook hands, & compromised us. Everybody could see that we knew him. To see those passengers stare! A nigger in heaven could not have created a profounder astonishment.
>
> However, Thompson didn't know anything was happening. He was right out of East Windsor, where the farmers had no prejudices about clothes, & where a person was correct enough as long as he had some on. I can still see him as he looked when we passed Sandy Hook & the winds of the big ocean smote us. He had not seen the big ocean ~~before,~~ ₊for a good while,₊ & he stood apart absorbed in it. ~~& comparing the majestic reality with his long-time dreams of it;~~ ₵Erect, & lofty, & grand he stood, ~~not~~ facing the blast, holding his plug on with both hánds, & his generous duster blowing out behind ₊level with his neck₊ & flapping & flopping like a loosed maintogallant royal in a gale. There were scoffers observing, but he didn't know it, & wasn't disturbed. (SLC 1909a, 9–12†)

To Charles Dudley Warner
17 May 1873 • SS *Batavia* en route
from New York, N.Y., to Liverpool, England
(MS: CU-MARK)

Under Way, Sat. AM¹

Dear Warner—

Ask House to tell you about Whitelaw Reid. He is a contemptible cur, & I want nothing more to do with him. I don't want the Tribune to have the book at all. Please tell Bliss *not to send a copy there under any circumstances*. If you feel at any time like explaining, you may tell Reid or any one that I desired this.²

I shall probably write some letters for Herald & possibly for Advertiser.[3]

We saw Boucicault, who, in some minor respects, is an ass. If you describe the outside of your trunk to him he can tell you what it's got in it.

I will not consent to his having more than one-third for dramatising the book.[4]

Yesterday I sued a New York fraud for $20,000 damages for violating my copyright.[5]

We send love,~to~

We are all well, & jolly.

Ys Ever

Sam*ˡ*. L. Clemens

[1]Clemens compressed this letter onto the two sides of his calling card (3½ by 2⅛ inches). He began it on the back and completed it on the front, writing across the printed facsimile of his signature as well as the address (see Appendix F).

[2]Reid had angered Clemens by refusing to allow Edward House to review *The Gilded Age* for the *Tribune*. In 1890 Clemens recalled that House read the manuscript during his visit to Hartford in late April 1873:

> I did not have to ~do~ ‚take‚ the initiative with House; he asked for the things himself, & cheerfully waded through them, & made useful corrections & suggestions. . . . Well, he liked the Gilded Age, & ~tried~ ‚wanted‚ to do it a favor. He proposed to review it in the New York Tribune before some other journal should get a chance to give it a start which might not be to its advantage. But the project failed. He said Whitelaw Reid abused him & charged him with bringing a dishonorable proposal from Warner & me. That seemed strange; indeed unaccountable, for there was nothing improper about ~the House~ the proposition, & would not have been if it really had come from ~House &~ Warner & me. Eight or ten years later I made ~the~ a like proposition to Col. John Hay when he was temporarily editing the Tribune, & when I [i.e., he] accepted it ~he~ I inquired into the former case. He said that the explanation of that case was, that Reid did not like House, & would not have entertained a proposition of any kind from him. However, I had taken House's report at its face value; & as his effort to do me a service had ~apparently~ gotten him into trouble I felt that the effort & the result placed me under a double obligation to him. I withdrew my smile from Reid, ~with a~ & did not speak to him again for twelve or thirteen years—1886; then I asked him to do a certain kindness for House, & he said he would, & kept his word. (SLC 1890, 6–9†)

The exchange with Hay occurred in 1881, when William D. Howells wanted to review *The Prince and the Pauper* for the *Tribune*. Hay published Howells's review on 25 October (Howells 1881), after requesting advice from Reid, who counseled:

> As to Twain. It isn't good journalism to let a warm personal friend & in some matters literary partner, write a critical review of him in a paper wh. has good reason to think little of his delicacy & highly of his greed. So, if you haven't published it yet, I wld. think of this point before doing so. If you have, there's no harm done. But, as you remember we agreed, years ago, a new book by Twain is *not* (as he modestly suggested) a literary event of such importance that it makes much difference whether we have our

dear friend Howells write the review, or whether indeed we have any review. (Reid to Hay, 25 Sept 81, RPB-JH; see also Monteiro and Murphy, 53)

The last sentence alluded to Clemens's letter of 20 April 1873 to Reid, which had clearly offended. In 1907, long after Clemens had quarreled with House over the dramatization of *The Prince and the Pauper,* Clemens expanded his account of his estrangement from Reid:

> Reid and Edward H. House had a falling out. House told me his side of the matter, and at second-hand I got Reid's side of it—which was simply that he considered House a "blatherskite," and wouldn't have anything to do with him. I ranged myself on House's side, and relations between Reid and me ceased; they were not resumed for twenty-two years; and then not cordially, but merely diplomatically, so to speak. . . . In justice to Reid I confess that . . . I found out that he was right concerning Edward H. House. Reid had labeled him correctly; he was a blatherskite. (AD, 28 Aug 1907, CU-MARK†)

Reid confided his own version of the matter to Kate Field, in a letter of 17 July 1873:

> [George W.] Smalley and yourself both speak of Mark Twain. I hear he says that he has a quarrel with *The Tribune.* If so, it is simply that *The Tribune* declined to allow him to dictate the person who should review his forthcoming novel. His modest suggestion was that Ned House should do it, he having previously interested House in the success of the book by taking him into partnership in dramatizing it. There is a nice correspondence on a part of the subject which would make pleasant reading; and if Twain gives us trouble, I'm very much tempted to make him a more ridiculous object than he has ever made anybody else. (Whitelaw Reid Papers, DLC)

The "nice correspondence" must have included Clemens's letter of 20 April 1873 to Reid. (For Clemens's planned revenge on Reid, see *N&J2,* 355–56, 417–25; for Smalley, see 11 June 73 to Miller, n. 2).

³Thompson noted in his autobiography, "Clemens, provoked about a certain New York editor and the 'Gilded Age,' was the more willing to write a series of letters for the 'New York Herald' on the visit of the Shah to England" (Thompson, 89). Clemens wrote five letters for the *Herald* about the state visit of Nasr-ed-Din, the shah of Persia (SLC 1873n–o, q–s; see 17 or 18 June 73 to Young, n. 1). A New York correspondent for the Chicago *Tribune,* who must have interviewed Clemens shortly before the *Batavia*'s departure, remarked:

> Who would have thought it? The extremely staid and dignified Boston *Advertiser* has actually engaged "Mark Twain" to contribute to its columns; and he will soon begin to be funny at so much per 1,000 words. I did not think this of the *Advertiser;* but then the world moves, and even the *Advertiser* must move with it. (Colstoun 1873b)

No 1873 travel letters from Clemens to the *Advertiser* have been found.

⁴On 19 May Clemens and Warner registered a copyright for a "Dramatic Composition" entitled *The Gilded Age: A Drama* (Copyright Office Receipt No. 5604D, CtHT-W). Dramatist Dion Boucicault was the well-known Irish-born author of *Arrah-na-Pogue* and other immensely popular plays. He did not collaborate on a stage version of *The Gilded Age.* In April 1874 an unauthorized dramatization of the book was performed in San Francisco. Clemens protested, purchased the script from its author, Gilbert S. Densmore, thoroughly revised it, and then first had it produced for the 1874–75 season, with John T. Raymond as Colonel Sellers, and Gertrude Kellogg (or, in several performances, Kate Field) as Laura Hawkins. It earned Clemens very substantial royalties for a few years (*L4,* 149 n. 3; *MTB,* 1:517–18; 5 May 74 to Charles Dudley Warner, CU-

MARK; 3 Nov 74 to the Hartford *Evening Post*, CU-MARK; Kiralis; see French, 242–55, and Schirer, 41–48).

[5]In a sworn affidavit written in his own hand and dated 16 May, Clemens claimed that a "month or so ago" he had been visited by Benjamin J. Such, who asked him to "write a sketch for an advertising pamphlet which he was about to publish." Clemens declined that request, but granted Such permission to reprint one sketch, free of charge, from "a London edition of certain sketches of mine":

> I made a mark in the index opposite to each of the ones I liked; gave him the book & told him I would prefer that he should use *one* of the sketches thus marked.
> Traveling on the Erie road yesterday (May 15) I found the newsman Blauvelt selling this pamphlet with this extraordinary feature in the title page: "Revised & selected *for this work*, by Mark Twain!" I never rev And furthermore, the pamphlet contained *five* of my sketches instead of one. And furthermore still, it contained ˄(with my name attached)˄ a bit of execrable rubbish entitled "A Self-Made Man," which I never wrote!—could not write, indeed, unless freighted with more
> My sketches are copyrighted in my own name.
> I consider a volume of them worth (to me) not less than $25,000, & certainly would not publish a volume of them unless I felt sure of getting that much for it—one of my reasons being that I consider that an author cannot bunch a mass of disconnected humorous sketches together & publish the same without sickening the public stomach & damaging his own reputation. (SLC 1873m, 2–4†)

The Such pamphlet had reprinted five sketches from *A Curious Dream; and Other Sketches* (SLC 1872a): "A Curious Dream," "My Late Senatorial Secretaryship," "The New Crime," "Back from 'Yurrup,'" and "More Distinction." It also included "A Self-Made Man" and several other sketches by unidentified authors. The sixty-three-page pamphlet bore the title *Fun, Fact & Fancy: A Collection of Original Comic Sketches and Choice Selections of Wit and Humor* on its paper cover. The title page read *A Book for an Hour, Containing Choice Reading and Character Sketches. A Curious Dream, and Other Sketches, Revised and Selected for This Work by the Author Mark Twain* (BAL 3352). In a bill of complaint prepared on 16 May by attorney Simon Sterne (to whom Clemens had been introduced by Edward House [House to Sterne, 16 May 73, CtHMTH]), Clemens sought an injunction to prevent any further sales of the pamphlet, payment to him of all profits realized, payment of $25,000 damages (not $20,000, as he told Warner), and reimbursement for "the costs and disbursements of this action" (Sterne, 4; Feinstein, 15–22). On 19 May a New York Supreme Court justice granted a temporary injunction, which was made permanent on 12 June. The case was resolved on 11 July, when the original injunction was modified to allow Such to publish *one* of the sketches that Clemens had originally selected. Clemens was awarded ten dollars in costs, but no profits or damages. Such was not allowed to use the nom de plume "Mark Twain" on the pamphlet's title page, and could merely state on its cover that it contained "amongst other things a Sketch by 'Mark Twain.'" Such understandably did not reissue his pamphlet under these new conditions (documents relating to *Clemens v. Such*, CtHMTH; Feinstein, 38–44).

🍂

No LETTERS written between 17 and 29 May 1873 have been found. The Atlantic crossing on board the *Batavia* with Captain Mouland was largely uneventful, except for several days of heavy weather during the first week, which sent Olivia and Clara to their berths with seasickness. Nellie, Susy's nursemaid, was even more severely afflicted. Olivia wrote her mother:

> Susie staid in her basket in the Capt.'s chart room all day—Nellie lying on the sofa there but Mr Clemens takin[g] the main care of her she slept most of the day. . . . Capt. Mouland is just about perfection, he has done every thing that he possibly could to make us comfortable and to make things pleasant for us, he and Clara take long walks on the deck together— . . .
> The table is very good indeed but we lack appetites some what. . . .
> We have had two or three very rough days, not stormy but the waves high so that the vessel rocks frightfully— . . .
> When I started to go to the dinner table yesterday afternoon there came a lunge of the ship and I took the curtain that hangs between the main saloon and our little passage with me into the saloon and went rushing headlong against the waiters— Clara who was coming just behind me was so convulsed with laughter that she was obliged to return to her state room and laugh it out— (23 and 26 May 73, CtHMTH)

The party disembarked at Liverpool on 27 May, and stayed over for one night, probably as guests of Captain and Mrs. Mouland, who lived in Linacre (a town on the Mersey slightly north of Liverpool), before taking the train to London (*Gore's Directory*, 351, 663; "Shipping Intelligence," London *Times*, 29 May 73, 6). Thompson recalled:

> Mr. and Mrs. Clemens paid a visit to Mrs. Mouland and the Captain at their suburban home. Some passengers had so spoken of Wales that it was determined that we should make a detour that way. But it was found inconvenient and postponed; so we soon left for London. (Thompson, 84)

Olivia wrote her sister that they

> left Liverpool at 11.30 and reached here [London] about 5.30 the ride was the most charming that I ever could imagine— . . . So many things that I had read were made plain to me as we rode along—the little thatched villages, the foot paths by the side of the road— It was like riding for all those hours through Central Park— (31 May 73, CtHMTH)

Upon the recommendation of a fellow passenger, the Clemenses took rooms at a private hotel, Edwards's Royal Cambridge Hotel in Hanover Square; Thompson "took lodging in a cheaper locality near by" (Thompson, 85; Baedeker 1878, 7). Thompson recalled:

> There was little routine in our daily life here. Sometimes Clemens would dictate in the morning. But there were callers, excursions and sightseeings.

He preferred to dictate when fresh from some outing[.] Otherwise he would forget what he wanted to record. He would light a cigar, walk back and forth and spin it out while I took it down, with an audible grin now and then, the ladies at their needlework. "How cosy this is," said Mrs. Clemens. (Thompson, 85)

The Clemenses were soon so busy with social engagements that they had little time for sightseeing. According to Albert Bigelow Paine, "It was a period of continuous honor and entertainment. If Mark Twain had been a lion on his first visit, he was little less than royalty now. His rooms at the Langham [to which he moved on 25 June] were like a court" (*MTB*, 1:484).

🍂

To Henry Watterson
29 May–15 June? 1873 • London, England
(Paraphrase: Watterson 1910, 70:373)

Once in London I was living with my family at 103 Mount Street.[1] Between 103 and 102 there was the parochial workhouse—quite a long and imposing building.[2] One evening, upon coming in from an outing, I found a letter he[3] had written on the sitting-room table and left with his card. He spoke of the shock he had received upon finding that next to 102—presumably 103—was the workhouse. He had loved me, but had always feared that I would end by disgracing the family—being hanged, or something—but the "work'us," that was beyond him; he had not thought it would come to that. And so on through pages of horse-play: his relief on ascertaining the truth and learning his mistake—his regret at not finding me at home—closing with a dinner invitation.[4]

[1] Henry Watterson (1840–1921) was the well-known and influential editor of the Louisville *Courier-Journal*. He was also Clemens's second cousin, by marriage: Clemens's uncle James J. Lampton (the prototype of Colonel Sellers) was the son of Lewis Lampton and Jennie Morrison, whose sister Mary Morrison was Watterson's maternal grandmother (Lampton 1990, 148). Watterson described the relationship in a 1910 reminiscence, which is also the source of his paraphrase of the present letter (the original is now lost):

Although Mark Twain and I called each other "cousin" and claimed to be blood-relatives, the connection between us was by marriage: a great uncle of his married a great aunt of mine; his mother was named after and reared by this great aunt; and the children of the marriage were, of course, his cousins and mine; and a large, varied and picturesque assortment they were. We were lifelong and very dear friends, however; passed much time together at home and abroad; and had many common ties and memories. (Watterson 1910, 372)

Watterson was born in Washington, D.C., while his father was a congressman from Tennessee. In 1858 he took a job reporting for the New York *Times*, but soon moved to the Washington *States*. During the Civil War he served in the Confederate army and edited the Chattanooga *Rebel*, and afterwards worked briefly on the Cincinnati *Evening Times* and the Nashville *Republican Banner*. In 1868 he became the editor of the Louisville *Journal*, soon to be the *Courier-Journal*, where he had a long and distinguished career, both as editor and owner. Watterson was known for his conviviality and conversational gifts as well as for his industry as a working journalist, and he spent much of his time traveling, both in this country and abroad, often writing political commentary for his newspaper. Although he may seem to imply that he and Clemens had known each other since childhood ("lifelong and very dear friends"), it is not certain when they first met. Their earliest known meeting was in New York, when Watterson attended the Lotos Club dinner in Clemens's honor, early in February 1873, but Clemens's remarks on that occasion suggest that he already knew Watterson (1 Feb 73 to Reid, n. 2). Watterson himself indicated in 1919 that "it was in the early seventies that Mark Twain dropped into New York, where there was already gathered a congenial group to meet and greet him." This group included John Hay, Thomas Nast, William A. Seaver, John Russell Young, Whitelaw Reid, Samuel Bowles, and Murat Halstead (Watterson 1919, 1:128–29). The occasion could have occurred in December 1870, when Clemens spent a week in New York and visited John Hay and other *Tribune* staff members. In 1865 Watterson married Rebecca Ewing of Nashville, and by mid-1873 they had a son and a daughter: Ewing (b. 1868) and Milbrey (b. 1871) (Wall, 6–7, 23–25, 35, 38, 51, 58–59, 64–65, 70–71, 84, 116; Lampton 1990, 149; *L4*, 269–70).

[2] St. George's Hanover Square Workhouse stood between 104 and 105 Mount Street, near the east end of Hyde Park (*London Directory*, 450; Weinreb and Hibbert, 529).

[3] Clemens.

[4] The Wattersons (with both children and a nurse) sailed from New York on the *Oceanic* on 10 May and arrived in London as early as 23 May, about a week before the Clemenses. Clemens left his card and this letter "not long after" the Wattersons' arrival (Wall, 116–17)—that is, as early as 29 May (presumably his first full day in London) and probably no later than mid-June ("Passengers Sailed," New York *Tribune*, 12 May 73, 2; "Ship News," London *Morning Post*, 23 May 73, 7).

To Henry Lee
1 or 2 June 1873 · London, England
(MS: ViU)

                                          Edwards' Hotel
                                George street, Hanover Square.[1]
My Dear Lee:
    Long life to you & yours!
                                    Saml. L. Clemens
                                        & family.

POST CARD

THE ADDRESS ONLY TO BE WRITTEN ON THIS SIDE.

TO

Henry Lee Esq
43 Holland street
Blackfriars Road
S. E.

[*postmarked:*] LONDON · W. 4 JU 2 73 5

[1] The postmark (JU 2 73) provides the sole evidence for the date of this post-card, which Clemens evidently sent just to apprise Lee of his return to London.

To Kate Field
9 June 1873 • London, England
(MS: MB)

(SLC)

Edwards' Hotel
George street Hanover Sq., Monday.[1]

Dear Miss Field:

ₚ̶ I see that it isn't your fault that you do not know me, & I'm sure it isnt mine that I do not know you. Plainly, then, ~~nobody~~ the party to blame is Providence, & therefore damages cannot be had in this vale. But we shall be glad to see & know you & likewise Lady Dilke;[2] & since you give us the privilege of naming the time, shall we say Wednesday about 5 PM? I do not know that we have another ~~day~~ disengaged day or hour for some little time to come, or I would of course offer a larger latitude. My small family of sight-seers keep themselves pretty busy—they never have been abroad before.

Very Truly Yrs
Sam¹. L. Clemens.

Miss Kate Field.

[1]Clemens replied to an invitation from Kate Field and her London hostess, Lady Dilke (see note 2). He must have written on 9 June—the first Monday that Field, who had arrived at Southampton on 4 June, was in London. Monday, 16 June, is not possible because the gathering Clemens proposed would then have come on Wednesday, 18 June, when both he and Field were to be in Ostend, reporting on the shah's visit. Monday, 23 June, is ruled out because Clemens and Field dined together at the Dilkes' the day before (see 23 June–18 July 73 to the Dilkes and Field). And all later Mondays are ruled out because after 24 June the Clemenses were no longer at Edwards's Hotel. Clemens had briefly met Field, a well-known author and lecturer, in Buffalo on 29 January 1871. Her most recent book, a collection of newspaper letters entitled *Hap-Hazard*, had just been published by James R. Osgood and Company. She had long corresponded for the New York *Tribune*, which in July published six of her letters about the shah's visit. On 17 July Whitelaw Reid complimented her on these letters, which he found superior to Clemens's: "You do not need to be told that most of the stuff he has done for *The Herald* is very poor, because you have seen it. It won't hurt you to know that your letters, on the other hand, have received more praise than any you ever wrote for us before" (Whitelaw Reid Papers, DLC; Smalley 1873b; Wilkie Collins to Anthony Trollope, 9 June 73, Trollope, 2:589; "Departures for

Europe," New York *Times,* 25 May 73, 8; "Foreign Ports," New York *Tribune,* 5 June 73, 2; Whiting 1900, 306, 308, 312, 314; *L4,* 322, 323–24 n. 3; "New Publications," Hartford *Evening Post,* 23 June 73, 1; Field 1873a–f).

[2] Lady Dilke, formerly Katherine Mary Eliza Sheil, had married Sir Charles Dilke in January 1872 (see 23 June–18 July 73 to the Dilkes and Field, n. 2). The orphaned daughter of an army captain, she was known for her "extreme attractiveness of appearance, her singing, and her wonderful power of mimicry," but also for "a violent temper" and "extraordinary powers of sarcasm" (reminiscence by Sir Charles, quoted in Roy Jenkins, 78). She died in September 1874, shortly after bearing her first child (Burke 1904, 483).

To Joaquin Miller
11 June 1873 • London, England
(MS: ViU)

(SLC)

Edwards' Hotel ⎱
June 11, '73. ⎰

My Dear Miller—[1]

I am exceedingly sorry that this previous engagement debars me from going with ~~you Sunday~~ you on the evening you mention, & I do hope that another opportunity may offer.[2]

Ys ⸓ Sincerely

Saml. L. Clemens.

P. S. I am keeping strictly before my memory the fact that I am to call on you at 4.45 Saturday on the way to the Savage—so don't *you* forget. And ~~tomorrow,~~ ˄Friday,˄ remember, you are to call here with one literary friend of yours, & we are then to go ~~alto~~ together & pay our respects to another. Haven I got that straight?[3]

Mark.

[1] Cincinnatus Hiner Miller (1837–1913) was born and spent his early years in Indiana, emigrating to Oregon with his family in 1852. After leaving home in 1854 he led a peripatetic existence as a miner, pony-express courier, Indian fighter, newspaper editor, lawyer, and county judge. He also lived for a time with Indians of the McCloud River region of Shasta County, California, fathering a daughter, Cali-Shasta, with Paquita, a member of the tribe. In 1862 he married

Theresa Dyer (d. 1883), who published poetry as "Minnie Myrtle," and with whom he had two children. (A third child, whose paternity he denied, was born in 1869.) They were divorced in 1870. In 1868 Miller published his first book of poetry, *Specimens*, followed by *Joaquin et al.* in 1869. In 1870 Ina Coolbrith suggested that Miller adopt the name "Joaquin," after a poem he had written in praise of the Mexican bandit Joaquin Murietta. After a second visit to the literary circles of San Francisco, in 1870 he went to London, where American writers had become popular. His *Pacific Poems* (privately printed in London in 1871) and *Songs of the Sierras* (published there by Longmans, Green, Reader, and Dyer in 1871) made him a celebrity with the English, who were charmed and fascinated by his exotic western exuberance and dress. By July 1871 he had returned to the United States, but he was back in England in early December 1872. In 1892 Miller recalled that he had once seen Mark Twain (among other local celebrities) in the offices of the San Francisco *Golden Era,* but was "never presented to any of these people" (Miller). Nevertheless, it is possible that he first met Clemens in May or June 1863, when both men were in San Francisco. It seems more likely, however, that they first became acquainted later, perhaps as late as 1873 in London (Frost, 11–12, 26–27, 32–37, 42–46, 51, 54–58, 63–64, 129, 132; *MTB*, 1:260; Marberry 1953, 31–32, 112; "Joaquin Miller's Crime," Hartford *Evening Post,* 4 Feb 73, 1; "Joaquin Miller," Boston *Evening Transcript,* 22 July 71, 2; "Personal," Hartford *Courant,* 25 Nov 72, 2). Clemens's secretary, Thompson, recalled that during the summer of 1873 Miller was

> with us often. . . . He was something unique. He was struck with how little mere wealth amounted socially. He would say to me "I'll take you round to Lord ———'s if you care to go. Come and see my little lodging. I am living mostly on milk and honey. I'll show you my saddle." I read that he sometimes dressed in Mexican style and rode swiftly about Hyde Park. He offered a wager to outdo anybody at rough riding. [W]ould break the other fellow's neck if he could find rough enough country. He wore long hair and beard, and was one of the kindest, mildest mannered men I ever met. . . . We dropped in to Bentley's, who was bringing out Miller's "Life among the Modocs[.]" He said to me "It will be a great experience when your first book comes out." (Thompson, 87)

Thompson alluded to Lord Houghton (see note 3).

[2]Clemens's mention of "this previous engagement" was probably an allusion to a dinner invitation for Sunday, 15 June, from George Washburn Smalley (1833–1916), the London correspondent for the New York *Tribune.* The invitation, which Smalley wrote on 11 June and probably delivered personally to Clemens at his hotel, was prepared "in case I don't find you in" (as Smalley noted in the margin):

> Dear Mr. Clemens,
> I don't know how it happens that I have always missed the pleasure of meeting you. Pray don't let it go on so. Will you do me the favour to dine with me on Sunday, the 15th at 7.30? Then I shall be sure that you are something more than a name[.] (Indeed I hear you have two names & I am not sure which you prefer. But come.) (CU-MARK)

Clemens probably enclosed this note in the present letter (and retrieved it a few days later). Smalley had been aware of Clemens's presence since at least 5 June, when he remarked in his "Notes from London": "Mark Twain has arrived also, but with that natural shyness which distinguishes him has omitted to let his friends know his address. A letter is waiting for him on my desk which, if he does not come for it, I shall have to advertise in *The Times*" (Smalley 1873a). On 14 June Smalley told his *Tribune* readers:

> I have found Mark Twain without advertising—indeed, it was my fault that I did not find him at once. He is at Edwards's Hotel, where he has Mr. Disraeli under his feet (and means to keep him there), with an Earl on one side of him and a Count on the other. In the midst of these aristocratic surroundings he preserves his loyalty to Republican institutions, and dislikes a joke as much as ever. (Smalley 1873b)

Smalley attended Yale and then Harvard Law School, and practiced law for five years. In 1861 he became a Civil War correspondent for the New York *Tribune*, where he took a regular staff position the following year. As the newspaper's foreign correspondent in Europe in 1866, he provided news dispatches by transatlantic cable, probably the first ever transmitted in this way. In 1867 he organized a London news bureau for the *Tribune*, and ensured its success by using the cable to an extent previously unknown. He remained in charge of the *Tribune*'s European correspondence until 1895, and his own letters from London earned him a wide reputation.

[3]On 11 June Miller wrote to Richard Monckton Milnes (1809–85), the first Baron Houghton, to arrange for him to meet Clemens (Gohdes, 297)—an indication that Houghton was probably the person to whom Miller and his unidentified "literary friend" planned to pay their respects, in company with Clemens, on Friday, 13 June. It is possible, but less likely, that Houghton was to join Clemens and Miller at the Savage Club on Saturday, 14 June. A poet, miscellaneous writer, and statesman, Houghton was the editor of Keats and an early champion of Swinburne. He enjoyed entertaining distinguished friends and acquaintances in all fields of endeavor, and was well known as a patron of literary talent, especially talent in distress. John Lothrop Motley described him as "a good speaker in Parliament, a good writer of poems, . . . a man of fashion, and altogether a swell of the first class" (Motley to Mary Motley, 28 May 58, Motley, 1:228). Thompson recalled that "Lord Houghton evidently enjoyed Jouquin Miller, and as Clemens drawled along in his grumpy way I have seen Lord Houghton sit on the sofa and shake with laughter till the tears rolled down his face" (Thompson, 94).

To George H. Fitzgibbon
12 June 1873 • London, England
(Henkels 1930a, lot 266, and two others)

Edw's Hotel, 12th.

My Dear Fitz Gibbon—

Thanks—many thanks, for that exceedingly kind article & the telegram.[1] I'm coming to the House of Commons soon (Monday evening, maybe) & shall hope to see you.

Oh, as to the article I wanted to write?—I wrote a good deal of it & then gave it up, partly because it was going to be too long, & partly because it was too essentially literary in its nature for such a grave, substantial, business-looking paper as the Observer.[2] Properly, it should be a magazine article. I wanted to seem deeply in earnest & greatly concerned, & one can't pretend all that with a good grace in a magazine where it is plain a writer has a month in which to "chaw over" a screed.

Mark.

[1] The telegram has not been found. Fitzgibbon published an article in the Darlington *Northern Echo* on 11 June, in which he described Clemens's growth as a humorist since his days on the Virginia City *Territorial Enterprise:*

> Since the advent to New York, Mr. CLEMENS has ceased to be a mere Californian celebrity. He has lived to prove that the fun which won the hearts of the rough miners of the Nevada has something more than the spice of the virgin soil in it. The free scope of a district which was allowed to develop its own literature no doubt gave it raciness, just as in ruder natures it would give license to horse-play. But the lively fancy, the quaint humour, the quick wit, the humane breadth of the man, and his penetrating insight withal, are gifts divine. . . . As a matter of taste, you may conclude his style to be at times too rollicking: you will never find it insincere. "When one has the disease that gives its possessor the title of humorist," is one of his remarks, "one must make oath to his statements, else the public will not believe him." Many a true word is spoken in jest. Many a true jest is truth hidden only to the blind. The essential quality of TWAIN'S fun—it should be of all fun—is that it *is* funny—that it provokes laughter. . . . But if you often laugh you must sometimes perforce reflect. There is a soul in this man's humor. He is no mere wearer of the cap and bells. His fun is iconoclastic. Its invariable moral is, that it is destructive of shams; or of what, to the humorist, are shams. . . . Right glad will we be to welcome to the North of England a humorist so healthy, an American cousin so worthy of his great country, a gentleman of the press who has done much to provoke the ever-growing interchange of sentiment and sympathy among the readers of our common language. (Fitzgibbon 1873a)

[2] The unfinished "literary" article has not been identified, nor is Clemens known to have written anything especially for the London *Observer*. His remarks here indicate that Fitzgibbon may have suggested a contribution, but no connection between Fitzgibbon and the *Observer* has been established. A Sunday newspaper founded in 1791, the *Observer* was "almost entirely of a *political* complexion," and dealt "chiefly with the more public topics of the day" (*Newspaper Press Directory*, 27). From 1870 until 1889 it was edited by Edward Dicey, formerly of the *Spectator, Macmillan's*, the London *Telegraph*, and the London *Daily News* (Griffiths, 200).

To Henry Lee
12 and 13 June 1873 • London, England
(MS: CtHSD and Schwalb)

Friday Eve[g].
ˏmidnight.ˏ[1]

My Dear Lee—

It was just like me. I wrote Sir Cordy Burrows[2] last Sunday that Miss Spaulding wouldn't be able to go again to Brighton, her sight-seeing time being so circumscribed, & therefore my wife couldn't go because she would be left forlorn & dreary in that Brighton hotel so long—consequently I would have to lose the pleasure of going myself, under the circumstances, & remain here & help the ladies do other sight-seeing. Then I said to myself, I will write Lee also—but I suppose I forgot it. No—now I remember, I *didn't* forget it. I argued that I would see you several times during the week & would tell you.

Don't you be offended, old friend, for I didn't mean to forget, & I've been moving night & day since I saw you. I want Mrs. Clemens to see the aquarium, & I mean that she shall see it, but I must not let her visit there be spoiled by a dreary & lonely interval in a hotel. So we want to go down some time when you are going & when I won't have to leave her lying around loose at all.[3]

When can you go to Hampton Court?[4] We have had a day or two open, but Mrs. Clemens & Miss Spaulding have both said pretty emphatically that they particularly wish to go when *you* can go & they are very ready to wait till you have leisure. So I have said, "All right, if you are more ~~satisfied~~ fascinated with that venerable naturalist than you are with the subscriber, *I* am willing to wait, too, because I find his company rather pleasant myself." Miss Spaulding said, several times, coming home, "I *do* think so much of Mr. Lee." I don't think you ever showed kindnesses to any lady that more heartily & gratefully appreciated them than she did.

Yrs Warmly
Sam[l]. L. Clemens.

Midnight ₣—Your note just arrived—sent you a telegram at once to say
I had written Sir Cordy last week.[5] ~~Saturday~~ I dine at the Savage to⸗
morrow night with Joaquin Miller—wish you could be there.[6]

Henry Lee Esq | 43 Holland st, Blackfriars Road | London, S.E. [*in up-
per left corner:*] *Personal* [*postmarked:*] LONDON · W 6 JU I3 73 [*and*] LONDON ·
SE LV JU I3 73[7]

[1] For the date of this letter, see note 7.

[2] John Cordy Burrows (1813–76), a surgeon, was a leading citizen and former
mayor of Brighton; he was knighted in February 1873 for his services on behalf
of that city. He had probably met Clemens through their mutual friend, Henry
Lee.

[3] Lee was the naturalist of the Brighton Aquarium, which Clemens had visited
in September 1872 (13 Sept–11 Nov 72 to Lee, n. 1). He soon accompanied the
Clemenses on a visit, for Thompson recalled: "The President of the Brighton
Aquarium took our party down in [a] special car, dined them and showed them
the Aquarium, the greatest in the world at that time I believe. I overslept and
was too late for that" (Thompson, 98). The "party" may well have included Clara
Spaulding after all. If so, the Brighton trip had to have occurred before she departed for the Continent on 26 June (6 July 73 to Fairbanks, n. 1).

[4] Hampton Court Palace, some fifteen miles southwest of London, is one of
the finest examples of Tudor architecture in Britain. Begun by Cardinal Wolsey
in 1514, it was greatly enlarged and embellished by the succession of monarchs
who resided there. Queen Victoria opened it to visitors, who enjoyed the art
treasures on display in the state apartments, as well as the extensive gardens
(Weinreb and Hibbert, 359–61).

[5] None of these communications survives.

[6] Clemens's dinner appointment with Miller at the Savage Club was for Saturday, 14 June (11 June 73 to Miller).

[7] Although the envelope and the letter manuscript are now in separate collections (see the textual commentary), the outgoing and incoming postmarks—
both for 13 June—together with Clemens's reference to his dinner engagement
with Miller "to-morrow night" (14 June), strongly suggest that the two belong
together. Clemens's apology was something he might well have marked "*Personal*" on the envelope. Furthermore, the reason for the apology—the failure to
write sooner—rules out the possibility that the envelope belonged to some other
letter, now lost, sent earlier the same day. Clemens's dateline implies that he
wrote before and after midnight, on Friday (13 June) and Saturday (14 June).
His revisions in the postscript (after the signature), however, offer ample evidence that he was confused about the day. On balance, it seems most likely that
he wrote the letter on 12 and 13 June and mailed it on the morning of 13 June.

To Adam Badeau
15 June 1873 • London, England
(MS: MH-H)

(*SLC*)

Edwards Hotel, June ~~13~~ 15.
Dear Gen. Badeau—[1]

Mrs. Clemens was frankly & sincerely sorry she had to deny herself the pleasure of seeing you, (she being very greatly fatigued because of sight-s/eeing)—& yet she would have cheerfully dressed & appeared, but that she feared to make such a draft upon your time.

I wish to call upon you, & will hunt out your office in town—for I judge I shall be more likely to catch you there than at your house.[2]

Ys Very Truly
Samˡ. L. Clemens.

[1] Badeau (1831–95) had been the American consul general in London since May 1870, and he remained so until 1881. Born in New York City, he wrote dramatic criticism for the *Sunday Times and Noah's Weekly Messenger*, which he collected in 1859 as *The Vagabond*. In 1862 he enlisted with the Union forces and was made an aide on the staff of General Thomas W. Sherman. Wounded in 1863, he became Ulysses S. Grant's military secretary in 1864, the beginning of a close friendship that lasted almost until Grant's death in 1885. In 1868 he published the first of three volumes in his *Military History of Ulysses S. Grant* (1868–81). In 1869 President Grant appointed him secretary of the legation in London, later raising him to consul general. The quarrel that ended his friendship with Grant concerned Badeau's role in helping to complete Grant's memoirs (see *N&J3*, 107, 127, 142, 205, 270).

[2] Badeau's office was in the United States Consulate, at 1 Dunster Court, Mincing Lane. The street address of his home, known as Little Boston House, has not been found (*London Directory*, 130, 279; Moran, 35:231).

To John Russell Young
17 or 18 June 1873 • Ostend, Belgium
(Transcript and paraphrase: Yates, 411)

A great likeness was said to exist between us. Mark Twain had written to Russell Young from Brussels, "They are selling portraits of Yates here at two francs apiece, & calling him the Shah. What does it mean?"[1]

[1]Clemens and Young met in June 1867, when Young was managing editor of the New York *Tribune*. After Young was replaced by Whitelaw Reid in May 1869, he founded the New York *Standard*, which he edited until it ceased publication in 1872. During those years he also traveled in Europe on missions for the secretary of the treasury and the secretary of state. In 1872 he accepted a position as foreign correspondent for the New York *Herald*, reporting primarily from Paris and London (*L2*, 55 n. 5; *L3*, 230 n. 6, 265 n. 1; "John Russell Young," New York *Herald*, 1 May 73, 3). Edmund Hodgson Yates (1831–94) was a novelist and journalist currently on the *Herald* staff. Born in London, he went to work at the London post office when only sixteen; in 1862 he became head of the missing-letter department, eventually resigning his position in 1872. In the 1850s he began writing poetry, humorous sketches, farces, and theatrical criticism, and in the 1860s edited two periodicals, *Temple Bar* and *Tinsley's Magazine*. His first novel, *For Better or Worse*, appeared in 1863. Between September 1872 and February 1873 he made a successful lecture tour in the United States. In April 1873 Yates and Young were assigned to report on the Vienna International Exhibition for the *Herald*. Clemens's letter may well have reached Young while he was still in Austria. The *Herald* also sent both Yates and Clemens to write about the shah's visit to England, which may have been the occasion of their first meeting: they were never in New York at the same time during Yates's 1872–73 tour, and no evidence has been found that they met in London in 1872, or between 1 and 15 June 1873 ("Edmund Yates," New York *Herald*, 1 May 73, 3; Yates 1885, 406–11). The text of the present fragment, allegedly written "from Brussels," is preserved only in Yates's footnote to his account of the shah assignment:

> I next donned the *Herald's* tabard on the 16th June, starting off with Mr. Forbes to Brussels, to meet the Shah of Persia, who was coming on a visit to England *via* Ostend. We put up at the Hôtel de l'Europe, where we found several of our journalistic *confrères*. On the 18th we were up at 3:30 A.M., and started at five o'clock for Ostend in the special train provided for his Persian majesty. Passage from Ostend to Dover was provided for the newspaper correspondents in H. M. S. *Lively*, where we were most graciously received and excellently entertained at luncheon by the officers. A comic scene occurred just before leaving Ostend. We were about to cast off from the pier, when suddenly there appeared, bearing an odd-looking bag, and looking a little seedy with early rising, a gentleman in whom we recognized Mark Twain, but for whom the stolid sailor at the gangway had no recognition.
>
> "I am coming on board," said Twain, persuasively.

"No, you ain't," said the stalwart A. B.—"no tramps here."
"What's that you say?" asked Twain.
"No tramps here," repeated the sailor.
"Well, now," said Twain, in his softest and longest drawl, "you are quite right, I am a 'tramp,'—I am the 'Tramp Abroad;'" and then we welcomed him with a shout. . . .
    Days and nights were now devoted to the pursuit of the Persian potentate, whom I followed everywhere, duly recording his doings. (Yates 1885, 411)

Yates's report is mistaken in at least two of its details: by Clemens's own account, he did not go to Brussels, but only to Ostend and back, on 17 and 18 June; and the reported allusion to *A Tramp Abroad* (1879) must have been a joking reference to *The Innocents Abroad* (1869) (SLC 1873n). Nasr-ed-Din (1829–96), the shah of Persia since 1848, was the first Persian monarch to undertake a state visit to Europe, during which he conferred with the governments of Russia, Germany, Belgium, England, France, Austria, Italy, and Turkey. In consequence he was responsible for bringing European ideas to his country, and granted trade concessions to Britain and Russia (*Annual Cyclopaedia 1873*, 637).

To Elisha Bliss, Jr.
18 June 1873 • London, England
(MS: NN-B)

Private.

London June 18.

Ɖ Friend Bliss—

    Have begun to write about the Shah to N. Y. Herald—don't want them copyrighted.

    You sieze them as they appear, & turn them into a 25 cent pamphlet (my royalty 10 per cent) & spread them over the land your own way, but be quick! Don't let it get cold before you are out. I suggest that you disseminate them by means of the news companies.[1]

Ys

Mark.

[*letter docketed:*] √ *M.T.*

---

[1] On 18 June Clemens wrote his first letter for the New York *Herald*, in which he described his trip to Ostend on 17 June, his overnight stay there, and his return on H.M.S. *Lively*, together with several of the shah's family members and retainers and some half-dozen fellow journalists, most of whom had accompanied the shah on the train from Brussels to Ostend (SLC 1873n). News compa-

nies were distributors of magazines and cheap paper-covered books, which they sold to the public primarily at newsstands and railroad stations. In 1867 Charles Henry Webb named the "AMERICAN NEWS CO., AGENTS"—one of the largest of these companies, located in New York—on the title page of the *Jumping Frog* book. And in 1874 Clemens published a small pamphlet, *Mark Twain's Sketches. Number One,* which was printed in Hartford but distributed through the American News Company (Tebbel, 106, 353, 393; Shove, 23, 32, 61).

To George H. Fitzgibbon
19 June 1873 • London, England
(MS: NN-B)

Edwards' Hotel

June 19.

My Dear Fitz Gibbon:

You must pardon my delay. I have been to ƀ Belgium to help write up the Shah for the N. Y. Herald—got back last evening & have already mailed 2 long letters & am starting in on a few more. Can't see Parliament or any place till I get the Shah off my hands & out of the country.

I have tried to make up my mind to deliver my New York lecture on the Sandwich Islands here, ₍in London₎, but I can't—so I have dismissed the subject from my mind at present & don't know whether I shall talk or not. But in any event, *I would not be likely to lecture outside of London* because I could not spare the time.

I had no idea of writing any newspaper letters while here, but I got fascinated with this Shah business & took a sudden notion to sally out for the Herald.

My novel ₍"The Gilded Age" (written by Chas. Dudley Warner & myself) will be published simultaneously here & in America in the coming autumn.[1]

These are all the facts in the case of yours truly. Hope to see you when this press of writing is over. We go to the Langham ₕHotel next Wednesday to live. My wife likes this awfully ~~quil~~ quiet place but I don't. I prefer a little more excitement.[2]

With warm regards,

Ys

S.L. Clemens.

[1]Clemens's first two letters on the shah, written on 18 and 19 June, appeared in the New York *Herald* on 1 and 4 July. The last three, written on 21, 26, and 30 June, were published on 9, 11, and 19 July (SLC 1873n–o, q–s). As the London correspondent for the Darlington *Northern Echo*, Fitzgibbon reported on the proceedings in Parliament; he had evidently invited Clemens to accompany him to a session. He must also have asked Clemens about his plans in order to report them for his newspaper. He used this letter to prepare the following paragraph, published on 21 June:

> I am very much afraid it will be some time before Mark Twain can lecture anywhere out of London. He has been interviewing the Shah, and accompanying him in Belgium, and from Belgium to London. He has only just returned to London. The result of his personal experience of the Shah is to be published in the *New York Herald*. He will be so busily occupied for some time, that he has given up for the present his idea of lecturing even in London. His new novel, "The Gilded Age," will be published next autumn, simultaneously in England and America. (Fitzgibbon 1873b)

[2]According to Thompson, Clemens and Olivia "foun[d] the private hotel, although about as expensive as a first class hotel, was not so convenient for some things; for instance there was no billiard room, and billiards was Clemens' chief exercise. . . . they moved to the Langham Hotel where he had stopped before" (Thompson, 99).

To Charles W. and Katherine M. Dilke
and Kate Field
23 June–18 July 1873 • London, England
(MS: Uk)

Mr. Clemens, called, representing in his person the family.[1]

For Ch Sir Chas.[2] & Lady Dilke
   & Miss Field.

[1]This note (written on a torn piece of paper rather than on a calling card) was presumably delivered when the Clemenses made their obligatory courtesy call on the Dilkes and Field after dining with them on 22 June. (It is possible, but less likely, that the call followed the social engagement proposed for 11 June: see 9 June 73 to Field.) In any event the call must have preceded the Clemenses' departure for York on 19 July, since Field left London on 31 July, well before they returned from Scotland. In a letter dated 24 June to the New York *Tribune*, Kate Field described a recent dinner party at which "an American by the singular name of Mark Twain" was present:

> Mr. Twain is endeavoring to instil civilization into the Shah by sitting on the floor and playing draw poker, and says that his august pupil makes wonderful progress in this

great American game, and will soon be able to play against the American Minister or the brilliant editor of *The Louisville Courier-Journal*, who now pines in May Fair for a partner worthy of his deal. (Field 1873d)

Robert C. Schenck was the U.S. minister in London; the editor of the *Courier-Journal* was Clemens's cousin, Henry Watterson. The date of Field's letter suggests that she may have been describing the Dilkes' 22 June dinner party, but their appointment book notes the presence only of the Clemenses and Field, making no mention of the shah. Still, she might have seen Clemens instructing the shah at another of the many official and private parties given for him, even though no independent corroboration of her report has so far been found (Additional MS 43902, folio 185, and Additional MS 43964, folio 46, Dilke Papers, Uk; Whiting, 315).

[2] Sir Charles Wentworth Dilke (1843–1911) was a liberal statesman, member of Parliament for Chelsea since 1868, and proprietor of the *Athenaeum*, a weekly journal of literary and artistic criticism. According to Dilke's biographers, Clemens had dined at the Dilkes' during his first visit to England in 1872, but no primary evidence for this has been found in the Dilke Papers. In mid-June 1873, Clemens's secretary entered the title of one of Dilke's books, *Greater Britain: A Record of Travel in English-Speaking Countries During 1866 and 1867* (1868), in his stenographic notebook—indicating that Clemens may have had some interest in Dilke's account of traveling in the western United States (*Newspaper Press Directory*, 18–19; Gwynn and Tuckwell, 1:160; *N&J1*, 529).

To Ellen D. Conway
25 June 1873 • London, England
(Transcripts and paraphrase: Anderson Galleries
1920a, lot 48, and AAA 1925b, lot 37)

Langham Hotel, June 25.

[*paraphrase: To Mrs. Conway.*[1] *Delightful and humorous letter, accepting an invitation for a visit, reading in part,—*] Pardon my dilatoriness . . . July 8, being one of the dates. . . . Mr. Charles suggests, we beg to take that for our visit to—to—I have forgotten the town's name . . . no matter so long as we get there . . . upon referring to my wife I learn . . . the town is . . . Hepworth & I see . . . she likes the ring of Mr. Charles's invitation[2] . . . so do I, after so many solemn "Mr. & Mrs . . . Jones's compliments & request the pleasure," &c.—precisely the language they used to use in Missouri in private invitations to funerals.

I date from the Langham, because we remove to that hotel today.

My wife likes Edwards' Hotel; & so would I if I were dead; I would not desire a more tranquil & satisfactory tomb.

.   .   .   .

Saml. L. Clemens.

[1] The former Ellen Davis Dana of Cincinnati (d. 1897), who had married Moncure Conway in 1858.

[2] In 1904 Conway described this visit:

> Clemens and his wife came to London, and Charles Flower of Avonbank, mayor of Stratford-on-Avon, begged me to bring them there for a visit. Mrs. Clemens was an ardent Shakespearian, and Mark Twain determined to give her a surprise. He told her that we were going on a journey to Epworth, and persuaded me to connive with the joke by writing to Charles Flower not to meet us himself but send his carriage. (Conway 1904, 2:145)

The name that Clemens and Conway chose to disguise "Stratford" was "Hepworth," a fictional town (10? July 73 to Warner, n. 2), not "Epworth," a real town in northern England. Conway was also mistaken in recalling that Charles Edward Flower (1830–92) was the mayor of Stratford in 1873: he served in that capacity from 1878 to 1880. (His father, Edward F. Flower, had served several terms as mayor before the 1870s.) Flower was the senior partner in the family brewery, Flower and Sons, from 1862 until his death. In 1874 he founded the Shakespeare Memorial Association, to which he donated thirty thousand pounds to construct a theater. Flower's widow bequeathed their home, Avonbank, to the Memorial in 1908 (Boase, 1:1071, 5:314; Trewin, 49; "Obituary," London *Times*, 4 May 92, 9; information from the Shakespeare Birthplace Trust).

To R. Cowley-Squier
per Samuel C. Thompson
25 June 1873 • (1st of 2) • London, England
(Stenographic draft: CU-MARK)

L June
Langah hotel[1]
Jn 25th

Dear sir;[2]

    I thk you very much for your kid offers, but I fear that ↔ I shall not have an op. of visiting Manchtr. I shall prob have no time to travel about any while I am here. I am dear sir yours fathfly,

    R. Cowly-Sq

[1] This and several other letters sent in late June and early July have been found only as Thompson took them down in his notebook from Clemens's dictation. Their texts are a pastiche of shorthand symbols and scrawled, sometimes nearly illegible, longhand, often including abbreviated or misspelled words. The fair copies that Thompson sent presumably corrected all or most of these errors: two such fair copies are extant, and they corroborate this assumption (16 July 73 to Bliss and 16 July 73 to Warner; see also 29 Apr 73 to Mouland, n. 1). In the absence of fair copies, however, the notebook texts have been transcribed without emendation.

[2] Cowley-Squier has not been identified, although he was apparently connected with the London *Examiner* (see the next letter).

~~To Henry Watterson~~
To R. Cowley-Squier
per Samuel C. Thompson
25 June 1873 • (2nd of 2) • London, England
(Stenographic draft: CU-MARK)

               ~~Langhan hotel~~ ‚London‚
               Jne 25th

~~Dear sir,~~
    ~~Dear Watterson,~~
Dear sir,
    You are under a misaprehns, I have not called at the Examiner office;[1] but all of have said in your note⊹ should go very well. Very truly,

    R. Cowley-Squier

[1] The London *Examiner* was a radical weekly launched in 1808 by John and Leigh Hunt. Its "political section gave great support to reform and was a frequent critic of the Prince of Wales" (Griffiths, 236).

To Lewis Sergeant, and
To Charles E. Seth-Smith
per Samuel C. Thompson
25 June 1873 • London, England
(Stenographic draft: CU-MARK)

L. L. Sergn:
Th Lagh hotel June 25

My dear sir,

I shall be very glad indeed to renew the acquaintance. I am usully at home about noon, but after that, like everybody else in London I am uncertain. With many thanks for your form kindnesses to me, I am yours very sincerly.

Lewis Sergeant Esq.
Chas. E. Seth Smith Esq.[1]

---

[1] Thompson added Seth-Smith's name when, presumably as an afterthought, Clemens decided that he, as well as Sergeant, should receive a fair copy of this dictated response. Lewis Sergeant (1841–1902) was educated at Cambridge. After working as a schoolmaster he became an editor, and was long associated with the *Athenaeum* and the London *Chronicle*. He wrote several books, among them *Introduction to English Composition* (1872) and *Elementary Mathematics in Connection with Science and Art Departments* (1873). Nothing has been learned about Sergeant's introduction to Clemens in 1872, except that as secretary of the Anti-Game-Law League he edited the society's circular, a copy of which Clemens acquired during his 1872 visit to England (CU-MARK). They clearly did renew their acquaintance in 1873, however, for in December, Sergeant, who was then editor of the London *Examiner,* wrote to Ambrose Bierce that he had obtained his

name & address through Mr Samuel L. Clemens. I desire to have for the Examiner a few articles on contemporary American literature, comprehending as much as possible of the whole field of printed literature; & Mr Clemens thought it possible that you might be willing to do it for me. (8 Dec 73, CtY-BR, in Grenander 1978, 469)

Bierce declined the request. In 1878 Sergeant published *New Greece* and became honorary secretary for the Greek committee in London, serving until his death. No record has been found, beyond this draft, of Clemens's acquaintance with Charles E. Seth-Smith (1847–94). In 1876 Seth-Smith was made a sublieutenant in the Royal Naval Artillery Volunteers, and from 1884 to 1892 was a lieutenant in command of the London corps. He became a barrister in 1887 and practiced in admiralty court. It is possible that Clemens's prior encounter with him was as recent as 23 June in Portsmouth, at the naval review organized for the shah (*BBA,* s.v. "Sergeant, Lewis"; Griffiths, 513; Boase, 3:496; SLC 1873r).

To William Stirling-Maxwell
28 June 1873 • London, England
(MS: UkGS)

(SLC)

The Langham Hotel ⎱
June 28. ⎰

Dear Sir:

Your note apprising me of the privilege which has been extended to me of visiting at the Cosmopolitan Club has been received & I desire to return my thanks & express my appreciation of the courtesy thus conferred upon me.[1]

These ~~acknow~~ my acknowledgments have not been delayed through forgetfulness, but by the turmoil & confusion of changing quarters & re-settling my family, & so I ask pardon with good confidence.

With great respect I am, sir,

Yours Very Truly
Sam*ⁱ*. L. Clemens

Sir William Stirling-Maxwell, Bart

⊠————————————————————————————————

Sir William Stirling-Maxwell, Bart. | 10 Upper Grosvenor street | W. [*postmarked:*] LONDON · W Y JU28 73

[1] In 1865, upon the death of his uncle, William Stirling-Maxwell (1818–78) became the ninth baronet of Pollok, County Renfrew (Scotland). He was a doctor of law, member of Parliament for Perthshire (1852–68, 1874–78), lord rector of the University of Edinburgh, and the author of several works of history. John Lothrop Motley described him as "mild, amiable, bald-headed, scholarlike, a Member of Parliament and a man of fortune" (Motley to Mary Motley, 28 May 58, Motley, 1:227–28). Stirling-Maxwell was a member of the Cosmopolitan Club, established in 1852 and described by Sir Wemyss Reid as

the most distinguished of the clubs given up to tobacco and talk. Membership is in itself a diploma. . . . In its comfortable room not a few of those who are concerned in the Government of the Empire meet to exchange their views, and to indulge in frank discussion of the questions of the hour. (Sims, 1:80)

Motley said in 1858 that it met "late in the evenings twice a week, Sundays and Wednesdays, in a large room which is the studio of the painter [Henry Wyndham] Phillips, in Charles Street, leading from Berkeley Square" (Motley, 1:227).

Ostensibly "free from party colour" and "diversely representative" (although exclusively male) in its membership, the club remained for half a century "the London paradise of the intelligent foreigner" (Escott, 167–69). Among the members Clemens had already met (or would soon meet) were Lord Houghton, John Lothrop Motley, Joaquin Miller, Thomas Hughes, Robert Browning, and Anthony Trollope. Clemens's reading notes about a two-volume unidentified work (possibly a reminiscence) include the following: "Cosmopolitan Club. 30 Charles St Berkeley □ went there with Lord Houghton several times 11 or 12 pm" (CU-MARK†; Burke 1904, 1056–57; Boase, 3:761; Trollope, 1:147; 1 and 2 July 73 to Miller, n. 1).

From Samuel L. and Olivia L. Clemens
to Joseph H. Twichell
29 June 1873 • London, England
(MS: CtY-BR)

London, June 29.

Dear Old Joe—

I consider myself *wholly* at liberty to decline to pay Chew anything, & at the same time strongly tempted to sue him into the bargain for coming so near ruining me. If he hadn't happened to send me that thing in print, I would have used ~~it~~ the story (like an innocent fool) & would straightway have been hounded to death as a plagiarist. It would have absolutely destroyed me. I cannot conceive of a man being such a hopeless ass ~~(hav~~ (after serving as a legislative reporter, too,) as to imagine that I or any other literary man in his senses would consent to chew over ~~a lot~~ old stuff that had already been in print. If that man weren't an infant in swaddling clothes, his only reply to our petition would have been "It has been in print." It makes me as mad as the very Old Harry every time I think of Mr. Chew & the frightfully narrow escape I have had at his hands. Con*found* Mr. Chew, with all my heart! I'm willing he should have ten dollars for his trouble of warming over his cold victuals—*cheer*fully willing to [pay] that—but no more. If I had had him near when his letter came, I would have got out my tomahawk & gone for him. He didn't tell the story half as well as you did, anyhow.[1] I wish to goodness you were here this moment—nobody in our parlor but Livy & me,—& a very good view of London to the fore. We have a luxuriously ample suite of apartments in Langham Hotel, 3ᵈ floor, our bedroom looking straight up Portland Place & our parlor having a noble array of great windows looking out upon both streets (Portland Place & the crook that joins it on to Regent street.)

ᴧ9 P.M. Full twilight—rich sunset tints lingering in the west.ᴧ

I am not going to write anything—rather tell it when I get back. I love you & Harmony,[2] & that is all the fresh news I've got, anyway. And I mean to *keep* that fresh, all the time.

Lovingly

Mark.

ᴧAm luxuriating ᴑⱼ in glorious old Pepys' Diary & smoking.[3]

Indeed it *is* fresh all the time, and we grow warm, and genial, and en-thusiastic when we speak of Joseph or Harmony— Bless your dear old hearts we love you

Livy—

---

[1] Albert Bigelow Paine explained this incident in 1917:

A man named Chew related to Twichell a most entertaining occurrence. Twichell saw great possibilities in it, and suggested that Mark Twain be allowed to make a story of it, sharing the profits with Chew. Chew agreed, and promised to send the facts, carefully set down. Twichell, in the mean time, told the story to Clemens, who was delighted with it and strongly tempted to write it at once, while he was in the spirit, without waiting on Chew. Fortunately, he did not do so, for when Chew's material came it was in the form of a clipping, the story having been already printed in some newspaper. Chew's knowledge of literary ethics would seem to have been slight. He thought himself entitled to something under the agreement with Twichell. Mark Twain, by this time in London, naturally had a different opinion. (*MTL*, 1:206)

Neither Chew, nor the story, has been further identified. It remains unclear whether Paine learned anything about the matter from Clemens or Twichell that could not be inferred from the letter itself, which Twichell lent to Paine for use in the official biography.

[2] Harmony C. Twichell.

[3] The diary of Samuel Pepys (1633–1703), written in shorthand between 1660 and 1669 but not deciphered until 1825, became one of Clemens's favorite books. In the guidebook he used during his 1872 London visit, across the section headed "Whitehall to Vauxhall," Clemens wrote: "Get Pepys" (*Pardon*, 109†; Gribben, 2:539–40).

To Moncure D. Conway
1 July 1873 • London, England
(MS: NNC)

The Langham
July 1.

My Dear Mr. Conway:

It is *too* bad, but I am called to Paris on business & ~~the chances are~~ ₐI am a little afraid, that I ~~shall~~ ₐmay, not get back in time for Hepworth on the 8th—I do wish we had ~~cos~~ chosen the later day, now.[1] I promised to ₐhelp, write up the Shah for the N. Y. Herald at £20 a column, gold, & have done him up pretty voluminously so far, but they insist upon my going to Paris & "doing" him there—& I *did* intimate that I would, in the first place, but had never thought of it since—never imagined they could want it, in fact.

Now I have a strong hope & belief that I can be back here Monday the 7th & thus save Hepworth. Four days of the Shah in Paris will be all of him that I can possibly need. Wherefore, won't it do to hold the engagement open till I can telegraph you from Paris? I go tomorrow & will telegraph you, say Thursday. Mrs. Clemens remains here, & so if the uncertainty won't do, you can communicate with her.

Ys Sincerely
Sam'. L. Clemens.

[1] See 25 June 73 to Ellen Conway.

To Joaquin Miller
1 and 2 July 1873 • London, England
(MS: ViU)

The Langham
July 1. P.M.

My Dear Miller—

I meant to go to Paris tomorrow, but am relieved of that necessity until next day. Am going to *try* to get to the Cosmopolitan Club about half past ˏten orˏ eleven tomorrow eve—if you intend to go there can you come by for me? Drop me a line, please.

Yrs Sincerely

S. L. Clemens.

July 2—Can't you drop in, to-night, say half past 10 or quarter to 11?[1]

Mark

---

[1] Miller did not get this invitation in time to accompany Clemens to the Cosmopolitan Club: his reply is transcribed in 5 July 73 to Miller, n. 1. Clemens evidently planned to go to the club late on 2 July, after he and Olivia dined with George Smalley and his wife, Phoebe Garnaut Smalley (1838?–1923)—Wendell Phillips's adopted daughter, who had married Smalley in 1862 (see also 14 Dec 73 to OLC, n. 1). Another guest of the Smalleys', Benjamin Moran, secretary of legation to U.S. Minister Robert C. Schenck (25 Oct 72 to OLC, n. 8), recorded the evening in his diary on 3 July:

> Last evening I dined at Geo. W. Smalley's, No. 8 Chester Place, Hyde Park Square, the first time I have ever been in this new residence of his. It is a comfortable, and good sized house, newly and tastefully furnished, Mr. Smalley evidently having taken some hints on the subject from Mr. Geo. H. Boughton, the artist, especially in the matter of oak and walnut furniture and Venetian glass.
>
> The company consisted of Mr. & Mrs. Smalley, a Miss White of New York, a pleasant girl and friend of Horace Greeley's daughters; Mrs. Mack, her sister; Mrs. Jones, an Irish literary lady; Mr. Herbert Spencer the political writer; Mr. Clemens (Mark Twain) and his pretty, dark eyed wife, myself, and Mr. & Mrs. Thomas Hughes. I sat between Mrs. Jones and Miss White. We were a small, but joyous party and had a great deal of fun, Mark Twain being our principal source of amusement. He speaks with an inconceivably comical drawl, which seems natural, but which one occasionally suspects is put on in order to turn over in his mind what he shall say before he utters it. His remarks were all shrewd, his language terse and appropriate, and his manner entirely free from affectation. His pretty wife has a girlish appearance, is lithe and graceful of figure, is a brunette of decided spirit and does not look to be more than 25 years old. She is evidently very fond of her lord.
>
> I found him familiar with the writings of all our early humorists, Jack Downing, Judge Longstreet and others; and judging from his good memory and familiarity with their best stories, I am sure that his wit received an impulse first from theirs.
>
> Mr. Herbert Spencer is a chippy sort of man, and is too deeply immersed in political speculation to be a good table talker. He dresses badly and wears a big black neckhandkerchief, which don't look well among white ties at a dinner table. (Moran, 35:217–20)

Moran alluded to painter and illustrator George Henry Boughton (1833–1905). Thomas Hughes (1822–96) and his wife, Anne Frances ("Fanny") Ford (b. 1826 or 1827), may have met the Clemenses for the first time on this occasion. Hughes was a novelist and biographer, best known for *Tom Brown's School Days* (1857), the story of a student at Rugby, which influenced English ideas on boarding schools. He had served as a member of Parliament for Lambeth, and as London correspondent for the New York *Tribune,* to which he still contributed occasional letters. Herbert Spencer (1820–1903) was already well known for his philosophical application of evolutionary principles to sociology, ethics, and education.

His most recent works were the second volume of *The Principles of Psychology* (1872) and *The Study of Sociology* (1873). In 1906 Clemens recalled meeting Hughes and Spencer at this time, the latter specifically at "a dinner at Smalley's" (AD, 22 Mar 1906, CU-MARK, in *MTA*, 2:232; Joseph J. Mathews, 17–18, 34, 36, 173; Trory, 44). It is not known whether Clemens went on to the Cosmopolitan Club as he had planned, but an autobiographical note among his papers reads simply: "The Cosmopolitan Club—Tom Hughes, Lord Houghton, Robert Browning, Lord Kimberley &c" (CU-MARK†).

To Adam Badeau
4 July 1873 • London, England
(MS: NRU)

(SLC)

The Langham Hotel
Independence Day

My Dear General:

Either the 11th or the 12th will suit us. I tell Mrs. Clemens things begin to look promising. She has been wanting to see Mr. Motley,[1] the Tower of London & Little Boston.[2] She has had a distant glimpse of the Tower, she came as near as anything to being at a luncheon at Lord Houghton's the other day where both Motley & Browning were present;[3] & now Little Boston is within her grasp. Providence still has the party under intermittent inspection, I reckon.

Ys very faithfully
Sam[l]. L. Clemens.

[1]Clemens had decided not to go to Paris (see the next letter). John Lothrop Motley (1814–77) entered Harvard University at the age of thirteen, and published his first serious historical paper in 1845, a review of two works on Russia. In 1856 he published *The Rise of the Dutch Republic*, and, between 1860 and 1868, the four-volume *History of the United Netherlands*. (Olivia wrote Clemens on 28 November 1871 that she had just finished reading this work [*L4*, 505 n. 8].) In 1861 President Lincoln appointed Motley minister to Austria, a post he held for six years. In 1869 President Grant made him minister to England, but recalled him (in spite of his protest) in late 1870. During July 1873 Motley was at work finishing the manuscript for *The Life and Death of John Barnevald, Advocate of Holland* (Motley, 2:373).

[2]Little Boston House was Badeau's residence (15 June 73 to Badeau, n. 2).

³Neither Clemens nor Olivia attended Lord Houghton's luncheon (6 July 73 to Fairbanks). Although Robert Browning (1812–89) published his first poem in 1833, his fame was not widespread until "The Ring and the Book," which appeared serially in 1868 and 1869. His most recent work was "Red Cotton Nightcap Country," published in June 1873. The Clemenses met him soon after this letter was written, when he called on them at the Langham. According to Thompson, Browning discussed a theory he had developed about the cause of seasickness, and was extremely sociable: "Considering the usual English deliberateness and Browning's profound style, I was surprised at his almost French like affability and rapid flow of conversation" (Thompson, 95).

To Moncure D. Conway
4 July 1873 • London, England
(MS: ICN)

Langham, July 4.

My Dear Mr. Conway—
  Good—I have given up Paris altogether for the present, because the Shah's movements are so uncertain. I don't think I shall go to France at all.¹

Ys Truly
Sam¹. L. Clemens

¹The note from Conway to which Clemens replied is now lost; it undoubtedly inquired about the upcoming trip to Stratford (1 July 73 to Conway; 10? July 73 to Warner, n. 2). On the evening of 4 July Clemens attended a dinner in celebration of Independence Day. Robert C. Schenck, the U.S. minister, presided, and "suppressed all speeches," to the annoyance of "a number of patriots" who "could not air their eloquence" (Moran, 35:232–33). According to Benjamin Moran,

> Mark Twain hit these disappointed orators off admirably. He said that his wife had told him the night before that he would be called upon to make a speech and at her instigation he sat up six hours and wrote one out. He then woke her up and read it. She said, very well, but you can't read that off—"you deliver it *extemporere*." He sat up six hours longer, got it by heart, and gave the manuscript to his wife to keep:—"and now," said he, "after all my labor and loss of sleep, you won't let me deliver that extemporere speech!" (Moran, 35:233–34)

Clemens did in fact preserve his manuscript (which is now at CtY-BR), and published it as "After-Dinner Speech" in *Sketches, New and Old* (SLC 1875, 180–81).

To Henry Lee
5 July 1873 • London, England
(Transcript and paraphrase: Parke-Bernet 1954c, lot 633)

· · · ·

[*paraphrase:*[1] *Accepts an invitation to the Whitefriars, but*] must leave again within an hour & a half in order to take my wife to a concert.

Clemens

✉️——

Henry Lee Esq | 43 Holland street | Blackfriars Road, S.E.

[1] The date is supplied by the Parke-Bernet catalog.

To Joaquin Miller
5 July 1873 • London, England
(MS: CtY-BR)

The Langham, July 5.

My Dear Miller:

Indeed I would exceedingly like to make that call with you, but we shall not be in town on Tuesday—going into the country for a 24 or 48 hours' visit. I'll get that book.[1] We think of running up to Lady Hardy's for an hour this evening—my wife has just received her hearty & inspiriting note.[2] Having Lady Hardy's es express permission to come at the early hour, we shall doubtless get there very soon after 8, inasmuch as Mrs. Clemens was a cooped-up invalid yesterday & shan't be allowed downstairs today until we start for North Bank this evening.

Simply reading your penmanship has distorted my own handwriting out of all shape; & so if you can't read this, remember it is your own fault.[3]

Yrs as Ever—,
Saml. L. Clemens.

¹Clemens replied to the following note from Miller (CU-MARK):

35 North Bank Regents Park
July 4—73

My Dear Mark I was down town the last two days and did not get your two letters addressed here till last night. This will explain why I did not call or write.
To day I drop a note to Locker to say you and I will call there Tuesday next at 5 or 6 P.M. I will call for you at 4 or 5.
Locker is the best humorous poet living. If you have time get a book made up of selections from Locker ~~Tenyny~~ Tennyson & Browning—I forget the name of it. Locker is certainly a first rate humorist as well as a first rate gentleman. He lives in Victoria Street; and at the top of a house like a true poet—though a man of fortune. His pictures curiosities & Autographs of great men will amuse you.—If you will be ready—or not ready to go with me Tuesday write me and I will send him the letter to put in his collection of Autographs.

Yours truly
Joaquin Miller

PS I open this to say come to Sir Thomases Saturday evening if not engaged. Hepworth Dixon, Wills and half a dozen great lights were here last Sat.

JM

William Hepworth Dixon (1821–79) wrote on historical and political subjects, and was the former editor of the *Athenaeum* (1853–69); for William Gorman Wills, see 6 July 73 to Fairbanks, n. 6. Clemens would be in Stratford on Tuesday, 8 July. He had evidently written to Miller at the Hardy mansion in North Bank, where he was a houseguest, but Miller had been "down town," in his rooms at 11 Museum Street. Only one of the two letters is known to survive (1 and 2 July 73 to Miller). Frederick Locker (1821–95), later Locker-Lampson, published his first book of verse, *London Lyrics*, in 1857, and an anthology of "vers de société and vers d'occasion" by several authors, entitled *Lyra Elegantiarum*, in 1867. The work containing "selections" from Locker, Tennyson, and Browning has not been identified; Clemens did, however, acquire a copy of an 1872 edition of *London Lyrics* (Gribben, 1:415). On 6 July Miller wrote to Locker: "You see Clemens happens also to be engaged on Tuesday; so we will drop in for you some other day and take our chances on finding you in. I enclose his letter which you may keep for your collection of letters if you like" (CtY-BR). Clemens's 5 July letter was preserved until recently in the Locker-Lampson Papers at the East Sussex Record Office in Lewes. (Frederick Locker was Arthur Locker's older brother: see 17 Sept 72 to Locker.)

²Mary Anne Hardy (1825?–91), the wife of Thomas Duffus Hardy (see 6 July 73 to Fairbanks, n. 15), had written several novels, the most recent being *A Woman's Triumph* (1872) (for Clemens's description of her, see the next letter; *BBA*, s.v. "Hardy, Lady Duffus"). In a letter to her mother also written on Saturday, 5 July, Olivia remarked, "I have just rec'd such an urgent pleasant note from Lady Hardy to spend the evening with them that we shall go there for an hour—you remember I wrote you about our being there before— They always receive Saturday evening—" (CtHMTH; neither Lady Hardy's invitation nor Olivia's previous letter to her mother is known to survive).

³Miller's notoriously illegible handwriting is evident in his 4 July letter, reproduced on the next two pages. Miller allegedly "had an alibi for his wretched scribbling. It was caused by the terrible wound he had received on the right

Joaquin Miller to Clemens, 4 July 1873, recto (manuscript pages 1 and 4). Mark Twain Papers, The Bancroft Library (CU-MARK). Clemens docketed the letter twice on page 4; "Jy 4/73" is written in the upper corner in an unidentified hand. Transcribed in 5 July 73 to Miller, n. 1; reproduced at 75 percent of actual size.

Miller to Clemens, 4 July 1873, verso (manuscript pages 2 and 3).

wrist, after he had been pinked by an arrow in one of his numerous battles against the Indians" (Marberry 1953, 124).

To Mary Mason Fairbanks
6 July 1873 • London, England
(MS: CSmH)

The Langham Hotel,
London, July 6.

My Dear Mother:

This is the letter which I have been intending to ~~answer~~ write this long time, but things have interfered constantly. We had a jolly time here for a month with Miss Clara, but now she has gone to the Continent to remain six weeks.[1]

We seem to ‸see‸ nothing but English social life; we seem to find no opportunity to see London sights. Tuesday we are to visit an English country gentleman & Friday dance at the Lord Mayor's.[2] But no "sights." No nothing, in fact, to make a book of. However, I mean to go to work presently, collecting material.[3] We have met many pleasant people at dinners—Tom Hughes, Herbert Spen¢cer,[4] Joaquin Miller, Hans Breitman,[5] ~~Willes~~ Wills (who wrote the two great dramatic successes of the period, Chas. I & Miss Bateman's Medea),[6] Anthony Trollope, Wilkie Collins,[7] Edmund Yates, Tom Hood, W. C. Bennett (you remember his poem "Baby May" in the ~~Whittier~~ Bryant Selections)[8] Douglas Jerrold, Jr,‸,[9] & *I* at my Lord —'s we were to have met Mr. Motley & Robert Browning, but business interfered & we did not go.[10] Tomorrow night I am to meet two or three of England's great men[11]—& I find that the *really* great ones are very easy to get along with, even when hampered with titles. But I will confess that mediocrity with a title is ‸(to me)‸ a formidable thing to encounter—*it* don't talk, & I'm afraid to.[12]

But I must tell you a secret, now, & mind you don't let me be discovered in divulging it. Joaquin Miller, at a date not yet fixed, is to marry the only daughter of Sir Thomas Hardy, Baronet. We see Miller every day or two, & like him better & better all the¢ time. He is just getting out his Modoc book here & I have made him go to my publishers in America with it (by letter) & they will make some money for him.[13]

§ His sweetheart is rather tall & slender, ₍about 26₎, good looking, good hearted, affectionate, frank, honest, cordial, unassuming, educated, intelligent, (she does a little in literature,) thoroughly English, & very much in love with Joaquin.[14]

Sir Thomas Hardy ₍aged 70₎, is grandson to that best beloved Captain of Nelson's who received the Admiral in his arms when he sank upon the bloody deck of the Victory upon that memorable day that England still glorifies & still mourns, & who heard the dying words "Kiss me, Hardy," that are a part of English history now.[15] And now I am reminded that I saw that colossal & superb old ship the other day, all beflagged in honor of the Shah, & with ~~the signal flying once more at her masthead~~ her old historical guns booming & her old historical signal flying at her masthead once more after all these lagging years, "England expects that every man will do his duty!"[16] God knows I wish we had some of England's reverence for the old & great.

Sir Thomas is a delightful specimen of the right & true Englishman. Loving, cordial, simple-hearted as a girl; fond of people of all ranks, if they are only good & have brains; devoting his house, his heart & his hospitalities four hours every Saturday night to a host of bright people that come & go as freely as if the house was theirs, & waiting for no formal invitation; & he is heartily aided & abetted in all this by his wife & daughter. He is keeper of the Queen's Records (these 53 years) & is very learned.

Lady Hardy (say 50) looks 40 & is stout & handsome—is even beautiful after one comes to know her—which is after four minutes acquaintanceship. She is a very volcano of warm-heartedness & is in a permanent state of irruption. Perhaps it is all set forth in a remark of Livy's yesterday when we started up there on her *second* & my third visit—she felt ⸕ as if she "were going home." And home it was, all the evening₍, & I smoked the ~~pla~~ premises all up before the company got there—not by permission, but command. Heaps of people came, & they were bright & talkative, too, having left their English reserve outside the gate.

Lady Hardy has written a number of novels & is well known here, but I think not in America. She told us the *facts* upon which her ~~"Chance~~ "Casual Acquaintance" was founded,—a thrilling recital & admirably done. Pity people can't always *talk* a book instead of writing it.[17]

The Hardy mansion is a modest, homelike one near Regent's Park. The grounds at its back are delightful with greensward & trees, & a broad ~~cam~~ canal or stream sweeping past its rear almost hidden with overhanging foliage—& all so still & so rural that one can hardly believe it is in the heart of the greatest city in the world. Miller is visiting there for a while at present & has a room in the house, & mighty cosy it is, too.

Some of the friends & relatives of the family oppose the match, but the family are satisfied.

There, now, you know as much about it, now, as I do,, & I have done a wicked thing to tell you; but then you have so warm a friendship & interest in Miller that one could not do less.[18]

But I must stop, for I do not approve of writing letters on the Sabbath day & am not a person who will do it.

Lovingly

Yr Son.

[*on back of letter as folded:*]

Livy & the Modoc are well & they love you—so they say.[19] The Modoc ~~st~~ is able to stand alone, now. She is getting into a habit of swearing when things don't suit. This gives us grave uneasiness.

---

[1] Clara Spaulding had left with her mother, and possibly her father as well, on 26 June. She rejoined the Clemenses in Edinburgh on 9 August (OLC to MEC, 23 June 73, CU-MARK; 2 and 6 Aug 73 to Langdon; Thompson, 99–100).

[2] The Clemenses' two-day visit to Charles E. Flower of Stratford-upon-Avon was scheduled for Tuesday and Wednesday, 8 and 9 July. Clemens had met the lord mayor of London, Sir Sydney Hedley Waterlow, the previous fall (28 Sept 72 to OLC, n. 1; 5 Nov 72 to Lee, n. 1). On Friday, 11 July, the Clemenses were presumably among the eight hundred guests who attended "a grand ball at the Mansion House" given by "the Lady Mayoress" (London *Pall Mall Gazette*, 12 July 73, 6).

[3] For the outcome of this resolve to resume research on a book about England, see 30 Dec 73 to Fitzgibbon, n. 2.

[4] See 1 and 2 July 73 to Miller, n. 1.

[5] Charles Godfrey Leland (1824–1903) was better known by his pen name, "Hans Breitmann." Like several other American humorists, since 1868 Leland had been successfully reprinted in England. Clemens knew him by September 1872, when he mentioned him in his English journal (Appendix C). Thompson described how Clemens and Leland met again in 1873:

> There called one day a large middle aged gentleman and his wife, returned from Egypt, elegantly and soberly dressed in black; serious, quiet and cultured. That was C. G. Leland, talented and learned essayest, etc. But, like most people, I had associated him with "Hans Breitman," the humorous Pennsylvania Dutch dialect poet. (Thompson, 89)

The first of the Hans Breitmann ballads, "Hans Breitmann's Barty," was published in 1857, but Leland did not collect it and his subsequent rhymes until July 1868, when T. B. Peterson published *Hans Breitmann's Party* in Philadelphia, the book that was reprinted in London and marked the start of his fame. Before that Leland had written for and edited a variety of magazines and newspapers, including *Vanity Fair* (1860–61), *The Knickerbocker* (1861–62), *Continental Magazine* (1862–63), and the Philadelphia *Evening Press* (1866–69) (Sloane, 259–61; Leland).

[6] William Gorman Wills (1828–91) was born in Ireland. He supported himself by writing stories and painting portraits, but his eccentricity and absent-mindedness jeopardized his promising career as a painter. In 1865 he began writing for the stage, and in 1872 was retained as a dramatist by Hezekiah L. Bateman, the American manager of the Lyceum Theatre in London. His first production for the Lyceum was *Medea in Corinth* (July 1872), in which Bateman's daughter Kate Josephine Bateman (1843–1917), a former child prodigy, achieved one of her greatest dramatic successes. His next effort, *Charles I* (September 1872), won great acclaim for Henry Irving in the title role; Clemens had seen this play in late September or early October 1872, and described it in his journal as "a curious literary absurdity" (Appendix C). He must have met Wills around the same time. In 1907 he recalled a dinner that had occurred "thirty-five years ago" at which he "told Irving and Wills, the playwright, about the whitewashing of the fence by Tom Sawyer, and thereby captured a chapter on cheap terms; for I wrote it out when I got back to the hotel while it was fresh in my mind" (AD, 19 Aug 1907, CU-MARK, in *MTE*, 331–32). This dinner must have taken place in 1872, not in the summer of 1873, since Clemens wrote the final version of the whitewashing episode, for chapter 2 of *The Adventures of Tom Sawyer*, in January 1873 (*TS*, 504–5; see also pp. 114 and 261). The occasion of Clemens's 1873 meeting with Wills has not been documented.

[7] It is not known when Clemens met novelists Anthony Trollope (1815–82) and William Wilkie Collins (1824–89). (Trollope and Collins were friends, dining together as recently as 10 June.) By 1873 Trollope had passed the peak of his popularity as a novelist. He had published *The Eustace Diamonds* in book form in October 1872, and a travel book, *Australia and New Zealand*, in February 1873. *Phineas Redux* was about to begin serial publication in the London *Graphic* on 19 July, and he had just completed writing *Harry Heathcote of Gangoil* on 28 June, allowing him to resume work on *The Way We Live Now* on 3 July. By 6 July Trollope had already invited Clemens to the dinner honoring Joaquin Miller the following evening (see note 11). Soon after meeting Clemens, Collins evidently provided him with complimentary tickets to his play *The New Magdalen*, which had opened on 19 May. According to Thompson, "Clemens wanted to see Wilkie Collins' new play, 'The New Magdalen.' I got choice seats (they were complimentary) but he was prevented, and we went without him" (Thompson, 99). Collins soon made a lecture tour in the United States, and when he was about to return home, he "received a select company of his most intimate friends at the St. James Hotel" in Boston. Clemens was among the guests and "gave a brief description of his reception in England, saying that he thought he was very successful in the object of his visit there, which was to teach the people good morals, and to introduce some of the improvements of the present century" ("Wilkie Collins," Boston *Evening Transcript*, 17 Feb 74, 1; Trollope, 1:xv, xxxvii, 2:xi–xii, 589).

[8] William Cox Bennett (1820–95) was a journalist and poet whose sentimental paean to his infant daughter was collected in William Cullen Bryant's *Library of*

Poetry and Song (1871). Clemens had met Bennett's brother John in London in 1872 (see 25 Sept 72 to OLC).

[9]Clemens referred to William Blanchard Jerrold (1826–84), not to his late father, playwright and journalist Douglas William Jerrold (1803–57). Upon his father's death the younger Jerrold succeeded him as editor of *Lloyd's Weekly London News*, holding that position until his own death. Jerrold had written successfully for the London stage and had also published a great variety of books, including collections of his own journalism, novels, a biography of his father, travel books, and, between 1871 and 1873, "charming descriptions, with portraits and facsimiles of handwriting, of six imaginary days spent respectively with Dickens, Scott, Lytton, Disraeli, Thackeray, and Douglas Jerrold" (*DNB*, 10:790). He was about to begin publishing what became his major work, *The Life of Napoleon III*, based in part on documents supplied by Napoleon's widow. Clemens seems to have met Jerrold on 1 July at a large party given by the Countess of Crawford and Balcarres "at the family mansion in Grosvenor-square," an event to which he was apparently invited by his old friend from Nevada, George Turner ("Fashionable Entertainments," London *Morning Post*, 2 July 73, 5). Clemens dictated his comments on the experience to Thompson on 2 July, noting that the company were not in the habit of introducing "anybody to anybody else except that they introduce person to one other person, and that was sufficient. I saw that in 2 or 3 other cases and my own case. Sat around among fine people ½ hour." Someone "took pity on our lonely condition" and introduced him to a lady who did not speak English, but tried instead to converse with him in French, German, Spanish, Italian, and, finally, Greek:

> Between us we spoke all the languages there are; I one and she all the rest. . . .
> Melancholy spectacle of the son of Douglas Jerrold sitting around in the hall of magnificent house. His turn to come out and speak or recite or imitate something, then be up and go about his business. 45 years old. (*N&J1*, 551–52)

Thompson recalled years later that Clemens "mentioned as rather pathetic, a well known writer [who] read selections from his more distinguished father's writings at grand receptions and recieved for it five guineas as he quietly left" (Thompson, 86). Clemens was sufficiently struck by this incident to remind himself to make use of it on at least three separate occasions, the first in early 1885: "Describe Judge Turner, Countess so-& so's rout; polyglot woman; poor Douglas Jerrold jr & his dirty shirt standing in hall with footmen" (*N&J3*, 87). Then, in 1888:

> & the awful spectacle of Douglas Jerrold's son at the grand evening blow-out of the noble bitch with the Italian name.
> I was [*one canceled word*] into that business through that ass Judge Turner.
> Polyglot woman there. (*N&J3*, 407)

And, finally, in 1897: "Douglas Jerrold's son at the grand evening party" (Notebook 41, TS p. 37, CU-MARK†).

[10]In his 4 July letter to Adam Badeau, Clemens referred to this same "luncheon at Lord Houghton's." He may have suppressed the name here to protect Houghton's privacy, anticipating that Fairbanks might publish his letter in her husband's Cleveland *Herald*.

[11]On 7 July Trollope hosted a dinner in honor of Joaquin Miller at the Garrick Club, to which he invited Clemens. The other guests were Thomas Hughes; Edward Levy, editor of the London *Telegraph;* and Granville George Leveson-

Gower (1815–91), the second Earl Granville, Liberal-party leader of the House of Lords since 1855 as well as minister for foreign affairs from 1870 to 1874. On 5 July Trollope teased his good friend Kate Field, "Two of the wildest of your countrymen, Joachim Miller & Mark Twain, dine with me at my club next week. Pity you have not yet established the rights of your sex or you could come and meet them, and be *as jolly as men*" (Trollope, 2:591; Griffiths, 362). In 1907 Clemens recalled this "long forgotten" occasion:

> Anthony Trollope was the host, and the dinner was in honor of Joaquin Miller, who was on the top wave of his English notoriety at that time. There were three other guests; one is obliterated, but I remember two of them, Tom Hughes and Levison-Gower. No trace of that obliterated guest remains with me—I mean the *other* obliterated guest, for I was an obliterated guest also. I don't remember that anybody ever addressed a remark to either of us; no, that is a mistake—Tom Hughes addressed remarks to us occasionally; it was not in his nature to forget or neglect any stranger. Trollope was voluble and animated, and was but vaguely aware that any other person was present excepting him of the noble blood, Levison-Gower. Trollope and Hughes addressed their talk almost altogether to Levison-Gower, and there was a deferential something about it that almost made me feel that I was at a religious service; that Levison-Gower was the acting deity, and that the illusion would be perfect if somebody would do a hymn or pass the contribution-box. All this was most curious and unfamiliar and interesting. Joaquin Miller did his full share of the talking, but he was a discordant note, a disturber and degrader of the solemnities. He was affecting the picturesque and untamed costume of the wild Sierras at the time, to the charmed astonishment of conventional London, and was helping out the effects with the breezy and independent and aggressive manners of that far away and romantic region. He and Trollope talked all the time and both at the same time, Trollope pouring forth a smooth and limpid and sparkling stream of faultless English, and Joaquin discharging into it, ~~and tumbling it, and disordering it,~~— his muddy and tumultuous mountain torrent, and— Well, there was never anything just like it except the Whirlpool Rapids under Niagara Falls. (AD, 19 Aug 1907, CU-MARK, in *MTE*, 332–33)

Edward Levy was presumably the other "obliterated" guest, for Miller mentioned him in a letter he wrote to Lord Houghton shortly after the dinner:

> Trollopes dinner at the Garrick was very pleasant indeed. My genial countryman— Mark Twain—was there; the editor of the *Telegraph* also. There was a member of the Cabinet I believe but not being familiar with your great politicians and being unfortunate in remembering names I cant tell you who he was. Also some members of Parliament all genial gentlemen. (Gohdes, 298)

According to Frederick Locker, Trollope was

> combative, and he was boisterous, but good-naturedly so. He was abrupt in manners and speech; he was ebullient, and therefore he sometimes offended people. . . . Some of Trollope's acquaintance used to wonder how so commonplace a person could have written such excellent novels; but I maintain that so honourable and interesting a man could not be commonplace. (Locker-Lampson, 331–32)

[12] Miller claimed that Clemens was "shy as a girl" and "could hardly be coaxed to meet the learned and great who wanted to take him by the hand" (Marberry 1953, 116).

[13] In late July 1873 Miller's London publisher, Richard Bentley and Son, issued his first major prose work, *Life amongst the Modocs: Unwritten History,* an ostensibly autobiographical narrative now regarded as largely a work of fiction. In it Miller described the customs of the California Indians with whom he had lived on the McCloud River in Shasta County. These Indians may or may not

have been Modocs (as Miller claimed), a tribe whose heroic war to reclaim their land from white settlers was much in the news in 1872 and 1873. The book was very popular, in part because of the sympathy aroused by the Modoc war, but not well received by critics. According to an unsympathetic biographer, Miller freely admitted that Prentice Mulford had been "hired to manufacture the volume after listening to Joaquin's tales of adventure" (Marberry 1953, 119–20, 129–30, 137–38; Frost, 68–72, 129; Hart 1987, 325, 469). For the edition issued by Clemens's American publisher, see 16 July 73 to Bliss, n. 2.

[14] Miller had evidently been engaged to marry Iza Duffus Hardy (d. 1922) since at least late May, when the Hartford *Evening Post* announced that "Joaquin Miller is to marry an English lady, daughter of Sir T. D. Hardy of London. She will be Mrs. Miller No. 2" ("Personal," 31 May 73, 3). In early June George Smalley told his *Tribune* readers, "I met him [Joaquin Miller] the other night at a club under Lord Houghton's wing—handsome as ever, and as unconventional, and engaged to be married to another wife" (Smalley 1873a). Iza Hardy began to write stories when quite young, starting work on a novel before she was fifteen. Her first book, *Not Easily Jealous*, was issued in 1872, and her second, *Between Two Fires*, in 1873. Her engagement to Miller was short-lived: in November the Elmira *Advertiser* announced that "Joaquin Miller has no present matrimonial engagement in England. It is broken off" ("Topics Uppermost," 5 Nov 73, 4). Miller had by then already developed an interest in another young lady, a kinswoman of Lord Houghton's wife, who rejected his attentions. On 9 September he wrote to Houghton:

> What you tell me of the lonely condition of Miss Crewe only makes me feel a deeper interest in her and if I had a home worthy of her and she would accept it I know of nothing that would stimulate me to offer it her more than this statement of yours. But her answer to my letter was brief and indifferent so that the matter ended almost as soon as it began. . . . I do confess to you that I was looking very seriously in the direction of Miss Crewe, for I am growing weary of this wandering about forever. I thought I saw a way to get on, but of course I was mistaken. (Gohdes, 300)

By all accounts, Miller was unconventionally free with his attentions to women: according to the Troy (N.Y.) *Press*, in January 1872 he had been "engaged to a lady of the Scottish nobility" ("Personal," 30 Jan 72, 2). In an undated note made late in life, Clemens himself recalled Miller's roving eye at this time: "Joaquin Miller . . . engaged to daughter of Sir Thomas Hardy & made love to Clara Spaulding" (CU-MARK). Although Iza Hardy never married, she and Miller remained friendly, and were still corresponding in 1912 (Black, 204; Kirk, 764; "Death of Miss I. Duffus Hardy," London *Times*, 31 Aug 1922, 9; Hardy to Miller, 9 Feb 1912, CU-BANC).

[15] Sir Thomas Duffus Hardy (1804–78) was descended from Vice-Admiral Sir Thomas Hardy (1666–1732), not from Sir Thomas Masterman Hardy (1769–1839), the flag-captain (and later vice-admiral) who was present at Lord Nelson's death at Trafalgar in October 1805. At age fourteen Thomas Duffus Hardy became a junior clerk in the Record Office, and in 1861 was appointed deputy keeper of the Public Records. He was knighted in 1873 in recognition of his long service in the archives, and of the many valuable historical publications he had edited and authored.

[16] The celebrated signal that Nelson hoisted on the *Victory*, his hundred-gun flagship, as the enemy approached at Trafalgar (Smith, 1036). Clemens had seen the ship at Portsmouth on 23 June, when he attended the naval review for the shah (SLC 1873r).

¹⁷ Lady Hardy's *A Casual Acquaintance: A Novel Founded on Fact* had been well received upon its publication in 1866. It told of a Frenchman who murdered his wife in order to marry an heiress, and deceived a stranger into unwittingly accompanying her corpse to Paris. Thompson recorded Clemens's retelling of the story after the Clemenses' 5 July visit with the Hardys (*N&J1*, 557–59).

¹⁸ See 6 Nov–10 Dec 72 to Fairbanks, n. 1.

¹⁹ In "A Record of The Small Foolishnesses of Susie & 'Bay' Clemens (Infants.),," Clemens recalled that Susy was nicknamed "'Modoc,' (from the cut of her hair.) This was at the time of the Modoc war in the lava beds of northern California" (SLC 1876–85, 3†).

To Elisha Bliss, Jr.
7 July 1873 • London, England
(MS and transcript: ViU and WU)

The Langham Hotel
London, July 7.

Friend Bliss:

Finally concluded not to go to Paris, &y So you can take the Herald letters & put them in a pamphlet along with the enclosed article about the Jumping Frog in French, (which is entirely new), & then add enough of my old sketches to make *a good fat 25 cent pamphlet* & let it slide—but don't charge *more* than 25^c nor less. If you haven't a Routledge edition of my sketches to select from you will find one at my house or Warner's.[1]

I don't expect to write any more Herald letters at present.

Yrs Truly
SL. Clemens

You can mention, if you choose, that the Frog article is has not been printed before.

I enclose Prefatory remarks, "To the Rel Reader"

[*enclosure:*]

To the Reader.

It is not my desire to republish these New York Herald letters in this form; I only do it to forestall some small pirate or other in the book trade.

If I do not publish some such person may, & I then become tacitly accessory to a theft. I have had a recent unpleasant experience of this kind.[2] I have copyrighted the letters here in London simply to prevent their republication in Great Britain in pamphlet form.[3] My objection to such republication, either in America or England, is, that I think everybody has already had enough of the Shah of Persia. I am sure I have.

To the letters I have added certain sketches of mine which are little known or not known at all in America, to the end that the purchaser of the pamphlet may get back a portion of his money & skip the chapters that refer to the Shah altogether.

With this brief apology, I am

Respectfully
Mark Twain

London, July 7

[1] The last three of Clemens's five letters to the New York *Herald* about the shah of Persia were unpublished when he wrote this letter (see SLC 1873n–o, q–s). He had told Olivia in April that he intended to make a literal retranslation of Thérèse Bentzon's "French version of the Jumping Frog" (26 Apr 73 to OLC). The manuscript of the resulting article—dated "London, June 30, 1873" and preserved with the present letter at the University of Virginia—does not include the text of the original "Jumping Frog" sketch, nor of the French translation. Instead Clemens wrote, "(Insert ~~pages A, B, C, D, E, F, G.~~ Jumping Frog in English.)," and then, on a new page, "[Translation of the above back from the French.]," indicating that he included a clipping (now lost) of Bentzon's French version from the *Revue des deux mondes* for 15 July 1872 (see SLC 1865c, 1873p, and Blanc, 313–35). The text of the enclosure was first published in *Sketches, New and Old* (SLC 1875, 28–43). The "Routledge edition" was *Mark Twain's Sketches,* issued in May 1872 (SLC 1872e). The pamphlet of sketches described here was never published (see 2 Aug 73 to Bliss). The shah letters were first reprinted by Paine in 1923 (SLC 1923, 31–86).

[2] See 17 May 73 to Warner, n. 5.

[3] No evidence has been found that Clemens applied in any formal way for British copyright. It is unlikely that he could have secured such a copyright, since the shah letters were being published in the New York *Herald* and British copyright required that publication occur first in England.

To Charles Dudley Warner
10? July 1873 • ?London, England
(MS: NjP)

[first 2 MS pages (about 150 words) missing]

Livy says—& I endorse it—that you cannot have our mother[1] at any price—but you can have an interest in her for nothing—which is cheap enough. But if you want to negotiate for our baby, any ~~suggestion~~ ˏproposition, (addressed to me) will meet with prompt attention. I am offered two twins & a cow by an English gentleman in Stratford ~~&~~ on Avon with whose family we have been staying a day or two,[2] & I am ready to trade but Livy continues to consider & is a good deal of an obstruction.

For goodness sake let no artist make of Sellers anything but a *gentleman*—he is always genial, always gentle, generous, hospitable, full of sympathy~~ies~~ with anything that any creature has at heart—he is always courtly of speech & manner & never descends to vulgarity. Even his dress (vide the scene where Washington first visits him at Hawkeye) is carefully kept & has the expression about it of being the latest charm in excellency of that kind. He always wears a stovepipe hat. He is never awkward in attitude or gesture, & is never ill at ease even in the company of the illustrious. He must not be *distorted or caricatured* in any way in order to make a "funny" picture. Make him plain & simple.[3] ˏ(The original was tall & slender.),[4] *[in margin:* However, I believe we have hinted that Sellers is portly, in one place—which is just as well.]

I have not lectured here & do not think I shall. One has no time to prepare. We only dine. We do nothing else.

Joaquin Miller & I are going to prowl through rural England "unbeknowns" to anybody, leaving Livy & the child in London.[5] However, Livy & I will "do" Scotland first. One can accomplish absolutely nothing when one is known.

With stores of love for Susie[6] & all of you.

Sam*ˡ*. L. Clemens.

[1] Olivia Lewis Langdon.
[2] The Clemenses' host was Charles E. Flower. On 7 July Moncure Conway had provided specific instructions for their trip (CU-MARK):

My dear Clements,

On the eve of the glorious and never-to-be-disremembered-or-underestimated day when we are to visit Hepworth, the birthplace of a great man, I take pleasure in writing that if tomorrow you will meet me at the great railway Station Paddington at two o'clock p. m. (I put in the p. m. lest in your morning enjoyments in the role of 'early bird' you should step in at 2 a. m. Do not.)—at *2 p*. m. precisely it will be well with us. Our train leaves at a quarter of an hour later: we go by way of Oxford and Honeybourne (a bourne at which Mrs. C. might naturally stop, but must not), and will soon be clasped in the arms of Mr. Charles [Flower] who will meet us at the Station.

Thine
M D Conway

By the evening of 10 July the Clemenses had returned to London (11 July 73 to unidentified; for details of the Stratford visit see 25 June 73 to Conway, n. 2; 14 July 73 to Flower; and Clemens's dictated remarks in *N&J1*, 561–64). It is possible that Clemens wrote this letter to Warner while still in Stratford, since he was vague about the length of their stay. It seems somewhat more likely, however, that he wrote it soon after returning to London, where he would have found Warner's letter reporting on the progress of the *Gilded Age* illustrations (see the next note).

[3] Warner was reviewing the initial drawings submitted to him as illustrations for *The Gilded Age*. The artists that Bliss had assigned to work from the manuscript were chiefly True W. Williams, Augustus Hoppin, and Henry Louis Stephens. The first illustration of Colonel Sellers in the body of the book, probably drawn by Williams, appears in chapter 5, followed by five more (two initialed by Williams) in chapters 7 and 8; all of them accord with Clemens's instructions (Hamilton, 155, 210, 221, 224; David, 168–69; SLC 1873–74, title page, 58, 77, 81, 85, 89, 91). The scene Clemens mentioned here occurs in chapter 7:

> The Colonel's "stovepipe" hat was napless and shiny with much polishing, but nevertheless it had an almost convincing expression about it of having been just purchased new. The rest of his clothing was napless and shiny, too, but it had the air of being entirely satisfied with itself and blandly sorry for other people's clothes. (SLC 1873–74, 78)

Several months after *The Gilded Age* was published, Clemens complained that it was "rubbishy looking" because it suffered, like *Roughing It*, from the "wretched paper & vile engravings" typical of subscription books (24 Mar 74 to Thomas Bailey Aldrich, MH-H, in *MTLP*, 81).

[4] The "original" of Colonel Sellers was James J. Lampton (1817–87), a first cousin of Jane Lampton Clemens's (*L1*, 135 n. 10; Lampton 1989). Clemens described him in an autobiographical reminiscence written in 1897–98:

> The real Colonel Sellers, as I knew him in James Lambton, was a pathetic & beautiful spirit, a manly man, a straight & honorable man, a man with a big, foolish, unselfish heart in his bosom, a man born to be loved; & he was loved by all his friends, & by his family worshiped. (SLC 1897–98, 21–22)

Lampton was also a kinsman of Henry Watterson's (see 29 May–15 June? 73 to Watterson, n. 1). Watterson recalled:

> Just after the successful production of his play, The Gilded Age, . . . I received a letter from him [Clemens] in which he told me he had made in Colonel Mulberry Sellers a close study of one of these kinsmen and thought he had drawn him to the life. "But for the love o' God," he said, "don't whisper it, for he would never understand or forgive me, if he did not thrash me on sight." . . .
>
> The original Sellers had partly brought him up and had been very good to him. A

second Don Quixote in appearance and not unlike the knight of La Mancha in character, it would have been safe for nobody to laugh at James Lampton, or by the slightest intimation, look or gesture to treat him with inconsideration, or any proposal of his, however preposterous, with levity.

He once came to visit me upon a public occasion and during a function. I knew that I must introduce him, and with all possible ceremony, to my colleagues. He was very queer; tall and peaked, wearing a black, swallow-tailed suit, shiny with age, and a silk hat, bound with black crepe to conceal its rustiness, not to indicate a recent death; but his linen as spotless as new-fallen snow. Happily the company, quite dazed by the apparition, proved decorous to solemnity, and the kind old gentleman, pleased with himself and proud of his "distinguished young kinsman," went away highly gratified. (Watterson 1919, 1:121–22)

Clemens had thought of using Lampton as a character as early as August 1870, when he wrote to his sister, Pamela Moffett, asking her to

get all the gossip you can out of Mollie [Clemens] about Cousin James Lampton & Family, *without her knowing it is I that want it*. I want every little trifling detail, about how they look & dress, & what they say, & how the house is furnished—& the various ages & characters of the tribe. (*L4*, 185)

[5] Thompson recalled that Miller and Clemens "wanted to take a tour together on English country roads. But he wanted to walk and Clemens wanted to ride horseback" (Thompson, 87). The plan was not fulfilled, but apparently was still alive on 15 August, when Olivia mentioned it to her mother in a letter from Edinburgh: "When I get back to London if Mr Clemens does some traveling through rural England with Mr Miller I shall go into apartments and live just as cheaply as possible so that I can have the money to spend" (10–15 Aug 73, CtHMTH).

[6] Warner's wife, Susan.

To Elisha Bliss, Jr.
10 July 1873 • London, England
(MS: Freedman)

London, July 10.

Friend Bliss—

Publish if you want to, or leave it alone, just as seems best. I am tired of the Shah & shall not write any more.[1]

Ys

Clemens

[1] Bliss had evidently written to Clemens soon after receiving his letter of 18 June, perhaps even before the first shah letter appeared in the New York *Herald* on 1 July. Bliss may have wanted to know how many shah letters Clemens planned to write.

To Mr. Smith
per Samuel C. Thompson
11 July 1873 • London, England
(Stenographic draft: CU-MARK)

July 11ᵗʰ

Dear Mr. Smith,[1]

We very particular not miss your Thu picnick party. We should
be at Mr. MᶜDonald's on the 16ᵗʰ.[2] And then, as you say, we can arrage
the date.

Sincerly Yours.

---

[1]Possibly George Smith (1824–1901), who in 1846 succeeded his father as
head of the London publishing firm of Smith, Elder and Company, and who
founded the *Cornhill Magazine* and the *Pall Mall Gazette*. Smith had published
two works by George MacDonald (see the next note), and was also a personal
friend of his (Raeper, 165, 178).

[2]On 10 July Louisa MacDonald wrote to Olivia, urging the Clemenses to attend a garden party on 16 July (a Wednesday) at her home, the Retreat, in Hammersmith. At this event, which she called her *"July Jumble,"* the MacDonald
family planned to enact a play, and the Jubilee Singers were to perform (CU-
MARK; 29 Sept 73 to MacDonald [1st], n. 1). George MacDonald (1824–1905)
was born in Scotland and educated at King's College, Aberdeen, and at the theological college at Highbury, outside London. In 1853 he resigned his formal ministry to devote himself to literature, publishing his first book—a poetic tragedy—two years later. In addition to verse he wrote fiction treating mystical and
religious themes and depicting humble Scottish life, as well as immensely popular stories for children. (Clemens had derided one of MacDonald's novels, *Robert Falconer*, to Mary Mason Fairbanks in September 1870: see *L4*, 187–89.)
Throughout his life he was an unorthodox but eloquent lay preacher. In 1872–
73 MacDonald—accompanied by his wife and one son—made a successful lecture tour in the United States, managed by Redpath and Fall. In late December
1872, and again in late January 1873, the MacDonalds stayed at Mrs. Langdon's
home in Elmira, both occasions when the Clemenses were in Hartford (Raeper,
295; "George MacDonald," Elmira *Advertiser*, 27 Jan 73, 4). According to Harriet Lewis, however, the MacDonalds were house guests of the Clemenses' during her own visit to Hartford in March and April 1873:

> Then there was George McDonald and his wife. They were with us a week. He had the
> simplicity of true greatness[.] Any one could sit down and talk to him as they would to
> an intimate friend and always find him responsive. His wife was a sweet gentle refined
> woman: the mother of eleven children, the oldest 21, the youngest 5. She looked the
> embodiment of a happy wife and mother without a care in the world. It was a rare treat
> to listen while he and Mr C. talked—for both were at their best. (Paff, 10–11)

To Unidentified
per Samuel C. Thompson
11 July 1873 • London, England
(Stenographic draft: CU-MARK)

July 11th.

Dear Sir,
Will Tuesdy evening 15th do? And if so, at what hour should we be at the Vic. station?[1] We were out of town, and did not get your note until last night.

[1] Neither the correspondent nor the occasion planned for 15 July has been identified.

To Charles E. Flower
14 July 1873 • London, England
(MS: DFo)

(SLC)

The Langham Hotel
July 14.

My Dear Mr. Flower:
The more we think of our visit the pleasanter it seems & the more gratified we are that we were allowed the opportunity to make it. No episode in our two months' sojourn in England has been so void of alloy & so altogether rounded & complete.[1] We do sincerely hope that no evil effects may follow it for Mrs. Flower[2]—we confess some uneasiness on that head.
It is a great thing to have seen three such beautiful homes & pleasant households & be able to associate them always in our recollections with the tangible realities of Shakspeare's abiding place. We desire to be remembered to all the Floral host & to thank each bud & blossom of the triple family for the enjoyment we have experienced.[3]

I may add here, that having learned all about how ~~all~~ ale is made, I now take a new & ferocious interest in consuming it.

Yours Sincerely

Sam*'*. L. Clemens & wife.

[1] Moncure Conway later recalled Olivia's response to the hoax he had helped Clemens plan (25 June 73 to Conway, n. 2):

> On arrival at the station we directed the driver to take us straight to the church. When we entered and Mrs. Clemens read on Shakespeare's grave "Good frend for Jesus sake forbeare," she started back exclaiming, "Heavens, where am I!" Mark received her reproaches with an affluence of guilt, but never did lady enjoy a visit more than that to Avonbank. Mrs. Charles Flower (*née* Martineau) took Mrs. Clemens to her heart and contrived that every social or other attraction of that region should surround her. (Conway 1904, 2:145)

Albert Bigelow Paine mistakenly implied that this incident took place in 1879 (*MTB*, 2:647).

[2] The former Sarah Martineau, of London, whom Flower had married in 1852 (Boase, 5:314).

[3] Charles and Sarah Flower were childless. The other two Flowers of the triple "Floral host" were Charles's father, Edward F. Flower (6 Oct 72 to Conway, n. 1), and his brother, Edgar Flower (1831?–1903), a junior partner in the family brewery business. Edgar and his wife, the daughter of T. M. Dennis, had five daughters and three sons (information from the Shakespeare Birthplace Trust; "Obituary," London *Times*, 30 July 1903, 8).

To Elisha Bliss, Jr.
per Samuel C. Thompson
16 July 1873 • London, England
(MS: CtY-BR)

Langham Hotel
London
July 16.

Friend Bliss,

We shall issue a copyright edition of the novel here in fine style—three volumes; and in order that there shall be no mistakes I wish you would be particular to send sheets and duplicate casts of the pictures by successive steamers always.[1] And send these casts and proofs along as fast as you get a signature done. Be sure to write on to Routledge and state as nearly as you can the exact day at which you can publish. Routledge will publish on that day or the day before. If you change the date of publication telegraph Routledge.

I told Joquin Miller to write you proposing 7½ per cent for his book.[2]

> Yours Truly,
> Sam*l*. L. Clemens.

✉—————————————————————

[*letter docketed:*] √ [*and*] Saml Clemens | July 16″ 73 [*and*] Joaquin Miller | July 16th 1873 | Author

[1] The English edition of *The Gilded Age*, published by George Routledge and Sons, was typeset from proofsheets of the American edition (27 July 73 to Bliss, n. 2) and illustrated with duplicate electrotypes ("casts") of the engravings. It included fewer than half the illustrations prepared for the American edition, however. All of the full-page engravings were omitted (evidently because they were too large for the English-edition page format), and as the book progressed, more and more of the small ones were absent as well, so that the third volume contained only three. Presumably the engravings for the last third of the book were completed too late for inclusion in the English edition.

[2] Bliss's American Publishing Company issued Miller's book as *Unwritten History: Life amongst the Modocs* (reversing the title and subtitle of the English edition) in late October 1874. In March 1874 Clemens told Thomas Bailey Aldrich: "Bliss had contracted to pay me 10 p.c. on my next book (contract made 18 months ago) so I made him pay that on ~~Roughing~~ Gilded Age. He paid 7½ p.c. on Roughing It & 5 p.c. on Innocents Abroad. I only made him pay 7½ on Joaquin Miller's Modoc book, because I don't think Miller much of a card in America" (24 Mar 74, MH-H, in *MTLP*, 81). Clemens alluded to the contract signed on 22 June 1872: see 11 June 72 to Sutro, n. 1, and Appendix D.

To Charles Dudley Warner
per Samuel C. Thompson
16 July 1873 • London, England
(MS: CtY-BR)

> Langham Hotel
> London
> July 16th

My Dear Warner,

I have just written Bliss asking him to send two ~~or~~ sets of sheets and two casts of the pictures always by successive steamers, so that if one set is ever lost it need not stop the book. I wish you would see that this is done, and don't let a sheet be carelessly kept back for a week or two, scaring a body to death with the idea that it is lost; but have the sheets sent in their regular order faithfully. Don't wait for a quantity, but send it right along, signature by signature. And I have told Bliss to name the day of publication and to write Routledge about it; and that if he should change that date to telegraph to Routledge; because if Routledge makes a mistake in the publishing day of Bliss it may cost us our copy-right.[1] Now you know what I have written Bliss, and you will know how to proceed.

> Yours Truly,
> Sam*[l]*. L. Clemens.[2]

[1] See 28 Feb 73 to Bliss, n. 1.

[2] Clemens dismissed Thompson shortly after dictating the present letter. In 1909 Thompson wrote to Clemens, recalling the circumstances of their parting and enclosing a money order as partial payment for a debt of ten pounds—a debt Clemens himself had forgotten, and quickly forgave. Thompson explained:

> After a few weeks in England you found the public and social tax on your time interfered with literary work and that you might as well dispense with my services. Your memory was that I was to expect less than ten dollars a week. However, you gave me twenty pounds and said I could owe you ten pounds. So I considered [it] a matter of circumstances—and no cause for complaint—was eager to repay as soon as I could. As I could live as cheaply in Europe as in New York with not a ghost of chance to do anything for just the remaining midsummer days, I tramped about some and came over in the Fall.

Thompson went on to recount, in painful detail, that in the intervening years he had become a minister and served for "twenty-two years without a vacation" in a small town in New York State, trying to pay his debts (20 Apr 1909, CU-MARK). Clemens, who regarded Thompson's letter as "tragic . . . & full of pathetic human interest," recalled how unsatisfactory this "first experience in dictating" had been, and how his "sentences came slow & painfully, & were clumsily phrased, & had no life in them" (SLC 1909a, 1, 12†; see also *N&J1*, 517, 525).

To Olivia Lewis Langdon
20 July 1873 • York, England
(MS: Tollett)

York, July 20.

Mother Dear—

I shall only just write a line to say that for full 24 hours no one has called, no cards have been sent up, no letters received, no engagements made, & none fulfilled. ~~That~~ All which is to say, we have been 24 hours out of London, & they have been 24 hours of *rest* & quiet. Nobody knows us here—we took good care of that. In Edinburgh we are to be introduced to nobody, & shall stay in a retired, private hotel, & go on resting.[1]

For the present we shall remain in this queer old walled town, with its crooked, narrow lanes that ~~remind us~~ tell us of ~~their~~ ,their, ,old, day that knew no wheeled vehicles; its plaster-&-timber dwellings with upper storieses far overhanging the street, & thus marking *their* date, say 300 years ago; the stately city walls, the castellated gates, the ivy-grown, foliage-sheltered, most noble & picturesque ruin of St. Mary's Abbey, suggesting *their* date, say 500 years ago, in the heart of Crusading times & the glory of English chivalry & romance;[2] the vast cathedral of York, with its worn carvings & quaintly pictured windows preaching of still remoter days;[3] the outlandish names of streets & courts & byways that stand as a record & a memorial, all these centuries, of Danish dominion here in still earlier times; the hint here & there of King Arthur & his knights & their bloody fights with ~~s~~Saxon oppressors round about this old city more than 1300 years gone by; & last of all, the melancholy old stone coffins & sculptured inscriptions, a venerable arch & a hoary tower of stone that still remain & are kissed by the sun & ~~carr~~ caressed by the shadows every day just as the sun & the shadows have kissed & caressed them every lagging day since the Roman Emperor's soldiers placed them here in the times when Jesus the Son of Mary walked the streets of Nazareth a youth with no more name or fame ~~that~~ than this Yorkshire boy that is loitering down this street this moment.

We are enjoying it, & shall go on enjoying it for several days yet (for

we have a delightful little hotel,) but we would like it ever so much better
~~of~~ if you & the rest of you were only with us. Goodbye, mother dear.

Yr loving son

Samˡ.

[1] On 19 July the Clemenses left London for Edinburgh, stopping for several
days in York. While there, Clemens purchased and annotated a copy of William
Combe's *History and Antiquities of the City of York, from Its Origin to the Present
Times* (3 vols., York: 1785), perhaps for use in his English book. By 25 July the
Clemenses had arrived in Edinburgh, where they settled at Veitch's Hotel (An-
derson Galleries 1920b, lot 10; Gribben, 1:155; OLC to Alice Day, 25 July 73,
CtHSD; 31 July 73 to unidentified, n. 1).

[2] St. Mary's Abbey was one of the first monasteries founded in Yorkshire after
the Norman Conquest; its principal remains date from about 1300. The seventh
(and last) Crusade for the recovery of the Holy Land took place in 1270–71
(Murray, 476; Smith, 294).

[3] York Minster, one of England's chief cathedrals and the seat of an archbish-
opric, was originally of Norman construction but was completely rebuilt in the
thirteenth through fifteenth centuries (Smith, 1077).

To Elisha Bliss, Jr.
27 July 1873 • Edinburgh, Scotland
(MS: CtY-BR)

Edinburgh, July 27.

Friend Bliss—

Confound it, I forgot to tell you not to advertise that pamphlet
(in case you publish it) or send a copy to any newspaper.[1] Bother the luck,
I wanted it to pass unnoticed.

Shall I look for Gilded Age sheets pretty soon?[2]

Ys

Clemens.

Care Routledge.
    London

[*letter docketed:*] √ [*and*] Mark Twain | Edinburgh July 27.

¹The proposed pamphlet of shah letters to the New York *Herald* (see 7 July 73 to Bliss).

²Although Clemens expected *The Gilded Age* to be published in Great Britain before his planned departure date of 25 October (see the next letter), Bliss had not yet forwarded any proofsheets for the English typesetters to work from. Clemens's contract with the Routledges guaranteed them typesetting copy at least three weeks before publication of the American edition (Appendix D). The first salesmen's prospectuses, comprising pages from the first fifteen chapters, came from the American Publishing Company bindery on 7 October, suggesting that proofsheets of those pages could have arrived in England at about that time. The cost of composition was entered in the Routledge ledger on 9 December, the probable date of completion of the English typesetting (APC, 95; Routledge Ledger Book 4:765, Routledge). Preliminary collations show that like the American edition, the bulk of the English edition incorporated revisions which Warner made in the manuscript after Clemens left for England in May, or on the early proofsheets, and which were then transmitted in the late proofsheets sent to England (13 May 73 to Warner). In the last nine chapters, however, the English edition accords more closely with the manuscript (only a fraction of which is extant), which suggests that Bliss was forced to forward unrevised proofs to speed up the production process. (An alternate—but less likely—possibility is that these late chapters were set from a fair copy of the manuscript, which of course also lacked Warner's revisions.) This procedure enabled the English publishers to issue their edition slightly before the American one, as required to secure a valid copyright (see Hill 1965).

~~To David Ross Locke~~
To T. B. Pugh
27 July 1873 • Edinburgh, Scotland
(MS: CtY-BR)

Edinburgh, July 27

My Dear ~~Locke—¹~~ ₐPugh—ₐ

I have got to remain in London till the 25ᵗʰ of October to see my book through the English press. As this is business & can't be avoided, I thought I had better ~~letter~~ let you know, so that you would be saved making any ~~apologies for no~~ advertisements with my name in them of the great lecture-jubilee if it is to come off before I get back. I want to appear in that caravan, according to my promise,² but it is now a fact beyond question that I shall have to remain in London till Oct. 25 & thus be able to secure English copyright.

Ys Truly
Sam*ˡ*. L. Clemens

[1] The occasion for Clemens's interrupted letter to David Ross Locke (Petroleum V. Nasby) is not known; no letter from Locke to Clemens from this period has been discovered. In 1873 Locke was managing editor of the New York *Evening Mail*, while retaining an interest in the Toledo *Blade* (Austin, 35, 39).

[2] The "great lecture-jubilee" in which Clemens had agreed to appear (without knowing the exact date) has not been identified. There survives in the Mark Twain Papers, however, an undated list of names in Pugh's hand, which could have been enclosed in a letter that is now lost. Under the first heading, entitled merely "The List," are twenty-six names, all of well-known lecturers, readers, or other performers—including Mark Twain himself, Charles Sumner, Wendell Phillips, Petroleum Nasby, Anna Dickinson, Josh Billings, Bret Harte, Frederick Douglass, Ralph Waldo Emerson, and three musical groups. Under a second heading, "*Invited,*" are six more names—including John B. Gough, Henry Ward Beecher, and Henry Wadsworth Longfellow. The third heading, "*Present,*" includes only "Gen. U.S. Grant & cabinet." The list cannot be dated with certainty, but must have been prepared between February 1871, when Harte arrived in the East, and March 1874, when Charles Sumner died. No record of any event involving the people listed has been discovered, suggesting that Pugh was unable to realize his plan.

To Unidentified
31 July 1873 • Edinburgh, Scotland
(MS: MHi)

Veitch's Hotel[1]
Edinburgh, July 31.

D*ʳ* Sir:[2]

I am afraid I am not able to help you. Mr. Bryant is not in any way connected with the N. Y. Times, but is a large owner in the N. Y. *Evening Post.*[3]

I should think Joaquin Miller might have that signature (Longmans, his publisher[4]—but his rooms are 11 Museum street). Or Robert Browning or Mr. Tennyson,[5] maybe. G. W. Smalley, of the N. Y. Tribune bureau might know his London friends—is almost *sure* to. Then there is a volume (issued by Scribner I think, some 3 or 4 years ago) of selections from the whole world's poets which contains Bryant's autograph— the collection *is compiled by ~~Wh~~ Bryant* but I forget its title.[6] Perhaps Mr. Trübner might know where to find a copy of that.[7] Of course Mr. John Lothrop Motley ~~must~~ (Long's Hotel) must have that signature, I should think. If he is not at Long's Hotel now, Lord Houghton (37 Berkeley Square,) will know his address. If poets have a fellow feeling for each other, Mr. Bryant has surely sent copies of the book I spoke of to members of the guild on this side.

I thank you very much for the offer of introductory letters, but shall not need them as I am too busy resting to go into company.

Ys Truly
Saml. L. Clemens.

---

[1] Veitch's was a first-class private hotel at 127 George Street, in the heart of the city (Baedeker 1901, 509–10).

[2] Clemens may have been writing to Grenville Howland Norcross (1854–1937), a lawyer and avid autograph collector who eventually bequeathed this letter to the Massachusetts Historical Society. Norcross was only nineteen years old in 1873, however, and still a student at Harvard, so it seems implausible that he would offer Clemens the "introductory letters" alluded to in the final paragraph. The greater likelihood is therefore that he purchased the letter from a dealer.

[3] William Cullen Bryant (1794–1878) had been the editor of the New York *Evening Post* since 1829, and a half-owner in it since 1836. For thirty years he took an active role in managing the paper, although by 1869 he had greatly relaxed his control over it.

[4] Miller had published *Songs of the Sierras* (1871) and *Songs of the Sun-Lands* (1873) through the London firm of Longmans, Green, Reader, and Dyer. His most recent work, *Life amongst the Modocs*, had just been issued by Richard Bentley and Son.

[5] Alfred Tennyson (1809–92) had been poet laureate since 1850, when he succeeded Wordsworth. It is not known whether Clemens had met him. Lord Houghton evidently introduced Tennyson, a close friend of his, to Joaquin Miller in the summer of 1873, and might have introduced him to Clemens as well (Pope-Hennessy, 56–59, 217, 236; Marberry 1953, 115; see 15 Dec 73 to Tennyson, and 16 Dec 73 to OLC, n. 3).

[6] *A Library of Poetry and Song* (New York: J. B. Ford and Co., 1871), which Bryant compiled, contained his portrait, with a facsimile of his signature, as a frontispiece.

[7]Nikolaus Trübner (1817–84) was a prominent London publisher, bibliographer, and oriental scholar who had taken an early interest in reprinting American writers, such as Charles Leland.

To Elisha Bliss, Jr.
2 August 1873 • (1st of 2) • Edinburgh, Scotland
(MS, draft telegram: CU-MARK)

> *American Telegram.*[1]
> E. Bliss,
>   Hartford, Conn.
> Stop that pamphlet.
>   Clemens.[2]

[1]This manuscript is a draft of the message that Clemens actually cabled to Bliss. The document Bliss received has not been found. For the date of this telegram, see the next letter.

[2]Appearing upside down and on the back of this sheet are notes Clemens made for his most recent version of the long-germinating "Noah's Ark" book, which he described in 1909:

> I began it in Edinburgh in 1873; I don't know where the manuscript is, now. It was a Diary, which professed to be the work of Shem, but wasn't. I began it again several months ago, but only for recreation; I hadn't any intention of carrying it to a finish— or even to the end of the first chapter, in fact. (SLC 1909b)

(For Clemens's earlier and later work on the project, see *L3*, 312, 313–14 n. 7; *L4*, 296 n. 3; and Baetzhold and McCullough, 91–110.) This draft telegram is among a group of sketchy notes, all on the same paper, which Clemens wrote in Edinburgh. Many of them refer explicitly to Exodus, chapters 19–22 and 34–35 (SLC 1873tt). On this particular sheet Clemens wrote "Edinburgh" four times, and several calculations to determine in what year various biblical characters died, based on figures from chapters 5–9 of Genesis, which recount the history of every generation from Adam's creation until the death of Noah—a total of 2006 years. Clemens also wrote "Meth died 1656," a conclusion he derived from Methuselah's birth 687 years after the creation, to which he added the 969 years of his life.

To Elisha Bliss, Jr.
2 August 1873 • (2nd of 2) • Edinburgh, Scotland
(Goodspeed's Book Shop 1926?, item 793c)

Edinburgh, Aug. 2.

Friend Bliss—
Have just telegraphed you to squelch that pamphlet (if you are publishing it). I find by reading over those Herald letters that I don't like
them at all—& besides, the Herald people have added paragraphs & in-
terlineations, & not pleasant ones, either.[1] So I know it will be better for
you & better for me to stop the pamphlet. I don't want to do anything
that can injure the novel.[2] We shall be in London during the month of
September. Curse those letters!

Yrs.

Clemens.

[1] In 1907 Clemens recalled the *Herald*'s editing of his letters:
I had been helping the London newspaper men fetch the Shah of Persia over from Ostend, I being for forty-eight hours in the service of Dr. Hosmer, London representative
of the New York *Herald.* I had dictated an account of the excursion covering two or three
columns of the *Herald,* and had charged and received three hundred dollars and expenses for it—a narrative which seemed to the *Herald* to lack humor, a defect which the
New York office supplied from its own resources, which were poor and coarse and silly
beyond imagination. (AD, 28 Aug 1907, CU-MARK†)
(For an example of these "poor and coarse" additions, see 4 Aug 73 to Yates.)
Clemens was well paid, however, for his five contributions. In a letter of 12 September 1873 to Whitelaw Reid, George Smalley commented: "The Herald
seems to be going in for all sorts of things, and money no object. I was wrong in
telling you Twain had $100, gold, a column, for the Shah; it was $125, or, actually, £25, and they counted in the display heads, wh. came to £69! This is what
Mark says" (Whitelaw Reid Papers, DLC). Thompson later recalled that Clemens said the first letter alone was worth $500, but Smalley's contemporary esti-
mate is probably more accurate (Thompson, 89).
[2] *The Gilded Age.*

From Olivia L. and Samuel L. Clemens
to Olivia Lewis Langdon
2 and 6 August 1873 • Edinburgh, Scotland
(MS: CtHMTH)

Edinburgh Aug 2nd 1873

Mother dear

I have been having a very lazy day lying on the sofa and just resting most of the day— Mr Clemens has gone out now for a little walk, it is a bright beautiful evening— I should so like it if we could chat together for a little while, so many things that I would like to talk with you about—

Susie trots all about the room of course she is not at all steady on her feet as yet but she enjoys it just as much apparently— I ~~shal~~ say to her ~~Shusie~~ Susie Shoo the flies and she makes her little ~~hads~~ hands go and says ⸢S⸣h! ⸢S⸣h! ⸢S⸣h!, ⸢S⸣he[1] has watched with the greatest interest two or three flies that have been on the window and would laugh when they would fly—she grows more and more interesting and entertaining all the time— She says baby very distinctly— The other day her father bought her a very pretty picture of a kitten and we ask her to say cat, she says tat, she says kitty quite distinctly— Every picture or anything that she particularly admires she say[s] something nearly like puddle, every time she comes into the room she points to the picture on the wall and says "puddle"—

Aug 6th

This afternoon at three o'clock Dr Brown is coming to take us for a drive, he is the most charming old gentleman and I believe grows more and more so all the time—[2] Being in bed and lying about on the sofa I had worn a net every time that he saw me, the other day he said to me I hope you do not put one of those horrid things ⸢(meaning the false hair extras)⸣ on the top of your head when you go out— I said I added a little something at the back— This morning when he came I had dressed my hair—very soon after he came in, he said "Oh you spoil your head with putting that thing on, but it is very modest compared to some of them⸶ —I have promised to show you in perfect simplicity." So I promised to do it up lower down— Wasn't it funny that he should notice so?—

Two or three day[s] ago Dr Brown's sister called, she is a very pleasant maiden lady of sixty five or seventy, I wish you could have seen her she is just like the characters that we see represented in books as lovable maiden aunts and so on—[3] She was speaking of some friends of theirs in America who lived in a boarding house and said to them it was such an odd idea that people should board— Said it was always a great mar to her in traveling if she was obliged to stop over night at a hotel—she at was really unhappy if she was not either under her own roof or that of some friend— She told of us ⁄us of a trip that she took when she was a young lady— She took ˌrodeˌ a pony and her two brothers (the present Dr Brown and a younger brother) walked by her side, in that way they traveled through the beautiful lake region of Scotland— She said they started from their father's manse after eating a hearty dinner breakfast, they got along without any dinner, having plenty of bread and butter with them and at night took a very frugal tea, she knew they could get along very economically ˌon their own foodˌ as the bread and butter they brought from home would last them some time—but it seemed to her that the feeding the pony would ruin them— Mother is n't that a pretty picture of the frugal habits of m which ministers children had in those days— Miss Brown said she did not think she could possibly enjoy a trip now about those regions as she did then, it seemed that the wild beauty of the scenery would be marred by the modern roads which had been made to facilitate travel— She knew it was selfish but she should dislike to see the lakes in their present changed condition, she prefered her vivid memory of them as they were when she was a young girl—[4] Oh Mother how I do wish that you could see these people they are so perfectly delightful—

Tomorrow evening we dine with Dr and Miss Brown and meet the younger brother, who was one of the foot passengers on in the journey around the lakes, and his wife, they are just now passing through the city on their way on to the continent—[5]

We were to meet there a Mr Russel, editor of the "Scotsman," the leading daily here—but he and his wife were unable to be there so they sent us the most cordial invitation to visit them in their country home and spend two or three days with them,[6] they are right near Melrose and Abbotsford and will drive us all about there.[7]

We shall go Friday noon afternoon returning Sat. evening, we should probably remain longer, but Clara comes Saturday night and it would be so forlorn for her not to find us that we shall return, what a *great* pity that she is not here to go with us, ⌃ she has missed so many things by being away.[8]

Mother I do love you and hope Minequa will do you a world of good.[9] I want to write more and perhaps I will ~~befoe~~ before I send off this letter but must stop now. Love to all—

With deepest love
Livy—

Ditto.—

Sam¹.

Our books have come—a rare thing we have been on the track of for ten days—got it at last—the famous "Abbotsford Edition" of Scott's works—12 huge volumes elaborately illustrated. Pretty scarce book.[10]

---

[1] Clemens wrote "Shoo" in the line above, where Olivia had left a space. Here he wrote over her four lowercase *s*'s, correcting them to capitals.

[2] In 1906 Clemens described the beginning of his family's warm friendship with Dr. John Brown:

> In 1873, when Susy was fourteen months old, we arrived in Edinburgh from London, fleeing thither for rest and refuge, after experiencing what had been to us an entirely new kind of life—six weeks of daily lunches, teas, and dinners away from home. . . . Straightway Mrs. Clemens needed a physician, and I stepped around to 23 Rutland Street to see if the author of "Rab and His Friends" was still a practising physician. He was. He came, and for six weeks thereafter we were together every day, either in his house or in our hotel. (AD, 2 Feb 1906, in *MTA*, 2:43–44)

Brown (1810–82), the son of a minister, was born in Biggar (Lanarkshire, Scotland), but educated in Edinburgh, where he became a practicing physician in 1833. He is best remembered as the author of essays and stories—collected in three volumes entitled *Horae Subsecivae* (1858, 1861, and 1882)—on topics ranging from medicine to human nature, the arts, and the scenery of his native country. In 1906 Clemens called his best-known dog story, "Rab and His Friends" (first published in 1858), a "pathetic and beautiful masterpiece," and remembered Brown's

> sweet and winning face—as beautiful a face as I have ever known. Reposeful, gentle, benignant—the face of a saint at peace with all the world and placidly beaming upon it the sunshine of love that filled his heart. Dr. John was beloved by everybody in Scotland; and I think that on its downward sweep southward it found no frontier. . . . We made the round of his professional visits with him in his carriage every day for six weeks. He always brought a basket of grapes, and we brought books. The scheme which we began with on the first round of visits was the one which was maintained until the end—and was based upon this remark, which he made when he was disembarking from the carriage at his first stopping place, to visit a patient: "Entertain yourselves while I go in here and reduce the population." (AD, 5 Feb 1906, in *MTA*, 2:44, 47–48)

Brown in turn developed a deep affection for the entire family, describing Olivia in a letter as "a quite lovely little woman, modest and clever," with "a girlie eighteen months old, her ludicrous miniature—and such eyes!" (*MTB*, 1:487). He soon became Susy's "worshiper and willing slave," happily romping and playing with her, and he nicknamed her "Megalopis" because her "large eyes seemed to him to warrant that sounding Greek epithet" (SLC 1876–85, 3†; AD, 2 Feb 1906 and 5 Feb 1906, CU-MARK, in *MTA*, 2:43, 45–46).

³Isabella Cranston Brown (1812–88), who had taken charge of the doctor's household in 1866 upon the marriage of his only daughter. Brown's wife had died in 1864 (M'Laren, 31, 60; John Brown, 135).

⁴Isabella Brown's fondly remembered trip through the picturesque Lake District of northwest England (not Scotland) probably took place in 1833: John Brown noted in an 1874 letter, "I walked from Edinburgh to Windermere and back in 1833, taking about a month to [do] it" (Brown to Susan Beever, 2 Apr 74, John Brown, 226–27). A family friend recalled the deep impression the experience had made:

> Her two brothers, John and William, and a companion of theirs, were with her. *They* walked, and she rode on a pony, lent her by a friend. . . . The weather was perfect.
> 'The gleam, the shadow, and the peace profound,'
> and all the loveliness sank into her heart, and dwelt there for evermore. When I went to the Lake District, though it must have been forty years after her visit, she wrote to me describing with perfect correctness every turn of the road, the position of the wooded crag, the little wayside inn, as if she had been there the week before. (M'Laren, 46–47)

⁵William Brown, also a physician, and his wife, Maggy, not further identified (John Brown, 38 n. 1, 139–40).

⁶Alexander Russel (1814–76) of Edinburgh, a friend of Brown's for at least twenty years, began his newspaper career as a printer, but soon began writing for *Tait's Magazine*. In 1839 he was appointed editor of the Berwick *Advertiser*, and three years later moved to the Cupar *Fife Herald*. He joined the staff of the Edinburgh *Scotsman* in 1845 and became its unofficial editor within a year, assuming the title formally in 1848. The *Scotsman* had been established in 1817 as a "sturdily independent newspaper," which "often angered the establishment" (Griffiths, 508). Since 1865 it had expanded its readership beyond Edinburgh by paying expensive rail costs for delivery, and by 1873 enjoyed a circulation of forty thousand. Russel's articles consistently and courageously defended liberal ideas and causes (Graham, 301–17; John Brown, 81; Griffiths, 499–500). Four years after his death a good friend recalled:

> The untiring vigour of his work, the clearness and pith of his style, his skill in political dialectics, his unsurpassed political knowledge, his remarkable powers of sarcasm, his rare sense of the ludicrous, his wit and mirthfulness, were familiar to all readers. The real generosity of his nature, the sterling honesty of purpose, the exquisite simplicity of character, the warm, genial, kindly, trustful nature, however, were known most to those who knew him best. (Graham, 316–17)

Russel "rejoiced in the presence of friends round his table"; he and his second wife, the former Mrs. Evans, also greatly enjoyed entertaining authors and other visitors of note (Graham, 314).

⁷Melrose, site of the late Gothic (ca. 1450) ruin of Melrose Abbey, was about thirty miles southeast of Edinburgh. Abbotsford, two miles above Melrose on the bank of the Tweed River, was the home of Sir Walter Scott from 1811 until his death in 1832. Several rooms in the picturesque mansion were open to public view, including the study and library (Baedeker 1901, 501). John Brown mentioned this visit in a letter to a friend:

There is a man here whom you would like in much, "Mark Twain"—Mr. Clemens; and he has a darling little wife, whom you had better not see, as it might disquiet your peace for life, not to speak of hers—such a startlingly pretty little creature, with eyes like a Peregrine's, and better than she looks. They were out seeing Russel and Abbotsford yesterday. (Brown to Alexander Nicolson, "*Sunday, August*" [10 Aug 73], John Brown, 224)

Olivia wrote her mother on 15 August that "last week" she and Clemens had visited Melrose and Abbotsford and "stopped with a Mr Russel editor of 'The Scotsman' and had a very pleasant time" (10–15 Aug 73, CtHMTH).

[8] See 6 July 73 to Fairbanks.

[9] Minnequa Springs, in Canton, Pennsylvania, was a summer resort known for its mineral waters (*L4*, 152 n. 1).

[10] Clemens evidently purchased two sets of this twelve-volume edition of Sir Walter Scott's thirty-two "Waverley" novels (Edinburgh: R. Cadell, 1842–47): one for his own library, and one as a gift for someone in the Langdon family. Charles and Ida Langdon's daughter donated the second set to the Mark Twain House in 1963 (Gribben, 2:618).

To Edmund H. Yates
4 August 1873 • Edinburgh, Scotland
(MS: CU-MARK)

Veitch's Hotel ⎫
Edinburgh, Monday. ⎬

My Dear Yates:[1]

I am sincerely grieved to see that the Herald people have added a paragraph to one of my letters which puts me in a bad light. They describe me & the London correspondents as cheering the Shah at Ostend & conducting ourselves in anything but a proper way. It was a careless thing in the Herald people to do, after the kindly & gentlemanly way in which those correspondents treated me on board the Lively.[2]

Whenever you meet one of those correspondents, I ~~would~~ wish you would do me the real kindness to explain this thing to him & say that I am as sincerely grieved about it as if I had done the deed myself. And in truth it has worried me more than I could tell in many pages of manuscript.

I don't think Hosmer could have done that. His ~~im~~ instincts would have been truer, I think.[3]

Ys Faithfully
Sam*ˡ*. L. Clemens.

¹See 17 or 18 June 73 to Young, n. 1. After seeing Clemens at Ostend in June, Yates had reported for the *Herald* on the shah's July visit to Paris, then made a quick trip to England: on 2 August he was in London. Shortly thereafter he returned to Vienna to report on the rewarding of prizes in the International Exhibition (Yates: 1885, 412; 1873, 10).

²The offensive remark was inserted into Clemens's first letter on the shah, which was published in the New York *Herald* on 1 July, but which he had only just seen in print (see 2 Aug 73 to Bliss [2nd]):

> The Shah walked back alongside his fine cabin, looking at the assemblage of silent, solemn Flounders; the correspondent of the London *Telegraph*, was hurrying along the pier and took off his hat and bowed to the "King of Kings," and the King of Kings gave a polite military salute in return. This was the commencement of the excitement. The success of the breathless *Telegraph* man made all the other London correspondents mad, every man of whom flourished his stovepipe recklessly and cheered lustily, some of the more enthusiastic varying the exercise by lowering their heads and elevating their coat-tails. Seeing all this, and feeling that if I was to "impress the Shah" at all, now was my time, I ventured a little squeaky yell, quite distinct from the other shouts, but just as hearty. His Shah ship heard and saw and saluted me in a manner that was, I considered, an acknowledgement of my superior importance. I do not know that I ever felt so ostentatious and absurd before. (SLC 1873n)

³George W. Hosmer (1830–1914), a practicing physician as well as a noted journalist, reported for the New York *Herald* during the Civil War and the Franco-Prussian War. As the London correspondent for the *Herald* he had supervised Clemens's assignment to report on the shah's visit (Joseph J. Mathews, 80; "Dr. George W. Hosmer Is Dead," New York *Times*, 14 June 1914, 11; see 2 Aug 73 to Bliss [2nd], n. 1).

❧

NO LETTERS written between 4 August and 10 September 1873 have been found. Several letters by Olivia, however, provide an outline of the Clemenses' movements during that time. On Friday, 15 August, she wrote her mother from Edinburgh, "We go next Monday up into the Trossacs for two days leaving Nellie and Susie here, then we expect to go to Glasgow on Thursday sailing for Belfast, Ireland, on Saturday then we shall get back to London in about two weeks—" (10–15 Aug 73, CtHMTH). The trip to the Trossachs, a "richly-wooded and romantic valley" east of Loch Katrine (about twenty miles north of Glasgow), was evidently abandoned, since Olivia wrote to Jane Clemens and Pamela Moffett, also on 15 August, "We are to be here until next week when we shall go to Glasgow for a day or two and then sail for Ireland where we shall be for about two weeks and then back to London—" (NPV; Baedeker 1901, 530). On 24 August Olivia wrote to Susan Crane: "We leave Edinburgh to-morrow with sincere regret; we have had such a delightful stay here—we do so regret leaving Dr. Brown and his sister, thinking that we shall probably never see them again" (*MTL*, 1:488). Her presentiment was correct: although the Clemenses corresponded affectionately with Brown, they never met him again.

After a brief stay in Glasgow, the Clemens party endured a rough ferry trip to Belfast on 28 August:

> We had a very disagreeable trip from Glasgow to Belfast, we were all except Mr Clemens wretchedly sick, Susie and all. I think we suffered more in that one day than in the ten days crossing the Atlantic.
>
> We reached Belfast about eight in the evening and before we had finished our supper a Mr Finlay son-in-law to the Mr Russel that we stoped with near Melrose called, he was a delightful man and did do everything he possibly could to make our stay in Belfast pleasant, his wife was absent from the city but we dined with him and through him were invited out to dinner twice beside to a most delightful house, an Irish gentlemans of great wealth and with a most charming home and delightful family— (OLC to Olivia Lewis Langdon, 31 Aug and 2 Sept 73, CtHMTH)

On 1 September the travelers proceeded to Dublin, where they stayed at the Shelbourne Hotel for several days (22 and 25 Sept 73 to Brown; London *Court Journal*, 6 Sept 73, 1055). From there they evidently traveled by ferry directly across the Irish Sea to Liverpool, and then south less than twenty miles to Chester, described in Baedeker's *Great Britain* as "perhaps the most quaint and mediæval-looking town in England" for a brief visit (Baedeker 1901, 284, 339; *MTB*, 1:488). From Chester they traveled another thirty-five miles further south to Shrewsbury, where they were the guests of Reginald Cholmondeley (1826–96) at nearby Condover Hall, a "fine Elizabethan house with characteristic gardens" (Murray, 374; see the next page) and by 9 September had returned to London. In chapter 15 of *Following the Equator* Clemens published an account of Cholmondeley's invitation (giving his name as "Bascom"):

> In 1873 I arrived in London with my wife and young child, and presently received a note from Naples signed by a name not familiar to me. . . . This note, of about six lines, was written on a strip of white paper whose end-edges were ragged. I came to be familiar with those strips in later years. Their size and pattern were always the same. Their contents were usually to the same effect: would I and mine come to the writer's country-place in England on such and such a date, by such and such a train, and stay twelve days and depart by such and such a train at the end of the specified time? A carriage would meet us at the station. . . .
>
> This first note invited us for a date three months in the future. It asked us

Condover Hall, Reginald Cholmondeley's Elizabethan mansion near Shrewsbury, England (Tipping, 166).

to arrive by the 4.10 p. m. train from London, August 6th. The carriage would be waiting. The carriage would take us away seven days later—train specified. And there were these words: "Speak to Tom Hughes."

I showed the note to the author of "Tom Brown at Rugby," and he said:— "Accept, and be thankful."

He described Mr. Bascom as being a man of genius, a man of fine attainments, a choice man in every way, a rare and beautiful character. He said that Bascom Hall [Condover] was a particularly fine example of the stately manorial mansion of Elizabeth's days, and that it was a house worth going a long way to see—like Knowle; that Mr. B. was of a social disposition, liked the company of agreeable people, and always had samples of the sort coming and going. (SLC 1897, 158–59)

Surviving letters, however, tell a different story. Clemens had evidently met Cholmondeley during his 1872 visit to England, since on 11 April 1873, before the Clemenses left for England, Cholmondeley wrote a letter offering them passage to Liverpool on his yacht in the first week in May, and reminding them, "I expect you all at Condover the first week in August" (CU-MARK). Cholmondeley renewed the invitation in a letter of 2 August (CU-MARK), which Clemens answered (in a letter now lost) from Edinburgh. On 6 August Cholmondeley wrote again, confirming their plan to arrive "at the end of August or beginning of September," and mentioning his intention to include Tom Hughes and his wife in the party (CU-MARK). Cholmondeley, a childless widower, was an alumnus of Trinity College, Cambridge, and an amateur naturalist. Many years later, after he had died impecunious, his niece described him as "sweet-tempered, genial, and of majestic appearance, but totally unaccustomed to small households and restricted means" (Cholmondeley, 23; Burke 1900, 292).

To William S. Andrews
10 September 1873 • London, England
(MS: VtMiM)

London, Sept. 10.

My Dear Andrews:

I am moving about all the time; I haven't the necessary documents

with me, & so I can't do [the] thing now, but I shall be back home plenty
time enough for you—so good-bye till then.[1]

Ys
Clemens

✉———————————————————————————————

W. S. Andrews Esq | Lotos Club | 2 Irving Place | New York [*in upper left
corner:*] America. | [*rule*] [*postmarked:*] LONDON · W 5 SP 11 73 [*and*] NEW
YORK SEP 22 PAID ALL

[1] This letter may be a response to a request from Andrews for help in preparing
for his upcoming appearance at Association Hall in New York City, on 24 November ("Amusements, etc., This Evening," New York *Tribune*, 24 Nov 73, 4).
Clemens planned to sail for home on 25 October.

To Thomas W. Knox
10 September 1873 • London, England
(MS: IGK)

The Langham Hotel
London, Sept. 10.

Dear Knox:[1]

God bless your heart, I have a wife with me; & a baby; & a nurse;
I have been here 4 months; I have already spent ten thousand dollars—
& the end is not yet! Is it to such a man that you blandly recommend
Vienna?[2] Shall I spend my remaining two months over there in that expensive Empire & return to my home an imposing pecuniary ruin? But
I know you will excuse me. No, Knox, I shall stay right here in this hos-
telry till Oct 24.

Oh, no, my hands are full. We are building a house in America, &
London is a good enough place to buy little odds & ends in for it, & so I
have sent for more money & am going to continue to collect the odds &
ends calmly & with courage.

Many thanks for the speech.[3] It is a mighty good one. The unl underlined remarks were some which I was about to make, once, but was interrupted.

I would like to write something for that Lotos book, but I can't do it, because I am just as busy as I can be, on work that *must* be done & cannot be avoided by any subterfuge. Therefore she must go to press without me.[4]

Come, now, when shall we see you here?

Truly Yrs

Sam*'*. L. Clemens

[1] Thomas W. Knox (1835–96)—a traveler, journalist, and author—was born in New Hampshire. He first worked as a teacher, but in 1860, after gold was discovered in Colorado, he went to Denver, where he worked on the *News*. He served as a volunteer aide during the Civil War, and also corresponded for the New York *Herald*. In 1866 he traveled five thousand miles by sledge and wagon across Siberia, in the employ of the *Herald*, with an American company that was establishing a telegraph line on behalf of the Russian government. His *Herald* letters formed the basis of his book *Overland through Asia* (1870), published by the American Publishing Company. In later years he produced nearly forty travel books for boys, as well as several biographies.

[2] Knox's letter is not known to survive.

[3] Unidentified.

[4] Knox, a director of the Lotos Club, had evidently asked Clemens to write something for an anthology entitled *Lotos Leaves*, currently being prepared by club members John Brougham and John Elderkin. In spite of Clemens's refusal here, he ultimately contributed "An Encounter with an Interviewer" to the volume, which issued in November 1874 and included articles by Knox and Andrews as well (see the previous letter; Elderkin, 23; Brougham and Elderkin, 27–32, 103–9, 263–75).

To Henry Lee
10 September 1873 • London, England
(MS: ViU)

Langham Hotel
Sep. 10.

Dear Lee—
We called yesterday in full force. What hour may we come
again tomorrow & get you to go with us to a fur establishment?[1]
Yrs
S.L. Clemens.

POST CARD

THE ADDRESS ONLY TO BE WRITTEN ON THIS SIDE.

TO

Henry Lee Esq
43 Holland street
Blackfriars Road,
S. E.

[*postmarked:*] LONDON · W. 3 SP 10 73 5

[1] Lee was in business as a "skinner, furrier & beaver cutter" (*London Directory*, 1053).

To Orion and Mary E. (Mollie) Clemens
12? September 1873 • London, England
(MS, *damage emended:* NPV)

[*one-fourth of MS page (between 6 and 20 words) missing*][1]

We got ma's & Pamela's seal-skin coats yesterday—£19 apiece—considerably more than double what they would have cost 2 years ago. I ordered a sealskin overcoat for Charley Langdon—price £50, which is just what mine cost me in Buffalo[2]—I suppose it would cost $500 there now. We also got ˄sealskin˄ muffs for ma & Pamela yesterday—24 shillings

[*one-fourth of MS page (about 20 words) missing*]

wholesale house, through an old friend of mine,[3] we saved about fifteen ~~dollars~~ or twenty dollars on each.

Livy & the baby are well. Indeed, the baby seems to have unfailing, robust health. She is on her feet all her waking hours, and always busy—generally in matters that would fare better without her help. She says a few trifling words in broken English.

Ys affly
Saml.

[1]The surviving text of this letter is on a single sheet (written on both sides), from which the top quarter has been torn away, presumably by some member of the family. It survives among the letters and documents now at Vassar which originally belonged to Pamela Moffett. If the original letter comprised only this sheet, then only the dateline and salutation (perhaps six words) are missing from the first side, and about twenty words from the second. The first five words have been supplied by emendation; only the bottoms of the original characters in the manuscript are still visible (see the textual commentary).

[2]As this letter indicates, Clemens had purchased his own sealskin coat in September 1871 ("2 years ago"). He was reported wearing it later that year, during his lecture tour (see *L4*, 518–19).

[3]Henry Lee (see the previous letter). The date of the present letter is based on the assumption that Lee responded positively and promptly to Clemens's request.

To John Brown
22 and 25 September 1873 • London, England
(MS: Sachs)

The Langham Hotel
Monday.

Dear Doctor & Dear Friend:

Of all the multitude of pretty things we have gathered together in these past few months for the adornment of our new home, these lovely pictures are the loveliest. Mrs Clemens is carried away with ~~em~~ enthusiasm over them, & I am sure I am too.[1] One can not even vaguely imagine the pleasure they are going to give, to in the years that are to come, to multitudes of people whom we do not even know yet. We do thank you the very best we know how—& that is still better than we can put in words. I am very glad—I am grateful—to know that I reached so high a place with you—& all the more so because we hold you in such love & reverence. Livy, my wife, has never conceived so strong & so warm an affection for any one since we were married as she has for you—& I take as much delight in her daily references to you, affectionate as they are, as if they were love-offerings to me. You were very kind to us in Edinburgh, Doctor, & I wish we could have you with us on the other side of the water so that we could show you how entirely we appreciated it.

Thursday.—The financial panic in America has absorbed about all my attention & anxiety since Monday evening when I laid down this pen.[2] However, I feel relieved, now—of £600 sterling, ~~& so~~—& so am able to take up my letter again & go on & finish it.[3] You ~~ask where you~~ ask how long we stay, ~~s~~ & where to write us?[4] Till Oct. 24 your letters will find us here at the Langham Hotel (we sail Oct 25)[5] & the more that come seeking us the better ~~wil~~ we shall like it. No, we didn't see St Mary's Church in Shrewsbury—we didn't have time there; but we heard enough about it to wish we *had* had.[6] I will be very glad & very willing, doctor, to take charge of the "collie," & will take every care of her. I have a good general idea of how to do it, because for a good while, in Esmeralda, a little mining camp far down in California, my neighbor in the next cabin kept them, professionally, & I have often followed them about with him, ~~for re~~ & given him a helping hand with a riat*l*a now & then when necessity demanded. He had one that used to come at his call & eat from his hand; but she finally fell down the well, in the night, & ~~kno~~ nobody knowing it she was not found until morning, & then her weight was such that she could not be got out. My mother had a favorite one that kicked the breath out of me once, but she gave very good milk. I will take charge of yours with a great deal of pleasure, Doctor, & I think a collie on shipboard would be a real treat; ~~but you~~ because one never gets cream there; but you seem to think they will let her go in the first cabin— which they won't by considerable; & that the baby can go around pulling & hauling at her tail—which Mrs. Clemens would never allow, I know perfectly well. But it ain't any difference—I will look after her myself; & if the collie has got a calf, send the calf along too. There is nothing I like better than a calf, on shipboard⁷

I sent to Dublin & got your letter from the Shelbourne Hotel— which reminds me that I forgot to go & see Swift's tomb—but I read Gulliver all over again at Condover (*first* edition)—which is perhaps as well. Still I am sorry I forgot to see the grave.⁸

Miss Clara says that though her voice was not heard much, she was ~~k~~ doing a world of affectionate thinking—& you were the object of it. I am sure she never says such pleasant things about me; & ~~yet I have known~~ yet she has known me for years. However, that may be the reason.

Yrs Affectionately

Sam'. L. Clemens

¹Two of these photographs, taken at the studio of John Moffat in Edinburgh, and sent by Brown in care of Routledge and Sons in London (see note 4), are known to survive. They are reproduced in Appendix F. One of them, a shot of the Clemens party together with Brown, shows Clara Spaulding holding Susy Clemens in her lap, and the other is of Susy alone. In 1882, after the doctor's death, Clemens wrote to his son, "Can you spare us a photograph of your father? We have none but the one taken in group with ourselves" (1 June 82 to John [Jock] Brown, UkENL†).

²On 18 September the failure of Jay Cooke and Company, a New York banking house that had helped finance the building of the Northern Pacific Railroad, precipitated a financial panic that spread through the entire banking system of the country, paralyzing monetary circulation. The value of securities and stocks plummeted, and foreign exchange was temporarily suspended. "It was generally regarded as the immediate cause of the crisis, that the money market had become overloaded with debt"—debt largely resulting from the stocks and bonds issued to pay for railroad construction (*Annual Cyclopaedia 1873*, 279, 285). The worst of the panic was over within a few weeks, during which New York banks paid each other with loan certificates. By January 1874 the U.S. Treasury had further

eased the crisis by restoring to circulation $26 million in retired greenbacks. During the six-year depression that followed, however, thousands of businesses failed and unemployment soared (Unger, 213–26).

[3] Six hundred pounds sterling were equivalent to about three thousand dollars. Clemens's New York bank, Henry Clews and Company, had been forced to suspend payments to depositors on 23 September after paying out "over a million and a quarter of dollars in cash" over the previous four days ("The Financial Crisis," New York *Times*, 24 Sept 73, 1; "The American Commercial Crisis," London *Times*, 25 Sept 73, 5). The Clemenses learned of the suspension on the evening of 24 September: see Olivia's letter to her mother about the crisis (25 or 26 Sept 73 to Lee, n. 1). On 4 October Clews announced that "as soon as the market grows more favorable for the negotiation of securities he will be able to tend to the demands of all his depositors," and by early January the company was able to resume business "with the ability to pay all obligations in full" (New York *Times:* "Affairs in Wall Street," 5 Oct 73, 1; "Local Miscellany," 6 Jan 74, 8). Nevertheless, Clemens persisted in believing that Clews had cheated him, as he wrote to Charles L. Webster on 17 November 1886: "He choused me out of a good deal of money, 13 years ago as coolly as ever any other crime was committed in this world" (NPV, in *MTLP*, 208–9).

[4] Since beginning this letter on 22 September, Clemens had received the following note from Brown, also written on 22 September:

> My dear friend— Thanks for yours. By this time you will have got my letter & I hope the photos—do you remain some time in London? let me know where it is safest to write to you. I am glad you saw something of life in Salop—did you see St Mary's Church in Shrewsbury? When are you thinking of crossing the sea? if I were 40 & not broken hearted, I would come with you. I may perhaps ask you to take some charge of a *Collie* which I hope to send to Professor Forsyth at West Point Academy. Baby will pull its ears & poke her fingers into its eyes, to pass the time on deck— I am glad you have so much good to tell of her & her Mother & the lealhearted Miss Spaulding—you will tell me if you got my Shelbourne letter. Isabella & "Jock" send their best regards
>
> Yrs. (all) affectly
>
> J. Brown

I sent my letter & the Photos to the Care of Routledge & Sons (CU-MARK)

John Forsyth (1810–86), a scholar and clergyman of Scottish ancestry, had been a chaplain and professor of geography, history, and ethics at West Point since 1871. He may have become acquainted with Brown while studying theology in Edinburgh in the early 1830s. Brown and his sister Isabella also made a home for Brown's son, John, known as "Jock" (John Brown, 135; John [Jock] Brown to SLC, 8 Mar 1906, CU-MARK). An envelope addressed by Brown to Clemens in care of the Routledges and postmarked 20 September survives in the Mark Twain Papers. It now contains only a sentimental poem, possibly by Brown himself, about a couple recalling their dead baby daughter, which is printed on a folder of stationery imprinted with his letterhead. This envelope may have contained a letter, now lost, but is almost certainly too small to have enclosed any photographs.

[5] The Clemenses had decided by 2 September to return home on 25 October, but in fact left four days earlier. Although Clemens's announced objective—to secure a British copyright on *The Gilded Age*—had thus far been thwarted by delays in the typesetting of the American edition, Olivia was growing homesick (OLC to Olivia Lewis Langdon, 31 Aug and 2 Sept 73, CtHMTH).

⁶The Clemenses had been guests at Condover Hall near Shrewsbury in early September. St. Mary's Church, in the center of the town, exhibits several architectural styles, "ranging from Norman to late-Perpendicular" (early sixteenth century), and contains "fine stained glass" (Baedeker 1901, 276).

⁷Brown responded to Clemens's teasing on 6 October:

> That *was* a joke about the Colly! you are an Innocent still. I have heard nothing of the doggie—& if it goes in the same vessel with you you must take no trouble with it—only let Susie just keep it in society by poking her forefinger into its eye. I have got the £5 for it from the good Professor. (CU-MARK)

⁸Clemens had read *Gulliver's Travels* as recently as 1869 (*L3*, 132). The first edition was published in 1726 by Benjamin Motte. Swift, who died in 1745, was buried in St. Patrick's Cathedral, of which he had been appointed dean in 1713.

To Shirley Brooks
23 September 1873 • London, England
(MS: NNPM)

                                          The Langham Hotel
                                          Sept. 23.

Dear Sir:

May I send you a brief article for acceptance or rejection?

                                          Ys Truly
                                          Samᶫ. L. Clemens
                                          (".Mark Twain")

To the Editor of Punch.¹

¹Charles William Shirley Brooks (1816–74) began his association with the illustrated comic weekly *Punch, or the London Charivari*, in 1851, and became its editor in 1870. He was trained in the law, and began his journalism career as the parliamentary reporter for the London *Morning Chronicle*. He contributed numerous articles and stories to the best periodicals, and wrote dramatic and comic works for the stage as well. Brooks's response to this letter has not been found, nor did any article by Clemens appear in *Punch*. It is possible, however, that an unpublished comic sketch about the Doré Gallery, which survives in the Mark Twain Papers, was the "brief article" that he wanted to submit. This piece, written in the form of a letter to an unidentified "Sir" and subscribed "London, September," mocks the importunate efforts of gallery employees to sell engravings to visitors (SLC 1873u†). It includes, in a humorous context, a description of Gustave Doré's *Christ Leaving the Praetorium*, an immense painting that Clemens praised in his English journal after first viewing it in 1872 (see Appendix C).

To Henry Lee
25 or 26 September 1873 • London, England
(MS: CLjC)

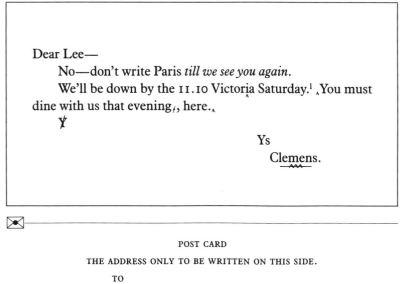

Dear Lee—
No—don't write Paris *till we see you again.*
We'll be down by the 11.10 Victoria Saturday.[1] ₐYou must
dine with us that evening,, here.ₐ
ɤ

                         Ys
                         Clemens.

✉

POST CARD

THE ADDRESS ONLY TO BE WRITTEN ON THIS SIDE.

TO

Henry Lee Esq
43 Holland street
Blackfriars Road, E.C.

[*postmarked:*] LONDON-W 7 SP26 73

[1] Before their bank suspended payment, the Clemenses had planned a trip to
Paris with Lee; they now wanted to assess their finances before deciding whether
to go (22 and 25 Sept 73 to Brown, nn. 2, 3). They had also accepted Lee's invitation for an excursion to the Brighton aquarium on Saturday, 27 September.
This was Olivia's second, and Clemens's third, tour of the aquarium as Lee's
guests (12 and 13 June 73 to Lee, n. 3). Olivia wrote her mother on 25
September:

> Last night when we returned from the theater we had a notification that our bank-
> ers had suspended payment— After we went to bed Mr Clemens could not sleep, he
> had to return to the parlor and smoke and try to get sleepy— He said the reason that he
> could not sleep was that he kept thinking how stupid he had been not to draw out our
> money after he heard that J. Cook & Co. had failed, said he kept thinking what the
> "boys" (meaning Mr Slee, Theodore, & Charlie) were saying at home—"Well it is 24
> hours since J. Cook suspended and Clemens will have drawn his money out of the
> bank—now it is 48 hours since J. Cook failed and of course Clemens is all safe, he will

have his money drawn out &c &c" I told him I thought he was mistaken I thought the people at home would feel certain that he had taken no steps in the matter, he laughed and thought I was in the right of it— We fortunately have by us the £200 that Charlie sent for you and £43 that Pamela sent—but we owe several quite heavy bills and shall have to have more money from home unless Clews & Co resume payment in a few days. Mr Clemens is inclined to think they will— If they do not you will probably get a dispatch from us before this reaches you— . . .

We do wish that we knew how you are all feeling at home financially, it seems as if this *terrible* panic must effect all business men. You know if the firm is cramped Mr Clemens can lecture and get money to pay our debts and get us home— Now Mother don't you and Charlie laugh at that, lecturing is what Mr C. always speaks of doing when their seems any need of money— Just think here we are among friends who would quickly lend us money if we needed it, think how many are seriously inconvenienced on this side now by this trouble.

The "boys"—partners in J. Langdon and Company—were John D. F. Slee, Theodore Crane, and Charles Langdon. Olivia continued her letter on Sunday, 28 September:

Yesterday we went to the Brighton Aquarium, that is a perfectly wonderful place I did enjoy it so very much, it was like an enchanted land—

Mr Clemens has one of his severe colds in the head, so is not feeling well— Susie is very well dear little trot   She tries to say aunt Clara—calls it "An Taal"—

On Tuesday of this week we go to Paris with Mr Lee. Mr Clemens wrote him after the loss of the money to wait, not to make the arrangements about Paris until he saw us again, but Mr Lee did not get the word and the arrangements were all made— I think probably it will not make any great difference. I am so very anxious to get word from home about financial affairs. Mr Clemens thinks perhaps it is best for us to borrow money from the Routledges— (25 and 28 Sept 73, CtHMTH)

To Louisa P. MacDonald
29 September 1873 • (1st of 2) • London, England
(MS: ViU)

Dear Mrs MacDonald,
    ~~Ou~~ We concluded to take a drive for an hour with the baby—that is how we came to be here after saying we couldn't come.[1]
                                                                          Ys Truly
                                                                  The Clemens family

[1] Clemens wrote this note on the front and back of his calling card, as he had done on 17 May, with his letter to Warner (reproduced in Appendix F). Louisa MacDonald (1822–1902), the former Louisa Powell, had married George in 1851. Although her time was largely occupied with rearing her eleven children (see the next letter), in 1870 she published *Chamber Dramas for Children*, a collection of pieces she had adapted for family theatrical performances. Since 1867

the MacDonalds had lived in the Retreat, in Hammersmith (the westernmost of London's inner boroughs), a large late-Georgian house with a long drawing-room facing the river and an orchard and vegetable gardens in the rear. Neither the invitation to the Retreat which Clemens alluded to, nor his response to it, is known to survive. Louisa MacDonald replied to the present note immediately, however, proposing an alternative:

> My dear Mrs Clemmans
>   I am so sorry we cannot have the pleasure of seeing you today—as we shall be going to Hastings on Tuesday, but as you are going to Paris we do not lose you that way only but I write now to beg you to come to us at Hastings on your way back just for a day or two— You could so easily come from Dover to Hastings it isn't much round to come that way back to London, and we could give you two rooms one for your nurse & a lot of young misses will be delighted to have a visit from that lovely little *Princess* that we saw just once—only once! we must see her again— Telegraph from Dover when you come & we will be in readiness for you— I know you'd like Hastings. (29 Sept 73, CU-MARK)

Since 1871 the MacDonalds had leased Halloway House, a brick house on Old London Road in Hastings, as a second home (MacDonald, 101, 561; Weinreb and Hibbert, 353; Raeper, 234–35, 270–71, 333, 335).

To Louisa P. MacDonald
29 September 1873 • (2nd of 2) • London, England
(MS: CtY-BR)

The Langham Hotel
Monday P.M¹

Dear Mrs MacDonald:
     Indeed we would be glad enough to ⸜ tarry a day or two with you in Hastings on our way back, but unfortunately we shall not be able to do it, for the reason that partly by gentle persuasion & partly by brute force I have prevailed upon Mrs. Clemens to leave the baby in London with Miss Spaulding & the nursemaid⸝ while we are away; & I know she will be frantic to see the child even before we are done with Paris. She says that if she thought she would not have another opportunity of seeing you, she believes she would return by Hastings; but I know her better than she knows herself, & so I know she ~~had~~ will find the separation ⸜ that is already provided for her all that she can endure. But I do hope we shall see you all again before we sail (Oct. ~~24~~ 25.) With our affectionate regards—

The Clemenses.

P. S. We sent the nursemaid off on a holiday to-day, & then we concluded to drive the baby out for an airing—& the drive ended at the Retreat, Hammersmith, & we just barely missed you both, & were so disappointed! And out of eleven children we couldn't scare up even one.[2] It was a great disappointment, but it was our own fault: we ought to have known we could go there.[3]

[1] Since mail was delivered in London several times a day, Clemens was able to respond to MacDonald's invitation on the same day she wrote it (see the previous letter, n. 1).

[2] The MacDonalds had five girls and six boys, born between 1852 and 1867 (MacDonald, 159, 187, 215–16, 255, 281, 296, 313, 345, 353, 379).

[3] That is, they ought to have accepted the MacDonalds' invitation to the Retreat.

🍃

NO LETTERS written between 29 September and 7 October 1873 have been found. On 30 September the Clemenses went to Paris with Henry Lee, and returned to London by 7 October, the date of the next letter, but nothing further is known about their trip. Clemens had by now agreed to lecture in London, and was scheduled to begin on 13 October. His appearances were arranged by George Dolby, who had tried unsuccessfully to persuade him to lecture during his 1872 visit (15 Sept 72 to OLC). According to Thompson, Dolby approached Clemens again, soon after his return to England in 1873, and said:

> "We want you to lecture[.] There is only one drawback. You've plenty of money and your wife is rich and you don't want to lecture." "I guess that's about the fact," said Clemens. "But," said Dolby "Just now you are the most widely read author in England, and people are eager to see you." Clemens wanted to lecture then and on the Sandwich Islands; because he had recently delivered it in New York, and it was fresh in mind and easier. He told me he wanted to get it over with the blessing and condemnation of it. But he consented to wait the Fall season. (Thompson, 86)

Dolby booked six London performances of Clemens's Sandwich Islands talk, the last on 18 October, and a final performance in Liverpool, on 20 October. He took charge of publicizing them, inserting the following advertisement in at least three newspapers:

> MARK TWAIN.—Mr. GEORGE DOLBY begs to announce that Mr. MARK TWAIN (the American Humorist) will DELIVER a LECTURE,

QUEEN'S CONCERT ROOMS,

HANOVER SQUARE.

Mr. GEORGE DOLBY begs to announce that

MR. MARK TWAIN

WILL DELIVER A

LECTURE

OF A

HUMOROUS CHARACTER,

AS ABOVE, ON

MONDAY EVENING NEXT, OCTOBER 13th, 1873,

AND REPEAT IT IN THE SAME PLACE, ON

TUESDAY EVENING, OCTOBER 14th,
WEDNESDAY ,, ,, 15th,
THURSDAY ,, ,, 16th,
FRIDAY ,, ,, 17th,

At Eight o'Clock,

AND

SATURDAY AFTERNOON, OCTOBER 18th,

At Three o'Clock.

SUBJECT :

"Our Fellow Savages of the Sandwich Islands."

As Mr. TWAIN has spent several months in these Islands, and is well acquainted with his subject, the Lecture may be expected to furnish matter of interest.

STALLS, 5s.   **UNRESERVED SEATS, 3s.**

Tickets may be obtained of CHAPPELL & Co. 50, New Bond Street; MITCHELL, 33, Old Bond Street; KEITH, PROWSE, & Co. 48, Cheapside; A. HAYS, Royal Exchange Buildings; Mr. GEORGE DOLBY, 52, New Bond Street; Mr. HALL, at the Hanover Square Rooms; and at Austin's Ticket Office, St. James's Hall, Piccadilly.

Broadside announcement of Clemens's first lecture series in London. Mark Twain Papers, The Bancroft Library (CU-MARK).

of a humorous character, at the Hanover-square Rooms, on MONDAY EVE-
NING next, the 13th inst., and repeat it in the same place on Tuesday,
Wednesday, Thursday, and Friday Evenings, at eight o'clock, and Saturday
Afternoon, at three o'clock, of the same week. Subject: "Our Fellow Savages
of the Sandwich Islands." As Mr. Twain has spent several months in these
islands, and is well acquainted with his subject, the lecture may be expected
to furnish matter of interest. (London *Morning Post*, 9 Oct 73, 1; also in London *Graphic* 335 [11 Oct 73]: 1; and London *Daily News*, 13 Oct 73, 4)

Dolby also arranged to have a broadside announcement printed (see the
previous page). And the 18 October issue of *Punch* (available by 15 October) published a comic quatrain in praise of Clemens, entitled "Welcome to a Lecturer" (*Punch* 65:154):

> " 'TIS time we Twain did show ourselves." 'Twas said
> By CÆSAR, when one MARK had lost his head:
> By MARK, whose head's quite bright, 'tis said again;
> Therefore, "go with me, friends, to bless this TWAIN."
>   PUNCH.

(See the enclosure with 13 and 15 Dec 73 to OLC.) To further spread the
word to his potential audience, Clemens wrote the following letter, addressed to the "Editor of the Standard" but clearly intended as a public
communication.

🌰

To the Editor of the London *Standard*
7 October 1873 • London, England
(London *Standard*, 9 Oct 73, and *MTB*, 1:490)

TO THE EDITOR OF THE STANDARD.

SIR,[1]—In view of the prevailing frenzy concerning the Sandwich
Islands, & the inflamed desire of the public to acquire information concerning them,[2] I have thought it well to tarry yet another week in England & deliver a lecture upon this absorbing subject. And lest it should
be thought unbecoming in me, a stranger, to come to the public rescue
at such a time, instead of leaving to abler hands a matter of so much
moment, I desire to explain that I do it with the best motives & the most
honorable intentions. I do it because I am convinced that no one can allay
this unwholesome excitement as effectually as I can, & to allay it, & allay

it as quickly as possible, is surely the one thing that is absolutely necessary at this juncture. I feel & know that I am equal to this task, for I can
allay any kind of an excitement by lecturing upon it. I have saved many
communities in this way. I have always been able to paralyze the public
interest in any topic that I chose to take hold of & elucidate with all my
strength.

Hoping that this explanation will show that if I am seeming to intrude I am at least doing it from a high impulse, I am, sir, your obedient
servant,

London. Oct. 7,   MARK TWAIN.

[1] The editor of the *Standard* was James Johnstone, Jr., the proprietor's son (see
5 Nov 73 to Bliss, n. 6); he was assisted by John Eldon Gorst (1835–1916), a
former Conservative member of Parliament—and, according to one of his colleagues, "a 'pig-headed' Tory" (Griffiths, 269, 627). No evidence has been found
that Clemens sent duplicate letters to other newspapers. On 11 October, however, a brief paraphrase of the letter appeared in the London *Court Journal*
("Metropolitan On Dits," 1194), which probably copied the text from the
Standard.

[2] William Lunalilo, king of the Sandwich Islands since January 1873, was
dying of tuberculosis, and had not chosen a successor (see 3 Jan 73 to Reid [2nd],
n. 1). Two brief notices had appeared in the London *Times*, on 25 September
and 2 October, announcing his illness and "expected death" ("The Sandwich
Islands," 5; Kuykendall and Gregory, 236).

To Henry Lee
7 October 1873 • London, England
(MS: CU-MARK)

Tuesday Night

Dear Lee—

I begin Monday at Hanover Square Rooms[1] & lecture every night
during the week. Talk it up with your friends! Come & see me when you
get a chance. We send warm regards.

Yrs
Mark.

[1] This concert hall, opened in 1774, was an elegant establishment famous for
its concerts, at which luminaries such as Haydn, Liszt, and Paganini had per-

formed. Its "ceiling was domed and the walls were decorated with paintings by West, Cipriani, Gainsborough and others" (Weinreb and Hibbert, 362–63). The building was demolished in 1900.

To Henry Lee
8? October 1873 • (1st of 3) • London, England
(Paraphrase: Rains Galleries, lot 109)

AUTOGRAPH POST CARD from Mark Twain, signed "Clemens" to Henry Lee, about tickets, and an invitation to dinner.[1]

[1] This brief paraphrase has been dated 8? October on the assumption that Lee responded immediately to the previous letter, requesting tickets to the upcoming Sandwich Islands lecture and inviting Clemens to dinner on Friday, 10 October (see the next two letters).

To Henry Lee
8 October 1873 • (2nd of 3) • London, England
(MS: MoSW)

Wednesday.[1]

Dear Lee—

Am writing to Dolby to send you the tickets.

I engage to dine Friday at 6 (I believe that is the hour) & if I fail to come you will know that it was *impossible* to come. Will you please drop me a line on *Friday* reminding me, for I have a whole world of things to think about now. We all send love.

Ys

Mark

⊠————————————————————————————————

Henry Lee Esq | 43 Holland street | Blackfriars Road, | S. E. [*postmarked:*] LONDON-W 7 OC 9 73 [*and*] LONDON-SE A O OC 9 73

[1] The date of this letter is established by the postmark on its envelope—9 October, a Thursday.

To Henry Lee
8 October 1873 • (3rd of 3) • London, England
(MS: ViU)

Wednesday.

P. S. I have ordered the 2 seats for 6 lectures, but you speak as if *you* meant to come 6 times! Bless your heart it is the same lecture *repeated word for word 6 times.* I thought I ought in simple kindness to tell you.[1]

Ys

Mark.

[1] This postscript, clearly an addendum to the previous letter to Lee, was probably mailed in a separate envelope. Clemens wrote it on a new sheet of paper, in spite of the fact that he had inscribed the earlier letter on the first page of a four-page folder, leaving three blank pages available for a postscript.

To Unidentified
11 October 1873 • London, England
(MS: CtHMTH)

Langham Hotel
London, 11th

Dear Sir:

I thank you very much for your kind invitation, but am engaged to lecture every night next week at Hanover Su Square Rooms, & leave for America *via* Liverpool on Sunday.[1]

Ys Truly
Sam*. L. Clemens.

[*letter docketed:*] Mark Twain. [*and*] Clemens | (Mark Twain).

[1] The Clemenses were scheduled to leave London on Sunday, 19 October, for Liverpool, where Clemens was to lecture the following evening. They sailed for

America on Tuesday, 21 October, on the *Batavia*, again commanded by their friend John Mouland ("Latest Ship News," New York *Tribune*, 3 Nov 73, 5).

To Olivia Lewis Langdon
12 October 1873 • London, England
(MS: CtHMTH)

. . . .

No indeedy, mother dear, let's not stop at the St. Nicholas if the new hotel is better—however, it don't matter—suit yourselves about that.[1]

I am lazying, to-day, in order to be rested for my first lecture tomorrow night,[2] so I won't write any more except to say that we love you & are ever so anxious to see you all.

Yr aff son
Sam[l]

[1] This fragment was written on one side of a single leaf; the number of pages now missing is unknown. Mrs. Langdon and her son, Charles, were planning to meet the Clemenses in New York upon their arrival, and stay at least one night in the city with them. The "new hotel" was almost certainly the Windsor on Fifth Avenue, completed in early September at a cost of over one million dollars. It occupied the entire block from Forty-sixth to Forty-seventh Street, and was an elegant and dignified hotel "far removed from the bustling business centres" ("A New Hotel," New York *Times*, 13 Aug 73, 2; OLC to Olivia Lewis Langdon, 31 Aug and 2 Sept 73, CtHMTH; OC to MEC, 3 Nov 73, CU-MARK). No record of the Langdons or the Clemenses has been found among the New York hotel arrivals for late October through early November.

[2] The date of this letter, written on the back in an unknown hand, is confirmed by Clemens's reference here to his first lecture, on 13 October. His lecture appearances on 13 through 18 October were very well received by audiences and critics alike. In a letter from London to the San Francisco *Chronicle*, Charles Warren Stoddard explained that Clemens

> had but three days to acquaint the public with the fact that he would lecture, and for one week only. Nobody expected him to draw an audience unless he could be advertised at least three months in advance. He drew. He drew better every night. The week's business was something astonishing. In this same hall Dickens used to read, and when Mark took it people were turned from the door on the last nights of his first week. (Stoddard 1874d)

The London correspondent for the Buffalo *Commercial* summed up for his readers:

> Mark Twain's success as a lecturer has been distinct and perfect. The general opinion is that he is not so essentially original a humorist as Art[e]mus Ward, but there are compensating qualities in his fun which render him as a whole as successful a "show"—he will pardon the expression—as was the poor fellow who came over here to make us laugh while he was coughing his way to an early grave. (Reprinted in the Elmira *Advertiser*, 7 Nov 73, 3)

On the morning after Clemens's first appearance, the London *Daily News* called his lecture "an odd and amusing mixture of solid fact and humorous extravagance," and concluded:

> Mr. Twain is a comparatively young man, small in form and feature, dark-haired and dark complexioned. He has a good deal of the nasal tone of some portion of the Americans. He possesses all that *insouciance* and *aplomb* which is generally ascribed to American lecturers, and apparently came upon the stage assured of the success which he so speedily obtained. (14 Oct 73, 2, clipping in Scrapbook 12:9, CU-MARK)

Clemens's friend George H. Fitzgibbon, the London correspondent for the Darlington *Northern Echo*, telegraphed his newspaper:

> Anything more thoroughly original and enjoyable than Mark Twain's lecture on our fellow savages of Sandwich Island has never been presented to the London public. If ever an entertainment had to be personally witnessed, to be fully enjoyed, it is Mark Twain's lecturing. No amount of verbatim reporting or glowing description could give you a fair idea of the charmingly novel mannerism and marvellously happy story-telling ability of this singularly eccentric American genius. . . . Judging by the attendance, applause, and laughter, the lecture was a great success. (Fitzgibbon 1873c)

The London *Graphic* noted that the

> description[s] of the manners and customs of the natives were interspersed with various witticisms, which were heartily appreciated and loudly applauded. Mr. Twain evidently has "the art of putting things." The lecture, which lasted rather more than an hour, . . . was listened to throughout with great interest. (18 Oct 73, 375)

And the London *Examiner* reported:

> This week we have had in Mark Twain (Mr S. L. Clemens) a genuine specimen of the American humorous lecturer. Although some of the more essentially American allusions were barely appreciated by an English audience, Mark Twain's dry manner, his admirable self-possession, and perfectly grave countenance formed a background that made the humorous portion of the lecture irresistible. Once or twice in the course of the evening the lecturer, partly on his credit as a man of humour and partly on the expectation that each sentence would prove to contain an artfully-hidden joke, was watched and listened to with almost breathless attention whilst he indulged in some rather bombastic prose-poetry descriptions of life in the islands that formed the subject of his lecture; and it was one of his boldest strokes to conclude, not with a quaint anecdote, but with one of those flowery performances that had been listened to in this way, and to make his exit in the most complete silence. (18 Oct 73, 10)

Favorable reviews also appeared in the London *Morning Post*, *Times*, *Evening Echo*, *Standard*, and *Sportsman*, as well as in several weeklies—the *Observer*, *Cosmopolitan*, *Spectator*, and *Saturday Review*, among others (Scrapbook 12:1, 7, 11, 13, 15, 19, 23, 25, 27, CU-MARK). Although Clemens was extremely gratified by his enthusiastic reception, he was probably not flattered by the remarks of a supercilious writer for the London *Daily News*, who called him "a leading professor" of "that school of jesting" that included humorists such as Artemus Ward, Petroleum V. Nasby, and Josh Billings:

> Fresh, original, and amusing this new kind of humor is; at its best, it is irresistible; even at its worst, it is popular. Its success here, as well as across the ocean, is beyond dispute. But we doubt whether it is destined to amuse the world for long; or whether anything more than ashes will be felt when its fire goes out.

This critic considered Bret Harte, however, to be "a true poet, . . . the discoverer of a new world for literature," and was also full of praise for James Russell Lowell, who

> belongs decidedly to the brotherhood of the great humourists whose works are among the ornaments of literature and the reforming agencies of society. He is of kin to the genuine poets who were satirists as well; his humour is always refined by high culture, intensified by its tinge of pathos, and strengthened by manly purpose. (17 Oct 73, 5, clipping in Scrapbook 12:3, 5, CU-MARK)

To George Bentley
13 October 1873 • London, England
(MS: ViU)

Langham Hotel Oct. 13.

My Dear Mr. Bentley:[1]

Did my ~late, turnip-headed~ clerk[2] take that French Jumping Frog Sketch to you some time ago? And could you read his writing? And are you proposing to use it? If not will you please post it to me here?[3]

Have called several times, but not been fortunate enough to catch you in.

Ys Truly
Mark Twain.

[1] George Bentley (1828–95) had become head of the London publishers Richard Bentley and Son upon his father's death in 1871. A businessman of energy and perseverance, he greatly improved the company's reputation and financial position. He had been the editor of *Temple Bar: A London Magazine for Town and Country Readers* since 1866, when the firm had purchased it.

[2] Samuel C. Thompson, whom Clemens had dismissed in mid-July (see 16 July 73 to Warner, n. 2).

[3] See 7 July 73 to Bliss, n. 1. Thompson's transcription of the sketch is not known to survive; it was never published in *Temple Bar*. Bentley had invited such

submissions, as Clemens recalled in an 1876 letter to him: "You remember a visit which Joaquin Miller & I paid you once. You asked me then to send you advance sheets of such sketches as I might write for magazines here, & I always purposed doing it, but continually forgot it" (26 Apr 76 to Richard [an error for George] Bentley, ViU†).

To George Bentley
15 and 30 October 1873 • London, England,
and SS *Batavia* en route from
Liverpool, England, to New York, N.Y.
(MS: ViU)

Oct. ~~14~~ 15.

My Dear Mr. Bentley:

Two engagements (both business) interfered, & I couldn't come. Am now (1 PM) starting out on another.

I'll think of the Mag. article, but probably cannot write it, I shall be so full of work as soon as I get home.[1] We sail next Tuesday.

Ys Truly

S. L. Clemens.

over.

ₐAT SEA, Oct. 30.ₐ[2]

P. S. My idea was to put ~~the~~ that French Jumping Frog into a book, in case you were done with it. Didn't want to take it away until you *were* done with it, tho[u]gh.

---

[1] So far as is known, Clemens never wrote the article Bentley had evidently requested specifically for *Temple Bar.*

[2] Clemens, Olivia, Susy, and Nellie (the nursemaid), accompanied by Clara Spaulding and her mother, embarked for New York on the *Batavia* on Tuesday, 21 October.

To Charles Warren Stoddard
19 October 1873 • London, England
(MS: CU-MARK)

Room 113.

Sunday:

Dear Stoddard:[1]

I am leaving a huge bundle of ⸠ "Standards" here in care of Mr. Firmin (in the hotel office).[2] Will you ~~get~~ drop him a line & tell him to send them to you by a messenger & charge to me? And will you please subscribe for the Standard dating back to Oct. 17 & continue to take it & preserve the Tichborne reports until the trial is ended. Charge these expenses to me, of course. When I get back I shall want ~~you~~ to get you [to] scrap-book these trial reports for me. I mean to ~~boul~~ boil the thing down into a more or less readable sketch some day.[3]

I shall sail from New York for Liverpool about Nov. 13.[4] Good bye, my boy. We hoped to see you once more before we sailed, but I have been too ill to go out today.

Ys

Mark.

---

[1] Stoddard (whose *South-Sea Idyls* had recently been issued by James R. Osgood) had arrived in London on 13 October, on a one-year assignment as a roving reporter for the San Francisco *Chronicle*. He settled into Joaquin Miller's rooms on Museum Street, while Miller was traveling on the Continent. Clemens later recalled, "He was refined, sensitive, charming, gentle, generous, honest himself & unsuspicious of other people's honesty, & I think he was the purest male I have known, in mind & speech" (SLC 1900, 33–34; Austen, 58–59, 65; Stoddard 1908, 273). Clemens also reportedly characterized Stoddard as "such a nice girl" (see, for example, Fatout 1960, 184), but the remark has not been confirmed.

[2] Firmin, a Langham Hotel employee, has not been further identified.

[3] In 1900 Clemens recalled his employment of Stoddard (see also pp. 476–78):

> Ostensibly Stoddard was my private secretary; in reality he was merely my comrade—I hired him ~~merely~~ in order to have his company. As secretary there was nothing for him to do except to scrap-book the daily reports of the great trial of the Tichborne Claimant for perjury. But he made a sufficient job out of that, for the reports filled six columns a day & he usually postponed the scrap-booking until Sunday: then he had 42 columns to cut out & paste in—a proper labor for Hercules. He did his work well, but if he had been older & feebler it would have killed him once a week. (SLC 1900, 32–33)

Stoddard cut out and pasted up six scrapbooks of clippings containing verbatim transcripts of the Tichborne trial from the London *Standard*, ranging in date from 23 April to 13 October 1873 (Scrapbooks 13–18, CU-MARK). The "Tichborne Claimant" was a butcher from Australia who claimed to be Roger Charles Tichborne (b. 1829), believed to have died at sea in 1854. Lady Henriette Tichborne refused to accept Roger's death, and after her husband died in 1862 she began advertising for news of her son's whereabouts. In late 1866 the claimant arrived from Australia, and Lady Tichborne (as well as several former associates and one other family member) soon identified him as Roger Tichborne, the rightful heir to the Tichborne baronetcy and estates. In 1872, four years after Lady Tichborne's death, the claimant lost an ejection suit against his nephew, the present baronet, and was subsequently charged with perjury. After the longest imposture trial in British history—lasting from April 1873 until February 1874—he was convicted, and declared to be Arthur Orton, a Cockney butcher who had emigrated to Australia. The claimant served ten years of a fourteen-year prison sentence. In 1895, when desperate for money, he admitted to being an impostor, but then recanted, claiming he had been paid for his confession. He died three years later. The notorious trial—which included testimony about a tattoo and a genital malformation, multiple aliases and assumed identities, and allegations of false testimony, forged documents, murder, seduction, and insanity—fascinated the public, and interest was briefly revived when new evidence supporting the claimant came to light during his prison term. A modern historian has concluded that he was almost certainly not Orton, and might well have been the actual Tichborne (Woodruff, 33–38, 51–66, 85–116, 123, 138–40, 166, 176, 180–85, 206, 213–17, 251–372, 395–96, 420–42, 448–62). Clemens was greatly intrigued by the case, in part because it reminded him of "the claimant in the Lampton family, who from time to time wrote him long letters, urging him to join in the effort to establish his rights to the earldom of Durham" (*MTB*, 1:497; *N&J1*, 546 n. 36, 550–51). Clemens may have attended the trial on 10 June, and apparently met the claimant in person at one of his "showy evenings" (SLC 1897, 157; *N&J1*, 527 n. 2). Nevertheless, he made little literary use of the story, devoting about two pages to it in chapter 15 of *Following the Equator.*

⁴On 19 October Clemens and his traveling party left London for Liverpool, where he lectured the following evening (see the next letter, n. 1). They departed for home the following morning, a few days earlier than they had originally anticipated. The Clemenses had known for some time that they would remain in England until late October (27 July 73 to Pugh). Dolby evidently pressed Clemens to extend his visit, to meet additional lecture engagements. Olivia, however, could not bear the thought of remaining any longer. "I am blue and cross and homesick," she wrote in an undated letter, probably to her mother or sister:

> I suppose what makes me feel the latter is because we are contemplating to stay in London another *month*. There has not one sheet of Mr. Clemens's proof come yet, and if he goes home before the book is published here he will lose his copyright. And then his friends feel that it will be better for him to lecture in London before his book is published, not only that it will give him a larger but a more enviable reputation. I would not hesitate *one moment* if it were simply for the money that his copyright will bring him, but if his reputation will be better for his staying and lecturing, of course he ought to stay. . . . The truth is, I can't bear the thought of postponing going home. (*MTB*, 1:489)

Olivia's yearning for home may have been reinforced by her suspicion that she was pregnant: she would give birth to her second daughter in June 1874. Clemens decided to accompany his family back to America, and then return to London alone for "a more extended course" of lectures (*MTL*, 1:209). After they reached New York on 2 November, Clemens escorted his wife and daughter to Hartford and returned almost immediately to New York, where he reembarked on 8 November (see pp. 460–61 and 7 Nov 73 to Bowen, n. 1).

To Unidentified
22 October 1873 • SS *Batavia* at
Queenstown, Ireland
(MS: CU-MARK)

CUNARD STEAM SHIP BATAVIA

At Sea, Oct. ~~30~~ ₗ22ₗ.[1]

Dear Sir:

Thanks for the books & the MS. Shall recreate with them on shipboard. I wish I could tell you about the Modoc man, but I cannot. I don't know as much about those people as Joaquin Miller.[2] All is hurry here.—In great haste,

Ys Truly
Sam*ˡ*. L. Clemens.

✉

[*letter docketed:*] Mark Twain

[1] This puzzling correction may have resulted from Clemens's haste in dispatching the letter at Queenstown, as the *Batavia* prepared to begin its Atlantic crossing, having left Liverpool the previous day. On 20 October, the night before his departure, Clemens gave a final performance of his Sandwich Islands lecture to an enthusiastic Liverpool audience. The Liverpool *Mercury* declared that Clemens's writings "fairly entitled him to rank amongst the keenest and most original of American humorists," and described his lecture as

> racy in its humour, artistic and powerful in its word painting, but somewhat deficient in arrangement. . . . His word-painting of a volcanic eruption was most striking, and at the end of his highly poetical peroration the audience cheered him to the echo, and recalled him to the platform. ("Mark Twain on the Sandwich Island Savages," 21 Oct 73, clipping in Scrapbook 12:29, 31, CU-MARK)

[2] See 6 July 73 to Fairbanks, n. 13.

To John Brown
30 October 1873 • SS *Batavia* en route
from Liverpool, England, to New York, N.Y.
(MS: CLjC)

CUNARD STEAM SHIP BATAVIA
Mid-Atlantic
Oct. 30.

Our dear friend the doctor:

We have plowed a long way over the ~~water~~, ˏsea,ˏ & there's twenty=
two hundred miles of restless water between us, now, beside the railway
stretch. And yet you are so

ˏ(run to fourth page),ˏ[1]

present with us, so close to us that a span & a whisper would bridge the
distance.[2]

The first three days were stormy, & wife, child, maid & Mrs. & Miss
Spaulding were all sea-sick 25. hours out of the 24, & I was sorry I ever
started. However, it has been smoothe, & balmy, & sunny & altogether
lovely for a day or two now, & at night there is a broad luminous highway
stretching over the sea to the moon, over which the spirits of the sea are
traveling up & down all through the secret night & having a genuine
good time, I make no doubt.

To-day they discovered a "collie" on board! I find (as per advertisement which I sent you) that they won't carry dogs in these ships at any
price. This one has been concealed up to this time. Now his owner has
to pay £10 or heave him overboard. Fortunately the doggie is a performing doggie & the money will be paid. So ~~y~~ after all it was just as well you
didn't ~~¢~~ entrust your collie to us.[3]

A poor little child died at midnight & was buried at dawn this morning—sheet⫽ed & shotted & sunk in the middle of the lonely ocean in
water ~~3,000~~ three thousand fathoms deep. Pity the poor mother.

With our love,
~~L~~ S. L. Clemens

---

[1] Clemens began this letter on the front of a four-page folder, then turned it
over and continued on the back before writing the last two pages on the inside.

² Possibly a quotation, although no source has been found.
³ See 22 and 25 Sept 73 to Brown.

🌿

No LETTERS written between 30 October and 5 November 1873 have been found. The *Batavia* reached New York on Sunday, 2 November. The Clemenses were met by Olivia's mother and brother, as well as by Orion Clemens, who had been in New York for some weeks looking for work. On 3 November Orion wrote to his wife, Mollie:

> Sam and Livy and Susie got ~~home~~ here last night about dusk, all right, after some sea sickness all round. Susie runs about and talks a little, and is exceedingly pretty, having a rather broad face with color in her cheeks. I enclose a notice of Sam's lecture which I cut from the world sometime ago. He had a fine large audience, who applauded him heartily in his descriptive portions, which his American audiences failed to do, seeming ~~to relish only non-sense, or rather~~ as if they did not allow him to talk anything but nonsense. He starts back next Saturday to lecture several weeks in England. The first lecture is to be the first of December in London. Whether he will go into the provinces or not is not yet decided. . . . They start for Hartford to-morrow at 3 o'clock in the afternoon. Mrs. Langdon is going with them. . . .
> Charlie Langdon was here, but left this afternoon. He got Sam's luggage ashore, had a suit of a large fine parlor and two other rooms engaged for him, and one for his mother, and attended to some other business about signing papers. (CU-MARK)

The suite of rooms that Charles Langdon had reserved for the Clemenses was probably at the Windsor Hotel (see 12 Oct 73 to Langdon, n. 1). (Clara Spaulding and her mother checked into Barnum's Hotel at Broadway and Twentieth Street, where Henry Spaulding had arrived the day before.) Orion reported to Mollie that the "president of the Mercantile Library Association sent up his card 'four times,'" in the hope of getting a chance to propose a lecture engagement. He also noted that on the evening of 3 November the Clemenses went to see Edwin Booth in *Hamlet*. Albert Bigelow Paine attributed to Orion a detail that does not appear in his letter to Mollie: "Booth sent for Sam to come behind the scenes, and when Sam proposed to add a part to *Hamlet*, the part of a bystander who makes humorous modern comment on the situations in the play, Booth laughed immoderately" (*MTB*, 1:495; "Passengers Arrived," New York *Times*, 3 Nov 73, 8; "Morning Arrivals," New York *Evening*

Express, 1 Nov 73 and 3 Nov 73, 3; Odell, 9:385). On 4 November the Clemenses returned to Hartford, accompanied by Mrs. Langdon, who planned to stay there for a visit, since Clemens was scheduled to embark again for England in less than a week.

❦

To Elisha Bliss, Jr.
5 November 1873 • Hartford, Conn.
(MS: ViU)

Nov. 5.

Friend Bliss:
    Please send very early copies of the Gilded Age (*Library style*) to[1]

✓ Tom Hood, 80 Fleet st. London[2]

✓ Henry Lee, 43 Holland st. Blackfriars Road, London.

✓ G. W. Smalley, (N. Y. Tribune Bureau,) 13 Pall Mall, London.[3]

✓ George Sauer, (N. Y. Herald Bureau,) 46 Fleet street.[4]

✓ Publisher Figaro, Fleet street.[5]

✓ Mr. Johnstone, Publisher Daily Standard, Shoe Lane, London.[6]

✓ Shirley Brooks, Editor Punch, London.[7]

✓ Mr. Russel, Editor Scotsman, Edinburgh.[8]

✓ G. Fitz Gibbon, 1 Wellesley Terrace, Upper Street, Islington, London.[9]

Ŗ⎯⎯⎯⎯⎯⎯⎯⎯⎯⎯⎯⎯⎯⎯⎯⎯

✓ Joseph T. Goodman, Virginia, Nevada.[10]

✓ Joseph Medill, ("Tribune,"[)] Chicago.[11]

✓ Frank Soulé & ⎫
            ⎬ Care "Alta" San Francisco.[13]
✓ John McComb ⎭

Middleton[12]

✓ Col. John Hay, Lotos Club, 2 Irving Place, N. Y.

✓ J. G. Croly, Daily Graphic, N. Y.[14]

✓ G. W. Hosmer, ‸"Herald,"‸ N. York.[15]

✓ Mr. Abel, Proprietor "Sun," Baltimore. Also, send extracts & advanced sheets to him—great friend of mine[16]

✓ The same to Donn Piatt, "Capital" Washington.[17]

✓ James Redpath, 36 Bromfield st. Boston.

✓ Clara Louise Moulton (Tribune Correspondent,[)] Boston.[18]

✓ D. W. Howells &
✓ T. B. Aldrich } Atlantic Monthly.[19]

✓ Mrs. Jane Clemens, Fredonia New York.

✓ George A. Hawes, Hannibal, Mo.[20]

✓ Thos. P. McMurry, Colony, Knox Co., Mo.[21]

✓ Fred. Quarles, Waco, Texas.[22]

✓ Mrs. A. W. Fairbanks, (care "Herald") Cleveland, Ohio.[23]

✓ Sam. Williams, ~~on,~~ "Bulletin," San Francisco.[24]

[bottom one-third of page left blank]

Middleton

See page 4.[25]

Also, send *half Turkey* copies of *Innocents, Roughing It & Gilded Age*, to

✓   Dr. Brown, 23 Rutland street, Edinburgh, Scotland.[26]

✓   Frank D. Finlay, 4 Royal Terrace, Belfast, Ireland.[27]

Charge them to me.

Send the *earliest* copies, & don't forget. They are promised.

Also, send a *half Turkey* Gilded Age to
✓ Judge Thomas Sunderland, 1 Rue Scribe, Paris, France.[28]

Don't fail.

Ys

Mark.

⊠————————————————————————————————

[letter docketed:] √

[1] Clemens furnished Bliss with this list several weeks before *The Gilded Age* was published, since this would occur after he had returned to England. The records of the American Publishing Company indicate that the first copies of the book bound in *"Library style"* arrived from the bindery on 12 December. Bliss must have sent out some of these before official publication on 23 December: one review appeared on 22 December, followed by at least two more the next day (APC, 97; American Publishing Company to George Routledge, 12 Dec 73, Agreement Book A–K:183, Routledge; see notes 14–15). Although many of the people Clemens listed were personal friends, he clearly hoped that the journalists among them would review the book. Bliss annotated Clemens's letter by checking off each name, presumably as he sent that person's book.

[2] The address of *Fun*, the humor magazine that Hood edited (*Newspaper Press Directory*, 134). *Fun* made no mention of *The Gilded Age*.

[3] Because Clemens had quarreled with Reid over House's offer to review *The Gilded Age*, he instructed Warner *"not to send a copy there under any circumstances"* (17 May 73 to Bliss). The copy for Smalley was presumably a personal gift, not intended to elicit a review. The *Tribune* did not review the book, but Smalley, in his 20 December letter from London to the *Tribune*, devoted a brief final paragraph, not to the American edition (which he could not yet have received), but to the appearance of the English edition in London:

> "The Gilded Age" by Mark Twain and Charles Warner appears to-day with Routledge's imprint on the title-page, and the copyright secured to the authors. It is more to establish this copyright than for his lectures that Mark Twain is here; he preferring, he declares, to make the voyage to England for that purpose rather than visit Canada. What the matter is with Canada I can't say. (Smalley 1874)

Smalley made no further mention of *The Gilded Age* in the *Tribune* letters he wrote from London in January or early February.

[4] George Sauer (1823–84), a former American consul in Brussels and an expert on telegraphy and European commerce, was an internationally known journalist. He had corresponded during the Franco-Prussian War for the New York *Times* and the New York *Herald*. When Clemens was writing about the shah, Sauer was also working in London for the *Herald*, in charge of telegraphing stories to New York. Since George Hosmer had by now returned to the United States (see note 15), Sauer may have already become head of the *Herald*'s London bureau, a position he certainly did assume in about 1874 ("George Sauer," New York *Times*, 18 July 84, 2; "Obituary Notes," New York *Herald*, 18 July 84, 10; 4 Aug 73 to Yates, n. 3; Yates 1885, 407).

[5] The London *Figaro*, whose correct address was 199 Strand, was a semiweekly illustrated "independent family journal," devoted to "politics, literature, art, criticism, and satire" (*Newspaper Press Directory*, 147). No copy of the *Figaro* was available to the editors, but Ambrose Bierce, who wrote for the magazine, inquired about Clemens of Charles Warren Stoddard on 15 January 1874 and reported, "I see that infallible sheet the 'Figaro' (of to-day) condemns his and Mr. 'Werner's' novel" (CSmH). The proprietor and editor of the *Figaro* was James Mortimer (1832–1911), who had founded the journal in 1868 with financ-

ing from Napoleon III. Mortimer was born in Virginia. He served in the navy and was later attached to the American embassy at St. Petersburg. Before starting the *Figaro,* he lived for many years in Paris, corresponding for American newspapers and writing about American affairs for Paris journals. Clemens dined with Mortimer on 12 September 1872, when he visited Brighton with Edmund Routledge, Henry Lee, and Tom Hood, as he recorded in his journal: "Mortimer of 'Figaro' dined with us & tried to crowd me into writing for his paper, but did not succeed" (Appendix C; Griffiths, 424).

⁶James Johnstone (1815–78) held an official appointment for many years in the Bankruptcy Court. In 1857 he purchased the London *Evening Standard* (together with the London *Morning Herald*) when its owner declared bankruptcy. By increasing its size and lowering the price, he succeeded in converting it into a highly successful morning newspaper. The paper's coverage of the Civil War (in which it supported the South) further increased its circulation, which reached a daily average of one hundred eighty-five thousand by early 1874 (Griffiths, 233–34, 341–42). The *Standard* published a favorable review of *The Gilded Age* on 29 December 1873, calling it "a satire of the bitterest kind, . . . a hardly overdrawn picture of the condition of society," which "every one should read" (clipping in CU-MARK). The unidentified reviewer, however, had not seen the American edition, but rather the simultaneously issued English edition.

⁷No mention of the book was found in *Punch,* which did not publish book reviews.

⁸An unidentified critic for the Edinburgh *Scotsman,* reviewing the Routledge edition of *The Gilded Age,* commented:

> The American writer calling himself Mark Twain, is in a high degree peculiar—his method or plan, his style, his humour, belong entirely, or very much, to himself; and it was not to be hoped that he could find some one else qualified in all respects to run with him in double harness. . . . Mark Twain by himself would have been more enjoyable, and probably so would Mr Warner. We should infer that they went into partnership in this matter because the one was supposed to have what the other had not—Mark Twain is not a good hand at a plot, and perhaps Mr Warner is, whilst, on the other hand, he may not have those qualities which have given Mark Twain celebrity and success. Those qualities are a quick, quaint, dry humour, very considerable powers of grave and even poetic description, a penetrating good sense, and an abhorrence of all shams and hypocrisy, especially of those most prevalent amongst his own countrymen. Possessing these qualities, Mark Twain has given to the world many books yielding much amusement, though no story interesting by its mere plot. It was to supply this supposed defect, we suppose, that Mr Warner was called in; but we were quite content to take Mark Twain by himself, and to read him for his fun and his good sense. ("Literature," 9 Jan 74, 2)

⁹No review of *The Gilded Age* appeared in Fitzgibbon's newspaper, the Darlington *Northern Echo.*

¹⁰Goodman's *Territorial Enterprise* did not usually print book reviews, and it made no exception for *The Gilded Age.*

¹¹Joseph Medill (1823–99) was born in Canada but grew up in Ohio, where he was trained as a lawyer. He turned to journalism in 1849, when—with three younger brothers—he purchased the Coshocton *Whig,* renaming it the *Republican.* In 1852 he established the Cleveland *Leader,* and then sold it in early 1855 to purchase an interest in the Chicago *Tribune,* with which he remained associated for the rest of his life. Under his editorial direction the newspaper was strongly antislavery, and during Reconstruction supported the Radical Republicans. Medill had been elected mayor of Chicago soon after the great fire of Oc-

tober 1871, but in August 1873, physically and emotionally exhausted, he resigned his position and departed for a year of European travel. Although Medill was in London in the fall of 1873, Clemens is not known to have seen him there (Protess, 2–3, 6–7, 12–14; "Foreign News," Cincinnati *Commercial,* 23 Oct 73, 1). An unidentified critic for the Chicago *Tribune* found little to praise in *The Gilded Age,* describing it "in terms of the severest censure":

> Every one . . . had a right to expect the book, when given to the world, though it should lack the unity and coherence of a work conceived and brought out by a single mind, should at least be redeemed with passages of the refined and delicate beauty which distinguishes the one writer, and with the quaint and fertile humor that has created for the other even a trans-Atlantic popularity. When, therefore, a book so utterly bald, so puerile, so vicious even, as "The Gilded Age," appears with the signatures of Mark Twain and Charles Dudley Warner to give it a passport among respectable readers, wrath and disgust may rightfully inspire the critic to chastise them with[out] mercy. . . . Their names had become a sort of certificate of high character. It is a fraud to the reading public to append them to a trashy book like the mongrel before us. Stupidity can be forgiven, but deliberate deceit—never. . . . Thousands will be deluded into its purchase, only to find themselves cheated and robbed. Mr. Clemens and Mr. Warner . . . have willfully degraded their craft, abused the people's trust, and provoked a stern condemnation. ("The Twain-Warner Novel," 1 Feb 74, 9)

See also note 14.

[12] Unidentified.

[13] Franklin Soulé (1810–82), a friend of Clemens's from his days in San Francisco, was born in Maine. After several years as a schoolteacher and journalist in Mississippi and Louisiana, he went to California in 1849. Soon thereafter he began a long career in California journalism, throughout which he also wrote (and occasionally published) poetry. In 1851 he joined the editorial staff of the San Francisco *Alta California,* but in 1853 began publishing his own short-lived newspaper, the *Chronicle.* When that failed he returned to the *Alta,* and later worked as an editor for the San Francisco *Times.* In 1861 he took a position in the U.S. customs house, and in 1864 became an editor on the *Morning Call,* where he met and worked with Clemens during Clemens's four-month stint as a *Call* reporter. Soulé resigned from the *Call* that same year to accept an appointment as collector for the Department of Internal Revenue. In 1869 and 1870 he was again employed on the *Call,* after which he once again returned to the *Alta,* where he remained until his death in 1882 ("The Late Frank Soulé," San Francisco *Alta California,* 5 July 82, 1; Guinn, 2:659–60; *L2,* 158 n. 3; Langley: 1869, 575; 1873, 571; Branch 1969, 18, 19, 304 n. 61). Soulé wrote to Clemens early in 1873 for advice about publishing his poetry, and received an encouraging response (not known to survive). In his reply to Clemens, written on 31 March from the "dull and dirty editorial room" of the *Alta,* Soulé recalled

> the time when we were scribbling in the same room for a little compensation—you with grand aspirations which I rejoice most sincerely you have found exchanged for, or transformed into grand realities. If my poor hopes and feebler anticipations have only brought the reverse, why, "sich is life," and let it go as a part of the game. (CU-MARK)

In a September 1880 letter to Howells, Clemens was still trying to help his friend publish his poetry:

> Frank Soulé *was* one of the sweetest and whitest & loveliest spirits that ever wandered into this world by mistake; I seem somehow to have got the impression that he has of late years become sour & querulous; cannot tell—it has been 13 years since I worked at his side in the Morning Call office, in San Francisco; but no matter, he has believed for 36 years, that he would next year, & then next year, & still next year, be recognized as

a poet—& all these slow years have come & gone, & each in its turn has lied to him. Soured?—why anybody would be, that had been served so. . . . Frank Soulé had that sort of a face which is so rare—I mean a face that is *always* welcome, that makes you happy all through, just to see it. And Lordy, to think that this fine & sensitive & beautiful & proud spirit had to grind, & grind, like a pitiful slave, on that degraded "Morning Call," whose mission from hell & politics was to lick the boots of the Irish & throw bold brave mud at the Chinamen. And he is a slave yet! (3 Sept 80, MH-H, in *MTHL*, 1:325–26)

Clemens had last seen his friend John McComb, supervising editor of the *Alta*, in early February (see pp. 296–97). The *Alta* published an unsigned review of *The Gilded Age* on 11 March 1874, which characterized the book as "excellent" in its conception, but "inferior" in its execution, with "much of the grotesque humor of Twain, and little of the elegant style of Warner." Although some chapters were deemed "almost trashy," the book was nevertheless recommended for its "many amusing passages" ("New Publications," 1).

[14] David G. Croly (17 Apr 73 to Croly, n. 1). Clemens soon regretted furnishing Croly with an early copy of *The Gilded Age*, as he recalled in 1906:

> When Charles Dudley Warner and I were about to bring out "The Gilded Age," the editor of the *Daily Graphic* persuaded me to let him have an advance copy, he giving me his word of honor that no notice of it should appear in his paper until after the *Atlantic Monthly* notice should have appeared. This reptile published a review of the book within three days afterward. I could not really complain, because he had only given me his word of honor, as security. I ought to have required of him something substantial. I believe his notice did not deal mainly with the merit of the book, or the lack of it, but with my moral attitude toward the public. It was charged that I had used my reputation to play a swindle upon the public—that Mr. Warner had written as much as half of the book, and that I had used my name to float it and give it currency—a currency which it could not have acquired without my name—and that this conduct of mine was a grave fraud upon the people. The *Graphic* was not an authority upon any subject whatever. It had a sort of distinction in that it was the first and only illustrated daily newspaper that the world had seen; but it was without character; it was poorly and cheaply edited; its opinion of a book or of any other work of art was of no consequence. Everybody knew this, yet all the critics in America, one after the other, copied the *Graphic's* criticism, merely changing the phraseology, and left me under that charge of dishonest conduct. Even the great Chicago *Tribune*, the most important journal in the Middle-West, was not able to invent anything fresh, but adopted the view of the humble daily *Graphic*, dishonesty-charge and all. (AD, 7 Feb 1906, CU-MARK, in *MTA*, 2:69 -70)

Clemens misremembered the source of the "dishonesty-charge," which was apparently the Chicago *Tribune* (note 11). The *Graphic's* review, published on 23 December, was far from complimentary, however, describing the book as a "rather dreary failure," despite "isolated passages" that were "clever and amusing":

> It is simply a rather incoherent series of sketches, from which the characteristic fun of Mr. Clemens and the subtle humor of Mr. Warner have been, for the most part, eliminated. . . . And so it has come to pass that the two most brilliant humorists in America—with the exception of "John Paul" [Charles Henry Webb]—have written a book in which we look almost in vain for the traces of either's pen. ("Literary Notes," 351)

Nor was the *Graphic* notice the first to appear: relatively favorable reviews were published in the New York *Herald* on 22 December and in the Boston *Evening Transcript* on 23 December (French, 16, 20).

[15] Hosmer had only recently returned to New York (reportedly "for financial reasons"), having served for some time as a London correspondent for the *Herald*

(Joseph J. Mathews, 80). The New York *Herald* printed an unsigned notice of *The Gilded Age* one day before its official publication:

> No reviewer would be in the right who handled this production in the same spirit in which he would handle a story pure and simple. . . . But as a clever though rude satire upon certain customs and institutions, many of which deserve contempt and reprobation, it will scarcely be too highly praised. ("American Satire," 22 Dec 73, clipping in CU-MARK)

[16] Arunah S. Abell (1806–88) was born in Rhode Island. He was trained as a printer, and in 1836 founded the Philadelphia *Public Ledger* with two associates. A year later he began the Baltimore *Sun* with the same partners, and served as its managing editor for the rest of his life, becoming its sole proprietor in 1868. He was known for his editorial independence, his thorough coverage of local news, and his innovative use of pony express riders, carrier pigeons, and the telegraph for speedy news delivery. No correspondence between Clemens and Abell has been found, nor is it known how Clemens came to regard him as a "great friend." The *Sun*'s review of *The Gilded Age* was complimentary, calling it "sparkling entertainment" and giving the entire credit to Clemens, with Warner mentioned only in passing:

> There is scarcely a phase of the diversified social state of America which he does not touch. He passes with graceful transition from the twilight of civilization in the far West to its full orbed splendors in the eastern cities, reminding us, however, as he lifts the veil from the surface of society in the Atlantic capitals that all is not gold that glitters, and that there is a good deal of barbarism even in the centers of civilization so-called. His sketches of society in Washington, including the antiques, the parvenues, and the middle aristocracy are admirable. The visit to the Wall street headquarters of improvement companies, and the restrictions that are put on members of Congress, male lobbyist, female lobbyist, high moral Senator, and country member, with the capital illustrations, are full of suggestiveness and merriment. The description of the steamboat race on the Mississippi, and of the explosion, is graphic and powerful. The whole story in its conception, exposition of characters and composition, will add new reputation to the author. ("Mark Twain's New Book," 6 Feb 74, 2)

Clemens's contract with the American Publishing Company, dated 8 May 1873, stipulated that a "sheet of extracts" from the text be "sent with copy of the book to editors, said extracts to be selected by the said Warner" (Appendix D). The stock ledger of the American Publishing Company contains the notation "60 sheets" next to the date of 13 December, indicating that sixty sets of unbound signatures may have been set aside then for reviewers (APC, 97).

[17] Donn Piatt had been the Washington correspondent for the Cincinnati *Commercial* since 1868, and was known for writing articles highly critical of corrupt politicians of both parties. He and Clemens had met—and liked each other immediately—at a dinner given in Clemens's honor in Washington in February 1871. Early that year Piatt helped establish *The Capital*, a weekly paper (*L4*, 328, 347). No file of *The Capital* has been searched for a *Gilded Age* review.

[18] Clemens meant Louise Chandler Moulton, whose notice of *Roughing It* had pleased him (18 June 72 to Moulton). He seems to have confused her name with the name of Clara Louise Kellogg, a renowned operatic soprano. Moulton made no mention of *The Gilded Age* in her correspondence from Boston for the New York *Tribune*.

[19] Thomas Bailey Aldrich had been the editor of *Every Saturday* since 1866; he replaced William Dean Howells on the *Atlantic Monthly*, but not until 1881.

Both journals were published by James R. Osgood and Company of Boston (*L4*, 304 n. 1, 489 n. 1). Aldrich did not comment on *The Gilded Age* in *Every Saturday*, nor did Howells review it for the *Atlantic*, which merely listed the book under "Other Publications" in March 1874 (33:374). Howells expressed reservations about reviewing the book in a letter to Warner dated 28 December 1873:

> Up to the time old Hawkins dies your novel is of the greatest promise—I read it with joy—but after that it fails to assimilate the crude material with which it is fed, and becomes a confirmed dyspeptic at last. Still it is always entertaining; and it kept me up till twelve last night, though I needed sleep. I was particularly sorry to have Sellers degenerate as he did, and none of the characters quite fulfill their early promise. I will withold my public opinion altogether if you like, and if on revision of the book, it does not strike me more favorably, I should prefer to do so; though I should be able to praise parts of it with heartiness and sincerity. (Howells 1979b, 46)

[20] George A. Hawes was a leading Hannibal merchant and a nephew of John Quarles, Clemens's uncle (*L2*, 132 n. 7).

[21] Thomas P. ("Pet") McMurry (d. 1886) was a printer in the office of the Hannibal *Missouri Courier* in the late 1840s, when Clemens was apprenticed there. He had renewed his acquaintance with Clemens by letter in July 1872 (CU-MARK):

Colony, Knox Co. Mo.
July 16th, 1872.

Dear Sam:

> You may call this a piece of presumption—but I can't help that—so few, so very *few*, of **my** boyhood acquaintances have become Literary Lights in the world, that I must not fail to keep up some kind of intercourse with those who have made their mark—"the cat you know, may smile at the King"—that is to say, I mean to keep up an intercourse, *if I kin*. If your memory extends so far back, you will recollect that when a boy, a little sandy-headed, curly-headed boy, nearly a quarter of a century ago, in the old Printing office at Hannibal, Mo, over the Brittingham Drug-Store, mounted upon a little box at the case, pulling away at a huge Cigar, or a diminutive pipe, you used to love to sing so well, the poor drunken man's expression, who was supposed to have fallen in the rut by the wayside: "If ever I *git up agin*, **I'll stay up,**—*if* **I kin!**" So with myself, I'll keep up my acquaintance with so distinguished a personage, **if I can.**
>
> Permit me to congratulate you upon the unprecedented success which has attended your efforts in the Literary world. It always affords me a great deal of pleasure to read your productions—consider them the natural offspring of that brain that was always so **chuck-full** of fun and mischief when a boy.
>
> Do you recollect any of the many serious conflicts that mirth-loving brain of yours used to get you into with that **diminutive** creature, (as compared to your own gigantic proportions) Wales McCormick—how you used to call upon me to hold your Cigar, or Pipe, as the case might be, whilst you went **entirely through** him? He "**still lives,**" and is a resident of the City of Quincy, Ills. but like myself, has never made a great deal of noise in the World.
>
> What has become of your mother & your brothers, Orion & Henry? Have never seen or heard of them since they left Muscatine, Iowa.
>
> Have been here since the Spring of 1860. Have been in the mercantile business ever since 1854. Quit the printing business in 1853, at Louisville, Kentucky. Am the happy father of 5 children—4 girls and one boy—the boy is a great book-worm, and a fond admirer of yours—never fails to read all the productions from your pen that his eye catches. If he should get hold of "**Roughing It,**" he would at once be of the same turn of mind that the Southern people were in '61, "want to be let alone" until he devoured it.
>
> Will not weary your patience farther at this time. As you are convenient to the

Artist, enclose your Photograph, when you write, & let us see how you look since you have **growed** up to be a man. Will take pleasure in giving it a conspicuous place in our Picture gallery.

Your old friend,
T. "Pet" McMurry

To Mark Twain,
Hartford, Conn.
P. S. Don't get vain of your reputation. Your reputation don't extend to **every** nook and corner yet. Wanted to show off a little this morning while penning this, and remarked to a lady acquaintance of some intelligence who stepped into the store, that I was engaged in the dignified task of writing a letter to that distinguished character, "**Mark Twain.**" "Who *is* Mark Twain?" was the reply. Had she been a man, should have taken her to be of that class who still persist in voting for Gen. Jackson. So you see there is a great work for you to do yet, before your name is a **universal** household word, particularly in the rural districts.

Yours,
"Pet."

It is not known whether Clemens replied to this letter, but in April 1873 he had ordered a copy of *The Innocents Abroad* sent to McMurry (bill from American Publishing Company dated 6 May 73, CU-MARK).

22 William Frederick S. Quarles (1833–98) was a first cousin of Clemens's—the son of Jane Clemens's sister (Selby, 23, 134).

23 The Cleveland *Herald*, the newspaper owned in part by Mary Mason Fairbanks's husband, Abel, reviewed *The Gilded Age* on 21 February 1874, describing it as "a biting satire on the men and principle—or absence of principles—of the age"; although it "contains some highly dramatic incidents and bits of good descriptive writing,"

> it is not what we had reason to expect from two authors of such unquestionable talent as Mr. Clemens and Mr. Warner. . . . It fearlessly lashes the frauds and humbugs who occupy prominent places in all ranks of society and in all positions of honor and profit. There is no mercy for such offenders. The mask of pretended piety and robe of assumed honesty are stripped off and the rascals exposed to the lash of the satirist and the scorn of the world. But, admitting this, it is not the work in which Messrs. Clemens and Warner feel most at home and in which their friends enjoy their company best. ("New Books," 2)

24 Samuel Williams had been an editor on the San Francisco *Evening Bulletin* since 1865, and was responsible for book reviews and dramatic criticism (*L2*, 209 n. 1). The *Bulletin* published an unsigned review on 7 March, which read in part:

> *The Gilded Age* is a little more coherent than the *Innocents Abroad*, but lacks the novelty of that veracious chronicle, while we search in vain for the charming pleasantry of *My Summer in a Garden*. The story is dreadfully attenuated, and the padding is so evident that one cannot help the suspicion that the dominant motive in writing the book was to make a "companion volume—price three dollars and a half." . . . Of course, there is much that is funny, and now and then a bit of pathos, with occasional sharp "cuts" at social and political life in Washington. . . . And yet one feels that the abundant material at hand has not been used in the most artistic manner, and the book fails of its purpose as a satire. ("The Gilded Age—A Tale of To-Day," 1)

25 After listing Williams, Clemens left the last third of the page (page 3 of the letter) blank, perhaps intending to add further names. He then wrote this direction at the bottom, to ensure that Bliss would not disregard the final leaf.

26 John Brown wrote Clemens on 12 February 1874: "I have been all too long

in thanking you for the 3 goodly volumes, so full of good sense & good feeling & good fun & good knowledge of men & things. I am quite surprised at the fulness of meaning in them" (CU-MARK). In an earlier letter to another friend, however, he was more candid: "Mark Twain is home—a queer fellow, but with excellent stuff in him—& his wife is simply delicious—beautiful & good. What do you think of his last novel? It is powerful but unequal—& lacks the true storytelling knack" (Brown to John Forsyth, 18 Jan 74, PHi).

[27] Clemens and his family had been entertained in Belfast by Francis Dalzell Finlay (1832?–1917), proprietor of the Belfast *Northern Whig* since 1857, when he inherited it from his father, its founder. Finlay began his career in the office of the Edinburgh *Scotsman* and was married to the daughter of its editor, Alexander Russel (see p. 432; London *Times:* "Mr. F. D. Finlay," 14 July 1917, 3; "Wills and Bequests," 6 Oct 1917, 9).

[28] Thomas Sunderland was an attorney and former chief justice of the California Supreme Court; Clemens had known him in Virginia City, where he maintained a lucrative law practice for many years. Presumably Clemens had seen Sunderland in early October in Paris, where he had been staying with his family since at least June. Sunderland had returned from abroad by early November (*L4,* 255–56 n. 1; "Californians Registered at the Office of Charles Le Gay," *California Mail Bag* 3 [July–Aug 73]: 59; New York *Times:* "Personal," 3 Nov 73, 5; "Obituary Notes," 11 Oct 86, 5).

To Jane Lampton Clemens
6 November 1873 • Hartford, Conn.
(Transcript: CU-MARK)

·   ·   ·

I meant to make a proposition to Orion in New York, but was hurried and lost the opportunity. It is this—you can tell him. He will never get a place in New York that will pay him more than $15 a week ($60 a month)—and if he got such a place he would soon lose it anyway.[1] ~~I loaned~~ I gave him $100 & will have to help him every now and then if he stays there. Now if he were in Fredonia he would be a comfort to your old age, and that is a better thing and a kinder thing than slaving night & day in [a] New York newspaper sty. So if he will live in Fredonia & will make no effort to leave there, I will pay him a pension of $15 a week as long as he is idle or can make no more than $10 a week. If he should be able at any time to make more than $10 a week I should expect him to release an equivalent portion of my $15.[2]

But I hamper this proposition with strict condition that *he is not to live in the same house with you or Pamela under any circumstances whatever,* I will not pay him a cent or *lend* him a cent while he is under your roof. I am willing that the pension shall be as high as $20 a week *if necessary while he is absolutely idle,* but not when at work. Let him work *for nothing* on the Fredonia paper, but keep diligently & faithfully at work every day of his life, & the pension shall cheerfully go on—but he must not stay idle a single day under the excuse that he cannot get *pay* for his work. No man can be contented unless he is hard at work—& happily Orion is not lazy, but is fond of work.

If Orion is a wise man he will accept this proposition, If he knows himself, he will accept it. Anybody who accurately knows him will certainly *advise* him to accept it. Anybody who knows what newspaper work in New York is, will say, In the name of God *accept any* proposition that will avoid that.

Orion may read my letter if he wants to. It has no harsh thought in it, but is kindly meant, as from brother to brother, & is simply a plain unvarnished common-sense view of the situation.

. . . .

[1] Mollie Clemens made this (partial) copy of Clemens's letter to his mother, identifying it as an "Extract of a letter from S L.C. to Ma, dated Hartford Nov 6. 1873," presumably to send to Orion in New York City. The original letter has not been found. In recent weeks Orion had been struggling to find employment in New York, applying at newspaper offices for work as an editorial writer, proof-reader, or typesetter, while Mollie stayed in Fredonia with Jane Clemens and Annie Moffett (Pamela was on a trip to the Midwest). On 5 November Orion described to Mollie a temporary position he had found, reading proof for the *Evening Post:*

> I had my hopes quite lifted up till to-night. I thought I should get a regular situation, at $25 a week, with hours from 9:30 to 4:30, and though that was an hour longer than the Telegram hours, I would rather take the place than risk waiting for the Telegram. But to-night I was informed that they count ten hours a days work at the Post for proofreaders, like their other weekly hands, and that they are paying me by the hour at that rate, paying $22 a week all round. For that sum, if employed regularly, I would be expected to commence at half past seven in the morning and work till five or half past six, as need may be for my services. . . . I am sadly disappointed, for I had begun to think of telegraphing you to-night to come on. Now as I shall be obliged to ask you to stay there till the first of January. (CU-MARK)

²On 3 November Orion wrote Mollie: "Sam gave me a check for $100 on the St. Nicholas Hotel which I am to collect day after to-morrow, and I will send you half. No, I believe it's Friday I am to collect it. He has to see to having money in the Hartford bank to respond" (CU-MARK). Since talking with Orion in New York Clemens had adopted a more generous policy than the one Orion reported in his 5 November letter to Mollie: "I am sorry Sam has announced his determination to let me have no more money. I do not think I would do so towards him. However, I might, under similar circumstances" (CU-MARK).

To William Bowen
7 November 1873 • Hartford, Conn.
(MS: TxU-Hu)

Hartford ⎱
Nov. 7. ⎰

Dear Will—

Have just got my wife & family home safe, & I start back to London tomorrow to finish talking.¹

I got your sad news in London & wrote you.² Yes, you must come & give us a good visit—but don't come till toward end of May, for we won't be in our new house till then.³ We will talk over old times & tell my wife about them.

Affectionately
Sam.

¹Clemens was to sail on the *City of Chester,* scheduled to depart at 8 A.M. on Saturday, 8 November (New York *Times:* "Shipping," 3 Nov 73 and 9 Nov 73, 7; "Passengers Sailed," 9 Nov 73, 8).

²Bowen had probably written Clemens about the death of his wife of sixteen years, Mary Cunningham Bowen (Hornberger, 7, 33). The exact date of her death in 1873 has not been found, and Clemens's letter of condolence (presumably written between June and late October) is not known to survive.

³Orion reported to Mollie on 3 November, "The roof is on Sam's house" in Hartford (CU-MARK). The new home was not ready for occupation, however, until the following fall.

To Olivia L. Clemens
10 and 17 November 1873 • SS *City of Chester* en route from New York, N.Y., to Liverpool, England; and Queenstown, Ireland
(MS: CU-MARK)

On Shipboard,
3 days out from N. Y,

L̶i̶y̶ Livy darling, you really don't know what a steamship is. The Batavia is 316 feet long. This ship is nearly 500. The great dining saloon is square, stretches from side to side of the vessel; has 8 tables in it (each seating only 14 people‚)₁; is brightly lighted by long rows of side-ports & by skylights; is elegantly "papered" with polished fancy wood. The two ends are just great mirrors framed in fluted columns of polished dark wood; there is a piano & elegant book cases; the ship does not rock & pitch,—so we do not need racks on the table; there are no staterooms anywhere near,—so you eat in peace & hear ⩫ no nasty sounds of vomiting in your vicinity. When we passed the Batavia she was wildly rolling & plunging, but our ship was as steady as a prairie.[1]

The smoking room is prettily upholstered & lighted with big windows, & has six marble-top card-tables in it.

My port is so large that I can lie in my berth (on a delicious spring mattrass) & read, as if out of doors.

At night I can read with perfect ease (& all night long,) for a swinging lamp hangs above my head. I can lie there & pull a knob & a flood of clean water gushes into my wash-bowl. At any hour of the whole night I can turn over & touch an electrical bell & a steward comes in a moment. My comb & tooth brush lie always on a smooth, level service & the trifling motion of the ship never disturbs them. Wherever I place my shoes or any other article, there they remain.

The ship & the smoking room & ladies' upper deck saloons are warmed by steam.

Our first day's run (simply under s̶t̶a̶ steam) was over 350 miles.

The hallways are wide & light & comfortable. The stairways are of elegant workmanship, & easy of ascent & descent. No danger of breaking one's neck, & no need to take hold of the balusters. The ship is thoroughly well ordered, officered & served. The captain has commanded steamers more than 20 years & never lost one.

The library is large & singularly well selected.

It is a charming ship. The times slides by in comfort & satisfaction & I seem to enjoy every hour of it. I do so regret taking you in the Batavia, for this captain would have been just as kind to you & would have put the thousand resources of the ship at the service of yourself & the Modoc. Your journey would have been a hundred times pleasanter.[2]

Mr. & Mrs. Nobles of Elmira are on board.[3] Methodist preacher. Very pleasant, companionable people they are—though when he gets to talking fine I suspect him of culling from old favorite sermons of his.

I love you, darling, & every day I grow more & more uneasy about you, for I have left you very short handed in nurse-help at a time when you cannot exert yourself without peril.[4] I shall immediately telegraph to ask how you are when I reach Queenstown & shall look for an answer at Liverpool or London. Good-bye my darling.

Telegraphed you. Also wrote from N. Y., & ALSO BY THE PILOT.[5]

✉—————————————————————————————

[*in ink:*] Mrs. Sam*l*. L. Clemens | Forest street | Hartford | Conn. [*in upper left corner:*] America | [*rule*] [*postmarked:*] QUEENSTOWN B NO18 73 [*and*] BOSTON DEC 3 PAID

---

[1] The *Batavia* had departed from New York on the same day as the *City of Chester* ("Shipping Intelligence," New York *Tribune*, 8 Nov 73, 5).

[2] The *City of Chester*, under Captain Kennedy, was a ship of the Inman Line, founded in 1854 by William Inman. This "canny young Englishman" had made his company a highly successful rival to Cunard by offering cheap and comfortable accommodation to British emigrants, as well as luxurious appointments for cabin passengers (Brinnin, 208–10, 259–60). Stoddard, who had arrived in England on the *City of Chester*, claimed in a letter to the San Francisco *Chronicle* that it was "a whole year coming to perfection, but has come very near to it at last" (Stoddard 1873). It may have been his recommendation that led Clemens to renounce his loyalty to Captain John Mouland and the Cunard Company.

[3] The Reverend John C. Nobles and his wife, not otherwise identified ("Passengers Sailed," New York *Times*, 9 Nov 73, 8).

[4] Olivia was now two months pregnant.

[5] Clemens added this brief marginal note upon arriving in Queenstown on 17 November, meaning that he had written from New York on the evening of 7 November, then entrusted a letter to the pilot of the boat that escorted the *City*

of Chester out of New York harbor on the morning of 8 November, and, finally, sent a telegram from Queenstown. None of these communications is known to survive.

To Olivia L. Clemens
14 November 1873 • SS *City of Chester* en route from New York, N.Y., to Liverpool, England
(MS: CU-MARK)

7th day out.

Livy darling, we have had a half-gale & a *very* tumultuous sea for 2 days & nights, & I found that this ship *could* roll, though nothing compared to the Batavia. The seas swept the ship several times & gushed through the saloon skylights in drowning volumes. Last night at dinner fifty dishes leaped clear off the table & fell in one common ruin. My dead⸗ light did not fit closely, & so all night the seas came in—my floor got as much as a barrel of water, altogether. Now the port is well caulked with tallow & is all right. I have read all night during this weather,—sleep would only tire me. Yesterday two or three people were hurt by being thrown down on the deck. A lurch ~~sent a~~ hurled a ~~d~~ steerage passenger across the ship & against a boat. People heard the concussion a great distance. He wilted down limp & senseless.

But she is a much more comfortable ship than any Cunarder.

Just been answering the enclosed rather difficult letter. The old man was in one of his childish moods I guess. The letter came to me Saturday as we were leaving port.[1]

Button gone from the shirt I brought in the satchel—Mrs. Slote sewed it on for me.[2] Cravat fell to pieces Tuesday—Mrs. Nobles recon- structed it. One suspender broke down to-day—& all the women sea⸗ sick. But no matter, there's only men to see that I *need* a suspender.

I *do* hope you are well & jolly, old chap. I don't believe I dare *ask* you by telegraph. I *am* afraid to do it. But you *must* be well, my darling— you *must*—I cannot have it otherwise. I *love* you.

Saml.

✉

[*in ink:*] Mrs. Sam*¹*. L. Clemens | Forest street | Hartford | Conn | [*flourish*] [*in upper left corner:*] America | [*rule*] [*postmarked:*] QUEENSTOWN B NO18
73 [*and*] BOSTON DEC 3 PAID

¹The enclosure, now lost, was probably a letter from John Mouland, whom Clemens referred to as the "old man" in his letters of 22 Jan 73 to Mouland and 26 Apr 73 to Greene.
²Clemens apparently spent the night before his departure with Daniel Slote and his family, at 110 East Fifty-fifth Street, the address to which they had recently moved. The household may have included Slote's elderly mother, Ann, but it was probably his wife who sewed on Clemens's button. Her first name has not been discovered, but at the time of Slote's death in 1882 she was identified as "the third daughter of ex-Alderman James Griffiths" ("Daniel Slote," New York *Tribune*, 14 Feb 82, 2; "Obituary Notes," New York *Times*, 14 Feb 82, 5; H. Wilson: 1869, 1023; 1872, 1122; 1873, 1212).

🌿

NO LETTERS written between 14 and 20 November 1873 have been found (except for the second portion of the 10 and 17 November letter to Olivia). The *City of Chester* arrived at Queenstown at 6 P.M. on 17 November, and presumably docked at Liverpool the following day ("Ship News," London *Morning Post*, 18 Nov 73, 3). It is not known whether Clemens stayed in that city one night, or immediately took the train for London, but by the evening of 19 November he had settled into his room at the Langham Hotel, where Stoddard joined him. In an 1876 letter asking William Dean Howells to recommend Stoddard for a consulship, Clemens wrote:

> Poor, sweet, pure-hearted, good-intentioned, impotent Stoddard, I have known him 12 years, now, & in all that time he has never been fit for anything but a consul. When I was at the Langham Hotel in London I hired him for 3 months, at $15 a week & board & lodging, to sit up nights with me & dissipate. At the end of the time he wouldn't take a cent. I had to finally smuggle it to him through Dolby after leaving England. (21 Sept 76, MH-H, in *MTHL*, 1:154)

Stoddard described his weeks as Clemens's companion and secretary in a 1903 collection of autobiographical sketches. After a late breakfast, the two enjoyed

> a lazy stroll through the London parks, or an hour in some picture-gallery, or a saunter among the byways of the city in search of the picturesque. . . . The

lazy hour before dinner was perhaps the pleasantest in the day—an exception to the general rule. There was chat or long intervals of dreamy silence by the fireside, or music at the piano, when to my amazement Mark would sing jubilee songs or "Ben Bowline" with excellent effect, accompanying himself and rolling his vowels in the Italian style.

After Clemens's evening lecture, they returned to the Langham for cocktails and talk:

> How the hours flew by, marked by the bell clock of the little church over the way! One—two—three in the morning, chimed on a set of baby bells, and still we sat by the sea-coal fire and smoked numberless peace-pipes, and told droll stories, and took solid comfort in our absolute seclusion. I could have written his biography at the end of the season. I believe I learned much of his life that is unknown even to his closest friends—of his boyhood, his early struggles, his hopes, his aims. I trust I am betraying no confidence when I state that a good deal of the real boy is blended with the "Story of Tom Sawyer." (Stoddard 1903, 64–65, 70)

Ina Coolbrith, a poet and close friend of Stoddard's, explained that it was one of Stoddard's duties "to help entertain Mr. Clemens and keep him cheerful":

> It was not required of Mr. Stoddard that he furnish any conversation—it was simply his duty to be, or at least to seem, amused at the conversation of Mr. Clemens and Mr. Dolby. This duty however he did not adequately perform. Instead of laughing boisterously at the conversation, he merely chuckled now and then, and in no wise earned his salary in this respect. It was expected of him that he should at least keep awake and listen. Again he failed. He did not listen and he did not keep awake. He went to sleep and interrupted the conversation with a species of snore which he had acquired in some foreign part. Aside from these trifling defects, Mr. Clemens found him a most delightful companion and comrade. (Coolbrith)

Stoddard himself wrote about the difficulty he had staying awake:

> And this thing kept up—Mark's speech getting slower and slower, and I growing sleepier and sleepier, until it was impossible for me to keep awake. Then I had to go to bed. "Mark, I'm going to bed. I cannot possibly keep awake," and to bed I'd go. As soon as I got into bed he'd come and sit right down by my side, his glass in his hand, now talking so slowly that the syllables came about every half minute and the last picture I'd have as I dropped off to sleep was of Mark bending over me, glass in hand, uttering the second syllable of a word he began a full minute ago. It was wonderfully funny.
>
> Very, very often these nightly talks became a lament. He was always afraid of dying in the poorhouse. The burden of his woe was that he would grow old and lose the power of interesting an audience, and become unable to write,

and then what would become of him? He had trained himself to do nothing else. He could not work with his hands. There could be no escape. The poorhouse was his destiny. And he'd drink cocktails and grow more and more gloomy and blue until he fairly wept at the misery of his own future. (James, 669–70)

For further reminiscences, see also Stoddard 1908, 262–63.

❦

To Olivia L. Clemens
20 November 1873 • London, England
(MS: CU-MARK)

Parlor 113
Langham Hotel
London, Nov. ~~19.~~ 20

Livy darling, it is close upon half past 9, now, the breakfast is on the table getting cold, & still you & Clara[1] do not come. The Modoc amused me for a while with a distant sound, down the hall, of uncertain footsteps & *abundance of "*Tah*-tah's" for benefits conferred by somebody out there—but *she* is gone, now, & I have nothing now but the ~~mor~~ Times, with Mr. ₍Lord Rector₎ Disraeli's speech in it.[2] I am not particularly hungry, but what I mind is the delay, & the lonesomeness of waiting. As far up Portland Place as I can see, the glittering Horse-Guards are filing in stately procession; out here on Langham Place that old "semi-detached" tooth-pick of a steeple stands up just as sharp & ₍a₎ ugly as ever;[3] that same beadle is behind a pillar "laying" for a tramp who has half a mind to venture inside the iron railings; that same one-legged crossing-sweeper is coming around the circle of the railings, & is humping himself too, to help a lady into a Hansom; that very same Punch & Judy man has arrived with a tap or two of his drum, a toot or two of his pipes & a ~~will~~ wild, shrill remark from Punch himself;—& the show is moving on again, the man taking off his hat humbly & beseechingly to people in various Langham Hotel windows—to no purpose. These sights are things that you & Clara always liked, heretofore, but now you do not ~~care for~~ come. Well, I will breakfast alone, then. Bacon, coffee & poached eggs are hardly worth sharing, anyhow.

But I love you my sweetheart & would give a great deal to divide these refreshments with you & have your company.

Sam*ˡ*.

✉———————————————————————

Mrs Sam*ˡ*. L. Clemens | Forest street | Hartford | Conn. [*in upper left corner:*] America. | [*flourish*] [*postmarked:*] LONDON-W ZB NO20 73 [*and*] LI [*and*] NEW YORK DEC ◇ PAID ALL

¹Spaulding.
²The renowned Conservative statesman and novelist Benjamin Disraeli (1804–81) was installed as Lord Rector of the University of Glasgow on 19 November. After the ceremony he gave a speech, reported in the London *Times* the next day, in which he asserted that two kinds of knowledge were important for success in life: an accurate understanding of one's own character and abilities, and a comprehension of the "spirit of the age" in which those abilities would be exercised ("Mr. Disraeli at Glasgow University," 20 Nov 73, 10).
³All Souls Church in Langham Place, designed by John Nash and built in 1822–24, featured a "combination of a Greek peristyle and a spire," which was "ridiculed at the time and the portly Nash was caricatured as impaled upon it," in a drawing by Cruikshank (Weinreb and Hibbert, 19–20).

To Olivia L. Clemens
21 November 1873 • London, England
(MS: CU-MARK)

Nov. 21.

Livy my darling, I have found the porcelain picture & am delighted. It stands open on the parlor clock, & the Modoc's picture is a background for it. You see the extra pictures from Edinburgh have come.¹ I bought an overcoat & some merschaum pipes, & have laid aside the seal-skin & cigars. I bought a ~~ni~~ particularly nice ~~upb~~ umbrella, a fancy merschaum for visitors to smoke, a hat, a hatbrush, a couple of razors, lost 2 games of billiards & ordered some patent leather shoes at a considerably higher price than one pays in Hartford for such things. And I have had my dress suit ironed by the tailor. Edmund Routledge sent in his card but I was out shopping.² Livy dear you must tell me *all* the gossip—everything the neighbors say about each other, & all that sort of thing. I mean our *friends,* mainly, though gossip of *any* kind, & about anybody is one of the most toothsomely Christian dishes I know of.

"James" is to sleep in the house 2 months, & then get some good reliable man to take his place. Mr. Hall recommends *his* man, & recommends him with all his whole might—so I ~~said~~ told him I wanted him to take James's place as soon as James left;[3] I said I would pay him $50 a month rather than run the risk of your sleeping a single night alone in the house—& mind you, I ~~w~~ command you, my dear, to pay whatever that man asks, clear up to $50 a month, but see that you secure him. Mr Hall's recommendation is entirely sufficient, & you must bear in mind that there will be such hard times this winter that there will be a multitude of tramps & prowlers about. Send Father Hawley a cheque for $50; have all ~~trea~~ tramps treated kindly but *sent to Hawley;* give them soup-tickets when they ask for food.

But my! I must not write all day. Good bye my darling.

Sam'.

✉——————————————————————————

Mrs Sam'. L. Clemens | Forest street | Hartford | Conn [*in upper left corner:*] America. | [*flourish*] [*postmarked:*] LONDON-W ZB NO20 73[4] [*and*] LI [*and*] NEW YORK ◊◊◊ ◊ PAID ALL

[1] The only known surviving images of Olivia for 1872 and 1873, one of which might have been the "porcelain picture" Clemens mentions, are reproduced in Appendix F. The "Modoc's picture" was presumably the one taken in Edinburgh in August by John Moffat (see 22 and 25 Sept 73 to Brown, n. 1); it too is reproduced in Appendix F.

[2] Edmund Routledge (1843–99), the second son of George Routledge, became a partner in his father's publishing firm in 1865. In 1862, at age nineteen, he founded *Every Boy's Magazine,* a highly successful publication devoted to the interests of "boys of cultivation and intelligence" (Mumby, 136). He edited this journal (which changed titles several times) until 1889. From 1867 to 1873 he was also the editor of the Routledge house journal, *The Broadway: A London Magazine,* which had printed an original article of Clemens's ("Cannibalism in the Cars") in November 1868 (SLC 1868e; *ET&S1,* 551; Mumby, 97, 98, 136–38, 147; Boase, 6:504–5).

[3] Ezra Hall (1835–77) was a neighbor of the Clemenses' on Forest Street, and a partner, with Franklin Chamberlin, in the law firm of Chamberlin and Hall. In 1863, and again in 1871, he was elected to the Connecticut State Senate (Geer 1873, 44, 74; Trumbull, 2:275). James has not been identified.

[4] This postmark is probably erroneous; the possibility remains, however, that Clemens misdated his letter.

To Henry Lee
per Charles Warren Stoddard
22 November 1873 • London, England
(MS: ViU)

Room 113
Langham's Hotel
22ᵈ Nov 1873.

My dear Lee

I am afraid I shall be so occupied with my Lecture business[1] that I cannot promise to go down to Croydon on Wednesday next ,;[2] but so I will wait a little, till I can decide, & then write you again.

Ys Ever

Mark

✉——————————————————————————

Henry Lee Esq | 43 Holland St | Blackfriars Road. | S. E. [*postmarked:*] LONDON · W X NO22 73 [*and*] LONDON · SE MM NO22 73

[1] Clemens was preparing to deliver a new series of lectures. His first London appearance took place on Monday, 1 December, and his last on 20 December. On 19 November the following announcement began to appear in every issue of the London *Daily News* (4):

MARK TWAIN.—Mr. GEORGE DOLBY has much pleasure in announcing that MARK TWAIN has this day arrived in London from America, and will make his RE-APPEARANCE at the Hanover-square Rooms on MONDAY EVENING, December 1, when he will deliver his Humorous Lecture, entitled "Our Fellow Savages of the Sandwich Islands." The lecture will be repeated every evening (except Saturday) at 8, and on Wednesday and Saturday afternoons at 3. Stalls, 5s.; second seats, 3s.; admission One Shilling.

The same notice appeared in the London *Morning Post, Pall Mall Gazette, Times, Graphic,* and no doubt other newspapers.

[2] Clemens altered the period after "next" to a semicolon, and then finished the letter.

To Olivia L. Clemens
23 November 1873 • London, England
(MS: CU-MARK)

Sunday, 23^d.

Sweetheart, it is a rather handsome day for London—very sunny & bright & cheery, & I heartily wish you were here to enjoy it. Stoddard & I walked through Regent's Park & up on top of Primrose Hill & back again.

Stoddard has been spending some days at Oxford with the students, & they swear that if I will come there & lecture they will entertain me like a duke, & will also cram the largest hall in the town for me.[1] I would like it—& at a *lecture* they would come in fu evening dress & behave with the utmost decorum—with that thorough & complete decorum which noblemen's sons know so well how to practise when they choose—but at a common theatre what a queer lot they are!—& ɖ how they do behave, these scions of the bluest aristocratic blood of Great Britain! Stoddard attended the theatre there—aʄ company of traveling actors. The house was full—both sexes—& all the students were there—or at least several hundred of them. They wore their hats all through the performance, & they all smoked pipes & cigars. Every individual devil of them had on an Ulster overcoat like mine, that came down to his heels; & every rascal of them brought a bull pup or a terrier pup under his arm, & they would set these creatures up on the broad-topped balustrades, & ~~leave~~ allow them to amuse themselves by barking at anybody or anything they chose to. ~~The~~ Some Davenport Brothers tied themselves up with ropes, & people were requested to come on the stage & examine the trick;[2] whereupon, several students, in their long coats, their hats on, their pups under their arms & their pipes in their mouths stepped out over the balustrades of private boxes, & gravely sauntered around & around the tied man on the stage examining the knots & expressing their opinions—& the audience never smiled or said a ~~work~~ word but took the whole thing as a matter of course.

(Am called away, sweetheart,)

Saml

Mrs. Sam*¹*. L. Clemens | Forest street | Hartford | Conn [*in upper left corner:*] America. | [*flourish*] [*postmarked:*] LONDON · W 7 NO 24 73 [*and*] NEW YORK DEC 8 PAID ALL

¹ Stoddard recounted his Oxford experiences in letters to the San Francisco *Chronicle* dated 10 December and 19 December (Stoddard 1874a–b). Clemens did not lecture there.
² The Davenport brothers—Ira Erastus (1839–1911) and William Henry Harrison (1841–77)—"created considerable stir in the United States, Great Britain, and other countries in the sixties and seventies." They "performed some remarkable Indian rope-tying and sack feats," effecting quick escapes from "rope bonds in which they were tied by representatives of the audience" ("Mr. I. E. Davenport," London *Times*, 10 July 1911, 11; "Ira E. Davenport Dead," New York *Times*, 9 July 1911, 9; Bryan, 1:330–31).

To Olivia L. Clemens
24 November 1873 • London, England
(MS: CU-MARK)

London, Nov. ~~23~~ 24.

Livy darling, ~~Dob~~ Dolby is ~~tha~~ the same jolly good fellow, & says heaps of ~~pla~~ pleasant things about you & Clara¹—among the rest that you, in face & nature & everything, are the most perfect woman he ever saw or knew—which is simply what any one would say, & so it does not surprise me. It is thoroughly & completely true, as I know of my own personal knowledge.

But ~~f~~ this reminds me of that Oxford theatrical performance. The students allowed their pups to roam about the stage at will, & occasionally the dogs would fight & then the performance had to wait till it was finished.

If a student desired to visit a friend opposite, he stepped over the balustrade of his box & took the near cut across the stage through the performers. Occasionally a student walked across the stage, borrowed a pup "off" of a friend, walked back & nursed & petted it at his leisure.

Dolby says he cannot take a great pianist there, because the boys won't stand a long, dreary, instrumental piece of music. They keep up their best decorum till nature breaks down under the pressure, & ~~they~~ then they begin to talk across the house at each other about the weather & the crops, & such things, & then if the dreary piece still goes on, they begin to talk to the pianist himself, & ask him about his family; & who ~~com~~ was the author of that piece of music; & what it costs to get a piece of music like that written; & *how* does a man go about composing a piece of music?—does he have to *understand* music, or does he just blast away, hit or miss, & set it down on a piece of paper as he goes along? &c. &c.

Dolby said that when he took Dickens there,[2] it was plain that there was going to be a fearful rush, & inasmuch as the seats were all sold, days before, there would doubtless be plenty of students on a lark, who would insist on going in anyhow & standing up. The authorities warned him that a squad of policemen would be necessary, but he wouldn't have them, but determined to stand at the door of entrance himself. Sure enough, by & by came two stalwart student-aristocrats who tried to shove by him; he barred the way; he said "Where are your tickets, gentlemen?" "Got no tickets—here's the money." "Can't admit you without tickets, gentlemen." "You can't, eh?—we'll show ~~th~~ you that that is a lie." Dolby said, "You are a blackguard." They were astounded at this familiarity. Then the speaker said to his friend, "Why this fellow's got some spirit"—then to Dolby, "My dear sir, I didn't mean any harm, & I'm very sorry; & to testify it, if there's anything I can do for you, just name it & I'll do it."

"You *can* do me a very great favor, sir. If you gentlemen will just stand at this door a quarter of an hour & not let anybody in without a ticket"—

"We're your men!—just stand aside."

And they kept the door most efficiently. When Dolby came back, by & by, the rush was done, the ~~rush~~ raid of the students had failed, with the two champions, & ~~Dobl~~ Dolby said, "I'm very much obliged, gentlemen, *now* you can go in without tickets," & in they went.

Douglas Straight has just called.

Good bye my darling, I do wish I were with you or you were with me.

Sam*ˡ*.

✉——————————————————————————————

Mrs. Sam*ˡ*. L. Clemens | Forest street | Hartford | Conn [*in upper left corner:*] America. | [*flourish*] [*postmarked:*] LONDON · W 7 NO24 73

¹Spaulding.
²A day-to-day chronology of Dickens's tours in 1866–69, when Dolby acted as his manager, records no engagement in Oxford (Page, 120–35; see 15 Sept 72 to OLC, n. 1). Dolby's own account of his years with Dickens, *Charles Dickens As I Knew Him* (Dolby 1885), likewise includes no mention of an Oxford appearance.

To Olivia L. Clemens
26 November 1873 • London, England
(MS: CU-MARK)

London, Nov. 26.

Livy darling, old sweetheart, tomorrow will be the birth-day of my own sweet wife;¹ & I shall think of her over & over & over again, all thro' the day & till the last thing at night; & shall bless her with all my heart all the whole time & wish that the day may speed along which shall bring me to her again.

The enclosed is from Charles Kingsley.² I have written & told him how greatly I regret that you did not see him. And I told him not to come all the way here again, but appoint a day & I would go to the Abbey.³ He don't know what *he* has missed in not seeing my darling old wife.

Saml.

[*enclosure:*]

The Cloisters   No*ᵇʳ* 26/73
Westminster

My dear Sir

I t̶r̶e̶ tried in vain, when you were last in London, to have the great pleasure of introducing myself to you. I called—hearing that you had returned—at the Langham Hotel today: but was too meek to intrude on you—even had you been at home.

But will you kindly let me know when I may have a chance of seeing you: I shall be absent from Town from *next Monday to next Thursday.*

Before & after that I am at your service. And may I say, that if you care to make a closer acquaintance than the multitude can make with our English Pantheon the old Abbey here—it would give me—& mine for my ladies[4] are even more fond of your work than I—extreme pleasure to act as cicerones to some strange & remote spots in our great Stone Mausoleum.[5]

Believe me with sincere respects

Yours vy truly

Charles Kingsley

Mrs. Sam*l*. L. Clemens | Hartford | Conn. [*in upper left corner:*] America. | [*flourish*] [*postmarked:*] LONDON · W 7 NO28 73 [*and*] L 28 II 1873 [*and*] NEW YORK DEC IO PAID ALL

[1] Olivia was twenty-eight years old on 27 November.

[2] Charles Kingsley (1819–75) was the canon of Westminster and the author of numerous historical novels, political pamphlets, poems, sermons, and essays. He had been a precocious child, writing poems and sermons at age four. After attending Cambridge University he was ordained a minister in 1842; in addition to his church positions, he held a professorship in history at Cambridge from 1860 to 1869. As a Christian Socialist, he was greatly concerned with social justice and the responsibilities of the wealthy. Clemens had tried to read Kingsley's *Hypatia* in 1869, and pronounced it "one of Kingsley's most tiresomest books" (*L3*, 413).

[3] Clemens's letter of 26 November to Kingsley is not known to survive. Kingsley replied on 28 November:

> Many thanks for your cordial letter. Will you & M*r*. Stoddard give me the pleasure of coming to luncheon tomorrow at 1 P.M.? I am sorry—& so will M*rs*. Kingsley be— that she is out of town. After our luncheon & our cigarette—we can look at the Abbey or not, as you may like. (CU-MARK)

[4] Kingsley married Fanny Grenfell in 1844. The couple had four children, of whom two were "ladies": Rose Georgina (b. 1845) and Mary St. Leger (b. 1852).

[5] In 1903 Stoddard recalled accompanying Clemens to lunch with Kingsley:

> My friend and I, by appointment, were in search of Canon Kingsley at the cloisters, Westminster. We passed out of the Abbey toward the chapter-house in a kind of dream. . . .
>
> With many a turn we come at last to a row of modest dwellings. Entering one of these we were welcomed by Miss Kingsley, and ushered at once into a pleasant room where the table was laid for dinner. There was a blessed absence of formality, a simple and hearty welcome. Canon Kingsley's table-talk sparkled with lively anecdotes, chiefly personal. A man of nervous organisation, animated, personally interested in the topics of the time, he glowed with enthusiasm and struck fire repeatedly, though he was then in ill-health and burdened with many cares. He looked forward with delight to his anticipated tour in America; wondered what sort of lecture the Americans would prefer. . . .

After the wholesome English dinner we lighted cigars; Canon Kingsley was confined to the medicated cigarette, which is supposed to discourage the bronchial disorder from which he was a sufferer. We entered a small garden by the bow-window of the dining-room. . . . Here we walked up and down, to and fro, under leafless trees—for it was winter,—smoking placidly, stopping now and again to hear the veritable tale of some monk or abbot who distinguished himself centuries ago on the very spot where we stood. . . .

When we left the cloisters it was sunset. The canon led us again into the Abbey, where the nave was flooded with that weird light which seems not of the earth and is but momentary. The long, low thunders of the world without broke at the sacred doors, which were at that moment closed to all save ourselves. We had indeed found sanctuary, but only for a little season. We hastened forth, and were instantly swallowed up in the eddies of the ceaseless tide of London life. (Stoddard 1903, 152–55, 160)

On 17 February 1874 Clemens introduced Kingsley when he lectured on West-minster Abbey to a Boston audience. Kingsley fondly recalled "wandering through Westminster Abbey" with Clemens the previous fall, and hearing him speak eloquently of his earlier "night visit there" (Reed, 692–93; see Appendix C).

To George H. Fitzgibbon
28 November 1873 • London, England
(MS and transcript: CtHMTH and NN-B)

Friday.

My Dear ~~F~~ Mr. Fitz Gibbon—

Thank you ever so much for your timely hints & suggestions. I shall make good use of them. I shall "lay" for that subscription ~~paper & make my~~ paper (as ~~we~~ the nobility say), & make my deposit there.[1]

And I have gone to work & written a speech for the occasion in order to be on the safe side (I enclose a copy.) It is not lost labor, even if I am not called upon, or even if I find it best to curtail it like ~~e~~ sin in the delivery, because it will easily find room in a future volume of Sketches as the impromptu speech which I *intended* to make.[2]

It will take me just ten minutes to deliver this speech (I have timed it,) but I do not know how to shorten it—every time I try, I only lengthen it.

I know Mr. Russel, editor of the Scotsman, very well, & I like him. My wife & I spent a day or so very delightfully at his country house near Edinburgh last summer. I know all of them. Finlay, proprietor of the Belfast "Northern Whig" is one of the closest friends I have. He is Russel's son-in-law. I would send him a copy of this speech to publish next morning "by telegraph" if I knew I was going to deliver it. Good advertisement, as I may possibly lecture in Belfast. You see, ∮ be the speech good, bad, or indifferent, I would like it to be published in full in as many papers as possible, because of its advertising qualities. ~~If you have~~

I shall have my Secretary make several copies, & I will carry them with me Monday night, so that if you see a reporter who would use the MS., we will let him have it—& welcome.[3]

Yes—I'm to be at the Salutation Saturday night & shall be precisely the reverse of sorry to meet you there.[4]

With kind regards to you all (ask Mrs. Fitz Gibbon if she does not think it is nothing against Miss Florence Stark[5] that she resembles Mrs. Clemens?)

> Ys Ever
> S.L. Clemens

[*enclosure, page 1 in SLC's hand:*][6]

~~I am~~

I am proud indeed of the distinction of being chosen to respond to this especial toast—"to the ladies",—or to Woman, if you please, for that is the preferable term, perhaps; it is certainly the older, & therefore the more entitled to reverence: I have noticed [*page 2, in unidentified hand:*] & probably you may have noticed that the bible with that plain blunt honesty which is such a conspicuous characteristic of the Scriptures is careful to never even refer to the illustrious mother of all mankind herself as a "lady" It is odd but I think you will find that it is so. I am peculiarly proud of this honour because I think that the toast of women should by right & every rule of gallantry take precedence of all others— of the Army the Navy of even royalty itself perhaps though the latter is not necessary this day & in this land for the reason that tacitly you do drink a broad general health to all good women when you drink to the health of the [*page 3, in Stoddard's hand:*] Queen of England and the Princess of Wales.

I have in mind a poem, just now, which is familiar to you all, familiar to every body. And what an inspiration that was (and how instantly the present toast recals the verses to all our minds), where the most noble, the most gracious, the purest and sweetest of all poets says, "Woman, O Woman—er—Wom—" however you remember the lines.

And you remember how feelingly, how daintily, [*page 4, in Stoddard's hand:*] how almost imperceptibly the verses raise up before you, feature by feature, the ideal of a true and perfect woman; and how, as you contemplate the finished marvel, your homage grows into worship of the intellect that could create so fair a thing out of mere breath, mere words.

And you call to mind, now, as I speak, how the poet with stern fidelity to the history of all humanity, delivers this beautiful child of his [*page 5, in Stoddard's hand:*] heart and his brain over to the trials and the sorrows that must come to all, sooner or later, that abide in the Earth; and how the pathetic story culminates in that apostrophe, so wild, so regretful, so full of mournful retrospection,—the lines run thus: "Alas! Alas!—a—Alas!— — —Alas!—["] and so on. I do not remember the rest. But taken altogether it seems to me that that poem is the noblest tribute to woman that human genius has ever [*page 6, in Stoddard's hand:*] brought forth; and I feel that if I were to talk hours I could not do my great theme completer or more graceful justice than I have now done in simply quoting that poets matchless words.

The phases of the womanly nature are infinite in their variety. Take any type of woman and you shall find in it something to respect, something to admire, something to love. And you shall find the whole world joining you [*page 7, in Stoddard's hand:*] heart and hand. Who was more patriotic than Joan of Arc? Who was braver? Who has given us a grander instance of self-sacrificing devotion? Ah, you remember, you remember well, what a throb of pain, what a great tidal-wave of grief swept over us all when Joan of Arc fell at Waterloo.— Who does not sorrow for the loss of Sappho the sweet singer of Israel? Who among us does not miss the gentle ministrations, [*page 8, in Stoddard's hand:*] the softening influences, the humble piety, of Lucretia Borgia?

Who can join in the heartless libel that says woman is extravagant in dress, when he can look back and call to mind our simple and lowly, Mother Eve arrayed in her modification of the Highland costume?

Sir, women have been soldiers, women have been painters, women have been poets. As long as language lives, [*page 9, in Stoddard's hand:*] the name of Cleopatra will live. And not because she conquered George III., but because she wrote those divine lines,

> "Let dogs delight to bark & bite
> For God hath made them so."[7]

The story of the world is adorned with the names of illustrious ones of our own sex, some of them sons of St Andrew, too,—Scott, Bruce, Burns, the warrior Wallace, Ben Nevis, the gifted Ben Lomond, & the great new Scotchman Ben Disraeli. [*page 10, in Stoddard's hand:*]

Out of the great plains of history tower whole mountain ranges of sublime women. The Queen of Sheba, Josephine, Semiramis, Sairey Gamp—the list is endless.

But I will not call the mighty roll—the names ris[e] up in your own memories at the mere [*page 11, in Stoddard's hand:*] ~~memories at the mere~~ suggestion, luminous with the glory of deeds that cannot die, hallowed by the loving worship of the good and the true of all epochs and all climes.

Suffice it for our pride and our honour that we in our day have added to it such names as those of Grace Darling & Florence Nightingale.[8]

Woman is all that she should be: gentle, patient, long-suffering, trustful, unselfish, full of [*page 12, in Stoddard's hand:*] generous impulses. It is her blessed mission to comfort the sorrowing, plead for the erring, encourage the faint of purpose, succor the distressed, uplift the fallen, befriend the friendless,—in a word, afford the healing of her sympathies and a home in her heart for all the bruised and persecuted children of misfortune that knock at its hospitable door. And when I say God bless her, [*page 12½ (inserted), in unidentified hand:*][9] there is none here present who has known the enobling affection of [*page 13, in SLC's hand:*] a wife or the steadfast devotion of a mother but in his heart will say Amen![10]

---

[1] Fitzgibbon's letter is not known to survive. The "subscription paper" was probably a fund-raising device for the Scottish Corporation (see the next note). No record of any contribution from Clemens has been found.

[2] Clemens was planning to attend a dinner on Monday, 1 December, commemorating the 209th anniversary of the Scottish Corporation, a benevolent society that provided pensions, allowances, and school grants for needy Scots in London. He went to the dinner after giving his eight o'clock lecture at the Hanover Square Rooms, and he responded to the toast to "The Ladies." According to the London *Times*, he "returned thanks in a characteristic and most humorous speech, which was loudly and repeatedly cheered" ("St. Andrew's Day" and "The Scottish Hospital," London *Times*, 2 Dec 73, 5, 10; Weinreb and Hibbert, 777; for Clemens's earlier toast on "Woman," see *L2*, 155–57). The London *Morning Post* published the speech on Tuesday, evidently from notes taken by its reporter ("Scottish Corporation of London," 2 Dec 73, 6, clipping in Scrapbook

12:33, CU-MARK). The text in the *Post* was reprinted by an unidentified London newspaper, a clipping of which Clemens ultimately used as printer's copy for the speech in *Mark Twain's Sketches, New and Old* (SLC 1875). Although he labeled the clipping "[From the London Observer.]," the *Observer* did not in fact publish it (TxU-Hu†).

[3] No printing of the speech based on any of these copies has been found.

[4] The day after he wrote this letter, Clemens attended a celebration given by the St. Andrew's Society of London, presided over by Tom Hood at the Salutation Tavern. The Hartford *Courant*, evidently reprinting an unidentified English newspaper, reported:

> One of the guests of the evening was Mr. Clemens, better known under the nom de plume of Mark Twain. The chairman gave the toast of the evening in appropriate terms, and Mark Twain in the course of his reply to the toast of "The Guests" said: I feel singularly at home in this Scotch society. I have spent so much time in Scotland that everything connected with Scotland is familiar to me. Last summer I passed five weeks in that magnificent city of Edinburgh, resting. I needed rest, and I did rest. I did not know anybody. I did not take any letters of introduction at all. I simply rested and enjoyed myself. From my experience of the Scotch everything belonging to them is familiar, the language, the peculiarities of expression, even the technical things that are national, are simple household words with me. I remember when in Edinburgh I was nearly always taken for a Scotchman. Oh, yes! (Laughter.) I had my clothes some part colored tartan, and I rather enjoyed being taken for a Scotchman. I stuck a big feather in my cap, too, and the people would follow me for miles. They thought I was a Highlander, and some of the best judges in Scotland said they had never seen a Highland costume like mine. What's more, one of those judges fined me for wearing it—out of mere envy, I suppose. (Laughter.) But any man may have a noble, good time in Scotland if they only think he's a native. (Laughter.) For breakfast you may have oatmeal poultice—I beg pardon, I mean porridge. (Laughter.) Then for dinner you may have fine Scotch game—the blackcock, the spatchcock, the woodcock, the moorcock. I have simply to return to you my acknowledgments, and to apologize for not being able to make a speech; but give me fair play, and I can make a speech that will astonish anybody and nobody more than myself. (Laughter.) My present position is a national one, if I may be regarded as representing the United States of America. On that side of the Atlantic there are 40,000,000 of people. They may be respectable, and I will say in conclusion that I do hope "a brother American" will soon cease to be simply a phrase meaning nothing, but will by and by become a reality, when Great Britain and the citizens of America will be brethren indeed. (Cheers.) (SLC 1873z)

[5] Unidentified. Stark is also mentioned in two other letters to Fitzgibbon: 5 Oct 72 and 30 Dec 73.

[6] The enclosure is comprised of two pages in Clemens's hand, ten pages in Charles Warren Stoddard's hand, and two in an unidentified hand. Clemens presumably recruited help from Stoddard and an amanuensis to create multiple copies of the text. Fitzgibbon's notes on the first and last pages of the manuscript indicate that he intended to publish it, probably in the newspaper for which he corresponded, the Darlington *Northern Echo*. It did not, however, appear there. At the beginning of the text he noted, "[Mark Twain responded for the Ladies. He said—". See also note 10.

[7] The first two lines of Isaac Watts's "Against Quarrelling and Fighting," in *Divine Songs* (1715). Watts was one of Clemens's perennial targets (*ET&S1*, 236, 237, 471, 472).

[8] Clemens alluded to the following in his romp through history: Princess Al-

exandra (1844–1925), the eldest daughter of Christian IX of Denmark, who in 1863 married Prince Albert Edward, Queen Victoria's eldest son and heir to the throne; Joan of Arc (1412–31); Napoleon's defeat at Waterloo on 18 June 1815; Sappho, a Greek poetess born on Lesbos in about 600 B.C.; King David of Israel (d. 973? B.C.), the "sweet singer of Israel"; Lucrezia Borgia (1480–1519); Cleopatra (69–30 B.C.); George III (1738–1820), crowned king of England in 1760; Sir Walter Scott (1771–1832); Robert Bruce (1274–1329), hero of the Scottish War of Independence; Robert Burns (1759–96); Sir William Wallace (1272–1305), patriot and soldier in the Scottish War of Independence; Ben Nevis and Ben Lomond, mountains in Scotland; Benjamin Disraeli (see 20 Nov 73 to OLC, n. 2); the Queen of Sheba (1 Kings 10:1–13); Marie Joséphine (1763–1814), the wife of Napoleon Bonaparte and empress of France; Semiramis (ninth century B.C.), a celebrated queen of Assyria; Sairey Gamp, the disreputable old nurse in Dickens's *Life and Adventures of Martin Chuzzlewit* (1843–44), which Clemens had read by November 1860 (*L1*, 104–5); Grace Horsley Darling (1815–42), who in 1838 helped her father, the keeper of a Farne Islands lighthouse, to rescue several shipwreck victims clinging to a rock and for her heroic deed was awarded a gold medal and £800; and Florence Nightingale (1820–1910).

⁹The words now on page 12½ were first jotted down, by the unidentified amanuensis, underneath Fitzgibbon's remarks on page 13 (see the next note), presumably to record that they were missing from the composite text. He then reinscribed them on a new page, numbered it 12½, and inserted it here.

¹⁰Immediately after Clemens's "Amen!" Fitzgibbon added, "(General cheering in the midst of which Mʳ Clemens resumed his seat.).".

🐦

No LETTERS written between 28 November and 3 December 1873 have been found. Clemens opened his second English lecture series on Monday, 1 December, delivering his popular Sandwich Islands talk to full and enthusiastic houses. One week later, on 8 December, he introduced a lecture that was new to English audiences, "Roughing It on the Silver Frontier," based in part on incidents recounted in *Roughing It*. (For reviews of both lectures see 6 Dec 73 to OLC, n. 1, and 9 Dec 73 to OLC [1st], n. 1.) Stoddard recalled:

> About three o'clock of each day Mark began to get nervous and irritable, as he always did when he was going to lecture, and from that time on it was my business to keep him as mentally occupied as I could. He was self-willed and obstinate, of course, and wanted to do what he wanted to do, and I had to fit into his moods as best I could. Dear old Mark! Those were trying times for him. A little before eight we would walk over to the Concert Rooms and up the stairs into the tiny room at the back, Mark getting more and more irritable and nervous all the while, looking at his watch, anxious to plunge in and have it over. The moment eight o'clock arrived he invariably said, "It's

time now. I'll not wait another moment," and then, as cool and deliberate as could be, he walked on to the platform, "washing his hands in invisible soap and water," slowly saying his first words. The moment he heard his own voice he began to feel better, and I knew he was all right. (James, 669)

Clemens was a consistent success, although there was some variation in the response of each audience:

> I found that a joke which took the house by storm one evening was not sure of a like success the following night. Some jokes took immediate effect and convulsed the house. The hearty laughter was as the laughter of one man with a thousand mouths. On another occasion the same joke caught feebly in one corner of the room, ran diagonally across the hall, followed by a trail of laughter, and exploded on the last bench. By this time the front seats had awakened to a sense of the ludicrous and the applause became general. (Stoddard 1903, 67–68)

After the lectures, according to Stoddard,

> Mark always felt amiable, and met the people who came to shake hands with his well-known suavity and grace, and cheerfully gave them autographs and all that kind of thing. Then we'd walk home. As soon as we arrived, he would bring out a bottle of Bourbon whiskey—he'd searched London over to find this—some Angostura bitters, sugar, lemons and the other "fixin's," and proceed to mix a cocktail for each of us, slowly talking to me the while. He was an adept at cocktail making—knew the art to perfection. As we drank it the constant drawl of his voice was heard, as he walked up and down the room. This was the only way he could get ready to sleep. Lecturing excited him and got him started and he would talk for hours. (James, 669)

❦

To Olivia L. Clemens
3 December 1873 • London, England
(MS: CU-MARK)

Dec. 3.

Livy darling, I am as busy as I can be, day & night, revamping & memorizing my "Roughing It" lecture, because I want to use it next week.[1] After that I want to try a reading here if I get time to prepare it.[2] I won't write you more, now, except to say that I love you with all my heart.

Sam*l.*

⊠——

Mrs. Sam*ˡ*. L. Clemens | Forest street | Hartford | Conn [*in upper left
corner:*] America. | [*rule*] [*postmarked:*] LONDON · W 1 DE 3 73 [*and*] NEW YORK
DEC 18 PAID ALL.

¹Clemens delivered "Roughing It on the Silver Frontier" from 8 through 20
December. He had previously used essentially the same lecture while on tour in
the East and Midwest in December 1871 and early 1872 ("Mark Twain's New
Humorous Lecture," London *Daily News*, 6, 15, 20 Dec 73, 4; 2 Jan 72 to Redpath, n. 1).
²No such "reading" took place.

To Olivia L. Clemens
6 December 1873 • London, England
(MS: CU-MARK)

Dec. 6.

Livy darling, I shall rest all day tomorrow (Sunday) except that I shall
be studying my new lecture, & on Monday evening I shall take a fresh
start. There was a mighty fine house there this afternoon, & I went
through all right, but I am unspeakably sick of the Sandwich Islands as
a topic to lecture on.¹ I shall get tired of the new one in a week I expect.

I am tired, but I do love you & I do long to see you.

Saml.

⊠——

Mrs. Sam*ˡ*. L. Clemens | Hartford | ~~Com~~ Conn | [*flourish*] [*in upper left
corner:*] America | [*flourish*] [*postmarked:*] LONDON-W. E 12 DE 8 73 [*and*]
NEW YORK DEC 20 PAID ALL

¹Despite Clemens's boredom with the Sandwich Islands lecture, he continued
to receive favorable notices. After his first return performance, for example, the
London *Telegraph* commented:

> The quaint American humourist, "Mark Twain," whose facetious lecture on "Our Fel-
> low Savages of the Sandwich Islands" was received with such distinguished favour on
> its first recital in October, has resumed his pleasant discourses, and a numerous audi-
> ence last night welcomed him back from a rapid trip across the Atlantic, which has had
> apparently no other effect than that of freshening the vivacity of the lecturer. To the odd
> fancies, amusing anecdotes, sly satirical comments, and graphic descriptions of the en-

tertainer, the assemblage listened with the same interest and sustained enjoyment which were so strongly manifested by the auditory on the previous occasions, and at the end "Mark Twain" was the recipient of one of those spontaneous tributes of hearty applause only given to those who have really honestly earned the thanks of an audience for an hour's genuine gratification. ("Hanover-square Rooms," 2 Dec 73, clipping in Scrapbook 12:33, CU-MARK)

On that same day the London *Morning Post* pointed out that Clemens's talents were greater than some critics gave him credit for:

It is a merit of the lecturer's that while . . . he is able to make his hearers very merry, he is competent to hold them well-nigh spell-bound as he describes in picturesque phraseology the thousand and one scenic beauties of the Sandwich Islands. Perhaps, as a rule, the audience are too apt to expect the lecturer to be "funny" the whole of the evening, instead of crediting him with a desire to be instructive as well as amusing. Of his ability to do both there is no question, as was abundantly proved last night. ("Mr. 'Mark Twain,'" 2 Dec 73, 6, clipping in Scrapbook 12:33, CU-MARK)

Stoddard preserved both of these notices in one of the scrapbooks he was keeping for Clemens.

To Olivia L. Clemens
7 December 1873 • London, England
(MS: CU-MARK)

Dec. 7.

Livy darling, I love you. I went thro' a rehearsal of my "Roughing It" lecture to-day (Sunday) & it seems to be all right. I think I shall enjoy delivering it. This is fatiguing work, my love—but in a day or two I hope I shall get to writing you regularly again. Did you never get a telegram from me at Queenstown? I sent one.[1]

Bliss must hurry up the book if I am to copyright it here.[2] I *love* you.

Sam*l*.

✉———————————————————————

Mrs. Sam*l*. L. Clemens | Hartford | Conn [*in upper left corner:*] America. | [*flourish*] [*postmarked:*] LONDON-W 7 DE 8 73 [*and*] NEW YORK DEC 20 PAID ALL

[1] See 10 and 17 Nov 73 to OLC, n. 5.
[2] *The Gilded Age.* See 22 Dec 73 to OLC (2nd), n. 2.

To a Member of the London Morayshire Club
per Charles Warren Stoddard
8 December 1873 • London, England
(MS: UkElgM)

Langham Hotel.
8th Dec 1873.

Dear Sir

Thanks for the tickets to the club dinner.[1]

I shall ~~try to~~ be[2] there about 10 P. M which is as early as I can get away from my Lecture.

Ys Truly
Saml. L. Clemens.

✉—————————————————————————————

[*letter docketed:*] London 8th Decr 1873 | Mark Twain | *Festival*

[1] An unidentified member of the London Morayshire Club had sent Clemens tickets to its second anniversary festival on 11 December. The club carried out charitable enterprises to benefit the people of Moray, a county in northeast Scotland ("London Morayshire Club," Elgin [Scotland] *Courant*, 16 Dec 73, no page).

[2] Clemens canceled Stoddard's "try to" and retraced his "be," possibly for emphasis. Clemens did in fact attend (11 and 12 Dec 73 to OLC).

To Olivia L. Clemens
9 December 1873 • (1st of 2) • London, England
(MS: CU-MARK)

Dec. 9,

Livy darling, I never enjoyed delivering a lecture, in all my life, more than I did tonight. It was ~~y~~ so perfectly jolly. ~~I~~ And it was such a stylish looking, bright ~~au~~ audience. There were people there who gave way entirely & just went on laughing, & I had to stop & wait for them to get through.[1] I wish you & Clara were here. You would enjoy it. I like this lecture ever so much better than the one on the Islands. I don't know why, but I do. And Stoddard does, & Dolby does, & they all do. I shan't *read*, in Hartford, for Alice Day, but will use this lecture. I believe I never have delivered it there yet. Ask Warner—he will know.[2] Those people almost made me laugh myself, tonight.

I got Warner's letter. Good. Let him tell Bliss I have put matters in motion about the Wood "Shells" & about canvassing Canada, & shall hear from the Routledges upon these matters tomorrow.[3] And I got a whole handful of letters from you, Livy dear,—Stoddard brought ~~then~~ them while I was still in bed, & I read them there, & I did enjoy them ever so much. I wished there were more.[4] Ma *is* a darling good old soul, & if she were only a Queen, her name would outlast that of any Monarch that ever wore a crown.[5] I wish I could see you & the Modoc. She is a pretty entertaining cub I think.

The fog was so thick to-day at noon that the cabs *went in a walk, & men went before the omnibuses carrying lanterns.* Give that item to Warner.[6] It was the heaviest fog seen in London in 20 years. And you know how the fog invades the houses & makes your eyes smart. To-night, the first thing I said on the stage was, "Ladies & gentlemen, I *hear* you, & so I know that you are here—& *I* am here, too, notwithstanding I am not visible." The audience did look so vague, & dim, & ghostly! The hall seemed full of a thick blue smoke.[7]

But I *must* quit, my eyes smart so. I do love you, sweetheart.
                                                                  Sam*l*.

P. S. I've written a *delicious* squib, if these ~~g~~ papers will only just dare to print it.[8] Love to our dear mother.[9]

Mrs. Sam*l*. L. Clemens | Hartford | Conn [*in upper left corner:*] America. | [*rule*] [*postmarked:*] LONDON-W 12 DE 10 73 [*and*] NEW YORK DEC 23 PAID ALL

---

[1] The "Roughing It" lecture (first delivered on 8 December) was as well received as the Sandwich Islands talk. The London *Morning Post* again emphasized Clemens's talent for descriptive writing (9 Dec 73 to Fitzgibbon, n. 1). The London *Times* found that Nevada Territory, "whether considered from a moral or a material point of view," seemed "the most objectionable place on the face of the earth":

> While we thus briefly indicate the matter of Mr. Mark Twain's discourse, we give no notion of the exquisite humour of his manner, or of the quiet irony with which he makes a narrative that might be exceedingly dismal a cause of perpetual mirth. A smile never appears on his lips and he makes the most startling remarks as if he were uttering the

merest common-place. At times, indeed, he rises into serious eloquence, as when, for instance, he describes in glowing terms the beauties of Lake Tahoe, but his great forte, like that of Artemus Ward, is his sustained irony, and this reaches its perfection when, at the end of his description of horrors, he grimly expresses a hope that he has not said anything which might tend to depopulate England, through a vast emigration to Nevada. ("Mr. Mark Twain," 12 Dec 73, 5, clipping in Scrapbook 12:45, CU-MARK)

The London *Evening Globe* was more critical, describing the new lecture as

> well received, but scarcely so heartily as the famous lecture on the Fiji Islands. The audience seemed to become accustomed to the speaker's tricks of style, and to find them less amusing the oftener they were repeated. He has some genuine humour; but it is of an elementary kind, consisting for the most part of grotesque exaggeration.

Still, this critic admitted that while "most of the 'points' of the lecture, if read, would seem outrageously absurd, if not contemptible," when

> delivered by Mark Twain they often excite hearty laughter. He is a capital speaker, free, sympathetic, and self-confident; and he has the first essential of a good platform orator—he never laughs at his own jokes. Last night he seemed more than once the only perfectly grave person in the hall. ("Mark Twain's Second Lecture," 9 Dec 73, clipping in Scrapbook 12:51, CU-MARK)

Favorable reviews also appeared in the London *Evening Echo* (9 Dec 73), *Telegraph* (9 Dec 73), *Standard* (10? Dec 73), *Observer* (14 Dec 73, 2), and *Figaro* (17 Dec 73) (clippings in Scrapbook 12:39–51, CU-MARK; see also 11 Dec 73 to OLC, n. 2).

[2] Nothing is known of the reading requested by the Clemenses' Hartford friend Alice Hooker Day. Clemens had not delivered "Roughing It" in Hartford, nor would he do so.

[3] Warner's letter has not been found. Bliss had evidently inquired through Warner about publishing an American edition of John George Wood's *Common Shells of the Sea-shore*, first published in London in 1865 by Frederick Warne and Company. Since Warne was George Routledge's brother-in-law, and from 1851 to 1865 had been his partner in the publishing business, Bliss probably hoped to use Clemens's offices with Routledge to negotiate for the American rights, but nothing ultimately came of the idea. No American Publishing Company edition of the book was ever issued. In 1870 Bliss had negotiated such an arrangement for another of Wood's works, *The Uncivilized Races, or Natural History of Man*, first published by Routledge (1868–70). Bliss seems also to have inquired through Warner whether Routledge would allow him to sell the American edition of *The Gilded Age* in Canada (Mumby, 51, 98; *RI 1993*, 605–6, 820–21; 13 and 15 Dec 73 to OLC).

[4] None of Olivia's letters to her husband for the period November 1873 through January 1874 has been found.

[5] Jane Lampton Clemens.

[6] No such item has been found in the Hartford *Courant*.

[7] Stoddard recalled this fog in 1903:

> It is dense, woolly, sticky, and full of small floating particles of smut, that settle upon your face, hands, collar and cuffs, and spoil your personal appearance inside of twenty minutes. It is yellow as furnace smoke—it is furnace smoke to a great degree. . . . The Concert Rooms were hermetically sealed during the day, but at night, when the audience gathered, the fog trailed in, dimming the gaslights and flooding the place with a vague gloom. . . .

There was an evening of fog at the close of a day during which the street-lamps had in vain struggled to light the bewildered citizens through the chaotic city. At high noon linkboys bore their flaming torches to and fro; and the air was burdened with the ceaseless cries of cabmen who were all adrift, and in danger of a collapse and total wreck at the imminent lamp-post. . . . Mark began his lecture on this occasion with a delicate allusion to the weather, and said: "Perhaps you can't see me, but I am here!" (Stoddard 1903, 67, 68–69)

[8] Possibly Clemens's letter of 10 December to the editor of the London *Morning Post*.

[9] Olivia Lewis Langdon.

To Olivia L. Clemens
9 December 1873 • (2nd of 2) • London, England
(MS: CU-MARK)

[on back of letter as folded:]

Dec. 9. Meant to enclose this, honey, but sealed the envelop before I thought.

Sam*l*.

8 Dec^br

23 RUTLAND STREET   EDINBURGH

My dear friend— Thanks for the M. Post—& the capital speech— You must have enjoyed it, as well as they you.[1] When are you coming here?— are you under a "former"?—surely you will give us a turn— I had a kind note from Mrs Clemens—she will enjoy your glory & prattle of it to Mel Megalopis Susie— What of the Novel?[2] We are all well & dull— I am dodging about from door to door—as usual— Don't trouble to write, only tell me when you know your time for invading us—& harrying the city—[3] Take care of your self—get 8 hours sleep out of every 24—& keep the Midland Counties regular—

Yrs ever

J. Brown

[1] Clemens had evidently sent Brown two clippings from the 2 December London *Morning Post*: the complimentary review of his 1 December lecture, and the text of his speech that evening on "The Ladies" (see 6 Dec 73 to OLC, n. 1, and 28 Nov 73 to Fitzgibbon, n. 2).

[2] The soon-to-be-published *Gilded Age.*
[3] Clemens was planning to lecture in the "provinces," including Edinburgh, after the close of his London engagement (17 Dec 73 to Redpath).

To George H. Fitzgibbon
9 December 1873 • London, England
(MS: MoSW)

                                          Dec. 9,

Dear Fitz Gibbon:

We had such a jolly nice audience, this foggy night, & I never en-joyed talking in all my life as I did on this occasion. It is a most excellent notice in the Post, & I am grateful for it.[1] Won't you & Mrs. Fitz Gibbon try to run down some night & hear this lecture? I wish you would. The people like it better than the other one.

Yes, I'm going to be at the Morayshire dinner[2]—but I haven't any highland costume but an undershirt & a striped cravat.

                                          Ys Ever
                                          S. L. Clemens.

[1] The critic for the London *Morning Post* wrote:

Of course Mr. Twain's *forte* is humour, often of the broadest kind, yet never going be-yond the line; but he must also be credited with possessing an extraordinary power of describing the wonders of those Western regions in picturesque language. He narrates with facility the splendours of mountain, valley, and lake scenery, conjuring up pan-orama after panorama matchless for its wealth of beauty. Evidently a very close observer of nature, Mr. Twain is also a nature-worshipper, for he dilates with what, for him, is enthusiasm upon the scenic charms which abound in California. This merit the audi-ence are too apt to overlook in their eagerness to hear "something funny," of which there is indeed a sufficiency. Few men can tell a story as well as Mr. Twain, who has an in-exhaustible stock of "yarns," and is never tired of spinning them. . . . There is nothing so broadly comic to be heard in London as "Roughing it on the Silver Frontier," and Mr. Twain ought to have crowded houses every night, as no doubt he will. His reception last night was exceedingly flattering, and the large concert-room was full. ("Mr. Mark Twain's New Lecture," 9 Dec 73, 2, clipping in Scrapbook 12:37, CU-MARK)

[2] See 8 Dec 73 to a member of the London Morayshire Club.

To Henry Lee
9 December 1873 • London, England
(MS: Dorn)

Dec. 9,

Dear Lee:

I like Hingston,[1] & I would do a good many things for him, but I couldn't do that for my brother—for the reason that a man isn't justified in telling an uproarious anecdote before an audience until he has led up to it with a lecture with things in it which show he is capable of better things. But Hingston will understand how a man naturally feels about these matters.[2]

Had a *jolly* good time with my ~~ad~~ audience to-night—& they were the nicest people in the world.

Ys Ever

Mark.

Henry Lee Esq | 43 Holland street | Blackfriars Road | S. E. [*post-marked:*] LONDON-W 3 DE10 73

[1] Edward P. Hingston, a well-known theatrical manager, had been Artemus Ward's agent and good friend. Clemens met him in late 1863, when he brought Ward to lecture in Virginia City, and in early 1867 tried to hire him as his own lecture agent. Clemens was no doubt familiar with Hingston's introduction to John Camden Hotten's pirated edition of *The Innocents Abroad* (1870), which included a brief (and somewhat inaccurate) biographical sketch of the author, as well as many compliments on his talent and personal appeal. And in the winter of 1871 Clemens had relied on Hingston's *The Genial Showman: Being Reminiscences of the Life of Artemus Ward* (1870) for some of the information in his "Artemus Ward, Humorist" lecture (*L1*, 269 n. 5; *L2*, 8–9; Hingston 1870; *ET&S1*, 554; *L4*, 480 n. 5).

[2] Hingston's friends, Lee presumably among them, were organizing a benefit for him, to be held on 15 and 16 December at the Opera Comique in London. Hingston had leased and managed this theater since October 1872, and was now about to resign. It is likely that Lee had asked Clemens to deliver a brief anecdote as part of the festivities, at which dozens of dancers, actors, and musicians had agreed to perform ("Opera Comique.—Mr. Hingston's Benefit," London *Times*, 15 Dec 73, 8; Boase, 1:1482–83).

To Moncure D. Conway
10 December 1873 • London, England
(Paraphrase: AAA 1925b, lot 27)

A. L. S. One page 12 mo, Dec. 10, no year. Signed,—"Mark." To Moncure D. Conway, saying his book will be issued soon and asking him to exchange.[1]

[1] Clemens replied to the following note from Conway, written on Wednesday, 10 December (CU-MARK):

My dear Clemens,

I would have liked much to have wrung your hand on Monday evening for that admirable speech of yours, but having a bonnetless lady along could not manage it. It (the lecture) is even better than the Sandwich one, and that is saying a great deal. Your audience was limited by Sir Sam Baker, who was to be welcomed that night by the Prince, but I have no doubt your lecture will be a favourite with the public—especially as the Baker and Tichborne affairs prevented the papers publishing all your best plums.

—I am under the most terrible persecution from printers and have been ever since your arrival; but my big book will be out this week; the dumb demon will be exorcised; I shall be a freeman. And when free it cannot be long before I get hold of S. L. C.

Meanwhile Mrs. Conway sends her thanks for the very pleasant note she has rec^d. from Mrs. Clemens; & hopes that after your lecture Monday you will be able to call in at the party given that night close to the Hanover Sq. rooms,—whereof a certain green ticket inviting you to a Club will inform you more particularly   It has been sent you.

Ever yours gratefully
M D Conway

For the club invitation see 16 Dec 73 to Colborne, n. 1. Conway's "big book" was *The Sacred Anthology: A Book of Ethnical Scriptures* (London: Trübner and Co.), announced in the *Publishers' Circular* for 17 January 1874 ("New Works," 8). It comprised a selection of writings from Eastern religions, intended, as Conway later explained, to "provide thoughtful readers with some idea of the ethical and religious geography, so to say, of the world; and also to provide myself with a book of ethnical scriptures from which to read lessons from my pulpit." The book was a popular success, earning Conway good profits even though he published it at his own expense (Conway 1904, 2:329, 332). Clemens acquired a copy of the book, presumably from Conway in exchange for *The Gilded Age* (*MTB*, 3:1584). Sir Samuel White Baker (1821–93), a well-known adventurer and explorer, had recently returned from a four-year term in the service of the Egyptian government as governor-general of the Equatorial Nile basin. He was honored at a reception by the Royal Geographical Society on the evening of 8 December, at which Albert Edward, the Prince of Wales, delivered "a few words of welcome" ("Sir Samuel Baker's Expedition," London *Morning Post*, 9 Dec 73, 5).

To the Editor of the London *Morning Post*
10 December 1873 • London, England
(London *Morning Post*, 11 Dec 73)

TO THE EDITOR OF THE MORNING POST.[1]

SIR,—Now that my lecturing engagement is drawing to its close, I find that there is one attraction which I forgot to provide, & that is, the attendance of some great member of the Government to give distinction to my entertainment. Strictly speaking, I did not really forget this or underrate its importance, but the truth was, I was afraid of it. I was afraid of it for the reason that those great personages have so many calls upon their time that they cannot well spare the time to sit out an entertainment, & I knew that if one of them were to leave his box & retire while I was lecturing it would seriously embarrass me. I find, however, that many people think I ought not to allow this lack to exist longer; therefore, I feel compelled to reveal a thing which I had intended to keep secret. I early applied to a party at the East-end who is in the same line of business as Madame Tussaud,[2] & he agreed to lend me a couple of kings & some nobility, & he said that they would sit out my lecture, & not only sit it out, but that they wouldn't even leave the place when it was done, but would just stay where they were, perfectly infatuated, & wait for more. So I made a bargain with him at once, & was going to ask the newspapers to mention, in the usual column, that on such-and-such an evening his Majesty King Henry VIII. would honour my entertainment with his presence, & that on such-&-such an evening his Majesty William the Conqueror would be present; & that on the succeeding evening Moses & Aaron would be there, & so on. I felt encouraged now, an attendance like that would make my entertainment all that could be desired, & besides, I would not be embarrassed by their going away before my lecture was over. But now a misfortune came. In attempting to move Henry VIII. to my lecture hall, the porter fell down stairs & utterly smashed him all to pieces; in the course of moving William the Conqueror, something let go & all the saw-dust burst out of him, & he collapsed & withered away to nothing before my eyes. Then we collared some dukes, but they were so seedy & decayed that nobody would ever have believed in their rank; & so I gave them up, with almost a broken heart. In my trouble I had nothing in the world left to depend on now but just Moses & Aaron, & I confess to you that it was all I could do to keep the tears back when I came to examine those two images & found that that man, in his unapproachable ignorance, had been exhibiting in Whitechapel for Moses & Aaron what any educated person could see at a glance, by the ligature, were only the Siamese Twins.[3]

You see now, sir, that I have done all that a man could do to supply a complained-of lack, & if I have failed I think I ought to be pitied, not blamed. I wish I could get a king somewhere, just only for a little while, & I would take good care of him, & send him home again, & pay the cab myself.

MARK TWAIN.

London, Dec. 10.[4]

[1] The editor of the *Morning Post*—considered "*the* fashionable chronicle and journal of the *Beau Monde*"—was William Hardman (1828–90). Educated at Cambridge and trained as a barrister, Hardman filled the position from 1872 until his death (*Newspaper Press Directory*, 17; Griffiths, 422–23; Boase, 1:1329–30). Clemens may not have known Hardman at this time, but both men attended a New Year's Eve party at Shirley Brooks's on 31 December (Layard, 576; see 29 Dec 73 to OLC, n. 3).

[2] Marie Tussaud (1760–1850) was a Swiss wax modeler who, as her uncle's apprentice, took death masks from heads severed by the guillotine during the French Revolution. After coming to England in 1802 she toured Britain with her life-size portrait waxworks of famous people, including royalty, and in 1833 set up a permanent exhibition on Baker Street in London. After her death her sons continued the business, which has remained a popular entertainment to this day.

[3] Whitechapel was a congested and poverty-ridden neighborhood in London's East End. In May 1869 Clemens had written a humorous article about Chang and Eng (1811–74), famous "Siamese Twins" who lived in North Carolina (Weinreb and Hibbert, 955; *L3*, 228).

[4] The *Morning Post* printed this letter on 11 December, with a brief introduction:

> We have received the following from Mr. Mark Twain, and give insertion to this singular advertisement as a curious specimen of Transatlantic puffery. We suppose that wag intends it to be funny; but it rather conveys the idea that the author of the "Jumping Frog" has become a prey to the sad melancholy which attacks foreigners in this country. ("Mark Twain's Lectures," 2)

The Belfast *Northern Whig* (Frank Finlay's newspaper) reprinted the letter on 13 December, remarking that

> MARK TWAIN has been audaciously poking fun at the snobbish tendencies of the great British public, by sending the following letter to the organ of fashionable society, the *Morning Post*. Jenkins publishes the letter, and gravely "supposes the writer intends it

to be funny," but is not at all sure. ("Mark Twain Again," clipping in Scrapbook 12:49, CU-MARK)
"Jenkins" was a general name for a "fawning, snobbish journalist" (Spielmann, 209–10, 289, 319–20).

To John L. Toole
per Charles Warren Stoddard
10 December 1873 • London, England
(MS: MH-H)

Langham Hotel
10 Dec 1873

My dear Toole[1]

I would gladly do what you wish to the fullest extent possible but I have been so little in New York or Boston of late years, & American News papers ship new crews so eternally that I hardly know any body on those papers now.

I think my best plan will be to give Mr Loveday[2] a letter to my old friend Sam Glenn who is on the New York Herald[3] & let him introduce Loveday to the best people for him to know. There are quite a lot of them in the Lotos Club & as you'r a member of the Savage, Loveday will find it easy to know them on that account.[4]

Ys Sincerely
Saml. L. Clemens.

J.L. Toole, Esq

[1] See 15 Sept 72 to OLC, n. 2. Toole was currently appearing at Prince's Theatre in Manchester, but would soon be engaged at London's Gaiety Theatre, from 15 to 20 December, in *The Hypocrite*, a comedy loosely based on Molière's *Tartuffe* (London *Times:* "Mr. J. L. Toole," 9 Dec 73, 8; "Gaiety," 15 Dec 73, 8; "Gaiety Theatre," 18 Dec 73, 5).

[2] George Loveday (1835–87) was Toole's business manager and traveling companion. In earlier years he had worked as a violinist and an operatic entrepreneur, in partnership with his brother. Upon his death a friend described him as a "quick, shrewd, courteous man of business" who was "always generous, courtly, and sincere" (Toole, 31–33).

[3] Samuel Relf Glen (1820–80) had known Clemens since at least the fall of 1867, when, as the "foreign-correspondence" editor for the New York *Herald*,

he managed to coax out of Clemens an incendiary letter about the *Quaker City* trip (*L2*, 107 n. 2, 122). Glen began his journalism career in 1834 as a compositor on the New York *Transcript*. He thereafter worked for several newspapers, including the New York *Herald*, in the same capacity. In about 1845 he became assistant editor and manager of the Boston *Times and Herald*, and in 1860 he took an editorial position with the New York *Herald*, remaining until his death. During the Civil War he corresponded for that paper, and did so again in 1866 while accompanying the Fenian expedition to Canada. According to his obituary, "He was a versatile writer upon political and social topics, possessed a wide knowledge of American public men and was especially noted for a rare fund of wit, humor and pathos. His was a genial character, and he seemed always in a happy mood" ("Samuel Relf Glen, Journalist," New York *Herald*, 14 May 80, 6).

⁴Toole was planning an American tour in 1874–75, and had evidently asked Clemens for his help. On 6 August 1874 the Lotos Club welcomed Toole with a dinner in his honor. Although Clemens did not attend, he sent a letter to be read to the assembled guests (Toole, 248–58; "Dinner to Mr. Toole," New York *Tribune*, 7 Aug 74, 5).

To Olivia L. Clemens
11 December 1873 • London, England
(MS: CU-MARK)

[*on back of letter as folded:*]

Dec. 11.

Livy darling, there's another thick fog. I have had the gas burning all day. Dressed by candle light at 10.30 this morning.

8, CHESTER PLACE, HYDE PARK SQUARE.W.

Dec 9 1873

Dear Mark Twain,

We have to thank you for your kindness in sending us tickets, & still more for the delight of hearing you. Mrs. Smalley¹ and I agreed in thinking the lecture capital, both in itself and in the manner of its delivery, which was simply inimitable. I admired your way of leading up to your points, & your great good sense in giving a slow witted English audience time to take them in. That they enjoyed so many of them was a proper tribute to you and some credit to them also, for the average Englishman does not take kindly to the peculiar humour in which you

excel. I was sorry to see you so wretchedly noticed in the *Daily News,—*
what a donkey the man must be to be able to spoil things so.[2]

Yours ever

G. W. Smalley

Conway sat beside us & laughed till the bench shook. I thought his
conduct most improper.[3]

---

[1] Phoebe Smalley (14 Dec 73 to OLC, n. 1).

[2] The unidentified critic for the London *Daily News* commented:

> Last evening Mr. Mark Twain delivered a new lecture at the Hanover-square Rooms,
> the title of which was "Roughing it on the Silver Frontier." When Mr. Twain announced
> a record of his adventures amidst the savages of the Sandwich Islands, the public got
> some idea of his whereabouts at least, although they could not anticipate the strange
> scenes he depicted nor the yet stranger mode of his portraiture. On the present occa-
> sion, though more familiar with his peculiar style, the London public have been left
> entirely in the dark as to the locality to which he intended to introduce them. Consid-
> ering the attraction that a little mystery has had at all times for the world, it would be
> unfair, perhaps, to Mr. Twain to find fault with him for shrouding himself in so much
> darkness as would lead people to the Hanover-square Rooms to ascertain what he
> meant. If such was his idea the result confirmed his expectation, for the large room was
> well filled by an audience many of whom were inquiring long before the lecturer's ap-
> pearance what was or where was the "Silver Frontier." Mexico was generally suggested,
> but Mr. Twain soon informed his hearers that by the "Silver Frontier" he meant a por-
> tion of Nevada. He lived in that part of the world for three years. It was inhabited when
> he was there by editors and thieves, blacklegs and lawyers, carters, miners, gamblers,
> and characters of that sort. On his journey he assisted at a Mormon marriage, but did
> not wait to see it all finished. They were very fond of card playing in Nevada. Their
> game was "Seven up," and he joined in; but he was sorry he did, for card playing was
> very sinful unless you won money at it. But though a place for gamblers he would not
> advise hunters to go there, for they might hunt for a whole year and find nothing. It was
> a country for desperadoes, and of one of these, named Jack Harris, the lecturer gave an
> amusing account. This man took refuge in Nevada from the justice of the United States,
> and lodged with the principal clergyman of the place, for there was no distinction in
> that country between classes. Harris was known for his expertness with the pistol and
> bowie-knife, but a change of life came over Harris, and he took to a doubled-barrel gun
> when he gave up the pistol and bowie-knife. Intermixed with his word-play and jests,
> Mr. Twain gave some very eloquent descriptions of the country. He began and con-
> cluded his lecture last evening amidst loud applause. ("Mr. Mark Twain," 9 Dec 73,
> clipping in Scrapbook 12:41, CU-MARK)

[3] Moncure Conway was a close friend of Smalley's, and often fulfilled his duties to the New York *Tribune* when Smalley was away from London (Joseph J.
Mathews, 36, 43). Conway had already expressed his approval of the lecture to
Clemens (10 Dec 73 to Conway, n. 1). He also alluded to it in his usual letter to
the Cincinnati *Commercial:*

> The talk of literary London just now is Mark Twain's account, in his new lecture of the
> "bucking" horse which he purchased in Nevada. It is impossible to put it on paper, as
> half of the effect produced by the story depends upon his manner of telling it. ("Mark
> Twain's Bucking Horse," Virginia City *Territorial Enterprise,* 21 Jan 74, 1, reprinting
> the Cincinnati *Commercial* of unknown date)

To Olivia L. Clemens
11 and 12 December 1873 • London, England
(MS, *damage emended:* CU-MARK)

(SLC/MT)   FARMINGTON AVENUE, HARTFORD.[1]

Dec. 11.

Livy my darling, I am just starting to the lecture hall, & O the dreadful fog still continues. The cattle are choking & dying in the great annual Cattle Show, & today they had to take some of the poor things out & haul them around on trucks to let them breathe the outside air & save their lives. I do wish it would let up.[2]

If I'm not homesick to see you, no other lover ever *was* homesick to see his sweetheart. And when I get there, remember, "Expedition's the word![""]3 *Most lovingly,*

Sam*l*.

[*new sheet:*]4

(SLC/MT)

2 A M.

Dec. 12.

My own dear little darling, it is 2 in the morning, & I had gone to my bedroom, but I thought, I will just go back to the parlor & look at Livy's picture once more before I go to bed. And so I am here, & your picture is before me (the same I have carried in my pocket so many many months) & I simply love it & I love you, Livy, my darling.[5]

Tonight, after my lecture, I went to the Scotch Morayshire dinner,—the lord Viscount MacDuff was in the chair[6]—& I made a speech which was received with prodigious applause—but I thought "if *L L* Livy were only here, I would enjoy it a thousand times more.[7] I do *love* you, Livy darling, & my last word is, (when I come) "*Expedition's* the word!"

Most Lovingly

Sam*l*.

✉

Mrs. Sam*l*. L. Clemens | Hartford | Conn. | [*rule*] [*in upper left corner:*] America. | [*flourish*] [*on flap:*] (SLC/MT) [*postmarked:*] LONDON-W 7 DE12 73 [*and*] L 12 12 1873 [*and*] NEW YORK DEC 26 PAID ALL

¹This is the first of several letters written on this stationery, evidently printed in anticipation of the Clemenses' move to their new home, which did not occur until the fall of 1874. Olivia had probably sent a sample of the stationery for her husband's approval.

²The "peculiar fog which has prevailed for an almost unprecedented number of days in succession has inflicted a loss of thousands of pounds upon the owners of animals" at the Smithfield Club Show at Agricultural Hall, the London *Times* reported ("Machinery at the Cattle Show," 13 Dec 73, 6). By the evening of 11 December, the fourth day of the show, ninety-one cattle had been removed from the hall. Some of them were "saved by being carried quickly into the clearer air of the country; but a very considerable number have been slaughtered, while several died before it was discovered that they were being poisoned by the smoke-laden atmosphere" ("Smithfield Club Show," London *Times*, 12 Dec 73, 5).

³This sentence is very heavily canceled in the manuscript, which remained in the Clemens family until it came to the Mark Twain Papers in 1952 as part of the Samossoud Collection. The cancellation was made with Clemens's typical looping line, but in an ink of a slightly different color and density from that used to write the letter. (The ink used to cancel the sentence was so thickly applied that it soaked through the paper and caused it to disintegrate in two places.) The last six words of the letter—"(when I come) '*Expedition's* the word!'"—were canceled in similar fashion. Although it is possible that Clemens made both cancellations before he sent the letter, the greater likelihood is that he did so only later, after it was received and reacted to by Olivia, who saved his letters with great care. "Expedition's the word!" is an unidentified quotation that Clemens is known to have used at least three times before, once in early 1867 and twice in late 1870 (*N&J1*, 272; *L4*, 251, 262). The present letter suggests, however, that the phrase had acquired a private significance for the Clemenses, perhaps one that they were unwilling, on reflection, to allow posterity even to guess at. The second cancellation in particular shows evidence also of a different hand (a distinct departure from Clemens's usual looping mark). On balance, therefore, it seems unlikely that Clemens canceled these phrases before he sent the letter, and they are therefore transcribed as he sent them. For a facsimile of the manuscript, see Appendix F.

⁴Clemens's usually clear handwriting became notably less clear and distinct by the time he wrote the following addition to this letter, perhaps the result of alcohol consumed at the Morayshire dinner, from which he had just returned.

⁵This picture has not been identified, although it may be one of those reproduced in Appendix F.

⁶Alexander William George Duff (1849–1912), known as Viscount Macduff (one of the lesser titles of his father, Earl Fife), was educated at Eton, and served as lord lieutenant of the county of Elgin (1872–1902) and as member of Parliament for Elgin and Nairnshire (1874–79). As of 1883 his estates totaled nearly one-quarter of a million acres, making him the fifth largest landowner in the United Kingdom. In 1889 he married Princess Louise, daughter of the Prince of Wales, and was created duke of Fife (Cokayne, 5:379–80).

⁷Clemens responded to the toast to "The Visitors." According to the Elgin (Scotland) *Courant,*

> He said he did not exactly know the wording of the toast, but he rather understood it to be a health drunk to the foreign visitors, and, with his name coupled with it, and he

was never so surprised at anything in his life, for he did not feel like a foreigner. . . .
He was going up into Scotland next week or the week after to lecture, and he was learning the language now—(laughter). He was only a small sort of a scholar, but he tried to
learn, and he had mastered six or eight of the words. However, he had got such a strong
foreign twang on him that he could not really understand the words himself. But he did
wish that when he was expected to respond to a toast, and it would be a great kindness
to him, if some one would tell him beforehand, because when he had to make an impromptu speech, he liked to have a week to think about it—(loud cheers). ("London
Morayshire Club," 16 Dec 73, no page)

To Shirley Brooks
12 December 1873 • London, England
(MS: ViU)

⬭ SLC/MT   FARMINGTON AVENUE, HARTFORD.

The Langham Hotel
Dec. 12.

My Dear Mr. Brooks:

The fog got so thick, & so depleted my audiences, that I got desperate. I *can't* talk to thin houses; I would so cheerfully have paid half a
crown to every man who would come—but I couldn't *say* that, & so I
had to talk, & go on suffering.

Then I thought maybe I was not advertised enough. So I wrote
the accompanying squib—the one which is not in my handwriting—&
sent it to all the morning dailies, hoping that maybe *one* out of the lot
would print it. But no—the first line was too plainly & sadly an advertisement, & then the gentle satirical vein—touching both the Prince &
the people—was a thing they were a bit afraid of, I fancy.

It is no longer an advertisement, because my lecturing will be at an
end a week & a day from now—& I have ˏjustˏ written 10 pages of remarks purposely to get in, very quietly & unobtrusively, the fact that I
mean no disrespect to the Prince, & that I believe he would appreciate
& smile at the joke as soon as anybody.

Still, you may not be favorably impressed, & if not, will you send it
back to me? There is nothing but good-nature in it—so I could send it
to America, & it would run there very well.[1]

Yrs Very Truly
Sam*l*. L. Clemens.

¹ Clemens evidently enclosed two brief manuscripts with his letter—neither of which survives. It is possible, however, that the one "not in my handwriting" was a copy, made by Stoddard, of his 10 December letter to the *Morning Post* (published on 11 December), which Clemens may not yet have seen in print. The other, comprising "10 pages of remarks," has not been identified. Brooks did not print it (or anything else by Clemens) in *Punch*, nor has a likely article been found in any American newspaper. For Brooks's response, see the enclosure with 13 and 15 Dec 73 to OLC.

To Robert W. Routledge
per Charles Warren Stoddard
12 December 1873 • London, England
(MS: Routledge)

(SLC/MT)

FARMINGTON AVENUE, HARTFORD.

Langham Hotel.

12. Dec 1873.

My dear Robert.¹

All right, any thing you say will be satisfactory to me. I am absolutely sure that you wont sell three hundred more copies at twenty five shillings than you will at thirty five. I dont fancy that you can popularize the high priced edition. I'm afraid it is only the low priced editions that will have a large sale; but as I say, the price is the publishers affair not the authors & I'll endorce what ever action you take²

> Yours Ever
> S. L. Clemens.
> per C.W.S.

¹ Robert Warne Routledge (1837–99), a partner in his father's publishing firm since 1858, was primarily concerned with the financial side of the business (Boase, 6:505; Mumby, 97, 136, 147).

² Routledge had written to Clemens earlier on 12 December:

> After giving the matter careful consideration and consulting people who can assist in the sale of "The Gilded Age" we have come to the conclusion that it will be best to publish the first edition at 25/6 instead of 31/6: the late Lord Lytton adopted this price for his last novel, and we think it a good one, the object being to attract *purchasers* and not throw the book entirely into the circulating libraries. The preface came to hand to-day & is now in the printers' hands. (Agreement Book A–K:183, Routledge)

The American Publishing Company's *Gilded Age* cost between $3.50 and $5.00, depending on the binding. Advertisements published before the three-volume Routledge edition was issued gave its price as 31s. 6d. ($7.88). By the time of publication, however, Routledge had lowered the price to 25s. 6d. ($6.38) (*Athenaeum:* "George Routledge & Sons' First List of New Books for the Coming Season," 4 Oct 73, 448; "Mark Twain and Charles Warner," 13 Dec 73, 788; "Mark Twain and Charles Warner," London *Morning Post,* 22 Dec 73, 8). This high price marked a new approach on Routledge's part: he sold his editions of *The Innocents Abroad* and *Roughing It*—each title divided into two volumes—for merely 1s. ($.25) per volume. Clemens wrote his new preface for the English edition on 11 December and sent it to Routledge on the same day; it is reproduced in Appendix E (see also 13 and 15 Dec 73 to OLC).

To Olivia L. Clemens
13 and 15 December 1873 • London, England
(MS: CU-MARK)

(SLC)

London, Dec. 13.

Livy darling, I am *so* tired of lecturing! I enjoy while I am on the stage, because the audience are such elegant looking people & are so heartily ~~responsible~~ responsive (heaps of fine carriages & liveries come,) but I don't take any interest in life during the day. I shall lecture only one week longer in London—closing Dec. 20—& then shall talk in 4 or 5 cities outside. I wish it would carry me home sooner. But that would not be fair to Dolby who long ago promised me to cities in January. I ought to keep on lecturing in London, but the fog nearly broke my heart, & on the foggiest night I lost faith & made Dolby advertised the early close of my season. It was rash & wrong, but I could not help it.[1] Day & night the streets were void of people; all day long the streets lamps burned, yet they only looked like rows of dull embers, half-dead sparks, extending up Portland Place—& you see them only *half way* up Portland Place, at that. There were but few cabs about. The steeple opposite the parlor window was visible only as a dreamy, unformed, spectral thing. My houses ~~f~~ fell right down till they contained only ~~£12~~ £14 & £17! It said

"It is going to last forever & ever—cut my season short!" But no matter. I would rather loaf & l than lecture, any time.

Why *don't* your letters come? It seems an age since I had one. I have been to[o] dreadfully busy to write you, often, but shall write oftener now.

I have been writing after-dinner speeches & a preface for the book. Read proof of the preface this evening. I state some plain facts in it,— so I have appended a postscript to say that Warner isn't to blame, because he don't know what I am writing.[2] The book is to be issued here at 25/ & a 2/ edition will be immediately shipped to Canada. The Routledges would not yield up Canada to Bliss—which is very well for Warᵱh-ner & W̶ me, because high-priced books don't extend one's reputation fast or far enough. I urge them to get out a cheap edition here just as soon as the libraries will consent.[3]

I have been getting up an elaborate speech to-day (expecting to be called upon, as usual,)̸ to respond to some toast or other at the Lord Mayor's dinner Tuesday night, after my lecture—I wrote him I could not come till 10 PM) purposely to wring in a word about International Copyright—but as it is at the end of the Speech I may conclude to cut it, at last.[4]

~~Preserve the en~~ The present Lord Mayor is an old brick—an old ᴬScotchᴬ brick—met him at the great St Andrews dinner.[5]

I *love* you, darling.

Sam*ˡ*.

[on back of enclosure as folded:][6]
Preserve all of these letters, Livy, in the green box, Sam*ˡ*.

14 Dec 1873

6, KENT TERRACE, REGENT'S PARK. N. W.

My dear Sir,

I feel desirous to do something more helpful to your lecture than perhaps the article would be,[7] and I have therefore written, and inserted in the new number of Punch a strong incitation to the public to make haste & go and see you, & I have put in quotations to attract the eye of the B. P.[8] I will send you an *early* copy ᴬtomorrowᴬ—it will appear on Wednesday & may do good for the brief time you mention it as your intention to remain.⁹ I will also send you my Almanac—Tenniel has done something which I am certain *you* will admire.¹⁰

Believe me
very sincerely yours
Shirley Brooks

S. L. Clemens Esq

✉—————————————————————————————

Mrs. Sam*ˡ*. L. Clemens | Hartford | Conn [*in upper left corner:*] America. | [*rule*] [*on flap:*] (SLC) [*postmarked:*] LONDON · W 7 DE 15 73 [*and*] NEW YORK · DEC 2◊ 13 · U.S. NOTES [*and*] INSUFFICIENTLY STAMPED [*and*] 13

¹In the early advertisements for Clemens's lectures, published between 19 November and 7 December, no ending date was mentioned. On 8 and 9 December the notice in the London *Daily News* included this advisory: "Mr. George Dolby begs to announce that Mark Twain's visit to England (London and the provinces included) is limited to a short period, important business calling him to America early in January." On 10 December, the second day of the fog (which cleared on 13 December), the words "Last Week but One" were added. On 11 December the notice stated: "Mr. George Dolby begs to announce that Mark Twain's Provincial Tour will commence on Monday, Dec. 22, and that his lectures in London will terminate Saturday, Dec. 20. Mark Twain returns to America on Monday, Jan. 12." This notice ran through 19 December (with one minor change on 15 December: "next" was added after "Monday" and "Saturday") (advertisements, London *Daily News,* 19 Nov–19 Dec 73, 4; "Meteorological Reports," London *Times:* 10 Dec 73, 7; 11 Dec 73, 6; 12 Dec 73, 4; 13 Dec 73, 7; 15 Dec 73, 7).

²The preface is reproduced in Appendix E. It contains no postscript exonerating Warner.

³It was customary for publishers to sell a book at a discounted price to lending libraries when they agreed to purchase a large quantity, and to keep the price to the public high to encourage borrowing.

> The economics of Victorian book production, especially of fiction, was much influenced by the large lending libraries, and there is no doubt either that they increased the reputations of many authors by widening the audience they reached. The best-known library was of course Mudie's, founded in 1842, and Mudie's order alone for a single title could, if the author were well-known, run into four figures. . . . The three-decker novels that they preferred were expensive, and obviously it was not in the interest either of the publisher or of the libraries to jeopardise the circulation of these or indeed of any library title by the premature issue of a cheap edition. (Welland, 43)

(For a full discussion of the relationship between publishers and lending libraries, see Griest, 58–86.) Routledge printed 500 copies of the 25*s*. 6*d*. edition in

December, and the following month printed 4,000 copies of a 2s. edition. No further reprintings were required until 1877. Routledge retained his contractual right to the Canadian market, and apparently sold his cheap edition there, withholding it from the English market until June 1874 (Routledge Ledger Book 4:765, Routledge; Routledge *Gilded Age* contract, Appendix D; "New Works Published from June 1 to 15," *Publishers' Circular* 37 [16 June 74]: 391; "The Times Column of New Books and New Editions," London *Times*, 9 June 74, 14; French, 264, mistakenly states that the edition advertised in June 1874 cost 12s.).

⁴Clemens's letter accepting the lord mayor's invitation for dinner on 16 December is not known to survive, but it elicited the following response (CU-MARK):

MANSION HOUSE, LONDON E.C.

Dec. 11. 1873.

Dear Sir.
   The Lord Mayor desires me to acknowledge the receipt of your letter of yesterday with thanks.
   Whilst regretting that the dinner will not be enlivened with your presence, His Lordship sincerely hopes you will not fail to put in an appearance at the finale, when his welcome will be none the less hearty.
   Should any other dinner be given here before you leave England, His Lordship will again request the honor of your acceptance of his hospitality & he trusts that timely notice of it will enable you to make arrangements for being present.

I am,
Dear Sir
yours faithfully
Jno. R. S. Vine
Private Secʸ

S. Clemans, Esq
(Mark Twain).

Clemens may have considered enclosing this note in the present letter (see the cancellation in the next paragraph) but refrained, since it would not easily fit in the envelope with the letter he evidently *did* enclose (see note 6). No text of Clemens's speech has been found, nor has his attendance at the dinner been confirmed.

⁵Andrew Lusk (1810–1909), elected lord mayor on 29 September 1873, had presided at the dinner of the Scottish Corporation of London on 1 December (see 28 Nov 73 to Fitzgibbon, n. 2). Lusk was born in Ayrshire, Scotland. In about 1835 he founded, with his brother, a wholesale grocery business in Greenock, whose success enabled him to open a similar business in London in 1840. He was highly active in city politics, serving as councilman, alderman, sheriff, and member of Parliament for Finsbury (1865–85), a large London constituency.

⁶Not only did Clemens put twice the usual amount of postage on this letter (six instead of three pence), it was assessed a thirteen-cent postage-due fee at New York, indicating that it must have contained an enclosure. The 15 Decem-

ber postmark suggests that a likely enclosure was this 14 December letter from Brooks: since 14 December was a Sunday, when there were no postal deliveries, Clemens could not have received Brooks's letter before 15 December. Presumably, he immediately inscribed and enclosed it with his letter to Olivia.

[7] See 12 Dec 73 to Brooks.

[8] The British Public (Partridge, 22).

[9] Brooks inserted the following announcement in the 20 December issue, which was evidently available for sale by Wednesday, 17 December, three days before Clemens's last London appearance:

"TWAIN CAN DO 'T."

Antony and Cleopatra.

AGAIN we have, as JACQUES PIERRE observes in the *Midsummer Night's Dream,*
"Twain, at large discourse;"
but, as the same eminent Frenchman says in the *Winter's Tale,* 'twill be only a case of
"Mark, a little while."
In fact, the distinguished humorist's stay is to be so brief that if we were not now upon such extraordinary sweet terms with America, we should write unpleasantly about such autoschediastic treatment of us. But for a few times MR. MARK TWAIN is to be visible to the naked eye, (fog permitting) in Hanover Square, and because his visit is so short, *Mr. Punch,* who extracts something good out of anything objectionable, performs the philanthropic act of hereby encouraging and inciting his friends to go and hear MR. TWAIN's new lecture. (*Punch* 65:248)

[10] *Punch's Almanack for 1874,* issued on 18 December 1873, contained one illustration signed with John Tenniel's distinctive monogram; it is reproduced on the next page. Tenniel (1820–1914) was a largely self-taught painter and illustrator. He had drawn illustrations for *Punch* since late 1850, and by the mid-1860s was its chief cartoonist. In recognition of his talent he was knighted in 1893. Professing no political opinions of his own, he nevertheless "dignified the political cartoon into a classic composition, and has raised the art of politico-humorous draughtsmanship from the relative position of the lampoon to that of polished satire" (Spielmann, 461–71; Wood, 468). Tenniel's illustrations for *Alice in Wonderland* (1865) and *Through the Looking Glass* (1871) remain his best-known works.

The painting tlentho about a Spanish boy,
So, followed by the hopes and numbers, and years,
The goblin Presence and the hunger's circles
Band making onward through surrounded Spare.—*Porphyrius Rolanus*, iv. 265.

Illustration by John Tenniel in *Punch's Almanack for 1874* (6–7).

To Olivia L. Clemens
14 December 1873 • London, England
(MS: CU-MARK)

(SLC)

London, Dec. 14.

My own little darling, my peerless wife, I am simply mad to see you. *You* don't know how I love you—you never will. Because you do all the gushing yourself, when we are together, & so there is no use in two of us doing it—& one gusher usually silences another—but an ocean is between us, now, & I *have* to gush. I simply worship you, Livy dear. You are all in all, to me. I went to Smalley's to-day, & in my secret heart I thanked Mrs. Smalley for reminding me of you, in her soft, undulating, unstudied grace.[1] But she fell a long way short of you, after all. There is no woman in the whole earth that is so lovely to me as you are, my child. You must forgive me for ɟ not talking all I feel when I am at home, honey. I *do* feel it, even if I don't talk it. Will you remember that? Will you remember it & not feel harshly when I do not utter it?

Finlay is my guest, for this week, & I warm up & am interested as soon as he takes you for a topic. I do so wish I were with you, my Livy.

Saml.

◙—————————————————————————————

Mrs. Sam*ˡ*. L. Clemens | Hartford | Conn. [*in upper left corner:*] America. | [*rule*] [*on flap:*] (SLC/MT) [*postmarked:*] LONDON · W 7 DE 16 73 [*and*] NEW YORK DEC 2◊ PAID ALL

[1] Phoebe Smalley was a diminutive brunette whom most observers considered "unusually attractive" (Joseph J. Mathews, 77). At her death in 1923, author Kate Douglas Wiggin recalled her as

> a rare spirit, very different from and superior to the ordinary woman. . . . I met her first in her London house, surrounded on her afternoons at home with clever, interesting, celebrated people. She was never strong and had, even then, the exquisite fragility of porcelain, but she was full of friendliness, hospitality and sympathy. (Wiggin)

To Alfred Tennyson
15 December 1873 • London, England
(MS: Jacobs)

(SLC)

The Langham Hotel

Dec. 15.

Dear Sir:

You have better things to think of & to do, & so I do not expect you to come to a lecture of mine—but still I wanted to send you the enclosed, ₍you to fill the blanks₎, just as I might say to any man, "What you have done has been a benefit, a pleasure, a *luxury* to me, & so what I am trying to ʃ do now is only homage, & therefore ought not to be offensive.["]¹

But I never would have ventured to do this thing, but that I saw my friend Moncure D. Conway last night & he said, "*Do* it—he probably won't come, but it's an inoffensive way of expressing ~~your~~ ₍a body's₎ appreciation—therefore do it."

~~Ad~~ And so, with all respect, I ₍"do it."₎²

Very Truly

₍Sam*ˡ*. L. Clemens₎

Mark Twain.

---

¹Clemens enclosed a complimentary ticket to his lecture, apparently valid for any date, which does not survive. For Tennyson's response, see 16 Dec 73 to OLC, n. 3.

To John Colborne
per Charles Warren Stoddard
16 December 1873 • London, England
(MS: TxU-Hu)

(SLC/MT)   FARMINGTON AVENUE, HARTFORD.

Langham Hotel
16 – Dec – 1873.

John Colborne. Esq
   Hon Sec. Temple Club.
   Dear Sir
        I thank you for the honor you have done me in electing me an
Honorary Member of your club and I hope to be able to be present on
the opening night.[1]

Very truly yours
S. L. Clemens.
per C.W.S.

✉ ——

[*letter docketed:*] S. L. Clemens | [*rule*] | 16 Dec.^r. | [*rule*] | Accepts Hon^y
Membership | [*rule*]

[1] Clemens answered the following note (CU-MARK):

TEMPLE CLUB   ARUNDEL STREET STRAND
15th December 1873

Dear Sir
        I have much pleasure in informing you that at a Committee Meeting of the above
Club held here this evening you were, on the nomination of Col^l. Rowland, unani-
mously elected an Honorary Member of the Club.
        I have further to state that the Club will open on the 1st of January next.
I am, Dear Sir
Yours faithfully
John Colborne
Major
Hon. Sec.
pp Q.A.L.

According to an announcement in the London *Times*, the newly formed Temple
Club was

   an institution which will be novel of its kind, comprehensive in the class of its supporters, and organized with a view to afford every comfort and the best accommodation to

its Members. The Club will be strictly non-political, and will be composed of Clergymen, Officers in the Army and Navy, Members of the Civil Service, Professional and
Private Gentlemen, who, untrammelled by party spirit, may enjoy a free and social exchange of ideas on subjects of Art, Literature, and Science. ("Temple Club," 15 Dec
73, 1)

The only committee member listed in the announcement known to be personally
acquainted with Clemens was Tom Hood. Moncure Conway was evidently planning to join, however, since he had told Clemens on 10 December to expect an
invitation (10 Dec 73 to Conway, n. 1). John Colborne (1830–90) was the fifth
son of the first Baron Seaton, who had been awarded his title in 1839 for distinguished military service. Colborne was a major in the Sixtieth Rifle Corps, and
had served in the Crimea, India, and China. Rowland may have been Andrew
Rowland (1800?–1878) of the Bombay Artillery, a colonel since 1858 (Burke
1904, 1389; Boase, 3:329).

To Olivia L. Clemens
16 December 1873 • London, England
(MS: CU-MARK)

(SLC/MT)   FARMINGTON AVENUE, HARTFORD.

Dec. 16.

Livy my darling, we did have a lovely audience tonight, such bright,
splendid people, & they sat as still as statues, for fear they might miss a
word, but they responded promptly & vigorou[s]ly to every single point.
I talked half a column or a column more of stuff than usual.

~~Then I read~~ Last night a portly lady very richly dressed, sat in the
second row & laughed as you never saw ~~a c~~ any creature laugh before
except Rev. Mr. Burton[1]—the tears streamed down her cheeks all the
time. Tonight a young English girl sat in the same row, & it seemed to
me that she would simply go into convulsions. Bully audiences, these
are.

Lunched with Mrs. Owen to-day—two *other* earl's daughters were
there, & I had a funny & a very queer adventure with ~~th~~ one of them
which I must tell you when I see you. Mrs. Owen was splendid. I am to
lunch there again, on Friday, & then we are to go to Westminster Abbey,
for she wants to show me the monument to the Owen who built Condover Hall.[2]

I have a pleasant note from Mr. Tennyson, to whom I sent a ticket.
An autograph note from *him* is a powerful hard thing to get.[3]
I love you, love you, love, you, Sweetheart.
                                                              Sam[.]

[✉]————————————————————————————————————

Mrs. Sam[.] L. Clemens | Hartford | Conn. [*in upper left corner:*] America.
| [*flourish*] [*on flap:*] (SLC/MT) [*postmarked:*] LONDON-W. O 7 DE 17 73 [*and*]
L 17 12 1873 [*and*] NEW YORK JAN 2 PAID ALL.

---

[1] The Reverend Nathaniel J. Burton (1824–87), a graduate of Wesleyan University, had been pastor of the Park Congregational Church in Hartford since 1870; prior to that (1857–70) he had served the Fourth Congregational Church of that city (Burpee, 1:520; Trumbull, 1:389, 393). He and Clemens were both members of the Hartford Monday Evening Club (see 15 Feb 73 to Trumbull, n. 2).

[2] Victoria Alexandrina Cotes Owen was the widow of Thomas Owen (1823–64), the older brother of Reginald Cholmondeley (see pp. 432, 434). Thomas had changed his name in 1863 when he inherited Condover Hall from his cousin, Edward William Smythe Owen, who had owned it since 1804. Thomas married in March 1864, but died in Florence less than two months later, leaving Condover to Reginald. Mrs. Owen's *mother* was the daughter of the third earl of Liverpool. The Clemenses probably met Mrs. Owen during their stay at Condover in early September. The "Owen who built Condover Hall" was Thomas Owen (d. 1598), a barrister and member of Parliament for Shrewsbury (1584–85); in 1594 he became a judge of the court of common pleas. He was buried in Westminster Abbey, on the south side of the choir, in a "Monument of Marble and Alabaster gilded," surmounted by a recumbent effigy in scarlet robes (Tipping, 166). Condover Hall, completed in 1598, was a great stone mansion whose exterior had remained relatively unchanged; its interior, however, had undergone alterations in the eighteenth and nineteenth centuries (Burke 1900, 292, 353; Tipping, 162, 165–68). See the illustration on p. 433.

[3] Tennyson wrote:

> 4 Seamore Place
> Park Lane
> Dec 16th/73
>
> Dear Sir,
> I saw some of your countrymen last Sunday, who spoke so highly of your Lectures, that I longed to come & hear you; but whether I come or not I am equally beholden to you for your kindness.
>
> Yours with all thanks
> A Tennyson.

Clemens noted on the back, "From Alfred Tennyson" (CU-MARK†).

To James Redpath
17 December 1873 • London, England
(MS: NHi)

(SLC/MT)   FARMINGTON AVENUE, HARTFORD.
                                    ͚Langham Hotel͚
                                    London, Dec. 17.

My Dear Redpath—

I shall go to the provinces about ten days hence, & lecture 2 or 3 times each in Glasgow, Edinburgh, Belfast, Dublin, Cork, Manchester, Liverpool, &c—that [is] if we can get halls upon dates that suit us— otherwise we'll talk in *other* big towns.

I sail for home in the Abysinnia Jan 17.[1] I find I don't like the idea of buckling in on another long siege in New York after this heavy one. So what I want to do, is, to talk in Steinway Hall on a Thursday, & Friday evenings, Saturday afternoon (& *possibly*) Saturday night. Then talk possibly Monday & Tuesday in Boston & *retire permanently* from the platform—for it is *my very last.* Any time in February will suit me. How does it strike you?[2]

Your answer can't reach me here, I think. Send it to Hartford.

                                    Yrs ever
                                    Sam͚. L. Clemens

⊠——————————————————————————————————

[*letter docketed:*] BOSTON LYCEUM BUREAU. JAMES REDPATH JAN 22 1874 [*and*] *Twain* Mark | London | Eng. | Dec. 17 1873

[1]Clemens ultimately changed both his lecture plans and his departure date: see 30 Dec 73 to Fitzgibbon.

[2]Clemens appeared on the platform only once in early 1874, on 5 March in Boston ("Roughing It—Lecture by Mark Twain," Boston *Evening Transcript,* 6 Mar 74, 8).

To Olivia L. Clemens
20 December 1873 • London, England
(MS: CU-MARK)

London, Dec. 20.

Livy darling, I am about to go to the hall, to deliver my last lecture in London. Presently I shall be free! All this time my health has been simply splendid. I never have taken such good care of myself before—& so my digestion is perfect.

I make this lecture go handsomely. I like it much better than the Sandwich Islands, & so does everybody.

Good bye my darling—shall see you by Feb. 1.! Hurrah!

Sam*l*.

⊠——————————————————————————————

Mrs. Sam*l*. L. Clemens | Hartford | Conn. [*in upper left corner:*] America. | [*rule*] [*on flap:*] ⟨SLC/MT⟩ [*postmarked:*] LONDON · W 7 DE 22 73 [*and*] NEW YORK JAN ◊ PAID ALL

To James Redpath
per Charles Warren Stoddard
21 December 1873 • London, England
(MS: ViU)

⟨SLC/MT⟩   ~~FARMINGTON AVENUE, HARTFORD.~~
                                    Langham Hotel.
                                    21ˢᵗ De 1873.

My dear Redpath

How would it do for me to deliver my "Sandwich Island" lecture with a reading of the "Jumping Frog" at Steinway Hall on Wednesday afternoon and evening and Thursday evening and my lecture "Roughing it" on Friday evening and Saturday afternoon and night.

Boston each lecture once and Baltimore ditto. I don't speak of Philadelphia because I've had a sort of arrangement with Pugh for some time for that town. Perhaps I might give "Roughing it" one night in Washington.[1]

Y~~r~~ Ys Ever
Mark.

Answer at *Hartford*.

>●|

[*letter docketed:*] BOSTON LYCEUM BUREAU. JAMES REDPATH JAN 22 1874 [*and*] *Twain* Mark | Dec. 21 1873

[1] See 17 Dec 73 to Redpath, n. 2.

To George H. Fitzgibbon
21 December 1873 • London, England
(MS: NN-B)

(SLC/MT)   FARMINGTON AVENUE, HARTFORD.

Dec. 21.

My Dear Fitz Gibbon:

I wish you *had* been there—it was a beautiful house; tho' piling the stage full of people made it pretty hard talking. I made no speech, because I had kept the audience there longer than I ever had before, & as I had had a jolly good time with them I didn't want to run the risk of spoiling the thing.

Besides, I was saving myself for tomorrow evening, when 6 or 8 personal friends of mine are to give me a quiet dinner, & I am to make a bit of a speech.[1] The speech itself won't amount to anything, but the enclosed paragraph will be a part of it. I *would* like to see it in print, because I want it to cross over & run through the American papers. But if you use it won't you please put it in *your* handwriting, & tear mine up? Remember the fate of that other thing![2]

Dolby is to let you know when I go north—which will be within the fortnight, I suppose.

With kind~~estnes~~ regar[d]s to you & all your family—

Ys faithfully

Sam[.] L. Clemens

[*enclosure:*]

In response to a toast to his health, at a dinner on Monday evening, Mark Twain said, among other things:

"I have lectured all through the fog & all through the fine weather, in London, & have completed my mission of instruction & moral elevation. ~~And~~ But now that it is all over, I am sorry rather than glad, for I never have seen audiences that were quicker to see a point & sieze it than those I have had in London & Liverpool—~~& there is where~~ ,& in this, the comfort of lecturing lies. I had always had an idea, before, that British risibles were hard to move."[3]

[1] Only three of these friends have been identified: Stoddard, Finlay, and Dolby (see 22 Dec 73 to OLC [1st]).

[2] The "other thing" may have been the speech on "The Ladies," a copy of which Clemens had sent Fitzgibbon on 28 November to use in the Darlington *Northern Echo*, where it did not, however, appear (see 28 Nov 73 to Fitzgibbon, n. 6).

[3] The second paragraph of this enclosure appeared in the Darlington *Northern Echo* on 23 December, with the following introduction:

> We saw to-night the last of Mark Twain. The ensuing fortnight he intends devoting to the enlightenment of the British public who live in North England and Scotland. At a private dinner given to-night to the distinguished American humorist by a few friends, he said, in response to the toast of his health, among other characteristically funny things:— (Fitzgibbon 1873d)

The entire item, with Fitzgibbon's introduction, was reprinted by the Edinburgh *Courant*, from which it was in turn reprinted by the Hartford *Courant* on 13 January 1874 ("Mark Twain's Last Night in London," 2).

To Olivia L. Clemens
21 December 1873 • London, England
(MS: CU-MARK)

(SLC/MT)   FARMINGTON AVENUE, HARTFORD.

Dec. 21.

Livy darling, I dined at Smalleys, last night‚, Finlay & I. His sister &
her ~~hun~~ husband (Mr. & Mrs. Hill, editor Daily News),[1] our Mrs. Jones,[2]
& John Russell Young, formerly of N. Y. Tribune, were present. Mrs.
Hill called upon you when you were here, but you were out. All the ladies
asked after you. Mrs. Jones said the Dilkes were on the Continent, but
will be back & take their Christmas dinner with her[3]—asked me to
come, but I was already engaged to go to the country, close to Stonehenge
& Salisbury, to stop with an English gentleman there.[4]

Mrs. Smalleys dinner was perfect. I ate heartily of every single
course, & then asked them to start some more along. All the glassware
was from Salviati's, & as dainty as it could be.[5] The flowers roosting
about the table in Venition glass vases before every plate were of the
choicest & newest pets of the hot-house. Livy dear, her mantel-pieces
are the things to have. You had better a long sight have yours that way
than the old conventional patterns, even though they be carved oak. And
mind you, these are Mrs. S.'s own invention. You can't find them in another house in the world. And they do look so bewitching with the dainty
glassware gems in their shelves & niches.[6] I propose to bring home one
or two Venetian ware jugs or vases. And the more I see of the colored
tiles for fire-places, the more I am out of conceit of cold white marble
ones or sullen brick or soapstone. You better order some for our fire-
places, hadn't you.

Well, Mrs. Smalley's dinner kept me awake the entire night & until
7 or 8 this morning, I ate so much of it. So now I'll say I *do* love you,
sweetheart, & go to bed.

                                                            Sam*l*.

✉—

Mrs. Sam*ˡ*. L. Clemens | Hartford | Conn. [*in upper left corner:*] America. | [*rule*] [*on flap:*] ⟨SLC/MT⟩ [*postmarked:*] LONDON-W 5 DE 22 73 [*and*] NEW YORK JAN 5 DUE 13 U.S. CURRENCY [*and*] INSUFFICIENTLY STAMPED [*and*] 13⁷

¹Jane Dalzell Finlay Hill (d. 1904), Frank Finlay's sister, wrote literary articles and reviews for the Belfast *Northern Whig*—the newspaper owned by her father until 1857 and thereafter by her brother—and, after her marriage in 1862, for other publications as well, among them the London *Saturday Review*. Frank Harrison Hill (1830–1910) was educated at Unitarian New College in Manchester and then at the University of London, and worked for a time as a private tutor. He edited the Belfast *Northern Whig* from 1861 until late 1865, when he took a position as assistant editor and political writer on the London *Daily News*, becoming its editor in chief in 1869. Although his keen understanding of politics helped make the newspaper an influential supporter of the Liberal party, his refusal to support Gladstone's home rule policy led to his abrupt dismissal in 1886. He thereafter worked for twenty years as the lead political reporter for the London *World*.

²Probably "Mrs. Inwood Jones (Lady Morgan's niece)," a friend of the Dilkes' and of Kate Field's but not further identified; possibly the same "Mrs. Jones, an Irish literary lady" who attended the dinner at the Smalleys' on 2 July (Gwynn and Tuckwell, 1:241; Whiting, 284; Moran, 35:218).

³The Dilkes had left for Monaco "late in autumn"; they remained abroad "until after Christmas" (Gwynn and Tuckwell, 1:168, 169).

⁴See 25 Dec 73 to OLC.

⁵A. Salviati and Company of Venice were famous manufacturers of glassware; especially admired were their fragile and richly decorated drinking glasses. During the second half of the nineteenth century, the company rediscovered many ancient secrets of glassmaking which had been lost since the industry's zenith in the Renaissance. The Clemenses purchased glassware from Salviati's in 1878, during the European trip that led to the writing of *A Tramp Abroad* (Baedeker 1895, 237, 289–90; *N&J2*, 219, 221, 340).

⁶Moncure Conway praised the recently decorated Smalley residence at 8 Chester Place in a December 1874 article on English homes in *Harper's Monthly*, giving primary credit to "Mrs. Smalley, whose taste has been the life of the ornamentation of her house":

> The wood used in Mr. Smalley's drawing-room is ebonized, and of it are several cabinets—one displaying some fine specimens of china—bracket-shelves, and two remarkably beautiful chimney-pieces supporting beveled mirrors, framed with shelves which display porcelain and other ornaments. (Conway 1874, 40)

For Benjamin Moran's description of the house see 1 and 2 July 73 to Miller, n. 1.

⁷This short letter was assessed thirteen cents for postage due, indicating that it originally contained an enclosure, now lost.

To Olivia L. Clemens
22 December 1873 • (1st of 2) • London, England
(MS: CU-MARK)

(SLC/MT)   FARMINGTON AVENUE, HARTFORD.

Dec. 22.

Livy my darling, this is Monday. Yesterday I said it had been more than a week since I had heard from you; Stoddard said, no, *just* a week; but that letters would come today. When I woke this morning & was going to turn over & take another nap, I remembered that there would doubtless be letters. So I got up at once & dressed. There were two, my child— one about Dʳ Browne's "Margaret"[1] & the other about Mrs. Cowan[2] & the private theatricals at the ladies club, & all that gossip—which is exactly what I like. I have always contended that Ma[3] was the best letter‐writer in the world, because she threw such an atmosphere of her locality & her surroundings into her letters that her reader was transported *to* her, & by the magic of her pen moved among creatures of living flesh & blood꜕, talked with them, hoped & feared & suffered with them.

I'll look up the Thackeray & Dickens.[4] And as Finlay leaves for Belfast tomorrow he shall take the order for the dragon, & then I will get it when I lecture there.[5]

I've got 7 razors all in one box, with the days of the week marked on them. That is to give each razor a week's rest, which is the next best thing to stropping it. Stoddard, Finlay & I are to dine with the Dolby to‐night at the Westminster Club & I reckon we'll have a pretty good time (now here's that Punch & Judy devil just struck up on his drum over by the church railings—but it is a dark, rainy day & he won't take a trick.)

Another Tichborne case—no, I mean a case of mistaken identity. Finlay & I started out for a walk yesterday afternoon—met a very young & very handsome [man] within 5 steps of the door, who looked at me as if he knew me, & I looked at him, not expecting to know him, but instantly recognizing the fact that I had seen the face somewhere before.

Very well. I kept telling Finlay I knew that face—& by & by, when we were well up Portland Place, I said "*Now* I've got it!—it is the young

Lord MacDuff ~~pre~~ who presided at a Morayshire Banquet in ʄ Regent street the other night."[6]

Very good again. Half an hour later, in Regent's Park we met a lady whom Finlay knew,—she was giving 3 or 4 of her children an airing. We walked with her an hour, then went to her house in Harley street (the "Long, unlovely street" of Tennyson In Memoriam)[7] to drink a glass of wine—sat there half an hour, when in comes that same man we met before the hotel (Finlay nodded to me as much as to say, "Here he is again") & then, lo & behold you he was introduced to us as ~~The~~ "Lord Arthur Hill," (and, in a whisper, "heir to the Marquis of Downshire.") I studied the fellow all over for more than half an hour, & there was *no* difference between the two men except that the hair of one was wavy & that of the other was not. The Mac Duff is a Scotchman, but this chap is Irish, born close to Belfast & is heir to one of those mighty estates there that Finlay ~~tell~~ told us of, with 40 miles extent & 60,000 population.[8] It was a curious case, all around, considering the exceeding scarcity of lords.

I *love* you, my child.

Sam*l*.

⊠

Mrs. Sam*l*. L. Clemens | Hartford | Conn [*in upper left corner:*] America. | [*flourish*] [*on flap:*] ⟨SLC/MT⟩ [*postmarked:*] LONDON-W 5 DE 22 73 [*and*] NEW YORK JAN ◊ DUE 13 U.S. CURRENCY [*and*] INSUFFICIENTLY STAMPED [*and*] 13

---

[1] John Brown, in a letter to Olivia not known to survive, may have asked for help in locating a copy of Sylvester Judd's *Margaret: A Tale of the Real and Ideal, Blight and Bloom*, first published in 1845. Clemens owned an 1871 edition of this work (Boston: Roberts Brothers) (Gribben, 1:361). In January 1874, shortly before leaving England, he sent Brown a volume of drawings inspired by the book, *Compositions in Outline, by Felix O. C. Darley, from Judd's Margaret* (first published in 1856), and in February, from Hartford, he forwarded a copy of the novel itself (28 Feb 74 to Brown, CtY).

[2] Mrs. Sidney J. Cowen was president of the Union for Home Work, a charity founded in 1872 "for the purpose of improving the condition and, in particular, the home life of the poorer women and children of the city" (Trumbull, 1:538–39; Geer 1873, 52, 296).

[3] Jane Lampton Clemens.

[4] Since Olivia's letters do not survive, nothing is known of her request regarding these authors.

[5] The "dragon," possibly an item of bric-a-brac for the Clemenses' Hartford house, has not been identified.

[6] See 11 and 12 Dec 73 to OLC, n. 6.

7 "In Memoriam" (1850), canto 7. Clemens owned an 1871 edition of Tennyson's complete works (Boston: J. R. Osgood) (Gribben, 2:693).

8 Clemens must have been mistaken, since the heir to the marquess of Downshire was only two years old at this time. Clemens evidently met his father, the present marquess, Arthur Wills Blundell Trumbull Sandys Roden Hill (1844–74). Both were born in London, not "close to Belfast." As of 1883 the family estates encompassed 114,621 acres in Ireland (in five different counties), as well as 5,568 acres in England. In all they yielded £96,691 a year, the eighth largest income from land in the United Kingdom (Burke 1904, 500–501; Cokayne, 4:460–61).

To Olivia L. Clemens
22 December 1873 • (2nd of 2) • London, England
(MS: CU-MARK)

[*on back of letter as folded:*][1]
Just wrote you a moment ago, Livy dear,

Dec. 22

Saml

> Halloway House, Hastings,
> Dec. 19, 1873.
>
> My dear M[r] Clemens,
>   Is there no chance of seeing you down here before you go? Anytime would do for us. Why not eat your Christmas Dinner with us? We are a merry party, & I don't think you would find it very dull. The shortest notice of your coming, or no notice at all will suffice.
>   Tell me, please, when you think of returning: I want to ask you to take out a watch for a friend of mine, if it would not be troublesome to you.
>   I long to see the novel—yours and Warner's: it is not out here yet. If you were living in London, or I in Hartford, I think we could make a good western play together. There are such elements in that book of yours![2]
>   All the best wishes of the season to you from us—
> > Yours most truly
> > George MacDonald.

Punch has frightened [us] as to your going away so soon.[3] I want you to take two bits of crockery for me to the dear Wife.

Yrs truly

Louisa M^cD.

[1] This note to Olivia was probably not enclosed with the previous letter, which was in itself sufficiently long to incur a thirteen-cent postage-due fee.

[2] The British edition of *The Gilded Age* was published on 22 December, one day before the American edition ("Mark Twain and Charles Warner," London *Morning Post*, 22 Dec 73, 8; "Brief Mention," Hartford *Courant*, 20 Dec 73, 2; American Publishing Company to George Routledge, 12 Dec 73, Agreement Book A–K:183, Routledge). MacDonald's proposed collaboration on a "western play," to be based on *Roughing It*, was never realized.

[3] See 13 and 15 Dec 73 to OLC, n. 9.

To Olivia L. Clemens
23 December 1873 • London, England
(MS: CU-MARK)

(SLC/MT)   FARMINGTON AVENUE, HARTFORD.

London, Dec. 23.

Livy darling, Finlay & I called on the Smalleys this evening. What nice children they have. The smallest reminded me a great deal of the Modoc.[1]

We all went last night to hear Burnand read his Happy Thoughts, & it made me a trifle nervous to find the opera glasses all leveled at *me*. I didn't mind it for a time, but when it had lasted an hour & a half I began to get a little fidgetty & ill at ease under it. Dolby said: "If I were Burnand, I would have you on the stage behind a curtain & charge these da-da-dam people an extra shilling for a sight."[2]

The photographs are so good, & they are around everywhere, so it seems as if 3 people out of every 5 I meet on the street recognize me. This in London! It seems incredible.[3]

Burnand reads mighty well. It is a wonderfully humorous, witty, bright, tip-top entertainment. I led the laughter, & the whole house followed suit. I went to the ante-room after it was over & congratulated him with all my heart. He said I was a whole audience by myself—& he wasn't far wrong.[4]

Come come—must stop.

I *love* you, sweetheart.

Sam*l*.

Mrs. Sam*l*. L. Clemens | Hartford | Conn [*on flap:*] ⟨SLC/MT⟩ [*post-marked:*] LONDON-W 7 DE 24 73 [*and*] NEW YORK JAN ◊ PAID ALL

[1] The Smalleys had five children, whose dates of birth have not been discovered: Eleanor, Phillips, Evelyn, Ida, and Emerson (Joseph J. Mathews, 173).

[2] Dolby had "a stutter which leads him to become suddenly stately in the middle of a homely phrase and to give a queer intonation to his voice" (Howe, 139).

[3] The photograph was almost certainly the one taken by Charles Watkins in September 1872 (see 5 Oct 72 to Fitzgibbon, n. 2). In mid-September a reporter for the South London *Press* mentioned having been "favoured" by Watkins with a copy of this portrait, which brought out "all the strong points in Mark's appearance: his well-shaped head—from which the thick stubbly hair rises as he has shown it in one of his own caricatures—the keen, eagle eye peering out from shaggy brows, and the firm square jaw indicative of power and determination" ("London Lounger," 14 Sept 72, 1). This photograph was also probably available for purchase by the public: on 1 November 1872 John Camden Hotten wrote Watkins to ask "your price per doz & per 100 to a poor but honest bookseller" of "Mark Twain's photograph" (CU-MARK). (Hotten also asked, "If you have an autograph of Mark Twain I wish you w^d send it to me by bearer. I WILL FAITH-FULLY RETURN it in the morning. *I am a student of caligraphy.*") Clemens was also photographed by Rogers and Nelson, art photographers and portrait painters at 215 Regent Street, in 1873. Three poses are known to be extant from that sitting. Clemens inscribed a print of one for Stoddard, who used it to illustrate a 1908 article about Clemens in the *Pacific Monthly* (Stoddard 1908, 270). He inscribed another to Lilian Aldrich in March 1874 (MH-H). A surviving print of the third bears no inscription. All are reproduced in Appendix F.

[4] Francis Cowley Burnand (1836–1917) attended Eton and Cambridge; he then prepared for a career in the church, and the law. In 1863 he submitted an article to *Punch* and was invited to join the staff. (In 1880 he became the editor of that journal, serving for twenty-six years.) He was also active as a playwright, writing many successful comedies and burlesques. On 22 December Burnand began a series of London readings from "Happy Thoughts," his popular comic series in *Punch*. The London *Pall Mall Gazette* described a November performance of a similar program in Brighton:

> Thus presented, the chapters, or chief divisions, of "Happy Thoughts" become so many little comedies, which lose nothing from the fact that hearers have already a reading acquaintance with their personages and incidents. Accordingly, without assuming the gestures and general demeanor of an actor, Mr. Burnand has to play parts throughout. . . . It says much for the author's art that his sketches and scenes of social life should bear so well being held up to the light. ("Mr. F. C. Burnand . . . ," 28 Nov 73, 11)

Burnand also published collections of his "Happy Thoughts" in 1868, 1871, and 1872, the last of which he illustrated himself (Griffiths, 135–36; *BBA*, s.v. "Burnand, Francis Cowley"; "Happy Thought Readings," London *Times*, 16 Dec 73, 8).

To Olivia L. Clemens
25 December 1873 • Salisbury, England
(MS: CU-MARK)

WHITE HART HOTEL   SALISBURY

Christmas Day, 1873.[1]

Livy my darling, I sent you a cable telegram from here last night to say "Merry Christmas!"

Today I attended the grand Christmas service in Salisbury Cathedral, in company with recumbent mail-clad knights who had lain there 650 years. What a fascinating building it is! It is the loveliest pile of stone that can be imagined—think of comparing it with that solemn barn at York.[2] And then we drove by Old Sarum[3]—all day I was thinking lovingly of my "Angel in the House,"—for Old Sarum & Salisbury naturally recal Coventry Patmore's books[4]—& then we went to Stonehenge. A wonderful thing is Stonehenge. It is one of the most mysterious & satisfactory ruins I have ever seen.[5]

Time to dress for dinner. With a world of love to you & to all,

Sam*l*.

✉—————————————————————————

Mrs. Sam*l*. L. Clemens | Hartford | Conn. [*in upper left corner:*] America | [*flourish*] [*on flap:*] WHITE HART HOTEL   SALISBURY [*postmarked:*] SALISBURY E DE 25 73 [*and*] L 2◊ 12 1873 [*and*] NEW YORK JAN 10 PAID ALL

[1] Clemens and Stoddard visited Salisbury for Christmas. They took rooms at the White Hart Hotel, near the cathedral, and were entertained during their stay by William Blackmore (1827–78), a native of the area. Blackmore was trained as a solicitor, and became wealthy from the commissions he earned helping European capitalists invest in American ventures. He traveled widely in the Ameri-

can West, acquiring interests in gold and salt mines, railroads, and real estate. As an amateur anthropologist he collected prehistoric artifacts from America and England and donated them to the city of Salisbury, building the Blackmore Museum (opened in 1867) to house them (Brayer, 29–33, 318; Willoughby, 317, 320–21). Stoddard described the Salisbury trip in a letter to the San Francisco *Chronicle:*

> Well, our Christmas mess took rail for Salisbury, and reached the "White Hart" hotel in good season. . . . The landlord "hoped we would find everything to our satisfaction," and we hurried into carriages at the door and went to our Christmas Eve dinner at a friend's house not far away. The dining-hall was as charming as possible; high and frescoed ceilings, paintings of defunct ancestry upon the walls; three great windows opening upon a faultless lawn. (Stoddard 1874c)

And to his family Stoddard wrote:

> On Wednesday, the 24th, Mark, Mr. Porton (of Arizona, etc.), and I, took train for Salisbury. We were to be entertained by Mr. Blackmore who has often been to America, chiefly to hunt Buffalo and to explore the unknown regions of the West. . . .
> After dinner we spent the evening in the beautiful museum of the Blackmore's, full of antiquities collected and housed at an expense of fifty thousand dollars—and it goes to the town as a free gift.
> We went to service Christmas morning in the old Salisbury cathedral, called the finest building in all Europe.
> After luncheon we drove over to Stonehenge, a curious old Druid ruin: then home across the Salisbury plains. . . . In the evening a grand dinner, with some invited guests. After it, snap-dragon, music, etc. etc. (Stoddard to "My Own Dear Ones at Home," 29 Dec 73, Bell, 278–79)

[2] Clemens and Stoddard attended "choral service" in the cathedral, and enjoyed the "lark-like carrol of the boy-soprano, who sent his notes off into the air like parti-colored sunbeams" (Stoddard 1874c). Salisbury Cathedral, whose foundation was laid in 1220, was one of the first and finest examples of early English Gothic architecture. Although its four-hundred-foot spire is the tallest in the country, the cathedral is considerably smaller than York Minster, the largest Gothic building in Great Britain (Murray, 355–56, 475).

[3] Old Sarum, about two miles north of Salisbury, was formerly the site of an ancient British camp, then a Roman station, a Saxon town, and finally a Norman town. From 1075 it was the seat of a bishopric, which was moved to Salisbury in 1220. All that remained of this formerly important settlement was a huge knoll, "encircled by two deep vertical entrenchments, with a central mound, the citadel of the fortress, peering above them" (Murray, 357).

[4] The Salisbury area was the setting for Coventry Patmore's four-volume verse narrative, *The Angel in the House,* which the Clemenses had enjoyed during their courtship (*L2,* 276 n. 7).

[5] Stonehenge, the largest megalithic monument in Britain, lies about eight miles north of Salisbury. It is thought to have been in continuous human use from about 3100 to 1100 B.C. (Gascoigne, 610).

To Olivia L. Clemens
29 December 1873 • London, England
(MS: CU-MARK)

⟨SLC/MT⟩   FARMINGTON AVENUE, HARTFORD.

Dec. 29,

Livy darling, I will only write a line, to accompany these enclosures. A moment ago I looked into the drawer & saw several letters, addressed to me, in a familiar handwriting—yours; & they brought you before me. No, not that exactly, b~~e~~ because nothing but *you*, yourself will do—but they so reminded me of you, & made me so long to see you & take you in my arms. Never mind the "gushing;" with one like me, that is nothing; I am not demonstrative, except at intervals—but I *always* love you—always admire you—am always your champion. In Salisbury when a gentleman[1] remarked upon my taking the trouble to telegraph a Merry Christmas to my *wife*, saying it was the sort of thing to do with a *sweetheart*, I closed him up very promptly, & ~~sad~~ said I did not allow any man to refer to my wife jestingly, however respectful he might intend to be. He apologized profusely—otherwise things would have been pretty unpleasant there, presently. I love you, my darling, whether I keep saying it or not—I *always* love you—*always*.

Sam*l*.

[*enclosure 1:*][2]
Preserve this, Livy, S. L. C.

6, KENT TERRACE, REGENT'S PARK. N. W.

Xmas day. 1873.

My dear Sir,

"After compliments", as the Orientals say, by which in this case I mean no compliments at all, but the heartiest good wishes of the season, I am to say to you, on the part of the partner of my expenses, that we shall assemble some friends here on *Wednesday*, New Year's Eve, at 9 o'clock, for frivolous conversation, to be atoned for by serious supper at 11, & so we hope to see in 1874 agreeably. It will much increase the chance of our doing so, if you will give us the pleasure of your company. Will you?

Always yours sincerely

Shirley Brooks.[3]

S. L. Clemens Esq

[*enclosure 2:*]
Preserve this.
    S. L. C.

Halloway House, Hastings

Dec. 27, 1873.

My dear Clemens,

The best wishes of this good time be yours and all its plentiful hopes.

Since it seems unhappily so doubtful whether you will be able to come and see us, can you tell me where you would be to be found in London any day between the 13th & ⁄ 16th of January.[4] We shall be up then, and I would bring to you the things you are so kind as [to] offer to take.

Some day perhaps we *may* write a play together. It would be great fun.[5]

Don't address me *Rev.* I'm not reverend. If you do I will return the compliment.

Yours ever,

George MacDonald.

[*in ink:*] Mrs. Sam*l*. L. Clemens | Hartford | Conn. | Forest street. | [*rule*] [*in upper left corner:*] America | [*rule*] [*on flap:*] ⟨SLC/MT⟩ [*postmarked:*] LONDON.W 3 DE 30 73 [*and*] BOSTON 14 JAN 12 U.S. NOTES [*and*] INSUFFICIENTLY STAMPED [*and*] 2 | [*flourish*] | Due 12

---

[1]Unidentified.

[2]The following two letters have been conjecturally identified as the enclosures mentioned in the first sentence of this letter.

[3]Clemens accepted this invitation, and spent New Year's Eve at the Brookses' with the Burnands, the Hardmans, the Jerrolds, the Yateses, and Tenniel, among others. Brooks recorded in his diary, "Somehow, . . . I did not fancy we were so jolly as usual," in spite of the fact that

Mark Twain proposed the host and hostess in a very funny little speech. . . . I believe that it was only my fancy that made me think our supper less effective than our other gatherings have been. To bed at 2.30, and all thanks where all should be paid for all the mercies of the year.

This entry constituted Brooks's last: he died, after a brief illness, on 23 February 1874 (Layard, 576–77, 580–86).

[4]Clemens sailed from Liverpool on 13 January.

[5]See 22 Dec 73 to OLC (2nd), n. 2.

To Tom Taylor
per Charles Warren Stoddard
29 December 1873 • London, England
(MS: Jacobs)

<u>SLC/MT</u>   ~~FARMINGTON AVENUE, HARTFORD.~~

Langham Hotel.

29 Dec 1873.

Dear Sir[1]

I went to Salisbury to spend Christmas and was persuaded to go on to Ventnor for a day.[2] My friend[3] told me I could get back to London in season to meet the engagement with you, but I found it impossible to do so and by this time it was too late to accomplish anything by telegraph.[4] I will call tomorrow about noon and shall by very glad if I find you at home but if not I shall consider that I am properly punished.

With a thousand apologies—

Ys Truly

Sam*[l]*. L. Clemens.

Tom Taylor, Esq

[1]Tom Taylor (1817–80) was educated at Glasgow and Cambridge universities. After sending his first contribution to *Punch* in 1844 he was invited to join the staff, where he served until his death, replacing Brooks as editor in early 1874. His greatest success, however, was as a playwright. Over the course of his career he created or adapted over seventy works for the London stage; although many were dramas, the most popular were domestic comedies. In addition, he wrote art criticism for the London *Times* and *Graphic,* and published several works of biography (Spielmann, 338–41).

²According to Stoddard, Clemens felt "rather ill" after all the dining over Christmas and "concluded to go down to the Isle of Wight to spend Sunday," 28 December (Stoddard to "My Own Dear Ones at Home," 29 Dec 73, Bell, 279). Ventnor was a resort on the southern coast of the island.

³Presumably William Blackmore, Clemens's host in Salisbury.

⁴For Clemens's business with Taylor see 30 Dec 73 to Warner, n. 1.

To George H. Fitzgibbon
30 December 1873 • London, England
(MS: NN-B)

(*SLC*)

Langham Hotel,
London, Dec. 30.

My Dear Mr. Fitz Gibbon:

After all, I find I am not going into the provinces—(I got the paragraph—many thanks.)¹ Every hall & theatre is full of holiday shows. We can't even get a church to talk in till near the end of January, & I can't wait that long. My chief business here is already accomplished (Eng (getting English copyright on my novel), so there is nothing to keep me from sailing at once, if I chose.² I lecture only 3 more times on British soil, & 3 nights in New York, & then I retire from the platform *permanently*.³ I think I will try to eke out a meagre subsistence upon my permanent annual income of £8,000, & try to sit at home & in peace & do nothing. (Don't tell anybody that.) But if there *is* a fool in the world, I think I am that person. A sensible man lectures only when butter & bread are scarce.

I am to appear on the scaffold 3 more times in England, as I remarked a moment ago—on the 8ᵗʰ of January at Leicester, & on the 9ᵗʰ & 10ᵗʰ at Liverpool—& then sail for home on the 13ᵗʰ in the *Parthia*.⁴ If you'll only run over there, the first time you get a chance, I'll treat you the best I know how, & give you the best bed in the house as long as you stay.

I was in Ventnor, Sunday, & hunted up Miss Florence.⁵ She is a most attractive & very natural & girlish sort of girl. (I hate artificial girls.) I saw all the family—exceedingly pleasant people they are, too.

Remember me kindly to Mrs. Fitz Gibbon & the family, & believe me—

Ys faithfully

Saml. L. Clemens.

[1] Evidently Fitzgibbon had sent a clipping from the 23 December Darlington *Northern Echo* of the item Clemens had asked him to publish (see 21 Dec 73 to Fitzgibbon, n. 3).

[2] Clemens's surviving letters since July make no mention of his other purpose (in addition to the publication of *The Gilded Age*) in revisiting England: to collect material for a book (see 6 July 73 to Fairbanks). It is not clear when he abandoned the project, but he had definitely put it aside by 25 June 1874, when he wrote to the New York *Evening Post* to deny a report that he was "at present engaged in writing a work on English manners & customs":

> Some day, but not just at present, I hope to write a book about England, but it will hardly bear so broad a title as the one suggested above. In such a book as that, I could not leave out the manners & customs which obtain in an English gentleman's household without leaving out the most interesting feature of the subject./ They are the next thing to perfection; ,admirable:, yet I would shrink from ,deliberately, describing them in a book, for I ẃ fear that such a course would be, after all, a violation of the liberal ,courteous, hospitality which furnished me the means of doing it. There may be no serious indelicacy about eating a gentleman's bread & then printing an appreciative & complimentary account of the ways of his family, but still it is a thing which one naturally dislikes to do. (Daley†)

In addition to the two pieces Clemens had probably written in the winter of 1872–73 (see pp. 258–59), he produced several manuscripts that originally could have been intended for the book. Two of these, "Rogers" and "Property in Opulent London," were included in *Mark Twain's Sketches. Number One*, where they were explicitly identified as "From the Author's Unpublished English Notes" (no such notes appear in the surviving English journals) (SLC 1874c, 13–16, 28–29; Appendix C). Two others, "The 'Blind Letter' Department, London P. O." and " 'Party Cries' in Ireland," survive in manuscript (the first at CtY-BR and the second at ViU) and were published in *Mark Twain's Sketches, New and Old* (SLC 1875, 262–63, 279–82). Clemens probably wrote the first of these shortly after visiting the post office, either in the company of Edmund Yates or through an introduction from him, since Yates had been head of the missing-letter department for a decade before his resignation in 1872. This visit may have taken place during the second half of June 1873, when Yates was in or near London reporting on the shah (17 or 18 June 73 to Young, n. 1). Clemens almost certainly wrote the second piece in Belfast, between 28 August and 1 September 1873. One last manuscript, "One Method of Teaching in England," remained unpublished: it was based on a visit Clemens made to an English school, apparently with Stoddard, sometime between late November 1873 and mid-January 1874. It includes a four-page introduction in Clemens's hand, together with thirteen pages of sample student essays copied by Stoddard. Clemens included this piece in the table of contents he drafted in February 1875 for *Sketches, New and Old*, but he later changed his mind and deleted it (*ET&S1*, 623, 626; SLC 1873w).

[3] The New York lectures did not take place (see 17 Dec 73 to Redpath, n. 2).

⁴ Fitzgibbon wrote the following item for the Darlington *Northern Echo*, where it appeared on 1 January:

> I regret having to inform you that the people of the North of England and Scotland are doomed not to make the personal acquaintance of "Mark Twain's" richly original humour. His agents have been prowling about the country endeavouring to get a place wherein he might lecture, and they report that every hall and theatre in the country has been pre-engaged for holiday shows till the end of January. "Mark Twain's" American engagements prevent him remaining so long in England. His chief business in England was to get copyright for his novel. That has been accomplished. As he cannot get any place in your neighbourhood or in Scotland to lecture, all that remains for him is to fulfil his remaining engagements. He sails for America in the *Parthia* on the 13th, and after lecturing three times in New York, he retires to private life. He has made up his mind, notwithstanding his splendid success, to never more appear on what he calls the public scaffold. So well he may, being in the enjoyment of a private annual income of 8,000*l.* The great surprise is that he ever bothered himself with lecturing. (Fitzgibbon 1874)

⁵ Florence Stark, not further identified.

To Charles Dudley Warner
30 December 1873 • London, England
(MS: CU-MARK)

(SLC)

London, Dec. 30.

My Dear Warner:

I have made 3 different appointments to meet Tom Taylor, & have failed to go, every time. He lives miles & miles away, in the edge of London—& that accounts for it. But on New Year's day, Dolby is to rout me out & *take* me there, by main force. Routledge sent me the book yesterday, & I do think it reads more & more bullier. I *know* it ought to dramatize well.[1] The editor of the Cosmopolitan told me he got a copy day before yesterday & read it entirely through, without laying it down. But he said he fell in love with Laura, & so he ripped & cursed when she died.[2]

Livy's letters are always full of your & Susie's[3] constant & unfailing kindnesses to her, & I am as grateful as she is, I can tell you. Lord knows I am glad that I am likely to see all of you 2 or 3 days sooner than I expected. I made a mistake: I sail for *Boston*, on the 13th, in the *Parthia*, instead of for New York the 17th in the Abysinnia. I ought to be home by the 25th.[4] I seem almost there now.

    With love to you both,

Sam*^l*. L. Clemens

✉︎————————————————————————————

Chas. Dudley Warner Esq | Editor "Courant" | Hartford | Conn. [*in upper left corner:*] Personal. | [*rule*] [*on flap:*] ⓈⓁⒸ [*postmarked:*] LONDON-W ZB DE 30 73 [*and*] LI [*and*] BOSTON JAN 14 PAID

[1]On 5 January 1874 Clemens wrote to Taylor to tell him he had called "the other day" and found only his wife at home. He concluded, "As I leave here on the 7th, the opportunity has gone by to speak to you upon the business I had in mind, of course, but I trust that it can never be too late for an erring man to offer an honest apology for his misdeeds—& this I am now moved to do" (Sturdevant, 8). Clemens evidently wanted Taylor's advice about dramatizing *The Gilded Age* (see also 17 May 73 to Warner, n. 4).

[2]The *Cosmopolitan*'s editor has not been identified. This weekly journal, "published simultaneously in London, Paris, and New York," contained "not only the news of both hemispheres, but also the political, commercial, literary, art, and social *on dits* of these capitals of civilization. A great feature is made of the opinions of the press on all subjects." The first number was published in October 1865, and the last appeared in 1876 (*Newspaper Press Directory*, 21, 143; *Tercentenary Handlist*, 104). Laura Hawkins dies in chapter 60 of *The Gilded Age* (see 16 Apr 73 to Fairbanks, n. 2).

[3]Susan Warner.

[4]The Cunard steamship *Parthia*, with Clemens aboard, departed from Liverpool on 13 January and arrived in Boston on 26 January ("Cunard Line," London *Times*, 31 Dec 73, 2; "Return of Mark Twain," Boston *Evening Transcript*, 26 Jan 74, 4).

To Olivia L. Clemens
31 December 1873 • London, England
(MS: CU-MARK)

London
Dec. 31

Livy my darling, I re-enclosed to you, today, the note of some Boston autograph hunter[1]—because I was in an ill humor. It occurs to me, now, that I have vented the ill humor on *you*, not on the autograph seeker. Well, never mind, I forgive you.

Thirteen more days in England, & then I sail! If I only *do* get home safe, & find my darling & the Modoc well, I shall be a grateful soul. And if ever I do have another longing to leave home, even for a week, please dissipate it with a club. Sometimes I get so homesick I don't know what to do.

Well, by & by it will all come right, no doubt. In the meantime I love you & honor you most sincerely

Saml.

Mrs. Saml. L. Clemens | Hartford | Conn. [*in upper left corner:*] America. | [*rule*] [*on flap:*] Ⓢ Ⓛ Ⓒ [*postmarked:*] LONDON-W ZB DE 30 73[2] [*and*] LI [*and*] BOSTON JAN 14 PAID

[1] The note is not known to survive, nor has the autograph hunter been identified.

[2] This postmark is probably erroneous; the possibility remains, however, that Clemens misdated his letter.

To James Redpath
31 December 1873 • London, England
(MS: MiD)

Ⓢ Ⓛ Ⓒ/MT   FARMINGTON AVENUE, HARTFORD.

London, Dec. 31.

Dear Redpath:

Shall sail in the Parthia Jan. 13 & arrive at *Boston* about the 23^d or 24th.[1] Want to see you.

Ys

Mark.

[*letter docketed:*] BOSTON LYCEUM BUREAU. JAMES REDPATH JAN 22 1874 [*and*] *Twain* Mark | London | Eng. | Dec. 31 ~~1874~~ 1873

[1] See 30 Dec 73 to Warner, n. 4.

Appendixes

Appendix A

Genealogies of the Clemens and Langdon Families

THESE GENEALOGIES are documented in *Mark Twain's Letters, Volume 1: 1853–1866* (379–81) and *Volume 2: 1867–1868* (375), respectively, where they were originally published. Pamela Clemens's first name is given here as before, in accord with her preferred usage, although in fact she was named for her paternal grandmother, Pamelia Goggin, and occasionally signed herself Pamelia (*MTBus*, 4–5; quit-claim deed from Pamelia A. Moffett to Charles L. Webster, 17 Oct 81, NPV).

Clemens Family

John Marshall Clemens
b. 11 Aug 1798
d. 24 Mar 1847

m. 6 May 1823 —————

Jane Lampton
b. 18 June 1803
d. 27 Oct 1890

Orion Clemens
b. 17 July 1825
d. 11 Dec 1897

m. 19 Dec 1854 ——————————

Mary Eleanor (Mollie) Stotts
b. 4 Apr 1834
d. 15 Jan 1904

Pamela Ann Clemens
b. 13 Sept 1827
d. 31 Aug 1904

m. 20 Sept 1851 ——————

William Anderson Moffett
b. 13 July 1816
d. 4 Aug 1865

Pleasant Hannibal Clemens
b. 1828 or 1829
d. aged 3 months

Margaret L. Clemens
b. 31 May 1830
d. 17 Aug 1839

Benjamin L. Clemens
b. 8 June 1832
d. 12 May 1842

SAMUEL LANGHORNE CLEMENS
b. 30 Nov 1835
d. 21 Apr 1910

m. 2 Feb 1870 ——————————

Olivia Louise (Livy) Langdon
b. 27 Nov 1845
d. 5 June 1904

Henry Clemens
b. 13 July 1838
d. 21 June 1858

548

Alice Jane (Jean) Webster
b. 24 July 1876
d. 11 June 1916

m. 7 Sept 1915 ——————— [1 child]

Glenn Ford McKinney
b. 15 Feb 1869
d. 15 Feb 1934

Jennie Clemens
b. 14 Sept 1855
d. 1 Feb 1864

Annie E. Moffett
b. 1 July 1852
d. 24 Mar 1950

m. 28 Sept 1875 ——————

Charles Luther Webster
b. 24 Sept 1851
d. 26 Apr 1891

William Luther Webster
b. 15 Oct 1878
d. ? Mar 1945

Samuel Charles Webster
b. 8 July 1884
d. 24 Mar 1962

m. 1920?

Doris Webb
b. ?
d. 9 July 1967

Samuel Erasmus Moffett
b. 5 Nov 1860
d. 1 Aug 1908

m. 13 Apr 1887 ——————

Mary Emily Mantz
b. 19 Aug 1863
d. 2 Oct 1940

Anita Moffett
b. 4 Feb 1891
d. 26 Mar 1952

Francis Clemens Moffett
b. 1 Oct 1895
d. 4 Mar 1927

Langdon Clemens
b. 7 Nov 1870
d. 2 June 1872

Olivia Susan (Susy) Clemens
b. 19 Mar 1872
d. 18 Aug 1896

Clara Langdon Clemens
b. 8 June 1874
d. 19 Nov 1962

m. 6 Oct 1909 ———————— Nina Gabrilowitsch
b. 18 Aug 1910
d. 16 Jan 1966

1) Ossip Gabrilowitsch
b. 7 Feb 1878
d. 14 Sept 1936

m. 11 May 1944

2) Jacques Alexander Samossoud
b. 8 Sept 1894
d. 13 June 1966

Jane Lampton (Jean) Clemens
b. 26 July 1880
d. 24 Dec 1909

Langdon Family

Jervis Langdon
b. 11 Jan 1809
d. 6 Aug 1870

m. 23 July 1832

Olivia Lewis
b. 19 Aug 1810
d. 28 Nov 1890

Susan Langdon (adopted)
b. 18 Feb 1836
d. 29 Aug 1924

m. 7 Dec 1858

Theodore W. Crane
b. 26 Sept 1831
d. 3 July 1889

Olivia Louise (Livy) Langdon
b. 27 Nov 1845
d. 5 June 1904

m. 2 Feb 1870

SAMUEL LANGHORNE CLEMENS
b. 30 Nov 1835
d. 21 Apr 1910

Charles Jervis Langdon
b. 13 Aug 1849
d. 19 Nov 1916

m. 12 Oct 1870

Ida B. Clark
b. 7 Mar 1849
d. 17 Dec 1934

[see Clemens genealogy]

Julia Olivia (Julie) Langdon
  b. 21 Nov 1871
  d. 15 July 1948

    m. 29 Nov 1902 —————————— [2 children]

Edward Eugene Loomis
  b. 2 Apr 1864
  d. 11 July 1937

Jervis Langdon
  b. 26 Jan 1875
  d. 16 Dec 1952

    m. 2 Oct 1902 —————————— [2 children]

Eleanor Sayles
  b. 10 Feb 1878
  d. 15 June 1971

Ida Langdon
  b. 15 Oct 1880
  d. 9 Oct 1964

Appendix B

Enclosures with the Letters

ENCLOSURES ARE transcribed here when they are too long to be presented with the letters themselves. The third item, Clemens's second Sandwich Islands letter to the New York *Tribune*, was presumably accompanied by a letter that is not known to survive. Textual commentaries for these enclosures appear following the commentaries for the letters.

Enclosure with 20 January 1872
To Olivia L. Clemens • Harrisburg, Pa.
(Longfellow 1871)

THE LEGEND BEAUTIFUL.
"HADST thou stayed, I must have fled!"
That is what the Vision said.

In his chamber all alone,
Kneeling on the floor of stone,
Prayed the Monk in deep contrition
For his sins of indecision,
Prayed for greater self-denial,
In temptation and in trial;
It was noonday by the dial,
And the Monk was all alone.

Suddenly, as if it lightened,
An unwonted splendor brightened
All within him and without him

In that narrow cell of stone;
And he saw the Blessed Vision
Of our Lord, with light Elysian
Like a vesture wrapped about him,
Like a garment round him thrown.

Not as crucified and slain,
Not in agonies of pain,
Not with bleeding hands and feet,
Did the Monk his Master see;
But as in the village street,
In the house or harvest-field,
Halt and lame and blind he healed,
When he walked in Galilee.

In an attitude imploring,
Hands upon his bosom crossed,
Wondering, worshipping, adoring,
Knelt the Monk in rapture lost.
Lord, he thought, in heaven that reignest,
Who am I, that thus thou deignest
To reveal thyself to me?
Who am I, that from the centre
Of thy glory, thou shouldst enter
This poor cell, my guest to be?

Then amid his exaltation,
Loud the convent bell appalling,
From its belfry calling, calling,
Rang through court and corridor,
With persistent iteration
He had never heard before.

It was now the appointed hour
When alike, in shine or shower,
Winter's cold or summer's heat,
To the convent portals came,
All the blind and halt and lame,

All the beggars of the street,
For their daily dole of food
Dealt them by the brotherhood;
And their almoner was he,
Who upon his bended knee,
Rapt in silent ecstasy
Of divinest self-surrender,
Saw the Vision and the Splendor.

Deep distress and hesitation
Mingled with his adoration;
Should he go, or should he stay?
Should he leave the poor to wait
Hungry at the convent gate,
Till the Vision passed away?
Should he slight his heavenly guest,
Slight this visitant celestial,
For a crowd of ragged, bestial
Beggars at the convent gate?
Would the Vision there remain?
Would the Vision come again?

Then a voice within his breast
Whispered, audible and clear
As if to the outward ear:
"Do thy duty; that is best;
Leave unto thy Lord the rest!"

Straightway to his feet he started,
And with longing look intent
On the Blessed Vision bent,
Slowly from his cell departed,
Slowly on his errand went.

At the gate the poor were waiting,
Looking through the iron grating,
With that terror in the eye
That is only seen in those

Who amid their wants and woes
Hear the sound of doors that close,
And of feet that pass them by;
Grown familiar with disfavor,
Grown familiar with the savor
Of the bread by which men die!
But to-day, they knew not why,
Like the gate of Paradise
Seemed the convent gate to rise,
Like a sacrament divine
Seemed to them the bread and wine.
In his heart the Monk was praying,
Thinking of the homeless poor,
What they suffer and endure;
What we see not, what we see;
And the inward voice was saying:
"Whatsoever thing thou doest
To the least of mine and lowest,
That thou doest unto me!"

Unto me! but had the Vision
Come to him in beggar's clothing,
Come a mendicant imploring,
Would he then have knelt adoring,
Or have listened with derision,
And have turned away with loathing?

Thus his conscience put the question,
Full of troublesome suggestion,
As at length, with hurried pace,
Towards his cell he turned his face,
And beheld the convent bright
With a supernatural light,
Like a luminous cloud expanding
Over floor and wall and ceiling.

But he paused with awe-struck feeling
At the threshold of his door,

For the Vision still was standing
As he left it there before,
When the convent bell appalling,
From its belfry calling, calling,
Summoned him to feed the poor.
Through the long hour intervening
It had waited his return,
And he felt his bosom burn,
Comprehending all the meaning,
When the Blessed Vision said,
"Hadst thou stayed, I must have fled!"
                                        Henry W. Longfellow.

Enclosure with 3 January 1873
To Whitelaw Reid • (2nd of 2) • Hartford, Conn.
(SLC 1873c)

To the Editor of The Tribune.

SIR: When you do me the honor to suggest that I write an article about the Sandwich Islands, just now when the death of the King has turned something of the public attention in that direction, you unkennel a man whose modesty would have kept him in hiding otherwise.[1] I could fill you full of statistics, but most human beings like gossip better, & so you will not blame me if I proceed after the largest audience & leave other people to worry the minority with arithmetic.

I spent several months in the Sandwich Islands, six years ago, &, if I could have my way about it, I would go back there & remain the rest of my days. It is paradise for an indolent man. If a man is rich he can live expensively, & his grandeur will be respected as in other parts of the earth; if he is poor he can herd with the natives, & live on next to nothing; he can sun himself all day long under the palm trees, & be no more troubled by his conscience than a butterfly would.

When you are in that blessed retreat, you are safe from the turmoil of life; you drowse your days away in a long deep dream of peace; the past is a forgotten thing, the present is heaven, the future you leave to

[1] See 3 Jan 73 to Reid (2nd), n. 1.

take care of itself. You are in the center of the Pacific Ocean; you are two thousand miles from any continent; you are millions of miles from the world; as far as you can see, on any hand, the crested billows wall the horizon, & beyond this barrier the wide universe is but a foreign land to you, & barren of interest.

The climate is simply delicious—never cold at the sea level, & never really too warm, for you are at the half-way house—that is, twenty degrees above the equator. But then you may order your own climate for this reason: the eight inhabited islands are merely mountains that lift themselves out of the sea—a group of bells, if you please, with some (but not very much) "flare" at their basis. You get the idea. Well, you take a thermometer, & mark on it where you want the mercury to stand permanently forever (with not more than 12 degrees variation) Winter & Summer. If 82 in the shade is your figure (with the privilege of going down or up 5 or 6 degrees at long intervals), you build your house down on the "flare"—the sloping or level ground by the sea-shore—& you have the deadest surest thing in the world on that temperature. And such is the climate of Honolulu, the capital of the kingdom. If you mark 70 as your mean temperature, you build your house on any mountain side, 400 or 500 feet above sea level. If you mark 55 or 60, go 1,500 feet higher. If you mark for Wintry weather, go on climbing & watching your mercury. If you want snow & ice forever & ever, & zero & below, build on the summit of Mauna Kea, 16,000 feet up in the air. If you must have hot weather, you should build at Lahaina, where they do not hang the thermometer on a nail because the solder might melt & the instrument get broken; or you should build in the crater of Kilauea, which would be the same as going home before your time. You cannot find as much climate bunched together anywhere in the world as you can in the Sandwich Islands. You may stand on the summit of Mauna Kea, in the midst of snow-banks that were there before Capt. Cook[2] was born, may be, & while you shiver in your furs you may cast your eye down the sweep of the mountain side & tell exactly where the frigid zone ends & vegetable life begins; a stunted & tormented growth of trees shades down into a taller & freer species, & that in turn, into the full foliage & varied tints of the temperate zone; further down, the mere ordinary green tone of a

[2]Captain James Cook (1728–79) was the first European to reach the Sandwich Islands, in 1778; he was killed by natives on the island of Hawaii (*RI 1993*, 490–91, 709).

forest washes over the edges of a broad bar of orange trees that embraces the mountain like a belt, & is so deep & dark a green that distance makes it black; & still further down, your eye rests upon the levels of the sea-shore, where the sugar-cane is scorching in the sun, & the feathery cocoa-palm glassing itself in the tropical waves: & where you know the sinful natives are lolling about in utter nakedness & never knowing or caring that you & your snow & your chattering teeth are so close by. So you perceive, you can look down upon all the climates of the earth, & note the kinds & colors of all the vegetations, just with a glance of the eye—& this glance only travels over about three miles as the bird flies, too.

The natives of the islands number only about 50,000, & the whites about 3,000, chiefly Americans. According to Capt. Cook, the natives numbered 400,000 less than a hundred years ago. But the traders brought labor & fancy diseases—in other words, long, deliberate, infallible destruction; & the missionaries brought the means of grace & got them ready. So the two forces are working along harmoniously, & anybody who knows anything about figures can tell you exactly when the last Kanaka will be in Abraham's bosom & his islands in the hands of the whites. It is the same as calculating an eclipse—if you get started right, you cannot miss it. For nearly a century the natives have been keeping up a ratio of about three births to five deaths, & you can see what that must result in. No doubt in fifty years a Kanaka will be a curiosity in his own land, & as an investment will be superior to a circus.

I am truly sorry that these people are dying out, for they are about the most interesting savages there are. Their language is soft & musical, it has not a hissing sound in it, & *all* their words end with a vowel. They would call Jim Fisk[3] *Jimmy Fikki*, for they will even do violence to a proper name if it grates too harshly in its natural state. The Italian is raspy & disagreeable compared to the Hawaiian tongue.

These people used to go naked, but the missionaries broke that up; in the towns the men wear clothing now, & in the country a plug hat & a breech-clout; or if they have company they put on a shirt collar & a

[3] James Fisk (1834–72) was a flashy and unscrupulous capitalist and speculator who, together with Jay Gould, had controlled the Erie Railroad. In January 1872 he was fatally shot by Edward Stokes, in a quarrel over his mistress and certain business transactions. A few days after Clemens wrote this article, Stokes was convicted of murder, his first trial having resulted in a hung jury (New York *Tribune:* "The Stokes Trial," 4 Jan 73, 2; "Stokes Convicted," 6 Jan 73, 1).

vest. Nothing but religion & education could have wrought these admirable changes. The women wear a single loose calico gown, that falls without a break from neck to heels.

In the old times, to speak plainly, there was absolutely no bar to the commerce of the sexes. To refuse the solicitations of a stranger was regarded as a contemptible thing for a girl or a woman to do; but the missionaries have so bitterly fought this thing that they have succeeded at least in driving it out of sight—& now it exists only in reality, not in name.

These natives are the simplest, the kindest-hearted, the most unselfish creatures that bear the image of the Maker. Where white influence has not changed them, they will make any chance stranger welcome, & divide their all with him—a trait which has never existed among any other people, perhaps. They live only for to-day; to-morrow is a thing which does not enter into their calculations. I had a native youth in my employ in Honolulu, a graduate of a missionary college, & he divided his time between translating the Greek Testament & taking care of a piece of property of mine which I considered a horse. Whenever this boy could collect his wages, he would go & lay out the entire amount, all the way up from fifty cents to a dollar, in *poi* (which is a paste made of the taro root, & is the national dish), & call in all the native ragamuffins that came along to help him eat it. And there, in the rich grass, under the tamarind trees, the gentle savages would sit & gorge till all was gone. My boy would go hungry & content for a day or two, & then some Kanaka he probably had never seen before would invite him to a similar feast, & give him a fresh start.

The ancient religion was only a jumble of curious superstitions. The shark seems to have been the god they chiefly worshiped—or rather sought to propitiate. Then there was Pele, a goddess who presided over the terrible fires of Kilauea; minor gods were not scarce. The natives are all Christians, now—every one of them; they all belong to the church, & are fonder of theology than they are of pie; they will sweat out a sermon as long as the Declaration of Independence; the duller it is the more it infatuates them; they would sit there & stew & stew in a trance of enjoyment till they floated away in their own grease if the ministers would stand watch-&-watch, & see them through. Sunday-schools are a favorite dissipation with them, & they never get enough. If there was physical as well as mental intoxication in this limb of the service, they would never draw a sober breath. Religion is drink & meat to the native. He can read his neatly printed Bible (in the native tongue—every solitary man, woman, & little child in the islands can), & he reads it over & over again. And he reads a whole world of moral tales, built on the good old Sunday-school book pattern exaggerated, & he worships their heroes—heroes who walk the world with their mouths full of butter, & who are simply impossibly chuckle-headed & pious. And he knows all the hymns you ever heard in your life, & he sings them in a soft, pleasant voice, to native words that make "On Jordan's stormy banks I stand"[4] sound as grotesquely & sweetly foreign to you as if it were a dictionary grinding wrong end first though a sugar-mill. Now you see how these natives, great & small, old & young, are saturated with religion—at least the poetry & the music of it. But as to the practice of it, they vary. Some of the nobler precepts of Christianity they have always practiced naturally, & they always will. Some of the minor precepts they as naturally do not practice, & as naturally they never will. The white man has taught them to lie, & they take to it pleasantly & without sin—for there cannot be much sin in a thing which they cannot be made to comprehend is a sin. Adultery they look upon as poetically wrong but practically proper.

These people are sentimentally religious—perhaps that describes it. They pray & sing & moralize in fair weather, but when they get into trouble, that is "business"—& then they are tolerably apt to drop poetry & call on the Great Shark God of their fathers to give them a lift. Their ancient superstitions are in their blood & bones, & they keep cropping out now & then in the most natural & pardonable way.

The natives make excellent seamen, & the whalers would rather have them than any other race. They are so tractable, docile & willing, & withal so faithful, that they rank first in the sugar-planters' esteem as laborers. Do not these facts speak well for our poor, brown Sunday-school children of the far islands?

There is a small property tax, & any native who has an income of $50 a year can vote.

The 3,000 whites in the islands handle all the money & carry on all the commerce & agriculture—& superintend the religion. Americans are largely in the majority. These whites are sugar-planters, merchants, whale-ship officers, & missionaries. The missionaries are sorry the most

[4] A hymn by Samuel Stennett (b. 1727?), set to music by George Kingsley, in Henry Ward Beecher's *Plymouth Collection* (Julian, 1091–92; Beecher, 412).

of the other whites are there, & these latter are sorry the missionaries don't migrate. The most of the belt of sloping land that borders the sea & rises toward the bases of the mountains, is rich & fertile. There are only 200,000 acres of this productive soil, but only think of its capabilities! In Louisiana, 200,000 acres of sugar land would only yield 50,000 tuns of sugar per annum, & possibly not so much; but in the Sandwich Islands, you could get at least 400,000 tuns out of it. This is a good, strong statement, but it is true, nevertheless. Two & a half tuns to the acre is a common yield in the islands; three & a half tuns is by no means unusual; five tuns is frequent; & I can name the man who took fifty tuns of sugar from seven acres of ground, one season. This cane was on the mountain-side, 2,500 feet above sea level, & it took it three years to mature. Address your inquiries to Capt. McKee, Island of Maui, S. I.[5] Few plantations are stuck up in the air like that, & so twelve months is ample time for the maturing of cane down there. And I would like to call attention to two or three exceedingly noteworthy facts. For instance, there you do not hurry up & cut your cane when it blossoms, but you just let it alone & cut it when you choose—no harm will come of it. And you do not have to keep an army of hands to plant in the planting season, grind in the grinding season, & rush in frantically & cut down the crop when a frost threatens. Not at all. There is no hurry. You run a large plantation with but a few hands, because you plant pretty much when you please, & you cut your cane & grind it when it suits your convenience. There is no frost, & the longer the cane stands the better it grows. Sometimes— often, in fact—part of your gang are planting a field, another part are cutting the crop from an adjoining field, & the rest are grinding at the mill. You only plant once in three years, & you take off two ratoon crops without replanting. You may keep on taking off ratoon crops about as long as you please, indeed; every year the bulk of the cane will be smaller, but the juice will grow regularly denser & richer, & so you are all right. I know of one lazy man who took off sixteen ratoon crops without replanting!

What fortunes those planters made during our war, when sugar went up into the twenties! It had cost them about ten or eleven cents a pound, delivered in San Francisco, & all charges paid. Now if any one

[5] Captain James Makee, a former whaling captain whose fifteen-thousand-acre Rose Ranch on the slopes of Haleakala was the most productive sugar plantation in the islands (Kuykendall and Day, 155; *N&J1*, 223 n. 101; Austen, 39, 41).

desires to know why these planters would probably like to be under our flag, the answer is simple: We make them pay us a duty of four cents a pound on refined sugars at present; brokerage, freights & handling (two or three times), costs three cents more; rearing the cane, & making the sugar, is an item of five cents more—total, 12 cents a pound, or within a cent of it, anyhow. And to-day refined sugar is only worth about 12½ cents (wholesale) in our markets. Profit—none worth mentioning. But if we were to annex the islands & do away with that crushing duty of four cents a pound, some of those heavy planters who can hardly keep their heads above water now, would clear $75,000 a year & upward. Two such years would pay for their plantations, & all their stock & machinery. It is so long since I was in the islands that I feel doubtful about swearing that the United States duties on their sugars was four cents a pound, but I can swear it was not under three.

I would like to say a word about the late King Kamehameha V. & the system of government, but I will wait a day. Also, I would like to know why your correspondents so calmly ignore the true heir to the Sandwich Islands throne, as if he had no existence & no chances; & I would like to heave in a word for him. I refer to our stanch American sympathizer, Prince William Lunalilo, descendant of eleven generations of sceptered savages—a splendid fellow, with talent, genius, education, gentlemanly manners, generous instincts, & an intellect that shines as radiantly through floods of whisky as if that fluid but fed a calcium light in his head. All people in the islands know that William—or "Prince Bill," as they call him, more in affection than otherwise—stands next the throne; & so why is he ignored?

MARK TWAIN.

Hartford, 3d January, 1873.

Enclosure with 6 January 1873
To Whitelaw Reid • Hartford, Conn.
(SLC 1873d)

To the Editor of The Tribune.

SIR: Having explained who the 3,000 whites are, & what sort of people the 50,000 natives are, I will now shovel in some information as to how this toy realm, with its toy population, is governed. By a con-

stable & six policemen? By a justice of the peace & a jury? By a mayor &
a board of aldermen? Oh, no. But by a King—& a Parliament—& a
Ministry—& a Privy Council—& a standing army (200 soldiers)—& a
navy (steam ferry-boat & a raft)—& a grand bench of supreme jus-
tices—& a lord high sheriff on each island. That is the way it is done. It
is like propelling a sardine dish with the Great Eastern's machinery.[1]

Something over 50 years ago the natives, by a sudden impulse which
they could not understand themselves, burned all their idols & over-
threw the ancient religion of the land. Curiously enough, our first invoice
of missionaries were sailing around the Horn at the time, & they arrived
just in season to furnish the people a new & much better means of grace.[2]
They baptized men, women, & children at once & by wholesale, & proceeded to instruct them in the tenets of the new religion immediately
afterward. They built enormous churches, & received into communion
as many as 5,000 people in a single day. The fame of it went abroad in
the earth, & everywhere the nations rejoiced; the unworldly called it a
"great awakening," & even the unregenerated were touched, & spoke of
it with admiration. The missionaries learned the language, translated
the Bible & other books into it, established schools, & even very complete colleges, & taught the whole nation to read & write; the princes &
nobles acquired collegiate educations, & became familiar with half a
dozen dead & living languages. Then, some twenty years later, the missionaries framed a constitution which became the law of the land. It
lifted woman up to a level with her lord; it placed the tenant less at the
mercy of his landlord; it established a just & equable system of taxation;
it introduced the ballot & universal suffrage; it defined & secured to
king, chiefs, & people their several rights & privileges; & it instituted a
parliament in which all the estates of the realm were to be represented,
&, if I remember rightly, it gave this parliament power to pass laws over
the King's veto.[3]

[1] When launched in 1859, the *Great Eastern* was five times larger than any
other steamship afloat. Built in England, the ship was nearly seven hundred feet
long and had "a propeller as big as a windmill" and "paddle boxes capacious
enough to contain Ferris wheels" (Brinnin, 216–17, 223).
[2] Mark Twain had recently described these events of 1819–20 in more detail
in *Roughing It* (*RI 1993*, 496–98, 732).
[3] Hawaii's first constitution was signed by Kamehameha III on 8 October
1840. Although the House of Representatives was granted the power to create
laws, as were the king and the Council of Chiefs, the king's veto "was absolute"
(Kuykendall, 12; Kuykendall and Day, 54–55).

Things went on swimmingly for several years, & especially under the reign of the late King's brother, an enlightened & liberal-minded prince; but when he died & Kamehameha V. ascended the throne, matters took a different turn.[4] He was one of your swell "grace of God" Kings, & not the "figure-head" some have said he was; indeed, he was the biggest power in the Islands all his days, & his royal will was sufficient to create a law any time or overturn one.

He was master in the beginning, & at the middle, & to the end. The Parliament was the "figure-head," & it never was much else in his time. One of his very first acts was to fly into a splendid passion (when his Parliament voted down some measure of his), & tear the beautiful Constitution into shreds, & stamp on them with his royal No. 18s! And his next act was to violently prorogue the Parliament & send the members about their business. He hated Parliaments, as being a rasping & useless incumbrance upon a king, but he allowed them to exist because as an obstruction they were more ornamental than real. He hated universal suffrage & he destroyed it—at least, he took the insides out of it & left the harmless figure. He said he would not have beggars voting industrious people's money away, & so he compelled the adoption of a cash qualification to vote.[5] He surrounded himself with an obsequious royal Cabinet of American & other foreigners, & he dictated his measures to them &, through them, to his Parliament; & the latter institution opposed them respectfully, not to say apologetically, & passed them.

This is but a sad kind of royal "figure-head." He was not a fool. He was a wise sovereign; he had seen something of the world; he was educated & accomplished, & he tried hard to do well by his people, & succeeded. There was no trivial royal nonsense about him; he dressed plainly, poked about Honolulu, night or day, on his old horse, unattended; he was popular, greatly respected, & even beloved. Perhaps the only man who never feared him was "Prince Bill," whom I have mentioned heretofore. Perhaps the only man who ever ventured to speak his whole mind about the King, in Parliament & on the hustings, was the

[4] Kamehameha IV (1834–63) ruled from 1855 until his death, when he was succeeded by his older brother, Kamehameha V (3 Jan 73 to Reid [2nd], n. 1; Alexander, 288, 339).

[5] Kamehameha's new constitution, which he signed on 20 August 1864, limited the voting privilege to literate males owning real estate valued at $150 or more, or having an income of not less than $75 a year (Kuykendall and Day, 111–13).

present true heir to the throne—if Prince Bill is still alive, & I have not heard that he is dead. This go-ahead young fellow used to handle His Majesty without gloves, & wholly indifferent to consequences; & being a shade more popular with the native masses than the King himself, perhaps, his opposition amounted to something. The foregoing was the common talk of Honolulu six years ago, & I set the statements down here because I believe them to be true, & not because I know them to be true.

Prince William is about 35 years of age, now, I should think. There is no blood relationship between him & the house of the Kamehamehas.[6] He comes of an older & prouder race; a race of imperious chiefs & princes of the Island of Maui, who held undisputed sway there during several hundred years. He is the eleventh prince in the direct descent, & the natives always paid a peculiar homage to his venerable nobility, which they never vouchsafed to the mushroom Kamehamehas. He is considered the true heir to the Hawaiian throne, for this reason, viz.: A dying or retiring king can name his own successor, by the law of the land—he can name any child of his he pleases, or he can name his brother or any other member of the royal family. The late king has passed away without leaving son, daughter, brother, uncle, nephew, or father (his father never was king—he died a year or two ago),[7] & without appointing a successor. The Parliament has power now to elect a king, & this king can be chosen from any one of the twelve chief families. This has been my understanding of the matter, & I am very sure I am right. In rank, Prince William overtops any chief in the Islands about as an English royal duke overtops a mere earl. He is the only Hawaiian, outside of the royal family, who is entitled to bear & transmit the title of Prince; & he is so popular that if the scepter were put to a popular vote he would "walk over the track."

He used to be a very handsome fellow, with a truly princely deportment, drunk or sober; but I merely speak figuratively—he never was drunk; he did not hold enough. All his features were fine, & he had a Roman nose that was a model of beauty & grandeur. He was brim full

[6] Prince William Lunalilo was the grandson of a half-brother of Kamehameha I and a cousin to Kamehameha V (*RI 1993*, 715).

[7] Clemens wrote a complimentary description of Mataio Kekuanaoa (1794–1868), the father of Kamehameha IV and Kamehameha V, in his manuscript for *Roughing It*, apparently before learning of his death. In the fall of 1871, when reading proofsheets for the book, he added a footnote to Kekuanaoa's name: "Since dead" (*RI 1993*, 457n, 714, 715).

of spirit, pluck & enterprise; his head was full of brains, & his speech was facile & all alive with point & vigor; there was nothing underhanded or two-faced about him, but he always went straight at everything he undertook, without caring who saw his hand or understood his game. He was a potent friend of America & Americans. Such is the true heir to the vacant throne—if he is not dead, as I said before.

I have suggested that William drinks. That is not an objection to a Sandwich Islander. Whisky cannot hurt them; it can seldom even tangle the legs or befog the brains of a practiced native. It is only water with a flavor to it, to Prince Bill; it is what cider is to us. *Poi* is the all-powerful agent that protects the lover of whisky. Whoever eats it habitually may imbibe habitually without serious harm. The late king & his late sister Victoria[8] both drank unlimited whisky, & so would the rest of the natives if they could get it. The native beverage, *awa*, is so terrific that mere whisky is foolishness to it. It turns a man's skin to white fish-scales that are so tough a dog might bite him, & he would not know it till he read about it in the papers. It is made of a root of some kind. The "quality" drink this to some extent, but the Excise law has placed it almost beyond the reach of the plebeians. After *awa*, what is whisky?

Many years ago the late King & his brother visited California,[9] & some Sacramento folks thought it would be fun to get them drunk. So they gathered together the most responsible soakers in the town & began to fill up royalty & themselves with strong brandy punches. At the end of two or three hours the citizens were all lying torpid under the table & the two princes were sitting disconsolate & saying what a lonely, dry country it was! I tell it to you as it was told to me in Sacramento.

The Hawaiian Parliament consists of half a dozen chiefs, a few whites, & perhaps thirty or forty common Kanakas. The King's ministers (half a dozen whites) sit with them & ride over all opposition to the King's wishes. There are always two people speaking at once—the member & the public translator. The little legislature is as proud of itself as any parliament could be, & puts on no end of airs. The wisdom of a Kanaka legislature is as profound as that of our ordinary run of State legislatures, but no more so. Perhaps God makes all legislatures alike in that respect. I remember one Kanaka bill that struck me: it proposed to con-

[8] See note 11.
[9] Kamehameha IV and Lot Kamehameha (later Kamehameha V) visited California and British Columbia in 1860 (Kuykendall and Day, 107–8).

nect the islands of Oahu & Hawaii with a suspension bridge, because the sea voyage between these points was attended with so much sea-sickness that the natives were greatly discommoded by it. This suspension bridge would have been 150 miles long!

I can imagine what is going on in Honolulu now, during this month of mourning, for I was there when the late King's sister, Victoria, died. David Kalakaua (a chief), Commander-in-Chief of the Household Troops (how is that, for a title?) is no doubt standing guard now over the closed entrances to the "palace" grounds, keeping out all whites but officers of State;[10] & within, the Christianized heathen are howling & dancing & wailing & carrying on in the same old savage fashion that obtained before Cook discovered the country. I lived three blocks from the wooden two-story palace when Victoria was being lamented, & for thirty nights in succession the mourning pow-wow defied sleep. All that time the christianized but morally unclean Princess lay in state in the palace.[11] I got into the grounds one night & saw some hundreds of half-naked savages of both sexes beating their dismal tom-toms, & wailing & caterwauling in the weird glare of innumerable torches; & while a great band of women swayed & jiggered their pliant bodies through the intricate movements of a lascivious dance called the hula-hula, they chanted an accompaniment in native words. I asked the son of a missionary what the words meant. He said they celebrated certain admired gifts & phys-

[10] David Kalakaua (1836–91), a descendant of two chiefs who aided Kamehameha I in the conquest of the kingdom, had also held the office of king's chamberlain under Kamehameha V. Because news from Hawaii took about three weeks to reach the United States, Clemens evidently did not know that Kalakaua was a rival candidate to Prince William Lunalilo for election as king. Although Lunalilo won both a people's referendum of 1 January 1873 and the official election by Legislative Assembly on 8 January, Kalakaua eventually succeeded him as king in February 1874, after Lunalilo's death (Kuykendall and Gregory, 230–33; "King Lunalilo," New York *Tribune*, 13 Feb 73, 5; *RI 1993*, 714–15, 717–18).

[11] Clemens stayed at the American Hotel on Beretania Street (*N&J1*, 192; *MTH*, 20, 80–81). Princess Victoria Kamamalu Kaahumanu (1838–66), sister of Kamehameha IV and Kamehameha V, was heir apparent to the Hawaiian throne when she died on 29 May 1866. In an 1866 letter to the Sacramento *Union*, Clemens publicly praised her accomplishments, her loyalty to the American missionaries who educated her, and her philanthropy, but privately he wrote in his notebook, "Pr. V. died in forcing abortion—kept half a dozen bucks to do her washing, & has suffered 7 abortions" (*N&J1*, 129; *RI 1993*, 720–21; SLC 1866f).

ical excellencies of the dead princess. I inquired further, but he said the words were too foul for translation; that the bodily excellencies were unmentionable; that the capabilities so lauded & so glorified had better be left to the imagination. He said the King was doubtless sitting where he could hear these ghastly praises & enjoy them. That is, the late King— the educated, cultivated Kamehameha V. And mind you, one of his titles was "the Head of the Church;" for, although he was brought up in the religion of the missionaries, & educated in their schools & colleges, he early learned to despise their plebeian form of worship, & had imported the English system & an English bishop, & bossed the works himself. You can imagine the saturnalia that is making the night hideous in the palace grounds now, where His Majesty is lying in state.

The late King was frequently on hand in the royal pew in the Royal Hawaiian Reformed Catholic Church, on Sundays; but whenever he got into trouble he did not fly to the cross for help—he flew to the heathen gods of his ancestors. Now this was a man who would write you a beautiful letter, in a faultless hand, & word it in faultless English; & perhaps throw in a few graceful classic allusions; & perhaps a few happy references to science, international law, or the world's political history; or he would array himself in elegant evening dress & entertain you at his board in princely style, & converse like a born Christian gentleman; & day after day he would work like a beaver in affairs of State, & on occasion exchange autograph letters with the kings & emperors of the old world. And the very next week, business being over, he would retire to a cluster of dismal little straw-thatched native huts by the sea-shore, & there for a fortnight he would turn himself into a heathen whom you could not tell from his savage grandfather. He would reduce his dress to a breech- clout, fill himself daily full of whisky, & sit with certain of his concubines while others danced the peculiar hula-hula. And if oppressed by great responsibilities he would summon one of his familiars, an ancient witch, & ask her to tell him the opinion & the commands of the heathen gods, & these commands he would obey. He was so superstitious that he would not step over a line drawn across a road, but would walk around it. These matters were common talk in the Islands. I never saw this King but once, & then he was not on his periodical debauch. He was in evening dress attending the funeral of his sister, & had a yard of crape depending from his stove-pipe hat.

If you will be so good as to remember that the population of the islands is but a little over 50,000 souls, & that over that little handful of people roosts a monarchy with its coat-tails fringed with as many mighty-titled dignitaries as would suffice to run the Russian Empire, you will wonder how, the offices all being filled, there can be anybody left to govern. And the truth is, that it is one of the oddest things in the world to stumble on a man there who has no title. I felt so lonesome, as being about the only unofficial person in Honolulu, that I had to leave the country to find company.

After all this exhibition of imperial grandeur, it is humiliating to have to say that the entire exports of the kingdom are not as much as $1,500,000, the imports in the neighborhood of that figure, & the revenues, say $500,000. And yet they pay the King $36,000 a year, & the other officials from $3,000 to $8,000—& heaven knows there are enough of them.

The National Debt was $150,000 when I was there—& there was nothing in the country they were so proud of. They would n't have taken any money for it. With what an air His Excellency the Minister of Finance[12] lugged in his Annual Budget & read off the impressive items & flourished the stately total!

The "Royal Ministers" are natural curiosities. They are white men of various nationalities, who have wandered thither in times gone by. I will give you a specimen—but not the most favorable. Harris, for instance. Harris is an American—a long-legged, vain, light-weight village lawyer from New-Hampshire. If he had brains in proportion to his legs, he would make Solomon seem a failure; if his modesty equaled his ignorance, he would make a violet seem stuck-up; if his learning equaled his vanity, he would make von Humboldt seem as unlettered as the backside of a tombstone;[13] if his stature were proportioned to his conscience, he would be a gem for the microscope; if his ideas were as large as his words, it would take a man three months to walk around one of them; if an audience were to contract to listen as long as he would talk, that audience would die of old age; & if he were to talk until he said something, he would still be on his hind legs when the last trump sounded. And he

[12] Charles Coffin Harris, whom Clemens goes on to discuss (see also 7 Apr 73 to unidentified, n. 3).
[13] Baron Alexander von Humboldt (1769–1859) was a German statesman and naturalist. His chief work was *Kosmos*, a description of the physical universe.

would have cheek enough to wait till the disturbance was over, & go on again.

Such is (or was) His Excellency Mr. Harris, his late Majesty's Minister of This, That, & The Other—for he was a little of everything; & particularly & always he was the King's most obedient humble servant & loving worshiper, & his chief champion & mouthpiece in the parliamentary branch of ministers. And when a question came up (it did n't make any difference what it was), how he would rise up & saw the air with his bony flails, & storm & cavort & hurl sounding emptiness which he thought was eloquence, & discharge bile which he fancied was satire, & issue dreary rubbish which he took for humor, & accompany it with contortions of his undertaker countenance which he believed to be comic expression!

He began in the islands as a little, obscure lawyer, & rose (?) to be such a many-sided official grandee that sarcastic folk dubbed him, "the wheels of the Government." He became a great man in a pigmy land— he was of the caliber that other countries construct constables & coroners of. I do not wish to seem prejudiced against Harris, & I hope that nothing I have said will convey such an impression. I must be an honest historian, & to do this in the present case I have to reveal the fact that this stately figure, which looks so like a Washington monument in the distance, is nothing but a thirty-dollar windmill when you get close to him.

Harris loves to proclaim that he is no longer an American, & is proud of it; that he is a Hawaiian through & through, & is proud of that, too; & that he is a willing subject & servant of his lord & master, the King, & is proud & grateful that it is so.

Now, let us annex the islands. Think how we could build up that whaling trade! [Though under our courts & judges it might soon be as impossible for whaleships to rendezvous there without being fleeced & "pulled" by sailors & pettifoggers as it now is in San Francisco—a place the skippers shun as they would rocks & shoals.] Let us annex. We could make sugar enough there to supply all America, perhaps, & the prices would be very easy with the duties removed. And then we would have such a fine half-way house for our Pacific-plying ships; & such a convenient supply depot & such a commanding sentry-box for an armed squadron; & we could raise cotton & coffee there & make it pay pretty well, with the duties off & capital easier to get at. And then we would own the mightiest volcano on earth—Kilauea! Barnum could run it—he understands fires now.[14] Let us annex, by all means. We could pacify Prince Bill & other nobles easily enough—put them on a reservation. Nothing pleases a savage like a reservation—a reservation where he has his annual hoes, & Bibles & blankets to trade for powder & whisky—a sweet Arcadian retreat fenced in with soldiers. By annexing, we would get all those 50,000 natives cheap as dirt, with their morals & other diseases thrown in. No expense for education—they are already educated; no need to convert them—they are already converted; no expense to clothe them—for obvious reasons.

We *must* annex those people. We can afflict them with our wise & beneficent government. We can introduce the novelty of thieves, all the way up from street-car pickpockets to municipal robbers & Government defaulters, & show them how amusing it is to arrest them & try them & then turn them loose—some for cash & some for "political influence." We can make them ashamed of their simple & primitive justice. We can do away with their occasional hangings for murder, & let them have Judge Pratt to teach them how to save imperiled Avery-assassins to society.[15] We can give them some Barnards to keep their money corporations out of difficulties.[16] We can give them juries composed entirely of the most simple & charming leatherheads. We can give them railway corporations who will buy their Legislatures like old clothes, & run over their best citizens & complain of the corpses for smearing their unpleasant juices on the track. In place of harmless & vaporing Harris, we can give them Tweed. We can let them have Connolly; we can loan them Sweeny; we can furnish them some Jay Goulds who will do away with

---

[14]On the morning of 24 December 1872, fire destroyed Phineas T. Barnum's newly renovated Hippotheatron in New York, containing the greater part of his circus, museum, and menagerie. The loss, for the most part uninsured, amounted to about three hundred thousand dollars (Saxon, 243; "A Carnival of Fire," New York *Tribune*, 25 Dec 72, 1).

[15]An allusion to William Foster's murder of Avery D. Putnam (7 Mar 73 to Reid [2nd]). New York Supreme Court Judge Calvin E. Pratt (1828–96) granted a stay of execution to Foster in July 1871, enabling his attorney to appeal the verdict (New York *Times:* "The Convict Foster," 6 July 71, 8; "Minor Topics," 20 Oct 71, 4; "Justice C. E. Pratt Dead," 4 Aug 96, 9).

[16]New York Supreme Court Judge George G. Barnard (1829–79), a tool of the Tammany Ring, was removed from office in August 1872 for corrupt conduct (New York *Times:* "Judge Barnard," 17 July 72, 4; "Exit Barnard," 20 Aug 72, 5; "Ex-Judge Barnard Dead," New York *Tribune*, 28 Apr 79, 5).

their old-time notion that stealing is not respectable.[17] We can confer Woodhull & Claflin on them. And George Francis Train.[18] We can give them lecturers! I will go myself.

We can make that little bunch of sleepy islands the hottest corner on earth, & array it in the moral splendor of our high & holy civilization. Annexation is what the poor islanders need. "Shall we to men benighted, the lamp of life deny?"[19]

Hartford, Jan. 6, 1873.   MARK TWAIN.

Enclosure with 25 January 1873
To Whitelaw Reid • Hartford, Conn.
(SLC 1873e)

To the Editor of The Tribune.

SIR: Some people do not do generous things by halves, even in the old "effete" monarchies. I returned from England (where I had been spending a sort of business holiday) in November, in the Cunard steamer Batavia, Capt. John E. Mouland. In mid-ocean we encountered a fearful

---

[17] William Marcy ("Boss") Tweed (1823–78) and his chief Tammany Hall cronies—Peter Barr ("Brains") Sweeny (1825–1911) and Richard B. ("Slippery Dick") Connolly (1810–80)—defrauded New York City of countless millions. Financier Jay Gould (1836–92) looted the Erie Railroad, abetted by Sweeny and Tweed ("At Three Score and Ten," New York *Times*, 1 June 80, 5; French, 119; see also 5 Dec 72 to the editor of the Hartford *Evening Post*).

[18] Clemens had satirized George Francis Train, a controversial shipping promoter and radical lecturer, in a letter to the New York *Tribune* in 1868. In December 1872 Train's political agitation on behalf of Victoria Woodhull led to his arrest on obscenity charges (SLC 1868a; *L2*, 157–58 n. 5; *L3*, 148 n. 5; "G. F. Train in Prison," New York *Times*, 21 Dec 72, 12; see 26 Nov 72 to JLC and PAM, n. 3).

[19] From the third verse of the hymn "From Greenland's Icy Mountains," written by Reginald Heber in 1819 (Wells, 28–29):

> Shall we, whose souls are lighted
>   With wisdom from on high,
> Shall we to men benighted
>   The lamp of light deny?
> Salvation, O salvation!
>   The joyful sound proclaim,
> Till earth's remotest nation
>   Has learned Messiah's name.
>   (Beecher, 299)

gale—a gale that is known to have destroyed a great many vessels, & is supposed to have made away with a great many more that have never been heard of to this day. The storm lasted two days with us; then subsided for a few brief hours; then burst forth again; & while this last effort was in full swing we came upon a dismasted vessel, the bark Charles Ward. She was nothing but a bursted & spouting hulk, surmounted with a chaos of broken spars & bits of fluttering rags—a sort of ruined flower-pot hung with last year's spider-webs, so to speak. The vast seas swept over her, burying her from sight, & then she would rise again & spew volumes of water through cracks in her sides & bows, & discharge white floods through the gateway that was left where her stern had been. Her captain & eight men were lashed in the remains of the main rigging. They were pretty well famished & frozen, for they had been there two nights & a part of two days of stormy wintry weather. Capt. Mouland brought up broadside to wind & sea, & called for volunteers to man the life-boat. D. Gillies, Third Officer; H. Kyle, Fourth Officer, & six seamen answered instantly.[1] It was worth any money to see that life-boat climb those dizzy mountains of water, in a driving mist of spume-flakes, & fight its way inch by inch in the teeth of the gale. Just the mere memory of it stirs a body so, that I would swing my hat & disgorge a cheer now, if I could do it without waking the baby. But if you get a baby awake once you can never get it asleep again, & then you get into trouble with the whole family. Somehow I don't seem to have a chance to yell, now, the way I used to. Well, in just one hour's time that life-boat crew had rescued those shipwrecked men; & during 30 minutes of the time, their own lives were not worth purchase at a sixpence, their peril was so great.

The passengers showed their appreciation of this thing as far as they were able, & we were so proud of our captain & our life-boat crew that we ventured to join in a communication to the Royal Humane Society of London, detailing the circumstances & petitioning that they would take notice of our sailors' gallant achievement.[2] I have just heard the result, & would like to communicate it to the passengers, & to all who take an interest in things nobler than the usual daily feast of Congress corruption & judicial rottenness.[3]

[1] See 22 Jan 73 to Mouland, n. 1.
[2] See 20 Nov 72 to the Royal Humane Society.
[3] The Crédit Mobilier investigation (7 Mar 73 to the staff of the New York *Tribune,* n. 1).

The Humane Society promptly conferred the gold medal & a vote of thanks upon Capt. Mouland; they also gave silver medals to Officers Gillies & Kyle, & a money reward suited to their official grade, & thanked them; & they likewise thanked the six seamen & gave £7 gold ($35), to each of them—say somewhere about two months' wages. We are a nation of forty millions, & we have some little money. Cannot we have a society like that? Why, it is the next most noblest thing to sending moral tracts to Timbuctoo. And would cost less money, too. Not that I object to sending moral tracts to Timbuctoo; far from it; I write the most of them myself, & gain the larger part of my living in that way. I would grieve to see Timbuctoo redeemed, & have to lose its custom. But why not start a Humane Society besides? We have got one man worthy to conduct it, & that is Mr. Bergh. If God did not make Bergh, He certainly did not make the insects that try to thwart his purposes—& do not succeed.[4]

We are the offspring of England; & so it is pleasant to reflect that the very first thing that astonishes a stranger when he arrives in that country is not its physical features, not the vastness of London, not the peculiarities of speech & dress of its people, but the curious lavishness with which that people pour money into the lap of any high & worthy object needing help. It is not done ostentatiously, but modestly. It comes from nobody knows where, about half the time, but it comes. Every few days you see a brief item like this in the papers: "The (such & such a charity) desire to acknowledge the receipt of £1,000 from X. Y. Z. This is the fifth £1,000 from the same source." X. Y. Z. don't give his name; he just gives his $25,000, & says no more about it. Some hospital will put up a contribution box by the door, & it will capture hundreds upon hundreds of pounds from unknown passers-by. The porter of the Charing-Cross hospital saw a gentleman stuff something into the contribution-box & pass on. He opened the box to see what it was; it was a roll of bank bills, amounting to $1,250. One day an unknown lady entered Middlesex Hospital & asked leave to go round & talk with the patients; it was found, after she was gone, that she had been distributing half sovereigns among them; she had squandered $750 there. But why

---

[4] Henry Bergh (1823–88) founded the American Society for the Prevention of Cruelty to Animals in 1866 and worked tirelessly as a lecturer and fundraiser to ensure its success and expansion. His tall, gaunt figure was a familiar sight in New York, where he patrolled the streets and reprimanded people who mistreated their animals (Sydney H. Coleman, 34–60).

go on? I got so worked up about charity matters in London that I was near coming away from there ignorant of everything else. I could reel off instances of prodigal charity conferred by stealth in that city till even THE TRIBUNE's broad columns would cry for quarter. "Ginx's Baby" could not satirize the national disposition toward free-handed benevolence—it could only satirize instances of foolish & stupid methods in the application of the funds by some of the charitable organizations.[5] But in most cases the great benevolent societies of England manage their affairs admirably.

It makes one dizzy to read the long list of enormous sums that individuals have given to the London hospitals. People die of want & starvation in that huge hive, just as they do in New-York, merely because nine people in ten who beg help are imposters—the worthy & the sensitive shrink from making their condition known, & perish without making an appeal. In either city a thousand hands would be stretched forth to save such if the need could be known in time. I have forgotten many things I saw in London, but I remember yet what an outburst there was, & what a pang seemed to dart through the whole great heart of England when a poor, obscure, & penniless American girl threw herself from Waterloo bridge because she was hungry & homeless & had no friend to turn to.[6] Everybody talked; everybody said "Shame, shame!" all the newspapers were troubled; one heard strong, honest regrets on every hand, & such expressions as, "What a pity, poor thing; she could have been smothered in money if a body could only have known of her case." You would have supposed an Emperor had fallen, & not a mere nameless waif from a far country. This mourning for the late Napoleon

[5] *Ginx's Baby: His Birth and Other Misfortunes*, a satire by John Edward Jenkins (1838–1910), recounts the early life of the thirteenth child born to wretchedly poor parents. Ginx, who vows to drown the child, abandons him instead. The boy's plight inspires endless and futile discussions of social reform among "philosophers, philanthropists, politicians, Papists and Protestants, poor-law ministers and parish-officers" (John Edward Jenkins, 125). Published anonymously in London in 1870, the book attracted immediate and widespread attention.

[6] Clemens pasted a clipping describing this incident, cut from the London *Morning Post* (10 Sept 72, 3), into the scrapbook he kept while in London in the fall of 1872. He presumably saved it as potential material for the English book he planned to write. The woman, Alice Blanche Oswald, had come to England as a governess and was then dismissed without receiving return fare to America. She drowned herself on 3 September 1872, a few days before her twentieth birthday ("The Suicide from Waterloo-Bridge," Scrapbook 9:29, CU-MARK).

is lifeless & empty compared to it.[7] That girl could have collected a whole fortune in London if she could have come alive again.

We know what the Royal Humane Society is; for it is always at work, & its fame is wide in the earth. Well, England is sown generously with just such institutions—not Government pets, but supported entirely by voluntary contributions of the people. And they make no pow-wow; one does not even see the names of their officers in print. Now there is the Royal National Life-Boat Institution, for instance. During the year 1869 it saved 28 vessels; its boats saved 1,072 human lives; it paid, in cash rewards for saving life, $12,000 gold. It keeps its own boats & boat stations; has its men on guard night & day, under regular salaries, & pays them an extra reward for every life saved. Since it first began its work it has saved a fraction under 19,000 lives; it has conferred 90 gold medals & 807 silver ones; it has given away $158,000 in cash rewards for saving life, & has expended $1,183,330 on its life-boat stations & life-saving apparatus. And all that money was obtained by voluntary subscriptions.[8]

To return to the life-boat crew of the "Batavia." The Cunard Steamship Company gave each of the six seamen £5 apiece, & promoted third officer Gillies & fourth officer Kyle to the rank & pay of *first* officers; the said rank & pay to commence, not upon the day we found the dismasted vessel, but upon the day our ship left Liverpool for America. Now how is that for "the clean white thing," as they say in the mountains?[9] I have italicized the word "first," for I ask you to understand that that is a perfectly dazzling promotion to achieve with just sixty minutes' work—it would have taken those men ten or twelve years of slow hard work in the Company's service to accomplish that, as matters usually go in that methodical old private navy. Indeed those practical, hard-headed, unromantic Cunard people would not take Noah himself as first mate till they had worked him up through all the lower grades & tried him ten years or such a matter. They make every officer serve an apprenticeship under

[7]Napoleon III (Charles Louis Napoleon Bonaparte, 1808–73) died on 9 January 1873, while in exile at Chiselhurst, England (*Annual Cyclopaedia 1873*, 69).

[8]Clemens copied his figures from a leaflet he pasted into his 1872 English scrapbook entitled "Royal National Life-boat Institution," which included a "General Summary for 1869." He calculated his dollar amounts by multiplying the number of pounds by a factor of five, rounding off in some cases (Scrapbook 9:11, CU-MARK).

[9]That is, the "honest, decent thing"—a western colloquialism (Mitford M. Mathews, 1:339, 2:1860).

their eyes in their own ships before they advance him or trust him. Capt. Mouland had been at sea 16 years, & was in command of a big 1,600-tun ship when they took him into their service; but they only made him fourth officer, & he had to work up tediously to earn his captaincy. He has been with them 18 years now. Officers Gillies & Kyle have suddenly jumped over a whole regiment of officers' heads & landed within one step of the captaincy, & all in good time they will be promoted that step, too. They hold the rank & receive the pay of first officers now, & will continue to do so, though there are no vacancies at present. But they will fill the first vacancies that occur.

It is a curious, self-possessed, old-fashioned Company, the Cunard. (Scotchmen they are.) It was born before the days of steamships; it inaugurated ocean steamer lines; it never has lost more than one vessel; it has never lost a passenger's life at all; its ships are never insured; great mercantile firms do not insure their goods sent over in Cunard ships; it is rather safer to be in their vessels than on shore. Old-fashioned is the word. When a thing is established by the Cunarders, it is there for good & all, almost. Before adopting a new thing the chiefs cogitate & cogitate & cogitate; then they lay it before their head purveyor, their head merchant, their head builder, their head engineer, & all the captains in the service, & *they* go off & cogitate about a year; then if the new wrinkle is approved it is adopted, & put into the regulations. In the old days, near 40 years ago, when this was an ocean line of sailing vessels, corpses were not permitted by the company to take passage, or go as freight, either— sailor superstition, you know. Very well; to this day they won't carry corpses. Forty years ago they always had stewed prunes & rice for dinner on "duff" days; well, to this present time, whenever duff day comes around, you will always have your regular stewed prunes & rice in a Cunarder. If you do n't get anything else, you can always depend on that— & depend on it with your money up, too, if you are that sort of a person.

It takes them about 10 or 15 years to manufacture a captain; but when they have got him manufactured to suit at last, they have full confidence in him. The only order they give a captain is this, brief & to the point: "Your ship is loaded, take her; speed is nothing; follow your own road, deliver her safe, bring her back safe—safety is all that is required."

The noted Cunard Company is composed simply of two or three grandchildren who have stepped into the shoes of two or three children who stepped into the shoes of a couple of old Scotch fathers; for Burns

& MacIver were the Cunard Company when it was born; it was Burns & MacIver when the originators had passed away; it is Burns & MacIver still in the third generation—never has been out of the two families. Burns was a Glasgow merchant, MacIver was an old sea-dog who sailed a ship for him in early times. That vessel's earnings were cast into a sinking fund; with the money they built another ship, & then another, & thus the old original packet line from Glasgow to Halifax was established. At that time the mails were slowly & expensively carried in English Government vessels. Burns & MacIver & Judge Haliburton ("Sam Slick") fell to considering a scheme of getting the job of carrying these mails in private bottoms. In order to manage the thing they needed to be quiet about it, & also they needed faster vessels. Haliburton had a relative who was not a shining success in practical life, but had an inventive head; name, Sam Cunard; he took his old jack-knife & a shingle & sat down & whittled out this enormous Royal Mail Line of vessels that we call the Cunarders—a great navy, it is—doing business in every ocean; owning forty-five steamships of vast cost; conducting its affairs with the rigid method & system of a national navy; promoting by merit, priority in routine, & for conspicuous service; using a company uniform; retiring superannuated & disabled men & officers on permanent pensions, & numbering its servants by hundreds & thousands. In its own private establishment in Liverpool it keeps 4,000 men under pay. That is what Sam. Cunard whittled out. That is to say, he whittled out a little model for a fast vessel; it was satisfactory; he was instructed to go & get the mail contract, simply under his own name; he did it, & the company became commonly known as the Cunard Company; then the Company tried steam & made it work; they prospered, & bought out Haliburton, & also Cunard's little interest; they removed Cunard to England & made him their London agent; he grew very rich & unspeakably respectable, & when he died he died not as a poor, dreaming provincial whittler of experimental models, but as the great Sir Samuel Cunard, K. C. B., or G. W. X., or something like that, for the sovereign had knighted him.[10]

[10] Abraham Cunard, a Philadelphian of German descent, emigrated to Halifax, Nova Scotia, in 1783. By 1812 the shipping business he founded there with his son Samuel (1787–1865) was well established. Clemens's history is inaccurate. Thomas C. Haliburton (1796–1865), a distinguished jurist, was a friend and compatriot of Samuel Cunard's from Halifax (his daughter Laura married Cunard's son William in 1851). He was best known for the humorous dialect sketches he wrote in the assumed character of a Yankee peddler named "Samuel

Well, the Cunard Company is a great institution, & has got more money than you & I both put together; & yet none of the family ever write editorials or deliver lectures. The Company have built school‑houses & they educate the children of their employés; they are going to build dwellings for their shore men that shall be cheap & clean & comfortable; when one of their men dies, a subscription list goes about in his ship or in whatever arm of the service his name is booked, & whatever sum is raised the Cunard Company add just a similar sum, & it all goes to the man's heirs. Their system of pensions—

But I have never been offered a cent for all this; I am not even acquainted with a member of the Cunard Company. I think I will wait awhile before I go on—it cramps my hand to write so much on a stretch. But it is all right, any way. So many thousands of Americans have traveled in those steamers that they will like to read about that Company.

Capt. Mouland has got the gold medal; but if I were to try to tell you how much fire & blood & peril a sailor will gladly go through to get that darling prize, I would have to write all night. I believe a captain would rather have that Royal Humane Society's gold medal for saving life at sea than be made a commodore & have a fleet of vessels under him.

The Cunard steamers always carry some casks of water & provisions

Slick," the first of which appeared in 1835. During a voyage to England in 1838 he learned an "object-lesson of being left behind by the power of steam to await the good-will of the wind" (Chittick, 219). Upon arrival, he supported an effort to convince the colonial secretary of the importance of establishing a transatlantic steam-powered mail service. Within a few months, the government advertised its intention to sponsor such a service, and "Haliburton never forgot, nor allowed others to forget, the part he thus played in securing to the old and new worlds the benefit of rapid intercommunication" (Chittick, 220). In 1839 Samuel Cunard went to England, where he won the government mail contract. At the urging of Robert Napier, an eminent marine engineer whom Cunard commissioned to build several new steamships, he formed a partnership with two major investors: George Burns (1795–1890) and David MacIver (d. 1845), co-owners since 1830 of the City of Glasgow Steam-Packet Company. The newly formed British and North American Royal Mail Steam Packet Company (commonly known as the Cunard Company) inaugurated its transatlantic service in 1840, when the *Britannia* sailed from Liverpool to Boston. The company, which had no enduring rival for over a hundred years, was soon entirely owned and run by three families: the Cunards in North America, the Burnses in Glasgow, and the MacIvers in Liverpool (Brinnin, 73–85, 89–90, 98, 101–2, 120–22; Haliburton, 145 n. 3, 157 n. 1; Herzberg, 419). Cunard was knighted by Queen Victoria in 1859 "for the services rendered by his ships in the Crimean campaign" (Brinnin, 271).

where they can be hoisted out at a moment's warning for the relief of distressed vessels at sea, & they—

But, really, I can't advertise these parties for nothing. It is n't "business."[11]

MARK TWAIN.

Hartford, &c.

[11] Much of this letter was in fact used in a Cunard Company advertising pamphlet issued in 1873 (PH in CU-MARK). It is not known whether Clemens gave his consent for the reprinting.

Appendix C

Mark Twain's 1872 English Journals

WHEN CLEMENS sailed for England in August 1872, he took with him two or more journals, or "manifold writers," purchased in New York, to draft text and record notes for his book about England. All of the surviving journal text—113 pages—is transcribed below. Only the last 12 pages of the first journal are extant, as cut-out loose sheets. The text of the second journal—written on 101 bound pages—is apparently complete (the last page ends in the middle of a word, and is followed by a blank leaf). In the front of the journal are three printed pages that identify it as a "Francis' Highly Improved Manifold Writer" manufactured by Francis and Loutrel, 45 Maiden Lane, New York, and give instructions in English, French, and Spanish, as well as the following claim:

> By this truly great invention, a Letter & duplicate can be written in One operation with more ease and greater facility than a single letter with an ordinary pen and Ink. To the Mercantile, Professional, and Traveling, part of the Community, it is of Infinite Value for its simplicity and dispatch in operation and portability in construction.

This manifold writer originally contained 202 blank ruled pages of tissue-thin, translucent paper, and it came equipped with a supply of carbon paper (both single- and double-sided), two styluses, and a "Tablet" (evidently a thin, hard board to place under the paper and carbon assemblage). Although the instructions explain that one could use carbon paper, journal pages, and even loose sheets of stationery in various combinations to produce as many as three copies, Clemens seems to have used the system in a simpler way: he inserted double-sided carbon paper between two bound journal pages and wrote on the top sheet with a stylus (not a pencil). This process produced duplicates of each page inscribed, the first with carbon adhering to the back (verso copy), and the second with carbon adhering to the front (recto copy).

Clemens evidently intended to send Olivia a copy of what he wrote in these journals, partly for safekeeping, and partly as an addition to his letters. For this purpose he carefully cut out about half the pages (all verso copies), leaving behind the page stubs interleaved with the sequence of recto pages. Sometimes both the cut-out copies and the bound copies survive; sometimes both copies survive still bound in the journal; and sometimes only the bound copies survive. On 29 August, having just crossed the Atlantic, Clemens forwarded to Olivia his first batch of notes: "I have given the purser a ten-dollar telegram of 3 words to send to you from Queenstown," he wrote, "& also my journal in 2 envelops." And on 1 September he wrote her from Liverpool, "I will put in another 20 minutes cutting out my journal to enclose with this. It seems to take a power of time to cut out those flimsy leaves." By 25 October, however, he was finding it difficult to write as much as he had intended: "I am using a note-book a little, now, & journalizing when I *can*," he wrote. (This "note-book" has not been found.) And on 6 November he confessed to his mother and sister, "I came here to take notes for a book, but I haven't done much but attend dinners & make speeches." No mention of the manifold writer has been found after this date, and it is not known how many he ultimately used.

Most of the material in the surviving pages is carefully composed narrative, virtually ready for publication. At one point Clemens even specified where he wanted an illustration to appear (594.19), and in another where he wanted the type set in "Diamond form" (595.29). In 1874, having set aside the English book, he used some of the verso copies cut from the second manifold writer as printer's copy for "A Memorable Midnight Experience," published for the first time in *Mark Twain's Sketches. Number One* (SLC 1874c), finding no need to alter the text beyond a single phrase and two spelling corrections (see the textual commentary). Albert Bigelow Paine also extracted several journal sketches for publication in his biography, with only minimal editing. Clemens himself made several alterations in pencil on the bound recto copies, presumably anticipating publication. Although these alterations may not have been made in 1872 or 1873, they are transcribed and identified in the notes as late changes. For alternate readings left standing, a slash (/) separates the two, with the first inscription on the left.

Before his trip to England, Clemens most likely planned to write a book that freely satirized English institutions and customs. In December 1871, for example, he commented on the Prince of Wales's recovery from typhoid in an interview with a reporter for the Chicago *Evening Post:*

> "I'm glad the boy's going to get well; I'm glad, and not ashamed to own it. For he will probably make the worst King Great Britain has ever had. And that's what the people need, exactly. They need a bad King. He'll be a blessing in disguise. He'll tax 'em, and disgrace 'em, and oppress 'em, and trouble 'em in a thousand ways, and they'll go into training for resistance. The best King they can have is a bad King. He'll cultivate their self-respect and self-reliance, and their muscle, and they'll finally kick him out of office and set up for themselves." ("Brevities," 21 Dec 71, 4)

The irreverence expressed in these remarks is conspicuously absent from the journals. Once in England, Clemens found himself reluctant to mock cherished beliefs or traditions for fear of offending his new English friends. As a result, he had difficulty finding suitable targets for his humor, as the journals demonstrate. He also clearly avoided lampooning— or even describing—English personal habits, and repeating information learned in confidence: "These English men & women take a body right into their inner sanctuary, as it were," he wrote Mrs. Fairbanks on 2 November 1872, "& when you have broken bread & eaten salt with them once it amounts to *friendship.* . . . Americans have the reputation here of not sufficiently respecting private conversations." This concern for propriety increased over time, ultimately causing Clemens to abandon the book altogether. In June 1874 he explained the problem in a letter to the New York *Post:*

> I could not leave out the manners & customs which obtain in an English gentleman's household without leaving out the most interesting feature of the subject. They are admirable; yet I would shrink from deliberately describing them in a book, for I fear that such a course would be, after all, a violation of the courteous hospitality which furnished me the means of doing it. (See 30 Dec 73 to Fitzgibbon, n. 2)

❧

There was once an American thief who fled his country & took refuge in England, & he dressed himself after the fashion of the Londoners & taught his tongue the peculiarities of the London pronunciation and did his best in all ways to pass himself for a native—but he did two fatal things: he stopped at the Langham hotel, & the first trip he took was to visit ~~the grave~~ Stratford-on-Avon & the grave of Shakspeare—& these things betrayed his nationality.

I find the English singularly cordial in their welcome & hearty in their hospitality. They make one feel very much at home.

Been around to see Stanley. He dined with the Queen last Saturday. He has just received the N.Y. Sun, & [is] naturally deeply troubled by the rascality of that paper.[1]

See the power a monarch wields! When I arrived here two weeks ago, the papers & geographers were in a fair way to eat poor Stanley up without salt or sauce. The Queen says Come ~~500~~ 400 miles up into Scotland & sit at my lunch table fifteen minutes—which, being translated, means, Gentlemen, I believe in this man & take him under my protection—& not another yelp is heard.

Regent's Park is a huge tract in the midst of London, adorned with great trees & luxuriantly carpeted with grass. And today (Sunday) Sept. 15) it was fine to look down the long perspective & see the hundreds of men, women & children moving hither & thither & in & out among the distant trees.

We entered the great Zoological Gardens with Mr. Henry Lee, a fellow & several royal societies, & he showed us through & through the mighty menagerie—& we saw the plaster cast which he & the great Buckland made of the infant hippopotamus that died. We were to call & get acquainted with Mr. Buckland but time pressed & we put it off, till another time.[2]

---

[1] See 25 Oct 72 to OLC, n. 4. Stanley, accompanied by Sir Henry Rawlinson of the Royal Geographical Society, traveled to Dunrobin Castle in Scotland, to be presented to Queen Victoria. They arrived on Monday, 9 September. Rawlinson actually dined with the queen, but Stanley was granted only a brief audience on 10 September, and saw her again for a moment before leaving on Wednesday, 11 September. The New York *Sun*, a rival of the New York *Herald* (which had sponsored Stanley's search for Livingstone), sought to embarrass and discredit Stanley by printing a series of articles on 24, 30, and 31 August 1872, based on information from his former manservant. The damaging revelations, although substantially true, were presented out of context. The articles asserted that Stanley, a Welshman who had changed his name when he came to America, had deserted from the United States Navy; that he had attempted to murder someone in Turkey; that he had brutally whipped the servant and forced him to steal food; and that he had written a worthless check in Constantinople (Hird, 115–18; Farwell, 88–90; Anstruther, 31–32).

[2] Francis Trevelyan Buckland (1826–80) was educated at Oxford and practiced medicine for several years. His primary interest, however, was natural his-

Half a dozen elephants, about as many hippopotami, & all sorts & ~~va~~ styles of lions & tigers & such cattle; among whom were many kangaroos playing leap-frog—which is to say, they place their little short fore-paws on the ground & then bring their haunches forward on either side of the forepaws, with a jump—the forepaws remaining stationary.

I wanted to find Mr. Darwin's baboon that plays mother to a cat, but did not succeed. So Darwin invented that.[3]

In the House of Monkeys there was one long, lean, active fellow that made me a convert to the theory of Natural Selection. He made a natural selection of monkeys smaller tha~~n~~n himself to sling around by the tail.

They have all possible birds & reptiles, & some that really seem impossible at a first glance. They have one building devoted to gorgeous birds of the parrot kind. The noise cannot be imagined.

Without reflection one might jump to the conclusion that Noah would consider the Zoo Gardens not much of a show, & look ~~twie~~ twice at his shilling before he bought a ticket; but it appears different to me. Noah could not get these animals into two arks like his. Though of course I do not ~~deny~~ wish to disparage Noah's collection. Far from it. Noah's collection was very well for his day.

In the Zoo Gardens (as in all public grounds here,) the people made perfectly free with the beautiful clean-shaven grass—walking over it, ~~loo~~ lolling on it, using it & enjoying it without let or hindrance. And the grass seems not least the worse for it. On our side of the water "Keep off the Grass" is as common a sign as we know—so common indeed, & so strictly obeyed by everybody ~~that~~ from babyhood up, that it has become a national trait to avoid grass; & so I never walk upon it here, though it is free to me, because I know that the ~~feeling of~~ sense of committing a sacrilege would destroy all the enjoyment. And up to this hour it keeps

---

tory, to the study of which he devoted his life, earning wide recognition for the entertaining articles he wrote for *Field* and, after 1866, for a weekly of his own, *Land and Water.* He was also active in pisciculture, and in 1867 was appointed inspector of salmon fisheries.

[3] In *The Descent of Man* Darwin described a "female baboon" with

so capacious a heart, that she not only adopted young monkeys of other species, but stole young dogs and cats, which she continually carried about. . . . An adopted kitten scratched the above-mentioned affectionate baboon, who certainly had a fine intellect, for she was much astonished at being scratched, and immediately examined the kitten's feet, and without more ado bit off the claws. (Darwin, 39–40)

Clemens penciled a mark in the margin next to this passage in his copy of this work, which survives in the Mark Twain Papers.

surprising me to see these people walking on the public grass. It is one of those things which I cannot reconcile myself to, it does seem such cold, deliberate villainy.

Tom Hood & I went down to Brighton (50 miles—1½ hours) one of the favorite better-class watering places (made popular by Geo. 4 when Prince Regent,)[4]—though in these days Scarborough is the boss ~~place~~ watering place. We went with Mr. Lee as his guests & Edmund Routledge preceded us.

Mr. Lee's father gave the eldest son a tremendous University education, & put Henry into trade. The said eldest son, with his costly & elaborate education, amounts to nothing at all, & accomplishes nothing, makes no figure in the world. Henry, snatching an hour here & there from his great factories & varied business employments, has given <u>himself</u> a profound & wide-reaching education (there's encouragement for you, Livy!) & has added to the sum of it, original researches & discoveries of his own, & contributed the same to the world's scientific possessions. He is fellow of this, that & the other learned body & his comrades are the great thinkers & creators of the day. His knowledge is not boxed up & labeled, but is <u>practical</u>. Knows all about birds, animals, architecture, fishes—can take off his coat & ~~beco~~ occupy the place of any officer in the Zoo Gardens or the great aquarium, or pretty much anywhere. (And he is mighty useful to me, because he does like Slote or Charley[5]— writes the notes, lays the plans, appoints the hours, delivers me at every needful place & assumes all the responsibilit[i]es.) God is good, & constantly raises up people to take care of the shiftless and helpless. Mr. Lee knows all the bosses of every place, & gets me in at tabooed hours & finds me entrance to the places that are forbidden to the general public.

Mr. Lord, naturalist, & certainly one of the gentlest, simplest & most ₗlovable &ₗ unassuming old children in the world, was appointed to construct the great (national) aquarium at Brighton. He had hardly got his work fairly & promisingly started when he ~~fee~~ fell sick & was thrown on his back with no present hope of getting on his feet again.[6]

---

[4] King George IV (1762–1830) was prince regent from 1811 (when his father became permanently deranged) until he ascended the throne in 1820.

[5] Langdon.

[6] John Keast Lord (1818–72) was trained as a veterinary surgeon and served with the British Army in the Crimea. He was sent to British Columbia after the discovery of gold there in 1858, and while residing on Vancouver Island collected valuable zoological specimens. He was on the staff of *Land and Water* from its

There were plenty who were ready & willing to undermine & oust the old gentleman, but he happened to be an old friend of Lee's—& so, hardly even waiting to be asked or permitted, Lee laid all his own affairs aside, left them to his clerks & subordinates & went down to Brighton, took off his coat & worked literally night & day, not only without pay, but at heavy personal expense, & built that wonderful aquarium & stocked it with its curious inhabitants—& the general public have not said Well done, & generously done, my boy, for the general public know nothing about it.

(Livy, I wish you would send, under cover to me, a note to Mr. Henry Lee, saying that you are aware of his kindnesses to me, & asking him to be sure & make our house his home as long as we can succeed in making it pleasant to him in case he chances to visit America—& send him pictures of Langdon & the baby, & go & get your own picture taken & send it to me & I will give it him myself, along with my own.)

The aquarium is a very large & handsome brick & stone structure whose top is on a level with the sea-front street of ᵽBrighton, & consequently one goes down a considerable flight of stairs to enter it. You first find yourself in a roomy hall (Pompeeiian style of architecture) ~~supporte~~ whose roof is supported by graceful columns whose capitals are carved into various kinds of fishes. On one side this opens into another roomy apartment where very complete & excellent breakfasts & dinners are served to all who desire them. On the other side you pass out into a spacious hall & on either side of you are ₍long,₎ tall walls of plate-glass through which one looks into roomy, comfortable chambers (or drawing rooms₍)₎ filled with limpid water, floored with clean sand & enclosed (on three sides) with rugged walls of rock that counterfeit the picturesque caves of the sea—& then the inhabitants! charming outlandish fishes that soar hither & thither as if in the transparent air, & fascinate one with their graceful forms & dainty colors; monster soldier-crabs & lobsters that go straddling about the sands & making the visitor's flesh crawl; hermit crabs traveling around in borrowed shells; ugly skates, that lie flat on the bottom & remind one of nothing within the possibilities of nature unless it be of a slice off some kind of a devil; still uglier cuttle=fish that remind one of an entire devil; prawns, in shoals & schools; fishes

inception, and subsequently traveled to Egypt for archaeological and scientific research. Lord was appointed the first manager of the Brighton Aquarium, but died in December 1872, only four months after it opened.

that have little slender legs, & walk on them; other fishes that are white when they lie asleep on the bottom, but turn red when they rise up & swim; specimens of a queer fish that takes the roe in his mouth when his wife is delivered of it, & carries it about with him, never allowing her to touch it—& circumstances have led to the belief that he washes down his dinner with ~~one or two of~~ a few dozen raw when nobody is looking, for the eggs seem to lose bulk under his protection; beautiful sea‹ anemones (some white, some pink & some purple) growing like the most natural of flowers, upon jutting headlands of the submerged rocks, & waiting for a chance to suck in & devour any small game that may wander above their treacherous blossoms; and, chief of the show, imposing sea turtles, big enough to carry passengers, go drifting airily about among the picturesque caverns of the glass-fronted ocean palace that contains a hundred & ten thousand gallons of water.

It is a wonderful place, the Brighton aquarium, & was a majestic curiosity to me, for I had never seen anything but our little toy affairs before, with half a dozen goldfish & a forlorn mud turtle.

We saw the architectural nightmare which Geo. 4 called his marine palace—but the less said i̶t̶ about it the better. It is probably the ugliest building above ground. Geo. built it for a menagerie of lewd women— the only kind of a zoological garden he took any interest in. It is said that its history is so repulsive to Queen Victoria that she will not visit it at all.[7]

Mortimer of "Figaro" dined with us & tried to crowd me into writing for his paper, but did not succeed. He has lived 17 years in France with a French wife (he is an American) & she does not know a single word of English. She was present. It was a queer conversation—she & Lee & Edmund Routledge clattering away in French & Mortimer & I clattering upon tabooed subjects in English with perfect freedom—he ripping out an oath occasionally & every now & then ʃ telling me to "cuss if you want to—she can't understand a word."[8]

She talked in her naive French way upon odd subjects. Inquired particularly into R's family affairs, & was full of sympathy when he told her (a fact) that he has been married 7 years & his wife b̶o̶ has had 5

---

[7]The Prince of Wales (later George IV), notorious for his profligate lifestyle, first built a Marine Pavilion at Brighton in 1787. In 1815–20 he employed John Nash to remodel and enlarge it at great expense, turning it into a lavish and "tasteless building in the Oriental style" (Baedeker 1901, 51). Queen Victoria made occasional visits there until 1844, and in 1850 it was sold to the town of Brighton (Gascoigne, 555; Murray, 58).

[8]See 5 Nov 73 to Bliss, n. 5.

children & 2 miscarriages—& that his brother's 7 children had but 11 months time between each. She asked if he could not prevent children, & said <u>she</u> could—said doubtless the Englishmen were more faithful than the ~~French~~—& added, with the sweetest simplicity that Routledge himself must be "ˌtrés <u>maladroit</u>."

Temple Bar, a small triple archway ˌwith heavy gates,ˌ over Fleet street, is the limit of the little "city" on one side, & Holborn Bars (the site of a former gate) is the limit on the other (say a mile or mile & a half ~~a p~~ apartˌ)ˌ (Inquire & make sure of this.ˌ)ˌ[9] A few months ago when the queen moved in state through ~~the city~~ London to offer thanksgivings at St Paul's for the Prince of Wales restoration to health, the Lord Mayor, in accordance with an ancient custom, stood by the closed gates of Temple Bar & denied her admission, or went through a ceremony of some kind or other before he would let her in to the "city."[10] They do not put people's heads on top of Temple Bar any more, now, & so they might as well pull it down, for that was all that made it attractive. It is not an architectural triumph.[11]

But as I was saying, the awful crookedness of London streets, the blending together of villages &c, make ~~all sorts of initials necessary, &~~ all sorts of combinations of names. ~~For instance:~~ necessary. For instance: 4, Upper-Terrace, Upper-street, Islington; 3, Cambridge-Gardens, Kensington Park, W.; 7, Dudley-place, Maida-Hill, Middle-

[9] The area encompassed by the City of London is slightly over one square mile. Temple Bar—torn down in 1878—stood on its western boundary, slightly north of the Thames (the southern boundary), and Holborn Bars—two stone obelisks surmounted by silver griffins—are situated about one-third of a mile further north, at its northwest corner (Weinreb and Hibbert, 172, 385, 857).

[10] This ancient ceremony, dating from the defeat of the Spanish Armada in 1588, is enacted on

> state occasions when the Sovereign wishes to enter the City: permission is asked of the Lord Mayor who offers his Sword of State as a demonstration of his loyalty. It is immediately returned to him and carried before the royal procession to show that the Sovereign is in the City under the Lord Mayor's protection. (Weinreb and Hibbert, 857)

It had most recently been performed by Lord Mayor Sir Sills John Gibbons on 27 February 1872, when Queen Victoria attended a National Thanksgiving service in St. Paul's Cathedral to offer thanks for the recovery of Albert Edward, the Prince of Wales, from typhoid fever (Kent, 653; "The National Thanksgiving Day," London *Times*, 28 Feb 72, 5).

[11] Temple Bar, consisting of a "central arch for carriages and a foot postern at either side," was built in the early 1670s by Sir Christopher Wren. From 1684 until 1746 it was "used to show the remains (usually the heads) of traitors to the populace" (Weinreb and Hibbert, 857).

sex; 141 St. George's Road, near Albany Road, Camberwell, S. E.; 7 Spencer-street, St John-street-road, Clerkenwell;

The great Lord Mayor is <u>nobody</u> outside the little "city" of London., By ancient custom no military company (except the Buffs—they belonging to the "city,") can march through the "city" with bands playing & colors flying, without a special permit from the Lord Mayor—so they generally march through in silence, with furled flags, rather than take the trouble to apply for the permit.[12]

J.L. Toole & the old clo' man of Dublin.[13]

We drove through Hyde Park, & all of a sudden a magnificent structure burst upon us. We got out & stood gazing at it in mute wonder. It was a tall, ornate pinnacle, of pierced with arches & flanked by noble groups of statuary; & this ᵽ airy, graceful pinnacle was splendid with guilding & richly-colored mosaics from its base to its summit. It was the brightest, freshest, loveliest bit of ˬgiganticˬ jewelry in all this battered & blackened old city. The fascinated sun, fondled it, petted it, glorified it. The very railings that enclosed the spacious marble platform it stood upon were sumptuously guilded. At the four corners of these railings, elevated upon great marble pedestals, were four groups of the groups of statuary I have mentioned—& the principal. All clean, & white & new. And all huge, imposing figures. And so perfectly wrought & so happily grouped that from whatever point you examined them they were ~~with-~~

---

[12] Originally raised in 1572, the regiment known as the "Buffs" (from its red uniforms with buff facings) had a series of names—the Holland Regiment, Prince George of Denmark's Regiment, Charles Churchill's Regiment—until 1751, when it officially became the Third Regiment of Foot. In 1782 it was additionally styled the East Kent Regiment, and in 1961 was incorporated into the Royal Kent Regiment, or Queen's Own Buffs. It is the only regiment with the privilege (which it has enjoyed since at least the mid-eighteenth century) of "marching through the City of London with drums beating and colours flying," although the origin of this custom is not known (Sibbald David Scott, 228–34; Oakley, 429).

[13] An anecdote apparently told by comic actor John L. Toole, with whom Clemens had lunch on 16 September 1872. Toole recounted in his *Reminiscences* that he had once played a trick on a used-clothing dealer who repeatedly importuned him for business, by inviting him to bid on some discarded clothes and then showing him the costume he habitually wore to portray Dickens's tatterdemalion Artful Dodger, from *Oliver Twist* (15 Sept 72 to OLC; Toole, 343–45).

out symmetrical, harmonious, guiltless of blemish. One group represented Asia—a stately female figure seated upon a prostrate elephant, & surrounded by Persians, Chinese, Indian warriors, & an Arab reading the Koran. Another group represents Europe—a woman seated upon a bull, & round about her other female figures typifying England & the States of the Continent. Another A third group represents America—an Indian woman seated upon a buffalo which is careering through the long prairie grass; & about her are half a dozen figures representing the United States, Canada, South America &c. The fourth group represents Africa—an Egyptian princess seated upon a Camel, & surrounded by other typical figures. One cannot convey, with words, the majesty of these stony creatures—the ease, the dignity, the grace, that sit upon them so royally. And there is no slurring over of anything—every little detail is perfect; The the fringes that depend from the camel's covering fall as limp & pliant as if they were woven instead of chiseled; no 'prentice work is visible anywhere.

We approached & entered the enclosure & mingled with the moving multitude, to make a close examination of the monumental spire. At its corners stood four more beautiful groups of statuary. All around its base ran a marble frieze—a procession of life-size figures of all the mighty poets, painters, architects the ages have given to the world—Shakspeare, Homer, ₁Virgil, Dante,₁ Michael Angelo, Raphael—all the world's supremely gifted men. Under the rich vault, stood a massy pedestal, & through the gilded arches the sunlight streamed upon it. We moved away again, & stood outside the railing to feast again upon the general view.

I said to my comrade,

"Tell me what it is."

"It is a monument—a memorial.["]

"Yes, I see—but to whom?"

"Guess."

"Guess—any one can guess it. There is only one name worthy of it—only just one. And I pay the humble homage of a stranger, & offer his gratitude, to the nation that so honors her great son, the world's great teacher—It is Shakspeare! Glory to old England!"

"Bah! What an innocent you are! It is Prince Albert!"[14]

[14]Clemens also poked fun at the Albert Memorial in his 21 September 1872 speech to the Savage Club (see 22 Sept 72 to Conway [2nd], n. 16).

~~Alas, it~~ It was too true. Napoleon's tomb at Paris has long-ranked as ~~the richest~~ the most sumptuous testimonial to departed greatness that Europe could show[15]—but it is ~~ima~~ insignificant compared to this memorial which England has erected to keep ~~in~~ green in the ~~affe ad~~ affectionate admiration of future generations a most excellent foreign gentleman who was a happy type of the Good, & the Kind, the Well-Meaning, the Mediocre, the Commonplace—~~amd~~ and who did no more for his country than five hundred tradesmen did in his own time, whose works are forgotten. The finest monument in the world erected to glorify—the Commonplace. It is the most genuinely humorous idea I have met with in this grave land. Presently the statue of the good, kind, well-meaning gentleman will be placed upon the monumental pedestal—& then what a satire upon human glory it will be to see Homer & Shakspeare ˏ& Milton, & Michael Angelo & all that long marble ~~proces~~ array of the world's demi-gods around the base, bracing their shoulders to the ˏgenial, work & supporting their brother in his high seat.

~~It~~ I still feel some lingering discomfort that this princely structure was not built for Shakspeare—but after all, maybe ˏhe, does not need it as much as the other. ˏ(Picture of Shak's grave.)ˏ

ˏ~~(End of Chapter.)~~[16]

We turned about & saw a prodigious building, constructed of cream colored stone—& every stone in the pile curiously & elaborately ornamented with the chisel—ˏ no end of flowers, & birds, & reptiles, all carved in painstaking detail. The building will seat ten thousand persons, ~~& great con~~ & great concerts are given there. ˏPrinces,ˏ Dukes, ⅋ Earls & bankers buy boxes there for 999 years, just as they would buy a piece of real estate, & they pay $5,000 for the said box & will transmit it

---

[15] The tomb of Napoleon I (1769–1821), in the Dôme des Invalides, is an open circular crypt, thirty-six feet in diameter, containing a sixty-seven-ton granite sarcophagus and decorated with numerous reliefs, sculptures, and mosaics. Napoleon's remains were placed there in 1840 (Baedeker 1884, 262–63).

[16] Clemens used a pencil to delete "(End of Chapter.)" and insert "(Picture of Shak's grave.)" on the recto copy remaining in his notebook. (He had earlier inserted, and then deleted, the same words in carbon at 595.5). Presumably the cut-out verso copy (now lost) lacked these revisions. Shakespeare's grave, in a niche in the Church of the Holy Trinity in Stratford-upon-Avon, is covered by a simple stone slab carved with an inscription (Murray, 390).

to their posterity. This palatial place is called Albert Hall, & was erected as just one more testimonial to departed mediocrity. Well, it is best to have a supply of memorials, to guard against accidents. I mean to have an assortment of tomb stones myself.

ₓ(~~Picture of Shak's grave.~~)ₓ

We passed into the International Exhibition & found several busts & pictures of Prince Albert.[17] Glory is a singular thing. I find only three individuals prodigiously glorified in monumental stone here, out of England's great long ~~illustrious~~ list of immortal names—ₓthe mighty, Wellington, ₓthe ~~gallant~~ peerless, Nelson, & the kindly foreign gentleman who ~~patiently acq~~ reared a large family of excellent children, dabbled in amateur agriculture, law & science, distributed prizes to mechanics' societies, & gave a notable impulse to industry by admiring it.

The inscription on the splendid monument yonder reads:

"Queen Victoria & her people to the memory of Albert, Prince Consort, as a tribute of their gratitude for a life devoted to the public good.["]

It is the oddest reversing of obligations that one can imagine. ~~It does~~ England found Albert very obscure & ~~by no means~~ rather stinted in worldly goods for one in his social position—~~& with him she found his numerous relatives, titled, respectable, but poor.~~ She gave ~~Albert~~ ₓhim, wealth, married him to a young & beautiful queen & ~~did honor to him~~ paid him homage all his life as the second personage in the greatest empire of this age. ~~The relatives were provided for & taken care of.~~ These were not trifles. ~~Now I think the carping stranger~~ There must be a mistake somewhere. Doubtless the Prince designed this monument himself, & intended to put on it this inscription:

"Prince Albert to the Queen & her people, as a tribute of his gratitude for incalculable benefits conferred upon him."

(Diamond form.)[18] (End of chapter.[)]

Saturdays the great reading room of the British Museum is full of

---

[17] The London International Exhibition of 1872, which opened on 1 May at Kensington, included a bust of Prince Albert executed by William Theed (1804–91), best known for sculpting the colossal group representing "Africa" on the pedestal of the Albert Memorial (London *Times:* "The International Exhibition," 30 Apr 72, 5; "The London Exhibition of 1872," 30 Apr 72, 8).

[18] The diagonal lines in the left margin and this parenthetical instruction indicate that Clemens wanted to have the quotation typeset in the shape of a diamond—that is, in lines of increasing and then decreasing length.

preachers, stealing sermons for next day! So said Mr. Woodward, chief of the geological department.[19] We were looking down from a gallery upon the busy scene—it <u>looked</u> busy, for there were one or two people scribbling & referring at every table, almost. But Mr. W. said "you ought to see it <u>Saturdays</u>!" They not only <u>copy</u> sermons, but tear them bodily out of the books. And Vandals of other kinds tear leaves out of valuable books for other purposes, although the Museum furnishes every possible convenience for its visitors.

As usual, Mr. Lee took me to headquarters & told the Museum people who I was, & straightway they treated me with every kindness & courtesy—& straightway, also, Mr. Woodward took us into the gold= room—one of those jealously-guarded places which one must usually go through some red tape to get into. Lee went to his business & Mr. W. showed me through some eighteen miles of tall book-cases—a labyrinth of circles & galleries. We have put off the rest of the library for the present.

But I, (upon recommendation of two householders of London,) am provided with a ticket to the Reading Room, & this is always open, whereas the rest of the Museum is only open 3 days in the week.[20] What a place it is!

Mention some very rare curiosity of a peculiar nature—a something which you have <u>read</u> about somewhere but never seen—they show you a dozen! They show you all the possible <u>varieties</u> of that thing! They show you curiously wrought & jeweled necklaces of beaten gold worn by the ancient Egyptians, Assyrians, Etruscans, Greeks, Britons—every people, of the forgotten ages, indeed. They show you the ornaments of all the tribes & peoples that live or ever did live. Then they show you a cast taken from Cromwell's face in death; then the venerable vase that once contained the ashes of Xerxes;[21] then you drift into some other room & stumble upon a world of ~~the~~ the flint hatchets ‚of pre-historic days;ᴧ & reindeer-horn handles; & pieces of bone with figures of animals delicately carved upon them; & long rows of bone fish-hooks & needles

[19] Geologist Henry Woodward (1832–1921), associated with the British Museum since 1858 and editor of *Geological Magazine* since 1864.
[20] See 22 Sept 72 to Conway (2nd), n. 12.
[21] Oliver Cromwell (1599–1658), lord protector of England in 1653–58; Xerxes I ("the Great," 519?–465 B.C.), king of Persia.

of the period—everything, indeed, connected with the household economy of the cave & lake dwellers—& every object, too, so repeated, &
multiplied, & remultiplied that they suddenly whisk away your doubts
& you find yourself accepting as a fact that these implements & ornaments are not scattering accidents, but deliberately designed & tediously
wrought, & of ₐin, very common use in some queer age of the world or
other. And the fact that many of them are found in ruined habitations in
the bottoms of Swiss Lakes, & ₰many in caverns in other parts of Europe
(buried under slowly-created & very thick layers of limestone) does not
encourage one to try to claim these parties as very recent kin. And then
you pass along & perhaps you ask if they have got such a thing as a
mummy about their cloᵗhes—& bless your heart & they rush you into
a whole Greenwood Cemetery[22] of them—old mummies, young mum-
mies, he mummies, she mummies, ~~starchy mummies,~~ high-toned mum-
mies, ragged mummies, old slouches, mummies in good whole coffins,
mummies on the half shell, mummies with money, mummies that are
"busted," Kings & Emperors, loafers & bummers, ~~all huddled together~~
p ₐall, straightened out as comfortable & happy in a Christian museum
as if they had brought their knitting with them & this was the very ~~place~~
hotel they had been hunting for for four thousand years & upwards. And
while you are wondering if these defunct had human feelings, human
sympathies, human emotions like your own, you turn pensively about
& find ~~your~~ an eloquent answer: an Egyptian woman's enormous chi-
gnon & the box she carried it in when she went out to a party! You want
to kiss that poor old half busheᵈl of curled & plaited hair; ⱨ you want to
uncover the glass case & shed some ~~ters~~ tears on it. You recognize the
fact that in the old, old times, woman was the same quaint, fascinating,
eccentric muggins she is in these.

They were strange, strange ₐpeople, in those old forgotten times.
But I wonder how the mummies walked, with all those bandages on.
Well, you pass on, & presently you come to

What a stupid regulation they have here in the American Consulate.
If you want to ship anything to America you must go there & swear to a

---

[22] A 178-acre cemetery in Brooklyn, New York, established in 1838 (Lossing,
579).

great long rigmarole, & kiss the book (years ago they found it was a dictionary) & you must fill & sign 3 blanks & pay a fee! All this infernal clog upon business in order to ~~sup~~ make the dirty Consulate pay for itself. We do hunt up more ways to save at the spigot & lose at the bung than any other idiotic government afloat.

(Speak of our diplomatic service)

Manner of oath:

"You do solemnlyswearthatthethingshereinsetfortharethetruth-thewholetruth&nothingbutthetruth~~sohes~~'elpyouGodkissthebookone-shil'nnochangemustgoout&getsome!"

Some of the oddest looking old cats browsing around here and writing out of books—one woman of 50—old maid—in tow linen, no hoops, dress rather short, ~~bottom~~ green hat like a lampshade—tilted forward in a gallus way[23]—pen behind her ear.

I am wonderfully thankful for the British Museum. Nobody comes bothering around me—nobody elbows me—all the room & all the light I want under this huge dome—no disturbing noises—& people standing ready to bring me a copy of pretty much any book that ever was printed under the sun—& if I choose to go wandering about the ~~great~~ long corridors & galleries of the great building, the secrets of all the Earth & all the ages are laid open to me. I am not capable of expressing my gratitude for the British Museum—it seems as if I do not know any but little words & weak ones.

They have just received the sculptured base of a great pillar of the temple of Diana at ~~Epe~~ Ephesus—the first ⌀ one unearthed in Modern times. Ancient historians describes the sculptures—& here in the 19th century they come to light. The figures are almost life size.[24]

---

[23] From "gallows," meaning "rakish, dashing" (Cassidy and Hall, 622).
[24] In 1869 British archaeologist John Turtle Wood (1820?–90), after six years of excavations at Ephesus (an ancient Greek city of Asia Minor, now in western Turkey), uncovered the remains of a magnificent Temple of Diana, probably the last of several temples to the goddess on the same site. This temple, built in the time of Alexander the Great and destroyed by Goths in 262 A.D., was described by several ancient writers (among them Vitruvius and Pliny). It comprised one hundred columns rising nearly sixty feet, and was considered one of the Seven Wonders of the World. Wood sent several shipments of excavated marble sculp-

"Come along—& hurry. Few people have got originality enough to think of the expedition I have been planning, & still fewer could carry it out, maybe, even if they did think of it. Hurry, now. Cab at the door."

It was past eleven o'clock & I was just going to bed. But this friend of mine was as reliable as he was eccentric, & so there was not a doubt in my mind that his "expedition" ~~would~~ had merit in it. I put on my coat & boots again, & we drove away.[25]

"Where is it? ~~Wha~~ Where are we going?"

"Don't worry. You'll see."

He was not inclined to talk. So I thought this must be a weighty matter. My curiosity grew with the minutes, but I kept it manfully under the surface. I watched the lamps, the signs, the numbers, as we thundered down the long streets, but it was of no use—I am always lost, in London, day or night. It was very chilly—almost bleak. People leaned against the gusty blasts as if it were the dead of winter. The crowds grew thinner & thinner & the noises waxed faint & seemed far away. The sky was overcast & threatening. We drove on, & still on, till I wondered if we were ever going to stop. At last we passed by a ~~bridge~~ spacious bridge, & a vast building with a lighted clock-tower, & presently entered a gateway, passed through a sort of tunnel & stopped in a court surrounded by the black outlines of a great edifice. Then we alighted, walked a dozen steps or so, & waited. In a little while footsteps were heard & a man emerged from the darkness & we dropped into his wake without saying anything. He led us ~~into~~ under an archway of masonry, & from that into a roomy tunnel, through a tall iron gate, which he locked behind us. We ~~proceeded~~ ₍followed him,₎ down this tunnel, guided more by his footsteps on the stone flagging than by anything we could very distinctly see. At the end of it we came to another iron gate, & our conductor stopped there & ~~made ready to~~ lit a little bull's-eye lantern. Then he unlocked the gate—& I wished he had oiled it first, it grated so dismally. The gate swung open & we stood on the threshold of what seemed a limitless domed & pillared cavern carved out of the solid darkness. ~~For the mo-~~

tures to his sponsor, the British Museum, including one in 1872 (Boase, 3:1472; "The Temple of Diana at Ephesus," London *Times*, 4 Apr 72, 6; John Turtle Wood, vii–viii, 192–97, 206, 208, 263–65, 277–78).

[25]Clemens's escort may have been Frank Buckland, son of the former dean of Westminster. Henry Lee evidently introduced Clemens to the younger Buckland (AD, 22 Mar 1906, CU-MARK; see note 37).

~~ment~~ The conduct͜o͜r͜e͜d ~~took~~ & my friend took off their hats reverently,
& I did likewise. For the moment that we stood there,/ˏthus,ˏ there was
not a sound; & the silence seemed ~~even~~ to add to the solemnity of the
gloom. ~~Speech was~~ I <u>looked</u> my inquiry.

"It is the tomb of the great dead of England—<u>Westminster
Abbey</u>."[26]
ˏ!

(One cannot express a start—in words.) ~~A little half-grown black &
white cat squeezed herself through the bars of the iron gate & came purring too affectionately about us unimpressed~~
Down among the columns—ever so far away, it seemed—a light revealed itself like a star, & a voice came echoing through the spacious
emptiness:

"Who goes there!"

"Wright!"

The star disappeared & the footsteps that accompanied it clanked
out of hearing in the distance. Mr. Wright held up his lantern & the
vague vastness ~~of~~ took something of form to itself—the stately columns
developed stronger outlines, & a dim pallor here & there marked the
places of lofty windows. We were among the tombs; & on every hand
dull shapes of men, ~~st~~ sitting, standing, or stooping, inspected us curiously out of the darkness—reached out their hands toward us—some
appealing, some beckoning, some warning us away. Effigies, they
were—statues over the graves; but they looked human & natural, in the
murky shadows. Now a little half-grown black-&-white cat squeezed
herself through the bars of the iron gate & came purring lovingly about
us, unawed by the time or the place—~~And she followed us about & never
left us while we pursued ou/r work.~~ unimpressed by the marble pomp
that sepulchres ~~the~~ a line of mighty dead that ends with a great author of
yesterday & began with a sceptred monarch away back in the dawn of
history ˏmore than,ˏ twelve hundred years ago.[27] And she followed us

[26] Westminster Abbey, or, more properly, the Collegiate Church of St. Peter
in Westminster, was the successor to a Norman church dedicated on the site in
1065. The present Gothic church was opened for service in 1269, but was not
completed until about 1740. For centuries it has been the scene of royal coro-
nations, marriages, and funerals, and the burial place of persons of note (Bradley
and Bradley, 3–5).

[27] See note 30.

about & never left us while we pursued our work. We wandered hither & thither, uncovered, & speaking in low voices, & stepping softly by instinct, for any little noise rang and echoed there in a way to make one shudder. Mr. Wright flashed his lantern first upon this object and then upon that, & kept up a running commentary that showed that there was nothing about the venerable Abbey that was trivial in his eyes or void of interest. He is a man in authority—being superintendent of the works—& his ‸daily‸ business keeps him familiar with every nook & corner of the great pile.[28] Casting a luminous ray now here, now yonder, he would say:

"Observe the height of the Abbey—103 feet to the base of the roof[29]—I measured it myself the other day. Notice the base of ~~the~~ this column—old, very old—hundreds & hundreds of ~~yeas~~ years; & how well they knew how to build in those old days. Notice it—every stone is laid horizontally—that is to say, just as nature laid it originally in the quarry—not set up edgewise; in our day some people set them on edge & then wonder why they split & flake. Architects cannot teach nature anything. Let me remove this matting—it is put there to preserve the pavement; now there is a bit of pavement that is seven hundred years old; you can see by these scattering clusters of colored mosaics how beautiful it ~~has~~ was before time & sacrilegious idlers marred it. Now there, in the border, was an inscription, once; see, follow the circle—you can trace it by the ornaments that have been pulled out—here is an A, & there is an O, & yonder another A—all beautiful old English capitals—there is no telling what the inscription was—no record left, now. Now move along in this direction, if you please. Yonder is where old King Sebert the Saxon, lies—his monument is the oldest one in the Abbey; Sebert died in 616, & that's as much as twelve hundred & fifty years ago—think of it!—twelve hundred & fifty years. Now yonder is the last one—~~about~~ Charles Dickens—there on the floor, with the brass letters on the slab—& to this day they ~~come &~~ people come & put flowers on it. Why along at first they almost had to <u>cart</u> the flowers out, there were

[28] Thomas Wright was "clerk of the works at the Abbey for thirty-seven years, and loved every stone of the building, which he knew so well." He died in 1906, at the age of eighty-three, and was buried in the south walk of the cloisters, close to his office (Bradley and Bradley, 88).

[29] The height of the nave, 103 feet, is "far higher than that of any other English church" (Weinreb and Hibbert, 944).

so many.[30] Could not <u>leave</u> them there, you know, because it's where everybody walks—& it a body wouldn't want them trampled on, anyway. All this place about here, now, is the Poets' Corner.[31] There is Garrick's monument; & Addison's, & Thackeray's bust—& Macaulay lies there. And here close to Dickens & Garrick, lie Sheridan, & D[r.] Johnson[32]—& here is old Parr—Thomas Parr—you can read the inscription:

"'Tho: Parr of y̆ covnty of Sallop borne A°: 1483. He lived in y̆ reignes of Ten Princes, viz: K. Edw. 4. K. Ed. 5. K. Rich 3. K. Hen. 7. K. Hen. 8. K. Edw. 6. Qu. Ma. Q. Eliz. K. I a. and K. Charles, aged 152 yeares. and was buryed here Novemb. 15. 1635.'[33]

"Very old man indeed, & saw a deal of life—come off the grave, Kitty, poor thing, she keeps the rats away from the office, & there's no harm in her—her & her mother. And here—this is Shakspeare's statue—leaning on his elbow & pointing with his finger at the lines on the scroll:

---

[30] Sebert (d. 616?), the first Christian king of the East Saxons, was the legendary founder of the first church dedicated to St. Peter on the site of Westminster Abbey (Bradley and Bradley, 4; Weinreb and Hibbert, 944). Charles Dickens's popularity extended to the entire English-speaking world. He died at age fifty-eight and was buried in the abbey on 14 June 1870.

[31] The first poet buried in the south transept, later known as the "Poets' Corner," was Geoffrey Chaucer (1340?–1400). After the burial nearby of Edmund Spenser (see note 35), the area was appropriated to writers, and later to those successful in other arts as well (Bradley and Bradley, 34; Arthur Penrhyn Stanley, 249–54).

[32] Actor David Garrick (1717–79); essayist Joseph Addison (1672–1719), whose monument was not erected until 1809; novelist William Makepeace Thackeray (1811–63), buried at Kensal Green and represented in the abbey by a bust carved by Carlo Marochetti; historian and poet Thomas Babington Macaulay (1800–1859), buried at the foot of Addison's statue; dramatist and orator Richard Brinsley Sheridan (1751–1816); and lexicographer and critic Samuel Johnson (1709–84) (Bradley and Bradley, 40–41).

[33] Thomas Parr allegedly lived in the reigns of ten monarchs: Edward IV (1442–83), reigned 1461–70, 1471–83; Edward V (1470–83), reigned 1483; Richard III (1452–85), reigned 1483–85; Henry VII (1457–1509), reigned 1485–1509; Henry VIII (1491–1547), reigned 1509–47; Edward VI (1537–53), reigned 1547–53; Mary I (1516–58), reigned 1553–58; Elizabeth I (1533–1603), reigned 1558–1603; James I (1566–1625), reigned 1603–25; and Charles I (1600–1649), reigned 1625–49. On 18 August 1871 Clemens wrote to Olivia, "One of these days I propose to write an Autobiography of Old Parr, the gentleman who lived to be 153 years old & saw the reigns of 8 English kings" (*L4*, 446).

[ᶜ]The cloud-capt towers, the gorgeous palaces,
The solemn temples, the great globe itself,
Yea, all which it inherit, shall dissolve,
And, like the base fabric of a vision,
Leave not a wreck behind.'[34]

"That stone there covers Campbell the poet. Here are names you know pretty well—Milton, & Gray who wrote the Elegy, & Butler who wrote Hudibras, & Edmund Spencer,[35] & Ben Johnson—there are three tablets scatt to him scattered about the Abbey, & all got 'O Rare Ben Jonson' cut on them—you were standing on one of them just now—he is buried standing up. There used to be a tradition here that explains it. The story goes that he did not dare ask to be buried in the ɟ Abbey, so he asked King James if he would make him a present of 18 inches of English ground, & the king said yes, & asked him where he would have it, & he said in Westminster Abbey. Well, the king wouldn't go back on his word, & so there he is, sure enough—stood up, on end.[36] Years ago,

[34] Shakespeare's statue, called a "preposterous monument" by Horace Walpole, was erected by subscription in 1740, 124 years after the great poet's death; his remains, however, were left in Stratford-upon-Avon (Bradley and Bradley, 38). The quotation, from *The Tempest*, act 4, scene 1, is not exact: in place of the correct fourth line ("And like this insubstantial pageant faded") the inscription substitutes the line immediately preceding those quoted: "And like the baseless fabric of a vision" (Brayley, 2:260–61). The editor of a variorum edition of the play commented that this transposition was one "which the needs of the case seem amply to justify" (Furness, 211). The substitution of "base" for "baseless" was Clemens's.

[35] Thomas Campbell (1777–1844), remembered primarily for his stirring patriotic lyrics; John Milton (1608–74), buried at St. Giles's, Cripplegate, and honored in the abbey by a bust erected in 1737; Thomas Gray (1716–71), buried at Stoke Poges, the scene of his famous "Elegy Written in a Country Churchyard" (1751), and memorialized in the abbey by a portrait medallion; Samuel Butler (1612–80), famous for his satirical mock-heroic poem "Hudibras" (1663–78), buried at St. Paul's, Covent Garden, and honored by a monument erected in 1721; and Edmund Spenser (1552?–99), whose monument was erected in 1620 and restored in 1778 (Bradley and Bradley, 36–38).

[36] According to "local tradition," Ben Jonson (1573?–1637) was granted his eighteen inches of "square ground" by King Charles I (not James I, his immediate predecessor). He was buried in the nave, with a stone (inscribed with the words Clemens quoted) marking his grave. When the nave was repaved in 1821, the original stone was removed, and the spot was thereafter marked by a copy. Dean Buckland (see the next note) later ordered the original stone fitted into the north wall of the nave. A memorial with the same inscription was set up in the poets' corner in the eighteenth century by Edward Harley, the second earl of Oxford (Arthur Penrhyn Stanley, 255–56; Bradley and Bradley, 36).

in Dean Buckland's time[37]—before my day—they were digging a grave close to Johnson & they uncovered him & his head fell off. Toward night the clerk of the works hid the head to keep it from being stolen, as the ground was to remain open till next day. Presently the dean's son came along, & he found a head, & hid it away for Johnson's. And by & by along comes a stranger, & he found a head, too, & walked off with it under his cloak & a month or so afterward he was heard to boast that he had Ben Jonson's head. Then there was a deal of correspondence about [it] in the Times, & everybody distressed. But Mr. Frank Buckland came out & comforted everybody by telling how he saved the true head, & so the stranger must have got one that wasn't of any consequence. And then up speaks the clerk of the works & tells how he saved the right head, & so Mr. Buckland must have got a wrong one. Well it was all settled satisfactorily at last, because the clerk of the works proved his head. And then I believe they got that head from the stranger—so now we have three. But it shows you what regiments of people you are walking over—been collecting here for twelve hundred years—in some places, no doubt, the bones are fairly matted together.[38]

"And here are some unfortunates. Under this place lies Anne, Queen of Richard III, & daughter of the king-maker, the great Earl of Warwick—murdered she was—poisoned by her husband.[39] And here is a slab which you see has once had the figure of a man in armor on it, in brass or copper, let into the stone. You can see the shape of it—but it is

[37] William Buckland (1784–1856), the father of Frank Buckland, was dean of Westminster from 1845 until his death. In addition, he was a renowned geologist, holding a chair of mineralogy at Oxford and serving twice as president of the Geological Society.

[38] Frank Buckland, in *Curiosities of Natural History* (a collection of previously published magazine articles), included a full account of the anecdote that Clemens alluded to. The controversy erupted when the London *Times* of 11 November 1865 printed the claim of an unidentified gentleman that he had "carried off" Jonson's skull from the abbey six years earlier. Buckland investigated the claim, and pieced together a complicated story involving two disinterments (the first in 1849, the second in 1859) and at least three skulls—one of which he himself had rescued on both occasions. Ultimately he determined that the correct skull (whose authenticity was proved by its red hair) had twice been rescued by the clerk of the works and replaced in Jonson's grave, where it remained (Buckland, 238–46).

[39] Richard III was suspected of contriving the murder of his queen, Anne (1456–85), because of her barrenness after the loss of their only son. She was the daughter of Richard Neville, the earl of Warwick.

all worn away, now, by people's feet—the man has been dead five hundred years that lies under it. He was a knight in Richard II's time. His
enemies pressed him close & he fled & took sanctuary here in the Abbey.
Generally a man was safe when he took sanctuary in those days, but this
man was not. The captain of the Tower & a band of men, pursued him
& his friends & they had a bloody fight here on this floor; but this poor
fellow did not stand much of a chance, & they butchered him right before the altar."[40]

We wandered over to another part of the Abbey, & came to a place
where the pavement was being repaired. Every paving stone is has an
inscription on it & covers a grave. Mr. Wright continued:

"Now, you are standing on William Pitt's grave—you can read the
name, though it is a good deal worn—& you, sir, are standing on the
grave of Charles James Fox.[41] I found a very good place here the other
day—nobody suspected it—been curiously overlooked, somehow—but
it is a very nice place indeed, & very comfortable" (holding his bull's-
eye to the pavement & searching around)—"Ah, here it is—this is the
stone—nothing under here—nothing at all—a very nice place indeed—
& very comfortable."

Mr. Wright spoke in a professional way, of course, & after the manner of a man who takes an interest in his business & is gratified at any
piece of good luck that fortune favors him with; & yet, with all that silence & gloom & solemnity about me, there was something about his
idea of a nice, comfortable place that made the cold chills creep up my
back. Presently we began to come upon little chamberlike chapels/ˌal-
covesˌ,[42] with solemn figures ranged around the sides, lying apparently
asleep, in on sumptuous marble alcoves ˌbedsˌ, with their hands placed

[40] The "large blue-coloured Slab, which exhibits the indent of a full-length
Brass figure of a Knight in armour," represents the "ill-fated ROBERT HAULE,
who, in the reign of Richard II., was murdered in the Choir, whilst resisting a
band of armed men, sent by John of Gaunt, to force him from sanctuary" (Brayley, 2:269; see note 46).

[41] William Pitt (1759–1806), probably England's greatest prime minister, and
his political rival, Whig orator Charles James Fox (1749–1806), were buried near
each other in the north transept (Bradley and Bradley, 21).

[42] Clemens interlined "alcoves" in pencil on the recto copy remaining in his
notebook. The revision does not appear on the cut-out verso copy for this passage, which survives as part of the printer's copy for "A Memorable Midnight
Experience," an extract of the text from "'Come along" at 599.1 to "work is
done." at 610.16 (SLC 1874c, 3–8).

together above their breasts—the figures & all their surroundings black with age. Some were dukes & earls, some were kings & queens,—~~all were noble.~~ some were ancient Abbots, whose effigies had lain there so many centuries & suffered such ~~defacement~~ disfigurement ~~their~~ that their faces were almost as ˬsmooth &ˬ featureless as the stony pillows their heads reposed upon. At one time, while I stood looking ~~up at~~ at a distant part𝑠 of the pavement, admiring the delicate tracery which the now flooding moonlight was casting upon it through a lofty,~~ pi~~ window, the party moved on & I lost them. The first step I made in the dark, holding my hands before me, as one does under such circumstances, I touched a cold object, & stopped to feel its shape. I made out a thumb, & then delicate fingers. It was the clasped, appealing hands of one of those reposing images—a lady, a queen. I touched the face—by accident, not design—& shuddered inwardly, if not outwardly; & then something rubbed against my leg, & I shuddered outwardly & inwardly both. It was the cat. The friendly creature meant well, but as the English say, she gave me "such a turn." I took her in my arms for company & wandered among the grim sleepers till I caught the ~~glinting~~ glimmer of the lantern again. Presently, in a little chapel, we were looking at the sarcophagus, let into the wall, which contains the bones of the infant princes whom were smothered in the Tower,;[43] ~~under them~~ behind us was the stately Monument of Queen Elizabeth, with her effigy dressed in the royal robes, lying as if ~~upon~~ at restˬ ~~upon a bed.~~ When we turned around, the cat, with stupendous simplicity, was ~~tran~~ coiled up & sound asleep upon the feet of the Great Queen! Truly this was reaching far toward the millennium, when the lion & the lamb shall lie down together.[44] The murdereṛss of Mary & Essex, the conqueror of the Armada, the imperious ruler of a turbulent Empire, become a couch, at last, for a tired kitten![45] ~~It~~ It was the most eloquent sermon upon the vanity of human

---

[43] In a small sarcophagus in the north aisle of Henry VII's chapel are bones that were found at the foot of a staircase in the Tower of London and are believed to be those of Edward V (b. 1470) and his brother Richard, the duke of York (b. 1472), who were murdered in 1483, allegedly by command of their uncle, Richard III (Bradley and Bradley, 62).

[44] A paraphrase from Isaiah 11:6.

[45] Also in the north aisle of Henry VII's chapel is the tomb of Elizabeth I, who signed the death warrant of her Roman Catholic rival, Mary, Queen of Scots (b. 1542), in 1587. This action led Philip of Spain to attempt to invade England with the Spanish Armada, which was defeated in 1588. In 1601 Elizabeth ordered the execution of Robert Devereux, earl of Essex (b. 1566), after he plotted against her (Bradley and Bradley, 61–62).

pride & human grandeur that inspired Westminster preached to us that night.

We would have turned puss out of the Abbey, but for the fact that her small body made light of railed gates, & she would have come straight back again. We walked up a flight of half a dozen steps, & stopping upon a pavement laid down in 1260, stood in the ~~midst of~~ core of English history, as it were—upon the holiest ground in the British Empire, if profusion of ~~renowned names & kingly names &~~ kingly bones & kingly names of old renown make holy ground. For here in this little space were the ashes, the monuments & the gilded effigies of ten of the most illustrious personages who have worn crowns & borne sceptres in this realm. This royal dust was the slow accumulation of ~~four~~ hundred$_\wedge$ of years. The latest comer entered into his rest four hundred years ago, & since the earliest was sepulchred, more than eight centuries have ~~passed~~ drifted by. Edward the Confessor, Henry the Fifth, Edward the First, Edward, the Third, Richard the Second, Henry the Third, Eleanor, ~~&~~ Phillippa, Margaret Woodville,—it was like bringing the colossal myths of history out of the forgotten ages & speaking to them face to face.[46] The gilded effigies were scarcely marred—the faces were comely & majestic; old Edward the first looked the king—one had no impulse to be familiar with him. ₵ While we were contemplating the figure of Queen Eleanor lying in state,—~~as the original had lain~~ & calling to mind how like an ordinary/ₐmere common,[47] human being the great king mourned for her six hundred years ago, we saw the vast illuminated clock-face of the Parliament-House tower ~~looking~~ glowering at us through a window of the Abbey & pointing with both hands to midnight. It was a derisive reminder that we were a part of this present sordid, plodding, commonplace time, & not august relics of a bygone age

[46] Clemens was in the most sacred part of the abbey, the Chapel of St. Edward, where the saint himself (known as Edward the Confessor, 1002?–1066) was buried. Crowned king in 1043, Edward founded the earlier Norman Westminster Abbey in 1065 (see note 26). Surrounding his tomb are the bodies of five kings and six queens. Of these are mentioned Henry V (1387–1422), crowned in 1413; Edward I (1239–1307), crowned in 1272; Edward III (1312–77), crowned in 1327; Richard II (1367–1400), crowned in 1377; Henry III (1207–72), crowned in 1216; Eleanor of Castile (d. 1290), first wife of Edward I; and Philippa (1314?–69), wife of Edward III. Margaret of York, the fourth daughter of Edward IV and Elizabeth Woodville, died in infancy in 1472 (Bradley and Bradley, 76–83; Lodge, 105).

[47] Clemens interlined "mere common" in pencil on the recto copy remaining in his notebook, but not on the surviving cut-out verso copy (see note 42).

& the comrades of kings—& then the booming of the great bell tolled twelve, & with the last stroke the mocking clock-face vanished in sudden darkness & left us with the past & its grandeurs again.

We descended, & entered the ʌnave of theʌ splendid chapel of Henry VII. Mr. Wright said:

"Here is where the order of knighthood was conferred for centuries; the candidates sat in these seats; these brasses bear their coats of arms; these are their banners overhead; torn & dusty, poor old things, for they have hung there many & many a long year/ʌgeneration,ʌ.[48] In the floor you see inscriptions—kings & queens that lie in the vault below. When this vault was opened in our time they found them lying there in beautiful order—all quiet & comfortable—the red velvet on the coffins hardly faded any.[49] And the bodies were sound—I saw them myself. They were embalmed, & looked natural, although they had been there such an awful time. One of them, though was in bad condition—he burst open & fell out on the floor—just a mess of stuff that looked like pitch, as á you may say. Now in this place here, which is called the Chantry, is a curious old group of statuary—the figures are mourning over George Villiers, duke of Buckingh\am, who was assassinated by Felton in Charles I's time. Yonder, Cromwell & his family used to lie.[50] Now we come to the south aisle, & this is the grand monument to Mary Queen

---

[48] Clemens interlined "generation" in pencil on the recto copy remaining in his notebook, but not on the surviving cut-out verso copy (see note 42). The chapel was the scene of the installation ceremony for the Knights of Bath only from 1725 until 1812. The number of knights was fixed to correspond with the number of stalls: "The banner of each knight hangs over the stall appointed for his use, to the back of which is attached a small plate of copper emblazoned with his arms" (Bradley and Bradley, 53; Arthur Penrhyn Stanley, 82–85).

[49] In February 1869 Dean Arthur Penrhyn Stanley undertook the excavation of the floor of Henry VII's chapel in a search for the coffin of James I. Several vaults were opened and found to contain remains in varying degrees of preservation before the object of the search was located, in the same vault that contained the body of Henry VII and his queen, Elizabeth of York (1465–1503) (Arthur Penrhyn Stanley, 499–526).

[50] A series of smaller chapels form the apse of Henry VII's chapel on the eastern end. In one of these is the tomb of George Villiers, duke of Buckingham (1592–1628), a favorite of Charles I's who was assassinated by a soldier named John Felton. Another once contained the remains of Oliver Cromwell (1599–1658) and other leaders of the Commonwealth, together with various members of Cromwell's family. In 1661, after the Restoration, the bodies of Cromwell and two of his followers were disinterred and taken to Tyburn, where they were hung and decapitated (Bradley and Bradley, 56, 59, 61; Arthur Penrhyn Stanley, 161).

of Scots, & her effigy—you easily see they get all the portraits from this effigy.[51] Here in the wall ~~is a bit of~~ of the aisle is a bit of a curiosity pretty roughly carved:

W^m WES T TOOME
SHOWER
1698

"'William West, tomb-shower, 1698.*'* That fellow carved his name around in several places about the Abbey."

This was a sort of revelation to me. I had been wandering through the Abbey never imagining but that its shows were created only for us— the people of the nineteenth century. But here is a man (become a show himself, now, & a curiosity,) to whom all these things were sights & wonders a hundred & seventy-five ⱨ years ago. When curious idlers from the country & from foreign lands came here to look, he showed them old Sebert's tomb & those of the other old worthies I have been speaking of, & called them ancient & venerable; & he showed them Charles II^s tomb as the newest & latest thing/ₐnovelty, he ~~has~~ had;[52] & he was doubtless present at the funeral. Three hundred ~~yeas~~ years before his time some ancestor of his, perchance, used to point out the ancient marvels, in the immemorial ₐway,[53] & then say "This, gentlemen, is the tomb ~~& the~~ of his late Majesty Edward the Third—& I wish I could see him alive & hearty again, as I saw him twenty years ago; yonder is the tomb of Sebert the Saxon king—he has been lying there well on to eight hundred years, they say." And three hundred years before this party, Westminster was still a show, & Edward the Confessor's grave was a novelty of some thirty years' standing—but old "Sebert" was hoary & ancient still, & people who spoke of Alfred the Great as a comparatively recent man, pondered over Sebert's ~~tomb~~ ₐgrave, & tried to take in all the tremendous meaning of it when the "toome-shower" said "This man has lain here wi well nigh five hundred years." It does seem as if all the generations that have lived

---

[51] Mary's beautifully carved white marble effigy "lies under an elaborate canopy, on a heavy sarcophagus. She wears a close-fitting coif, a laced ruff, and a long mantle fastened by a brooch. At her feet sits the Scottish lion crowned" (Bradley and Bradley, 55).

[52] Charles II (1630–85) was restored to the throne in 1660 and crowned in 1661; he was buried in the south aisle of Henry VII's chapel.

[53] Clemens interlined "novelty" (two lines above) and "way" in pencil on the recto copy remaining in his notebook. Presumably the cut-out verso copy (now lost) lacked this revision.

& died since the world was created, have visited Westminster to stare & wonder—& still found ancient things there. And some day a curiously clad company may arrive here in a balloon-ship from some remote corner of the globe, & as they follow the verger among the monuments they may hear him say: "This is the tomb of Victoria the Good Queen; battered & uncouth as it looks, it once was a wonder of magnificence—but twelve hundred years work a deal of damage to these things."[54]

~~As we were leaving~~

As we turned toward the door, the moonlight was beaming in at the windows; & it gave to the sacred place such an air of restfulness & peace, that Westminster ~~seemed~~ ₐwas, no longer a grisly museum of mouldering vanities, but ~~a home & a refuge for the toil-worn architects of England's greatness~~ her better & worthier self—the deathless mentor of a great nation, the guide & encourager of right ambitions, the preserver of ~~well-earned~~ ₐjust, fame, & the home & refuge for the nation's ~~rest &~~ best & bravest when their work is done.

At noon we reached the ancient Guildhall & cut our way through the cordon of police with our cards of invitation.[55] On a throne on a high & spacious platform sat the Lord Mayor in his robes of office,[56] & on ~~one side~~ his right sat, in their robes all the aldermen who had been Lord Mayor—& on his left the rest of the aldermen. The performance was about to begin. We went up & were introduced to the Lord Mayor & the new sheriffs,[57] & then I got a position where I could see everything, & held, it. The Sheriffs were ~~their~~ there, in their dazzling red robes, & the great many-stranded gold chain which is festooned about their shoulders & breast & supports the large jeweled coat of arms they wear on their breast. Every officer & every servant wore clothes of ancient pattern— knee breeches & stocking, low shoes with great buckles, lace wristbands & bosom ruffles, white, curled wigs, ₐcourt swords,ₐ & cocked hats. And all the costumes were exceedingly rich & costly, & perfectly new—they are renewed every year. The costumes were various, & all picturesque.

[54] Queen Victoria (1819–1901), crowned in 1837, was buried at Windsor.
[55] Clemens attended the installation of the new sheriffs of London and the election of the lord mayor on 28 September 1872 as the guest of John Bennett, a retiring sheriff (25 Sept 72 to OLC, n. 5, and 28 Sept 72 to OLC).
[56] Sills John Gibbons.
[57] Thomas White and Frederick Perkins.

The common crier in black,—of 2 or 3 centuries ago—he did the yelling. One short man wore embroidered black silk robes, with a great ~~hat~~ fur hat or muff on his head, shaped like a reversed gallon measure—& he was the only man who never took off his hat. He supported with his two hands the Sword of State, a weapon heavily enriched with gold, & just about the man's own height. But of all the gorgeous costumes, those of the coachmen & footmen of the sheriffs beat everything—& the carriages were beautified & decorated as if for a spectacular play. Mr. Sheriff Perkins's coachman wore [a] green silk velvet coat of ancient pattern, knee breeches of some splendid red stuff (cherry, I think the color was,) white silk stockings, low shoes with large silver buckles, ~~white,~~ ˏgrayˏˏ close-curled wig, & a great cocked hat. And from the top of his ~~cocked hat~~ ˏhigh coat collarˏ clear down ~~down to his heels he was~~ to the bottom of the broad tails—all up & down the back, & ˏfront &ˏ around the margins, & the flap pockets & the wristbands he was just one blinding conflagration of gold bullion embroidery. Not thin gimp & ribbons of it,~~but~~ pasted to the surfaces, but ropes & pads of it, piled on like stucco. I heard an official mention the cost of this coat as being a hundred & twenty guineas—that is to say, six hundred & thirty dollars. I have procured one like it for my coachman. The two footmen who stood where the trunks belong, behind the carriage, were just as splendid as the coachman—dressed in the same general fashion & with equal magnificence. I thought to myself that I would rather be one of those footmen than a rainbow. I overheard a man say, "Those three liveries cost 600 pound."

Next year the next sheriffs will buy these ˏstateˏ carriages & refurnish them; but they will buy new liveries out & out. It costs something to be a sheriff of London—& there is no salary, & no emoluments. It is a post of high honor & great consequence—but it would wreck a poor man in twenty-four hours. The under-sheriffs, however, have certain perquisites that make their office very fairly remunerative.

Very well. The Lord Mayor gets no salary & has no perquisites—holds office a year & is thought mean & stingy if he does not render the hospitalities of the Mansion House of a splendor befitting the dignity & greatness of London. And so, during his year, my lord mayor usually spends quite a fortune. When he goes to church in state, for instance—& that may be fiftyˏ-twoˏ times a year—that church expects a contribution for its poor; & as the lord mayor is always & necessarily a very rich man, it is expected that this contribution will amount to several hundred dollars every time.[58]

There have been lord mayors of ↓London for a thousand years; & some of their customs & the language of some of their ceremonials has not altered in that time. (Drinking the "loving-cup" at the banquet, &c.)[59] They represent the people & their liberties, & are a check upon encroachments of the crown. They are elected by the livery of the city, of the several guilds, & if I understand it rightly they cannot be mayor till they have served 7 years of their life-term of alderman, & so they come to the office with a good official education. By courtesy the office falls to the alderman who has been longest in office; & so the election of Lord Mayor by the assembled guilds & liveries seems a useless & empty ceremony—but it is nevertheless a very important ceremony because it keeps in constant exercise & in unquestioned authority a power which may be needed some day—that of ~~electing~~ setting aside the customary ~~to the~~ heir to the lord Mayor's chair & electing some other alderman in his place. It has occurred once. Venerable custom was overridden & the unworthy & obnoxious heir defeated & a good man ~~put~~ ˄chosen˄ in his stead.[60]

[58] As of 1870, the lord mayor received "an allowance of £8000 for his year, but he spends £4000 or £5000 out of his own pocket in addition" (*Black's Guide*, 204).

[59] London's first lord mayor, Henry Fitzailwyn, served from 1192 to 1212 (Weinreb and Hibbert, 480). Clemens explained the tradition of the loving-cup in a historical note to *The Prince and the Pauper:*

> The loving-cup, and the peculiar ceremonies observed in drinking from it, are older than English history. It is thought that both are Danish importations. As far back as knowledge goes, the loving-cup has always been drunk at English banquets. Tradition explains the ceremonies in this way: in the rude ancient times it was deemed a wise precaution to have both hands of both drinkers employed, lest while the pledger pledged his love and fidelity to the pledgee, the pledgee take that opportunity to slip a dirk into him! (*P&P*, 338)

Clemens took his information from John Timbs's *Curiosities of London* (*P&P*, 20, 386).

[60] The seven-year requirement seems to be Clemens's misunderstanding. Since there were twenty-six life-term aldermen, however, and the office of mayor usually went to the most senior of them (who must also have served as sheriff), an alderman would have many years of experience before becoming eligible for the mayoralty. The "unworthy & obnoxious heir" has not been identified. Clemens may have heard something about the disputed elections of 1739 and 1740, when the senior aldermen were passed over in favor of John Salter and Humphrey Parsons (*Black's Guide*, 203; Sharpe, 41–46).

Well, as I was saying, the common crier walked forward to the railing & made a quaint old time proclamation. Then the new sheriffs & under-sheriffs[61] were sworn in with great ceremony, (& in the simplest & prettiest old-time language some of the oaths were worded)—each read an oath himself & signed it in the book; & then he repeated another after an officer & signed that, too—& all the oaths were as long as a country p̶ minister's city prayer, & covered as much ground, too. Then the gorgeous footmen brought the splendid new robes & chains & jewels & swords, & officers invested the new sheriffs with them.

Then in procession the company marched to church, & heard a sermon; then returned, & at one oclock, there being now some five or six hundred voters present, the common crier made proclamation that this "common hall" was this day held for the d̶ election of Lord Mayor of London. Everybody k̶n̶o̶ knew that by the usual rotation, Sir Sidney Watterlo[62] was now heir to the mayoralty & that nobody would vote against him—still, they went through the ceremony of an elaborate election. The vote being called upon Sir Sidney, ‚(& he showing himself,)‚ every man in the house held up his hand—contrary, no hands up. ‚Jones questioned both these men, & his parasite put in his jaw.‚[63] Then they brought forward another r̶o̶b̶ crimson-robed alderman & called a vote upon him—but no hands were held up, & he retired. Then half a dozen boards containing aldermanic names, were elevated, i̶n̶ ̶q̶u̶i̶c̶k̶ ̶s̶u̶c̶c̶e̶s̶ one at a time, & the common crier called a vote upon each—but nobody voted.

Then a̶d̶m̶ amid great enthusiasm Sir Sidney was declared elected, & he made a slashing good speech[·]

[61] Solicitors Alexander Crosley (1827–76) and Arthur Turner Hewitt (*London Directory*, 967, 2240; "Election of Lord Mayor," London *Times*, 30 Sept 72, 11; Boase, 1:770).

[62] Sydney Hedley Waterlow.

[63] John Jones, one of the liverymen charged with electing the new mayor, directed questions about matters of policy to both Sir Sydney Waterlow and Alderman Andrew Lusk, who was "next in rotation" after Waterlow to be mayor ("Election of Lord Mayor," London *Morning Post*, 30 Sept 72, 2; "Election of Lord Mayor," London *Times*, 30 Sept 72, 11). Jones's "parasite" was mentioned, but not named, in the London *Telegraph*:

> Mr. Jones and another public-spirited gentleman, who may be regarded as a sort of Jonesian Satellite, . . . have not failed, at any mayoral election for some years past, to interrogate sternly, but with a certain urbanity bordering on *bonhomie*, the alderman whom rotation and choice combine to seat on the civic throne. ("Civic Changes," 30 Sept 72, 3)

ₐAnd if you could see the turf in the quadrangles of some of the colleges, & the Virginian creeper that pours its ~~lavish~~ ₐrichₐ cataract of green & golden & crimson leaves down a quaint old gothic tower of Magdalen College;—[64] clear from the topmost pinnacle it comes flooding down over pointed windows, & battered statues, & grotesque stone faces projecting from the wall—a wasteful, graceful, gorgeous little Niagara—& whosoever looks upon it will miss his train, sure.ₐ

What curious people customs officers are. Mr. Seymour of Hartford[65] was telling me this evening that after traveling all over Europe without having his luggage examined, he was stopped at the gates of Paris or some French port, & after rummaging among the thousand fancy things he had bought in various countries they passed the whole lot with demur till they came to [a] forlorn piece of Bologna sausage six inches long, & they charged him fifteen centimes on that! He wanted to make them a present of it—they wouldn't accept it. He insisted on their confiscating it—they wouldn't do it. Said if he didn't snake it off the ~~pres~~ premises & stop bothering, they'd have him arrested.

I believe the Dorè gallery has fascinated me more than anything I have seen in London yet. I spent the day there. The main feature is the enormous ~~pi~~ oil painting 20 by 30 feet, "Christ Leaving the Pretorium" (after judgment has been passed upon him.) What a marvelous creation it is! And how insignificant, & lifeless & artificial the works of almost <u>all</u> other artists are compared to its greatness & its <u>intense</u> <u>reality</u>. They don't seem to be mere representations of men & women, they seem alive.[66]

[64] Clemens inserted this entire paragraph in pencil on a page he had left blank and unnumbered in his notebook. He visited Magdalen College, Oxford, sometime between 29 September and 3 October 1872 (3 Oct 72 to OLC).

[65] Daniel F. Seymour, vice-president of the Hartford Life and Annuity Insurance Company ("Personal," Hartford *Courant*, 26 Oct 72, 2; Geer: 1870, 258; 1872, 119, 288).

[66] Clemens was fond of the work of French painter and book illustrator Gustave Doré (1833–83). In January 1870, shortly before his marriage to Olivia, he gave her an edition of Milton's *Paradise Lost* with pictures by Doré, and he later purchased several of his other illustrated editions. The Doré Gallery, which opened in 1869 at 35 New Bond Street, was until 1892 devoted entirely to the exhibition and sales of Doré's works. On 3 June 1872 the gallery advertised Doré's recently completed *Christ Leaving the Praetorium* with a quote from the artist himself, who called it "le plus grand effort de ma vie d'artiste" ("Doré's Great Work," London *Times*, 1). The painting was an immense critical and pop-

And to think that a man can paint the wind—you can look at the middle distance of this picture & see it blow!

It is the greatest work of art that ever I have seen—by long odds. Your first glance—your first sudden sweep of the eye, without taking note of details shows a vast crowd of life-size people, shouldering & struggling, swaying & crowding each other, fiercely, eagerly, anxiously, to get a sight of some important object, & no man caring who he hurts or crowds out so he gets the best view—hundreds & hundreds of these people—they fairly swarm ˌdown the sides &ˌ at the foot of a broad marble stairway, (on both sides of it)—the soldiers pressing them back with their halberts to keep the road clear in the middle—& they swarm on top of the spacious landing at the top of the stairs—a broad space between some stately, pillared temples—they fairly overflow the edges of the great landing—one girl, stands up conspicuously & leans so far over to get a sight that the touch of a feather would topple her over—they swarm among the pillars & the windows of the temples & crane their necks for a sight—they swarm to confusion the middle background—& all these turbulent, eager surroundings have their eyes fixed upon one majestic Figure in the centre of the stairway—clad in a flowing white garment—a figure that is a little isolated from the other people—a Figure with a glory about the head & such a divine sorrow in the face—a face that is saying only one thing, so long as you look—"Father, forgive them",." —they know And this general glance of the eye gives you a vague stately statue towering out of the crowd behind the Savior—& beyond that the murky fronts of further (though adjoining temples,)— murky with the coming storm—& statues pinnacled on the airy height of the porticoes, & that look about them of a strong wind blowing—& still beyond you catch a glimpse of a distant blue sky & the whitest & softest of tumbling, billowy clouds—& under them a little of ſ Jerusalem on a far hill, bathed in light.

When youʃ get your breath again, after this first grand surprise & astonishment, you come to consider details. Then you find that that mul-

ular success in London: "The Doré Gallery was crowded from morning to night; preachers, painters, connoisseurs, art-critics, press-men, and the public in general kept up a constant talk and excitement about the work" (Macchetta, 336–37). Ultimately, however, critics denounced this painting, as well as Doré's other works in oil, citing faults of color and composition and "mawkish and anecdotal" subject matter (Gosling, 26, 80; *L4*, 1; Gribben, 2:823; Macchetta, 330–32; Williamson, 2:82).

titude has in it Copts, Syrians, Jews, Romans, Greeks,—all sorts of nationalities—& clad in such a rich profusion of eastern costumes. Brilliant!—where the sun strikes the mass in the foreground it is as if it
clothed the multitude in rainbows. And the strength of those dark
faces!—the intense malignity & hate in many—the exultation in some—
the strong curiosity—the wonder, the excitement—& in some the pity,
the compassion—in some the grief—in some the broken heart speaking
from face & attitude. Caiaphas,[67] in exquisite vestments—a noble figure—almost at the Savior's elbow turns a sneering face upon him. Pilate,
in the background, is protesting that it is no work of his & he washes his
hands of the condemnation of this just man. Judas, off to one side, hangs
his head—the only man who is not trying to see the Savior. Near the foot
of the steps the three Marys[68]—the virgin, pale, stricken, helpless, hopeless, paralysed—the saddest face, the most pathetic face, that was ever
put upon canvas. It strongly reminds one of the Mater Dolorosa[69]—
seems almost a likeness of it—but it moves one more than that.

The Christ is the only Christ I ever saw that was divine, except Leo-
nardo da Vinci's.[70] When you look upon it you say, I always [thought]
that what one missed in a Christ's face was the absence of godlike intellect, but here I care not a straw whether it is absent or present—the real
thing necessary to portray a god is here—not inane gentleness, or sweet-
ness or namby-pamby want of spirit, but that divine forgiveness—all
mortal attributes, intellect, power, majesty, are poor & mean & human
in presence of it. It is the one thing that a mortal cannot have. Pictured
Christs are always exasperating—but one feels reconciled to this one—
one can say, this is not a man. Always I shall see that stately figure, moving among those lowering faces—I shall never forget it.

You may look that picture through—or any other of Dore's pictures—& you will never find an ungraceful attitude—every creature he
makes is as lithe & easy, & undulating, & just as natural & graceful and
picturesque as it can be.

The original studies for this great picture are there—there are

67 The Jewish high priest who presided at the trial of Jesus.
68 The Virgin Mary, Mary Magdalene, and Mary the mother of apostles James
and Joses.
69 Presumably Clemens meant the famous painting by Titian (1554), which
depicts the Virgin Mary mourning her son with her hands upraised.
70 Probably an allusion to da Vinci's masterpiece *The Last Supper* (1498).

four—& one can trace in them the unfolding of the conception from its half-formed crudity to its ripe perfection—& he never began his work till he had wrought a study that satisfied him. I could not beat it into an American that they were not copies of the big picture—he persisted in saying—"but they are not alike—they are all different—here in this one the fellows that are lugging the cross lug it one way, & they don't lug it the same way in any oth of the others; & in the big picture they don't lug it at all like they do in the small ones;—& in this little mud-colored one they are not even the same fellows that are lugging it in the others." I suppose that man will go through life worrying his poor soul about the discrepancies in the manner of "lugging" the Savior's cross.

This is the greatest picture that ever was painted—& has got more sense in it. And what do you think Doré was paid for it? A beggarly $31,500.[71] We pay Bierstadt $10,000 for his nightmares;[72] A. T. Stewart paid $20,000 for that vast artistic outrage that hangs in his house[73]—&, God forgive us, Congress paid $20,000 apiece for some of the horrors that hang in the Capitol[74]—to say nothing of the $10,000 paid to Vinnie

[71] Doré received £6,000 for the painting (Macchetta, 339).

[72] Painter Albert Bierstadt (1830–1902) was known primarily for his idealized western landscapes, many of which commanded high prices (Wilson and Fiske, 1:259–60).

[73] Alexander T. Stewart (1803–76), a wealthy New York merchant and philanthropist, had one of the most valuable art collections in the country in his two-million-dollar marble mansion on Fifth Avenue. Clemens was undoubtedly alluding to a "large work painted to Mr. Stewart's order, for $20,000," by French artist Adolphe Yvon (1817–93) ("The Art Gallery," New York *Times*, 12 Apr 76, 8). Completed in 1870 and exhibited in Paris the same year, the painting was "severely criticised by European critics, and the Paris correspondents of some American newspapers . . . made it the subject of unsparing ridicule." The work allegorically represented the thirty-four states of the Union, "grouped around the symbolic figure of the Republic, whose hand rests in that of Wisdom" ("The United States," *Harper's Weekly* 14 [9 July 70]: 440). Stewart himself was "not proud of" the unsuccessful work, hanging it in his bathroom instead of his art gallery ("The Art Gallery," New York *Times*, 12 Apr 76, 8; Kouwenhoven, 23, 372; H. Wilson 1872, 1162; Bénézit, 10:858). Clemens may well have seen an engraving of the picture printed in *Harper's Weekly* for 9 July 1870 (14:440–41).

[74] This opinion echoed one expressed in the "Editor's Easy Chair" in *Harper's New Monthly Magazine* for August 1872:

Is it because Congress thinks that nobody knows or can know any thing about art, or perceive differences between one picture or statue and another, that such extraordinary commissions are given? . . . On the east front of the Capitol is Persico's [statue of] Columbus, the most comical work in the world. . . . And in the old hall of the House of

Ream for her queer effigy of Lincoln contemplating with just indignation a folded napkin in his hand (intended to represent the Emancipation proclamation) & apparently saying, "Mrs. L., I can put up with a
good deal, but I will be d—d if I will pay 75 cents a dozen for any such
washing as that."[75]

If Doré had lived in the time of those infernal Old Masters the
people would have worshipped him. He would have utterly el eclipsed
that absurd Raphael, & he would have made it warm for the Rev. Michael
G. Angelo himself.[76] (Quotation from a critical American.)

A dapper Englishman about 30, came in & screwed a disk of window glass into his left eye & hove the rest of his face around it to hold it
there, & contemplated the imperial picture a moment & then said,
"Capetal, by Jove—capetal thing!" The English use that word constantly, & always pronounce it with fond distinctness—they apply it to
everything & use it on all occasions—but I never heard it before when
it seemed so preposterously out of place. The man who can stand up
before so grand a creation as the Christ Leaving the Pretorium & call it
a "capetal thing," would screw his window glass into his eye & admire
the day of judgment.

One fat, elderly, kindly old Englishwoman planted herself before
the picture & gazed upon it a quarter of an hour with the most absorbing
interest. There was nothing odd about that, of course—but all this time

---

Representatives is Mistress Vinnie Ream's Lincoln! In the Rotunda hangs Mr. [George
William H.] Powell's picture of De Soto discovering the Mississippi; and now there is
a proposition to buy another picture by the same hand. . . . During the winter a reso-
lution was offered to order a group of sculpture commemorative of the war. . . .
    Tens of thousands of dollars are to be paid for each of these pictures and statues. No
less than twenty-five thousand dollars have been appropriated for Mr. Powell's picture
of the battle of Lake Erie, and thirty thousand dollars was the pretty "figure" mentioned
for the sculpture. (Curtis, 461–62)

[75] Vinnie Ream (1847–1914) was a clerk in the Post Office Department in
Washington during the Civil War when she discovered her talent for clay mod-
eling. She "made a bust from sittings by LINCOLN. This bore such a striking
resemblance to LINCOLN that Congress ordered from her a statue of life size,"
which was unveiled on 25 January 1871 in the Rotunda of the Capitol. Ream
portrayed Lincoln with a "pensive expression," as if he were "burdened with
thought" ("The Lincoln Statue," New York *Times*, 26 Jan 71, 1). The statue
"met with a storm of adverse criticism which generally included the insinuations
that Miss Ream had not made it herself" (*NCAB*, 1:443; Fairman, 234–36).

[76] Raphael (or Raffaello) Santo (1483–1520); Michelangelo Buonarroti (1475–
1564).

she held a motionless little contemptible <u>poodle-dog</u> under her arm as if it were a book—held it there with its weak eyes blinking & its indolent legs hanging down. Finally she said, apparently to herself, "Well it's 'ansome," & waddled contentedly away, the gentle old goose. An old dowager, richly dressed, arrived in her coach, with an gorgeous footmen & coachman, a lavishly buttoned page & I don't know how many more accessories to nobility & greatness, & <u>she</u> came in to look. There is nothing strange about that—true enough, but the she was as blind as a bat! A Her servant piloted her around, carefully, saying all the time, "Take care, your ladyship, there is a chair bef in your way—be careful, your ladyship, here is a step"—& so on. And when they went out I heard the old lady say, "Well, I would have liked to see it, but I suppose there isn't much use in my coming to such places." I should think so. She absolutely could not have seen the picture if it had been at the end of her nose. But it is fashionable to visit the Doré gallery, & possibly that may excep account for the preposterous visit.

One man pointed to a large painting, & said, "I wonder what that is, now—oh, yes, I see; it is a jury—& a rum lot they are, too." It was about a dozen Carmelite friars sitting on a couple of benches, holding a religious service of some kind. If you can imagine the look of these robed & cowled & sandalled & shaven-pated old worthies, you will confess that as a petit jury, they <u>would</u> stand for "a rum lot."

All the fine array of great oil paintings in the gallery are by Doré— & one can look his head off & never get enough. They are all full of Doré—there is no need of his name being signed in the corner. One large picture represents a bit of prairie—just a little patch of its tall grasses & flowers the same as if you were standing in the midst—& consequently every little detail of every slender weed & flower is minutely represented, although there is an infinite profusion of them—& the gaudy butterflies—they are of every species. Very well, one may say, many artists could counterfeit a couple of square yards of prairie. True enough; but while they were filling your heart with the careless delight of the transfer from the smoky city to the charm & the solace of the tranquil field, & to the gentle companionship of the butterflies, would they startle you out of your pretty dreams with just a little touch of unobtrusive pathos? Such as, by and by, you all at once observe a <u>scythe</u> lying there half hidden by the luxuriant grasses! All beauty must fade—all that is precious must pass away—all that live must die. Who but Doré could have written so beautiful a sermon with such a simple little touch of the brush?[77]

You know Susie's picture of the child among the meadow grasses & flowers. That man could paint Doré's picture, but he would never think of that scythe—because <u>he</u> is a mere genius, but Doré is <u>inspired</u>.

I am afraid I shall never entirely enjoy a Doré engraving again. A Doré engraving is to the painted original as a fire-fly is to the sun, as a dull wooden image is to Cleopatra in the glory of life & ablaze with the splendors of oriental costume. True I have ordered ~~first-proof~~ artist's-proof No. 306 of the line engraving of the great Pretorium picture—price eighty dollars, gold,—but then it is going to take two years & a half to engrave it & by that time I shall be ready to prize <u>any</u> reminder of to-day's delight.[78]

The Pretorium is the <u>greatest</u> picture extant, but the strangest & the loveliest, is the Christian Martyrs. Scene, midnight; a vast Roman amphitheatre—the coliseum—no roof to it, of course—the stars glinting in the placid sky—the huge, gloomy array of circling seats tenantless, lifeless, solemn—in the centre of the arena, in a shadowy, soft twilight, a group of men & women mingled together in various attitudes of death, pain, ~~ex~~ insensibility, ~~&~~—all with a pathetic forsaken look about them—blood upon them & here & there upon the ground—gaunt imposing forms of lions & tigers tugging at them with their teeth—in the vague distances of the receding circle of the arena other such groups of men & beasts. And overhead comes floating silently down through the roofless edifice a wonderful vision of angels with outspread wings—of the most wierd, ethereal, pallid blue color—it is simply a rich, sheeny, bluish <u>glow</u>, in the loveliest, strangest contrast with the solemn twilight—& so ethereal, so substanceless, so spiritual are these wonderful forms that through the arms & wings of one angel <u>can be seen the</u> ~~body~~ <u>bodies of the others</u>. The huge dusky lions cast duskier shadows on the

---

[77] *The Prairie* (1867), measuring four by ten feet (Jerrold, 408).

[78] These artist's proofs were large prints (measuring twenty-two by thirty-three inches) of an engraving by Herbert Bourne, signed in pencil by Doré himself, for which the gallery charged £15 15s. In an unpublished manuscript, Clemens described a return visit he made to the gallery in September 1873, during which he told an importunate salesman that he had ordered an artist's proof of the painting "a year ago" (SLC 1873u; see 23 Sept 73 to Brooks, n. 1). The print did not retain its value: by 1918 it was worth only 35s. (Slater, 280–81).

ground, but in place of shadows the bodies of the angels send down rich pale emanations of bluish light—& where it falls, upon statues over the emperor's stall & upon the men & beasts in the centre of the arena, it suffuses them with an exquisite <u>suspicion</u> of luminosity. It is certainly the wierdest, the most unearthly, the most spiritual, the *l* most lovely & altogether the most deeply silent & impressive picture I have ever seen.[79]

I could describe in detail every picture in the gallery they so marvellously impressed themselves upon the vacancy which by courtesy I call my memory. And all the walls *&* are hung with Dorès original studies for his Tennyson[80] & other books—& how much more bewitching they are than the dead & soulless engravings.

Old Saint Paul's.[81]

Who can look upon this venerable edifice, with its clustering memories & old traditions, without emotion! Who can contemplate its scarred & blackened walls without drifting insensibly ~~in about &~~ ~~through~~ into dreams of the historic past! Who can hold to be trivial even the least detail or appurtenance of this stately national altar! It is with diffidence that I approach the work of description, it is with humility that I offer the thoughts that crowd upon me.

Upon arriving at Saint Paul's; the first thing that bursts upon the beholder/ˌattracts the beholder's attentionˌ is the back yard.[82] This ~~noble~~ fine work of art is forty-three feet long by thirty-four & a half feet wide— & all enclosed with real iron railings. The pavement is of fine oolite, or skylight, or some other stone of that geologic period, & is laid almost flat on the ground, in places. The stones are ~~almost~~ ˌexactlyˌ square, & it is thought that they were made so by design; though of course, as in all matters of antiquarian science, there are wide differences of opinion about this. The architect of the pavement was Morgan Jones, of No. 4,

---

[79] *Christian Martyrs—Reign of Diocletian* (1869 or 1870), a painting measuring about five by seven and one-half feet (Jerrold, 281–83, 408).

[80] *Idylls of the King, by Alfred Tennyson, Illustrated by Gustave Doré* (London: E. Moxon and Co., 1868).

[81] See 11 Sept 72 to OLC, n. 6.

[82] In the margin of his London guidebook, four pages after the section on St. Paul's Cathedral, Clemens noted, "Make a sham guide-book, for fun"—an intention he began to carry out in the passage that follows (Pardon, 79†). The names of the craftsmen are, of course, his own creation.

Piccadilly, Cheapside, Islington,̯–& He died in the reign of Richard III, of the prevailing disorder. An axe fell on his neck. The coloring of the pavement is very beautiful, & will immediately attract the notice of the visitor. Part of it is white & the other part black. The part that is white, has been washed. This was done upon the occasion of the coronation of George II, & the person who did it was knighted, as the reader will already have opined. The iron railings cannot be too much admired. They were designed & constructed by Ralph Benson, of No. 9, Gracechurch-street, Fenchurch-street, Upper-Terrace, Tottenham=court-road, Felter-lane, London, C. E., by special appointment black-smith to his royal Majesty, George III,[83] of gracious memory, & were done at his own shop, by his own hands, & under his own personal su-pervision. Specimens/ˌRelicsˏ of this greates artist's inspiration are ex-ceedingly rare, & are valued at enormous sums; however, two shovels & a horse-shoe made by him are on file at the British Museum, & no stranger should go away from London without seeing them. One of the shovels is undoubtedly genuine, but ~~many~~ ˌallˏ authorities ~~consider~~ ˌagree thatˏ the other one [is] spurious. It is not known which is the spu-rious one, & this is unfortunate, for nothing connected with this great man can be deemed of trifling importance. It is said that he was buried at Westminster Abbey, but was taken up & hanged in chains at Tyburn, ˌat the time of the restoration,ˏ under the impression that he was ¢ Crom-well. But this is considered doubtful, by some, because he was not ˌyetˏ born at the time of the restoration. The railings are nine feet three inches high, from the top of the stone pediment to the spear-heads ~~on th~~ that form the apex, & twelve feet four inches high from the ground to the apex, the stone pediment being three feet one inch high, all of solid stone. The railings are not merely stood up on the pediment, but are mortised in, in the most ravishing manner. It was originally intended to make the railings two inches higher than they are, but the idea was finally abandoned, for some reason or other. This is greatly to be regretted, be-cause it makes the fence out of proportion to the rest of ~~the~~ St Paul's, & seriously ˌmarsˏ the general effect. The spear-heads upon the tops of the railings were gilded upon the death of Henry VIII, out of respect for the memory of that truly great king. The artist who performed the work was knighted by the regency, & hanged by Queen Mary when she came into

[83] George II (1683–1760), crowned in 1727; George III (1738–1820), grandson and successor of George II.

power. No charge is made for contemplating the railings, or looking through them or climbing over them—which is in marked & generous contrast to some of the other sights of London. All you have to do is to apply to a member of the Common Council & get a letter to the Lord Mayor, ~~w~~ who will give you a note to the Lord High Chamberlain of the Exchequer, who will grant you a pass, good for two days, together with a return ticket. This is much simpler than the system observed by the custodians of some of the other sights of London. You can walk, but it is best to go in a cab, for there is no place in London which is less than two miles & a half from any other place. I am not speaking heedlessly, but from experience. At all the other public buildings & parks in London, there is an arched ,& prodigious, gateway which is special & sacred to the queen, who is ~~doubt~~ either sixty feet high or the gateways don't fit—but at St. Paul's the case is different. There is no special gate for the queen, & so I do not know how she gets in there. It ~~is~~ must be very inconvenient to go through a common highway when one is not used to it.

The stone ~~pede~~ pediment upon which the iron railings stand was designed & erected by William Marlow, of 14, ⌀ Threadneedle-street, Paternoster Row, St. Giles's, Belgravia, W. C., & is composed of alternate layers of rock, one above the other, & all cemented together in the most compact & impressive manner. The style of its architecture is a combination of the pre-raphaelite & the renaissance,—just enough of the pre-rapha[e]lite to make it firm & substantial, & just enough of the renaissance to ~~make the~~ impart to the whole a calm & gracious expression. There is nothing like this stone wall in England. We have no such artists now-a-days. To find true art, we must go back to the past. Let the visitor note the tone of this wall, & the feeling. No work of art can be intelligently & enjoyably contemplated unless you know about ~~the~~ tone & feeling; unless you know all about tone & feeling, & can tell at a glance which is the tone & which is the feeling—& can talk about it with the guide-book shut up. I will venture to say that there is more tone in that stone wall than was ever hurled into a stone wall before; & as for feeling, it is just suffocated with it. As a whole, this fence is absolutely without its equal. If Michael Angelo could have seen this fence, ~~If it~~ would ~~hav~~ he have wasted his years sitting on a stone worshiping the ~~Duomo of~~ cathedral of Florence? No; he would have spent his life gazing at this fence, & ~~wh~~ he would have taken a wax impression of it with him when he died. Michael Angelo & I may be considered extravagant, but as for me, if you simply mention art, I cannot be calm. I can go down on my knees before one of those decayed & venerable old Masters that you ⱪ have to put a sign on to tell which side of it you are looking at, & I do not want any bread, I do not want any meat, I do not want any air to breathe—I can live, in the tone & the feeling of it. Expression—expression is the thing—in art. I do not care what it expres[s]es, & I cannot most always sometimes tell, generally, but expression is what I worship, it is what I glory in, with all my impetuous nature. All ~~my traveling~~ the traveling world are just like me.

Ϯ Marlow, the architect & builder of the stone pediment I was speaking of, was the favorite pupil of the lamented Hugh Miller, & worked in the same quarry with him. Specimens of the stone, for the cabinet, can be easily chipped off by the tourist with his hammer, in the customary way. I will observe that the stone was brought from a quarry on the Surrey side, near London. ~~a trifling,~~ You can go either by Blackfriars bridge, or Ⱡ Westminster ᵬ bridge or the Thames tunnel[84]— fare, two shillings in a cab. It is best seen at sunrise, though many prefer moonlight.

The front yard of St Paul's is just like the back yard, except that it is adorned with a very noble & imposing statue of a black woman which is said to have resembled queen Anne, in some respects.[85] It is five feet four inches high from the top of the figure to the pedestal, & nine feet seven inches from the top of the ᵽ figure to the ground, the pedestal being four feet three inches high—all of solid stone. The figure measures eleven inches around the arm, & fifty three inches around the body. The rigidity of the drapery has been much admired.

I will not make any description of the rest of Old Saint Paul's, for that has already been done in every book upon London that has thus far been written, & therefore the reader must be measurably familiar with it. My only object is to instruct the reader upon matters which have been

---

[84] This twelve-hundred-foot tunnel, from Wapping on the north bank to Rotherhithe on the south, was designed by Marc Isambard Brunel (1769–1849). The world's first underwater tunnel, it took eighteen years to complete, opening to foot traffic in 1843. In 1865 it was closed to pedestrians and converted to railway use (Gascoigne, 96, 633, 636; Pardon, 151–52).

[85] Clemens's guidebook stated, "In the Yard facing the Western gate, the principal entrance, there is a full-length *Statue of Queen Anne*, supposed to be in white marble, but black with dust and grime, as, indeed, are many parts of the Cathedral" (Pardon, 75).

strangely neglected by other tourists; & if I have supplied a vacuum which must often have been painfully felt, my reward is sufficient. I have endeavored to furnish the exact ~~de~~ dimensions of everything in feet & inches, in the customary exciting way, & likewise to supply names & dates & gushingses upon art which will instruct the future tourist how to feel, & what to think, & how to tell it when he gets home.

Write up Bummer & Lazarus & Emperor Norton.[86]

Also Toole's park ranger that "had to keep himself up" (on about 17 meals a day.)[87]

A solemn waiter in a white neck-tie & a swallow-tailed coat offered the bill of fare, & I told him to select a dinner for me himself, & bring it—which he did. He stood by, & when I had begun to make fair progress, he tilted himself into a deferential attitude, & said impressively:

"I am afraid, sir, your soul is a tough one."

I laid down my knife & fork & looked at him a little surprised—& even hurt. I said:

"Although you are a stranger to me, I will not deny that it is not what it ought to be, though 'tough' is ~~pr~~ putting it rather strongly—but since you have offered the assertion, how should you know?"

[86] For several years in the early 1860s two vagrant dogs named Bummer and Lazarus roamed the streets of San Francisco; they became the town's pets, and were granted the freedom of the city by special ordinance. When Bummer died in November 1865 Clemens eulogized him in a letter to the Virginia City *Territorial Enterprise*, which survives as reprinted in the *Californian* (SLC 1865b). Joshua A. Norton (d. 1880) was a wealthy San Franciscan who became a kindly lunatic after losing his fortune in 1853, calling himself "Norton I, Emperor of the United States." He was supported for more than twenty years by the townspeople, who treated him with affectionate tolerance (*ET&S2*, 323; *L1*, 324–25 n. 2). On 3 September 1880 Clemens wrote to William Dean Howells:

> What an odd thing it is, that neither Frank Soulé, nor Charley Warren Stoddard, nor I, nor Bret Harte the Immortal Bilk, nor any other professionally literary person of S.F., has ever "written up" the Emperor Norton. Nobody has ever written him up who was able to see any but his ~~ludicrous or his~~ grotesque side; but I think that with all his dirt & unsavoriness there was a pathetic side to him. . . . I have seen him in *all* his various moods & tenses & there was always more room for pity than laughter. (MH-H, in *MTHL*, 1:326)

Clemens is not known to have written anything further about Bummer, Lazarus, or Emperor Norton.

[87] Unidentified.

"I "Oh, they're all tough that comes to this house here lately—awful tough, sir."

"Indeed,?", they are sir

"Indeed they are, sir. Now there's that lady at the next table—the fat one—she's got a soul that to it leather would be nowheres."

"It seems to me that you are not only a close observer, but rather personal. Do you know the character of all these people's souls?"

"Yes, sir. All tough."

"All tough. And mine along with the lot. Now if you had a soul as tough as mine, what would you do with it? You would not preach about a trouble without being able to suggest a remedy. As a lost man I ask you, what would you do with it,?"

"Do with it, sir? I'd burn it!"

"You would what?"

[*in top margin:* ["O, give a man time to knock a man down"—Sailor's song.)][88]

"My!"

"Yes indeed, sir, I'd burn it—roast it—nothing but roasting will tone down a real tough soul, sir."

"Well, you are orthodox, anyway. There are a very, very great many intelligent people that believe just as you do. But you wouldn't have me apply the process now?"

"Oh no, sir, by no means—it's too far gone."

"The mischief it is!"

"O, Yes indeed sir. It ought to been done sooner."

"Well, this goes ahead of anything I ever heard of. Perhaps it would have been better if I never had a soul?"

"Yes indeed, sir. Kidneys is much better, sir. If you'd a had 3 or 4 kidneys—"

"Monstrous heresy! Can a multiplicity of kidneys supply the place of a soul?"

"Some thinks they do, sir. Kidneys, with gravy on 'em?."

When the awful gloom of this stupendous proposition began to clear away, a gathering comprehension ,suspicion that there was a misapprehension somewhere,, worked its gradual way through. I said:

[88] A variant of the refrain of "Blow the Man Down," a nineteenth-century chantey (Palmer, 221–23; Hugill, 200).

"My friend, look me in the eye. What is the thing you refer to when you speak of my soul?"

"Why the fish, sir, on your plate!"

"Oh, now I understand. S-o-l-e, <u>sole</u>! To be sure. O, certainly. I was just chaffing you. I knew what you ~~meam~~ meant, all the time. S-o-l-e,╱ soul. Certainly, ~~le~~ certainly. We have plenty of them in America. We have all kinds—cork-soles, double-soles, half-soles, human soles—<u>all</u> kinds. ~~Bring me the kidneys, please.~~ Ah, yes—all kinds. You get <u>your</u> fish of this description from America. No explanations—no apologies—no discussion—debate is barred! Bring the kidneys, please."

I never had seen a sole before. I believe it is a fish that is not known in American seas. But it is a delicious creature, & as ~~ugly~~ ˏ"homely"ˏ as any human being that ever was born in salt water, except the cuttle-fish. The sole is ~~shaped like~~ flat, & is shaped like the sole of a shoe—hence the name. It is a one-sided fish like the skate, is white on its stomach side & ~~g~~ muddy-white on its back; & it probably spends all its time lying on the bottom of the ocean, like the other fishes of that ilk, till it is wanted. ~~I have eaten soles e~~ In the last month I have eaten soles enough to sandal a nation,ˏ or less. He is the most conveniently arranged fish I know of. He has his spine & radiating bones ~~just~~ laid neatly in the middle of his person, like a fern-spray in a hymn-book, & you just open him the same as if you were hunting for the page, & there you are. Lay that bony spray aside, trim off the selvedge edges of your soul (for they contain a comb of little bones), & all you have now got to do is to hurl the dainty into your system.

English breakfast,ˏ—tea, potatoes, bread, &,ˏ—what ˏmeat (cold)ˏ was left over from supper. ⟨ English luncheon—(at the B'way) boiled mutton or roast beef, & bread, (they ˏthe English)ˏ never bring butter on till they bring the cheese) sherry, claret, & ˏ"bitter-beer" (ale;)[89] English dinner—<u>every</u>thing, except <u>vegetables</u>; never have seen anything but tasteless boiled potatoes & those execrable French lentils on a British table. (I am perishing for some vegetables.) They serve hock, then sherry, then claret, & then they drop on to shampagne as a <u>steady</u> thing the rest of the way. They finish with a glass of old port, then maraschino,

[89]Clemens probably referred to lunches in "a private room up-stairs in the publishing house" of George Routledge and Sons, located on "The Broadway, Ludgate Hill" (p. 154; 28 Mar 73 to Bowen; *London Directory*, 198).

curaçoa, or some other digester whose name is strange to me & I have forgotten it. And along about here somewhere comes the cheese—the more stinkinger it is, the better—& with it little pats of butter; then black coffee. Then the ladies leave the table, the cloth is removed, & the gentlemen smoke cigars & sip brandy & water. I ~~dir~~ drink <u>nothing</u> but shampagne, & not much of that. I never have seen an English gentleman or lady even stirred out of their natural grave geniality & comfortableness by what they had drank. The children usually drink only one kind of wine, I believe, but they can choose that ˄one˄ themselves.

The origin of the custom of the ladies leaving the table ˄it is˄ said by some, was, that they might be out of reach of the brawls & violence that ensued anciently when the postprandial bowl went round. (Now <u>there</u> is an expression we all use just as naturally & easily—when the "<u>bowl</u> <u>went round</u>"—but none of us ever saw a bowl go round—we drink out of our own glass, & it remains by us. But I see what it comes from now—as illustrated by the ancient "loving-cup" at the Sheriff's dinner.) And it is said by others that it was done for a reason which shall not be specified. It is likely that both are right. Possibly it began for the first reason & was continued for the latter. Supper is sometimes a stately affair, when there is company, otherwise not. After a state dinner, they merely bring tea into the drawing room & pass it around, after the gentlemen have joined the ladies.

"Do you want to go up stairs & wash your hands?" (Mem.)

They have gas all over the dwellings, but not in hotel bedrooms. I ~~sen~~ They give you a candle five inches long, & so I send out & buy a ton & burn fifteen at a time. I endeavor to make the place cheerful. I think the chambermaids consider me a nice, pleasant sort of lunatic who will burn the house down, some time. But they <u>do</u> give you a power of coal on a cold day. In American ~~hold~~ hotels they send it to you in a spoon.

Livy, I am going to send that cloak to you in a day or two, instead of waiting to bring it myself. The weather will make you need it presently. Shall send it through Routledge & Sons of 416 Broome street, New York.[90]

I do like these English people—they are perfectly splendid—& so says every American who has staid here any length of time. Hans Breitmann has tried it a year & has taken up his residence permanently, he

---

[90] See 3 Oct 72 and 12 Oct 72 to OLC.

told me. ~~Geo~~ Judge Turner & family & Gov. Stanford's brother[91] & family hailed me from a box in the Lyceum theatre last night, where I had gone by invitation of Mr. Bateman, the manager to see the new piece Chas. I, which is faultlessly put on the stage but is a curious literary absurdity[92]—¢ the queen is with Charles a moment before the execution, instead of in France, & the king, instead of saying his ¢ mysterious & celebrated "Remember!" on the scaffold & to nobody in particular, says it as a sort of idiotic good-bye to his wife as he passes out of the fatal window of Whitehall![93] There are other queer al breaches of history & also of consistency in the piece, but I have forgotten, now, what they were.

A little actor who called in our box told me how he cured himself of consumption

[91] Leland Stanford (1824–93), governor of California from 1861 to 1863, was president of the Central Pacific Railroad. One of his older brothers, Asa Phillip (1822–1903), had been living in London since 1868. Born in New York State, he went to California in 1852 and engaged in selling general merchandise with his brothers, first in Sacramento and later in San Francisco, where they established the Pacific Oil and Camphene Works. In 1868 he withdrew from the firm and moved to London, where he remained for about five years before relocating to New York. His business in London has not been identified; according to one of his brothers he "was a stock operator in the mines"—perhaps an agent or broker (Stanford, 20; Tutorow, 20–23, 185; Langley: 1861, 267, 316; 1862, 306, 364; 1863, 337; 1864, 372; 1872, 613; "Brother of Stanford Dies in New York City," San Francisco *Morning Call*, 7 May 1903, 5; *London Directory*, 336, 2158).

[92] Hezekiah L. Bateman (1812–75) was born in Maryland and began his theatrical career as an actor, becoming manager of a St. Louis theater in 1855. After devoting several years to furthering the career of his daughter, actress Kate Bateman, he assumed the management of the Lyceum Theatre in London in 1870. On 28 September 1872 he opened his 1872–73 winter season with *Charles I*, a drama by William G. Wills, starring Henry Irving in the title role ("Lyceum Theatre," London *Times*, 30 Sept 72, 8; see 6 July 73 to Fairbanks, n. 6).

[93] Queen Henrietta Maria (1609–69) last saw her husband, Charles I, almost five years before his execution on 30 January 1849. Edmund Ludlow (1617–92) recorded in his *Memoirs* that the king, who was beheaded in front of the palace at Whitehall, stepped onto the scaffold from a window in a small building north of the banqueting house (Timbs, 834).

Appendix D

Book Contracts

Revised Contract for Diamond Mine Book

WHEN IT BECAME clear that John Henry Riley was too ill to collaborate with Clemens on a book about the African diamond fields, Elisha Bliss wrote a new contract between Clemens and the American Publishing Company, revising the terms of the existing contract of 6 December 1870 (see *L4*, 566–68). Clemens's copy was prepared from Bliss's original by an amanuensis, then corrected by Bliss, and signed on 22 June 1872 by both Clemens and Bliss; it is in the Mark Twain Papers (CU-MARK) and is transcribed below. Bliss's copy is in the Beinecke Rare Book and Manuscript Library, Yale University (CtY-BR). There are several trivial variants between the two copies; they have not been recorded.

❦

 This Agreement entered into on the twenty second day of June 1872 by the American Publishing Company of the City of Hartford ˏConn.ˏ as party of the first part and Samuel L. Clemens ˏof same city & stateˏ as party of the second part witnesseth that whereas a certain contract for the writing of a book by the sd party of the second part and to be published by the said party of the first part was entered into by both parties by̶ ˏinˏ a written agreement dated Dec 6ᵗʰ 1870 and whereas a part of said contract has been fulfilled viz so much of it as related to the sending of the party to Africa by the said Clemens and also that portion of it which related to the advance of $2000. to sd Clemens by sd company and whereas circumstances render it doubtful whether the information to be received from Mr J. H Riley the party sent to Africa will on account of his ill health be sufficient to enable the sd ¢Clemens to write a book on the subject, or if ˏitˏ is sufficient for that purpose whether it will be sufficient for him to write a book which he will be satisfied to put his own nom de plume (Mark Twain) to, now it is agreed by the parties hereto that sd Clemens shall have the privilege of substituting the following agreement in the place of those in sd contract. To wit. He shall go on and write up the book as proposed on the Diamond Fields if it is possible to do it, and if he shall conclude to substitute another name as its author for his nom-de-plume (Mark Twain) then the copyright on said book shall be 5% instead of 8½% to be paid him; and in that case the sd Clemens in consideration of this privilege and of the following further agreements on the part of the American Publishing Co shall write for them another book to follow the *Diamond Fields* book on such subject as may be mutually agreed upon,, Ţthe manuscript for which shall be ready within a reasonable time after the issue of the other it being understood that the sd Clemens shall go to work upon it without unnecessary delay after the other book is ready and devote his time to its preparation. This book to have the nom de plume of (Mark Twain) on its title page as author and the sd Company shall pay for such book to said Clemens a copyright of 10% per cent. The $2000. advanced already by said company under provision of the contract of Dec 6 1870 to be repaid to said company by their deducting it from the 1st copyright coming sd to the sd Clemens on sd books.

In case the health of sd Riley should be such as to render it utterly impossible for the said Clemens to write the book on the Diamond Fields at all, then he shall be freed from his agreement to write a book on that subject but shall proceed to prepare the other book at once—viz the one upon which he is to appear as author and on which he is to receive 10% copyright. It is understood the Diamond Fields Book is to be written if practicable & in no wise shall the information or memorandum given by sd Riley go into the hands of other parties. All other agreements, provisions[,] exemptions, restrictions, specifications as to size of books[,] time of payment of copyright &c ,&c, contained in said contract of Dec 6th 1870 to apply to both of above mentioned books and to remain in force under this new agreement.

All matters of difference as to ,the, meaning or private understanding of contracts heretofore made between sd. parties are hereby settled and adjusted and such contracts are recognized and agreed to be valid on their face & satisfactory to all parties as they stand.

[*in Bliss's hand:*]
Should the said Clemens write the book on the Diamond Fields under his own nom-de-plume as arranged for in the contract of December 6th 1870. then the book is to be published by sd Company under that contract & on the terms specified therein

It is agreed that while either of the above books are being written, published & sold that the sd Clemens shall not furnish manuscript to any other party for any other book or allow his name to be used as author on any other book until such time as the publication of another book with his name shall not be an injury to the sale of either of the above mentioned books.

Saml. L. Clemens

E. Bliss Jr Sy

The Mss for book contracted for by within Contract by S. L Clemens has been delivered to us—& entitled "Tom T Sawyer"

Am Pub Co

per E Bliss Jr pres[1]

[*on back as folded:*]

Contract between

Am Pub. Co

&

S L Clemens

June 22. 1872

[1] Elisha Bliss succeeded E. G. Hastings as president of the American Publishing Company in 1873, probably at the annual meeting of the company in early April, not by July 1870 as previously stated (*L4*, 127 n. 1). Frank Bliss became secretary as well as treasurer. By 1 May the company's letterhead stationery reflected the change. Bliss, however, did not add this endorsement to Clemens's contract until late June 1879, when the stipulations of the diamond mine contracts of 1870 and 1872 were finally resolved. Clemens instructed his lawyer, Charles Perkins, to offer *Tom Sawyer* (published in 1876) as a substitute for the never-written diamond mine book, and to have the American Publishing Company "endorse all my contracts as completed & deduct $2000 from copyrights now due, in satisfaction of the Riley debt" (10 June 79 to Francis E. Bliss [1st], WU, in *MTLP*, 116). Perkins replied on 26 June, "I have had the Am Pub Co. indorse on all the contracts with you that your part thereof has been performed" (CU-MARK; Elisha Bliss, Jr., to SLC, 1 May 73, CU-MARK; Geer: 1870, 57; 1871, 123, 282; 1872, 34, 288; 1873, 34, 291).

[*in the hand of Charles Perkins:*]
Tom Sawyer
===

[*in pencil:*]

2nd Riley
in place of African Contract

Contract for the American Publishing Company Gilded Age

On 8 May 1873 Elisha Bliss produced an original and two copies of a contract for *The Gilded Age* between coauthors Clemens and Warner and the American Publishing Company. Clemens's copy, signed by all three men, is in the Mark Twain Papers (CU-MARK); it is transcribed below. Warner's copy is in the Henry W. and Albert A. Berg Collection, New York Public Library (NN-B). Bliss's draft is in the Beinecke Rare Book and Manuscript Library at Yale (CtY-BR). There are numerous insignificant variants between the three copies; they have not been recorded here. Bliss's copy, however, does include two important addenda. On the last page Bliss wrote—almost certainly in 1879, when he thus endorsed all of Clemens's contracts—"The mss. on this contract has been delivered to us" (see the previous contract, n. 1). In addition, Bliss's copy is accompanied by an undated endorsement on a separate sheet, probably also written in 1879—but certainly sometime after March 1875, when Clemens delivered the manuscript for *Mark Twain's Sketches, New and Old*, contracted for on 29 December 1870 (*ET&S1*, 621):

> We have received from S. L. Clemens the Mss. for book contracted for in contract dated Dec. 29—1870—& also recd from S L Clemens & C Dudley Warner, the Mss for book contracted for in contract dated May 8. 1873—& we have endorsed the receipt by us of same on the respective contracts—
>   There is no contract existing between S. L. Clemens & the Am. Pub Co. for a book or books, made prior to the latest above mentioned dates, on which the mss. contracted for has not been delivered to us.
>
> Am Pub Co
per E Bliss Jr prest

Despite Bliss's statement above that he had "endorsed the receipt" of the manuscripts on their "respective contracts," Clemens's copy of the *Gilded Age* contract carries no such endorsement.

❦

This agreement made between Samuel L. Clemens & Charles Dudley Warner both of City of Hartford & State of Connecticut as parties of the first part & The American Publishing Co. of said city of Hartford as party of the second part Wittnesseth—

The said parties of the first part, being the authors of a manuscript for a proposed book, to be called *"The Gilded Age"*; in consideration of the agreements hereinafter made by the party of the second part, stipulate to furnish to the said party of the second part the said manuscript as soon as they desire it, in sufficient quantity to make a volume of about 600 pages printed octavo pages (small pica) & that they will not use or suffer any portion of the matter of said mss. to be used by others, but give the said party of the second part full control of it with full & exclusive right to publish the same so long as they the said party of the second part shall fulfill their part of this contract, & the copyright of said matter, having been or to be taken out in the names of said authors, it shall be held by them subject to their stipulations in this contract. The said party of the first part also agree to do all necessary proof reading & render other or-dinary & usual assistance in bringing out the book, & to give all possible aid in its sale—

The party of the second part agrees to publish said book as soon as practicable for them to do so, commencing upon the work without un-necessary delay. The book is to be after the style of "The Innocents Abroad" & to equal it in the quality of its paper, binding, engravings & printing— The engravings inserted to be mutually acceptable to the said Warner & to E. Bliss Jr. Prest. of said American Publishing Co.

The said party of the second part also agrees to use their best efforts to sell said book, to print & distribute among their agents notices of the book, reviews &c & in large cities they shall instruct their agents to use introductory cards & or circulars stating the object of their visit—

A sheet of extracts to be sent with copy of the book to editors, said extracts to be selected by the said Warner who shall also furnish a list of newspapers, from which he in connexion with the said E. Bliss. Jr. shall select such as they may deem proper, (say 500 more or less as they may agree,) to whom the said party of the second part shall within 12 months from issue of the book send free copies at their own expense, with sheets of extracts, Copies of the book with extracts to be sent to the leading papers and periodicals of the great cities from first edition printed—

And the party of the second part farther agrees to pay to the parties of

the $ first part a royalty upon all books sold, of *Ten* per cent on the sub-
scription price, one half of said sum or *Five* (5) per cent of the same to
be paid to the said Clemens, and one half or *Five* (5) per cent of the same
to be paid to the said Warner, a statement of sales & settlement of royalty
to be made every three months after the issue of the book, said settlement to be made at office of said Company or sent upon the order of the
respective parties.

No royalty is to be paid upon any book given by said party of the second part or their agents to editors or others to advance the sale of the of
the book—a list of such gifts to be rendered to parties of the first part if
it is required by them—

It is farther agreed that no books shall be issued to any party (except
to editors as above provided, to parties for reviews & reccommendation—and to agents as sample copies to canvass with)—until enough are
printed & bound to fill all orders on hand at once unless it be with the
consent of said Warner.

This contract executed
at Hartford May 8. 1873.   Sam*. L. Clemens.
                                          Chas. D. Warner
                                          E Bliss Jr. prest.
                                          American Publishing Co.

[*on back as folded, in the hand of Charles Perkins:*]
Agreement as to Golden Age

S. L. Clemens Copy
Gilded Age

May 8ᵗʰ 1873

Contract for the *Routledge* Gilded Age

The contract for the English edition of *The Gilded Age* was signed in
London on 18 October 1873, just two days before Clemens left London.
Clemens's copy of the contract has not been found. Warner's copy, which
is in the Watkinson Library, Trinity College, Hartford (CtHT-W), was
signed by the Routledges and by Clemens, whose signature was wit-

nessed at the Langham Hotel by Ellen Bermingham, Susy's nursemaid. This copy was then sent to Hartford, where Warner added his signature, witnessed by his brother George. The Routledges' copy, signed only by Clemens "for himself & Chas Dudley Warner," is in the company archives (Routledge and Kegan Paul, London), and is transcribed below. There are a number of trivial variants between the two copies; they have not been recorded.

🌿

An Agreement made on the ˏ18ᵗʰˏ day of ˏOctoberˏ One thousand eight hundred and seventy three[1] between Samuel Langhorne Clemens (who is better known to the Public as "Mark Twain[ʺ]) now of Hartford Connecticut in the United States of America ₍₍Author) on behalf of himself and Charles Dudley Warner ₍₍also of Hartford aforesaid Author) of the one part and George Routledge, Robert Warne Routledge, Edmund Routledge, and William Routledge[2] all of the Broadway Ludgate Hill in the City of London Wholesale Booksellers and publishers (who are hereinafter referred to as "George Routledge and Sons") of the other part   Whereas the said Samuel Langhorne Clemens and Charles Dudley Warner are about to write a new and original Book or work to be entitled "The Gilded Age" or some equally suitable name   And whereas the said Samuel Langhorne Clemens and Charles Dudley Warner have proposed to sell to the said George Routledge and Sons the exclusive copyright in and right to publish the said work when completed in Great Britain the Dominion of Canada and The British Colonies and Dependencies at the price and upon the conditions hereinafter appearing   Now it is hereby agreed that the said Samuel Langhorne Clemens doth for himself and the said Charles Dudley Warner, hereby

[1] The Routledges apparently prepared this contract in 1873 sometime before 18 October and later inserted the day and month in the first line. It could not, however, have been drafted when Clemens and Warner were "about to write . . . 'The Gilded Age,' " as stated later in this paragraph. They began the book in late December 1872 or early January 1873, but did not give it a title until April (17? Apr 73 to Reid, n. 1; 21 Apr 73 to Spofford).
[2] William Routledge, whose name appeared on company contracts in the mid-1870s, was probably, like Edmund and Robert, one of the eight children of George Routledge's first marriage. George's brother William, a clergyman and headmaster, was not connected with the firm (Mumby, 9–10, 97–98; *Routledge Archives*).

agree with the said George Routledge and Sons their executors administrators and assigns And the said George Routledge and Sons do hereby agree with the said Samuel Langhorne Clemens and Charles Dudley Warner in manner following that is to say

1. The said Samuel Langhorne Clemens and Charles Dudley Warner shall as soon as possible write and the said George Routledge and Sons ˏshallˏ on fulfilment of the second clause herein on the part of the said Samuel Langhorne Clemens and Charles Dudley Warner contained print and publish the above mentioned work of such suitable size and appearance as they shall consider to be adapted to the British public.

2. Three weeks at least before the said Work or any part thereof shall be published in America or elsewhere the said Samuel Langhorne Clemens and Charles Dudley Warner shall provide the said George Routledge and Sons with a complete copy of the manuscript of the said work ready in all respects for immediate publication and such period of three weeks shall date from the actual delivery of the said Copy ˏManuscriptˏ to the said George Routledge and Sons.

3. The types for the introduction text and notes respectively the quality of the paper and the mode of binding of the said work shall be such as may be considered by the said George Routledge and Sons their executors administrators or assigns as best adapted for the purpose

4. The said George Routledge and Sons their executors administrators and assigns shall bear the whole expense and risk of the paper and printing of the said work and of the publication thereof and shall be entitled to the entire copyright thereof in Great Britain and Ireland the Dominion of Canada the Colonies and Dependencies of the British Empire at or for the price or consideration mentioned in the eighth clause of this agreement.

5. In order to secure such copyright to the said George Routledge and Sons the said Samuel Langhorne Clemens and Charles Dudley Warner shall arrange with them on what day the said work shall be first published in England and three days before such day shall go to and from thence until four days after such day shall reside in some part of the Dominion of Canada or some other parts of the British Empire to be previously agreed upon by the parties hereto

6. Immediately after the publication of the said work the said Samuel Langhorne Clemens and Charles Dudley Warner shall make a solemn declaration before some competent authority of the fact of their having so resided during such seven days in the Dominion of Canada or such other part of the British Empire as aforesaid and shall forthwith sign and forward to the said George Routledge and Sons the documents necessary to procure the entry of their names as Proprietors of the copyright in the said work in the Books kept at Stationers' Hall in the City of London and for assigning their copyright therein to the said George Routledge and Sons pursuant to the thirteenth section of the 5 and 6 Vic: Cap:45.[3]

7. The said George Routledge and Sons ‸their executors administrators and assigns‸ shall (if and so long as the said copyright shall be obtained and exist) introduce and make known the said work to their Customers and the Public by including the same in their several Catalogues of books published by them and shall otherwise promote the Sale of the said work in such manner as they shall deem most expedient and also shall (if and so long as the said copyright shall be obtained and shall exist) keep just and true accounts of all copies of the said work which shall be sold and disposed of by them and of the times when the same shall be sold and also from time to time on the thirtieth day of June and the thirtieth day of December in every year or within seventy eight days after each of the said days make out and render to the said Samuel Langhorne Clemens and Charles Dudley Warner true and correct statements and accounts of the number of the said Copies of the said work which shall have been sold by the said George Routledge and Sons their executors administrators or assigns during the six calendar months immediately preceding each of the said days and the prices at which the same shall have been sold

8. The said George Routledge and Sons their executors administrators or assigns shall (if and so long as the said Copyright shall be

[3] The Literary Copyright Act passed by Parliament in 1842 (Copinger, 18–19, xxi–xxxv). Clemens and Warner evidently considered traveling to Canada to fulfill this copyright requirement. Sometime in the spring of 1873 they drew up a formal document to attest to their residency there, leaving spaces to be filled in later with the date and place of their sojourn. This document remained incomplete and unsigned (CtHT-W; French, 259–60, 339 n. 4).

obtained and shall exist) pay or cause to be paid to the said Samuel
Langhorne Clemens and Charles Dudley Warner within three calendar months after each thirtieth day of June and thirtieth day of
December on receiving their approval of the accounts rendered to
those days respectively a sum equal to twenty per cent on the retail
price of all copies of the said work which shall have been sold by
them during the period in respect of which the aforesaid statements or accounts shall have been rendered if the retail price or
sum shall have exceeded ten shillings for each copy and a sum equal
to ten per cent on the retail price of all copies of the said work which
shall have been sold by them during the like period at a retail price
of ten shillings or under for each copy—for the purpose of such
accounts every thirteen copies sold shall be counted as twelve and
the respective per centage above mentioned shall be paid only on
twelve

9. In case the exclusive right of the said George Routledge and Sons
    their executors administrators and assigns to publish the said Work
    in Great Britain the Dominion of Canada and the British Colonies
    and Dependencies shall at any time be called in question or dis-
    puted in any action suit or proceeding at law or in Equity which
    may be brought or commenced by or against the said George Rout-
    ledge and Sons their executors administrators or assigns in respect
    thereof the per centage payable to the said Samuel Langhorne
    Clemens and Charles Dudley Warner by the last preceding clause
    shall thereupon immediately cease to be payable until the said right
    of the said George Routledge and Sons shall have been fully
    established.

10. The said George Routledge and Sons shall be at liberty to use the
    names or name of the said Samuel Langhorne Clemens and Charles
    Dudley Warner or either of them their or either of their executors
    and administrators or the name "Mark Twain" in promoting the
    sale of the said work or in any proceedings at Law or in equity
    which may be brought by or against them in consequence of any
    infringement of the said copyright. The said George Routledge
    and Sons their executors administrators and assigns effectually in-
    demnifying and saving harmless the said Samuel Langhorne
    Clemens and Charles Dudley Warner their executors administra-

tors and assigns of and from all costs losses charges and expences which may be incurred by them by reason of such proceedings.

11. The said Samuel Langhorne Clemens and Charles Dudley Warner their executors administrators and assigns shall ˌat any time or times hereafter˰ (if and so long as the said copyright shall be obtained and exist) at the request and costs of the said George Routledge and Sons their executors administrators or assigns or any of them execute such a deed of Assignment of the said copyright (which Deed shall contain all of the foregoing provisions which may then be applicable and all covenants which are usually entered into in assignments of a like nature) and do such other acts for effectually assuming the said copyright to the said George Routledge and Sons their executors administrators and assigns as may by them be reasonably required   In witness whereof the said parties have hereunto set their hands.

                                        Sam*ˡ*. L. Clemens
                        for himself & Chas Dudley Warner.

Witness:
   Ellen Bermingham[4]

[4]Clemens not only signed his name for himself and Warner, he wrote "Witness:" above Ellen (Nellie) Bermingham's signature. The Clemenses hired Nellie as a nursemaid in May 1872, and took her with them to England in May 1873. She left their employ in January 1874, "amicably," according to Olivia, "on account of her sister's health (the sister will not probably live longer than March)—but I assure you I was not sorry to have her go, and from things Margaret has said I know that she was disrespectful about me in the kitchen" (OLC to MEC, 11 and 14 Jan 74, NPV). Olivia apparently maintained some contact with Bermingham for several years: a notebook she used in 1878 and 1879 to record gifts and purchases listed "Nellie Birmingham" below the names of current household staff (OLC; *N&J2*, 42–43; 17 May 72 to Moffett; 17 May 73 to Langdon, n. 1).

Appendix E

Preface to the Routledge Gilded Age

CLEMENS WROTE Olivia on 13 December 1873, "I have been writing after-dinner speeches & a preface for the book," referring to *The Gilded Age*, which Routledge and Sons would publish in England on 22 December: "Read proof of the preface this evening. I state some plain facts in it,—so I have appended a postscript to say that Warner isn't to blame, because he don't know what I am writing" (13 and 15 Dec 73 to OLC). Robert Routledge noted on the following day, "The preface came to hand to-day & is now in the printers' hands" (12 Dec 73 to Routledge, n. 2). The text transcribed below appeared in the first volume of the three-volume English edition. Clemens evidently revised it after writing to Olivia, since it contains no "postscript" exonerating Warner.

🍂

AUTHOR'S PREFACE TO THE LONDON EDITION.

IN America nearly every man has his dream, his pet scheme, whereby he is to advance himself socially or pecuniarily. It is this all-pervading speculativeness which we have tried to illustrate in "The Gilded Age." It is a characteristic which is both bad and good, for both the individual and the nation. Good, because it allows neither to stand still, but drives both for ever on, toward some point or other which is a-head, not behind nor at one side. Bad, because the chosen point is often badly chosen, and then the individual is wrecked; the aggregation of such cases affects the nation, and so is bad for the nation. Still, it is a trait which it is of course better for a people to have and sometimes suffer from than to be without.

We have also touched upon one sad feature, and it is one which we found little pleasure in handling. That is the shameful corruption which lately crept into our politics, and in a handful of years has spread until the pollution has affected some portion of every State and every Territory in the Union.

But I have a great strong faith in a noble future for my country. A vast majority of the people are straightforward and honest; and this late state of things is stirring them to action. If it would only keep on stirring them until it became the habit of their lives to attend to the politics of the country personally, and put only their very best men into positions of trust and authority! That day will come.

Our improvement has already begun. Mr. Tweed (whom Great Britain furnished to us), after laughing at our laws and courts for a good while, has at last been sentenced to thirteen years' imprisonment, with hard labour.[1] It is simply bliss to think of it. It will be at least two years before any governor will dare to pardon him out, too. A great New York judge, who continued a vile, a shameless career, season after season, defying the legislature and sneering at the newspapers, was brought low at last, stripped of his dignities, and by public sentence debarred from ever again holding any office of honour or profit in the State.[2] Another such judge (furnished to us by Great Britain) had the grace to break his heart and die in the palace built with his robberies when he saw the same blow preparing for his own head and sure to fall upon it.[3]

MARK TWAIN.

THE LANGHAM HOTEL,
LONDON, *Dec.* 11th, 1873.

[1] Tweed, whose great-grandfather emigrated from Scotland, was convicted on 19 November 1873 and sentenced to twelve years' imprisonment and a fine of $12,750 (see Appendix B, enclosure with 6 Jan 73 to Reid, n. 17; New York *Evening Express:* "The Tweed Verdict," 19 Nov 73, 3; "The Sentence," 24 Nov 73, 4).

[2] George G. Barnard (see Appendix B, enclosure with 6 Jan 73 to Reid, n. 16).

[3] John H. McCunn (1824–72), an Irish immigrant, was elected judge of the Superior Court of New York City in 1864. He was removed from the bench in July 1872 for "malfeasance in office." He died a few days later, reportedly of nervous and physical prostration, in his modest three-story brick house on West Twenty-first Street. He also owned a "fine country residence in New Jersey" and an estate in Ireland, in addition to a "fortune estimated at $3,000,000" ("Death of Ex-Judge McCunn," Buffalo *Courier,* 8 July 72, 1; "Obituary," New York *Tribune,* 8 July 72, 8; Hershkowitz, 229–30).

Appendix F

Photographs and Manuscript Facsimiles

REPRODUCED HERE are thirty-six contemporary images, many of them never before published, of Samuel and Olivia Clemens and their families, friends, associates, and places of residence during the period of these letters. Immediately following these images are six of Clemens's holograph letters, reproduced in facsimile. We provide these documents partly for their inherent interest, and partly to afford readers a chance to see for themselves what details of the manuscript the transcription includes, as well as what it omits. Because of the imperfect nature of these facsimiles, close comparison with the transcription may turn up apparent discrepancies between the two.

Olivia L. Clemens, 1872 or 1873. Photograph by Horace L. Bundy, Hartford. Mark Twain House, Hartford, Connecticut (CtHMTH).

Langdon Clemens, 1872 (aged eighteen months). From Olivia L. Clemens's photograph album, pages 15 and 24. Huntington Library, San Marino, California (CSmH).

Olivia Susan (Susy) Clemens, 1872 (aged six and one-half months). From Olivia L. Clemens's photograph album, page 14. Huntington Library, San Marino, California (CSmH).

Samuel L. Clemens, September 1872. Photograph by Charles Watkins, London. "Mr. Sandifer" has not been identified (see 13–18 Sept 72 to Osgood, n. 3). Mark Twain Papers, The Bancroft Library (CU-MARK).

Samuel L. Clemens, 1872. Photograph probably by Charles Watkins, but not from the same sitting as the image to the left. Printed on an oval silk doily with looped fringe (see the frontispiece). Mark Twain Papers, The Bancroft Library (CU-MARK).

Langham Hotel, London. From a postcard in the Mark Twain Papers, The Bancroft Library (CU-MARK).

Henry Lee. Photograph possibly by
Charles Watkins in 1872. Printed
on an oval silk doily identical to
Clemens's (previous page, top right).
Mark Twain Papers, The Bancroft
Library (CU-MARK).

John L. Toole. Photograph possibly
by Charles Watkins in 1872. Printed
on a doily identical to Lee's and
Clemens's, above. Mark Twain
Papers, The Bancroft Library
(CU-MARK).

Charles Godfrey Leland (Hans
Breitmann) (London *Graphic*,
5 Oct 72, 324).

Samuel L. Clemens, 12 September 1872. Photographs by W. and A. H. Fry, Brighton. Mark Twain Papers, The Bancroft Library (CU-MARK).

Henry Lee, Samuel L. Clemens, and Edmund Routledge, 12 September 1872. Photograph by W. and A. H. Fry, Brighton. Addressed on the verso to Olivia (see 5 Oct 72 to Fitzgibbon, n. 4). Henry Lee autographed his picture, but Routledge signed Clemens's name and Clemens signed Routledge's, presumably as a prank. Two other prints of this photograph survive in the Mark Twain Papers, one signed only by Lee and one autographed correctly by all three men. Mark Twain Papers, The Bancroft Library (CU-MARK).

Nasr-ed-Din, shah of Persia (*Harper's Weekly* 17 [12 July 73]: 616).

Edmund Yates, early 1880s (Yates 1885, frontispiece).

George MacDonald (*Scribner's Monthly* 2 [May 71]: frontispiece).

Henry Watterson (*Harper's Weekly* 16 [6 July 72]: 525).

"AMERICAN HUMOUR."

Caricature of Samuel L. Clemens by Frederick Waddy for the London magazine *Once a Week* (14 Dec 72, 519; *MTH*, 188–89; Houfe, 487). The brief accompanying biography called Mark Twain the "best living exponent of American humour" (521).

Joaquin Miller, 1874. Inscribed
to Walt Whitman (Traubel,
facing 49).

James R. Osgood, 1870s? (Howells 1900, facing 122).

Mary Anne Hardy (Black, facing 198).

Iza Duffus Hardy (Black, facing 204).

Sir Charles Dilke (*Harper's Weekly* 16 [20 Apr 72]: 317).

Reginald Cholmondeley, 1860s? Mark Twain Papers, The Bancroft Library (CU-MARK).

Moncure D. Conway, 1870s? (Conway 1904, facing 1:108).

Henry M. Stanley (*Harper's Weekly* 16 [27 July 72]: 581).

Shirley Brooks (*Illustrated London News*, 7 Mar 74, 225).

Tom Hood (*Once a Week*, 3 Aug 72, 101).

Samuel L. Clemens, 1873. Photograph by Rogers and Nelson, London. Inscribed to Charles Warren Stoddard. Mark Twain Papers, The Bancroft Library (CU-MARK).

Samuel L. Clemens, 1873. Photograph by Rogers and Nelson, London. "Copyright" is written in an unidentified hand. Mark Twain House, Hartford, Connecticut (CtHMTH).

Samuel L. Clemens, 1873. Photograph by Rogers and Nelson, London. Inscribed on the verso to Lilian W. Aldrich. "Copyright" is written in an unidentified hand. Houghton Library (Autograph file), Harvard University, Cambridge, Massachusetts (MH-H).

661

Clara Spaulding with Olivia Susan (Susy) Clemens in her lap, Olivia L. Clemens, Samuel L. Clemens, and John Brown, August 1873. Photograph by John Moffat, Edinburgh. Inscribed by Clemens. Mark Twain House, Hartford, Connecticut (CtHMTH).

Olivia L. Clemens, 1872 or 1873. Photo-
graph by Prescott and White, Hartford.
Mark Twain Papers, The Bancroft Library
(CU-MARK).

Samuel E. Moffett, early 1870s. Photo-
graph by S. S. Washburn, Louisville,
Kentucky. Mark Twain Papers, The
Bancroft Library (CU-MARK).

Olivia Susan (Susy) Clemens, August
1873 (aged seventeen months). Photograph by John Moffat, Edinburgh. Mark
Twain Papers, The Bancroft Library
(CU-MARK).

Clemens to Jane Lampton Clemens, 11 June 1871, postscript, Elmira, N.Y. Collection of Chester L. Davis, Jr. Manuscript scrap 10, recto and verso, reproduced at 78 percent of actual size. Transcribed on p. 689. The body of the letter, written on the rectos and versos of nine scraps, was transcribed and photographically reproduced in *L4*, 403–5, 581–84.

FENWICK HALL.

D. A. Rood, Proprietor.

New Saybrook, Conn., Jul 30 1872

Dear Mollie —

The Satchel arrived.
But we are often on short
allowance of condensed
milk. Send us about 10
cans, now, & after that send
us a can or two whenever you
send clothes — & this will
keep us supplied.

All flourishing.

Yr's aff
Sam

Clemens to Mary E. (Mollie) Clemens, 30 July 1872, New Saybrook, Connecticut. Mark Twain Papers, The Bancroft Library (CU-MARK). Transcribed on p. 136; reproduced at 75 percent of actual size.

m on this page)
plagiarist, but I'm not sure that the author
g page 637 of the "Innocents Abroad," at
a deliberate plagiarism is seldom made by
any person who is not an ass; but unconscious &
blameless plagiarisms are made by the best of people
every day: Considering the fact that billions of people have
been thinking & writing every day for 5 or 6,000 years, I wonder
that any man of the present day (ever) dar

up in "most admired disorder." The first half of the book is occupied by chronicles of their misdeeds and misfortunes, in the narrative of which their several characters are clearly disclosed. This part of the story is almost undiluted fun, while in the latter half there is a strong infusion of pathos. Such enterprising and ingenious little chits as these children were! They ran over the whole gamut of mischief with flying feet; free as air, when away from Aunt Izzie's subduing presence, honest, truthful, affectionate, but untamed and irrepressible. Not only children alone will laugh over their pranks, but men and women, remembering what they did, or what they longed to do, in their youth, will render the tribute of hearty merriment to the author's marvellous comprehension of child-nature, and her rare power of describing its manifestations. Hardly anything in the book pleased us more than the account of Katy's friendships: how she struck up sudden intimacies with all sorts of people, to the annoyance of her friends, and her own frequent discomfiture—an affectional experience which falls to the lot of most little girls, we believe. Equally admirable, in another vein, is the story of the reconciliation between Katy and Elsie, whose pathos will bring tears into many eyes. But we cannot refer to a tithe of the beautiful or funny things that crowd the book, and make it thoroughly interesting from beginning to end. There is no preaching in it, unless Cousin Helen's soft suggestions may be called such; but its moral cannot fail to impress the dullest reader, or its influence to reach and stir many hearts. We give two extracts which illustrate the author's pleasant humor, and her power of personal portraiture. The first is an extract from the journal of Dorry, a boy of six years:—

false front, which was just the color of a dusty Newfoundland dog's back. Her eyes were dim, and she used spectacles; but for all that, she was an excellent worker. Every one liked Miss Petingill, though Aunt Izzie *did* once say that her tongue 'was hung in the middle.' Aunt Izzie made this remark when she was in a temper, and was by no means prepared to have Phil walk up at once and request Miss Petingill to 'stick it out,' which she obligingly did; while the rest of the children crowded to look. They couldn't see that it was different from other tongues, but Philly persisted in finding something curious about it; there must be, you know,—since it was hung in that queer way!

"Wherever Miss Petingill went, all sorts of treasures went with her. The children liked to have her come, for it was as good as a fairy story, or the circus, to see her things unpacked. Miss Petingill was very much afraid of burglars; she lay awake half the night listening for them, and nothing on earth would have persuaded her to go anywhere, leaving behind what she called her 'plate.' This stately word meant six old tea-spoons, very thin and bright and sharp, and a butter-knife, whose handle set forth that it was 'A testimonial of gratitude, for saving the life of Ithuriel Jobson, aged seven, on the occasion of his being attacked with quinsy sore throat.' Miss Petingill was very proud of her knife. It and the spoons travelled about in a little basket which hung on her arm, and was never allowed to be out of her sight, even when the family she was sewing for were the honestest people in the world."

NOTES AND QUERIES.

—"*A. H. C.*," *Providence, R. I.*, writes: "Can the *Literary World*, or any of its readers, describe to me a 'high oak-dresser,' such as Mrs. A. D. T. Whitney alludes to in 'Hitherto,' where Anstiss says: 'I was putting away the last of the pink-edged cups and

—"*B.*," *Salem, Mass.*, sends us a copy of some sentimental verses, written many years ago by some inconsiderate youth, with the request that we will publish them. We have no spite against the author, and it would be unkind to punish him at this late day for the follies of his youth. We will retain the verses subject to "B.'s" order.

—"*F. B. P.*," *Boston*, inquires: "Is Mark Twain a plagiarist? The sin of plagiarism has been charged upon most great writers, both of prose and poetry—usually with no particular justice. I propose to convict Mark Twain of the said sin—with about as little justice as in any of their cases. His celebrated scene of mourning at the grave of Adam, because he had never seen Adam, and more particularly because Adam had never seen him, is one of his best. Will it be believed that he imitated it from an old French story? I guess not;—but here is the story just the same: Chapelle, the French wit, used often to dine or sup with a certain lady of good position, who liked good eating and set forth good wine. One evening when as it happened there was no other company, the lady's maid, coming in during the latter part of the meal, found her mistress in tears, and Chapelle himself overwhelmed with grief. Upon her inquiring what was the matter, Chapelle replied with many sighs, that they were lamenting the death of the poet Pindar, a victim to the ignorance of his physicians, who murdered him by giving him the wrong medicine. He proceeded to deliver so powerful a eulogium upon the poet, such an elaborate account of his good qualities and poetical talents, that the kind-hearted serving-woman, deeply affected, mingled her tears with those of her mistress, and all three wept together for a long time over the untimely

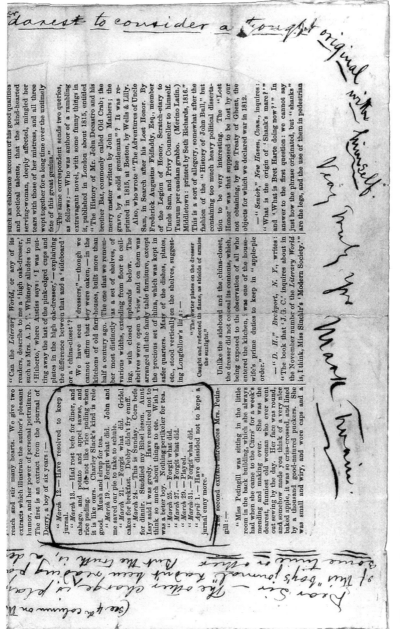

Clemens to the editor of the *Literary World*, December 1872, Hartford, Connecticut. Beinecke Rare Book and Manuscript Library, Yale University, New Haven, Connecticut (CtY-BR). Clemens wrote in the margins of page 106 of the December 1872 issue of the *Literary World*. Transcribed on p. 232; reproduced at 68 percent of actual size.

Clemens to David G. Croly, 17 April 1873, Hartford, Connecticut. This facsimile of the letter, reproduced by photolithography, appeared in the New York *Graphic* for 22 April 1873. The manuscript pages were spliced together for the engraving, so that the text ran continuously, filling one and a half columns. The page breaks of the original have been conjecturally restored here: the indented lines at the top left of the second and last pages show that Clemens was writing around an embossment. The paper was probably of the type embossed with "E. H. MFG. CO.," measuring $4\frac{15}{16}$ by 8 inches, which he is known to have used during this period. The short first page suggests that he may have begun his letter with a personal salutation and message, which were not reproduced in the *Graphic*. Transcribed on pp. 341–43; reproduced at actual size.

to sing, the zephyrs to sigh, the flowers to bloom, & the stagnation, the pensive melancholy, the lagging weariness of summer to threaten, I grow restless, I get the fidgets; I want to pack off somewhere where there's something going on. But you know how that is — you must have felt that way. This very day I saw the signs in the air of the coming dulness, & I said to myself, "How glad I am that I have already chartered ~~a steamship~~ to tow me & my party over on my life-raft." There was absolutely nothing in the morning papers. You can see for yourself what the telegraphic headings were

BY TELEGRAPH.

A Colored Congressman in Trouble.

Excitement at Albany.

Five Years' Imprisonment.

Wall Street Panicky.

Two Failures, and Money at 150 Per Cent.

Two Criminal Cases.

Arrested for Highway Robbery.

RIDDLE'S WARNING.

A Father Killed by His Son.

A Bloody Fight in Kentucky.

An Eight-Year Old Murderer.

A Grave-Yard Floating Off.

A LOUISIANA MASSACRE.

A Court House Fired, and Negroes Therein Shot While Escaping.

Two to Three Hundred Men Roasted Alive!

669

The Assault on the Gas Collector.

A Striker Held for Murder in the Second Degree.

The Murderer King Dangerously Sick.

Lusignani, the Wife Murderer, to be Hung.

Two Would-be Murderers to be Hung.

Incendiarism in a Baptist Flock.

A Fatal Mistake.

Washing Away of a Railroad.

Ku-Klux Murders.

A SHOCKING DISASTER.

A Chimney Falls and Buries Five Children— Two of them Already Dead.

The Modoc Massacre.

A Lively Skirmish in Indiana.

A TOWN IN A STATE OF GENERAL RIOT.

A PARTY OF MINERS BESIEGED IN A BOARDING HOUSE.

TROOPS AND POLICE FROM INDIANAPOLIS ASKED FOR.

BLOODY WORK EXPECTED.

Furious Amazon Leaders.

A HORRIBLE STORY.

A NEGRO'S OUTRAGE.

A SUFFERING AND MURDERED WOMAN TERRIBLY AVENGED.

A Man 24 Hours Burning, and Carved Piecemeal.

The items under these headings all bear date yesterday, Apl. 16, — *(refer to your own paper.)* & & I give you my word of honour that that string of commonplace stuff was everything there was in the telegraphic columns that a body could call news. Well, said I to myself, this is getting pretty dull; this is getting pretty dry; there don't appear to be anything going on anywhere; has this progressive nation gone to sleep? Have I got to stand another month of this torpidity before I can begin to browse among the lively capitals of Europe? But never mind — things may revive while I am away.

During the last two months my next-door neighbor, Chas. Dudley Warner, has dropped his "Back-Log Studies," & he & I have written a bulky novel in partnership. He has worked up the fiction & I have ~~shoveled~~ hurled in the facts. I consider it one of the most astonishing novels that ever was written. Night after night I sit up reading it over & over again & crying. It will be published early in the fall, with plenty of pictures. (Do you consider this an advertisement? — & if so, do you charge for such things, when a man is your friend & is an orphan?

Drooping, now, under the solemn peacefulness, the general stagnation, the profound lethargy that broods over the land, I am

Yours truly

Saml L. Clemens.
Mark Twain.

Clemens to Charles Dudley Warner, 17 May 1873, on board the SS *Batavia* en route from New York, N.Y., to Liverpool, England. Mark Twain Papers, The Bancroft Library (CU-MARK). Clemens began the letter on the back of his calling card, and finished it on the front, writing across the facsimile of his signature and the address. Transcribed on pp. 367–68; reproduced at actual size.

Farmington Avenue,
Hartford.

Dec. 11.

Livy my darling, I am just starting to the lecture hall, & O the dreadful fog still continues. The cattle are choking & dying in the great annual Cattle Show, & to-day they had to take some of the poor things out & haul them

Clemens to Olivia L. Clemens, 11 and 12 December 1873, London. Mark Twain Papers, The Bancroft Library (CU-MARK). The letter is written on two folders; page 1 is written on the front of the first, which is blank inside. Transcribed on p. 508; reproduced at 90 percent of actual size.

around on trucks
to let them breathe
the outside air &
save their lives.
I do wish it would
let up.

If I am not home-
sick to see you, no
other lover ever _was_
homesick to see
his sweet heart. —

Most

lovingly

Sam.

Manuscript page 2, to Olivia L. Clemens, 11 and 12 December 1873. Written on the back of the first folder.

2 A.M.
Dec. 12.

My own I dear little
darling, it is 2 in
the morning, & I had
gone to my bedroom,
but I thought I will
just go back to the

Manuscript page 3, to Olivia L. Clemens, 11 and 12 December 1873. Written on the front of the second folder.

parlor & look at
Livy's picture once
more before I go to
bed. And so I am
here, & your picture
is before me (the same
I have carried in
my pocket so many
many months) & I
simply love it & I love
you, Livy my darling.

Manuscript page 4, to Olivia L. Clemens, 11 and 12 December 1873. Written on the back of the second folder.

Tonight, after my lecture I went to to the Scotch Moray. Club's dinner, — the lord Viscount MacDuff was in the chair, — & I made a speech which was received with prodigious ap-plause — & I thought

Manuscript page 5, to Olivia L. Clemens, 11 and 12 December 1873. Written on the third page of the second folder.

were only here, I would enjoy it a thousand times more. I do love _you_, Livy darling, & my last word is, (~~████████~~) "

Most Lovingly
Saml

Manuscript page 6, to Olivia L. Clemens, 11 and 12 December 1873. Written on the second page of the second folder.

Appendix G

Newly Discovered Letters, 1865–1871

THE ELEVEN LETTERS (or portions of letters) in this appendix, written between 1865 and 1871, were discovered too late for inclusion in the first four volumes of *Mark Twain's Letters*. They are therefore published here outside of their correct chronological sequence.

To William Wright (Dan De Quille)
14 July 1865 • San Francisco, Calif.
(MS: Morris and Anderson)

San francisco
July 14, 1865

Dear Dan—

This is to make you acquainted with Dan Setchell, Esq. You are to do anything & everything you can to secure his comfort & forward his interest—especially the latter.[1]

By order of
Sam. L. Clemens.

Why don't you write me.

P.S. Jo is at the Warm Springs.[2]

[1] Daniel E. Setchell (1831–66), an actor and comedian, made his debut in Boston in 1853, thereafter performing in New York with great popular success, primarily in comic roles, until August 1863. He arrived in San Francisco on 27 April 1865, and appeared from 8 May through 24 June at Maguire's Opera House as a featured player with a theatrical troupe that included the popular actor Frank Mayo, earning for the most part highly favorable notices. On 27 May Clemens published an endorsement of Setchell in the *Californian*, which stated in part:

I have experienced more real pleasure, and more physical benefit, from laughing naturally and unconfinedly at his funny personations and extempore speeches than I have from all the operas and tragedies I have endured, and all the blue mass pills I have swallowed in six months. As a comedian, this man is the best the coast has seen, and is above criticism; and therefore one feels at liberty to laugh at any effort of his which seems funny, without stopping to undergo that demoralizing process of first considering whether some other great comedian, somewhere else, hasn't done the same thing a shade funnier, some time or other, years ago. (SLC 1865a)

Setchell arrived in Virginia City on 17 July, and presumably hand delivered Clemens's letter to Wright. He appeared with his traveling company at Maguire's Virginia City Opera House from 18 through 28 July, and left the following day. The files of the *Territorial Enterprise*—where Wright served as the local editor— are lost, so any plug he might have given Setchell in his column has not been preserved. After a return engagement in San Francisco in early 1866, Setchell sailed for New Zealand, but his ship disappeared en route, and he was presumed dead. In 1895 Clemens again praised him, noting that he had perfected the technique that Artemus Ward (and later he himself) adopted, of telling a humorous story "gravely": "then when the belated audience presently caught the joke he would look up with innocent surprise, as if wondering what they had found to laugh at" (SLC 1895; T. Allston Brown, 333; Ireland, 2:661; *ET&S2*, 169–71; "Opera House," San Francisco *Evening Bulletin*, 9 May 65, 3; San Francisco *Dramatic Chronicle:* "Maguire's Opera House," 25 May 65, 3, and 24 June 65, 2; San Francisco *Alta California*, 22 Jan 66, 1; Gold Hill [Nev.] *Evening News:* "Arrivals and Departures," 17 July 65, 3; "Opera House," 19 July 65, 3; "Opera House," 28 July 65, 3; "Arrivals and Departures," 29 July 65, 2; Berkove, 6; see *L1*, 277 n. 4).

    [2] No response from Wright has been found. Joseph T. Goodman, chief editor and Wright's boss at the *Territorial Enterprise*, had evidently been visiting San Francisco. Warm Springs (now Fremont), in Alameda County, was thirty-seven miles from San Francisco by ferry (Gudde, 108, 340; *Appletons' Hand-Book*, 242).

To Joseph T. Goodman
per Denis E. McCarthy and Telegraph Operator
26 October 1866 • Meadow Lake, Calif.

(Goodman, 2)

CALIFORNIA STATE TELEGRAPH COMPANY

Meadow Lake, October 26, 186 6.⎫
Via Cisco, 27—7:50 A. M.   ⎬

TO J. T. Goodman, Editor Enterprise:

Our circus is coming. Sound the hewgag.[1]
Mark Twain [Mac.][2]

---

[1] A toy instrument resembling a kazoo, dating from the 1850s, which produced a doleful sound. Used humorously, the word was understood to mean "an imaginary musical instrument feigned to be loudly sounded on occasions of special jubilation" (Whitney and Smith, 3:2818–19).

[2] Clemens, who was traveling with his friend and lecture manager Denis E. McCarthy ("Mac"), had delivered his Sandwich Islands lecture in You Bet (Nevada County, California) on 25 October, and planned to lecture next in Virginia City, Nevada. En route, they stopped in Meadow Lake (Nevada County) on 26 October and remained overnight, traveling south early the next morning to Cisco (formerly Heaton Station, Placer County). From there they took the Pioneer stage to Virginia City, arriving that same evening. To advertise Clemens's lecture, the Virginia City *Territorial Enterprise* reprinted his latest Sandwich Islands letter to the Sacramento *Union* on 27 October, "How, for Instance?" from the New York *Weekly Review* on 28 October, and the telegram itself on 28 October, noting:

MARK TWAIN COMING.—"Mark Twain," who stands at the head of American humorists, is dignifiedly wending his way toward Virginia, as will be seen by the following characteristic dispatch: . . .
The "circus" alluded to is "Mark's" lecture on the Sandwich Islands—a stupendously amusing affair, if we are to credit the California journals. "Mac.," which follows the signature of the lecturer, represents our old *confrere*, D. E. McCarthy, who, we take it, is preceding Mark in his journeyings and making the crooked paths straight. Of course the whole of Virginia will turn out to see Sam. Clemens and his "show" when he makes his appearance here.
P. S.—Since the foregoing was written Mark Twain and D. E. McCarthy have arrived. (Goodman, 2)

On 30 October the *Enterprise* first announced that Clemens would lecture in Virginia City the following evening, adding the comment, "We expect to see the very mountains shake with a tempest of applause" ("Mark Twain," 3; "Arrival," Meadow Lake *Weekly Sun*, 27 Oct 66, 3; Gudde, 62; *L1*, 361–62; Doten, 2:900; SLC 1866g, i).

To George L. Hutchings
15 October 1868 • Hartford, Conn.
(MS: CLSU)

☞ AGENTS WANTED FOR THE "PERSONAL HISTORY OF U. S. GRANT," "BEYOND THE MISSISSIPPI," AND "FIELD, DUNGEON AND ESCAPE," BY A. D. RICHARDSON. "GREAT REBELLION," BY HEADLEY, "BIBLE HISTORY," ILLUSTRATED, AND OTHER STANDARD WORKS SOLD BY SUBSCRIPTION ONLY. THE MOST LIBERAL COMMISSION PAID. SEND FOR CIRCULAR.

AMERICAN PUBLISHING COMPANY,

S. DRAKE, PRES'T.
E. BLISS, JR., SEC'Y.   148 Asylum st.
F. E. BLISS, TREAS.   HARTFORD, CONN., Oct. 15 186 8

G. L. Hutchings, Esq
        Dear Sir:
                Your favor of Sept 23 is just to hand. I have been absent &-f in the West & failed to send to the Everett House for my letters.
        My terms are $100. Thus far, my only subject is, "*American Vandals Abroad.*" I do not expect to use my old lectures. I have just written this.[1]
                                        Yrs Truly
                                        Mark Twain

P.S.

✉

G. L. Hutchings Esq | Chairman C. L. Soc. | 42 Wall street | New York [*return address:*] FROM AMERICAN PUBLISHING CO., HARTFORD, CONN. IF NOT CALLED FOR WITHIN TEN DAYS, PLEASE RETURN. [*postmarked:*] HARTFORD CONN. OCT 15 [*docketed:*] Ans'd Oct. 19th | Mark Twain

---

[1]George Long Hutchings (1843?–1937), born in London, was a banker with the Merchants' National Bank at 42 Wall Street in New York City, where this

letter was directed. He had written Clemens in his capacity as the lecture committee chairman of the Clayonian Society of Newark, New Jersey, a position he
held at least through 1871. Clemens was in Cleveland and St. Louis from 9 to 26
September, and in Elmira from 27 to 29 September, before returning to Hartford
by way of New York, where he arrived on the morning of 30 September. He may
have stopped overnight at the Everett House, where he had directed his mail
since mid-August. Clemens had finished writing his "American Vandal Abroad"
lecture by 7 October. He delivered it exclusively throughout his 1868–69 tour,
appearing successfully before the Clayonian Society in Newark on 9 December
1868. His usual fee was $100 during the season, although he evidently had to pay
his own expenses ("George L. Hutchings," New York *Times*, 5 Dec 1937, sec.
2:9; H. Wilson 1869, 758; 21 Sept 69 and 1 Jan 70 to Hutchings, Appendix G;
Redpath and Fall, 5–6; *L2*, 240, 242 n. 1, 246, 247 n. 1, 249 n. 1, 252–54 n. 1,
256, 257–58 n. 1, 262–65, 294, 320–21, 323–24 n. 4; *L3*, 44 n. 2, 481).

To Elisha Bliss, Jr.
10 May–1 June 1869 • Elmira, N.Y., or Hartford, Conn.
(Paraphrase and transcript: AAA 1926b, lot 79)

[*paraphrase: Sheet of Note Paper, containing an Autograph Note, consisting
of about 35 words, being instructions to his printer regarding the word "tabu"
in one of his books, and of which he writes,*—] If he does not know the
meaning of "tabu" let him look it up in a dictionary.

[*paraphrase: On the verso of the sheet are two columns of figures, being
the number of words in one of his works; in each case he has marked the chapter number and the number of words contained therein. A note, in the Autograph of Clemens, at the end of the final column reads,*—] After knocking
as much as possible out, there must still be 200,000 words left.[1]

[1] Clemens almost certainly directed his remark about "tabu" to the "infernally
unreliable" printer's proofreader who so exasperated him in April 1869, when
he was reading proofs of *The Innocents Abroad*, by failing to follow his instructions (*L3*, 197–98). This proofreader had evidently either written a query on the
proofs themselves, or relayed it through Bliss. By 15 April Clemens suspected,
and by 29 April had confirmed, that the manuscript for *The Innocents Abroad* was
too long. He returned to Hartford from Elmira on 8 May to continue proofreading, planning to make cuts in the material that was not yet typeset, and even on
the typeset pages that were not yet electroplated (*L3*, 196, 199–200, 202 n. 1,
206). By 10 May he had finished reading "500 pages of proof"—possibly
through chapter 47, which ends on page 502—and believed he would have
"about 200 more to read" (*L3*, 212, 218). That day or the next he received another set of proofs, which may have included chapters 51 and 52, where he used
the words "tabooed" and "*tabu*" (pages 539 and 551 of the book). The earliest
likely date for Clemens to receive a query about "tabu" was therefore 10 May.

On 13 May he wrote Olivia that he had "just finished going over the last of the Book MSS. & scratching out for the last time. No proofs have come in since Monday or Tuesday" (*L3*, 225). He must have made his word count by chapter and his estimate of "200,000 words left" around this time, to determine the consequences of his cuts. If he did not receive chapters 51 and 52 in the 10 May batch (or the next, a small batch received on or before 17 May), he probably had them in hand by 24 May, when he wrote that the remaining proof included "all the *vital* part of the Holy Land"—the account of which ended in chapter 57 (*L3*, 239, 251–52). He had certainly completed reading them by 1 June, when he wrote to a friend from Elmira that he had "several chapters to read yet," probably chapters 58–61 and the "Conclusion" (*L3*, 254).

To George L. Hutchings
21 September 1869 • Buffalo, N.Y.
(MS: CLSU)

MORNING EXPRESS $10 PER ANNUM.   OFFICE OF THE EXPRESS PRINTING COMPANY,
EVENING EXPRESS $8 PER ANNUM.   NO. 14 EAST SWAN STREET,
WEEKLY EXPRESS $1.50 PER ANNUM.
                                    BUFFALO, Sept. 21 18 69.

Mr. Hutchings—

   Dear Sir—

         I'll not be able to tell for two or three weeks, yet, what the subject will be—shan't go to work at it before then. I'll not have *two* subjects, though—only one. I have written Medbery not to lecture me for Y. M. C. A. *before* I talk for the Clayonians. (I have two agents, & by this means I am enabled not to know anything whatever about my own business, with unfailing promptness. I suppose it is all right.)[1]

                                        Resignedly Yrs.

                                             Clemens.

Personal. | G. L. Hutchings Esq | Merc. Nat. Bank | 42 Wall st | New York [*postmark cut away*]

[1] After attempting to withdraw from his partially scheduled lecture tour of 1869–70, Clemens advertised in a public letter dated 9 September 1869 that he would fulfill his engagements after all, "it being too late, now, to find lecturers to fill them" (*L3*, 351). Hutchings had apparently written for the subject of his

new lecture, which Clemens began preparing in Elmira in early October. He delivered "Our Fellow Savages of the Sandwich Islands," his only title of the season, before the Clayonians on 29 December 1869, to mixed reviews. He made no other appearance in Newark. During this season he was represented by James K. Medbery, of the American Literary Bureau, as well as by James Redpath (*L3*, 216, 297–98, 367, 483–86; "Mark Twain on the Sandwich Islanders," Newark *Journal*, 30 Dec 69, 2; "Mark Twain Last Night," Newark *Advertiser*, 30 Dec 69, 2; 22 Mar 73 to Larned, n. 2).

To George L. Hutchings
1 January 1870 • Elmira, N.Y.
(MS: CLSU)

Elmira, ~~De~~ Jan. 1.

Friend Hutchings—

I am in a desperate hurry, but I *must* take time to ask you to pardon me for showing such unmannerly temper the other morning about that synopsis. Those things always make me angry, & the fact that I had sat up until 5 AM talking,—then got up at 7, did not improve my temper. Still, it was shameful in me to intrude such a spirit upon you who had never done me any but the kindest offices—& so I have now siezed upon the very first opportunity to apologize—I have had no earlier chance than this.[1]

Truly Yrs.

Saml. L. Clemens.

Happy N. Y.'s to you!

✉

[*in ink:*] *Personal.* | G. L. Hutchings Esq | Bank—42 WALL ST | New York. [*return address:*] RETURN TO J. LANGDON, ELMIRA, N. Y., IF NOT DELIVERED WITHIN 10 DAYS. [*postmarked:*] ELMIRA N.Y. JAN 3 [*docketed:*] Mark Twain | apology

[1] On the morning of 30 December 1869 Hutchings may have shown Clemens a copy of that day's Trenton *True American*, which published a lengthy synopsis of his Sandwich Islands lecture in Trenton on 28 December ("Mark Twain," 3, reprinted in Lane). (On the afternoon of 30 December the Newark *Journal* printed a long excerpt from his 29 December Clayonian Society lecture, but by then he had left for his next engagement, in Wilkes-Barre, Pennsylvania ["Mark

Twain on the Sandwich Islanders," 30 Dec 69, 2].) Clemens again lectured for
the Clayonian Society on 29 November 1871 (*L3*, 485; *L4*, 515 n. 5).

To George L. Hutchings
13 August 1870 • Elmira, N.Y.
(MS: CLSU)

OFFICE EXPRESS PRINTING COMPANY,

BUFFALO, Aug. 13 187 0 .

DEAR SIR:

IN ANSWER, I HAVE TO SAY THAT I AM NO LONGER IN THE LECTURE
FIELD, AND HAVE, AT PRESENT, NO EXPECTATION OF ENTERING IT THE
PRESENT SEASON. IF ANYTHING SHOULD OCCUR TO CHANGE MY MIND,
HOWEVER, YOU WILL HAVE EARLY NOTICE THROUGH MY AGENTS, THE
BOSTON LYCEUM BUREAU, NO. 20 BROMFIELD STREET, BOSTON.

VERY TRULY YOURS,

SAMUEL L. CLEMENS

(MARK TWAIN.)

Friend Hutchings—

    For 5 months I have been declining as per above formula. I
haven't the slightest idea of ever talking again on a platform. Congrat-
ulate me on my emancipation! With sincere esteem

    I remain

Yrs

Clemens.

✉—————————————————————————————————

Personal. | G. L. Hutchings, Esq. | Bank, 42 Wall st. | New York. [*return
address:*] RETURN TO J. LANGDON, ELMIRA, N. Y., IF NOT DELIVERED WITHIN 10
DAYS. [*postmarked:*] ELMIRA N.Y. AUG 13 [*docketed:*] Mark Twain Aug 13. '70
[*and on flap:*] Mac | Headly | Albert | Rogers | Rindell | Hutchings | Ran-
dolph | Nesbitt[1]

    [1] None of these men, except Hutchings, has been identified. They may have
been members of the Clayonian Society lecture committee, of which Hutchings
was chairman (15 Oct 68 to Hutchings, n. 1, Appendix G).

To Unidentified
6 January 1871 • Buffalo, N.Y.
(MS: IU-R)

[*on the back:*]

BRADY'S

NATIONAL PHOTOGRAPHIC PORTRAIT

GALLERIES,

BROADWAY AND TENTH ST., NEW YORK.

———

627 PENNSYLVANIA AVENUE,

WASHINGTON, D. C.

Buffalo, Jan 6/71.

This is the latest—taken last July in Washington. Haven't succeeded in ~~ga~~ getting my wife to a photographic gallery yet, but shall some day, & then we'll send you one.[1]

Your friend

Mark Twain.

[1] Clemens sat for this photograph by Mathew Brady on 8 July 1870. It is reproduced here at 90 percent of actual size. No photographs of Olivia are known to have been taken in 1870 or 1871 (*L4*, 167, 168 n. 3, 374, 375 n. 2, 398 n. 1, 496).

To Jane Lampton Clemens
11 June 1871, postscript • Elmira, N.Y.
(MS: Davis, Jr.)

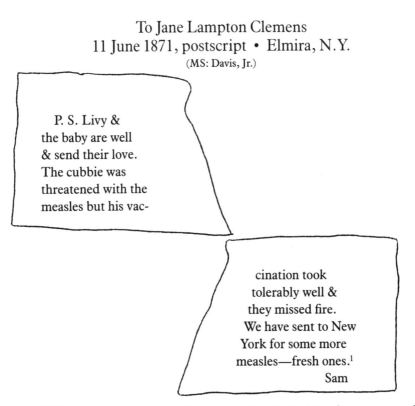

P. S. Livy &
the baby are well
& send their love.
The cubbie was
threatened with the
measles but his vac-

cination took
tolerably well &
they missed fire.
We have sent to New
York for some more
measles—fresh ones.[1]
Sam

[1] This undated postscript, written in pencil on both sides of a torn scrap of paper, is almost certainly an addendum to Clemens's letter of 11 June 1871 to Jane Lampton Clemens, which he wrote on nine scraps as a joke (*L4*, 403–6). The postscript was not previously associated with the letter, in part because it had become separated from the other scraps. The form of the letter is unique, however, and the paper of this scrap apparently matches the paper of two of the other nine scraps. Moreover, the subject is Langdon Clemens (the "cubbie"), and mid-1871 is one of the few periods in Langdon's short life when he was robust enough for Clemens to joke about his health (*L4*, 398 n. 1). Although the measles vaccine was not introduced into North America until 1963, in the 1750s a Scottish doctor, Francis Home (1710–1801), experimented with measles inoculation by transferring blood from an infected patient to an uninfected patient, thereby causing a "much milder" form of the disease (Cliff, Haggett, and Smallman-Raynor, 62; Kurstak, 70). Although some form of measles inoculation may have been practiced in 1871, no report of it has been found. Smallpox vaccine was certainly available, and some doctors believed that it also provided protection from measles, or resulted in milder cases. Clemens himself was vaccinated or revaccinated for smallpox in Chicago in late December 1871 and

thereafter urged Olivia, "Get vaccinated—*right away*—no matter if you were vaccinated 6 months ago—the theory is, *keep* doing it" (*L4*, 521; Jones, 434–35; Strout).

To Elisha Bliss, Jr.
11 July 1871 • Elmira, N.Y.
(Christie 1994, lot 221)

Elmira, 11 July.

Friend Bliss:

Shipped Mss. (up to & including Chapter 55,) this evening.[1] Let me know if you receive it.[2]

Yours

Mark.

It goes by Express.

✉——————————————————————————————————

[*letter docketed:*] 1871

[1]Clemens did not submit his manuscript for *Roughing It* to Bliss all at once, but forwarded it in several batches. On 10 July 1871 he promised to "fix up & forward" his fourth batch the next day (*L4*, 431). The editors of the 1993 edition of *Roughing It* showed that since Clemens added out-of-sequence chapters both before and during typesetting, his manuscript chapter numbers did not match those in the printed book. They conjectured that after July four chapters (36, 49, 52, and 53) were added, while one (the Mountain Meadows massacre narrative) was removed to an appendix: the difference between manuscript and book numbers was therefore four minus one, or three. The batch of manuscript transmitted on 11 July was thought to include book chapters 54–57, numbered 51–54 in the manuscript. This conjecture was based in part on a variation in the printed chapter headings for chapters 58–75, 77, and 79—evidence that chapter 57 was probably the last in a batch, and that chapter 58 began another batch, typeset at a later date. The present letter, discovered in 1994, suggests that book chapter 57 corresponded to Clemens's "Chapter 55"—the last in his batch—rather than to manuscript chapter 54, as previously conjectured. If only three chapters, instead of four, were added late (36, 49, and 53), the difference between manuscript and book chapter numbers would have been only two. It now seems likely that the 11 July batch comprised five chapters, numbered 51–55 in the manuscript, 52 and 54–57 in the book (53 was probably a late addition) (see *RI 1993*, 814–15, 852–62; *L4*, 432 n. 4).

[2]No reply is known to survive.

To the Staff of the Virginia City
Territorial Enterprise
7–8? December 1871 • Warsaw, N.Y., or Buffalo, N.Y.
(Paraphrase: Virginia City *Territorial Enterprise*, 18 Jan 72)

Our business yesterday was more particularly—though we had an eye to all new developments—the safe guidance of an old newspaper man through the mine, Mr. Kean, of the Buffalo *Courier*. Thomas arrived here armed with a letter of introduction from Mark Twain, the substance of which was: "Boys, show Tom the elephant."[1]

---

[1] Thomas Kean was the city editor and drama critic of the Buffalo *Courier* from 1861 to 1883. Clemens presumably met him in 1869 while living in Buffalo. Kean may have obtained the letter of introduction on 7 December 1871, when Clemens lectured in Warsaw, New York (David Gray, managing editor of the *Courier*, attended the lecture, and Kean may have accompanied him), or the next day, when Clemens stopped in Buffalo. Kean was traveling to the West as agent and companion to phrenologist Orson Squire Fowler (1809–87), who lectured in Virginia City, Nevada, from 13 to 17 January 1872. According to the Gold Hill (Nev.) *News*, Kean, having come "recommended as a respectable and resolute individual by Mark Twain," was welcomed by Dan De Quille (William Wright) of the *Enterprise* and taken on a tour of the rich Belcher silver mine on 17 January ("Personal," Gold Hill *News*, 18 Jan 72, 3). De Quille insisted that Kean descend "into the very bowels of the mine" and enjoyed his discomfiture when he had to strip "to the buff" and don special garb ("A Look into the Belcher," Virginia City *Territorial Enterprise*, 18 Jan 72, 3). "To see the elephant," an expression current in America by the mid-nineteenth century, meant "to view the sights in a city," or "to gain experience of the world, generally at some cost to the investigator" (Cassidy and Hall, 286; Virginia City *Territorial Enterprise:* "The Belcher Mine" and "Belcher and Crown Point Bullion," 11 Jan 72, 3; "Professor Fowler's Lectures and Examinations," 14 Jan 72, 3; "Prof. Fowler—His Special Lectures," 17 Jan 72, 3).

Editorial Apparatus

Guide to Editorial Practice

THE AIM OF *Mark Twain's Letters* is to publish, in chronological order, the most reliable and the most legible text possible for every personal and business letter written by (or for) Samuel L. Clemens, and to publish the letters he received, selectively, as a part of the annotation. The editorial aim for that annotation is to explain whatever requires explanation, either in notes appended to the letters, or in editorial narrative between them, with cross-references and reidentifications accomplished (as necessary) largely through the index. Three further matters, about which it is useful to be informed only as the need arises, are treated in the textual commentaries at the back of the volume: (a) when and where a letter has been previously published, if at all; (b) where and by whom the original documents have been preserved, or not, as the case may be; and (c) how and on what evidence the text of each letter has been established for this edition.

Fundamentally, the text of any letter is a matter of historical fact, determined for all time by the original act of sending it. Its text therefore includes everything that was originally sent, from the envelope to the enclosures: all nonverbal elements, all words and word fragments, numerals, punctuation, and formal signs—whether canceled or standing, inscribed or adopted, written or stamped by others during the time of original transmission and receipt. There is no necessary or obvious hypothetical limit on which of these elements may be significant. We must begin, in fact, with the assumption that almost any aspect of an original letter might be significant, either to the writer or the recipient, or both—not to mention those for whom the letters are now being published. In principle, therefore, the text of any letter properly excludes only such additions, revisions, and corrections as were made in the documents after the original transmission and receipt—even if such changes were made by the writer or the original recipient, or someone acting on their behalf.

But while there are few limits on what properly constitutes the text of a letter, there are many limits on what constitutes a satisfactory transcription of it. Most of Clemens's letters that survive in the original holograph, for example, lack the original envelope. Some lack one or more of the enclosures, or have been deliberately censored with the scissors, and not a few have been accidentally damaged and partly lost in one way or another, subsequent to their original transmission. All such accidents, however, limit only how much of the letter may be said to survive in its original documents, not how much of it ought to be, or even can be, transcribed. It is commonplace for a letter to survive partly in its original documents, and partly in a copy of originals otherwise lost: any transcription that did not rely on *both* could scarcely be called complete, let alone reliable. The hard question is not how transcriptions may be limited because parts of a letter no longer survive in any form, but rather what sorts of details in a letter text the editor may change or deliberately *omit* and still produce a reliable transcription.

We assume that the purpose of publishing letters is to make them easier to read than they are in the original documents. On that assumption, a successful transcription must include enough of the text to enable someone to rely on *it*, rather than the original, and it must exclude enough to make the transcribed text easier to read (or at least not more difficult to read) than the original. Thus, when the documents originally sent are intact and available, we transcribe them as fully and precisely as is compatible with a highly inclusive *critical text*—not a literal, or all-inclusive one, but a typographical transcription that is optimally legible and, at the same time, maximally faithful to the text that Clemens himself transmitted.[1] Original documents are therefore emended (changed) *as little as possible*, which means only in order to alter, simplify, or omit what would otherwise threaten to make the transcription unreadable, or less than fully intelligible in its own right. When, however, the original

---

[1] The transcription is not a *literal text*, even though it is probably as inclusive as most texts for which that claim is made, nor is it a *noncritical text*, as defined by G. Thomas Tanselle, since even though it "aims at reproducing a given earlier text [i.e., the original letter] as exactly as possible," the editor essentially defines what *is* possible by deciding what can be transcribed legibly. The editor is therefore "making decisions about how the new text will differ from the text in the document," with the result that the transcription necessarily "becomes a critical text" ("Textual Scholarship" in *Introduction to Scholarship in Modern Languages and Literatures*, edited by Joseph Gibaldi [New York: Modern Language Association, 1981], 32, 47).

documents are lost, we necessarily rely on the most authoritative *copy* of them. Since copies by their nature contain errors, nonoriginal documents are emended *as much as necessary*, partly for the reasons we emend originals, but chiefly to restore the text of the lost original, insofar as the evidence permits. The only exceptions (each discussed below) are letters which survive (a) only in the author's draft, (b) only in someone else's paraphrase of the original, (c) only in damaged originals or unique non-originals, and (d) in originals that, wholly or in part, can be faithfully reproduced only in photographic facsimile. But whether or not a letter survives in its original documents, every departure from the text of the documents used (designated the copy-text) is recorded as an emendation in the textual commentary for that letter, barring only the most trivial kinds of change, which are instead categorized and described here.

Mark Twain's Letters, Volume 1 (1988), first applied this basic rationale for emendation while also deploying a new system of manuscript notation. We called the result "plain text," partly to denominate its straightforward clarity, but partly also to distinguish it from the two alternative methods commonly used to publish letters, so-called "clear text" and the now much rarer "genetic text."[2] We require two things of every transcription in plain text: (a) it must be sufficiently faithful to the text of the

[2] According to Fredson Bowers, "General methods of transcription divide neatly in two," which is to say (a) *clear texts*, with supplementary apparatus containing all details of revision, and (b) *genetic texts*, without supplementary apparatus because the text itself contains all such details. A clear text transcribes the revised form of a manuscript "diplomatically," meaning that the "transcription exactly follows the forms of the manuscript in spelling, punctuation, word-division, italics (for underlining), and capitalization, but not in matters of spacing or in line-division, nor is a facsimile visual presentation of alterations attempted." A genetic text, on the other hand, includes authorial alterations in the text "by means of a number of arbitrary symbols like pointed brackets to the left or right, arrows, bars, and so on," with the common result that it is often "difficult to read the original text consecutively" and "impossible to read the revised text at all in a coherent sequence" ("Transcription of Manuscripts: The Record of Variants," *Studies in Bibliography* 29 [1976]: 213–14, 248). *Plain text*, however, descends from a kind of transcription not mentioned by Bowers, in which the myriad details of a manuscript (particularly the author's alterations to it) are systematically divided between the text and its apparatus, precisely in order to make the text as complete and informative as possible without destroying its legibility (see *N&J1*, 575–84). The practical result of this division is radically improved by adopting a less obtrusive and more readable system of notation than has been used in the past: plain text manages simultaneously to increase both overall legibility *and* the amount of detail that can be included in the transcription.

letter to serve as the most *reliable substitute* now possible for it; and (b) it must be *easier to read* than the original letter, so long as its reliability is preserved intact. To the extent that maximum fidelity and maximum legibility come into conflict, this way of linking them ensures that neither goal is maximized at undue expense to the other. The linkage works well for Clemens's letters, in part because they (like many people's letters) were intended to be read in manuscript, and his manuscripts are typically very legible to begin with. But in no small part, the linkage succeeds because the new system of notation is able to make legible in transcription many aspects of manuscript which would otherwise pose the necessity of choosing between maximum fidelity and maximum legibility. The consequence is that a typical letter transcription in plain text, though obviously not a replacement for the original, can still be read, relied on, and quoted from, as if it were the original.

While the notation system is admittedly new, it makes as much use as possible of editorial conventions that are familiar, traditional, and old. We have, for instance, deliberately kept the number of new conventions to a minimum, modifying or adding to them only very gradually, and only as the letters themselves demand it. When editorial conventions are new, they often adapt familiar conventions of both handwriting and typography. New conventions are in general called for by the effort to include, or at least to include more legibly, what has tended to be problematic, or simply ignored, in earlier methods of transcription. Two examples here will suffice. To transcribe printed letterhead in a way that is practical, inclusive, and fully intelligible, plain text uses EXTRA-SMALL SMALL CAPITALS for the printed words and a dotted underscore below whatever the writer put in the printed blanks, such as the date and place. Likewise, to transcribe all cancellations and identify all insertions (even of single characters) where they occur in the text, but without making the result illegible, plain text uses ~~line-through~~ cross-out rules, ⫽ slashes, and ˏinferiorˏ carets.ˏ

Most of these devices can now be produced with the type itself, making them economical both to set and to print. And many can fairly be characterized as type-identical with their handwritten counterparts. A line or a slash through type, crossing it out, needs no interpretation: it simply *means* canceled, just as it would in manuscript. The overall effect therefore contrasts favorably with the effect of arbitrary symbols, such as ⟨pointed⟩ brackets to the left ⟨a⟩ or right, ↑arrows,↓ | bars↑,↓ and so on—editorial conventions that today will seem both new and numerous, that will almost certainly mean something different from one edition to the next, and that in any case must be consciously construed at each occurrence.

A related risk of type-identical signs, on the other hand, is that their editorial function as *signs* will be forgotten—that they will be seen to picture, rather than to transcribe (re-encode), the original manuscript. It thus bears repeating that plain text, despite its greater visual resemblance to the handwritten originals, is emphatically not a type facsimile of them. Like all diplomatic transcription *except* type facsimile, plain text does not reproduce, simulate, or report the original lineation, pagination, or any other formal aspect of the manuscript, save where the writer intended it to bear meaning and that meaning is transcribable— which is exactly why it does reproduce or simulate many formal elements, such as various kinds of indention and purposeful lineation. In fact, it is usually the case that these formal (nonverbal) aspects of manuscript already have more or less exact *equivalents* in nineteenth-century typographical conventions.

Clemens's letters lend themselves to such treatment in part because his training as a printer (1847–53) began a lifelong fascination with all typographical matters, and in part because he lived at a time when the equivalents between handwriting and type were probably more fully developed and more widely accepted than they had ever been before (or are likely ever to be again). The consequence for his handwritten letters was that, while he clearly never intended them to be set in type, he still used the handwritten forms of a great many typographical conventions as consistently and precisely in them, as he did in literary manuscripts that were intended for publication. This habitual practice makes it possible to transcribe his letters very much as if they were intended for type—to use, in other words, the system of equivalents employed by nineteenth-century writers to tell the typesetter how the manuscript should appear in type—but in reverse, to tell those who rely on the typographical transcription just how the letter manuscript appears. In short, Clemens's typographical expertise makes his letters easier to transcribe fully and precisely, as well as easier to read in transcription, than they otherwise would be, assuming that we understand the meaning of his signs and the code for their typographical equivalents exactly as he did—an assumption that cannot always be taken as granted.

1. The Author's Signs

A few of the typographical signs in these letters may seem a bit unfamiliar, if not wholly exotic. Others may seem familiar, even though they in fact no longer have the precise and accepted meaning they had when Clemens used them. Especially because some signs have fallen into disuse and (partly for that reason) been adapted by modern editors for their own purposes, it is the more necessary to emphasize that here they bear only the meaning given them by Clemens and his contemporaries. Purely editorial signs in the transcription are identified on pages xxxiii–xxxv above, and since they sometimes adapt typographical conventions, they must not be confused with authorial signs. They have, in fact, been designed to avoid such confusion, and especially to avoid usurping the normal, typographical equivalents for authorial signs.

Still, authorial signs present two related but distinct problems for successful transcription: (a) how to explicate those signs whose authorial meaning differed from the modern meaning, but can still be recovered, at least in part; and (b) how to represent authorial signs whose earlier typographical equivalent, if any, remains unknown—at least to the editors. The glossary of SPECIAL SORTS and table of EMPHASIS EQUIVALENTS which follow here are intended to solve these problems—to alert the reader to those changes in meaning which we can identify, and to describe the handwritten forms for which the typographical forms are taken to be equivalent—or, in a few cases, for which they have been *made* equivalent because we lack a better alternative.

The glossary includes signs that do not appear in every volume of *Mark Twain's Letters*, much less in every letter, and it omits some signs that will only be added as they become relevant in subsequent volumes. Like the glossary, the table provides some information that was, and often still is, regarded as common knowledge, which may explain why the contemporary equivalent for some authorial signs has proved so elusive. That no table of comparable detail or completeness has so far been found in any grammar, printer's handbook, dictionary, or encyclopedia, would appear to indicate that the system of emphasis was almost completely taken for granted, hence rarely made fully explicit or published, even by those who relied upon it. The particular meaning for Clemens of all such equivalents between manuscript and type, at any rate, has had to be deduced or inferred from the letters themselves, and from his numerous literary manuscripts, with his instructions for the typist and typesetter (sometimes with the further evidence of how they responded to his instructions), as well as from the consistent but usually partial evidence in a variety of printer's handbooks, encyclopedias, manuals of forms, and other documents bearing on what we take to be the system of equivalents between handwriting and type (*L1*, xlvi n. 3).

SPECIAL SORTS

asterisks * * * Always called "stars" by Clemens and by printers generally, asterisks appear in his manuscript as simple "Xs" or crosses (X), or in a somewhat more elaborate variant of the cross (✳), often when used singly. In letters (and elsewhere) he used the asterisk as a standard reference mark, either to signal his occasional footnotes, or to refer the reader from one part of a text to another part. (The conventional order of the standard reference marks was as follows: *, †, ‡, §, ‖, ¶, and, by the end of the century, ☞.) He also used asterisks for a kind of ellipsis that was then standard and is still recognizable, and for one now virtually obsolete—the "line of stars"—in which evenly spaced asterisks occupy a line by themselves to indicate a major omission of text, or—for Clemens, at any rate—the passage of time not otherwise represented in a narrative. For the standard ellipsis, we duplicate the number of asterisks in the source, thus: * * * * (see also *ellipsis*, below). In transcribing the line of stars, however, the exact number of asterisks in the original becomes irrelevant, since the device is intended to fill the line, which is rarely the same length in manuscript as it is in the transcription. The line of stars in the original is thus always transcribed by seven asterisks, evenly separated and indented from both margins, thus:

*   *   *   *   *   *   *

braces ⌣   Clemens drew the brace as a wavy vertical line that did not much resemble the brace in type, except that it clearly grouped two or three lines of text together. He drew braces intended for three or more lines as straight (nonwavy) lines with squared corners, like a large bracket, usually in the margin. He occasionally used the two- and three-line braces in pairs, vertically and horizontally, to box or partly enclose one or more words, often on a single line. The one-line brace ({ }) was evidently not known to him, and would

probably have seemed a contradiction in terms. It appears to be a modern invention, but has sometimes proved useful in the transcription
when the original lineation could not be reproduced or readily simulated
(see *L1*, 219). Otherwise, the transcription always prints a brace and preserves, or at least simulates, the original lineation.

dashes – —   Clemens used the dash in all four of its most common
—— ———   typographical forms (en, em, two-em, and three-em), as
= =   well as a parallel dash, usually but not invariably shorter
             than an em dash. The parallel dash appears to be used
interchangeably with the much more frequently used em dash, but almost always at the end of a line (often a short line, such as the greeting).
Its special meaning, if any, remains unknown. Clemens occasionally
used dashes visibly longer than his em dash, presumably to indicate a
longer pause: these are transcribed as two-, three-, or (more)-em dashes,
by relying on the length of em dashes in the manuscript as the basic
unit. That Clemens thought in terms of ems at all is suggested by his
occasional sign for a dash that he has interlined as a correction or revision
(   ), which was then the standard proofreader's mark for an em dash.
Clemens used the dash as *terminal* punctuation only to indicate abrupt
cessation or suspension, almost never combining it with a terminal period. Exceptions do occur (*L3*, 78), but most departures from this rule
are only apparent or inadvertent. For instance, Clemens frequently used
period and dash together in the standard typographical method for con-
necting sideheads with their proper text ('P.S.—They have'), a recognized decorative use of period-dash that does not indicate a pause. The
em, two-em and, more rarely, the en and the parallel dash were also used
for various kinds of ellipsis: contraction ('d—n'); suspension ('Wash = ');
and ellipsis of a full word or more ('until ——.'). Despite some appearance to the contrary, terminal punctuation here again consists solely in
the period. On the other hand, Clemens often did use the period and
dash combined when the sentence period fell at the end of a slightly short
line in his manuscript ("period.— | New line"), a practice derived from
the typographical practice of justifying short lines with an em dash.
These dashes likewise do not indicate a pause and, because their function at line ends cannot be reproduced in the transcription, are always
emended, never transcribed. Clemens used en dashes in their familiar
role with numerals to signify "through" ('Matt. xxv, 44–45'). And he
used both the em dash and varying lengths and thicknesses of *plain*

rule—in lists, to signify "ditto" or "the same" for the name or word above, and in tables to express a blank. See also *ellipsis* and *rules*, below.

ellipsis - - - - - Nineteenth-century typography recognized an enviably
. . . . . . * * * * large variety of ellipses (or leaders, depending on the use
– – – – – – – to which the device was being put). Clemens himself de-
— — — — monstrably used hyphens, periods, asterisks, en dashes, and em dashes to form ellipses or leaders, in his letters and literary manuscripts. The ellipsis using a dash of an em or more is also called a "blank" and may stand for characters ('Mr. C—'s bones') or a full word left unexpressed. In the second case, the dash is always separated by normal word space from the next word on *both* sides ('by — Reilly'), thereby distinguishing it from the dash used as punctuation ('now— Next'), which is closed up with the word on at least one side, and usually on both ('evening—or'). When any of these marks are used as leaders, the transcription does not necessarily duplicate the number in the manuscript, using instead only what is needed to connect the two elements linked by the leaders. But for any kind of ellipsis except the "line of stars" (see *asterisks*), the transcription duplicates exactly the number of characters used in the original.

fist ☞ Clemens used the "fist," as it was called by printers (also
☜ "hand," "index," "index-mark," "mutton-fist," and doubtless other names), not as the seventh of the standard reference marks, but for its much commoner purpose of calling special attention to some point in a text. As late as 1871 the *American Encyclopaedia of Printing* characterized the device as used "chiefly in handbills, posters, direction placards, and in newspaper work,"[3] but Clemens used it often—and without apology—in his letters. We transcribe it by a standard typographical device, either right- or left-pointing, as appropriate, except in special circumstances. The following case, for instance, requires facsimile of the original, since Clemens clearly meant to play upon the term "fist" by drawing the device as a distinctly *open hand:*

"Put it *there*, Charlie!" (*L2*, 331)

---

[3] *American Encyclopaedia of Printing*, edited by J. Luther Ringwalt (Philadelphia: Menamim and Ringwalt, J. B. Lippincott and Co., 1871), 217.

paragraph ¶   The paragraph sign is both a mark of emphasis and the
sixth of the reference marks. It is actually "P" reversed
(left for right, and white for black) to distinguish it from that character.
Clemens, however, commonly miswrote it as a "P," drawing the hollow
stem with large, flat feet, but not the left/right or white/black reversal
in the loop. Whenever the sign is used in a letter, we transcribe it by the
standard typographical device, with a record of emendation when it has
been misdrawn. Clemens used the paragraph sign as a reference mark
and as shorthand for the word "paragraph," but most commonly in letters to indicate a change of subject within a passage, one of its original
meanings. When he inserted the paragraph sign in text intended for a
typesetter, he was doubtless specifying paragraph indention. But when
he used it in a letter, he was usually invoking that original meaning. The
transcription always prints the sign itself, even when it was inserted (¶)
or was manifestly an instruction to a typesetter. In the textual commentary, however, the paragraph sign in brackets [¶] is *editorial* shorthand
for "paragraph indention."

rules   *Double rules* (a), *parallel rules* (b), and *plain rules* (c), or
═══ (a) ═══ rule dashes, in manuscript are usually, but not invari-
═══ (b) ═══ ably, centered on a line by themselves, serving to sepa-
─── (c) ─── rate sections of the text. When used within a line of text,
they are positioned like an ordinary em dash and may
serve as a common form of ellipsis, or to mean "ditto," or simply to fill
blank space in a line. This last function may be compared with the original purpose of the eighteenth-century flourish, namely to prevent
forged additions in otherwise blank space. But as with the flourish, this
function had in Clemens's day long since dissolved into a mainly decorative one. Rules appear in Clemens's manuscript in three distinguish-
able species, each with two variant forms. We construe wavy lines in
manuscript as "thick" rules, and straight lines as "thin" rules, regular-
izing length as necessary. (a) *Double rules* appear in manuscript as two
parallel lines, one wavy and the other straight, in either order. (b) *Parallel rules* appear in manuscript as two parallel lines, either both wavy or
both straight (thick or thin). (c) *Plain rules* appear as single lines, either
wavy or straight (thick or thin).

EMPHASIS EQUIVALENTS

Clemens used the standard nineteenth-century system of underscoring
to indicate emphasis, both within and between words. He indubitably

understood the equivalents in type for the various kinds of underscore, but even if he had not, they could probably be relied on for the transcription of his underscored words, simply because the handwritten and the typographical systems were mutually translatable. Although we may not understand this system as well as Clemens apparently did, it is still clear that he used it habitually and consistently, and that anomalies are much more likely to result from our, rather than his, ignorance or error.

Occasionally Clemens used what appear to be two variations of a single underscore—a broken underscore (*not* prompted by descenders from the underscored word) and a wavy underscore (more distinctly wavy than normally occurs with any hand-drawn line). If these are in fact variations of a single underscore, they evidently indicate a more deliberate, or a slightly greater, emphasis than single underscore would imply. They have been transcribed in *l e t t e r s p a c e d   i t a l i c* and **boldface** type, respectively, even though we do not know what, if any, typographical equivalent existed for them (both are marked ★ in the table). Clemens occasionally used letterspacing, with or without hyphens, as an a-l-t-e-r-n-a-t-i-v-e to italic, but he seems not to have combined it with italic, so that this editorial combination may always signify broken underscore. Wavy underscore in manuscript prepared for a printer did mean boldface, or some other fullface type, at least by 1900, but it is not clear for how long this convention had been in place. And in any case, boldface would now ordinarily be used for a level of emphasis higher than CAPITALS or *ITALIC CAPITALS*, so that the use of boldface type to represent wavy underscore is necessarily an editorial convention.

Clemens also sometimes emphasized capital letters and numerals in ways that appear to exceed the normal limits of the typographical system as we know it. For instance, when in manuscript the pronoun 'I' has been underscored twice, and is not part of an underscored phrase, we do not know what typographical equivalent, if any, existed for it. Since the intention is clearly to give greater emphasis than single underscore, rendering the word in small capitals (ı) would probably be a mistake, for that would indicate *less* emphasis than the absence of any underscore at all (I). In such cases (also marked ★ in the table), we extend the fundamental logic of the underscoring system and simulate one underscore for each manuscript underscore that exceeds the highest known typographical convention. 'I' in manuscript is therefore transcribed as an italic capital with one underscore (*I*). Otherwise, underscores in the original documents are simulated only (a) when Clemens included in his letter

MANUSCRIPT	TYPE
lowercase	roman lowercase
Capitals and Lowercase	Roman Capitals and Lowercase
<u>lowercase</u>	*italic lowercase*
<u>Capitals and Lowercase</u>	*Italic Capitals and Lowercase*
*<u>Capitals and Lowercase</u>	**Italic Letterspaced*
*<u>Capitals and Lowercase</u>	***Boldface Capitals and Lowercase**
lowercase	ROMAN SMALL CAPITALS
<u>Capitals and Lowercase</u>	ROMAN CAPITALS AND SMALL CAPITALS
CAPITALS or <u>lowercase</u>	ROMAN CAPITALS
CAPITALS or <u>lowercase</u>	*ITALIC CAPITALS*
*<u>CAPITALS</u>	*<u>ITALIC CAPITALS</u>*
*<u>1, 2, 3, 4, 5</u>	*<u>1, 2, 3, 4, 5</u>*

something he intended to have set in type, in which case his instructions to the typesetter must be reproduced, not construed, if they are to be intelligibly transcribed; and (b) when he deleted his underscore, in which case the transcription simulates it by using the standard manuscript convention for deleting an underscore.

Since underscores in manuscript may be revisions (added as an afterthought, even if not demonstrably so), one virtue of the system of equivalents is that it allows the transcription to encode exactly how the manuscript was marked without resorting to simulation. There are, however, some ambiguities in thus reversing the code: for example, a word inscribed initially as 'Knight' or 'knight' and then underscored three times would in either case appear in type as 'KNIGHT'. Clemens also sometimes used block or noncursive capitals or small capitals, simulating 'KNIGHT' or 'KNIGHT', rather than signaling them with underscores. Ambiguities of this kind do not affect the final form in the text, but whenever Clemens used block or noncursive letters, or when other uncertainties about the form in the manuscript arise, they are noted or clarified in the record of emendations.

2. Revisions and Self-Corrections

The transcription always represents authorial *revisions* where they occur in the text, just as it does all but the most ephemeral kinds of *self-correction*. Either kind of change is wholly given in the transcription, except when giving all details of an individual occurrence or all cases of a particular phenomenon would destroy the legibility of the transcription. For *revisions*, the transcription always includes at least the initial and the final reading, with intermediate stages (if any) described in the record of emendations. But in letters, revisions are rarely so complicated as to require this supplemental report.

Self-corrections are sometimes omitted by emendation, and are more frequently simplified by emendation than are revisions, chiefly because if fully transcribed in place they often could not be distinguished from revisions, except by consulting the textual commentary—even though the distinction is perfectly intelligible in the original letter. This limitation comes about in part because causal evidence of errors, such as a line ending ("misspel- | ling") or a physical defect in the pen or paper, cannot be represented in the text without adding a heavy burden of arbitrary editorial signs. Thus a word miswritten, then canceled and reinscribed because of such a defect would, in the transcription, look like a revision, or at least like hesitation in the choice of words. In part, however, the problem with transcribing self-corrections lies in the sheer number that typically occur in manuscript. Self-corrections internal to a word, for example, are so frequent that more than one kind of emendation has had to be invoked to bring their presence in the transcription within manageable, which is to say readable, limits.

Another limitation of the present system is that the transcription does not distinguish between *simple deletions*, which may have been made either before or after writing further, and *deletions by superimposition*, in which the writer deleted one word by writing another on top of it, hence certainly before writing further. Because we have no way to make this distinction legible in the transcription, we represent all deletions as simple deletions. In the first volume, we supplemented the transcription in this respect by recording as emendations "each instance of deletion by superimposition" (*L1*, xxxiv), thereby enabling anyone to ascertain the method of cancellation used, since deletions by superimposition were always described ('x' *over* 'y'), whereas simple deletions were not. The advantage of this procedure was that, while clumsy and expensive, it meant the transcription with its apparatus could always be relied on to indicate the method of cancellation, whether or not the editors thought this information was useful in any given case. Its great disadvantage was that it caused the record of emendations to be nearly overwhelmed by reports of superimposition, only a small percentage of which were of any interest.

Pending the invention of an affordable, reliable way to signal this distinction in the transcription, subsequent volumes record deletion by superimposition *only* when it is judged to be useful information—chiefly where the timing of a cancellation can be established as immediate from this evidence in the manuscript, although in the transcription the timing appears indeterminate. For example, where the transcription reads 'Dont you', the manuscript might show either (a) that 'you' followed 'Dont' (a simple deletion, hence indeterminate), or (b) that 'you' was superimposed on 'nt' (deletion by superimposition, hence certainly immediate). Since the record of emendation gives *only* those cases where cancellation by superimposition establishes the immediate timing of a change, and only where this fact is deemed relevant, readers are entitled to infer from the *absence* of an entry for two such words ('& at', for example) that simple deletion has occurred. Where it is deemed irrelevant ('in order that so that'), the method of deletion is neither transcribed, nor recorded as an emendation.

All transcribed deletions are, with minor exceptions, fully legible to the editors, and were therefore arguably so to the original recipient of the letter. But Clemens clearly did make some deletions easier or more difficult to read than others. His occasional addition of false ascenders and descenders to his normal deletion marks, for instance, has the intended effect of making it quite difficult to read what was canceled, at least so long as the presence of these false clues remains undetected. Such cases show, in fact, that Clemens must have known that his normal methods of cancellation did not prevent most readers from reading what he crossed out. Indeed, we know from certain letters that he enjoyed teasing his fiancée about her practice of reading his cancellations—even going so far as to challenge her to read a deletion he made "impenetrable" (*L3*, 126).

It is clear that Clemens experimented with a wide variety of cancellations more or less actively *intended* to be read, but even apart from these deliberate and relatively rare cases, his methods of cancellation in letters ranged across a full spectrum of difficulty. The transcription does not, however, attempt routinely to discriminate among these, simply because we lack any conventional means for representing the differences legibly. Cancellations thus actively intended to be read—or not, as the case may be—are identified in the notes when their special character is not otherwise apparent from the transcription. But deletions accomplished by unusual methods *are* simulated whenever possible, for the methods themselves often convey some such intention (see, for example, *L3*, 337). And in some letters, Clemens used two methods of cancellation which occupy opposite ends of the spectrum of difficulty, and which the transcription therefore simulates.

Mock, or pretended, cancellations are words crossed out so lightly that they are easily read, visibly distinct from normal deletions, as well as being (for the most part) deletions of words still necessary to the sense. Clemens used various methods for creating mock cancellations, but the transcription renders them uniformly as struck through by a hairline rule, which is visibly thinner and rides higher on the x-height than the half-point rule used for normal deletions. (Compare 'Well, *I* pass.' with 'Well, *I* pass.'). Clemens also deleted parts of some letters by tearing away portions of the manuscript page, which he then sent, visibly mutilated. By their very nature, such deletions are unlikely to be read by anyone, but occasionally Clemens left enough evidence in the torn page to permit as much as the first or last line of the suppressed passage to be reconstructed. Yet even if the entire excision somehow survived, it would not be included in the transcription, simply because it was not part of the letter he sent. When text canceled in this fashion can be reconstructed, therefore, it is transcribed with wholly missing characters as diamonds and partly missing characters as normal alphabetical characters, bracketed as *interpolations:* 'I [j◇◇◇] ros[◇ ◇p] &' (*L3*, 115). The result is not, in the ordinary sense, readable—any more than the original manuscript at this point was, except where one or two characters or words left standing could still be read, out of context. The fully legible reconstructed reading is, therefore, given only in the notes.

It may be added here that some deletions in manuscript, especially of punctuation, were indicated there only by methods not themselves transcribable. For instance, when Clemens added a word or more to a sentence already completed, he rarely struck out the original period. Instead, he signaled his intention simply by leaving only the usual word space between the original last word and the first word of his addition, rather than the larger space always left following a sentence period. Whenever someone reading the manuscript would have *understood* something as canceled, even though it was not literally struck out, the transcription represents it as if it had been deleted in the normal fashion, and the record of emendations reports the fact as an *implied deletion*.

DELETIONS

■ Single characters and underscores are deleted by slash marks—occasionally even when the deletion is internal to the final form of the word ('privile̸dge'). Single characters include the symbol for illegible character (∅) and, more rarely, Clemens's own deleted caret (ʌ), when that alone testifies to his having begun a change.

, , ; ! ( ) “ ” ‘ ’ ! ? — + + a̸ b̸ c̸ d̸ j̸ k̸ l̸ t̸ w̸ x̸ y̸ z̸ 1̸ 2̸ 3̸ 4̸ ∅
A̸ B̸ C̸ D̸ E̸ F̸ G̸ H̸ I̸ J̸ K̸ L̸ M̸ N̸ O̸ P̸ Q̸ R̸ S̸ T̸ U̸ V̸ W̸ X̸ Y̸ Z̸ $̸ &̸

■ Two or more characters are deleted by a horizontal rule ('~~have written~~') —occasionally even when they are internal to the word ('examin~~ed~~ation').

■ Separate, successive deletions of two or more characters are signified by gaps in the horizontal rule ('~~that dwell in~~ all ~~the hearts~~'). These gaps *never* coincide with line ends in the transcription. Thus, horizontal rules that continue from the end of one line to the next ('~~it by any wilful act of her own~~') *always* signify a single, continuous deletion, never separate ones.

■ Deletions *within* deletions are shown by combining the horizontal rule with the slash mark for single characters ('~~though̸~~'), or two horizontal rules for two or more characters ('~~I was sail~~'). The earlier of the two deletions is always represented by the shorter line: to read the first stage, mentally *peel away* the longer line, which undeletes the second stage.

INSERTIONS

■ Insertions are defined as text that has been placed between two previously inscribed words or characters, or between such a word or character and a previously fixed point (such as the top of the page), thus written *later than* the text on either side of it. Insertions may be interlined (with or without a caret), squeezed in, or superimposed on deleted characters—methods not distinguished in the transcription and not recorded as emendations except when pertinent.

■ Single characters (including punctuation marks) are shown inserted by a caret immediately beneath them ('& I̬ desire').

■ Two or more characters are shown inserted, either between words or within a word, by a pair of carets ('in̬t̬o').

INSERTIONS WITH DELETIONS

■ Insertions may be combined with deletions of one or more words, and in various sequences:

'worth knowing,̬ ~~the King included, I believe.~~'

'~~Eighteen months~~ ̬A short time,̬ ago'

'intended to say, Aunt Betsey, ̬~~that~~,̬'

■ Insertions may be combined with deletions within a word:

'Malcolm̬b̸'

'ṃ̬May-tree'

'wishe̬s̬~~ing~~'

In the last two cases here, the carets indicating insertion designate characters that have been superimposed on the characters they delete. Superimposition is, in such cases, a kind of insertion designed to place new characters next to older, standing characters. Clemens might have achieved much the same thing, albeit with greater trouble, by crossing out the old and literally interlining the new characters. The timing of insertions combined with deletions internal to a word must, in any case, be understood as pertaining only to the sequence of change to that word, not as later than any other part of the text.

With the one class of exceptions noted at the end of this paragraph, alterations within a word are transcribed in the text only (a) if the rejected form was a complete word, even though not a possible word in context, or (b) if it was a recognizable start on, or misspelling of, a word possible in context. Thus the reader will find 'litera/ture' in the text because it contains the beginning of 'literary', which was possible in context, but will not find 'excursi/on' except in the report of emendations because it contains no other word or part of a word possible in context, nor is it a genuine misspelling. This rule of thumb has been devised partly because the notation for internally altered words is unconventional, and partly because such internal self-corrections occur very frequently in manuscript, so that if always transcribed they would introduce a large number of trivial puzzles throughout the text, threatening its legibility. In fact, to reduce the impediment further, the editors *may* simplify internally altered words, (c) whether or not the original form was a word, or start of a word possible in context, *whenever Clemens reused three or fewer characters* (counting quotation marks, parentheses, dollar signs, and the like). In such cases the transcription gives the canceled and the final form in succession, just as if they had been separately inscribed. Thus we transcribe 'and any' for what could be accurately, but not as legibly, transcribed as 'anyd' or 'andy'—forms which are used to record the emendation. Altered numerals of more than one digit must always be simplified in this way, even if the writer reused more than three characters.

To quote the letters without including the author's alterations, omit carets and crossed-out matter, closing up the space left by their omission. Compound words divided at the end of a line in this edition use the double hyphen (⸗) if and only if the hyphen should be retained.

3. Emendation of the Copy-Text

We emend original documents as little as possible, and nonoriginal documents as much as necessary, but we emend both kinds of copy-text for two fundamental reasons: to avoid including an error, ambiguity, or puzzle that (a) is *not in* the original, or (b) *is* in the original, but cannot be intelligibly transcribed without altering, correcting, resolving, or simplifying it.

Errors made by the writer are not emended if they can be intelligibly transcribed. Some few errors may be corrected by *interpolation*—supplying an omitted character or word within editorial square brackets— but only if the editor is confident that the writer has inadvertently omitted what is thus supplied. Interpolated corrections may be necessary to construe the text at all, let alone to read it easily, and would therefore be supplied by any reader if not supplied by the editor. Permitting interpolated corrections in the text is thus a logical extension of transcribing errors when, and only when, they can be intelligibly transcribed. Interpolated corrections, at any rate, do not conceal the existence of error in the original, and are therefore not *emendations* of it: like editorial description, or superscript numbers for the notes, they are always recognizably editorial, even when they enclose a conjecture for what the writer meant to but did not, for whatever reason, include in the letter sent. Interpolations are therefore not normally recorded in the textual commentaries. Interpolations are not always supplied, even if what is missing seems beyond serious doubt, nor could they be used to correct all authorial errors of omission: mistaken 'is' for 'it', for example, or a missing close parenthesis that must remain missing because it might belong equally well in either of two places.

Most errors in a *nonoriginal* copy-text, such as a contemporary newspaper, are attributable not to the writer, but to the typesetter, and are therefore emended. Yet even here, certain grammatical errors and misspellings may be recognizably authorial, and therefore not emended. On the whole, however, Clemens's precise and meticulous habits, which were well known in editorial offices even before he left the West, make it more rather than less likely that errors in such a printing are the typesetter's—especially because editors and typesetters were typically committed by their professions not to a literal transcription, but to a "correct" form of any document they published. Typesetting errors are self-evident in such things as transposition ('strated' for 'started'), wrong font ('carriEd'), and some kinds of misspelling ('pouud'). In addition, we know that by 1867 Clemens consistently wrote '&' for 'and' in his letters—except where the word needed to be capitalized, or the occasion was somewhat more formal than usual (for example, see *L2*, 35–37). In any nonoriginal copy-text, therefore, 'and' is sure to be a form imposed by the typesetter, who had good professional reasons for excluding '&' as an unacceptable abbreviation. The word is therefore always emended as an error in nonoriginal copy-texts.

But if authorial errors are preserved uncorrected, it may well be asked why it is ever necessary to emend *originals* to avoid including them, not to mention how this can be done without changing the meaning of the original letter, and therefore the reliability of the transcription.[4] The general answer to these questions is that in a transcription which does not reproduce the text line for line with the original, some forms in the original must *be* changed if they are not to assume a different meaning

[4]G. Thomas Tanselle, "Historicism and Critical Editing," *Studies in Bibliography* 39 (1986): 8 n. 15.

in the transcription—in other words, if they are not to become errors in it. Clemens's characteristic period-dash combination at the end of a line is a classic example of something that must be emended because it would become an error if literally transcribed. The period-dash apparently combined as terminal punctuation in Clemens's manuscripts virtually always occurs at a line end, at least until about the mid-1880s, when he seems to have trained himself not to use the dash there, probably because contemporary typesetters so often misinterpreted his manuscript by including it in the type, where it would appear as an intralinear dash between sentences. The typographical origin of this device was probably as an inexpensive way to justify a line of type (especially in narrow measure, as for a newspaper), but Clemens would certainly have agreed with the majority view, which frowned upon the practice.[5] As already suggested (p. 702), when Clemens used a dash following his period, he indicated simply that the slightly short line was nevertheless full, and did not portend a new paragraph. The device may owe something to the eighteenth-century flourish used to prevent forged additions in otherwise blank space, since it sometimes occurs at the end of short lines that *are* followed by a new paragraph. At any rate, he never intended these dashes to be construed as punctuation. Yet that is precisely what happens if the typesetter or the reader does not recognize the convention and reads it as a pause. Any dash following terminal punctuation at the end of a line is therefore not transcribed, but emended. When "period.— | New line" occurs in a newspaper or other transcription of a lost letter, it doubtless reflects the typesetter's own use of this method for right justification, and is necessarily emended. And when "period.— Dash" occurs within a line in such a printing, it is almost certainly the result of the typesetter's misunderstanding the convention in Clemens's manuscript, and is likewise emended.

    Ambiguities left by the writer are also not emended if they can be intelligibly transcribed. But both original and nonoriginal copy-texts will inevitably contain ambiguous forms that, because the transcription is not line for line, must be resolved, not literally copied. Am-

---

[5] The dash "is totally inadmissible as something to fill out a line, when that ends with a period and there is hardly enough matter" ([Wesley Washington Pasko], *American Dictionary of Printing and Bookmaking* [New York: Howard Lockwood and Co., 1894; facsimile edition, Detroit: Gale Research Company, 1967], 132).

biguously hyphenated compounds ("water-|wheel"), for example, cannot be transcribed literally: they must be transcribed unambiguously ("waterwheel" *or* "water-wheel"), since their division at a line end cannot be duplicated. Using the editorial rule (|) to show line end would introduce a very large number of editorial signs into the text, since consistency would oblige the editor to use the symbol wherever line endings affected the form in the transcription. Even noncompound words divided at the end of a line may sometimes be ambiguous in ways that cannot be legibly preserved in the transcription: "*wit*-|ness" in the copy-text must be either "*witness*" or "*wit*ness." Dittography (of words as well as punctuation) likewise occurs most frequently at line ends—physical evidence that makes it readily intelligible as an error in the source, but that is lost in a transcription which abandons the original lineation. Dittography becomes more difficult to construe readily when it is simply copied, because the result is at least momentarily ambiguous. It is therefore emended, even in intralinear cases, in order not to give a distorted impression of this overall class of error. The general category of manuscript forms affected by their original position at line ends, however, is even larger than can be indicated here.

Puzzles created by the writer are likewise preserved if they can be intelligibly transcribed. On the other hand, we have already described several aspects of the author's alterations in manuscript which would, if transcribed, introduce puzzles in the transcription: the method of cancellation, errors with a physical cause, implied deletions, self-corrections that would masquerade as revisions, and changes internal to a word which the editor may simplify. These alone show that holograph manuscripts invariably contain many small details which we simply have no adequate means to transcribe. But with the system of notation used in plain text, it is technically feasible to include many more of these details in the transcription than we do. For instance, when Clemens wrote 'yourself' in an 1853 letter, he corrected an error that can be transcribed as 'yourseflf' (Clemens wrote the necessary 'l' over the mistaken 'f', thereby canceling it). The transcription, following the rules of thumb already described, omits this self-correction, which is recorded as an emendation (*L1*, 17, 470). It does so because the superseded form ('yoursef') is not a complete word, does not begin a possible word in context, is not a genuine misspelling, and cannot be simplified, since Clemens reused *more* than three characters.

The question posed by such details is not simply whether including them would make the text more reliable or more complete (it would), but whether they *can* be intelligibly and consistently included without creating a series of trivial puzzles, destroying legibility, while not adding significantly to information about the writer's choice of words or ability to spell. There are, in fact, a nearly infinite variety of manuscript occurrences which, if transcribed, would simply present the reader with a puzzle that has no existence in the original. For instance, a carelessly placed caret, inserting a phrase to the left instead of the right of the intended word, is readily understood in the original, but can be transcribed literally only at the cost of complete confusion. And when Clemens writes off the right edge of the page and must then reinsert words he has just deleted on the right, but now in the left margin, literal transcription which did not also represent the cause of the changes would create a puzzle where there simply is none in the original.

Exceptional Copy-Texts. When the original documents are lost, and the text is therefore based on a nonoriginal transcription of one kind or another, the normal rules of evidence for copy-text editing apply. When, however, two transcriptions descend independently from a common source (not necessarily the lost original itself, but a single document nearer to the original than any other document in the line of descent from it), each might preserve readings from the original which are not preserved in the other, and these cannot be properly excluded from any text that attempts the fullest possible fidelity to the original. In such cases, no copy-text is designated; all texts judged to have derived independently from the lost original are identified; and the text is established by selecting the most persuasively authorial readings from among all variants, substantive and accidental. Before this alternative method is followed, however, we require that the independence of the variant texts be demonstrated by at least one persuasively authorial variant occurring uniquely in each, thereby excluding the possibility that either text actually derives from the other. If independent descent is suspected, even likely but not demonstrable in this way, the fact is made clear, but whichever text has the preponderance of persuasively authorial readings is designated copy-text, and the others are treated *as if* they simply derived from it, whether or not their variants are published.

Damaged texts (usually, but not necessarily, the original letters) are emended as much as possible to restore the original, though now invisible, parts of the text that was in fact sent. This treatment of an original document may seem to be an exception to the general rule about emending originals as little as possible, but a damaged manuscript is perhaps best thought of in this context as an imperfect copy of the original. And despite some appearance to the contrary, emendation in such cases is still based on documentary evidence: sometimes a copy of the original made before it was damaged, or damaged to its present extent—more commonly, evidence still in the original documents but requiring interpretation, such as fragments of the original characters, the size and shape of the missing pieces, the regularity of inscribed characters (or type) and of margin formation, the grammar and syntax of a partly missing sentence, and, more generally, Clemens's documented habits of spelling, punctuation, and diction. This kind of evidence cannot establish beyond a reasonable doubt how the text originally read. Its strength lies instead in its ability to *rule out* possible readings, often doing this so successfully and completely that any conjecture which survives may warrant some confidence. At any rate, we undertake such emendations even though they are inevitably conjectural, in part because the alternative is to render the text even less complete and more puzzling than it is in the damaged original (since sentence fragments are unintelligible without some conjecture, however tentative), and in part because only a specific, albeit uncertain, conjecture is likely to elicit any effort to improve upon what the editors have been able to perform. For this same reason, a facsimile of any seriously damaged document is always provided, either in an appendix with other manuscript facsimiles or in the textual commentary for that letter.

Letters and, more frequently, parts of letters that survive in the original but cannot be successfully transcribed constitute another exception and will be published in facsimile. For example, two letters that Clemens typed in 1874 (joking the while about his difficulties with the typewriter) clearly exceed the capacity of transcription to capture all their significant details, particularly the typing errors to which he alludes in them. Partly because they were typed, however, the original documents are relatively easy to read and therefore can be published in photographic facsimile, which preserves most of their details without at the same time making them any harder to read than the originals. These are true exceptions in the sense that most of Clemens's typed letters can and will be transcribed. But it is generally the case that facsimile cannot provide an optimally reliable and readable text, even of Clemens's very legible holograph letters, which comprise at least eight thousand of the approximately ten thousand known letters.

Yet by the same principles which justify transcription of most letters into type, facsimile should serve to represent within a transcription most elements of a manuscript which would (a) not be rendered more clearly, or (b) not be rendered as faithfully by being transcribed (newspaper clippings, for instance)—or that simply cannot be faithfully transcribed, redrawn, or simulated (drawings, maps, rebuses, to name just a few of the possibilities). It follows that if an original newspaper clipping enclosed with a letter cannot, for any reason, be reproduced in legible facsimile, it will be transcribed line for line in what approximates a type facsimile of the original typesetting. If the text of an enclosed clipping survives, but no example of the original printing is known, it is transcribed without simulating the newspaper format. And long or otherwise unwieldy, or doubtful, enclosures may be reproduced in an appendix, rather than immediately following the letter.

Letters which survive only in the author's draft, or in someone else's paraphrase of the original, are also exceptions. In the first case, the source line of the editorial heading always alerts the reader that the text is a draft. In such cases, emendation is confined to those adjustments required for any original manuscript, and is not designed to recover the text of the document actually sent, but to reproduce the draft faithfully as a draft. Likewise, if a letter survives only in a paraphrase, summary, or description, it is included in the volume only if the nonoriginal source is judged to preserve at least some words of the original. And like the author's draft, it is not necessarily emended to approximate the original letter text more closely, since its nonauthorial words usually provide a necessary context for the authorial words it has, in part, preserved. When it is necessary to interlard paraphrase with transcription, the paraphrase appears in italic type and within editorial brackets, labeled as a paraphrase, in order to guarantee that there will be no confusion between text which transcribes the letter and text which does not pretend to. When nonoriginal sources use typographical conventions that are never found in Clemens's manuscripts—word space on both sides of the em dash, for instance, or italic type for roman and vice versa—the normal forms of the lost manuscript are silently restored.

Silent Emendations. In addition to the method of cancellation, which is usually omitted from the transcription and the record of emendations, several other matters may involve at least an element of unitemized, which is to say silent, change. To save space, we transcribe only routine addresses on envelopes by using the vertical rule (|) to signify line end; nonroutine text on envelopes is transcribed by the same principles used elsewhere. The text of preprinted letterhead is reproduced in EXTRA-SMALL SMALL CAPITALS, usually in its entirety, but as fully as possible even when unusually verbose, and never to an extent less than what Clemens may be said to adopt or refer to ("I'm down here at the office"). Only substantive omissions from letterhead are reported as emendations, since the decorative variations of job type are literally indescribable. Postmarks are also transcribed in EXTRA-SMALL SMALL CAPITALS, but only unusual postage stamps are transcribed or described. Whenever Clemens used any of the following typographical conventions in his original letter (hence also whenever they occur in nonoriginal copy-texts and are deemed authorial), the transcription reproduces or simulates them, even when it is necessary to narrow the measure of the line temporarily, which is done silently: diagonal indention; hanging indention; half-diamond indention; squared indention; the flush-left paragraph and the half line of extra space, which is its collateral convention; text centered on a line, positioned flush right, or flush left; and quotations set off by quotation marks, indention, reduced space between lines (reduced leading in type), extra space above or below (or both), smaller characters in manuscript (smaller type in nonoriginals), or any combination of these conventions.

In this volume, as in the previous four, normal paragraph indention is standardized at two ems, with variations of one em and three ems often occurring in the same letter. We silently eliminate minor, presumably unintended variation in the size of all indentions, and we place datelines, complimentary closings, and signatures in a default position, unless this position is contradicted by the manuscript, as when extra space below the closing and signature show that Clemens intended them to appear on the same line. But unmistakably large variation in the size of indention is treated as deliberate, or as an error, and reproduced or simulated, not corrected or made uniform. Notes which Clemens specifically did *not* insert within the letter text but wrote instead in its margin are nevertheless transcribed at the most appropriate place within the text, and identified by editorial description: '[*in margin:*] All well', or '[*in bottom margin:* over]'. The editorial brackets in these cases may enclose just the editorial description, or both the description and the text described, depending on which conveys the original most economically. The only alternative to transcribing these notes where they are deemed "appropriate" is to transcribe them in a *completely* arbitrary location, such as the end of the letter. We likewise transcribe postscripts in the order they occur, even if this differs from the order they were intended to be read, so long as the intended order remains clear. Thus a marginal 'P.P.S.' can intelligibly precede a 'P.S.', just as a 'P.S.' inserted at the top of a letter can precede the letter proper, whether or not it was actually intended to be read first. But if, for example, a postscript inserted at the top is written across or at right angles to the main text—a sign it was *not* intended to be read before or with the text it crosses—the intended order must prevail over the physical order, and the postscript is therefore moved to the end of the letter. Only *changes* in writing media are noted where they occur in the text, as in '[*postscript in pencil:*]', from which it may also be reliably inferred that all preceding text was in ink. Line endings, page endings, and page numbers are silently omitted from the transcription, but where they affect the text or its emendation, they are given in the record of emendation.

4. Textual Commentaries

The *headings* to these commentaries serve collectively as a calendar of letters: they repeat the facts given in the letter headings themselves, but start with the date and end with the letter's record number from the *Union Catalog of Clemens Letters* (*UCCL*). Each commentary may have as many as five sections (sections are omitted when there are no facts to report). ■ *Copy-text* identifies the document or documents that serve as the basis for the transcription, and from which the editors depart only in the specific ways listed as emendations. ■ *Previous publication* cites, in chronological order, all published forms of the letter known to the editors, indicating which of these (if any) are notably incomplete or erroneous. The record of publication given here is not necessarily exhaustive, since the aim is to identify where and when a letter was first made generally accessible. Publications frequently referred to are described in the prefatory section called Description of Texts. ■ *Provenance* reports what the editors have been able to learn about an original letter's history of ownership. The reader may often be referred to the history of the relevant collection of manuscripts, as given in Description of Provenance. ∎*Emendations and textual notes* lists all deliberate departures from the copy-text (barring only changes categorized here as *silent emendations*). But the list may also include (a) editorial *refusals* to emend, identified by '[*sic*]', and (b) textual notes (always italicized and within square brackets) which explain the reasoning behind particular editorial decisions to emend, or not, as the case may be. When no copy-text has been designated because two or more documents descend independently from the lost original, *all variants* are recorded and identified by abbreviations defined under *Copy-text*, and this section is renamed *Emendations, adopted readings, and textual notes*, to signify that variant readings have been chosen on their merits from two or more authoritative texts. ∎*Historical collation* lists variants between two or more nonoriginal documents that may have descended independently from a common source, but have yielded no conclusively authorial variants.

All entries in these lists begin with a page and line cue (for example, 120.3, meaning page 120, line 3), followed by the word or passage to be documented, exactly as it stands in the transcription, except where indention [¶], line ending (|), or abbreviation ('Write . . . is') is necessary. As far as possible, entries are confined to the words and punctuation being documented. Line numbers include every line of letter text on a page, even when the page contains text for more than one letter, including all *rules*, all enclosures, and all lines that are wholly editorial, such as '[*about one page (150 words) missing*]', '[*in pencil*]', the editorial ellipsis (. . . .), or the full-measure envelope rule. Line numbers *exclude* all editorial matter in the letter headings and in the notes. Each reading is separated by a centered bullet (•) from the corresponding reading of the copy-text, *transcribed* without change or emendation, insofar as our notation permits, or *described* within brackets and in italic type, as necessary.

EDITORIAL SIGNS AND TERMS

[¶]	Paragraph indention.
~	A word identical to that on the left of the bullet (hyphenated compounds are defined as one word).
∧	Punctuation absent from text to the right of the bullet.

‖	End of a line at the end of a page.
[t◊◊t wi]thin brackets	Text within brackets is missing from, or obscured in, a damaged copy-text, and therefore can be identified only conjecturally. Diamonds stand for missing and invisible characters; normal characters stand for partly visible characters; and word space is conjectural, not actually visible. Thus the following notation shows which characters have been emended into the copy-text, and how they must have been configured in the *un*damaged original *if and only if* the conjecture is correct.

120.5–6   did not mean • di[◊ ◊◊◊ ◊◊◊◊] [*torn*]

Alternative conjectures are almost always possible, and may be more or less plausible, insofar as they too are consistent with the physical and syntactical evidence.

above	Interlined or written in the space above something else. Compare '*over*' and '*across*'.
across	Written over and at an angle to previously inscribed text.
conflated	Sharing an element, usually a minim.
false start	Start anticipated, requiring a new beginning, as in a race.
implied	Understood as intended, even though not literally or completely inscribed.
miswritten	Malformed, misshapen—*not* mistaken in any other sense.
over	Superimposed on something, thereby deleting it. Compare '*above*' and '*across*'.
partly formed	Not completed, hence conjectural.

R. H. H.
Revised, January 1997

Descriptions and Commentaries

THE CONTENT and purpose of the textual commentaries, as well as the special symbols and terms used in them, are described in the last part of the Guide to Editorial Practice, pp. 720–22. The siglum (C) identifies editorial emendations: readings adopted by the editors because they are thought to correspond better than the variant source readings to the most likely reading of the MS. In what follows here we summarize information about prior publication and provenance which would otherwise have to be frequently repeated in the commentaries for letters in this volume.

1. Description of Texts

Individual commentaries may designate as copy-text one or both of the following publications. When the information given here is pertinent for any reason, the reader is specifically referred to it.

MTB   *Mark Twain: A Biography. The Personal and Literary Life of Samuel Langhorne Clemens by Albert Bigelow Paine, with Letters, Comments and Incidental Writings Hitherto Unpublished; Also New Episodes, Anecdotes, etc.* 3 vols. New York and London: Harper and Brothers, 1912. *BAL,* p. 251. *Copy used:* copy #1, CU-MARK. Where *MTB* has served as copy-text, copy #1 (publisher's code H-M on the copyright page of volume 1, signifying the first impression, ordered in August 1912) has been collated against copy #2 (code K-K, signifying an impression ordered in October 1935, which is the latest impression located). In 1935 Paine made a few corrections in the plates, but no variants in the texts of the letters collected in the present volume have been found.

    MTB was first issued in three volumes, then in four and later in two, all with the same pagination. Paine said that he had "obtained his data from direct and positive sources: letters, diaries, account-books, or other immediate memoranda" (*MTB*, 1:xv). His industry in this respect was such that several letters he published have not since been found in their original form and are therefore known only from his transcriptions (or occasional facsimiles) in *MTB* and *MTL*. Although the printer's copy for *MTB* has not been found, it is known that Paine's general method of acquiring letter texts was to borrow the original whenever possible, presumably transcribe it himself, probably on a typewriter, and then return the manuscript to its owner. He presumably had full access both to the documents (now in the Mark Twain Papers) that Clemens himself defined and set aside for his official biography, and to those now in the McKinney Family Papers. He also had access to at least some of the letters in the Moffett Collection, but it is not known whether these were ever fully in his hands or transcribed for him. Although he published many of the letters now in the McKinney Family Papers, he published relatively few of those in the Moffett Collection. *MTB* is copy-text for a few letters not republished in *MTL*. But letter texts in *MTB* are generally excerpts and, judging from collation with letters that are still extant in manuscript, they were more freely edited than the corresponding passages published in *MTL*. Excerpts from *MTB* appeared in *Harper's Monthly Magazine* in thirteen installments, running from November 1911 through November 1912, hence, largely before *MTB* appeared in September 1912. Collation shows that when the book and the magazine both include text for a letter, they sometimes contain evidence of having each derived independently from a common source (very likely a typescript and its carbon copy), even though each has been separately copy-edited. Whenever persuasively authorial variants are found uniquely in both texts, the transcription is based on both. When such variants cannot be found, *MTB* is designated copy-text and the magazine, which was generally edited more heavily than the book, is treated as if it simply derived from *MTB* instead of their common source.

MTL   *Mark Twain's Letters, Arranged with Comment by Albert Bigelow Paine.* 2 vols. New York and London: Harper and Brothers Publishers, 1917. *BAL* 3525. *Copy used:* copy #1, CU-MARK. As indicated under *MTB*, the letters published in *MTL* are generally more complete as well as more reliable than those extracted or published in full in *MTB*. Because printer's copy for *MTL* has likewise not been found, it is not always clear what relation it bore to the printer's copy for *MTB*. Transcriptions are based on both *MTL* and *MTB* only when persuasively authorial variants occur uniquely in both, thus establishing their independent derivation from the lost manuscripts. Otherwise, if a letter appears both in *MTL* and *MTB*, *MTL* is chosen as copytext and *MTB* treated as if it simply derived from *MTL* instead of their common source.

Most of the letters published in *MTL* survive as original manuscripts. Collation of these documents with their transcriptions in *MTL* shows, in addition to the expected errors and omissions, that the *MTL* transcription always spelled out ampersands, and always imposed a uniform style on the dateline, greeting, complimentary closing, and signature lines. The uniformity of this house styling is established by a very large body of letter manuscript, and Clemens's consistency in using certain forms is likewise established by an even larger body of evidence. When the copy-text is *MTL*, this evidence is considered sufficient to permit the conjectural restoration of the likely forms in the original letter, at least in these uniformly styled elements. All emendations to remove this nonauthorial styling in *MTL* are, of course, published.

2. Description of Provenance

Brownell   The George H. Brownell Collection is housed in the
Collection   Rare Book Department of the Memorial Library of the
University of Wisconsin (WU). George H. Brownell (1875–1950) was a midwestern newspaperman who eventually became a full-time Mark Twain scholar, devoted especially to the task of obtaining photocopies (or originals) of Clemens's uncollected journalism and letters. In 1935 he helped found the Mark Twain Society of Chicago and, in 1941, the Mark Twain Association of America. In January 1939 he became the first editor of the *Twainian*, a position he held until his death. In October 1936, Brownell acquired an unusual collection of Clemens material from a Mark Twain collector, Irving S. Underhill (who died in 1937, in Buffalo). According to Brownell,

> the aged, bed-ridden Irving S. Underhill had begun his preparations for death by shipping the more valuable items in his Twain collection to a New York

auction concern. To me, at that time, he shipped two large cartons of miscellaneous Twainiana of no sale value, but having for me an almost inestimable bibliographical value.

Contained in one of those cartons was a box of Mark Twain letters—not the originals, but copies of the originals made by typewriter, pen and pencil. I never learned from Mr. Underhill how he acquired this strange collection of fully 200 Twain letters. My guess is that the copies were made by some dealer, long ago, at a time when the originals were passing through his hands to the purchaser. Mr. Underhill might then have bought or traded something to the dealer for the copies. (Brownell 1943, 2)

Brownell's conjecture was correct. The copies had been made by Dana S. Ayer of Worcester, Massachusetts, a book and manuscript dealer who had been a salesman (as of the late 1890s) for the American Publishing Company (*BAL* 3521; Second Life Books, lot 764; Samuel R. Morrill to Clifton W. Barrett, 24 Apr 1957, ViU). Brownell compiled a list of Underhill's documents, which included 158 Ayer transcriptions of Clemens letters (Brownell 1941). None of these letters was written earlier than 1867, when Clemens first corresponded with Elisha Bliss of the American Publishing Company. More than half of them were addressed to Bliss or to his son, Francis E. Bliss, who were both officers of the American Publishing Company. Most of the remaining letter transcriptions were addressed to Frank Fuller, Clemens's business agent from the spring of 1867 until sometime in 1868, when Clemens presumably placed Bliss in charge of past as well as his then current business correspondence (Brownell 1941). In the fall of 1942, Brownell loaned the Ayer transcriptions to Bernard DeVoto, who in turn had the majority of them retranscribed, depositing these retranscriptions in the Mark Twain Papers (described below). Brownell ultimately bequeathed the documents to the University of Wisconsin, where they now reside.

The original manuscripts for most of the letter transcriptions in the Brownell Collection have been found and are accessible to the editors, but a few letters are known only by the copy Ayer made of the original. By assessing the overall accuracy of Ayer's transcriptions and identifying the kinds of errors he introduced into them, it is possible to emend the texts of those few letters or parts of letters for which no manuscript survives, in order to restore the likely reading of the lost original. Three letters in this volume, all to Elisha Bliss, Jr., derive from Ayer transcriptions: one of them wholly (3 May 1873), and two in part (20 March 1872 and 7 July 1873).

Huntington   Henry E. Huntington (1850–1927), financier, railway
Library   executive, and heir to Collis Potter Huntington's railroad fortune, bequeathed his San Marino, California,
estate as an endowed public museum and art gallery for his enormous
collection of rare books, manuscripts, and paintings. The Clemens material at the Huntington Library includes literary manuscripts and
nearly two hundred autograph letters. Over half of these letters are addressed to Mary Mason Fairbanks, and were bought by Henry Huntington from William K. Bixby in 1918 (not from the Fairbanks family,
as stated in *L2*, 512, and *L3*, 583). Charles Mason Fairbanks, Mary Mason Fairbanks's son, had sold the letters in 1911 to "a collector in the
West," probably Bixby (Robert H. Dodd to Charles Mason Fairbanks,
8 Mar 1911, CtHMTH). Six letters in this volume to Mary Mason Fairbanks belong to the Huntington Library.

McKinney   The Jean Webster McKinney Family Papers, housed in
Family Papers the Francis Fitz Randolph Rare Book Room, Helen D.
Lockwood Library, Vassar College, Poughkeepsie, New
York (NPV). This collection was given to Vassar in 1977 by Jean and
Ralph Connor, of Tymor Farm, LaGrangeville, New York. Jean Connor
inherited the papers from her mother, Jean Webster McKinney, who
had in turn inherited them from her mother, Annie Moffett Webster,
Clemens's niece and the wife of Charles L. Webster, his business partner
from 1884 to 1888. The letters and other Clemens materials in the collection represent one of the three principal caches of family letters,
which passed from Clemens to his mother, Jane Lampton Clemens (d.
1890), his brother Orion (d. 1897) and sister-in-law Mollie Clemens (d.
January 1904), and ultimately to his sister, Pamela A. Moffett (d. August
1904). Some of these documents went eventually to Pamela's son, Samuel E. Moffett (see Moffett Collection, below), and some to her daughter,
Annie Moffett Webster. Not surprisingly, therefore, several manuscript
letters are now found partly in the McKinney Family Papers and partly
in the Moffett Collection.

 Mollie Clemens wrote her nephew Samuel Moffett on 31 July 1899,
"We never destroyed Sams letters—*excepting* by his request, or a few no
one should see" (CU-MARK). At least one partly destroyed (censored)
letter survives in this collection (see *L1*, 347–49), but by far the larger
toll was probably taken by accidental physical damage or loss, and by the

deliberate destruction, following Mollie Clemens's death, of most of Clemens's letters to his mother. As early as 1881, Orion Clemens had assembled a number of his brother's letters written between about 1853 and 1865 as part of a sprawling manuscript for his own never-published autobiography, finding even then that not all the letters had been preserved intact. On 6 October 1899, Pamela Moffett sent an unknown number of original letters to her son, Samuel Moffett, then a journalist in California, saying in part that she "was sorry to see that parts of some of the letters were missing" (CU-MARK). He tried to publish at least a few of these letters in biographical sketches of Clemens, but was eventually told to preserve them for publication after Clemens's death. Some, if not all, of these letters must eventually have become part of the Moffett Collection.

But in 1904, according to a 1935 Associated Press story in an unidentified newspaper clipping, Mollie Clemens's executor, John R. Carpenter, burned "almost four trunks" of Clemens's letters to his mother, "as requested by the famous humorist." Carpenter confided his story, according to this report, to Dr. G. Walter Barr of Keokuk, who gave this account:

> When Mrs. Clemens died [in 1890], . . . her carefully preserved personal and family treasures went into the possession of her son, Orion. When Orion died, his wife had the succession and kept it inviolate until her own death in 1904.
>
> John R. Carpenter was administrator of Orion's wife's estate and the treasured archives of Mother Clemens were delivered to him. One item was a collection of letters from Mark Twain to his mother, running through many decades, from youth to worldwide fame.
>
> But with those three or four trunks of letters was an admonition. Mark Twain had enjoined his mother that she always burn his letters to her. She had not done so, but had passed on the mandamus to Orion and to the wife of the latter, and Carpenter was familiar with it.
>
> He had a treasure of incalculable value and an imperative order to destroy it.
>
> Carpenter realized fully the value of the material he was about to burn in his library grate. When I exclaimed that to destroy all those letters was a monstrous crime against biography, history and the record of a man who belonged to the whole world, he answered that he agreed with me—but what could be done under the circumstances?
>
> Mark Twain had written those letters to his mother in perfect candor—and about the whole sum of his candid writing was in them—intending and believing that nobody else would ever see them, and had ordered them burned.

And so Carpenter burned every one. It took him several long evenings to complete the job thoroughly. ("Mark Twain Letters to Mother Burned at Direction of Author," unidentified clipping, datelined 14 Dec [1935], PH in CU-MARK; the New York *Times* also published an abbreviated version of this story on 15 Dec 1935, 2)

That this story was not a fiction is suggested by the postscript of Clemens's 14 February 1904 letter to Carpenter, the original draft of which survives in the Mark Twain Papers: "If there are any letters of mine, I beg that you will destroy them."

The McKinney Family Papers consist of Clemens documents typically left by him, at various times, with his sister. They include his earliest surviving notebook (probably written in 1855; see *N&J1*, 11–39); half a dozen literary manuscripts, incomplete and unpublished, written principally between 1859 and 1868 (see *ET&S1–3*); more than six hundred letters and telegrams from Clemens to various members of his family, and to business associates like Webster, as well as family photographs and mementoes, and letters and documents by other family members and close associates (Simpson, 6–14). Six letters in this volume belong to the McKinney Family Papers: 17 May 1872 to Annie E. Moffett; 6 November 1872 and 26 November 1872, both to Jane Lampton Clemens and Pamela A. Moffett; 5 December 1872 and 20 December 1872, both to Jane Lampton Clemens and family; and 12? September 1873 to Orion and Mary E. (Mollie) Clemens.

Mark Twain The Mark Twain Papers, The Bancroft Library, Univer-
Papers sity of California, Berkeley (CU-MARK). The core of
this collection consists of the original documents that Clemens made available to Albert Bigelow Paine for the official biography Paine was to produce, and from which (in part) Paine eventually published his selected editions of letters, notebooks, and the autobiography. Since Clemens's death in 1910, these papers were successively in the care of Paine (1910–37); Bernard DeVoto at Harvard (1938–46); Dixon Wecter at the Huntington Library, San Marino, California, and later at the University of California in Berkeley (1946–50); Henry Nash Smith (1953–63); and Frederick Anderson (1963–79), both of the latter at the University of California in Berkeley, and both successors to Paine, DeVoto, and Wecter as the official literary executor of the Clemens estate. Upon the death of Clara Clemens Samossoud in 1962, the papers were bequeathed to the University of California, and

in 1971 they became part of The Bancroft Library, where they now reside.

The original collection segregated by Clemens for Paine included forty-five of the approximately fifty extant notebooks kept between 1855 and 1910; approximately seventeen thousand letters received by Clemens or his family; an estimated six hundred literary manuscripts, most of them unpublished, including the autobiographical dictations; as well as photographs, clippings, contracts, and a variety of other documents originally owned by Clemens. Twenty-four letters (or parts of letters) in this volume are definitely from this original collection: 7 March 1872, 19 March 1872 (1st), and 19 March 1872 (2nd), all to Orion Clemens; 15 May 1872, 22 May 1872, and 5 May 1873, all to Orion and Mary E. (Mollie) Clemens; 16 or 17 August 1872 to Orion or Mary E. (Mollie) Clemens; 20 May 1872, 20–23 July 1872, 22 or 23 July 1872, 24 or 25 July 1872, 25–27? July 1872, 30 July 1872, 2 August 1872, 5 August 1872, 8 August 1872 (1st), 8 August 1872 (2nd), 16 August 1872, all to Mary E. (Mollie) Clemens; 20 March 1872 (draft) and 2 August 1873 (1st), both to Elisha Bliss, Jr.; 6 November 1873 to Jane Lampton Clemens; 9 December 1873, 11 December 1873, and 22 December 1873, all to Olivia L. Clemens. Two letters may belong either to the Mark Twain Papers or to the Moffett Collection: 11 August 1872 to Orion Clemens, and 22 January 1873 to Pamela A. Moffett. Since Paine's tenure, primary and secondary documents have been added in various ways to the Papers—ranging from gifts of both photocopied and original manuscripts and documents, to large purchases and bequests comprising many hundreds of documents, to the systematic compilation of a secondary archive of photocopies, collected from institutions and private owners of original documents around the world, for the specific purpose of publishing a comprehensive scholarly edition of Mark Twain's Works and Papers.

Samossoud Collection (1952), The Mark Twain Papers. Among the documents in Clemens's possession at the time of his death, but not included in the Mark Twain Papers or made wholly available to Paine, were the letters written to his fiancée and wife, Olivia L. Langdon, and later to their daughters, Susie, Clara, and Jean. Dixon Wecter was permitted to transcribe most of these letters, as well as some others that were still owned and separately housed by Clara. He used these transcriptions as the basis for his selected edition, *The Love Letters of Mark Twain*

(*LLMT*), published in 1949, and ultimately deposited all of them in the Mark Twain Papers. On 21 March 1952, however, the University of California purchased from Clara's husband Jacques Samossoud (d. 1966) approximately five hundred original letters written to Olivia between September 1868 and her death in 1904. Other parts of the large cache of family letters still held by Clara and her husband were sold or given at various times between 1949 and 1962 to other persons and institutions, including Chester L. Davis, Sr., and the Mark Twain Research Foundation of Perry, Missouri. This volume contains forty-three letters in the Samossoud Collection, all to Olivia.

Moffett Collection (1954), The Mark Twain Papers. This collection represents the portion of Pamela Moffett's papers which passed to her son, Samuel, instead of her daughter, Annie (see McKinney Family Papers, above). The collection became the property of Samuel Moffett's daughter Anita Moffett (d. 1952), either upon his death in 1908, or upon the death of Anita's younger brother, Francis Clemens Moffett, in 1927. The papers were discovered in 1953 by Paul P. Appel, a Mamaroneck, New York, book dealer (not in 1954 by Jacob Zeitlin, as reported in *L2*, 516), in a warehouse sale that included some of Anita Moffett's effects: sixteen hundred letters by Clemens, his family, and associates (including Pamela's letters to her son and daughter); ten scrapbooks of newspaper clippings for the period 1858–98, evidently compiled by Orion and Mollie Clemens, and containing original printings of Clemens's (and Orion's) western journalism, which had been largely unknown to Paine and all subsequent scholars (see *MTEnt*); deeds to 1860s Nevada mining claims owned by Clemens or his brother; family photographs; and a family Bible. The collection was purchased for the University of California in 1954 by a group of anonymous donors. The inventory of Clemens letters made at the time is not always specific enough to enable the editors to be certain whether some letters were part of the Moffett acquisition or were already part of the Mark Twain Papers in 1954. This volume contains two letters that belong either to the Moffett Collection or to the Mark Twain Papers: 11 August 1872 to Orion Clemens, and 22 January 1873 to Pamela A. Moffett.

Mendoza Collection (1957), The Mark Twain Papers. In January 1957 the University of California purchased a collection of one hundred sixteen Clemens letters written between 1867 and 1905 (all but one of them to Elisha Bliss or Henry H. Rogers), as well as eleven other miscellaneous items. This collection was offered for sale to the University by Aaron Mendoza of the Isaac Mendoza Book Company, New York City. The letters came from the collection of C. Warren Force (1880–1959), who had bought the letters to the Blisses in 1938 at the sale of the collection of George C. Smith, Jr. (Parke-Bernet 1938a, lot 126). In 1939 Force had given Bernard DeVoto transcripts of the letters to the Blisses. The Mark Twain Papers now contain about eighty-five letters to Rogers (or members of his family) and fifty-three original letters to Elisha Bliss or Francis E. Bliss. Of the total, all but roughly twenty-four letters were part of the Mendoza Collection, which contributes two letters to this volume: 26 February 1873 and 26 March 1873, both to Elisha Bliss, Jr.

    Appert Collection (1973 and 1977), The Mark Twain Papers. The gift of Mr. and Mrs. Kurt E. Appert of Pebble Beach, California, this collection includes more than fifty letters by Clemens to various correspondents, literary manuscripts, photographs, letters from various hands to Clemens, first editions of his works, and books from his library. This volume contains five letters that belong to the Appert Collection: 28 September 1872 to Elisha Bliss, Jr.; March 1873 to Louisa I. Conrad; 7 October 1873 to Henry Lee; 19 October 1873 to Charles Warren Stoddard; and 22 October 1873 to Unidentified.

3. Textual Commentaries

■ 2 January 1872 · To James Redpath · Logansport, Ind. · *UCCL* 00701

■ *Copy-text:* None. The text is based on four transcriptions, each of which derives independently from the MS:

P1	Will M. Clemens, 29
P2	*MTB,* 1:444
P3	*MTL,* 1:193–94
P4	Anderson Galleries 1922, lot 236

The independence of P1 is assured by its date of publication, 1900. P2 and P3 (published respectively in 1912 and 1917) each include text not found in P1, and therefore must derive independently from the MS (see the Description of Texts). Two later printings—Horner in 1926 (170–71), and Cyril Clemens in 1942 (21)—both derive from P1, not from the MS. ■ *Provenance:* The MS may have been owned (or merely borrowed) by Will Clemens before he published it in 1900. By 1922 it belonged to George H. Hart, who offered it for sale through Anderson Galleries. ■ *Emendations, adopted readings, and textual notes:*

1.1   Logansport, Ind. Jan. 2. (C) • LOGANSPORT, IND., Jan. 2, 1872.
        (P¹); LOGANSPORT, IND. *Jan. 2, 1872.* (P³); [*not in*] (P²,⁴)

1.2   [*no* ¶] Friend Redpath— (C) • [*no* ¶] *Friend Redpath:* (P¹); [¶]
        FRIEND REDPATH,— (P³); to Mr. Redpath of the Boston Ly-
        ceum Bureau [*reported, not quoted*] (P⁴); [*not in*] (P²)

1.3–4   [¶] Had . . . here. (P²) • [¶] Had . . . here and (P¹); [*no* ¶] Had
        . . . here. (P³); [*not in*] (P⁴)

1.4   night— (P¹,³) • ~; (P²)

1.4   house, (P²,³) • ~∧ (P¹)

1.4   have (P¹,²) • have had (P³)

1.4–6   I like . . . more. (P¹,³) • ~ ~ . . . ~∧ (P⁴); [*not in*] (P²)

1.5   the new (P¹,³) • this new (P⁴)

1.5   lecture (P¹,³) • ~, (P⁴)

1.5   "Artemus Ward" (P³) • '~ ~' (P¹); ∧~ ~∧ (P⁴)

1.5   & (C) • and (P¹,³,⁴)

1.6–7   No . . . think. (P¹,³) • [*not in*] (P²,⁴)

1.8–9   Give . . . house? (P³) • [*not in*] (P¹,²,⁴)

1.9   I . . . canceled. (P²) • I . . . cancelled. (P³); [*not in*] (P¹,⁴)

1.10   I'll . . . lecture. (P²,³) • ~ . . . ~∧ (P⁴); [*not in*] (P¹)

1.10   "fetch" (P²,³) • ∧~∧ (P⁴)

1.11–12 Have . . . again. (P²,³) • [*not in*] (P¹,⁴)

1.11 $4,000 (P²) • $4000 (P³)

1.12   days (P³) • ~, (P²)

1.12   & (C) • and (P²,³)

1.13–14 Yours, | Mark. (C) • Yours, | MARK. (P¹,³); signed "Mark."
        (P⁴); [*not in*] (P²)

■ 4 January 1872 · To John Henry Riley · Dayton, Ohio · *UCCL*
00706

■ *Copy-text:* MS, Henry W. and Albert A. Berg Collection, The New York Public
Library, Astor, Lenox and Tilden Foundations (NN-B). ■ *Provenance:* The MS
was offered for sale in 1924 as part of the collection of businessman William F.
Gable (1856–1921) (AAA 1924c, lot 94). It later belonged to lawyer and corporate official Owen D. Young (1874–1962), whose collection NN acquired in
about 1940 through purchase and donation. ■ *Emendations and textual notes:*

3.7   ~~Baby~~ Babe • Babȳe

■ 4 January 1872 · To Olivia L. Clemens, enclosing a letter (not sent) to
J. H. Barton · Dayton, Ohio · *UCCL* 00704 and 00705

■ *Copy-text:* MS, Mark Twain Papers, The Bancroft Library, University of California, Berkeley (CU-MARK). ■ *Previous publication: MFMT*, 52, excerpt;

LLMT, 162–63, excerpt, mistakenly as part of 31 Oct 71 to OLC. ▪*Provenance:* see Samossoud Collection in Description of Provenance. ▪*Emendations and textual notes:*

5.7	~~der~~ dreads • derreads [*underscored after revision*]
5.19	henchmen • hench-|men
6.4	~~just be~~ • ~~just be~~|

▪ 7 January 1872 · To William Dean Howells, *per* Telegraph Operator · Wooster, Ohio · *UCCL* 00707

▪*Copy-text:* MS, copy received, telegram blank filled out by the receiving telegraph operator, Houghton Library, Harvard University (MH-H). ▪*Previous publication: LLMT,* 171; *MTHL,* 1:9. ▪*Provenance:* The MS is one of 225 letters from Clemens to William Dean Howells, dating from 1872 to 1909, purchased by MH in 1937 from Howells's children, Mildred Howells and John Mead Howells. ▪*Emendations and textual notes:*

8.9	~~11~~ • [*possibly* '10']
8.27	Twx • [*possibly* 'Iwx' *or* 'Tax']

▪ 7 January 1872 · To Olivia L. Clemens · Wooster, Ohio · *UCCL* 00708

▪*Copy-text:* MS, Mark Twain Papers, The Bancroft Library, University of California, Berkeley (CU-MARK). ▪*Previous publication: MFMT,* 46, excerpt, mistakenly as part of 9 Nov 71 to OLC; *LLMT,* 171–72. ▪*Provenance:* see Samossoud Collection in Description of Provenance. ▪*Emendations and textual notes:*

11.2	~~th~~ • ['h' *partly formed*]
11.10	~~wh~~ well • w|hell ['h' *partly formed*]
11.15	hereafter • here-|after
11.26	wooster • w[oo]ster [*badly inked*]

▪ 7 January 1872 · To James Redpath · Wooster, Ohio · *UCCL* 00710

▪*Copy-text:* MS, collection of Todd M. Axelrod. ▪*Previous publication:* Bangs 1902, lot 83, brief excerpt. ▪*Provenance:* The MS was sold in 1902. By 1918, when it was offered by Anderson Galleries (lot 306), it belonged to E. B. Clare-Avery and was laid in a first edition copy of *Punch, Brothers, Punch! And Other Sketches* (Slote, Woodman and Co., 1878). It belonged to Alan N. Mendleson when it was again offered for sale in 1956 by Parke-Bernet Galleries (lot 108). Subsequently, it may have belonged to Jim Williams. By 1983 the MS—no longer laid in the book—belonged to Todd M. Axelrod, who gave the editors access to it. ■*Emendations and textual notes:*

12.1 ⨍ 7 • ['⨍' *partly formed; possibly* '⨍' *partly formed*]
12.6 i̶n̶ • ['n' *partly formed*]

■ **8 January 1872 · To Olivia L. Clemens · Salem, Ohio · *UCCL* 00711**
■*Copy-text:* MS, Mark Twain Papers, The Bancroft Library, University of California, Berkeley (CU-MARK). ■*Previous publication: LLMT,* 362, brief paraphrase. ■*Provenance:* see Samossoud Collection in Description of Provenance.

■ **10 January 1872 · To Olivia L. Clemens · Steubenville, Ohio · *UCCL* 00712**
■*Copy-text:* MS, Mark Twain Papers, The Bancroft Library, University of California, Berkeley (CU-MARK). ■*Previous publication: LLMT,* 172–73. ■*Provenance:* see Samossoud Collection in Description of Provenance. ■*Emendations and textual notes:*

15.4 steamboats • steam-|boats
15.8 Railroad • Rail-|road
15.24 Hartford • Hartfo𝑑rd

■ **10 and 11 January 1872 · To Olivia L. Clemens · Wheeling, W. Va., and Pittsburgh, Pa. · *UCCL* 00714**
■*Copy-text:* MS, Mark Twain Papers, The Bancroft Library, University of California, Berkeley (CU-MARK). ■*Previous publication: LLMT,* 362, brief paraphrase. ■*Provenance:* see Samossoud Collection in Description of Provenance. ■*Emendations and textual notes:*

18.4 M̶ • [*possibly* 'W̶']
18.8 b̶a̶ • [*possibly* 'b̶r̶'; 'r' *partly formed*]
18.15 you/ • [*deletion implied*]
19.2 Hawthorne • Hawthorn[◊] [*torn*]
19.2 Conn. • Con[n◊] [*torn*]
19.4 PITTSBURGH PA. JAN 1◊ • PIT[◊◊◊◊◊◊]H PA. JAN 1[◊] [*badly inked*]

■ **12 January 1872 · To Olivia L. Clemens · Kittanning, Pa. · *UCCL* 00715**
■*Copy-text:* MS, Mark Twain Papers, The Bancroft Library, University of California, Berkeley (CU-MARK). ■*Previous publication: LLMT,* 173. ■*Prove-*

nance: see Samossoud Collection in Description of Provenance. ▪Emendations and textual notes:

22.1	P̶u̶t̶t̶ Pittsburgh • P⁀h̬itt̬s̬burgh
22.6	Conn. • Conn[◊] [torn]
22.8	PITTSBURGH PA. JAN 1◊ • PITTS[◊◊◊◊◊] PA. JA[◊] 1[◊] [badly inked]

▪ 13 January 1872 · To Olivia L. Clemens · Pittsburgh, Pa. · UCCL 00716

▪Copy-text: MS, Mark Twain Papers, The Bancroft Library, University of California, Berkeley (CU-MARK). A clipping from the Pittsburgh Gazette (12 Jan 72, 4) survives with the letter and is photographically reproduced at actual size. ▪Previous publication: LLMT, 362, brief paraphrase. ▪Provenance: see Samossoud Collection in Description of Provenance. ▪Emendations and textual notes:

22.9	Livy • ['iv' conflated]
24.2	Conn. • Conn[◊] [torn]
24.4	PITTSBURGH PA. JAN 1◊ • P[◊◊◊◊◊◊◊◊◊] PA. [◊A◊ 1◊] [badly inked]

▪ 13 January 1872 · To James Redpath and George L. Fall · Pittsburgh, Pa. · UCCL 00717

▪Copy-text: MS, James S. Copley Library, La Jolla, California (CLjC). ▪Previous publication: Christie 1988, lot 1187. ▪Provenance: The MS was for many years in the Estelle Doheny Collection at The Edward Laurence Doheny Memorial Library of St. John's Seminary, Camarillo, California. John L. Feldman purchased it in October 1988 and sold it to the Copley Library in 1990.

▪ 16 January 1872 · To Olivia L. Clemens · Pittsburgh, Pa. · UCCL 00718

▪Copy-text: MS, Mark Twain Papers, The Bancroft Library, University of California, Berkeley (CU-MARK). ▪Previous publication: LLMT, 362, brief paraphrase. ▪Provenance: see Samossoud Collection in Description of Provenance. ▪Emendations and textual notes:

27.2	L̬ivy • ['y' miswritten]
27.2	ƀ • [possibly 'h̬']
27.9	Hawthorne • Hawthorn[◊] [torn]
27.9	Conn. • Conn[◊] [torn]

■ 17 January 1872 · To James Redpath · Lock Haven or Milton, Pa. · *UCCL* 00719

■ *Copy-text:* MS, University of Iowa, Iowa City (IaU). ■ *Previous publication:* Will M. Clemens, 29; Horner, 171; Cyril Clemens 1942, 21. ■ *Provenance:* The MS may have been owned (or merely borrowed) by Will Clemens before he published it in 1900. Sometime before 1922, "Dr. F[rank] W[akeley] Gunsaulus found this letter while on a lecture tour in the East and presented it to Harry P. Harrison, general manager of the Redpath Bureau, Chicago" (notation accompanying MS at IaU). The MS was donated to IaU in 1973 by Carl Backman, then manager of the Chicago bureau.

■ 20 January 1872 · To Olivia L. Clemens · Harrisburg, Pa. · *UCCL* 00720

■ *Copy-text:* MS, Mark Twain Papers, The Bancroft Library, University of California, Berkeley (CU-MARK). ■ *Previous publication: LLMT,* 363, brief paraphrase. ■ *Provenance:* see Samossoud Collection in Description of Provenance. ■ *Emendations and textual notes:*

29.9	Mr. •	Mr[◊] [*written off edge*]
29.11	∅ •	[*possibly* '∅']
29.11	overlooked •	overlooₐked
29.16	*promise* •	*prom-|ise*

■ 26 January 1872 · To James Redpath · Hartford, Conn. · *UCCL* 00721

■ *Copy-text:* AAA 1924c, lot 98, which describes the letter as an "Autograph Letter Signed, '*Mark,*' 2pp. 12mo, '*Home, 26th*' [1872]. To James Redpath," and states that it was accompanied by a "portrait of Mark Twain." The portrait was almost certainly not enclosed with the original letter, but furnished by a dealer or collector as an adornment. There undoubtedly was, however, an enclosure not mentioned by the catalog, yet clearly implied by the text, which refers to "this notice." The notice referred to appeared originally in the New York *Tribune* (25 Jan 72, 5), and was reprinted verbatim in the Hartford *Courant* (26 Jan 72, 2), attributed to the *Tribune.* The text here is a line-for-line resetting of the *Tribune* notice. Copy-text is a microfilm edition of the newspaper in the Newspaper and Microcopy Division, University of California, Berkeley (CU-NEWS). ■ *Provenance:* When offered for sale in 1924 the MS was part of the collection of businessman William F. Gable (1856–1921). ■ *Emendations and textual notes:*

33.3	$150, •	~.
33.6	and •	[*possibly* '&' *in the original MS, but not emended here because the transcriber of this and several other Clemens letters in the catalog,*]

while not completely literal or error free, was demonstrably careful to preserve both 'and' and '&' even when both occurred in the same letter, as they presumably did in this one: see '&' at 33.8 and 33.9]

33.8–9 authoritatively • authoratively
33.12 Mark • ~,

■ 27 January 1872 · To James Redpath · Hartford, Conn. · *UCCL* 00722

■ *Copy-text:* MS, Houghton Library, Harvard University (MH-H). ■ *Provenance:* bequeathed to MH by Evert Jansen Wendell (1860–1917), a Harvard alumnus and collector of theater memorabilia (Dickinson, 332–33).

■ 3 February 1872 · To Alvin J. Johnson · Hartford, Conn. · *UCCL* 00724

■ *Copy-text:* Wingate 1872, 67. ■ *Emendations and textual notes:*

39.1   Hartford . . . 3d, • HARTFORD, CONN., *Feb. 3d,*
39.2   Mr. A. J. Johnson • MR. A. J. JOHNSON
39.2   Dear Sir: • *Dear Sir:*
39.4–5 family. | Mark Twain. • family. [*extra space*] MARK TWAIN.

■ 13 February 1872 · To Mary Mason Fairbanks · Hartford, Conn. · *UCCL* 00725

■ *Copy-text:* MS, Henry E. Huntington Library, San Marino (CSmH, call no. HM 14276). ■ *Previous publication: MTMF,* 158–61. ■ *Provenance:* see Huntington Library in Description of Provenance. ■ *Emendations and textual notes:*

44.6   twelve • ['we' *conflated*]
44.12–13 seel seems • seelms
44.13   fatl • ['l' *partly formed*]
44.17   del development • delvelopment
44.21   Irishwoman • Irish-|woman

■ 13 February 1872 · To James Redpath · Hartford, Conn. · *UCCL* 00726

■ *Copy-text:* None. The text is based on three fragmentary transcriptions, each of which derives independently from the MS:

P¹   Will M. Clemens, 28
P²   Libbie, lot 62
P³   AAA 1926a, lot 132

The independence of P[1] is assured by its date of publication (1900), although it contains only one sentence, 'Success . . . returns.' (45.7), mistakenly included with the text of 10 July 71 to Redpath (the MS of that letter does not contain the sentence). According to both P[2] and P[3], the MS consists of four pages, octavo. P[2] does not identify the addressee but describes the letter as "regarding a lecturing tour"; P[3] describes it as "To Redpath, referring to 'Mark's' lecture tour." ■*Provenance:* The MS may have been owned (or merely borrowed) by Will Clemens before he published it in 1900. When sold in 1905 (Libbie), it was part of the collection of Arthur Mason Knapp, custodian of Bates Hall, Boston Public Library. ■*Emendations, adopted readings, and textual notes:*

45.1–5	Hartford . . . Boston (P[2,3]) • [*not in*] (P[1])	
45.1	Hartford, Feb. 13. (C) • Hartford, Feb. 13, 1872 (P[2]); Hartford, Feb. 13 [1872] [*reported, not quoted*] (P[3])	
45.5	triumph. (P[2]) • success (P[3]); [*not in*] (P[1])	
45.7	Success . . . returns. (P[1]) • ~ . . . ~, (P[3]); [*not in*] (P[2])	
45.7	& (P[3]) • and (P[1])	

■ 23 February 1872 · To James Redpath · Hartford, Conn. · *UCCL* 11920

■*Copy-text:* Transcript and paraphrase, AAA/Anderson 1935, lot 121. ■*Provenance:* When offered for sale in 1935 the MS was laid in a first edition copy of *Mark Twain's Autobiography* (Harper and Brothers, 1924) from the collection of Waldo Leon Rich. ■*Emendations and textual notes:*

47.4	Allyn • Aleyn

■ 26 February 1872 · To James Redpath and George L. Fall, *per* Telegraph Operator · Hartford, Conn. · *UCCL* 00727

■*Copy-text:* MS, copy received, telegram blank filled out by the receiving telegraph operator, Reed College, Portland (OrPR). ■*Previous publication:* Will M. Clemens, 29, with omission; *MTB*, 1:452, with omission; *MTL*, 1:194, brief quotation; brief excerpts in the following: John Anderson, Jr., lot 49; Anderson Auction Company 1910, lot 180; AAA 1925a, lot 109 (also erroneously quoted as part of lot 108 in the same sale). ■*Provenance:* The MS, which may have been owned (or merely borrowed) by Will Clemens before he published it in 1900, was offered for sale at least three times: in 1903 by John Anderson, Jr., from an unidentified collection; in 1910 as part of the collection of George Bentham; and in 1925 as part of the collection of businessman William F. Gable (1856–1921). It was eventually acquired by Portland banker Charles Francis Adams (1862–1943), who donated it to Reed College in 1940 or 1941 (*Reed College Notes* 7 [Apr 1945]: 1). ■*Emendations and textual notes:*

48.15   me. • me[◇] [*torn*]
48.20   Hdx • [*possibly* 'Hdw']

■ 2? March 1872 · To Mary Mason Fairbanks · Hartford, Conn. ·
UCCL 00728
■ *Copy-text:* MS, Henry E. Huntington Library, San Marino (CSmH, call no.
HM 14277). ■ *Previous publication: MTMF*, 161–62. ■ *Provenance:* see Huntington Library in Description of Provenance. ■ *Emendations and textual notes:*

49.1   Hartford • [*miswritten; possibly* 'Hartfor^d']
49.9   to the • tøhe
49.10   rh • [*partly formed*]
50.8   to-day • to-|day

■ 3 March 1872 · To James Redpath · Hartford, Conn. · *UCCL* 00729
■ *Copy-text:* MS, Clifton Waller Barrett Library, Alderman Library, University
of Virginia, Charlottesville (ViU). ■ *Provenance:* deposited at ViU by Clifton
Waller Barrett on 17 December 1963. ■ *Emendations and textual notes:*

52.3–4   with a will • withll ɑ ['a' *partly formed*]
52.4   The They • Thɛey [*possibly* 'Thɛey']

■ 7 March 1872 · To James Redpath and George L. Fall · Hartford,
Conn. · *UCCL* 00731
■ *Copy-text:* MS, Houghton Library, Harvard University (MH-H). ■ *Provenance:*
bequeathed to MH by Evert Jansen Wendell (1860–1917), a Harvard alumnus
and collector of theater memorabilia (Dickinson, 332–33). ■ *Emendations and
textual notes:*

54.7   happily • [*false ascenders/descenders*]
54.11   fe fat • fɛat

■ 7 March 1872 · To Orion Clemens · Hartford, Conn. · *UCCL* 00730
■ *Copy-text:* MS, Mark Twain Papers, The Bancroft Library, University of California, Berkeley (CU-MARK). ■ *Provenance:* see Mark Twain Papers in Description of Provenance. ■ *Emendations and textual notes:*

55.14   it • [*sic; someone, probably OC, has corrected* 'it' *to* 'in' *in pencil*]

■ 16 March–28 May 1872 · To Unidentified · Elmira, N.Y. · *UCCL* 08200

■*Copy-text:* MS, collection of David Howland. The upper portion of the MS page has been torn away. The extant portion is one leaf (torn from a folder) of white laid paper, ruled in blue, measuring 5 by 5⅜ inches. A portion of the watermark ("& Sons | 71") is visible, which clearly identifies the stationery as that used by Clemens in four letters written from Elmira between 27 March and 17 May 1872. ■*Provenance:* The MS descended to Howland from his paternal grandfather, Judge Henry Elias Howland (1835–1913), an acquaintance of Clemens's in the 1890s and later, who acquired it under unknown circumstances (see *HHR*, 139, 464–66).

■ 18 March 1872 · To William Dean Howells · Elmira, N.Y. · *UCCL* 00732

■*Copy-text:* MS, Houghton Library, Harvard University (MH-H). ■*Previous publication: MTHL,* 1:9–10. ■*Provenance:* The MS is one of 225 letters from Clemens to William Dean Howells, dating from 1872 to 1909, purchased by MH in 1937 from Howells's children, Mildred Howells and John Mead Howells.

■ 19 March 1872 · To Orion Clemens · (1st of 2) · Elmira, N.Y. · *UCCL* 00734

■*Copy-text:* MS, Mark Twain Papers, The Bancroft Library, University of California, Berkeley (CU-MARK). ■*Provenance:* see Mark Twain Papers in Description of Provenance.

■ 19 March 1872 · To Orion Clemens · (2nd of 2) · Elmira, N.Y. · *UCCL* 00733

■*Copy-text:* MS, Mark Twain Papers, The Bancroft Library, University of California, Berkeley (CU-MARK). ■*Provenance:* see Mark Twain Papers in Description of Provenance. ■*Emendations and textual notes:*

60.1   ~~18~~ 19 · 1~~8~~9

■ 19–22 March 1872 · To Frank Mayo · Elmira, N.Y. · *UCCL* 11847

■*Copy-text:* MS facsimile. The editors have not seen the MS, which was in the Alice Fischer (Frank Mayo) Papers, The New York Public Library, Astor, Lenox and Tilden Foundations (NN), but has been missing since 1979. ■*Provenance:* The papers of the actress Alice Fischer (1869–1947) at NN include the letters, diaries, and other papers of actor Frank Mayo (1839–96).

■ 19–22 March 1872 · To Joseph H. and Harmony C. Twichell · Elmira, N.Y. · *UCCL* 00735

■ *Copy-text:* MS, Robert B. Honeyman Collection, Linderman Library, Lehigh University, Bethlehem, Pennsylvania (PBL). ■ *Provenance:* The Honeyman Collection was donated to PBL in March 1957.

■ 19 March–8 May 1872 · To Unidentified · Elmira, N.Y. · *UCCL* 09046

■ *Copy-text:* MS, Ford Collection, Personal (Miscellaneous) Papers, Manuscripts and Archives Division, The New York Public Library, Astor, Lenox and Tilden Foundations (NN). The surviving letter fragment is cut or torn from a folder of white laid paper bearing a "P & P" embossment. ■ *Provenance:* The MS belonged to journalist and businessman Gordon Lester Ford (1823–91), and was probably donated to NN in 1899. ■ *Emendations and textual notes:*

64.4   unusually well, nowadays • unusu[all◊] well$_{[,]}$ now-| [*cut or torn away*]

■ 20 March 1872 · To Elisha Bliss, Jr. · (draft, not sent) · Elmira, N.Y. · *UCCL* 00737

■ *Copy-text:* MS, Mark Twain Papers, The Bancroft Library, University of California, Berkeley (CU-MARK). ■ *Previous publication: MTLP,* 70–71, with omissions. ■ *Provenance:* see Mark Twain Papers in Description of Provenance. ■ *Emendations and textual notes:*

65.3   ſ • [*partly formed*]
65.14   been • ['be' *canceled, then restored*]
66.5   ~~consequence.~~ Any • ~.—|~
66.10   ~~complicated~~ • c[◊◊◊]|plicated [*obscured by inkblot*]
66.17   *reason* • *rea-*|son
66.25   ~~25~~ 23 • 2ſ3 ['5' *partly formed; possibly malformed* '3']
66.25   ~~morr~~ moroccos • morſoccos

■ 20 March 1872 · To Elisha Bliss, Jr. · Elmira, N.Y. · *UCCL* 11848

■ *Copy-text:* None. The text is based on three sources:

P[1]   Clemens's MS draft (CU-MARK)
P[2]   Typescript (WU)
P[3]   Anderson Galleries 1917, lot 85

P[1] is a draft in CU-MARK of the fair copy letter Clemens sent Bliss (see pp. 65–66 and the previous commentary). P[2] and P[3] each derive independently from the fair copy MS, whose present location is not known. P[2] is a typewritten transcript—probably made by George Brownell from a hand transcription of the fair copy by Dana S. Ayer (now lost)—in the Rare Book Department, Memorial Library, University of Wisconsin, Madison (WU). P[3] is a partial transcript published in a 1917 catalog, when the MS was offered for sale. The catalog describes the letter as an "A. L. S., 4 pp. 8vo. Elmira, Mar. 20, 1872. Signed 'Clemens.' Marked 'Private.'" ■*Provenance:* The MS evidently remained among the American Publishing Company's files until it was sold (and may have been copied at that time by Ayer; see Brownell Collection in Description of Provenance).

■*Emendations, adopted readings, and textual notes:*

68.1	Private. (C) • Marked "Private." [*placement inferred from other letters of the period, such as 20 Jan 73 to Pugh and 9 Apr 73 to Reid*] (P[3]); [*not in*] (P[1,2])
68.2	Mch. 20 / 72 (P[1,2]) • Mar. 20, 1872 [*reported, not quoted*] (P[3])
68.3	Friend Bliss— (P[1]) • Friend Bliss:— (P[2]); To Frank Bliss [*reported, not quoted*] (P[3])
68.4–69.8	[¶] The more . . . book. (P[1,2]) • [*not in*] (P[3])
68.4	copyright (P[1]) • copy-|right (P[2])
68.5	deal, (P[1]) • ~$_\wedge$ (P[2])
68.9–10	perplexities, (P[1]) • ~$_\wedge$ (P[2])
68.10	& figures (P[1]) • and figures (P[2])
68.12	net (P[1]) • nett (P[2])
69.2	open, (P[1]) • ~$_\wedge$ (P[2])
69.3	all over (P[2]) • over (P[1])
69.7	it. (P[2]) • it. | $_\wedge$See page 6., (P[1])
69.9	testimony, (P[1,2]) • ~$_\wedge$ (P[3])
69.9	derived . . . friends, (P[1,2]) • [*not in*] (P[3])
69.11–12	otherwise (P[1,2]) • other-|wise (P[3])
69.12	*reason* (P[2]) • *rea-*|son (P[1]); reason (P[3])
69.14	country. (P[2]) • country," etc. (P[3]); country. Miss Anna Dickinson says the book is unprecedentedly popular—a strong term, but I believe that was it. (P[1])
69.15–16	We . . . Yrs (P[2]) • We . . . Ys (P[1]); [*not in*] (P[3])
69.15	well (P[2]) • all well (P[1])
69.15	& (P[1]) • and (P[2])
69.17–18	Clemens | [*list missing*] (C) • Clemens (P[2]); Signed "Clemens." (P[3]); Clemens. [¶] (Request added to send ~~25~~ 23 ½ ~~morr~~ moroccos to friends of mine named.) [*on back as folded:*] ½ profit letter to Bliss. | [*rule*] (P[1])

■ 21 March 1872 · To Elisha Bliss, Jr. · Elmira, N.Y. · *UCCL* 00738

■*Copy-text:* MS, Willard S. Morse Collection, Collection of American Literature, Beinecke Rare Book and Manuscript Library, Yale University (CtY-BR).

■*Previous publication: MTLP,* 72–73. ■*Provenance:* The Morse Collection was donated to CtY in 1942 by Walter F. Frear. ■*Emendations and textual notes:*

| 69.23–24 | it. Don't • ~.—\|~ |
| 70.1 | s̶h̶e̶ should • shǿould |

■ 27 March 1872 · To John Henry Riley · Elmira, N.Y. · *UCCL* 00740

■*Copy-text:* Clifton Waller Barrett Library, Alderman Library, University of Virginia, Charlottesville (ViU). ■*Provenance:* deposited at ViU by Clifton Waller Barrett on 16 January 1963. ■*Emendations and textual notes:*

71.14	work, • [*deletion implied*]
71.18	s̶ ̶t̶o̶ ̶n̶ • ['n' *partly formed*]
71.19	*copying,* • [*possibly 'copying,'*]
71.22	*listener—* • ~—|—

■ 31 March 1872 · To James R. Osgood · Elmira, N.Y. · *UCCL* 00739

■*Copy-text:* MS, General Manuscripts (Misc.), Princeton University (NjP). Published with permission of the Princeton University Libraries. ■*Previous publication: MTLP,* 73. ■*Emendations and textual notes:*

| 72.15 | countrymen • country-\|men |
| 72.16 | "suffer . . . strong" • [*quotation marks possibly inserted*] |

■ 19 April 1872 · To Francis E. Bliss · Elmira, N.Y. · *UCCL* 00741

■*Copy-text:* MS, collection of Mr. and Mrs. Fred D. Bentley, Sr. ■*Provenance:* The MS evidently remained among the American Publishing Company's files until it was sold, and may have been copied at that time by Dana S. Ayer. A handwritten Ayer transcription is at WU (see Brownell Collection in Description of Provenance). In 1988 the MS belonged to Arthur L. Scott of San Diego. ■*Emendations and textual notes:*

| 76.4 | o̶n̶ old • oǿld |

■ 20 April 1872 · To James Redpath · Elmira, N.Y. · *UCCL* 00742

■*Copy-text:* MS, Clifton Waller Barrett Library, Alderman Library, University of Virginia, Charlottesville (ViU). ■*Provenance:* deposited at ViU by Clifton Waller Barrett on 17 December 1963. ■*Emendations and textual notes:*

| 77.8 | Jubilee. I • ~.—\|~ |

■ 22 April 1872 · To Charles Dudley and Susan L. Warner · Elmira, N.Y. · *UCCL* 00744

■*Copy-text:* MS, Mark Twain Papers, The Bancroft Library, University of California, Berkeley (CU-MARK), is copy-text for the letter and envelope. MS, Mathilde Victor to SLC, 18 Apr 72, CU-MARK (*UCLC* 31803), and MS, David Ross Locke to Victor, 15 Apr 72, CU-MARK (*UCLC* 39059), are copy-texts for the enclosures. There is some evidence of repair to the first leaf of Clemens's MS (79.1–20). ■*Previous publication: LLMT*, 173–74, with omission. ■*Provenance:* The letter and enclosures were donated to CU-MARK in January 1950 by Mary Barton of Hartford, a close friend of the Warners', who had owned them since at least 1938. ■*Emendations and textual notes:*

79.6	Mrs. •	[*period somewhat obscured by repair to the MS*]
79.9	"humping • ⁴ "∼	[*quotation marks rewritten for clarity*]
79.19	~~Ys~~ Yrs. •	Y⌀rs.
81.9	it⌀ •	[*deletion implied*]
81.11	th[e] •	['h' *partly formed*]

■ 23 April–14 May 1872 · To Francis E. Bliss · Elmira, N.Y. · *UCCL* 09424

■*Copy-text:* Parke-Bernet 1954b, lot 290. The lot included a first edition copy of *Roughing It*, accompanied by a copy of a *Roughing It* prospectus and an unidentified letter from Redpath to Clemens, "apparently regarding the present work." Clemens's note to Frank Bliss was written "at the foot" of Redpath's letter. ■*Provenance:* When offered for sale in 1954 the MS was part of the collection of Jean Hersholt. ■*Emendations and textual notes:*

82.2–5	oblige	Yrs	Mark.	Address •	oblige Yrs Mark. Address

■ 8 May 1872 · To Charles E. Perkins · Elmira, N.Y. · *UCCL* 00745

■*Copy-text:* MS, Mark Twain House, Hartford (CtHMTH) is copy-text for the letter. MS, Francis E. Bliss to SLC, 1 May 72, CtHMTH (*UCLC* 31804), is copy-text for the enclosure. ■*Provenance:* Clemens's letter and its enclosure were among ninety-two items found in the files of the Hartford law firm of Howard, Kohn, Sprague and Fitzgerald; they were donated to the Mark Twain House as the Perkins Collection in January 1975 by William W. Sprague. Charles Perkins was a partner in this law firm (then called Perkins and Perkins) until his death in 1917 ("Large File of Twain Letters Discovered in Area Law Firm," Hartford *Courant*, 11 Mar 1975).

■ 9 May 1872 · To Olivia Susan (Susy) Clemens · Cleveland, Ohio · *UCCL* 00746

■*Copy-text:* MS, Mark Twain House, Hartford (CtHMTH). ■*Previous publication: LLMT*, 174–75. ■*Provenance:* donated to CtHMTH in 1962 or 1963 by Ida Langdon. ■*Emendations and textual notes:*

85.4	grandmother • grand-|mother
85.6	an • an | an
85.19	place. My • ~.—|~

■ 15 May 1872 · To Orion and Mary E. (Mollie) Clemens · Elmira, N.Y.
· *UCCL* 00747

■ *Copy-text:* MS, Mark Twain Papers, The Bancroft Library, University of California, Berkeley (CU-MARK). ■ *Previous publication: MTMF,* 162, brief excerpt. ■ *Provenance:* see Mark Twain Papers in Description of Provenance.
■ *Emendations and textual notes:*

86.3	ℬ • [*partly formed*]
86.5	cleer cheeringly • cleḥeŕeringly
86.11	ju journey • júourney
86.15	Mary Margaret's • Marŷgaret's
87.13	$44. $40. • $4ʌ0.
87.17	OVER. • [*simulated small capitals underscored twice*]
87.19	notice • notiḉce
87.25	ELMIRA N Y. MAY • ELMI[RA] N [Y◊] [M]AY [*badly inked*]

■ 15 May 1872 · To James Redpath · Elmira, N.Y. · *UCCL* 00748

■ *Copy-text:* MS, Boston Public Library and Eastern Massachusetts Regional Public Library, Boston (MB). ■ *Provenance:* The MS is laid in a first edition copy of *Roughing It* (American Publishing Company, 1872), bound in half-morocco, which bears the bookplate of the "Boston Public Library Memorial Collection of the Books of Louise Chandler Moulton." Moulton's extensive collection of autographed books went to the library after her death in 1908 (Whiting 1910, 281). ■ *Emendations and textual notes:*

90.2	Redpath • Redpaḥth

■ 15 May 1872 · To Francis E. Bliss · Elmira, N.Y. · *UCCL* 00749

■ *Copy-text:* MS, Willard S. Morse Collection, Collection of American Literature, Beinecke Rare Book and Manuscript Library, Yale University (CtY-BR).
■ *Provenance:* The Morse Collection was donated to CtY in 1942 by Walter F. Frear. ■ *Emendations and textual notes:*

91.6	him • ['m' *partly formed; possibly* 'hu']

■ 17 May 1872 · From Olivia L. and Samuel L. Clemens to Annie E. Moffett · Elmira, N.Y. · *UCCL* 00750

■ *Copy-text:* MS, Jean Webster McKinney Family Papers, Vassar College Library (NPV). ■ *Provenance:* see McKinney Family Papers in Description of Provenance. ■ *Emendations and textual notes:*

92.19   ~~Livy~~ • ['y' *partly formed*]

■ 20 May 1872 · To Mary E. (Mollie) Clemens · Elmira, N.Y. · *UCCL* 00751

■ *Copy-text:* MS, Mark Twain Papers, The Bancroft Library, University of California, Berkeley (CU-MARK). ■ *Provenance:* see Mark Twain Papers in Description of Provenance. ■ *Emendations and textual notes:*

93.5   ~~ca~~ cot • c⁄ot
94.2   Conn. • Conn[◊] [*torn*]
94.4   ELMIRA N Y. • [E◊]MIRA [◊ ◊.] [*badly inked*]

■ 22 May 1872 · To Orion and Mary E. (Mollie) Clemens · Elmira, N.Y. · *UCCL* 00752

■ *Copy-text:* MS, Mark Twain Papers, The Bancroft Library, University of California, Berkeley (CU-MARK). ■ *Provenance:* see Mark Twain Papers in Description of Provenance. ■ *Emendations and textual notes:*

94.6   Wednesʸ • ['y' *partly formed*]
94.8   ~~one~~ only • on⁄ly
94.18   N Y. MAY • N [Y]. MA[Y] [*badly inked*]

■ 22–29? May 1872 · To William Dean Howells · Elmira, N.Y. · *UCCL* 00754

■ *Copy-text:* Broadley, 229. ■ *Previous publication: MTHL*, 1:10–11 (misdated June 1872). ■ *Provenance:* The MS presumably belonged at one time to journalist and lawyer Alexander Meyrick Broadley (1847–1916). ■ *Emendations and textual notes:*

95.3   & . . . & • and . . . and [*here and hereafter*]
95.6   N. Y. • N. of
95.8–9   thanks | Twain • thanks [*extra space*] TWAIN

■ 26 May 1872 · To Francis E. Bliss · Elmira, N.Y. · *UCCL* 00753

■ *Copy-text:* MS, collection of Robert Daley. ■ *Provenance:* The MS was one of nineteen letters to Elisha and Frank Bliss (dating from 1868 to 1902) owned by

David G. Joyce, which were sold in 1923 (Anderson Galleries 1923, lot 138).
Daley bought the letters in 1974 and sold them again in December 1993 (Sotheby
1993, lot 214).

■ 11 June 1872 · To Adolph H. Sutro · Hartford, Conn. · *UCCL* 00755
■ *Copy-text:* MS, collection of Victor and Irene Murr Jacobs, on deposit at Roesch
Library, University of Dayton (ODaU). ■ *Provenance:* The MS was offered for
sale in 1960 (De Laney, lot 6), and again in May 1962 by Seven Gables Bookshop,
when the Jacobses purchased it. They deposited their collection at ODaU in
1984. ■ *Emendations and textual notes:*

101.2   *Ł* • [*partly formed; possibly 'Đ' or 'Ħ'*]

■ 15 June 1872 · To William Dean Howells · Hartford, Conn. · *UCCL*
00756
■ *Copy-text:* MS, Henry W. and Albert A. Berg Collection, The New York Public
Library, Astor, Lenox and Tilden Foundations (NN-B). The enclosed clipping
was cut from the Salt Lake City *Tribune* (27 May 72, 1); it survives with the letter,
glued to the top of the first page—probably not by Clemens—and is photographically reproduced at 85 percent of actual size. ■ *Previous publication:* Paine 1917,
781; *MTL*, 1:194–95; *MTHL*, 1:11–12; enclosure omitted from all. ■ *Provenance:* The MS belonged to lawyer and corporate official Owen D. Young (1874–
1962), whose collection NN acquired in about 1940 through purchase and donation. ■ *Emendations and textual notes:*

103.3   be*ł* • ['*ł* *partly formed; possibly 'ł' or 'Ħ'*]
103.8   humbled • ~~hum-~~ | humbled [*rewritten for clarity*]
103.13   ~~tha~~ • ['a' *partly formed*]

■ 18 June 1872 · To Louise Chandler Moulton · Hartford, Conn. ·
UCCL 00757
■ *Copy-text:* MS, Papers of Ellen Louise Chandler Moulton, Library of Congress
(DLC). ■ *Provenance:* After Moulton's death in 1908, her daughter gave the
"bulk of her correspondence," comprising autograph letters from a great many
distinguished persons, to DLC (Whiting 1910, 292–93).

■ 21 June 1872 · To Joseph L. Blamire · Hartford, Conn. · *UCCL*
00758
■ *Copy-text:* MS, Clifton Waller Barrett Library, Alderman Library, University
of Virginia, Charlottesville (ViU). ■ *Provenance:* The MS was almost certainly

one of four letters from Clemens to Blamire, the property of Frances H. S. Stallybrass, offered for sale in 1950 by Sotheby's in London (Sotheby 1950, lot 186). Stallybrass was the daughter of William Swan Sonnenschein, a director of Routledge and Sons after the company's reorganization in 1902 (Mumby, 148–49; Mumby and Stallybrass, 5, 20). Clifton Waller Barrett deposited the MS at ViU on 16 April 1960.

■ 23 June 1872 · To Joseph L. Blamire · Hartford, Conn. · *UCCL* 00759

■ *Copy-text:* MS, Clifton Waller Barrett Library, Alderman Library, University of Virginia, Charlottesville (ViU), is copy-text for the letter and its enclosure. ■ *Provenance:* The letter was almost certainly one of four letters from Clemens to Blamire, the property of Frances H. S. Stallybrass (see the commentary for 21 June 72 to Blamire), offered for sale in 1950 by Sotheby's in London (Sotheby 1950, lot 186). It is not clear whether the enclosure was included in that sale. Information from an unidentified catalog, now with the MS at ViU, suggests that Clifton Waller Barrett purchased the letter and its enclosure at a later sale. He deposited both items at ViU on 16 April 1960. ■ *Emendations and textual notes:*

110.12	~~coy~~ copyright • coýpy-|right [*canceled* 'y' *partly formed*]
111.2	steal. ~~at J. C. H.~~ • ~. ‖ ~ ~. ~. ~.
111.3	firm. ~~Other~~ • ~.—|~
111.7	~~this~~ the • thiṣe
111.8	~~their~~ the • theiᵣ
111.15	any • ~~any~~ ‚any‚ [*rewritten for clarity*]

■ 9–12 July 1872 · To Francis E. Bliss · New Saybrook, Conn. · *UCCL* 00767

■ *Copy-text:* MS, Saint Mary's Seminary, Perryville, Missouri (MoPeS). ■ *Provenance:* donated to MoPeS before 1955 by Estelle Doheny. ■ *Emendations and textual notes:*

114.1	Mrs. • Mrs[◊] [*obscured by inkblot*]

■ 10 July 1872 · To Joseph L. Blamire · New Saybrook, Conn. · *UCCL* 00764

■ *Copy-text:* MS, Routledge and Kegan Paul, London. The MS is in Volume A–H of George Routledge and Sons' "Agreement and Copyright Receipts," folio 186. ■ *Previous publication:* Grenander 1975, 1. ■ *Provenance:* Blamire presumably forwarded the MS to the Routledges in London.

■ 11 July 1872 · To Francis E. Bliss · New Saybrook, Conn. · *UCCL*
00765

■*Copy-text:* Henkels 1930c, lot 351, which describes the letter as an "A. L. S.
8vo, Fenwick Hall (with view of the Hotel), New Saybrook, Conn. July 11,
1872." ■*Emendations and textual notes:*

118.1–2   FENWICK . . . 187 2 • [*reported, not quoted; text of letterhead
           adopted from 30 July 72 to MEC*]
118.3   Friend Frank— • To Friend Frank.
118.5–7   Harte | . . . . | but • Harte *** but
118.8   Mark. • Signed "Mark."

■ 12 July 1872 · To Colt's Patent Fire Arms Manufacturing Company ·
New Saybrook, Conn. · *UCCL* 00768

■*Copy-text:* MS, Connecticut State Library, Hartford (Ct). ■*Previous publication:*
Davis 1951. ■*Provenance:* The MS was in the Colt company museum as late as
1951; it was donated to Ct sometime between 1951 and 1976. ■*Emendations and
textual notes:*

118.14   Gattling • [*sic*]

■ 16 or 17 July 1872 · To Joseph L. Blamire · New Saybrook, Conn. ·
UCCL 11894

■*Copy-text:* MS, Clifton Waller Barrett Library, Alderman Library, University
of Virginia, Charlottesville (ViU). ■*Previous publication:* University of Virginia,
70–71; Welland, 35–36. ■*Provenance:* The MS, the property of Frances H. S.
Stallybrass, was offered for sale in 1950 by Sotheby's in London (Sotheby 1950,
lot 186; see the commentary for 21 June 72 to Blamire). The catalog misidenti-
fied it as a "Holograph Preface to the English edition of 'Roughing It,' *dated Hartford, July,* 1872, *4 pp.*, *8vo.*" Information from an unidentified catalog, now with
the MS at ViU, suggests that Clifton Waller Barrett purchased the MS at a later
sale, at which time it was pinned, probably by the owner or a dealer, to Clemens's
letter of 21 July 72 to Blamire. Barrett deposited the MS at ViU on 16 April 1960.

■ 18 July 1872 · To James Redpath · New Saybrook, Conn. · *UCCL*
00769

■*Copy-text:* MS, Henry W. and Albert A. Berg Collection, The New York Public
Library, Astor, Lenox and Tilden Foundations (NN-B). ■*Provenance:* The MS
was owned by businessman William T. H. Howe (1874–1939); in 1940 Dr. A. A.
Berg bought and donated the Howe Collection to NN. ■*Emendations and textual
notes:*

121.21   season • seasoℏn

■ 20 July 1872 · To Elisha Bliss, Jr. · New Saybrook, Conn. · *UCCL* 00770

■ *Copy-text:* MS, Clifton Waller Barrett Library, Alderman Library, University of Virginia, Charlottesville (ViU). ■ *Provenance:* deposited at ViU by Clifton Waller Barrett on 17 December 1963.

■ 20 or 21 July 1872 · From Samuel L. and Olivia L. Clemens to Mary E. (Mollie) Clemens · New Saybrook, Conn. · *UCCL* 00775

■ *Copy-text:* MS facsimile is copy-text for the letter. The editors have not seen the MS, which was owned in 1977 by Chester L. Davis, Sr. (1903–87), who provided a photocopy to the Mark Twain Papers. The photocopy is of poor quality; many of the characters in Olivia's portion of the letter are illegible. Davis 1977b, 3, is copy-text for the envelope. ■ *Previous publication:* Davis 1977b, 3; Christie 1993, lot 24, Clemens's portion only. ■ *Provenance:* Chester L. Davis, Sr., probably acquired the MS from Clara Clemens Samossoud between 1949 and 1962 (see Samossoud Collection in Description of Provenance). After Davis's death in 1987, the MS was owned by Chester L. Davis, Jr., who sold it through Christie's in June 1993. ■ *Emendations and textual notes:*

[*MS facsimile is copy-text for* 'Dear . . . closet?——' *(125.1–126.23)*]

125.14	⊬ Mr •	[*deletion implied*]
125.15	going •	[◊]oing [*illegible*]
125.15	trouble •	t[◊]ouble [*illegible*]
125.16	black •	[◊]lack [*illegible*]
125.16	hangs •	[◊◊]ngs [*illegible*]
125.25	of •	[◊]f [*illegible*]
125.29	care •	[◊]are [*illegible*]
126.6	bottom •	b[◊◊]tom [*illegible*]
126.7	it, •	it[,] [*illegible*]
126.14	go •	[◊]o [*illegible*]
126.14	with •	[◊◊]th [*illegible*]
126.14–15	~~se~~ such •	sⱡuch
126.15	~~hap~~ habit •	haⱡbit
126.17	should have •	[◊]hould h[◊◊]e [*illegible*]

[*Davis 1977b is copy-text for* 'O.K. . . . 1872' *(126.25–26)*]

126.25	O.K. . . . Conn. •	O.K. at Clemens, Cor. Forest & Hawthorne, Hartford, Conn.
126.26	NEW . . . 1872 •	"New Saybrook, Conn." and "Jul." [*text of postmark adopted in part from* 30 *July* 72 *to MEC; since Davis 1977b reported that the postmark was* 'very dim,' *with* 'no day or year,' *it was probably badly inked*]

■ 20–23 July 1872 · To Mary E. (Mollie) Clemens · New Saybrook, Conn. · *UCCL* 00771

■ *Copy-text:* MS, Mark Twain Papers, The Bancroft Library, University of California, Berkeley (CU-MARK). ■ *Provenance:* see Mark Twain Papers in Description of Provenance. ■ *Emendations and textual notes:*

127.4	your bedroom • your bed-|room
127.12	Conn. • Conn[◇] [*torn*]
127.14	SAYBROOK CONN. JUL 2◇ 1872 • SAYBROO[K] CO[N]N[◇] JUL 2[◇] 1[8]7[2] [*badly inked*]
127.16	~~12~~ 13 • 1$\cancel{2}$3
127.17	~~30~~ 35 • 3$\cancel{0}$5
127.18	~~90~~ 95 • 9$\cancel{0}$5

■ 21 July 1872 · To Joseph L. Blamire · New Saybrook, Conn. · *UCCL* 00772

■ *Copy-text:* MS, Clifton Waller Barrett Library, Alderman Library, University of Virginia, Charlottesville (ViU), is copy-text for the letter and the two enclosures. ■ *Previous publication:* Sotheby 1950, lot 186, brief quotation from letter; University of Virginia, 71, first enclosure only; Welland, 33–34, brief quotation from letter, and texts of both enclosures. ■ *Provenance:* The letter, the property of Frances H. S. Stallybrass (see the commentary for 21 June 72 to Blamire), was offered for sale in 1950 by Sotheby's in London (Sotheby 1950, lot 186). It is not clear whether the enclosures were included in that sale. Information from two unidentified catalogs, now with the MSS at ViU, suggests that Clifton Waller Barrett purchased the letter and the enclosures separately at two later sales. He deposited them at ViU on 16 April 1960. ■ *Emendations and textual notes:*

128.7	either • [*sic*]
128.10	~~in~~ • ['n' *partly formed*]
129.7	republication • re-|publication
129.20	Edition • [◇◇◇◇◇◇]n [*torn*]
129.23	overestimated • overestima$\cancel{/}$ted
129.30	midsummer • mid-|summer

■ 22 or 23 July 1872 · To Mary E. (Mollie) Clemens · New Saybrook, Conn. · *UCCL* 00773

■ *Copy-text:* MS, Mark Twain Papers, The Bancroft Library, University of California, Berkeley (CU-MARK). ■ *Provenance:* see Mark Twain Papers in Description of Provenance.

■ 24 or 25 July 1872 · To Mary E. (Mollie) Clemens · New Saybrook, Conn. · *UCCL* 00774

■*Copy-text:* MS, Mark Twain Papers, The Bancroft Library, University of California, Berkeley (CU-MARK). ■*Provenance:* see Mark Twain Papers in Description of Provenance. ■*Emendations and textual notes:*

131.10   washerwoman • washer-|woman
132.7   ~~Cor~~ Clemens's • Corlemens's
132.8   SAYBROOK CONN. JUL 25 • [◊◊◊◊]ROOK CONN. JU[L] 2[5] [*badly inked*]

■ 25–27? July 1872 · To Mary E. (Mollie) Clemens · New Saybrook, Conn. · *UCCL* 00762

■*Copy-text:* MS, Mark Twain Papers, The Bancroft Library, University of California, Berkeley (CU-MARK). ■*Provenance:* see Mark Twain Papers in Description of Provenance.

■ 28 July 1872 · To Elisha Bliss, Jr. · New Saybrook, Conn. · *UCCL* 00781

■*Copy-text:* MS, Arents Tobacco Collection, The New York Public Library, Astor, Lenox and Tilden Foundations (NN). ■*Provenance:* George Arents (1885–1960) donated his collection of items relating to the history of tobacco to NN in 1944, together with a sizable endowment for further purchases. NN bought the MS, laid in a first edition copy of *Roughing It* (American Publishing Company, 1872), no later than 1981. ■*Emendations and textual notes:*

133.4   copyright • copy-|right

■ 30 July 1872 · To Mary E. (Mollie) Clemens · New Saybrook, Conn. · *UCCL* 00782

■*Copy-text:* MS, Mark Twain Papers, The Bancroft Library, University of California, Berkeley (CU-MARK). ■*Provenance:* see Mark Twain Papers in Description of Provenance. ■*Emendations and textual notes:*

136.7   All • [*possibly '⌀ All'*]
136.12   SAYBROOK • S[A◊]BROOK [*badly inked*]

■ 2 August 1872 · To Mary E. (Mollie) Clemens · New Saybrook, Conn. · *UCCL* 00784

■*Copy-text:* MS, Mark Twain Papers, The Bancroft Library, University of California, Berkeley (CU-MARK). ■*Provenance:* see Mark Twain Papers in Description of Provenance. ■*Emendations and textual notes:*

136.23   Ɬ • [*partly formed*]
137.5   Ḿ • [*partly formed*]
137.10   Clemens • Clem[◊◊◊] [*torn*]

■ 5 August 1872 · To Mary E. (Mollie) Clemens, *per* Telegraph Operator
 · Saybrook Point, Conn. · *UCCL* 00785

■ *Copy-text:* MS, copy received, telegram blank filled out by the receiving telegraph operator, Mark Twain Papers, The Bancroft Library, University of California, Berkeley (CU-MARK). ■*Provenance:* see Mark Twain Papers in Description of Provenance. ■*Emendations and textual notes:*

137.23   10 • [*circled by the telegraph operator*]
137.25   collect • [*partly circled by the telegraph operator*]
138.2   Hawthorn • Haw[t◊◊◊◊] [*torn*]
138.2   PRES'T. • [◊◊◊◊◊◊◊] [*torn*]
138.3   CO. • c[◊◊] [*torn*]

■ 6 August 1872 · To Charles M. Underhill · New Saybrook, Conn. ·
 UCCL 08840

■ *Copy-text:* MS, Henry W. and Albert A. Berg Collection, The New York Public
Library, Astor, Lenox and Tilden Foundations (NN-B). ■*Provenance:* The MS
was owned by businessman William T. H. Howe (1874–1939); in 1940 Dr. A. A.
Berg bought and donated the Howe Collection to NN. ■*Emendations and textual
notes:*

138.15   believeing • ['g' *partly formed*]

■ 7 August 1872 · To Elisha Bliss, Jr. · New Saybrook, Conn. · *UCCL*
 00787

■ *Copy-text:* MS, Willard S. Morse Collection, Collection of American Literature, Beinecke Rare Book and Manuscript Library, Yale University (CtY-BR).
■*Previous publication: MTLP,* 73–74. ■*Provenance:* The Morse Collection was
donated to CtY in 1942 by Walter F. Frear.

■ 8 August 1872 · To Mary E. (Mollie) Clemens, *per* Telegraph Operator
 · (1st of 2) · Saybrook Point, Conn. · *UCCL* 00788

■ *Copy-text:* MS, copy received, telegram blank filled out by the receiving telegraph operator, Mark Twain Papers, The Bancroft Library, University of Cali-

fornia, Berkeley (CU-MARK). ▪*Provenance:* see Mark Twain Papers in Description of Provenance. ▪*Emendations and textual notes:*

141.13 infernal • inf~~er~~n̂ern̂al [*rewritten for clarity*]
142.2 NO. . . . CHARGES. • [◇◇◇] . . . [◇◇◇]RGES. [*torn; text adopted from envelope with 5 Aug 72 to MEC*]

▪ 8 August 1872 · To Mary E. (Mollie) Clemens · (2nd of 2) · New Saybrook, Conn. · *UCCL* 00789

▪*Copy-text:* MS, Mark Twain Papers, The Bancroft Library, University of California, Berkeley (CU-MARK). ▪*Provenance:* see Mark Twain Papers in Description of Provenance. ▪*Emendations and textual notes:*

142.11 Conn. • Con[n◇] [*torn*]

▪ 11 August 1872 · To Orion Clemens · New Saybrook, Conn. · *UCCL* 00791

▪*Copy-text:* MS, Mark Twain Papers, The Bancroft Library, University of California, Berkeley (CU-MARK). Clemens's drawing is photographically reproduced at actual size. ▪*Previous publication: MTB,* 1:457, paraphrase; *MTL,* 1:196–97; Davis 1977c, 1; Davis 1987, 3; Clemens's drawing omitted from all. ▪*Provenance:* either Mark Twain Papers or Moffett Collection (see Description of Provenance). ▪*Emendations and textual notes:*

143.8 ~~whch~~ which • wh~~ch~~ĥich
143.8–9 scrap-book • scrap-\book
143.12 tragicanth • [*sic*]
143.16 ~~dap~~ • ['p' *partly formed*]
144.2 ~~brs~~ broad • br‰oad
144.7 evidence/ • [*deletion implied*]
144.18–19 SAYBROOK CONN. AUG 1◇ • SA[Y◇◇◇◇K] CONN. [A◇◇] 1[◇] [*badly inked*]

▪ 11 August 1872 · To Mary Mason Fairbanks · New Saybrook, Conn. · *UCCL* 00792

▪*Copy-text:* MS, Henry E. Huntington Library, San Marino (CSmH, call no. HM 14278). ▪*Previous publication: MTMF,* 163–64; Grenander 1975, 1, excerpt; Davis 1977b, 3, excerpt. ▪*Provenance:* see Huntington Library in Description of Provenance.

■ 16 August 1872 · To Mary E. (Mollie) Clemens, *per* Telegraph Operator · Saybrook Point, Conn. · *UCCL* 00794

■*Copy-text:* MS, copy received, telegram blank filled out by the receiving telegraph operator, Mark Twain Papers, The Bancroft Library, University of California, Berkeley (CU-MARK). ■*Provenance:* see Mark Twain Papers in Description of Provenance.

■ 16 or 17 August 1872 · To Orion or Mary E. (Mollie) Clemens · New Saybrook, Conn. · *UCCL* 10727

■*Copy-text:* MS, Mark Twain Papers, The Bancroft Library, University of California, Berkeley (CU-MARK). ■*Provenance:* see Mark Twain Papers in Description of Provenance.

■ 19 August 1872 · To Olivia L. Clemens · Hartford, Conn. · *UCCL* 00795

■*Copy-text:* MS, Henry W. and Albert A. Berg Collection, The New York Public Library, Astor, Lenox and Tilden Foundations (NN-B). ■*Provenance:* purchased in 1972 from Seven Gables Bookshop. ■*Emendations and textual notes:*

| 148.14 | ~~na~~ near • n⟨a⟩ear |
| 149.6 | accumulated • accumul⟨f⟩ated |

■ 20 August 1872 · To Olivia L. Clemens · New York, N.Y. · *UCCL* 00796

■*Copy-text:* MS, collection of Chester L. Davis, Jr., is copy-text for the letter and envelope. The letter was written on the backs of two related flyers, one green and one blue, advertising the "Williams and Packard Patent Copy-book" and penmanship system. The flyers were printed by Slote, Woodman and Company, publishers of the copy-book. MS, Mark Twain Papers, The Bancroft Library, University of California, Berkeley (CU-MARK), is copy-text for the enclosure; it is photographically reproduced at 50 percent of actual size. ■*Previous publication: LLMT*, 363, brief paraphrase of letter only; Davis 1977c, 2, and Davis 1987, 4, letter only; Christie 1991b, lot 187, excerpt from letter. ■*Provenance:* The letter MS, part of the Samossoud Collection in the late 1940s when it was transcribed by Dixon Wecter, was acquired by Chester L. Davis, Sr., from Clara Clemens Samossoud between 1949 and 1962 (see Samossoud Collection in Description of Provenance). After Davis's death in 1987, the letter MS was owned by Chester L. Davis, Jr., who sold it through Christie's in December 1991. For the enclosure see Mark Twain Papers in Description of Provenance. ■*Emendations and textual notes:*

149.18   bath-tub • bath-|tub
150.2   tomorrow • to-|morrow
150.3   b̶a̶l̶ • ['l' *partly formed*]

■ 29 August 1872 · To Olivia L. Clemens · SS *Scotia* en route from New York, N.Y., to Liverpool, England · *UCCL* 00800

■ *Copy-text:* MS, Mark Twain Papers, The Bancroft Library, University of California, Berkeley (CU-MARK). ■ *Previous publication: LLMT,* 176; Davis 1977a, 1, brief excerpt. ■ *Provenance:* see Samossoud Collection in Description of Provenance.

■ 1 September 1872 · To Olivia L. Clemens · Liverpool, England · *UCCL* 00803

■ *Copy-text:* MS, Mark Twain Papers, The Bancroft Library, University of California, Berkeley (CU-MARK). ■ *Previous publication: LLMT,* 363, brief paraphrase. ■ *Provenance:* see Samossoud Collection in Description of Provenance. ■ *Emendations and textual notes:*

153.10   sts • s[ts] [*torn*]

■ 11 September 1872 · To Olivia L. Clemens · London, England · *UCCL* 00805

■ *Copy-text:* MS, Mark Twain Papers, The Bancroft Library, University of California, Berkeley (CU-MARK). ■ *Previous publication: LLMT,* 177, with omission; Davis 1977a, 1, brief excerpt. ■ *Provenance:* see Samossoud Collection in Description of Provenance. ■ *Emendations and textual notes:*

154.4   f̶r̶ first • f/irst
155.6   Chrystal • [*sic*]
155.9   Londay • [*sic*]
155.18   T̶o̶m̶ Thomas • Thomas ['as' *added*]
155.32 $̶5̶0̶0̶ $600 • $/600 ͵600ͅ ['600' *rewritten for clarity; added above the revised figure and circled, with an arrow indicating its position*]
155.34   YORK • [Y]ORK [*badly inked*]

■ 13 September–11 November 1872 · To Henry Lee · London, England · *UCCL* 09891

■ *Copy-text:* Dawson's Book Shop 1938, item 161.

■ 13–18 September 1872 · To James R. Osgood · London, England · *UCCL* 00937

■ *Copy-text:* Rendell 1970, item 35, which describes the letter as an "ALS, 1p., 8vo, The Langham, undated. On his crested stationery, to 'Dear Osgood.'" ■ *Emendations and textual notes:*

158.5–6   (SLC) . . . Langham • [*reported, not quoted*]

■ 15 September 1872 · To Olivia L. Clemens · London, England · *UCCL* 00807

■ *Copy-text:* MS, collection of Chester L. Davis, Jr. ■ *Previous publication: MTB,* 1:469, excerpt; *MTL,* 1:199; Christie 1991b, lot 188, with omission. ■ *Provenance:* Chester L. Davis, Sr., probably acquired the MS from Clara Clemens Samossoud between 1949 and 1962 (see Samossoud Collection in Description of Provenance). After Davis's death in 1987, the MS was owned by Chester L. Davis, Jr., who sold it through Christie's in December 1991. ■ *Emendations and textual notes:*

159.4   present. Mr. • ~.—|~.
159.4   D̶o̶b̶ Dolby • Dob̶lby
159.5   tomorrow • to-|morrow
160.1   day. And • ~.—|~

■ 17 September 1872 · To Arthur Locker · London, England · *UCCL* 00808

■ *Copy-text:* MS, Mark Twain Archives and Center for Mark Twain Studies at Quarry Farm, Elmira College (NElmC). ■ *Provenance:* The MS was donated to NelmC in 1974 by William T. Love, Jr., who purchased it from B. Altman, a New York City department store.

■ 20 September 1872 · To the Editor of the London *Spectator* · London, England · *UCCL* 00809

■ *Copy-text:* "Mark Twain and His English Editor," London *Spectator,* 21 Sept 72, 1201–2. ■ *Previous publication: Every Saturday,* n.s. 3 (2 Nov 72): 504; Kozlay, 48–51; Johnson, 160–62; Neider 1961, 157–58; Grenander 1975, 2, brief excerpt. ■ *Emendations and textual notes:*

163.1   To . . . "SPECTATOR." • [~ . . . "~."]
163.3   & • and [*here and hereafter, except at 164.22, where copy-text reads* '&c.']

■ 22 September 1872 · To Olivia L. Clemens · London, England · *UCCL* 00810

■*Copy-text:* MS, Mark Twain Papers, The Bancroft Library, University of California, Berkeley (CU-MARK). ■*Previous publication: LLMT,* 178. ■*Provenance:* see Samossoud Collection in Description of Provenance. ■*Emendations and textual notes:*

169.3	sight-seeing • sight-|seeing
169.17	sweetheart • sweet-|heart
169.17	assure • assure assure
169.23	LONDON · W 6 • [◊]ONDON · W [6] [*badly inked*]
169.23	NEW YORK OCT 5 PAID • [◊]EW [Y]ORK [◊◊]T 5 [◊]AID [*badly inked*]

■ 22 September 1872 · To Moncure D. Conway · (1st of 2) · London, England · *UCCL* 11873

■*Copy-text:* Anderson Galleries 1920a, lot 47. ■*Provenance:* The MS belonged to Moncure D. Conway's son, Eustace Conway, when it was sold in 1920. ■*Emendations and textual notes:*

171.1	47. CLEMENS (SAMUEL L.). • 47. —— [*lot 47 was the second of three Clemens lots in the sale; the author's name was provided only with the first lot and has been supplied here in place of the dash*]

■ 22 September 1872 · To Moncure D. Conway · (2nd of 2) · London, England · *UCCL* 00811

■*Copy-text:* MS, Conway Papers, Columbia University (NNC), is copy-text for the letter. The MS for the enclosure has not been found. The source for it is "Mark Twain in London," Cincinnati *Commercial,* 10 Oct 72, 4 (Conway 1872). Copy-text is a microfilm edition of the newspaper in the Library of Congress (DLC). ■*Previous publication:* numerous newspapers, including "Mark Twain in London," Newark (N.J.) *Advertiser,* 14 Oct 72, 2; Cleveland *Leader,* 15 Oct 72, 3; Cleveland *Herald,* 19 Oct 72; *MTS* 1910, 417–21; *MTB,* 3:1630–32; *MTS* 1923, 37–41; Fatout 1976, 69–72; all enclosure only. ■*Provenance:* The Conway Papers were acquired by NNC sometime after Conway's death in 1907. ■*Emendations and textual notes:* The quotation marks added by Conway for his printing of Clemens's speech in the Cincinnati *Commercial* have been silently removed, and the internal single quotation marks silently restored to double ones, as they presumably were in the MS. The explanatory remarks that Conway inserted into the speech (at Clemens's suggestion) have been removed from the text and quoted verbatim in the notes, rather than being recorded here as emendations.

172.20	[¶] Mr. Chairman & gentlemen, it • [*no* ¶] "Mr. Chairman and gentlemen," he began, "it

172.21   & • and [*here and hereafter*]
174.5–37   Memorial.* . . . [¶] *Sarcasm . . . obscurity. • Memorial. [¶]
            [Sarcasm . . . obscurity.] [*footnote moved to bottom of page to accord
            with SLC's usual style*]

■ 23 September 1872 · To T. B. Pugh · London, England · *UCCL*
00812

■ *Copy-text:* MS, Historical Society of Pennsylvania, Philadelphia (PHi). ■ *Provenance:* The MS is in the section of American Prose Writers in the wide-ranging
Dreer Collection, donated to PHi by collector Ferdinand Julius Dreer (1812–
1902). Dreer acquired the MS sometime before 1890 (Dreer, 1:123).

■ 25 September 1872 · To Olivia L. Clemens · London, England ·
UCCL 00814

■ *Copy-text:* MS, Mark Twain Papers, The Bancroft Library, University of California, Berkeley (CU-MARK). ■ *Previous publication: LLMT*, 363, brief paraphrase. ■ *Provenance:* see Samossoud Collection in Description of Provenance.
■ *Emendations and textual notes:*

178.12   st sleepy • s⁄leepy ['t' *partly formed*]
179.16   Baily⁄ey • ['y' *partly formed*]
179.17   na made • m⁄made
179.28   Sob Somebody • Sob⁄mebody [*canceled* 'b' *partly formed*]
180.4   YORK OCT 7 PAID ALL • YO[◇◇] OC[T 7 ◇◇◇◇ ◇◇◇]

■ 28 September 1872 · To Elisha Bliss, Jr. · London, England · *UCCL*
00816

■ *Copy-text:* MS, Mark Twain Papers, The Bancroft Library, University of California, Berkeley (CU-MARK). The MS, a single leaf, has been mounted on
paper so that some letters and punctuation at the right and bottom edges of the
verso are partially obscured. ■ *Previous publication: MTB*, 1:462–63, excerpt;
MTL, 1:199–200, with omission; Anderson Galleries 1916, lot 22, excerpt.
■ *Provenance:* see Appert Collection in Description of Provenance. ■ *Emendations
and textual notes:*

182.4   tonight • to-|night
182.6   being . . . being • [*sic*]
182.6   bet being • be⁄ing ['t' *partly formed*]
182.8   called. • called[.] [*obscured by mounting*]
182.10   assistance • assi⁄stance
182.10   want • wan[t] [*obscured by mounting*]

182.11	enclosed • enclose[d] [*obscured by mounting*]
182.12	It, • [*deletion implied*]
182.18	they are coming. • the[y] a[re] co[◊◊◊◊◊] [*obscured by mounting*]

■ 28 September 1872 · To Olivia L. Clemens · London, England · UCCL 00815

■ *Copy-text:* MS, Mark Twain Papers, The Bancroft Library, University of California, Berkeley (CU-MARK). Both enclosures survive with the letter. Straight's note was written on a scrap of paper measuring 7 by 3 inches, torn from a larger sheet, conceivably a menu or program for the event (a small section of printed box is visible on the back of the note). Bennett's calling card is photographically reproduced at actual size. ■ *Previous publication: LLMT,* 178–79. ■ *Provenance:* see Samossoud Collection in Description of Provenance. ■ *Emendations and textual notes:*

183.7	Tonight • To-|night
183.8	news • [*sic*]
183.10–11	me. There • ~.—|~
183.16	such • ~~such~~ such [*corrected miswriting*]
184.3	unlocked-for • [*sic*]
184.4	~~my~~ • ['y' *partly formed*]
184.6	nothing • nothiny̨g
184.9	~~rep~~ respond • rep̨spond [*canceled* 'p' *partly formed*]
185.10	◊◊ PAID • [◊◊] P[◊◊]D [*badly inked*]

■ 3 October 1872 · To Olivia L. Clemens · London, England · UCCL 00817

■ *Copy-text:* MS, Mark Twain Papers, The Bancroft Library, University of California, Berkeley (CU-MARK). ■ *Previous publication:* Wecter, 85–86, with omission; *LLMT,* 180–81. ■ *Provenance:* see Samossoud Collection in Description of Provenance. ■ *Emendations and textual notes:*

188.21	~~upo~~ unto • up̨onto
189.2	~~el~~ • ['l' *partly formed*]
189.3	spinning • ~~spinnn~~ ‖ sp̨inning [*corrected miswriting*]
189.5	~~ad~~ • ad-|
189.22–23	~~graceful~~ . . . Niagara • grace-|~~ful little Niagara~~|ful, gorgeous little Niagara
189.24	loveliest • loveli~~s~~test
189.32	America • Americ[◊] [*obscured by postage stamp*]

■ 4 October 1872 · To Henry Lee · London, England · *UCCL* 00818

■*Copy-text:* MS, collection of Todd M. Axelrod. The letter was written on a halfpenny postcard printed in violet ink and measuring 4¾ by 3 inches, of a type in use from November 1870 until January 1875 (Marshall, 43, 46). The royal coat of arms appearing under the words 'POST CARD' (191.9) has not been reproduced here. ■*Previous publication:* Current Company, item 29; Todd M. Axelrod, 124. ■*Provenance:* The MS was sold in 1977 by the Current Company of Rhode Island. It was acquired—perhaps then, certainly before 1981—by Jim Williams, a collector. Axelrod owned it by June 1983.

■ 5 October 1872 · To Charles Dudley Warner · London, England · *UCCL* 00819

■*Copy-text:* MS, Mark Twain Papers, The Bancroft Library, University of California, Berkeley (CU-MARK), is copy-text for the letter. The enclosure does not survive. The source for it is "The Scottish Corporation and Mr. Stanley and Mark Twain," Darlington *Northern Echo*, 3 Oct 72, 3 (Fitzgibbon 1872). The text printed here is a line-for-line resetting of the article. Copy-text is a microfilm edition of the newspaper at the Georgia State University Library (GASU). ■*Provenance:* The MS was donated to CU-MARK in January 1950 by Mary Barton, a close friend of the Warners', who had owned it since at least 1938. ■*Emendations and textual notes:*

192.36   Sheriff's · [*sic*]

193.11   OCT 20 PAID ALL · [◊◊T] 2[0] PAID [◊]LL [*badly inked*]

■ 5 October 1872 · To George H. Fitzgibbon · London, England · *UCCL* 00820

■*Copy-text:* MS, Cyril Clemens Collection, Mark Twain House, Hartford (CtHMTH). The MS was written entirely in pencil. Sometime later an unidentified person, using ink, attempted to trace over the pencil exactly, often obliterating the pencil beneath. The tracer occasionally missed punctuation and the crossbars on *t*'s, and in one case mistraced entirely, so that Clemens's 'kindest' (194.19) became 'kindact' in the ink version. ■*Previous publication:* Henkels 1930b, lot 380; AAA /Anderson 1934a, lot 127; Parke-Bernet 1946, lot 88; all brief excerpts. ■*Provenance:* The MS was apparently purchased in 1930 by Edmund W. Evans, Jr., of Oil City, Pennsylvania, who offered it for sale again in April 1934. In 1946 it was sold as part of the collection of W. W. Cohen. Cyril Clemens donated it to CtHMTH in 1984.

■ 6 October 1872 · To Moncure D. Conway · London, England · *UCCL* 00821

■*Copy-text:* MS, Conway Papers, Columbia University (NNC). ■*Provenance:* The Conway Papers were acquired by NNC sometime after Conway's death in 1907. ■*Emendations and textual notes:*

195.5–6   offered • offerϕed

■ 12 October 1872 · To Olivia L. Clemens · London, England · *UCCL* 00822

■*Copy-text:* MS, James L. Copley Library, La Jolla, California (CLjC). ■*Previous publication: MTB*, 1:469–70, brief paraphrase; Davis 1978, 1; Christie 1991a, lot 88, with omissions. ■*Provenance:* Chester L. Davis, Sr., probably acquired the MS from Clara Clemens Samossoud between 1949 and 1962 (see Samossoud Collection in Description of Provenance). After Davis's death in 1987, the MS was owned by Chester L. Davis, Jr., who sold it through Christie's in May 1991 to CLjC. ■*Emendations and textual notes:*

196.9   be╪ • be-| [*deletion implied*]
196.13   ~~their~~ there • the╪rre [*canceled* 'r' *partly formed*]
197.6   Routledge's • [*sic*]
197.10   ~~con~~ • con-|
197.14   NEW YORK OCT 2◊ PAID ALL • N[◊]W YORK OCT [2◊] PAID A[LL]
          [*badly inked*]

■ 18 October 1872 · To Unidentified · London, England · *UCCL* 11320

■*Copy-text:* MS facsimile. The editors have not seen the MS, which was owned in 1985 by Todd M. Axelrod, who provided a photocopy to the Mark Twain Papers. ■*Emendations and textual notes:*

197.19   indefinite • indefinite╪ [*deletion of second* 'e' *implied by retracing of first*]

■ 25 October 1872 · To Henry Lee · London, England · *UCCL* 00824

■*Copy-text:* MS, Clifton Waller Barrett Library, Alderman Library, University of Virginia, Charlottesville (ViU). The letter was written on a halfpenny postcard identical to the one described in the commentary for 4 Oct 72 to Lee. ■*Provenance:* The MS was at one time in the autograph collection of Dr. Max Thorek of Chicago. It was later acquired by Clifton Waller Barrett, who deposited it at ViU on 15 May 1962. ▪*Emendations and textual notes:*

198.4	ĭ • [*partly formed*]
198.18	◊◊ 3 OC25 • [◊◊] 3 OC2[5] [*badly inked*]

▪ 25 October 1872 · To Olivia L. Clemens · London, England · *UCCL* 00823

▪*Copy-text:* MS, Mark Twain Papers, The Bancroft Library, University of California, Berkeley (CU-MARK). Clemens's drawing is photographically reproduced at actual size. ▪*Previous publication: LLMT*, 363, brief paraphrase. ▪*Provenance:* see Samossoud Collection in Description of Provenance. ▪*Emendations and textual notes:*

199.4	second-hand • second-|hand
199.13	sieze • [*sic*]
199.21	~~And be as~~ As • ~~And be~~ ⱯAs
199.31	snarling • snar⫿ling
201.3	gla⌀d • ['d' *over partly formed character, possibly* 'ŋ' *or* 'ɲ']
201.21	YORK NOV 6 PAID ALL • YO[RK] N[OV 6] [P◊◊◊ ◊◊◊] [*badly inked*]

▪ 2 November 1872 · To Mary Mason Fairbanks · London, England · *UCCL* 00825

▪*Copy-text:* MS, Henry E. Huntington Library, San Marino (CSmH, call no. HM 14279). Clemens's drawing is photographically reproduced at actual size. ▪*Previous publication: MTMF*, 165–68. ▪*Provenance:* see Huntington Library in Description of Provenance. ▪*Emendations and textual notes:*

205.2	English • Ɇ English ['Ɇ' *partly formed; corrected miswriting*]
205.26	days. I • ~.—|~
205.27	pigskin-breeched • pig-|skin-breeched
205.36	Ɉ • [*partly formed*]
206.12	There • Therere [*corrected miswriting; possibly* 'Theirere']
206.36	ʂ • [*partly formed*]

▪ 3 November 1872 · To James Redpath · London, England · *UCCL* 00828

▪*Copy-text:* None. The text is based on two transcriptions, each of which derives independently from the MS:

P¹	Typescript (CtLHi)
P²	Will M. Clemens, 29

P¹, an unidentified typescript in the Litchfield Historical Society (CtLHi), contains the entire text of the letter and is the only source that records the docket of the Boston Lyceum Bureau (209.9). Although nothing is known about the origin of P¹, it appears to be relatively modern and it is clear that it was based on the MS. P² omits several passages but is the only source for 'Langham Hotel' (208.1). Five other partial texts, listed below under *Previous publication*, may derive independently from the MS, but contain no persuasively authorial variants. The three catalogs describe the MS as consisting of four pages, and the Anderson and Swann catalogs mention that it was written in pencil. ■*Previous publication:* Bangs 1901, lot 118 (misdated 1871); Anderson Auction Company 1909, lot 303; *MTB,* 1:473; Paine 1912, 107; and Swann, lot 234; all excerpts. ■*Provenance:* The MS may have been owned (or merely borrowed) by Will Clemens before he published it in 1900. It was sold by an unnamed consignor in 1901, and in November 1909 was again offered for sale as part of the collection of Frank Maier, by which time it was laid in a first edition copy of *Roughing It* (American Publishing Company, 1872). By 1977 the MS was part of the K. Benjamin DeForest Curtiss Collection of Watertown Library (Watertown, Conn.), which sold it in that year—still in the copy of *Roughing It*—through Swann Galleries. The unidentified typescript was also in the Curtiss Collection, before it went to Litchfield. ■*Emendations, adopted readings, and textual notes:* Handwritten changes on P¹ deemed to be simple corrections of typing errors or omissions are not reported, but the handwritten deletions of typed underscores at 208.19, 208.20, and 208.21 are reported because they may in some way reflect the appearance of the missing MS.

208.1–2	Langham . . . 3 (C) • Langham Hall | London Nov. 3 (P¹); LANGHAM HOTEL, LONDON, Nov. 3, 1872. (P²)
208.3	Dear Redpath— (C) • Dear Redpath (P¹); *Dear Redpath:* (P²)
208.4–11	Good . . . of (P¹) • " * * * I was down for a speech at (P²)
208.10	Whitefriars Club (P¹) • Whitefriar's Club, (P²)
208.10	& (C) • and (P¹,²) [*here and hereafter*]
208.11	right hand (P¹) • right, (P²)
208.11	know (P²) • knew (P¹)
208.11	all of (P¹) • all (P²)
208.12	Whitefriars (P¹) • ∼, (P²)
208.12	time. But (P¹) • time, but (P²)
208.13	head (P¹) • ∼, (P²)
208.13	Thursday & (C) • Thursday and (P¹); Thursday, (P²)
208.13	staid (P¹) • stayed (P²)
208.14	night (P¹) • ∼, (P²)
208.15	*the night before* (P¹) • the night before (P²)
208.18	[¶] I (P¹) • [*no* ¶] ∼ (P²)
208.18	revamping (P¹) • re-vamping (P²)
208.18	polishing & otherwise (C) • polishing and otherwise (P¹); polishing, in other words (P²)

208.19	Roughing It (C) • Roughing It (P¹); 'Roughing It' (P²)
208.19	times (P¹) • ~, (P²)
208.20–23	Have . . . homewards. (P¹) • [*not in*] (P²)
208.20	large offers (C) • large offers (P¹)
208.21	all (C) • all (P¹)
208.21–22	declined, (C) • ~∧ (P¹)
208.24	*should* (P¹) • should (P²)
208.25	2 (P¹) • two (P²)
208.25	15 (P¹) • fifteen (P²)
208.25	minutes, (P¹) • ~∧ (P²)
208.26	charged (P²) • charge (P¹)
208.26	squawk, (P¹) • squeak (P²)
209.1	*fashion* (P¹) • fashion (P²)
209.1	hear us (P¹) • ~ ~— (P²)
209.2	*always* (P¹) • always (P²)
209.3	[¶] When (P¹) • [*no* ¶] ~ (P²)
209.4	intentions (P¹) • intention (P²)
209.5	How . . . news. (P¹) • [*not in*] (P²)
209.6	Ys (C) • As (P¹); Yours (P²)
209.7	Mark (C) • Mark (P¹); MARK. (P²)
209.9	BOSTON . . . 1872 (C) • BOSTON LYCEUM BUREAU RED-PATH & FALLS NOV 25 1872 [*facsimile of docket drawn by hand*] (P¹); [*not in*] (P²)

■ 3 November 1872 · To W. A. Turner · London, England · *UCCL* 00827

■*Copy-text:* MS, Cyril Clemens Collection, Mark Twain House, Hartford (CtHMTH). ■*Provenance:* donated to CtHMTH in 1984 by Cyril Clemens. ■*Emendations and textual notes:*

212.4–213.1	lie literarily • li⊄terarily
213.1	overlook • over-|look

■ 4–11 November 1872 · To Susan L. Crane · London, England · *UCCL* 00826

■*Copy-text: MTB*, 1:470. Albert Bigelow Paine also quoted this portion of the letter in *MTL* (1:200–201), omitting two sentences (213.13–15). Letters printed in *MTL* are usually more complete than those excerpted in *MTB*, and preserve details of the MS more accurately (see the discussion in the Description of

Texts). In this case, however, *MTB* has the fuller text and, in the few instances where it differs from *MTL*, seems to contain readings closer to Clemens's usage of the period. It seems probable that the text in *MTL* derives from that in *MTB*, but since it is possible that both derive from the MS or from a lost transcription, the rejected readings of *MTL* are reported. ■*Emendations, adopted readings, and textual notes:*

213.11	& . . . & . . . & (C) • and . . . and . . . and	(*MTB*, *MTL*)
	[*here and hereafter*]	
213.11	spring (*MTB*) • Spring (*MTL*)	
213.12	summer, (*MTB*) • ~∧ (*MTL*)	
213.12	shall (*MTB*) • will (*MTL*)	
213.13	fairy-land (*MTB*) • Fairyland (*MTL*)	
213.13–15	There . . . nature. (*MTB*) • [*not in*] (*MTL*)	
213.16	[¶] And (*MTB*) • [*no* ¶] and (*MTL*)	

■ 5 November 1872 · To Henry Lee · London, England · *UCCL* 11069

■*Copy-text:* MS facsimile. The editors have not seen the MS, which was owned in 1984 by Todd M. Axelrod, who provided a photocopy to the Mark Twain Papers. ■*Emendations and textual notes:*

214.7	spend • spenŕd
214.8	O.K.. • [*sic*]

■ 5 November 1872 · To the Editor of the London *Daily News* · London, England · *UCCL* 11068

■*Copy-text:* "Mark Twain," London *Daily News*, 6 Nov 72, 2. Copy-text is a microfilm edition of the newspaper in the British Library (Uk). ■*Previous publication:* "Mark Twain," London *Morning Post*, 7 Nov 72, 6; "Mark Twain," London *Times*, 7 Nov 72, 8. ■*Emendations and textual notes:* The copy-text reading 'greatest,' which was probably an error introduced by the *Daily News*, has been emended to 'greater'—the reading in the amanuensis copy of 8 Nov 72, as well as in the London *Morning Post* and *Times* printings.

215.3	& • and [*here and hereafter*]
215.5	greater • greatest

■ 6 November 1872 · To Jane Lampton Clemens and Pamela A. Moffett · London, England · *UCCL* 00829

■*Copy-text:* MS, Jean Webster McKinney Family Papers, Vassar College Library (NPV). ■*Previous publication: MTB*, 1:470, excerpt; *MTL*, 1:201–2, with omis-

sion. ■*Provenance:* see McKinney Family Papers in Description of Provenance.
■*Emendations and textual notes:*

215.13   everlasting • ever-|lasting
216.3   Guildhall • Guild-|hall

■ **6 November–10 December 1872 · To Mary Mason Fairbanks · London, England · *UCCL* 11817**

■*Copy-text:* Transcript, handwritten by Julia Beecher in Thomas K. Beecher to Ella L. Wolcott, 13 Dec 72, Harriet Beecher Stowe Center, Hartford (CtHSD). ■*Provenance:* Thomas K. Beecher's letters to Ella Wolcott are part of the extensive Beecher family collection at CtHSD, whose holdings were originally collected by Katharine Seymour Day (1870–1964), grandniece of Harriet Beecher Stowe.

■ **8 November 1872 · To the Editor of the London *Telegraph*, *per* Unidentified · London, England · *UCCL* 00830**

■*Copy-text:* MS, Clifton Waller Barrett Library, Alderman Library, University of Virginia, Charlottesville (ViU). ■*Provenance:* deposited at ViU by Clifton Waller Barrett on 15 May 1962. ■*Emendations and textual notes:*

220.12   DLJ • [*possibly* 'DSJ']

■ **10 November 1872 · To Olivia L. Clemens · London, England · *UCCL* 00831**

■*Copy-text:* MS, Mark Twain Papers, The Bancroft Library, University of California, Berkeley (CU-MARK). ■*Previous publication: LLMT,* 181–82; Davis 1978. ■*Provenance:* see Samossoud Collection in Description of Provenance. ■*Emendations and textual notes:*

221.10   ~~be-g~~ be-wigged • be-g̸wigged
221.21   23 • 2[3] [*badly inked*]

■ **20 November 1872 · To the Royal Humane Society · SS *Batavia* en route from Liverpool, England, to Boston, Mass. · *UCCL* 00833**

■*Copy-text:* "A Daring Deed," Boston *Advertiser,* 26 Nov 72, 4, clipping in the Mark Twain Papers, The Bancroft Library, University of California, Berkeley (CU-MARK). Since the clipping is slightly damaged, the editors have also consulted a microfilm edition of the newspaper in the Library of Congress (DLC). ■*Previous publication:* numerous newspapers, including "Perils of the Sea," New

York *Times,* 26 Nov 72, 1; "A Daring Deed," Boston *Evening Transcript,* 26 Nov 72, 1; "Perils of the Sea," Hartford *Courant,* 27 Nov 72, 1; "Perils of the Sea," Cleveland *Leader,* 30 Nov 72, 3; "Disasters at Sea," London *Times,* 12 Dec 72, 7; "Perils of the Sea," London *Morning Post,* 27 Dec 72, 8; *MTB,* 1:471, brief excerpt; Brownell 1949, 1–2. ■ *Emendations and textual notes:*

222.5	& • and [*here and hereafter*]
222.10	staterooms • state-|rooms
224.16	quartermasters • quarter-|masters
226.2	Denmead • Demmead

■ 23 November 1872 · From Samuel L. Clemens and Others to John E. Mouland · SS *Batavia* en route from Liverpool, England, to Boston, Mass. · *UCCL* 00834

■ *Copy-text:* MS, Clifton Waller Barrett Library, Alderman Library, University of Virginia, Charlottesville (ViU). ■ *Previous publication:* numerous newspapers, including "A Daring Deed," Boston *Advertiser,* 26 Nov 72, 4; "A Daring Deed," Boston *Evening Transcript,* 26 Nov 72, 1; "Perils of the Sea," Hartford *Courant,* 27 Nov 72, 1; Brownell 1949, 2–3. ■ *Provenance:* deposited at ViU by Clifton Waller Barrett on 16 April 1960. ■ *Emendations and textual notes:*

227.2	O̶f̶ On • Ofn ['f' *partly formed; possibly* 'l']
228.1	t̶h̶e̶ those • thŕose
228.11	exercise • e̶x̶ ‖ exercise
228.14	d̶e̶a̶d̶ deed • deḁed

■ 26 November 1872 · From Mary E. (Mollie) Clemens and Samuel L. Clemens to Jane Lampton Clemens and Pamela A. Moffett · Hartford, Conn. · *UCCL* 00835

■ *Copy-text:* MS, Jean Webster McKinney Family Papers, Vassar College Library (NPV). Mollie Clemens wrote on the first three pages of a folder; Clemens filled the fourth page. ■ *Provenance:* see McKinney Family Papers in Description of Provenance. ■ *Emendations and textual notes:*

230.1	terriffic • [*sic*]
230.7	Fejeee • Tejeee [*crossbar omitted*]
230.11	∮ or • ∮ o̶r̶ or ['∮' *partly formed; corrected miswriting*]
230.21	$̶4̶ $140 • $⁄140

■ December 1872 · To the Editor of the *Literary World* · Hartford, Conn. · *UCCL* 00836

■ *Copy-text:* MS, Beinecke Rare Book and Manuscript Library, Yale University (CtY-BR). Clemens wrote his letter in the margins of page 106 of the 1 December

1872 issue of the *Literary World: A Review of Current Literature.* The page is photographically reproduced, at 68 percent of actual size, in Appendix F. ∎*Provenance:* The MS was formerly laid in a first edition copy of *The Innocents Abroad*
(American Publishing Company, 1869) owned by Owen F. Aldis (1852–1925),
who donated his collection of American literature to CtY in 1911 (Cannon, 180).
∎*Emendations and textual notes:*

232.9   dares to • dares͓ to [*false start*]

∎ 3 December 1872 · To the Editor of the San Francisco *Alta California*
 · Hartford, Conn. · *UCCL* 00837
∎*Copy-text:* MS, Houghton Library, Harvard University (MH-H). The MS was
annotated in pencil, apparently by someone on the *Alta* editorial staff: at the top
of the first page was written "City 1x"; "x" was added to Clemens's own page
numbering on the next two pages. Also at the top of the first page was written
"Appeal for Capt. Ned Wakeman," the title under which the letter was published
in the newspaper, and Clemens's "To the Editor of the Alta:" was revised to read
"Editors Alta:"—again matching the published text. ∎*Previous publication:* "Appeal for Capt. Ned Wakeman—Letter from 'Mark Twain,'" San Francisco *Alta
California*, 14 Dec 72, 1. ∎*Provenance:* bequeathed to MH by Evert Jansen Wendell (1860–1917), a Harvard alumnus and collector of theater memorabilia
(Dickinson, 332–33). ∎*Emendations and textual notes:*

233.2 $ • [*partly formed; possibly* 'E']

∎ 3 December 1872 · To Olivia Lewis Langdon · Hartford, Conn. ·
UCCL 00838
∎*Copy-text:* MS, Mark Twain House, Hartford (CtHMTH). ∎*Provenance:* donated to CtHMTH in 1962 or 1963 by Ida Langdon. ∎*Emendations and textual
notes:*

235.8   *daylight* • *day-|light*
235.12   *prepaid* • *pre-|paid*
235.20   on • [*possibly* 'ori']
236.8   th • ['h' *partly formed*]
236.18   the that • th͓at
236.22   Henry • Hen͓ry

∎ 3 December 1872 · To John E. Mouland · Hartford, Conn. · *UCCL*
00839
∎*Copy-text:* MS, Clifton Waller Barrett Library, Alderman Library, University
of Virginia, Charlottesville (ViU). ∎*Provenance:* deposited at ViU by Clifton
Waller Barrett on 16 April 1960. ∎*Emendations and textual notes:*

239.4   ~~dow~~ • ['w' *partly formed*]
239.9   papers • pap[e]rs [*torn*]
239.13   ~~she~~ the • ⱥthe

■ 5 December 1872 · To Jane Lampton Clemens and Family · Hartford, Conn. · *UCCL* 00840

■*Copy-text:* MS, Jean Webster McKinney Family Papers, Vassar College Library (NPV). ■*Previous publication: MTBus,* 121–22, with omission. ■*Provenance:* see McKinney Family Papers in Description of Provenance. ■*Emendations and textual notes:*

240.9   move • ~~mo~~ move [*corrected miswriting*]
241.3–4   presently. It • ~.—|~

■ 5 December 1872 · To Whitelaw Reid · Hartford, Conn. · *UCCL* 00841

■*Copy-text:* "The Missouri Disaster," New York *Tribune,* 7 Dec 72, 5. With his letter, Clemens enclosed a portion of a New York *Tribune* editorial (5 Dec 72, 4). The actual clipping does not survive; the text printed here is a line-for-line resetting of the article. Copy-text for the letter and enclosure is a microfilm edition of the newspaper in the Newspaper and Microcopy Division, University of California, Berkeley (CU-NEWS). ■*Emendations and textual notes:*

241.14   & • and [*here and hereafter*]

■ 5 December 1872 · To the Editor of the Hartford *Evening Post* · Hartford, Conn. · *UCCL* 11892

■*Copy-text:* "Concerning an Insupportable Nuisance," Hartford *Evening Post,* 6 Dec 72, 2. Copy-text is a microfilm prepared for the Mark Twain Papers from the original newspaper at the Connecticut Historical Society, Hartford (CtHi). ■*Emendations and textual notes:*

244.2   & • and [*here and hereafter*]

■ 5 December 1872 · To Albert W. Whelpley · Hartford, Conn. · *UCCL* 00842

■*Copy-text:* MS, Cincinnati Historical Society, Cincinnati (OCHP). ■*Provenance:* The MS is in the Whelpley Autograph Collection, donated to OCHP in 1906 by Mrs. Albert Whelpley. ■*Emendations and textual notes:*

248.12   ◊◊◊ • [◊◊◊] [*badly inked*]

■ 10 December 1872 · To Thomas Nast · Hartford, Conn. · *UCCL* 00843

■ *Copy-text:* MS, Princeton University (NjP). Published with permission of the Princeton University Libraries. The MS is now accompanied by a red calling card bearing a photographic portrait of Mark Twain, published by the "Happy Hours Company" in 1872. The card was almost certainly not enclosed with the original letter, but furnished by a dealer or collector as an adornment. ■ *Previous publication:* Paine 1904, 263, brief excerpt; Merwin-Clayton, lot 242, brief excerpt; *MTB*, 1:472, brief excerpt; *MTL*, 1:202, brief excerpt (misdated November 1872); Freeman, lot 103, brief paraphrase; *MTMF*, 169, with omission. ■ *Provenance:* The MS was among the papers and drawings from Nast's estate sold in April 1906 (Merwin-Clayton). It was sold again in 1932 as part of the collection of businessman William F. Gable (1856–1921) (Freeman). In 1961 James Rankin donated it to Princeton, where it is part of the Rankin Autograph Collection. ■ *Emendations and textual notes:*

249.6   H̶r̶ Her • H⸍er
249.10   deal • [d]eal [*torn*]
249.19   ⱷ • [*possibly* 'ⱡ']

■ 10 December 1872 · To Mary Hunter Smith · Hartford, Conn. · *UCCL* 11669

■ *Copy-text:* MS, collection of Nicholas Karanovich. ■ *Previous publication:* Lilly Library, 13. ■ *Emendations and textual notes:*

250.16   HARTFORD CONN. DEC 11 ◊◊◊ • HARTFO[RD] C[ONN.] DEC 11
           [◊◊◊] [*badly inked*]

■ 17 December 1872 · To Thomas Nast · Hartford, Conn. · *UCCL* 00846

■ *Copy-text:* MS facsimile. The editors have not seen the MS, which was owned in 1992 by Jean Thompson, who provided a photocopy to the Mark Twain Papers. ■ *Previous publication:* Paine 1904, 263, excerpts, text rearranged somewhat; Merwin-Clayton, lot 244, brief quote; "For Twain Letter, $43," New York *Tribune*, 3 Apr 1906, 7, brief excerpt; Christie 1992, lot 164. ■ *Provenance:* The MS was among the papers and drawings from Nast's estate sold in April 1906 (Merwin-Clayton). In 1992 Jean Thompson discovered the MS laid in an unidentified volume in an edition of Mark Twain's works, purchased at auction for one dollar; she resold it in November 1992 (Christie 1992, lot 164). ■ *Emendations and textual notes:*

251.5–6   Charley. [¶] The • ~.—| [¶] ~
251.6   m̶ • [*partly formed*]

251.9   idiots. Pity • ~.—|~
251.10   acquaintance • acqua~~in~~tintance
251.12   ⍴ • [*partly formed*]

■ **20 December 1872 · From Olivia L. and Samuel L. Clemens to Jane Lampton Clemens and Family · Hartford, Conn. · UCCL 00847**
■ *Copy-text:* MS, Jean Webster McKinney Family Papers, Vassar College Library (NPV). ■ *Previous Publication: MTBus*, 122–23. ■ *Provenance:* see McKinney Family Papers in Description of Provenance. ■ *Emendations and textual notes:*

254.24   so • [*possibly* 'as']
254.24   ~~the~~ that • th⍀at
255.1   hand-glass • hand-|glass
255.2   justing • [*sic*]

■ **20–22 December 1872 · To Joseph H. Twichell · Hartford, Conn. · UCCL 00848**
■ *Copy-text:* MS, Joseph H. Twichell Collection, Beinecke Rare Book and Manuscript Library, Yale University (CtY-BR), is copy-text for the letter and envelope. MS, Horace Bushnell to SLC, 20 Dec 72 (*UCLC* 31840), Mark Twain Papers, The Bancroft Library, University of California, Berkeley (CU-MARK), is copy-text for the enclosure. ■ *Provenance:* It is not known when Twichell's papers were deposited at Yale, although it is likely that he bequeathed them to the university upon his death in 1918 (*L2*, 570). For the enclosure see Mark Twain Papers in Description of Provenance. ■ *Emendations and textual notes:*

255.18   flavor • fla⍀vor

■ **3 January 1873 · To Whitelaw Reid, *per* Telegraph Operator · (1st of 2) · Hartford, Conn. · UCCL 00851**
■ *Copy-text:* MS, copy received, telegram blank filled out by the receiving telegraph operator, Whitelaw Reid Papers, Library of Congress (DLC). ■ *Provenance:* The Whitelaw Reid Papers (part of the Papers of the Reid Family) were donated to DLC between 1953 and 1957 by Helen Rogers Reid (Mrs. Ogden Mills Reid). ■ *Emendations and textual notes:*

263.15   OK • [*possibly* 'OKr']

■ **3 January 1873 · To Whitelaw Reid · (2nd of 2) · Hartford, Conn. · UCCL 00852**
■ *Copy-text:* MS, Whitelaw Reid Papers, Library of Congress (DLC). ■ *Provenance:* The Whitelaw Reid Papers (part of the Papers of the Reid Family) were

donated to DLC between 1953 and 1957 by Helen Rogers Reid (Mrs. Ogden Mills Reid). ■*Emendations and textual notes:*

264.4   it. I • ~.—|~
264.17   ~~1872.~~ *1873.* • *1872.3. [docket written in pencil, then corrected in ink]*

■ 6 January 1873 · To Whitelaw Reid, *per* Telegraph Operator · Hartford, Conn. · *UCCL* 00853

■*Copy-text:* MS, copy received, telegram blank filled out by the receiving telegraph operator, Whitelaw Reid Papers, Library of Congress (DLC). ■*Provenance:* The Whitelaw Reid Papers (part of the Papers of the Reid Family) were donated to DLC between 1953 and 1957 by Helen Rogers Reid (Mrs. Ogden Mills Reid). ■*Emendations and textual notes:*

266.14   6pdx • [*possibly* '6pd4']
266.14   Jos • [*possibly* 'Jrs']

■ 12 January 1873 · To Ira F. Hart, *per* Olivia L. Clemens · Hartford, Conn. · *UCCL* 00855

■*Copy-text:* MS facsimile, Tollett and Harman, item 29. ■*Previous publication:* Parke-Bernet 1944, lot 96, handwritten portion only; Christie 1988, lot 1188. ■*Provenance:* The MS was for many years in the Estelle Doheny Collection at The Edward Laurence Doheny Memorial Library of St. John's Seminary, Camarillo, California. Heritage Bookshop purchased it in 1988, and Tollett and Harman offered it for sale in 1991.

■ 12 January 1873 · To John M. Hay · Hartford, Conn. · *UCCL* 00856

■*Copy-text:* MS, Samuel Mather Family Papers, Western Reserve Historical Society, Cleveland (OClWHi). ■*Provenance:* donated to OClWHi in 1969 by Dr. and Mrs. Jonathan Bishop. Dr. Bishop is the grandson of Samuel Mather and Flora Stone, whose sister, Clara Stone, was married to John Hay. ■*Emendations and textual notes:*

268.13–14   figures) • figures)). [*closing parenthesis written accidentally over the* 's' *and then rewritten*]
268.21   Editorial • Editorial[
268.23   HARTFORD • HART[◊◊◊◊] [*torn; remainder of postmark torn away*]

■ 13 and 17 January 1873 · To Whitelaw Reid · Hartford, Conn. · *UCCL* 00857

■*Copy-text:* MS, Whitelaw Reid Papers, Library of Congress (DLC). ■*Provenance:* The Whitelaw Reid Papers (part of the Papers of the Reid Family) were donated to DLC between 1953 and 1957 by Helen Rogers Reid (Mrs. Ogden Mills Reid). ▪ *Emendations and textual notes:*

269.3   ~~12~~ ₌13₌ • 1⁄3

269.12   ~~$12,000.~~ • [*period doubtful*]

▪ 14 January 1873 · To Whitelaw Reid · Hartford, Conn. · *UCCL* 11835

▪ *Copy-text:* "The Sandwich Islands," New York *Tribune*, "Lectures and Letters—Extra Sheet," undated, at least one issue printed after 15 Jan 73, 4. Copytext is a microfilm edition of the newspaper in the Newspaper and Microcopy Division, University of California, Berkeley (CU-NEWS). The letter is a paragraph inserted in the issue or issues of the "Extra Sheet" printed after 15 January, of an article first printed in the daily *Tribune* on 6 January (SLC 1873c). ▪ *Emendations and textual notes:*

272.2   & • and [*here and hereafter*]

▪ 17 January 1873 · To William Bowen · Hartford, Conn. · *UCCL* 00858

▪ *Copy-text:* MS, Harry Ransom Humanities Research Center, University of Texas, Austin (TxU-Hu). ▪ *Previous publication:* Hornberger, 21. ▪ *Provenance:* purchased by TxU in 1940 from Eva Laura Bowen (Mrs. Louis Knox), daughter of William Bowen. ▪ *Emendations and textual notes:*

273.6   feel. Otherwise • ~.—|~

▪ 17 January 1873 · To James Redpath · Hartford, Conn. · *UCCL* 09230

▪ *Copy-text:* None. The text is based on two incomplete transcriptions, each of which derives independently from the MS:

          P¹   Anderson Galleries 1926, lot 413
          P²   AAA/Anderson 1929, lot 22

P¹ describes the letter as an "A. L. s., 1 p., 8vo. Hartford, Jan. 17, 1873. To Mr. Redpath." P² describes the letter identically, except for the variants noted below, but its text is less complete. ▪ *Provenance:* The MS was offered for sale in 1926 as part of the autograph collection of Emanuel Hertz, and in 1929 as part of the collection of John M. Geddes. ▪ *Emendations, adopted readings, and textual notes:*

274.1   Home, (C) • Home [Hartford], (P²); Hartford, (P¹) [*both reported, not quoted*]

274.1   Jan. 17, 1873. (P¹) • Jan. 17, 1773. (P²) [*both reported, not quoted*]
274.3   re-deliver (P²) • re-|deliver (P¹)
274.4–5   —besides . . . Library (P¹) • [*not in*] (P²)

■ 20 January 1873 · To T. B. Pugh · Hartford, Conn. · *UCCL* 00860

■ *Copy-text:* MS, Samuel M. Clement, Jr., Collection, Historical Society of Pennsylvania, Philadelphia (PHi). ■ *Provenance:* donated to PHi in 1930 by Mrs. Samuel M. Clement, Jr. ■ *Emendations and textual notes:*

275.6   ~~witte~~ with • witteh
275.13   circus. They • ~.—|~

■ 22 January 1873 · To John E. Mouland · Hartford, Conn. · *UCCL* 00862

■ *Copy-text:* MS, Clifton Waller Barrett Library, University of Virginia, Charlottesville (ViU). ■ *Provenance:* deposited at ViU by Clifton Waller Barrett on 16 April 1960. ■ *Emendations and textual notes:*

277.7   make • ~~make~~ | make [*rewritten for clarity*]

■ 22 January 1873 · To Pamela A. Moffett · Hartford, Conn. · *UCCL* 00861

■ *Copy-text:* MS, Mark Twain Papers, The Bancroft Library, University of California, Berkeley (CU-MARK). ■ *Provenance:* either Mark Twain Papers or Moffett Collection (see Description of Provenance). ■ *Emendations and textual notes:*

279.5–6   expensive. I • ~.—|~

■ 24 January 1873 · To James Redpath · Hartford, Conn. · *UCCL* 00864

■ *Copy-text:* MS, Anthony Collection, Manuscripts and Archives Division, The New York Public Library, Astor, Lenox and Tilden Foundations (NN). ■ *Previous publication:* AAA 1924a, lot 215, brief excerpt. ■ *Provenance:* The MS was offered for sale in 1924 as part of the collection of businessman William F. Gable (1856–1921). It later belonged to educator and Baptist clergyman Alfred Williams Anthony (1860–1939), whose collection NN probably acquired after his death. ■ *Emendations and textual notes:*

280.12   indignant • indigṁnant
280.15   ~~not, entirel~~ • ['l' *partly formed*]

■ 25 January 1873 · To Whitelaw Reid · Hartford, Conn. · *UCCL* 00865

■*Copy-text:* MS, Whitelaw Reid Papers, Library of Congress (DLC). ■*Provenance:* The Whitelaw Reid Papers (part of the Papers of the Reid Family) were donated to DLC between 1953 and 1957 by Helen Rogers Reid (Mrs. Ogden Mills Reid). ■*Emendations and textual notes:*

282.2	~~24~~ 25ᵗʰ· • 25ᵗʰ·
282.5	tomorrow's • to-|morrow's

■ 27 and 28 January 1873 · To Michael Laird Simons · Hartford, Conn. · *UCCL* 00868

■*Copy-text:* MS, Henry W. and Albert A. Berg Collection, The New York Public Library, Astor, Lenox and Tilden Foundations (NN-B), is copy-text for the letter. The enclosures are not known to survive. The source for the first is the *Aldine* 4 (Apr 71): 52; the second is from Duyckinck and Duyckinck, 2:951. Both are photographically reproduced at actual size. ■*Previous publication:* AAA 1924b, lot 552, paraphrase and brief excerpts. ■*Provenance:* The MS was offered for sale in 1924 as part of the collection of businessman William F. Gable (1856–1921). It was later owned by businessman William T. H. Howe (1874–1939); in 1940 Dr. A. A. Berg bought and donated the Howe Collection to NN. ■*Emendations and textual notes:*

283.6	~~wise~~ will • wisell
284.13	~~th~~ • ['h' *partly formed*]
284.21	~~di~~ descriptive • dₑscriptive
284.23	background • backgroⱴund
284.23	earnestness • earnestness
284.25	reader. Will • ~.—|~

■ 28 January 1873 · To the Public · Hartford, Conn. · *UCCL* 00869

■*Copy-text:* "A Card," Hartford *Evening Post*, 28 Jan 73, 2, clipping in Scrapbook 6:125, Mark Twain Papers, The Bancroft Library, University of California, Berkeley (CU-MARK). ■*Previous publication:* "The Poor of Hartford and the Sandwich Islands," Hartford *Courant*, 29 Jan 73, 2; "The Poor of Hartford—a Card from Mark Twain," Hartford *Times*, 29 Jan 73, 2. ■*Emendations and textual notes:*

287.5	& . . . & . . . & • and . . . and . . . and [*here and hereafter*]
288.20	&c. • etc.
288.27	great • great | great
288.30	Brown & • Brown
289.22	some • so me

■ 30 January 1873 · To the Staff of the New York *Tribune* · Hartford, Conn. · *UCCL* 00870

■ *Copy-text:* MS, Ford Collection, Personal (Miscellaneous) Papers, Manuscripts and Archives Division, The New York Public Library, Astor, Lenox and Tilden Foundations (NN). ■ *Provenance:* The MS belonged to journalist and businessman Gordon Lester Ford (1823–91), and was probably donated to NN in 1899. ■ *Emendations and textual notes:*

291.3   ~~letter~~ • ['r' *partly formed*]

■ 1 February 1873 · To Whitelaw Reid, *per* Telegraph Operator · Hartford, Conn. · *UCCL* 00871

■ *Copy-text:* MS, copy received, telegram blank filled out by the receiving telegraph operator, Whitelaw Reid Papers, Library of Congress (DLC). ■ *Provenance:* The Whitelaw Reid Papers (part of the Papers of the Reid Family) were donated to DLC between 1953 and 1957 by Helen Rogers Reid (Mrs. Ogden Mills Reid).

■ 2 February 1873 · To Olivia L. Clemens · New York, N.Y. · *UCCL* 00872

■ *Copy-text:* MS, Mark Twain Papers, The Bancroft Library, University of California, Berkeley (CU-MARK). ■ *Previous publication: MFMT,* 47, excerpt; *LLMT,* 363, brief paraphrase. ■ *Provenance:* see Samossoud Collection in Description of Provenance. ■ *Emendations and textual notes:*

293.14   ~~th~~ • ['h' *partly formed*]
293.14   whirlwind • whirl-|wind
294.2   ~~o◊~~ one • o⊘ne
294.10   ~~God~~ Gold • Go⊄ld
294.16–17   MAILED ST. NICHOLAS HOTEL, FEB 2 ◊◊◊◊ • [◊◊◊L]E[◊] ST.
             NIC[HOLAS HOT◊◊◊ ◊E]B 2 [◊◊◊◊] [*badly inked*]

■ 15 February 1873 · To James Hammond Trumbull · Hartford, Conn. · *UCCL* 00873

■ *Copy-text:* MS, Connecticut Historical Society, Hartford (CtHi). ■ *Provenance:* acquired by CtHi in about 1897 from the James Hammond Trumbull estate. ■ *Emendations and textual notes:*

297.8   Sanscrit*ℓ* • ['ℓ' *partly formed*]

■ 17 February 1873 · Olivia L. and Samuel L. Clemens to Olivia Lewis Langdon · Hartford, Conn. · *UCCL* 00879

■*Copy-text:* MS, Mark Twain House, Hartford (CtHMTH). ■*Provenance:* donated to CtHMTH in 1962 or 1963 by Ida Langdon. ■*Emendations and textual notes:*

298.24   by • [*sic*]

■ 18 February 1873 · To Whitelaw Reid · Hartford, Conn. · *UCCL* 00874

■*Copy-text:* "Mark Twain's success . . . ," New York *Tribune*, 22 Feb 73, 6, is the source for the first three lines of the letter. Copy-text is a microfilm edition of the newspaper in the Newspaper and Microcopy Division, University of California, Berkeley (CU-NEWS). MS, Whitelaw Reid Papers, Library of Congress (DLC), is copy-text for the remainder of the letter. ■*Provenance:* The Whitelaw Reid Papers (part of the Papers of the Reid Family) were donated to DLC between 1953 and 1957 by Helen Rogers Reid (Mrs. Ogden Mills Reid). ■*Emendations and textual notes:*

[Tribune *is copy-text for* 'Mark . . . season.' *(299.1–3)*]
299.3   & • and
[*MS is copy-text for* 'Private . . . *1873*' *(300.1–12)*]
300.9   faithly • [*extra ascender left standing after* 't']

■ 25 February 1873 · To Elisha Bliss, Jr. · Hartford, Conn. · *UCCL* 00875

■*Copy-text:* MS, Willard S. Morse Collection, Collection of American Literature, Beinecke Rare Book and Manuscript Library, Yale University (CtY-BR). ■*Provenance:* The MS is laid in a first edition copy of *The Celebrated Jumping Frog of Calaveras County* (C. H. Webb, 1867); the Morse Collection was donated to CtY in 1942 by Walter F. Frear. ■*Emendations and textual notes:*

300.15   S̶t̶r̶ Stir • St/ir

■ 26 February 1873 · To Elisha Bliss, Jr. · Hartford, Conn. · *UCCL* 00876

■*Copy-text:* MS, Mark Twain Papers, The Bancroft Library, University of California, Berkeley (CU-MARK). ■*Previous publication: MTLP*, 85. ■*Provenance:* see Mendoza Collection in Description of Provenance.

■ 28 February 1873 · To Elisha Bliss, Jr. · Hartford, Conn. · *UCCL* 09999

■ *Copy-text:* Transcript and paraphrase, Heritage, item 199, which describes the letter as an "A.L.S. by Twain to his publisher, Elisha Bliss, Jr. of the American Publishing Company, dated 'Hartford, Feb. 28 [1873]', addressed 'Friend Bliss.' . . . The letter is signed 'Clemens.'" ■ *Provenance:* When offered for sale in 1982 (Heritage) the MS was laid in a first edition copy of *What Is Man?* (New York: De Vinne Press, 1906). ■ *Emendations and textual notes:*

302.1   28. • ~ ∧
302.2   Bliss— • ~.

■ March 1873 · To Louisa I. Conrad · Hartford, Conn. · *UCCL* 00878

■ *Copy-text:* MS, Mark Twain Papers, The Bancroft Library, University of California, Berkeley (CU-MARK). A bow of blue ribbon, now preserved with the letter, was almost certainly not part of the original letter. If the letter was preserved in Conrad's scrapbook, as seems likely, it had been removed by 1977, when it was donated as part of the Appert Collection. ■ *Provenance:* see Appert Collection in Description of Provenance. ■ *Emendations and textual notes:*

303.6–7   RECIPE . . . PA PLAN • Recipe for Making a Scrapbook upon the Customary Pɬlan [*underscored with three short lines like a literary title*]
303.18   tragicanth • [*sic; also at 303.32*]
303.23   time. Now • ~.—|~

■ March? 1873 · To Henry Wheeler Shaw (Josh Billings) · Hartford, Conn. · *UCCL* 00877

■ *Copy-text:* Shaw 1873, 4. Copy-text is a microfilm edition of Street and Smith's *New York Weekly* for 28 July 1873 in The New York Public Library, Astor, Lenox and Tilden Foundations (NN). ■ *Previous publication:* Shaw 1874, 573–75; Cyril Clemens 1932, 124–27; Brownell 1944, 3. ■ *Emendations and textual notes:*

304.16   Dear Josh • DEAR JOSH
304.16   I • "~
305.1   Therefore • Tharefore
305.1   believe • beleave
305.1   don't • dont
305.2   there • thare
305.4   & • and [*here and hereafter*]
305.6   debarred • debared
306.16   Mark Twain • MARK TWAIN

■ 3 March 1873 · To Willard M. White · Hartford, Conn. · *UCCL* 00880

■*Copy-text:* Printed transcript in an advertising circular (*BAL* 3356), Willard S. Morse Collection, Collection of American Literature, Beinecke Rare Book and Manuscript Library, Yale University (CtY-BR). ■*Provenance:* The Morse Collection was donated to CtY in 1942 by Walter F. Frear. ■*Emendations and textual notes:* The dateline is in boldface italic type, and the rest of the text is in italic type, a convention not adopted here.

307.2	Mr. White	• *MR. WHITE*
307.3	&	• *and* [*here and hereafter*]
308.3	Mark Twain	• *MARK TWAIN*

■ 4 March 1873 · To Elisha Bliss, Jr. · Hartford, Conn. · *UCCL* 00881

■*Copy-text:* MS, Clifton Waller Barrett Library, University of Virginia, Charlottesville (ViU). ■*Previous publication: MTLP,* 74–75. ■*Provenance:* deposited at ViU by Clifton Waller Barrett on 17 December 1963. ■*Emendations and textual notes:*

309.7	~~wh~~ will	• w⸜ill ['h' *partly formed*]
309.11	~~the~~ this	• th⸜is

■ 7 March 1873 · To Whitelaw Reid, *per* Telegraph Operator · (1st of 2) · Hartford, Conn. · *UCCL* 00882

■*Copy-text:* MS, copy received, telegram blank filled out by the receiving telegraph operator, Whitelaw Reid Papers, Library of Congress (DLC). ■*Provenance:* The Whitelaw Reid Papers (part of the Papers of the Reid Family) were donated to DLC between 1953 and 1957 by Helen Rogers Reid (Mrs. Ogden Mills Reid).

■ 7 March 1873 · To Whitelaw Reid · (2nd of 2) · Hartford, Conn. · *UCCL* 00883 and 00884

■*Copy-text:* MS, Whitelaw Reid Papers, Library of Congress (DLC), is copy-text for the letter and the dockets. MS, Ford Collection, Personal (Miscellaneous) Papers, Manuscripts and Archives Division, The New York Public Library, Astor, Lenox and Tilden Foundations (NN), is copy-text for the enclosure. ■*Previous publication:* "Foster's Case," New York *Tribune,* 10 Mar 73, 5; Willson, 3; Neider 1961, 166–67; Budd 1992a, 549–50, all enclosure only. ■*Provenance:* The Whitelaw Reid Papers (part of the Papers of the Reid Family) were donated to DLC between 1953 and 1957 by Helen Rogers Reid (Mrs. Ogden Mills Reid). The enclosure belonged to journalist and businessman Gordon

Lester Ford (1823–91), and was probably donated to NN in 1899. ■ *Emendations and textual notes:*

311.6	penalty • penalt̸y
311.25	~~read Foster's Plea in T~~ • ['T' *partly formed*]
312.3	¢ • [*partly formed*]
312.14	seem • ~~seem~~ ₓseem, [*obscured by inkblot and rewritten for clarity*]
312.22	maccaronian • [*sic*]
312.25	~~whe~~ why • wh̸y
312.29	~~ut~~ • ['t' *partly formed*]

■ 7 March 1873 · To the Staff of the New York *Tribune* · Hartford, Conn. · *UCCL* 00885

■ *Copy-text:* MS, Ford Collection, Personal (Miscellaneous) Papers, The New York Public Library, Astor, Lenox and Tilden Foundations (NN). ■ *Provenance:* The MS belonged to journalist and businessman Gordon Lester Ford (1823–91), and was probably donated to NN in 1899.

■ 10 March 1873 · To Tom Hood and George Routledge and Sons · Hartford, Conn. · *UCCL* 00886

■ *Copy-text:* Pike, 14–15. ■ *Previous publication: Fun*, 26 Apr 73, 172, excerpts. The letter was probably also printed in the first edition of Pike (London: 1874), but the editors were unable to examine a copy. ■ *Emendations and textual notes:*

315.1	Hartford, March • *Hartford, March*
315.2	Tom Hood • Tᴏᴍ Hᴏᴏᴅ
315.2	Esq., & • Esq., and
315.2	Messrs. George Routledge & Sons • Mᴇssʀs. Gᴇᴏʀɢᴇ Rᴏᴜᴛ-ʟᴇᴅɢᴇ & Sᴏɴs
315.4	& • and [*here and hereafter*]
316.8–9	Saml. L. Clemens. | Mark Twain. • Sᴀᴍʟ. L. Cʟᴇᴍᴇɴs. Mᴀʀᴋ Tᴡᴀɪɴ.

■ 13 March 1873 · To William Dean Howells · Hartford, Conn. · *UCCL* 00887

■ *Copy-text:* MS, Clifton Waller Barrett Library, University of Virginia, Charlottesville (ViU). ■ *Previous publication:* Anderson, Gibson, and Smith, v, 10–12. ■ *Provenance:* deposited at ViU by Clifton Waller Barrett on 17 December 1963. ■ *Emendations and textual notes:*

317.4	baseley • [*sic*]
318.15	~~than~~ that • thaɡ́t ['n' *partly formed*]

■ 20 March 1873 · To William Bowen · Hartford, Conn. · *UCCL*
00888

■*Copy-text:* MS, Harry Ransom Humanities Research Center, University of
Texas, Austin (TxU-Hu). ■*Previous publication:* Hornberger, 21–22. ■*Provenance:* purchased by TxU in 1940 from Eva Laura Bowen (Mrs. Louis Knox),
daughter of William Bowen. ■*Emendations and textual notes:*

319.5	lecture. Can't • ~.—|~
319.5	detest • detecsst
319.8	*No* • ~N̶o̶~ *No* [*rewritten for clarity*]
320.1	s̶a̶i̶d̶ sail • saiḑl

■ 22 March 1873 · To Josephus N. Larned · Hartford, Conn. · *UCCL*
00889

■*Copy-text:* MS facsimile. The editors have not seen the MS, which is in the Buffalo and Erie County Historical Society Archives (A64-1, Mark Twain Letters),
Buffalo (NBuHi).

■ 26 March 1873 · To Elisha Bliss, Jr. · Hartford, Conn. · *UCCL*
00890

■*Copy-text:* MS, Mark Twain Papers, The Bancroft Library, University of California, Berkeley (CU-MARK). ■*Provenance:* see Mendoza Collection in Description of Provenance.

■ 28 March 1873 · To William Bowen · Hartford, Conn. · *UCCL*
00891

■*Copy-text:* MS, Harry Ransom Humanities Research Center, University of
Texas, Austin (TxU-Hu). ■*Previous publication:* Hornberger, 22. ■*Provenance:*
purchased by TxU in 1940 from Eva Laura Bowen (Mrs. Louis Knox), daughter
of William Bowen.

■ 28 March 1873 · To Whitelaw Reid · Hartford, Conn. · *UCCL* 00892

■*Copy-text:* MS, Whitelaw Reid Papers, Library of Congress (DLC). ■*Previous
publication:* Cortissoz, 1:273, excerpts. ■*Provenance:* The Whitelaw Reid Papers
(part of the Papers of the Reid Family) were donated to DLC between 1953 and
1957 by Helen Rogers Reid (Mrs. Ogden Mills Reid). ■*Emendations and textual
notes:*

324.7	S̶l̶ Self • S̶l̶elf

■ 30 March 1873 · To the Editor of the Hartford *Courant* · Hartford, Conn. · *UCCL* 00893

■ *Copy-text:* "A Horrible Tale. Fearful Calamity in Forest Street," Hartford *Courant*, 31 Mar 73, 2. Copy-text is a microfilm edition of the newspaper in the Newspaper and Microcopy Division, University of California, Berkeley (CU-NEWS). ■ *Emendations and textual notes:*

325.5	& • and [*here and hereafter, except at 326.30, where copy-text reads* 'Johnson &']
325.12	Chamberlin's • Chamberiln's
326.12	life-boat • life-|boat [*also at 326.14*]
327.5	castaways • cast-|aways
328.8	M. T. • ~∧ ~.

■ 2 April 1873 · To Charles F. Wingate · Hartford, Conn. · *UCCL* 00896

■ *Copy-text:* MS, Cyril Clemens Collection, Mark Twain House, Hartford (CtHMTH). ■ *Previous publication:* Richards, item 102, excerpts. ■ *Provenance:* donated to CtHMTH in 1984 by Cyril Clemens. ■ *Emendations and textual notes:*

328.14	at • ['t' *partly formed*]

■ 5–15? April 1873 · To William C. Cornwell · Hartford, Conn. · *UCCL* 00894

■ *Copy-text:* "A Letter from Mark Twain," *Globe* 1 (May 73): 28–29. ■ *Emendations and textual notes:*

329.3	& • and
329.5	isn't • is'nt

■ 7 April 1873 · To Unidentified · Hartford, Conn. · *UCCL* 00897

■ *Copy-text:* MS, Amherst College, Amherst, Massachusetts (MA). ■ *Previous publication: MTH*, 176 and facing page, transcription of letter and facsimile of enclosure. ■ *Provenance:* The MS is laid in a copy of *The Sandwich Islands by Mark Twain* (New York: 1920). William F. Gable (1856–1921), who purchased the book from James F. Drake, inscribed it, "William F. Gable (Altoona,) Pa. \| November 1920." It is not clear when the MS was laid in the book, but it was certainly there by 1938 when the MS was offered for sale from the collection of George C. Smith, Jr. (Parke-Bernet 1938, lot 162). It may have been purchased at that time by Arthur F. Brown, whose widow donated it to MA in 1947. ■ *Emen-*

dations and textual notes: Except for the final paragraph, the MS sheet was originally inscribed, and revised here and there, in brown ink; all revisions in pencil
are noted below.

331.8–9	~~but~~ . . . ~~success.~~	• [*canceled in pencil*]
331.9	* • [*in pencil*]	
331.10	~~besides these,~~	• [*canceled in pencil*]
331.11	is it	• i$\cancel{s}$t
331.11–12	~~we~~ . . . termed	• ['we might term' *inscribed and altered to* 'we might ₍be₎ termed' *in ink, then altered to the final reading in pencil*]
331.12–13	₍Officers . . . go.₎	• [*interlined without a caret, in pencil*]
331.13	₍But . . . cch.₎	• [*in pencil*]
331.14	scowl	• sco$\cancel{u}$wl
331.14	₍nondescript₎	• [*in pencil*]
331.15	₍& . . . ships₎	• [*in pencil*]
331.16–17	~~It~~ . . . ~~religions,~~	• [*canceled in pencil*]
331.17–18	₍In . . . wild₎	• [*in pencil*]
331.23	₍Harris . . . popular.₎	• [*in pencil*]
331.24	~~was a S &~~	• ['&' *partly formed*]

■ 7–30? April 1873 · To Unidentified #1 · Hartford, Conn. · *UCCL*
10821

■*Copy-text:* MS, Houghton Library (Autograph file), Harvard University (MH-
H). ■*Provenance:* bequeathed to MH-H in 1951 by engineer and bibliophile William B. Osgood Field (1870–1949). ■*Emendations and textual notes:*

333.14	Original	• Origin$\cancel{f}$al

■ 7–30? April 1873 · To Unidentified #2 · Hartford, Conn. · *UCCL*
00895

■*Copy-text:* MS, Henry W. and Albert A. Berg Collection, The New York Public
Library, Astor, Lenox and Tilden Foundations (NN-B). ■*Previous publication:*
Anderson Galleries 1924, lot 191, personal note only. ■*Provenance:* The MS,
owned at one time by Irving S. Underhill, was sold in 1924 as part of the collection of William Harris Arnold (1854–1923). It was later owned by businessman
William T. H. Howe (1874–1939); in 1940 Dr. A. A. Berg bought and donated
the Howe Collection to NN.

■ 9 April 1873 · To Whitelaw Reid · Hartford, Conn. · *UCCL* 00898
and 00899

■*Copy-text:* MS, Whitelaw Reid Papers, Library of Congress (DLC), is copy-
text for the letter. The enclosure does not survive. The source for it is "Life-

Rafts. How the Atlantic's Passengers Might Have Been Saved," New York *Tribune,* 11 Apr 73, 5. Copy-text is a microfilm edition of the newspaper in the Newspaper and Microcopy Division, University of California, Berkeley (CU-NEWS). ■*Provenance:* The Whitelaw Reid Papers (part of the Papers of the Reid Family) were donated to DLC between 1953 and 1957 by Helen Rogers Reid (Mrs. Ogden Mills Reid). ■*Emendations and textual notes:*

| 335.20 | & • and [*here and hereafter*] |
| 336.24 | gunwales • gun-\|wales |

■ **16 April 1873 · To Mary Mason Fairbanks · Hartford, Conn. ·** *UCCL* 00900

■*Copy-text:* MS, Henry E. Huntington Library, San Marino (CSmH, call no. HM 14280). ■*Previous publication: MTMF,* 170–72; Davis 1977c, 3, excerpt. ■*Provenance:* see Huntington Library in Description of Provenance. ■*Emendations and textual notes:*

339.3	~~ham~~ • ham-|
339.4	Every • [*sic*]
339.11	$ • [*partly formed*]

■ **17 April 1873 · To David G. Croly · Hartford, Conn. ·** *UCCL* 00901

■*Copy-text:* MS facsimile, "'Mark Twain' to the Editor of 'The Daily Graphic.' An Autograph Letter," New York *Graphic,* 22 Apr 73, 8, is copy-text, except for the headlines at 342.1–43. These headlines, which Clemens cut from the Hartford *Evening Post* for 16 Apr 73 (3) and pasted into his letter, were not photographically reproduced in the *Graphic* as the letter was, but were retypeset, with slight alterations in punctuation and lineation. For the headlines, therefore, copy-text is a photograph of a page of the original *Evening Post* at the Connecticut Historical Society, Hartford (CtHi). ■*Previous publication: MTL,* 1:204–5, with omissions; Johnson, 20–22. ■*Emendations and textual notes:*

| 341.21 | ~~tell~~ telegraphic • tel\|egraphic [*canceled* 'l' *partly formed*] |
| 342.46 | commonplace • common-\|place |

■ **17? April 1873 · To Whitelaw Reid · Hartford, Conn. ·** *UCCL* 00902

■*Copy-text:* MS, Whitelaw Reid Papers, Library of Congress (DLC). ■*Provenance:* The Whitelaw Reid Papers (part of the Papers of the Reid Family) were donated to DLC between 1953 and 1957 by Helen Rogers Reid (Mrs. Ogden Mills Reid). ■*Emendations and textual notes:*

| 344.3 | title • ~~tiltle~~ title [*corrected miswriting*] |

■ 20 April 1873 · To Whitelaw Reid · Hartford, Conn. · *UCCL* 00903

■ *Copy-text:* MS, Whitelaw Reid Papers, Library of Congress (DLC), is copy-text for the letter. Clemens cut the enclosed clipping from the New York *Christian Union* for 16 Apr 73 (7:301); it survives with the letter, glued to the top of the first page—probably not by Clemens—and is photographically reproduced at actual size. ■ *Provenance:* The Whitelaw Reid Papers (part of the Papers of the Reid Family) were donated to DLC between 1953 and 1957 by Helen Rogers Reid (Mrs. Ogden Mills Reid). ■ *Emendations and textual notes:*

346.5	us. I • ~.—|~
347.2	2,000 1000 • 2,1000
347.4	let literature • l¢it-|erature
347.12	after • [*possibly* 'after ₍']
347.24	Metropolisville • Metropo/lisville
347.31	an other another • [*ligature added to connect the two words*]
347.32	an am • aⁿm
348.1	sa • ['a' *partly formed*]

■ 21 April 1873 · Samuel L. Clemens and Charles D. Warner to Ainsworth R. Spofford · Hartford, Conn. · *UCCL* 00904

■ *Copy-text:* MS, Papers of Ainsworth Rand Spofford, Library of Congress (DLC). ■ *Provenance:* The Papers of Ainsworth Rand Spofford were donated to DLC between 1923 and 1982 by Barbara Spofford Morgan. ■ *Emendations and textual notes:*

350.3	Spofford • Spoff/ord

■ 22 April 1873 · To Whitelaw Reid · (1st of 3) · Hartford, Conn. · *UCCL* 00905

■ *Copy-text:* MS, Whitelaw Reid Papers, Library of Congress (DLC), is copy-text for the letter. Warner cut the enclosure from the Springfield *Republican* for 22 Apr 73 (7) and forwarded it to Clemens; it survives with the letter, glued to the top of the first page—probably not by Clemens—and is photographically reproduced at actual size. ■ *Previous publication:* Cortissoz, 1:274. ■ *Provenance:* The Whitelaw Reid Papers (part of the Papers of the Reid Family) were donated to DLC between 1953 and 1957 by Helen Rogers Reid (Mrs. Ogden Mills Reid). ■ *Emendations and textual notes:*

351.4	ahead • aheaⁿdd
351.4	notice. Bilious? • ~.—|~?
351.7	up us • up̸s ['p' *partly formed*]

■ 22 April 1873 · To Whitelaw Reid · (2nd of 3) · Hartford, Conn. ·
UCCL 00906

■ *Copy-text:* MS, Whitelaw Reid Papers, Library of Congress (DLC). ■ *Provenance:* The Whitelaw Reid Papers (part of the Papers of the Reid Family) were donated to DLC between 1953 and 1957 by Helen Rogers Reid (Mrs. Ogden Mills Reid). ■ *Emendations and textual notes:*

352.9   ⸘ • [*partly formed*]

■ 22 April 1873 · To Whitelaw Reid · (3rd of 3) · Hartford, Conn. ·
UCCL 00907

■ *Copy-text:* MS, Whitelaw Reid Papers, Library of Congress (DLC). ■ *Provenance:* The Whitelaw Reid Papers (part of the Papers of the Reid Family) were donated to DLC between 1953 and 1957 by Helen Rogers Reid (Mrs. Ogden Mills Reid). ■ *Emendations and textual notes:*

353.6   time. So • ~.—|~

■ 25 April ?1873 · To Unidentified · Hartford, Conn. · UCCL 09691

■ *Copy-text:* Parke-Bernet 1971, lot 207, which describes the letter as an "A.L.s., 1 page 8vo, Hartford, April 25, n.y., to an unnamed recipient." ■ *Emendations and textual notes:*

354.1   Hartford, April 25. • ~, ~ ~, [*reported, not quoted*]

■ 25 and 26 April 1873 · To Olivia L. Clemens · Hartford, Conn. ·
UCCL 00908

■ *Copy-text:* MS, collection of Chester L. Davis, Jr. ■ *Previous publication:* Davis 1977c, 3; Christie 1991a, lot 89, excerpts. ■ *Provenance:* The MS, part of the Samossoud Collection in the late 1940s when it was transcribed by Dixon Wecter, was acquired between 1949 and 1962 by Chester L. Davis, Sr., from Clara Clemens Samossoud (see Samossoud Collection in Description of Provenance). After Davis's death in 1987, the MS was owned by Chester L. Davis, Jr., who sold it through Christie's in May 1991. ■ *Emendations and textual notes:*

354.6   Ɖ • [*partly formed*]
354.8   ᴡᴇ the • ᴡᵗhe
354.10   revamping • re-|vamping
354.12   to-wit: When • ~-~:—|~
355.3   a • ɑ̸ | a [*corrected miswriting*]
355.17   little • lᵻittlᴇłᴇ

355.23–24   IF . . . TO • [*torn away; text adopted from envelope with 26 Apr 73 to OLC*]

355.24   2◊ • 2[◊] [*badly inked*]

■ 26 April 1873 · To Colton Greene · Hartford, Conn. · *UCCL* 11885

■*Copy-text:* MS, Lyman L. Pierce Collection, Mark Twain Home Foundation, Hannibal, Missouri (MoHH). ■*Provenance:* donated to MoHH in 1995 by Lyman L. Pierce.

■ 26 April 1873 · To Olivia L. Clemens · Hartford, Conn. · *UCCL* 00909

■*Copy-text:* MS, Mark Twain Papers, The Bancroft Library, University of California, Berkeley (CU-MARK). ■*Previous publication:* Wecter, 86–87; *LLMT*, 182–83; Davis 1977c, 4, excerpt. ■*Provenance:* see Samossoud Collection in Description of Provenance. ■*Emendations and textual notes:*

358.7   phaze • [*sic*]
358.14   *literary`ally* • [*sic*]
358.16   ₩ • [*partly formed*]
358.19   muggins. It • ~.—|~
358.24   CT. APR ◊◊ II • [CT◊] APR [◊◊ II] [*badly inked*]

■ 29 April 1873 · To John E. Mouland · Hartford, Conn. · *UCCL* 00910

■*Copy-text:* Typed transcript in the autobiography of Samuel Chalmers Thompson, 79, Mark Twain Papers, The Bancroft Library, University of California, Berkeley (CU-MARK). ■*Provenance:* Thompson's autobiography was purchased by CU-MARK in 1978 with funds donated by Elinor R. Heller. ■*Emendations and textual notes:* Changes deemed to be simple corrections of typing errors or omissions are not reported.

359.4   May • Mey
359.7   wife • Wife

■ 1 May 1873 · To Olivia L. Clemens · Hartford, Conn. · *UCCL* 00911

■*Copy-text:* Typed transcript, Mark Twain Papers, The Bancroft Library, University of California, Berkeley (CU-MARK). The transcript as corrected by Dixon Wecter (presumably by comparing it with the MS) serves as copy-text. Changes deemed to be simple corrections of typing errors or omissions are not reported. ∎*Provenance:* The MS was part of the Samossoud Collection in the late 1940s when it was transcribed by Wecter; its present location is not known (see Samossoud Collection in Description of Provenance).

∎ 3 May 1873 · To Elisha Bliss, Jr. · Hartford, Conn. · *UCCL* 00912

∎*Copy-text:* Transcript facsimile. The editors have not seen the original hand-written transcript, made by Dana S. Ayer during the late 1890s or later, which is in the Rare Book Department, Memorial Library, University of Wisconsin, Madison (WU). ∎*Previous publication: MTLP,* 75–76. ∎*Provenance:* The MS evidently remained among the American Publishing Company's files until it was sold (and may have been copied at that time by Ayer; see Brownell Collection in Description of Provenance). The Ayer transcription was in turn copied by a typist, and this typed transcription is also at WU. ∎*Emendations and textual notes:*

361.6	& • and [*here and hereafter, except at 361.7, where copy-text reads* 'Sheldon & Co']
361.6	too— • ~.—
361.8–9	subscription. • ~∧ [*written off edge*]

∎ 5 May 1873 · To Orion and Mary E. (Mollie) Clemens · Hartford, Conn. · *UCCL* 00913

∎*Copy-text:* MS, Mark Twain Papers, The Bancroft Library, University of California, Berkeley (CU-MARK). ∎*Provenance:* see Mark Twain Papers in Description of Provenance. ∎*Emendations and textual notes:*

363.3	May • [*possibly* 'J May'; 'J' *partly formed*]
363.5	Quinzy • [*sic*]
363.11	Vermont • Verm[◊◊◊] [*torn*]
363.13	CT. MAY 6 I PM • [CT]. [M◊Y] 6 [I P]M [*badly inked*]

∎ 12 May 1873 · To James Redpath · Elmira, N.Y. · *UCCL* 00914

∎*Copy-text:* "Letters to James Redpath," *Mark Twain Quarterly* 5 (Winter–Spring 1942): 19. ∎*Emendations and textual notes:* The house style of the *Mark Twain Quarterly* employed boldface type, rather than italic, for emphasis. In the present instance, however, the boldface styling of "Batavia" almost certainly does not reflect an underline in the MS: Clemens rarely underlined ship names in his letters, and the *Quarterly* made an analogous styling change in at least one other letter for which MS is extant: see 8 Dec 71 to Redpath and Fall, published in the same issue (5:20).

364.3	Batavia • **Batavia**
364.3	shan't • Shan't
364.8	& • and

■ 13 May 1873 · To Charles Dudley Warner · Elmira, N.Y. · *UCCL* 00915

■*Copy-text:* MS facsimile. The editors have not seen the MS, which is in the Robert B. Honeyman Collection, Linderman Library, Lehigh University, Bethlehem, Pennsylvania (PBL). ■*Provenance:* The Honeyman Collection was donated to PBL in March 1957. ■*Emendations and textual notes:*

| 365.6 | ʜ • [*partly formed*] |
| 365.8 | ~~aut~~ • ['t' *partly formed*] |

■ 17 May 1873 · From Olivia L. and Samuel L. Clemens to Olivia Lewis Langdon · SS *Batavia* at New York, N.Y. · *UCCL* 00916

■*Copy-text:* MS, Mark Twain House, Hartford (CtHMTH). ■*Provenance:* donated to CtHMTH in 1962 or 1963 by Ida Langdon. ■*Emendations and textual notes:*

| 366.3 | news • ~~news~~ news [*corrected miswriting*] |

■ 17 May 1873 · To Charles Dudley Warner · SS *Batavia* en route from New York, N.Y., to Liverpool, England · *UCCL* 00917

■*Copy-text:* MS, Mark Twain Papers, The Bancroft Library, University of California, Berkeley (CU-MARK). ■*Previous publication: MTLP,* 76–77. ■*Provenance:* donated to CU-MARK in January 1950 by Mary Barton of Hartford, a close friend of the Warners', who had owned it since at least 1938. ■*Emendations and textual notes:*

| 368.9 | copyright • copy-|right |

■ 29 May–15 June? 1873 · To Henry Watterson · London, England · *UCCL* 11801

■*Copy-text:* Paraphrase, Watterson 1910, 70:373. ■*Previous publication:* Watterson: 1911, 26; 1919, 1:126–27; 1927, 612.

■ 1 or 2 June 1873 · To Henry Lee · London, England · *UCCL* 00922

■*Copy-text:* MS, Clifton Waller Barrett Library, University of Virginia, Charlottesville (ViU). The letter was written on a halfpenny postcard identical to the one described in the commentary for 4 Oct 72 to Lee. ▪*Previous publication:* Parke-Bernet 1959, lot 62. ▪*Provenance:* deposited at ViU by Clifton Waller Barrett on 15 May 1962. ▪*Emendations and textual notes:*

374.9   SIDE. • SIDE[◇] [*obscured by postmark*]

▪ 9 June 1873 · To Kate Field · London, England · *UCCL* 00920
▪*Copy-text:* MS, Boston Public Library and Eastern Massachusetts Regional Public Library System, Boston (MB). ▪*Previous publication:* Whiting 1900, 289. ▪*Provenance:* donated to MB in 1898 by T. Sanford Beaty, Field's chief legatee.

▪ 11 June 1873 · To Joaquin Miller · London, England · *UCCL* 00923
▪*Copy-text:* MS, Clifton Waller Barrett Library, University of Virginia, Charlottesville (ViU). ▪*Provenance:* deposited at ViU by Clifton Waller Barrett on 17 December 1963. ▪*Emendations and textual notes:*

376.6   ~~you Sunday~~ • [*false ascenders/descenders*]
376.12   ~~tomorrow,~~ • to-|morrow,

▪ 12 June 1873 · To George H. Fitzgibbon · London, England · *UCCL* 00925
▪*Copy-text:* None. The text is based on three transcriptions, each of which derives independently from the MS:

P[1]   Henkels 1930a, lot 266
P[2]   Bloomfield ca. 1954, item 23
P[3]   Bloomfield post 1954, item 19

P[1] and P[3] each preserve portions of text not present in the other. Since P[2] contains text not found in P[1], it must also have derived directly from the MS, since it preceded P[3] in date of publication. All three sources describe the letter as "2pp., 8vo." The composite text that results from drawing on all sources appears to be complete, but the possibility remains that some portion of the original was neither quoted nor paraphrased in any of them. Two additional catalog listings contain no distinctly authorial variants and have contributed no readings to the present text. ▪*Previous publication:* Parke-Bernet 1945, lot 137, brief paraphrase; Parke-Bernet 1954a, lot 63, brief paraphrase. ▪*Emendations, adopted readings, and textual notes:*

378.1   Edw's Hotel, 12th. (P[2,3]) • Edwards Hotel, London, (June 12, 1873). [*reported, not quoted*] (P[1])
378.2   My Dear Fitz Gibbon— (C) • My Dear Fitz Gibbon. (P[2,3]); To G. Fitz-|Gibbon. [*reported, not quoted*] (P[1])

378.3–4	Thanks . . . telegram. (P[1]) • Thanks for that exceedingly kind article. (P[2]); [*not in*] (P[3])
378.4	House of Commons (P[1,3]) • HOUSE OF COMMONS (P[2])
378.4	evening (P[2]) • Evening (P[1,3])
378.5	& . . . you. (P[1,3]) • [*not in*] (P[2])
379.1	[¶] Oh (P[1]) • [*no* ¶] ~ (P[2,3])
379.3	literary (P[1,2]) • LITERARY (P[3])
379.3–4	substantial, (P[2,3]) • ~∧ (P[1])
379.4	the Observer (P[1,2]) • THE OBSERVER (P[3])
379.4–5	Properly . . . article. (P[1]) • [*not in*] (P[2,3])
379.5–6	I . . . magazine (P[3]) • [*not in*] (P[1,2])
379.7	where . . . to (P[2,3]) • [*not in*] (P[1])
379.7	"chaw over" a screed. (C) • 'CHAW OVER' a screed. (P[2,3]); [*not in*] (P[1])
379.8	Mark (P[1]) • MARK (P[2,3])

■ 12 and 13 June 1873 · To Henry Lee · London, England · *UCCL* 00924

■ *Copy-text:* MS, Harriet Beecher Stowe Center, Hartford (CtHSD), is copy-text for the letter. MS facsimile is copy-text for the envelope; the editors have not seen the MS, which is in the collection of Bruce Schwalb. ■ *Emendations and textual notes:*

380.7	be left • bel left [*false start; first* 'l' *partly formed*]
380.9	sight-seeing • sight-|seeing
380.10	myself • myse¢lf
380.11	it. I • ~.—|~
381.1	F̧ • [*partly formed*]
381.2–3	to-morrow∧night • [*originally* 'to-night']
381.6–7	LONDON·SE • LONDON·s[◊] [*badly inked*]

■ 15 June 1873 · To Adam Badeau · London, England · *UCCL* 00927

■ *Copy-text:* MS, Houghton Library (Autograph file), Harvard University (MH-H). ■ *Provenance:* bequeathed to MH by Evert Jansen Wendell (1860–1917), a Harvard alumnus and collector of theater memorabilia (Dickinson, 332–33). ■ *Emendations and textual notes:*

382.1	(SLC) • [◊◊◊] [*cut away*]
382.2	+3 15 • 1⁄5
382.6	sight-s⁄eeing • sight-|s⁄eeing

■ 17 or 18 June 1873 · To John Russell Young · Ostend, Belgium ·
UCCL 11802

■*Copy-text:* Yates, 411. ■*Emendations and textual notes:*

383.3   & · and

■ 18 June 1873 · To Elisha Bliss, Jr. · London, England · *UCCL* 00928

■*Copy-text:* MS, Henry W. and Albert A. Berg Collection, The New York Public
Library, Astor, Lenox and Tilden Foundations (NN-B). ■*Provenance:* NN-B
acquired the MS in 1970. It is laid in a copy of *The Innocents Abroad,* in the Autograph Edition of The Writings of Mark Twain (American Publishing Company, 1899–1907), signed "Julia S. Field (Mrs. Eugene Field)." ■*Emendations
and textual notes:*

384.6   sieze · [*sic*]

■ 19 June 1873 · To George H. Fitzgibbon · London, England ·
UCCL 00929

■*Copy-text:* MS, Henry W. and Albert A. Berg Collection, The New York Public
Library, Astor, Lenox and Tilden Foundations (NN-B). ■*Provenance:* The MS
was owned by businessman William T. H. Howe (1874–1939); in 1940 Dr. A. A.
Berg bought and donated the Howe Collection to NN. ■*Emendations and textual
notes:*

385.4   ♭ · [*partly formed*]
385.21   ~~quil~~ quiet · quiʃet

■ 23 June–18 July 1873 · To Charles W. and Katherine M. Dilke and
Kate Field · London, England · *UCCL* 03718

■*Copy-text:* MS, Dilke Papers, British Library, London (Uk). ■*Provenance:* The
Dilke Papers were deposited at the British Library in 1939 by Gertrude Tuckwell, the niece of the second Lady Dilke.

■ 25 June 1873 · To Ellen D. Conway · London, England · *UCCL*
00932

■*Copy-text:* None. The text is based on two transcriptions, each of which derives
independently from the MS:

P[1]   Anderson Galleries 1920a, lot 48
P[2]   AAA 1925b, lot 37

P¹ and P² each preserve portions of text not present in the other, although P² is much more complete. P¹ describes the letter as "3 pp. 12mo.," whereas P² describes it as "3pp. 8vo." ▪*Provenance:* The MS belonged to Moncure D. Conway's son, Eustace Conway, when it was sold in 1920, and was offered for sale again in 1925 as part of the collection of businessman William F. Gable (1856–1921). ▪*Emendations, adopted readings, and textual notes:*

387.1	Langham Hotel, June 25. (C) • Langham Hotel, June 25, n. y. (P¹); Langham Hotel, June 25, no year. (P²) [*both reported, not quoted*]
387.3–10	Pardon . . . funerals. (P²) • [*not in*] (P¹)
387.11	Langham, because (P¹) • Langham . . . (P²)
387.11	today (P²) • to day (P¹)
388.1	& (P¹) • [*not in*] (P²)
388.1	dead; (P²) • ∼, (P¹)
388.1–2	I . . . tomb. (P²) • [*not in*] (P¹)
388.4	Saml. L. Clemens. (P²) • [*not in*] (P¹)

▪ 25 June 1873 · To R. Cowley-Squier, *per* Samuel C. Thompson · (1st of 2) · London, England · *UCCL* 00931

▪*Copy-text:* Dictation recorded by Samuel C. Thompson in his stenographic notebook, Mark Twain Papers, The Bancroft Library, University of California, Berkeley (CU-MARK). ▪*Previous publication: N&J1*, 545. ▪*Provenance:* Thompson's notebook was purchased by CU-MARK in 1958 from Dawson's Book Shop (Los Angeles). ▪*Emendations and textual notes:* As with all letters transcribed from Thompson's notebook, the words inscribed in longhand are noted; the balance of the text was written in shorthand symbols. All the draft letters were canceled, probably by Thompson when he had completed his fair copies.

388.5–7	L̶ ̶J̶u̶n̶e̶ . . . Jn 25ᵗʰ • [*longhand*]
388.9	thk • [*longhand*]
388.9	kid offers • [*longhand*]
388.9	⚬̶ ̶⚬̶ • [*two canceled shorthand symbols*]
389.1	op. • [*longhand*]
389.1	Manchtr • [*longhand*]
389.1	prob • [*longhand*]
389.2	travel • [*longhand*]
389.2	fathfly • [*longhand*]
389.3	R. Cowly-Sq • [*longhand*]

▪ 25 June 1873 · To R. Cowley-Squier, *per* Samuel C. Thompson · (2nd of 2) · London, England · *UCCL* 00933

▪*Copy-text:* Dictation recorded by Samuel C. Thompson in his stenographic notebook, Mark Twain Papers, The Bancroft Library, University of California,

Berkeley (CU-MARK). ▪*Previous publication: N&J1,* 546. ▪*Provenance:* Thompson's notebook was purchased by CU-MARK in 1958 from Dawson's Book Shop (Los Angeles). ▪*Emendations and textual notes:* see the commentary for 25 June 73 to Cowley-Squier (1st of 2).

389.4	L̶a̶n̶g̶h̶a̶n̶ • [*longhand*]
389.5	Jne 25ᵗʰ • [*longhand*]
389.7	W̶a̶t̶t̶e̶r̶s̶o̶n̶ • [*longhand*]
389.9	misaprehns • [*longhand*]
389.9	I have • I̶ ̶h̶a̶v̶e̶ I have [*shorthand; corrected miswriting*]
389.9–10	Examiner office • [*longhand*]
389.10	of • [*shorthand; possibly* 'that']
389.11	R. Cowley-Squier • R. Cowley-S̬-Squier	[*longhand*]

▪ 25 June 1873 · To Lewis Sergeant, and to Charles E. Seth-Smith, *per* Samuel C. Thompson · London, England · *UCCL* 00935

▪*Copy-text:* Dictation recorded by Samuel C. Thompson in his stenographic notebook, Mark Twain Papers, The Bancroft Library, University of California, Berkeley (CU-MARK). ▪*Previous publication: N&J1,* 546. ▪*Provenance:* Thompson's notebook was purchased by CU-MARK in 1958 from Dawson's Book Shop (Los Angeles). ▪*Emendations and textual notes:* see the commentary for 25 June 73 to Cowley-Squier (1st of 2). Thompson's self-corrections at 390.4 and 390.8, reported below, have not been transcribed in the text.

390.1	L. L. Sergn: • [*longhand*]
390.2	Th Lagh • [*longhand*]
390.2	June 25 • [*longhand*]
390.4	indeed • i̶n̶t̶ indeed [*corrected miswriting of shorthand symbol*]
390.4	renew • ɟ̶ renew [*longhand*]
390.4	usully • [*longhand*]
390.5	noon • [*longhand*]
390.6	uncertain • [*longhand*]
390.6	thanks • [*longhand*]
390.6	form kindnesses • [*longhand*]
390.7	sincerly • [*longhand*]
390.8	Lewis Sergeant Esq. • L̶o̶u̶ Lewis Sergeant Esq. [*longhand; written at bottom of first page following* 'home' *(390.5)*]
390.9	Chas. E. Seth Smith Esq. • [*longhand*]

■ 28 June 1873 · To William Stirling-Maxwell · London, England · *UCCL* 09201

■ *Copy-text:* MS facsimile. The editors have not seen the MS, which is in the Stirling of Keir Papers, Strathclyde Regional Archives, Glasgow, Scotland (UkGS). ■ *Emendations and textual notes:*

391.8–9   me. [¶] These · ~.—| [¶] ~

■ 29 June 1873 · From Samuel L. and Olivia L. Clemens to Joseph H. Twichell · London, England · *UCCL* 00936

■ *Copy-text:* MS, Joseph H. Twichell Collection, Beinecke Rare Book and Manuscript Library, Yale University (CtY-BR). ■ *Previous publication:* Paine, 109, excerpt; *MTB*, 1:483–84, excerpt; *MTL*, 1:206–7. ■ *Provenance:* It is not known when Twichell's papers were deposited at Yale, although it is likely that he bequeathed them to the university upon his death in 1918 (*L2*, 570). ■ *Emendations and textual notes:*

392.5   near ruining · near⸍ ruining [*false start; 'ⱡ' partly formed*]
392.16   cheerfully · *cheer-|fully*
393.15   ⸔l · [*possibly 'gl'*]

■ 1 July 1873 · To Moncure D. Conway · London, England · *UCCL* 00940

■ *Copy-text:* MS, Conway Papers, Columbia University (NNC). ■ *Provenance:* The Conway Papers were acquired by NNC sometime after Conway's death in 1907. ■ *Emendations and textual notes:*

394.6   c̶o̶s̶ chosen · c̶o̶shosen

■ 1 and 2 July 1873 · To Joaquin Miller · London, England · *UCCL* 00941

■ *Copy-text:* MS, Clifton Waller Barrett Library, University of Virginia, Charlottesville (ViU). ■ *Provenance:* deposited at ViU by Clifton Waller Barrett on 17 December 1963. ■ *Emendations and textual notes:*

395.6   say · s̶a̶y̶ | say [*rewritten for clarity*]

■ 4 July 1873 · To Adam Badeau · London, England · *UCCL* 00942
■*Copy-text:* MS, Department of Rare Books and Special Collections, Rush Rhees Library, University of Rochester, Rochester, N.Y. (NRU). ■*Provenance:* The MS is in the Charles A. Brown Collection of Autographs, donated to NRU in 1914.

■ 4 July 1873 · To Moncure D. Conway · London, England · *UCCL* 00943
■*Copy-text:* MS, Stone and Kimball Collection, Newberry Library, Chicago (ICN). ■*Provenance:* The MS, laid in a first edition copy of *Life on the Mississippi* (James R. Osgood and Co., 1883), was donated to ICN in 1962 by Howard Ellis.

■ 5 July 1873 · To Henry Lee · London, England · *UCCL* 00944
■*Copy-text:* Transcript and paraphrase, Parke-Bernet 1954c, lot 633, which describes the letter as "CLEMENS, S.L.-A.L.s. '*Clemens*'. 1 p., 12mo [London, July 5, 1873]. With envelope addressed to '*Henry Lee . . . Blackfriars Road, S.E.*'" ■*Emendations and textual notes:*

398.6   Esq | 43 Holland street • [*not in; address adopted from five enve-
           lopes or postcards addressed to Lee in 1873, all identical*]

■ 5 July 1873 · To Joaquin Miller · London, England · *UCCL* 00945
■*Copy-text:* MS facsimile. The editors have not seen the MS, which is in the Locker-Lampson Papers in the Osborn Collection, Beinecke Rare Book and Manuscript Library, Yale University (CtY-BR). ■*Provenance:* The MS was preserved in the Locker-Lampson Papers—a collection of some two thousand letters, most of them addressed to Frederick Locker—at the East Sussex Record Office, Lewes, England, until 1993, when CtY-BR acquired them. ■*Emendations and textual notes:*

398.13   e̶s̶ express • eᶠxpress

■ 6 July 1873 · To Mary Mason Fairbanks · London, England · *UCCL* 00947
■*Copy-text:* MS, Henry E. Huntington Library, San Marino (CSmH, call no. HM 14281). ■*Previous publication: MTMF,* 172–77; Harnsberger, 64, brief excerpt. ■*Provenance:* see Huntington Library in Description of Provenance. ■*Emendations and textual notes:*

402.11   of. However • ~.—|~
402.13   Spenₑcer • ['*s*' *partly formed*]

402.18–19   Motley • M̸ Motley [*corrected miswriting*]
402.23   formidable • formi̸dable
404.1   c̶a̶m̶ canal • car̸nal

■ 7 July 1873 · To Elisha Bliss, Jr. · London, England · *UCCL* 00948
■ *Copy-text:* MS, Clifton Waller Barrett Library, University of Virginia, Charlottesville (ViU), is copy-text for the letter. A transcript facsimile is copy-text for
the enclosure. The editors have not seen the original handwritten transcript,
made by Dana S. Ayer during the late 1890s or later, which is in the Rare Book
Department, Memorial Library, University of Wisconsin, Madison (WU). (A
second enclosure, the MS of "The 'Jumping Frog.' In English. Then in French,"
survives at ViU with the MS for the letter; it is described in the notes.) ■ *Previous
publication:* Parke-Bernet 1954d, lot 12, excerpts; *MTLP,* 79–80 n. 1, enclosure
only. ■ *Provenance:* The MS for the letter was deposited at ViU by Clifton Waller
Barrett on 16 April 1960. The enclosure evidently remained among the American Publishing Company's files until it was sold (and may have been copied at
that time by Ayer; see Brownell Collection in Description of Provenance). The
Ayer transcription was in turn copied by a typist and this typed transcription is
also at WU. ■ *Emendations and textual notes:*

[*MS is copy-text for* 'The . . . Reader" ' *(409.1–15)*]
409.4   Paris‸ &̶ y̶ • [*insertion and cancellation doubtful*]
409.7   sketches • sketc[h◊]s [*obscured by inkblot*]
409.13   article • [a◊]ticle [*obscured by inkblot*]
409.13   been • bee[n] [*obscured by inkblot*]
409.15   R̶e̶l̶ Reader • Re̸ader
             [*Transcript is copy-text for* 'To . . . 7' *(409.17–410.13)*]
409.21   & • and [*also at 410.8*]
410.5   Shah • Shas
410.5   Persia. • ~‸
410.7   not known • not know

■ 10? July 1873 · To Charles Dudley Warner · ?London, England ·
UCCL 00951
■ *Copy-text:* MS, Sinclair Hamilton Collection, Princeton University (NjP). Published with permission of the Princeton University Libraries. ■ *Provenance:* The
MS, which lacks the letter's first two pages, is laid in a first edition copy of *The
Gilded Age* (American Publishing Company, 1874). Sinclair Hamilton (1884–
1978) donated much of his collection (primarily woodcuts and wood engravings)
to NjP in 1945, and continued to supplement his gift until shortly before his
death (Dickinson, 148–49). ■ *Emendations and textual notes:*

411.13   Hawkeye · Hawk-|eye
411.18–19   original · originale

■ 10 July 1873 · To Elisha Bliss, Jr. · London, England · *UCCL* 10976
■*Copy-text:* MS facsimile. The editors have not seen the MS, which was owned
in 1984 by Russell Freedman of Second Life Books (Lanesborough, Mass.), who
provided a photocopy to the Mark Twain Papers. ■*Provenance:* When offered
for sale in 1984 the MS was laid in a volume of the Autograph Edition of The
Writings of Mark Twain, almost certainly *The Innocents Abroad* (American Publishing Company, 1899–1907).

■ 11 July 1873 · To Mr. Smith, *per* Samuel C. Thompson · London,
England · *UCCL* 00949
■*Copy-text:* Dictation recorded by Samuel C. Thompson in his stenographic
notebook, Mark Twain Papers, The Bancroft Library, University of California,
Berkeley (CU-MARK). ■*Previous publication: N&J1*, 564, with omission.
■*Provenance:* Thompson's notebook was purchased by CU-MARK in 1958 from
Dawson's Book Shop (Los Angeles). ■*Emendations and textual notes:* see the com-
mentary for 25 June 73 to Cowley-Squier (1st of 2).

414.1   *July 11ᵗʰ* · [*longhand*]
414.2   Smith · [*longhand*]
414.3   particular · par- [*longhand*] | ticular [*shorthand*]
414.3   Thu · [*longhand*]
414.3   picnick · [*longhand*]
414.4   MᶜDonald's · [*longhand*]
414.4   16ᵗʰ · [*longhand*]
414.4   arrage · [*longhand*]
414.6   Sincerly Yours · [*longhand*]

■ 11 July 1873 · To Unidentified, *per* Samuel C. Thompson · London,
England · *UCCL* 00950
■*Copy-text:* Dictation recorded by Samuel C. Thompson in his stenographic
notebook, Mark Twain Papers, The Bancroft Library, University of California,
Berkeley (CU-MARK). ■*Previous publication: N&J1*, 564. ■*Provenance:*
Thompson's notebook was purchased by CU-MARK in 1958 from Dawson's
Book Shop (Los Angeles). ■*Emendations and textual notes:* see the commentary
for 25 June 73 to Cowley-Squier (1st of 2). Thompson's self-correction at 415.4,
reported below, has not been transcribed in the text.

415.1   July 11ᵗʰ · [*longhand*]
415.2   Sir · [*longhand*]

415.3   Tuesdy • [*longhand*]
415.3   15th do • [*longhand*]
415.4   Vic. • Ẇ Vic. [*longhand*]

■ 14 July 1873 · To Charles E. Flower · London, England · *UCCL* 00952

■ *Copy-text:* MS, Folger Shakespeare Library, Washington, D.C. (DFo). ■ *Provenance:* purchased in 1924 by businessman and collector Henry Clay Folger (1857–1930) from Maggs Bros., London. ■ *Emendations and textual notes:*

415.11   it. No • ~.—‖~
415.17   households • house-|holds
416.1   all ale • al/e

■ 16 July 1873 · To Elisha Bliss, Jr., *per* Samuel C. Thompson · London, England · *UCCL* 00953

■ *Copy-text:* MS, Willard S. Morse Collection, Collection of American Literature, Beinecke Rare Book and Manuscript Library, Yale University (CtY-BR). Thompson made this fair copy from the stenographic version of the letter that he had recorded in his notebook from Clemens's dictation (CU-MARK; see *N&J1*, 567). ■ *Previous publication: MTLP,* 77. ■ *Provenance:* The Morse Collection was donated to CtY in 1942 by Walter F. Frear. ■ *Emendations and textual notes:*

416.10   volumes • [*possibly* 'volum∮es']
416.12   and • and ‖ and

■ 16 July 1873 · To Charles Dudley Warner, *per* Samuel C. Thompson · London, England · *UCCL* 00954

■ *Copy-text:* MS, Willard S. Morse Collection, Collection of American Literature, Beinecke Rare Book and Manuscript Library, Yale University (CtY-BR). Thompson made this fair copy from the stenographic version of the letter that he had recorded in his notebook from Clemens's dictation (CU-MARK; see *N&J1*, 567–68). ■ *Previous publication: MTLP,* 78. ■ *Provenance:* The MS is laid in a first edition copy of *The Gilded Age* (American Publishing Company, 1873); the Morse Collection was donated to CtY in 1942 by Walter F. Frear.

■ 20 July 1873 · To Olivia Lewis Langdon · York, England · *UCCL* 00955

■ *Copy-text:* MS, collection of Robert Tollett. ■ *Previous publication: MTB,* 1:485–86; *MTL,* 1:207–8; Jervis Langdon, 8–9; Jerome and Wisbey, 206–7, all with omissions. ▪*Provenance:* The MS probably remained in the Langdon family until at least 1938, when it was published by Jervis Langdon (Olivia Lewis Langdon's grandson). Robert Tollett purchased it in the late 1960s from an unidentified owner. ▪*Emendations and textual notes:*

419.5   ~~That~~ • ['t' *partly formed*]
419.16   chivalry • chival‸ry
419.18   byways • by-|ways
419.24   ~~carr~~ caressed • car‸essed
419.28   ~~that~~ than • tha‸n
420.2   ~~of~~ if • ‸if

▪ 27 July 1873 · To Elisha Bliss, Jr. · Edinburgh, Scotland · *UCCL* 00956

▪*Copy-text:* MS, Beinecke Rare Book and Manuscript Library, Yale University (CtY-BR). ▪*Previous publication: MTLP,* 79. ▪*Provenance:* The MS was formerly laid in a first English edition copy of *The Gilded Age* (Routledge, 1874) owned by Owen F. Aldis (1852–1925), who donated his collection of American literature to CtY in 1911 (Cannon, 180).

▪ 27 July 1873 · ~~To David Ross Locke~~ To T. B. Pugh · Edinburgh, Scotland · *UCCL* 00957

▪*Copy-text:* MS, Willard S. Morse Collection, Collection of American Literature, Beinecke Rare Book and Manuscript Library, Yale University (CtY-BR). ▪*Previous publication: MTLP,* 78–79. ▪*Provenance:* The MS is laid in a first English edition copy of *The Gilded Age* (Routledge, 1874); the Morse Collection was donated to CtY in 1942 by Walter F. Frear. ▪*Emendations and textual notes:*

421.2   ~~Locke—~~ • [*deletion of dash implied*]

▪ 31 July 1873 · To Unidentified · Edinburgh, Scotland · *UCCL* 00958

▪*Copy-text:* MS, Norcross Collection, Massachusetts Historical Society, Boston (MHi). ▪*Previous publication:* AAA 1924b, lot 549, excerpts. ▪*Provenance:* The MS, offered for sale in 1924 as part of the collection of businessman William F. Gable (1856–1921), was bequeathed to MHi in 1937 by Grenville Howland Norcross. ▪*Emendations and textual notes:*

423.2   maybe. G. • ~.—|~.
423.6   ~~Wh~~ • ['h' *partly formed*]
423.11   Mr. • ~~Mr~~ Mr. [*corrected miswriting*]

■ 2 August 1873 · To Elisha Bliss, Jr. · (1st of 2) · Edinburgh, Scotland · *UCCL* 08826

■ *Copy-text:* MS, draft telegram on a page of untitled notes (SLC 1873t), Mark Twain Papers, The Bancroft Library, University of California, Berkeley (CU-MARK). ■ *Provenance:* see Mark Twain Papers in Description of Provenance.

■ 2 August 1873 · To Elisha Bliss, Jr. · (2nd of 2) · Edinburgh, Scotland · *UCCL* 05816

■ *Copy-text:* Goodspeed's Book Shop 1926?, item 793c. The transcription published in Goodspeed's later catalog, Goodspeed's Book Shop 1927?, item 4633b, is identical except for a corrected typographical error, 'that' for 'than' at 425.4. Both catalogs describe the letter as an "A. l. s., 2 pp., Edinburgh, Aug. 2, n.y." ■ *Emendations and textual notes:*

425.1	Edinburgh, Aug. 2. • [*reported, not quoted*]
425.3	[¶] Have • [*no* ¶] ~
425.4	that • than

■ 2 and 6 August 1873 · Olivia L. and Samuel L. Clemens to Olivia Lewis Langdon · Edinburgh, Scotland · *UCCL* 00959

■ *Copy-text:* MS, Mark Twain House, Hartford (CtHMTH). ■ *Provenance:* donated to CtHMTH in 1962 or 1963 by Ida Langdon. ■ *Emendations and textual notes:*

426.9	s̶h̶a̶l̶ • ['l' *partly formed*]
426.10	h̶a̶d̶s̶ hands • h̶a̶d̶s̶n̶d̶s̶ hands [*rewritten for clarity*]
426.11	s̶She • [*possibly* 's̶She'; *that is, OLC may have written only the* 's', *which SLC then altered to* 'S' *before completing the word*]
427.29	o̶n̶ in • ɸin

■ 4 August 1873 · To Edmund H. Yates · Edinburgh, Scotland · *UCCL* 10703

■ *Copy-text:* MS, Mark Twain Papers, The Bancroft Library, University of California, Berkeley (CU-MARK). ■ *Previous publication:* Waiting for Godot Books, item 6, with omissions. ■ *Provenance:* The MS, owned at an unknown date by Raphael King (London) and in 1969 by Paul H. North of Second Life Books (Columbus, Ohio), was purchased by CU-MARK in January 1995 from Waiting for Godot Books through the James F. and Agnes R. Robb Memorial Fund. ■ *Emendations and textual notes:*

430.9   treated • trea/ted
430.12   myself. And • ~.—|~
430.15   im̶ • im̶-|

■ 10 September 1873 · To William S. Andrews · London, England ·
UCCL 00960

■ *Copy-text:* MS, Middlebury College, Middlebury, Vermont (VtMiM). ■ *Provenance:* purchased from William F. Kelleher in March 1944. ■ *Emendations and textual notes:*

435.2   good-bye • good-|bye
435.6   Place • Plac[◊] [*torn*]
435.7–8   NEW YORK • NE[◊ ◊◊◊◊] [*torn*]

■ 10 September 1873 · To Thomas W. Knox · London, England ·
UCCL 04137

■ *Copy-text:* MS, Special Collections and Archives, Knox College Library, Galesburg, Illinois (IGK). ■ *Provenance:* The MS was owned by George Steele Seymour (1878–1945), whose papers were donated to IGK in 1952 by the Bookfellow Foundation. ■ *Emendations and textual notes:*

435.13   ten • t̶e̶n̶ ten [*corrected miswriting*]
435.16   ruin? • r̶u̶i̶n̶?̶ ruin? [*corrected miswriting*]
435.21   continue • ['nu' *conflated*]
435.23–436.1 un̶l̶ underlined • un/derlined

■ 10 September 1873 · To Henry Lee · London, England · *UCCL*
00961

■ *Copy-text:* MS, Clifton Waller Barrett Library, University of Virginia, Charlottesville (ViU). The letter was written on a halfpenny postcard identical to the one described in the commentary for 4 Oct 72 to Lee. ■ *Previous publication:* Parke-Bernet 1959, lot 62. ■ *Provenance:* deposited at ViU by Clifton Waller Barrett on 15 May 1962.

■ 12? September 1873 · To Orion and Mary E. (Mollie) Clemens · London, England · *UCCL* 00962

■ *Copy-text:* MS, *damage emended,* Jean Webster McKinney Family Papers, Vassar College Library (NPV). The letter was written on both sides of a single sheet, the top of which has been torn away. See the illustration below of the top of the torn page, reproduced at actual size. ■*Provenance:* see McKinney Family Papers in Description of Provenance. ■*Emendations and textual notes:*

438.2	We got ma's & Pamela's •	[We got ma◇s & P◇◇◇◇◇◇◇] [*torn away*]
438.4	sealskin • sealḳskin ['ḳ' *partly formed*]	
438.7	shillings • shil-‖ [*torn away*]	

■ 22 and 25 September 1873 · To John Brown · London, England · *UCCL* 03362

■*Copy-text:* MS facsimile. The editors have not seen the MS, which was owned in 1981 by Charles W. Sachs of the Scriptorium (Beverly Hills), who provided a photocopy to the Mark Twain Papers. ■*Previous publication:* Christie 1981, lot 69, excerpts; Kelleher, lot 19, excerpts. ■*Emendations and textual notes:*

439.6–7	e̶m̶ enthusiasm • er̸hnthusiasm	
439.8	come • com[e] [*torn*]	
439.21	pen. However • ~.—|~	
439.23	us? Till • ~?—|~	
439.25	w̶i̶l̶ we • wi̶le ['l' *partly formed*]	
439.26	Shrewsbury • ['ws' *conflated*]	

■ 23 September 1873 · To Shirley Brooks · London, England · *UCCL* 00963

■*Copy-text:* MS, Pierpont Morgan Library, New York City (NNPM). ■*Provenance:* The MS was in the collection of financier J. Pierpont Morgan (1837–1913), which his son conveyed to the state of New York in 1924 for use as a public reference library.

■ 25 or 26 September 1873 · To Henry Lee · London, England · *UCCL* 00965

■*Copy-text:* MS, James S. Copley Library, La Jolla, California (CLjC). The letter was written on a halfpenny postcard identical to the one described in the commentary for 4 Oct 72 to Lee. ■*Previous publication:* Christie 1988, lot 1189. ■*Provenance:* The MS was for many years in the Estelle Doheny Collection at The Edward Laurence Doheny Memorial Library of St. John's Seminary, Camarillo, California. John L. Feldman purchased it in October 1988 and sold it to the Copley Library in 1990.

■ 29 September 1873 · To Louisa P. MacDonald · (1st of 2) · London, England · *UCCL* 00966

■*Copy-text:* MS on calling card, Clifton Waller Barrett Library, University of Virginia, Charlottesville (ViU). The card was enclosed in an envelope, on which nothing was inscribed. ■*Provenance:* deposited at ViU by Clifton Waller Barrett on 17 December 1963.

■ 29 September 1873 · To Louisa P. MacDonald · (2nd of 2) · London, England · *UCCL* 11830

■*Copy-text:* MS, George MacDonald Collection, Beinecke Rare Book and Manuscript Library, Yale University (CtY-BR). ■*Previous publication:* Raeper, 333, excerpt. ■*Provenance:* The George MacDonald Collection was purchased by CtY in 1976. ■*Emendations and textual notes:*

445.14   2̶4̶ 25 · 2⁄5 ['4' *partly formed*]

■ 7 October 1873 · To the Editor of the London *Standard* · London, England · *UCCL* 00969

■*Copy-text:* None. The text is based on two transcriptions, each of which may derive independently from the manuscript:

P¹	"Mark Twain on the Sandwich Islands," London *Standard*, 9 Oct 73
P²	*MTB*, 1:490

P¹, a clipping in Scrapbook 12:1, Mark Twain Papers, The Bancroft Library, University of California, Berkeley (CU-MARK), was probably typeset from Clemens's original manuscript. Although it is possible that Paine took his text (P²) from P¹, incorporating his own revisions, several of P²'s variants appear to be authorial, suggesting that it may well have been typeset from Clemens's own fair copy of the manuscript—made for security when he wrote the letter, and preserved among his papers. The occurrence of 'SIR,—' in both texts does not necessarily suggest that P² derives from P¹, since it may reflect the missing manuscript, or editorial styling applied independently by the *Standard* and by Paine, who consistently used this form when publishing Clemens's letters (see the Description of Texts). ■*Provenance:* for the scrapbook see Mark Twain Papers in Description of Provenance. ■*Emendations, adopted readings, and textual notes:*

448.3	& (C) • and (P¹,²) [*here and hereafter*]
448.4–5	England (P²) • ∼, (P¹)
448.5–6	should be (P²) • be (P¹)
448.8	best (P²) • best of (P¹)
448.9	honorable (P²) • honourable (P¹)
449.1	the one (P¹) • one (P²)
449.4	paralyze (P²) • paralyse (P¹)
449.8	sir (P²) • Sir (P¹)
449.8–9	obedient servant (P²) • obedient obedient (P¹)
449.10	London. Oct. 7, (P¹) • [*not in*] (P²)
449.10	Mark Twain (P²) • MARK TWAIN (P¹)

■ 7 October 1873 · To Henry Lee · London, England · *UCCL* 00968

■ *Copy-text:* MS, Mark Twain Papers, The Bancroft Library, University of California, Berkeley (CU-MARK). ■ *Provenance:* The MS was sold by John Howell Books in 1972 and donated to CU-MARK in 1973. See Appert Collection in Description of Provenance.

■ 8? October 1873 · To Henry Lee · (1st of 3) · London, England · *UCCL* 11921

■ *Copy-text:* Paraphrase, Rains Galleries, lot 109. The letter was written on a postcard, presumably identical to the one described in the commentary for 4 Oct 72 to Lee. ■ *Provenance:* When offered for sale in 1937 (Rains Galleries) the MS was laid in a first edition copy of *Is Shakespeare Dead? From My Autobiography* (Harper and Brothers, 1909).

■ 8 October 1873 · To Henry Lee · (2nd of 3) · London, England · *UCCL* 00970

■ *Copy-text:* MS, George N. Meissner Collection, Washington University, St. Louis (MoSW). ■ *Previous publication:* Chicago, lot 35. ■ *Provenance:* donated to MoSW in about 1960 by the family of businessman and collector George N. Meissner (1872–1960). ■ *Emendations and textual notes:*

450.14	LONDON-W • LON[D◊]N-W [*badly inked*]

■ 8 October 1873 · To Henry Lee · (3rd of 3) · London, England · *UCCL* 11812 (formerly part of 00970)

■ *Copy-text:* MS, Clifton Waller Barrett Library, University of Virginia, Charlottesville (ViU). ■ *Previous publication:* City Book Auction, lot 144. ■ *Provenance:* The MS, laid in a first edition copy of *Mark Twain's Speeches* (Harper and

Brothers, 1910), was sold in 1954 to Seven Gables Bookshop (New York City) as part of the collection of Byron Price (City Book Auction); it was deposited at ViU by Clifton Waller Barrett on 16 April 1960.

■ 11 October 1873 · To Unidentified · London, England · *UCCL* 00971

■*Copy-text:* MS, Cyril Clemens Collection, Mark Twain House, Hartford (CtHMTH). ■*Provenance:* donated to CtHMTH in 1984 by Cyril Clemens. ■*Emendations and textual notes:*

451.11   S̶u̶ Square • S͟q̶uare

■ 12 October 1873 · To Olivia Lewis Langdon · London, England · *UCCL* 00973

■*Copy-text:* MS, Mark Twain House, Hartford (CtHMTH). ■*Provenance:* donated to CtHMTH in 1962 or 1963 by Ida Langdon. ■*Emendations and textual notes:*

452.4   to-day • to-|day
452.5   tomorrow • to-|morrow

■ 13 October 1873 · To George Bentley · London, England · *UCCL* 00974

■*Copy-text:* MS, Clifton Waller Barrett Library, University of Virginia, Charlottesville (ViU). ■*Provenance:* deposited at ViU by Clifton Waller Barrett on 17 December 1963.

■ 15 and 30 October 1873 · To George Bentley · London, England, and SS *Batavia* en route from Liverpool, England, to New York, N.Y. · *UCCL* 00975

■*Copy-text:* MS, Clifton Waller Barrett Library, University of Virginia, Charlottesville (ViU). ■*Provenance:* deposited at ViU by Clifton Waller Barrett on 17 December 1963. ■*Emendations and textual notes:*

455.1   1̶4̶ 15 • 1͟45
455.3   interfered • interfer͟ded
455.11   t̶h̶e̶ that • th͟eat

■ 19 October 1873 · To Charles Warren Stoddard · London, England · *UCCL* 00976

■ *Copy-text:* MS, Mark Twain Papers, The Bancroft Library, University of California, Berkeley (CU-MARK). ■ *Provenance:* The MS was sold by James F. Drake in 1929 (note by Dixon Wecter in CU-MARK copy of *MTB*, 1:497), and by John Howell Books in 1972; it was donated to CU-MARK in 1973. See Appert Collection in Description of Provenance. ■ *Emendations and textual notes:*

456.8   ended. Charge • ~.—|~
456.9   course. When • ~.—|~
456.10   b̶o̶u̶l̶ boil • boulil [*canceled* 'l' *partly formed*]

■ 22 October 1873 · To Unidentified · SS *Batavia* at Queenstown, Ireland · *UCCL* 00977

■ *Copy-text:* MS, Mark Twain Papers, The Bancroft Library, University of California, Berkeley (CU-MARK). ■ *Provenance:* donated to CU-MARK in 1977. See Appert Collection in Description of Provenance.

■ 30 October 1873 · To John Brown · SS *Batavia* en route from Liverpool, England, to New York, N.Y. · *UCCL* 00978

■ *Copy-text:* MS, James S. Copley Library, La Jolla, California (CLjC). ■ *Previous publication:* Paine 1912, 112, brief excerpt; *MTB*, 1:494, brief excerpt; *MTL*, 1:209–10; Christie 1981, lot 69, excerpts; Sotheby 1983, lot 4, excerpts. ■ *Provenance:* The MS was sold by Christie in May 1981, by Charles W. Sachs of the Scriptorium (Beverly Hills) after July 1981, and then by Sotheby Parke-Bernet in April 1983. It was purchased by CLjC in May 1983 from an unidentified dealer. ■ *Emendations and textual notes:*

459.2   Mid-Atlantic • Mid-Atlan∉tic
459.13   smoothe • [*sic*]
459.21   overboard • over-|board
459.22   y̸ • [*partly formed*]

■ 5 November 1873 · To Elisha Bliss, Jr. · Hartford, Conn. · *UCCL* 00979

■ *Copy-text:* MS, Clifton Waller Barrett Library, University of Virginia, Charlottesville (ViU). ■ *Provenance:* deposited at ViU by Clifton Waller Barrett on 17 December 1963. ■ *Emendations and textual notes:*

461.10   Bureau,) • Bureau,,) [original comma accidentally obscured by closing parenthesis] ^
461.13–14 Shoe Lane, • ~~Shoe~~ Shoe ~~Lane,~~ Lane, [corrected miswriting]

■ 6 November 1873 · To Jane Lampton Clemens · Hartford, Conn. · UCCL 00980

■Copy-text: Transcript, handwritten by Mollie Clemens, Mark Twain Papers, The Bancroft Library, University of California, Berkeley (CU-MARK). ■Provenance: see Mark Twain Papers in Description of Provenance. ■Emendations and textual notes: Mollie's revisions and self-corrections, reported below, have not been transcribed in the text. The revision '~~I loaned~~ I gave' at 470.6 most likely preserves Clemens's own change of wording, and therefore has been included in the text.

470.3   opportunity. • ~,.
470.4 $15 • $15
470.10   pension^ • ẃ pension
470.10–11 $15 . . . $10 • $15 . . . $10
471.1   more • ∅ more^ ^
471.1 $10 • ~~10~~ $10
471.3   condition • condition$
471.7   absolutely • abso╪lutely|
471.9   pension • ~~th~~ pen_∧|sion
471.11   contented • conten╪ted
471.11   & • & ∦
471.13   proposition, If • pro_∧|position, If [sic]
471.19   but • ~,
471.20   common-sense • common-|sense

■ 7 November 1873 · To William Bowen · Hartford, Conn. · UCCL 00981

■Copy-text: MS, Harry Ransom Humanities Research Center, University of Texas, Austin (TxU-Hu). ■Previous publication: Hornberger, 22–23. ■Provenance: purchased by TxU in 1940 from Eva Laura Bowen (Mrs. Louis Knox), daughter of William Bowen.

■ 10 and 17 November 1873 · To Olivia L. Clemens · SS City of Chester en route from New York, N.Y., to Liverpool, England; and Queenstown, Ireland · UCCL 00982

■Copy-text: MS, Mark Twain Papers, The Bancroft Library, University of California, Berkeley (CU-MARK). ■Previous publication: LLMT, 363, brief para-

phrase. ▪*Provenance:* see Samossoud Collection in Description of Provenance.
▪*Emendations and textual notes:*

473.3	~~Liy~~ Livy • Li∮vy	
473.7	skylights • sky-|lights	
473.11	∮ • [*partly formed*]	
473.22	service • [*sic*]	
473.27	~~sta~~ steam • st∮eam	
474.14	left • [*possibly ' ᴬleft'*]	
474.21	QUEENSTOWN • QUEENSTOW[N] [*badly inked*]	
474.22	BOSTON • [B◊◊◊◊N] [*badly inked*]	

▪ **14 November 1873 · To Olivia L. Clemens · SS *City of Chester* en route from New York, N.Y., to Liverpool, England · *UCCL* 00983**

▪*Copy-text:* MS, Mark Twain Papers, The Bancroft Library, University of California, Berkeley (CU-MARK). ▪*Previous publication: LLMT*, 363, brief paraphrase. ▪*Provenance:* see Samossoud Collection in Description of Provenance.
▪*Emendations and textual notes:*

475.5	skylights • sky-|lights
475.5	drowning • ~~drown~~ drowning [*corrected miswriting*]
476.3	QUEENSTOWN • QUEENSTOW[N] [*badly inked*]
476.4	BOSTON • B[OST]O[N] [*badly inked*]

▪ **20 November 1873 · To Olivia L. Clemens · London, England · *UCCL* 00984**

▪*Copy-text:* MS, Mark Twain Papers, The Bancroft Library, University of California, Berkeley (CU-MARK). ▪*Previous publication: LLMT*, 184. ▪*Provenance:* see Samossoud Collection in Description of Provenance. ▪*Emendations and textual notes:*

478.6	footsteps • foot-|steps
478.9	Disraeli's • Disrael∮i's
478.18	~~will~~ wild • wil∮d
479.6	LONDON-W • LONDO[◊-]W [*badly inked*]
479.7	NEW YORK DEC ◊ PAID ALL • [NE◊ ◊O◊K ◊◊]C [◊] PAID [◊◊◊] [*badly inked*]

▪ **21 November 1873 · To Olivia L. Clemens · London, England · *UCCL* 00985**

▪*Copy-text:* MS, Mark Twain Papers, The Bancroft Library, University of California, Berkeley (CU-MARK). ▪*Previous publication: MFMT*, 53, brief excerpt; *LLMT*, 363, brief paraphrase. ▪ *Provenance:* see Samossoud Collection in Description of Provenance. ▪ *Emendations and textual notes:*

479.12	merschaum • [*sic; also at 479.13*]
479.13	u̶p̶b̶ • ['b' *partly formed*]
480.8	w̶ • [*partly formed*]
480.9	him. Mr • ~.—|~
480.13	t̶r̶e̶a̶ tramps • treaamps
480.15	day. Good • ~.—|~
480.20	NEW YORK ◊◊◊ ◊ PAID ALL • [NEW YOR]K [◊◊◊ ◊] PAID [◊◊◊] [*badly inked*]

▪ **22 November 1873 · To Henry Lee · London, England · *UCCL* 00986**

▪ *Copy-text:* MS, Clifton Waller Barrett Library, University of Virginia, Charlottesville (ViU). ▪ *Provenance:* purchased by ViU on 4 January 1963.

▪ **23 November 1873 · To Olivia L. Clemens · London, England · *UCCL* 00987**

▪ *Copy-text:* MS, Mark Twain Papers, The Bancroft Library, University of California, Berkeley (CU-MARK). ▪ *Previous publication:* Wecter, 87; *LLMT*, 185. ▪ *Provenance:* see Samossoud Collection in Description of Provenance. ▪ *Emendations and textual notes:*

482.8	for • [f]or [*torn*]
482.8	me. I • ~.—|~
482.12	lot • [l]ot [*obscured by inkblot*]
482.14	a̶t̶ • ['t' *partly formed; possibly* 'I']
482.28	w̶o̶r̶k̶ word • worḳd
483.3	LONDON·W • LONDON·[W] [*badly inked*]
483.4	YORK DEC 8 PAID • Y[ORK ◊◊◊] 8 P[◊◊D] [*badly inked*]

▪ **24 November 1873 · To Olivia L. Clemens · London, England · *UCCL* 00988**

▪ *Copy-text:* MS, Mark Twain Papers, The Bancroft Library, University of California, Berkeley (CU-MARK). ▪ *Previous publication:* *LLMT*, 364, brief paraphrase. ▪ *Provenance:* see Samossoud Collection in Description of Provenance. ▪ *Emendations and textual notes:* A smudge of red ink—probably a badly inked New York postmark—appears on the flap of the envelope, but is not legible enough to transcribe.

483.5	~~23~~ 24 • 2↕4
483.6	~~Dob~~ Dolby • Do↕lby
483.6	~~tha~~ the • th↓e
483.7	~~pla~~ pleasant • pl↓easant
483.12	↕ • [*possibly* '↕']
484.3–4	~~they~~ then • the↕n
484.8	about • abo↕ut
484.20	~~th~~ • ['h' *partly formed*]
484.22	familiarity • familiar↕ity ['↕' *partly formed*]
484.31	~~rush~~ • ['h' *partly formed*]
484.32	~~Dobl~~ Dolby • Do~~bl~~lby [*canceled* 'l' *partly formed*]
485.3	LONDON • [L]ONDON [*badly inked*]

■ 26 November 1873 · To Olivia L. Clemens · London, England · *UCCL* 00989

■ *Copy-text:* MS, Mark Twain Papers, The Bancroft Library, University of California, Berkeley (CU-MARK), is copy-text for the letter and envelope. MS, Charles Kingsley to SLC, 26 Nov 73, CU-MARK (*UCLC* 31896), is copy-text for the enclosure. ■ *Previous publication: LLMT*, 364, brief paraphrase of letter only. ■ *Provenance:* see Samossoud Collection (letter) and Mark Twain Papers (enclosure) in Description of Provenance. ■ *Emendations and textual notes:*

[*MS, Kingsley to SLC, is copy-text for* 'The . . . Kingsley' *(485.16–486.9)*]
485.19	~~tre~~ tried • tr↓ied

[*MS, SLC to OLC, is copy-text for* 'Mrs. . . . . ALL' *(486.11–13)*]
486.12	LONDON·W 7 NO28 73 • [L]ONDON·W 7 NO28 [7]3 [*badly inked*]
486.12	II • [◇◇] [*badly inked*]
486.13	PAID ALL • [◇◇◇◇ ◇◇◇] [*badly inked*]

■ 28 November 1873 · To George H. Fitzgibbon · London, England · *UCCL* 00990

■ *Copy-text:* MS, Cyril Clemens Collection, Mark Twain House, Hartford (CtHMTH), is copy-text for the letter. No enclosure survives with the letter, but a manuscript that is clearly one of several copies prepared for the occasion, and might well have been the one enclosed, is in the Henry W. and Albert A. Berg Collection, The New York Public Library, Astor, Lenox and Tilden Foundations (NN-B), and is copy-text for the enclosure. It comprises two MS pages in Clemens's hand, and twelve pages of transcription, ten in the hand of Charles Warren Stoddard and two in an unidentified hand. One other page from Clemens's original MS survives in the Beinecke Rare Book and Manuscript Library, Yale University (CtY-BR); it is numbered '4' and contains the text for '(and

. . . how,' (488.34–489.3), with no significant variants. ■*Previous publication:* AAA/Anderson 1934a, lot 127; Parke-Bernet 1946, lot 88, excerpts from the letter only. The enclosed MS has never been published, but a verbatim text of the speech as delivered by Clemens was published in "Scottish Corporation of London," London *Morning Post*, 2 Dec 73, 6. Later texts apparently derived from it or another verbatim transcription: "Mark Twain on Woman," *Hornet*, 13 Dec 73, clipping in Scrapbook 12:43, 45, CU-MARK; "Mark Twain's Best," San Francisco *Illustrated Press* 2 (Sept 74): 29; SLC 1875, 213–14; *MTS* 1910, 94–98; *MTS* 1923, 42–45; Fatout 1976, 78–80; Budd 1992a, 559–61. ■*Provenance:* The letter MS, owned at one time by Charles Retz (New York), later belonged to Edmund W. Evans, Jr. (of Oil City, Pennsylvania), who offered it for sale in April 1934. It was again offered for sale in 1946, when it was apparently the property of W. W. Cohen. Cyril Clemens donated it to CtHMTH in 1984. The enclosure was owned by businessman William T. H. Howe (1874–1939); in 1940 Dr. A. A. Berg bought and donated the Howe Collection to NN. ■*Emendations and textual notes:*

> [*MS is copy-text for* 'Friday . . . noticed' *(487.1–488.21)*]

487.5   ~~we~~ the • ᴠ̌the

> [*Transcript is copy-text for* '& . . . of' *(488.22–490.23)*]

488.35   recals • ~~recals~~ ‚recals‚ [*corrected miswriting*]

489.30   lowly • ~~loẉly~~ lowly [*corrected miswriting*]

■ 3 December 1873 · To Olivia L. Clemens · London, England · UCCL 00991

■*Copy-text:* MS, Mark Twain Papers, The Bancroft Library, University of California, Berkeley (CU-MARK). ■*Previous publication: LLMT,* 364, brief paraphrase. ■*Provenance:* see Samossoud Collection in Description of Provenance. ■*Emendations and textual notes:*

493.4   it. I • ~.—|~

■ 6 December 1873 · To Olivia L. Clemens · London, England · UCCL 00992

■*Copy-text:* MS, Mark Twain Papers, The Bancroft Library, University of California, Berkeley (CU-MARK). ■*Previous publication: LLMT,* 364, brief paraphrase. ■*Provenance:* see Samossoud Collection in Description of Provenance. ■*Emendations and textual notes:*

494.14   ~~Com~~ Conn • Coɳ́nn

■ 7 December 1873 · To Olivia L. Clemens · London, England · UCCL 00993

■*Copy-text:* MS, Mark Twain Papers, The Bancroft Library, University of California, Berkeley (CU-MARK). ■*Previous publication: LLMT,* 364, brief para-

phrase. ▪*Provenance:* see Samossoud Collection in Description of Provenance.
▪*Emendations and textual notes:*

495.2	rehearsal • rehears~l~sal
495.7	copyright • copy-|right
495.11–12	YORK DEC 20 PAID ALL • YOR[K] DEC [20 P◊◊◊ ◊]LL [*badly inked*]

▪ 8 December 1873 · To a Member of the London Morayshire Club, *per* Charles Warren Stoddard · London, England · *UCCL* 09207
▪*Copy-text:* MS facsimile. The editors have not seen the MS, which is in the Technical and Leisure Services Department, The Moray Council, Elgin, Scotland (UkElgM).

▪ 9 December 1873 · To Olivia L. Clemens · (1st of 2) · London, England · *UCCL* 00994
▪*Copy-text:* MS, Mark Twain Papers, The Bancroft Library, University of California, Berkeley (CU-MARK). ▪*Previous publication: LLMT*, 364, brief paraphrase. ▪*Provenance:* see Samossoud Collection in Description of Provenance.
▪*Emendations and textual notes:*

496.13	tonight • to-|night
496.13	ⱡ • [*partly formed*]
496.14	~au◊~ audience • au∕dience
497.9–10	~then~ them • the∕m
497.29	LONDON-W • [◊]ONDON-W [*badly inked*]
497.29	NEW YORK DEC 23 PAID ALL • [◊◊◊ ◊◊◊◊ ◊◊◊ 23 ◊AID A◊◊] [*badly inked*]

▪ 9 December 1873 · To Olivia L. Clemens · (2nd of 2) · London, England · *UCCL* 11803
▪*Copy-text:* MS, on the back of John Brown to SLC, 8 Dec 73 (*UCLC* 31901), Mark Twain Papers, The Bancroft Library, University of California, Berkeley (CU-MARK). ▪*Provenance:* see Mark Twain Papers in Description of Provenance. ▪*Emendations and textual notes:*

499.10–11	~Mel~ Megalopis • Me∕galopis

▪ 9 December 1873 · To George H. Fitzgibbon · London, England · *UCCL* 00995
▪*Copy-text:* MS, George N. Meissner Collection, Washington University, St. Louis (MoSW). ▪*Provenance:* donated to MoSW in about 1960 by the family of businessman and collector George N. Meissner (1872–1960).

■ 9 December 1873 · To Henry Lee · London, England · *UCCL* 00996

■*Copy-text:* MS facsimile. The editors have not seen the MS, which was owned in 1943 by Robert M. Dorn, who provided a photocopy to the Mark Twain Papers. ■*Emendations and textual notes:*

501.9   ad audience • aďudience
501.15   LONDON-W • [◊]ONDON-[◊] [*badly inked*]

■ 10 December 1873 · To Moncure D. Conway · London, England · *UCCL* 11887

■*Copy-text:* Paraphrase, AAA 1925b, lot 27. ■*Emendations and textual notes:*

502.3   exchange. • ∼;

■ 10 December 1873 · To the Editor of the London *Morning Post* · London, England · *UCCL* 00997

■*Copy-text:* "Mark Twain's Lectures," London *Morning Post*, 11 Dec 73, 2. Copy-text is a microfilm edition of the newspaper in the British Library Newspaper Library, London (Uk). ■*Previous publication:* numerous newspapers, including "Mark Twain Again," Belfast *Northern Whig*, 13 Dec 73, Scrapbook 12:49, CU-MARK; "Mark Twain and the Nobility": San Francisco *Evening Bulletin*, 3 Jan 74, 4, and San Francisco *Alta California*, 11 Jan 74, 4; Grenander 1975, 3. ■*Emendations and textual notes:*

503.3   & • and [*here and hereafter*]
503.7   those • tho[s]e [*broken type*]

■ 10 December 1873 · To John L. Toole, *per* Charles Warren Stoddard · London, England · *UCCL* 00998

■*Copy-text:* MS, Theatre Collection, Houghton Library, Harvard University (MH-H). ■*Provenance:* preserved in Toole's autograph album.

■ 11 December 1873 · To Olivia L. Clemens · London, England · *UCCL* 00999

■*Copy-text:* MS, on the back of George W. Smalley to SLC, 9 Dec 73 (*UCLC* 31902), Mark Twain Papers, The Bancroft Library, University of California, Berkeley (CU-MARK). ■*Provenance:* see Mark Twain Papers in Description of Provenance.

■ 11 and 12 December 1873 · To Olivia L. Clemens · London, England
· *UCCL* 01000 (formerly *UCCL* 01000 and 01001)

■*Copy-text:* MS, Mark Twain Papers, The Bancroft Library, University of California, Berkeley (CU-MARK). ■*Previous publication: LLMT,* 185–86. ■*Provenance:* see Samossoud Collection in Description of Provenance. ■*Emendations and textual notes:* The words 'when' and 'Expedition's' at 508.9 have been so heavily canceled that some of the paper has disintegrated (see p. 509 n. 3).

508.8	homesick • home-|sick
508.9	sweetheart. And • ~.—|~
508.9	when • [◊]hen [*damaged*]
508.9	"Expedition's • "[◊◊]pedition's [*damaged*]
508.21	to • to | to
508.32	NEW YORK DEC 26 PAID ALL • [◊]EW YO[◊◊] DE[C ◊6] P[A◊◊] A[◊◊] [*badly inked*]

■ 12 December 1873 · To Shirley Brooks · London, England · *UCCL* 01002

■*Copy-text:* MS facsimile. The editors have not seen the MS, which is in Clifton Waller Barrett Library, University of Virginia, Charlottesville (ViU). ■*Provenance:* deposited at ViU by Clifton Waller Barrett on 17 December 1963. ■*Emendations and textual notes:*

510.5–6	desperate. I • ~.—|~
510.12	it. But • ~.—|~
510.18	disrespect • disrespe/ct

■ 12 December 1873 · To Robert Routledge, *per* Charles Warren Stoddard · London, England · *UCCL* 01003

■*Copy-text:* MS, Routledge and Kegan Paul, London. ■*Provenance:* preserved in the Routledge archives since receipt.

■ 13 and 15 December 1873 · To Olivia L. Clemens · London, England
· *UCCL* 01004

■*Copy-text:* MS, Mark Twain Papers, The Bancroft Library, University of California, Berkeley (CU-MARK), is copy-text for the letter and envelope. MS, Shirley Brooks to SLC, 14 Dec 73, CU-MARK (UCLC 31907), is copy-text for the enclosure. ■*Previous publication: LLMT,* 364, brief paraphrase. ■*Provenance:* see Samossoud Collection (letter) and Mark Twain Papers (enclosure) in Description of Provenance. ■*Emendations and textual notes:*

512.4   elegant • ele | elegant [corrected miswriting]
512.5   responsive • responsivｅe
512.8   sooner • soomerner
512.11   advertised • [sic]
512.18   £12 £14 • £14
512.18   It • [sic]
513.9   writing. The • [possibly a paragraph break; 'writing.' written short
            of right margin at bottom of page and 'The' written at top of new page]
513.12   W̶ • [partly formed; possibly 'T']
513.18–19   Copyright • Copy-|right
514.9–10   NEW YORK · DEC 2◇ 13 · U.S. NOTES • [NE]W YORK · D[E]C [◇◇]
            13 · [U◇]S. N[OTE]S [badly inked]
514.10   INSUFFICIENTLY STAMPED • INSUF[F]ICIENTLY S[T]AMPED [badly
            inked]

■ 14 December 1873 · To Olivia L. Clemens · London, England ·
UCCL 01005

■ Copy-text: MS, Mark Twain Papers, The Bancroft Library, University of California, Berkeley (CU-MARK). ■ Previous publication: LLMT, 186–87. ■ Provenance: see Samossoud Collection in Description of Provenance. ■ Emendations and textual notes:

518.20–21   NEW YORK DEC 2◇ PAID ALL • [◇E]W YO[◇◇ ◇◇◇ ◇◇ ◇◇◇◇ ALL]
            [badly inked]

■ 15 December 1873 · To Alfred Tennyson · London, England ·
UCCL 01006

■ Copy-text: MS, collection of Victor and Irene Murr Jacobs, on deposit at Roesch Library, University of Dayton, Dayton, Ohio (ODaU). ■ Previous publication: Sotheby 1980, lot 363, facsimile of pages 3 and 4. ■ Provenance: The Jacobses purchased the MS from Sotheby's in 1980; they deposited their collection at ODaU in 1984. ■ Emendations and textual notes:

519.9–10   offensive.["] [¶] But • ~.—| [¶] ~
519.14   Ad And • Adnd

■ 16 December 1873 · To John Colborne, per Charles Warren Stoddard
· London, England · UCCL 01008

■ Copy-text: MS, Harry Ransom Humanities Research Center, University of Texas, Austin (TxU-Hu).

■ 16 December 1873 · To Olivia L. Clemens · London, England ·
UCCL 01007

■*Copy-text:* MS, Mark Twain Papers, The Bancroft Library, University of California, Berkeley (CU-MARK). ■*Previous publication: LLMT,* 364, brief paraphrase. ■*Provenance:* see Samossoud Collection in Description of Provenance.
■*Emendations and textual notes:*

521.14   th̶ • ['h' *partly formed*]
522.7   17 • [◇7] [*badly inked*]
522.8   1873 • [◇]873 [*badly inked*]
522.8   YORK JAN 2 PAID ALL. • [YOR◇] JAN [2 ◇◇◇◇ A]LL. [*badly inked;*
            '2' *doubtful*]

■ 17 December 1873 · To James Redpath · London, England · *UCCL*
01009

■*Copy-text:* MS, New York Historical Society, New York City (NHi). ■*Emendations and textual notes:*

523.6   Edinburgh • Edin*f*burgh
523.9   Abysinnia • [*sic*]

■ 20 December 1873 · To Olivia L. Clemens · London, England ·
UCCL 01010

■*Copy-text:* MS, Mark Twain Papers, The Bancroft Library, University of California, Berkeley (CU-MARK). ■*Previous publication: LLMT,* 364, brief paraphrase. ■*Provenance:* see Samossoud Collection in Description of Provenance.
■*Emendations and textual notes:*

524.12–13   NEW YORK JAN ◇ PAID ALL • [NE◇ ◇◇RK ◇◇◇ ◇ ◇◇◇◇ ALL] [*badly
            inked*]

■ 21 December 1873 · To James Redpath, *per* Charles Warren Stoddard
· London, England · *UCCL* 01013

■*Copy-text:* MS, Clifton Waller Barrett Library, University of Virginia, Charlottesville (ViU). ■*Provenance:* deposited at ViU by Clifton Waller Barrett on 15 May 1962.

■ 21 December 1873 · To George H. Fitzgibbon · London, England ·
UCCL 01012

■*Copy-text:* MS, Henry W. and Albert A. Berg Collection, The New York Public Library, Astor, Lenox and Tilden Foundations (NN-B). ■*Provenance:* The MS was owned by businessman William T. H. Howe (1874–1939); in 1940 Dr. A. A. Berg bought and donated the Howe Collection to NN. ■*Emendations and textual notes:*

525.19	tomorrow • to-|morrow
525.24	tear • ~~te~~ tear [*corrected miswriting*]
526.2	fortnight • fort-|night
526.4	faithfully • fa~~lly~~ithfully [*corrected miswriting*]
526.10–11	elevation. ~~And~~ • ~.—|~
526.12	sieze • [*sic*]

■ **21 December 1873 · To Olivia L. Clemens · London, England · UCCL 01011**

■*Copy-text:* MS, Mark Twain Papers, The Bancroft Library, University of California, Berkeley (CU-MARK). ■*Previous publication: LLMT,* 364, brief paraphrase. ■*Provenance:* see Samossoud Collection in Description of Provenance. ■*Emendations and textual notes:*

527.4	~~hun~~ husband • hu#sband
527.7	Jones • [*possibly* 'Jo#nes'; '#' *partly formed*]
527.14	Venition • [*sic*]
527.20	glassware • glass-|ware
528.4	JAN 5 • JAN [5] [*badly inked*]
528.4	STAMPED • S[T]AMPED [*badly inked*]

■ **22 December 1873 · To Olivia L. Clemens · (1st of 2) · London, England · UCCL 01014**

■*Copy-text:* MS, Mark Twain Papers, The Bancroft Library, University of California, Berkeley (CU-MARK). ■*Previous publication: LLMT,* 187–88. ■*Provenance:* see Samossoud Collection in Description of Provenance. ■*Emendations and textual notes:*

529.22	drum • ~~dr◊~~ drum [*corrected miswriting*]
529.26	5 • $ 5 [*corrected miswriting*]
530.22	NEW YORK JAN ◊ DUE 13 U.S. CURRENCY • [N◊◊ ◊◊◊◊ ◊◊◊ ◊] DUE 13 U.S. CURREN[◊◊] [*badly inked*]

■ **22 December 1873 · To Olivia L. Clemens · (2nd of 2) · London, England · UCCL 11878**

■*Copy-text:* MS, on the back of George and Louisa MacDonald to SLC, 19 Dec 73 (*UCLC* 31912), Mark Twain Papers, The Bancroft Library, University of

California, Berkeley (CU-MARK). ▪*Provenance:* see Mark Twain Papers in Description of Provenance.

▪ 23 December 1873 · To Olivia L. Clemens · London, England · *UCCL* 01015

▪*Copy-text:* MS, Mark Twain Papers, The Bancroft Library, University of California, Berkeley (CU-MARK). ▪*Previous publication: LLMT,* 364, brief paraphrase. ▪*Provenance:* see Samossoud Collection in Description of Provenance. ▪*Emendations and textual notes:*

532.20   tip-top • tip-|top

▪ 25 December 1873 · To Olivia L. Clemens · Salisbury, England · *UCCL* 01017

▪*Copy-text:* MS, Mark Twain Papers, The Bancroft Library, University of California, Berkeley (CU-MARK). ▪*Previous publication: LLMT,* 364, brief paraphrase. ▪*Provenance:* see Samossoud Collection in Description of Provenance. ▪*Emendations and textual notes:*

534.7   is! It • ~!—|~
534.19   2◊ 12 • 2[◊ 12] [*badly inked*]
534.19   NEW YORK • N[◊◊ ◊◊◊◊] [*badly inked*]

▪ 29 December 1873 · To Olivia L. Clemens · London, England · *UCCL* 01018

▪*Copy-text:* MS, Mark Twain Papers, The Bancroft Library, University of California, Berkeley (CU-MARK), is copy-text for the letter and envelope. MS, Shirley Brooks to SLC, 25 Dec 73, CU-MARK (*UCLC* 31915) and MS, George MacDonald to SLC, 27 Dec 73, CU-MARK (*UCLC* 31917), are copy-texts for the enclosures. ▪*Previous publication: LLMT,* 188–89, letter only. ▪*Provenance:* see Samossoud Collection (letter) and Mark Twain Papers (enclosures) in Description of Provenance. ▪*Emendations and textual notes:*

536.5   handwriting • hand-|writing
536.6   b̶e̶ because • b̸ecause
536.13   s̶a̶d̶ said • sa̸did
537.28   U.S. • U.[s.] [*badly inked*]

▪ 29 December 1873 · To Tom Taylor, *per* Charles Warren Stoddard · London, England · *UCCL* 01019

▪*Copy-text:* MS, collection of Victor and Irene Murr Jacobs, on deposit at Roesch Library, University of Dayton, Dayton, Ohio (ODaU). ▪*Previous publication:*

Sotheby 1964, lot 475, excerpt. ▪*Provenance:* The Jacobses owned the MS by 1967; they deposited their collection at ODaU in 1984.

▪ **30 December 1873 · To George H. Fitzgibbon · London, England · UCCL 01020**

▪*Copy-text:* MS, Henry W. and Albert A. Berg Collection, The New York Public Library, Astor, Lenox and Tilden Foundations (NN-B). ▪*Previous publication:* AAA/Anderson 1934b, lot 130, excerpts; AAA/Anderson 1936, lot 127, excerpts. ▪*Provenance:* The MS was offered for sale in 1936 as part of the collection of Abel Cary Thomas. By 1939 it was owned by businessman William T. H. Howe (1874–1939); in 1940 Dr. A. A. Berg bought and donated the Howe Collection to NN. ▪*Emendations and textual notes:*

539.14   think • thin⌀k

▪ **30 December 1873 · To Charles Dudley Warner · London, England · UCCL 01021**

▪*Copy-text:* MS, Mark Twain Papers, The Bancroft Library, University of California, Berkeley (CU-MARK). ▪*Provenance:* donated to CU-MARK in January 1950 by Mary Barton of Hartford, a close friend of the Warners', who had owned it since at least 1938. ▪*Emendations and textual notes:*

541.15   that • tha$t
542.1   Abysinnia • ['ni' *conflated; sic*]
542.7   LONDON-W • LON[◊◊]N-W [*stamped off edge*]
542.8   BOSTON JAN 14 PAID • B[◊]ST[◊]N JAN [14] PAI[D] [*badly inked*]

▪ **31 December 1873 · To Olivia L. Clemens · London, England · UCCL 01022**

▪*Copy-text:* MS, Mark Twain Papers, The Bancroft Library, University of California, Berkeley (CU-MARK). ▪*Previous publication: LLMT*, 364, brief paraphrase. ▪*Provenance:* see Samossoud Collection in Description of Provenance. ▪*Emendations and textual notes:*

542.12   humor. It • ~.—|~
543.10   Conn. • ['nn' *conflated*]
543.12   BOSTON JAN 14 PAID • BO[◊◊◊◊ ◊◊◊ 14] PAI[◊] [*badly inked*]

▪ **31 December 1873 · To James Redpath · London, England · UCCL 01023**

▪*Copy-text:* MS, Detroit Public Library, Detroit (MiD). ▪*Previous publication:* Duschnes, item 104, paraphrase. ▪*Provenance:* MiD purchased the MS from Philip C. Duschnes in 1967. ▪*Emendations and textual notes:*

543.21   BOSTON   LYCEUM   BUREAU.   JAMES   REDPATH   JAN   22   1874 •
                [◊◊◊◊◊N] LYCEUM BUR[◊◊◊ ◊◊◊◊◊ ◊◊◊◊◊◊◊] JAN 22 [◊◊◊◊] [*badly
                inked*]
543.22   ~~1874~~ 1873 • 187₄3

■ Appendix B: Enclosure with 20 January 1872 • To Olivia L. Clemens
  • Harrisburg, Pa.

■ *Copy-text:* "The Legend Beautiful," *Atlantic Monthly* 28 (Dec 71): 657–60
(Longfellow 1871).

■ Appendix B: Enclosure with 3 January 1873 • To Whitelaw Reid •
  (2nd of 2) • Hartford, Conn.

■ *Copy-text:* "The Sandwich Islands," New York *Tribune*, 6 Jan 73, 4–5 (SLC
1873c). Copy-text is a microfilm edition of the newspaper in the Newspaper and
Microcopy Division, University of California, Berkeley (CU-NEWS). ■ *Previous
publication:* numerous newspapers, including the Hartford *Courant*, 7 Jan 73, 1;
Elmira *Advertiser*, 9 Jan 73, 2; Rochester (N.Y.) *Democrat and Chronicle*, 7 Jan
73, clipping in CU-MARK; "Lectures and Letters—Extra Sheet," New York
Tribune, issues printed on and after 15 Jan 73, 4; *MTH*, 489–94. ■ *Emendations
and textual notes:* The *Tribune* text does not represent Clemens's lost manuscript
with complete accuracy, since it includes some apparent transcription errors as
well as certain unidentified revisions volunteered by Reid: see 13 and 17 Jan 73
to Reid. The text was first reprinted by the *Tribune* about 15 January in an undated "Lectures and Letters—Extra Sheet." Soon thereafter it was revised and
reprinted in a second issue of the "Extra Sheet" (ExS2). Collation reveals that
this second issue contains a new paragraph, which Clemens evidently submitted
to Reid in a now-lost letter (see 14 Jan 73 to Reid, n. 1). It also includes two
corrections—probably restorations of manuscript readings corrupted in the first
Tribune typesetting. Clemens may have suggested these corrections to Reid in
the lost letter; both have been adopted in the present text (at 562.30 and 563.19).
The centered subtitle and subheadings, undoubtedly supplied by a *Tribune* editor, have been excluded, as noted below.

557.13   *To* • VIEWS OF MARK TWAIN. | A CHARACTERISTIC LET-
                TER FROM THE HUMORIST. | *To*
557.18   & • and [*here and hereafter*]
557.20   arithmetic. • arithmetic. | A PARADISE FOR ALL SORTS.
558.26   Kilauea • Kileaua
559.11   too. • too. | ABOUT THE NATIVES.
560.26   start. • start. | CURIOUS, MORAL, AND RELIGIOUS ASPECTS.
560.30   Kilauea • Kileauea

561.32   vote. • vote. | THE WHITES AND SUGAR.
562.30   regularly (ExS2) • ~,
563.14   three. • three. | THE TRUE PRINCE.
563.19   stanch (ExS2) • staunch

■ Appendix B: Enclosure with 6 January 1873 · To Whitelaw Reid ·
Hartford, Conn.

■*Copy-text:* "The Sandwich Islands," New York *Tribune*, 9 Jan 73, 4–5 (SLC
1873d). Copy-text is a microfilm edition of the newspaper in the Newspaper and
Microcopy Division, University of California, Berkeley (CU-NEWS). ■*Previous
publication:* numerous newspapers, including the Hartford *Courant*, 10 Jan 73,
1; Elmira *Advertiser*, 11 Jan 73, 2; "Lectures and Letters—Extra Sheet," New
York *Tribune*, issues printed on and after 15 Jan 73, 4; *MTH*, 494–500. ■*Emendations and textual notes:* The centered subtitle and subheadings, undoubtedly
supplied by a *Tribune* editor, have been excluded, as noted below.

563.29   *To* • CONCLUDING VIEWS OF MARK TWAIN. | THE
           GOVERNMENT—PRINCE BILL—WHISKY AND AWA—A SPECIMEN
           MINISTER—REASONS FOR ANEXATION. | *To*
563.30   & • and [*here and hereafter*]
564.30   veto. • veto. | THE ROYAL "FIGURE-HEAD."
565.5   figure-head • figure-|head [*also at 565.9*]
566.7   true. • true. | A WORD ABOUT "PRINCE BILL."
567.6   before. • before. | WHISKY'S ANTIDOTE.
567.26   Sacramento. • Sacramento. | THE PARLIAMENT.
568.4   long! • long! | FUNERAL FESTIVITIES.
568.14   mourning • morning
569.12   state. • state. | A ROYAL CURIOSITY.
569.37   stove-pipe hat. • stove-|pipe hat. | GRANDEUR IN MINIATURE.
570.20   total! • total! | A SPECIMEN MINISTER.
571.27   so. • so. | WHY WE SHOULD ANNEX.

■ Appendix B: Enclosure with 25 January 1873 · To Whitelaw Reid ·
Hartford, Conn.

■*Copy-text:* "British Benevolence," New York *Tribune*, 27 Jan 73, 4–5 (SLC
1873e), clipping in the Mark Twain Papers, The Bancroft Library, University of
California, Berkeley (CU-MARK). ■*Previous publication:* Cunard Company advertising circular, undated, reprinted in Boston *Journal*, 7 Feb 73, which was in
turn reprinted in Martin, 1–2, all with omissions; Brownell 1949, 3–5; Neider
1961, 159–65. ■*Emendations and textual notes:* The centered subtitle and subheadings, undoubtedly supplied by a *Tribune* editor, have been excluded, as
noted below.

573.9	*To* • THE GOLD MEDAL AWARDED.	MARK TWAIN ON THE ENGLISH WAY OF REWARDING A PLUCKY ACT—WHAT HAS COME TO THE MEN WHO RESCUED THE CREW OF THE BARK CHARLES WARD.	*To*
573.13	mid-ocean • mid-|ocean
574.1	& • and [*here and hereafter, except at 579.9, where copy-text reads* 'Burns &']
575.15	succeed. • succeed.	ENGLISH GOOD-HEARTEDNESS.
577.2	again. • again.	THE ROYAL NATIONAL LIFE-BOAT INSTI-TUTION.
577.16	subscriptions. • subscriptions.	WHAT THE CUNARD CO. DID FOR OUR HEROES.
577.18	apiece • a piece
578.10	occur. • occur.	ORIGIN AND QUEER OLD WAYS, ETC., OF A PIO-NEER STEAMSHIP COMPANY.
579.1	MacIver • MacIvor [*also at 579.2* ('& MacIver') *and 579.9*]
579.30	when he • when de
580.14	Company. • Company.	VALUE OF THE GOLD MEDAL.

■ Appendix C: Mark Twain's 1872 English Journals

■ *Copy-text:* MS, Mark Twain Birthplace State Historic Site, Department of Natural Resources, Division of State Parks, Stoutsville, Missouri (MoSMTB), is copy-text for 'There . . . better.' (585.1–590.19). The twelve pages of this MS were cut from a journal, the rest of which does not survive. This lost journal was presumably identical to the holograph journal preserved in the Mark Twain Papers, The Bancroft Library, University of California, Berkeley (CU-MARK), which is copy-text for the balance of the text. The journal is a "Manifold Writer," which enabled Clemens to make two bound carbon copies of every page, using a stylus, as described in detail in the headnote to this appendix. The journal once contained 202 tissue-thin pages: 200 carbon copies, one unnumbered page inscribed in pencil, and one blank page at the end. It now contains only 126 pages, numbered 100–199 (of which 24 are duplicates), interleaved with 76 stubs for pages that have been cut out. MS pages 88–99, cut from a journal that is otherwise lost, are "verso" copies. The MS pages in the second occur in a variety of forms. The following pages survive only as bound "recto" copies: pp. 100–119, 'It . . . size.' (590.19–598.29); pp. 137–38, 'behind . . . Margaret' (606.21–607.17); and pp. 141–74, 'although . . . engravings.' (608.14–621.12). Both "recto" copies (bound pages) and "verso" copies (loose pages) survive of MS pp. 120–36, '"Come . . . ~~them~~' (599.1–606.21); pp. 139–40, 'Woodville . . . natural,' (607.17–608.14); and p. 181, 'Paul's . . . renais-||' (623.14–24). Both types of copies, still bound in the journal, survive of MS pp. 175–80, 'Old . . . St.' (621.13–623.14); and pp. 182–99, '||sance . . . consump-||' (623.24–629.13; see the emendation at 629.13). The passage '‚And . . . sure.‚' (614.1–7) was written in pencil on an unnumbered page following MS page 153, and presumably did not appear in any other version of the text. ∎*Previous publication:* "A Memorable Midnight Experience" (599.1–610.16) in SLC 1874c, 3–8, and SLC 1923, 1–13; "An Expatriate" (585.1–586.2), "Stanley and the Queen" (586.8–13), "At the British Museum" (596.20–29, 598.16–24), and "Westminster Abbey by Night" (599.4–600.6, 600.20–31, 601.4–602.6, 603.6–16) in *MTB*, 1:465–69; "The Albert Memorial" (592.13–595.28), "The British Museum" (595.30–597.30, 598.16–24), and "Old Saint Paul's" (621.14–625.6) in *LE*, 171–80; MS pages 88–99 (585.1–590.17) in Davis 1977a. ∎*Provenance:* In 1874 Clemens used loose MS pages 120–36 and 139–40 as part of the printer's copy for "A Memorable Midnight Experience" in *Mark Twain's Sketches. Number One* (SLC 1874c); the other printer's copy pages (MS pages 137–38 and 141–45) have not been found. On the extant printer's copy he wrote several revisions in pencil: he added the title at the top (above 599.1), altered 'Wright' to 'W——' (600.15), canceled the 'h' in 'Johnson' (603.8), and altered 'again.' to 'again, & then put her down' (606.19). These revision were incorporated into the printed text. Evidently sometime before *MTB* was published in 1912, Albert Bigelow Paine made marks and notes on several passages in the MS, which are recorded below as insertions. Several of the marked passages, identified below by asterisks, correspond—albeit in some cases only roughly—to those printed in *MTB*. A comparison with the information in *Previous publication* will clarify the correspondence between marked and published passages.

592.13–21	ₐ4 /ₐ We . . . gₕilded. ₐ/4ₐ
593.28–	
594.19	ₐ4 /ₐ "Tell . . . other. ₐ/4ₐ
*596.20–	
597.10	ₐ5 /ₐ What . . . kin. ₐ/5ₐ
*598.16–24	ₐ5 /ₐ I . . . ones. ₐ/5ₐ
*599.4–600.7	ₐ6 /ₐ It . . . ! ₐ/6 (cont to p 124)ₐ
*600.20–31	ₐ6 /ₐ We . . . ago. ₐ/6.0 Contₐ
*601.4–32	ₐ6- /ₐ Mr. . . . it. ₐ/6ₐ
602.3–6	ₐ6 /ₐ There . . . old Parr— ₐ/6ₐ
*603.6–16	ₐ6 /ₐ "That . . . end. ₐ/6ₐ
623.8–37	ₐ/ₐ You . . . died. ₐ/ₐ

After Clemens's death, Clara Clemens Samossoud retained MS pages 88–99 until at least the late 1940s, when Dixon Wecter made a typescript from them. Chester L. Davis, Sr., probably acquired the pages from her between 1949 and 1962 (see Samossoud Collection in Description of Provenance). Davis apparently placed them in his Mark Twain Research Foundation collection. In 1993, six years after his death, this collection was donated to the state of Missouri. For MS pages 100–199, see Mark Twain Papers. ∎*Emendations and textual notes:*

586.10	~~500~~ 400 • ₕ400
586.15–16	(Sunday) . . . 15) • [*two closing parentheses*]
586.20	fellow & • [*sic*]

586.23	off, • [*deletion implied*]
587.15	~~twie~~ twice • twi¢ce
587.21–22	~~loo~~ lolling • lo∅lling
588.3	villainy • ['ny' *conflated*]
588.10	Henry • ['en' *conflated*]
588.31	~~fee~~ fell • fe¢ll
589.19	roomy • ['my' *conflated*]
589.19	Pompeeiian • [*sic*]
589.34–35	cuttle-fish • cuttle-|fish
590.4	to • to | to
590.13	the • [◊◊◊] [*smudged and obscured by fold*]
590.17	goldfish • gold-|fish
590.19	better. It • ~.—‖~
590.33	~~bo~~ • ['o' *partly formed; possibly* 'r']
591.10	~~a p~~ apart • apart ∅ [*canceled* 'p' *partly formed*]
591.17	attractive • attra∫ctive
591.21	names.~~For~~ • [*deletion of period implied*]
592.2	Clerkenwell; • [*sic*]
592.16	∅ • [*partly formed*]
592.17	guilding • [*sic*]
594.1	~~Alas, it~~ It • ~~Alas, i~~It
594.3	~~ima~~ insignificant • ~~ima~~nsignificant
594.7	~~amd~~ and • ~~amd~~nd
594.14	~~proces~~ • ~~proces~~-|
594.15	demi-gods • demi-|gods
596.25	Egyptians • ['yp' *conflated*]
596.32	fish-hooks • fish-|hooks
597.14–15	mummies, she mummies, ~~starchy mummies,~~ high-toned mummies • ['mm' *conflated (four times)*]
597.16	mummies on . . . mummies with . . . mummies that • ['mm' *conflated (three times)*]
597.26	~~ters~~ tears • ter̄sars
597.32–33	Consulate. If • ~.—|~
598.8–10	solemnly . . . some! • solemnly . . . that the | things . . . nothing | but . . . no | change . . . some!
598.9	wholetruth • wholettr̄truth
598.27	~~Epe~~ Ephesus • Ep¢hesus
598.28	sculptures • ~~sculp~~ sculptures [*corrected miswriting; canceled* 'p' *partly formed*]
599.3	now. Cab • ~.—|~
599.8	~~Wha~~ Where • Wh∥ere
599.17	overcast • over-|cast

599.22	footsteps • foot-‖steps
599.24	anything. He • ~.—|~
601.13	~~yeas~~ years • yea$\not$rs
601.16	people • peo-|~~peop~~ ple [*second canceled 'p' partly formed*]
601.17	split & • split & | &
601.17	cannot • ['nn' *conflated*]
603.8	Spencer . . . Johnson • [*sic*]
604.20	king-maker • king-|maker
605.25	chamberlike • chamber-‖like
605.27	~~in~~ on • $\not$on
606.4	~~defacement~~ disfigurement • de-is-|~~facement~~ figurement
606.29	~~It~~ • ['t' *partly formed*]
607.25	clock-face • clock-|face
608.21	monument • ['um' *conflated*]
609.13	~~h~~ • [*partly formed; doubtful*]
609.17	~~has~~ had • ha$\not$d
609.18	~~yeas~~ years • yea$\not$rs
609.29	~~wi~~ well • w$\not$ell
610.25	held, • [*deletion implied*]
610.25	~~their~~ there • thei~~r~~re
611.15	wristbands • wrist-|bands
613.14	~~kno~~ knew • kn$\not$ew
613.14–15	Sidney Watterlo • [*sic*]
613.15	mayoralty • mayor$\not$alty
613.17	Sidney • [*sic*]
613.20	~~rob~~ • ['b' *partly formed*]
614.16–17	~~pres~~ premises • pre$\not$mises
614.17	& • & ‖ &
614.19	Dorè • [*sic*]
615.11	middle— • ~— ‖ —
615.13	some • some some
615.19	flowing • ['ng' *conflated*]
615.29	$\not$ • [*partly formed*]
616.11	condemnation • ['mn' *conflated*]
616.22	namby-pamby • namby-|pamby
616.28	Dore's • [*sic*]
617.7	~~oth~~ • ['h' *partly formed*]
618.7	~~el~~ eclipsed • e$\not$clipsed
618.9	Angelo himself • Angelo him-‖gelo himself
619.8	~~the~~ she • $\not$she
619.10	~~bef~~ • ['f' *partly formed*]

619.36	and • & and
620.10	~~first-proof~~ • [*second* 'f' *partly formed*]
620.27	wierd • [*sic*]
620.30–31	~~body~~ bodies • bod~~y~~ies [*underscored after revision*]
621.5	wierdest • [*sic*]
621.5	I̶ • [*partly formed*]
621.10	Dorès • [*sic*]
621.16	~~in about~~ • [*doubtful*]
621.24	oolite • ~~oo-|~~ oolite [*rewritten for clarity*]
622.22	time • ['me' *conflated*]
622.25	~~th~~ • ['h' *partly formed*]
623.5	w̶ • [*partly formed*]
623.13	gateways • gate-|ways
623.17	~~pede~~ pediment • ped~~d~~iment
623.33	suffocated • ~~su~~ suffocated [*rewritten for clarity*]
623.34–35	~~hav~~ he • ha~~ve~~
623.37	~~wh~~ • ['h' *partly formed*]
624.16	B̶ • [*partly formed*]
624.16	tunnel • ['nn' *conflated*]
625.3	~~de~~ dimensions • d~~e~~imensions
625.5	which • which	~~whi~~
625.20	deny • de-|~~ny~~ ny [*corrected miswriting*]
625.21	~~pr~~ putting • p~~r~~utting
626.1	"I̶ • ['I' *doubtful*]
626.12	it, • [*deletion implied*]
626.28	Kidneys • Kid-|ny̶eys ['y̶' *partly formed*]
626.35	through. I • ~.—|~
627.5	~~meam~~ meant • meam~~t~~nt
627.6	le • [*possibly* 'te']
627.13	cuttle-fish • cuttle-|fish
627.21	hymn-book • hymn-|book
627.23	of your • of your ‖ of your
627.28–29	English) . . . cheese) • [*two closing parentheses*]
627.33	shampagne • [*sic; also at 628.6*]
628.1	curaçoa • [*sic*]
628.5	~~dir~~ drink • di~~r~~rink
628.10	table ₐit is, • table is ‖ ₐit is,
628.29	~~hold~~ hotels • hol~~d~~tels
629.5	absurdity • absurd~~y~~ity
629.13	consumption • consump-‖

■ Appendix D: Revised Contract for Diamond Mine Book · 22 June 1872 · Hartford, Conn.

■ *Copy-text:* MS of Clemens's copy, in the hand of an amanuensis with revisions by Elisha Bliss, Jr., Mark Twain Papers, The Bancroft Library, University of California, Berkeley (CU-MARK). ■ *Provenance:* see Mark Twain Papers in Description of Provenance. ■ *Emendations and textual notes:*

632.23   Diamond · Dia∧|mond
632.28   no wise · [*possibly enclosed by single quotation marks*]

■ Appendix D: Contract for the American Publishing Company *Gilded Age* · 8 May 1873 · Hartford, Conn.

■ *Copy-text:* MS of Clemens's copy, drafted by Elisha Bliss, Jr., Mark Twain Papers, The Bancroft Library, University of California, Berkeley (CU-MARK). ■ *Provenance:* see Mark Twain Papers in Description of Provenance. ■ *Emendations and textual notes:*

635.4   Wittnesseth · [*sic*]
636.13–14   reccommendation · [*sic*]

■ Appendix D: Contract for the Routledge *Gilded Age* · 18 October 1873 · London, England

■ *Copy-text:* MS of Routledge copy, Routledge and Kegan Paul, London. ■ *Emendations and textual notes:*

639.10   copyright · copy-|right

■ Appendix G: 14 July 1865 · To William Wright (Dan De Quille) · San Francisco, Calif. · *UCCL* 11610

■ *Copy-text:* MS facsimile. The editors have not seen the MS, which is owned by Rosemary Morris and Marjory Anderson, descendants of William Wright. With the permission of their brother, the late Evans Morris, a photocopy was provided to the Mark Twain Papers in October 1988. Preserved with the letter, but no doubt not originally enclosed with it, is Setchell's calling card, on which was written "Barnum's Hotel"—presumably by Setchell. The inscription has not been explained: no hotel of that name is listed in either the San Francisco or the Virginia City directories of the period. ■ *Previous publication:* Berkove, 7. ■ *Provenance:* The MS is one of nine letters from Clemens to Wright which after Wright's death "were left with his daughter, Mell Evans. She, in turn, passed them on to her daughter, Irma Evans Morris. Effie Mona Mack learned of them while doing research for *Mark Twain in Nevada* (1947), and purchased photographic negatives of them. . . . When Mrs. Morris died, she passed the letters on to her son, Evans Morris." Copies of the collection are on deposit in the Morris Family Collection of De Quille Papers at the State Historical Society of Iowa (IaHi) (Berkove, 4, 18 n. 1).

■ Appendix G: 26 October 1866 · To Joseph T. Goodman, *per* Denis E. McCarthy and Telegraph Operator · Meadow Lake, Calif. · *UCCL* 11613

■ *Copy-text:* Goodman, 2. Copy-text is a microfilm edition of the Virginia City *Territorial Enterprise* for 28 October 1866 in the Newspaper and Microcopy Division, University of California, Berkeley (CU-NEWS). The California State Telegraph Company form is recreated from Dixon Wecter's transcription of a 1 Nov 66 telegram to Abraham V. Z. Curry and others (*L1*, 363, 544–45). The California State Telegraph Company was the only telegraph company operating in California in 1866 (Langley 1865, 628–29; 1867, 693–94). ■ *Previous publication:* Salt Lake City *Union Vedette*, 3 Nov 66, 2. ■ *Emendations and textual notes:*

681.1	CALIFORNIA . . . COMPANY • [*not in*]
681.2	Meadow Lake • MEADOW LAKE
681.2	186 6. • 1866.
681.3	Via Cisco • VIA CISCO
681.4	TO • To
681.4	Goodman, Editor Enterprise • GOODMAN, EDITOR ENTERPRISE
681.6	Mark Twain [Mac.] • MARK TWAIN [MAC.]

■ Appendix G: 15 October 1868 · To George L. Hutchings · Hartford, Conn. · *UCCL* 11875

■ *Copy-text:* MS, University Library, University of Southern California, Los Angeles (CLSU). ■ *Provenance:* donated, as part of a collection of 150 letters from the George Long Hutchings Lecture Club, to CLSU in 1986 by Mrs. Jeanne Hutchings, George Long Hutchings's daughter. ■ *Emendations and textual notes:*

682.14	$100. Thus • ~.—|~
682.22	HARTFORD • HAR[◊◊◊R]D [*stamped off edge*]

■ Appendix G: 10 May–1 June 1869 · To Elisha Bliss, Jr. · Elmira, N.Y., or Hartford, Conn. · *UCCL* 09924

■ *Copy-text:* Paraphrase and transcript, AAA 1926b, lot 79. An earlier dealer catalog text is less complete and shows no significant variants (Dawson's Book Shop

1925, item 113). ■*Provenance:* After its sale in 1925 the MS was offered again in 1926, in a sale that included the library of Hannah M. Standish.

■ Appendix G: 21 September 1869 · To George L. Hutchings · Buffalo, N.Y. · *UCCL* 11876

■*Copy-text:* MS, University Library, University of Southern California, Los Angeles (CLSU). ■*Provenance:* donated, as part of a collection of 150 letters from the George Long Hutchings Lecture Club, to CLSU in 1986 by Mrs. Jeanne Hutchings, George Long Hutchings's daughter. ■*Emendations and textual notes:*

684.16   st • s[t] [*torn*]
684.16–17   New York • New Yor[◊] [*torn*]

■ Appendix G: 1 January 1870 · To George L. Hutchings · Elmira, N.Y. · *UCCL* 11877

■*Copy-text:* MS, University Library, University of Southern California, Los Angeles (CLSU). This letter is written on a leaf torn from the same notebook as ten other surviving letters that Clemens wrote in October, November, and December 1869 (*L3*, 381–82 n. 1). ■*Provenance:* donated, as part of a collection of 150 letters from the George Long Hutchings Lecture Club, to CLSU in 1986 by Mrs. Jeanne Hutchings, George Long Hutchings's daughter. ■*Emendations and textual notes:*

685.8   siezed • [*sic*]
685.18   ELMIRA • E[◊M]IRA [*badly inked*]

■ Appendix G: 6 January 1871 · To Unidentified · Buffalo, N.Y. · *UCCL* 11887

■*Copy-text:* MS facsimile, on the front and back of a photograph of Clemens. The editors have not seen the MS, which is in the Franklin J. Meine Collection, Rare Book and Special Collections Library, University of Illinois, Urbana (IU-R). The front of the photograph is reproduced at 90 percent of actual size. ■*Provenance:* purchased in 1969 from the widow of Franklin J. Meine (1896–1968), a Chicago editor and publisher. ■*Emendations and textual notes:*

688.11   ~~ga~~ getting • g⧸etting

■ Appendix G: 11 June 1871, postscript · To Jane Lampton Clemens · Elmira, N.Y. · *UCCL* 00615

■*Copy-text:* MS, collection of Chester L. Davis, Jr. See *L4*, 405–6 nn. 1, 2, 4, 581–4, and 670, for a physical description and photofacsimile of the nine scraps that form the body of the letter to which this postscript apparently belongs, and for the rationale for transcribing the text line-by-line with an editorially supplied outline. For a photofacsimile of this postscript scrap, see Appendix F. The paper appears to match that of scraps 5 and 9; Clemens's inscription on this scrap is in pencil, whereas the body of the letter is in purple ink. ■*Previous publication:* Davis 1978, 3. ■*Provenance:* The postscript scrap, like the other nine scraps, was returned to Clemens, presumably after the death of his mother or sister. It was among those letters which, in the 1950s, Clara Clemens Samossoud gave or sold to Chester L. Davis, Sr. Because the scrap had been separated from the other nine scraps, he did not recognize it as an addendum to the 11 June 1871 scrap letter. After Davis's death in 1987, it became part of the collection of Chester L. Davis, Jr.

■ Appendix G: 11 July 1871 · To Elisha Bliss, Jr. · Elmira, N.Y. · *UCCL* 11888

■*Copy-text:* Christie 1994, lot 221, which indicates that the letter is "to 'Friend Bliss' and discusses the sending of a manuscript. Elmira, 11 July [docketed 1871]. *One page, 8vo, written in purple ink."* ■*Provenance:* The MS is tipped into the first volume of set 227 of the 25-volume Author's Edition De Luxe of Mark Twain's works (London: Chatto and Windus, 1899–1903), sold in 1994 as part of the estate of lyricist Johnny Burke. ■*Emendations and textual notes:*

690.1   Elmira, 11 July. • [*reported, not quoted*]
690.3   [¶] Shipped • [*no* ¶] ~
690.9   [*letter docketed:*] 1871 • [*reported, not quoted*]

■ Appendix G: 7–8? December 1871 · To the Staff of the Virginia City *Territorial Enterprise* · Warsaw, N.Y., or Buffalo, N.Y. · *UCCL* 11905

■*Copy-text:* Paraphrase, "A Look into the Belcher. We Escort Tom Kean into the Depths Profound," Virginia City *Territorial Enterprise*, 18 Jan 72, 3. Copy-text is a microfilm edition of the newspaper in the Newspaper and Microcopy Division, University of California, Berkeley (CU-NEWS).

References

THIS LIST defines the abbreviations used in this book and provides full bibliographic information for works cited by the author's name and publication date, or by a short title. Alphabetization is word-by-word: i.e., *"Men of the Time"* precedes "Menefee, C. A."

AAA.
1924a. *The Collection of the Late William F. Gable of Altoona, Pennsylvania.* Part 3. Sale of 13 and 14 February. New York: American Art Association.

1924b. *The Renowned Collection of the Late William F. Gable of Altoona, Pennsylvania.* Part 4. Sale of 10 and 11 March. New York: American Art Association.

1924c. *The Renowned Collection of the Late William F. Gable of Altoona, Pennsylvania.* Part 5. Sale of 24 and 25 November. New York: American Art Association.

1925a. *The Renowned Collection of the Late William F. Gable of Altoona, Pennsylvania.* Part 6. Sale of 8 and 9 January. New York: American Art Association.

1925b. *The Collection of the Late William F. Gable of Altoona, Pennsylvania.* Part 8. Sale of 16 April. New York: American Art Association.

1926a. *Books and Autographs: Selections from the Private Libraries of the Late Edmund Penfold and William Hall Penfold . . . the Late Dr. William W. Walker also the Late W. W. C. Wilson. . . .* Sale of 11 and 12 January. New York: American Art Association.

1926b. *Library Sets of Standard Authors . . . Also Autographs of Celebrities, &c. Including the Private Library of the Late Mrs. Hannah M. Standish of Pittsburgh, Pa.* Sale of 3 and 4 March. New York: American Art Association.

AAA/Anderson.
1929. *American Autographs from the Collection of Gertrude Emerson, New York City; American & Foreign Autographs from the Collection of John M. Geddes, Williamsport, Pa.* Sale no. 3781 (30 October). New York: American Art Association, Anderson Galleries.

1934a. *First Editions and Manuscripts Collected by the Late Mr. and Mrs. William*

K. Bixby . . . and Other Literary Property. . . . Sale no. 4098 (4 and 5 April). New York: American Art Association, Anderson Galleries.

1934b. *The Fine Library of the Late Mrs. Benjamin Stern Together with Autograph Letters from the Collections of William L. Clements and E. W. Evans, Jr.* Sale no. 4111 (9, 10, and 11 May). New York: American Art Association, Anderson Galleries.

1935. *The Library Formed by Abraham Goldsmith . . . Books, Autographs, and Mementos from the James Whitcomb Riley Homestead; Selections from the Collections of George B. Thummel and Jahu Dewitt Miller; and Other Properties.* Sale no. 4150 (7 and 8 February). New York: American Art Association, Anderson Galleries.

1936. *The Library of Abel Cary Thomas.* Sale no. 4221 (14 and 15 January). New York: American Art Association, Anderson Galleries.

Adams, William Henry Davenport. 1877. *Great Shipwrecks: A Record of Perils and Disasters at Sea, 1544–1877.* London: T. Nelson and Sons.

Adamson, Hans Christian. 1961. *Rebellion in Missouri: 1861. Nathaniel Lyon and His Army of the West.* Philadelphia and New York: Chilton Company.

Alexander, W. D. 1891 and 1899. *A Brief History of the Hawaiian People.* New York: American Book Company.

Anderson, Frederick, and Kenneth M. Sanderson, eds. 1971. *Mark Twain: The Critical Heritage.* New York: Barnes and Noble.

Anderson, Frederick, William M. Gibson, and Henry Nash Smith, eds. 1967. *Selected Mark Twain–Howells Letters, 1872–1910.* Cambridge: Belknap Press of Harvard University Press.

Anderson, John, Jr. 1903. *Catalogue of a Fine Collection of American Historical Autograph Letters.* Sale no. 168 (15 April). New York: John Anderson, Jr.

Anderson Auction Company.

1909. *First Editions of American Authors Forming the Library of Frank Maier of New York.* Part 1. Sale no. 782 (16 and 17 November). New York: Anderson Auction Company.

1910. *Library and Art Collection of George Bentham of New York City.* Part 1. Sale no. 867 (28 and 29 November). New York: Anderson Auction Company.

1911. *Two Hundred Books from the Library of Richard Butler Glaenzer.* Sale no. 924 (28 November). New York: Anderson Auction Company.

Anderson Galleries.

1916. *Autograph Letters and Lincolniana.* Sale no. 1248 (13 and 14 November). New York: Anderson Galleries.

1917. *Letters to Mrs. Sarah Josepha Hale and Maj.-Gen. David Hunter and Other Rare Autographs.* Sale no. 1270 (25 and 26 January). New York: Anderson Galleries.

1918. *Choice Books from the Library of E. B. Clare-Avery.* Sale no. 1372 (25 November). New York: Anderson Galleries.

1920a. *Selections from the Library of Mr. Eustace Conway of New York, Including Books and Manuscripts Formerly Belonging to the Late Moncure D. Conway.* Sale no. 1510 (7 June). New York: Anderson Galleries.

1920b. *Association Books Collected by Edwin W. Coggeshall of New York City.* Sale no. 1525 (4 November). New York: Anderson Galleries.

1922. *The Library of the Late George H. Hart of New York City.* Part 1. Sale no. 1669 (16, 17, 18, and 19 October). New York: Anderson Galleries.

1923. *Choice Books from the Library of David G. Joyce of Chicago, Ill.* Sale no. 1709 (13 and 14 February). New York: Anderson Galleries.

1924. *Catalogue of the William Harris Arnold Collection of Manuscripts, Books & Autograph Letters.* Sale no. 1873 (10 and 11 November). New York: Anderson Galleries.

1926. *The Autograph Collection Formed by Mr. Emanuel Hertz, New York City.* . . . Sale no. 2086 (19 and 20 October). New York: Anderson Galleries.

Andrews, Kenneth R. 1950. *Nook Farm: Mark Twain's Hartford Circle.* Cambridge: Harvard University Press.

Annual Cyclopaedia 1871. 1875. *The American Annual Cyclopaedia and Register of Important Events of the Year 1871.* Vol. 11. New York: D. Appleton and Co.

Annual Cyclopaedia 1873. 1877. *The American Annual Cyclopaedia and Register of Important Events of the Year 1873.* Vol. 13. New York: D. Appleton and Co.

Annual Cyclopaedia 1890. 1891. *Appletons' Annual Cyclopaedia and Register of Important Events of the Year 1890.* N.s. vol. 15. New York: D. Appleton and Co.

Anstruther, Ian. 1956. *I Presume: Stanley's Triumph and Disaster.* London: Geoffrey Bles.

APC (American Publishing Company). 1866–79. "Books received from the Binderies, Dec 1ˢᵗ *1866* to Dec 31. *1879,*" the company's stock ledger, NN-B.

Appletons' Hand-Book. 1867. *Appletons' Hand-Book of American Travel.* New York: D. Appleton and Co.

Austen, Roger. 1991. *Genteel Pagan: The Double Life of Charles Warren Stoddard.* Edited by John W. Crowley. Amherst: University of Massachusetts Press.

Austin, James C.
1953. *Fields of "The Atlantic Monthly."* San Marino, Calif.: Huntington Library.
1965. *Petroleum V. Nasby (David Ross Locke).* Twayne's United States Authors Series, edited by Sylvia E. Bowman, no. 89. New York: Twayne Publishers.

Axelrod. Collection of Todd M. Axelrod, American Museum of Historical Documents, Las Vegas, Nevada.

Axelrod, Todd M. 1986. *Collecting Historical Documents: A Guide to Owning History.* Rev. ed. Neptune City, N.J.: T. F. H. Publications.

Baedeker, Karl.
1874. *Paris and Its Environs.* 4th ed. Leipzig: Karl Baedeker.
1878. *London and Its Environs.* Leipzig: Karl Baedeker.
1884. *Paris and Environs.* Leipzig: Karl Baedeker.
1893. *The United States, with an Excursion into Mexico.* Leipzig: Karl Baedeker.

1895. *Italy. . . . First Part: Northern Italy.* Leipzig: Karl Baedeker.

1900. *London and Its Environs.* Leipzig: Karl Baedeker.

1901. *Great Britain.* Leipzig: Karl Baedeker.

Baehr, Harry W., Jr. 1936. *"The New York Tribune" since the Civil War.* New York: Dodd, Mead and Co.

Baetzhold, Howard G., and Joseph B. McCullough. 1995. *The Bible According to Mark Twain: Writings on Heaven, Eden, and the Flood.* Athens: University of Georgia Press.

BAL. 1957. *Bibliography of American Literature.* Compiled by Jacob Blanck. Vol. 2. New Haven: Yale University Press.

Bangs.
1901. *Catalogue of American and English Literature.* Sale of 9, 10, and 11 December. New York: Bangs and Co.
1902. *Catalogue of an Interesting Collection of Autograph Letters and Documents.* Sale of 24 January. New York: Bangs and Co.

Baring-Gould, Sabine. 1910. *Family Names and Their Story.* London: Seeley and Co.

Barnum, Phineas T. 1865. *The Humbugs of the World.* New York: G. W. Carleton and Co. Citations are to the 1970 reprint edition, Detroit: Singing Tree Press.

Bates, Alan. 1968. *The Western Rivers Steamboat Cyclopoedium; or, American Riverboat Structure & Detail, Salted with Lore, with a Nod to the Modelmaker.* Leonia, N.J.: Hustle Press.

BBA. 1990. *British Biographical Archive. A One-Alphabet Cumulation of 324 of the Most Important English-Language Biographical Reference Works Originally Published between 1601 and 1929.* Edited by Laureen Baillie and Paul Sieveking. London: K. G. Saur. Microfiche.

Beecher, Henry Ward, ed. 1864. *Plymouth Collection of Hymns and Tunes; for the Use of Christian Congregations.* New York: Barnes and Burr.

Beecher Trial. 1875. *The Beecher Trial: A Review of the Evidence. Reprinted from the New York Times of July 3, 1875.* 4th ed. New York: n.p. Copy owned by Clemens, CU-MARK.

Bell, Mary. 1896. "The Essayist of the West." *University of California Magazine* 2 (November): 272–87.

Bénézit, E. 1976. *Dictionnaire critique et documentaire des peintres, sculpteurs, dessinateurs et graveurs.* Rev. ed. 10 vols. Paris: Librairie Gründ.

Bentley. Collection of Mr. and Mrs. Fred D. Bentley, Sr.

Berkove, Lawrence I. 1988. " 'Nobody Writes to Anybody Except to Ask a Favor': New Correspondence between Mark Twain and Dan De Quille." *Mark Twain Journal* 26 (Spring): 2–21.

Berkshire Directory. 1877. *The Post Office Directory of Berkshire, Buckinghamshire and Oxfordshire.* Edited by E. R. Kelly. London: Kelly and Co.

Bierce, Ambrose. 1872. "Letter from England." Letter dated 3 October. San Francisco *Alta California,* 30 October, 1.

Black, Helen C. 1893. *Notable Women Authors of the Day.* Glasgow: David Bryce and Son.

Black's Guide. 1870. *Black's Guide to London and Its Environs.* Edinburgh: Adam and Charles Black.

Blair, Walter. 1960. *Native American Humor.* San Francisco: Chandler Publishing Company.

Blair, Walter, and Hamlin Hill. 1978. *America's Humor, from Poor Richard to Doonesbury.* New York: Oxford University Press.

Blanc, Marie-Thérèse [Thérèse Bentzon, pseud.]. 1872. "Les humoristes américains: I. Mark Twain." *Revue des deux mondes* 100 (15 July): 313–35.

Bloomfield, Ben.
ca. 1954. *Autographs of Distinction. List: DM-1.* New York: Ben Bloomfield.
post 1954. *Autographs of Distinction. List: DM-6.* New York: Ben Bloomfield.

Blunt, John Henry, ed. 1868. *The Annotated Book of Common Prayer: Being an Historical, Ritual, and Theological Commentary on the Devotional System of the Church of England.* 3d ed. London: Rivingtons.

Boase, Frederic. 1892–1921. *Modern English Biography, Containing Many Thousand Concise Memoirs of Persons Who Have Died since the Year 1850.* 6 vols. Truro: Netherton and Worth.

Boone, H., comp.
1871. *Directory of Pittsburgh & Allegheny Cities, . . . for 1871–72.* Pittsburgh: George H. Thurston.
1872. *Directory of Pittsburgh & Allegheny Cities, . . . for 1872–73.* Pittsburgh: George H. Thurston.

Boyd, Andrew, comp. 1871. *Boyd's Paterson Directory, 1871–72.* Paterson, N.J.: Andrew Boyd.

Boyd, Andrew, and W. Harry Boyd, comps. 1872. *Boyds' Elmira and Corning Directory: Containing the Names of the Citizens, a Compendium of the Government, and Public and Private Institutions. . . . 1872–3.* Elmira: Andrew and W. Harry Boyd.

Bradley, M. C., and E. T. Bradley. 1910. *The Westminster Abbey Guide, Sold at the Abbey by Permission of the Dean.* 18th ed. London: Pall Mall Press.

Branch, Edgar Marquess.
1950. *The Literary Apprenticeship of Mark Twain.* Urbana: University of Illinois Press.
1969. *Clemens of the "Call": Mark Twain in San Francisco.* Berkeley and Los Angeles: University of California Press.

Brayer, Herbert O. 1949. *William Blackmore: The Spanish-Mexican Land Grants of New Mexico and Colorado, 1863–1878.* A Case Study in the Economic Development of the West, vol. 1. Denver: Bradford-Robinson.

Brayley, Edward Wedlake. 1818–23. *The History and Antiquities of the Abbey Church of St. Peter, Westminster.* 2 vols. London: J. P. Neale, and Hurst, Robinson, and Co.

Brinnin, John Malcolm. 1971. *The Sway of the Grand Saloon: A Social History of the North Atlantic*. New York: Delacorte Press.

Broadley, A. M. 1910. *Chats on Autographs*. New York: Frederick A. Stokes Company.

Brooks, Noah. 1898. "Mark Twain in California." *Century Illustrated Monthly Magazine*, n.s. 57 (November): 97–99.

Brougham, John, and John Elderkin, eds. 1875. *Lotos Leaves*. Boston: William F. Gill and Co.

Brown, John. 1907. *Letters of Dr. John Brown. With Letters from Ruskin, Thackeray, and Others*. Edited by John Brown and D. W. Forrest. London: Adam and Charles Black.

Brown, T. Allston. 1870. *History of the New York Stage*. New York: Dick and Fitzgerald.

Browne, J. Ross. 1969. *J. Ross Browne: His Letters, Journals, and Writings*. Edited by Lina Fergusson Browne. Albuquerque: University of New Mexico Press.

Brownell, George H.
1944. "Everybody's Friend." *Twainian* 3 (February): 1–4.
1949. "Twain's Tale in 'The Bazaar Record' Based on Actual Heroic Rescue at Sea." *Twainian* 8 (November–December): 1–5.

Bryan, George B., comp. 1991. *Stage Deaths: A Biographical Guide to International Theatrical Obituaries, 1850 to 1990*. 2 vols. Bibliographies and Indexes in the Performing Arts, no. 9. Westport, Conn.: Greenwood Press.

Buckland, Francis T. 1868. *Curiosities of Natural History. Third Series*. 2d ed. 2 vols. London: Richard Bentley.

Budd, Louis J., ed.
1992a. *Mark Twain: Collected Tales, Sketches, Speeches, & Essays, 1852–1890*. The Library of America. New York: Literary Classics of the United States.
1992b. *Mark Twain: Collected Tales, Sketches, Speeches, & Essays, 1891–1910*. The Library of America. New York: Literary Classics of the United States.

Buffalo Directory.
1869. *Buffalo City Directory*. Buffalo: Warren, Johnson and Co.
1871. *Buffalo City Directory for the Year 1871*. Buffalo: Warren, Johnson and Co.
1872. *Buffalo City Directory for the Year 1872*. Buffalo: Warren, Johnson and Co.

Burke, Bernard.
1900. *A Genealogical and Heraldic History of the Landed Gentry of Great Britain*. 10th ed. London: Harrison and Sons.
1904. *A Genealogical and Heraldic Dictionary of the Peerage and Baronetage, the Privy Council, Knightage and Companionage*. 66th ed. London: Harrison and Sons.

Burpee, Charles W. 1928. *History of Hartford County, Connecticut, 1633–1928*. 3 vols. Chicago: S. J. Clarke Publishing Company.

Burtis, Mary Elizabeth. 1952. *Moncure Conway: 1832–1907*. New Brunswick, N.J.: Rutgers University Press.

Byng, Carl [pseud.?].
1870a. "Review of Holiday Literature." Buffalo *Express*, 24 December, 2. Reprinted as "Holiday Literature" in SLC 1871e, 9–13.
1870b. "Advice to Parents." Buffalo *Express*, 31 December, 2. Reprinted as "How to Train up a Child" in SLC 1871c, 49–55, and SLC 1871e, 151–55.
1871. " 'Train up a Child, and Away He Goes.['] " Buffalo *Express*, 28 January, 2. Reprinted in SLC 1871c, 56–60, and SLC 1871e, 156–58.

Cannon, Carl L. 1941. *American Book Collectors and Collecting*. New York: H. W. Wilson Company.

Carkeet, David. 1979. "The Dialects in *Huckleberry Finn*." *American Literature* 51 (November): 315–32.

Carleton, Will M.
1871a. "Betsey and I Are Out." *Harper's Weekly* 15 (27 May): 473.
1871b. "Out of the Old House, Nancy." *Harper's Weekly* 15 (3 June): 497.
1871c. "Over the Hill to the Poor-House." *Harper's Weekly* 15 (17 June): 545.
1871d. "Gone with a Handsomer Man." *Harper's Weekly* 15 (15 July): 641.
1873. *Farm Ballads*. New York: Harper and Brothers.

Cassidy, Frederic G., and Joan Houston Hall. 1991. *Dictionary of American Regional English*. Vol. 2, D–H. Cambridge: Belknap Press of Harvard University Press.

CCamarSJ. Estelle Doheny Collection, The Edward Laurence Doheny Memorial Library, Saint John's Seminary, Camarillo, California.

Chatto and Windus. Chatto and Windus, London.

Cheney, Howell, ed. 1954. *The List of Members of the Monday Evening Club Together with the Record of Papers Read at Their Meetings, 1869–1954*. Hartford: Privately printed.

Chester, Giraud. 1951. *Embattled Maiden: The Life of Anna Dickinson*. New York: G. P. Putnam's Sons.

Chicago. 1934. *American Autographs and Americana*. Sale no. 45 (27 November). Chicago: Chicago Book and Art Auctions.

Cholmondeley, Mary. 1918. *Under One Roof: A Family Record*. London: John Murray.

Chowder, Ken, ed. 1991. *Gold Miners & Guttersnipes: Tales of California by Mark Twain*. San Francisco: Chronicle Books.

Christie.
1981. Catalog for sale of 22 May. New York: Christie, Manson and Woods International.
1988. *The Estelle Doheny Collection . . . Part IV*. Sale of 17 and 18 October. New York: Christie, Manson and Woods International.
1991a. *Printed Books and Manuscripts Including Americana. . . . The Estates of*

Henry Bowen, Chester Davis, William Salloch. Sale no. 7286 (17 and 18 May). New York: Christie, Manson and Woods International.

1991b. *Printed Books and Manuscripts Including Americana and Bookbindings. . . . The Estates of Chester L. Davis, Augustus Maxwell, and from Various Sources.* Sale no. 7378 (5 December). New York: Christie, Manson and Woods International.

1992. *Printed Books and Manuscripts Including Americana. . . .* Sale no. 7574 (20 November). New York: Christie, Manson and Woods International.

1993. *Printed Books and Manuscripts Including Americana. . . . The Estate of Chester L. Davis. . . .* Sale no. 7700 (9 June). New York: Christie, Manson and Woods International.

1994. *Printed Books, Autographs, Maps and Decorative Graphics. . . . The Properties of . . . the Late Lyricist Johnny Burke. . . .* Sale no. 7545 (20 April). New York: Christie, Manson and Woods International.

Cincinnati Public Library. 1899. "In Memoriam." In the "Historical Sketch, 1855–1900," included in the *Annual Report of the Board of Trustees of the Public Library of Cincinnati, Ohio,* 85–88.

City Book Auction. 1954. *The Byron Price Library.* Sale no. 656 (1 December). New York: City Book Auction.

Clark, Clifford E., Jr. 1978. *Henry Ward Beecher: Spokesman for a Middle-Class America.* Urbana: University of Illinois Press.

Clemens, Cyril.
   1932. *Josh Billings, Yankee Humorist.* Webster Groves, Mo.: International Mark Twain Society.
   1942. "Letters to James Redpath." *Mark Twain Quarterly* 5 (Winter–Spring): 19–21.

Clemens, Olivia Susan (Susy). 1885–86. "Biography of Mark Twain." MS of 131 pages, edited and annotated by SLC, ViU. Published in Neider 1985, 83–225; in part in *MTA,* vol. 2, passim; and in Salsbury, passim.

Clemens, Samuel L. See SLC.

Clemens, Will M. 1900. "Mark Twain on the Lecture Platform." *Ainslee's Magazine* 6 (August): 25–32.

Cleveland Directory. 1871. *Cleveland Directory, 1871–72. Comprising an Alphabetical List of All Business Firms and Private Citizens; a Classified Business Directory; and a Directory of the Public Institutions of the City.* Compiled by A. Bailey. Cleveland: W. S. Robison and Co.

Cliff, Andrew, Peter Haggett, and Matthew Smallman-Raynor. 1993. *Measles: An Historical Geography of a Major Human Viral Disease, from Global Expansion to Local Retreat, 1840–1990.* Oxford, England, and Cambridge, Mass.: Blackwell Publishers.

CLjC. The James S. Copley Library, La Jolla, California.

CLSU. University of Southern California, Los Angeles.

CLU-S/C. Department of Special Collections, University Research Library, University of California, Los Angeles.

Cokayne, George Edward. 1910–59. *The Complete Peerage of England, Scotland, Ireland, Great Britain, and the United Kingdom.* New ed., rev. and enl., ed. Vicary Gibbs and H. Arthur Doubleday. 13 vols. in 14. London: St. Catherine Press.

Coleman, Albert E. 1873. "Life in the Diamond Fields." *Harper's New Monthly Magazine* 46 (February): 321–36.

Coleman, Sydney H. 1924. *Humane Society Leaders in America.* Albany, N.Y.: American Humane Association.

Colstoun [pseud.].
  1873a. "New York." Letter dated 19 February. Chicago *Tribune*, 23 February, 7.
  1873b. "New York." Letter dated 22 May. Chicago *Tribune*, 25 May, 12.

Congressional Globe.
  1872. *The Congressional Globe: Containing the Debates and Proceedings of the Second Session Forty-Second Congress; with an Appendix, Embracing the Laws Passed at That Session.* 6 vols. Washington, D.C.: Office of the Congressional Globe.
  1873. *The Congressional Globe: Containing the Debates and Proceedings of the Third Session Forty-Second Congress; with an Appendix, Embracing the Laws Passed at That Session.* 3 vols. Washington, D.C.: Office of the Congressional Globe.

Conway, Moncure Daniel.
  1872. "Mark Twain in London." Letter dated 24 September. Cincinnati *Commercial*, 10 October, 4.
  1873. "Letter from London." Letter dated 9 September. Cincinnati *Commercial*, 24 September, 2.
  1874. "Decorative Art and Architecture in England." *Harper's New Monthly Magazine* 50 (December): 35–49.
  1904. *Autobiography: Memories and Experiences of Moncure Daniel Conway.* 2 vols. Boston: Houghton, Mifflin and Co.

Coolbrith, Ina. n.d. Untitled two-page reminiscence, CU-BANC.

Copinger, Walter Arthur. 1870. *The Law of Copyright, in Works of Literature and Art.* London: Stevens and Haynes.

Cortissoz, Royal. 1921. *The Life of Whitelaw Reid.* 2 vols. New York: Charles Scribner's Sons.

Cotton, Michelle L. 1985. *Mark Twain's Elmira, 1870–1910.* Elmira: Chemung County Historical Society.

Crocker, Samuel R.
  1871. "Mark Twain's Autobiography." *Literary World* 1 (April): 165.
  1872. "What Katy Did." *Literary World* 3 (December): 105–6.
  1873. "Notes and Queries." *Literary World* 3 (January): 122.

CSfCP. Society of California Pioneers, San Francisco.

CSmH. Henry E. Huntington Library, San Marino, California.

Ct. Connecticut State Library, Hartford.

CtHi. Connecticut Historical Society, Hartford.

CtHMTH. Mark Twain House, Hartford, Connecticut.

CtHSD. Harriet Beecher Stowe Center, Hartford, Connecticut.

CtHT-W. Watkinson Library, Trinity College, Hartford, Connecticut.

CtLHi. Litchfield Historical Society, Litchfield, Connecticut.

CtRe. Mark Twain Library Association, Redding, Connecticut.

CtY. Yale University Library, New Haven, Connecticut.

CtY-BR. Beinecke Rare Book and Manuscript Library, Yale University, New Haven, Connecticut.

CU-BANC. The Bancroft Library, University of California, Berkeley.

CU-MARK. Mark Twain Papers, CU-BANC.

Cummins, Ella Sterling. 1893. *The Story of the Files: A Review of Californian Writers and Literature.* San Francisco: World's Fair Commission of California, Columbian Exposition.

CU-NEWS. Newspaper and Microcopy Division, University of California, Berkeley.

Current Company. 1977. *The Current Company's Pen & Pencil.* Bristol, R.I.: Current Company.

Curtis, George William. 1872. "Editor's Easy Chair." *Harper's New Monthly Magazine* 45 (August): 458–62.

CY. 1979. *A Connecticut Yankee in King Arthur's Court.* Edited by Bernard L. Stein, with an Introduction by Henry Nash Smith. The Works of Mark Twain. Berkeley, Los Angeles, London: University of California Press.

DAB. 1928–36. *Dictionary of American Biography.* Edited by Allen Johnson and Dumas Malone. 20 vols. New York: Charles Scribner's Sons.

DAH. 1940. *Dictionary of American History.* Edited by James Truslow Adams and R. V. Coleman. 5 vols. New York: Charles Scribner's Sons.

Daley. Collection of Robert Daley.

Darwin, Charles. 1871. *The Descent of Man, and Selection in Relation to Sex.* Vol. 1. New York: D. Appleton and Co. Copy owned by Clemens, with marginalia, CU-MARK.

Davis, Chester L., Sr.
1951. "'Roughing It' and Firearms." *Twainian* 10 (November–December): 4.
1956. "Letters from Susan Crane." *Twainian* 15 (November–December): 3–4.
1967. "Letters to Paine from Clara (Spaulding) Stanchfield." *Twainian* 26 (May–June): 1–3.
1977a. "The Book That Was Never Written (England in 1872)." *Twainian* 36 (March–April): 1–4.

1977b. "Family Letters of the 1870's." *Twainian* 36 (July–August): 1–4.

1977c. "Family Letters of the 1870's (Mark's Inventions and 'The Gilded Age.')" *Twainian* 36 (September–October): 1–4.

1978. "The Book That Was Never Written (Another Unpublished Letter)." *Twainian* 37 (May–June): 1–2.

1987. "Mark's Inventions and *The Gilded Age*." *Twainian* 46 (July–August): 3–4.

Davis, Jr. Collection of Chester L. Davis, Jr.

Dawson's Book Shop.
1925. *A Catalogue of Rare Books*. No. 37 (February). Los Angeles: Dawson's Book Shop.

1938. *Catalogue 131*. October. Los Angeles: Dawson's Book Shop.

De Laney, Norman. 1960. "Books for Sale by Norman De Laney." *Antiquarian Bookman* 25 (14 March): 1062.

DFo. Folger Shakespeare Library, Washington, D.C.

Dickinson, Donald C. 1986. *Dictionary of American Book Collectors*. Westport, Conn.: Greenwood Press.

Disturnell, John, comp. 1876. *New York As It Was and As It Is*. New York: D. Van Nostrand.

DLC. United States Library of Congress, Washington, D.C.

DNA. United States National Archives and Record Service, National Archives Library, Washington, D.C.

DNB. 1959. *The Dictionary of National Biography, 1941–1950*. Edited by L. G. Wickham Legg and E. T. Williams. London: Oxford University Press.

Dolby, George. 1885. *Charles Dickens As I Knew Him: The Story of the Reading Tours in Great Britain and America (1866–1870)*. London: T. Fisher Unwin.

Dorn. Collection of Robert M. Dorn.

Doten, Alfred. 1973. *The Journals of Alfred Doten, 1849–1903*. Edited by Walter Van Tilburg Clark. 3 vols. Reno: University of Nevada Press.

Dreer, Ferdinand Julius. 1890. *A Catalogue of the Collection of Autographs Formed by Ferdinand Julius Dreer*. 2 vols. Philadelphia: Privately printed.

Duckett, Margaret. 1964. *Mark Twain and Bret Harte*. Norman: University of Oklahoma Press.

Duncan, Bingham. 1975. *Whitelaw Reid: Journalist, Politician, Diplomat*. Athens: University of Georgia Press.

Duncan, Edmondstoune. 1905. *The Minstrelsy of England*. London: Augener.

Dunn, Waldo Hilary. 1961–63. *James Anthony Froude: A Biography*. 2 vols. Oxford: Clarendon Press.

Durfee, Charles A. 1886. *Index to Harper's New Monthly Magazine. Alphabetical, Analytical, and Classified. Volumes I. to LXX. Inclusive, from June, 1850, to June, 1885*. New York: Harper and Brothers.

Duschnes. 1967. *First Editions of American & British Authors.* New York: Philip C. Duschnes.

Duyckinck, Evert A., and George L. Duyckinck, eds. 1875. *Cyclopaedia of American Literature: Embracing Personal and Critical Notices of Authors, and Selections from Their Writings, from the Earliest Period to the Present Day; with Portraits, Autographs, and Other Illustrations.* Edited to date by M. Laird Simons. 2 vols. Philadelphia: William Rutter and Co. Citations are to the 1965 reprint edition, Detroit: Gale Research Company.

Eder, Josef Maria. 1945. *History of Photography.* Translated by Edward Epstean. New York: Columbia University Press.

Edgar, Neal L. 1986. "James R. Osgood and Company (Boston: 1871–1878; 1880–1885); Houghton, Osgood and Company (Boston: 1878–1880); Ticknor and Company (Boston: 1885–1889)." In *American Literary Publishing Houses, 1638–1899, Part 2: N–Z,* edited by Peter Dzwonkoski. Vol. 49 of *Dictionary of Literary Biography.* Detroit: Gale Research Company.

Edwards, E. J. 1910. "How Mark Twain and Charles Dudley Warner Came to Write 'The Gilded Age.'" New York *Evening Mail,* 5 May, 8.

Edwards, Richard. 1869. *Edwards' Eleventh Annual Directory to the Inhabitants, Institutions, Incorporated Companies, Manufacturing Establishments, Business, Business Firms, etc., etc., in the City of St. Louis, for 1869.* St. Louis: Charless Publishing and Manufacturing Company.

Eggleston, George Cary.
1902. "Distinguished Americans in Conversational Duets, No. 1: Secy. of State Hay and George Cary Eggleston Discuss Pike County Ballads and the Future of American Literature." New York *Herald,* 27 April, 5:1.
1910. *Recollections of a Varied Life.* New York: Henry Holt and Co.

Elderkin, John. 1895. *A Brief History of the Lotos Club.* New York: Lotos Club.

Escott, T. H. S. 1914. *Club Makers and Club Members.* New York: Sturgis and Walton Company.

ET&S1. 1979. *Early Tales & Sketches, Volume 1 (1851–1864).* Edited by Edgar Marquess Branch and Robert H. Hirst, with the assistance of Harriet Elinor Smith. The Works of Mark Twain. Berkeley, Los Angeles, London: University of California Press.

ET&S2. 1981. *Early Tales & Sketches, Volume 2 (1864–1865).* Edited by Edgar Marquess Branch and Robert H. Hirst, with the assistance of Harriet Elinor Smith. The Works of Mark Twain. Berkeley, Los Angeles, London: University of California Press.

Eubank, Marjorie Harrell. 1969. *The Redpath Lyceum Bureau from 1868 to 1901.* Ph.D. diss., University of Michigan, Ann Arbor.

Facts. 1881. *Facts. By a Woman.* Oakland, Calif.: Pacific Press Publishing House.

Fairbairn, James. 1905. *Book of Crests of the Families of Great Britain and Ireland.* 4th ed., rev. and enl. 2 vols. London: T. C. and E. C. Jack.

Fairbanks, Lorenzo Sayles. 1897. *Genealogy of the Fairbanks Family in America, 1633–1897.* Boston: American Printing and Engraving Company.

Fairman, Charles E. 1927. *Art and Artists of the Capitol of the United States of America.* Washington, D.C.: Government Printing Office.

Farington, Frank [Chandler, pseud.]. 1872. "Notes from a Rolling Stone." Correspondence dated "London, April 23, 1872." Virginia City *Territorial Enterprise,* 12 May, 1.

Farwell, Byron. 1957. *The Man Who Presumed: A Biography of Henry M. Stanley.* New York: Henry Holt and Co.

Fatout, Paul.
   1960. *Mark Twain on the Lecture Circuit.* Bloomington: Indiana University Press.
   1976. *Mark Twain Speaking.* Iowa City: University of Iowa Press.

Feinstein, Herbert Charles Verschleisser. 1968. "Mark Twain's Lawsuits." Ph.D. diss., University of California, Berkeley.

Feldman. Collection of John L. Feldman.

Field, Kate.
   1873a. "The Shah of Persia. His Reception in England." Letter dated 19 June. New York *Tribune,* 1 July, 1.
   1873b. "The Guildhall Banquet." Letter dated 21 June. New York *Tribune,* 4 July, 1.
   1873c. "The Sojourn in England." Letter dated 23 June. New York *Tribune,* 7 July, 1.
   1873d. "Receiving the Shah." Letter dated 24 June. New York *Tribune,* 9 July, 4.
   1873e. "The Shah of Persia. Public Demonstrations in His Honor." Letter dated 26 June. New York *Tribune,* 12 July, 1.
   1873f. "The Shah at Windsor. Reviewing His Majesty's Troops." Letter dated 27 June. New York *Tribune,* 14 July, 1.
   1873g. "London Gossip." Letter dated 4 July. New York *Tribune,* 1 August, 2.

Fitzgibbon, George H.
   1872. "The Scottish Corporation and Mr. Stanley and Mark Twain.—Mark Twain at the Sheriffs' Dinner. (From Our London Correspondent.)" Dispatch dated "London, Wednesday Evening" [2 October]. Darlington (England) *Northern Echo,* 3 October, 3.
   1873a. "Mark Twain in England." Darlington (England) *Northern Echo,* 11 June, 2–3.
   1873b. "The Shah in the City.—Mark Twain. [From Our London Correspondent.]" Dispatch dated "London, Friday Night" [20 June]. Darlington (England) *Northern Echo,* 21 June, 3.
   1873c. "Mark Twain in London. [From Our London Correspondent.]" Dispatch dated "London, Monday Night" [13 October]. Darlington (England) *Northern Echo,* 14 October, 3, clipping in Scrapbook 12:1, CU-MARK.

1873d. "Mark Twain.—Royal Naval Artillery Volunteers. (From Our London Correspondent.)" Dispatch dated "London, Monday Night" [22 December]. Darlington (England) *Northern Echo*, 23 December, 3.

1874. "The Projected Visit of 'Mark Twain' to the Provinces. [From Our London Correspondent.]" Dispatch dated "London, Wednesday Night" [31 December 1873]. Darlington (England) *Northern Echo*, 1 January, 3.

Forbes, Edward W., and John H. Finley, Jr., eds. 1958. *The Saturday Club: A Century Completed, 1920–1956.* Boston: Houghton Mifflin Company.

Franklin, Benjamin. 1987. *Writings.* Edited by J. A. Leo Lemay. The Library of America. New York: Literary Classics of the United States.

Freedman. Collection of Russell Freedman, Second Life Books, Lanesborough, Massachusetts.

Freeman. 1932. *Valuable Autographs, Rare Books, First Editions, Presentation Copies: The Collection of the Late William F. Gable.* Sale of 3 May. Philadelphia: Samuel T. Freeman and Co.

Fremont, Jessie Benton. 1993. *The Letters of Jessie Benton Frémont.* Edited by Pamela Herr and Mary Lee Spence. Urbana: University of Illinois Press.

French, Bryant Morey. 1965. *Mark Twain and* The Gilded Age: *The Book That Named an Era.* Dallas: Southern Methodist University Press.

Frost, O. W. 1967. *Joaquin Miller.* New York: Twayne Publishers.

Furness, Horace Howard, ed. 1920. *A New Variorum Edition of Shakespeare.* Vol. 9, *The Tempest.* 11th ed. [1st printing, 1892]. Philadelphia: J. B. Lippincott Company.

Gabler, Edwin. 1988. *The American Telegrapher: A Social History, 1860–1900.* New Brunswick, N.J.: Rutgers University Press.

Gascoigne, Bamber. 1993. *Encyclopedia of Britain.* New York: Macmillan Publishing Company.

GASU. Georgia State University, Atlanta.

Geer, Elihu, comp.

1870. *Geer's Hartford City Directory; For 1870–71: Containing Every Kind of Desirable Information for Citizens and Strangers; Together with a Classified Business Directory, and a Newly Engraved Map of the City.* Hartford: Elihu Geer.

1871. *Geer's Hartford City Directory, for 1871–72: Containing Every Kind of Desirable Information for Citizens and Strangers; Together with a Classified Business Directory.* Hartford: Elihu Geer.

1872. *Geer's Hartford City Directory, for 1872–73: Containing Every Kind of Desirable Information for Citizens and Strangers; Together with a Classified Business Directory.* Hartford: Elihu Geer.

1873. *Geer's Hartford City Directory, for 1873–74: Containing Every Kind of Desirable Information for Citizens and Strangers; Together with a Classified Business Directory.* Hartford: Elihu Geer.

1874. *Geer's Hartford City Directory, for 1874–75: and Hartford Illustrated: Containing a Classified Business Directory.* Hartford: Elihu Geer.

1875. *Geer's Hartford City Directory, for the Year Commencing July, 1875: and*

Hartford Illustrated: Containing a Classified Business Directory. Hartford: Elihu Geer.

1876. *Geer's Hartford City Directory; for the Year Commencing July, 1876: and Hartford Illustrated: Containing a Classified Business Directory.* Hartford: Elihu Geer.

1877. *Geer's Hartford City Directory, for the Year Commencing July, 1877; and Hartford Illustrated: Containing a Classified Business Directory.* Hartford: Elihu Geer.

1878. *Geer's Hartford City Directory, for the Year Commencing July, 1878; and Hartford Illustrated: Containing a Classified Business Directory.* Hartford: Elihu Geer.

1879. *Geer's Hartford City Directory, for the Year Commencing July, 1879; and Hartford Illustrated: Containing a Classified Business Directory.* Hartford: Elihu Geer.

1880. *Geer's Hartford City Directory and Hartford Illustrated; for the Year Commencing July, 1880: Containing a Classified Business Directory.* Hartford: Elihu Geer.

1881. *Geer's Hartford City Directory and Hartford Illustrated; for the Year Commencing July, 1881: Containing a General Directory of Citizens, Corporations, Etc.* Hartford: Elihu Geer.

1882. *Geer's Hartford City Directory and Hartford Illustrated; for the Year Commencing July 1st, 1882: Containing a New Map of the City; New Street Guide; General Directory of Citizens, Corporations, Etc.* Hartford: Elihu Geer.

Gohdes, Clarence. 1942. "Some Letters of Joaquin Miller to Lord Houghton." *Modern Language Quarterly* 3 (June): 297–306.

Goodman, Joseph T. 1866. "Mark Twain Coming." Virginia City *Territorial Enterprise*, 28 October, 2.

Goodspeed's Book Shop.
1926? *Catalogue of Autographs No. 169.* Boston: Goodspeed's Book Shop.
1927? *Goodspeed's Catalogue No. 174. Autographs of Famous Men & Women.* Boston: Goodspeed's Book Shop.

Gore's Directory. 1872. *Gore's Directory for Liverpool and Its Environs.* Liverpool: J. Mawdsley and Son.

Gosling, Nigel. 1974. *Gustave Doré.* New York: Praeger Publishers.

Graham, H. G. 1880. "Russel of 'The Scotsman.'" *Fraser's Magazine*, n.s. 22 (September): 301–17.

Green, Paul M., and Melvin G. Holli, eds. 1987. *The Mayors: The Chicago Political Tradition.* Carbondale: Southern Illinois University Press.

Gregory, Winifred, ed. 1937. *American Newspapers, 1821–1936: A Union List of Files Available in the United States and Canada.* New York: H. W. Wilson Company.

Grenander, M. E.
1975. "Mark Twain's English Lectures and George Routledge & Sons." *Mark Twain Journal* 17 (Summer): 1–4.

1978. "California's Albion: Mark Twain, Ambrose Bierce, Tom Hood, John Camden Hotten, and Andrew Chatto." *The Papers of the Bibliographical Society of America* 72 (Fourth Quarter): 455–75.

Greve, Charles Theodore. 1904. *Centennial History of Cincinnati and Representative Citizens*. 2 vols. Chicago: Biographical Publishing Company.

Gribben, Alan. 1980. *Mark Twain's Library: A Reconstruction*. 2 vols. Boston: G. K. Hall and Co.

Griest, Guinevere L. 1970. *Mudie's Circulating Library and the Victorian Novel*. Bloomington: Indiana University Press.

Griffiths, Dennis, ed. 1992. *The Encyclopedia of the British Press, 1422–1992*. New York: St. Martin's Press.

Gudde, Erwin G. 1962. *California Place Names: The Origin and Etymology of Current Geographical Names*. 2d ed., rev. and enl. Berkeley and Los Angeles: University of California Press.

Guinn, J. M. 1907. *History of the State of California and Biographical Record of Oakland and Environs*. 2 vols. Los Angeles: Historic Record Company.

Gwynn, Stephen, and Gertrude M. Tuckwell. 1917. *The Life of the Rt. Hon. Sir Charles W. Dilke*. 2 vols. London: John Murray.

Haliburton, Thomas Chandler. [Samuel Slick, pseud.]. 1988. *The Letters of Thomas Chandler Haliburton*. Edited by Richard A. Davies. Toronto: University of Toronto Press.

Hamilton, Sinclair. 1958. *Early American Book Illustrators and Wood Engravers, 1670–1870*. Princeton, N.J.: Princeton University Library.

Hammond, Barbara L., ed. 1993. *Edgar County, Illinois: An Extraction of the 1870 Census*. Paris, Ill.: Tresearch.

Hardinge, Emma. 1872. *Modern American Spiritualism: A Twenty Years' Record of the Communion between Earth and the World of Spirits*. 4th ed. [1st printing, 1870]. New York: Published by the author.

Harlow, Samuel R., and S. C. Hutchins. 1868. *Life Sketches of the State Officers, Senators, and Members of the Assembly, of the State of New York, in 1868*. Albany: Weed, Parsons and Co.

Harnsberger, Caroline Thomas. 1960. *Mark Twain, Family Man*. New York: Citadel Press.

Hart, James D.
1983. *The Oxford Companion to American Literature*. 5th ed. New York: Oxford University Press.
1987. *A Companion to California*. Rev. ed. Berkeley, Los Angeles, London: University of California Press.

Harte, Bret.
1866. *Outcroppings: Being Selections of California Verse*. Compiled by Bret Harte. San Francisco: A. Roman and Co.
1870. "Plain Language from Truthful James." *Overland Monthly* 5 (September): 287–88.

1871. *Poems*. Boston: Fields, Osgood, and Co.

1872. "Bret Harte and His Lecture Engagement." Letter dated 16 November. Boston *Advertiser*, 20 November, 2.

1926. *The Letters of Bret Harte*. Edited by Geoffrey Bret Harte. Boston: Houghton Mifflin Company.

1997, forthcoming. *Selected Letters of Bret Harte*. Edited by Gary Scharnhorst. Norman: University of Oklahoma Press.

"Hartford Residents." 1974. Unpublished TS by anonymous compiler, CtHSD.

Hassard, John Rose Greene. 1871. "The New York Mercantile Library." *Scribner's Monthly* 1 (February): 353–67.

Hay, John M.
1870. "Little-Breeches." New York *Tribune*, 19 November, 5.

1871a. *Pike County Ballads and Other Pieces*. Boston: James R. Osgood and Co.

1871b. "Jim Bludso, (of the Prairie Belle.)" New York *Tribune*, 5 January, 5.

1872. "Mark Twain at Steinway Hall." New York *Tribune*, 25 January, 5.

1908. *Letters of John Hay and Extracts from Diary*. Edited by Clara Louise Hay. 3 vols. Washington, D.C.: Privately printed.

Heitman, Francis B. 1903. *Historical Register and Dictionary of the United States Army, from Its Organization, September 29, 1789, to March 2, 1903*. 2 vols. Washington, D.C.: Government Printing Office.

Henderson, Archibald. 1910. "The International Fame of Mark Twain." *North American Review* 192 (December): 805–15. In Anderson and Sanderson, 302–12.

Henkels.
1930a. Catalog for sale no. 1439 (31 January). Philadelphia: Stan. V. Henkels.

1930b. *Autographs, Letters, Documents, Manuscripts from the Correspondence of Charles Thomson . . . with Additions from Other Private Sources*. Sale no. 1442 (10 April). Philadelphia: Stan. V. Henkels.

1930c. *Autographs, Letters, Documents, Manuscripts Belonging to J. Fred Osterstock, Easton, Penna, and for Other Accounts*. Sale no. 1447 (16 October). Philadelphia: Stan. V. Henkels.

Heritage. 1982. *Mark Twain. Catalogue 130*. Los Angeles: Heritage Bookshop.

Hershkowitz, Leo. 1977. *Tweed's New York: Another Look*. Garden City, N.Y.: Anchor Press/Doubleday.

Hertzberg, Max J. 1962. *The Reader's Encyclopedia of American Literature*. New York: Thomas Y. Crowell Company.

HF. 1988. *Adventures of Huckleberry Finn*. Edited by Walter Blair and Victor Fischer, with the assistance of Dahlia Armon and Harriet Elinor Smith. The Works of Mark Twain. Berkeley, Los Angeles, London: University of California Press.

HHR. 1969. *Mark Twain's Correspondence with Henry Huttleston Rogers, 1893–1909*. Edited by Lewis Leary. The Mark Twain Papers. Berkeley and Los Angeles: University of California Press.

Hibben, Paxton. 1942. *Henry Ward Beecher: An American Portrait.* 2d ed. New York: Readers Club.

Hill, Hamlin.
1962. "Escol Sellers from Uncharted Space: A Footnote to *The Gilded Age.*" *American Literature* 34 (March): 107–13.
1964. *Mark Twain and Elisha Bliss.* Columbia: University of Missouri Press.
1965. "Toward a Critical Text of *The Gilded Age.*" *Papers of the Bibliographical Society of America* 59 (Second Quarter): 142–49.

Hingston, Edward P.
1870. "Introduction." In SLC 1870b, 3–8.
1871. *The Genial Showman: Being Reminiscences of the Life of Artemus Ward and Pictures of a Showman's Career in the Western World.* London: John Camden Hotten. First published in 1870 in two volumes.

Hird, Frank. 1935. *H. M. Stanley: The Authorized Life.* London: Stanley Paul and Co.

Hirst, Robert H. 1975. "The Making of *The Innocents Abroad:* 1867–1872." Ph.D. diss., University of California, Berkeley.

History of Edgar County. 1879. *The History of Edgar County, Illinois.* Chicago: William Le Baron, Jr., and Co.

Holland, Josiah Gilbert [Timothy Titcomb, pseud.].
1865. "The Popular Lecture." *Atlantic Monthly* 15 (March): 362–71.
1871. "Lecture-Brokers and Lecture-Breakers." *Scribner's Monthly* 1 (March): 560–61.
1872a. "Triflers on the Platform." *Scribner's Monthly* 3 (February): 489.
1872b. "Hepworth and Heterodoxy." *Scribner's Monthly* 3 (April): 745–46.
1872c. "The Literary Bureaus Again." *Scribner's Monthly* 4 (July): 362–63.

Holman, Mabel Cassine. 1930. *The Western Neck: The Story of Fenwick.* Hartford: Privately printed.

Hood, Tom.
1872a. "A Grave Lecture." *Fun,* 9 November, 190.
1872b. *Tom Hood's Comic Annual for 1873. With Twenty-three Pages of Illustrations by the Brothers Dalziel.* London: Published at the Fun Office.
1873. "Coming Events." *Fun,* 26 April, 172.

Hooker, John. 1899. *Some Reminiscences of a Long Life.* Hartford: Belknap and Warfield.

Hornberger, Theodore, ed. 1941. *Mark Twain's Letters to Will Bowen.* Austin: University of Texas.

Horner, Charles F. 1926. *The Life of James Redpath and the Development of the Modern Lyceum.* New York and Newark: Barse and Hopkins.

Hotten, John Camden.
1870a. *The Piccadilly Annual of Entertaining Literature, Retrospective and Contemporary.* London: John Camden Hotten.

1870b. *A 3rd Supply of Yankee Drolleries: The Most Recent Works of the Best American Humourists*. London: John Camden Hotten. Reprints SLC 1870c.

1871. Introduction to "Holiday Literature." In SLC 1871e, 9.

1872a. *Practical Jokes with Artemus Ward, Including the Story of the Man Who Fought Cats*. London: John Camden Hotten. Includes several pieces erroneously attributed to Clemens.

1872b. "Mr. Hotten's Edition of 'Mark Twain.' [To the Editor of the 'Spectator.']" Letter dated 5 June. London *Spectator*, 8 June, 722.

1872c. " 'Mark Twain' and His English Editor. [To the Editor of the 'Spectator.']" Undated letter. London *Spectator*, 28 September, 1237.

1873. "Mark Twain: A Sketch of His Life." Dated "PICCADILLY, *March 12th, 1873.*" In SLC 1873a, vii–xxxix.

Houfe, Simon. 1978. *The Dictionary of British Book Illustrators and Caricaturists, 1800–1914*. Woodbridge, England: Antique Collectors' Club.

Howe, M. A. DeWolfe. 1922. *Memories of a Hostess: A Chronicle of Eminent Friendships, Drawn Chiefly from the Diaries of Mrs. James T. Fields*. Boston: Atlantic Monthly Press.

Howells, William Dean.
1872. "Recent Literature." *Atlantic Monthly* 29 (June): 754–55.

1874. "Recent Literature." *Atlantic Monthly* 33 (June): 745–53.

1881. "New Publications. A Romance by Mark Twain." New York *Tribune*, 25 October, 6.

1900. *Literary Friends and Acquaintance*. New York: Harper and Brothers.

1910. *My Mark Twain: Reminiscences and Criticisms*. New York: Harper and Brothers.

1928. *Life in Letters of William Dean Howells*. Edited by Mildred Howells. 2 vols. Garden City, N.Y.: Doubleday, Doran and Co.

1979a. *W. D. Howells, Selected Letters, Volume 1: 1852–1872*. Edited and annotated by George Arms, Richard H. Ballinger, Christoph K. Lohmann, and John K. Reeves. Textual editors Don L. Cook, Christoph K. Lohmann, and David Nordloh. Boston: Twayne Publishers.

1979b. *W. D. Howells, Selected Letters, Volume 2: 1873–1881*. Edited and annotated by George Arms and Christoph K. Lohmann. Textual editors Christoph K. Lohmann and Jerry Herron. Boston: Twayne Publishers.

Howland. Collection of David Howland.

Hugill, Stan, comp. 1984. *Shanties from the Seven Seas*. 2d ed. London: Routledge and Kegan Paul.

Hunter, Louis C. 1949. *Steamboats on the Western Rivers: An Economic and Technological History*. Cambridge: Harvard University Press.

IaHi. State Historical Society of Iowa, Iowa City.

IaU. University of Iowa, Iowa City.

ICN. Newberry Library, Chicago, Illinois.

ICU. University of Chicago, Chicago, Illinois.

IGK. Knox College, Galesburg, Illinois.

Inds. 1989. *Huck Finn and Tom Sawyer among the Indians, and Other Unfinished Stories.* Foreword and notes by Dahlia Armon and Walter Blair. Texts established by Dahlia Armon, Paul Baender, Walter Blair, William M. Gibson, and Franklin R. Rogers. The Mark Twain Library. Berkeley, Los Angeles, London: University of California Press.

Ireland, Joseph N. 1866–67. *Records of the New York Stage, from 1750 to 1860.* 2 vols. New York: T. H. Morrell.

IU-R. Rare Book and Special Collections Library, University of Illinois, Urbana.

Jacobs. Collection of Victor and Irene Murr Jacobs, on deposit at ODaU.

James, George Wharton. 1911. "Charles Warren Stoddard." *National Magazine* 34 (August): 659–72.

Jenkins, John Edward. 1871. *Ginx's Baby: His Birth and Other Misfortunes.* 2d ed. Boston: James R. Osgood and Co.

Jenkins, Roy. 1958. *Sir Charles Dilke: A Victorian Tragedy.* London: Collins.

Jerome, Robert D., and Herbert A. Wisbey, Jr. 1977. *Mark Twain in Elmira.* Elmira: Mark Twain Society.

Jerrold, Blanchard. 1891. *Life of Gustave Doré.* London: W. H. Allen and Co.

JLC. Jane Lampton Clemens.

Johnson, Merle. 1935. *A Bibliography of the Works of Mark Twain, Samuel Langhorne Clemens.* 2d ed., rev. and enl. New York: Harper and Brothers.

Jones, Joseph. 1890. *Medical and Surgical Memoirs: Containing Investigations on the Geographical Distribution, Causes, Nature, Relations and Treatment of Various Diseases, 1855–1890.* New Orleans: Printed for the author by L. Graham and Son.

Julian, John, ed. 1908. *A Dictionary of Hymnology Setting Forth the Origin and History of Christian Hymns of All Ages and Nations.* 2d ed. London: John Murray.

Kelleher. 1982. Catalog for sale no. 555 (22 July). Boston: Daniel F. Kelleher Company.

Kelly, J. Wells, comp. 1863. *Second Directory of Nevada Territory.* San Francisco: Valentine and Co.

Kendall, W. A.
1868. *The Voice My Soul Heard.* San Francisco: H. H. Bancroft and Co.
1869a. "Better Cheer." *Overland Monthly* 2 (March): 247.
1869b. "Invitation." *Overland Monthly* 2 (May): 441.
1869c. "Crowned." *Overland Monthly* 3 (August): 124.
1869d. "Renewed." *Overland Monthly* 3 (September): 220.
1870. "Good-Night." *Overland Monthly* 4 (June): 549.
1872. "Frank Bret Harte." San Francisco *Chronicle,* 15 December, 1.

Kent, William, ed. 1937. *An Encyclopaedia of London*. New York: E. P. Dutton and Co.

Kerr, Howard. 1972. *Mediums, and Spirit-Rappers, and Roaring Radicals: Spiritualism in American Literature, 1850–1900*. Urbana: University of Illinois Press.

Kesterson, David B. 1973. *Josh Billings (Henry Wheeler Shaw)*. New York: Twayne Publishers.

King, Clarence. 1874. "John Hay." *Scribner's Monthly* 7 (April): 736–39.

King, Moses.
1885. *King's Hand-Book of Boston*. 7th ed. Boston: Moses King.
1893. *King's Handbook of New York City*. 2d ed. Boston: Moses King.

Kiralis, Karl. 1970–71. "Two Recently Discovered Letters by Mark Twain." *Mark Twain Journal* 15 (Winter): 1–5.

Kirk, John Foster. 1892. *A Supplement to Allibone's Critical Dictionary of English Literature and British and American Authors*. 2 vols. Philadelphia: J. B. Lippincott Company.

Kouwenhoven, John A. 1953. *The Columbia Historical Portrait of New York*. Garden City, N.Y.: Doubleday and Co.

Kozlay, Charles Meeker, comp. 1909. *The Lectures of Bret Harte*. Brooklyn, N.Y.: Charles Meeker Kozlay.

Kuhlmann, Charles Byron. 1929. *The Development of the Flour-Milling Industry in the United States*. Boston and New York: Houghton Mifflin Company.

Kurstak, Edouard, and Raymond G. Marusyk, eds. 1984. *Control of Virus Diseases*. New York and Basel: Marcel Dekker.

KU-S. Kenneth Spencer Research Library, University of Kansas, Lawrence.

Kuykendall, Ralph S. 1940. "Constitutions of the Hawaiian Kingdom: A Brief History and Analysis." *Papers of the Hawaiian Historical Society*, no. 21. Honolulu: Hawaiian Historical Society.

Kuykendall, Ralph S., and A. Grove Day. 1961. *Hawaii: A History*. Rev. ed. Englewood Cliffs, N.J.: Prentice-Hall.

Kuykendall, Ralph S., and Herbert E. Gregory. 1927. *A History of Hawaii*. New York: Macmillan Company.

L1. 1988. *Mark Twain's Letters, Volume 1: 1853–1866*. Edited by Edgar Marquess Branch, Michael B. Frank, Kenneth M. Sanderson, Harriet Elinor Smith, Lin Salamo, and Richard Bucci. The Mark Twain Papers. Berkeley, Los Angeles, London: University of California Press.

L2. 1990. *Mark Twain's Letters, Volume 2: 1867–1868*. Edited by Harriet Elinor Smith, Richard Bucci, and Lin Salamo. The Mark Twain Papers. Berkeley, Los Angeles, London: University of California Press.

L3. 1992. *Mark Twain's Letters, Volume 3: 1869*. Edited by Victor Fischer, Michael B. Frank, and Dahlia Armon. The Mark Twain Papers. Berkeley, Los Angeles, London: University of California Press.

L4. 1995. *Mark Twain's Letters, Volume 4: 1870–1871*. Edited by Victor Fischer, Michael B. Frank, and Lin Salamo. The Mark Twain Papers. Berkeley, Los Angeles, London: University of California Press.

Lampton, Lucius M.

1989. "Hero in a Fool's Paradise: Twain's Cousin James J. Lampton and Colonel Sellers." *Mark Twain Journal* 27 (Fall): 1–56.

1990. *The Genealogy of Mark Twain*. Jackson, Miss.: Diamond L Publishing.

Landau, Sarah Bradford. 1979. *Edward T. and William A. Potter: American Victorian Architects*. New York: Garland Publishing.

Landon, Melville De Lancey [Eli Perkins, pseud.]. 1872. *Saratoga in 1901*. New York: Sheldon and Co. Copy owned by Clemens, with marginalia, CtRe.

Lane, Sally. 1984. "Then and Now." Trenton (N.J.) *Sunday Times Magazine*, 8 April, 18.

Langdon, Jervis. 1938. *Samuel Langhorne Clemens: Some Reminiscences and Some Excerpts from Letters and Unpublished Manuscripts*. [Elmira, N.Y.]: Privately printed.

Langdon, Jervis, Jr. 1992. "How Twain Traveled between Hartford and Elmira." *Mark Twain Society Bulletin* 15 (January): 3–4.

Langley, Henry G., comp.

1861. *The San Francisco Directory for the Year Commencing September, 1861*. San Francisco: Valentine and Co.

1862. *The San Francisco Directory for the Year Commencing September, 1862*. San Francisco: Valentine and Co.

1863. *The San Francisco Directory for the Year Commencing October, 1863*. San Francisco: Towne and Bacon.

1864. *The San Francisco Directory for the Year Commencing October, 1864*. San Francisco: Towne and Bacon.

1865. *The San Francisco Directory for the Year Commencing December, 1865*. San Francisco: Towne and Bacon.

1867. *The San Francisco Directory for the Year Commencing September, 1867*. San Francisco: Henry G. Langley.

1869. *The San Francisco Directory for the Year Commencing December, 1869*. San Francisco: Henry G. Langley.

1872. *The San Francisco Directory for the Year Commencing March, 1872*. San Francisco: Henry G. Langley.

1873. *The San Francisco Directory for the Year Commencing March, 1873*. San Francisco: Henry G. Langley.

Layard, George Somes. 1907. *Shirley Brooks of Punch: His Life, Letters, and Diaries*. New York: Henry Holt and Co.

LE. 1962. *Mark Twain: Letters from the Earth*. Edited by Bernard DeVoto, with a Preface by Henry Nash Smith. New York: Harper and Row.

Lehmann-Haupt, Hellmut. 1951. *The Book in America: A History of the Making and Selling of Books in the United States*. 2d ed. New York: R. R. Bowker Company.

Leland, Charles Godfrey [Hans Breitmann, pseud.]. 1857. "Hans Breitmann's Barty." *Graham's Illustrated Magazine* 50 (May): 458.

"Lewis Genealogy." 1995. Unpublished TS, CU-MARK.

Libbie. 1905. *Catalogue of the Valuable Private Library of the Late Arthur Mason Knapp*. . . . Sale of 14, 15, and 16 February. Boston: C. F. Libbie and Co.

Lilly Library. 1991. *Mark Twain: Selections from the Collection of Nick Karanovich*. Exhibition prepared and described by Nick Karanovich, William Cagle, and Joel Silver. Bloomington: The Lilly Library, Indiana University.

Liverpool Shipwreck and Humane Society.
1873. "34th Annual Report, Year Ended 1st July, 1873." Liverpool: Liverpool Shipwreck and Humane Society.
1994. "155th Annual Report, 1993/94." Liverpool: Liverpool Shipwreck and Humane Society.

LLMT. 1949. *The Love Letters of Mark Twain*. Edited by Dixon Wecter. New York: Harper and Brothers.

Lloyd's Register. 1869. *Lloyd's Captains' Register, Containing the Names and Services of Certificated Masters of the British Mercantile Marine Now Afloat*. Under the superintendence of B. C. Stephenson. London: J. D. Potter.

Locker, Arthur. 1872. "Two American Humorists—Hans Breitmann and Mark Twain." London *Graphic*, 5 October, 310, 324.

Locker-Lampson, Frederick. 1896. *My Confidences. An Autobiographical Sketch Addressed to My Descendants*. London: Smith, Elder, and Co.

Lodge, Edmund. 1907. *The Peerage, Baronetage, Knightage & Companionage of the British Empire for 1907*. London: Kelly's Directories.

London Directory. 1872. *The Post Office London Directory, 1873*. . . . Printed and Published for Frederic Kelly, Proprietor. London: Kelly and Co.

Longfellow, Henry Wadsworth.
1871. "The Legend Beautiful." *Atlantic Monthly* 28 (December): 657–60.
1902. *The Complete Poetical Works of Henry Wadsworth Longfellow*. Household Edition. Boston: Houghton, Mifflin and Co.

Lorch, Fred W. 1968. *The Trouble Begins at Eight: Mark Twain's Lecture Tours*. Ames: Iowa State University Press.

Lossing, Benson J. 1884. *History of New York City, Embracing an Outline Sketch of Events from 1609 to 1830, and a Full Account of Its Development from 1830 to 1884*. New York and Chicago: A. S. Barnes and Co.

Lounsbury, Thomas R. 1904. "Biographical Sketch." In *The Complete Writings of Charles Dudley Warner*. Vol. 15. Hartford: American Publishing Company.

Lyceum.
1869. *The Lyceum*. Boston: [Redpath and Fall].
1870. *The Lyceum: Containing a Complete List of Lecturers, Readers, and Musicians for the Season of 1870–71*. Boston: Redpath and Fall.
1871. *The Lyceum Magazine: Edited by the Boston Lyceum Bureau, and Con-*

taining Its Third Annual List. For the Season of 1871–1872. Boston: Redpath and Fall.

1872. *The Lyceum Magazine: Edited by the Boston Lyceum Bureau, and Containing Its Fourth Annual List. Season of 1872–1873.* Boston: Redpath and Fall.

1873. *The Lyceum Magazine: Edited by the Boston Lyceum Bureau, and Containing Its Fifth Annual List. Season of 1873–1874.* Boston: Redpath's Lyceum Bureau.

1876. *The Redpath Lyceum: Circular of the Redpath Lyceum Bureau. Season of 1876–1877.* Boston and Chicago: [Redpath's Lyceum Bureau].

Lysons, Daniel, and Samuel Lysons. 1813. *Magna Britannia; Being a Concise Topographical Account of the Several Counties of Great Britain. Vol. I.—Part II. Containing Berkshire.* London: T. Cadell and W. Davies.

MA. Amherst College, Amherst, Massachusetts.

Macchetta, Blanche Roosevelt Tucker. 1885. *Life and Reminiscences of Gustave Doré.* New York: Cassell and Co.

MacDonald, Greville. 1924. *George MacDonald and His Wife.* London: George Allen and Unwin Ltd.

McIlwaine, Shields. 1948. *Memphis Down in Dixie.* New York: E. P. Dutton and Co.

M'Laren, Elizabeth T. 1889. *Dr. John Brown and His Sister Isabella.* Edinburgh: David Douglas. Copy owned by Olivia Clemens, inscribed "Hartford 1890," CU-MARK.

MacMinn, G. R. 1936. " 'The Gentleman from Pike' in Early California." *American Literature* 8 (May): 160–69.

Malmquist, O. N. 1971. *The First 100 Years: A History of "The Salt Lake Tribune," 1871–1971.* Salt Lake City: Utah State Historical Society.

Marberry, M. M.
1953. *Splendid Poseur: Joaquin Miller—American Poet.* New York: Thomas Y. Crowell Company.
1967. *Vicky: A Biography of Victoria C. Woodhull.* New York: Funk and Wagnalls.

Marcus, Steven. 1966. *The Other Victorians: A Study of Sexuality and Pornography in Mid-Nineteenth-Century England.* New York: Basic Books.

Margolis, Anne Throne, ed. 1979. *The Isabella Beecher Hooker Project: A Microfiche Edition of Her Papers and Suffrage-Related Correspondence Owned by The Stowe-Day Foundation.* Hartford: The Stowe-Day Foundation.

Marshall, C. F. Dendy. 1926. *The British Post Office from Its Beginnings to the End of 1925.* London: Humphrey Milford, Oxford University Press.

Martin, Willard E., Jr. 1975–76. "Letters and Remarks by Mark Twain from the Boston Daily Journal." *Mark Twain Journal* 18 (Winter): 1–5.

Masters, David. 1955. *The Plimsoll Mark.* London: Cassell and Co.

Mathews, Joseph J. 1973. *George W. Smalley: Forty Years a Foreign Correspondent.* Chapel Hill: University of North Carolina Press.

Mathews, Mitford M., ed. 1951. *A Dictionary of Americanisms on Historical Principles.* 2 vols. Chicago: University of Chicago Press.

MB. Boston Public Library and Eastern Massachusetts Regional Public Library System, Boston.

MEC. Mary E. (Mollie) Clemens.

Men of the Time. 1872. *Men of the Time: A Dictionary of Contemporaries, Containing Biographical Notices of Eminent Characters of Both Sexes.* 8th ed., rev. by Thompson Cooper. London: George Routledge and Sons.

Menefee, C. A. 1873. *Historical and Descriptive Sketch Book of Napa, Sonoma, Lake and Mendocino, Comprising Sketches of Their Topography, Productions, History, Scenery, and Peculiar Attractions.* Napa City, Calif.: Reporter Publishing House.

Mercantile Library. 1872. *Fifty-first Annual Report of the Board of Direction of the Mercantile Library Association of the City of New York.* New York: James Sutton and Co.

Merwin, Henry Childs. 1911. *The Life of Bret Harte.* Boston: Houghton Mifflin Company.

Merwin-Clayton. 1906. *Catalogue of the Library, Correspondence and Original Cartoons of the Late Thomas Nast.* Sale of 2 and 3 April. New York: Merwin-Clayton Sales Company.

MFMT. 1931. *My Father, Mark Twain.* By Clara Clemens. New York and London: Harper and Brothers.

MH-H. Houghton Library, Harvard University, Cambridge, Massachusetts.

MHi. Massachusetts Historical Society, Boston.

MiD. Detroit Public Library, Detroit, Michigan.

Mieder, Wolfgang, Stewart A. Kingsbury, and Kelsie B. Harder, eds. 1992. *A Dictionary of American Proverbs.* New York: Oxford University Press.

Miller, Cincinnatus Hiner [Joaquin Miller, pseud.]. 1892. "Joseph E. Lawrence." San Francisco *Morning Call,* 4 September, 13.

MnU. University of Minnesota, Minneapolis.

MoHH. Mark Twain Home Foundation, Hannibal, Missouri.

Monteiro, George, and Brenda Murphy, eds. 1980. *John Hay–Howells Letters: The Correspondence of John Milton Hay and William Dean Howells, 1861–1905.* Boston: Twayne Publishers.

MoPeS. Saint Mary's Seminary, Perryville, Missouri.

Moran, Benjamin. 1872–73. Journals. Papers of Benjamin Moran, Manuscript Division, DLC.

Morris and Anderson. Collection of Rosemary Morris and Marjory Anderson.

MoSMTB. Mark Twain Birthplace State Historic Site, Department of Natural Resources, Division of State Parks, Stoutsville, Missouri.

MoSW. Washington University, St. Louis, Missouri.

Motley, John Lothrop. 1889. *The Correspondence of John Lothrop Motley.* Edited by George William Curtis. 2d ed. 2 vols. London: John Murray.

Mott, Frank Luther.

1938. *A History of American Magazines, 1850–1865.* Cambridge: Harvard University Press.

1950. *American Journalism: A History of Newspapers in the United States through 260 Years: 1690 to 1950.* Rev. ed. New York: Macmillan Company.

1957. *A History of American Magazines, 1865–1885.* 2d printing [1st printing, 1938]. Cambridge: Belknap Press of Harvard University Press.

Moulton, Louise Chandler. 1872. "Boston. Literary Notes." New York *Tribune,* 10 June, 6.

MS. Manuscript.

MTA. 1924. *Mark Twain's Autobiography.* Edited by Albert Bigelow Paine. 2 vols. New York: Harper and Brothers.

MTB. 1912. *Mark Twain: A Biography.* By Albert Bigelow Paine. 3 vols. New York: Harper and Brothers. [*Volume numbers in citations are to this edition; page numbers are the same in all editions.*]

MTBus. 1946. *Mark Twain, Business Man.* Edited by Samuel Charles Webster. Boston: Little, Brown and Co.

MTE. 1940. *Mark Twain in Eruption.* Edited by Bernard DeVoto. New York: Harper and Brothers.

MTH. 1947. *Mark Twain and Hawaii.* By Walter Francis Frear. Chicago: Lakeside Press.

MTHL. 1960. *Mark Twain–Howells Letters.* Edited by Henry Nash Smith and William M. Gibson, with the assistance of Frederick Anderson. 2 vols. Cambridge: Belknap Press of Harvard University Press.

MTHL(S). 1967. *Selected Mark Twain–Howells Letters, 1872–1910.* Edited by Frederick Anderson, William M. Gibson, and Henry Nash Smith. Cambridge: Belknap Press of Harvard University Press.

MTL. 1917. *Mark Twain's Letters.* Edited by Albert Bigelow Paine. 2 vols. New York: Harper and Brothers.

MTLP. 1967. *Mark Twain's Letters to His Publishers, 1867–1894.* Edited by Hamlin Hill. The Mark Twain Papers. Berkeley and Los Angeles: University of California Press.

MTMF. 1949. *Mark Twain to Mrs. Fairbanks.* Edited by Dixon Wecter. San Marino, Calif.: Huntington Library.

MTS.

1910. *Mark Twain's Speeches.* With an introduction by William Dean Howells. New York: Harper and Brothers.

1923. *Mark Twain's Speeches.* With an introduction by Albert Bigelow Paine and an appreciation by William Dean Howells. New York: Harper and Brothers.

MTTB. 1940. *Mark Twain's Travels with Mr. Brown.* Edited by Franklin Walker and G. Ezra Dane. New York: Alfred A. Knopf.

Mumby, Frank Arthur. 1934. *The House of Routledge, 1834–1934*. London: George Routledge and Sons.

Mumby, Frank Arthur, and Frances H. S. Stallybrass. 1955. *From Swan Sonnenschein to George Allen & Unwin Ltd*. London: George Allen and Unwin.

Munson, James E. 1892. *The Complete Phonographer, and Reporters' Guide: An Inductive Exposition of Phonography, with Its Application to All Branches of Reporting, and Affording the Fullest Instruction to Those Who Have Not the Assistance of an Oral Teacher; Also Intended as a School-Book*. Rev. ed. New York: Harper and Brothers.

Murray, John. 1890. *Handbook for England and Wales*. 2d ed. London: John Murray.

N&J1. 1975. *Mark Twain's Notebooks & Journals, Volume I (1855–1873)*. Edited by Frederick Anderson, Michael B. Frank, and Kenneth M. Sanderson. The Mark Twain Papers. Berkeley, Los Angeles, London: University of California Press.

N&J2. 1975. *Mark Twain's Notebooks & Journals, Volume II (1877–1883)*. Edited by Frederick Anderson, Lin Salamo, and Bernard L. Stein. The Mark Twain Papers. Berkeley, Los Angeles, London: University of California Press.

Nast, Thomas.
1871. *Th. Nast's Illustrated Almanac for 1872*. New York: Harper and Brothers.
1872. *Th. Nast's Illustrated Almanac for 1873*. New York: Harper and Brothers.

NBuHi. Buffalo and Erie County Historical Society, Buffalo, New York.

NBuU-PO. Poetry Library, State University of New York at Buffalo, Buffalo, New York.

NCAB. 1898–1984. *The National Cyclopedia of American Biography*. Volumes 1–62 and A–M plus index. New York: James T. White and Co.

Neider, Charles, ed.
1961. *Mark Twain: Life As I Find It*. Garden City, N.Y.: Hanover House.
1985. *Papa: An Intimate Biography of Mark Twain, by Susy Clemens, His Daughter, Thirteen*. Garden City, N.Y.: Doubleday and Co.

NElmC. Mark Twain Archives and Center for Mark Twain Studies at Quarry Farm, Elmira College, Elmira, New York.

Newman, Mary Richardson [May Wentworth, pseud.], ed. 1867. *Poetry of the Pacific: Selections and Original Poems from the Poets of the Pacific States*. San Francisco: Pacific Publishing Company.

Newspaper Press Directory. 1873. *The Newspaper Press Directory and Advertisers' Guide. Containing Full Particulars Relative to Each Journal Published in the United Kingdom and the British Isles*. London: C. Mitchell and Co.

NHi. New York Historical Society, New York City.

NHyF. General Services Administration National Archives and Record Service, Franklin D. Roosevelt Library, Hyde Park, New York.

NjP. Princeton University, Princeton, New Jersey.

NN. The New York Public Library, Astor, Lenox and Tilden Foundations, New York City.

NN-B. Henry W. and Albert A. Berg Collection, NN.

NNC. Columbia University, New York City.

NNPM. Pierpont Morgan Library, New York City.

"Nook Farm Genealogy." 1974. TS by anonymous compiler, CtHSD.

NPV. Jean Webster McKinney Family Papers, Francis Fitz Randolph Rare Book Room, Vassar College Library, Poughkeepsie, New York.

NRU. Rush Rhees Library, University of Rochester, Rochester, New York.

Oakley, Maureen, comp. 1969. *General Index: Volumes I–XL, 1921–1962,* for *Journal of the Society for Army Historical Research.* London: Robert Stockwell.

OC. Orion Clemens.

OCHP. Cincinnati Historical Society, Cincinnati, Ohio.

OClWHi. Western Reserve Historical Society, Cleveland, Ohio.

ODaU. Roesch Library, University of Dayton, Dayton, Ohio.

Odell, George C. D. 1927–49. *Annals of the New York Stage.* 15 vols. New York: Columbia University Press.

OED. 1989. *The Oxford English Dictionary.* 2d ed. Prepared by J. A. Simpson and E. S. C. Weiner. 20 vols. Oxford: Clarendon Press.

Official Gazette. 1872. *Official Gazette of the United States Patent Office.* Vol. 2, no. 23 (19 November).

OLC (Olivia Langdon Clemens). 1878–79. Notebook containing shopping and gift lists compiled by Olivia Clemens before and during the Clemens family's 1878–79 European trip. The lists occupy about 38 pages—written from back to front—of the notebook Clemens used during his 1871–72 lecture tour: see Redpath and Fall.

Oliver, Leon. 1873. *The Great Sensation. A Full, Complete and Reliable History of the Beecher-Tilton-Woodhull Scandal.* Chicago: The Beverly Company.

Ollé, James G. 1958. "Dickens and Dolby." *Dickensian* 54 (Winter): 27–35.

OrPR. Reed College, Portland, Oregon.

Paff, Harriet Lewis. 1897. "What I Know about Mark Twain." MS of twelve pages, CtY-BR.

Page, Norman. 1988. *A Dickens Chronology.* Houndmills, Basingstoke, England: Macmillan Press.

Page, William, and P. H. Ditchfield, eds. 1924. *The Victoria History of the County of Berkshire.* 4 vols. London: St. Catherine Press.

Paine, Albert Bigelow.
    1904. *Th. Nast: His Period and His Pictures.* New York: Harper and Brothers.
    1912. "Mark Twain: Some Chapters from an Extraordinary Life. Eighth Paper." *Harper's Monthly Magazine* 125 (June): 104–19.

1917. "Some Mark Twain Letters to William Dean Howells and Others." *Harper's Monthly Magazine* 134 (May): 781–94.

Palmer, Roy, ed. 1986. *The Oxford Book of Sea Songs*. Oxford: Oxford University Press.

PAM. Pamela Ann Moffett.

P&P. 1979. *The Prince and the Pauper.* Edited by Victor Fischer and Lin Salamo, with the assistance of Mary Jane Jones. The Works of Mark Twain. Berkeley, Los Angeles, London: University of California Press.

Pardon, George Frederick. 1866. *Routledge's Guide to London and Its Suburbs: Comprising Descriptions of All Its Points of Interest.* New rev. ed. London: George Routledge and Sons. Copy owned by Clemens, with marginalia, CU-MARK.

Park Church. 1896. *The Park Church. 1846–1896.* Elmira: Park Church.

Parke-Bernet.
1938. *William Blake . . . Samuel L. Clemens: Manuscripts, Autographs, First Editions . . . Collected by the Late George C. Smith, Jr.* Sale no. 59 (2 and 3 November). New York: Parke-Bernet Galleries.

1944. *Autograph Letters, Documents, Manuscripts: The Stock of the American Autograph Shop, Merion, Pa.* Sale no. 611 (4 and 5 December). New York: Parke-Bernet Galleries.

1945. *Autograph Letters, Documents, Manuscripts: The Stock of the American Autograph Shop, Merion, Pa.* Sale no. 635 (19 February). New York: Parke-Bernet Galleries.

1946. *Rare First Editions, Historical Americana, Autograph Letters and Manuscripts . . . Collected by the Late Hon. W. W. Cohen. . . .* Sale no. 802 (4, 5, and 6 November). New York: Parke-Bernet Galleries.

1954a. *Autograph Letters, Manuscripts, Documents of . . . James B. Pond and Other Owners.* Sale no. 1496 (23 and 24 February). New York: Parke-Bernet Galleries.

1954b. *English & American First Editions and Other Books; Americana Relating to California and the West Collected by Jean Hersholt.* Sale no. 1503 (23 and 24 March). New York: Parke-Bernet Galleries.

1954c. Catalog for sale no. 1552 (23 and 24 November). New York: Parke-Bernet Galleries.

1954d. *The Distinguished Collection of First Editions, Autograph Letters & MSS. of American Authors . . . Formed by Walter P. Chrysler, Jr.* Sale no. 1556 (7 and 8 December). New York: Parke-Bernet Galleries.

1956. *Books, Autographs and Mss of Samuel L. Clemens: The Splendid Collection Formed by the Late Alan N. Mendleson, New York.* Sale no. 1719 (11 and 12 December). New York: Parke-Bernet Galleries.

1959. Catalog for sale no. 1920 (27 and 28 October). New York: Parke-Bernet Galleries.

1971. *Autographs: Historical, Literary, Scientific, Artistic, Musical. . . . The Property of Various Owners, Including Charles N. Owen.* Sale no. 3151 (2 and 3 February). New York: Parke-Bernet Galleries.

Partridge, Eric. 1972. *A Dictionary of Slang and Unconventional English.* 7th ed. New York: The Macmillan Company.

Pasko, Wesley Washington. 1894. *American Dictionary of Printing and Bookmaking.* New York: Howard Lockwood and Co. Citations are to the 1967 reprint edition, Detroit: Gale Research Company.

Pattee, Fred Lewis. 1917. *A History of American Literature since 1870.* New York: Century Company.

PBL. Robert B. Honeyman Collection, Linderman Library, Lehigh University, Bethlehem, Pennsylvania.

PHi. Historical Society of Pennsylvania, Philadelphia.

Pike, Gustavus D. 1875. *The Singing Campaign for Ten Thousand Pounds; or, The Jubilee Singers in Great Britain.* Rev. ed. New York: American Missionary Association.

Pond, James B. 1900. *Eccentricities of Genius: Memories of Famous Men and Women of the Platform and Stage.* New York: G. W. Dillingham Company.

Pope-Hennessy, James. 1951. *Monckton Milnes: The Flight of Youth, 1851–1885.* London: Constable and Co.

PPAmP. American Philosophical Society, Philadelphia, Pennsylvania.

Protess, David L. 1987. "Joseph Medill: Chicago's First Modern Mayor." In Green and Holli, 1–15.

Raeper, William. 1987. *George MacDonald.* Tring, England: Lion Publishing.

Rains Galleries. 1937. *Americana—First Editions, Dramatic and Theatrical Literature, Autographs, and Signed Photographs from Various Collections.* Sale no. 528 (25 and 26 January). New York: Rains Galleries.

Ramsay, Robert L., and Frances G. Emberson. 1963. *A Mark Twain Lexicon.* New York: Russell and Russell.

Redpath, James.
1871. "Reply." In *Lyceum* 1871, 9–11.
1872a. "The Americans Who Laugh." New York *Independent*, 11 July, 2.
1872b. "Mr. Bret Harte's Explanation." Boston *Advertiser*, 22 November, 4.
1875. "'Warrington.'" In Harriet J. H. Robinson, 153–55.
1876. "To Our Patrons." In *Lyceum* 1876, unnumbered prefatory page.

Redpath, James, and George L. Fall. 1871–72. Notebook containing Clemens's lecture itinerary for 1871–72 in the hand of George H. Hathaway of the Boston Lyceum Bureau. MS of sixteen pages entitled "Lecture-route, winter of 1871" and annotated by Clemens. Accompanied by its own black leather wallet, which is engraved in gold on an interior flap "Sam'l L. Clemens," CU-MARK.

Reed, Thomas B., ed. 1901. *Modern Eloquence. Volume V: Lectures, F–M.* Philadelphia: John D. Morris and Co.

Reid, James D. 1886. *The Telegraph in America.* New York: John Polhemus.

Reid, Whitelaw. 1872. "Schools of Journalism." *Scribner's Monthly* 4 (June): 194–204.

Reigstad, Tom. 1989. "Twain's Langdon-Appointed Guardian Angels in Buffalo: 'Mac,' 'Fletch,' and 'Dombrowski.'" *Mark Twain Society Bulletin* 12 (July): 1, 3–6, 8.

Rendell, Kenneth W. 1970. *Autographs Manuscripts Documents Catalogue 53*. Somerville, Mass.: Kenneth W. Rendell.

Return of Owners of Land, 1873. 1875. *England and Wales. (Exclusive of the Metropolis.) Return of Owners of Land, 1873. Vol. I. Counties. England*. London: Printed by George Edward Eyre and William Spottiswoode . . . for Her Majesty's Stationery Office.

RI 1993. 1993. *Roughing It*. Edited by Harriet Elinor Smith, Edgar Marquess Branch, Lin Salamo, and Robert Pack Browning. The Works of Mark Twain. Berkeley, Los Angeles, London: University of California Press.

Richards, Paul C. 1971. *Catalogue No. 61*. Brookline, Mass.: Paul C. Richards, Autographs.

Richardson, Albert Deane. 1867. *Beyond the Mississippi: From the Great River to the Great Ocean*. Hartford: American Publishing Company.

Ripley, George. 1873. "New Publications." New York *Tribune*, 31 January, 6.

Robinson, Harriet J. H. (Mrs. W. S. Robinson), ed. 1877. *"Warrington" Pen-Portraits: A Collection of Personal and Political Reminiscences, from 1848 to 1876, from the Writings of William S. Robinson*. Boston: Lee and Shepard.

Robinson, William Stevens [Warrington, pseud.]. 1872. "Warrington's Letters." Letter dated 21 March from Boston. Springfield *Republican*, 22 March, 5–6.

Rose, William Ganson. 1950. *Cleveland: The Making of a City*. Cleveland and New York: World Publishing Company.

Routledge. Routledge and Kegan Paul, London.

Routledge Archives. 1973. *The Archives of George Routledge and Co., 1853–1902*. 14 vols. Bishops Stortford, England: Chadwyck-Healey. Microfilm.

Rowell, George P. 1869. *Geo. P. Rowell & Co's American Newspaper Directory*. New York: George P. Rowell and Co.

Royal Humane Society. 1845. *The Seventy-first Annual Report of the Royal Humane Society, Instituted 1774*. London: Printed for the Society.

RPB-JH. John Hay Library of Rare Books and Special Collections, Brown University, Providence, Rhode Island.

Sachs. Collection of Charles W. Sachs, Scriptorium, Beverly Hills, California.

St. Louis Census. [1850] 1963. "Free Inhabitants in . . . St. Louis." *Population Schedules of the Seventh Census of the United States, 1850. Roll 416. Missouri: St. Louis County (pt.), St. Louis City (pt.), Ward 3*. National Archives Microfilm Publications, Microcopy no. 432. Washington, D.C.: General Services Administration.

Salsbury, Edith Colgate, ed. 1965. *Susy and Mark Twain: Family Dialogues*. New York: Harper and Row.

Saxon, A. H. 1989. *P. T. Barnum: The Legend and the Man.* New York: Columbia University Press.

Schirer, Thomas. 1984. *Mark Twain and the Theatre.* Nuremberg: Hans Carl.

Schwalb. Collection of Bruce Schwalb.

Schwinn, Walter. 1982. *The Hartford House.* 2 vols. Unpublished typescript, CU-MARK.

Scott, Arthur L. 1953. "Mark Twain's Revisions of *The Innocents Abroad* for the British Edition of 1872." *American Literature* 25 (March): 43–61.

Scott, Sibbald David. 1880. *The British Army: Its Origin, Progress, and Equipment.* Vol. 3, *From the Restoration to the Revolution.* London: Cassell, Petter, Galpin, and Co.

Selby, P. O., comp. 1973. *Mark Twain's Kinfolks.* Kirksville, Mo.: Missouriana Library, Northeast Missouri State University.

Severance, Frank H., comp. 1915. "The Periodical Press of Buffalo, 1811–1915." *Publications of the Buffalo Historical Society* 19:177–280.

Shaplen, Robert. 1954. *Free Love and Heavenly Sinners: The Story of the Great Henry Ward Beecher Scandal.* New York: Alfred A. Knopf.

Sharpe, Reginald R. 1895. *London and the Kingdom.* 3 vols. London: Longmans, Green and Co.

Shaw, Henry Wheeler [Josh Billings, pseud.].
    1866. *Josh Billings, Hiz Sayings.* New York: G. W. Carleton.
    1868. *Josh Billings on Ice, and Other Things.* New York: G. W. Carleton and Co.
    1873. "Spice-Box." Street and Smith's *New York Weekly* 28 (14 July): 4.
    1874. *Everybody's Friend; or, Josh Billings' Encyclopedia and Proverbial Philosophy of Wit and Humor.* Hartford: American Publishing Company.

Shove, Raymond Howard. 1937. "Cheap Book Production in the United States, 1870 to 1891." M.A. thesis, University of Illinois, Urbana.

Sims, George R., ed. 1901. *Living London: Its Work and Its Play, Its Humour and Its Pathos, Its Sights and Its Scenes.* 3 vols. London: Cassell and Co.

Slater, J. Herbert. 1929. *Engravings and Their Value.* 6th ed., rev. and enl. by F. W. Maxwell-Barbour. New York: Charles Scribner's Sons.

SLC (Samuel Langhorne Clemens).
    1865a. "A Voice for Setchell." *Californian* 3 (27 May): 9. Reprinted in *ET&S2,* 169–73.
    1865b. "Exit 'Bummer.'" *Californian* 3 (11 November): 12. Reprinted in *ET&S2,* 323–25.
    1865c. "Jim Smiley and His Jumping Frog." New York *Saturday Press* 4 (18 November): 248–49. Reprinted in *ET&S2,* 282–88.
    1866a. "Mark Twain among the Spirits." San Francisco *Golden Era* 14 (4 February): 5, reprinting the Virginia City *Territorial Enterprise* of 26–27 January. Reprinted in Chowder, 170–73.
    1866b. "'Mark Twain' among the Spirits." *Californian* 4 (10 February): 12,

reprinting the Virginia City *Territorial Enterprise* of 4 February. Also reprinted in the San Francisco *Golden Era* 14 (11 February): 5, as "Mark Twain a Committee Man.—Ghostly Gathering—Down among the Dead Men.—A Phantom Fandango." Reprinted in Chowder, 176–81.

1866c. "Mark Twain on Spiritual Insanity." San Francisco *Golden Era* 14 (18 February): 8, reprinting the Virginia City *Territorial Enterprise* of 8–11 February.

1866d. "Mark Twain on the New Wild Cat Religion." San Francisco *Golden Era* 14 (4 March): 5, reprinting the Virginia City *Territorial Enterprise* of 22–28 February. Reprinted in Chowder, 173–74.

1866e. "More Spiritual Investigations by Mark Twain." San Francisco *Golden Era* 14 (11 March): 5, reprinting the Virginia City *Territorial Enterprise* of late February or early March. Reprinted in Chowder, 174–76.

1866f. "Scenes in Honolulu—No. 13." Letter dated 22 June. Sacramento *Union*, 16 July, 3, clipping in Scrapbook 6:118–19, CU-MARK. Reprinted in *MTH*, 328–34.

1866g. "How, for Instance?" New York *Weekly Review* 17 (29 September): 1. Reprinted in the Virginia City *Territorial Enterprise*, 28 October, 1.

1866h. Miscellaneous Sandwich Islands lecture notes and drafts. MS of eighty-seven pages, written for the 2 October lecture in San Francisco, CU-MARK.

1866i. "From the Sandwich Islands." Letter dated June. Sacramento *Union*, 25 October, 1. Reprinted as "Letter from Mark Twain" in the Virginia City *Territorial Enterprise*, 27 October, 1; also reprinted in *MTH*, 408–15.

1867a. *The Celebrated Jumping Frog of Calaveras County, And other Sketches.* Edited by John Paul. New York: C. H. Webb.

1867b. "Jim Wolf and the Tom-Cats." New York *Sunday Mercury*, 14 July, 3. Reprinted in Budd 1992a, 235–37.

1867c. "Letter from 'Mark Twain.' [Number 26.]" Letter dated 6 June. San Francisco *Alta California*, 18 August, 1. Reprinted in *MTTB*, 270–79.

1868a. "Information Wanted." Undated letter to the editor. New York *Tribune*, 22 January, 2.

1868b. "My Late Senatorial Secretaryship." *Galaxy* 5 (May): 633–36.

1868c. "Remarkable Sagacity of a Cat." MS of four pages, probably written in June, catalogued as A4, NPV.

1868d. "Letter from Mark Twain." Letter dated 17 August. Chicago *Republican*, 23 August, 2.

1868e. "Cannibalism in the Cars." *Broadway: A London Magazine*, n.s.1 (November): 189–94.

1869a. *The Innocents Abroad; or, The New Pilgrims' Progress.* Hartford: American Publishing Company.

1869b. "Letter from Mark Twain." Letter dated July. San Francisco *Alta California*, 25 July, 1.

1869c. "The Latest Novelty. Mental Photographs." Buffalo *Express*, 2 October, 1.

1869d. "Back from 'Yurrup.'" In "Browsing Around," letter dated November, Buffalo *Express*, 4 December, 2.

1869e. "Around the World. Letter Number 5." Undated letter. Buffalo *Express*, 18 December, 2.

1870a. *The Celebrated Jumping Frog of Calaveras County, And other Sketches*. London: George Routledge and Sons.

1870b. *The Innocents Abroad. . . . The Voyage Out*. London: John Camden Hotten.

1870c. *The Jumping Frog and Other Humourous Sketches*. London: John Camden Hotten.

1870d. *The New Pilgrim's Progress. . . . The Journey Home*. London: John Camden Hotten.

1870e. "Anson Burlingame." Buffalo *Express*, 25 February, 2.

1870f. "The New Crime." Buffalo *Express*, 16 April, 2.

1870g. "Curious Dream." Buffalo *Express*, 30 April, 2.

1870h. "The Story of the Good Little Boy Who Did Not Prosper." *Galaxy* 9 (May): 724–26.

1870i. "More Distinction." Buffalo *Express*, 4 June, 2.

1871a. *Eye Openers: Good Things, Immensely Funny Sayings & Stories That Will Bring a Smile upon the Gruffest Countenance*. London: John Camden Hotten.

1871b. *Mark Twain's (Burlesque) Autobiography and First Romance*. New York: Sheldon and Co.

1871c. *Mark Twain's (Burlesque) 1. Autobiography. 2. Mediæval Romance. 3. On Children*. London: John Camden Hotten. Includes two pieces erroneously attributed to Clemens (see "Byng, Carl").

1871d. *Mark Twain's Pleasure Trip on the Continent*. London: John Camden Hotten. Reprints SLC 1870b, d.

1871e. *Screamers: A Gathering of Scraps of Humour, Delicious Bits, & Short Stories*. London: John Camden Hotten. Includes three pieces erroneously attributed to Clemens (see "Byng, Carl").

1871f. "An Autobiography." *Aldine* 4 (April): 52.

1871g. "A New Beecher Church." *American Publisher* 1 (July): 4. Reprinted in SLC 1872a, 24–38, and SLC 1872e, 30–39.

1871h. "The Revised Catechism." New York *Tribune*, 27 September, 6. Reprinted in Vogelback 1955, 72–76, and Budd 1992a, 539–40.

1871i. "A Brace of Brief Lectures on Science." Part 2. *American Publisher* 1 (October): 4.

1871j. Untitled MS fragments, twenty-two pages, written in December, miscellaneous notes for the "Roughing It" lecture, CU-MARK.

1872a. *A Curious Dream; and Other Sketches*. Selected and Revised by the Author. Copyright. London: George Routledge and Sons.

1872b. "How I Escaped Being Killed in a Duel." In Hood 1872b, 90–91.

1872c. *The Innocents Abroad*. Author's English Edition. Rev. ed. London: George Routledge and Sons.

1872d. *Mark Twain's Celebrated Jumping Frog of Calaveras County And other*

Sketches. With the Burlesque Autobiography and First Romance. London: George Routledge and Sons.

1872e. *Mark Twain's Sketches.* Selected and Revised by the Author. Copyright Edition. London: George Routledge and Sons.

1872f. *The New Pilgrims' Progress.* Author's English Edition. Rev. ed. London: George Routledge and Sons.

1872g. *Roughing It.* Hartford: American Publishing Company.

1872h. *"Roughing It"* and *The Innocents at Home.* Copyright Edition. 2 vols. London: George Routledge and Sons.

1872i. Speech at the *Aldine* dinner of 23 February, as reported in "A Model Impromptu Speech," Elmira *Advertiser*, 18 March, 3. Variant texts published in *MTS* 1910 (as "Cats and Candy," a partial text), 262–64, and Fatout 1976, 65–68.

1872j. "To the English Reader." Fragmentary MS preface of three and one-half pages, written in July, a discarded draft of the preface for the second volume of the 1872 English edition of *The Innocents Abroad* (SLC 1872f), CU-MARK.

1872k. "An Appeal from One That Is Persecuted." MS of nineteen pages, written ca. 18 July. W. T. H. Howe Collection, NN-B.

1872*l*. "The Secret of Dr. Livingstone's Continued Voluntary Exile." Hartford *Courant*, 20 July, 2. Reprinted in Budd 1992a, 541–42.

1872m. Fragments of a script, MS of three leaves, inscribed on both sides and numbered 3, 7, 8, 13, 14, and 18, written for Clemens's performance as Mrs. Jarley, the wax-works exhibitor in Dickens's *Old Curiosity Shop*, at Fenwick Hall, New Saybrook, Connecticut, on 29 July, CU-MARK.

1872n. Speech at the Whitefriars Club dinner of 6 September, as reported in "Mark Twain at the Whitefriars Club," South London *Press*, 14 September, 4. Variant texts published in *MTS* 1910, 154–65; *MTS* 1923, 133–34; and Fatout 1976, 72–74.

1872o. "To the Superintendent of the Zoological Gardens." MS of six pages, written between 15 September and 11 November, a denunciation of John Camden Hotten, CU-MARK.

1872p. "Mark Twain and His English Editor." Letter dated 20 September. London *Spectator*, 21 September, 1201–2.

1872q. Speech at the London sheriffs' inauguration dinner of 28 September, as reported in "Election of Lord Mayor & Swearing in of Sheriffs," London *Observer*, 29 September, 6, clipping in CU-MARK.

1872r. Speech at the Savage Club dinner of 21 September, as reported in Conway 1872. Reprinted in *MTS* 1910, 417–21; *MTS* 1923, 37–41; and Fatout 1976, 69–72.

1872s. "Mark Twain." Departure announcement dated 5 November. London *Daily News*, 6 November, 2. Sent to several additional London newspapers.

1872t. "A Daring Deed." Letter dated 20 November to the Royal Humane Society. Boston *Advertiser*, 26 November, 4.

1872u. "Concerning an Insupportable Nuisance." Letter dated 5 December. Hartford *Evening Post*, 6 December, 2.

1872v. "The Missouri Disaster." Letter dated 5 December. New York *Tribune*, 7 December, 5.

1872w. "Appeal for Capt. Ned Wakeman—Letter from 'Mark Twain.'" Letter dated 3 December. San Francisco *Alta California*, 14 December, 1.

1872x. Fragment of a burlesque protest against foreign copyright. MS of five and one-third pages, written ca. mid-December, CU-MARK.

1872y. "Petition. (Concerning Copyright.)" and "Circular to American Authors & Publishers." MS of eight pages, written ca. mid-December, CU-MARK. Published as "Petition. Concerning Copyright" in Appendix N of *MTB*, 3:1637–39, where it is dated 1875.

1872z. "The New Cock-Robin." Poem dated 23 December. Hartford *Evening Post*, 24 December, 2, clipping in CU-MARK. Reprinted in Vogelback 1954, 377–80.

1872–73. "John Camden Hotten, Publisher, London." MS of nineteen pages, written between 26 November 1872 and June 1873, a denunciation of Hotten, CU-MARK.

1873a. *The Choice Humorous Works of Mark Twain*. Now First Collected. With Extra Passages to the "Innocents Abroad," Now First Reprinted, and a Life of the Author. Illustrations by Mark Twain and other Artists; also Portrait of the Author. London: John Camden Hotten.

1873b. A set of sheets from the unauthorized *Choice Humorous Works* (SLC 1873a) revised and annotated by Mark Twain for an authorized edition (SLC 1874a), NN.

1873c. "The Sandwich Islands." Letter dated 3 January. New York *Tribune*, 6 January, 4–5. Reprinted in Appendix B.

1873d. "The Sandwich Islands." Letter dated 6 January. New York *Tribune*, 9 January, 4–5. Reprinted in Appendix B.

1873e. "British Benevolence." Undated letter. New York *Tribune*, 27 January, 4–5. Reprinted in Appendix B.

1873f. "Samuel Langhorne Clemens." MS of eleven pages, written ca. 27 January, NNPM.

1873g. "A Card." Letter dated 28 January. Hartford *Evening Post*, 28 January, 2, clipping in Scrapbook 6:125, CU-MARK.

1873h. "Foster's Case." Letter dated 7 March. New York *Tribune*, 10 March, 5. MS (at NN) transcribed as an enclosure with letter of 7 Mar 73 to Reid (2nd).

1873i. "A Horrible Tale. Fearful Calamity in Forest Street." Letter dated 30 March. Hartford *Courant*, 31 March, 2.

1873j. "Life-Rafts. How the Atlantic's Passengers Might Have Been Saved." Letter dated 8 April. New York *Tribune*, 11 April, 5. Reprinted as an enclosure with letter of 9 Apr 73 to Reid.

1873k. Statement dated 15 April, forming part of Letters Patent No. 140,245, "Samuel L. Clemens, of Hartford, Connecticut. Improvement in Scrap-Books," in the records of the United States Patent Office, Department of Commerce, Washington, D.C.

1873*l*. "'Mark Twain' to the Editor of 'The Daily Graphic.' *An Autograph Letter*." Letter dated 17 April. New York *Graphic*, 22 April, 8.

1873m. Affidavit of Samuel L. Clemens, dated 16 May, in "Samuel L. Clemens agst Benjamin J. Such," Supreme Court of the State of New York, City and County of New York, PH in CU-MARK. Transcribed in Feinstein, 18–21.

1873n. "The Man of Mark Ready to Bring Over the O'Shah." Letter dated 18 June. New York *Herald*, 1 July, 3. Reprinted in SLC 1923, 31–46.

1873o. "Mark Twain Executes His Contract and Delivers the Persian in London." Letter dated 19 June. New York *Herald*, 4 July, 5. Reprinted in SLC 1923, 46–57.

1873p. "The 'Jumping Frog.' In English. Then in French. Then clawed back into a civilized language once more, by patient, unremunerated toil." MS of thirty-nine pages, dated 30 June, ViU. Published in SLC 1875, 28–43; reprinted in Budd 1992a, 588–603.

1873q. "Mark Twain Takes Another Contract." Letter dated 21 June. New York *Herald*, 9 July, 3. Reprinted in SLC 1923, 57–69.

1873r. "Mark Twain Hooks the Persian out of the English Channel." Letter dated 26 June. New York *Herald*, 11 July, 3. Reprinted in SLC 1923, 69–78.

1873s. "Mark Twain Gives the Royal Persian a 'Send-Off.'" Letter dated 30 June. New York *Herald*, 19 July, 5. Reprinted in SLC 1923, 78–86.

1873t. Untitled notes about the Old Testament for the "Noah's Ark" book. MS of thirteen pages, written between late July and late August in Edinburgh; preserved (probably by Clemens) together with fourteen pages of related notes from the later 1870s, CU-MARK.

1873u. Untitled MS of fourteen pages, written in September, about a visit to the Doré Gallery in London, CU-MARK.

1873v. "Mark Twain on the Sandwich Islands." Letter dated 7 October. London *Standard*, 9 October, clipping in Scrapbook 12:1, CU-MARK.

1873w. "One Method of Teaching in England." MS of four pages in Clemens's hand, and thirteen pages in the hand of Charles Warren Stoddard, written between 20 November 1873 and 12 January 1874, CU-MARK.

1873x. Speech in response to the toast to "The Ladies" at the Scottish Corporation dinner of 1 December. MS (at NN-B) transcribed as an enclosure with 28 Nov 73 to Fitzgibbon. Variant texts published in SLC 1875, 213–14; Fatout 1976, 78–80; and Budd 1992a, 559–61.

1873y. "Mark Twain's Lectures." Letter dated 10 December. London *Morning Post*, 11 December, 3.

1873z. Speech in response to the toast to "The Guests" at the St. Andrew's Society dinner of 29 November, as reported in "Mark Twain on Scotland," Hartford *Courant*, 20 December, 2. Variant text published in Fatout 1976, 82–83.

1873–74. *The Gilded Age: A Tale of To-day.* Charles Dudley Warner, coauthor. Hartford: American Publishing Company. [*Early copies bound with 1873 title page, later ones with 1874 title page: see BAL 3357.*]

1874a. *The Choice Humorous Works of Mark Twain.* Revised and Corrected by the Author. With Life and Portrait of the Author, and Numerous Illustrations. London: Chatto and Windus.

1874b. *The Gilded Age: A Novel*. Charles Dudley Warner, coauthor. 3 vols. London: George Routledge and Sons.

1874c. *Mark Twain's Sketches. Number One*. Authorised Edition. New York: American News Company.

1874d. "Sociable Jimmy." New York *Times*, 29 November, 7.

1875. *Mark Twain's Sketches, New and Old*. Now First Published in Complete Form. Hartford: American Publishing Company.

1876. "Some Recollections of a Storm at Sea." Cleveland *Bazaar Record*, 18 January, no page. Reprinted in Storkan.

1876–85. "A Record of The Small Foolishnesses of Susie & 'Bay' Clemens (Infants.)" MS of 111 pages, ViU.

1877. *A True Story, and the Recent Carnival of Crime*. Boston: James R. Osgood and Co.

1879a. *The Innocents Abroad; or, The New Pilgrims' Progress*. 2 vols. Collection of British Authors, vols. 1812 and 1813. Leipzig: Bernhard Tauchnitz.

1879b. Speech delivered at a breakfast honoring Oliver Wendell Holmes's seventieth birthday, on 3 December in Boston, as reported in "The Holmes Breakfast," Boston *Advertiser*, 4 December, 1. Variant texts published in the Supplement to the *Atlantic Monthly* 45 (February 1880); *MTS* 1910, 56–58; *MTS* 1923, 77–79; and Fatout 1976, 134–36.

1882. Draft of chapter 48 of *Life on the Mississippi*. MS of thirty-four pages, NNPM.

1883. *Life on the Mississippi*. Boston: James R. Osgood and Co.

1890. "Concerning the Scoundrel Edward H. House." MS of fifty-two pages, CU-MARK.

1890–99. "The Christening Yarn. On Telling a Story. The 'Bram Stoker Surprise.'" MS of eleven pages, titled and dated "90s" by A. B. Paine, CU-MARK.

1895. "How to Tell a Story." *Youth's Companion*, 3 October, 464. Reprinted in Budd 1992b, 201–6.

1897. *Following the Equator: A Journey around the World*. Hartford: American Publishing Company.

1897–98. "My Autobiography. [Random Extracts from it.]" MS of seventy-five pages, CU-MARK. Published, with omissions, as "Early Days" in *MTA*, 1:81–115.

1898. "Ralph Keeler." MS of twenty-four pages, CU-MARK. Published in *MTA*, 1:154–64.

1900. "Playing 'Bear.' Herrings. Jim Wolf and the Cats." MS of forty-two pages, CU-MARK. Published in *MTA*, 1:125–43.

1907. "First Day in England." TS of six pages, dictated 19 February, CU-MARK. Published in Watson, 131–35.

1909a. "To Rev. S. C. Thompson." MS of seventeen pages, dated 23 April, incorporating a letter of Thompson to SLC dated 20 April, CU-MARK. Published in part in *MTB*, 1:482–83.

1909b. "*Notes*." Autobiographical reminiscence. MS of three pages (numbered 5–7), dated 30 April, appended to unsent four-page letter of 14 May 1887 to Jeannette Gilder, both in CU-MARK. Published in *MTL*, 2:487–88.

1923. *Europe and Elsewhere*. With an Appreciation by Brander Matthews and an Introduction by Albert Bigelow Paine. New York: Harper and Brothers.

1982. *The Adventures of Tom Sawyer . . . A Facsimile of the Author's Holograph Manuscript*. Introduction by Paul Baender. 2 vols. Frederick, Md., and Washington, D.C.: University Publications of America and Georgetown University Library.

Sloane, David E. E. 1982. "Charles G. Leland." In *American Humorists, 1800–1950, Part 1: A–L*, edited by Stanley Trachtenberg. Vol. 11 of *Dictionary of Literary Biography*. Detroit: Gale Research Company.

Smalley, George W.
1873a. "Notes from London." Letter dated 5 June. New York *Tribune*, 20 June, 8.
1873b. "Transatlantic Mails." Letter dated 14 June. New York *Tribune*, 28 June, 3.
1874. "Foreign Literature. Publications in England." Letter dated 20 December 1873. New York *Tribune*, 17 January, 3.

Smith, Benjamin E. 1894. *The Century Cyclopedia of Names*. New York: Century Company.

Sotheby.
1950. *Catalogue of Valuable Printed Books, Fine Bindings, Drawings for Book Illustrations, Autograph Letters and Historical Documents, Etc.* Sale of 26 June. London: Sotheby and Co.
1964. *Catalogue of English Literature, Science and Medicine, and Other Valuable Printed Books, Autograph Letters and Historical Documents*. Sale of 25, 26, and 27 May. London: Sotheby and Co.
1980. *Catalogue of Valuable Autograph Letters, Literary Manuscripts and Historical Documents*. Sale no. 9341 (21 and 22 July). London: Sotheby Parke Bernet.
1983. *Fine Printed and Manuscript Americana*. Sale no. 5031 (26 April). New York: Sotheby Parke-Bernet.
1993. *Fine Books and Manuscripts*. Sale no. 6515 (10 and 11 December). New York: Sotheby's.

Spielmann, M. H. 1895. *The History of "Punch."* New York: Cassell Publishing Company.

Stanford, Josiah. 1889. TS of thirty pages, dictation dated 19 September, CU-BANC.

Stanley, Arthur Penrhyn. 1882. *Historical Memorials of Westminster Abbey*. 5th ed., with the author's final revisions. London: John Murray.

Stanley, Henry M. 1867. "Mark Twain at the Mercantile Library Hall Tuesday Night." St. Louis *Missouri Democrat*, 28 March, 4.

Stern, Madeleine B., ed. 1974. *The Victoria Woodhull Reader*. Weston, Mass.: M & S Press.

Sterne, Simon. 1873. Bill of complaint, dated 16 May, in "Samuel L. Clemens agst Benjamin J. Such," Supreme Court of the State of New York, City and County of New York, PH in CU-MARK.

Stewart, George R., Jr. 1931. *Bret Harte: Argonaut and Exile.* Boston and New York: Houghton Mifflin Company.

Stewart, Robert E. 1958. "Adolph Sutro: A Study of His Early Career." Ph.D. diss., University of California, Berkeley.

Stewart, Robert E., and Mary Frances Stewart. 1962. *Adolph Sutro: A Biography.* Berkeley: Howell-North Books.

Stoddard, Charles Warren.
1873. "Stoddard's Letter . . . Number Five." Letter dated 13 October. San Francisco *Chronicle,* 16 November, 2.

1874a. "Oxford, Ho! . . . Number XI." Letter dated 10 December 1873. San Francisco *Chronicle,* 11 January, 1.

1874b. "'Dear Old Oxford.' . . . Number XII." Letter dated 19 December 1873. San Francisco *Chronicle,* 19 January, 1.

1874c. "Christmas in New Sarum. . . . Number XIII." Letter dated 26 December 1873. San Francisco *Chronicle,* 25 January, 2.

1874d. "An Anglo-American City. Chas. Warren Stoddard's Notes in Liverpool. . . . Number Fourteen." Letter dated 10 January. San Francisco *Chronicle,* 8 February, 1.

1903. *Exits and Entrances: A Book of Essays and Sketches.* Boston: Lothrop Publishing Company.

1907. "In Old Bohemia: Memories of San Francisco in the Sixties." *Pacific Monthly* 18 (December): 638–50.

1908. "In Old Bohemia. II. The 'Overland' and the Overlanders." *Pacific Monthly* 19 (March): 261–73.

Storkan, Charles J. 1949. "That Tall Twain Tale, 'A Storm at Sea,' at Last Traced to Its Printed Origin." *Twainian* 8 (July–August): 1–2.

Stowe, Lyman Beecher. 1934. *Saints Sinners and Beechers.* Indianapolis: Bobbs-Merrill Company.

Strong, Leah A. 1966. *Joseph Hopkins Twichell: Mark Twain's Friend and Pastor.* Athens: University of Georgia Press.

Strout, A. O. 1881. "Vaccination and Measles." *Medical and Surgical Reporter* 44 (14 May): 558.

Sturdevant, James R. 1967–68. "Mark Twain's Unpublished Letter to Tom Taylor—an Enigma." *Mark Twain Journal* 14 (Winter): 8–9.

Swann. 1977. *Rare Books, Autographs, Graphics.* Sale no. 1077 (20 October). New York: Swann Galleries.

Sweets, Henry H. 1987. "Two Related Works of Art?" *The Fence Painter* 7 (Spring): 1, 4.

Taylor, Eva. 1973. "Langdon-Clemens Plot in Woodlawn." *Chemung Historical Journal* 18 (June): 2273–81.

Tebbel, John. 1975. *A History of Book Publishing in the United States. Volume II: The Expansion of an Industry, 1865–1919.* New York: R. R. Bowker.

Tenney, Thomas Asa. 1977. *Mark Twain: A Reference Guide.* Boston: G. K. Hall and Co.

Tercentenary Handlist. 1920. *Tercentenary Handlist of English & Welsh Newspapers, Magazines & Reviews.* London: The Times.

Thompson. Collection of Jean Thompson.

Thompson, Samuel C. 1918–21. Untitled reminiscences. TS of 224 pages, CU-MARK.

Thomson, Mortimer Neal [Q. K. Philander Doesticks, pseud.]. 1855. *Doesticks: What He Says.* New York: Edward Livermore.

Timbs, John. 1867. *Curiosities of London.* London: John Camden Hotten. Citations are to the 1968 reprint edition, Detroit: Singing Tree Press.

Tipping, H. Avray. 1922. *English Homes. Period III—Vol. 1: Late Tudor and Early Stuart, 1558–1649.* London: Offices of Country Life and George Newnes.

Tollett. Collection of Robert Tollett.

Tollett and Harman. 1991. *Catalogue 11: Autographs, Signed Books, First Editions, Signed Photographs, Vintage Photographs.* New York: Tollett and Harman.

Toole, J. L. 1889. *Reminiscences of J. L. Toole, Related by Himself, and Chronicled by Joseph Hatton.* 3d ed. London: Hurst and Blackett.

Traubel, Horace. 1906. *With Walt Whitman in Camden.* Boston: Small, Maynard and Co.

Trewin, J. C. 1950. *The Story of Stratford upon Avon.* London: Staples Press.

Trollope, Anthony. 1983. *The Letters of Anthony Trollope.* Edited by N. John Hall. 2 vols. Stanford, Calif.: Stanford University Press.

Trory, Ernie. 1993. *Truth against the World: The Life and Times of Thomas Hughes, Author of "Tom Brown's School Days."* Hove, East Sussex, England: Crabtree Press.

Trumbull, J. Hammond, ed. 1886. *The Memorial History of Hartford County, Connecticut, 1633–1884.* 2 vols. Boston: Edward L. Osgood.

TS. Typescript.

TS. 1980. *The Adventures of Tom Sawyer; Tom Sawyer Abroad; Tom Sawyer, Detective.* Edited by John C. Gerber, Paul Baender, and Terry Firkins. The Works of Mark Twain. Berkeley, Los Angeles, London: University of California Press.

Tutorow, Norman E. 1971. *Leland Stanford: Man of Many Careers.* Menlo Park, Calif.: Pacific Coast Publishers.

TxU. University of Texas, Austin.

TxU-Hu. Harry Ransom Humanities Research Center, TxU.

UCCL. 1986. *Union Catalog of Clemens Letters.* Edited by Paul Machlis. Berkeley, Los Angeles, London: University of California Press. [*In a few cases, UCCL catalog numbers cited in this volume supersede those assigned in 1986 and reflect corrections or additions to the catalog since publication.*]

UCLC. 1992. *Union Catalog of Letters to Clemens.* Edited by Paul Machlis, with the assistance of Deborah Ann Turner. Berkeley, Los Angeles, Oxford: University of California Press.

Uk. British Library, London.

UkElgM. Archives of the Moray District Council, Elgin, England.

UkENL. National Library of Scotland, Edinburgh.

UkGS. Strathclyde Regional Archives, Glasgow, Scotland.

Unger, Irwin. 1964. *The Greenback Era: A Social and Political History of American Finance, 1865–1879.* Princeton, N.J.: Princeton University Press.

University of Virginia. 1969. *The American Writer in England: An Exhibition Arranged in Honor of the Sesquicentennial of the University of Virginia.* With a foreword by Gordon N. Ray and an introduction by C. Waller Barrett. Charlottesville: University Press of Virginia.

Van Why, Joseph S. 1975. *Nook Farm.* Rev. ed. Edited by Earl A. French. Hartford: Stowe-Day Foundation.

Vincent, James Edmund. 1919. *Highways and Byways in Berkshire.* London: Macmillan and Co.

ViU. Clifton Waller Barrett Library, Alderman Library, University of Virginia, Charlottesville.

Vogelback, Arthur L.
1954. "Mark Twain and the Fight for Control of the *Tribune.*" *American Literature* 26 (November): 374–83.
1955. "Mark Twain and the Tammany Ring." *PMLA* 70 (March): 69–77.

VtMiM. Middlebury College, Middlebury, Vermont.

Waiting for Godot Books. 1995. *Mark Twain: Books by and About. Special List Number 1.* Hadley, Mass.: Waiting for Godot Books.

Wakeman-Curtis, Minnie, ed. 1878. *The Log of an Ancient Mariner. Being the Life and Adventures of Captain Edgar Wakeman.* Written by himself, and edited by his daughter. San Francisco: A. L. Bancroft and Co.

Wall, Joseph Frazier. 1956. *Henry Watterson: Reconstructed Rebel.* New York: Oxford University Press.

Warner, Charles Dudley.
1872. "Back-Log Studies.—IV." *Scribner's Monthly* 3 (April): 693–700.
1873. *Backlog Studies.* Boston: James R. Osgood and Co.
1875. "Samuel Langhorne Clemens." In Duyckinck and Duyckinck, 2:951–55.

Warner, Elisabeth G. (Lilly). 1872–79. Untitled diary. MS of 130 pages, inscribed in a blank book bound in leather, with numerous photographs of the children of George and Lilly Warner, CU-MARK.

Watson, Aaron. 1907. *The Savage Club. A Medley of History, Anecdote and Reminiscence. . . . With a Chapter by Mark Twain.* London: T. Fisher Unwin.

Watterson, Henry.
1910. "Mark Twain—An Intimate Memory." *American Magazine* 70 (July): 372–75.
1911. Address in "Public Meeting under the Auspices of the Academy in Memory of Samuel Langhorne Clemens (Mark Twain) Held at Carnegie Hall, New York, November 30, 1910." *Proceedings of the American Academy of Arts and Letters* 1 (November): 24–29.
1919. *"Marse Henry": An Autobiography.* 2 vols. New York: George H. Doran Company.
1927. "Memories of Mark Twain." *Master Mason,* August, 610–14.

Way, Frederick, Jr. 1943. *Pilotin' Comes Natural.* New York: Farrar and Rinehart.

Weber, Carl J. 1959. *The Rise and Fall of James Ripley Osgood: A Biography.* Waterville, Me.: Colby College Press.

Wecter, Dixon. 1948. "The Love Letters of Mark Twain." *Atlantic Monthly* 181 (January): 83–88.

Weinreb, Ben, and Christopher Hibbert. 1983. *The London Encyclopaedia.* London: Macmillan London. Citations are to the 1986 reprint edition, Bethesda, Md.: Adler and Adler.

Weisenburger, Francis P. 1941. *The Passing of the Frontier, 1825–1850.* Vol. 3 of *The History of the State of Ohio.* Columbus: Ohio State Archaeological and Historical Society.

Welland, Dennis. 1978. *Mark Twain in England.* London: Chatto and Windus.

Wells, Amos R. 1945. *A Treasure of Hymns: Brief Biographies of One Hundred and Twenty Leading Hymn-Writers and Their Best Hymns.* Boston: W. A. Wilde Company.

Westby-Gibson, John. 1887. *The Bibliography of Shorthand.* London: Isaac Pitman and Sons.

Western Union. 1867. *The Western Union Telegraph Company. Pacific Division. Rules, Regulations, and Instructions.* San Francisco: Alta California General Printing House.

Whiting, Lilian.
1900. *Kate Field: A Record.* Boston: Little, Brown, and Co.
1910. *Louise Chandler Moulton: Poet and Friend.* Boston: Little, Brown, and Co.

Whitney, William Dwight, and Benjamin E. Smith, eds. 1889–91. *The Century Dictionary: An Encyclopedic Lexicon of the English Language.* 6 vols. New York: Century Company.

Wiggin, Kate Douglas. 1923. "Phoebe Garnaut Smalley." *New York Times,* 12 February, 12.

Williamson, George C., ed. 1903–5. *Bryan's Dictionary of Painters and Engravers.* New ed., rev. and enl. 5 vols. London: George Bell and Sons.

Willoughby, R. W. H. 1960. "The Blackmore Museum." *Wiltshire Archaeological and Natural History Magazine* 57: 316–21.

Willson, Frank C. 1955. "Mark Twain and the Foster Case." *Twainian* 14 (March–April): 2–3.

Wilson, H., comp.
1869. *Trow's New York City Directory, . . . Vol. LXXXIII. For the Year Ending May 1, 1870.* New York: John F. Trow.
1870. *Trow's New York City Directory, . . . Vol. LXXXIV. For the Year Ending May 1, 1871.* New York: John F. Trow.
1871. *Trow's New York City Directory, . . . Vol. LXXXV. For the Year Ending May 1, 1872.* New York: John F. Trow.
1872. *Trow's New York City Directory, . . . Vol. LXXXVI. For the Year Ending May 1, 1873.* New York: Trow City Directory Company.
1873. *Trow's New York City Directory, . . . Vol. LXXXVII. For the Year Ending May 1, 1874.* New York: Trow City Directory Company.

Wilson, James Grant, and John Fiske, eds. 1887–89. *Appletons' Cyclopaedia of American Biography.* 6 vols. New York: D. Appleton and Co.

Wilson, Mark K. 1974. "Mr. Clemens and Madame Blanc: Mark Twain's First French Critic." *American Literature* 45 (January): 537–56.

Wingate, Charles F. [Carlfried, pseud.].
1872. "Sketch of the Celebration of the Sixty-first Birthday of the Hon. Horace Greeley, LL.D." New York: Printed, not published.
1875. *Views and Interviews on Journalism.* New York: F. B. Patterson.

Wise, Stephen R. 1988. *Lifeline of the Confederacy: Blockade Running During the Civil War.* Columbia: University of South Carolina Press.

Wolcott, Samuel. 1881. *Memorial of Henry Wolcott, One of the First Settlers of Windsor, Connecticut, and of Some of His Descendants.* New York: Anson D. F. Randolph and Co.

Wood, C. F. 1875. *A Yachting Cruise in the South Seas.* London: Henry S. King and Co.

Wood, Christopher. 1978. *The Dictionary of Victorian Painters.* 2d ed. Woodbridge, England: Antique Collectors' Club.

Wood, John Turtle. 1877. *Discoveries at Ephesus, Including the Site and Remains of the Great Temple of Diana.* London: Longmans, Green, and Co.

Woodhull, Victoria C. 1872? *Victoria C. Woodhull's Complete and Detailed Version of the Beecher-Tilton Affair.* Washington, D.C.: J. Bradley Adams. In Stern. A "verbatim" reprinting of "The Beecher-Tilton Scandal Case," *Woodhull and Claflin's Weekly*, 2 November 1872, 9–13.

Woodruff, Douglas. 1957. *The Tichborne Claimant: A Victorian Mystery.* New York: Farrar, Straus and Cudahy.

WU. Memorial Library, University of Wisconsin, Madison.

Yates, Edmund.
1873. "English Watering Places." Letter dated 2 August. New York *Herald*, 16 August, 10.
1885. *Fifty Years of London Life: Memoirs of a Man of the World.* New York: Harper and Brothers.

Index

THE FOLLOWING have not been indexed: fictional characters, Editorial Signs, Description of Texts, Description of Provenance, and Textual Commentaries. Place names are included when they refer to locations that Clemens lived in, visited, or commented upon, but are excluded when mentioned only in passing.

Alphabetizing is *word-by-word,* except for the following. (1) When persons, places, and things share the same name, they are indexed in that order. (2) Formal titles (Mr., Mrs., Dr., and so forth) may be included with a name, but are ignored when alphabetizing. (3) The subheadings "letters to," "notes to," "letters by," and "letters from" *precede* all other subheadings.

Recipients of Clemens's letters are listed in **boldface type;** boldface numbers (**304n1**) designate principal identifications. Numbers linked by an ampersand (98 & 100n1) indicate that the allusion in the letter text is not explicit, and can best be located by reading the note first. Works written by Mark Twain are indexed separately by title *and* under "Clemens, Samuel Langhorne: works," as well as, when appropriate, under the publishing journal. Works written by others are indexed both by title and by author's name. Newspapers are indexed both by title and by author's name. Newspapers are indexed by their location (city or town), other periodicals by title.

The text of this book is set in Mergenthaler Linotype Plantin. Headings are in Plantin Light. Plantin was originally designed for the Monotype Company by F. H. Pierpont in 1913. The paper is Glatfelter Offset, Natural B31, acid-free. The book was composed by Wilsted & Taylor Publishing Services of Oakland, California, using Data General Nova 4c and Nova 4x computers, Penta software, and a Linotron 202 typesetter. It was printed and bound by Maple-Vail Book Manufacturing Group in Binghamton, New York.